A Textbook of

PHYSICAL CHEMISTRY

A Textbook of
PHYSICAL CHEMISTRY

Second Edition

A.S. Negi
S.C. Anand

PUBLISHING FOR ONE WORLD

NEW AGE INTERNATIONAL (P) LIMITED, PUBLISHERS
New Delhi • Bangalore • Chennai •Cochin • Guwahati • Hyderabad
Jalandhar • Kolkata • Lucknow • Mumbai • Ranchi
Visit us at www.newagepublishers.com

Branches:

- No. 37/10, 8th Cross (Near Hanuman Temple), Azad Nagar, Chamrajpet, **Bangalore**- 560 018.
  Tel.: (080) 26756823, Telefax: 26756820, E-mail: bangalore@newagepublishers.com
- 26, Damodaran Street, T. Nagar, **Chennai**- 600 017. Tel.: (044) 24353401, Telefax: 24351463
  E-mail: chennai@newagepublishers.com
- CC-39/1016, Carrier Station Road, Ernakulam South, **Cochin**- 682 016. Tel.: (0484) 2377004, Telefax: 4051303
  E-mail: cochin@newagepublishers.com
- Hemsen Complex, Mohd. Shah Road, Paltan Bazar, Near Starline Hotel, **Guwahati**- 781 008.Tel.: (0361) 2513881
  Telefax: 2543669, E-mail: guwahati@newagepublishers.com
- No. 105, 1st Floor, Madhiray Kaveri Tower, 3-2-19, Azam Jahi Road, Nimboliadda, **Hyderabad**- 500 027.
  Tel.: (040) 24652456, Telefax: 24652457, E-mail:hyderabad@newagepublishers.com
- RDB Chambers (Formerly Lotus Cinema)106A, 1st Floor, S.N. Banerjee Road, **Kolkata**- 700 014.
  Tel.: (033) 22273773, Telefax: 22275247, E-mail:kolkata@newagepublishers.com
- 16-A, Jopling Road, **Lucknow**- 226 001. Tel.: (0522) 2209578, 4045297, Telefax: 2204098
  E-mail: lucknow@newagepublishers.com
- 142C, Victor House, Ground Floor, N.M. Joshi Marg, Lower Parel, **Mumbai**- 400 013. Tel.: (022) 24927869
  Telefax: 24915415, E-mail: mumbai@newagepublishers.com
- 22, Golden House, Daryaganj, **New Delhi**- 110 002. Tel.: (011) 23262370, 23262368, Telefax: 43551305
  E-mail: sales@newagepublishers.com

ISBN (10) : 81-224-2005-2
ISBN (13) : 978-81-224-2005-0

Rs. 395.00

C-10-06-4717

Printed in India at Sanjeev Offset, Delhi.
Typeset at Pagitek Graphics, Delhi.

PUBLISHING FOR ONE WORLD
NEW AGE INTERNATIONAL (P) LIMITED, PUBLISHERS
4835/24, Ansari Road, Daryaganj, New Delhi-110002
Visit us at **www.newagepublishers.com**

Preface to the Second Edition

In this second revised edition of the book several modifications have been made. Some chapters have been substantially reshuffled, rewritten and rearranged. New sections have been incorporated in many chapters. The chapter dealing with Physical Properties and Molecular Structure has been divided into two chapters viz., Molecular Spectroscopy and Electrical and Magnetic Properties. A new chapter on Macromolecules has been introduced. Some of the conventional problems have been removed and many thought-provoking worked-out examples are included. These should expose the students to practical applications of various concepts and fundamentals of the subject. The logical approach, coherent and adequate coverage, simple style and lucid language should meet the requirements of students of science, engineering and other professional courses of Indian universities.

We are grateful to our students and colleagues for their constructive suggestions which have helped us in improving the present edition. We would welcome comments and suggestions for further improvement of the book.

AUTHORS

Preface to the First Edition

This book is intended for the degree students of various Indian universities. Due to the introduction of ten-plus-two system of education at the school level, the syllabi of our Universities have undergone drastic changes. A greater emphasis has now been made on theoretical and conceptual approach and the application of underlying basic concepts and principles.

As teachers of physical chemistry for over a decade, the authors have observed that the performance of students has been far from satisfactory in physical chemistry. The main reason for such poor performance appears to be mainly due to the wrong approach to the subject by the students. In spite of the fact that sufficiently large number of books are available on the subject, the idea behind writing this book is to provide the students with the latest trends and developments in various fields of physical chemistry in a simpler manner.

Thus, the book will meet the basic requirements of the students. The subject matter has been presented in a sound, logical and lucid manner. There are 25 chapters in all. In each of them the fundamental principles have been illustrated with the help of suitable examples, diagrams and description of experimental techniques. The mathematical deductions have been given in sufficient detail in a simple manner.

Physical chemistry is incomplete if greater importance is not given to the problems which are the aids to the understanding of the concepts and fundamentals of physical chemistry. With this objective, a number of problems of general and objective type have been given at the end of each chapter.

A major step in the book has been the introduction of SI (International System of Units) units. However, other non-SI units have been retained wherever their necessities have been felt.

Thus, we believe that the book will enable the students to grasp the subject rather easily and more clearly. It will also help students to gain confidence in the subject.

We wish to acknowledge our greatest indebtedness to our teacher, late Prof. R.P. Mitra, who inculcated in us the spirit of scientific inquiry. We also express our thanks to all our colleagues for comments and valuable suggestions towards the improvement of the book. The authors duly acknowledge the subsidy for the book from the National Book Trust of India.

We would gratefully welcome suggestions for the improvement of the book. All possible care has been taken to avoid any printing error, still we would be grateful if the omissions, errors and misprints detected in the book are brought to the notice of the authors.

A.S. NEGI
S.C. ANAND

Contents

Chapter 13 Electrolytic Conduction   504

Chapter 14 Ionic Equilibria   553

Introduction

1.1 PHYSICAL CHEMISTRY AND ITS SIGNIFICANCE

Rapid development of the study of external universe lead to the separation of chemistry as a special branch of natural science. Chemistry deals essentially with the composition and behaviour of natural world. It may be regarded as a molecular science involving an integrated study of the preparation, properties, structure and reactions of elements and their compounds. It is closely related to other physical and natural sciences.

Chemical changes are always associated with a number of diversified physical changes like heat transfer, absorption or emission of electromagnetic radiations, electrical and surface phenomena. The correlation between physical and chemical processes and systematization of the theories underlying the behaviour of matter in terms of molecular structure constitute the subject matter of physical chemistry. Although chemists have been giving due attention to these problems from the beginning of nineteenth century, it was only in the last half of the century that such studies became formalized into physical chemistry. Among the important investigations and generalizations which laid the foundation of physical chemistry, mention may be made of the kinetic molecular theory of gases, studies of dilute solutions, laws of electrolysis and the mechanism of conduction of electricity in solutions of electrolytes, laws of thermodynamics, principle of chemical equilibrium, dynamics of chemical reactions, discovery of electron, x-rays, radioactivity, interaction of matter with radiations, laws of quantum mechanics and statistical mechanics, etc. These and a number of other investigations provided a great impetus to the study of physical chemistry. Physical chemistry lies between physics and chemistry and uses the theoretical principles and experimental techniques of both the sciences to investigate the chemical transformations and physical changes accompanying them. The main concern of physical chemists is the problem of chemical equilibrium, the extent and rate of chemical reactions. The former is the problem of thermodynamics while the latter is the problem of chemical kinetics. Both these problems are intimately connected with the interactions between molecules, their structures and the strength of bonds between atoms in the molecules. Structures of atoms and molecules and a study of their properties is an important aspect of physical chemistry. Experimental techniques like x-ray analysis, electron diffraction, spectroscopy, mass spectroscopy and magnetic methods lead to an insight into the problem of structure elucidation of many complex and complicated systems. On the basis of structure and properties of molecules of a combining system, physical chemists can predict how the reactions can proceed with time.

Many industrial processes that have been developed are the results of physico-chemical investigations of the underlying processes. Physico-chemical investigations are increasingly employed by organic, inorganic and analytical chemists in solving many complicated and complex problems confronting them. Physico-chemical principles have played significant roles in applied fields like agriculture, engineering, metallurgy, ore mining, medicines, petroleum industries etc., and have given man control over nature to alleviate human sufferings and enhance the comforts of modern living.

1.2 INTERNATIONAL SYSTEM OF UNITS (SI)

Units form an integral part of any measurement. The numerical values of different properties of substances obtained as a result of experimental investigation can be expressed in different units. Chemists have traditionally used the metric system in all the measurements. It is simple and scientific. In this system all larger and smaller version of each basic unit could be obtained by multiplying or dividing the unit by 10. It is a decimal system or a base-10 system. In October 1960, the General Conference on Weights and Measures made an extensive revision of the metric system and adopted a new system of units called "*Le System International d'Units* (International System of Units)" to report scientific facts. It is based on seven basic units as given in Table 1.1.

Table 1.1 The Seven Basic SI Units

Physical quantity	Name of SI unit	Symbol for SI unit
Length	metre	m
Mass	kilogram	kg
Time	second	s
Temperature	kelvin	K
Amount of substance	mole	mol
Electric current	ampere	A
Luminous intensity	candela	cd

There are certain conventions regarding the use of SI units. Periods are not used with any symbol. Numbers are organised in groups of three but commas are not used to separate these groups and only spaces are used. For example, a figure like 7, 813.342, 83 is written as 7 813.342 83. Exponents ( )^2 and ( )^3 are used with symbols instead of square and cube. The symbols for all units are written identical in both singular and plural. Thus 100 metres is written as 100 m.

All other quantities may be expressed in these units or in terms of derived units obtained algebraically by multiplication or division. For example, the SI units for area and volume are m^2 and m^3 respectively. The unit of force, the newton (N), is the force imparting an acceleration of 1 ms^{-2} to a mass of one kilogram and is equal to 10^5 dynes. The principal derived units used in physical chemistry are listed in Table 1.2.

Though the SI units are slowly replacing the older metric (CGS) units, however, one should be familiar with both the old and the new systems of units. In this text we have largely emphasised on the use of SI units but in a number of cases the common CGS units have been retained. Decimal multiples and fractions of these units are designated by means of prefixes as shown in Table 1.3.

Table 1.2 Some Principal Derived SI Units

Quantity	Unit	Symbol	Definitions
Force	newton	N	$kg\ ms^{-2}$
Work, energy, quantity of heat	joule	J	Nm
Pressure	pascal	Pa	Nm^{-2}
Electric charge	coulomb	C	As
Power	watt	W	$J\ s^{-1}$
Magnetic flux density	tesla	T	$kg\ s^{-2}\ A^{-1}\ (= V\ m^{-2}\ s)$
Frequency	hertz	Hz	s^{-1} (cycle per second)
Electrical potential difference	volt	V	$kg\ m^2\ s^{-3}\ A^{-1}\ (= JA^{-1}\ s^{-1} = JC^{-1})$

Table 1.3 Prefixes that Modify the Size of Metric System of Units

Name	Symbol	Factor	Name	Symbol	Factor
atto	a	10^{-18}	deci	d	10^{-1}
femto	f	10^{-15}	kilo	k	10^{3}
pico	p	10^{-12}	mega	M	10^{6}
nano	n	10^{-9}	giga	G	10^{9}
micro	μ	10^{-6}	tera	T	10^{12}
milli	m	10^{-3}	peta	P	10^{15}
centi	c	10^{-2}	exa	E	10^{18}

Definition of Basic SI Units

The metre: It is the SI unit of length and is defined as 1650 763.73 wavelengths of orange red radiation in vacuum of krypton 86 corresponding to the unperturbed transition between the $2p_{10}$ and $5d_5$ levels. Prior to 1960 the metre was simply the distance between two scratches on a bar of platinum iridium alloy stored at Sevres, France. The advantage of the new reference is that the wavelength of orange red light of krypton is not affected by pressure, temperature and humidity.

The kilogram: It is the unit of mass and is equal to the mass of the International Prototype of the Kilogram, a block of platinum iridium alloy stored at the International Chamber of Weights and Measures.

Mass should be differentiated from weight. The mass of an object is defined as the amount of material contained in it as compared from a reference standard mass while weight is the gravitational force it exerts. In spite of the difference, mass and weight are used almost interchangeably.

The second: It is equal to the duration of 9 192 631 770 cycles of the radiation associated with a specific transition of caesium 133 atoms.

The kelvin: It is the fraction of $\dfrac{1}{273.16}$ (exactly) of the thermodynamic temperature of the triple point of water. The thirteenth General Conference on Weights and Measures in 1967 recommended that for the kelvin, symbol K be used for the thermodynamic temperature and the symbols °K or degree be abandoned.

The candela: It is the unit of luminous intensity and is equal to the luminous intensity in the perpendicular direction of a surface $\dfrac{1}{600000}$ m² of a black body at the temperature of solidification of platinum (2046.2 K) under a pressure of 101 325 Nm⁻².

The ampere: It is that constant current which if maintained in two straight parallel conductors of infinite lengths and of negligible cross section and placed one metre apart in vacuum would produce between these conductors a force equal to 2×10^{-7} N per metre of length.

The mole: It is the amount of substance of a system which contains as many elementary entities as there are C atoms in 0.012 kg. The elementary entities may be atoms, molecules, electrons or any specified group of particles. Mole is an extremely useful concept for counting particles present and takes a very specified significance because numerous properties depend on the number of particles present in the sample.

Those are the Physical Chemistry

$P_1 V_1 = P_2 V_2$ (Temperature and mass of the gas constant)

CHAPTER

2

Gases

2.1 INTRODUCTION

In general, matter is known to exist in one of the three states, solid, liquid or gas. A solid may be defined as a body possessing definite volume and shape at a given temperature and pressure. Solids are orderly arrays of atoms, molecules or ions having definite geometry depending upon the arrangements of these atoms, molecules or ions in a solid. Solids are relatively rigid. The constituents are held close together by strong attractive forces. A liquid, on the other hand, has a definite volume, but no definite shape. Molecules constituting a liquid are held by molecular forces which are not so strong as in solids. A gas has neither shape nor volume and the molecular forces of attraction are very much weaker. Gaseous state is the simplest state of matter and the laws and theories of gaseous behaviour are more uniform and better understood. In this chapter, we shall discuss some of the properties associated with the gaseous state.

Gases are conveniently classified into two types, namely, (a) ideal gases, and (b) nonideal or real gases. An ideal gas is one that obeys certain laws which will be dealt with shortly, while a real gas is one that obeys these laws at low pressures and relatively high temperatures. In ideal gases, the volume occupied by the molecules themselves is negligible as compared with the total volume at all pressures and temperatures. The intermolecular attraction is almost absent under all conditions. In case of real gases, both these factors are appreciable and the magnitude of each depends on the temperature and pressure of the gas and the nature of the gas.

2.2 IDEAL GAS BEHAVIOUR

(i) **Boyle's Law:** As early as 1660, Robert Boyle performed a series of experiments in which he determined the effect of pressure on the volume of a given amount of air at a constant temperature. He found that the volume of any definite quantity of a gas at constant temperature varied inversely to the pressure of the gas. Mathematically,

$$V \propto \frac{1}{P} \text{ (Temperature and mass of the gas constant)}$$

or $\hspace{3cm} PV = \text{constant} \hspace{4cm}$ ...(2.1)

where V is the volume and P the pressure of the gas. Thus if V_1 is the volume occupied by a given quantity of the gas at pressure P_1 and V_2 is its volume when the pressure changes to P_2, then at constant temperature it follows that

$$P_1V_1 = P_2V_2 \text{ (Temperature and mass of the gas constant)}$$

or

$$\frac{P_1}{P_2} = \frac{V_2}{V_1}$$

When the pressure of the gas is plotted against the volume in accordance with Eq. (2.1), we obtain curves (hyperbola) such as shown in Fig. 2.1. These curves are known as isotherms. The upper curve corresponds to the higher temperature.

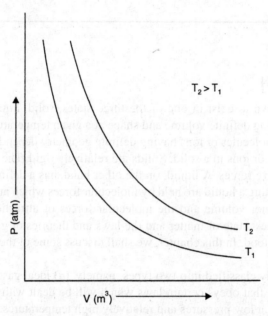

Fig. 2.1 *P–V* plots for a given amount of gas at two temperatures

(*ii*) **Charles' Law:** Charles in 1787 studied the variations in volume of a gas with temperature at constant pressure and observed that the volume of a certain mass of the gas increases or decreases by 1/273.16 of its value at 0°C. If V_0 is the volume of a gas at 0°C and V_t its volume at t°C, then mathematically,

$$V_t = V_0 + \frac{t}{273.16}V_0$$

$$= V_0\left(1 + \frac{t}{273.16}\right)$$

$$= V_0\left(\frac{273.16 + t}{273.16}\right) \qquad \qquad ...(2.2)$$

We may define now a new temperature scale such that any temperature 't' on this scale will be given by $T = 273.16 + t$, and 0°C by $T_0 = 273.16$. Then Eq. (2.2) becomes

$$V_t = V_0 \frac{T}{T_0}$$

or

$$\frac{V_t}{V_0} = \frac{T}{T_0}$$

or generally,

$$\frac{V_2}{V_1} = \frac{T_2}{T_1} \qquad \qquad ...(2.3)$$

This new temperature scale is known as the Absolute or Kelvin scale of temperature and is of fundamental importance in all sciences. In terms of this scale, Eq. (2.3) predicts that the volume of a definite quantity of a gas at constant pressure is directly proportional to the absolute temperature. Stated mathematically,

$$V \propto T$$

or

$$\frac{V}{T} = \text{constant} \qquad \qquad ...(2.4)$$

According to Eq. (2.4) the volume of a gas should be a linear function of absolute temperature at constant pressure. Such a plot of V versus T at two pressures P_1 and P_2 $(P_2 > P_1)$ is shown in Fig. 2.2. Each constant pressure line is called an isobar. For every isobar the slope is greater, lower the pressure.

Equation (2.4) suggests that if we wish to cool a gas to 0 K (−273.16°C), its volume should become zero. However, no such phenomenon is ever encountered, for usually long before 0 K is approached the gas first liquefies and then solidifies.

If the volume of a gas is maintained constant and its temperature is raised the pressure will increase. The increase in pressure per degree rise in temperature relative to its pressure P_0 at 0°C is again found to be $(1/273.16) P_0$. Hence the pressure P_t of the gas at temperature t is given as

$$P_t = P_0 \left(1 + t/273.16\right)$$

$$= P_0 \left(\frac{273.16 + t}{273.16}\right) = \frac{P_0 T}{T_0}$$

or

$$\frac{P_t}{P_0} = \frac{T}{T_0} \qquad \qquad ...(2.5)$$

It is clear from this equation that P is directly proportional to the absolute temperature at constant volume of the gas. One can therefore write

$$P \propto T$$

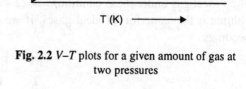

Fig. 2.2 V–T plots for a given amount of gas at two pressures

or
$$\frac{P}{T} = \text{constant} \qquad \qquad ...(2.6)$$

A plot of pressure against temperature for a given amount of gas at two volumes V_1 and V_2 ($V_1 > V_2$) is shown in Fig. 2.3.

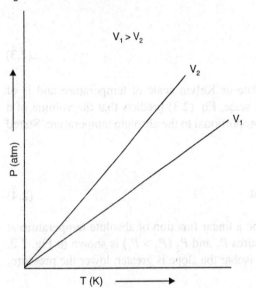

Fig. 2.3 *P–T* plots for a given amount of the gas at two volumes

From Eq. (2.6), it is apparent that at $T = 0$ K the pressure of a gas should be equal to zero. In actual practice this condition can never be achieved as all gases will liquefy or solidify before the absolute zero is attained.

(*iii*) **Avogadro's Law:** Avogadro in 1811 suggested that "equal volumes of different gases at the same temperature and pressure contain equal number of molecules." It will be recalled here that 1 mole of any substance contains the same number of molecules and this number is known as the Avogadro constant. It is represented by N_A and has a value 6.023×10^{23}. Hence, we can write

$$V \propto n \text{ (at constant temperature and pressure) } ...(2.7)$$

where n is the number of moles of the gas.

(*iv*) **Equation of State of an Ideal Gas:** Boyle's law, Charles' law and Avogadro's law can be combined to give a general relation between the volume, pressure, temperature and the number of moles of a gas.

Equation (2.1) describes the variation of P with V at constant T and Eq. (2.4) represents the variation of V with T at constant P, *i.e.*,

$$PV = \text{constant } (T \text{ constant})$$

$$\frac{V}{T} = \text{constant } (P \text{ constant})$$

On combining these equations, we get

$$\frac{PV}{T} = \text{constant} \qquad \qquad ...(2.8)$$

The combined Eq. (2.8) relating the variables P, V and T of an ideal gas is known as the equation of state. It is clear from Eq. (2.8) that the product PV divided by T is always constant for all specified states of the gas. Hence, if we know these values for any one state the constant can be computed. In the standard state (STP), the pressure is 1 atm and temperature 273.16 K. The volume occupied by a mole of an ideal gas under these conditions is 22 414 cm^3 (22.414 litres). According to Avogadro's law this volume is the same for all ideal gases. If we consider n moles of an ideal gas at STP, then Eq. (2.8) becomes

$$\frac{PV}{T} = \frac{P_0 V_0}{T_0} = nR$$

or
$$PV = n RT \qquad \qquad ...(2.9)$$

where R is a universal constant known as the gas constant per mole. Equation (2.9) is known as the ideal gas equation and it connects directly the volume, temperature, pressure and the number of moles of a gas and permits all types of calculations as soon as the constant R is known.

Since $n = \dfrac{w}{M}$, where w is the mass of the gas and M is its molar mass, Eq. (2.9) allows us to calculate the molar mass of the gas from P–V measurements. Therefore, from Eq. (2.9) we have

$$M = \frac{w RT}{PV} \qquad \qquad ...(2.10)$$

For 1 mole of a gas ($n = 1$), Eq. (2.9) reduces to
$$PV = RT$$

Dimensions of R: From the general Eq. (2.9)

$$R = \frac{PV}{nT} \qquad \qquad ...(2.11)$$

$$= \frac{\text{Pressure} \times \text{Volume}}{\text{Mole} \times \text{Temperature}}$$

Since P is defined as force per unit area, hence

$$R = \frac{(\text{Force/Area})(\text{Volume})}{(\text{Mole})(\text{Temperature})}$$

But
$$\text{Area} = (\text{Length})^2$$
and
$$\text{Volume} = (\text{Length})^3$$

therefore,
$$R = \frac{\left(\dfrac{\text{Force}}{(\text{Length})^2} \right)(\text{Length})^3}{(\text{Mole})(\text{Temperature})}$$

$$= \frac{(\text{Force})(\text{Length})}{(\text{Mole})(\text{Temperature})}$$

But
$$\text{Force} \times \text{Length} = \text{Work}$$

hence
$$R = \frac{\text{Work}}{(\text{Mole})(\text{Temperature})}$$

The physical significance of R is work per degree per mol. It may be expressed in any set of units representing work or energy.

Numerical value of R: Numerical value of the gas constant can be obtained readily at 1 atm and 273.16 K. Since 1 mole of an ideal gas occupies a volume of 22.414 litres at STP, therefore

$$R = \frac{(1 \text{ atm})(22.414 \text{ L})}{(1 \text{ mol})(273.16 \text{ K})}$$

$$= 0.0821 \text{ L atm K}^{-1} \text{mol}^{-1}$$

If the volume is expressed in cubic centimetres instead of litres, the value is

$$R = 82.1 \text{ cc atm K}^{-1} \text{mol}^{-1}$$

When the pressure is expressed in dynes/cm^2 and volume in cubic centimetres, R can be expressed in units of erg K^{-1} mol^{-1}. A pressure of 1 atm is the pressure of a column of mercury 76 cm high and 1 square centimetre of cross section at 273.16 K. Since the density of mercury is 13.6 g/cm^3, the mass of the column is 76×13.6 g. The pressure in dynes/cm^2 will be its mass multiplied by the acceleration due to gravity, 981 cm/s^2. Inserting these values, we get pressure as

$$1 \text{ atm} = hdg$$

$$= (76 \text{ cm}) \ (13.6 \text{ g/cm}^3) \ (981 \text{ cm/s}^2)$$

$$= 1.0133 \times 10^6 \text{ dynes/cm}^2 \ \left(\text{where 1 dyne} = \frac{1 \text{ g cm}}{s^2} \right)$$

Volume of the gas can be expressed in cubic centimetre, e.g., 1 L = 1000 cm^3. Substituting these values of P and V in Eq. (2.11), we get

$$R = \frac{\left(1.0133 \times 10^6 \text{ dynes/cm}^2 \right) \left(22414 \text{ cm}^3 \right)}{(1 \text{ mol}) \ (273.16 \text{ K})}$$

$$= 8.314 \times 10^7 \text{ erg K}^{-1} \text{mol}^{-1} \qquad\qquad (\because \text{ dyne} \times \text{cm} = \text{erg})$$

$$= 8.314 \text{ joule K}^{-1} \text{mol}^{-1} \qquad\qquad \left(10^7 \text{ ergs} = 1 \text{ J} \right)$$

$$= 1.987 \text{ cal K}^{-1} \text{mol}^{-1} \qquad\qquad (1 \text{ cal} = 4.184 \text{ J})$$

In the SI units, pressure is expressed in pascal Pa, which is defined as the pressure produced by a force of 1 N on an area of 1 m^2. Hence, the pressure corresponding to 1 atm in Pa is given by

$$P = (0.76 \text{ m}) \left(13.6 \times 10^3 \text{ kg m}^{-3} \right) \left(9.81 \text{ ms}^{-2} \right)$$

$$= 101\,325 \text{ Pa} = 101\,325 \text{ Nm}^{-2}$$

Thus the gas constant R is expressed as

$$R = \frac{PV}{nT} = \frac{\left(101\,325 \text{ Nm}^{-2} \right) \left(22.414 \times 10^{-3} \text{ m}^3 \right)}{(1 \text{ mol}) \ (273.16 \text{ K})}$$

$$= 8.314 \text{ Nm K}^{-1} \text{mol}^{-1}$$

$$= 8.314 \text{ J K}^{-1} \text{mol}^{-1}$$

Hence the **value of R in different units is**

$$R = 0.0821 \text{ L atm K}^{-1} \text{mol}^{-1}$$

$$= 8.314 \times 10^7 \text{ erg K}^{-1} \text{mol}^{-1}$$

$$= 8.314 \text{ J K}^{-1} \text{ mol}^{-1}$$

$$= 1.987 \text{ cal K}^{-1} \text{ mol}^{-1}$$

It should be clearly understood that although R may be expressed in different units, for pressure-volume calculations involving gases R must be taken in the same units as those used for pressure and volume.

(v) **Dalton's Law of Partial Pressures:** The law states, "if two or more than two gases which do not react chemically at constant temperature are enclosed in a vessel, the total pressure exerted by the gaseous mixture is the sum of the individual partial pressures which each gas will exert if present alone in that volume." If $p_1, p_2, p_3, ..., p_n$ are the partial pressures of the individual gases in a mixture then according to the Dalton's law of partial pressure the total pressure, P is given by

$$P = p_1 + p_2 + p_3 + ... + p_n \qquad ...(2.12)$$

The ideal gas equation can be applied to each component of the gas

$$p_1 = \frac{n_1 RT}{V} \qquad ...(2.13a)$$

$$p_2 = \frac{n_2 RT}{V} \qquad ...(2.13b)$$

$$p_3 = \frac{n_3 RT}{V} \qquad ...(2.13c)$$

or

$$P = n_1 \frac{RT}{V} + n_2 \frac{RT}{V} + n_3 \frac{RT}{V} + ...$$

$$= \frac{RT}{V}(n_1 + n_2 + n_3 + ...)$$

$$= n_t \frac{RT}{V} \qquad ...(2.14)$$

where $n_t = n_1 + n_2 + ... + n_n$ and is the total number of moles of the gas mixture in volume V.

The above equation shows that the expression $PV = n_t RT$ can be used for mixtures of gases as well as for pure gases.

Dividing Eq. (2.13a) to (2.13c) by Eq. (2.14), we get

$$p_1 = \frac{n_1}{n_t} P \qquad ...(2.15a)$$

$$p_2 = \frac{n_2}{n_t} P \qquad ...(2.15b)$$

and

$$p_3 = \frac{n_3}{n_t} P \qquad ..(2.15c)$$

Equations such as (2.15a) to (2.15c) are important as they relate the partial pressure of a gas to the total pressure of the gaseous mixture. Since the fractions $\frac{n_1}{n_t}, \frac{n_2}{n_t}$ and $\frac{n_3}{n_t}$ represent the moles of a particular constituent present in the mixture divided by the total number of moles of all the gases present; these quantities are called the mole fractions and are denoted by X_1, X_2, X_3, etc., respectively. A noteworthy property of mole fractions is that the sum of the mole fractions of all the components of the system is unity,

$$X_1 + X_2 + X_3 + \ldots = 1 \qquad \ldots(2.16)$$

(vi) **Amagat's Law of Partial Volume:** "The total volume of a nonreacting mixture of gases at constant temperature and pressure is equal to the sum of the individual partial volumes of the constituents." If $V_1, V_2, \ldots V_n$ are the partial volumes of components in the gaseous mixture, then the total volume V is given by

$$V = V_1 + V_2 + \ldots V_n = \sum_i V_i \qquad \ldots(2.17)$$

Problem 2.1: 1.0×10^{-2} kg of hydrogen and 6.4×10^{-2} kg of oxygen are contained in a 10×10^{-3} m^3 flask at 473 K. Calculate the total pressure of the mixture. If a spark ignites the mixture, what will be the final pressure?

Solution: The number of moles of hydrogen, $n_{H_2} = \dfrac{1.0 \times 10^{-2}}{2.0 \times 10^{-3}} = 5.0$

and the number of moles of oxygen, $n_{O_2} = \dfrac{6.4 \times 10^{-2}}{3.2 \times 10^{-2}} = 2.0$

$$P = p_{O_2} + p_{H_2}$$

$$= \left(n_{O_2} + n_{H_2}\right)\frac{RT}{V}$$

$$= \frac{(7.0 \text{ mol})\left(8.314 \text{ Nm K}^{-1} \text{ mol}^{-1}\right)(473 \text{ K})}{\left(10 \times 10^{-3} \text{ m}^3\right)}$$

∴   Total pressure of the mixture = **27.54×10^5 Nm^{-2}**

The reaction occurring on sparking is

$$2H_2(g) + O_2(g) \rightarrow 2H_2O(g)$$

Since 2 moles of oxygen and 5 moles of hydrogen were initially present, the net result of the reaction is that 4 moles of H$_2$O (g) are formed, leaving 1 mole of H$_2$ unreacted. The volume and temperature are constant, hence the total pressure after the reaction is

$$P = p_{H_2O} + p_{H_2}$$

$$= \frac{(5 \text{ mol})\left(8.314 \text{ Nm K}^{-1} \text{ mol}^{-1}\right)(473 \text{ K})}{\left(10 \times 10^{-3} \text{ m}^3\right)}$$

$$= 19.66 \times 10^5 \text{ Nm}^{-2}.$$

(*vii*) **Graham's Law of Diffusion:** Different gases diffuse at different rates depending on their densities. The law governing such diffusions was given by Graham in 1829, which states that "at constant temperature and pressure, the rates of diffusion of different gases are inversely proportional to the square roots of their densities." If the rates of diffusion of two gases are denoted by r_1 and r_2 and their densities by d_1 and d_2, then

$$\frac{r_1}{r_2} = \sqrt{\frac{d_2}{d_1}} \qquad \qquad ...(2.18)$$

Since the gas densities are directly proportional to their molar masses, we can also write

$$\frac{r_1}{r_2} = \sqrt{\frac{d_2}{d_1}} = \sqrt{\frac{M_2}{M_1}}$$

Problem 2.2: A teacher enters a classroom from the front door while a student from the back door. There are 13 equidistant rows of benches in the classroom. The teacher releases N_2O, the laughing gas from the first bench while the student releases the weeping gas, $C_6H_{11}OBr$ from the last bench. At which row will the student start laughing and weeping simultaneously?

Solution: The rates of diffusion of N_2O and $C_6H_{11}OBr$ are given by

$$\frac{r_{N_2O}}{r_{C_6H_{11}OBr}} = \sqrt{\frac{M_{C_6H_{11}OBr}}{M_{N_2O}}} = \sqrt{\frac{179}{44}} \simeq 2$$

Thus, N_2O diffuses at a rate twice as fast as $C_6H_{11}OBr$.

Let x be the row from the front where the students start laughing and weeping simultaneously, then

$$\frac{x}{13-x} = 2$$

or $x \simeq 9.$

Problem 2.3: When 2g of gaseous A is introduced into an initially evacuated flask kept at 298 K, the pressure is found to be 1 atmosphere. 3 g of gaseous substance B is then introduced to 2 g of A and the pressure is now found to be 1.5 atmosphere. Calculate the ratio of molar mass of A is to B, (M_A/M_B).

Solution: At constant temperature and volume, pressure exerted by the gas will be proportional to the number of moles of the gas, *i.e.*,

$$P \propto n \, (T, V)$$

Number of moles of $A = \dfrac{2}{M_A}$

and the number of moles of $B = \dfrac{3}{M_B}$

So total number of moles of A and $B = \dfrac{2}{M_A} + \dfrac{3}{M_B}$

Pressure due to A alone = 1 atm

and pressure due to A and B both = 1.5 atm

Since $P \propto n$, so we have

$$1 \text{ atm} \propto \dfrac{2}{M_A} \text{ and } 1.5 \text{ atm} \propto \left(\dfrac{2}{M_A} + \dfrac{3}{M_B} \right)$$

Hence

$$\dfrac{\dfrac{2}{M_A} + \dfrac{3}{M_B}}{\dfrac{2}{M_A}} = \dfrac{1.5}{1}$$

or,

$$\dfrac{M_A}{M_B} = \dfrac{1}{3}$$

Problem 2.4: A flask 'A' of unknown volume V containing oxygen gas at 5 atm was connected to a 2L flask 'B' containing helium at 3 atm. Analysis showed that the mole fraction of oxygen in the resulting mixture was 0.2. Calculate the volume of flask A.

Solution: We are given

Pressure of oxygen, $P_{O_2} = 5$ atm

Pressure of helium, $P_{He} = 3$ atm

Volume of flask B = 2 L

Mole fraction of oxygen $\left(X_{O_2} \right)$ in the mixture = 0.2

So, Number of moles of oxygen, $n_{O_2} = \dfrac{5V}{RT}$

and the number of moles of helium, $n_{He} = \dfrac{3 \times 2}{RT} = \dfrac{6}{RT}$

Hence the mole fraction of oxygen $X_{O_2} = 0.2 = \dfrac{5V/RT}{\dfrac{5V}{RT} + \dfrac{6}{RT}}$

Hence $V = 0.3$ L

2.3 THE KINETIC THEORY OF IDEAL GASES

All the laws of gas behaviour which have been discussed previously are only empirical and were derived through experiments. They are not based on any theory. Attempts had been made to elucidate the behaviour of gases from theoretical considerations. Kinetic theory, first proposed by Bernoulli in 1738 and considerably elaborated and extended by Boltzmann, Maxwell, Clausius, van der Waals and others provides a beautiful and important illustration of the relationship of theory to experiments. A number of statements, known as assumptions, are made regarding the behaviour of gas molecules. On the basis of these assumptions a model is suggested for the description of the behaviour of gases. The essential postulates are:

(i) A gas consists of large number of minute discrete particles called molecules. Molecules of a gas are identical in all respects but differ from the molecules of the other gases. The molecules are so small that their actual volume is negligible in comparison to the total volume occupied by the gas.

(ii) The molecules within a container are in a random or chaotic motion, during which they collide with each other and with the walls of the container.

(iii) Collisions between the molecules and between the molecules and the walls of the container are perfectly elastic, *i.e.*, there is no loss of kinetic energy.

(iv) The pressure which a gas exerts is due to continuous bombardment by its molecules on the walls of the container.

(v) At a particular instant molecules in a gas have different speeds and hence different kinetic energies. However, the average kinetic energy of the molecules is directly proportional to the absolute temperature.

(vi) There is no interaction between the gas molecules and their behaviour is completely independent of one another.

(vii) Gravity has no effect on the motion of the gas molecules.

The Kinetic Gas Equation: Let us consider a cube of volume V with side l being filled with a gas having n' as the total number of molecules. The mass of each molecule is m. To begin with, only one of the n' molecules will be considered. The speed c_1 of the molecule can be resolved into its three components c_{1x}, c_{1y} and c_{1z} along x, y and z axes which are perpendicular to the walls of the container as shown in Fig. 2.4. These components are related to the speed c_1 by the following relation:

$$c_1^2 = c_{1x}^2 + c_{1y}^2 + c_{1z}^2 \qquad ...(2.19)$$

Each of the components of motion in Eq. (2.19) may now be treated as a single molecule of mass m moving independently with each of the component velocities along the direction x, y or z. The motion along x direction will be considered now.

Along x direction the molecule will collide on face A of the container, which is perpendicular to the x-axis. The momentum of the molecule before collision with the face A is mc_{1x}. After collision the

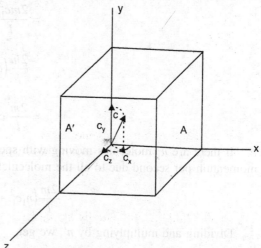

Fig. 2.4 Cubical container showing molecular collisions along x-axis

molecule bounces back and moves away from the wall with the velocity component $-c_{1x}$ and momentum $-mc_{1x}$.

The change in momentum per molecule per collision on face A along x direction is $mc_{1x} - (-mc_{1x})$ $= 2\,mc_{1x}$. Before the molecule can strike the same face again, it must travel to the opposite face A', collide with it, rebound and return. To do this, it must travel a distance of 2 l, where l is the length of the cube. Hence, the number of collisions per second per molecule on face A is $\dfrac{c_{1x}}{2l}$.

The rate of change of momentum per molecule, *i.e.*, the change of momentum per second is

$$= \left(2mc_{1x}\right)\left(\frac{c_{1x}}{2l}\right)$$

$$= \frac{mc_{1x}^2}{l}. \qquad \qquad ...(2.20)$$

The same change in momentum will also be experienced by the same molecule at the opposite face A'. Therefore, the total change in momentum per molecule per second in the x direction is twice the quantity in Eq. (2.20), or

change in momentum per molecule per second along x direction $= \dfrac{2mc_{1x}^2}{l}$

Similarly the total change in momentum per molecule per second due to the impact of the single molecule along the y and z axes will be $\dfrac{2mc_{1y}^2}{l}$ and $\dfrac{2mc_{1z}^2}{l}$ respectively.

Hence the total change in momentum per molecule per second on all the six faces of the cube will be

$$= \frac{2mc_{1x}^2}{l} + \frac{2mc_{1y}^2}{l} + \frac{2mc_{1z}^2}{l}$$

$$= \frac{2m}{l}\left(c_{1x}^2 + c_{1y}^2 + c_{1z}^2\right)$$

$$= \frac{2m}{l}c_1^2 \qquad \left(\because \quad c_1^2 = c_{1x}^2 + c_{1y}^2 + c_{1z}^2\right) \qquad ...(2.21)$$

If there are n_1 molecules moving with speed c_1, n_2 with speed c_2 and so on, then the change in momentum per second due to all the molecules in the container is given by

$$\frac{2m}{l}\left(n_1 c_1^2 + n_2 c_2^2 + \ldots\ldots n_n\, c_n^2\right)$$

Dividing and multiplying by n', we get,

$$\frac{2mn'}{l} = \frac{\left(n_1 c_1^2 + n_2 c_2^2 + \ldots\ldots n_n\, c_n^2\right)}{n'}$$

$$= \frac{2mn'}{l}\bar{c}^2 \qquad \qquad ...(2.22)$$

where $\bar{c}^2$ is termed as the mean square speed of the gas molecules. Since the rate of change of momentum is the force acting on the walls of the container (Newton's second law of motion), therefore, the pressure (force per unit area) on the walls of the container is given by

$$P = \frac{f}{A} = \frac{2mn'\bar{c}^2}{lA}$$

where P is the pressure and A is the total area over which the force is acting. For a cube, $A = 6\,l^2$, and hence,

$$P = \frac{2mn'\bar{c}^2}{6l^3}$$

$$= \frac{mn'\bar{c}^2}{3V} \qquad \left(\because l^3 = V \right)$$

or

$$PV = \frac{1}{3}mn'\bar{c}^2 \qquad \qquad ...(2.23)$$

This equation is known as the kinetic gas equation. According to this equation, the product PV for any gas should be equal to one third of the mass of all the molecules (mn') multiplied by the square of the root mean square speed.

2.4 KINETIC ENERGY AND TEMPERATURE

The average translational kinetic energy $\bar{\varepsilon}_k$ of a molecule of a gas of mass m and moving with a speed $\bar{c}$ is given by

$$\bar{\varepsilon}_k = \frac{1}{2}m\bar{c}^2$$

Equation (2.23) can be rewritten as

$$PV = \frac{2}{3}n'\left(\frac{1}{2}m\bar{c}^2 \right)$$

$$= \frac{2}{3}n'\bar{\varepsilon}_k$$

$$= \frac{2}{3}E_k \qquad \qquad ...(2.24)$$

where E_k is the total kinetic energy of n' molecules of the gas.

At this stage it is necessary to recall the empirical result for one mole of the gas,

$$PV = RT$$

and from Eq. (2.24), the kinetic energy per mol ($E_{k,\,m}$) is given as

$$PV = RT = \frac{2}{3} E_{k,m}$$

or,

$$E_{k,\,m} = \frac{3}{2} RT \qquad \qquad ...(2.25)$$

For n moles of the gas the total translational kinetic energy of the molecules is

$$E_k = \frac{3}{2} nRT = \frac{3}{2} PV$$

or

$$PV = \frac{2}{3} E_k \qquad \qquad ...(2.26)$$

Thus the kinetic energy of an ideal gas is a function of its absolute temperature [$E_k = f(T)$] and is independent of its volume or pressure and molar mass or type of molecules.

The average kinetic energy per molecule follows from Eq. (2.25) on division by Avogadro's constant gives

$$\frac{E_{k,\,m}}{N_A} = \frac{3}{2} \cdot \frac{RT}{N_A}$$

$$\bar{\varepsilon}_k = \frac{3}{2} kT \qquad \qquad ...(2.27)$$

where $k = R/N_A$ is called the Boltzmann constant and its value is given by

$$k = \frac{R}{N_A} = \frac{8.314 \times 10^7 \text{ erg K}^{-1}\text{mol}^{-1}}{6.023 \times 10^{23} \text{ mol}^{-1}}$$

$$= 1.381 \times 10^{-16} \text{ erg K}^{-1}$$

$$= 1.381 \times 10^{-23} \text{ JK}^{-1}$$

$$= 3.30 \times 10^{-24} \text{ cal K}^{-1}$$

The average translational kinetic energy of a gas molecule at 298 K is

$$\bar{\varepsilon}_k = \frac{3}{2}\left(1.381 \times 10^{-23} \text{ JK}^{-1}\right)(298 \text{ K})$$

$$= 6.17 \times 10^{-21} \text{ J}$$

It is worthwhile to consider a related and more readily visualised molecular property, the speed with which molecules travel. Since the translational kinetic energy

$$E_k \propto \bar{c}^2$$

it follows that

$$\bar{c}^2 \propto T$$

or

$$c_{rms} = \sqrt{\bar{c}^2} \propto \sqrt{T}$$

where c_{rms} is the root mean square speed and is proportional to the square root of the absolute temperature. To calculate the root mean square speed (c_{rms}) of gas molecules, kinetic gas Eq. (2.23) may be used.

$$PV = \frac{1}{3}mn'\bar{c}^2 = nRT$$

Since

$$n' = nN_A,$$

hence

$$PV = \frac{1}{3}nN_A m\bar{c}^2 = nRT$$

$$= \frac{nM\bar{c}^2}{3} = nRT$$

where $M = mN_A$ is the molar mass of the gas.

From the above equation, we get

$$c_{rms} = \sqrt{\bar{c}^2} = \sqrt{\frac{3RT}{M}} \qquad \text{...(2.28)}$$

Since $RT = PV/n$ and $nM/V = d$, the density of the gas at temperature T and pressure P, Eq. (2.28) may be written as

$$c_{rms} = \sqrt{\bar{c}^2} = \sqrt{\frac{3P}{d}} \qquad \text{...(2.29)}$$

By either of these equations the root mean square speed may be calculated from directly measurable quantities. It is necessary to note that this term implies that the magnitude of each of the molecular speeds is squared then the average value of the squared term is taken and finally the square root of this average is determined. This procedure leads to a quantity which is different from the simple average speed, as we shall see later, by about 10 per cent.

Problem 2.5: Calculate the root mean square speed of hydrogen molecules at 273 K.

Solution:

Since

$$c_{rms} = \sqrt{\frac{3RT}{M}}$$

and

$$R = 8.314 \times 10^7 \text{ erg K}^{-1} \text{ mol}^{-1}$$

$$= 8.314 \text{ kg m}^2 \text{ s}^{-2} \text{ K}^{-1} \text{ mol}^{-1} \left(1 \text{ erg} = 10^{-7} \text{ kg m}^2 \text{ s}^{-2}\right)$$

$$T = 273 \text{ K}$$

$$M = 2 \text{ g mol}^{-1} = 0.002 \text{ kg mol}^{-1}.$$

Putting these values in the above equation, we get

$$c_{rms} = \sqrt{\frac{3(8.314 \text{ kg m}^2 \text{ s}^{-2} \text{ K}^{-1} \text{ mol}^{-1})(273 \text{ K})}{(0.002 \text{ kg mol}^{-1})}}$$

$$= 1840 \text{ ms}^{-1}$$

Problem 2.6: Calculate the root mean square speed of oxygen molecules having density of 1.429 kg/m^3 at STP.

Solution:

$$c_{rms} = \sqrt{\frac{3P}{d}}$$

Here
$$P = 1 \text{ atm} = 1.013 \times 10^5 \text{ Jm}^{-3} = 1.013 \times 10^5 \text{ kg m}^{-1} \text{ s}^{-2}$$

$$d = 1.429 \text{ kgm}^{-3}$$

$$c_{rms} = \sqrt{\frac{3(1.013 \times 10^5 \text{ kg m}^{-1} \text{ s}^{-2})}{1.429 \text{ kg m}^{-3}}}$$

$$= 461 \text{ ms}^{-1}$$

2.5 DEDUCTION OF GAS LAWS FROM THE KINETIC GAS EQUATION

All the empirical gas laws can be derived from the kinetic gas Eq. (2.23) as follows:

(i) **Boyle's Law:** From Eq. (2.26), we have

$$PV = \frac{2}{3} E_k$$

At constant temperature kinetic energy is constant and is unchanged by elastic collisions. Hence the above expression is equivalent to Boyle's law.

(ii) **Charles's Law:** At constant pressure, Eq. (2.26) reduces to

$$V = \frac{2}{3}\left(\frac{E_k}{P}\right)$$

Since $E_k = f(T)$, hence the above equation becomes
$$V = \text{constant } T$$

which is the Charles's law.

(iii) **Avogadro's Law:** For any two gases the kinetic gas Eq. (2.23) may be written as

$$P_1 V_1 = \frac{2}{3}\frac{1}{2} m_1 n_1' \bar{c}_1^2$$

and
$$P_2 V_2 = \frac{2}{3} \frac{1}{2} m_2 n_2' \bar{c}_2^2$$

When pressures and volumes of two gases are same, *i.e.*, $P_1 = P_2$ and $V_1 = V_2$, it follows

$$\frac{1}{2} m_1 n_1' \bar{c}_1^2 = \frac{1}{2} m_2 n_2' \bar{c}_2^2$$

If the gases are also at the same temperature, the average kinetic energies of these molecules will also be equal,

$$\frac{1}{2} m_1 \bar{c}_1^2 = \frac{1}{2} m_2 \bar{c}_2^2$$

Therefore, from the above equations, we get

$$n_1 = n_2$$

(*iv*) **Graham's Law of Diffusion:** From Eq. (2.29)

$$c_{\text{rms}} = \sqrt{\frac{3P}{d}}$$

The rate of diffusion of a gas (r) evidently depends upon the speed of its molecules

$$r \propto c_{\text{rms}}$$

$$r \propto \sqrt{\frac{3P}{d}}$$

or
$$r \propto \sqrt{\frac{1}{d}} \qquad \text{(at constant pressure)}$$

This is Graham's law of diffusion.

(*v*) **Dalton's Law of Partial Pressures:** For a mixture of ideal gases the kinetic energy of the mixture is equal to the sum of the individual kinetic energies

$$E_k = E_{k_1} + E_{k_2} + \ldots\ldots + E_{k_n}$$

From Eq. (2.26) we have

$$E_{k_1} = \frac{3}{2} p_1 V$$

$$E_{k_2} = \frac{3}{2} p_2 V, \text{ etc.}$$

where p_1, p_2, etc., are the partial pressures of gas 1, gas 2, etc. Adding the above equations, we obtain

$$E_k = \frac{3}{2} PV = \frac{3}{2} p_1 V + \frac{3}{2} p_2 V + \frac{3}{2} p_3 V + \ldots\ldots$$

or
$$P = p_1 + p_2 + p_3 + \ldots$$

This is the Dalton's law of partial pressures.

2.6 DISTRIBUTION OF MOLECULAR SPEEDS

In the derivation of the kinetic gas equation it was considered that all the molecules of a gas at a given temperature are moving with a constant root mean square speed. Actually, however, all the molecules do not have the same speed because they are continually colliding with each other and with the sides of the container. During collisions a transfer of momentum takes place between the molecules. As a result of this transfer of momentum, some of the molecules may move with increased speeds while the others may have low speeds or may even stop completely. It is further possible that the molecules with increased speeds may again collide with other molecules attaining even higher speeds. When a steady state is attained each molecule will experience a continuous change in speed, it is obvious that the individual speeds of the molecules are not known. One can only obtain a distribution of molecular speeds at a given temperature. Thus the collisions result in a redistribution of both energy and speeds. The speeds will vary from zero to very high values. Maxwell and Boltzmann utilising probability considerations have shown that the actual distribution of molecular speeds depends on the temperature and molar mass of the gas. The expression derived by Boltzmann and Maxwell is written as

$$\frac{dn_c}{n'} = 4\pi \left(\frac{m}{2\pi kT}\right)^{3/2} \exp\left(-mc^2/2kT\right) c^2 dc \qquad \qquad ...(2.30)$$

where $\dfrac{dn_c}{n'}$ is the fraction of the total number of molecules having speeds between c and $c + dc$, m is the mass of a gas molecule, T is the temperature and k, the Boltzmann constant.

Dividing Eq. (2.30) by dc, we get

$$p = \frac{1}{n'}\frac{dn_c}{dc} = 4\pi \left(\frac{m}{2\pi kT}\right)^{3/2} \exp\left(-mc^2/2kT\right) c^2 \qquad \qquad ...(2.31)$$

Since $k = R/N_A$ and $mN_A = M$, hence the above equation can be rewritten as

$$p = \frac{1}{n'}\frac{dn_c}{dc} = 4\pi \left(\frac{M}{2\pi RT}\right)^{3/2} e^{-MC^2/2RT} c^2 \qquad \qquad ...(2.31a)$$

The expression on the left hand side of this equation gives the fraction of molecules in the speed range c and $c + dc$ per unit interval of speed and is thus the probability, p, of finding molecules having the speeds between c and $c + dc$.

The distribution of molecular speeds is shown in Fig. 2.5 in which p is plotted against c for several temperatures T_1, T_2, T_3 such that $T_3 > T_2 > T_1$.

The plot is approximately parabolic near the origin. It can be seen from these curves that the fraction of the molecules which remain motionless or have zero speeds at any instant is very small. Further, the fraction of the molecules having speeds greater than zero goes on increasing with c, passes through a maximum and then falls more or less rapidly towards zero again for very high speeds. The fall in probability towards zero at higher speeds is because the exponential term decreases more rapidly than c^2 increases. It is, therefore, evident that molecules both with very low and very high speeds are highly improbable. The number of molecules within the range of c and $c + dc$ is determined from the area given by the product of the ordinate $\left(\dfrac{1}{n'}\dfrac{dn_c}{dc}\right)$ and the speed range dc and is equal to $\dfrac{dn_c}{n'}$ the fraction of the molecules within the said range. Hence the area under the whole curve gives the total number of molecules. Most of the molecules have speeds corresponding to the maximum of the curve at each temperature. This speed is known as the most probable speed (c_{mp}).

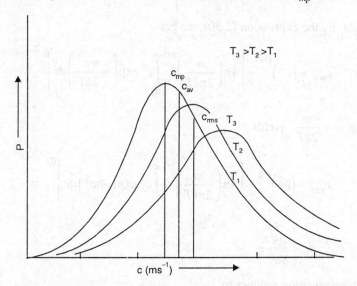

Fig. 2.5 Distribution of molecular speeds in a gas at different temperatures

One further notices that as the temperature is raised the general form of the distribution curve changes slightly as shown in Fig. 2.5. The maximum of the curve is shifted to the right corresponding to the increase of molecular speed with increasing temperature. The maximum shifts towards higher speed at higher temperature. The curve becomes broader near the maximum for higher temperature than for the lower temperature indicating that the number of molecules possessing higher speeds have increased. This effect is mainly due to the presence of the exponential term which increases rapidly with temperature.

From Eq. (2.30), the distribution of speed depends on the value of $\dfrac{m}{T}$. The distribution for a gas with molar mass $2M$ and at a temperature $2T$ will be the same as for a gas with molar mass M and at a temperature T. At a given temperature, heavier gases would have a narrower distribution of speed than the lighter ones.

2.7 CALCULATIONS OF MOLECULAR SPEEDS

Maxwell-Boltzmann distribution can be used to calculate the root mean square speed, the average speed and the most probable speed.

(a) **Root Mean Square Speed,** c_{rms}: To obtain the root mean square speed from the distribution expression, one multiplies the number of molecules that have a particular value of the quantity to be averaged by that value of the quantity. Then one sums or integrates over all possible values of this quantity and finally divides by the total number of molecules in the sample. Thus c_{rms} is given by

$$c_{rms} = \left(\overline{c^2}\right)^{1/2} = \left[\frac{1}{n'}\int_0^\infty c^2 \, dn_c\right]^{1/2}$$

Replacing dn_c by the expression (2.30), we get

$$c_{rms} = \left(\overline{c^2}\right)^{1/2} = \left[4\pi\left(\frac{m}{2\pi kT}\right)^{3/2}\int_0^\infty c^4 \exp\left(-\frac{mc^2}{2kT}\right)dc\right]^{1/2}$$

Substituting, $a = \dfrac{m}{2kT}$, yields

$$c_{rms} = \left(\overline{c^2}\right)^{1/2} = \left[4\pi\left(\frac{m}{2\pi kT}\right)^{3/2}\int_0^\infty c^4 \exp\left(-ac^2\right)dc\right]^{1/2}$$

Since $\displaystyle\int_0^\infty c^4 e^{-ac^2} \, dc = \frac{3\sqrt{\pi}}{8a^{5/2}}$

Thus the above equation reduces to

$$c_{rms} = \left(\overline{c^2}\right)^{1/2} = \left[4\pi\left(\frac{m}{2\pi kT}\right)^{3/2}\frac{3}{8}\frac{\sqrt{\pi}}{\left(\dfrac{m}{2kT}\right)^{5/2}}\right]^{1/2}$$

$$= \left[4\pi\left(\frac{m}{2\pi kT}\right)^{3/2}\frac{3}{8}\sqrt{\pi}\left(\frac{2kT}{m}\right)^{5/2}\right]^{1/2}$$

$$= \sqrt{\frac{3kT}{m}}$$

$$= 1.7\sqrt{\frac{RT}{M}} \qquad\qquad ...(2.32)$$

(b) **Average Speed** c_{av} : In a similar way, as mentioned above, one obtains the average speed as

$$c_{av} = \frac{1}{n'}\int_0^\infty c \, dn_c$$

Putting the value of dn_c from Eq. (2.30) yields

$$c_{av} = 4\pi\left(\frac{m}{2\pi kT}\right)^{3/2}\int_0^\infty c^3 \exp\left(-\frac{mc^2}{2kT}\right)dc$$

Putting $\qquad a = \dfrac{m}{2kT}$ gives

$$c_{av} = 4\pi \left(\frac{m}{2\pi kT}\right)^{3/2} \int_0^\infty c^3 \exp\left(-ac^2\right) dc$$

Since $\qquad \displaystyle\int_0^\infty c^3 \exp\left(-ac^2\right) dc = \dfrac{1}{2a^2}$, therefore

$$c_{av} = 4\pi \left(\frac{m}{2\pi kT}\right)^{3/2} \frac{4k^2 T^2}{2m^2}$$

or, $\qquad\qquad\qquad c_{av} = \sqrt{\dfrac{8kT}{\pi m}}$

$$= 1.6 \sqrt{\frac{RT}{M}} \qquad\qquad\qquad\dots(2.33)$$

(c) **Most Probable Speed, c_{mp}** : The most probable speed can be calculated by differentiating the function on the right hand side of Eq. (2.30) with respect to c and equating the result to zero, *i.e.*, applying the condition for maximum or minimum. Thus we get

$$2c \exp\left(-\frac{mc^2}{2kT}\right) + c^2 \exp\left(-\frac{mc^2}{2kT}\right)\left(-\frac{2mc}{2kT}\right) = 0$$

$$2c \exp\left(-\frac{mc^2}{2kT}\right) - \frac{mc^3}{kT}\exp\left(-\frac{mc^2}{2kT}\right) = 0$$

$$c \exp\left(-\frac{mc^2}{2kT}\right)\left[2 - \frac{mc^2}{kT}\right] = 0$$

Two possible solutions of this equation are for c to be 0 and ∞ corresponding to the minima as there are no molecules having speed equal to zero or infinity. The other solution is obtained by putting the quantity in bracket, *i.e.*, $2 - \dfrac{mc^2}{kT}$ equal to zero. This condition determines c_{mp}, *i.e.*,

$$2 - \frac{mc_{mp}^2}{kT} = 0$$

$$c_{mp} = \sqrt{\frac{2kT}{m}} = \sqrt{\frac{2RT}{M}}$$

$$= 1.4 \sqrt{\frac{RT}{M}} \qquad \qquad \text{...(2.34)}$$

These three speeds c_{rms}, c_{av} and c_{mp} are not very different from each other and from Eqs. (2.32), (2.33) and (2.34) one gets the ratio as

$$c_{rms} : c_{av} : c_{mp} = 1.7 : 1.6 : 1.4$$

$$\text{or} \qquad 1.0 : 0.92 : 0.82$$

One or other of these usually provides sufficient information on the molecular speeds in any given problem.

Distribution of Energy Amongst the Molecules—If ε represents the kinetic energy of a molecule of the gas having speed c, *i.e.*, $\varepsilon = \frac{1}{2} mc^2$, then

$$c = \sqrt{\frac{2\varepsilon}{m}}$$

Differentiation of the above equation gives

$$dc = \sqrt{\frac{2}{m}} \cdot \frac{1}{2} \varepsilon^{-1/2} d\varepsilon$$

$$= \frac{1}{\sqrt{2m}} \varepsilon^{-1/2} d\varepsilon$$

Substitution in Eq. (2.31), yields

$$\frac{1}{n'} \cdot \frac{dn_\varepsilon}{d\varepsilon} = 2\pi \left(\frac{1}{\pi kT} \right)^{3/2} e^{-\frac{\varepsilon}{kT}} \varepsilon^{\frac{1}{2}} \qquad \qquad \text{...(2.35)}$$

or

$$\frac{1}{n'} \cdot \frac{dn_\varepsilon}{d\varepsilon} = 2\pi \left(\frac{1}{\pi RT} \right)^{3/2} e^{-\frac{E}{RT}} E^{\frac{1}{2}} \qquad \qquad \text{...(2.35a)}$$

Equation (2.35) gives the distribution of energy amongst the molecules. A plot similar to that for the distribution of molecular speeds can be obtained when $\dfrac{1}{n'} \dfrac{dn_\varepsilon}{d\varepsilon}$ is plotted against ε. The fraction of molecules having energy greater than ε is given by

$$\frac{n_\varepsilon}{n'} = \int_\varepsilon^\infty \frac{dn_\varepsilon}{n'}$$

Putting the value of $\dfrac{dn_\varepsilon}{n'}$ from Eq. (2.35), we get

$$\frac{n_\varepsilon}{n'} = 2\pi \left(\frac{1}{\pi kT} \right)^{3/2} \int_\varepsilon^\infty \varepsilon^{\frac{1}{2}} e^{-\varepsilon/kT} d\varepsilon$$

Solving the integral under the assumption that $\varepsilon \gg kT$, we get

$$\frac{n_\varepsilon}{n'} = 2\left(\frac{\varepsilon}{\pi kT}\right)^{\frac{1}{2}} e^{-\frac{\varepsilon}{kT}} \qquad \qquad ...(2.36)$$

Thus energy is distributed amongst the molecules and the fraction of molecules having energy between (ε) and $\varepsilon + d\varepsilon$ varies exponentially with temperature.

Problem 2.7: Calculate the average, the root mean square and the most probable speeds for oxygen molecules at 298 K. At what temperature would hydrogen have the same values of these speeds?

Solution: The average speed is given by

$$c_{av} = \sqrt{\frac{8RT}{\pi M}}$$

$$= \sqrt{\frac{8\left(8.314 \text{ kgm}^2\text{s}^{-2}\text{ K}^{-1}\text{mol}^{-1}\right)(298 \text{ K})}{\pi\left(0.032 \text{ kg mol}^{-1}\right)}}$$

$$= 448 \text{ ms}^{-1}$$

The root mean square speed is given as

$$c_{rms} = \sqrt{\frac{3RT}{M}}$$

$$= \sqrt{\frac{3\left(8.314 \text{ kgm}^2\text{s}^{-2}\text{ K}^{-1}\text{mol}^{-1}\right)(298 \text{ K})}{\left(0.032 \text{ kg mol}^{-1}\right)}}$$

$$= 476 \text{ ms}^{-1}$$

The most probable speed is given by

$$c_{mp} = \sqrt{\frac{2RT}{M}}$$

$$= \sqrt{\frac{2\left(8.314 \text{ kgm}^2\text{s}^{-2}\text{K}^{-1}\text{mol}^{-1}\right)(298 \text{ K})}{\left(0.032 \text{ kg mol}^{-1}\right)}}$$

$$= 392 \text{ ms}^{-1}$$

To find the temperature, T_{H_2}, at which hydrogen gas has the same values of the speeds it is only necessary to equate the constant factor $\sqrt{RT/M}$ and solve for T_{H_2}.

$$\sqrt{\left(\frac{RT}{M}\right)_{O_2}} = \sqrt{\left(\frac{RT}{M}\right)_{H_2}}$$

$$T_{H_2} = \left(\frac{RT}{M}\right)_{O_2}\left(\frac{M_{H_2}}{R}\right)$$

$$= \frac{T_{O_2}}{M_{O_2}}M_{H_2}$$

$$= \frac{(298 \text{ K})\left(2 \times 10^{-3} \text{ kg mol}^{-1}\right)}{\left(32 \times 10^{-3} \text{ kg mol}^{-1}\right)} = 18.6 \text{ K}$$

2.8 THE BAROMETRIC DISTRIBUTION LAW

In the foregoing discussion we have ignored the influence of gravitational field on the motion of gas molecules. The approximation is correct in the absence of force fields. The effect of gravity on motion of lighter gases may be small but for heavier gases it may be quite pronounced. As a consequence, the pressure will be different at different heights in a vertical column. To derive an expression for the variation of pressure with height in a vertical column due to the influence of gravitational field, consider a vertical column of fluid (Fig. 2.6) with cross-sectional area A and density ρ maintained at a uniform temperature T. The pressure at the ground level, $h = 0$, is P_0 and the pressure at any height h in the column is determined by the total weight of the fluid in the column above that height. The pressure decrease $(-dP)$ between heights h and $h + dh$ is equal to the weight per unit area of a layer of fluid of thickness dh. The mass of the fluid between heights h and $h + dh$ is $\rho A\,dh$ and the weight of the fluid between these heights is $\rho Adhg$. Hence

$$-dP = \frac{\text{Weight}}{\text{area}} = \frac{(\rho Adh)g}{A} = \rho gdh \qquad \qquad ...(2.37)$$

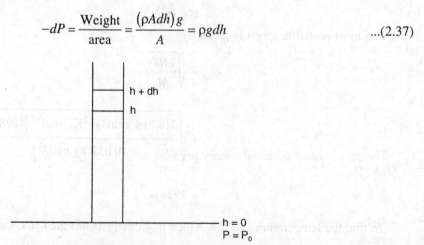

Fig. 2.6 Column of a fluid in a gravitational field

In the case of liquids, density is independent of pressure, hence the pressure (P) at any height is given by the integration of above equation.

$$\int_{P_0}^{P} -dP = \rho g \int_{0}^{h} dh$$

$$(P - P_0) = -\rho g h \qquad ...(2.38)$$

To apply Eq. (2.37) to a gas, it must be remembered that the density of the gas depends on the pressure. For an ideal gas, we have

$$PV = nRT = \frac{w}{M} RT$$

But density ρ is given by

$$\rho = \frac{w}{V}$$

or

$$\rho = \frac{PM}{RT}$$

With this Eq. (2.37) becomes

$$dP = -\frac{Mgdh}{RT} P$$

Separating variables, we get

$$\frac{dP}{P} = -\frac{Mgdh}{RT} \qquad ...(2.39)$$

which on integration gives

$$\int_{P_0}^{P} \frac{dP}{P} = -\int_{0}^{h} \frac{Mg}{RT} dh$$

$$\ln \frac{P}{P_0} = -\frac{Mgh}{RT} \qquad ...(2.40)$$

or

$$P = P_0 e^{-\frac{Mgh}{RT}} \qquad ...(2.41)$$

The gravitational potential energy per mole ($E_{p,\,m}$) at any point at a height h from the ground level is Mgh. Then

$$P = P_0 e^{-E_{p,\,m}/RT}$$

Since density of a gas is directly proportional to its pressure and the number of molecules per unit volume is proportional to pressure, Eq. (2.41) can be written in other forms as

$$\rho = \rho_0 e^{-\frac{Mgh}{RT}} \qquad \qquad ...(2.42)$$

or

$$n = n_0 e^{-\frac{Mgh}{RT}} \qquad \qquad ...(2.43)$$

where ρ and ρ_0 are the densities and n and n_0 are the number of molecules per unit volume at height h and at the ground level respectively. Equations (2.41) and (2.43) are expressions for the barometric distribution law or the gravitational distribution law as they describe the distribution of the gas in a vertical column under the influence of gravitational field.

Equation (2.43) is a form of the well known Boltzmann distribution law which describes the distribution of molecules among various energy levels with respect to some reference level. Boltzmann distribution law may be written as

$$n_i = n_0 e^{-\Delta E/RT}$$

where n_i is the number of molecules in the ith level whose energy differs from those in the reference level by an amount equal to ΔE.

Effect of Temperature on Distribution: From Eq. (2.41) it is clear that the value of P/P_0 at a given height is larger at higher temperature than at lower temperature. It means the variation of pressure with height will be less pronounced at higher temperature and if the temperature were infinite, the pressure would be the same everywhere in the column as shown in Fig. 2.7.

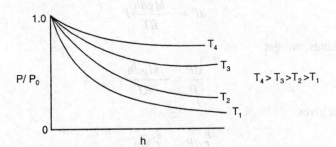

Fig. 2.7 Plot of P/P_0 versus height at different temperature

Effect of Height on Distribution: From Eq. (2.38) it is clear that for a given gas at a specified temperature, the relative decrease in pressure $(-dP/P)$ is directly proportional to dh. It follows that the relative decrease is the same at all positions in the column. Thus if the pressure decreases to one-half at a height 5 km from the ground level then for the same gas at a height $(5 + x)$ km it will be one half of the value of the pressure at a height x km. This aspect is shown in Fig. 2.8.

Effect of Molar Mass on Distribution: From Eq. (2.38) the relative decrease in pressure is directly proportional to the molar mass of the gas. It means at a given temperature, the relative decrease is larger for heavier gases and smaller for lighter gases. For example carbon dioxide would show a larger decrease in pressure than hydrogen at a given temperature.

For a mixture of ideal gases, each of the gases obeys the distribution law independently of the others, so that

$$P_i = P_i^0 \, e^{-\frac{M_i gh}{RT}} \qquad \qquad ...(2.44)$$

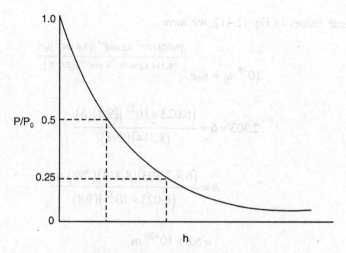

Fig. 2.8 Plot of P/P_0 versus height

where P_i and P_i^0 are the partial pressures at any height h and at the ground level. The partial pressures of lighter gases decrease less rapidly with height than those of heavier gases. This is why the proportion of lighter gases in air is more at greater heights.

Problem 2.8: Calculate the molar mass of a gas if the pressure of the gas is to fall to one-half of its value in a vertical distance of 1000 m at 300 K.

Solution: $P = P_0/2$, $h = 1000$ m, $g = 9.8$ ms^{-2}

Substituting these quantities in Eq. (2.41), we get

$$\frac{P_0}{2} = P_0 e^{-\dfrac{M\left(9.8\,ms^{-2}\right)(1000\ m)}{\left(8.314\ kg\ m^2\ s^{-2}\ K^{-1}\ mol^{-1}\right)(300\ K)}}$$

$$\frac{1}{2} = e^{-\dfrac{M(9.8)(1000)}{\left(8.314\ kg\ mol^{-1}\right)(300)}}$$

$$M = \frac{(2.303)(0.3010)(8.314)(300)}{(9.8)(1000)}\ kg\ mol^{-1}$$

$$= 0.1764\ kg\ mol^{-1}$$

Problem 2.9: Consider a hypothetical gas having the following characteristics: it obeys the ideal gas laws, the individual molecules weigh 0.1 kg, but occupy no volume, *i.e.*, they are point masses. (*a*) At 298 K compute the height at which the number of particles per unit volume falls to one-millionth of its ground level value. (*b*) Calculate the time taken by a molecule to cover a distance of 10^{-2} m.

Solution: (*a*) $n = 10^{-6}n_0$, $M = 0.1 \times 6.023 \times 10^{23}$ kg mol^{-1}

$$= 6.023 \times 10^{22}\ kg\ mol^{-1}$$

Substituting these values in Eq. (2.41), we have

$$10^{-6} n_0 = n_0 e^{-\frac{\left(6.023 \times 10^{22} \text{ kg mol}^{-1}\right)\left(9.8 \text{ ms}^{-2}\right)(h)}{\left(8.314 \text{ kg m}^2 s^{-2} \text{K mol}^{-1}\right)(298 \text{ K})}}$$

$$2.303 \times 6 = \frac{\left(6.023 \times 10^{22}\right)(9.8)(h)}{(8.314)(298)}$$

$$h = \frac{(6 \times 2.303)(8.314)(298) \text{ m}}{\left(6.023 \times 10^{22}\right)(9.8)}$$

$$= 5.8 \times 10^{-20} \text{ m}$$

(b) The average speed (c_{av}) of the gas molecules is obtained from the relation

$$c_{av} = \sqrt{\frac{8RT}{\pi M}}$$

$$= \sqrt{\frac{(8)\left(8.314 \text{ kg m}^2 \text{ s}^{-2} \text{ mol}^{-1}\right)(298 \text{ K})(7)}{(22)\left(6.023 \times 10^{22} \text{ kg mol}^{-1}\right)}}$$

$$= 3.236 \times 10^{-10} \text{ ms}^{-1}$$

Hence the time taken by the gas molecules to cover a distance of 10^{-2} m is

$$\frac{10^{-2}}{3.236 \times 10^{-10}} \text{s} = 3.1 \times 10^{7} \text{s}$$

$$= 1 \text{ year}$$

2.9 COLLISION PROPERTIES

In the derivation of kinetic gas equation we have not taken into account collisions between the molecules. However, molecules in a gas are constantly colliding with each other many times during the course of their movement. These collisions do not change the net momentum of the colliding molecules but involve a transfer of momentum and energy from one part to another in the gas. Transport properties like heat conduction, diffusion, viscosity and mean free path depend on the molecular collisions; it is therefore essential to introduce the concept of molecular size.

We shall derive an approximate relation for the frequency of intermolecular collisions. In the derivation, it will be assumed that molecules are rigid nonreacting spheres. When two identical molecules approach one another, there is certain distance beyond which they cannot come closer. *The distance of closest approach between the centres of molecules is known as the collision diameter* (Fig. 2.9). It is denoted by σ. Whenever the distance between the centres of two molecules is σ, a collision results.

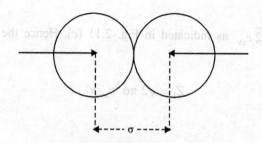

Fig. 2.9 Collision diameter of molecules.

Collision Frequency: It is the number of collisions per unit time per unit volume. To derive an expression for the collision frequency let us consider that all the molecules except one, say A, are at rest. Molecule A moves with an average speed of c_{av} ms^{-1} in the direction as indicated in Fig. 2.10. In one second molecule A will travel a distance of c_{av} m and will sweep out a cylindrical volume $\pi\sigma^2 c_{av}$ where $\pi\sigma^2$ is known as the collision cross section.

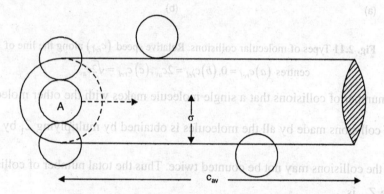

Fig. 2.10 Path swept out by a molecule of a gas in unit time.

In one second molecule A will collide with all those molecules that have their centres with the cylinder. If n' is the number of molecules per unit volume then the total number of molecules in the cylinder is $\pi\sigma^2 c_{av}\, n'$. Molecule A will collide with these molecules in one second. The number of collisions made by molecule A per second is the collision frequency of A and is given by

$$Z_1 = \pi\sigma^2 c_{av}\, n' \qquad\qquad ...(2.45)$$

In this derivation it has been assumed that only molecule A is moving and others are at rest. In fact all the molecules are moving with an average speed c_{av} and all types of molecular collisions ranging from glancing to head on collisions will occur. A more correct value of the number of collisions per second is obtained by considering the speed relative to the stationary molecules.

For this consider two molecules which have their velocity vectors oriented as shown in Fig. 2.11. The magnitude of relative speed depends on the angle between these velocity vectors. For molecules moving in the same direction with the same average speed c_{av}, the relative speed of approach is zero. [Fig. 2.11 (a)]. When the molecules approach head on, the relative speed of approach is $2c_{av}$ [Fig. 2.11 (b)]. On an average molecules approach at 90° to each other and the relative speed of approach is given by $\frac{1}{2}\sqrt{2}\,c_{av} + \frac{1}{2}\sqrt{2}\,c_{av} = \sqrt{2}\,c_{av}$ as indicated in Fig. 2.11 (c). Hence the number of collisions per second is

$$Z_1 = \sqrt{2}\,\pi\sigma^2 c_{av}\,n' \qquad\qquad ...(2.46)$$

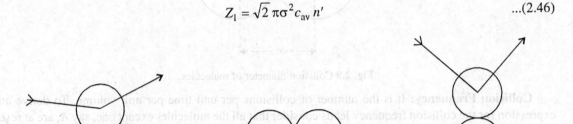

$$\qquad\qquad\qquad (a) \qquad\qquad\qquad\qquad\qquad\qquad (b) \qquad\qquad\qquad\qquad\qquad\qquad (c)$$

Fig. 2.11 Types of molecular collisions. Relative speed (c_{rel}) along the line of

centres $(a)\,c_{rel} = 0,\,(b)\,c_{rel} = 2c_{av},\,(c)\,c_{rel} = \sqrt{2}c_{av}.$

This is the number of collisions that a single molecule makes with the other molecules. Hence the total number of collisions made by all the molecules is obtained by multiplying Z_1 by $\frac{1}{2}n'$. The factor

$\frac{1}{2}$ ensures that the collisions may not be counted twice. Thus the total number of collisions per second per unit volume Z_{11} is

$$Z_{11} = \frac{1}{2}n'Z_1$$

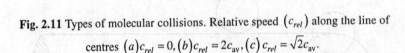

$$= \frac{1}{2}\sqrt{2}\,\pi\sigma^2 c_{av}\left(n'\right)^2 \qquad\qquad ...(2.47)$$

The number of collisions occurring per second per unit volume of the gas is of considerable importance in understanding the rate of chemical reactions. For a mixture of two gases A and B, the number of binary collisions Z_{12} per unit time per unit volume is given by

$$Z_{12} = n'_A\,n'_B\,\sigma_{AB}^2\left(\frac{8\pi kT\left(m_A + m_B\right)}{m_A\,m_B}\right)^{1/2} \qquad\qquad ...(2.48)$$

where n'_A and n'_B are the number of molecules per unit volume and m_A and m_B are the molecular masses of two gases A and B respectively and $\sigma_{AB} = \dfrac{\sigma_A + \sigma_B}{2}$ is the collision diameter.

Dependence of Z_1 and Z_{11} on Temperature and Pressure

From Eqs. (2.46) and (2.47), we have

$$Z_1 = \sqrt{2}\pi \ \sigma^2 \ c_{av} \ n'$$

or

$$Z_1 \propto c_{av} \ n'$$

and

$$Z_{11} = \frac{1}{\sqrt{2}} \pi \sigma^2 c_{av} \left(n'\right)^2$$

or

$$Z_{11} \propto c_{av} \left(n'\right)^2$$

The number of molecules per unit volume is given by (assuming ideal behaviour for the gas)

$$n' = \frac{nN_A}{V} = \frac{nN_A}{nRT} P = \frac{P}{kT}$$

or

$$n' \propto \frac{P}{T}$$

Also

$$c_{av} = \sqrt{\frac{8RT}{\pi m}}$$

or

$$c_{av} \propto \sqrt{T}$$

Hence,

$$Z_1 \propto \sqrt{T} \cdot \frac{P}{T}$$

$$\propto \frac{P}{\sqrt{T}}$$

and

$$Z_{11} \propto \sqrt{T} \cdot \left(\frac{P}{T}\right)^2$$

$$\propto \frac{P^2}{T^{3/2}}$$

Mean Free Path (λ): A molecule moves along a straight line with a constant speed before colliding with other molecules. The distance traversed by a molecule between two successive collisions is referred to as the free path. Free path varies from time to time. The average distance travelled by a molecule before colliding with other molecules is known as the mean free path λ. It depends on the molecular size and concentration (number of molecules per unit volume) of the gas molecules. Larger the molecular size more frequent would be the collisions and consequently shorter will be the mean free path. Also, more the number of molecules larger will be the number of collisions and hence shorter will be the mean free path.

Calculations of collision frequency can be used to derive an expression for the mean free path. If a molecule is moving with a speed c_{av} and collides with a frequency Z_1, the mean free path would be given by

$$\lambda = \frac{c_{av}}{Z_1} = \frac{c_{av}}{\sqrt{2}\,\pi\sigma^2 \bar{c}\, n'} = \frac{1}{\sqrt{2}\,\pi\sigma^2 n'} \qquad \text{...(2.49)}$$

Equation (2.49) shows how far a molecule on an average travels between collisions. λ is inversely proportional to the concentration of the gas molecules and molecular size.

Using the ideal gas equation $PV = nRT$, the number of molecules per unit volume n' is given as

$$n' = \frac{nN_A}{V} = \frac{nN_A P}{nRT} = \frac{P}{kT}$$

Substituting the value of n' in the Eq. (2.49), we get

$$\lambda = \frac{kT}{\sqrt{2}\,\pi\sigma^2 P} \qquad \text{...(2.50)}$$

Equation (2.50) gives the dependence of λ on temperature and pressure. Mean free path at any given temperature will be higher at lower pressures as molecules will be relatively far apart at these pressures and would collide less frequently.

Let us calculate the mean free path for a gas ($\sigma = 2 \times 10^{-10}$ m) at STP. The number of molecules in a mole of the gas is given by Avogadro's constant, 6.023×10^{23} and the number of molecules per unit volume at STP is given by

$$n' = \frac{6.023 \times 10^{23}}{22.414 \times 10^{-3}} = 2.7 \times 10^{25} \text{ molecules m}^{-3}$$

Hence the mean free path is

$$\lambda = \frac{1}{\sqrt{2}\,\pi\left(2 \times 10^{-10}\,\text{m}\right)^2 \left(2.7 \times 10^{25}\ \text{m}^{-3}\right)} = 1.32 \times 10^{-7}\,\text{m}$$

Thus under normal conditions the molecules in a gas travel only short distances of the order of 10^{-7} m between two successive collisions.

Both the mean free path and the collision numbers have been expressed by the equations that involve the molecular diameter σ. Since the molecular speeds and the number of molecules per unit volume of a gas can be determined, only molecular diameter needs to be known to calculate λ, Z_1 and Z_{11}. Many methods are available for the determination of the size of the molecules. Determination of coefficient of viscosity of gases provides a convenient method of calculating the value of collision diameter.

2.10 VISCOSITY OF GASES

This property is exhibited by both gases and liquids and is a measure of the frictional resistance that a fluid in motion offers to an applied shearing force. In gases, viscosity is due to the exchange of molecules from one layer to other. As a result of continuous exchange of molecules, there is a transfer of momentum of molecules from one layer to the other and consequently, their velocities. The exchange of molecules from the faster moving layer to the slower moving layer results in a decrease in the speed of the molecule in the faster layer and an increase in the speed of the molecules in the slower moving layer. The net result of this exchange of molecules is a tendency towards equalizing the flow rate of the different parts of the gas.

To define viscosity, let us consider a gas flowing in parallel planes along the x direction with a velocity v (Fig. 2.12). These layers are separated by a distance λ from each other. The layer adjacent to the x axis has a velocity $v \simeq 0$ and it increases with increasing distance along y axis. If the velocity gradient is given by $\dfrac{dv}{dy}$ along y-axis; then if the gradient is uniform the average velocity of flow at any distance λ above a layer AA' is given by $v + \lambda \dfrac{dv}{dy}$. Similarly the average velocity of flow at any distance λ below it is equal to $v - \lambda \dfrac{dv}{dy}$ as shown in the figure. The flow of gas can be understood in terms of a force required to move a layer of gas relative to another layer. The force F required to maintain a steady velocity difference dv between any two parallel layers is directly proportional to the area A of the layers and the velocity gradient, $\dfrac{dv}{dy}$. Consequently

$$F = -\eta A \frac{dv}{dy} \qquad \qquad ...(2.51)$$

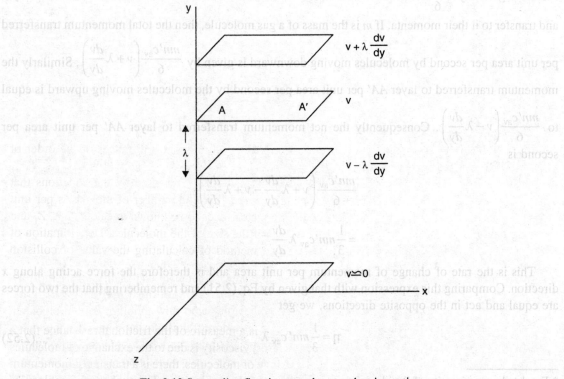

Fig. 2.12 Stream line flow in gases due to a shearing action

where η is the constant of proportionality and is called the coefficient of viscosity. The negative sign indicates that the frictional force is opposite to the direction of flow. The coefficient of viscosity may be defined as the force per unit area per unit velocity gradient between layers unit distance apart. The dimension of η is (mass) (length)$^{-1}$ (time)$^{-1}$. In CGS units, the viscosity coefficient of a fluid is expressed in poise (1 poise = 1 g cm^{-1} s^{-1}) or micropoise (1 micropoise = 10^{-6} poise). In SI system, it is expressed in pascal second (Pa s), where 1 Pa s = 1 kg m^{-1} s^{-1} = 10 poise*. Thus a fluid has a viscosity of 1 Pa s, if a force of 1 newton is required to move a plane of 1 m^2 at a velocity of 1 ms^{-1} with respect to a plane surface a metre away and parallel to it.

In order to derive an expression for the coefficient of viscosity, let us assume that the number of molecules of a gas per unit volume is n' and the average velocity of gas molecules is c_{av}. Since the motion of the gas molecules is completely random, it may be assumed that $\dfrac{n'}{3}$ molecules are moving along each axis. Of these $\dfrac{n'}{3}$ molecules, half $\left(\dfrac{n'}{6}\right)$ would be moving in one direction (say along y-axis) and $\dfrac{n'}{6}$ in the opposite direction ($-y$ axis). Referring to Fig. 2.12 and remembering that viscosity in gases arises due to transfer of momentum from one layer to another, we calculate the net momentum transferred per unit area per second to a layer (say AA') by the molecules from adjacent layers separated by a distance λ. The number of molecules moving upward (or downward) through unit area in one second is given by $\dfrac{n'c_{av}}{6}$. All those molecules which are at a distance λ from AA' will strike this layer and transfer to it their momenta. If m is the mass of a gas molecule, then the total momentum transferred per unit area per second by molecules moving downward is given by $\dfrac{mn'c_{av}}{6}\left(v+\lambda\dfrac{dv}{dy}\right)$. Similarly the momentum transferred to layer AA' per unit area per second by the molecules moving upward is equal to $\dfrac{mn'c_{av}}{6}\left(v-\lambda\dfrac{dv}{dy}\right)$. Consequently the net momentum transferred to layer AA' per unit area per second is

$$\frac{mn'c_{av}}{6}\left(v+\lambda\frac{dv}{dy}-v+\lambda\frac{dv}{dy}\right)$$

$$=\frac{1}{3}mn'c_{av}\,\lambda\frac{dv}{dy}$$

This is the rate of change of momentum per unit area and is therefore the force acting along x direction. Comparing this expression with that given by Eq. (2.51) and remembering that the two forces are equal and act in the opposite directions, we get

$$\eta=\frac{1}{3}mn'\,c_{av}\,\lambda \qquad\qquad\qquad ...(2.52)$$

---

* For details, see viscosity of liquids.

However, a more rigorous derivation is obtained by taking into account the distribution of molecular speeds. The resulting expression is

$$\eta = \frac{1}{2} m n' c_{av} \lambda \qquad ...(2.53)$$

Since λ is given by Eq. (2.49), therefore Eq. (2.53) reduces to

$$\eta = \frac{1}{2} m n' c_{av} \frac{1}{\sqrt{2}\, \pi \sigma^2 n'}$$

$$= \frac{c_{av}\, m}{2\sqrt{2}\, \pi \sigma^2} \qquad ...(2.54)$$

Equation (2.54) suggests that the viscosity of a gas is independent of its density or pressure. This result was predicted by Maxwell and its experimental verification was regarded as one of the triumphs of kinetic theory of gases. At lower pressures, fewer molecules jump from one layer to the other but because of larger mean free paths, each jump carries proportionately greater momentum. This important result allows the calculation of collision diameter of a gas molecule from the measurement of viscosity of the gas.

Substituting the value of c_{av} in Eq. (2.54), we get

$$\eta = m \sqrt{\frac{8kT}{\pi m}} \frac{1}{2\sqrt{2}\, \pi \sigma^2}$$

$$= \sqrt{\frac{RTM}{\pi}} \frac{1}{N \pi \sigma^2} \qquad ...(2.55)$$

It is clear from Eq. (2.55) that the viscosity of a gas is proportional to the square root of the absolute temperature. In actual practice, it is found that it increases more rapidly than implied by this relationship. The increase in η with temperature is due to the fact that the momentum is transported more rapidly through a given area and a greater force has to be applied to maintain the motion of the layer of the gas.

Table 2.1 shows the transport properties for some gases at 273 K and 1 atm.

Table 2.1 Transport Properties of Some Gases at 273 K and 1 Atm

Gas	Collision diameter, σ ($m \times 10^{10}$)	Mean free path, λ ($10^{10} \times m$)	Viscosity, η ($Pa\ s \times 10^5$)	Collision per second ($Z_1 \times 10^{-9}$)	Collision per second per m^3 ($Z_{11} \times 10^{-34}$)
He	2.18	18.00	1.86	6.6	8.1
H_2	2.73	11.23	0.84	14.2	17.4
O_2	3.57	6.47	1.92	6.0	7.3
N_2	3.74	6.00	1.67	7.1	8.8
CO_2	4.54	3.98	1.38	8.4	10.3

Problem 2.10: For nitrogen gas at 1 atm and 298 K, calculate (*a*) the number of collisions each nitrogen molecule encounters in one second, (*b*) the total number of collisions in a volume of 1 m³ in one second, and (*c*) the mean free path of a nitrogen molecule. The collision diameter of a nitrogen molecule is 3.74×10^{-10} m.

Solution: The number of molecules in 1 m³ at 298 K and 1 atm is given by

$$n' = \frac{N_A}{V} = \frac{N_A P}{RT}$$

$$= \frac{(1 \text{ atm})(6.023 \times 10^{23} \text{ molecules mol}^{-1})(10^3 \text{ L m}^{-3})}{(0.0821 \text{ atm L K}^{-1}\text{mol}^{-1})(298 \text{ K})}$$

$$= 2.462 \times 10^{25} \text{ molecules m}^{-3}$$

The average speed, c_{av} is given by

$$c_{av} = \sqrt{\frac{8RT}{\pi M}}$$

$$= \sqrt{\frac{8(8.314 \text{ kg m}^2\text{s}^{-2}\text{ K}^{-1}\text{mol}^{-1})(298 \text{ K})}{\pi(28 \times 10^{-3} \text{ kg mol}^{-1})}}$$

$$= 4.75 \times 10^2 \text{ ms}^{-1}$$

(*a*) The number of collisions per second is given as

$$Z_1 = \sqrt{2} \, \pi \sigma^2 \, c_{av} \, n'$$

$$= \sqrt{2}\pi(3.74 \times 10^{-10}\text{m})^2 (4.75 \times 10^2 \text{ ms}^{-1})(2.462 \times 10^{25} \text{ m}^{-3})$$

$$= 7.26 \times 10^9 \text{ s}^{-1}$$

(*b*) The total number of collisions per unit volume per second is given as

$$Z_{11} = \frac{1}{\sqrt{2}} \pi \sigma^2 \, c_{av} \, (n')^2$$

$$= \frac{1}{2} n' Z_1$$

$$= \frac{1}{2} (2.462 \times 10^{25}\text{ m}^{-3})(7.26 \times 10^9 \text{ s}^{-1})$$

$$= 8.93 \times 10^{34} \text{ m}^{-3} \text{ s}^{-1}$$

(*c*) The mean free path is given as

$$\lambda = \frac{1}{\sqrt{2}\,\pi\sigma^2 n'}$$

$$= \frac{1}{\sqrt{2}\,\pi\left(3.74 \times 10^{-10}\ \text{m}\right)^2\left(2.462 \times 10^{25}\ \text{m}^{-3}\right)}$$

$$= 6.54 \times 10^{-8}\ \text{m}$$

Problem 2.11: Calculate (*a*) the number of collisions per second per molecule (Z_1), (*b*) the total number of collisions per second per cubic metre (Z_{11}), and (*c*) the mean free path (λ) at 1 atm pressure for oxygen molecules and 298 K. Given the coefficient of viscosity of oxygen as 2.08×10^{-5} Pascal second.

Solution: The number of molecules in 1 m^3 at 298 K and 1 atm

$$n' = \frac{N_A}{V} = \frac{N_A P}{RT} = \frac{(1\ \text{atm})\left(6.023 \times 10^{23}\ \text{mol}^{-1}\right)\left(10^3\ \text{L}^3\ \text{m}^{-3}\right)}{\left(0.0821\ \text{L atm K}^{-1}\text{mol}^{-1}\right)(298\ \text{K})}$$

$$= 2.46 \times 10^{25}\ \text{m}^{-3}$$

The average speed c_{av} is given as

$$c_{av} = \sqrt{\frac{8RT}{\pi M}}$$

$$= \sqrt{\frac{8\left(8.314\ \text{kg m}^2\text{s}^{-2}\text{mol}^{-1}\right)(298\ \text{K})}{\pi\left(32 \times 10^{-3}\text{kg mol}^{-1}\right)}}$$

$$= 444\ \text{ms}^{-1}$$

The mass of an oxygen molecule is

$$m = \frac{\left(32 \times 10^{-3}\ \text{kg mol}^{-1}\right)}{\left(6.023 \times 10^{23}\ \text{mol}^{-1}\right)}$$

$$= 5.31 \times 10^{-26}\ \text{kg}$$

Since

$$\eta = \frac{c_{av}\,m}{2\sqrt{2}\,\pi\sigma^2}$$

or

$$\sigma = \sqrt{\frac{c_{av}\,m}{2\sqrt{2}\,\pi\eta}}$$

$$= \sqrt{\frac{\left(444 \text{ m s}^{-1}\right)\left(5.31 \times 10^{-26} \text{ kg}\right)}{2\sqrt{2} \ \pi \left(2.08 \times 10^{-5} \text{ kg m}^{-1} \text{ s}^{-1}\right)}}$$

$$= 3.57 \times 10^{-10} \text{ m}$$

With this value of molecular diameter, Eqs. (2.36), (2.37) and (2.39) can be used to calculate the number of collisions per second per molecule, the total number of collisions per second per m^3 and the mean free path respectively. Thus

$$Z_1 = \sqrt{2} \ \pi \sigma^2 c_{av} \, n'$$

$$= \sqrt{2} \ \pi \left(3.57 \times 10^{-10} \text{ m}\right)^2 \left(444 \text{ ms}^{-1}\right)\left(2.46 \times 10^{25} \text{ m}^{-3}\right)$$

$$= 6.3 \times 10^9 \text{ s}^{-1}$$

$$Z_{11} = \frac{1}{2} n' Z_1$$

$$= \frac{1}{2}\left(2.46 \times 10^{25} \text{ m}^{-3}\right)\left(6.3 \times 10^9 \text{ s}^{-1}\right)$$

$$= 7.51 \times 10^{34} \text{ s}^{-1} \text{ m}^{-3}$$

$$\lambda = \frac{1}{\sqrt{2} \ \pi \sigma^2 n'}$$

$$= \frac{1}{\sqrt{2} \ \pi \left(3.57 \times 10^{-10} \text{ m}\right)^2 \left(2.46 \times 10^{25} \text{ m}^{-3}\right)}$$

$$= 7.1 \times 10^{-8} \text{ m}$$

Problem 2.12: At 273 K and 1 atm pressure the coefficient of viscosity of hydrogen is 8.41×10^{-6} Pa s. Its density is 9×10^{-2} kg m^{-3} and the average speed is 1.69×10^3 ms^{-1}. Calculate the mean free path.

Solution: The mean free path and the coefficient of viscosity are related by

$$\eta = \frac{1}{2} mn' c_{av} \, \lambda$$

Now $\qquad\qquad mn' = d(\text{density})$

therefore, $\qquad\qquad \lambda = \dfrac{2\eta}{d \, c_{av}}$

$$= \frac{2\left(8.41 \times 10^{-6}\,\text{kg}\,\text{m}^{-1}\text{s}^{-1}\right)}{\left(9 \times 10^{-2}\,\text{kg}\,\text{m}^{-3}\right)\left(1.69 \times 10^{3}\ \text{ms}^{-1}\right)}$$

$$= 1.11 \times 10^{-7}\ \text{m}.$$

2.11 DEGREE OF FREEDOM

The degree of freedom of a particle may be defined *as the number of co-ordinates necessary to describe the position of a particle*. To describe the motion of a particle moving along a line, only one coordinate (say x coordinate) is necessary to specify its position. The other coordinate (y) is known from the equation of the line. The particle is said to possess one degree of freedom. On the other hand, a particle moving on a two-dimensional plane both x and y coordinates are essential to locate its position. The particle is said to have two degrees of freedom. When the particle moves unrestricted in a three-dimensional space, all the three coordinates x, y and z are necessary in order to specify its position in space. The particle has three degrees of freedom.

A spherical monatomic gas molecule will have three degrees of freedom. A diatomic molecule will have six degrees of freedom (three coordinates for each atom). In general, a molecule containing N atoms has 3N degrees of freedom because 3N coordinates are required to locate the atoms in space. As the atoms in the molecule are not capable of moving independently of one another therefore the molecule executes translational motion as a whole. Three coordinates are necessary to locate the position of the centre of mass of the molecule. The centre of mass of a molecule is the point where the whole mass can be assumed to be concentrated. So there remain 3N–3 degrees of freedom. These are attributed to other modes of internal motions, viz., rotation and vibration which are possessed by diatomic or polyatomic molecules.

A diatomic or a linear polyatomic molecule behaving as a rigid rotator can rotate about only two axes [Fig. 2.13 (a)] and two additional degrees of freedom are required to describe the rotational motion of such molecules. Hence for diatomic or linear polyatomic molecules there are 3N–3–2 = 3N–5 vibrational degrees of freedom. In case of nonlinear molecules three independent modes of rotations are possible about all the three mutually perpendicular axes passing through the centre of mass of the molecule [Fig. 2.13 (b)]. So the vibrational degrees of freedom for nonlinear molecules are 3N–3–3 = 3N – 6. In vibration, the bonds between the atoms are regarded as weightless and frictionless springs and the atoms are assumed to execute simple harmonic motions about the mean positions. The bonds are alternately stretched and compressed. In the equilibrium position, potential energy is zero and kinetic energy is maximum while in the maximum stretched or maximum compressed positions atoms come to rest; kinetic energy is zero and potential energy is maximum. Between these two positions energy is partly kinetic and partly potential. Vibrational motion is thus associated with both kinetic and potential energies, kinetic energy being proportional to the square of the relative velocity of the atoms along the internuclear axis while the potential energy is proportional to the square of the displacement from the equilibrium internuclear distance.

The energy associated with different modes of motions are given by the expressions:

Translational kinetic energy, $(E_k)_{\text{trans}} = \dfrac{1}{2}mv_x^2$

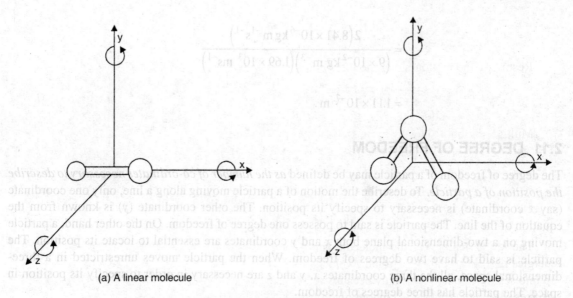

(a) A linear molecule   (b) A nonlinear molecule

Fig. 2.13 Rotational modes of motions

Rotational kinetic energy, $(E_k)_{rot} = \dfrac{1}{2} I\omega_x^2$

Vibrational kinetic energy, $(E_k)_{vib} = \dfrac{1}{2} \mu v^2$

Potential energy, $(E_p)_{vib} = \dfrac{1}{2} kx^2$

where m is the mass of the molecule, v_x is the component of velocity along x-axis, I is the moment of inertia about the x-axis, ω_x is the angular velocity along x-axis, v is the vibrational velocity of atoms and μ is the reduced mass (defined as $\dfrac{1}{\mu} = \dfrac{1}{m_1} + \dfrac{1}{m_2}$ for a diatomic molecule), x is the displacement of atoms from equilibrium internuclear distance and k is the force constant of the bond. When dealing with a large collection of molecules, the average value of energy for each mode of motion is the same and depends on temperature only.

2.12 PRINCIPLE OF EQUIPARTITION OF ENERGY

The principle states that *the total energy possessed by a molecule is equally distributed amongst its different degrees of freedom*. In translational motion it is distributed in three ways, in rotational motion in two ways for linear molecules and in three ways for nonlinear molecules. For vibrational motion, the distribution of energy can take place in 2 (3N – 5) ways for linear and 2 (3N – 6) for nonlinear molecules. The factor of two implies that each vibrational motion is associated with both the kinetic and the potential energies.

The magnitude of energy for each mode of motion can be calculated by considering the translational motion of a monatomic molecule. The average kinetic energy per molecule is given by

$$\overline{\varepsilon}_k = \frac{1}{2} m \overline{c}^2 = \frac{3}{2} kT$$

Resolving the motion along the three coordinate axes x, y and z, we have

$$\overline{c}^2 = \overline{c}_x^2 + \overline{c}_y^2 + \overline{c}_z^2$$

Multiplying both sides by $\frac{1}{2} m$, we get

$$\frac{1}{2} m \overline{c}^2 = \frac{1}{2} m \overline{c}_x^2 + \frac{1}{2} m \overline{c}_y^2 + \frac{1}{2} m \overline{c}_z^2$$

$$\overline{\varepsilon}_k = \left(\overline{\varepsilon}_k \right)_x + \left(\overline{\varepsilon}_k \right)_y + \left(\overline{\varepsilon}_k \right)_z$$

The kinetic energy of the molecule can therefore be regarded as being made up of the kinetic energies resulting from the x, y and z velocity components. It is to be noted that kinetic energy breaks up into separate components only because velocities can be resolved along three mutually perpendicular axes. Since the motion is random, there is no directional preference, hence we have

$$\overline{c}_x^2 = \overline{c}_y^2 = \overline{c}_z^2$$

Consequently,

$$\left(\overline{\varepsilon}_k \right)_x = \frac{1}{2} kT$$

$$\left(\overline{\varepsilon}_k \right)_y = \frac{1}{2} kT$$

$$\left(\overline{\varepsilon}_k \right)_z = \frac{1}{2} kT$$

Thus the total translational kinetic energy of $\frac{3}{2} kT$ per molecule or $\frac{3}{2} RT$ per mole is distributed equally in three translational degrees of freedom.

Similarly, it can be shown that rotational mode of motion contributes $1/2\ kT$ to the total energy of the molecule. In vibration, each mode contributes kT to the total energy of the molecule as each mode has two energy terms associated with it and each contributes $1/2\ kT$.

2.13 HEAT CAPACITIES OF GASES

Heat capacity (C) of a substance is defined *as the heat required to raise its temperature through 1 degree.* It is often convenient to talk about the heat capacity of a given amount of the material. The amount that is usually taken is a mole of the substance. The heat capacity of a mole of the substance is called *the molar heat capacity* and is defined *as the heat required to raise the temperature of a mole of the substance through one degree.*

Since heat capacities vary with temperature and may be defined as

$$C = \frac{\delta Q}{dT}$$

where δQ is the infinitesimally small amount of heat absorbed by the system when its temperature rises by dT.

Heat capacity depends on the conditions under which heat is transferred to the system. Two types of heat capacities are (a) molar heat capacity at constant volume ($C_{V,\,m}$) and, (b) molar heat capacity at constant pressure ($C_{P,\,m}$). These are defined as

$$C_{V,\,m} = \frac{\delta Q_V}{dT} \qquad \qquad ...(2.56)$$

and

$$C_{P,\,m} = \frac{\delta Q_P}{dT} \qquad \qquad ...(2.57)$$

where δQ_v and δQ_p are infinitesimal amounts of heat absorbed at constant volume and at constant pressure respectively. For gases these quantities differ appreciably while for solids or liquids the difference is small. Let us see how these two heat capacities are related to each other.

(a) **Molar Heat Capacity at Constant Volume** ($C_{V,\,m}$): Here the absorption of heat takes place in a rigid container at constant volume. Since there is no change in volume, no external work is done by the gas molecules. Heat that is taken up by the system is used completely in increasing the kinetic energy of the gas molecules. Under these conditions

$$\delta Q_V = dE$$

where dE is the increase in energy of the system. Hence the heat capacity $C_{V,\,m}$ at constant volume is given by

$$C_{V,\,m} = \frac{\delta Q_V}{dT} = \left(\frac{\partial E}{\partial T} \right)_V$$

The heat capacity at constant volume is thus equal to the rate of change of energy with temperature at constant volume. Since the translational kinetic energy per mole of an ideal gas is given as

$$E_{k,\,m} = \frac{3}{2} RT$$

and

$$C_{V,m} = \left(\frac{\partial E_{k,m}}{\partial T} \right)_V = \frac{3}{2} R = 12.48 \text{ J K}^{-1}\text{mol}^{-1}$$

The molar heat capacity at constant volume is thus $\frac{3}{2} R$ and is true in case of monatomic gases like He, Ne, Ar, etc. In case of diatomic or polyatomic gases some of the heat supplied may be used in causing rotation and vibration of the molecules besides translation. Thus in raising the temperature through 1 degree more heat would be required in such cases and the molar heat capacity at constant volume will then be $(12.48 + x)$ JK^{-1} mol^{-1} where x denotes the increase in value due to rotation and vibration of the molecules.

(b) **Molar Heat Capacity at Constant Pressure** ($C_{P,\,m}$): Consider a mole of the gas enclosed in a cylinder fitted with a weightless and frictionless piston. The pressure on the piston is maintained at a constant value usually at one atmosphere pressure. When heat is supplied to the cylinder, a part of it is used in pushing the piston, i.e., in performing P–V work of expansion and the remaining part is used in increasing the energy of the molecules as in the case at constant volume. Thus for an increase of temperature through 1 degree more heat would be required. Hence the mean molar heat capacity at constant pressure is always larger than that at constant volume. If δQ_P is the heat absorbed at constant pressure then

$$\delta Q_P = \delta Q_v + (-\delta w)$$

$$= \delta Q_V + PdV$$

where PdV represents the pressure-volume work. The molar heat capacity $C_{P,m}$ is given by

$$C_{P,m} = \frac{\delta Q_P}{dT} = \frac{\delta Q_V}{dT} + P\left(\frac{dV}{dT}\right)_P$$

$$= C_{V,m} + P\left(\frac{dV}{dT}\right)_P$$

For a mole of an ideal gas $P\left(\dfrac{dV}{dT}\right)_P = R.$ Hence we have

$$C_{P,m} = C_{V,m} + R \qquad\qquad ...(2.58)$$

$$C_{P,m} - C_{V,m} = R = 8.314 \ J \ K^{-1} mol^{-1}$$

For a monatomic gas, $\qquad C_{V,m} = \frac{3}{2} R$

$$C_{P,m} = \frac{3}{2}R + R = \frac{5}{2}R$$

and the ratio $\qquad\qquad \gamma = \dfrac{C_{P,m}}{C_{V,m}} = \dfrac{5}{3} = 1.67$

Values of $C_{P,m}$ and $C_{V,m}$ at 298 K are given in Table 2.2 for various gases.

Table 2.2 Molar Heat Capacities for Several Gases at Constant Volume and Pressure in $JK^{-1} \ mol^{-1}$ at 298 K

Gas	$C_{V,m}$	$C_{P,m}$
He	12.54	20.92
H_2	20.59	28.87
N_2	20.92	29.28
O_2	21.10	29.46
CO	20.78	29.14
Cl_2	25.10	33.46
NH_3	27.30	35.66

It is seen that only for monatomic gases, the experimental values are in agreement with the predicted values. For diatomic and polyatomic molecules the observed heat capacities are always higher than those predicted by the theory and increase with temperature. These deviations can be accounted for if one considers the contributions of the internal modes of motion to the total energy of the molecule. This can be illustrated by the actual calculations of $C_{P,m}$, $C_{V,m}$, and $\dfrac{C_{P,m}}{C_{V,m}}$ values for a few typical molecules.

A diatomic molecule has three translational, two rotational and one vibrational degrees of freedom. The average molar energy $E_{k,m}$ of the molecule according to the principle of equipartition of energy is given by

$$E_{k,m} = \left(E_{k,m}\right)_{\text{trans}} + \left(E_{k,m}\right)_{\text{rot}} + \left(E_{k,m}\right)_{\text{vib}}$$

$$= \frac{3}{2}RT + RT + RT$$

$$= \frac{7}{2}RT$$

Hence
$$C_{V,m} = \left(\frac{\partial E_{k,m}}{\partial T}\right)_V = \frac{7}{2}R$$

and
$$C_{P,m} = \frac{7}{2}R + R = \frac{9}{2}R$$

Therefore,
$$\gamma = \frac{C_{P,m}}{C_{V,m}} = \frac{9}{7} \simeq 1.3$$

For a linear triatomic molecule translational and rotational degrees of freedom are the same as for the diatomic molecule but the vibrational degrees of freedom is four ($3 \times 3 - 5 = 4$). The average molar energy is given as

$$E_{k,m} = \frac{3}{2}RT + RT + 4RT = \frac{13}{2}RT$$

Hence
$$C_{V,m} = \left(\frac{\partial E_{k,m}}{\partial T}\right)_V = \frac{13}{2}R \text{ and } C_{P,m} = \frac{13}{2}R + R = \frac{15}{2}R$$

and
$$\gamma = \frac{C_{P,m}}{C_{V,m}} = \frac{15}{13} = 1.15$$

For a nonlinear triatomic molecule, there are three translational and three rotational degrees of freedom. The vibrational degrees of freedom are ($3 \times 3 - 6 = 3$). The energy of the molecule is

$$E_{k,m} = \frac{3}{2}RT + \frac{3}{2}RT + 3RT = 6RT$$

and
$$C_{V,m} = \left(\frac{\partial E_{k,\,m}}{\partial T}\right)_V = 6R \text{ and } C_{P,\,m} = 7R$$

Therefore,
$$\gamma = \frac{C_{p,\,m}}{C_{V,\,m}} = \frac{7}{6} = 1.16$$

A comparison of these values with those given in Table 2.2 shows that the calculated values are higher than the experimental values. This is due to the fact that at ordinary temperature vibrational modes are inactive. For gases like Cl_2, the higher values of $C_{V,\,m}$ or $C_{P,\,m}$ suggest that vibrational modes are active even at ordinary temperatures. The vibrational modes become active only at high temperatures.

Problem 2.13: 11.2×10^{-3} m^3 of a certain gas at STP requires 104.6 J to raise its temperature by 10 degree. Calculate $C_{V,\,m}$ for the gas. Assuming that the vibrational modes are inactive, what can be concluded about the structure of the gas molecules?

Solution: 11.2×10^{-3} m^3 of the gas at STP corresponds to ½ mole of the gas. Total heat supplied to the gas at constant volumes is

$$Q_v = nC_{V,\,m}\,\Delta T$$

$$n = \frac{1}{2}\,\text{mol}, \ T = 10 \text{ degree}, \ Q_V = 104.6 \text{ J}$$

Hence
$$C_{V,\,m} = \frac{(104.6 \text{ J})}{\left(\dfrac{1}{2}\,\text{mol}\right)(10 \text{ degree})} = 20.92 \text{ J deg}^{-1}\text{ mol}^{-1}$$

Now translational contribution to $C_{V,\,m}$ is 12.62 J deg^{-1} mol^{-1}, the remaining 8.30 J deg^{-1} mol^{-1} are contributed by only two rotational modes of motion. Hence the molecule is linear.

Problem 2.14: 418.4 J of heat is added to a 4×10^{-3} m^3 rigid container containing a diatomic gas at STP. Calculate the final temperature and pressure of the gas assuming ideal behaviour. The vibrational contributions may be neglected.

Solution:

Here
$$Q_v = nC_{V,\,m}\Delta T \text{ and } C_{V,\,m} = \frac{3}{2}R + R = \frac{5}{2}R$$

$$n = \frac{4 \times 10^{-3}}{22.414 \times 10^{-3}} \text{ mol}$$

$$Q_v = 418.4 \text{ J}$$

Hence
$$\Delta T = \frac{Q_V}{nC_{V,\,m}} = \frac{(418.4 \text{ J})}{(20.92 \text{ JK}^{-1}\text{mol}^{-1})}\left(\frac{22.414}{4 \text{ mol}}\right)$$

$$= 112 \text{ K}.$$

The final temperature is 273.16 + 112 = 385.16 K and the final pressure is given by

$$P = \frac{nRT}{V} = \left(\frac{4}{22.414}\,\text{mol}\right)\frac{\left(8.314\ \text{kg m}^2\text{s}^{-2}\ \text{K}^{-1}\text{mol}^{-1}\right)(385.16\ \text{K})}{\left(4 \times 10^{-3}\,\text{m}^3\right)}$$

$$= 1.416 \times 10^5\ \text{kg m}^{-1}\text{s}^{-2}$$

$$= 1.416 \times 10^5\ \text{Nm}^{-2}$$

2.14 REAL GASES — DEVIATIONS FROM IDEAL BEHAVIOUR

A gas is termed as an ideal gas or a perfect gas if it obeys gas laws or the gas equation PV = nRT under all conditions of temperatures and pressures. However, no gas is ideal; almost all gases show significant deviations from the ideal behaviour. The ideal behaviour with such gases is observed only under certain conditions of temperatures and pressures. These gases are thus termed as *real* or *nonideal gases.* The magnitude and the nature of deviation may be seen from the examination of the variation of product PV for a given quantity of gas at constant temperature with pressure. For an ideal gas the plot of PV versus P at constant temperature should give a straight line parallel to abscissa. The data for hydrogen and nitrogen at 273 K, for carbon dioxide at 313 K are given in Table 2.3 and are plotted in Fig. 2.14. At a given temperature and 1 atm pressure, the volume of the gas taken in each case is one litre and the product PV at 1 atm pressure is unity.

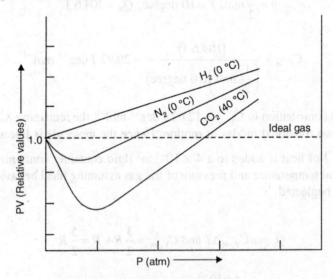

Fig. 2.14 *PV versus P plot for various gases*

(*a*) **Effect of Pressure on Deviations from the Ideal Behaviour:** It is clear from Fig. 2.14 as well as from Table 2.3 that the real gases show considerable deviations from the ideal behaviour at higher pressures. Further examination of the figure reveals that there are two types of curves. For gases like H_2, He, Ne, etc., the curves start at the value of PV as required by the ideal gas equation, and then increases continuously with pressure.

In the second case, the plot for gases like N_2, CO_2 etc., starts again at the same point, shows a decrease in the product PV with pressure, passes through a minimum, characteristics of each gas and then increases continuously with pressure. In both cases, the gases approach ideal behaviour only in the limiting case when $P \to 0$.

A more convenient way of showing the deviations from ideality is in terms of *compressibility factor*, denoted by Z. It is defined as

$$Z = \frac{PV}{nRT} = \frac{PV}{(PV)_{ideal}}$$

Table 2.3 Variation of PV with Pressure

Pressure (in atm)	Value of PV of different gases		
	N_2 at 273 K	N_2 at 273 K	CO_2 at 313 K
1	1.000	1.000	1.000
50	1.033	0.985	0.741
100	1.064	0.985	0.270
200	1.134	1.037	0.409
400	1.277	1.256	0.718
800	1.566	1.796	1.299

For an ideal gas $Z = 1$ and is independent of temperature and pressure. For a real gas, Z depends on both the temperature and pressure. The deviations from ideality will be measured by the deviation of compressibility factor from unity. Some results on the determination of compressibility factor for H_2, N_2 and CO_2 over a range of pressure at constant temperature are shown in Fig. 2.15. At very low pressures for all these gases, Z is approximately equal to one, indicating the ideal behaviour. As the

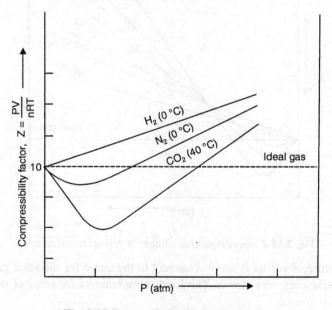

Fig. 2.15 Z versus P plot for various gases

pressure is increased, gases like H_2, He, etc., show a continuous increase in Z (from $Z = 1$), whereas for gases like N_2, CO_2, etc., it first decreases, ($Z < 1$), passes through a minimum and then increases continuously with pressure ($Z > 1$). In case of carbon dioxide the minimum is more pronounced than for nitrogen indicating that carbon dioxide is more compressible than nitrogen. The greater compressibility of carbon dioxide means that for a given increase in pressure, there is a large volume decrease in carbon dioxide than in nitrogen. Further increase in pressure would cause smaller decrease in volume and PV will now become more than RT and hence Z would be greater than 1.

From the Fig. 2.15 one can also say whether a gas is easily liquefiable or not. Those gases in which there is a sharp decrease in Z can be easily liquefied. Thus carbon dioxide gas can be easily liquefied than nitrogen. In case of hydrogen or other inert gases there is no dip in the plot at ordinary temperature and hence these gases cannot be easily liquefied.

(*b*) **Effect of Temperature on Deviations from the Ideal Behaviour:** Figure 2.16 shows the plot of Z versus P for nitrogen gas at different temperatures. Change in the shape of the curve with temperature is clearly seen in the figure. At lower temperature dip in the curve is large and the slope of the curve is negative, *i.e.*, $Z < 1$. As the temperature is raised, dip in the curve decreases and the position of the minimum moves to the left. At a certain temperature the minimum in the curve vanishes and the curve

remains horizontal for which $\dfrac{PV}{nRT}$ is about unity for an appreciable range of pressures. Within this

range Boyle's law is obeyed and hence the temperature is called the Boyle temperature. This temperature is characteristic of each gas. Above Boyle temperature slope of the curve increases continuously, *i.e.*, $Z > 1$. Below Boyle temperature, increase of pressure causes the value of Z first to decrease to a minimum and then increase.

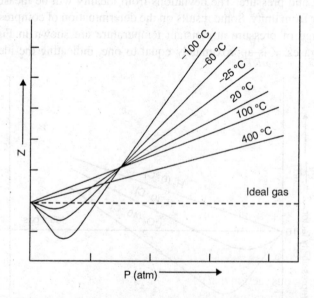

Fig. 2.16 Z versus P plot for nitrogen at various temperatures

At Boyle temperature, Z versus P curve is tangent to the curve for the ideal gas at $P = 0$ and rises above the ideal gas curve only very slowly. The Boyle temperatures for some of the gases are given in Table 2.4.

Table 2.4 Boyle temperature for some gases

Gas	H_2	He	N_2	NH_3	CH_4
Temperature (K)	117	24	332	860	497

From the above discussions it is clear that real gases approach ideal behaviour at low pressures and fairly high temperatures. Under these conditions all gases lose their individualistic behaviour and obey the ideal gas equation $PV = nRT$.

Problem 2.15: The compressibility factor, $Z = PV/nRT$ for CO_2 at 273 K and 100 atm (101.325 × 10^5 Nm^{-2}) pressure is 0.2007. Calculate the volume occupied by 0.1 mole of the gas at 100 atm and 273 K (a) by the ideal gas equation, and (b) by making use of the compressibility factor.

Solution: (a) For an ideal gas

$$PV = nRT$$

or

$$V = \frac{nRT}{P}$$

$$= \frac{(0.1 \text{ mol})(8.314 \text{ Nm K}^{-1} \text{ mol}^{-1})(273.0 \text{ K})}{(101.325 \times 10^5 \text{ Nm}^{-2})}$$

$$= 22.4 \times 10^{-6} \text{ m}^3$$

(b) Since,

$$Z = \frac{PV}{nRT}$$

$$V = \frac{ZnRT}{P}$$

$$= \frac{(0.2007)(0.1 \text{ mol})(8.314 \text{ Nm K}^{-1} \text{ mol}^{-1})(273.0 \text{ K})}{(101.325 \times 10^5 \text{ Nm}^{-2})}$$

$$= 4.5 \times 10^{-6} \text{ m}^3$$

2.15 THE VAN DER WAALS EQUATION

It has been shown in the previous section that gases show significant deviations from the ideal behaviour at high pressures and low temperatures. The extent of deviation depends on the nature of the gas, pressure and temperature at which the behaviour is studied. These results are contrary to those predicted by the kinetic theory of gases where it was postulated that the behaviour of gases were alike under all conditions of temperatures and pressures. Hence the model suggested by the kinetic theory of gases must be modified in order to study the behaviour of real gases.

The deviations of gases from ideal behaviour are due to two faulty assumptions made in the kinetic theory of gases, *viz.*,

(*a*) the volume of the molecules is negligible in comparison to the total volume of the gas, and

(*b*) there are no forces of attraction between the molecules.

The fact that the molecules have appreciable collision diameters means that they possess an effective volume. Under normal conditions, the volume of the molecules is very small. However, at high pressures (about 100 atm) the volume occupied by the gas molecules is appreciable and hence cannot be neglected. Furthermore, the volume of a gas can be decreased by lowering the temperature and increasing the pressure until the gas liquefies and finally solidifies. Solids cannot be further compressed. This further confirms that the molecules of a gas do occupy some definite volume.

The existence of a collision diameter shows that there are repulsive and attractive forces between the molecules. Also, the fact that the gases can be liquefied shows the presence of attractive forces between the gas molecules. Decrease in the compressibility factor with pressure and a large decrease in volume of the gas with pressure can now be explained in a better way in terms of the attractive forces operating between the gas molecules. On increasing the pressure, molecules of a gas are brought closer and the attractive forces become significant. These attractive forces would be more effective at lower temperatures.

Van der Waals in 1873 introduced two correction terms to the ideal gas equation $PV = nRT$ and obtained an equation of state for real gases. The first correction is made for the volume occupied by the molecules themselves and the second one is for the forces of attraction between the molecules.

(*a*) **Correction due to Volume:** When n moles of a gas are placed in a container of volume V, the space in which the molecules are free to move is equal to V if the volume occupied by the molecules themselves is negligible. Since the molecules have a finite size, the actual volume available to them for their movement would not be V but less than V. If b is *the effective volume per mole of the gas* then this volume must be subtracted from the total volume in order to get the actual volume for their movement. Therefore

$$V_{ideal} = V - b$$

For n moles of the gas

$$V_{ideal} = (V - nb) \qquad\qquad ...(2.59)$$

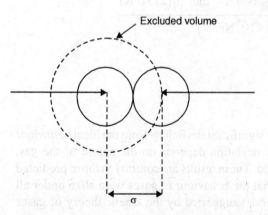

Excluded volume

Fig. 2.17 Excluded volume for impenetrable spheres

b is also sometimes called the excluded volume and is usually treated as a constant and characteristic for each gas. The excluded volume is not equal to the actual volume of the gas molecules but four times the actual volume of the molecules. It can be calculated by assuming bimolecular collisions between two impenetrable spherical gas molecules (Fig. 2.17). Suppose r is the radius and σ ($= 2r$) is the collision diameter of the gas molecules, then the space indicated by the dotted sphere having a radius σ will not be available to the pair of the colliding molecules. This space is the excluded volume for the pair of molecules and is given as

$$V_{\text{pair}} = \frac{4}{3}\pi\sigma^3$$

$$= \frac{4}{3}\pi(2r)^3$$

$$= 8\left(\frac{4}{3}\pi r^3\right)$$

The excluded volume per molecule (V_e) is therefore

$$V_e = \frac{1}{2}\, 8\left(\frac{4}{3}\pi r^3\right)$$

$$= 4\left(\frac{4}{3}\pi r^3\right)$$

$$= 4 v_m$$

where v_m is the volume of a single gas molecule.

(b) **Correction due to Molecular Attraction:** Consider a molecule in the interior of a gas (Fig. 2.18). It is surrounded uniformly by other molecules so that there is no resultant attractive force on this molecule. However, as it approaches the wall of the vessel, the uniform distribution of molecules around it is disturbed and it is now attracted by molecules from one side only. The molecule will thus experience a net inward pull (Fig. 2.18). Hence, it will strike the wall of the vessel with lower velocity and will exert a lower pressure than it would have done if there were no forces of attraction. The measured pressure P will thus be less than the ideal pressure. It is therefore necessary to add a correction term (P_a) to the observed pressure in order to obtain the ideal pressure.

Corrected (ideal pressure) $P_{\text{ideal}} = P + P_a$

The net inward pull experienced by the molecules about to strike the wall of the vessel is proportional to (i) the number of molecules in the bulk of the gas, and (ii) the number of molecules striking the wall per unit area at any given instant. Both these factors are proportional to the number of molecules per unit volume (n/V), where V is volume occupied by n moles of the gas. Hence, the correction term P_a is

$$P_a \propto \left(\frac{n}{V}\right)^2$$

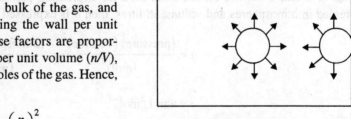

Fig. 2.18 Intermolecular forces in a gas

or

$$P_a = \frac{an^2}{V^2}$$

where a is the constant of proportionality.

Therefore, the corrected (ideal) pressure,

$$P_{\text{ideal}} = P + \frac{an^2}{V^2}$$ ...(2.60)

Hence the product of ideal pressure and ideal volume given by Eqs. (2.59) and (2.60) respectively should be equal to nRT

$$\left(P + \frac{an^2}{V^2}\right)(V - nb) = nRT$$ ...(2.61)

This is known as the van der Waals equation for n moles of a gas. For 1 mole of a gas, van der Waals equation becomes

$$\left(P + \frac{a}{V^2}\right)(V - b) = RT$$ ...(2.62)

For a gas with finite molecular size and no attractive forces between the molecules, Eq. (2.61) reduces to

$$P = \frac{nRT}{V - nb}$$

The pressure is greater than the ideal value as $\dfrac{nRT}{V - nb} > \dfrac{nRT}{V}$.

Thus size effect alone increases the pressure above the ideal value. On the other hand, for a gas involving only the attractive forces between the molecules, Eq. (2.61) becomes

$$P = \frac{nRT}{V} - \frac{an^2}{V^2}$$

The attractive forces reduce the pressure below the ideal value.

The constants a and b are known as the van der Waals constants and are characteristic of each gas. Values of a and b depend on the units used for expressing pressure and volume. If the pressure is expressed in atmospheres and volume in litres, then a is expressed as

$$a = \frac{(\text{pressure})(\text{volume})^2}{(\text{mol})^2} = \frac{(\text{atmosphere})(\text{L})^2}{(\text{mol})^2}$$

$$= \text{atm L}^2\text{mol}^{-2}$$

and b as

$$b = \frac{(\text{volume})}{(\text{mol})} = \frac{(\text{L})}{(\text{mol})} = \text{L mol}^{-1}$$

In SI units, $$a = \frac{(\text{pressure})(\text{volume})^2}{(\text{mol})^2}$$

$$= \frac{\left(Nm^{-2}\right)\left(m^3\right)^2}{\left(mol\right)^2} = Nm^4 mol^{-2}$$

or
$$\frac{\left(1\ atm\right)\left(L\right)^2}{\left(mol\right)^2} = \frac{\left(1.013 \times 10^5\ Nm^{-2}\right)\left(10^{-3}\ m^3\right)^2}{\left(mol\right)^2}$$

$$= 1.013 \times 10^{-1}\ Nm^4\ mol^{-2}$$

and
$$b = Volume\ mol^{-1}$$

$$= m^3\ mol^{-1}$$

or,
$$1\ litre\ mol^{-1} = 10^{-3}\ m^3 mol^{-1}$$

Values of these constants can be determined either from P–V–T relation or from critical constants. These constants are assumed to be temperature independent. The values of the van der Waals constants for some gases are given in Table 2.5.

Table 2.5 van der Waals Constants for Some Gases

Gas	a (atm L² mol⁻²)	a (Nm⁴ mol⁻²)	b (L mol⁻¹)	b (10³ m³ mol⁻¹)
H_2	0.245	0.0247	0.0266	0.0266
He	0.034	0.0035	0.0237	0.0237
O_2	1.360	0.1378	0.0318	0.0318
N_2	1.390	0.1408	0.0391	0.0391
Cl_2	6.493	0.6577	0.0562	0.0562
CO_2	3.590	0.3637	0.0428	0.0428
NH_3	4.170	0.4210	0.0371	0.0371
SO_2	6.710	0.6780	0.0564	0.0564
CH_4	2.250	0.2279	0.0428	0.0428

Gases which can be easily liquefied have large values of a.

The van der Waals equation is an improvement over the ideal gas equation and explains qualitatively the deviations of real gases from ideal behaviour. It is valid over a wide range of temperatures and pressures. However, van der Waals equation fails to give the perfect agreement at very high pressures and low temperatures particularly near the critical temperatures. Therefore numerous attempts have been made to modify the van der Waals equation.

Problem 2.16: Calculate the pressure in atmospheres exerted by 2.0 moles of chlorobenzene vapours confined to 10.0 litre vessel at 298 K using (a) the ideal gas equation, and (b) the van der Waals equation. $a = 25.43\ L^2\ atm\ mol^{-2}$, $b = 0.1453\ L\ mol^{-1}$.

Solution: (a) From ideal gas law

$$PV = nRT$$

$$P = \frac{nRT}{V} = \frac{(2.0 \text{ mol})\left(8.314 \text{Nm K}^{-1}\text{mol}^{-1}\right)(298 \text{ K})}{\left(10 \times 10^{-3} \text{m}^3\right)}$$

$$= 4.994 \times 10^5 \text{ Nm}^{-2}.$$

(b) From the van der Waals equation,

$$\left(P + \frac{an^2}{V^2}\right)(V - nb) = nRT$$

$$P = \frac{nRT}{V - nb} - \frac{an^2}{V^2}$$

$$P = \frac{(2.0 \text{ mol})\left(8.314 \text{ Nm K}^{-1}\text{mol}^{-1}\right)(298 \text{ K})}{\left(10 \times 10^{-3} \text{m}^3\right) - (2 \text{ mol})\left(0.1453 \times 10^{-3} \text{m}^3\text{mol}^{-1}\right)}$$

$$- \frac{(2.0 \text{ mol})^2 \left(2.576 \text{Nm}^4 \text{mol}^{-2}\right)}{\left(10 \times 10^{-3} \text{m}^3\right)^2}$$

$$= \frac{(2.0 \text{ mol})\left(8.314 \text{Nm K}^{-1}\text{mol}^{-1}\right)(298 \text{ K})}{10^{-3}(10 - 0.2906) \text{m}^3} - \frac{4\left(2.576 \text{ Nm}^4\right)}{100 \times 10^{-6} \text{m}^6}$$

$$= 5.105 \times 10^5 \text{Nm}^{-2} - 1.03 \times 10^5 \text{Nm}^{-2}$$

$$= 4.075 \times 10^5 \text{ Nm}^{-2}$$

2.16 IMPLICATIONS OF THE VAN DER WAALS EQUATION

The van der Waals equation, as shown above, does not reproduce the exact behaviour of real gases but it is certainly an improvement over the ideal gas equation. It is in agreement with the general properties of gases as represented by Fig. 2.15. For a mole of the gas van der Waals equation may be written as

$$PV = RT + Pb - \frac{a}{V} + \frac{ab}{V^2} \qquad \qquad ...(2.63)$$

(a) **At Low Pressures:** When P is small, V is large, both the terms Pb and $\dfrac{ab}{V^2}$ in Eq. (2.63) may

be neglected in comparison to a/V, hence Eq. (2.63) reduces to

$$PV = RT - \frac{a}{V}$$

Under these conditions, PV should be less than RT by $\frac{a}{V}$ and this difference increases as V decreases, that is, as the pressure increases. The dip in plot Z versus P in Fig. 2.15 for nitrogen and carbon dioxide can thus be correlated with the effect of a/V^2, i.e., the molecular attraction term of the van der Waals equation. This is in agreement with the statement made earlier that when the molecules are relatively far apart, as at low pressure, the attractive forces predominate over the repulsive forces.

(b) **At High Pressures:** At high pressures, the last two terms in Eq. (2.63) being of opposite sign and approximately equal in magnitude and may be neglected in comparison to the other two terms. Thus Eq. (2.63) becomes

$$PV = RT + Pb$$

It is seen that PV is greater than RT by an amount equal to Pb and it increases linearly with the pressure. This accounts for the rising part of the curves in Fig. 2.15 which is largely due to the influence of the 'b' term, i.e., the effective volume of the molecules. At high pressures, the molecules are close to one another and the crowding leads to significant repulsive forces.

(c) **At Extremely Low Pressures and High Temperatures:** At very low pressures, V will be quite large and thus the term $\frac{a}{V^2}$ and b in the van der Waals equation are negligible in comparison to P and V. Equation (2.63) therefore reduces to $PV = RT$. Similarly at very high temperatures, volume will be large ($V \propto T$) and hence the pressure will be very small and again the equation $PV = RT$ is obtained. Thus, at extremely low pressures and very high temperatures all real gases tend to approach the ideal behaviour.

At low temperatures where P and V are small, both the correction terms are appreciable and the deviations would be quite pronounced.

For most gases, at ordinary temperature, the effect of $\frac{a}{V^2}$ term in the van der Waals equation is predominant at low pressures while that of b is important at high pressures. With hydrogen, helium, neon, etc., the molecular attraction is small and the size effect predominates over the intermolecular attraction effect at ordinary temperatures. It is for this reason that the PV curve for hydrogen shows no dip at ordinary temperature (Fig. 2.15).

Calculation of the Boyle Temperature: At the Boyle temperature a real gas behaves ideally over an appreciable range of pressure. The Boyle temperature (T_B) of a gas can be readily obtained from the van der Waals equation. For one mole of a gas we can write

$$P = \frac{RT}{V-b} - \frac{a}{V^2}$$

$$PV = \frac{VRT}{V-b} - \frac{a}{V}$$

Dividing by RT, we get

$$Z = \frac{PV}{RT} = \frac{V}{V-b} - \frac{a}{VRT}$$

$$= \frac{1}{1 - \dfrac{b}{V}} - \frac{a}{VRT}$$

At low pressures $V \gg b$ and $\dfrac{b}{V}$ is small in comparison to unity therefore $\left(1 - \dfrac{b}{V}\right)^{-1}$ can be expanded into a power series yielding

$$Z = 1 + \frac{b}{V} + \left(\frac{b}{V}\right)^2 + \ldots - \frac{a}{VRT}$$

$$= 1 + \frac{1}{V}\left(b - \frac{a}{RT}\right) + \left(\frac{b}{V}\right)^2 + \ldots \qquad \ldots(2.64)$$

As an approximation, V may be replaced by $\dfrac{RT}{P}$ to give

$$Z = 1 + \frac{1}{RT}\left(b - \frac{a}{RT}\right)P + \left(\frac{b}{RT}\right)^2 P^2 + \ldots \qquad \ldots(2.65)$$

Differentiating Eq. (2.65) with respect to P at constant temperature, we get

$$\left(\frac{dZ}{dP}\right)_T = \frac{1}{RT}\left(b - \frac{a}{RT}\right) + 2P\left(\frac{b}{RT}\right)^2 + \ldots$$

At $P = 0$, all the higher terms drop out and the above equation reduces to

$$\left(\frac{dZ}{dP}\right)_T = \frac{1}{RT}\left(b - \frac{a}{RT}\right)$$

At the Boyle temperature, initial slope of Z versus P plot is zero. Hence

$$b - \frac{a}{RT_B} = 0$$

or

$$T_B = \frac{a}{Rb}$$

At the Boyle temperature a real gas behaves ideally over an appreciable range of pressure. The two effects, viz., finite size and the intermolecular attractions roughly compensate each other. Above Boyle temperature the slope of Z versus P plot is positive; hence $b > \dfrac{a}{RT}$ or the size effect dominates the behaviour of the gas. Below the Boyle temperature the slope is negative; $b < \dfrac{a}{RT}$ or the intermolecular forces dominate the behaviour of the gas.

2.17 OTHER EQUATIONS OF STATE

A large number of equations have been proposed from time to time to express P–V–T relations of gases. Some of these are based on theoretical considerations, while others are entirely empirical. A brief description of some of these equations are given below.

(*i*) **Virial Equation:** The most general equation for the variation of pressure, volume and temperature of a gas is that of H.K.Onnes (1901). It is written as

$$PV = RT\left(1 + \frac{B}{V} + \frac{C}{V^2} + ...\right) \qquad ...(2.66)$$

where B, C etc., are temperature dependent constants and are called the second, third, etc., virial coefficients. The values of the coefficients B, C, etc., can be calculated from the experimental P–V–T measurements. In general, the coefficient B is negative at low temperature, becoming zero and then positive as the temperature is increased. The temperature at which B is zero is called the Boyle temperature, since the gas obeys Boyle's law.

The expression is also more often written as

$$PV = A + B'P + C'P^2 + ... \qquad ...(2.67)$$

In this form the virial equation is known as **Kammerlingh Onnes equation**. Only the first virial coefficient is significant at very low pressure, and is equal to RT.

Any equation can be expressed in the virial form. From Eq. (2.64) or (2.65) the second virial coefficient in the van der Waals equation is equal to $b - \dfrac{a}{RT}$.

(*ii*) **Berthelot Equation:** Berthelot derived an empirical relation for the behaviour of real gas as

$$\left(P + \frac{an^2}{TV^2}\right)(V - nb) = nRT \qquad ...(2.68)$$

where a and b are constants referred to as Berthelot constants and the appearance of $\dfrac{1}{T}$ term with $\dfrac{an^2}{V^2}$ takes into account the dependence of intermolecular attractions with temperature.

(*iii*) **Dieterici Equation:** Dieterici suggested the following equation of state

$$P(V - nb) = nRTe^{-an/VRT} \qquad ...(2.69)$$

For a mole of the gas, the equation becomes

$$P(V - b) = RT\,e^{-\frac{a}{VRT}} \qquad ...(2.70)$$

At low pressure, the volume of the gas will be large hence b may be neglected in comparison to V.

Also $\dfrac{a}{VRT}$ will have a small value and the expansion of $e^{-a/VRT}$ yields

$$e^{-a/VRT} = 1 - \frac{a}{VRT}$$

and Eq. (2.70) becomes

$$P = \frac{RT}{V}\left(1 - \frac{a}{RTV}\right)$$

$$= \frac{RT}{V} - \frac{a}{V^2}$$

which is identical with the van der Waals equation at low pressure. Thus the Dieterici equation agrees with van der Waals equation at low and moderate pressures but at high pressure the difference becomes quite appreciable.

Problem 2.17: Express Berthelot and Dieterici equations in the virial form and obtain an expression for the Boyle temperature in each case.

Solution: Berthelot equation for a mole of the gas is

$$\left(P + \frac{a}{TV^2}\right)(V - b) = RT$$

$$P = \frac{RT}{V - b} - \frac{a}{TV^2}$$

$$PV = \frac{RTV}{V - b} - \frac{a}{TV}$$

Dividing by RT, we get

$$\frac{PV}{RT} = \frac{V}{V - b} - \frac{a}{VRT^2}$$

$$Z = \left(1 - \frac{b}{V}\right)^{-1} - \frac{a}{VRT^2}$$

$$= 1 + \frac{b}{V} + \frac{b^2}{V^2} + \ldots\ldots - \frac{a}{VRT^2}$$

$$= 1 + \frac{1}{V}\left(b - \frac{a}{RT^2}\right) + \ldots\ldots$$

The second virial coefficient is $b - \dfrac{a}{RT^2}$. At the Boyle temperature it is zero, hence the Boyle

temperature

$$T_B = \left(\frac{a}{Rb}\right)^{1/2}$$

(*ii*) Dieterici equation for a mole of the gas is

$$P = \frac{RT}{V - b}e^{-a/VRT}$$

$$Z = \frac{PV}{RT} = \frac{V}{V-b} e^{-\frac{a}{VRT}}$$

$$= \left(1 - \frac{b}{V} + \ldots\right)^{-1} \left(1 - \frac{a}{VRT} + \ldots\right)$$

$$= \left[1 + \frac{b}{V} + \left(\frac{b}{V}\right)^2 + \ldots\right] \left[1 - \frac{a}{VRT} + \ldots\right]$$

Ignoring higher order terms in $\frac{1}{V}$, we get

$$Z = 1 + \frac{1}{V}\left(b - \frac{a}{RT}\right) + \ldots$$

Thus the second virial coefficient in this case is $b - a/RT$ and the Boyle temperature would be

$$T_B = \frac{a}{Rb}$$

2.18 CRITICAL PHENOMENA

During the early part of nineteenth century, a number of gases such as carbon dioxide, sulphur dioxide, ammonia, etc., were liquefied by subjecting the gas to decrease in temperature and increase in pressure. The effect of temperature is rather more important than that of pressure. The essential conditions for liquefaction of gases were discovered by Andrews in 1869 as a result of his study of $P-V-T$ relationships for carbon dioxide. It was found that above a certain temperature it was impossible to liquefy a gas no matter what pressure was applied. This temperature is called *the critical temperature* (T_c). The pressure required to liquefy a gas at this temperature is called *the critical pressure* (P_c). The volume occupied by one mole of the substance at the critical temperature and pressure is called *the critical volume* (V_c). A gas or liquid in this condition is said to be at the critical point. T_c, P_c and V_c taken together are known as *the critical constants* for a gas. At the critical temperature and pressure, physical properties of a gas are indistinguishable from its liquid form and no distinction can be observed between the two. The phenomenon of smooth merging of a gas with its liquid form is called the critical phenomenon. It is a reversible process.

The results of Andrews experiments are shown in Fig. 2.19 in which the pressure is plotted against volume at various temperatures for carbon dioxide. Each $P-V$ plot is called an isotherm. Consider an isotherm at 13.1°C. At low pressures, carbon dioxide is entirely gaseous and is represented by the point A in the isotherm (Fig. 2.19). On increasing the pressure, volume decreases as shown by the portion AX of the isotherm, approximately in accordance with Boyle's law. At X, deviations from Boyle's law begin to appear and the volume decreases rapidly as the gas is converted into the liquid. At point Y carbon dioxide has been completely liquefied. Between X and Y, pressure remains constant and both the gas and the liquid phases are in equilibrium. As the volume is decreased, the amount of liquid increases as the gas condenses. The pressure corresponding to the horizontal portion XY of the isotherm is the vapour pressure of the liquid at the temperature of the isotherm.

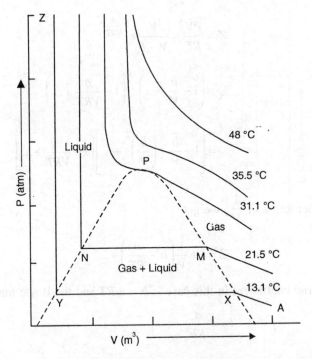

Fig. 2.19 Isotherms for carbon dioxide showing the critical region

The pressure volume curve at 21.5°C shows a similar behaviour except that liquefaction starts at higher pressure and the horizontal portion MN is shorter. As the temperature is raised, the horizontal portion of the isotherm becomes smaller and smaller until at 31.1°C it reduces to a point P. At this point the boundary between the two phases disappears indicating that both the phases have identical characteristics. Above 31.1°C there is no indication of liquefaction. Andrews concluded that if the temperature of carbon dioxide was above 31.1°C, carbon dioxide could not be liquefied even at pressures of several hundred atmospheres. This temperature of 31.1°C is the critical temperature for carbon dioxide. The isotherm at the critical temperature is known as *the critical isotherm*.

It may be concluded from this explanation that in the area to the left of the dotted line below the critical isotherm, only liquid carbon dioxide exists. To the right of the dotted line exists only gaseous carbon dioxide. Within the dotted area, obtained by joining the ends of the horizontal portions of the isotherms, two phases, viz., liquid and gas exist in equilibrium.

Above the critical temperature, no horizontal portion of the curve is obtained and the isotherms are parabolic and almost similar to those demanded by Boyle's law.

2.19 PRINCIPLE OF CONTINUITY OF STATES

At the critical temperature a gas becomes indistinguishable from its liquid indicating that the transition from a gas into the liquid or the reverse is not a sharp and discontinuous process, but is rather continuous. The fact that it is not possible to distinguish between a liquid and a gas is the principle of *continuity of states*. The idea of continuity from a gas to liquid or the reverse can be shown from the following considerations.

In Fig. 2.20, the end points of the horizontal plateau of the isotherms of Fig. 2.19 have been connected by a dotted line. Points A and B lie on the same isotherm below the critical temperature T_c.

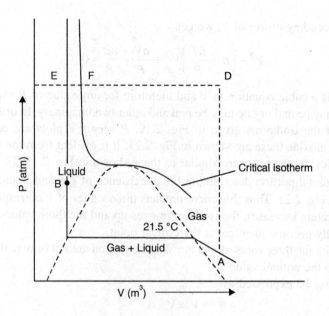

Fig. 2.20 Continuity of state

Point A represents a gaseous state while B represents the liquid obtained by compressing the gas. To convert carbon dioxide gas at a temperature 21.5°C to liquid carbon dioxide without any discontinuity, *i.e.*, without having more than one phases present, let us consider the gas at A and heat it at constant volume until its temperature increases to a value D above the critical temperature. During this isochoric heating pressure rises along the line AD. The pressure of the gas at D is now held constant while the temperature is lowered until the volume decreases from D to E. The system which was entirely gaseous at A is now completely liquid at E. At point F, the intermolecular attractive forces are large enough to cause condensation. Thus at the point F the state can be thought of as a highly compressed gas or a liquid. The change has been made from gas to liquid at the same temperature without any discontinuity. The change in the state actually occurs during compression along DE. The process of transition from gas to liquid or vice versa is regarded as continuous.

2.20 THE VAN DER WAALS EQUATION AND THE CRITICAL CONSTANTS

The van der Waals equation for 1 mole of a gas is given by

$$\left(P + \frac{a}{V^2}\right)(V - b) = RT$$

This equation may be written as

$$PV + \frac{a}{V} - Pb - \frac{ab}{V^2} = RT$$

or

$$PV^3 + aV - PbV^2 - ab = RTV^2$$

or

$$PV^3 + aV - PbV^2 - ab - RTV^{2^{\cdot}} = 0$$

Arranging in descending power of V, we get

$$V^3 - \left(b + \frac{RT}{P}\right)V^2 + \frac{aV}{P} - \frac{ab}{P} = 0 \qquad \qquad ...(2.71)$$

Equation (2.71) is a cubic equation in V and therefore for any value of P and T it will have three values, all of which may be real or one may be real and other two imaginary. In order to see if Eq. (2.71) predicts the shape of the isotherms given in Fig. 2.19, P versus V plots are constructed using this equation. For carbon dioxide these are shown in Fig. 2.21. It is evident from the figure that the curves at and above the critical temperature are similar to those shown in Fig. 2.19. However, below critical temperature the horizontal portion determining the coexistence of gas and liquid is replaced by an ~ shaped curve ABC in Fig. 2.21. Thus this curve predicts three values of V corresponding to points A, B and C. As the temperature increases, the isotherm moves up and the three values of volume approach one another and finally become identical at the critical point.

At the critical point the three roots of van der Waals equation are not only real and positive but also identical and equal to the critical value V_c.

This condition may be expressed as

$$V = V_c$$

or

$$V - V_c = 0$$

and consequently,

$$(V - V_c)^3 = 0$$

Expanding this, we get

$$V^3 - 3V_c V^2 + 3V_c^2 V - V_c^3 = 0 \qquad \qquad ...(2.72)$$

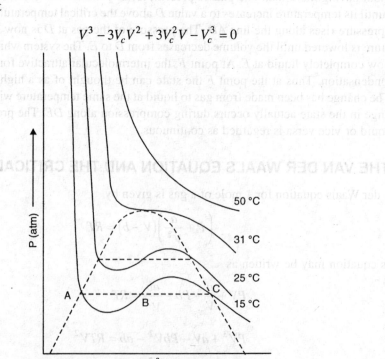

Fig. 2.21 Isotherms of carbon dioxide according to van der Waals equation

At the critical point, Eqs. (2.71) and (2.72) must become identical. Comparing and equating the coefficients of like powers of V gives

$$3V_c = b + \frac{RT_c}{P_c} \qquad \text{...(2.73)}$$

$$3V_c^2 = \frac{a}{P_c} \qquad \text{...(2.74)}$$

$$V_c^3 = \frac{ab}{P_c} \qquad \text{...(2.75)}$$

Dividing Eq. (2.75) by Eq. (2.74), we get

$$V_c = 3b \qquad \text{...(2.76a)}$$

Substituting this value of V_c in Eq. (2.74), we obtain

$$P_c = \frac{a}{27b^2} \qquad \text{...(2.76b)}$$

Finally, substituting the values of P_c and V_c in Eq. (2.73), we get

$$T_c = \frac{8a}{27 Rb} \qquad \text{...(2.76c)}$$

We can express the constants a, b and R in terms of P_c, V_c and T_c as

$$b = \frac{V_c}{3}; \quad a = 3P_c\, V_c^2; \quad R = \frac{8P_c V_c}{3T_c} \qquad \text{...(2.77)}$$

Since experimentally it is difficult to determine V_c accurately, it would be better if a and b could be obtained from P_c and T_c only.

Since

$$V_c = \frac{3RT_c}{8P_c}$$

and substituting the value of V_c in the first two Eq. of (2.77) gives

$$b = \frac{RT_c}{8P_c} \qquad \text{...(2.78)}$$

$$a = \frac{27\left(RT_c\right)^2}{64 P_c} \qquad \text{...(2.79)}$$

Thus the values of a and b can be calculated from Eqs. (2.78) and (2.79).

If the van der Waals equation is obeyed by gases at their critical points then the critical compressibility factor $Z_c \left(= \dfrac{P_c V_c}{nRT_c} \right)$ should be equal to $\dfrac{3}{8}$ or 0.375. Table 2.6 lists the values of critical constants and the critical compressibility factor (Z_c) for a number of substances.

Table 2.6 Critical Constants of Gases

Gas	P_c (atm)	V_c (cm^3 mol^{-1})	T_c (K)	$Z_c = \dfrac{P_c V_c}{nRT_c}$
He	2.3	57.8	5.3	0.306
H_2	12.8	65.0	33.2	0.304
Ne	26.9	41.7	44.4	0.302
N_2	33.6	90.1	126.1	0.291
O_2	50.3	74.4	154.5	0.302
CO_2	72.7	95.0	304.2	0.275
H_2O	218.0	55.6	647.3	0.227
NH_3	112.0	72.0	405.5	0.243
CH_4	45.8	99.0	191.0	0.290
C_2H_6	48.2	139.0	305.5	0.267
C_2H_4	50.5	124.0	417.2	0.275

It is evident from the table that the calculated and experimental values generally disagree and the difference between the two values varies from gas to gas. It may be due to the fact that the van der Waals equation although an improvement over the ideal gas equation but does not adequately describe the behaviour of the gas near the critical state.

Problem 2.18: The van der Waals constant for gaseous HCl are $a = 0.367$ N m^4 mol^{-2}, and $b = 0.0408 \times 10^{-3}$ m^3 mol^{-1}. Calculate the critical constants of the gas.

Solution: $V_c = 3b$

$$= 3\left(0.0408 \times 10^{-3}\,\text{m}^3\text{mol}^{-1}\right)$$

$$= 0.1224 \times 10^{-3}\,\text{m}^3\text{mol}^{-1}$$

$$P_c = \frac{a}{27b^2} = \frac{\left(0.367\,\text{N m}^4\text{mol}^{-2}\right)}{27\left(0.0408 \times 10^{-3}\,\text{m}^3\text{mol}^{-1}\right)^2}$$

$$= 8.1 \times 10^6\,\text{Nm}^{-2}$$

and　　　　　$T_c = \dfrac{8a}{27\,Rb}$

$$= \frac{8\left(0.367\,\text{Nm}^4\text{mol}^{-2}\right)}{27\left(8.314\,\text{N m K}^{-1}\text{mol}^{-1}\right)\left(0.0408 \times 10^{-3}\,\text{m}^3\text{mol}^{-1}\right)}$$

$$= 321\,\text{K}$$

Problem 2.19: The critical temperature and the critical pressure of a gas are 393 K and 50 atmospheres respectively. Calculate the van der Waals constants.

Solution: $b = \dfrac{RT_c}{8P_c}$

$$= \frac{\left(8.314\,\mathrm{N\,m\,K^{-1}mol^{-1}}\right)(393\ \mathrm{K})}{8\left(50 \times 1.013 \times 10^5\ \mathrm{N\,m^{-2}}\right)}$$

$$= 8.07 \times 10^{-5}\ \mathrm{m^3\ mol^{-1}}$$

and $\quad a = \dfrac{27\left(RT_c\right)^2}{64P_c}$

$$= \frac{27\left(8.314\,\mathrm{N\,m\,K^{-1}mol^{-1}}\right)^2 (393\mathrm{K})^2}{64\left(50 \times 1.013 \times 10^5\mathrm{N\,m^{-2}}\right)}$$

$$= 0.276\ \mathrm{N\,m^4mol^{-2}}$$

2.21 THE LAW OF CORRESPONDING STATES

It was shown by van der Waals that instead of using volume, pressure and temperature of a gas, the ratio of these quantities to the corresponding critical quantities could be used in his equation. Thus,

$$\frac{P}{P_c} = P_r, \ \frac{V}{V_c} = V_r \ \text{and} \ \frac{T}{T_c} = T_r$$

where P_r, V_r and T_r are known as *the reduced pressure, the reduced volume* and *the reduced temperature* respectively.

Substituting these values in the van der Waals equation

$$\left(P + \frac{a}{V^2}\right)(V - b) = RT$$

we get

$$\left(P_c P_r + \frac{a}{V_c^2 V_r^2}\right)(V_c V_r - b) = RT_c T_r \qquad \qquad ...(2.80)$$

Since

$$P_c = \frac{a}{27b^2}, \ V_c = 3b \ \text{and} \ T_c = \frac{8a}{27\,Rb}$$

Substituting these values in Eq. (2.80), we get

$$\left(P_r \frac{a}{27b^2} + \frac{a}{9V_r^2 b^2}\right)(3V_r b - b) = RT_r \frac{8a}{27\,Rb}$$

or

$$\frac{a}{27b^2}\left(P_r + \frac{3}{V_r^2}\right)(3V_r - 1)b = \frac{8aT_r}{27b}$$

or

$$\frac{a}{27b}\left(P_r + \frac{3}{V_r^2}\right)(3V_r - 1) = \frac{8aT_r}{27b}$$

or

$$\left(P_r + \frac{3}{V_r^2}\right)(3V_r - 1) = 8T_r \qquad \qquad ...(2.81)$$

This is known as the reduced equation of state. It does not involve constants characterizing the individuality of substances and should be applicable to all substances. According to Eq. (2.81), it is clear that if two or more substances have the same reduced pressures and reduced temperatures, then their reduced volumes should be equal. Substances under these conditions are said to be in the corresponding states. This statement is called the law of corresponding states.

One can investigate the utility of these reduced variables by making plots of $Z\left(\dfrac{PV}{nRT}\right)$ for a

number of gases expressed as a function of their reduced pressures for various values of reduced temperatures (Fig. 2.22). It is found that the values of Z are approximately the same for a large number of gases under wide range of conditions indicating that all gases behave nearly alike in terms of these variables. Gases having the same values of their reduced variables deviate almost equally from ideality.

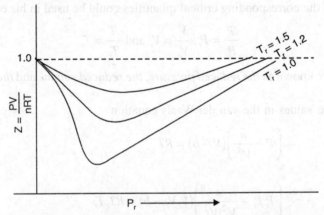

Fig. 2.22 Compressibility factor as a function of reduced pressure

2.22 LIQUEFACTION OF GASES

Presence of intermolecular forces between gas molecules suggests that all gases can be liquefied if subjected to high pressures and low temperatures. Discovery of critical phenomenon by Andrews in 1861 showed that gases cannot be liquefied by the application of pressure alone; they must first be cooled below their critical temperatures and then subjected to adequate pressures to cause liquefaction. The principles involved in the liquefaction are (*i*) A gas must be at or below its critical temperature. Lower the temperature below the critical value, easier would be the liquefaction and less would be the pressure required for liquefaction; and

(*ii*) The gas is cooled either by doing external work or by expanding against the internal forces of molecular attractions.

Low temperature for the liquefaction of gases may be attained by the following techniques:

(*a*) Use of freezing mixtures

(*b*) Cooling by rapid evaporation of a volatile liquid

(*c*) Cooling by Joule-Thomson effect

(*d*) Cooling by adiabatic expansion involving mechanical work

(*e*) Cooling by adiabatic demagnetization

(*a*) **Use of Freezing Mixtures:** Freezing mixtures such as ice with various salts, and solid carbon dioxide with ether, alcohol or acetone were the earliest to be employed for the liquefaction of gases. Addition of a salt to ice results in the melting of some ice and lowering of temperature. The added salt dissolves in water forming the solution. Both these processes, *viz.*, melting of ice and dissolution of salt are endothermic processes; the temperature of the mixture progressively decreases and continues up to a temperature where the solution becomes saturated with respect to both the salt and ice. This is the lowest temperature that can be attained with any freezing mixture.

(*b*) **Cooling by Rapid Evaporation of a Volatile Liquid:** This method was first employed by Pictet and Cailletet. An easily volatile liquid is rapidly evaporated which gets cooled and is used to liquefy less volatile liquid. This is the principle underlying the Cascades process for the liquefaction of O_2.

(*c*) **Cooling by Joule-Thomson Method:** When a compressed gas is allowed to expand into a region of low pressure or vacuum under adiabatic conditions, a lowering of temperature is observed. This is known as the Joule-Thomson effect. In the expansion, molecules of the gas move far apart from one another. Work is done by the gas molecules in overcoming the intermolecular forces. As the system is thermally insulated, work is done at the cost of the kinetic energy of the gas molecules. Consequently, a cooling effect is observed. For each gas there is a characteristic temperature above which a gas on expansion shows a heating effect while below it the gas cools on expansion. This temperature is known as *the inversion temperature of the gas*. This temperature is related to the van der Waals constants '*a*' and '*b*' by the expression

$$T_i = \frac{2a}{Rb}$$

where T_i is the inversion temperature of the gas.

Gases which show a cooling effect under ordinary temperatures have fairly high inversion temperatures. Gases like H_2 and He have low inversion temperatures, $(T_{i,H_2} = 193\ K$ and $T_{i,H_e} = 33\ K)$ and they show heating effects in Joule-Thomson expansion under ordinary temperatures. If these gases are cooled below their inversion temperatures they also show cooling effects.

(*d*) **Cooling by Adiabatic Expansion Involving Mechanical Work:** When a gas is allowed to expand adiabatically against a pressure, it does some external work at the cost of its kinetic energy, due to which its temperature falls. This principle is used in Claudes process for the liquefaction of air.

(*e*) **Cooling by Adiabatic Demagnetization:** Giauque and Debye independently suggested a new technique for the production of low temperature by using adiabatic demagnetization of paramagnetic salts like, cerium fluoride, gadolinium sulphate and other rare earth salts. In this technique, the paramagnetic salt is first cooled with liquid helium in the presence of a strong magnetic field. Liquid helium is then pumped away leaving the chilled magnetised salt thermally isolated from the surroundings. The magnetic field is then switched off, the salt then undergoes a reversible adiabatic transformation in which the atomic spins become disordered, *i.e.*, the entropy of the salt increases. The energy for this transformation must come from the crystal lattice and hence the temperature must fall. A temperature of 0.001 K was obtained by Lerden et al. Demagnetization of nuclear spins can be used to obtain a temperature of about 2×10^{-5} K.

EXERCISES

1. Correct the following statements:
   (*i*) A given quantity of a gas is heated from 20°C to 40°C at constant pressure. The gas will expand to twice its original volume.
   (*ii*) The rate of diffusion of a gas is directly proportional to its molar mass.
   (*iii*) At a given temperature, average kinetic energy per mole for hydrogen and SO_2 will be different.
   (*iv*) The difference between root mean square and the most probable speeds remains constant with increase in temperature.
   (*v*) All the molecules of a gas move with the same speed and the average speed of the molecules is zero.
   (*vi*) Mean free path of gas molecules is directly proportional to the pressure of the gas.
   (*vii*) The coefficient of viscosity of a gas varies linearly with the pressure of the gas.
   (*viii*) The number of collisions between gas molecules decreases with increase of temperature.
   (*ix*) An equimolar mixture of hydrogen and oxygen is at STP, the number of collisions per second on the walls of the container are equal for both hydrogen and oxygen.
   (*x*) A real gas does not behave ideally even at the Boyle temperature.
   (*xi*) Size effect decreases the pressure above the ideal value.
   (*xii*) The attractive forces between the molecules of a gas are higher at higher temperatures.
   (*xiii*) A gas can be liquefied at
       (*a*) $T = T_c$ and $P < P_c$ or
       (*b*) $T < T_c$ and $P = P_c$
   (*xiv*) The critical temperature of a gas is greater than its Boyle temperature.
   (*xv*) A gas with $a = 0$ and $b \neq 0$ can be liquefied.
   (*xvi*) An ideal gas can be liquefied below its critical temperature.

2. Explain, giving reasons, the following statements:
   (*i*) The kinetic energy of a gas increases with increasing temperature.
   (*ii*) The mean free path of gas molecules increases and the number of collisions per unit time decreases with the lowering of temperature.
   (*iii*) Viscosity of gas molecules increases with increasing temperature but is independent of the pressure.
   (*iv*) In an ideal gas, the mean free path is infinite.
   (*v*) Heat capacity of a diatomic gas is greater than that of a monatomic gas.
   (*vi*) Expected values of heat capacities for gases are observed only at high temperatures.
   (*vii*) Nonideal gases approach ideal behaviour at low pressures and high temperatures.
   (*viii*) The compressibility factor is unity at Boyle temperature of a gas.
   (*ix*) The molecular attractions between gas molecules are pronounced at low temperatures.
   (*x*) Gases cannot be liquefied merely by the application of pressure above their critical temperatures.
   (*xi*) A nonideal gas below its inversion temperatures shows a cooling effect in Joule-Thomson expansion.
   (*xii*) Information whether a gas is monatomic or diatomic can be obtained from heat capacity measurements.

(xiii) Fraction of molecules $\left(\dfrac{dn_c}{n'}\right)$ with speeds between c and $c + dc$ for oxygen gas at a temperature T is equal to that of sulphur dioxide at temperature $2T$.

(xiv) An ideal gas cannot be liquefied.

3. In the derivation of $PV = kT$ from Boyle's law, the following steps are followed:

(i) $PV = k_1$ (ii) $\dfrac{V}{T} = k_2$ (iii) $\dfrac{k_1}{P} = V$

(iv) $V = k_2 T$ (v) $\dfrac{k_1}{P} = k_2 T$ (vi) $\dfrac{k_1}{k_2} = k_3 = PT$

The conclusion is obviously wrong. What is the error? At what step is it introduced?

4. From the relations between the variables for two ideal gases A and B, given below on the left, what can be concluded regarding the variables on the right?

Given	Inference ($>$ or $=$ or $<$)
(i) Equal $P, V, T, M_A > M_B$	$\bar{c}_A \ldots \ldots \bar{c}_B$
(ii) Equal $P, V, T, M_A > M_B$	$n_A \ldots \ldots n_B$
(iii) Equal $P, V, n_A > n_B$	$T_A \ldots \ldots T_B$
(iv) Equal $T, n, P_A > P_B, M_A > M_B$	$V_A \ldots \ldots V_B$
(v) Equal $V, n, \bar{c}, M_A > M_B$	$P_A \ldots \ldots P_B$

Ans. (i) $\bar{c}_A < \bar{c}_B$, (ii) $n_A = n_B$, (iii) $T_A < T_B$, (iv) $V_A < V_B$, (v) $P_A > P_B$

5. Explain whether a gas approaches ideal behaviour or deviates from ideal behaviour if
   (i) it is compressed to a smaller volume at constant temperature,
   (ii) its temperature is raised keeping the volume constant.
   (iii) more gas is introduced into the same volume and at the same temperature.

6. Two flasks A and B have equal volumes. A is maintained at 300 K and B at 600 K. A contains hydrogen and B contains an equal mass of methane. Assuming ideal behaviour for both the gases, answer the following questions:
   (i) Which flask contains greater number of molecules? How many times as great?
   (ii) In which flask is the pressure greater? How many times as great?
   (iii) In which flask are the molecules moving faster? How many times as fast?
   (iv) In which flask are the number of collisions (X) with the walls greater? How many times as great?
   (v) In which flask is the mean free path of molecules greater? How many times as great? (Assume $= 2\sigma_{H_2} = \sigma_{CH4}$)
   (vi) In which flask is the viscosity greater? How many times as great?
   (vii) In which flask is the kinetic energy per mole ($\bar{E}$) greater? How many times as great?
   (viii) In which flask is the total kinetic energy (E) greater? How many times as great?
   (ix) In which flask is the compressibility factor (Z) greater? How many times as great?

Ans. (i) $\dfrac{N_{H_2}}{N_{CH_4}} = 8$, (ii) $\dfrac{P_{H_2}}{P_{CH_4}} = 4$, (iii) $\dfrac{\bar{c}_{H_2}}{\bar{c}_{CH_4}} = 2$, (iv) $\dfrac{X_{H_2}}{X_{CH_4}} = 16$, (v) $\dfrac{\lambda_{H_2}}{\lambda_{CH_4}} = \dfrac{1}{2}$,

(vi) $\dfrac{\eta_{H_2}}{\eta_{CH_4}} = 1$, (vii) $\dfrac{\overline{E}_{H_2}}{\overline{E}_{CH_4}} = \dfrac{1}{2}$, (viii) $\dfrac{E_{H_2}}{E_{CH_4}} = 4$, (ix) $\dfrac{Z_{H_2}}{Z_{CH_4}} = 1$.

7. Suppose that we change the root mean square speed of the gas molecules in a closed container of fixed volume from 5×10^2 m s^{-1} to 10×10^2 m s^{-1}. Which one of the following statements might correctly explain how this change was accomplished:

   (i) By heating the gas we double the temperature.

   (ii) By removing 75% of the gas at constant volume, we decrease the pressure to one-quarter of its original value.

   (iii) By heating the gas we quadruple the pressure.

   (iv) By pumping in more gas at constant temperature, we quadruple the pressure.

   (v) None of the above.   **Ans.** (iii).

8. Under what conditions will a pure sample of an ideal gas not only exhibit a pressure of 1 atm but also a concentration of 1 mole dm^{-3}?   **Ans.** $T = 12$ K.

9. A mixture of hydrogen and oxygen is prepared such that the number of wall collisions per second by molecules of each gas is the same. Which gas has a higher concentration?   **Ans.** O_2.

10. Explain why gaseous helium is a better conductor of heat than Xe? If hydrogen and deuterium both have same molecular diameters, which would be expected to be a better conductor of heat?   **Ans.** H_2.

11. Starting from the postulates of kinetic theory of gases, derive the kinetic gas equation, $PV = \dfrac{1}{3}mn'\overline{c}^2$.

    Deduce from this (a) the Boyle's law, (b) the Graham's law of diffusion, and (c) the Daltons's law of partial pressures.

12. State Maxwells's law of distribution of molecular speeds amongst the molecules of a gas. Explain from this the effect of temperature on the distribution of speeds. Can the molecules of a gas have high and almost zero

    speeds? Show that the most probable speed is given by $c_{mp} = \sqrt{\dfrac{2RT}{M}}$.

13. (a) Derive a relation between the mean free path of gas molecules and its collision diameter.

    (b) Define the terms, collision diameter and collision frequency. Derive the expression for the number of collisions per unit time per unit volume, Z_{11}.

14. Explain the variation of compressibility factor Z with pressure for nitrogen and hydrogen (i) at a given temperature and (ii) at different temperatures.

15. What are believed to be the chief causes of deviations of real gases from ideal behaviour? How are they accounted for in the van der Waals equation of state?

16. (a) What is the physical significance of 'a' and 'b' in the van der Waals equation?

    (b) Show that the excluded volume is four times the actual volume of molecules.

    (c) Comment on the nature of the gas whose equation of state for a mole is

    (i) $P(V - b) = RT$ and (ii) $(P + a/V^2)V = RT$

17. Comment on the statement "the van der Waals equation is an improvement over the ideal gas equation." Derive the expressions for the critical constants in terms of van der Waals constants 'a' and 'b'.

18. Deduce the law of corresponding states from the van der Waals equation. What is the significance of the law?

19. Write notes on:

    (a) Viscosity of gases;   (b) Degrees of freedom;

    (c) Law of equipartition of energy and   (d) Continuity of state.

20. Estimate the number of gas molecules left in a volume of 10^{-3} cm^3 if the gas is pumped out to give a vacuum of 10^{-5} mm Hg at 298 K. **Ans.** 3.243×10^8.

21. An iron tank of helium at 298 K contains the gas at 200 atmospheres. The tank will hold upto a pressure of about 700 atmospheres. If the tank is in a building that catches fire, will the tank blow up before it melts? The m.p. of iron is 1808 K. **Ans.** It will blow up.

22. A 2 m long tube is provided with inlets at both the ends so that HCl and NH$_3$ gases can be admitted simultaneously. Calculate the distance from the HCl inlet end of the tube at which NH$_4$Cl will first appear if two gases are admitted at the same time, one from one end and the other from the other end. **Ans.** 0.811 m.

23. The pressure of a certain gas at 293.2 K contained in 0.5×10^{-3} m^3 flask was 1 atm. The mass of the flask and the gas was found to be 25.178×10^{-3} kg. The gas was allowed to escape until the final pressure was 0.83 atm and the flask was found to weigh 25.053×10^{-3} kg. Calculate the molar mass of the gas. **Ans.** 32×10^{-3} kg mol^{-1}.

24. A gas sample is known to be a mixture of ethane and butane. A bulb of 2×10^{-4} m^3 capacity is filled with the gas to a pressure of 750 mm at 293.2 K. If the mass of the gas in the bulb is 0.3846×10^{-3} kg, what is the mole percent of C$_4$H$_{10}$ in the mixture? **Ans.** 60.4%.

25. Calculate the pressure exerted by 10^{23} gas molecules each with mass 10^{-25} kg in a container of volume 1 dm^3. The root mean square speed is 10^3 m s^{-1}. What is the total kinetic energy (KE) of these gas molecules? Calculate the temperature of the gas. **Ans.** $P = 32.91$ atm, $KE = 5.0$ kJ, $T = 2415$ K.

26. Kinetic theory was once criticised on the grounds that it should apply even to potatoes. Compute the average speed of a potato at 298 K weighing 0.1 kg. Assuming that gravity has no effect on the motion of the potatoes, how long would a potato take to traverse a distance of 10^{-2} m. **Ans.** 1 yr.

27. If all the translational kinetic energy of 1 mole of hydrogen gas at 300 K is transferred to 10 moles of water vapours at 300 K, what will be the final temperature of water vapours? **Ans.** 330 K.

28. Calculate the kinetic energy of a mole of an ideal gas at 273 K. At what temperature will three moles of the ideal gas have the same kinetic energy? **Ans.** $KE = 3.405$ kJ mol^{-1}, $T = 91$ K.

29. The molecular diameter of CO is 3.19×10^{-10} m. At 300 K and a pressure of 100 mm Hg, what will be (a) the number of molecules colliding per unit volume, (b) the number of collisions per metre cube per second and (c) the mean free path of the gas molecules? **Ans.** (a) 3.22×10^{24}, (b) 1.06×10^{23} and (c) 6.87×10^{-5} m.

30. If the molecular diameter of H$_2$ is 1.9×10^{-10} m, calculate the number of collisions by a hydrogen molecule in 1 second (a) if $T = 300$ K and $P = 1$ atmosphere, (b) if $T = 500$ K and $P = 1$ atmosphere, (c) if $T = 300$ K and $P = 10^{-4}$ cm Hg, (d) compute the total number of collisions per second occurring in one m^3 for each case in (a), (b) and (c).

Ans. (a) 7.03×10^9 s^{-1}, (b) 1.71×10^{10} s^{-1}, (c) 9.2×10^1 s^{-1} and (d) 8.61×10^{34} m^{-3} s^{-1}, 1.25×10^{35} m^{-3} s^{-1} and 1.5×10^{19} m^{-3} s^{-1}.

31. Specific heat of a monatomic gas at constant volume is 315 J kg^{-1} deg^{-1} and that at constant pressure is 525 J kg^{-1} deg^{-1}. What is the molar mass of the gas. **Ans.** 40×10^{-3} kg mol^{-1}.

32. Which one would be expected to have higher heat capacity, an ideal gas or a van der Waals gas? Discuss.

33. Two separate bulbs are containing gases A and B respectively. The pressure and volume are such that PV product is the same for both the gases. However, gas A is ideal while gas B is nonideal and is at a pressure and temperature less than the critical values. Explain whether the temperature of the gas B should be the same, more or less than that of A.

34. Two gases A and B are confined in separate containers under identical conditions. The gas A has the van der Waals constants $a = 0.0248$ N m^4 mol^{-2} and $b = 0.267 \times 10^{-3}$ m^3 mol^{-1}; while the corresponding values of the constants 'a' and 'b' for gas B are 0.227 N m^4 mol^{-2} and 0.0428×10^{-3} m^3 mol^{-1} respectively. Explain
   (a) Which gas will have the greater pressure correction term?
   (b) Which gas has the larger molecular size?

      (c) Which gas would have a higher value of T_c?   **Ans.** (a) Gas B, (b) gas A and (c) gas A.

35.   Calculate the pressure exerted by 22×10^{-3} kg of CO_2 in 0.5×10^{-3} m³ capacity at 298 K using (a) the van der Waals equation and (b) the ideal gas equation (a and b are 0.0368 N m⁴ mol⁻² and 0.4267×10^3 m³ mol⁻¹ respectively.)   **Ans.** (a) 21.95 atm. (b) 24.43 atm.

36.   The van der Waals constant 'b' for helium is 2.433×10^{-5} m³ mol⁻¹, calculate the diameter of a helium atom.
                                                        Ans. 2.68×10^{-10} m.

37.   (i) Two van der Waals gases have the same value of 'b' but different 'a' values, which of these would occupy greater volume under identical conditions?

      (ii) If the gases have same 'a' values but different values of 'b' which would be more compressible?

                        Ans. (i) Gas with larger value of 'a' would occupy smaller volume, and
                                (ii) the gas with smaller 'b' value would be more compressible.

38.   A nonideal gas of molar mass 1.50×10^{-1} kg mol⁻¹ obeys the van der Waals equation; its critical pressure and temperature are 100 atm and 373 K respectively. The compressibility factor $\dfrac{PV}{nRT}$ will be greater than unity at 500 atm and 353 K or 500 atm and 393 K or 50 atm and 333 K or 50 atm and 393 K or none of these.
                                                   Ans. 500 atm and 393 K.

39.   The equation of state for 1 mole of a certain gas is

$$P = \frac{RT}{V-b} - \frac{a}{V}$$

where a and b are constants distinct from zero. Ascertain whether the gas has a critical point or not.
                                                   Ans. No.

40.   Assuming that air has a mean molar mass of 0.0289 kg mol⁻¹ and that the atmosphere is an isothermal at 298 K, compute the pressure at a height of 1600 m above the sea level. The sea level pressure may be taken as 1 atmosphere.   **Ans.** 0.8329 atm.

41.   4 g of argon in a bulb at temperature TK had a pressure P. When the bulb was placed in a hotter bath at temperature 50°C more than the first one, 0.8 g of argon had to be removed to get the original pressure P. Calculate the original temperature of the gas.   **Ans.** 200 K.

42.   At room temperature the following reactions proceed nearly to completion:

$$2NO + O_2 \rightarrow 2\,NO_2 \rightarrow N_2O_4$$

The dimer, N_2O_4, solidifies at 262 K. A 250 ml flask and a 100 ml flask are separated by a stop-cock. At 300 K, NO in larger flask exerts a pressure of 1.053 atmospheres and the smaller one containing O_2 had a pressure of 0.789 atmosphere. The gases are mixed by opening the stop-cock and after the end of the reaction, the flasks are cooled to 220 K. Neglecting the vapour pressure of the dimer, calculate the final pressure (P_f) and the composition of the gas mixture at 220 K. (Assume gases to behave ideally).
                                                   Ans. P_f = 0.2216 atm.

43.   A 100 dm³ flask contains 10 moles each of N_2 and H_2 at 777 K. The two gases were made to react and at equilibrium partial pressure of hydrogen was 1 atmosphere. At this point 5L water was injected into the flask and the gas mixture was cooled to 298 K. Find the gas pressure.   **Ans.** 2.25 atm.

44.   The pressure in a bulb dropped from 2000 mm Hg to 1500 mm Hg in 47 minute. When the contained O_2 leaked through a small hole, the bulb was completely evacuated and a mixture of oxygen and another gas of molar mass 79 g mol⁻¹, in the molar ratio 1:1 at a total pressure of 4000 mm mol⁻¹ Hg was introduced. Find the molar ratio of two gases remaining in the bulb after 74 min.
                                               Ans. mole ratio 1:1.24 in favours of oxygen.

CHAPTER

3

The Liquid State

3.1 INTRODUCTION

In the last chapter we have studied that in gases the molecules are in a state of random motion and furthermore, there are no appreciable forces of attractions amongst them. On the other hand, in crystalline solids due to strong attractive forces, the constituents are arranged in a perfect ordered manner in fixed positions. The liquid state lies between the gaseous and the solid state in the sense that there is neither the ordered arrangement of constituents nor the complete disorder as in gases. It is generally observed that some of the properties of liquids closely resemble those of gases while some of the properties approach those of the solids. In the light of the kinetic molecular theory, liquids may be considered as a continuation of gases into the region of small volumes and high intermolecular attraction. The cohesive forces in a liquid are stronger than those in gases even at high pressures, and are sufficiently high to keep the molecules confined to a definite volume. The positions of the molecules in liquids are not rigidly fixed. These forces are not strong enough to entirely eliminate the movements of the molecules in the liquid. Thus the molecules in the liquid state have much shorter mean free path as compared to gas molecules.

Properties of liquids can be explained on the basis of their following characteristics:

(a) There are appreciable forces of attractions between the molecules of a liquid. These are about 10^6 times as strong as in gases. The forces amongst the constituents of a liquid prevent them from separating spontaneously from each other, but they are not strong enough to hold the molecules in fixed positions. Surface tension, viscosity, fairly high heat of vapourisation and vapour pressure of liquids can be explained in terms of these attractive forces.

(b) The molecules in a liquid are in a state of random motion although the extent of randomness is small in comparison to gases. The molecules are relatively close together. Most of the space in the liquid is occupied by its molecules and only a small fraction of the space is available to them for their free movement. This explains the higher density, incompressibility and slow diffusion of liquids in comparison to gases.

(c) The average kinetic energy of the molecules in a liquid is proportional to the absolute temperature. Increase in temperature increases the proportion of the energized molecules, lowers the attractive forces between the molecules, and consequently increases the vapour pressure of the liquid.

From the above arguments, it is concluded that most of the characteristic properties of the liquid arise due to the nature and magnitude of the intermolecular forces between the molecules. The important properties which will be dealt with in this chapter are: (*i*) Vapour pressure; (*ii*) Surface tension; and (*iii*) Viscosity.

3.2 LIQUID-VAPOUR EQUILIBRIUM—VAPOUR PRESSURE

Molecules of a liquid, like those of a gas, exhibit a distribution of energies. The molecules that have sufficient energy to overcome intermolecular attractions can escape from the bulk into the gas phase (or vapour phase) provided they are close to the surface. This happens during evaporation. Since the average kinetic energy of molecules in vapour state is more than that in liquid state, the temperature of the liquid falls on evaporation. The rate of evaporation of a liquid depends upon (*a*) the temperature of the liquid, (*b*) attractive forces in the liquid, (*c*) surface area, and (*d*) pressure above the liquid.

If we examine the evaporation of a liquid in an enclosed space (at constant temperature), we find that some of the molecules of the liquid will spontaneously pass from the surface into the space above it (Fig. 3.1). Since the space is closed, the molecules in the vapour state are unable to escape from the container. The molecules in the vapour phase collide with each other and with the sides of the container. Some of the molecules on collision pass on their energy to other molecules and come back to the liquid phase.

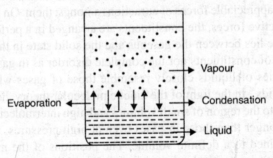

Fig. 3.1 Liquid-vapour equilibrium

This phenomenon is known as condensation. The rate of condensation of molecules in the vapour phase is proportional to the concentration of molecules in the vapour phase. A stage is ultimately reached when the rate of condensation equals the rate of evaporation. This situation corresponds to that of a dynamic equilibrium between the liquid and its vapour, e.g.,

$$H_2O(l) \underset{\text{condensation}}{\overset{\text{evaporation}}{\rightleftharpoons}} H_2O(g)$$

Thus a state of equilibrium is attained at which two opposing processes occur simultaneously at the same rate. At this point there is no further change in the number of molecules in either the liquid or in the vapour state.

Molecules of a liquid in the vapour state exert some pressure. At equilibrium this pressure is characteristic of the liquid at a given temperature and is called *the vapour pressure* of the liquid. The vapour pressure of a liquid is therefore defined as *the pressure exerted by the vapours that are in equilibrium with the liquid at a given temperature*. The vapour pressure depends on

(*i*) the nature of the intermolecular forces in the liquid, and

(*ii*) the temperature of the liquid.

(*i*) **The Nature of the Liquid:** If in a liquid the attractive forces between the molecules are strong then the tendency of the molecules to escape from the surface of the liquid would be low. Hence, such a liquid will have low vapour pressure. However, liquids with low intermolecular forces would have a high escaping tendency and consequently high equilibrium vapour pressure.

(*ii*) **Effect of Temperature:** As the temperature of a liquid is increased the average kinetic energy of the molecules increases. The increased kinetic energy partly overcomes the attractive forces between the molecules and thus raises the escaping tendency of the molecules. This results in an increase in the equilibrium vapour pressure. The values of vapour pressure when plotted against temperature, a curve of the type shown in Fig. 3.2 is obtained. The curve indicates that the vapour pressure increases exponentially with the increase of temperature. The temperature at which the vapour pressure of a liquid becomes equal to the atmospheric pressure is called the boiling point of the liquid. The *boiling point of a liquid is the temperature at which its vapour pressure is equal to the external pressure*. When the external pressure is 1 atmosphere the term *normal boiling* point is used.

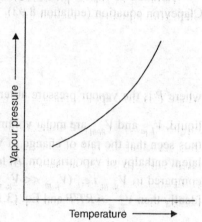

Fig. 3.2 Variation of vapour pressure of a liquid with temperature

The vapour pressures of some commonly used liquids are given in Table 3.1.

Table 3.1 Vapour Pressures of Liquids (10^{-3} N m^{-2})

Temperature (°C)	Water	Ethanol	Acetone	Carbon tetrachloride	Chloroform	Acetic acid
10	1.226	3.17	15.41	7.46	13.40	–
20	2.333	5.79	24.63	12.13	23.95	1.56
30	4.240	10.46	47.44	19.06	32.80	2.67
40	7.372	18.04	56.19	30.10	48.85	4.64
50	12.331	29.62	81.68	48.93	70.13	7.55
60	19.920	47.02	–	60.10	98.60	11.73
70	31.158	72.33	–	89.99	–	18.13
80	47.320	–	–	–	–	26.97
90	70.115	–	–	–	–	31.16
100	101.330	–	–	–	–	55.59

3.3 VARIATION OF VAPOUR PRESSURE WITH TEMPERATURE

The vapour pressure of a liquid increases exponentially with increase of temperature up to the critical point of the liquid. In terms of kinetic theory, the increase in vapour pressure with temperature is easily understandable. As the temperature increases, a greater proportion of the molecules acquires sufficient energy to overcome the cohesive forces and escapes from the liquid. Consequently, a higher pressure is necessary to establish the equilibrium between vapours and the liquid. Above the critical temperature the escaping tendency of the molecules is so high that only the vapours exist.

Variation of vapour pressure with temperature (Fig. 3.2) is expressed mathematically by Clausius-Clapeyron equation (equation 8.92).

$$\frac{dP}{dT} = \frac{\Delta H_{vap,\,m}}{T\left(V_{g,m} - V_{l,m}\right)} \qquad \qquad ...(3.1)$$

where P is the vapour pressure at temperature T, $\Delta H_{vap,m}$ the molar enthalpy of vapourisation of the liquid, $V_{l,\,m}$ and $V_{g,\,m}$ are molar volumes of the liquid and the vapour respectively at temperature T. It is thus seen that the rate of change of vapour pressure with temperature (dP/dT) is dependent upon the latent enthalpy of vapourisation. At temperatures not too near the critical temperature, $V_{l,\,m}$ is small as compared to $V_{g,\,m}$ i.e., ($V_{l,\,m} \ll V_{g,\,m}$) and it may be neglected. Furthermore, if the vapours behave ideally then $V_{g,\,m} = RT/P$ and Eq. (3.1) becomes

$$\frac{dP}{dT} = \frac{\Delta H_{vap,\,m}}{TV_g} = \frac{\Delta H_{vap,\,m}}{RT^2}P$$

or

$$\frac{1}{P}\frac{dP}{dT} = \frac{\Delta H_{vap,\,m}}{RT^2}$$

or

$$\frac{d\ln P}{dT} = \frac{\Delta H_{vap,\,m}}{RT^2}$$

or

$$d\ln P = \frac{\Delta H_{vap,\,m}}{RT^2}dT \qquad \qquad ...(3.2)$$

Integration of Eq. (3.2) gives

$$\ln P = -\frac{\Delta H_{vap,\,m}}{R}\left(\frac{1}{T}\right) + \text{constant}$$

$$\log P = -\frac{\Delta H_{vap,\,m}}{2.303R}\left(\frac{1}{T}\right) + \text{constant} \qquad \qquad ...(3.3)$$

Equation (3.3) predicts that the logarithm of the vapour pressure should be a linear function of the reciprocal of the absolute temperature. Comparison of Eq. (3.3) with the equation of a straight line, viz., $y = mx + c$, suggests that a plot of log P against $1/T$ should be a straight line with slope $[= -\Delta H_{vap,\,m}/(2.303R)]$ and the intercept equal to a constant. This is shown in Fig. 3.3. From the slope of the line the enthalpy of vapourisation can be calculated as

$$\text{slope, } m = -\frac{\Delta H_{vap,m}}{2.303\,R}$$

or

$$\Delta H_{vap,\,m} = -2.303\,Rm$$

To obtain the value of the constant in Eq. (3.3), the value of $\Delta H_{vap, m}$ calculated above and a value of log P and $1/T$ corresponding to a point on the line are substituted in the equation and solved for the constant. Once $\Delta H_{vap, m}$ and constant for a given liquid are known, the vapour pressure of the liquid at any temperature can be calculated.

Equation (3.3) can also be written in a more convenient form by integrating Eq. (3.2) between the limits P_1 and P_2 corresponding to the temperature T_1 and T_2. Thus

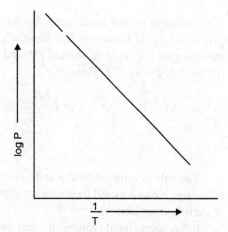

Fig. 3.3 log P versus $1/T$ plot for a liquid

$$\int_{P_1}^{P_2} d\ln P = \frac{\Delta H_{vap, m}}{R} \int_{T_1}^{T_2} \frac{dT}{T^2}$$

Assuming that $\Delta H_{vap, m}$ remains constant in the temperature range T_1 and T_2, we have

$$\ln \frac{P_2}{P_1} = \frac{\Delta H_{vap, m}}{R} \left[-\frac{1}{T} \right]_{T_1}^{T_2}$$

$$= \frac{\Delta H_{vap, m}}{R} \left[\frac{T_2 - T_1}{T_2 T_1} \right]$$

$$\log \frac{P_2}{P_1} = \frac{\Delta H_{vap,m}}{2.303 R} \left[\frac{T_2 - T_1}{T_1 T_2} \right] \qquad \qquad ...(3.4)$$

Equation (3.4) is known as the Clausius-Clapeyron equation and can be used to calculate $\Delta H_{vap, m}$ from the values of the vapour pressure at two temperatures. Alternatively, knowing $\Delta H_{vap, m}$ the boiling point of a liquid at a certain pressure can be calculated when the value at another pressure is known. Similarly, one can employ Eq. (3.4) in evaluating the vapour pressure of a liquid at a certain temperature provided $\Delta H_{vap, m}$ and the vapour pressure at some temperature is known. Equation (3.4) can also be applied to solid vapour equilibrium provided $V_{g,m} \gg V_{s,m}$.

Trouton's Rule

From Eq. (3.3), we get,

$$\log P = -\frac{\Delta H_{vap,m}}{2.303 \, RT} + \text{constant}$$

If we consider a liquid at its normal boiling point (T_b), *i.e.*, the temperature at which the vapours of the liquid attain a value of one atmosphere ($P = 1$ atm), the above equation becomes

$$\frac{\Delta H_{vap, m}}{T_b} = \text{constant}$$

The ratio of the molar enthalpy of vapourization to the normal boiling point is constant. This generalisation is known as the *Trouton's rule*. From experimental results, he found that the value of the constant for most of the simple and non-associated liquids is approximately 21 cal deg^{-1} mol^{-1} (87.86 J deg^{-1} mol^{-1}). Thus

$$\frac{\Delta H_{vap, m}}{T_b} = 21 \text{ cal deg}^{-1}\text{mol}^{-1}$$

$$= 87.86 \text{ J deg}^{-1} \text{mol}^{-1}$$

The rule is only empirical and is not obeyed by associated or low boiling or high boiling liquids. However, it can be used to obtain an approximate value of the heat of vapourization of normal liquids at their boiling points.

It has been found empirically that the normal boiling point of a liquid is approximately two-thirds of its critical temperature (T_c), *i.e.*,

$$T_b = \frac{2}{3} T_c$$

Problem 3.1: Calculate the rate of change of boiling point with pressure (dT/dP) for water. Given $\Delta H_{vap, m}$ = 40.67 kJ mol^{-1}, molar volumes of liquid water and water vapours at 100°C are respectively 1.872×10^{-2} dm^3 mol^{-1} and 30.33 dm^3 mol^{-1}. Also calculate (*i*) the boiling point of water when the pressure is raised by 1 atmosphere, (*ii*) the vapour pressure of water when the boiling point is increased by 1 degree.

Solution: From Clapeyron equation we have

$$\frac{dP}{dT} = \frac{\Delta H_{vap,m}}{T\left(V_{g, m} - V_{l, m}\right)}$$

or

$$\frac{dT}{dP} = \frac{T\left(V_{g, m} - V_{l, m}\right)}{\Delta H_{vap, m}}$$

Now,

$$\left(V_{g, m} - V_{l, m}\right) = \left(30.33 - 1.872 \times 10^{-2}\right) \text{dm}^3\text{mol}^{-1} = 30.311 \text{ dm}^3\text{mol}^{-1}$$

Hence

$$\frac{dT}{dP} = \frac{(373.16 \text{ K})\left(30.311 \text{ dm}^3 \text{ mol}^{-1}\right)}{40650 \text{ J mol}^{-1}}$$

$$= 2.78 \times 10^{-1} \text{dm}^3 \text{ KJ}^{-1}$$

$$= 2.78 \times 10^{-1} \times 10^{-3} \text{m}^3 \text{ KJ}^{-1} \qquad \left(\because 10^{-3}\text{m}^3 = 1 \text{ dm}^3\right)$$

$$= 2.78 \times 10^{-4} \text{m}^3\text{K}\left(\text{Nm}\right)^{-1} \qquad \left(\because 1 \text{ J} = 1 \text{ Nm}\right)$$

$$= 2.78 \times 10^{-4} \text{ K}\left(\text{Nm}^{-2}\right)^{-1}$$

$$= 2.78 \times 10^{-4} \times 1.013 \times 10^5 \ \text{K atm}^{-1} \quad \left(\because 1 \ \text{atm} = 1.013 \times 10^5 \ \text{Nm}^{-2} \right)$$

$$= 28.08 \ \text{K atm}^{-1}$$

(i) The boiling point of water for one atmospheric increase in pressure

$$= 373.16 + 28.08 = 401.24 \ \text{K}$$

Now, $\dfrac{dP}{dT} = \dfrac{1}{28.08} \ \text{atm K}^{-1} = 27.05 \ \text{mm Hg K}^{-1}$

Therefore, the vapour pressure for 1 degree rise in temperature is $760 + 27.05 = 787.05$ mm Hg

Problem 3.2: At 373.6 K and 372.6 K the vapour pressures of H_2O (l) are 1.03×10^5 N m^{-2} and 0.9947×10^5 N m^{-2} respectively. What is the enthalpy of vapourization of water?

Solution: $T_1 = 372.6 \ \text{K}$ $\qquad\qquad P_1 = 0.9947 \times 10^5 \ \text{N m}^{-2}$

$T_2 = 373.6 \ \text{K}$ $\qquad\qquad P_2 = 1.03 \times 10^5 \ \text{N m}^{-2}$

Using Eq. (3.4), we have

$$\log \frac{P_2}{P_1} = \frac{\Delta H_{vap,m}}{2.303R} \left[\frac{T_2 - T_1}{T_1 T_2} \right]$$

$$\log \frac{1.03 \times 10^5}{0.9947 \times 10^5} = \frac{\Delta H_{vap,m}}{2.303 \times 8.314 \ \text{J K}^{-1} \text{mol}^{-1}} \left[\frac{373.6 \ \text{K} - 372.6 \ \text{K}}{373.6 \ \text{K} \times 372.6 \ \text{K}} \right]$$

or $\qquad\qquad \Delta H_{vap,m} = 40.24 \ \text{kJ mol}^{-1}$

$$= 2.236 \times 10^3 \ \text{kJ kg}^{-1}.$$

Problem 3.3: At what temperature will water boil when the elevation is such that the barometric pressure is 500 mm Hg? $\Delta H_{vap,m} = 40670 \ \text{J mol}^{-1}$.

Solution: From Clausius-Clapeyron equation

$$\log \frac{P_2}{P_1} = \frac{\Delta H_{vap,m}}{2.303 \ R} \left[\frac{1}{T_1} - \frac{1}{T_2} \right]$$

Here $\quad P_2 = 1.013 \times 10^5 \ \text{N m}^{-2}$ $\qquad\qquad T_2 = 373.16 \ \text{K}$

$P_1 = 6.665 \times 10^4 \ \text{N m}^{-2}$ $\qquad\qquad T_1 = ?$

$$\Delta H_{vap,m} = 40670 \ \text{J mol}^{-1}$$

Therefore $\quad \log \dfrac{1.013 \times 10^5 \ \text{Nm}^{-2}}{6.665 \times 10^4 \ \text{Nm}^{-2}} = \dfrac{40670 \ \text{J mol}^{-1}}{2.303 \times 8.314 \text{J mol}^{-1} \text{K}^{-1}} \left(\dfrac{1}{T_1} - \dfrac{1}{373.16} \right)$

or $\qquad\qquad\qquad T_1 = 365 \ \text{K}.$

3.4 SURFACE TENSION

Surface tension is another important property of liquids related to the intermolecular forces. This phenomenon may be explained by reference to Fig. 3.4.

Consider a molecule A within the liquid. It is completely surrounded by other molecules, and so on the average, it is attracted equally in all directions by other molecules. The molecule B on the surface,

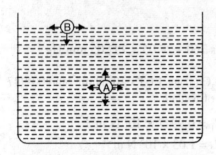

however, is partially surrounded by other molecules and experiences only a downward force of attraction. This unbalanced attractive force tends to draw the surface molecules inward, and the surface of a liquid tends to contract to the smallest possible area. As a result of the tendency to contract, a liquid surface behaves as if it were in a state of tension. This effect is called the *surface tension* which is defined as *the force in dynes (newton) acting at right angles along the surface of a liquid one centimetre (1 metre) in length.* It is generally represented by γ and is expressed in *dynes* cm^{-1} in CGS system and as Nm^{-1} in SI system.

Fig. 3.4 Forces on a molecule at the surface and in the interior of a liquid

Surface tension of liquids accounts for the spherical shape of drops of a liquid or bubbles of a gas in a liquid. It is also responsible for the rise or fall of liquids in capillary tubes. For example, water rises in a capillary tube while mercury level falls in a capillary. The concave meniscus that we observe (while handling liquids in burettes and pipettes) also arises from the surface tension of liquids.

Surface Energy: As a result of the inward pull, surface of the liquid always tends to contract to the smallest possible surface area. In order to increase the surface area it is necessary to do work to bring molecules from the bulk of the liquid on to the surface against the inward attractive forces. *The work required to increase the surface area by unity is called the surface energy.* To obtain an expression for this work, consider a liquid film contained within a rectangular wire frame ABCD as shown in Fig. 3.5. The side CD = l, is fitted with a movable piston. If the wire CD is pulled out by a distance dl, the surface energy of the film is increased by the amount of work done against the surface tension. The increase in surface energy is given by $\gamma\, dA$, where γ is the surface energy per unit area and dA is the increase in the area of the film. Since there are two surfaces of the film, therefore the increase in the area is

$$dA = 2\,(l \times dl)$$

Hence, the total increase in the surface energy is equal to $\gamma \times 2\,(l \times dl)$. This increase in surface energy is opposed by a force F applied perpendicular to the movable side to move it against the surface tension. If the wire moves a distance dl from position CD to XY, the work done W, is given by

$$W = F \times dl$$

Since increase in surface energy = work done

therefore, $\gamma \times 2\,(l \times dl) = F \times dl$

or $F = \gamma 2l$

$$\gamma = \frac{F}{2l} = \frac{\text{Force}}{\text{Length}} \qquad ...(3.5)$$

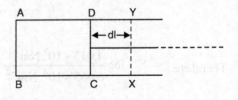

Fig. 3.5 Surface energy

$$= \frac{W}{2l\,dl} \qquad\qquad (\because \text{ work} = \text{force} \times \text{distance})$$

$$= \frac{W}{\Delta A} \qquad\qquad ...(3.6)$$

where $\Delta A = 2\,ldl$ is the area of new surface of liquid generated by CD. Thus, it is evident that surface tension is defined *as the work required to enlarge the surface area by unity and is, therefore, frequently referred to as the surface energy of a liquid per unit area.* The surface tension (Nm^{-1}) is numerically equal to the rate of increase of surface energy with area ($J\ m^{-2}$).

The surface tension is a characteristic property of each liquid and differs largely in magnitude for different liquids. Table 3.2 lists the values of surface tension of a few liquids.

Table 3.2 Surface Tension of Liquids at 293 K

Liquid	γ		Liquid	γ	
	dynes cm^{-1}	*Nm^{-1} × 10^2*		*dynes cm^{-1}*	*Nm^{-1} × 10^2*
Methanol	22.60	2.260	Toluene	28.50	2.850
Ethanol	22.75	2.275	Benzene	28.85	2.885
Acetone	23.70	2.370	Nitrobenzene	41.80	4.180
Ethyl acetate	23.90	2.390	Water	72.80	7.280
Carbon tetrachloride	26.95	2.695			

*1 dyne cm^{-1} = 10^{-5} N × 10^2 m^{-1}

$\qquad\qquad\quad$ = 10^{-3} N m^{-1}

Rise and Fall of liquids in capillary tubes: The rise or fall of liquid levels in a container depends on the interaction between the liquid surface and the walls of the container. If the intermolecular forces between liquid molecules are weaker than the forces between the liquid and the solid surface, the liquid will rise and wet the solid surface. If the solid-liquid interactions are weaker than the intermolecular forces in the liquid its level will fall and the liquid will not wet the solid surface. *The angle between the tangent to the liquid surface at the point of contact and the solid surface inside the liquid is known as the contact angle* (θ) *for the pair of liquid and solid surface* (Fig. 3.6). The contact angle can have any value between 0 and 180°. For liquids which wet the solid surface, θ is less than 90° while those which do not wet the solid surface, θ is more than 90°.

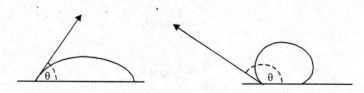

Fig. 3.6 Contact angle

3.5 DETERMINATION OF SURFACE TENSION

There are many methods which can be employed for the measurement of surface tension. We shall, however, discuss here briefly two of the commonly used methods.

(a) **The Capillary Rise Method:** If a capillary tube is placed in a liquid, it is found that the liquid usually rises in the tube (except for mercury in which it falls). Consider a capillary tube of radius 'r' immersed in a vessel containing a liquid that wets the glass (Fig. 3.7).

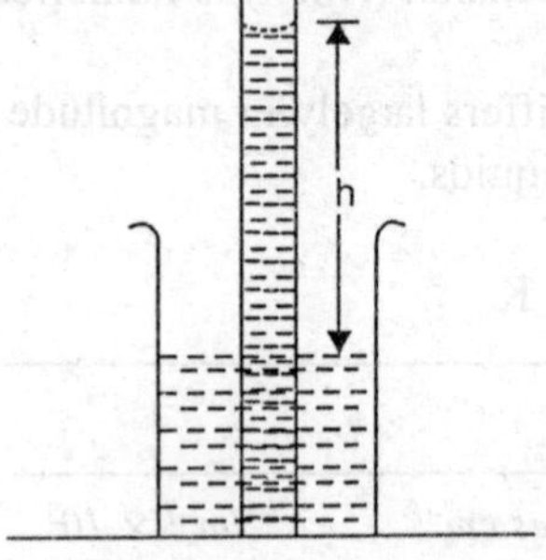

Let the liquid rise to a height 'h' above the level of the liquid and 'd' be the density of the liquid.

The force due to surface tension acting upwards on the inner side of the capillary raising the liquid column upward is equal to $\gamma \cos \theta \times$ inner circumference of the capillary, *i.e.*,

$$\text{Force} = \gamma \cos \theta \times 2 \pi r$$

where γ is the surface tension of the liquid and θ is the contact angle.

Force of gravity pulling the liquid downward = weight of the liquid column = vdg

where v is the volume of the liquid in the tube.

But $v = \pi r^2 h$

Hence the weight of the liquid column = $\pi r^2 hdg$

Fig. 3.7 Surface tension measurement by capillary rise method

At equilibrium,

$$\gamma \cos \theta \, 2\pi r = \pi r^2 hdg$$

or
$$\gamma = \frac{rhdg}{2\cos\theta} \qquad \qquad ...(3.7)$$

If the angle of contact θ between the glass and liquid is zero then $\cos \theta$ is unity and Eq. (3.7) reduces to

$$\gamma = \frac{rhdg}{2} \qquad \qquad ...(3.8)$$

For the determination of surface tension of a liquid, it is required to measure the height (h) upto which the liquid rises and the radius (r) of the capillary tube. The height 'h' is measured by cathetometer and the radius of the capillary tube by a travelling microscope.

A modification of this method is the differential capillary rise method. Two capillary tubes of different radii r_1 and r_2 are taken and dipped into a liquid. If h_1 and h_2 are heights upto which the liquid rises, then from Eq. (3.8)

$$\gamma = \frac{1}{2} h_1 dg r_1$$

or
$$\frac{\gamma}{r_1} = \frac{1}{2} h_1 dg$$

and
$$\gamma = \frac{1}{2} h_2 dg r_2$$

or

$$\frac{\gamma}{r_2} = \frac{1}{2} h_2 dg$$

On subtraction, we have

$$\gamma \left(\frac{1}{r_1} - \frac{1}{r_2} \right) = \frac{1}{2}(h_1 - h_2) dg = \frac{1}{2} \Delta h dg$$

or

$$\gamma = \frac{\frac{1}{2} \Delta h dg}{\left(\dfrac{1}{r_1} - \dfrac{1}{r_2} \right)} \qquad \qquad ...(3.8(a))$$

If the same set of capillary tubes is dipped in two different liquids A and B, then we have

$$\gamma_A = \frac{1}{2} \frac{\Delta h_A d_A g}{\left(\dfrac{1}{r_1} - \dfrac{1}{r_2} \right)}$$

and

$$\gamma_B = \frac{1}{2} \frac{\Delta h_B d_B g}{\left(\dfrac{1}{r_1} - \dfrac{1}{r_2} \right)}$$

On dividing, we get

$$\gamma_A = \gamma_B \frac{\Delta h_A}{\Delta h_B} \frac{d_A}{d_B} \qquad \qquad ...(3.8(b))$$

from which γ_A can be determined if the quantities on the right hand side of Eq. 3.8(b) are known.

Problem 3.4: The surface tension of toluene at 293 K is 0.0284 Nm^{-1} and its density at this temperature is 0.866 g cm^{-3}. What is the largest radius of the capillary that will permit the liquid to rise 2×10^{-2} m?

Solution: Since $\gamma = \dfrac{1}{2} rhdg$

therefore

$$r = \frac{2\gamma}{hdg}$$

Here $\quad h = 2 \times 10^{-2}$ m

$\qquad r = ?$

$\qquad \gamma = 0.0284$ N m^{-1}

$d = 0.866$ g cm^{-3}

$\quad = 8.66 \times 10^2$ kg m^{-3}

$g = 9.8$ ms^{-2}

Substituting these values in the above equation, we get

$$r = \frac{2\left(0.0284 \text{ Nm}^{-1}\right)}{\left(2 \times 10^{-2} \text{m}\right)\left(8.66 \times 10^2 \text{ kg m}^{-3}\right)\left(9.8 \text{ ms}^{-2}\right)}$$

$$= 3.347 \times 10^{-4} \, \text{N} \, \text{kg}^{-1} \text{s}^2 \text{m}^2$$

$$= 3.347 \times 10^{-4} \, \text{m} \quad \left(1 \, \text{N} = 1 \, \text{kg} \, \text{ms}^{-2}\right)$$

$$= 0.03347 \, \text{cm}$$

Problem 3.5: At 303 K, the surface tension of ethanol in contact with its vapour is $2.189 \times 10^{-2} \, \text{Nm}^{-1}$, and its density is $0.780 \, \text{g} \, \text{cm}^{-3}$. (a) How far up a tube of internal radius 0.2 mm will it rise? (b) What pressure is needed to push the meniscus level back with the surrounding liquid?

Solution: (a) Since

$$\gamma = \frac{1}{2} rhdg$$

$$\therefore \qquad h = \frac{2\gamma}{rdg}$$

Here
$$\gamma = 2.189 \times 10^{-2} \, \text{Nm}^{-1} \qquad\qquad r = 0.2 \, \text{mm}$$
$$d = 0.780 \, \text{g} \, \text{cm}^{-3} \qquad\qquad\qquad = 2 \times 10^{-4} \, \text{m}$$
$$\quad = 7.8 \times 10^2 \, \text{kg} \, \text{m}^{-3} \qquad\qquad g = 9.8 \, \text{ms}^{-2}$$

Therefore,
$$h = \frac{2\left(2.189 \times 10^{-2} \, \text{N} \, \text{m}^{-1}\right)}{\left(2 \times 10^{-4} \, \text{m}\right)\left(7.8 \times 10^2 \, \text{kg} \, \text{m}^{-3}\right)\left(9.8 \, \text{m} \, \text{s}^{-2}\right)}$$

$$= 0.02864 \, \text{m}$$

$$= 28.64 \, \text{mm}$$

(b) The downward force $= \pi r^2 \, hdg$

The pressure needed to push the meniscus level back $= \dfrac{\pi r^2 hdg}{\pi r^2} = hdg$

$$= (0.02864 \, \text{m})\left(7.8 \times 10^2 \, \text{kg} \, \text{m}^{-3}\right)\left(9.8 \, \text{ms}^{-2}\right)$$

$$= 214.0 \, \text{kg} \, \text{m}^{-1} \text{s}^{-2}$$

$$= 214 \, \text{Nm}^{-2}.$$

Problem 3.6: How much effect would doubling the cross-sectional area of a capillary tube have on the height to which a liquid would rise in the capillary?

Solution: Since the cross-sectional area of the capillary tube is $A = \pi r^2$. For one capillary

$$A_1 = \pi r_1^2 \text{ or } r_1 = \sqrt{\frac{A_1}{\pi}}$$

and for other capillary
$$A_2 = 2A_1 = \pi r_2^2 \text{ or } r_2 = \sqrt{\frac{A_2}{\pi}} = \sqrt{\frac{2A_1}{\pi}}$$

So

$$\frac{r_1}{r_2} = \frac{1}{\sqrt{2}}$$

The surface tension γ is given by

$$\gamma = \frac{1}{2}hdgr$$

or

$$h = \frac{2\gamma}{gdr}$$

The height h upto which the liquid rises is inversely proportional to r

Hence

$$\frac{h_2}{h_1} = \frac{r_1}{r_2} = \frac{1}{\sqrt{2}} = 0.707$$

The liquid rises 0.707 times that in the narrower capillary.

(b) (i) **Drop Weight Method:** The weight of a drop falling from a capillary depends on the radius of the capillary and on the surface tension of the liquid. It was first thought that the weight of a drop falling from a capillary of radius r is equal to the surface tension acting along the circumference of the capillary bore. However, this relationship is not so simple.

This method is generally used for the comparison of surface tension of a liquid with another liquid of which the absolute value of surface tension is already known.

The instrument used is called a stalagmometer and consists of a bulbed capillary tube as shown in Fig. 3.8. The tube is first cleaned thoroughly with chromic acid, and then with distilled water and dried. It is filled up to the mark A with the liquid whose surface tension is to be measured by sucking in the liquid. A weighing tube is placed under the stalagmometer and a certain number of drops (say 10) are allowed to fall into it. The rate at which the drops fall is adjusted in such a way that each drop falls after about three seconds. The mass of 10 drops is found. The apparatus is then washed and the experiment is repeated with the other liquid. If m_1 and m_2 are the masses of 10 drops of the liquids and γ_1 and γ_2 are their surface tensions, then

$$\frac{\gamma_1}{\gamma_2} = \frac{m_1}{m_2} \qquad \qquad ...(3.9)$$

If the surface tension of one liquid is known, that of the other is readily calculated. Thus, if it is required to find out the surface tension of toluene, the masses of same number of drops of water and toluene would be compared. The surface tension of water being known, hence the surface tension of toluene may be calculated.

Fig. 3.8 Stalagmometer for surface tension measurement

(b) (ii) **Drop Number Method:** It is sometimes more convenient to determine the number of drops formed by a certain volume of the liquid, instead of finding the mass of a drop. In this case, the stalagmometer is filled up to the mark A with the liquid under examination. The liquid is allowed to flow completely through the stalagmometer. The number of drops being counted carefully. The purpose graduated portion of the tube is to enable fractions of a drop to be judged. The same procedure is repeated with the other liquid, say water. Let

n_1 = number of drops of one liquid in a certain volume V
n_2 = number of drops of second liquid (say water) in the same volume)
d_1 = density of first liquid
d_2 = density of water

Then the average weight of liquid drops is given by

$$w_1 = \frac{m_1 g}{n_1} = \frac{V d_1 g}{n_1}$$

and

$$w_2 = \frac{V d_2 g}{n_2}$$

Hence

$$\frac{\gamma_1}{\gamma_2} = \frac{w_1}{w_2} = \frac{\dfrac{V}{n_1} d_1 g}{\dfrac{V}{n_2} d_2 g}$$

$$\frac{\gamma_1}{\gamma_2} = \frac{n_2 d_1}{n_1 d_2} \qquad \qquad ...(3.10)$$

If the surface tension of water is known, that of the other liquid can be easily calculated.

Problem 3.7: Equal volumes of an organic liquid and water gave 55 drops and 35 drops respectively. The densities of water and the organic liquid are 0.996 and 0.80 g cm^{-3} and the surface tension of water is 7.2×10^{-2} Nm^{-1}. Calculate the surface tension of the organic liquid. How many times a water drop is heavier than a drop of the organic liquid?

Solution: $\dfrac{\gamma_1}{\gamma_2} = \dfrac{n_2 d_1}{n_1 d_2}$

or $\gamma_1 = \dfrac{\gamma_2 n_2 d_1}{n_1 d_2}$

Since $n_1 = 55$ $n_2 = 35$

$d_1 = 0.80$ g cm^{-3} $d_2 = 0.996$ g cm^{-3}

$= 8.0 \times 10^2$ kg m^{-3} $= 9.96 \times 10^2$ kg m^{-3}

$\gamma_1 = ?$ $\gamma_2 = 7.2 \times 10^{-2}$ Nm^{-1}

Therefore, $\gamma_1 = \dfrac{\left(7.2 \times 10^{-2} \, Nm^{-1}\right)(35)\left(8.0 \times 10^2 \, kg\,m^{-3}\right)}{(55)\left(9.96 \times 10^2 \, kg\,m^{-3}\right)}$

$= 2.63 \times 10^{-2}$ Nm^{-1}

Now,
$$\frac{m_{\text{water}}}{m_{\text{organic liquid}}} = \frac{\gamma_{\text{water}}}{\gamma_{\text{organic liquid}}}$$

$$= \frac{7.2 \times 10^{-2} \, \text{Nm}^{-1}}{2.63 \times 10^{-2} \, \text{Nm}^{-1}}$$

$$= 2.74.$$

3.6 EXCESS PRESSURE INSIDE A BUBBLE

Bubble formation is due to surface tension and the pressure inside the bubble is larger than the pressure outside the bubble. The excess pressure inside a bubble is related to the radius of the bubble and the surface tension. To obtain a relationship between these, consider a bubble of radius r. If γ is surface tension acting on it, then the surface energy is given by $4\pi r^2 \gamma$. If the radius of bubble increases by dr then the increase in the surface energy is given by

$$4\pi\gamma\left[(r+dr)^2 - r^2\right]$$

$$= 4\pi\gamma\left[r^2 + dr^2 + 2rdr - r^2\right]$$

$$= 8\pi\gamma\, r\, dr$$

The term involving dr^2 being small and hence neglected.

If P_1 and P_2 be the pressure inside and outside the bubble, then the work done during expansion of the bubble is $(P_1 - P_2)\,\Delta V$, where ΔV is the change in volume and is given by $4\pi r^2\, dr$. At equilibrium, the work done must be equal to the increase in surface energy, *i.e.*,

$$(P_1 - P_2)4\pi r^2\, dr = 8\pi\gamma\, r\, dr$$

or
$$\Delta P = P_1 - P_2 = \frac{2\gamma}{r} \qquad\qquad\qquad ...(3.11)$$

The excess pressure inside a spherical bubble is thus inversely proportional to its radius. In case of a soap bubble since there are two surfaces hence the excess pressure is given by

$$\Delta P = \frac{4\gamma}{r} \qquad\qquad\qquad ...(3.12)$$

The inverse relationship between ΔP and the radius indicates that formation and maintenance of smaller bubble requires larger excess pressures than larger ones.

3.7 INTERFACIAL TENSION

When two immiscible or partially miscible liquids are in contact, the force operative at the surface of separation between the two liquids is referred to as the interfacial tension. It may be defined as the work required to enlarge the surface of separation between two immiscible liquids by unity. Interfacial tension between two liquids A and B is generally less than the larger of the two surface tensions and is given as

$$\gamma_{AB} = \gamma_A - \gamma_B \qquad \qquad ...(3.13)$$

Mutual attraction across the interface between molecules of one liquid and those of the other tend to reduce the inward pull of the molecules in the surface by those of its own kind.

3.8 VARIATION OF SURFACE TENSION WITH TEMPERATURE

Surface tension decreases with increase of temperature and vanishes at the critical temperature. Increase in temperature of the liquid is accompanied by an increase in the energy of the molecules; the intermolecular forces decrease with rise of temperature. The environment of the molecules in the bulk tend to become similar to that on the surface at higher temperatures. Consequently, less work would be required to bring molecules from the bulk of the liquid on to the surface.

Ramsay and Shields suggested an empirical relationship between the surface tension and temperature as

$$\gamma \left[\frac{M}{d} \right]^{2/3} = k\left(T_c - T - 6\right) \qquad \qquad ...(3.14)$$

where M is the molar mass of the liquid; d = density; T_c = critical temperature; T = temperature of observation; and k = a constant.

The quantity $\left(\dfrac{M}{d} \right)$ is molar volume and hence $\left[\dfrac{M}{d} \right]^{2/3}$ represents the molar surface. Since the

surface tension measures the surface energy, hence $\gamma \left[\dfrac{M}{d} \right]^{2/3}$ is the molar surface energy. If we plot

$\gamma \left[\dfrac{M}{d} \right]^{2/3}$ versus temperature a straight line not passing through the origin is obtained. For many non

associated liquids, the constant k has a value of about 2.1. In case of water, alcohols, carboxylic acids etc., the value of k is less than 2.1 and this value rises with temperature. The deviations in the value of k are attributed due to the associated state of the molecules.

According to Ramsay's equation, if $T = T_c - 6$, $\gamma = 0$, i.e., the surface tension vanishes at a temperature 6 degree below the critical temperature.

Another equation which relates the surface tension with temperature is given by Eötvös and is known as Eötvös equation which is given as

$$\gamma \left[\frac{M}{d} \right]^{2/3} = k'\left(T_c - T\right) \qquad \qquad ...(3.15)$$

In this equation, at critical temperature, i.e., when $T = T_c$, $\gamma = 0$. This is in accordance with the earlier studies that the surface tension of a liquid at its critical temperature is zero.

MacLeod in 1923 proposed an empirical relationship between the surface tension and density of a liquid in the form

$$\gamma = C\left(D - d\right)^4 \qquad \qquad ...(3.16)$$

where D is the density of the liquid, d is the density of the vapour and C is a constant and is independent of temperature over a wide range for non associated liquids. For associated liquids, C is found to increase with increasing temperature.

Table 3.3 shows the results obtained for the surface tension of a number of liquids at various temperatures.

Table 3.3 Surface Tensions of Some Liquids (Nm^{-1} × 10^2)

Liquids	273 K	293 K	313 K	333 K
Water	7.564	7.275	6.956	6.618
Ethanol	2.405	2.230	2.060	1.900
Acetone	2.620	2.370	2.120	1.860
Benzene	3.160	2.890	2.630	2.370
Toluene	3.070	2.840	2.610	2.380

3.9 PARACHOR

From MacLeod Eq. (3.16), we have

$$C^{1/4} = \frac{\gamma^{1/4}}{D-d} \qquad ...(3.17)$$

Multiplying both sides by the molar mass M, we get

$$MC^{1/4} = \frac{M\gamma^{1/4}}{D-d} \qquad ...(3.18)$$

At temperatures, far below the critical temperature, density of the liquid is much greater than that of its vapour, *i.e.*, $D >> d$. Hence Eq. (3.18) reduces to

$$MC^{1/4} = \frac{M\gamma^{1/4}}{D}$$

$$= [P] \qquad ...(3.19)$$

$\left(\dfrac{M}{D}\right)$ is the molar volume of the liquid at the same temperature at which surface tension is measured.

The quantity $MC^{1/4}$ is a constant characteristic of the liquid and is called *the parachor*. It is denoted by $[P]$. If $\gamma = 1$ then

$$MC^{1/4} = \frac{M}{D}$$

$$= V_m = [P] \qquad ...(3.20)$$

Hence parachor may be defined as *the molar volume of the liquid at a temperature where its surface tension is unity*. From Eq. (3.20), it is clear that a comparison of parachor values of two liquids in effect means a comparison of their molar volumes under conditions such that their surface tensions are equal. Thus,

$$\frac{[P_1]}{[P_2]} = \frac{V_{m_1}}{V_{m_2}}$$

Since molar volume is an additive property, parachor would also be expected to be an additive property.

3.10 APPLICATIONS OF SURFACE TENSION

(*i*) Soaps and detergents are used as cleansing agents and their cleansing actions are due to their property of lowering the interfacial tension between water and oily and greasy substances. It thus becomes possible to detach oil or grease from a soiled surface and bring it into a finely divided state, dispersed throughout water, with the surface of each globule protected by a layer of detergent ion.

(*ii*) Synthetic detergents on account of their strong effect in decreasing surface tension of water, are being incorporated in preparations like tooth paste, toilet creams, complexion improving milks and medicinal emulsions, etc.

(*iii*) Surface tension measurements may be used for elucidating molecular structure through parachor values.

3.11 VISCOSITY

The resistance to flow exhibited by liquid is known as viscosity. Because of this property some liquids flow slowly than others. For example, glycerine, castor oil, honey etc., which flow slowly are said to have high viscosity while water, alcohol and ether which flow rapidly are said to have low viscosity. The phenomenon of viscosity may be further elucidated by considering the flow of a liquid through a narrow pipe (Fig. 3.9).

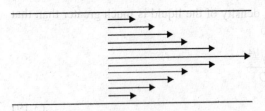

Fig. 3.9 Flow of liquid

When a liquid flows through a pipe, all parts of the liquid do not move with the same velocity. A thin layer immediately in contact with the wall of the pipe is almost stationary. The velocity of flow of each successive layer of the liquid gradually increases as we move towards the centre of the pipe. Each layer of the liquid moving with higher velocity over the other layer with low velocity will experience a retarding effect due to the friction between two layers. The resistance that one part of a liquid flowing with one velocity offers to another part of a liquid flowing with different velocity is known as the viscosity.

, As with gases, the coefficient of viscosity η may be defined as *the force per unit area required to maintain unit difference of velocity between two layers unit in the liquid distance apart*. If A is the area of the layer, *dx* the distance between them and *du* the velocity difference of the layer, then the tangential force required to maintain a constant velocity difference *du* is directly proportional to A and *du* and inversely proportional to *dx*. Consequently,

$$F \propto A \frac{du}{dx}$$

$$F = -\eta A \frac{du}{dx} \qquad \qquad ...(3.21)$$

where η is the proportionality constant called the coefficient of viscosity of the liquid. The reciprocal

of the coefficient of viscosity is called the *fluidity* and is denoted by ϕ, that is, $\phi = \dfrac{1}{\eta}$.

Units of η: From Eq. (3.21), we get

$$\eta = \frac{F}{A}\frac{dx}{du}$$

In CGS system, F is measured in dynes, dx in cm, du in cm s^{-1} and A in cm^2, so that η is expressed as

$$\eta = \frac{(\text{dynes})(\text{cm})}{(\text{cm}^2)(\text{cm/s})}$$

$$= \text{dynes cm}^{-2}\text{s}$$

$$= \text{g cm s}^{-2}\text{ cm}^{-2}\text{ s} \qquad \left(\because 1 \text{ dyne} = 1 \text{ g cm s}^{-2} \right)$$

$$= \text{g cm}^{-1}\text{ s}^{-1}$$

The unit of viscosity is thus dyne cm^{-2} s (g cm^{-1} s^{-1}) and is known as *poise*. In SI system force is expressed in newton, dx in metre, area in metre^2, and η is therefore given by

$$\eta = \frac{\text{N m}}{\left(\text{m}^2\right)\left(\text{m s}^{-1}\right)}$$

$$= \text{N m}^{-2}\text{s}^1$$

Since $1\text{N} = 1 \text{ kg m s}^{-2}$

hence $\eta = \left(1\text{ kg m s}^{-2}\right)\left(\text{m}^{-2}\text{ s}^1\right)$

$$= 1\text{ kg m}^{-1}\text{s}^{-1}$$

This is equal to 1 *pascal-second* (1 Pa s)

Relation between poise and pascal second:

Since $1 \text{ poise} = 1 \text{ g cm}^{-1}\text{ s}^{-1}$

$$= 10^{-3}\text{ kg } 10^2\text{ m}^{-1}\text{ s}^{-1}$$

$$= 10^{-1}\text{ kg m}^{-1}\text{ s}^{-1}$$

$$= 0.1 \text{ kg m}^{-1}\text{s}^{-1}$$

$$= 0.1 \text{ Pa s}$$

3.12 MEASUREMENT OF VISCOSITY

The rate of laminar flow of a liquid through a capillary tube at a constant pressure is related to the viscosity of the liquid. This relationship was first derived by Poiseuille in 1844 and is given by the equation

$$\eta = \frac{\pi P r^4 t}{8lV} \qquad \qquad ...(3.22)$$

where V is the volume of the liquid of viscosity η which flows in time t through a capillary of radius r and length l under a driving pressure P. Since $P = hdg$, where h is the height of the liquid column, d the density of the liquid and g the acceleration due to gravity. Substituting these values in Eq. (3.22), we get

$$\eta = \frac{\pi h d g r^4 t}{8lV}$$

$$= \frac{\pi r^4 t h d g}{8lV} \qquad \qquad ...(3.23)$$

If equal volumes of two liquids are allowed to flow through the same capillary under similar conditions, then we have

$$\frac{\eta_1}{\eta_2} = \frac{\pi r^4 t_1 h d_1 g}{8lV} \times \frac{8lV}{\pi r^4 t_2 h d_2 g}$$

or

$$\frac{\eta_1}{\eta_2} = \frac{t_1 d_1}{t_2 d_2} \qquad \qquad ...(3.24)$$

If d_1, d_2 and η_2 are known, determination of t_1 and t_2 enables us to calculate η_1, the coefficient of viscosity of the liquid under investigation.

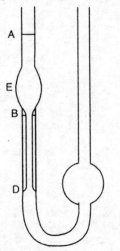

Fig. 3.10 Ostwald viscometer

Ostwald Viscometer Method: As mentioned above, the quantities t_1 and t_2 are most conveniently measured with an Ostwald viscometer shown in Fig. 3.10. It consists of a capillary tube BD through which a definite volume of liquid (between the marks A and B) is allowed to flow under the force of its own weight. To start with, a definite quantity of a liquid is introduced into the viscometer and is then drawn up by suction into the bulb E until the liquid level is above the mark A. The liquid is then allowed to drain, and the time necessary for the liquid level to fall from A to B is measured with a stop watch. The viscometer is now washed, dried and the whole operation is repeated with the reference liquid, usually water. Knowing the times of flow for both the liquids, the viscosity of the unknown liquid can be calculated using Eq. (3.24).

Falling Sphere Viscometer: The motion of a body moving through a viscous medium is opposed by the frictional resistance of the medium. In order to maintain a uniform velocity, a driving force has to be applied to overcome the frictional forces. The magnitude of the frictional force (F_r) depends on the velocity of the body and is given by the Stokes relation

$$F_r = 6\pi r \eta u$$

where r is the radius of the spherical body and u its velocity through the medium having coefficient of viscosity η.

If d is the density of the spherical body and d_0 the density of the medium, then the gravitational force, F_g

$$F_g = \frac{4}{3}\pi r^3 (d - d_0) g$$

When the rate of settling of the sphere in the liquid is constant, then the gravitational and frictional forces are equal, *i.e.*,

$$6\pi r \eta u = \frac{4}{3}\pi r^3 (d - d_0) g$$

or
$$\eta = \frac{2r^2 (d - d_0) g}{9u} \qquad \qquad ...(3.25)$$

This equation is known as *Stokes' law* and is applicable to the fall of spherical bodies in fluids. By measuring the velocity u of the spherical body of known r and d, through a vertical column of liquid of density d_0, η may be calculated. This method is generally used for solutions of high viscosities.

If the same spherical body is allowed to fall through the same distance in two liquids then the ratio of the two viscosities is given by

$$\frac{\eta_1}{\eta_2} = \left(\frac{d - d_0'}{d - d_0''}\right)\left(\frac{t_1}{t_2}\right) \qquad \qquad ...(3.26)$$

where d_0' and d_0'' are the densities of the media and t_1 and t_2 are the times taken by the spherical body to fall through the same distance in the two media.

3.13 EFFECT OF TEMPERATURE ON VISCOSITY

The effect of temperature on the viscosity of a liquid is strikingly different from that of a gas. The coefficient of viscosity of gases increases with the increase of temperature, while those of liquids decreases due to weakening of intermolecular attractions. Various empirical equations relating viscosity with temperature have been proposed, but the expression given by Arrhenius and Guzman is the most satisfactory and is given by

$$\eta = A e^{E_a/RT}$$

$$\ln \eta = \ln A + \frac{E_a}{RT}$$

$$\log \eta = \text{constant} + \frac{E_a}{2.303 \, RT} \qquad \qquad ...(3.27)$$

where A is a constant and E_a is the activation energy for the viscous flow and R is the gas constant and T the temperature in degree absolute. It follows from Eq. (3.27) that a plot of log η against $1/T$ will be straight line with slope $E_a/2.303\ R$, from which E_a can be calculated. Table 3.4 gives the viscosity coefficients in centipoise of several liquids at various temperatures.

Table 3.4 Viscosity Coefficients of Liquids (Centipoise)*

Liquid	Temperature (K)					
	273	293	313	333	353	373
Water	1.792	1.005	0.656	0.469	0.356	0.284
Ethanol	1.773	1.200	0.834	0.592	–	–
Benzene	0.912	0.652	0.503	0.392	0.329	–
Carbon tetrachloride	1.329	0.969	0.739	0.585	0.468	0.384
Mercury	1.685	1.554	1.450	1.367	1.298	1.240

*1 centipoise = 10^{-2} poise = 10^{-3} Pa s.

Problem 3.8: Water requires 120.5 seconds to flow through a viscometer and the same volume of acetone requires 49.5 seconds. If the densities of water and acetone at 293 K are 9.982×10^2 kg m^{-3} and 7.92×10^2 kg m^{-3} respectively and the viscosity of water at 293 K is 10.05 pascal second, calculate the viscosity of acetone at 293 K.

    Solution: Since,

$$\frac{\eta_{water}}{\eta_{acetone}} = \frac{t_1 d_1}{t_2 d_2}$$

$$\eta_{acetone} = \frac{\eta_{water} t_2 d_2}{t_1 d_1}$$

$$= \frac{\left(1.005 \times 10^1\,\text{Pa s}\right)\left(49.5\text{s}\right)\left(7.92 \times 10^2\ \text{kg m}^{-3}\right)}{\left(120.5\ \text{s}\right)\left(9.982 \times 10^2\ \text{kg m}^{-3}\right)}$$

$$= 3.275\ \text{Pa s}$$

Problem 3.9: A steel ball ($d = 7.86 \times 10^3$ kg m^{-3}) with 2×10^{-3} m in diameter falls 0.1 m through a viscous liquid ($d_0 = 1.50 \times 10^3$ kg m^{-3}) in 25 seconds. What is the absolute viscosity of liquid?

    Solution: From Eq. (3.25)

$$\frac{dx}{dt} = \frac{2}{9}\frac{r^2(d - d_0)g}{\eta}$$

$$\eta = \frac{2}{9}\frac{r^2(d - d_0)g}{dx/dt}$$

$$= \frac{2}{9} \frac{\left(1 \times 10^{-3} \, \text{m}\right)^2 \left(6.36 \times 10^3 \, \text{kg m}^{-3}\right)\left(9.8 \, \text{m s}^{-2}\right)}{\left(\dfrac{0.1}{25} \, \text{ms}^{-1}\right)}$$

$$= 3.462 \, \text{kg m}^{-1}\text{s}^{-1}$$

$$= 3.462 \, \text{Pa s}$$

Problem 3.10: How long will a spherical air bubble 0.5 mm in diameter take to rise 10 cm through water ($d = 0.994$ g cm^{-3}) at 298 K? The coefficient of viscosity of water at 298 K is 8.95×10^{-4} Pa s.

Solution:

$$r = 0.25 \, \text{mm} = 2.5 \times 10^{-4} \, \text{m}$$

$$dx = 10 \, \text{cm} = 10^{-1} \, \text{m}$$

$$d_{H_2O} = 0.994 \, \text{g cm}^{-3} = 9.94 \times 10^2 \, \text{kg m}^{-3}$$

$$\eta_{H_2O} = 8.95 \times 10^{-4} \, \text{kg m}^{-1}\text{s}^{-1}$$

Since

$$\frac{dx}{dt} = \frac{2}{9} \frac{r^2 (d - d_0) g}{\eta}$$

Here density of air bubble is very small in comparison to that of water and hence can be neglected, *i.e.*, $d - d_0 \cong -d_0$. The negative sign indicates that the bubble will rise. Therefore, the time taken by the bubble is

$$\frac{9\left(10^{-1}\text{m}\right) \times \left(8.95 \times 10^{-4} \, \text{kg m}^{-1}\text{s}^{-1}\right)}{2 \times \left(2.5 \times 10^{-4}\text{m}\right)^2 \left(9.94 \times 10^2 \, \text{kg m}^{-3}\right)\left(9.8 \, \text{ms}^{-2}\right)} = 0.66 \, \text{s}$$

3.14 SOME OTHER VISCOSITY FUNCTIONS

The ratio of η to the density of a liquid is called kinematic viscosity. Molecular viscosity is defined as

$$\eta \left[\frac{M}{d}\right]^{2/3}$$

Since M/d is the molar volume and $(M/d)^{2/3}$ would be the molar surface. Hence molar viscosity may be regarded as a function of molar surface area.

Rheochor (R) is defined as

$$R = \frac{M}{d} \eta^{1/8} \qquad \qquad ...(3.28)$$

If $\eta = 1$, then $R = \dfrac{M}{d} = V_m$

that is, rheochor may be defined as *the molar volume of a liquid at a temperature where its viscosity is unity.* Use of rheochor as an additive and constitutive property in elucidating the structure of compounds has met with little success.

3.15 STRUCTURE OF LIQUIDS

In a perfect crystal there is a complete ordered arrangement of the atoms, ions or molecules constituting the crystal. The intermolecular forces are strong enough to hold them together. The constituents vibrate about their mean positions but cannot execute translational motion. Thus both the short range as well as the long range orders exist in crystals. The molecules in a gas possess complete random motion and the intermolecular forces between the molecules are small and are effective only at short distances. There is no possibility of any kind of ordered structure in gases. In liquids, on the other hand, the situation is somewhat in between the two. The cohesive forces in liquids are stronger than those in gases. These forces, however, are not strong enough to prevent considerably the translational motion of the individual molecules. In terms of the arrangement of the constituents a liquid has *short range order* but lacks *long range order.*

When a crystal melts there is, in general, an increase about 10% in volume of or about 3% in intermolecular spacings. The molecules in the liquid state still remain in the vicinity of the other molecules surrounding them. The intermolecular forces decreases as the distance between the molecules increases. In other words, the short range forces exist while the long range forces are negligible. The thermal motion introduces a disorder in the structure but the motion is not as random as in a gas. Some ordered arrangement still persists. The ordered arrangement in the crystal is not completely destroyed on melting. As the temperature is further increased, the thermal motions of the molecules increase the kinetic energy, decrease the order until at the boiling point it completely vanishes.

The sharpness of the melting point can be explained by a two dimensional model for solids, liquids and gases as shown in Fig. 3.11. Introduction of a small region of disorder into a crystal causes the disturbance of the long range order and destroys the crystalline arrangement. This explains the abrupt variation in the properties between solids and liquids. J.D. Bernal suggested that an atom is surrounded by five atoms (Fig. 3.11) instead of normal six atoms as is the requirement for a closest packed structure for solids. The remaining atoms (circles in the figure) are drawn in the utmost possible ordered arrangement. One point of abnormal coordination number is sufficient to cause a long range disorder. That is, when the normal motion causes a disorder in one region, it spreads in all directions destroying the entire regular structure. Liquids, therefore, may be assumed to have structure like that of a crystal with a difference that the ordered arrangement extends over a short region instead of over the whole mass. This is called the short range order or long range disorder. It should be noted that the short range order in a liquid structure is continuously changing due to the thermal motions.

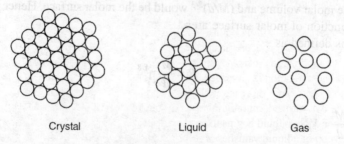

Crystal   Liquid   Gas

Fig. 3.11 Two dimensional models of states of matter

X-ray Diffraction of Liquids: It is possible to calculate the distribution of atoms or molecules in a liquid by the analysis of the intensity of the scattered x-rays. The diffraction pattern of a liquid resembles a powder photograph with a difference that in place of sharp lines a few broad bands are observed. This indicates the existence of a regular order. From the intensities of these bands, it is possible to construct the radial distribution function which is interpreted in terms of the average number of atoms around a central atom at a certain distance. As the temperature of the liquid is raised, the bands become less pronounced and the pattern resembles those of a gas indicating a more disordered arrangement at higher temperatures.

The Vacancy Model for a Liquid: This model for the structure of liquids was given by Eyring (1933) who assumed the liquids more or less similar to a gas. In the liquid, most of the space is occupied by the molecules and only a small fraction (about 3% of the total volume at ordinary temperature and pressure) of the total volume is free or void. This void space in which the molecules can move is called the *free volume*. This is shown in Fig. 3.12. The vapours contain only a few molecules moving randomly and thus has large free volume. With a rise in temperature, the concentration of the molecules in the vapour phase increases causing an increase in the vacancies of the liquid. The density of the vapour increases while that of the liquid decreases until they become equal at the critical temperature. At the critical temperature the liquid and vapour become indistinguishable. Eyring further assumed that the free volume is distributed randomly and the vacancies are of approximately molecular size. Molecules

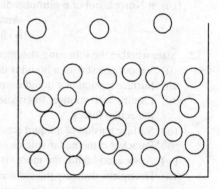

Fig. 3.12 Eyring's vacancy model of liquids

adjacent to a vacancy would be expected to possess gas-like properties and show maximum disorder. But a molecule away from the vacancy would be having solid-like properties and possessing a more ordered arrangement. Based on this model, they were able to show a fairly good agreement between the observed and predicted values of the properties.

EXERCISES

1. Explain, giving reasons, the following:
    (i) Rate of diffusion in liquids is less than that in gases.
    (ii) Liquids evaporate faster at higher temperatures.
    (iii) Evaporation leads to a lowering of temperature.
    (iv) Clothes dry more rapidly on a dry day than on a humid day.
    (v) Liquids with strong intermolecular attractive forces have higher boiling points than liquids with weak intermolecular attractive forces.
    (vi) In a homologous series boiling points generally increase with increasing molar masses.
    (vii) Enthalpy of vapourization decreases in the series H_2O, H_2S, H_2Se and H_2Te.
    (viii) Enthalpy of vapourization increases from F_2 to I_2.
    (ix) Enthalpy of vapourization is larger for H_2O than for HF.
    (x) Steam at 373 K produces more severe burns than an equivalent amount of water at 373 K.
    (xi) When a liquid is warmed, initially many small bubbles begin to form.
    (xii) When a super cooled liquid begins to freeze, its temperature rises.
    (xiii) Surface tension of a liquid vanishes at its critical temperature.
    (xiv) Water is more viscous than ethanol.

    (*xv*) Rain drops and mercury drops are spherical.

  (*xvi*) Viscosity of a liquid decreases with rise in temperature.

 (*xvii*) Liquids exhibit only a few diffraction maxima in their x-ray patterns.

2.   Which one in the following pairs would be expected to have higher viscosity and higher surface tension? Give reasons.

     (*i*) Ether or ethanol.

    (*ii*) Ethyl bromide or ethyl iodide.

   (*iii*) Pure water or aqueous sodium chloride solution.

   (*iv*) Liquid pentane or liquid hexane.

    (*v*) Liquid hexane or 2, 3 dimethyl butane.

   (*vi*) Ethylene glycol or glycerine.

  (*vii*) o-Nitrophenol or p-nitrophenol.

                  Ans. (*i*) Ethanol, (*ii*) ethyl iodide, (*iii*) aqueous sodium chloride solution, (*iv*) liquid hexane, (*v*) liquid hexane, (*vi*) glycerine, and (*vii*) p-nitrophenol.

3.   State whether the following statements are true or false:

     (*i*) Vapour pressure of a liquid is the measure of the strength of intermolecular attractive forces.

    (*ii*) Surface tension of a liquid decreases with rise in temperature and is zero at its critical temperature.

   (*iii*) Liquids with stronger intermolecular attractive forces are more viscous than those with weaker intermolecular forces.

   (*iv*) Surface tension of a liquid acts perpendicular to the surface of the liquid.

    (*v*) Parachor is the molar volume of a liquid at temperature at which surface tension is unity.

   (*vi*) Associated liquids are more viscous than non associated liquids.

  (*vii*) Detergents decrease the surface tension of water.

 (*viii*) Surface tension is the force acting per unit area of the surface.

   (*ix*) Long chain molecules are less viscous than smaller spherical molecules.

    (*x*) Viscosity of a liquid increases with rise in temperature.

                  Ans. True: (*i*), (*ii*), (*iii*), (*v*), (*vi*), (*vii*). False: (*iv*), (*viii*), (*ix*), (*x*).

4.   The intermolecular attractive forces in liquid A are greater than those in liquid B. Predict which liquid will have the greater critical temperature (T_c), greater viscosity, (η) and greater surface tension (γ).

                  Ans. T_c, η and γ for liquid A will be greater.

5.   Predict the effect of changes in temperature and pressure on equilibria (*i*) $s \rightleftharpoons l$ and (*ii*) $l \rightleftharpoons g$ for (*a*) water and (*b*) carbon dioxide.

6.   When a liquid is in dynamic equilibrium with its vapour, the following conditions could exist:

     (*i*) There is no transfer of molecules between liquid and vapour.

    (*ii*) The vapour pressure has a unique value.

   (*iii*) The opposing processes proceed at equal rates.

   (*iv*) The concentration of vapour is dependent on time.

    Which of the above choices are most appropriate? Explain.   **Ans.** (*ii*) and (*iii*).

7.   Vapour pressure of all the liquids ....

     (*i*) is the same at 373 K, or

    (*ii*) is the same at their freezing points, or

   (*iii*) increases with the volume of the liquid, or

   (*iv*) decreases with increasing volume of the container, or

    (*v*) increases with the rise in temperature.

    Select the most appropriate statement.

                  Ans. (*v*) is the correct statement.

8.   Discuss the origin of surface tension of liquids. Indicate the direction along which it acts. Show that surface tension and surface energy have the same dimension. Derive the relation

$$\gamma = \frac{1}{2}(\pm h)dgr$$

where the plus and minus signs refer to wetting and nonwetting liquids.

9. How does the viscosity of a liquid arise? What are its units? How does it depend on temperature? Describe methods commonly used for the measurement of viscosity of a liquid.

10. At 298 K, liquid X has a vapour pressure of 100 torr while liquid Y has a vapour pressure of 200 torr. The enthalpy of vapourization of liquid X is 43.57 kJ mol^{-1} while that of Y is 16.74 kJ mol^{-1}. Calculate the temperature at which both X and B will have the same vapour pressure. **Ans. 328 K.**

11. A liquid which is used in a manometer has a density of 0.87×10^3 kg m^{-3}. Calculate the pressure in (*i*) cm, (*ii*) atm, (*iii*) newton per metre square if the liquid rises upto a height of 53.6 cm. **Ans. (*i*) 3.43 cm Hg, (*ii*) 0.0452 atm, (*iii*) 4.58×10^3 N m^{-2}.**

12. The enthalpy of vapourization of water is 40.67 kJ mol^{-1} at 373 K. Calculate the pressure required to boil water at 348 K. **Ans. 0.390 atm.**

13. Calculate the change in pressure necessary to increase the normal boiling point of water by one degree. $\Delta H_{vap,\,m}$ = 40.67 kJ mol^{-1} at 373 K. **Ans. 1.035 atm.**

14. An excess pressure of 364 Pa is required to produce a hemispherical bubble at the end of a capillary tube of 0.300 mm diameter immersed in acetone. Calculate γ. **Ans. 0.0273 N m^{-1}**

15. Surface tension of water at 293 K is 72.75×10^{-3} N m^{-1}. A 33.24 vol% solution of ethanol has $\gamma = 33.24 \times 10^{-3}$ N m^{-1} at this temperature. If $d = 0.9614 \times 10^3$ kg m^{-3} for the solution and 0.9982×10^3 kg m^{-3} for water, how much less in the same capillary tube will the alcohol solution rise? **Ans. 47.4% as far as pure water.**

16. Calculate the work done in creating a surface at 293 K for a film of (*a*) water and (*b*) ethanol in a rectangular wire with a movable bar. The movable bar is 5 cm long and is pulled to a distance of 4 cm. **Ans. (*a*) 1.456×10^{-2} N, (*b*) 0.446×10^{-3} N.**

17. A U-tube, containing water at 293 K, has capillary arms of different radii, one equal to 5 mm and the other 2 mm. (*a*) Calculate the difference in the levels of the two arms. Density of water is 0.998×10^{-3} kg m^{-3} at 293 K. (*b*) Calculate the difference in the levels of the U-tube containing acetone at 293 K. Density of acetone is 0.792×10^3 kg m^{-3} at 293 K. **Ans. (*a*) 0.44 cm, (*b*) 0.18 cm.**

18. How high will sap rise in a plant if the capillaries are 0.01 mm in diameter, the density of the fluid is 1.3×10^3 kg m^{-3} and its surface tension being 65.0×10^{-3} N m^{-1}? Assume that the latter property accounts for this rise. **Ans. 2.04 m.**

19. At 293 K, water rises in a capillary upto a height of 8.37 cm. Using the same capillary a sample of mercury was depressed by 3.67 cm. If the densities of water and mercury at this temperature are 0.9982×10^3 kg m^{-3} and 13.60×10^2 kg m^{-3} respectively, calculate the surface tension of mercury. Surface tension of water at 293 K is 72.75×10^{-3} N m^{-1}. Evaluate γ_{Hg} and radius (*r*) of the capillary. **Ans. $\gamma_{Hg} = 0.434$ N m^{-1}, $r = 1.78 \times 10^{-4}$ m.**

20. In measuring the surface tension of a liquid A by the drop number method using stalagmometer for equal volumes. A gave 60 drops while water gave 20 drops 293 K. Water and A have densities of 0.996×10^3 kg m^{-3} and 0.664×10^3 kg m^{-3} respectively. (*a*) Calculate the surface tension of liquid A. (*b*) How many times is the water drop heavier than a drop of A? $\gamma_{H_2O} = 72.75 \times 10^{-3}$ Nm^{-1} at 293 K. **Ans. (*a*) 24.24×10^{-3} N m^{-1}, (*b*) 3 times.**

21. Find the capillary depression of mercury in a tube of diameter 1 mm. Assume that the contact angle is zero. The density of mercury is 13×10^3 kg m^{-3} and the surface tension of mercury 0.460 N m^{-1}. **Ans. 1.38×10^{-2} m.**

22. From the following data on the measurement of surface tension of a liquid (molar mass 60.1 g mol^{-1}), determine the constant k in the Ramsay-Shields equation and critical temperature of the liquid

T (°C)	20.0	75.0
$\gamma \left(\text{Nm}^{-1}\right) \times 10^3$	27.4	22.3
$d_{\text{liquid}} \left(\text{kg m}^{-3}\right) \times 10^{-3}$	1.049	0.9892

Ans. $k = 1.15$, $T_c = 380°C$.

23. 10 ml of water and isopropyl alcohol weigh 9.982 g and 7.887 g respectively. At 293 K, isopropyl alcohol flowed through a viscometer in 624s and an equal volume of water flowed through the same viscometer in 200s. If the viscosity of water at 293 K is 1.009×10^{-3} N s m^{-2}, calculate the viscosity of isopropyl alcohol at 293 K.   **Ans.** $2.487 \times 10^{-3} \text{ Nsm}^{-2}$.

24. The time required to drop a steel ball (density = 7.8×10^3 kg m^{-3}) through water was 1s, and that through a commercial sample of shampoo was 7s. If the density of water was 1.0×10^3 kg m^{-3} and that of the sample was 1.03×10^3 kg m^{-3}, calculate the coefficient of viscosity of the sample. $\eta_{\text{H}_2\text{O}} = 8.9 \times 10^{-4}$ Nsm^{-2}.

Ans. $\eta_{\text{sample}} = 6.23 \times 10^{-3}$ N s m^{-2}.

25. The viscosity of molten sodium is 4.5×10^{-4} N s m^{-2} at 473 K and 2.12×10^{-4} N s m^{-2} at 873 K. Calculate the activation energy (E_a) for the viscous flow. Also calculate the viscosity at 673 K.

Ans. $E_a = 6.46 \text{kJ mol}^{-1}$, $\eta_{673} = 2.76 \times 10^{-4}$ N s m^{-2}.

26. Consider two liquids A and B such that A has half the surface tension and twice the density of B. If liquid A rises to a height of 2.0 cm in a capillary, what will be the height to which liquid B will rise in the same capillary?   **Ans. 8.0 cm.**

27. Two liquids A and B are completely immiscible. The normal boiling points of A and B are T_A and T_B respectively ($T_A > T_B$). The two liquids are taken together and heated. Assess the temperature at which the boiling will start.   **Ans.** Slightly less than T_B.

CHAPTER 4

The Solid State

4.1 INTRODUCTION

In Chapter 2, the structure of a gas was simply described in terms of the chaotic motion of molecules which are separated from one another by distances larger than their own diameter. The volume actually occupied by the gas molecules is small in comparison to the volume of the container. In liquids, the motion of the molecules is still largely chaotic. However, the molar volume of a liquid is smaller than the molar volume of its vapour, a larger fraction of the space is occupied by the molecules in the liquid state. A less randomness in the space distribution of molecules and probably some partial and transient ordered arrangement may be expected for the liquid state. Ease of flow and generally low density in comparison to the corresponding solid indicates the irregular arrangement of molecules in the liquid and creates void space in its structure.

The constituents of crystalline solids, on the other hand, *are arranged spatially in a regular and repetitive manner yielding a completely ordered structure.* The highly ordered arrangement is always accompanied by a lowering of potential energy, so that energy is required to convert a solid into a liquid. The ordered arrangement usually has a smaller volume and low compressibility than the liquid.

Solids are usually classified as either *crystalline* or *amorphous.* The term solid is generally employed for substances which are crystalline in nature. In these crystalline solids, the constituents may be atoms, ions or molecules. The definite and ordered arrangement of the constituents extends over a large distance in the crystal and is called a *long-range order.* Crystalline solids such as sodium chloride, ice or sugar etc. possess a sharp melting point. Amorphous solids like glass, pitch, rubber, plastics etc. although possessing many characteristics of crystalline solids such as definite shape, rigidity and hardness, but are devoid of a regular internal structure and melt gradually over a range of temperature. For this reason, they are not considered as true solids but rather highly supercooled liquids.

An amorphous solid exhibits the same value of any property in all the directions and is said to be *isotropic.* For example, refractive index, thermal and electrical conductivities, coefficient of thermal expansion, solubility characteristics are independent of the direction along which they are measured. Crystalline solids (other than those belonging to the cubic class), on the other hand are, *anisotropic.* In these cases, the magnitude of the property depends on the direction along which it is measured. Isotropy arises due to the fact that the amorphous solids have the same arrangement in all the directions.

The size and shape of a crystal depends on the conditions under which crystallization takes place. The angle between any two faces is the inter-facial angle. The corresponding angles in different crystals of the same substance are the same. This is known as *the law of constancy of inter-facial angle.*

4.2 SYMMETRY ELEMENTS AND SYMMETRY OPERATIONS

Symmetry is a peculiar regularity observed in arrangement of atoms, ions or molecules in a crystal. Crystals can be classified according to their symmetry aspects. This could help us to understand the molecular properties such as, dipole moment, optical activity and spectral characteristics. Before trying to classify molecules on the basis of symmetry, we must understand the terms, symmetry elements and symmetry operations.

Symmetry operation is the movement of an object which leaves the object looking the same. A symmetry operation brings the molecule into the equivalent or identical configuration. Consider a cardboard shaped like an equilateral triangle (Fig. 4.1). Label the three vertices of the triangle as 1, 2

and 3. If we rotate the cardboard through an angle $120°$ $\left(\dfrac{2\pi}{3}\right)$, an equilateral configuration (Fig. 4.1(*b*)) is obtained.

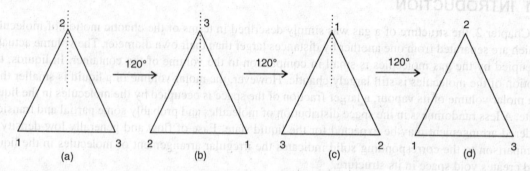

Fig. 4.1 (*a*) Configuration before rotation, the dotted line shows the axis of rotation in a direction perpendicular to the plane of the molecule; (*b*) and (*c*) equivalent configuration after anticlockwise rotation through $\left(\dfrac{2\pi}{3}\right)$ and $\left(\dfrac{4\pi}{3}\right)$ degree; (*d*) identical configuration of (*a*)

Further rotation through $120°$ $(2\pi/3)$ will again give an equilateral configuration (*c*), whereas the rotation of (*a*) through $360°$ (2π) will result in an identical configuration (*d*). In the equivalent configuration, the positions of the atoms are the same as before applying symmetry operation. The rotation

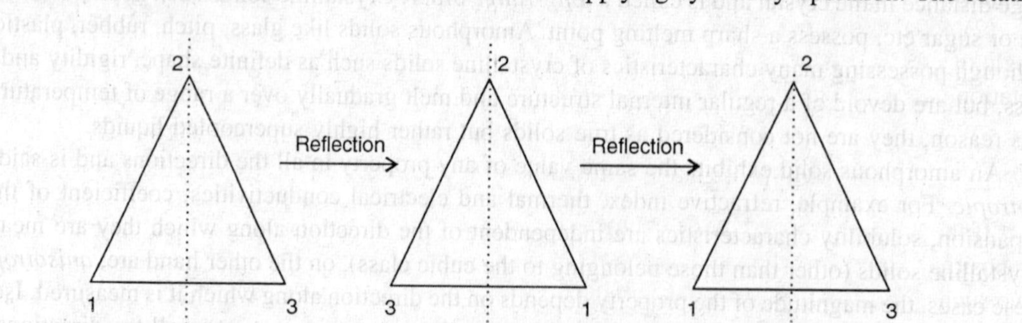

Fig. 4.2 (*a*) Original configuration (before reflection); (*b*) equivalent configuration resulting from reflection through a perpendicular plane; (*c*) identical configuration

through 120° (2p/3) once, twice and thrice can be denoted by C_3^1, C_3^2 and C_3^3. C_3 also represents three fold axis of symmetry.

Similarly, reflection across a plane passing through the vertex 2 of an equilateral triangle shaped molecule (the perpendicular plane is shown by dotted lines) results in equivalent configuration (Fig. 4.2).

Another reflection through this plane results in an identical configuration [Fig. 4.2(c)].

Table 4.1 lists the various symmetry operations, corresponding to each symmetry operation, there is a symmetry element. The symmetry element is a point, line, or plane with respect to which a symmetry operation is carried out.

Table 4.1 Symmetry Elements and Symmetry Operations

S.No.	Symmetry element	Symmetry operation
1.	Identity element (E)	Doing nothing to the object
2.	Proper axis of symmetry or n-fold axis of symmetry (C_n)	Rotation about the axis. Once or several time by an angle $\left(\dfrac{2\pi}{n}\right)$ or $\dfrac{360°}{n}$; n must be an integer
3.	Centre of symmetry (i)	Inversion of all atoms through the centre of symmetry
4.	Plane of symmetry (σ)	Reflection plane passing through the molecule
5.	Improper rotation axis of symmetry or rotation reflection axis (S_n)	Rotation about an axis by an angle $\left(\dfrac{2\pi}{n}\right)$ or $\dfrac{360°}{n}$, followed by reflection in a plane perpendicular to the axis of rotation

(1) **Identity:** It is denoted by E and is indistinguishable from itself if nothing is done on it. In other words, it leaves each point of the crystal unchanged when a rotation of 360° about any axis is performed. Every object possesses at least this type of symmetry.

(2) **Axis of symmetry:** An axis of symmetry is a line about which the crystal if rotated through an angle of 360°/n brings the molecule into a configuration indistinguishable from the original one. This rotation operation is denoted by C_n, where n is the order of rotation. The order of an axis is defined as

$$n = \frac{2\pi}{\text{Minimum angle of rotation for obtaining equivalent configuration}}$$

If the crystal is rotated in the counter-clockwise direction then the rotation is conventionally taken as positive. When a rotation about the axis by π leads to a result indistinguishable from the original one, two such equivalent arrangements will occur in a complete rotation, *i.e.*, through 2π, the axis is said to be a two-fold (diad) axis of symmetry (C_2). For example in water molecule, rotation about the axis by

180°($2\pi/2$) leads to an equivalent configuration, *i.e.*, $n = \dfrac{360°}{180°} = 2$. Thus, water molecule has a two-fold axis of rotation (C_2). This is shown in Fig. 4.3.

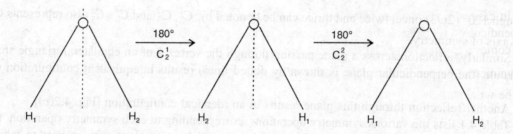

Fig. 4.3 The two-fold axis of symmetry (C_2) in water molecule

If the rotation through 120° $\left(\dfrac{2\pi}{3}\right)$ about its axis leads to an equivalent configuration, the axis is

called a three-fold (triad) axis of symmetry (C_3). The ammonia molecule [Fig. 4.4(a)] has a three-fold axis of symmetry (C_3), passing through the nitrogen atom.

This is shown as follows.

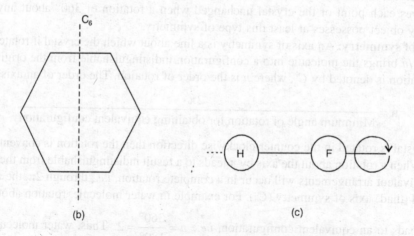

Fig. 4.4 (a) Axis of symmetry for ammonia molecule

The rotation through 120° (C_3^1) and 240° (C_3^2) results in equivalent configurations while 360° (C_3^3) leads to identical configuration. This three-fold axis of symmetry can be written as

$$C_3^1 \, C_3^2 = C_3^3 = E$$

Fig. 4.4 (b) Axis of symmetry for regular hexagon; (c) Hydrofluoric acid molecule

In case of a regular hexagon [Fig. 4.4(b)], it can be turned into the same configuration about a perpendicular axis passing through its centre; i.e., the point of intersection of its diagonals. The hexagon comes into coincidence six times in a complete rotation. This is said to possess a six-fold axis (C_6) of symmetry. In general, an n-fold axis of symmetry (C_n) gives rise to $C_n^1, C_n^2, \ldots C_n^n$ operations and can be written as

$$C_n^n = E$$

where E is the identity operation. C_n^n means n times rotation about C_n axis.

If the rotation of $2\pi/3$, i.e., by thirds of a complete revolution leads to the same result as the original one, the axis is called a three-fold (triad) axis of symmetry (C_3).

A linear molecule such as hydrofluoric acid [Fig. 4.4(c)] has C_∞ axis of symmetry because the rotation about the internuclear axis by any amount (∞ in numbers) would leave the molecule unchanged.

(3) **Centre of symmetry:** It is denoted by i. Centre of symmetry or inversion centre of a molecules is a point such that any line drawn through it intersects the surface of the crystal at equal distances in both the directions. To investigate the centre of symmetry, one changes coordinates (x, y, z) of each atom into −x, −y, −z, if a configuration indistinguishable from the original one is obtained, then the point of origin (0, 0, 0) is the centre of symmetry. A crystal can have only one centre of symmetry. If inversion process is applied twice, the original configuration is obtained, i.e.,

$$i.i = E$$

The successive application of i an even number of times produces the identity E. All homonuclear diatomic molecules (H_2, O_2, N_2 etc.) possess the centre of symmetry. Also CO_2, C_2H_4, C_6H_6, SF_6 and staggered confirmation of ethane possess centre of symmetry.

(4) **Plane of symmetry:** A molecule is said to possess a plane of symmetry if it can be divided by an imaginary plane into two parts such that one is the exact *mirror image* of the other. The plane of symmetry is usually designated by σ. When the mirror plane is perpendicular to the direction of the principal axis (axis of highest order), it is called the *horizontal mirror plane* and is denoted by σ_h. On the other hand, when a mirror plane contains the principal axis of symmetry, it is known as the *vertical mirror plane* and denoted by σ_v.

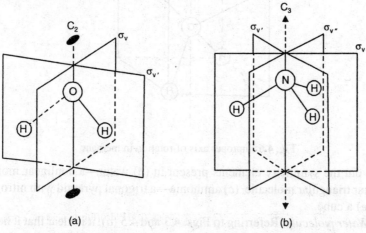

(a)   (b)

Fig. 4.5 Planes of symmetry in the molecules of (a) water and (b) ammonia

Water molecule has two vertical planes of symmetry, σ_v and $\sigma_{v'}$, which are perpendicular to each other [Fig. 4.5(a)]. One of these mirror planes $\sigma_{v'}$ contains the plane of the molecule and the other is perpendicular to it. In ammonia molecule, there are three vertical planes of symmetry, σ_v, $\sigma_{v'}$ and $\sigma_{v''}$ planes [Fig. 4.5(b)]. In Benzene all the six carbon atoms and six hydrogen atoms are in the horizontal plane. This is perpendicular to the C_6 principal axis and hence has a C_6 axis and one σ_h and six σ_v planes. A linear molecule like hydrochloric acid has an infinite number of vertical mirror planes, all of which include C_∞ rotation axis.

(5) **Improper rotation about an axis of improper rotation:** The improper rotation consists of a rotation by $\left(\dfrac{2\pi}{n}\right)$ about an axis followed by reflection through a plane perpendicular to the axis (horizontal reflection). It is denoted by S_n. Thus, the improper rotation operator S_n is the product of two operators.

$$S_n = \sigma C_n$$

This implies that two operations C_n and σ are applied successively.

An S_1 is equivalent to plane of symmetry (σ). It involves first rotation by 360° followed by reflection across the symmetry plane perpendicular to the axis of rotation. This can be simply represented as reflection across the mirror plane.

An S_2 is equivalent to a centre of symmetry. (*i*) It consists of a counter-clockwise rotation about an axis through $\dfrac{2\pi}{2}$ or 180°, followed by reflection across a horizontal symmetry plane perpendicular to this axis yield the original configuration. Similarly an S_3 axis has C_3 axis and a horizontal symmetry plane σ_h. Methane has three equivalent S_4 axis at right angles to each other (Fig. 4.6).

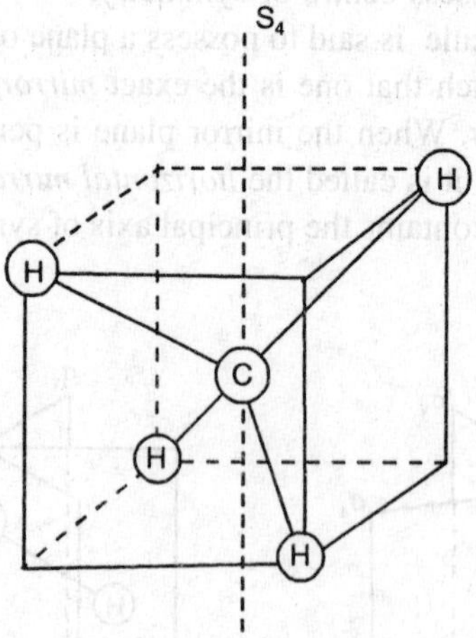

Fig. 4.6 Improper axis of rotation in methane

Problem 4.1: List out the symmetry elements present in (*a*) water—a nonlinear molecule, (*b*) boron trichloride—a planar triangular molecule, (*c*) ammonia—a trigonal pyramid with nitrogen at the vertex, (*d*) benzene, and (*e*) a cube.

Solution: (*a*) *Water molecule:* Referring to Figs. 4.3 and 4.5 (*a*), it is clear that it has a two-fold axis of symmetry (C_2) and two vertical planes of symmetry (σ_v and $\sigma_{v'}$). There is no centre of symmetry.

(b) Boron trichloride: The molecule possesses a C_3 and three C_2 axes of symmetry; C_3 axis is perpendicular to the plane of the molecule while a C_2 axis contains a chlorine and boron atom and bisects the angle between the other two chlorine atoms [Fig. 4.6 (*a*)]. There are four planes of symmetry. Three of these lie along each of the C_2 axis and are normal to the plane of the molecule and the fourth one is coincident with the plane of the molecule. It is also perpendicular to the C_3 axis and is therefore the σ_h plane. The other three planes encompass it and are consequently σ_v planes. There is no centre of symmetry.

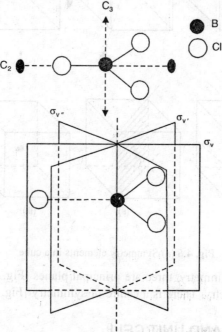

Fig. 4.6 (*a*) Symmetry elements in boron trichloride

(c) Ammonia: There is a C_3 axis of symmetry and three σ_v planes containing nitrogen and one hydrogen and bisecting the angle between the other two hydrogen atoms [Fig. 4.4(*a*)]. There is no centre of symmetry.

(d) Benzene: From Fig. 4.6 (*b*), the different symmetry elements are—one C_6 axis of symmetry and three C_2 symmetry axes which pass through the centre of the molecule and through two carbons and two hydrogens. There are three additional two-fold axes of symmetry (C_2') which pass through centre of the molecule and bisect the C-C bonds.

There is a σ_h plane and $3\sigma_v$ and $3\sigma_{v'}$ planes which bisect the angles formed by the C_2 and C_2' axes, respectively. There is a centre of symmetry.

(e) A cube: From Fig. 4.6 (*c*), the various symmetry elements are three C_4 axes of symmetry at right angles to each other, four C_3 axes of symmetry passing through the opposite corners of the cube and six C_2 axes of symmetry emerging from the opposite edges.

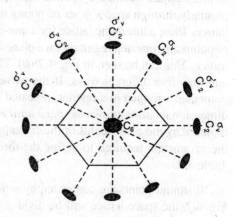

Fig. 4.6 (*b*) Symmetry elements in benzene

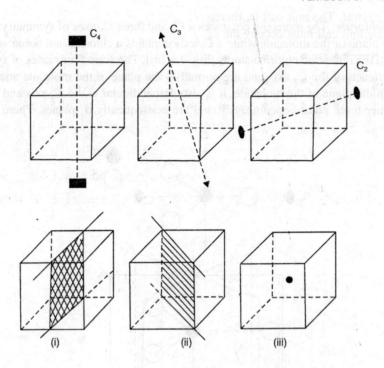

Fig. 4.6 (*c*) Symmetry elements in a cube

There are nine planes of symmetry, three are principal planes [Fig. 4.6*c* (*i*)] and six are diagonal planes [Fig. 4.6*c* (*ii*)] of symmetry. There is a centre of symmetry [Fig. 4.6*c* (*iii*)].

4.3 CRYSTAL LATTICE AND UNIT CELL

The idea of the lattice was developed from the internal regularity of the crystal structure. Lattice is defined as an arrangement of geometrical points in a definite pattern in space. *A highly ordered three-dimensional structure formed by atoms, molecules or ions is called a crystal lattice.* If the constituents of a crystal are denoted by points then a lattice may be regarded as an infinite set of points repeated regularly through space. A set of points repeated at a regular interval along a line is a one-dimension lattice. Thus, a line is the lattice for a one-dimensional pattern. This is shown in Fig. 4.7 (*a*). When a set of points are repeated regularly on a plane (along any two coordinate axes) it is called a *two-dimensional lattice*. This can be seen in Fig. 4.7 (*b*). The points in a two-dimensional plane can be arranged in five and only five different ways. If the two-dimensional lattice is extended in three-dimension, *i.e.*, the points are arranged in a regular, repeated manner along the three coordinate axes, it results in a three-dimensional lattice known as *space lattice or point lattice* [Fig. 4.7 (*c*)]. If the points in space lattice are replaced by the constituents of the crystal (atoms, molecules or ions), a crystal lattice is obtained. Thus, the parameters required to define the three types of lattices in their most general forms are given in Table 4.2.

If similar points are connected by sets of parallel lines along the three coordinate axes as shown in Fig. 4.7, the space lattice will be divided into a large number of small symmetrical units. These basic units of the space lattice are known as the *unit cells*. Thus, *a unit cell is the smallest fundamental building unit of crystal*. The unit cell is, therefore, the essential feature of the crystal structure. Any point placed in the unit cell must occupy the same relative position in every unit cell.

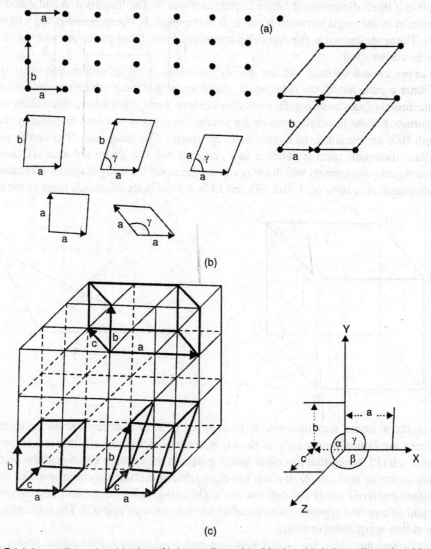

Fig. 4.7 (*a*) A one-dimensional lattice; (*b*) A two-dimensional lattice; (*c*) A three-dimensional lattice

Table 4.2 Unit Cell Parameters in One, Two and Three-dimensional Lattices

Lattice	Lattice translation (repeated distance)	Interaxial angle
One-dimensional	*a*	–
Two-dimensional	*a*, *b*	γ
Three-dimensional	*a*, *b*, *c*	γ, α, β

4.4 CRYSTAL SYSTEMS

The unit cell in a three-dimensional lattice is characterized by the lengths a, b and c and the angles α, β and γ, where α is the angle between b and c, β is the angle between a and c and γ between a and b respectively. These are known as the unit cell parameters. From these parameters a total of seven crystal lattices can be constructed.

Of the seven crystal systems, we are mainly interested in cubic system due to its simplicity and symmetry. Since a cube has all the sides equal, therefore, all the three lattice parameters ($a = b = c$) are same. A cube has six faces and each face has four corners. Each point where three faces of a cube meet is called a *corner*. A cube has eight corners. By joining the corners of a face diagonally, two face diagonals (AC and BD) are obtained. In a cube there are twelve face diagonals. The centre point of a face where two face diagonals meet is called a *face centre* (Point O). There are total six face centres in a cube. By joining any two corners which are not in the same face, a body diagonal is obtained. There are four body diagonals in a cube (AG, BH, FD and EC). All the body diagonals meet at the body centre.

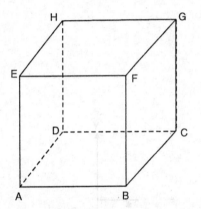 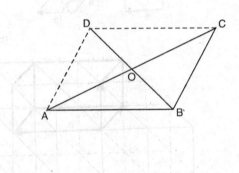

Some crystal systems, may have one or more types of lattices depending on the number of lattice points. If there are lattice points only at the eight corners of a unit cell, this is known as *simple* or *primitive unit cell* (P). A cell that has eight lattice points at the corners and one at the body centre, it is called a *body-centered unit cell* (I). If a cell has eight lattice points at the corner and the six face centres is called as *face-centered cell* (F). A cell that has eight lattice points at the corners and two more at the centre of a pair of any two opposite faces is called an *end-centered cell* (C). The unit cells of the type F, C and I are called non-primitive cells.

Bravais showed that there are 14 different unit cells to account for the lattice points at the corners of the unit cell as well as those at the centres and on some of the faces. These 14 unit cells (Fig. 4.8 and Table 4.2) are known as the *Bravias lattices*.

The set or combination of symmetry elements associated with a point in a regular pattern is called a *point group*. In a two-dimensional lattice, there are 10 point groups. However, in a three-dimensional lattice, 32 *point groups* result from the various possible combinations of symmetry elements with each Bravais lattice. These symmetry operations do not include rotation-translation (screw axis) and reflection-translation (glide plane) operations. When these symmetry operations are included a total of 230 *space groups*, *i.e.*, a possible group of symmetry operations of infinite objects are obtained. A three-dimensional crystal must belong to any one of these space groups.

Table 4.3 lists the various crystal systems with their axial characteristics, the minimum symmetry elements necessary for each system and some typical examples of substances in the various systems.

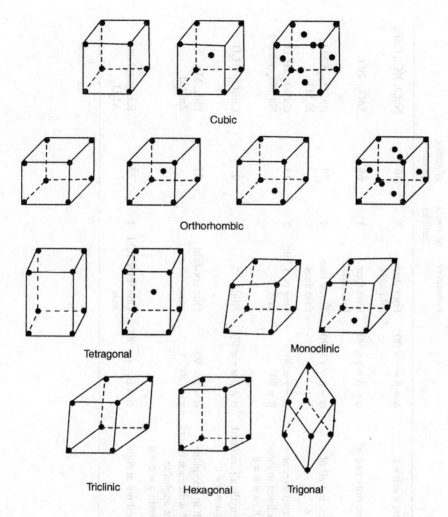

Fig. 4.8 The 14 Bravais lattices

4.5 LATTICE PLANES AND THEIR DESIGNATIONS

The points in a space lattice may be arranged in a large number of ways in a series of parallel and equidistant planes known as the *lattice planes*. In terms of these planes, it is convenient to describe a crystal lattice. The faces of a complete crystal are parallel to these planes containing the largest number of points. To illustrate this statement, consider a simple two-dimensional rectangular crystal lattice as shown in Fig. 4.9. The planes will appear as lines parallel to the z axis. A large number of planes with different orientations AA', BB', CC', DD' etc., are possible with each plane containing some of the lattice points.

The lattice planes are designated in terms of their intercepts on x, y and z axes measured from an arbitrarily-chosen origin. For the set of parallel and equidistant planes AA' (Fig. 4.9), the first plane, makes intercepts of a and b on the x and y axes. Since it is parallel to the z axis, therefore, the intercept on the z axis is infinity. The ratio of the intercepts is a:b:∞. The next plane makes the intercepts, $2a$, $2b$ and ∞. The ratio is again a simple multiple of a, b and ∞. Hence, this set of planes is designated as

Table 4.3 Crystal Systems, Bravais Lattices and Space Groups in Crystals

System	Axial characteristic	Angles	Minimum symmetry	Number of space lattices	Number of space groups	Examples
1. Cubic	Three axes at right angles; $a = b = c$	$\alpha = \beta = \gamma = 90°$	Four three fold axes	3	36	NaCl, KCl, CaF_2
2. Tetragonal	Three axes at right angles, only two of equal length; $a = b \neq c$	$\alpha = \beta = \gamma = 90°$	One four fold axis	2	68	SnO_2, TiO_2
3. Orthorhombic	Three axes at right angles, but all of different length; $a \neq b \neq c$	$\alpha = \beta = \gamma = 90°$	Three two fold axes	4	59	$BaSO_4$, KNO_3, K_2SO_4
4. Monoclinic	Three axes, all unequal, two axes at right angles, the third inclined to these at an angle other than 90°; $a \neq b \neq c$	$\alpha = \gamma = 90°$ $\beta \neq 90°$	One two fold axis	2	13	$CaSO_4 \cdot 2H_2O$ $Na_2SO_4 \cdot 10H_2O$
5. Triclinic	Three axes of unequal length, all inclined at angles other than 90°; $a \neq b \neq c$	$\alpha \neq \beta \neq \gamma \neq 90°$	None	1	2	$CuSO_4 \cdot 5H_2O$
6. Hexagonal	Two axes of equal length in one plane making an angle of 120° with each other and the third axis at right angles to these and of unequal length; $a = b \neq c$	$\alpha = \beta = 90°$ $\gamma = 120°$	One six-fold axis	1	27	PbI_2, Mg, Zn, Cd
7. Rhombohedral	Three axes equal, inclined not at right angles; $a = b = c$	$\alpha = \beta = \gamma \neq 90°$	One three fold axis	1	25	Ice, graphite, Al_2O_3

$a:b:\infty$ planes. Now consider another set of planes BB' (Fig. 4.9), in which the intercepts on the x, y and z axes are simple integral multiples of $3a$, $2b$ and ∞, respectively. These planes can be denoted as $3a:2b:\infty$ planes. Similarly, for the set of planes CC' (Fig. 4.9) the intercepts on x axis are multiples of 'a' while the intercepts on y and z axes are infinity as the planes are parallel to these two axes. These planes can be represented as $a:\infty:\infty$ planes.

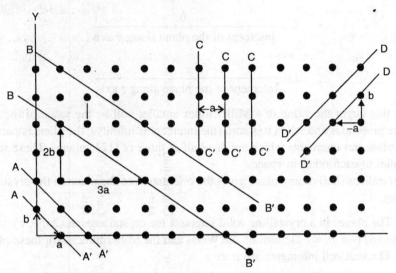

Fig. 4.9 End view of two-dimensional lattice planes

If one moves in the negative direction along an axis from the arbitrarily chosen point, the intercept is given a negative sign. For example, in the set of planes DD' (Fig. 4.9), the intercepts on x axis in the negative direction are multiples of a while on y axis, these are multiples of b. These planes are referred to as—$a:b:\infty$ planes.

From the above discussions, we see that the intercepts of any plane along the three crystallographic axes are either equal to the ratio of the unit cell intercepts a, b, c or some integral multiples of them, i.e., la, mb and nc where l, m and n are small whole numbers. This is known as *the law of rational indices*. The coefficients of a, b and c are known as the *Weiss indices* and characterize the given set of parallel and equidistant planes in the Weiss system of indexing the planes. The appearance of ∞ in the Weiss system is rather inconvenient and is avoided in the Miller system of indexing the lattice planes. The various steps involved in the inversion of Weiss indices into Miller indices are as follows:

(*i*) The reciprocals of the Weiss coefficients are taken.

(*ii*) The reciprocals are cleared of the fractions, if any.

(*iii*) These are then reduced to the smallest set of integers.

For examples, in the planes $a:b:\infty$, the reciprocals of Weiss indices are $\dfrac{1}{1}, \dfrac{1}{1}, \dfrac{1}{\infty}$ and the Miller indices are written as (110). Similarly, for the set of planes $3a:2b:\infty$, the reciprocals of Weiss indices are $\dfrac{1}{3}, \dfrac{1}{2}, \dfrac{1}{\infty}$ and the Miller indices would be (230). The Miller indices for the set of planes $-a:b:\infty$ are $(\bar{1}10)$ where a bar sign above the number means a negative sign.

In general, the Miller indices of a plane can be expressed as (hkl) where h, k and l refer to the reciprocals of the intercepts expressed in units of the lattice distance, *i.e.*,

$$h = \frac{a}{\text{Intercepts of the plane along } x \text{ axis}}$$

$$k = \frac{b}{\text{Intercept of the plane along } y \text{ axis}}$$

and

$$l = \frac{c}{\text{Intercept of the plane along } z \text{ axis}}$$

It is clear that larger the value of a Miller index smaller will be the value of the intercept of that plane along the given axis and when it is zero (the intercept is infinity), the plane is parallel to that axis. Thus, a (222) plane has intercepts which are one-half of those of (111) planes. These sets of planes are, however, parallel to each other in space.

The Miller indices (hkl) of any plane gives the orientation of the plane in the crystal with reference to its three axes.

Problem 4.2: The planes in a crystalline solid intersect the crystal axes at ($2a$, b, c), ($-a$, b, c), (a, $2b$, $3c$), ($3a$, $2b$, ∞) and ($-a$, b, ∞). Determine the Weiss and the Miller indices for these planes.

Solution: The unit cell intercepts are a, b, c

Intercepts	$2a$	b	c	$-a$	b	c	a	$2b$	$3c$	$3a$	$2b$	c	$-a$	b	∞
Weiss indices	2	1	1	-1	1	1	1	2	3	3	2	1	-1	1	∞
Reciprocal of Weiss indices	$\frac{1}{2}$	$\frac{1}{1}$	$\frac{1}{1}$	$-\frac{1}{1}$	$\frac{1}{1}$	$\frac{1}{1}$	$\frac{1}{1}$	$\frac{1}{2}$	$\frac{1}{3}$	$\frac{1}{3}$	$\frac{1}{2}$	1	$-\frac{1}{1}$	$\frac{1}{1}$	$\frac{1}{\infty}$
Clear fractions	1	2	2	-1	1	1	6	3	2	2	3	6	-1	1	0
Miller indices	(122)			($\bar{1}$11)			(632)			(236)			($\bar{1}$10)		

4.6 LATTICE PLANES IN CUBIC CRYSTALS

A cubic system is the simplest type of crystal system where the intercepts on the three axes are equal and all the angles are equal to 90°. In the primitive cubic lattice, the lattice points are present at each corner of the cube. The planes that can pass through the lattice points have Miller indices (100), (110) and (111) as shown in Fig. 4.10 (*a*). The (100) planes have intercepts only on these axis but are parallel to the y and z axes. The other planes (110) and (111) have intercepts on x and y axes and x, y and z axes, respectively. The perpendicular distance between the adjacent planes is known as *the interplanar spacing* and is denoted by d_{hkl}. For (100) planes, the interplanar spacing

$$d_{100} = a$$

where a is side of the cube.

The spacing between (110) planes, d_{110} is one-half of the diagonal of he square base of the cube as shown in the Fig. 4.10 (*a*). Thus, $d_{110} = \frac{\sqrt{2}a}{2} = \frac{a}{\sqrt{2}}$. The spacings between (111) planes d_{111} can be calculated from the fact that two planes pass through the body diagonal of the cube dividing it into three

equal parts. The body diagonal of the cube is given as $\left(\sqrt{2}a\right)^2 + (a)^2 = \sqrt{3}a$. Hence, $d_{111} = \dfrac{\sqrt{3}a}{3} = \dfrac{a}{\sqrt{3}}$.

The ratio of the inter-planar spacings, $d_{100} : d_{100} : d_{111} = a : \dfrac{a}{\sqrt{2}} : \dfrac{a}{\sqrt{3}} = 1 : \dfrac{1}{\sqrt{2}} : \dfrac{1}{\sqrt{3}}$.

In the face-centered cubic (*fcc*) lattice, the points are present at the centre of each face in addition to those at the corners of the primitive cubic lattice. Hence, parallel planes can be drawn midway between (100) and (110) planes in the primitive cubic lattice [Fig. 4.10 (*b*)]. The Miller indices of these

planes are (200) and (220) and the interplanar spacings are $d_{200} = \dfrac{a}{2}$ and $d_{220} = \dfrac{a}{2\sqrt{2}}$. Points on faces

of the cube are contained in (111) planes of the simple cubic lattice and therefore no additional planes are required.

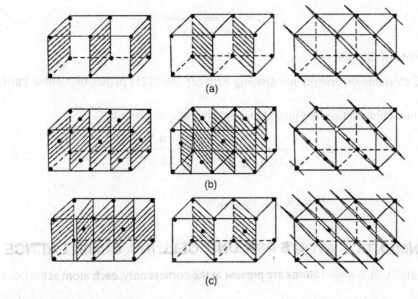

(a)

(b)

(c)

Fig. 4.10 Planes in the three types of cubic lattices (*a*) Planes in simple cubic lattice; (*b*) Planes in face centered cubic lattice; (*c*) Planes in body centered cubic lattice.

Finally in the body-centered cubic (*bcc*) lattice-additional points are present at the centre of each cubic lattice. As can be seen from the [Fig. 4.10 (*c*)], parallel planes with Miller indices (200) can be drawn midway between (100) planes; (222) planes can be drawn half-way between (111) planes in the simple cubic lattice. No additional plane is required in (110) planes as the body centered point is contained in this plane. The inter-planar spacings between d_{200} and d_{222} are

$$d_{200} = \frac{a}{2}$$

and

$$d_{222} = \frac{a}{2\sqrt{3}}$$

Table 4.4 gives the ratios of d_{hkl} for different cubic lattices.

Table 4.4 Ratios of d_{hkl} for Cubic Lattices

Simple cubic lattice	$d_{100} : d_{110} : d_{111} = 1 : \dfrac{1}{\sqrt{2}} : \dfrac{1}{\sqrt{3}} = 1 : 0.707 : 0.577$
Face-centered cubic lattice	$d_{200} : d_{220} : d_{111} = \dfrac{1}{2} : \dfrac{1}{2\sqrt{2}} : \dfrac{1}{\sqrt{3}} = 1 : 0.707 : 1.154$
Body-centered cubic lattice	$d_{200} : d_{110} : d_{222} = \dfrac{1}{2} : \dfrac{1}{\sqrt{2}} : \dfrac{1}{2\sqrt{3}} = 1 : 1.414 : 0.577$

In general, the interplanar spacing (d_{hkl}) between the planes hkl in a cubic lattice in given as

$$d_{hkl} = \frac{a}{\sqrt{h^2 + k^2 + l^2}} \qquad \qquad ...(4.1)$$

where a is the side of the cube.

Problem 4.3: Determine the interplanar spacing between the (221) planes of a cubic lattice of length 4.5Å (450 pm).

  Solution: In a cubic lattice, the interplanar spacing d_{221} is given by

$$d_{221} = \frac{a}{\left(h^2 + k^2 + l^2\right)^{1/2}} = \frac{4.5}{\left(4 + 4 + 1\right)^{1/2}} \text{Å}$$

$$= 1.5 \text{ Å} = 150 \text{ pm}$$

4.7 ASSIGNMENT OF ATOMS PER UNIT CELL IN A CUBIC LATTICE

In a primitive cubic lattice where atoms are present at the corners only, each atom at the corner is shared

equally by eight other units cells. Hence the contribution of each atom to the unit cell is $\dfrac{1}{8}$ and the total

number of atoms per unit cell is $8 \times \dfrac{1}{8} = 1$.

  A face atom is shared equally between two unit cells and therefore a face atom contributes only $\dfrac{1}{2}$

to the unit cell. The number of atoms per unit cell in an *fcc* lattice is

contribution of 6 face atoms = $6 \times \dfrac{1}{2} = 3$

contribution of 8 corner atom $= 8 \times \dfrac{1}{8} = 1$

thus giving a total of 4 atoms per unit cell.

In a *bcc* lattice, the body-centered atom belongs exclusively to the unit cell. The total number of atoms per unit cell is two as shown below:

Contribution from corner atoms $= 8 \times \dfrac{1}{8} = 1$

and from the body centre $= 1$

An edge atom is common to four unit cells and there are twelve edges of the unit cell. The

contribution from each edge atom is therefore $\dfrac{1}{4}$ and the total from 12 edges is $12 \times \dfrac{1}{4} = 3$. The number

of atoms per unit cell in such cases is therefore four (three from 12 edges and 1 from eight corners).

The summary of the above results is given in Table 4.5.

Table 4.5 Number of Atoms per Unit Cell in Cubic Lattices

Types of lattice	Location of atoms	Portion in the unit cell	Number of atoms in the unit cell
Primitive	Corner	$\dfrac{1}{8}$	1
Face centered	Face centre	$\dfrac{1}{2}$	4
Body centered	Body centre	1	2
Edge centered	Edge centre	$\dfrac{1}{4}$	4

Problem 4.4: In an *fcc* arrangement, the corner atoms are *A* type and those at the face centres are *B* type. What is the simplest formula of the compound?

Solution: Number of *A* type atoms in the unit cell = 1
Number of *B* type atoms in the unit cell = 3
Hence, the formula is AB_3

Problem 4.5: In an *fcc* lattice of *A* and *B*, *A* type atoms are present at the corners while *B* types are at face centres. If in each unit cell, one of the *A* type atom is missing from the corner, what is the simplest formula of the compound?

Solution: Number of atoms of *A* type in the unit cell $= \dfrac{7}{8}$

Number of atoms of *B* type in the unit cell = 3

Hence, the formula is $A_{7/8}B_3$ or A_7B_{24}

4.8 DIFFRACTION OF X-RAYS BY CRYSTALS

Ewall in 1911 showed that when light falls on an object which is of the same size as the wavelength of radiation, it is diffracted. This fact is usually investigated by means of a diffraction grating which consists of a large number of fine, equidistant and parallel lines drawn on the metal or some other material. When monochromatic radiation falls on a diffraction grating, it is diffracted and a large number of images of different intensities are formed. If two diffracted waves are in the same phase, a constructive interference results and a series of bright spots would be observed on a screen placed on the path of the diffracted waves. On the other hand, if the waves are out of phase, a destructive interference would result and dark spots would be observed on the screen (Fig. 4.11). The condition for constructive interference is that the path difference for the two waves must be an integral multiple of wavelength.

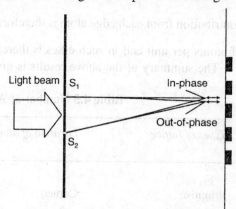

Fig. 4.11 In-phase and out-of-phase waves

X-rays are electromagnetic radiations of short wavelength of the order of 0.1 nm. The wavelength is comparable with the spacings of atoms in crystals. This led M. von Laue to suggest that crystals can act as three-dimensional diffraction grating to X-rays. This was confirmed experimentally by Friendrich and Knipping. They passed a beam of homogeneous X-ray through a crystal of zinc blende. The resulting radiation when allowed to fall on a photographic plate, a definite diffraction pattern was obtained.

If there are two waves starting from a common source, their phase difference will be directly proportional to their path difference. A pattern of this type is generally referred to as a Laue photograph or Laue pattern. From the Laue's pattern it is possible to arrive at the size, shape and the detailed information regarding the position of atoms in a crystal.

The important discovery that a crystal could behave as a three-dimensional diffraction grating to X-rays led W.H. Bragg and W.L. Bragg to use X-ray for the purpose of studying the internal structure of crystals.

4.9 THE BRAGG EQUATION

Since a crystal may be regarded as consisting of a large numbers of parallel and equidistant atomic planes, Bragg considered that the diffraction effects observed for X-ray could be represented as reflection of X-ray by successive planes of atoms in the crystal. Thus, when X-rays are incident on a crystal face they penetrate into the crystal and are scattered by the atoms or ions. Consider a set of parallel and equidistant planes AA, BB, etc. in the crystal as shown in Fig. 4.12. These planes characterize the arrangement of the atoms or ions in the crystal. A parallel beam of monochromatic X-ray of wavelength λ strikes these planes at an angle of incidence θ. Some of the rays will be reflected by atoms from the upper layer AA, with angle of reflection being equal to the angle of incidence. Some of the rays will be absorbed and some will be reflected from the second layer BB and so on with the successive layers. When the rays reflected from the successive layers are in phase, constructive interference will occur and a bright diffraction spot would be obtained from these planes. The condition for the constructive interference is that the path difference between the reflected rays from successive planes must be an integral multiple of wavelength, λ. The condition for reinforcement can be obtained as follows.

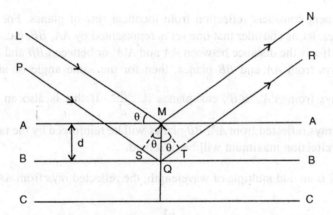

Fig. 4.12 X-ray reflection from equidistant planes

The path difference for *LMN* and *PQR* is equal to *SQ* + *QT*, where *MS* and *MT* are perpendiculars drawn from *M* to *PQ* and *QR*, respectively. If *d* is the interplanar spacing between the successive planes, then both SQ and QT are equal to $d \sin\theta$, since the angles *SMQ* and *QMT* are each equal to θ. The total path difference in thus $2d \sin\theta$. For a reflection of maximum intensity, this quantity must be an integral number (n) of wavelength (λ), as stated above. Hence, the condition for maximum reflection is

$$n\lambda = 2 \, d_{hkl} \sin\theta \qquad \qquad ...(4.2)$$

Equation 4.2 is known as the *Bragg equation* and gives the relationship between the interplanar spacing d_{hkl} and the angle at which the reflected radiation has maximum reflection for a given wavelength λ. The value of n gives the order of reflection. If $n = 1$, the order of reflection is one, if $n = 2$, the reflection is second order and so on. For a given value of d and λ, there may be a number of values of angle of incidence, $\theta_1, \theta_2...$ corresponding to $n = 1, 2...$at which maximum reflection will occur. From eq. (4.2), it is clear that higher-order reflection will be obtained for larger values of θ. In case $\lambda \gg 2d$, there is no solution for n and hence no diffraction would result. In other words, the light would pass through the crystal without diffraction by the planes. If $\lambda \ll d$, the rays are diffracted through small angles, and thus the Bragg equation does not indicate the intensities of the various diffracted rays. For higher intensities of diffracted rays, the angle of reflection should be small.

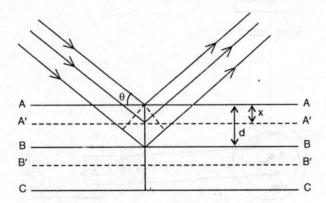

Fig. 4.13 Reflection of X-ray from dissimilar planes

The above treatment considers reflection from identical sets of planes. For reflection from two different sets of planes, let us consider that one set is represented by AA, BB, etc. and another by $A'A'$, $B'B'$ etc. (Fig. 4.13). If x is the distance between AA and $A'A'$ or between BB and $B'B'$ and $n\lambda$ the path difference for the rays from AA and BB planes, then for the same angle of incidence θ, the path

difference for the rays from $A'A'$, $B'B'$, etc. planes is $\dfrac{xn\lambda}{d}$. If this is also an integral multiple of

wavelength, then the rays reflected from AA, BB planes will be reinforced by the rays from $A'A'$ or $B'B'$ planes and a strong reflection maximum will be observed.

However, if $\dfrac{xn\lambda}{d}$ is an odd multiple of wavelength, the reflected rays from AA will be opposed by

those from $A'A'$. If $x = d/2$ the path difference is $\dfrac{n\lambda}{2}$, it means odd order spectra will be missing; and

if $x = \dfrac{d}{4}$, the path difference is $\dfrac{n\lambda}{4}$ indicating that second, sixth, tenth, etc. order spectra will also be

weak.

4.10 EXPERIMENTAL METHODS OF CRYSTAL ANALYSIS

(*a*) **Bragg X-ray spectrometer:** It is evident from Bragg equation that if the angles of incidence θ are measured for the various orders of maximum reflection, the interplanar spacing d between the successive planes of a given type of crystal can be calculated, provided the wavelength λ of the X-ray is known. The reflection angle θ and the intensities of the reflected beams corresponding to these angles can be determined with a Bragg X-ray spectrometer shown in Fig. 4.14. The X-rays generated in X-ray tube are passed through a series of slits to give a sharp and monochromatic beam. The beam is then directed to strike the face of a crystal which is mounted on a graduated rotating table. The latter may be rotated to any desired angle of incidence. The rays reflected from the crystal are then allowed to pass through a detector known as an *ionizing chamber* filled with vapours of methyl bromide. The chamber is rotated

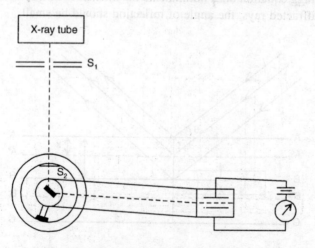

Fig. 4.14 Bragg X-ray spectrometer

coaxially with the crystal table. The crystal table and the chamber are so adjusted that when the crystal rotates through any angle, the chamber rotates at twice that angle so that the reflected rays always enter the chamber. The extent of ionization produced by the reflected beam is measured by the electrometer.

The value of incident angle θ is gradually increased by rotating the table. The intensities of the reflected X-rays for various angles are determined. Strong reflections are obtained from those planes which contain larger number of atoms and for those values of θ which satisfy the Bragg equation. The process is repeated for each plane of the crystal. The intensities of the reflected rays are plotted against twice the angle of incidence of the beam to the crystal and the lines are indexed.

(b) **The Powder Method:** This simple method for obtaining X-ray diffraction data was developed by Debye and Scherrer in 1916 and later by Hull in 1917. In this method instead of scattering X-rays from a single crystal, a finely-powdered sample is taken in a thin-walled glass capillary tube and is irradiated by a monochromatic beam of X-rays. In the powder, the crystal planes are randomly oriented in all possible directions. The sample is considered to be equivalent to a large number of single crystals

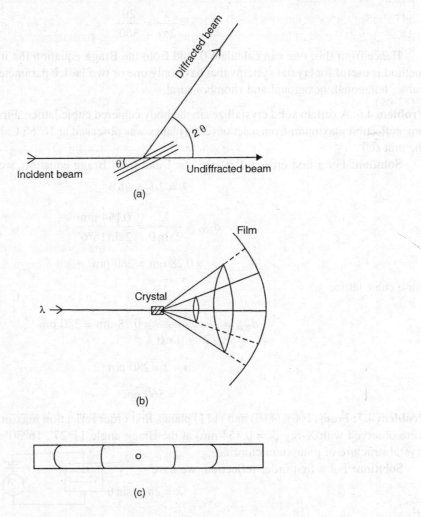

Fig. 4.15 Powder method (a) Angle between the diffracted and undiffracted beams; (b) Cone of diffracted beams; (c) Appearance of the photographic film

with all possible orientations. Out of these, some will be so oriented so as to satisfy the Bragg equation for a given set of planes. Another set of crystals will be oriented so that the Bragg condition is satisfied for another set of planes, and so on. Consider a set of parallel planes making an angle θ with the incident beam of X-rays as shown in Fig. 4.15(a). The reflected ray from these planes will make an angle of 2θ with the unreflected beam. When a given set of planes satisfying the Bragg equation is rotated about the axis of the beam, the reflected ray will outline a cone of scattered radiation. These reflections may be recorded on a photographic film. If the strip of the film is curved into a cylinder, then the different planes will intercept the film as curved or straight lines [Fig. 4.15(c)]. On a flat film, the observed pattern consists of a series of concentric circles.

After obtaining the powder pattern the lines are indexed. The distance x of each line from the central spot in measured, usually by halving the distance between the two reflections on either side of the centre. If r is the radius of the film, then its circumference $2\pi r$ corresponds to a scattering angle of 360°. Then

$$\frac{x}{2\pi r} = \frac{2\theta}{360}$$

Hence from this, one can calculate θ, and from the Bragg equation the interplanar spacings. This method is useful for crystal systems that have only one or two lattice parameters to be determined e.g., cubic, tetragonal, hexagonal and rhombohedral.

Problem 4.6: A certain solid crystallizes in the body centered cubic lattice. First order X-ray ($\lambda = 0.154$ nm) reflection maximum from a set of (200) planes was observed at 16°6'. Calculate the edge length of the unit cell.

Solution: For a first order reflection, $n = 1$ and from Bragg equation, we have

$$\lambda = 2d_{200} \sin\theta$$

or
$$d_{200} = \frac{\lambda}{2\sin\theta} = \frac{0.154 \text{ nm}}{2\sin 16°6'}$$

$$= 0.28 \text{ nm} = 280 \text{ pm}$$

For a cubic lattice

or
$$d_{200} = \frac{a}{\sqrt{2^2 + 0 + 0}} = 0.28 \text{ nm} = 280 \text{ pm}$$

$$a = 2 \times 280 \text{ pm}$$

$$= 560 \text{ pm}$$

Problem 4.7: From (100), (110) and (111) planes first order reflection maxima for potassium chloride were observed with X-ray ($\lambda = 0.154$ nm) at the Bragg angle 11°27', 16°30' and 20°7'. Ascertain the crystal structure of potassium chloride.

Solution: For a first order reflection, we have

$$\lambda = 2d_{hkl} \sin\theta$$

$$d_{hkl} = \frac{\lambda}{2\sin\theta}$$

For a given value of λ, d_{hkl} is therefore inversely proportional to $\sin\theta$. Hence,

$$d_{100}:d_{110}:d_{111} = \frac{1}{(\sin\theta)_{100}} : \frac{1}{(\sin\theta)_{110}} : \frac{1}{(\sin\theta)_{111}}$$

$$= \frac{1}{\sin 11°27'} : \frac{1}{\sin 16°30'} : \frac{1}{\sin 20°7'}$$

$$= \frac{1}{0.1986} : \frac{1}{0.2840} : \frac{1}{0.3440}$$

$$= 5.035 : 3.522 : 2.907$$

$$= 1.0 : 0.707 : 0.577$$

As the ratio corresponds to that for a simple cubic lattice hence potassium chloride belongs to a simple cubic lattice.

4.11 INDEXING OF LATTICE PLANES IN A CUBIC SYSTEM – STRUCTURE OF SODIUM AND POTASSIUM CHLORIDES

From external geometry, it is known that sodium and potassium chlorides belong to the cubic system. The experimental data can be used to investigate whether a cubic crystal is primitive, body centered, or face centered. For this purpose, intensity of the reflected X-ray beam is plotted against twice the angle of incidence (θ). A series of reflection maxima (Fig. 4.16) are obtained. The planes in the crystal responsible for producing these maxima are then indexed. The results are compared with those expected for these three types of lattices. This is done as follows:

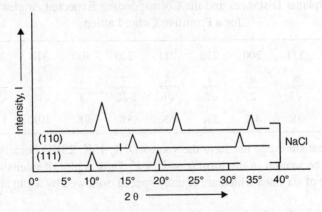

Fig. 4.16 Typical diffraction pattern; plot of I versus 2θ

For a cubic crystal, the interplanar spacing, d_{hkl} is given by

$$d_{hkl} = \frac{a}{\sqrt{h^2 + k^2 + l^2}}$$

or
$$d_{hkl}^2 = \frac{a^2}{h^2 + k^2 + l^2}$$ ...(4.3)

From the Bragg law we have

or
$$\lambda = 2 d_{hkl} \sin \theta$$

$$d_{hkl}^2 = \frac{\lambda^2}{4 \sin^2 \theta}$$ ...(4.4)

From Eq. (4.3) and (4.4), we obtain

$$\frac{\lambda^2}{4 \sin^2 \theta} = \frac{a^2}{h^2 + k^2 + l^2}$$

or
$$\sin^2 \theta = \left(\frac{\lambda}{2a}\right)^2 \left(h^2 + k^2 + l^2\right) = K\left(h^2 + k^2 + l^2\right)$$ ...(4.5)

where
$$K = \frac{\lambda^2}{4a^2}$$

Equation 4.5 can be used to predict the diffraction patterns for the three types of cubic system. These are discussed below:

(1) **Primitive cubic lattice:** By assigning consecutive integral values (0, 1, 2,...) to h, k and l, we can calculate a series of values of d_{hkl} and $\sin^2\theta$ from equations 4.3 and 4.5, respectively. These are listed in Table 4.6.

Table 4.6 Interplanar Distances and the Corresponding Expected Angles of Diffraction for a Primitive Cubic Lattice

hkl	100	110	111	200	210	211	220	300	310	311	222	320
d_{hkl}	a	$\dfrac{a}{\sqrt{2}}$	$\dfrac{a}{\sqrt{3}}$	$\dfrac{a}{2}$	$\dfrac{a}{\sqrt{5}}$	$\dfrac{a}{\sqrt{6}}$	$\dfrac{a}{2\sqrt{2}}$	$\dfrac{a}{3}$	$\dfrac{a}{\sqrt{10}}$	$\dfrac{a}{\sqrt{11}}$	$\dfrac{a}{\sqrt{12}}$	$\dfrac{a}{\sqrt{13}}$
$\sin^2\theta$	K	2K	3K	4K	5K	6K	8K	9K	10K	11K	12K	13K

It may be noted that $\sin^2\theta$ can not have the value of 7K, 15K, 23K... because there is no way the integers 7, 15, 23 can be written in the form $h^2 + k^2 + l^2$. Thus, a plot of intensity of reflected X-rays versus $\sin^2\theta$ yield a set of six lines which are equally spaced, followed by a gap and then another series of lines.

(2) **Body-centered lattice:** In the case of a body centered cubic crystal (Fig. 4.10), midway between (100) planes are (200) planes. X-rays reflected from (100) planes will be in phase and reinforce each other. However, the rays reflected from the planes lying midway between the (100) planes are opposed by half a wave-length and are exactly out of phase with those originating from (100) planes. If all the lattice atoms are identical or have equal scattering power, the observed intensity from (100) planes will be zero and a reflection maximum from (100) would be missing.

The (200) and (110) planes however include all the atoms and hence produce sharp reflection maxima.

In case of (111) planes, no reflection maximum will be observed as midway between them are planes which destructively interfere with the reflections from (111) planes. The (222) planes will reinforce each other. It may be stated that for a body-centered cubic crystal, reflection from planes for which $h + k + l$ is odd are *not observed*. The observed diffraction lines at angles are given in table 4.7.

Table 4.7 Angles at which Diffraction Lines are Observed for a Body-centered Cubic Lattice

hkl	100	110	111	200	210	211	220	300 221	310	311	222	320
d_{hkl}	–	$\dfrac{a}{\sqrt{2}}$	–	$\dfrac{a}{2}$	–	$\dfrac{a}{\sqrt{6}}$	$\dfrac{a}{2\sqrt{2}}$	–	$\dfrac{a}{\sqrt{10}}$	–	$\dfrac{a}{\sqrt{12}}$	–
$\sin^2\theta$	–	2K	–	4K	–	6K	8K	–	10K	–	12K	–

(3) **Face-centered lattice:** For a face-centered lattice, it may be seen (Fig. 4.10) that the reflection maxima from (100), (110) planes will be missing in the case of a face-centered cubic crystal. However, reflection maxima will be observed for rays from planes (200), (220), (111) etc. In fact, reflection maxima will be observed from planes for which hkl are **either all odd or all even.** The observed diffraction lines at angles are given in table 4.8.

Table 4.8 Angles at which Diffraction Lines are Observed for a Face-centered Cubic Lattice

hkl	100	110	111	200	210	211	220	221 300	210	311	222
d_{hkl}	–	–	$\dfrac{a}{\sqrt{3}}$	$\dfrac{a}{2}$	–	–	$\dfrac{a}{2\sqrt{2}}$	–	–	$\dfrac{a}{\sqrt{11}}$	$\dfrac{a}{\sqrt{12}}$
$\sin^2\theta$	–	–	3K	4K	–	–	8K	–	–	11K	12K

Table 4.9 Calculated and Observed Diffraction Maxima for Cubic Crystals

	100	110	111	200	210	211		220	300	310	311
$h^2 + k^2 + l^2$	1	2	3	4	5	6	Missing	8	9	10	11
Primitive cubic	√	√	√	√	√	√		√	√	√	√
Body centred cubic	×	√	×	√	×	√		√	×	√	×
Face centred cubic	×	×	√	√	×	×		√	×	×	√
Potassium chloride	×	×	×	√	×	×		√	×	×	×
Sodium chloride	×	×	√	√	×	×		√	×	×	√

The calculated reflection maxima for the three types of cubic lattices and the observed reflection maxima obtained by comparing sin θ values are given in Table 4.9. The (√) mark indicates that a reflection maximum will be observed while the cross (×) shows the absence of reflection maximum.

It is found that sodium chloride belongs to the face-centered cubic lattice while potassium chloride has a simple cubic lattice. The reason why identical alkali halides such as sodium and potassium chlorides should differ in their crystal structure is due to the fact that both K^+ and Cl^- ions contain 18 electrons and thus have identical scattering powers. X-rays, therefore, do not distinguish these ions. On the other hand, in sodium chloride, the scattering power of Na^+ (having 10 electrons) is different from that of chloride ion (18 electrons).

The crystal lattice of sodium chloride is shown in Fig. 4.17. It consists of two interpenetrating face centered cubic lattices of sodium and chloride ions. Each sodium ion is surrounded octahedrally by six chloride ions and each chloride ion in turn is surrounded octahedrally by six sodium ions. Thus, the chloride ion at the centre of the unit cell is surrounded by six equidistant sodium ions: four in the same plane one above and one below it. In this structure (100) or (110) planes contain equal number of both types of ions but (111) planes have either all sodium or chloride ions. The X-rays reflected from successive (111) planes containing sodium ions are destructively interfered by the rays from successive (111) planes containing chloride ions. Hence, the first order reflection from (111) planes will be comparatively weak in sodium chloride. In the case of potassium chloride reflection maximum from (111) planes would be missing as mid-way between (111) planes is another set of planes which would cause destructive interference.

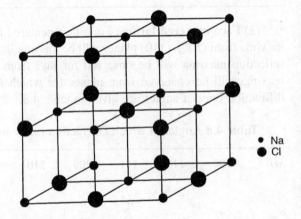

Fig. 4.17 Face-centred cubic lattice of sodium chloride

Caesium chloride structure: CsCl has a body-centered cubic structure in which each Cs^+ ion is surrounded by eight Cl^- ions which is turn is surrounded by eight Cs^+ ions (Fig. 4.18).

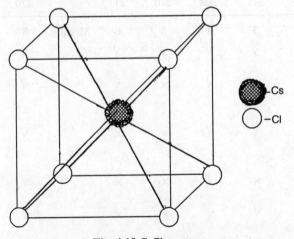

Fig. 4.18 CsCl structure

Problem 4.8: An X-ray ($\lambda = 0.1785$ nm or 178.5 pm) powder photograph of a cubic crystalline solid was taken. Reflection maxima were observed at the following Bragg angles: 18.5°, 27.0°, 33.7°, 40.0°, 45.9° and 51.9°. Index the planes and indicate the type of the cubic lattice. Calculate the unit cell dimension, a.

Solution: For a cubic lattice we have, $\sin^2\theta = \dfrac{\lambda^2}{4a^2}\left(h^2 + k^2 + l^2\right)$

θ	18.5	27.0	33.7	40.0	45.9	51.9
$\sin\theta$	0.3173	0.4540	0.5534	0.6428	0.7181	0.7869
$\sin^2\theta$	0.1007	0.2062	0.3062	0.4132	0.5157	0.6193

Dividing by the common factor 0.0515, we get the values of $h^2 + k^2 + l^2$ which are approximately as

2	4	6	8	10	12

These correspond to hkl values of (110), (200), (211), (220), (310) and (222). The sum of h, k and l values is even in each case showing that the unit cell belongs to the body-centered cubic arrangement.

The larger Bragg angles can be measured more accurately than the smaller one, so a more accurate value for θ is 51.9°; the value of $\dfrac{\lambda^2}{4a^2}$ may be found by dividing $\sin^2\theta$ by 12

$$\frac{\lambda^2}{4a^2} = \frac{0.6193}{12}$$

Hence,

$$a^2 = \frac{(0.1785 \text{ nm})^2}{4 \times 0.6193}$$

$$= 0.3928 \text{ nm}$$

$$= 392.8 \text{ pm}$$

4.12 DENSITY FROM CUBIC LATTICE DIMENSION

The density of the crystal can be measured accurately from experiments and it can be compared calculated for its structure. The density based on the structure can be calculated from the mass contained in a unit cell and its volume. If a is the edge length of the unit cell, then its volume is a^3.

The mass of an atom of substance is obtained by dividing the mass of one mole atom (M) by Avogadro constant, N_A i.e.

$$\text{Mass of an atom} = \frac{M}{N_A}$$

The density of the crystal $d = \dfrac{Mz}{N_A a^3}$

where z is the number of atoms per unit cubic cell.

(i) For a simple (primitive) cubic cell, atoms are present at the corners of the cube. There are eight corners of a cube and thus eight atoms are present at these corners. Therefore, the number of atoms associated with a single primitive unit cell is $8 \times \frac{1}{8} = 1$. Therefore the density of a primi-

tive cubic cell is $\frac{M}{N_A a^3}$.

(*ii*) In a body-centered cubic unit cell (bcc), there are atoms at the eight corners and one atom in the centre of the cube. Therefore, the number of atoms per unit cell are $\left[\left(8 \times \frac{1}{8}\right) + 1\right] = 2$. Thus, the

density of a body-centered cubic cell $= \frac{2M}{N_A a^3}$.

(*iii*) In a face-centered cubic cell (*fcc*), besides eight atoms at the corners, there are six atoms at the centres of six faces. Each of these atoms is shared between two such unit cells. Therefore, the

net atoms per unit cell is $\left(8 \times \frac{1}{8}\right) + \left(6 \times \frac{1}{2}\right) = 4$. Hence, the density of an *fcc* cell $= \frac{4M}{N_A a^3}$.

Problem 4.9: Copper crystallizes in the *fcc* pattern. From X-ray diffraction the edge length of the unit cell has been found to be 0.360 nm (360 pm). If the density of copper is 8.94×10^3 kg m^{-3}, calculate the value of N_A.

Solution: The lattice is *fcc*, hence the number of atoms per unit cell is 4. The edge length of the unit cell is 0.360 nm and its volume is

$$...(360 \times 10^{-12} m)^3 = 4.66 \times 10^{-29} m^3$$

Now mass of 4 copper atoms is

$$\frac{4 \times 63.54}{N_A} \times 10^{-3} \text{ kg mol}^{-1}$$

Hence, the density $= \dfrac{4 \times 63.54 \times 10^{-3} \text{kg mol}^{-1}}{N_A \times 4.66 \times 10^{-29} \text{ m}^3}$

But the density is $\quad 8.94 \times 10^3 \text{kg m}^{-3}$

Therefore, $\quad 8.94 \times 10^3 \text{ kg m}^{-3} = \dfrac{4 \times 63.54 \times 10^{-3}}{N_A \times 4.66 \times 10^{-29}} \text{kg mol}^{-1} \text{m}^{-3}$

$$N_A = \frac{4 \times 63.54 \times 10^{23}}{8.94 \times 4.666} \text{mol}^{-1}$$

or $\quad = 6.095 \times 10^{23} \text{mol}^{-1}$

Problem 4.10: Silver crystallizes in the cubic lattice. The density is found to be 10.7 g cm^{-3}. If the unit cell length is 0.406 nm, calculate the number of atoms per unit cell. Suggest the unit cell type.

Solution: If z is the number of atoms of silver per unit cell, then the density is given by

$$\frac{z \times 108 \times 10^{-3}\,\text{kg mol}^{-1}}{\left(6.023 \times 10^{23}\,\text{mol}^{-1}\right)\left(406 \times 10^{-12}\,\text{m}\right)^{3}}$$

and it is equal to 10.7×10^{3} kg m^{-3}.

Hence

$$z = \frac{\left(10.7 \times 10^{3}\,\text{kg m}^{-3}\right)\left(6.023 \times 10^{23}\,\text{mol}^{-1}\right)\left(4.06 \times 10^{-10}\,\text{m}\right)^{3}}{\left(108 \times 10^{-3}\,\text{mol}^{-1}\right)}$$

$$= 4.024$$

The number of atoms per unit cell is 4. The lattice is therefore an *fcc* type.

Problem 4.11: A certain solid X (at. mass 27) crystallizes in the *fcc* arrangement. if the density of X is 27 g cm^{-3}. What is the unit cell length?

Solution: There are four atoms of X in the unit cell and the mass of these atoms is given by

$$\frac{4 \times 27}{N_A}\,\text{g}$$

If a is the unit cell length, then the volume of the unit cell is a^3 and its density is

$$\frac{4 \times 27}{N_A a^3}\,\text{g cm}^{-3}$$

But the density as given is 2.7 g cm^{-3}, hence

$$\frac{4 \times 27}{N_A a^3} = 2.7$$

or

$$a^3 = \frac{27 \times 4}{2.7\,N_A}$$

or

$$a = \left(\frac{27 \times 4}{2.7 \times 6.023 \times 10^{23}}\right)^{1/3}\,\text{cm}$$

$$= 4.049 \times 10^{-8}\,\text{cm}$$

$$= 4.049 \times 10^{-10}\,\text{m} = 404.9\,\text{pm}$$

Problem 4.12: A closed-packed structure of uniform spheres has a cubic unit cell with side 0.8 nm. What is the radius of the spherical molecule?

Solution: The unit cell has an *fcc* structure. Here the spheres are touching each other along the face diagonal. If f is the radius of the sphere and a the side of the unit cell, then

$$(4r)^2 = a^2 + a^2$$

$$r = \frac{a}{2\sqrt{2}} = \frac{0.8\,\text{nm}}{2\sqrt{2}} = 0.2828\,\text{nm} = 282.8\,\text{pm}$$

4.13 CLOSEST PACKING

In crystals, the atoms, ions or molecules are arranged in a regular way in three-dimensional space. The arrangement has minimum energy and hence maximum stability. For maximum stability, a constituent in the aggregate must be surrounded by the maximum number of neighbours. For maximum number of contacts, each constituent of the crystal must by packed as closely as possible. However, if the constituents are spheres of the uniform size, then the problem reduces to arranging the uniform spheres in three-dimensional space. In a two-dimensional plane, the closest arrangement being that in which each sphere is in contact with six other spheres (Fig. 4.19). Let us denote this layer of spheres by A. To obtain the closest packing in space, the spheres are placed over the layer A in a regular manner. There are six vacant sites or triangular pockets around any sphere in layer A. In Fig. 4.19 around a sphere X these sites are labelled as 1, 2, 3, 4, 5 and 6. We can place only three spheres touching each other in alternate vacant sites, e.g., either in 1, 3 and 5 or in 2, 4 and 6. Suppose the second layer is constructed by placing the spheres in the vacant sites labelled as 1, 3 and 5 then the sites marked 2, 4 and 6 are left unoccupied. Let us denote the second layer of spheres by B. The second layer again has two types of vacant sites. Around any atom in the second layer (Fig. 4.19), one set of vacant sites lies just above the vacant sites 2, 4 and 6 of the first layer and the other set lies above the centres of the spheres of the first layer. Thus, after the second layer is complete, there are two different ways of placing the spheres in the third layer. If the spheres in the third layer are placed in the vacant sites which are above the centres of the spheres

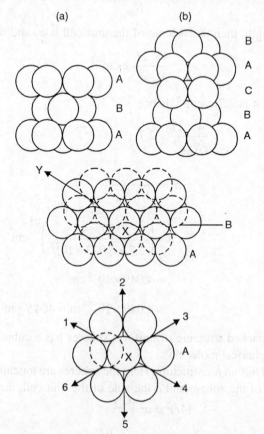

Fig. 4.19 Close-packed structures (*a*) Hexagonal closest packing; (*b*) Cubical closest packing

of the first layer, then the third layer repeats the arrangement of the first layer and we have only two types of layers, viz., *ABAB*......etc. This is called *a hexagonal closest packing, hcp* [Fig. 4.19(*a*)]. On the other hand, if the spheres are placed in the vacant sites above 2, 4 and 6, a new arrangement (*C*) of the spheres is produced [Fig. 4.19(*b*)]. The entire arrangement is now of the type *ABCABC*......etc., and is referred to as *a cubical closest packing, ccp or face-centered cubical closest packing, fcc.*

The number of nearest neighbours (known as the *coordination number*) in each arrangement is twelve: six in the same layer, three in the layer above and three in the layer below it.

In the *fcc* structure, there are two types of vacant sites or holes: *tetrahedral and octahedral.* A tetrahedral hole is surrounded by four spheres while an octahedral hole is the empty space surrounded by six spheres. These vacant sites can accommodate other smaller atoms or molecules giving rise to a variety of different structures.

In an *fcc* structure, there are eight tetrahedral holes per unit cell as shown in Fig. 4.20 (*a*). The number of octahedral holes in the unit cell of the *fcc* structure is four as can be deduced from the following considerations. In Fig. 4.20(*b*), each (X) mark represent a vacant site and there are twelve such vacant sites at the edges of unit cubic lattice. The vacancy at an edge is common to four unit cells and hence the number of such vacant sites per unit cell is $\frac{12}{4} = 3$. In addition to these vacancies, there is one octahedral hole at the centre of the unit cell. Thus, the total number of octahedral holes per unit cell is four.

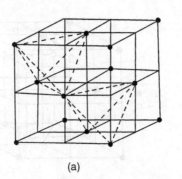 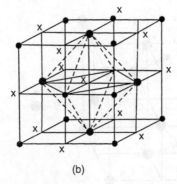

(a)   (b)

Fig. 4.20 (*a*) Tetrahedral holes and (*b*) octahedral holes in an *fcc* structure

Another less-packed arrangement of spheres is the body-centered cubic arrangement (Fig. 4.21) in which each sphere has eight nearest neighbours: four in the same plane, two above and two below it in the adjacent layers. Since the coordination number in *fcc* or *hcp* structures is greater than that in the *bcc* structures, the latter are therefore less denser.

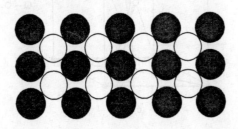

Fig. 4.21 Body centered cubical close-packed structure

4.14 PACKING IN IONIC SOLIDS

The packing of spheres in ionic solids involves cations and anions. If the cations and anions have equal but opposite charges, then a stable electrically neutral structure requires that the number of cations surrounding an anion should be equal to the number of anions surrounding a cation. An electrically neutral structure with twelve coordination number is not possible with ions of the same size. A most closely-packed stable structure of like charged ions in a *bcc* arrangement in which the ion at the body centre is surrounded by eight oppositely charged ions at the corners of the cube. This the structure of caesium chloride, the coordination number of each ion is 8.

Sodium chloride has an *fcc* structure (Fig. 4.17) and may be considered as a face-centered arrangement of Cl^- ions in which the Na^+ ions occupy the octahedral sites resulting in a 6-6 coordination number.

Zinc blende (ZnS) structure may be regarded as an *fcc* arrangement of S^{2-} ions in which half of the tetrahedral holes are alternatively occupied by the Zn^{2+} ions. Each Zn^{2+} ion [Fig. 4.22(a)] is surrounded by four S^{2-} ions at the corner of a tetrahedron. Similarly, each S^{2-} ion is surrounded by four Zn^{2+} ions tetrahedrally giving 4-4 coordination number.

In fluorite (CaF_2), calcium ions have the *fcc* arrangement [Fig. 4.22(b)] where all the tetrahedral holes are occupied by F^- ions. Each F^- ion is tetrahedrally coordinated to four Ca^{2+} ions and each Ca^{2+} ion is surrounded by eight F^- ions at the corners of a cube. This gives a cation:anion ratio of 1:2 or a 8-4 coordination number.

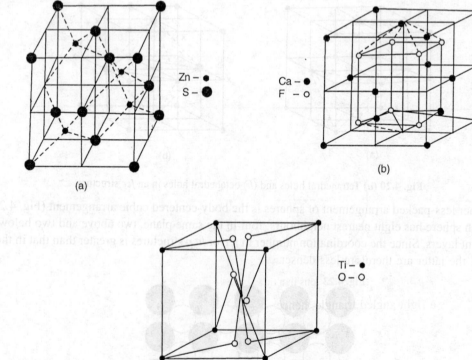

Zn – ●
S – ◉

Ca – ●
F – ○

(a)

(b)

Ti – ●
O – ○

(c)

Fig. 4.22 Unit cells in (*a*) zinc blende; (*b*) fluorite and (*c*) rutile

Rutile (TiO_2) [Fig. 4.22(c)], on the other hand, has a 6-3 coordination number. Hence, each Ti^{4+} ion is octahedrally coordinated to O^{2-} while each O^{2-} is surrounded by three Ti^{4+} ions at the corners of a triangle.

4.15 EFFECT OF ION SIZE ON CRYSTAL STRUCTURE—RADIUS RATIO

In close-packed arrangements of like charged ions, the oppositely-charged ions touch one another. The difference in the crystal structure depends on the size of the ions. Larger the size of a given ion, greater will be the number of oppositely-charged ions which can be packed around it. The geometrical requirement for a given structure in terms of the size of the two ions is expressed by *radius ratio* which is defined as

$$R = \frac{r_s}{r_l} \qquad \qquad ...(4.7)$$

where r_s and r_l are the radii of the smaller (usually a cation) and the larger ions (anion), respectively. Let us calculate the radius ratio for 3, 4, 6 and 8 coordinate structures.

Radius ratio for three coordinate structures: A three coordinate structure gives rise to an equilateral triangular arrangement as shown in Fig. 4.23.

The perpendicular distance CD is given by

$$\frac{r_l}{\sqrt{3}}$$

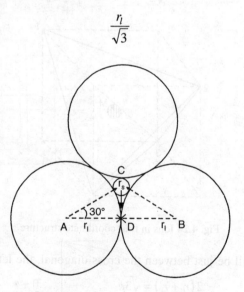

Fig. 4.23 Ions in a three coordinate structure

Since ACD is a right angled triangle, hence

$$AC^2 = AD^2 + CD^2$$

$$(r_l + r_s)^2 = (r_l)^2 + \frac{r_l^2}{3}$$

$$r_l^2 + 2r_l r_s + r_s^2 = r_l^2 + \frac{r_l^2}{3}$$

$$3\left(\frac{r_s}{r_l}\right)^2 + 6\left(\frac{r_s}{r_l}\right) - 1 = 0$$

$$\frac{r_s}{r_l} = \frac{-6 \pm \sqrt{36 + 12}}{6} = \frac{2\sqrt{3}}{3} - 1 = 0.155$$

If the ratio falls below this value, then the large ions can no longer touch the central small ion and this arrangement becomes unstable. If r_s increases, the larger ions are no longer in contact with each other, and when the ratio approaches a value of 0.225 it is possible to accommodate four larger ions around the central ion at the vertices of a regular tetrahedron.

Radius ratio for four coordinate structures: A tetrahedral arrangement can be drawn with in a cube as shown in Fig. 4.24. The anions 1 and 3 (or 1 and 2, 2 and 4, 2 and 3, etc.) will touch each other and lie on the face-diagonal, the length of which is $\sqrt{2}a$. Thus,

$$r_l + r_s = \sqrt{2}a$$

or

$$r_l = \frac{a}{\sqrt{2}}$$

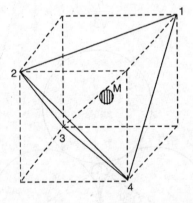

Fig. 4.24 Ions in four coordinate structure

The central cation M will be just between the cross diagonal, the length of which is $\sqrt{3}a$. Thus,

$$2(r_l + r_s) = \sqrt{3}a$$

or

$$r_l + r_s = \frac{\sqrt{3}}{2}a$$

Dividing the above equation by r_l, we get

$$1 + \frac{r_s}{r_l} = \left(\frac{\sqrt{3}}{2}a\right)\left(\frac{\sqrt{2}}{a}\right)$$

$$= \sqrt{\frac{3}{2}} = \frac{1.73}{1.41}$$

or

$$\frac{r_s}{r_l} = \frac{1.73}{1.41} - 1$$

$$= 0.225$$

Radius ratio for six coordinate structures: In these structures, the ions are in contact along the face diagonal of a cube. Fig. 4.25 shows a view of the square planar cross section of an octahedron. From the geometry, it is clear that

$$(2r_l)^2 + (2r_l)^2 = \left[2(r_s + r_l)\right]^2$$

$$4r_l^2 + 4r_l^2 = 4r_s^2 + 4r_l^2 + 8r_l\, r_s$$

$$\left(\frac{r_s}{r_l}\right)^2 + 2\left(\frac{r_s}{r_l}\right) - 1 = 0$$

$$\frac{r_s}{r_l} = \frac{-2 \pm \sqrt{8}}{2} = 0.414$$

This is the lowest value of the radius ratio in which six larger ions could be arranged octahedrally about the central smaller ion. The structure becomes unstable as r_s decreases or r_l increases.

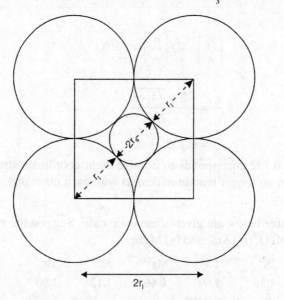

Fig. 4.25 Ions on the face of a unit cell

Radius ratio for eight coordinate structures: In an eight coordinate structure, oppositely-charged ions are touching each other along the body diagonal of the cube (Fig. 4.26), while the ions with

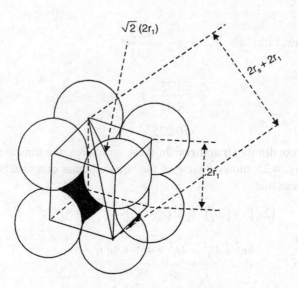

Fig. 4.26 Ions in *bcc* structure

radius r_l are in contact with each other along the sides of the cube. The body diagonal has a length of $2r_l + 2r_s$ and the face diagonal being $2\sqrt{2}r_l$. For a cube, the body diagonal is given by

$$...(\text{Body diagonal})^2 = (\text{Face diagonal})^2 + (\text{Side of the cube})^2$$

$$(2r_s + 2r_l)^2 = (2\sqrt{2}r_l)^2 + (2r_l)^2$$

$$\left(\frac{r_s}{r_l}\right)^2 + 2\left(\frac{r_s}{r_l}\right) - 2 = 0$$

$$\frac{r_s}{r_l} = \frac{-2 \pm \sqrt{4-8}}{2}$$

$$= 0.732.$$

Thus, the value of 0.732 corresponds to a stable eight coordinate structure. If r_s decreases or r_l increases, eight ions can no longer remain in contact with each other and an unstable structure would result.

Problem 4.13: In the table below are given some ionic radii. Suggest the most probable structures for (*i*) KBr, (*ii*) CsBr, (*iii*) MgO, (*iv*) SrS, and (*v*) MgSe.

Ions	K^+	Cs^+	Mg^{2+}	Sr^{2+}	Br^-	O^{2-}	S^{2-}	Se^{2-}
Ionic radii A	1.33	1.69	0.66	1.12	1.96	1.40	1.84	1.98

Solution: (*i*) The radius ratio for KBr is given as

$$\frac{r_{K^+}}{r_{Br^-}} = \frac{1.33}{1.96} = 0.678$$

The ratio is less than 0.73 therefore KBr has an *fcc* lattice.
(*ii*) For CsBr, the radius ratio is

$$\frac{r_{Cs^+}}{r_{Br^-}} = \frac{1.69}{1.96} = 0.863$$

The lattice is thus *bcc*.
(*iii*) For MgO,

$$\frac{r_{Mg^{2+}}}{r_{O^{2-}}} = \frac{0.66}{1.40} = 0.472$$

The lattice is an *fcc*.
(*iv*) For SrS,

$$\frac{r_{Sr^{2+}}}{r_{S^{2-}}} = \frac{1.12}{1.84} = 0.609$$

It corresponds to an *fcc* lattice.
(*v*) For MgSe,

$$\frac{r_{Mg^{2+}}}{r_{Se^{2+}}} = \frac{0.66}{1.98} = 0.333$$

The ratio corresponds to a tetrahedral structure.

Problem 4.14: An ionic compound AB has Na^+Cl^- structure. If the radius of A^+ ion is 414 pm then (*a*) what is the ideal radius of B^- ion? (*b*) If the radius of A^+ ion decreases and becomes equal to 30 pm, then what type of structure AB would have? What would be the co-ordination number of A^+ ion?

Solution: (*a*) For $Na^+ Cl^-$ structure the radius ratio, $\dfrac{r_+}{r_-} = 0.414$

Therefore,
$$r_{B^-} = \frac{r_+}{0.414} = \frac{414 \text{ pm}}{0.414} = 100 \text{ pm}$$

(*b*) If the radius of A^+ ion is 30 pm, then the radius ratio would become

$$\frac{r_+}{r_-} = \frac{30}{100} = 0.3$$

and AB would have zinc sulphide type of structure and the co-ordination number of A^+ ion would be 4.

4.16 VOID OR EMPTY SPACE IN CUBIC LATTICES

In the preceding section it has been shown that uniform spheres can be packed in a number of ways, namely, a primitive unit cell, *fcc* (or *hcp*) and *bcc*. In these close-packed structures, some space is always left unoccupied. This is known as the *void* or *empty space*. In the closest-packed structures, *fcc* or *hcp*, the void space would be less in comparison to a *bcc* or a primitive unit cell. Let us calculate the fraction of the total volume occupied by the spheres in these lattices.

(*a*) **Primitive cubic lattice:** In a primitive unit cell of length *a*, the spheres are present only at the corners of the cube. Each corner atom is shared by eight other unit cells. Hence, the contribution from a sphere at the corner of the cube is 1/8, and the total number of spheres per unit cell is $8 \times \dfrac{1}{8} = 1$. In a primitive unit cube, the spheres are touching each other along the side of the unit cell [Fig. 4.27(*a*)]. The distance between the centres of the two spheres is *a*, and the radius of the sphere is *a*/2. The volume of the sphere is $\dfrac{4}{3}\pi\left(\dfrac{a}{2}\right)^3$. The volume of the unit cell is a^3, and there is only one sphere in the unit cell. Therefore, the fraction of the total volume occupied by the sphere is

$$\frac{\dfrac{4}{3}\pi\left(\dfrac{a}{2}\right)^3}{a^3} = 0.523 \text{ or } 52.3\%$$

It is clear that the void space is 47.7%.

(*b*) **Face centered cubic lattice:** In an *fcc* structure, there are spheres at the centres of each face in addition to those at the corners. A face sphere is common to two unit cells, therefore the contribution of the spheres from the faces is $6 \times \dfrac{1}{2} = 3$. The contribution from the spheres at the corners of the unit cell is $8 \times \dfrac{1}{8} = 1$. The total number of spheres per unit cell in an *fcc* structure is, therefore, 4. In the *fcc* arrangement the spheres are touching each other along the face diagonal [Fig. 4.27 (*b*)].

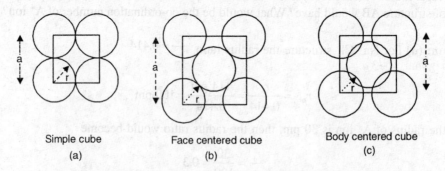

Simple cube
(a)

Face centered cube
(b)

Body centered cube
(c)

Fig. 4.27 Arrangement of spheres in cubic lattices (*a*) simple, (*b*) *fcc*, and (*c*) *bcc*

The face diagonal is given by $\sqrt{2}\,a$, and the distance between centres of any two nearest spheres would be $\dfrac{a}{\sqrt{2}}$.

The radius of the sphere $= \dfrac{a}{2\sqrt{2}}$.

The volume of the sphere of radius $\dfrac{a}{2\sqrt{2}}$ is $\dfrac{4}{3}\pi\left(\dfrac{a}{2\sqrt{2}}\right)^3$

Since there are four atoms per unit cell, therefore the volume occupied by four spheres

$$= 4 \times \dfrac{4}{3}\pi\left(\dfrac{a}{2\sqrt{2}}\right)^3$$

Hence, the fraction of the total volume occupied by the spheres of the unit cell is

$$\dfrac{4 \times \dfrac{4}{3}\pi\left(\dfrac{a}{2\sqrt{2}}\right)^3}{a^3} = \dfrac{\sqrt{2}}{6}\pi = 0.74 \text{ or } 74\%$$

So, we notice that in the closest-packed structure only 74% of the space is actually occupied by the spheres. It means that 26% is the void space.

(c) **Body-centered cubic lattice:** In a body-centered arrangement, the sphere present at the centre of the unit cell exclusively belongs to it. In addition to this the contribution of the spheres from the

corners to the unit cell is $8 \times \dfrac{1}{8} = 1$. Therefore, the total number of spheres per unit cell of a *bcc* lattice

is 2. In this arrangement, the spheres are touching each other along the body diagonal [Fig. 4.27(c)] which is given by

(Body diagonal)^2 = (Face diagonal)^2 + (Side of the unit cell)^2

$$= \left(\sqrt{2}a\right)^2 + a^2$$

$$= 3a^2$$

Body diagonal $= \sqrt{3}\,a$.

The distance between the centres of two nearest spheres would be $\dfrac{\sqrt{3}}{2}a$.

The radius of the sphere would be $\dfrac{\sqrt{3}a}{4}$

The volume of a sphere $= \dfrac{4}{3}\pi\left(\dfrac{\sqrt{3}}{4}a\right)^3$

As there are two spheres per unit cell, therefore the volume occupied by these spheres

$$= 2 \times \dfrac{4}{3}\pi\left(\dfrac{\sqrt{3}}{4}a\right)^3$$

Hence, the fraction of the total volume occupied by the spheres $= \dfrac{2 \times \dfrac{4}{3}\pi \left(\dfrac{\sqrt{3}}{4}a\right)^3}{a^3}$

$$= \frac{\sqrt{3}}{8}\pi = 0.68 = 68\%$$

Evidently, the body-centered cubic lattice is less closely packed than the *hcp* or *fcc* lattice as 32% is the void space.

4.17 TYPES OF CRYSTALS

A number of different types of bonding forces operate in the crystals to hold them together. Properties of the crystals depend on the nature of these binding forces. Based on this, it is possible to classify them into four categories.

(*a*) **Ionic crystals:** In ionic crystals like sodium chloride, the structural units are held in position by electrostatic forces between the oppositely charged ions. This leads to a regular three-dimensional structure. Due to these electrostatic forces, the ionic crystals usually have high lattice energy. The ionic bond is spherically symmetrical and has no direction. The number of nearest neighbours surrounding a given ion in a crystal is known as the co-ordination number of the ion. The co-ordination numbers commonly encountered in ionic crystals are 4, 6 and 8. In a 4 co-ordinated structure, the arrangement is tetrahedral with the anions at the corners and cation at the centre. In 6 co-ordination number, an octahedral arrangement with the anions at the corners of the octahedral and a cation at the centre. For 8 co-ordination number, the arrangement is like a body-centered cube with cation at the centre and anions at the corners. Ionic crystals are brittle, have very little elasticity and can not be easily bent. The melting points of ionic crystals are usually high. Their solutions in polar solvents conduct electricity.

(*b*) **Covalent crystals:** A covalent crystal results from the overlapping of valence orbitals between the atoms. When extended in three-dimension, it leads to a variety of crystal structures depending on the number of electrons available for bonding. Structure of diamond is an example of this type. There is a tetrahedral arrangement (sp^3 hybridization) and every carbon atom is covalently bonded to four equidistant carbon atoms [Fig. 4.28(*a*)]. The crystal is therefore a three-dimensional molecule without any limit on its extension giving rise to a giant molecule, a polymer of carbon. The structure may be looked as an *fcc* lattice of carbon atoms where alternate four out of eight tetrahedral holes are occupied by carbon atoms. The bonds in diamond are similar to the C—C bonds in the saturated hydrocarbons such as ethane. The C—C bond distance is 1.54 Å (0.154 nm). Since the bonding orbitals are fully occupied, the crystal is an insulator. The hardness of diamond is probably due to the strength of the bonds and their uniformity in all the directions throughout the crystal.

Silicon carbide, silver iodide and zinc sulphide also form crystals of the diamond type and the bonding is essentially covalent in character.

In graphite, each carbon atom is bonded to three other carbon atoms through sp^2 hybridization forming the hexagonal network sheets like those in benzene rings. The structure is shown in Fig. 4.28(*b*). The π electrons are mobile contributing to electrical conductivity in the direction parallel to the sheets. The distance between the atoms is 1.42 Å (0.142 nm). The layers are held by weak van der Waals forces. The distance between the adjacent layers is 3.35 Å (0.335 nm). Weak binding between the layers results the graphite crystals slipper and flaky conferring on graphite its valuable lubricating property. The crystals are strong and hard and have high melting points. The covalent compounds have low melting points and boiling points. Hence, the covalent compounds are often gases liquids or soft solids.

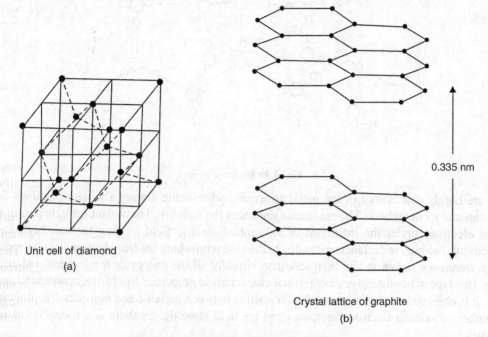

Unit cell of diamond
(a)

0.335 nm

Crystal lattice of graphite
(b)

Fig. 4.28 (*a*) Diamond lattice; (*b*) Graphite lattice

(*c*) **Molecular crystals:** These crystals have short range forces that attract all discrete species like atoms, molecules or ions to each other. They arise from dipole-induced dipole and dispersion forces and are relatively weak but sufficiently strong to hold the species (usually molecules) together in liquids and solids. Crystals held by these forces, are called *molecular crystals*. Crystals of nitrogen, carbon tetrachloride, benzene etc., are examples of molecular crystals. In these crystals, the molecules tend to pack as closely as their size and shape allow. Because of weak forces in molecular crystals they possess comparatively low melting points and are soft.

(*d*) **Hydrogen bonding:** Such crystals are held together by the sharing of protons between electronegative atoms. Many inorganic and organic acids, salt hydrates, water, glycols and ice are examples of crystals where hydrogen bonds are involved. In ice, each oxygen is tetrahedrally surrounded by four hydrogens. Two are covalently bonded to it. The other two, one from each of the two neighbouring molecules, are held by hydrogen bonds (Fig. 4.29). The bond lengths of these bonds is more than twice that of OH bonds in water molecule. Each water molecule is then bonded to four other water molecules giving a very strong structure with large numbers of hydrogen bonds. Strong orientation of hydrogen atoms towards oxygen atoms causes less efficient packing in the crystal and thus gives rise to open structure which is less denser than the liquid water. Hydrogen bonds are comparatively weak but play an important role in the structures of proteins, polypeptides, etc.

(*e*) **Metallic crystals:** Atoms with fewer and loosely-held electrons form metallic crystals. Each metal atom forms covalent bonds with its nearest neighbour through the overlap of valence orbitals. The

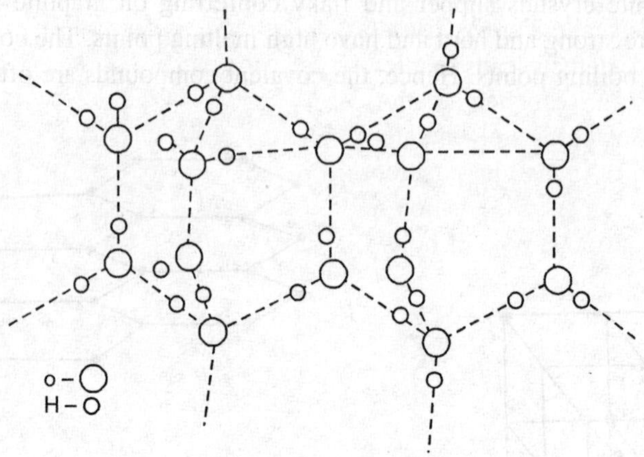

o – ◯
H – ○

Fig. 4.29 Structure of ice

bonds are highly delocalized in the metal structure and resonate among alternate positions between each atom and its neighbour. The resonance enhances the stability. The vacant orbitals permit a ready flow of electrons under the influence of an applied electric field leading to their high electrical conductivity. The high reflectance arises due to the ease with which the free electrons can be accelerated by high frequency radiation and then reradiate virtually all the energy of the incident radiation they absorb. This type of bonding gives metals their characteristic properties like lustre, opaque and malleable nature. It is observed that there is a gradual transition between metallic and non-metallic properties. As the number of valence electrons increases and are held more tightly there is a transition to covalent properties.

4.18 DEFECTS IN CRYSTALS

A crystal with perfect lattice is very rare and they usually suffer from imperfection or defects of various kinds. The defect may be at a point or along a line or over a surface. The defects may modify the physical and chemical properties of the crystals.

Two types of defects may be observed in stoichiometric compounds, called *Schottky* and *Frenkel defects* respectively. Crystals have a perfectly ordered arrangement at absolute zero. As the temperature increases, the amount of thermal vibrations of ions in their lattice sites increases. If the vibration of a particular ion becomes large enough, it may jump out of its lattice site. This constitute a point defect. At higher temperatures, the chances of lattice sites to be unoccupied are greater.

Schottky defects: A Schottky defect consists of a pair of holes in the crystal lattice. One cation and one anion (pair-wise) are absent (Fig. 4.30). This type of defect occurs mainly in highly ionic

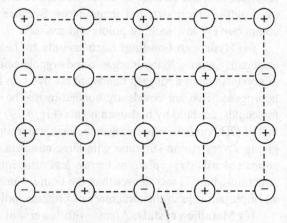

Fig. 4.30 Schottky defects

compounds where the cations and anions are of a smaller size, e.g., NaCl, KCl, CsCl and KBr etc. (coordination number usually 8 or 6). Crystals with Schottky defects have holes from both positive and negative ions. Schottky defects leads to a lowering of the density of the crystal.

Frenkel defects: It arises when a cation leaves its normal lattice site and occupies an interstitial position (Fig. 4.31). Metal ions are generally smaller than the ions and therefore it is easier to squeeze cation (+) into alternative interstitial positions. This type of defect is generally observed when there is a large size difference between the cation and anion, e.g., ZnS, AgCl, AgBr, AgI etc. Crystals with Frankel defects have only one type of hole. Frankel defects donot change the density of the crystal.

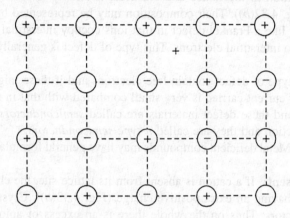

Fig. 4.31 Frenkel defects

Metal excess: This may occur in two ways.

F-centres (Colour Centres)

An anion may be absent from its lattice site, leaving a hole which is occupied by an electron, thereby maintaining the electrical balance (Fig. 4.32(a)). This is rather similar to a Schottky defect but only with one hole rather than a pair. This type of defect is formed by crystals which would be expected to from Schottky defects. When compounds like NaCl, KCl, LiH etc. are heated with excess of their constituent metal vapours, or treated with high energy radiation, they become deficient in the anions

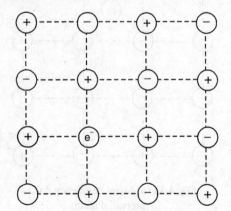

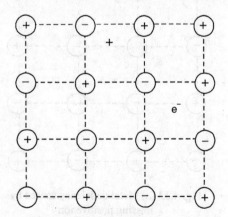

Fig. 4.32 (*a*) Metal excess defect because of absence of anions

Fig. 4.32 (*b*) Metal excess defects caused by interstitial cations

and their formulae may be represented by $AX_{i-\delta}$ where δ is a small fraction. The non-stoichiometric form of NaCl is yellow, non-stoichiometric form of KCl is blue-lilac in colour.

The crystal lattice has vacant anion sites which are occupied by electrons. Anion sites occupied by electrons in this way are called *colour centres*. These colour centres are associated with the colour of the compound. More the colour centres present greater will be the intensity of colour. Solids containing colour centres are paramagnetic because the electrons occupying the vacant sites are unpaired.

Interstitial ions and electrons: Metal excess defects also occur when an extra positive ion occupies an interstitial position in the lattice and electrical neutrality is maintained by the inclusion of interstitial electron (Fig. 4.32(*b*)). Their composition may be represented by the formula $A_{i+\delta}X$. This type of defect is rather like a Frankel defect in that ions occupy interstitial position, but there are no holes, and there are also interstitial electrons. This type of defect is generally observed in ZnO, Fe_2O_3, CdO etc.

Crystals with this type of defect contain free electrons and if these migrate they conduct electric current. The amount of current carried is very small compared with that in metals, fused salts or salts in aqueous solutions, and these defect materials are called *semiconductors*. Since the mechanism is normal electron conduction and they are called *n-type semiconductors*.

Metal deficiency: Metal deficient compounds may have general formula $A_{i-\delta}X$. It can occur in two ways.

(*i*) **Positive ion absent:** If a cation is absent from its lattice site, the charges can be balanced by an adjacent metal ion having an extra positive charge (Fig. 4.33(*a*)). Crystals with metal deficiency defects are semiconductors. Thus on the whole there is an excess of anion and the lattice remains deficient of cations. Considering FeO crystal, we notice some Fe^{3+} ions in the defective crystals in addition to Fe^{2+} ions. Some other compounds that show this defect are FeS, NiO etc. Suppose a lattice contains A^+ and A^{2+} metal ions. If an electron 'hops' from A^+ ion to the positive centre (A^{2+}), then A^+ becomes a new positive centre. There has been an apparent movement of A^{2+} ion. With a series of similar hops, an electron may be transferred in one direction across the structure. At the same time the positive hole migrates in the opposite direction across the structure. This is called *positive hole*, or p-type semiconduction.

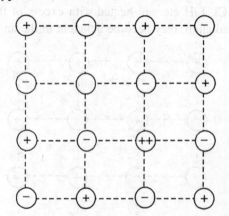

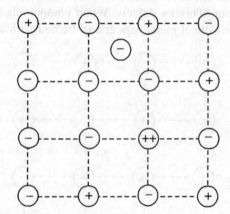

Fig. 4.33 (*a*) Metal deficiency caused by missing positive ion

Fig. 4.33 (*b*) Metal deficiency due to interstitial anion

(*ii*) **Defect due to interstitial anion:** In this type of defect an anion is trapped in between the lattice sites. This extra negative ion is in the interstitial position and the balance of charge takes place by means of an extra charge on an adjacent metal ion (Fig. 4.33(*b*)). In crystals possessing this defect, the anions are relatively small when compared to the size of cation, thus allowing the anion to find a place in the interstitial site.

EXERCISES

1. Explain, giving reasons, the following:
   (*i*) Solids are essentially incompressible whereas gases are easily compressed.
   (*ii*) Diffusion in solids is slower than in liquids.
   (*iii*) Density of a solid is generally greater than its liquid.
   (*iv*) Covalent crystals are hard while molecular crystals are soft.
   (*v*) Attractive forces in metals are non directional.
   (*vi*) Metals are malleable (easily flattened into sheets) are ductile.
   (*vii*) A long range order exists in crystals.
   (*viii*) Centre of symmetry can be represented by rotation inversion axis.
   (*ix*) Crystalline solids are anisotropic while amorphous solids are isotropic.
   (*x*) Solids with *ccp* structures are more dense than those with *bcc* structures.

2. Explain why it is not possible
   (*i*) to deduce the position of hydrogen atoms from X-ray diffraction studies,
   (*ii*) to use too large or too small crystals in the Debye-Scherrer method,
   (*iii*) to distinguish K$^+$ ions from Cl$^-$ ions by X-ray diffraction studies,
   (*iv*) to replace X-ray by UV of 10 nm wavelength in the diffraction studies of crystals,
   (*v*) to use polychromatic X-rays in the debye-Scherrer powder method.

3. State which of the following statements are true and which are false:
   (*i*) All crystalline solids are isotropic.
   (*ii*) Tetrahedral methane molecule has a centre of symmetry and a four fold axis of symmetry.
   (*iii*) Amorphous solids are supper cooled liquids with high viscosity.
   (*iv*) In crystals short range order exists.
   (*v*) Unit cell is the smallest building unit in the crystals.
   (*vi*) Every object possesses an identity element.
   (*vii*) There are five and only five possible lattices in a two-dimensional plane.
   (*viii*) *n* in the Bragg's equation can have any value—positive or negative integer or fraction.
   (*ix*) In the closest packed structure, 26% of the space is vacant.
   (*x*) The number of atoms per unit cell in an *fcc* structure is 4 while in a *bcc* structure it is 2.
                                   Ans. True: (*iii*), (*v*), (*vi*), (*vii*), (*ix*), (*x*).
                                                   False: (*i*), (*ii*), (*iv*), (*viii*).

4. What types of crystals would be expected to be (*i*) the hardest, (*ii*) the softest, (*iii*) the highest melting, (*iv*) the lowest melting, (*v*) good conductors of heat and electricity, (*vi*) having directional lattice forces, (*vii*) having non directional lattice forces.
                       Ans. (*i*) Covalent, (*ii*) molecular, (*iii*) covalent, (*iv*) molecular, (*v*) metallic,
                                                   (*vi*) ionic and metallic, (*vii*) covalent and molecular.

5. What types of crystals are given by (*i*) diamond, (*ii*) KCl, (*iii*) Au, (*iv*) anthracene and (*v*) H$_2$O?
                       Ans. (*i*) Covalent, (*ii*) ionic, (*iii*) metallic, (*iv*) and (*v*) molecular.

6. LiBr, NaBr, KBr, RbBr all have the same crystal structure. However, X-ray analysis indicates that RbBr is a simple cubic while all others are face centered. Explain.
                       Ans. Rb$^+$ and Br$^-$ ions have the same number of electrons.

7. SnCl$_4$ is a colourless liquid (b. pt. 114°C and m. pt.–33°C) while SnCl$_2$ is a white solid melting at 246°C. What type of solid (ionic, covalent, etc.) is most likely to be formed when SnCl$_2$ solidifies?   **Ans.** Ionic.

8. In the table below are given unit cell parameters. Identify the crystal system in each case.

	a (nm)	b (nm)	c (nm)	α	β	γ
(i)	5	5	5	90°	90°	90°
(ii)	6.5	6.5	10.5	90°	90°	90°
(iii)	7	7	7	96°	96°	96°
(iv)	6	6	5	90°	90°	120°

Ans. (i) Cubic, (ii) tetragonal, (iii) rhombohedral, (iv) hexagonal.

9. Sketch the following crystal structures:
    (i) Diamond—tetrahedral covalent lattice
    (ii) NaCl—face centered cubic lattice
    (iii) CsCl—body centered cubic lattice

10. Suppose you have a face centered cubic arrangement of A and B atoms where A atoms are at the corners of the unit cell and B atoms at the face centres. (a) What is the formula of the compound? (b) What would be the simplest formula if (i) one of the A atoms were missing from a corner in each unit cell and (ii) two A atoms were missing from two corners? **Ans.** (a) AB_3, (b) (i) A_7B_{24}, (ii) AB_4.

11. A certain compound of X and Y (both monovalent ions) crystallizes in the *bcc* lattice with X at the corners and Y at the body centre. (a) What is the formula of the compound? (b) If one of the X atoms from a corner be replaced by Z (also a monovalent ion) what would be the simplest formula of the resulting compound?
    Ans. (a) XY, (b) ZX_7Y_3

12. What is meant by symmetry operations and symmetry elements? Explain the following symmetry elements: (i) Proper and improper rotation axes, (ii) mirror plane, and (iii) centre of symmetry.

13. (i) List out the symmetry elements is (a) H_2O, (b) NH_3, (c) C_2H_4, (d) CH_4, (e) letter 'M', and (f) football, (ii) Which of the following molecules have a centre of symmetry?
    (i) C_6H_6, (ii) SF_6, (iii) CO_2, (iv) C_2H_4, (v) NH_3.
    Ans. (i): (a) C_3, σ_v, $\sigma_{v'}$, E, (b) C_3, $3\sigma_{v'}$, E, (c) $3C_2$, σ_v, $\sigma_{v'}$, σ_h, i, E, (d) $4C_3$, E, S_4; (e) C_2, σ_v, $\sigma_{v'}$, E, (f) $C\infty$, ∞C_2, $\infty\sigma_v$, σ_h, i, E

14. How many unit cells are possible in a planar lattice? Sketch a two-dimensional lattice of closest packed identical spheres indicating a suitable unit cell.

15. What are the seven crystal systems? What parameters are used to describe a particular system? Write down the characteristics of each system. Name the Bravais lattices of each class.

16. What is the law of rational indices? How are the rational indices arrived at for a crystal plane. The Weiss indices of some crystal planes are (i) a:b:∞c, (ii) a:b:c, (iii) a:∞b:c, (iv) a:2b:2c, (v) a:−b:∞c, (vi) $\dfrac{a}{2} : \dfrac{2}{3} b : \infty$,

    (vii) $\dfrac{2a}{3} : 2b : \dfrac{1c}{3}$. What are the corresponding Miller indices of these planes?

    Ans. (i) (110), (ii) (111), (iii) (101), (iv) (211), (v) $(1\overline{1}0)$, (vi) (430), (vii) (316).

17. Prepare sketches showing the planes that have Miller indices (011), (111), (222), (010), $(1\overline{1}0)$ and (200).

18. (a) Derive the Bragg's equation, $n\lambda = 2d \sin \theta$ and show that it can be written as $\lambda = d_{hkl}\sin\theta$. What is the physical significance of n in this equation? Under what conditions reflection of X-rays from dissimilar planes can give rise to reflection maxima?
    (b) On what factors does the intensity of reflected X-ray beams depend?

(c) Explain why one should employ monochromatic X-rays in studying the reflections from the faces of crystals?

19. Define the following terms:
    (i) Unit cell (primitive and non-primitive), (ii) space lattice, (iii) lattice planes, (iv) law of rational indices, (v) interfacial angle, (vi) space and point groups, (vii) centre and planes of symmetry.

20. (a) Prove that the interplanar spacing (d_{hkl}) in a cubic system is given by

$$d_{hkl} = \frac{a}{\left(h^2 + k^2 + l^2\right)^{1/2}}$$

where a is edge length of the cube.

(b) Calculate the interplanar spacing (d_{hkl}) for a cubic system between the following sets of planes: (i) (100), (ii) (200), (iii) (110), (iv) (220), (v) (111), (vi) (222). Assume 'a to be the edge length of the cube.

Ans. (i) $d_{100} = a$, (ii) $d_{200} = \dfrac{a}{2}$, (iii) $\dfrac{a}{\sqrt{2}}$, (iv) $\dfrac{a}{2\sqrt{2}}$, (v) $\dfrac{a}{\sqrt{3}}$, (vi) $\dfrac{a}{2\sqrt{3}}$.

21. What are the three types of cubic crystals? How are they distinguished from each other? Calculate the number of atoms per unit cell in each case.

22. Illustrate, with the help of diagrams, the following planes with Miller indice (i) (100), (110) and (111) in a simple cube, (ii) (200), (220) and (111) in a face centered cubic, and (iii) (200), (100) and (222) in a body centered cubic cell.

23. CsCl has a body centered cubic lattice. How many Cs^+ and Cl^- ions are there in the unit cell?
    Ans. $Cs^+ = 1$, $Cl^- = 1$.

24. NaCl has an *fcc* structure. How many Na^+ and Cl^- ions are there in the unit cell?
    Ans. $Na^+ = 4$, $Cl^- = 4$.

25. NaCl has a face-centered cubic lattice. What is the coordination number of (a) the sodium (b) the chlorine? (c) What are the individual lattice structures of sodium and chlorine in sodium chloride? (d) Calculate the number of Na^+ and Cl^- ions is the unit cell'of sodium chloride.
    Ans. (a) 6, (b) (c) face-centered, (d) 4 Na^+ ions and 4 Cl^- ions.

26. (a) Calculate the number of atoms per unit cell of (i) a simple cube, (ii) face centered cube, (iii) body centered cube, (iv) an edge centered cube, (v) face centered tetragonal and (vi) simple orthorhomic.
    Ans. (i) 1, (ii) 4, (iii) 2, (iv) 4, (v) 4, (vi) 1.

(b) A hexagonal cell contains three unit cells. (i) How many atoms are there in the hexagonal cell? How many atoms are there in the unit cell?
    Ans. (i) 6, (ii) 2.

27. What is understood by the closest packing of identical spheres? What is meant by the stacking sequences ABAB... and ABC ABC...? How do these structures differ from each other? Can we have a pattern like ABC ACB AB AC...? Show that number of octahedral holes per unit atom in an *fcc* structure is one and in a *bcc* structure it is 1.5. How many tetrahedral holes per unit atom are there in an *fcc* structure?
    Ans. 2 holes per atom.

28. Show that the maximum proportion of available volume which may be filled by hard spheres in various structures is (i) simple cube $= \dfrac{\pi}{6} = 0.52$, (ii) body centered cube $= \dfrac{\pi\sqrt{3}}{8} = 0.68$, (iii) face centered cube $= \dfrac{\pi\sqrt{2}}{6} = 0.74$, (iv) hexagonal closest packed structure $= \dfrac{\pi\sqrt{2}}{6} = 0.74$, (v) diamond $= \dfrac{\pi\sqrt{3}}{6} = 0.34$. What is the percentage of void space in each case?   **Ans.** (i) 48%, (ii) 32%, (iii) & (iv) 26%, (v) 66%.

29. (a) What is the radius ratio? What is its significance? Calculate the limiting radius ratio of cation (smaller) to that of anion (larger) in the following arrangements:

      (*i*) Triangular, (*ii*) face centered cubic structures, (*iii*) body centered cubic arrangements.

      (*c*) Account for the fact that LiCl, KCl, RbCl have face centered cubic structures while CsCl has a body centered cubic structure.

30. Three uni-univalent ionic crystal, AX, AY and AZ are composed of ions having the following radii (arbitrary units):

	A^+	X^-	Y^-	Z^-
	1.0	1.0	2.0	3.0

Assuming that ions are hard spheres, predict (*a*) whether each crystal will have the sodium chloride or the caesium chloride structure, explain. (*b*) Calculate the volume of the unit cell in each case.

                               Ans. (*a*) AX will have CsCl structure, AY, and AZ will have NaCl structure,

                                             (*b*) AX = 12.3 AY = 216, AZ = 609.8.

31. Describe the crystal structure of zinc blende. What is the cation to anion ratio in this structure? What geometric arrangement of cations is there about each anion?

32. Calculate the interplanar spacings that correspond to reflections at $\theta = 20°$, 27.4°, and 35.8° by X-rays of wavelength 0.141 nm. Assume $n = 1$.   **Ans.** 0.206 nm, 0.153 nm and 0.121 nm.

33. Silver has an atomic radius of 0.144 nm. What would be the density of silver if it were to crystallize in the following structures: (*a*) simple cubic, (*b*) body centered cubic, (*c*) face centered cubic, (*d*) If the density of silver is 10.6×10^3 kg m^{-3}, which of these correspond to the correct structure?

                Ans. (*a*) 7.5×10^3 kg m^{-3}, (*b*) 9.7×10^3 kg m^{-3} (*c*) 10.6×10^3 kg m^{-3}, (*d*) *fcc*.

34. CsCl forms a simple cubic lattice in which there are Cs$^+$ ions at the corners of the unit cell and Cl$^-$ ions at the centre of the unit cell. The cation/anion contact occurs along the body diagonal of the unit cell. The length of unit cells is 0.4123 nm and the radius of the Cl$^-$ ion is 0.81 nm. Calculate the radius of the Cs$^+$ ion.

                                                 Ans. 0.176 nm.

35. Copper (at. mass 63.54 and density 8.936 g cm^{-3}) crystallizes is the *fcc* pattern. If the edge length of the unit cell is 0.3615 nm, calculate the Avogadro constant.   **Ans.** 6.02×10^{23}

36. Metal X (at. mass 55.8) crystallizes in body centered cubic pattern. The unit cell dimension is 0.286 nm. (*i*) How many atoms are there per unit cell? (*ii*) What is the number of nearest neighbours? (*iii*) What is the volume of the unit cell? (*iv*) Determine the density of the metal?

        Ans. (*i*) 2, (*ii*) 8, (*iii*) 2.34×10^{-2} nm^3 = 2.34×10^{-23} cm^3, (*iv*) 7.91×10^3 kg m^{-3}.

37. KF crystallizes in the NaCl type structure. If the radius of K$^+$ ion is 0.132 nm and F$^-$ ion is 0.135 nm, what is the shortest K-F distance? (*ii*) What is the edge length of the unit cell? (*iii*) What is the closest K-K distance? (*iv*) What is the volume of the unit cell?

                Ans. (*i*) 0.267 nm, (*ii*) 0.534 nm, (*iii*) 0.378 nm (*iv*) 1.52×10^{-22} cm^3.

38. The observed densities of NaF, AgCl and CsI are respectively 2.79, 5.56 and 4.51 g cm^{-3} while the corresponding theoretical densities are 2.84, 5.57 and 4.53 g cm^{-3}. Calculate the percentage of unoccupied sites in the crystal lattices of these compounds.   **Ans.** 2%, 0.2%, 0.4%.

39. NaF and KF form crystals having the same cubic lattice. The strongest X-ray reflection occurs from crystal surfaces (200) at angles 8° 47′ and 7° 40′. Calculate the ratio of the molar volumes of both the crystalline fluorides.   **Ans.** 1: 1.5

40. Copper has a face-centered cubic lattice with a unit cell edge length of 0.361 nm. What is the size of the largest atom which could fit into (*i*) octahedral holes and (*ii*) tetrahedral holes of this lattice without disturbing the lattice?   **Ans.** (*i*) 0.053 nm, (*ii*) 0.029 nm.

41. KCl has a simple cubic lattice with K$^+$ and Cl$^-$ ions taken as identical and the (100) plane spacings as 0.3152 nm. At what angle would first and second order reflections from (100) and (110) planes be observed if X-rays of wavelength 0.1537 nm are used?

                      Ans. First order: 14°7′ for (100) planes, 20°10′ for (110) planes,

                            Second order: 29°12′ for (100) planes, 48°36′ for (110) planes.

CHAPTER
5

The First Law of Thermodynamics

5.1 INTRODUCTION

Scope and limitations of thermodynamics: Thermodynamics, literally speaking, means flow of heat and deals with the quantitative relationship between heat and other forms of energy in physico-chemical transformations. It is sometimes called *energetics*. The subject matter of thermodynamics is based on three fundamental laws. They are applicable to all the phenomena in nature. These laws are not based on any theory but are based on experimental facts. The laws have been subjected to rigorous mathematical treatment and have yielded correlations between different observable properties of matter. These have been proved to be very convenient and useful in describing the states of systems in chemical and physical transformations. The results of thermodynamic deductions have been proved to be correct by experiments and found to be rigidly valid. Thermodynamics is, therefore, an exact science.

Thermodynamics has a great predicting power. It can predict whether a given process will occur spontaneously or not under a given set of conditions. The laws provide necessary criteria for predicting the feasibility of a process. However, it gives no information with regard to the rate at which a given change will proceed. Thermodynamics deals only with the states of the system and makes no mention of the mechanism of how the change is accomplished. Thermodynamics answers to why a change occurs but not to how it occurs.

Classical thermodynamics is based on the behaviour of bulk or macroscopic properties of the systems, *i.e.*, systems having many molecules and is independent of the atomic and molecular structure. Consequently, no information can be obtained regarding the molecular structure. This difficulty is, however, obviated in statistical thermodynamics where the laws of mechanics are applied to the behaviour of individual molecules and then a suitable statistical average is taken. The results obtained from classical and statistical thermodynamics are, however, complementary to each other.

The first law deals with the equivalence between various forms of energy, but does not say anything about the conditions under which such an equivalence is achieved. The second law places a restriction on the first law and is concerned with the directions of physico-chemical transformations and the relationships between the properties of the systems at equilibrium. The third law attempts to evaluate the thermodynamic functions. The zeroth law provides an operational definition of temperature.

In this text, we shall be applying the laws of thermodynamics to systems at equilibrium and hence time as a variable will not appear in all our discussions.

5.2 THERMODYNAMIC TERMS

In the study of thermodynamics, it is essential to understand the meaning of terms employed in thermodynamics. These terms have definite meanings. Some of the most commonly used terms are:

(a) **System and surroundings:** A thermodynamic system is defined as *the part of the universe which is selected for thermodynamic considerations.* A system usually has a definite amount(s) of a specific substance(s). It is separated from the rest of the universe called *surroundings* by a definite boundary. The boundary may be real or imaginary. A system is *homogeneous if it is uniform throughout in all respects and is heterogeneous if it is not uniform throughout and consists of more than one phase separated from each other by sharp boundaries.* A system consisting of a pure mixture of gases or a liquid or a solid, etc. are examples of homogeneous systems while a liquid and its vapour or a mixture of two immiscible liquids or two different solids, etc. constitute heterogeneous systems.

The *boundary* (wall) between the system and the surroundings differs in its ability to allow the passage of energy and matter through it. A *permeable wall* allows the passage of both matter and energy, a *diathermal wall* prevents the passage of matter but allows the flow of energy while an *adiabatic wall* neither allows the passage of energy nor matter.

(b) **Types of systems:** In thermodynamics, we deal mainly with three different types of systems depending on the interactions between the system and the surroundings. These are (*i*) *open systems,* (*ii*) *closed systems* and (*iii*) *isolated systems.*

   (*i*) **Open systems:** *A system which can exchange both matter and energy with the surroundings is known as an open system* [Fig. 5.1 (*a*)]. Due to these exchanges, matter and energy do not remain constant in open systems.

   (*ii*) **Closed systems:** *These are systems in which exchange of energy with the surroundings is possible while the transfer of matter to and from the surroundings does not take place* [Fig. 5.1 (*b*)]. Consequently, in a closed system mass remains constant and only the energy changes.

   (*iii*) **Isolated systems:** *It is a system that prevents any interaction between the system and the surroundings* [Fig. 5.1(*c*)]. Both mass and energy of the system remains constant as there is no interaction of the system with the surroundings.

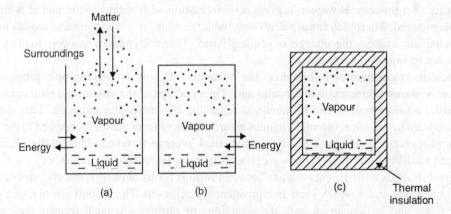

Fig. 5.1 Different types of systems (*a*) open system; (*b*) closed system; (*c*) isolated system

(c) **Properties of a system:** Measurable properties of a system may be divided into two classes, viz., *extensive and intensive.* An extensive property of a system depends upon the total amount of material in the system. Mass, volume, internal energy, heat contents, free energy, entropy, heat capacity are some examples of extensive properties. An intensive property, on the other hand, is defined as a *property which is independent of the amount of material in the system*. Density, molar properties, (molar volume, molar energy, molar entropy, molar heat capacity etc.), surface tension, viscosity, specific heat, thermal conductivity, refractive index, pressure, temperature, boiling and freezing points, vapour pressure of a liquid, etc., are some examples of intensive properties.

(*d*) **State of a system:** A thermodynamic system is said to be in a definite state when the properties have definite values. Various measurable properties of a system which completely define the state of a system are pressure, volume, temperature and concentration. These are known as the *state variables* or *thermodynamic variables*. Any change in the property due to a change in the state of the system depends only on the initial and the final states of the system. These variables are directly measureable from experiments and do not require any assumption regarding the structure of matter and related to one another by an equation called the *equation of state*. For an ideal gas, the equation of state for *n* moles

is $PV = nRT$ while for a van der Waals gas, the equation of state is $\left(P + \dfrac{an^2}{V^2} \right)(V - nb) = nRT$. The

thermodynamic state of a system in such cases can be defined completely by specifying any two of the three variables. Any change in the value of these variables will change the state of the system which will attain a new state. If it is desired to bring the system back to its initial state, the variables will have their original values.

(*e*) **Change in state:** Change in the state of the system is completely defined when the initial and final states are specified.

(*f*) **Path:** *It is the sequence of intermediate steps or stages arranged in order, followed by the system in going from its initial to the final state.*

(*g*) **Thermodynamic equilibrium**: *A system is said to be in a state of thermodynamic equilibrium if none of the observable properties of the system appears to change with time.* Actually, the term thermodynamic equilibrium assumes the existence of three types of equilibria in the system. They are (*i*)*thermal equilibrium, (ii) mechanical equilibrium* and (*iii*) *chemical equilibrium.*

    (*i*) **Thermal equilibrium**: *A system is said to be in thermal equilibrium if the temperature remains the same in all parts of the system.* Systems in thermal equilibrium with each other will have the same temperature while systems not in thermal equilibrium with each other will have different temperatures. This state is known as the *zeroth law of thermodynamics.*

    (*ii*) **Mechanical equilibrium:** *It implies the uniformity of pressure throughout the whole system.*

    (*iii*) **Chemical equilibrium:** *If the composition of the system remains constant and uniform throughout, the system is said to be in chemical equilibrium.*

An equilibrium may be stable, metastable or unstable. If after displacement to a new state and release of the constraint causing displacement, it goes back to its original state, the system is said to be in a state of stable equilibrium. But if the system fails to return to its original state, it is said to be in a state of unstable equilibrium. In metastable equilibrium, the system is stable for smaller displacements and unstable for larger displacements.

(*h*) **Process:** A thermodynamic process is defined *as the method of operation with the help of which a change in the state of a system is effected.* The various processes are:

    (*i*) **Cyclic process:** If a system after undergoing through a series of changes in its state comes back to its initial state, then the process is termed as a *cyclic process* and the path followed is known as the *cyclic path.*

(*ii*) **Isothermal process:** *A process that is carried out under conditions of constant temperature is called as isothermal process.* The constancy of temperature is achieved either by extracting heat from the system or supplying heat to it.

(*iii*) **Adiabatic process:** *A process in which there is no exchange of heat between the system and the surroundings is known as an adiabatic process.* The system is enclosed by adiabatic walls which do not permit heat exchanges with the surroundings. In an adiabatic process, there is a change in the temperature of the system.

(*iv*) **Isochoric process:** *A process in which volume of the system remains constant.*

(*v*) **Isobaric or isopiestic process:** *A process that is carried out under conditions of constant pressure.*

(*vi*) **Reversible process:** *A process is said to be reversible if at any instant during the transformation, the system does not deviate from equilibrium by more than an infinitesimal amount.* A reversible process must be carried out extremely slowly so that the properties of the system virtually remain unchanged at any stage of the change. In a reversible process, all the changes occurring in any part of the process are exactly reversed when the process is carried out in the reverse direction. On completing a reversible cyclic path, the system and the surroundings are both restored exactly to their original states. A reversible process is, therefore, always in a state of equilibrium at each of the small stages. As an example of a reversible process, consider a case in which a system absorbs heat from the surroundings. Reversibility in this case implies that the temperature of the surroundings should be infinitesimally higher than that of the system. If heat is to flow from the system to the surroundings, the temperature of the latter must be only infinitesimally lower than that of the system. Similarly, the expansion of a gas at constant temperature enclosed in a cylinder fitted with a weightless and frictionless piston will be reversible only if the pressure on the gas during expansion is reduced by an infinitesimal amount. During compression, the pressure on the gas at each stage is increased by a very small amount.

A truly reversible process has to be carried out in an infinite number of steps or stages and would thus require infinite time for its completion. In actual practice, the small changes in a process have definite magnitudes and are only approximately closer to a strictly reversible process. A reversible process has, therefore, only a conceptual importance. It is an ideal process and extremely useful in dealing with problems related to energy transfers.

(*vii*) **Irreversible process:** *A process that occurs rapidly or spontaneously such that it does not remain in equilibrium during the transformation is called an irreversible process.* Such processes do not involve a succession of equilibrium states of the system. After undergoing a change, such processes do not return themselves to their initial states but can be reversed only with the help of external agencies. Expansion of a gas against zero applied pressure, dissolution of a solute in a solvent, mixing of gases, flow of liquid from higher to lower levels, etc. are examples of irreversible processes. All irreversible processes take finite time for their completion and are real processes in actual practice.

5.3 COMPLETE DIFFERENTIALS AND HOMOGENEOUS FUNCTIONS

Thermodynamic functions like pressure, volume, temperature, energy, entropy, etc. are state functions. The change in the values of these quantities does not depend on how the change is carried out but depends only on the initial and final states of the system. If Z is any thermodynamic property of a homogeneous system of constant composition then its value is completely determined by the three thermodynamics variables, pressure, volume and temperature. They are related to one another by an equation of state. Any two of these three variables are sufficient to define any thermodynamic property. We can write

$$Z = f(P, T)$$

where Z may be energy, volume, enthalpy content or any other property to be considered in details at a later stage. Any change in Z resulting from changes in the values of P and T is given by

$$\Delta Z = Z_{\text{final state}} - Z_{\text{initial state}} \qquad ...(5.1)$$

Utilising the principle of calculus, we may write for an infinitesimal change dZ in the property Z as

$$dZ = \left(\frac{\partial Z}{\partial P}\right)_T dP + \left(\frac{\partial Z}{\partial T}\right)_P dT \qquad ...(5.2)$$

where the partial derivatives $(\partial Z/\partial P)_T$ represents the rate of change of Z with pressure at constant temperature and $(\partial Z/\partial T)_P$ denotes the rate of change of Z with temperature at constant pressure. In Eq. (5.2), the first term on the right hand side denotes the contribution of changes in pressure and the second term indicates the contribution for changes in temperature to Z. The differential dZ of a function Z as defined by Eq. (5.2) is called a *complete* or *exact differential*. If we put $(\partial Z/\partial P)_T = L(P, T)$ and $(\partial Z/\partial T)_P = M(P, T)$ in Eq, (5.2), we get

$$dZ = L(P, T)\, dP + M(P, T)dT$$

on differentiating $L(P, T)$ $[= (\partial Z/\partial P)_T]$ with respect to T keeping P constant and $M(P, T)$ $[= (\partial Z/\partial T)_P]$ with respect to P maintaining T constant, we get

$$\left(\frac{\partial L}{\partial T}\right)_P = \frac{\partial^2 Z}{\partial T \partial P}$$

and

$$\left(\frac{\partial M}{\partial P}\right)_T = \frac{\partial^2 Z}{\partial P \partial T}$$

Since

$$\frac{\partial^2 Z}{\partial T \partial P} = \frac{\partial^2 Z}{\partial P \partial T}$$

we have

$$\left(\frac{\partial L}{\partial T}\right)_P = \left(\frac{\partial M}{\partial P}\right)_T \qquad ...(5.3)$$

Hence, if Z is any thermodynamic function, dZ is an exact differential then the cross derivatives,

$\left(\dfrac{\partial L}{\partial T}\right)_P$ and $\left(\dfrac{\partial M}{\partial P}\right)_T$ must be equal. This is known as *Euler's theorem of exactness*. Another characteristic of an exact differential is that its value for a cyclic transformation is zero, *i.e.*,

$$\oint dZ = 0$$

where $\oint$ denotes the cyclic integral.

We can, therefore conclude that dZ will be an exact differential when

(i) Z is a single-valued function depending entirely on the values of temperature and pressure; or,

(ii) dZ between two specified states is independent of the path of the transformation; or,

(iii) for a cyclic process $\oint dZ = 0$: or,

(iv) $\dfrac{\partial^2 Z}{\partial T\, \partial P} = \dfrac{\partial^2 Z}{\partial P\, \partial T}$

As an example, suppose we have a system containing an ideal gas. The pressure for a given quantity, say one mole, of the gas is a function of temperature and volume of the gas, *i.e.*,

$$P = f(T, V)$$

For dP to be an exact differential, we have

$$dP = \left(\frac{\partial P}{\partial T}\right)_V dT + \left(\frac{\partial P}{\partial V}\right)_T dV$$

and

$$\frac{\partial^2 P}{\partial T\, \partial V} = \frac{\partial^2 P}{\partial V\, \partial T}$$

These can be evaluated using the ideal gas equation $PV = RT$. Thus

$$\left(\frac{\partial P}{\partial T}\right)_V = \frac{R}{V}, \text{ and } \frac{\partial^2 P}{\partial V\, \partial T} = -\frac{R}{V^2} \qquad \ldots(5.4)$$

$$\left(\frac{\partial P}{\partial V}\right)_T = -\frac{RT}{V^2}, \text{ and } \frac{\partial^2 P}{\partial T\, \partial V} = -\frac{R}{V^2} \qquad \ldots(5.5)$$

From Eqs. (5.4) and (5.5), we see that

$$\frac{\partial^2 P}{\partial V\, \partial T} = \frac{\partial^2 P}{\partial T\, \partial V} = -\frac{R}{V^2}$$

Hence dP is an exact differential.

There are other thermodynamic functions which depend only on the state of the system and are therefore state functions.

Cyclic rule: Considering any thermodynamic function Z as a function of volume V and temperature T, we can write

$$Z = f(V, T)$$

Since Z is a state function dZ is given by

$$dZ = \left(\frac{\partial Z}{\partial V}\right)_T dV + \left(\frac{\partial Z}{\partial T}\right)_V dT$$

If $\qquad\qquad\qquad dZ = 0$

then

$$\left(\frac{\partial Z}{\partial V}\right)_T dV = -\left(\frac{\partial Z}{\partial T}\right)_V dT$$

$$\left(\frac{\partial Z}{\partial V}\right)_T \left(\frac{\partial V}{\partial T}\right)_Z = -\left(\frac{\partial Z}{\partial T}\right)_V$$

Rearranging we get

$$\left(\frac{\partial Z}{\partial V}\right)_T \left(\frac{\partial V}{\partial T}\right)_Z \left(\frac{\partial T}{\partial Z}\right)_V = -1 \qquad \qquad ...(5.6)$$

Equation (5.6) expresses the cyclic rule. Similar types of expressions can be deduced for any other thermodynamic quantity. For example, Z is the pressure of a gas, Eq. (5.6) would be

$$\left(\frac{\partial P}{\partial V}\right)_T \left(\frac{\partial V}{\partial T}\right)_P \left(\frac{\partial T}{\partial P}\right)_V = -1 \qquad \qquad ...(5.7)$$

Homogeneous Functions

A function $f(x, y, z, ...)$ is homogeneous of degree n, if upon replacement of each independent variable by an arbitrary parameter λ times the variable, the function is multiplied by λ^n, that is

$$f(\lambda_x, \lambda_y, \lambda_z, ...) = \lambda^n f(x, y, z, ...)$$

As a simple example, consider the function

$$f(x, y) = ax^2 + bxy + cy^2$$

If we replace the variable x by λx and y by λy, we can write

$$f(\lambda x, \lambda y) = a\lambda^2 x^2 + b\lambda^2 xy + c\lambda^2 y^2$$

$$= \lambda^2 \left(ax^2 + bxy + cy^2\right)$$

$$= \lambda^2 f(x, y)$$

The net result is a change in the function by a factor of λ^2. The function is called a *homogeneous function*. In the above equation, the exponent of λ gives the degree of homogeneity. All extensive variables are homogeneous functions of first degree in moles and intensive variables are functions of zero degree with respect to moles. Volume is a homogeneous function of first degree in mole because at constant pressure and temperature doubling the number of moles doubles the volume, *i.e.*,

$$V = f(P, T, n)$$

$$V_1 = f(P, T, 2n) = 2f(P, T, n) = 2V$$

Euler's theorem: According to the theorem, if $f(x, y, z)$ is a homogeneous function of degree n, then

$$x\frac{\partial f}{\partial x} + y\frac{\partial f}{\partial y} + z\frac{\partial f}{\partial z} = nf(x, y, z)$$

It is useful in the discussions of partial molar quantities.

Problem 5.1: If the equation of state for 1 mole of a gas is

$$P(V - b) = RT$$

prove that P is a state function, dP is an exact differential and

$$\left(\frac{\partial V}{\partial P}\right)_T \left(\frac{\partial P}{\partial T}\right)_V \left(\frac{\partial T}{\partial V}\right)_P = -1$$

Solution: dP would be exact differential if

$$\frac{\partial^2 P}{\partial V \partial T} = \frac{\partial^2 P}{\partial T \partial V}$$

From the equation of state we have

$$P = \frac{RT}{V - b}$$

Hence,

$$\left(\frac{\partial P}{\partial T}\right)_V = \frac{R}{V - b}; \quad \frac{\partial^2 P}{\partial V \partial T} = -\frac{R}{(V - b)^2} \qquad \qquad ...(i)$$

and

$$\left(\frac{\partial P}{\partial V}\right)_T = \frac{RT}{(V - b)^2}; \quad \frac{\partial^2 P}{\partial T \partial V} = -\frac{R}{(V - b)^2} \qquad \qquad ...(ii)$$

From (i) and (ii) we see that

$$\frac{\partial^2 P}{\partial V \partial T} = \frac{\partial^2 P}{\partial T \partial V}$$

therefore, dP is an exact differential.

The differential $\left(\dfrac{\partial V}{\partial T}\right)_P$ from the above equation of state is

$$\left(\frac{\partial V}{\partial T}\right)_P = \frac{R}{P} \qquad \qquad ...(iii)$$

and

$$\left(\frac{\partial V}{\partial P}\right)_T \left(\frac{\partial P}{\partial T}\right)_V \left(\frac{\partial T}{\partial V}\right)_P = -\frac{(V - b)^2}{RT} \frac{R}{(V - b)} \frac{P}{R}$$

$$= -\left(\frac{V - b}{RT}\right) P$$

$$= -\frac{1}{P} P \left(\because \frac{V - b}{RT} = \frac{1}{P} \right)$$

$$= -1$$

The change in P will depend only on the initial and the final states of the system. Hence P is a state function.

Problem 5.2: The coefficient of thermal expansion, α is defined as

$$\alpha = \frac{1}{V}\left(\frac{dV}{dT}\right)_P$$

while the compressibility coefficient k is defined as

$$k = -\frac{1}{V}\left(\frac{dV}{dP}\right)_T$$

Evaluate them for an ideal gas and prove that

$$\left(\frac{dP}{dT}\right)_V = \frac{\alpha}{k}$$

Solution: For a mole of an ideal gas $PV = RT$

Differentiating V with respect to T at constant P yields

$$P\left(\frac{dV}{dT}\right)_P = R$$

$$\left(\frac{dV}{dT}\right)_P = \frac{R}{P}$$

$$\alpha = \frac{1}{V}\left(\frac{dV}{dT}\right)_P = \frac{1}{V}\frac{R}{P} = \frac{R}{RT} = \frac{1}{T}$$

Differentiation of V with respect to P at constant T gives

$$\left(\frac{dV}{dP}\right)_T = -\frac{RT}{P^2}$$

and

$$k = -\frac{1}{V}\left(\frac{dV}{dP}\right)_T = \frac{RT}{VP^2} = \frac{RT}{RT \cdot P} = \frac{1}{P}$$

From the cyclic rule, we have

$$\left(\frac{dV}{dT}\right)_P\left(\frac{dT}{dP}\right)_V\left(\frac{dP}{dV}\right)_T = -1$$

$$\alpha V\left(\frac{dT}{dP}\right)_V \frac{1}{-kV} = -1$$

$$\frac{\alpha}{k}\left(\frac{dT}{dP}\right)_V = 1$$

$$\left(\frac{dP}{dT}\right)_V = \frac{\alpha}{k}$$

Problem 5.3: Show that $\left(\dfrac{\partial \alpha}{\partial P}\right)_T + \left(\dfrac{\partial k}{\partial T}\right)_P = 0$

Solution: Since

$$\alpha = \frac{1}{V}\left(\frac{dV}{dT}\right)_P$$

$$\left(\frac{\partial \alpha}{\partial P}\right)_T = \frac{\partial}{\partial P}\left(\frac{1}{V}\right)_T \left(\frac{\partial V}{\partial T}\right)_P + \frac{1}{V}\frac{\partial^2 V}{\partial P\,\partial T}$$

$$= -\frac{1}{V^2}\left(\frac{\partial V}{\partial P}\right)_T \left(\frac{\partial V}{\partial T}\right)_P + \frac{1}{V}\frac{\partial^2 V}{\partial P\,\partial T} \qquad \ldots(i)$$

and

$$k = -\frac{1}{V}\left(\frac{\partial V}{\partial P}\right)_T$$

$$\left(\frac{\partial k}{\partial T}\right)_P = \frac{\partial}{\partial T}\left(-\frac{1}{V}\right)\left(\frac{\partial V}{\partial P}\right)_T - \frac{1}{V}\frac{\partial^2 V}{\partial T\,\partial P}$$

$$= \frac{1}{V^2}\left(\frac{\partial V}{\partial T}\right)_P \left(\frac{\partial V}{\partial P}\right)_T - \frac{1}{V}\frac{\partial^2 V}{\partial T\,\partial P} \qquad \ldots(ii)$$

Adding (i) and (ii) yields

$$\left(\frac{\partial \alpha}{\partial P}\right)_T + \left(\frac{\partial k}{\partial T}\right)_P = \frac{1}{V}\left(\frac{\partial^2 V}{\partial P\,\partial T} - \frac{\partial^2 V}{\partial T\,\partial P}\right) = 0$$

5.4 WORK, HEAT AND ENERGY

The concepts of work and heat are of fundamental importance in thermodynamics. Work and heat are algebraic quantities and can be positive or negative. They appear only during a change in the state of the system and appear only at the boundary of the system. They are manifestations of energy.

Work

If an object is displaced through a distance dx against a force $F(x)$ then the amount of work which has to be done is defined as

$$W = -F(x)\,dx$$

In SI system of units, work is expressed in Joule or kilojoule; 1 J = 1 Nm. When work is done on the system W is positive and when work is done by the system W is negative. There are many types of work and all of them could be expressed as the product of two factors; (*i*) an intensity factor, and (*ii*) a capacity factor. Some of these types are:

Gravitational work: Gravitational work is said to be done when a body is raised through a certain height against the gravitational field. If a body of mass *m* is raised through a height *h* against the gravitational field, the magnitude of the gravitational work is *mg*. In this expression mg, the force required to overcome the gravity is the intensity factor and height *h* is the capacity factor.

Electrical work: Electric work is said to be done when a charged body is moved from one potential region into another. If the charge is expressed in coulombs and the potential difference in volts, then the electrical work is given by *QV*. Here potential difference (*V*) is the intensity factor and the quantity of electricity (*Q*) is the capacity factor.

Mechanical work: Work associated with the change in volume of a system against an external pressure is referred to as the mechanical or pressure-volume work. The magnitude of this work in an isothermal expansion of a gas can be obtained as follows. Consider a certain quantity of a gas enclosed in a cylinder fitted with a weightless and frictionless piston. The gas is held in position by a constant external pressure, P_{ext}. The force acting on the piston is given by the product of the external pressure and the cross-sectional area of the piston ($P_{ext} \cdot A$), where *A* is its area of cross section. The cylinder is immersed in a thermostat to ensure constant temperature during the expansion of the gas. The initial state of the system is described by P_1, V_1 and *T* [Fig. 5.2(*a*)]. By lowering the external pressure, the gas tends to expand. During expansion, the piston moves to a new position where the variables of the system are P_2, V_2 and *T*. This is shown in Fig. 5.2 (*b*). Let the height upto which the piston has moved be *h*. The work done by the gas during expansion is given by

$$W = -(\text{Force} \times \text{distance})$$

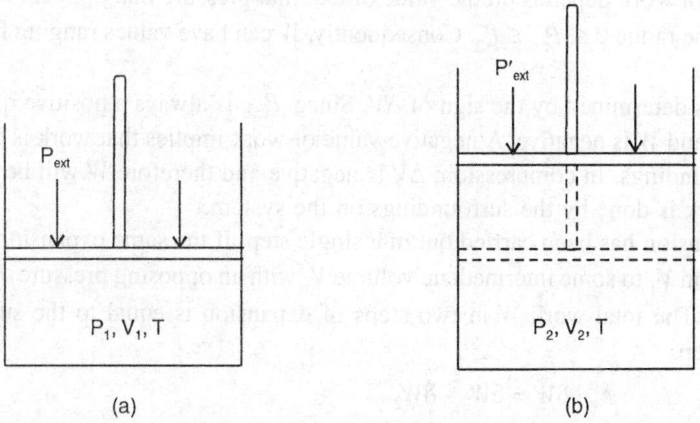

Fig. 5.2 Isothermal expansion of a gas (*a*) Initial state; (*b*) Final state

Since the work is being done by the system on the surroundings, it decreases the internal energy of the system and consequently, the work is given a negative sign. Similarly, if work is being done on the system, it increases the internal energy of the system, and, therefore, work is given a positive sign. The work of expansion is given as

$$W = -P_{ext}\, Ah \qquad \left(\because \text{Force} = \frac{P_{ext}}{A} \right)$$

But (Ah) is the change in volume, ΔV during the expansion and is equal to $(V_2 - V_1)$. Hence the work of expansion is

$$W = -P_{ext}\,\Delta V \qquad \qquad ...(5.8)$$

It may be mentioned that P_{ext} is not the pressure of the gas, it is the pressure that resists the expansion of the gas. The work done as given by Eq. (5.8) is indicated by the shaded area in Fig. 5.3 (a). The dashed curve A is the usual isotherm of the gas.

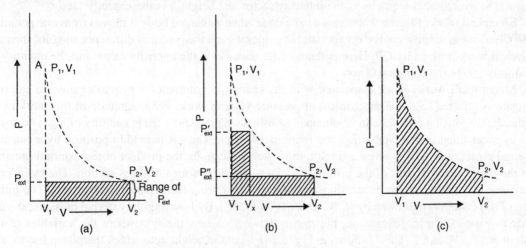

Fig. 5.3 Work done in (a) one-step expansion; (b) two-step expansion and (c) multi step expansion of an ideal gas

The magnitude of work depends on the value of external pressure that opposes expansion and can have any values in the range $0 \le P_{ext} \le P_2$. Consequently, W can have values ranging from zero to some upper limit.

The sign of W is determined by the sign of ΔV. Since P_{ext} is always a positive quantity. In expansion, ΔV is positive and W is negative. A negative value of work implies that work is being done by the system on the surroundings. In compression, ΔV is negative and therefore W will be positive meaning thereby that the work is done by the surroundings on the system.

The above expansion has been carried out in a single step. If the same expansion were carried out in two steps, first from V_1 to some intermediate volume V_x with an opposing pressure P'_{ext} and then from V_x to V_2 with P''_{ext}. The total work W in two steps of expansion is equal to the sum of the amount produced in each step.

$$\delta W = \delta W_1 + \delta W_2$$

or

$$-W = P'_{ext}\left(V_x - V_1\right) + P''_{ext}\left(V_2 - V_x\right) \qquad \qquad ...(5.9)$$

Fig. 5.3 (b) shows the graphical representation of this two-step expansion work and its magnitude is obviously more than the single-step expansion for the same change in the state of the system. If the expansion is carried out in infinite number of steps with a constant external pressure such that the volume increases by a very small amount dV, then the quantity of work for each step is given by

$$-\delta W = P_{ext}\,dV \qquad \qquad ...(5.10)$$

and the total work of expansion is

$$-W = \int_{V_1}^{V_2} P_{ext}\, dV \qquad \qquad ...(5.11)$$

Work done in free expansion of the gas: If the external pressure is zero, *i.e.*, the gas expands in vacuum, no work is done by the system

$$-\delta W = P_{ext}\, dV = 0$$

Work Involved in Reversible Expansion of a Gas

As seen above, in a two-step expansion the magnitude of the work produced is more than that involved in a single-step expansion. If the expansion were carried out in an infinite number of steps such that the external pressure at each stage of the expansion is only infinitesimally less than the pressure of the gas, the magnitude of the work goes on increasing and attains a maximum value. This is given by integrating Eq. (5.10).

$$W_{rev} = -\int_{V_1}^{V_2} P_{ext}\, dV$$

For expansion of the gas, P_{ext} should be less than the pressure (P) of the gas *i.e.*, $P_{ext} = P - dP$, where dP is infinitesimally small. Therefore the magnitude of work involved is

$$W_{rev} = -\int_{V_1}^{V_2} (P - dP)\, dV$$

Since dP is exceedingly small and in the limit $P - dP \approx P$, hence

$$W_{rev} = -\int_{V_1}^{V_2} P\, dV$$

If the gas behaves ideally, then

$$P = \frac{nRT}{V}$$

and

$$-W_{rev} = \int_{V_1}^{V_2} \frac{nRT}{V}\, dV$$

Since the temperature is constant therefore integration of the above equation yields

$$-W_{rev} = nRT \ln \frac{V_2}{V_1} \qquad \qquad ...(5.12)$$

$$= nRT \ln \frac{P_1}{P_2} \qquad \qquad ...(5.13)$$

Figure 5.3 (c) gives the graphical representation of work in a reversible isothermal expansion. The work as given by Eq. (5.12) or (5.13) is obtained only under reversible conditions such that the system does not deviate from its equilibrium state. This is the maximum amount of work that can be derived from the system. If the expansion is carried out rapidly the equilibrium of the system will be disturbed and the process will be irreversible. Consequently, the magnitude of work would be less. This can be seen from the following comparison in which an ideal gas expands reversibly and irreversibly from state P_1, V_1 to state P_2, V_2 under isothermal conditions

$$-W_{rev} = nRT \ln \frac{V_2}{V_1} = nRT \ln \frac{P_1}{P_2}$$

$$= nRT \ln \left[1 - \left(1 - \frac{P_1}{P_2} \right) \right]$$

Expanding $\ln \left[1 - \left(1 - \frac{P_1}{P_2} \right) \right]$ and neglecting higher terms we get

$$-W_{rev} = nRT \left(\frac{P_1}{P_2} - 1 \right) \qquad \qquad ...(5.14)$$

When the gas expands irreversibly at constant pressure P_2, we have

$$-W_{irr} = P_2 \left(V_2 - V_1 \right)$$

$$= P_2 \left(\frac{nRT}{P_2} - \frac{nRT}{P_1} \right)$$

$$= nRT \left(1 - \frac{P_2}{P_1} \right)$$

Therefore, the difference in the magnitude of W_{rev} and W_{irr} is

$$\left| W_{rev} \right| - \left| W_{irr} \right| = nRT \left[\frac{P_1}{P_2} - 1 - 1 + \frac{P_2}{P_1} \right]$$

$$= nRT \left[\frac{P_1^2 - 2 P_1 P_2 + P_2^2}{P_1 P_2} \right]$$

$$= \frac{nRT}{P_1 P_2} \left(P_1 - P_2 \right)^2 \qquad \qquad ...(5.16)$$

Since $(P_1 - P_2)^2$ is always positive irrespective of whether P_1 is less than, equal to or greater than P_2, hence

$$\left| W_{rev} \right| - \left| W_{irr} \right| > 0$$

or

$$|W_{rev}| > |W_{irr}|$$

This shows that the magnitude of work in a reversible process is more than that in an irreversible process.

In compression, the external pressure should be larger than the pressure of the gas. If the compression of the gas is done from P_2, V_2 to P_1, V_1 in one step, then the minimum value of external pressure should be P_1 and the work done on the system would be given by

$$-W = P_{ext}(V_1 - V_2) = P_1(V_1 - V_2)$$

It is equal to the area of the shaded rectangle in Fig. 5.4 (a). If larger external pressure is used, the surroundings will have to do more work in bringing about the desired change. If the compression is done in two stages — from P_2, V_2 to some intermediate value P_2', V_2' and then to P_1, V_1, lesser amount of work will be done by the surroundings (Fig. 5.4 (b)). By carrying out compression in a large number of steps taking P_{ext} at each stage only, slightly greater than the pressure (P) of the gas, i.e., $P_{ext} = P + dP$, then the work involved is given by

$$-W_{min} = \int_{V_2}^{V_1} P_{ext}\, dV = \int_{V_2}^{V_1} (P + dP)\, dV$$

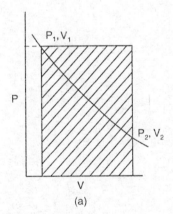
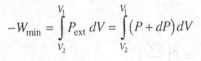
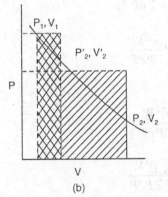
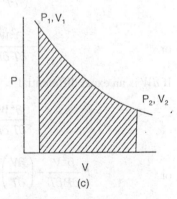

Fig. 5.4 Work done in (a) one-step compression; (b) two-step compression and (c) multi-step compression of an ideal gas

Since dP is very small and can be neglected, therefore the work done on the ideal gas is given by

$$-W_{min} = nRT \ln \frac{V_1}{V_2} \qquad ...(5.17)$$

This is the limiting minimum value of the work which the surroundings will perform on the system during compression and is obviously the area under the curve (Fig. 5.4 (c)). The magnitudes of the reversible work of expansion and compression as may be seen from Eqs. (5.13) and (5.17) are equal.

Nature of work: W is not a thermodynamic quantity. Its value as seen from Eqs. (5.8), (5.9) and (5.12) for the same change in state depends on the path followed for the isothermal transformation of the system. Mathematically, one can prove that W is not an exact differential. If W is an exact differential for mechanical work, one may write

$$-dW = PdV$$

Considering V as a function of P and T, *i.e.*,

$$V = f(P, T)$$

$$dV = \left(\frac{\partial V}{\partial P}\right)_T dP + \left(\frac{\partial V}{\partial T}\right)_P dT$$

Hence

$$-dW = P\left(\frac{\partial V}{\partial P}\right)_T dP + P\left(\frac{\partial V}{\partial T}\right)_P dT$$

If $dP = 0$, then

$$-\left(\frac{\partial W}{\partial T}\right)_P = P\left(\frac{\partial V}{\partial T}\right)_P$$

or

$$-\frac{\partial^2 W}{\partial P \partial T} = P\frac{\partial^2 V}{\partial P \partial T} + \left(\frac{\partial V}{\partial T}\right)_P$$

and at constant temperature $dT = 0$ and

$$-\left(\frac{\partial W}{\partial P}\right)_T = P\left(\frac{\partial V}{\partial P}\right)_T$$

or

$$-\frac{\partial^2 W}{\partial T \partial P} = P\frac{\partial^2 V}{\partial P \partial T}$$

If dW is an exact differential

$$\frac{\partial^2 W}{\partial T \partial P} = \frac{\partial^2 W}{\partial P \partial T}$$

or

$$P\frac{\partial^2 V}{\partial P \partial T} + \left(\frac{\partial V}{\partial T}\right)_P = P\frac{\partial^2 V}{\partial T \partial P}$$

$$\left(\frac{\partial V}{\partial T}\right)_P = 0$$

The conclusion is obviously incorrect which mean dW is not an exact differential.

For a cyclic transformation carried out reversibly and irreversibly, the value of W for two different processes would be different. This can be shown as follows:

(*i*) **Isothermal reversible transformation:** Suppose the gas is expanded from V_1 to V_2 with $P_{ext} = P$, the pressure of the gas and then compressed from V_2 to V_1 with $P_{ext} = P$. The network for the complete reversible cycle is

$$W_{cyc} = W_{exp} + W_{comp}$$

$$= -\int_{V_1}^{V_2} P dV - \int_{V_2}^{V_1} P dV$$

$$\oint \delta W = W_{cyc} = -\int_{V_1}^{V_2} PdV + \int_{V_1}^{V_2} PdV = 0$$

Hence, in an isothermal reversible process

$$\oint \delta W = 0$$

(*ii*) **Isothermal irreversible transformation:** The expansion of the gas is carried out from V_1 to V_2 with $P_{ext} = P_2$. The gas is then compressed from V_2 to V_1 with $P_{ext} = P_1$. Both the steps are irreversible and the network (W'_{eye}) is given as

$$\oint \delta W = W'_{cyc} = -P_2(V_2 - V_1) - P_1(V_1 - V_2)$$

$$= (P_1 - P_2)(V_2 - V_1)$$

Since $V_2 > V_1$ and $P_2 < P_1$, therefore, W'_{cyc} is positive indicating that work has been done on the system. In other words, the surroundings have to do more work in bringing the system back to its original state than the work done by the system during expansion. From this one can state that W is not a state function or δW is an inexact differential.

If the system contains n moles of a real gas obeying van der Waals equation

$$\left(P + \frac{an^2}{V^2}\right)(V - nb) = nRT$$

then the work ($-W_{vd}$) in isothermal reversible expansion is given by

$$-W_{vd} = \int_{V_1}^{V_2} PdV = \int_{V_1}^{V_2} \left(\frac{nRT}{V - nb} - \frac{an^2}{V^2}\right)dV$$

$$= \left[nRT \ln(V - nb) + \frac{an^2}{V}\right]_{V_1}^{V_2}$$

$$= 2.303\, nRT \log \frac{V_2 - nb}{V_1 - nb} + an^2\left(\frac{1}{V_2} - \frac{1}{V_1}\right) \qquad \ldots(5.18)$$

The difference in the magnitude of work of expansion for an ideal and a van der Waals gas is given by

$$|W_{id}| - |W_{vd}| = nRT \ln \frac{V_2}{V_1} - nRT \ln \frac{V_2 - nb}{V_1 - nb} + an^2\left(\frac{1}{V_1} - \frac{1}{V_2}\right)$$

If $nb << V$, so that $V - nb \approx V$, then

$$|W_{id}| - |W_{vd}| = an^2\left(\frac{1}{V_1} - \frac{1}{V_2}\right) = an^2\left(\frac{V_2 - V_1}{V_1 V_2}\right)$$

$$= \frac{an^2 \Delta V}{V_1 V_2} = \text{a positive quantity}$$

The magnitude of reversible work of expansion for an ideal gas is always greater than that for a van der Waals gas as work has to be done in overcoming the attractive forces between the molecules of a van der Waals gas.

Energy

Energy is defined as *the capacity to do work*. Every system containing some quantity of matter possesses a store of energy. It may occur in various forms such as kinetic energy due to the motion of the body; potential energy by virtue of its position in a force field; thermal energy due to the temperature of the body; chemical energy due to constitution of the compounds; nuclear energy; mechanical energy, electrical energy, etc.

The energy possessed by a system due to translational, vibrational and rotational motions of the molecules along with the energy of the electrons, nuclei and molecular interactions is known as its *internal* or *intrinsic energy* or *energy content* of the system. The energy acquired by a system in a force field like electrical, magnetic, gravitational surface, etc., are termed as *external energies* and are usually not considered as part of the internal energy of the system. The energy content of a system is denoted by E and depends on the internal structure and the constitution of the material composing the system. It is independent of the previous history of the system. The magnitude of energy is determined by the state of the system and in turn by the variables of the system like pressure, volume and temperature. As these variables are related to one another by an equation of state, the energy of a system of fixed composition may be described in terms of any two of these state variables, *i.e.*,

$$E = f_1(P, T) = f_2(V, T) = f_3(P, V)$$

Energy is an extensive property, *i.e.*, its magnitude depends upon the quantity of material in the system. In SI system, it is expressed in J or kJ.

If in a transformation the system changes from state A to some other state B, the energy change $\Delta E = (E_B - E_A)$ is determined by the values of variables in the two states. The change in the state of the system can be brought about by a number of paths but the change in E is always the same, viz., $E_B - E_A)$ is determined by the values of variables in the two states. The change in the state of the system can be brought about by a number of paths but the change in E is always the same, viz., $E_B - E_A$ and is independent of the paths by which the transformation is carried out. Energy is, therefore, a state function. In a cyclic process, the initial state of the system is restored and the energy change would be zero. These facts can be stated mathematically as

(*i*) energy is a state function;

(*ii*) dE is an exact differential;

(*iii*) $\oint dE = 0$; and

(*iv*) Euler's theorem of exactness applied to dE yields

$$\frac{\partial^2 E}{\partial V \, \partial T} = \frac{\partial^2 E}{\partial T \, \partial V}$$

Heat

Heat is a form of energy and can be produced from work or can be partly converted into work. It appears only during a change in the state of the system and flows from a region of higher temperature to a region of lower temperature. The flow ceases when the thermal equilibrium is attained. Heat is different from other forms of energy. All other forms of energy can be quantitatively converted into work but heat cannot be completely converted into work without producing permanent changes either in the system or in the surroundings.

Heat is an algebraic quantity and is denoted by Q. Q is taken as positive when the system absorbs it from the surrounding and negative when it leaves the system. Like work, Q is not a state function, its value depends on the path which is followed for carrying out the transformation in the state of the system. Heat is, therefore, a path-dependent quantity.

Problem 5.4: Calculate the work required to raise a body of mass 2 kg through a height of 0.5 m on the surface of (a) the earth where $g = 9.8$ ms^{-2}, and (b) the moon where $g = 1.6$ ms^{-2}.

Solution: The work required to raise a body against gravitational force is given by

$$W = mgh$$

(a) on the surface of earth,

$$W = (2 \text{ kg})(0.5 \text{ m})(9.8 \text{ ms}^{-2}) = 9.8 \text{ J} \qquad (\because 1 \text{ J} = 1 \text{ kg m}^2 \text{ s}^{-2})$$

(b) On the moon's surface,

$$W = (2 \text{ kg})(0.5 \text{ m})(1.6 \text{ ms}^{-2}) = 1.6 \text{ J}$$

Problem 5.5: One mole of oxygen at 300 K expands isothermally from 3 atmospheres to 1 atmosphere. Assuming that oxygen behaves ideally, calculate W, if the expansion is (i) reversible and (ii) single step against a constant pressure of 1 atmosphere.

Solution: The initial volume of the gas, V_1 is given by

$$V_1 = \frac{RT}{P} = \frac{(1 \text{ mol})(0.0821 \text{ dm}^3 \text{ atm K}^{-1} \text{ mol}^{-1})(300 \text{ K})}{3 \text{ atm}}$$

$$= 8.21 \text{ dm}^3$$

The final volume V_2 would be 24.63 dm^3 $\left(\dfrac{1 \times .0821 \times 300}{1} \right)$

For process (i), the expansion is reversible and work involved is given by

$$-W_{rev} = nRT \ln \frac{V_2}{V_1} = nRT \ln \frac{P_1}{P_2}$$

$$= (1 \text{ mol})(8.314 \text{ JK}^{-1} \text{ mol}^{-1})(300 \text{ K}) \times 2.303 \log \frac{3}{1}$$

$$= 2.74 \text{ kJ}$$

For the single-step expansion in (ii), W is given by

$$-W = P\Delta V = P(V_2 - V_1)$$

$$= \left(1.013 \times 10^5 \ \text{Nm}^{-2}\right)\left(24.63 \times 10^{-3} \text{m}^3 - 8.21 \times 10^{-3} \text{m}^3\right)$$

$$= 1.013 \times 10^5 \text{Nm}^{-2} \times 16.42 \times 10^{-3} \text{m}^3$$

$$= 1.013 \times 1.642 \times 10^3 \ \text{Nm}$$

$$W = -1.663 \text{ kJ} \qquad\qquad\qquad (\because 1 \ \text{Nm} = 1\text{J})$$

Problem 5.6: Calculate the work involved when 0.06538 kg of zinc dissolves in hydrochloric acid in (*i*) an open beaker and (*ii*) a closed beaker at 300 K.

Solution: In the dissolution of zinc in hydrochloric acid

$$\text{Zn (s)} + 2\,\text{HCl (aq)} = \text{ZnCl}_2 \text{(aq)} + \text{H}_2(\text{g})$$

1 mole of hydrogen gas is generated for each mole of zinc dissolved. The liberated gas pushes the surrounding atmosphere and thereby performs work equal to $P\Delta V$. If the gas behaves ideally and the initial volume of the system is neglected in comparison to the volume of the gas produced then the work in the open beaker is

$$-W = P\Delta V \approx PV_{\text{H}_2} = n_{\text{H}_2} RT$$

$$= (1 \text{ mol}) \left(8.314 \text{JK}^{-1}\text{mol}^{-1}\right)(300 \text{ K})$$

$$= 2.4942 \text{ kJ}$$

If the reaction occurs in a closed beaker, there is no change in the volume, *i.e.*, $\Delta V = 0$, hence work involved is zero.

Problem 5.7: Calculate the work done when one mole of sulphur dioxide gas expands isothermally and reversibly at 300 K from 2.46×10^{-3} m^3 to 24.6×10^{-3} m^3, assuming that the gas obeys (*a*) ideal gas equation, and (*b*) van der Waals equation ($a = 0.6799$ Nm^4 mol^{-2}, $b = 0.0564 \times 10^{-3}$ m^3 mol^{-1}).

Solution. (*a*) The reversible work done by 1 mole of gas when it expands from 2.46×10^{-3} m^3 to 24.6×10^{-3} m^3 is given by

$$W_{id} = -2.303 \, nRT \log \frac{V_2}{V_1}$$

$$= -(2.303)\,(1 \text{ mol}) \left(8.314 \text{ JK}^{-1}\text{mol}^{-1}\right)(300 \text{ K}) \times \log 10 \qquad \left(\because \log \frac{V_2}{V_1} = \log 10\right)$$

$$= -(2.303)\left(8.314 \text{ JK}^{-1}\text{mol}^{-1}\right)(300 \text{ K})\log(10)$$

$$= -5744 \text{ J mol}^{-1}$$

$$= -5.744 \text{ kJ mol}^{-1}$$

(*b*) Work done by 1 mole of gas when it obeys van der Waals equation

$$W_{vd} = -2.303 \, RT \log \frac{V_2 - b}{V_1 - b} - a\left[\frac{1}{V_2} - \frac{1}{V_2}\right]$$

On substituting the values of various quantities and solving, the work done is

$$= -5794 \text{ J mol}^{-1} + 252.4 \text{ J mol}^{-1}$$

$$= -5541.6 \text{ J mol}^{-1}$$

$$= -5.542 \text{ kJ mol}^{-1}$$

Problem 5.8: A system consisting of 1 mole of an ideal diatomic gas absorbs 200 J of heat and does 50 J of work on the surroundings. Calculate the change in temperature of the gas if the vibrational modes of motion are inactive.

Solution: $Q = 200$ J, $W = -50$ J

From first law we have

$$\Delta E = Q + W$$

$$= (200 - 50) \text{J} = 150 \text{ J}$$

As the vibrational modes are inactive so the change in internal energy ΔE is given by the translational and rotational contributions, *i.e.*,

$$\Delta E = \frac{3}{2} R\Delta T + R\Delta T$$

$$\Delta E = \frac{5}{2} R\Delta T$$

$$\Delta T = \frac{150 \text{ J mol}^{-1}}{\left(8.314 \text{ JK}^{-1} \text{ mol}^{-1}\right)\left(\dfrac{5}{2}\right)}$$

or

$$= 7.2 \text{ K}$$

Problem 5.9: At low temperatures, a non-ideal gas follows the relation $PV = RT - \dfrac{a}{V}$, where $a = 0.3636$ Nm^{4}mol^{-2}. Calculate the work done by one mole of this gas in expanding from 2.24×10^{-4}m^3 to 2.24×10^{-2}m^3 at 400 K. Compare this result with the work done in the correspondings expansion of an ideal gas.

Solution: For an ideal gas, reversible work done $= -2.303 \, nRT \log \dfrac{V_2}{V_1}$

Here

$$V_2 = 2.24 \times 10^{-2} \text{ m}^3\text{mol}^{-1}$$

$$V_1 = 2.24 \times 10^{-4} \text{ m}^3\text{mol}^{-1}$$

$$-W_{\text{rev}} = (2.303)(1 \text{ mol})\left(8.314 \text{ JK}^{-1}\text{mol}^{-1}\right)(400 \text{ K}) \log \frac{2.24 \times 10^{-2}}{2.24 \times 10^{-4}}$$

$$= (2.303)(1 \text{ mol})(8.314 \text{ JK}^{-1}\text{mol}^{-1})(400 \text{ K})\log(100)$$

or

$$= 15320 \text{ J mol}^{-1}$$

$$W_{rev} = -15.32 \text{ kJ mol}^{-1}$$

For the non-ideal gas, $\qquad PV = RT - \dfrac{a}{V}$

Therefore, the work done $= (-W) = \displaystyle\int_{V_1}^{V_2} PdV = \int_{V_1}^{V_2}\left(\dfrac{RT}{V} - \dfrac{a}{V^2}\right)dV$

$$= 2.303 RT \log\dfrac{V_2}{V_1} + a\left[\dfrac{1}{V_2} - \dfrac{1}{V_1}\right]$$

Now the first term is equal to 15.32 kJ mol^{-1} and the second term is given as

$$0.3636 \text{ Nm}^4\text{mol}^{-2}\left[\dfrac{1}{2.24 \times 10^{-2}\,\text{m}^3\,\text{mol}^{-1}} - \dfrac{1}{2.24 \times 10^{-4}\,\text{m}^3\text{mol}^{-1}}\right]$$

$$= 1.604 \text{ kJ mol}^{-1}$$

Hence work done $(-W)$ is $\qquad = 15.320 \text{ kJ mol}^{-1} - 1.604 \text{ kJ mol}^{-1}$

$$= 13.716 \text{ kJ mol}^{-1}$$

5.5 ZEROTH LAW OF THERMODYNAMICS

Zeroth law of thermodynamics is also referred to as the law of thermal equilibrium. It was formulated after the enunciation of the first and the second laws of thermodynamics. But it was considered to be of primary importance so it was placed before the first law of thermodynamics, hence the unusual name zeroth law. The law, like other laws of thermodynamics is based on experience. The law states that two systems A and B which are in thermal equilibrium with a third system C, are in thermal equilibrium with each other and will have the same temperature. The temperature concept can be stated as — systems in thermal equilibrium with each other have the same temperature and systems not in thermal equilibrium with each other have different temperatures. The zeroth law therefore provides operational definition of temperature.

5.6 CONSERVATION OF ENERGY—THE FIRST LAW OF THERMODYNAMICS

The first law of thermodynamics is the law of conservation of energy. It is the result of our experience and is not derivable from any principle. The law has been stated in various forms but the fundamental implication is that although *energy may be transformed from one form into another, it can neither be created nor destroyed.* In other words, whenever energy of a particular form disappears an exactly equivalent amount of another form must be produced. The first law rules out the possibility of constructing a perpetual motion machine of the first kind — a machine operating in cycles and producing work without any expenditure of energy on it. According to the first law, the total energy of a system and its surroundings, *i.e.*, the universe is conserved. Gain or loss in energy by the system is exactly compensated by the loss or gain in energy of the surroundings. The law is universally valid for all processes. In reactions between atomic nuclei, the change in energy is always accompanied by the corresponding change of mass. In these cases the total energy and mass of the isolated system is conserved.

Change in energy of a system: mathematical formulation of the First Law. Consider a system in state A with internal energy E_A. It absorbs from the surroundings a certain amount of heat Q and undergoes a change in its state to B where its energy is E_B. The change may be physical, chemical or mechanical. The increase in energy of the system ΔE is given by

$$\Delta E = E_B - E_A \qquad \qquad ...(5.19)$$

The change is independent of the path or manner in which the change has been brought about.

If W is the work involved in this transformation, the net gain of energy is $Q + W$. From the first law of thermodynamics, this must be equal to the increase in energy ΔE of the system, *i.e.*,

$$\Delta E = E_B - E_A = Q + W$$

or $$Q = \Delta E - W \qquad \qquad ...(5.20)$$

for an infinitesimally small change

$$\delta Q = dE - \delta W \qquad \qquad ...(5.21)$$

Equations (5.20) and (5.21) are the mathematical forms of the first law of thermodynamics. The heat absorbed is equal to increase in energy of the system plus the work done by the system. If the system loses heat to the surroundings, its energy decreases, ΔE would be negative and work will be done on the system by the surroundings.

The above change can be brought about by a large number of paths (Fig. 5.5). Since E is a state function, its magnitude depends only on the state of the system, the change ΔE will be independent of the path followed. However, the quantities Q and W are path functions, they adjust themselves in such a manner that $Q + W$ is always equal to ΔE.

Energy change in an isolated system: If the transformation is carried out under adiabatic conditions such that heat neither enters nor leaves the system then $Q = 0$ and therefore

$$\Delta E = W$$

or $$\Delta E - W = 0 \qquad \qquad ...(5.22)$$

The work done by the system would be at the cost of its internal energy and is equal to the decrease in its energy content or the algebraic sum or difference of the changes in energy and the work performed in an isolated system is zero.

Energy change in a cyclic process: If the system after undergoing a change in its state is brought back to its initial state,

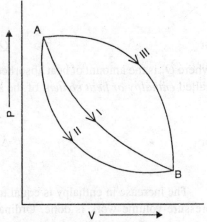

Fig. 5.5 Energy change independent of the path

$$\Delta E = 0$$

and $$Q = -W \qquad \qquad \qquad ...(5.23)$$

The heat absorbed by the system from the surroundings is exactly equal to the work done by the system on the surroundings. Equation (5.23) establishes the impossibility of a perpetual motion of the first kind, viz., work cannot be produced without withdrawing heat from an external source.

Energy change in a non-isolated system: Such a system permits heat exchange with the surroundings. If the system absorbs heat Q and performs work, the increase in energy of the system is given by

$$\Delta E = Q + W$$

The surroundings loses this heat and receives W units of work, the energy change of the surroundings $\Delta E'$ is

$$\Delta E' = Q + W$$

and consequently, $$\Delta E = \Delta E'$$

The gain in energy of the system is equal to the loss in energy of the surroundings. The energy of the system plus the energy of the surroundings is conserved in any transformation.

5.7 HEAT CONTENT OR ENTHALPY

Heat changes at constant volume and constant pressure: When a process is carried out at constant volume, no mechanical work is done, since V = constant, $dV = 0$, $W = 0$. It follows from the first law of thermodynamics Eq. (5.20) that

$$E_2 - E_1 = \Delta E_V = Q_V \qquad \qquad ...(5.24)$$

This equation shows that the increase in internal energy of a system is equal to the heat absorbed at constant volume (Q_v).

If the process is carried out at constant pressure, the volume of the system changes and if only pressure-volume work, $P\Delta V$ is done, Eq. (5.20) may be written as

$$\Delta E = E_2 - E_1 = Q_P - P\Delta V \qquad \qquad (\because W = -P\Delta V)$$

$$= Q_P - P(V_2 - V_1)$$

or $$Q_P = (E_2 + PV_2) - (E_1 + PV_1) \qquad \qquad ...(5.25)$$

where Q_P is the amount of heat absorbed at constant pressure. We define a new thermodynamic function called *enthalpy or heat content* of the system as

$$H = E + PV \qquad \qquad ...(5.26)$$

or $$\Delta H = H_2 - H_1 = (E_2 - E_1) + P(V_2 - V_1) = Q_P$$

$$= \Delta E + P\Delta V \qquad \qquad ...(5.27)$$

The increase in enthalpy is equal to the heat absorbed in a process at constant pressure when only pressure-volume work is done. Ordinarily, heat effects are measured at constant pressure, therefore these heat effects indicate the changes in enthalpy contents of a system and not changes in its internal energy. Since E is a state function, and so are P and V, therefore H is a state function and is independent of the path by which the transformation is carried out, consequently dH is an exact differential.

5.8 HEAT CAPACITY

Heat capacity of a substance is defined as the *amount of heat required to raise its temperature through one degree or the ratio of the heat absorbed to the resulting increase in temperature.* If δQ is a very small quantity of heat absorbed by the substance and dT is its rise in temperature then the heat capacity, C is defined as

$$C = \frac{\delta Q}{dT}$$

From the first law of thermodynamics we have

$$\delta Q = dE - \delta W$$

and if only pressure-volume work is involved $(-\delta W = P\Delta V)$

$$\delta Q = dE + PdV$$

or
$$C = \frac{\delta Q}{dT} = \frac{dE + PdV}{dT} \qquad ...(5.28)$$

If the absorption of heat takes place at constant volume, $dV = 0$, Eq. (5.28) reduces to

$$C_V = \frac{\delta Q_V}{dT} = \left(\frac{\partial E}{\partial T}\right)_V \qquad ...(5.29)$$

where C_v is the heat capacity at constant volume and gives the rate of change of internal energy with temperature at constant volume.

At constant pressure, Eq. (5.28) takes the form

$$C_P = \frac{\delta Q_P}{dT} = \left(\frac{dE}{dT}\right)_P + P\left(\frac{dV}{dT}\right)_P \qquad ...(5.30)$$

Since
$$H = E + PV$$

differentiating this equation with respect to T at constant pressure gives

$$\left(\frac{\partial H}{\partial T}\right)_P = \left(\frac{\partial E}{\partial T}\right)_P + P\left(\frac{\partial V}{\partial T}\right)_P \qquad ...(5.31)$$

Therefore,
$$C_P = \left(\frac{\partial H}{\partial T}\right)_P \qquad ...(5.32)$$

Thus, heat capacity C_P is the rate of change of enthalpy with temperature at constant pressure. The symbols $C_{P, m}$ and $C_{V, m}$ are used to denote the heat capacities per mole. Therefore, we have $C_P = nC_{P, m}$ and $C_V = nC_{V, m}$ where n is the number of moles of the substance in the system. Heat capacities are extensive properties but heat capacities per mole are intensive quantities.

Relation between C_P and C_V: The two heat capacities are not equal; C_P is greater than C_V. The difference is on account of the work involved in changing the size of the system. At constant pressure, a part of the heat absorbed is utilised in performing external work while at constant volume all the heat is utilised in increasing the internal energy of the system. It follows therefore that the temperature rise at constant pressure will be less for a given quantity of heat transferred. More heat would be required at constant pressure to cause the same temperature rise and C_P will be greater than C_V. The difference is greater for gases and smaller for solids or liquids, because the latter change their volumes only slightly when heated and therefore do little work.

The difference between the two heat capacities can be deduced from thermodynamic considerations. From Eqs. (5.29) and (5.32) we have

$$C_P - C_V = \left(\frac{\partial H}{\partial T}\right)_P - \left(\frac{\partial E}{\partial T}\right)_V \qquad \text{...(5.33)}$$

Substituting the value of $\left(\dfrac{\partial H}{\partial T}\right)_P$ from Eq. (5.31) in Eq. (5.33) we get

$$C_P - C_V = \left(\frac{\partial E}{\partial T}\right)_P + P\left(\frac{\partial V}{\partial T}\right)_P - \left(\frac{\partial E}{\partial T}\right)_V \qquad \text{...(5.34)}$$

The internal energy E, in general, is a function of any two of the three variables, pressure, volume and temperature. If temperature and volume are taken as the independent variables, then

$$E = f(T, V)$$

Since E is a state function, the differential dE is given by

$$dE = \left(\frac{\partial E}{\partial T}\right)_V dT + \left(\frac{\partial E}{\partial V}\right)_T dV \qquad \text{...(5.35)}$$

$$= C_V dT + \left(\frac{\partial E}{\partial V}\right)_T dV \qquad \text{...(5.36)}$$

On dividing both sides of Eq. (5.35) by dT and then imposing the condition that pressure is constant we get

$$\left(\frac{\partial E}{\partial T}\right)_P = \left(\frac{\partial E}{\partial T}\right)_V + \left(\frac{\partial E}{\partial V}\right)_T \left(\frac{\partial V}{\partial T}\right)_P \qquad \text{...(5.37)}$$

Substituting the value of $\left(\dfrac{\partial E}{\partial T}\right)_P$ in Eq. (5.34) gives

$$C_P - C_V = \left(\frac{\partial E}{\partial T}\right)_V + \left(\frac{\partial E}{\partial V}\right)_T \left(\frac{\partial V}{\partial T}\right)_P + P\left(\frac{\partial V}{\partial T}\right)_P - \left(\frac{\partial E}{\partial T}\right)_V$$

$$= \left(\frac{\partial V}{\partial T}\right)_P \left[\left(\frac{\partial E}{\partial V}\right)_T + P\right] \qquad \text{...(5.38)}$$

This equation is general and is applicable to all substances solids, liquids and gases. In Eq. (5.38), the term $\left(\dfrac{\partial V}{\partial T}\right)_P$ is the change of volume caused by a rise in temperature at constant pressure, and multiplication by P converts this into work. Thus, $P\left(\dfrac{\partial V}{\partial T}\right)_P$ is the work produced per unit increase in

temperature in a constant pressure process. The term $\left(\dfrac{\partial E}{\partial V}\right)_T$ represents the change in energy with

changes in volume at constant temperature and is known as the *internal pressure*. It is, therefore, a measure of interactions between the molecules. The magnitude of this term is quite large for solids and liquids. For gases, the term is usually very small and for ideal gases it is zero, *i.e.*,

$$\left(\frac{\partial E}{\partial V}\right)_T = 0$$

Hence, Eq. (5.38) reduces to

$$C_P - C_V = P\left(\frac{\partial V}{\partial T}\right)_P \qquad \qquad ...(5.39)$$

For a mole of an ideal gas

$$\left(\frac{\partial V}{\partial T}\right)_P = \frac{R}{P} \qquad \qquad (\because PV = RT)$$

Therefore, $\qquad\qquad\qquad\qquad C_{P,\,m} - C_{V,\,m} = R \qquad\qquad\qquad ...(5.40)$

This relation holds good only for ideal gases. In case of non-ideal gases, the difference will not be equal to R.

5.9 JOULE'S EXPERIMENT — MEASUREMENT OF $\left(\dfrac{\partial E}{\partial V}\right)_T$

In order to calculate the change in energy with changes in temperature and volume Eq. (5.36) can be

employed. The change in energy is the sum of two terms, $C_V dT$ and $\left(\dfrac{\partial E}{\partial V}\right)_T dV$. Knowing the values of

these terms, the total change in energy of the system can be calculated by integrating Eq. (5.36). Since

the heat capacity at constant volume can be measured experimentally but the term $\left(\dfrac{\partial E}{\partial V}\right)_T dV$ cannot be

easily identified with measurable quantities. For gases, it can be done by an experiment known as *Joule's experiment*.

Joule's experimental set up is shown in Fig. 5.6. It consists of two bulbs A and B connected by means of a stopcock S. One of the bulbs is filled with a gas at a certain pressure while the other is evacuated. The bulbs are kept in a well-stirred water thermostat the temperature of which is recorded by a sensitive thermometer. When the stopcock S is opened, the gas expands into the evacuated bulb. The system is allowed to attain thermal equilibrium and the temperature of the bath is recorded. Joule observed no change in temperature of the thermostat.

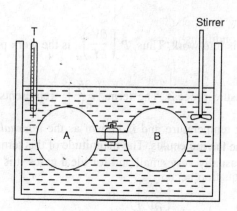

Fig. 5.6 Joule's experiment

· The thermodynamic interpretation of this experiment is as follows: Since the gas expands against zero pressure, consequently, no work is done by the gas; therefore $W = 0$. Because the temperature of the thermostat does not change, *i.e.*, $dT = 0$, it has not exchanged heat with the system; hence $Q = 0$. Consequently, $\Delta E = 0$. It follows that E does not vary when the gas expands isothermally. Therefore, E is independent of volume at constant temperature. Mathematically, we can write

$$\left(\frac{\partial E}{\partial V}\right)_T = 0$$

This behaviour is known as Joule's law and is valid for ideal gases. For non-ideal gases, the quantity $\left(\dfrac{\partial E}{\partial V}\right)_T$ is different from zero.

Joule's experiment was not capable of detecting small temperature changes due to the high heat capacity of water bath compared to that of the gas. The quantity $\left(\dfrac{\partial T}{\partial V}\right)_E$ is called *Joule's coefficient* (μ_J) and is defined as *the rate of change of temperature with change in volume at constant internal energy*. For ideal gases, $\mu_J = 0$. The relation between $\left(\dfrac{\partial E}{\partial V}\right)_T$ and μ_J is obtained from the equation

$$\left(\frac{\partial E}{\partial V}\right)_T\left(\frac{\partial V}{\partial T}\right)_E\left(\frac{\partial T}{\partial E}\right)_V = -1$$

Since

$$\left(\frac{\partial E}{\partial T}\right)_V = C_V \text{ and } \left(\frac{\partial T}{\partial V}\right)_E = \mu_J$$

Hence,

$$\left(\frac{\partial E}{\partial V}\right)_T = -C_V\mu_J \qquad \qquad \dots(5.41)$$

Joule's experiment is not suitable for solids and liquids. At constant temperature, very large pressure is required to bring even a very small change in volume of solids or liquids. The change in energy of a solid or liquid under these conditions is obtained by integrating Eq. (5.35).

$$\int_{E_1}^{E_2} dE = \int_{V_1}^{V_2} \left(\frac{\partial E}{\partial V}\right)_T dV \qquad ...(5.42)$$

Since the change in volume is very small ($V_1 \approx V_2$) so that $\left(\frac{\partial E}{\partial V}\right)_T$ is constant over the small range of volume; hence the above equation becomes

$$\Delta E = \left(\frac{\partial E}{\partial V}\right)_T \Delta V \qquad ...(5.43)$$

Although $\left(\frac{\partial E}{\partial V}\right)_T$ is fairly high for solids and liquids, but the change in volume ΔV is exceedingly small such that the product is approximately equal to zero. From the above arguments it can be stated that energy of all substances may be regarded approximately as a function of temperature only.

Problem 5.10: If $\left(\frac{\partial E}{\partial V}\right)_T = 0$, show that $\left(\frac{\partial E}{\partial P}\right)_T = 0$.

Solution:
$$E = f(P, V)$$

$$dE = \left(\frac{\partial E}{\partial P}\right)_V dP + \left(\frac{\partial E}{\partial V}\right)_P dV$$

$$\left(\frac{\partial E}{\partial V}\right)_T = \left(\frac{\partial E}{\partial P}\right)_V \left(\frac{\partial P}{\partial V}\right)_T + \left(\frac{\partial E}{\partial V}\right)_P \qquad ...(a)$$

Also, one can write

$$\left(\frac{\partial E}{\partial P}\right)_T = \left(\frac{\partial E}{\partial P}\right)_V + \left(\frac{\partial E}{\partial V}\right)_P \left(\frac{\partial V}{\partial P}\right)_T \qquad ...(b)$$

If $\left(\frac{\partial E}{\partial V}\right)_T = 0$, then from Eq. (a)

$$-\left(\frac{\partial E}{\partial P}\right)_V \left(\frac{\partial P}{\partial V}\right)_T = \left(\frac{\partial E}{\partial V}\right)_P$$

or

$$\left(\frac{\partial E}{\partial P}\right)_V = -\left(\frac{\partial E}{\partial V}\right)_P \left(\frac{\partial V}{\partial P}\right)_T$$

Substituting the value of $\left(\dfrac{\partial E}{\partial P}\right)_V$ in Eq. (b),

$$\left(\frac{\partial E}{\partial P}\right)_T = -\left(\frac{\partial E}{\partial V}\right)_P\left(\frac{\partial V}{\partial P}\right)_T + \left(\frac{\partial E}{\partial V}\right)_P\left(\frac{\partial V}{\partial P}\right)_T = 0$$

Specific applications of the First Law: Calculations of W, Q, ΔE and ΔH for an ideal gas in reversible and irreversible isothermal processes: The internal energy and heat content of an ideal gas are functions of temperature only. Therefore, under isothermal conditions

$$\Delta E = 0$$

$$\Delta H = \Delta E + \Delta(PV) = \Delta E + \Delta(nRT) = 0$$

for both reversible and irreversible changes. The reversible work of expansion is given by

$$-W_{rev} = Q_{rev} = nRT\ln\frac{V_2}{V_1} = nRT\ln\frac{P_1}{P_2}$$

and

$$-W_{irr} = Q_{irr} = P_{ext}(V_2 - V_1)$$

W and Q being the path-dependent functions will, however, have different values for reversible and irreversible isothermal changes.

Problem 5.11: Three moles of an ideal monatomic gas at 300 K expand isothermally and reversibly from 10 dm^3 to 30 dm^3. Calculate W, Q, ΔE and ΔH. Would these quantities change if the gas were diatomic?

Solution: $V_1 = 10$ dm^3, $V_2 = 30$ dm^3 and $n = 3$ moles.

For isothermal expansion, temperature remains constant hence ΔE and ΔH are zero. The reversible work of expansion is given by

$$-W_{rev} = nRT\ln\frac{V_2}{V_1}$$

$$= (3 \text{ mol})(8.314\,\text{JK}^{-1}\text{mol}^{-1})(300 \text{ K})\left(2.303 \log\frac{30}{10}\right)$$

$$= 8.22 \text{ kJ}$$

Since $\Delta E = 0$

Therefore, $Q_{rev} = -W_{rev} = 8.22$ kJ

Thus, $\Delta E = 0$

$$\Delta H = 0$$

$$Q_{rev} = -W_{rev} = 8.22 \text{ kJ}$$

In case of a diatomic gas, these quantities remain unchanged.

Problem 5.12: Calculate Q, W, ΔE and ΔH for the conversion of a mole of water at 373 K and 1 atmosphere pressure to steam. Given $\Delta H_{vap, m} = 40.67$ kJ mol^{-1}, molar volume of liquid water and steam are 1.872×10^{-5} m^3 mol^{-1} and 3.033×10^{-2} m^3 mol^{-1} respectively.

Solution: At constant pressure

$$Q = Q_P = \Delta H_{vap, m}$$

$$= 40.67 \text{ kJ mol}^{-1}$$

and work involved during vapourisation is given by

$$-W = P\Delta V$$

$$= \left(1.013 \times 10^5 \text{ Nm}^{-2}\right)\left(3.033 \times 10^{-2} \text{ m}^3 \text{mol}^{-1} - 1.872 \times 10^{-5} \text{ m}^3 \text{mol}^{-1}\right)$$

$$= -3.07 \text{ kJ mol}^{-1}$$

From the first law of thermodynamics

$$\Delta E = Q + W$$

$$= 40.67 \text{ kJ mol}^{-1} - 3.07 \text{ kJ mol}^{-1}$$

$$= 37.60 \text{ kJ mol}^{-1}$$

Problem 5.13: A certain solid X exists in two solid modifications X_1 and X_2, X_2 is stable at higher temperature and X_1 at lower temperature. The transition temperature at 1 atmospheric pressure is 859 K. The molar volumes of X_2 and X_1 are 5.309×10^{-5} and 4.95×10^{-5} m^3 mol^{-1} respectively and the heat of transition is 27.2 kJ mol^{-1}. Calculate W, Q, ΔE and ΔH for the transformation of X_1 into X_2.

Solution: For solid-solid transformation, $\Delta E = \Delta H$.

Here
$$Q = \Delta H = \Delta E = 27.2 \text{ kJ mol}^{-1}$$

$$-W = P\Delta V$$

$$= \left(1.013 \times 10^5 \text{ Nm}^{-2}\right)\left(5.309 \times 10^{-5} \text{ m}^3 \text{mol}^{-1} - 4.95 \times 10^{-5} \text{ m}^3 \text{mol}^{-1}\right)$$

$$= 0.364 \text{ J mol}^{-1}$$

Problem 5.14: Calculate ΔE and ΔH when 100 dm^3 of Helium at STP are heated to 373 K in a closed container. Assuming that the gas behaves ideally and its $C_{V, m}$ is 12.55 Jmol$^-$ K^{-1}.

Solution:
$$\Delta E = nC_{V, m}\Delta T$$

$$= \left(\frac{100}{22.414} \text{ mol}\right)\left(12.55 \text{ J K}^{-1}\text{mol}^{-1}\right)(100 \text{ K})$$

$$= 5226 \text{ J}$$

and
$$= 5.226 \text{ kJ}$$

$$\Delta H = nC_{P, m}\Delta T$$

$$= \left(\frac{100}{22.414} \text{ mol}\right)\left(20.864 \text{ JK}^{-1} \text{ mol}^{-1}\right)(100 \text{ K})$$

$$= 9317 \text{ J}$$

$$= 9.317 \text{ kJ}$$

Problem 5.15: Show that

$$C_P - C_V = \left[V - \left(\frac{\partial H}{\partial P} \right)_T \right] \left(\frac{\partial P}{\partial T} \right)_V$$

Solution: From Eq. (5.38), we have

$$C_P - C_V = \left[P + \left(\frac{\partial E}{\partial V} \right)_T \right] \left(\frac{\partial V}{\partial T} \right)_P$$

Since

$$H = E + PV$$

$$dH = dE + PdV + VdP \qquad \qquad ...(i)$$

and

$$dH = C_P \, dT + \left(\frac{\partial H}{\partial P} \right)_T dP \qquad \qquad ...(ii)$$

$$dE = C_V \, dT + \left(\frac{\partial E}{\partial V} \right)_T dV \qquad \qquad ...(iii)$$

Substituting the values of dE and dH in Eq. (i)

$$C_P \, dT + \left(\frac{\partial H}{\partial P} \right)_T dP = C_V \, dT + \left(\frac{\partial E}{\partial V} \right)_T dV + PdV + VdP$$

If $dT = 0$

$$\left(\frac{\partial H}{\partial P} \right)_T dP = \left(\frac{\partial E}{\partial V} \right)_T dV + PdV + VdP$$

or

$$\left(\frac{\partial H}{\partial P} \right)_T = \left[\left(\frac{\partial E}{\partial V} \right)_T + P \right] \left(\frac{\partial V}{\partial P} \right)_T + V \qquad \qquad ...(iv)$$

$$\left[\left(\frac{\partial E}{\partial V} \right)_T + P \right] \left(\frac{\partial V}{\partial P} \right)_T = \left(\frac{\partial H}{\partial P} \right)_T - V$$

From cyclic rule

$$\left(\frac{\partial V}{\partial P} \right)_T \left(\frac{\partial P}{\partial T} \right)_V \left(\frac{\partial T}{\partial V} \right)_P = -1$$

$$\left(\frac{\partial V}{\partial P} \right)_T = -\left(\frac{\partial V}{\partial T} \right)_P \left(\frac{\partial T}{\partial P} \right)_V \qquad \qquad ...(v)$$

Substituting the value of $\left(\dfrac{\partial V}{\partial P}\right)_T$ in Eq. (*iv*), we get

$$-\left[\left(\frac{\partial E}{\partial V}\right)_T + P\right]\left(\frac{\partial V}{\partial T}\right)_P \left(\frac{\partial T}{\partial P}\right)_V = \left(\frac{\partial H}{\partial P}\right)_T - V$$

or

$$\left[\left(\frac{\partial E}{\partial V}\right)_T + P\right]\left(\frac{\partial V}{\partial T}\right)_P = \left[V - \left(\frac{\partial H}{\partial P}\right)_T\right]\left(\frac{\partial P}{\partial T}\right)_V$$

But the quantity on the left is equal to $(C_P - C_V)$ hence

$$C_P - C_V = \left[V - \left(\frac{\partial H}{\partial P}\right)_T\right]\left(\frac{\partial P}{\partial T}\right)_V$$

5.10 JOULE-THOMSON EFFECT

In the Joule experiment, the gas expands in vacuum and the temperature-drop of the system is zero if the gas were ideal. But Joule-Thomson investigated the change in temperature of a gas when it passes through a porous plug from a higher pressure to a lower pressure. The experimental set up is shown in Fig. 5.7. It consists of a thermally-insulated tube fitted with a porous plug and two weightless and frictionless pistons X and Y. Two sensitive thermometers (not shown in the figure) are placed on both sides of the porous plug to record the temperature. The whole apparatus is thermally insulated such that no heat enters or leaves the system. As the gas expands, a drop in temperature was observed. This drop in temperature was found to be proportional to the pressure difference maintained, *i.e.*, $\Delta T \propto \Delta P$.

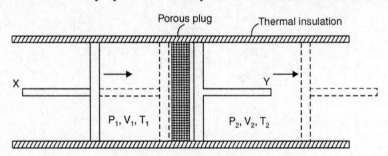

Fig. 5.7 The Joule-Thomson experiment

The thermodynamic interpretation of the experiment is as follows:

Consider that a certain amount of the gas is passed through the porous plug. The pressure and temperature on the left side of the porous plug are P_1 and T_1 and it occupies a volume V_1. On its right, same amount of the gas will be at a pressure P_2, temperature T_2 and will occupy a volume V_2. As the gas is compressed, work done on the gas is $P_1 V_1$ and the work done by the gas during expansion is $P_2 V_2$. Therefore, the total work done by the gas is

$$-W = P_2 V_2 - P_1 V_1 \qquad\qquad ...(5.44)$$

Since the expansion takes place adiabatically, $Q = 0$; the system therefore performs work at the cost of its internal energy.

From the first law of thermodynamics, we have

$$\Delta E = E_2 - E_1 = Q + W = W$$

or

$$E_2 - E_1 = -(P_2 V_2 - P_1 V_1)$$

or

$$E_2 + P_2 V_2 = E_1 + P_1 V_1$$

$$H_2 = H_1$$

or

$$\Delta H = H_2 - H_1 = 0 \qquad \qquad \text{...(5.45)}$$

It follows from Eq. (5.45) that in the expansion of the gas through the porous plug the enthalpy content remains unchanged, *i.e.*, the process is carried out at constant enthalpy (it is an isoenthalpic change).

The enthalpy of a system may be regarded as a function of temperature and pressure

$$H = f(P, T)$$

Since H is a state function, the differential dH is given by

$$dH = \left(\frac{\partial H}{\partial T}\right)_P dT + \left(\frac{\partial H}{\partial P}\right)_T dP \qquad \qquad \text{...(5.46)}$$

In Joule-Thomson experiment enthalpy remains constant, $dH = 0$ therefore

or

$$C_P \, dT + \left(\frac{\partial H}{\partial P}\right)_T dP = 0$$

$$\left(\frac{\partial T}{\partial P}\right)_H = \frac{-\left(\dfrac{\partial H}{\partial P}\right)_T}{C_P} \qquad \qquad \text{...(5.47)}$$

$$\mu_{JT} = -\left(\frac{\partial H}{\partial P}\right)_T \Big/ C_P \qquad \qquad \text{...(5.48)}$$

The quantity $\left(\dfrac{\partial T}{\partial P}\right)_H$ is known as the *Joule-Thomson coefficient* and is denoted by the symbol μ_{JT}. It gives the rate of change of temperature with pressure in isoenthalpic processes. Now, if we measure μ_{JT} and C_P, the value of $\left(\dfrac{\partial H}{\partial P}\right)_T$ can be calculated. Since

$$H = E + PV$$

Therefore,
$$\left(\frac{\partial H}{\partial P}\right)_T = \left(\frac{\partial E}{\partial P}\right)_T + \left(\frac{\partial(PV)}{\partial P}\right)_T$$

Substituting the value of $\left(\dfrac{\partial H}{\partial P}\right)_T$ in Eq. (5.47), we get

$$\mu_{JT} = -\frac{1}{C_P}\left[\left(\frac{\partial E}{\partial P}\right)_T + \left(\frac{\partial(PV)}{\partial P}\right)_T\right]$$

$$= -\frac{1}{C_P}\left[\left(\frac{\partial E}{\partial V}\right)_T\left(\frac{\partial V}{\partial P}\right)_T + \left(\frac{\partial(PV)}{\partial P}\right)_T\right] \qquad ...(5.49)$$

$$= -\frac{1}{C_P}\left(\frac{\partial E}{\partial V}\right)_T\left(\frac{\partial V}{\partial P}\right)_T - \frac{1}{C_P}\left(\frac{\partial(PV)}{\partial P}\right)_T \qquad ...(5.50)$$

Equation (5.50) is perfectly general and is applicable to all gases. For ideal gases, $\left(\dfrac{\partial E}{\partial V}\right)_T = 0$ and

$\left(\dfrac{\partial(PV)}{\partial P}\right)_T = 0$, hence

$$\mu_{JT} = 0 \qquad ...(5.51)$$

It is seen from above that in case of expansion of an ideal gas through a porous plug, there is no change in temperature of the gas.

In case of real gases, μ_{JT} is different from zero. In Eq. (5.49), the derivative, $\left(\dfrac{\partial E}{\partial V}\right)_T$ for a van der

Waals gas is approximately equal to a/V^2 and is usually positive. The factor $\left(\dfrac{\partial V}{\partial P}\right)_T$ is always negative

because the volume of a gas decreases with increase of pressure. As a result, the first term in Eq. (5.49)

is always positive. The term $\left(\dfrac{\partial(PV)}{\partial P}\right)_T$ is equal to slope of the *PV* versus *P* plot (Fig. 2.11); its

magnitude may be positive or negative depending upon the temperature and pressure of the gas. At low

temperatures and low pressures, $\left(\dfrac{\partial(PV)}{\partial P}\right)_T$ is negative. Under such conditions, both the terms in

Eq. (5.49) are positive. Consequently, μ_{JT} has a positive value; a cooling effect would be observed. At ordinary temperatures, $\left(\dfrac{\partial(PV)}{\partial P}\right)_T$ is negative at lower pressures except for Hydrogen and Helium. As

the pressure of the gas is increased, the quantity $\left(\dfrac{\partial(PV)}{\partial P}\right)_T$ decreases, passes through a minimum and

then increases, and eventually becomes positive. If its value exceeds that of the first term, μ_{JT} becomes

negative; a heating effect would be observed. At high temperatures $\left(\dfrac{\partial(PV)}{\partial P}\right)_T$ for all gases is positive

and so μ_{JT} is negative and the gases will show heating effects at these temperatures.

We may conclude that all gases show cooling effect at low temperatures, while a heating effect at high temperatures. The temperature at which neither heating nor cooling effect is observed in Joule-Thomson experiment is called the inversion temperature (T_i). At this temperature, $\mu_{JT} = 0$. The inversion temperature is characteristic of a gas. Gases like Hydrogen and Helium which at room temperature show a heating effect also show a cooling effect when the Joule-Thomson experiment is carried out at temperatures below their inversion temperatures.

Calculation of μ_{JT} and inversion temperature for a van der Waals gas: For a van der Waals gas, one can calculate the Joule-Thomson coefficient (μ_{JT}) using the treatment given above.

For a mole of van der Waals gas

$$\left(P + a/V^2\right)(V - b) = RT$$

or

$$PV + \frac{a}{V} - Pb - \frac{ab}{V^2} = RT$$

When pressure is not too large, the term ab/V^2 can be neglected, hence

$$PV + \frac{a}{V} - Pb = RT$$

$$PV = RT + Pb - \frac{a}{V} \qquad \qquad \dots(5.52)$$

As an approximation, we may replace V by RT/P, therefore,

$$V = \frac{RT}{P} - \frac{a}{RT} + b \qquad \qquad \dots(5.53)$$

Differentiating Eq. (5.53) with respect to T at constant pressure, we get

$$\left(\frac{\partial V}{\partial T}\right)_P = \frac{R}{P} + \frac{a}{RT^2} \qquad \qquad \dots(5.54)$$

Replacing $\dfrac{a}{V}$ by $\dfrac{aP}{RT}$ in Eq. (5.52) and rearranging we obtain

$$RT = P(V - b) + \frac{aP}{RT}$$

Dividing both sides by PT, gives

$$\frac{R}{P} = \frac{V - b}{T} + \frac{a}{RT^2}$$

Substituting the value of R/P in Eq. (5.54), we get

$$\left(\frac{\partial V}{\partial T}\right)_P = \frac{V - b}{T} + \frac{a}{RT^2} + \frac{a}{RT^2}$$

$$= \frac{V - b}{T} + \frac{2a}{RT^2}$$

$$T\left(\frac{\partial V}{\partial T}\right)_P = (V - b) + \frac{2a}{RT}$$

or

$$T\left(\frac{\partial V}{\partial T}\right)_P - V = \frac{2a}{RT} - b \qquad \text{...(5.55)}$$

Using the thermodynamic equation of state

$$\left(\frac{\partial H}{\partial P}\right)_T = V - T\left(\frac{\partial V}{\partial T}\right)_P \qquad \text{...(5.56)}$$

and substituting the value of $(\partial H/\partial P]_T$ in Eq. (5.47) we obtain

$$\left(\frac{\partial T}{\partial P}\right)_H = -\frac{1}{C_{P,m}}\left[V - T\left(\frac{\partial V}{\partial T}\right)_P\right] \qquad \text{...(5.57)}$$

On comparing Eqs. (5.55) and (5.57), we get

$$\left(\frac{\partial T}{\partial P}\right)_H = \mu_{JT} = \frac{1}{C_{P,m}}\left[\frac{2a}{RT} - b\right] \qquad \text{...(5.58)}$$

From Eq. (5.58), it is clear that μ_{JT} for a gas depends on $C_{P,m}$, a, b, R and T. Since all other quantities except T are constants for a gas, therefore the Joule-Thomson coefficient (μ_{JT}) depends upon the temperature of the gas. At low temperature, the term $2a/RT$ involving attractive forces between the molecules predominates $\left(\frac{2a}{RT} > b\right)$, hence μ_{JT} is positive. At high temperatures, $\frac{2a}{RT} < b$, and μ_{JT} is negative. For Hydrogen or Helium, where a is small, $\frac{2a}{RT}$ even at ordinary temperatures is less than b and so a heating effect is observed in Joule-Thomson experiment.

At the inversion temperature $(T = T_i)$, $\mu_{JT} = 0$ therefore, we have

$$\frac{2a}{RT_i} - b = 0$$

or

$$T_i = \frac{2a}{Rb}$$

Thus, the inversion temperature of a gas depends upon the values of van der Waals constants a and b.

Problem 5.16: Prove that if $\left(\dfrac{\partial E}{\partial V}\right)_T = 0$, then it does not necessarily follow that

$$\left(\frac{\partial H}{\partial V}\right)_T = 0$$

Solution:

$$H = E + PV$$

$$dH = dE + d(PV)$$

$$\left(\frac{\partial H}{\partial V}\right)_T = \left(\frac{\partial E}{\partial V}\right)_T + \left[\frac{\partial (PV)}{\partial V}\right]_T$$

If

$$\left(\frac{\partial E}{\partial V}\right)_T = 0, \text{ then}$$

$$\left(\frac{\partial H}{\partial V}\right)_T = \left[\frac{\partial (PV)}{\partial V}\right]_T$$

Now $\left[\dfrac{\partial (PV)}{\partial V}\right]_T = 0$, only if $(PV)_T$ is constant, *i.e.*, the gas is ideal. Hence

$$\left(\frac{\partial H}{\partial V}\right)_T = 0$$

only if the gas is ideal.

Problem 5.17: Prove that $\left(\dfrac{\partial C_P}{\partial P}\right)_T = -\mu_{JT}\left(\dfrac{\partial C_P}{\partial T}\right)_P - C_P\left(\dfrac{\partial \mu_{JT}}{\partial T}\right)_P$

Solution:

$$C_P = \left(\frac{\partial H}{\partial T}\right)_P$$

Differentiating with respect to pressure at constant temperature, we get

$$\left(\frac{\partial C_P}{\partial P}\right)_T = \frac{\partial}{\partial P}\left(\frac{\partial H}{\partial T}\right)_P$$

$$= \frac{\partial^2 H}{\partial P \partial T} = \left[\frac{\partial}{\partial T}\left(\frac{\partial H}{\partial P}\right)_T\right] \qquad \dots(a)$$

From Eq. (5.47)

$$\left(\frac{\partial T}{\partial P}\right)_H = \frac{-\left(\frac{\partial H}{\partial P}\right)_T}{C_P}$$

$$\left(\frac{\partial H}{\partial P}\right)_T = -C_P\left(\frac{\partial T}{\partial P}\right)_H$$

$$= -C_P\,\mu_{JT}$$

Substituting the value of $\left(\frac{\partial H}{\partial P}\right)_T$ in Eq. (a), we get

$$\left[\frac{\partial C_P}{\partial P}\right]_P = \frac{\partial}{\partial T}\left[-C_P\mu_{JT}\right]$$

$$= -\mu_{JT}\left(\frac{\partial C_P}{\partial T}\right)_P - C_P\left(\frac{\partial \mu_{JT}}{\partial T}\right)_P$$

Problem 5.18: Calculate μ_{JT} for a certain gas at 300 K and 100 atmospheres taking $C_{P,m}$ as 35.15 JK^{-1} mol^{-1}. The van der Waals constants a and b are respectively 0.139 Nm^4 mol^{-2} and 3.92×10^{-5}m^3 mol^{-1}. Also predict the inversion temperature of the gas.

Solution:
$$\mu_{JT} = \frac{1}{C_{P,m}}\left[\frac{2a}{RT} - b\right]$$

$$= \frac{1}{\left(35.15\,\text{JK}^{-1}\text{mol}^{-1}\right)}\left[\frac{2 \times 0.139\,\text{N m}^4\text{mol}^{-2}}{\left(8.314\,\text{JK}^{-1}\text{mol}^{-1}\right)(300\,\text{K})} - 3.92 \times 10^{-5}\,\text{m}^3\text{mol}^{-1}\right]$$

$$= \frac{1}{\left(35.15\,\text{N m K}^{-1}\text{mol}^{-1}\right)}\left[\frac{0.278\,\text{N m}^4\text{mol}^{-1}}{2494.2\,\text{N m}} - 3.92 \times 10^{-5}\,\text{m}^3\text{mol}^{-1}\right]$$

$$= \frac{1}{35.15\,\mathrm{N\,m\,K^{-1}mol^{-1}}}\left[0.722 \times 10^{-4}\,\mathrm{m^3\,mol^{-1}}\right]$$

$$= 2.054 \times 10^{-6}\,\mathrm{K}\left(\mathrm{N\,m^{-2}}\right)^{-1}$$

$$= 2.054 \times 10^{-6} \times 1.013 \times 10^{5}\,\mathrm{K\,atm^{-1}}$$

$$= 0.2081\,\mathrm{K\,atm^{-1}}$$

At the inversion temperature $\mu_{JT} = 0$, therefore

$$T_i = \frac{2a}{Rb}$$

$$= \frac{2\left(0.139\,\mathrm{N\,m^4\,mol^{-2}}\right)}{\left(8.314\,\mathrm{N\,m\,K^{-1}mol^{-1}}\right)\left(3.92 \times 10^{-5}\,\mathrm{m^3\,mol^{-1}}\right)}$$

$$= 853\,\mathrm{K}$$

Problem 5.19: The Joule-Thomson co-efficient for a van der Waals gas is given by

$$\mu_{JT} = \frac{1}{C_{P,\,m}}\left[\frac{2a}{RT} - b\right] = \left(\frac{\partial T}{\partial P}\right)_H$$

Calculate the value of ΔH for the isothermal compression of 1 mole of nitrogen from 1 to 500 atmospheres at 300 K; $a = 0.1353\,\mathrm{Nm^4\,mol^{-2}}$, $b = 0.039 \times 10^{-3}\,\mathrm{m^3\,mol^{-1}}$.

Solution:
$$\mu_{JT} = \frac{1}{C_{P,m}}\left[\frac{2a}{RT} - b\right] = \left(\frac{\partial T}{\partial P}\right)_H$$

Also
$$\left(\frac{\partial T}{\partial P}\right)_H = -\frac{1}{C_{P,\,m}}\left(\frac{\partial H}{\partial P}\right)_T$$

Therefore,
$$-\frac{1}{C_{P,\,m}}\left(\frac{\partial H}{\partial P}\right)_T = \frac{1}{C_{P,\,m}}\left[\frac{2a}{RT} - b\right]$$

$$-\left(\frac{\partial H}{\partial P}\right)_T = \left[\frac{2a}{RT} - b\right]$$

$$= \frac{\left(2 \times 0.1353\,\mathrm{Nm^4\,mol^{-2}}\right)}{\left(8.314\,\mathrm{JK^{-1}mol^{-1}}\right)\left(300\,\mathrm{K}\right)} - \left(0.039 \times 10^{-3}\,\mathrm{m^3\,mol^{-1}}\right)$$

$$= \frac{0.2706\,\mathrm{N\,m^4\,mol^{-1}}}{\left(8.314\,\mathrm{J} \times 300\right)} - \left(0.039 \times 10^{-3}\,\mathrm{m^3\,mol^{-1}}\right)$$

$$= \frac{0.2706 \text{ Nm}^4\text{mol}^{-1}}{2494.2 \text{ Nm}} - \left(0.039 \times 10^{-3}\text{m}^3\text{mol}^{-1}\right) \qquad \left[\because 1\text{J} = 1 \text{ Nm}\right]$$

$$= \left(1.084 \times 10^{-4}\text{m}^3\text{mol}^{-1}\right) - \left(0.039 \times 10^{-3}\text{m}^3\text{mol}^{-1}\right)$$

$$= 0.694 \times 10^{-1}\text{m}^3\text{mol}^{-1}$$

$$-\left(\frac{\partial H}{\partial P}\right)_T = -\left(\frac{\Delta H}{\Delta P}\right)_T = 0.694 \times 10^{-4}\text{m}^3\text{mol}^{-1}$$

Now
$$\Delta P = (500 - 1) = 499 \text{ atm}$$

$$= 499 \times 1.01 \times 10^5 \text{ Nm}^{-2}$$

Therefore,
$$-\Delta H = \left(0.694 \times 10^{-1}\text{m}^3\text{mol}^{-1}\right)\left(499 \times 1.01 \times 10^5\text{Nm}^{-2}\right)$$

$$= 3497 \text{ J mol}^{-1}$$

or,
$$\Delta H = -3497 \text{ J mol}^{-1}$$

$$= -3.497 \text{ kJ mol}^{-1}$$

5.11 ADIABATIC CHANGES IN STATE

Reversible adiabatic changes: In an adiabatic change, there is no transfer of heat between the system and the surroundings, *i.e.*, δQ for an infinitesimal change is zero. Hence, from the first law, we have

$$dE = \delta W \qquad \qquad ...(5.59)$$

For a finite change

$$\Delta E = W \qquad \qquad ...(5.60)$$

Any work done by the system will be at the expense of the internal energy of the system, while work done on the system will increase the internal energy of the system. Since internal energy is a function of temperature, consequently, the temperature of the system will change during the adiabatic transformation. When the system expands, it performs work and the final temperature will be less than the initial temperature. In compression, on the other hand, work is done on the system and its final temperature will increase. If the work is only pressure-volume work of expansion or compression, then Eq. (5.59) becomes

$$dE = -P_{\text{ext}} dV \qquad \qquad ...(5.61)$$

It is clear from Eq. (5.61) that dV is positive in expansion and therefore dE is negative. In compression, dV is negative, hence dE is positive. If the process is carried out reversibly, the actual pressure (P) of the system is virtually identical with the external pressure P_{ext}. For a mole of an ideal gas, $dE = nC_{V,m}dT$ and hence Eq. (5.59) becomes

$$dE = nC_{V,m} dT = -PdV \qquad \qquad ...(5.62)$$

The sign of dT and dV in adiabatic reversible changes are opposite. For example, when the gas expands, temperature of the gas will fall, whereas if it contracts its temperature will rise. The total energy change ΔE or W can be calculated by integrating Eq. (5.62) within the specified limits.

$$\int_{E_1}^{E_2} dE = nC_{V,m} \int_{T_1}^{T_2} dT$$

$$\Delta E = E_2 - E_1 = nC_{V,m}(T_2 - T_1)$$

For a mole of an ideal gas $T = \dfrac{PV}{R}$ and therefore,

$$\Delta E = C_{V,m}\left(\frac{P_2 V_2}{R} - \frac{P_1 V_1}{R}\right)$$

$$= \frac{C_{V,m}}{R}(P_2 V_2 - P_1 V_1)$$

$$= C_{V,m}\frac{(P_2 V_2 - P_1 V_1)}{C_{P,m} - C_{V,m}} \qquad (\because C_{P,m} - C_{V,m} = R)$$

$$= \frac{P_2 V_2 - P_1 V_1}{\dfrac{C_{P,m}}{C_{V,m}} - 1}$$

$$= \frac{P_2 V_2 - P_1 V_1}{\gamma - 1} \qquad \left(\because \frac{C_{P,m}}{C_{V,m}} = \gamma\right) \qquad ...(5.63)$$

Therefore, we have

$$\Delta E = nC_{V,m}(T_2 - T_1) = W \qquad ...(5.64)$$

for n moles of an ideal gas.

The enthalpy change, ΔH in a reversible adiabatic transformation is given by

$$\Delta H = H_2 - H_1$$

$$= (E_2 + P_2 V_2) - (E_1 + P_1 V_1)$$

$$= (E_2 - E_1) + (P_2 V_2 - P_1 V_1)$$

$$= \Delta E + (nRT_2 - nRT_1)$$

For an ideal gas, we have

$$\Delta H = nC_{V,\,m}\left(T_2 - T_1\right) + nR\left(T_2 - T_1\right)$$

$$= \left(nC_{V,\,m} + nR\right)\left(T_2 - T_1\right) \qquad \qquad ...(5.65a)$$

Hence, for an ideal gas

$$\Delta H = nC_{P,\,m}\left(T_2 - T_1\right) \qquad \qquad ...(5.65b)$$

Thus the magnitudes of W, ΔE and ΔH can be calculated provided we know P_1, V_1, T_1 and P_2, T_2 and the heat capacities $C_{P,\,m}$ and $C_{V,\,m}$.

Relationship between temperature and volume in reversible adiabatic changes: For a mole of an ideal gas $P = \dfrac{RT}{V}$ and from Eq. (5.62), we have

$$C_{V,\,m}\, dT = -\frac{RT}{V}\, dV$$

$$C_{V,\,m}\, \frac{dT}{T} = -R \frac{dV}{V}$$

If $C_{V,\,m}$ is assumed to be temperature independent, then it is possible to integrate the above equation within the specified limits. The result is

$$C_{V,m}\int_{T_1}^{T_2} \frac{dT}{T} = -R\int_{V_1}^{V_2} \frac{dV}{V}$$

$$C_{V,\,m}\, \ln\frac{T_2}{T_1} = -R\ln\frac{V_2}{V_1} \qquad \qquad ...(5.66)$$

$$= R\ln\frac{V_1}{V_2}$$

$$\ln\frac{T_2}{T_1} = \frac{R}{C_{V,\,m}}\ln\frac{V_1}{V_2}$$

$$\frac{T_2}{T_1} = \left(\frac{V_1}{V_2}\right)^{R/C_{V,\,m}} = \left(\frac{V_1}{V_2}\right)^{\gamma-1} \qquad \left[\because r - 1 = \frac{R}{C_{V,m}}\right] \qquad ...(5.67)$$

or
$$TV^{\gamma-1} = \text{constant} \qquad \qquad ...(5.68)$$

Pressure-volume relation in reversible adiabatic changes: For an ideal gas

$$\frac{P_1 V_1}{T_1} = \frac{P_2 V_2}{T_2}$$

or
$$\left(\frac{T_2}{T_1}\right) = \frac{P_2 V_2}{P_1 V_1}$$

Substituting the value of T_2/T_1 in Eq. (5.67), we get

$$\frac{P_2 V_2}{P_1 V_1} = \left(\frac{V_1}{V_2}\right)^{R/C_{V,m}} = \left(\frac{V_1}{V_2}\right)^{\gamma-1}$$

$$\frac{P_2}{P_1} = \left(\frac{V_1}{V_2}\right)^{(R/C_{V,m})-1} = \left(\frac{V_1}{V_2}\right)^{\gamma} \qquad \qquad ...(5.69)$$

$$PV^r = \text{constant} \qquad \qquad ...(5.70)$$

In an isothermal process, PV = constant, while for an adiabatic change PV^r is constant. As $\gamma = \dfrac{C_{P,m}}{C_{V,m}}$ and is always greater than one, it follows therefore that if the pressure of a gas be reduced to the same extent isothermally and adiabatically the final volume in an adiabatic process would be less than that in the isothermal process. This is indicated in Fig. 5.8. Since the area under P-V curve is equal to the work done, it is obvious that the magnitude of work is more in isothermal expansion than in adiabatic expansion for the same change in pressure or volume.

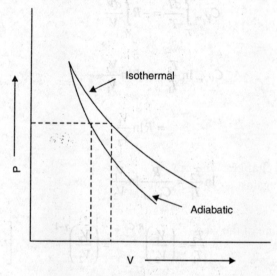

Fig. 5.8 Isothermal and adiabatic reversible expansions of an ideal gas from the same initial pressure and volume

Pressure temperature relation in reversible adiabatic changes: From ideal gas laws, we have

$$\frac{V_1}{V_2} = \frac{P_2 T_1}{P_1 T_2}$$

Substituting the value of V_1/V_2 in Eq. (5.67), we get

$$\frac{T_2}{T_1} = \left(\frac{P_2 T_1}{P_1 T_2}\right)^{R/C_{V.m}} = \left(\frac{P_2 T_1}{P_1 T_2}\right)^{\gamma-1}$$

$$\left(\frac{T_2}{T_1}\right)\left(\frac{T_2}{T_1}\right)^{\gamma-1} = \left(\frac{P_2}{P_1}\right)^{\gamma-1}$$

$$\left(\frac{T_2}{T_1}\right)^{\gamma} = \left(\frac{P_2}{P_1}\right)^{\gamma-1}$$

$$\left(\frac{T_2}{T_1}\right) = \left(\frac{P_2}{P_1}\right)^{\gamma-1/\gamma}$$

Hence

$$\left(\frac{T_2}{T_1}\right) = \left(\frac{P_2}{P_1}\right)^{R/C_{P,m}} \qquad \left(\because \frac{\gamma-1}{\gamma} = \frac{R}{C_{P,m}}\right) \qquad \text{...(5.71)}$$

$$\frac{T_2}{P_2^{R/C_{P,m}}} = \frac{T_1}{P_1^{R/C_{P,m}}} = \text{constant} \qquad \text{...(5.72)}$$

From Eqs. (5.67), (5.69) and (5.71), we can summarise the results as

$$\frac{T_2}{T_1} = \left(\frac{V_1}{V_2}\right)^{R/C_{V.m}} = \left(\frac{P_2}{P_1}\right)^{R/C_{P,m}}$$

or

$$\frac{1}{R}\ln\frac{T_2}{T_1} = \frac{1}{C_{V,m}}\ln\frac{V_1}{V_2} = \frac{1}{C_{P,m}}\ln\frac{P_2}{P_1}$$

Adiabatic irreversible changes: The irreversible work of expansion or compression for an ideal gas in an adiabatic change against a constant external pressure is given by

$$-W_{\text{irr}} = P_{\text{ext}}\Delta V$$

If $P_{\text{ext}} = P_2 =$ the final pressure of the gas

$$-W_{\text{irr}} = P_2(V_2 - V_1)$$

and

$$\Delta E = W_{\text{irr}} = -P_2(V_2 - V_1) = nC_{V,m}(T_2 - T_1)$$

But

$$V_2 = \frac{nRT_2}{P_2} \quad \text{and} \quad V_1 = \frac{nRT_1}{P_1}$$

Therefore,
$$\Delta E = W_{irr} = -P_2 \left(\frac{nRT_2}{P_2} - \frac{nRT_1}{P_1} \right)$$

$$= nC_{V,\,m}(T_2 - T_1)$$

or
$$RT_1 \frac{P_2}{P_1} - RT_2 = C_{V,m}(T_2 - T_1)$$

Hence
$$T_2 = T_1 \frac{R\left(\dfrac{P_2}{P_1}\right) + C_{V,\,m}}{C_{P,\,m}} \qquad \qquad ...(5.73)$$

ΔE can therefore be calculated once T_2 is known. The enthalpy change ΔH is given by

$$\Delta H = nC_{P,\,m}(T_2 - T_1)$$

Adiabatic free expansion: Here the gas expands against zero external pressure, *i.e.*, in vacuum and hence no work is done by the gas during expansion. So

$$W_{irr} = 0$$

$$Q = 0$$

$$\Delta E = W_{irr} = nC_{V,\,m}(T_2 - T_1) = 0$$

$$\Delta H = nC_{P,\,m}(T_2 - T_1) = 0$$

and
$$T_1 = T_2$$

Hence, all the quantities W, Q, ΔE and ΔH are zero in adiabatic free expansion of an ideal gas. If we compare these quantities with those in isothermal expansion, we observe that adiabatic free expansion is identical with isothermal free expansion. Hence, we conclude that every adiabatic free expansion has to be isothermal and vice versa.

Unlike isothermal changes, the final states for reversible and irreversible adiabatic transformations are different; hence ΔE and ΔH in each case are different.

5.12 CALCULATIONS OF W, Q, ΔE AND ΔH FOR A VAN DER WAALS GAS

We shall consider the calculations of these quantities for reversible and irreversible isothermal and adiabatic transformations.

(*i*) **Reversible isothermal changes:** The work of expansion or compression for isothermal transformations as given by Eq. (5.18) is

$$-W_{rev,\,vd} = nRT \ln \frac{V_2 - nb}{V_1 - nb} + an^2 \left(\frac{1}{V_2} - \frac{1}{V_1} \right)$$

Since
$$dE = nC_{V,\,m}dT + \left(\frac{\partial E}{\partial V} \right)_T dV$$

and for a van der Waals gas, the quantity $\dfrac{an^2}{V^2}$ is a measure of internal pressure, *i.e.*, $\left(\dfrac{\partial E}{\partial V}\right)_T$, hence

$$dE = \left(\frac{\partial E}{\partial V}\right)_T dV = \frac{an^2}{V^2} dV \qquad \qquad ...(5.74)$$

($\because dT = 0$ for isothermal processes)

The total change in energy is obtained by integrating the above equation

$$\Delta E = \int_{V_1}^{V_2} \frac{an^2}{V^2} dV$$

$$= an^2 \left[\frac{1}{V_1} - \frac{1}{V_2}\right] \qquad \qquad ...(5.75)$$

The enthalpy change is given by

$$\Delta H = \Delta E + \Delta (PV)$$

$$= \Delta E + P_2 V_2 - P_1 V_1$$

But PV for a van der Waals gas is

$$PV = \frac{nRTV}{V - nb} - \frac{an^2}{V}$$

Hence,

$$\Delta H = an^2 \left(\frac{1}{V_1} - \frac{1}{V_2}\right) + nRT \left(\frac{V_2}{V_2 - nb} - \frac{V_1}{V_1 - nb}\right) + an^2 \left(\frac{1}{V_1} - \frac{1}{V_2}\right)$$

$$= nRT \left(\frac{V_2}{V_2 - nb} - \frac{V_1}{V_1 - nb}\right) + 2an^2 \left(\frac{1}{V_1} - \frac{1}{V_2}\right) \qquad \qquad ...(5.77)$$

But $\dfrac{V_2}{V_2 - nb} - \dfrac{V_1}{V_1 - nb}$ on simplification yields

$$\frac{V_1 nb - V_2 nb}{(V_2 - nb)(V_1 - nb)}$$

Partial factorisation of the above expression gives

$$\frac{V_1 nb - V_2 nb}{(V_2 - nb)(V_1 - nb)} = nb \left[\frac{1}{V_2 - nb} - \frac{1}{V_1 - nb}\right]$$

Hence,
$$\Delta H = n^2 bRT \left[\frac{1}{V_2 - nb} - \frac{1}{V_1 - nb} \right] + 2an^2 \left(\frac{1}{V_1} - \frac{1}{V_2} \right)$$

Now
$$Q = \Delta E - W$$

$$= an^2 \left(\frac{1}{V_1} - \frac{1}{V_2} \right) + nRT \ln \frac{V_2 - nb}{V_1 - nb} + an^2 \left(\frac{1}{V_2} - \frac{1}{V_1} \right)$$

$$= nRT \ln \frac{V_2 - nb}{V_1 - nb} \qquad \qquad ...(5.77)$$

It may be noted that ΔE and ΔH are not zero for a van der Waals gas in isothermal changes.

(ii) **Adiabatic reversible transformations:** Since $Q = 0$ and $\Delta E = W$ and

$$dE = C_V dT + \left(\frac{\partial E}{\partial V} \right)_T dV$$

$$= nC_{V,\,m} dT + \frac{an^2}{V^2} dV$$

Integrating we get

$$\Delta E = nC_{V,\,m} (T_2 - T_1) + an^2 \left(\frac{1}{V_1} - \frac{1}{V_2} \right) = W \qquad \qquad ...(5.78)$$

and
$$\Delta H = \Delta E + \Delta (PV) \qquad \qquad ...(5.79)$$

Relation between temperature and volume for a van der Waals gas in reversible adiabatic transformations: Since

$$dE = C_{V,\,m} dT + \left(\frac{\partial E}{\partial V} \right)_T dV$$

and
$$\left(\frac{\partial E}{\partial V} \right)_T = \frac{a}{V^2} \text{ (for a mole of the gas)}$$

Therefore,
$$dE = C_{V,\,m} dT + \frac{a}{V^2} dV$$

In adiabatic changes, $Q = 0$ and $\Delta E = W$, hence

$$dE = C_{V,\,m} dT + \frac{a}{V^2} dV = -PdV$$

But
$$P = \frac{RT}{V - b} - \frac{a}{V^2}$$

for a mole of van der Waals gas. Substituting the value of P in the above equation, we get

$$C_{V,m} dT + \frac{a}{V^2} dV = -\frac{RT dV}{V-b} + \frac{a}{V^2} dV$$

or

$$C_{V,m} \frac{dT}{T} = -R \frac{dV}{V-b}$$

Integrating the above equation, we get

$$C_{V,m} \ln \frac{T_2}{T_1} = -R \ln \frac{V_2 - b}{V_1 - b}$$

$$(T_2)^{C_{V,m}/R} (V_2 - b) = (T_1)^{C_{V,m}/R} (V_1 - b)$$

or

$$T_2 = T_1 \left(\frac{V_1 - b}{V_2 - b} \right)^{R/C_{V,m}} \qquad ...(5.80)$$

(iii) **Isothermal irreversible changes:** Since E and H are state functions, ΔE and ΔH would be the same as for the reversible changes but Q and W would be different from the reversible isothermal values. $(-W_{irr})$ is given by

$$-W_{irr} = P_{ext}(V_2 - V_1); \text{ if } P_{ext} = P_2, \text{ then}$$

$$-W_{irr} = P_2(V_2 - V_1) = \left(\frac{nRT}{V_2 - nb} - \frac{an^2}{V_2^2} \right)(V_2 - V_1) \qquad ...(5.81)$$

As

$$\Delta E = an^2 \left(\frac{1}{V_1} - \frac{1}{V_2} \right)$$

$$Q = \Delta E - W_{irr} = P_{ext}(V_2 - V_1) + an^2 \left(\frac{1}{V_1} - \frac{1}{V_2} \right)$$

$$= \left(\frac{nRT}{V_2 - nb} - \frac{an^2}{V_2^2} \right)(V_2 - V_1) + an^2 \left(\frac{1}{V_1} - \frac{1}{V_2} \right) \qquad ...(5.82)$$

(iv) **Adiabatic irreversible changes:** Q will be zero and

$$\Delta E = nC_{V,m}(T_2 - T_1) + an^2 \left(\frac{1}{V_1} - \frac{1}{V_2} \right) = W_{irr} = P_2(V_2 - V_1)$$

and

$$\Delta H = \Delta E + \Delta(PV)$$

Problem 5.20: One mole of air at 750 K is expanded reversibly and adiabatically from 1 dm³ to 10 dm³. Taking $C_{V,m}$ for air as 20.92 JK⁻¹ mol⁻¹ and assuming ideal behaviour, calculate the final temperature, ΔE, ΔH and ΔW.

Solution: $V_1 = 1 \text{ dm}^3$, $V_2 = 10 \text{ dm}^3$, $T_1 = 750 \text{ K}$, $T_2 = ?$

$$C_{v,m} = 20.92 \text{ JK}^{-1} \text{ mol}^{-1}, \ R = 8.314 \text{ JK}^{-1}\text{mol}^{-1}$$

$$C_{V,m} = C_{P,m} + R = 29.234 \text{ JK}^{-1}\text{mol}^{-1}$$

We have

$$\frac{T_2}{750} = \left(\frac{1}{10}\right)^{\frac{8.314}{20.92}}$$

$$\log T_2 = \log 750 + \frac{8.314}{20.92} \log\left(\frac{1}{10}\right)$$

On simplification, we get

$$T_2 = 300.2 \text{ K}$$

$$\Delta E = C_{V,m}\left(T_2 - T_1\right) = -W$$

$$= 20.92 \text{ JK}^{-1}\text{mol}^{-1}(300.2 - 750) \text{ K}$$

$$= -9406 \text{ J mol}^{-1} = -9.406 \text{ kJ mol}^{-1}$$

$$-W = 9.406 \text{ kJ mol}^{-1}$$

$$\Delta H = C_{P,m}\left(T_2 - T_1\right)$$

$$= 29.234(300.2 - 750)\text{J mol}^{-1}$$

$$= -13140 \text{ J mol}^{-1} = -13.140 \text{ kJ mol}^{-1}$$

Problem 5.21: 0.084 kg of Nitrogen initially at 300 K and 10 atmospheres expands adiabatically against a constant pressure of 1 atmosphere.

Assuming that the gas behaves ideally, calculate the final temperature, final volume, W, ΔE and ΔH. Molar heat capacity ($C_{p,m}$) of the gas is 29.13 JK^{-1} mol^{-1}.

Solution: Number of moles of the gas is $\dfrac{0.084 \text{ kg}}{0.028 \text{ kg mol}^{-1}} = 3$ moles

$$C_{P,m} = 29.13 \text{ JK}^{-1}\text{mol}^{-1}$$

and $C_{V,m} = 20.816 \text{ JK}^{-1}\text{mol}^{-1}$

Initial pressure is 10 atm and initial temperature is 300 K.

Hence, the initial volume is given by

$$V_1 = \frac{nRT_1}{P_1}$$

$$= \frac{(3 \text{ mol})(0.0821 \text{ dm}^3 \text{ atm K}^{-1} \text{ mol}^{-1})(300 \text{ K})}{(10 \text{ atm})}$$

$$= 7.389 \text{ dm}^3$$

The final temperature (T_2) is given by

$$T_2 = T_1 \frac{C_{V,m} + R\dfrac{P_2}{P_1}}{C_{P,m}}$$

$$= 300 \text{ K} \frac{20.816 \text{ JK}^{-1}\text{mol}^{-1} + 8.314 \text{ JK}^{-1}\text{mol}^{-1}(1/10)}{29.13 \text{ JK}^{-1}\text{mol}^{-1}}$$

$$= 223.0 \text{ K}$$

The final volume V_2 is given by

$$V_2 = \frac{P_1 V_1}{T_1} \times \frac{T_2}{P_2}$$

$$= \frac{(10 \text{ atm})}{(1 \text{ atm})}(7.389 \text{ dm}^3)\frac{(230 \text{ K})}{(300 \text{ K})}$$

$$= 54.93 \text{ dm}^3$$

Now

$$\Delta E = nC_{V,m}(T_2 - T_1)$$

$$= (3 \text{ mol})(20.816 \text{ JK}^{-1}\text{mol}^{-1})(223 \text{ K} - 300 \text{ K})$$

$$= -4.809 \text{ kJ}$$

and

$$\Delta H = nC_{P,m}(T_2 - T_1)$$

$$= (3 \text{ mol})(29.13 \text{ JK}^{-1}\text{mol}^{-1})(223 - 300)\text{K}$$

$$= -6.613 \text{ kJ}$$

Problem 5.22: One mole of an ideal gas $(C_{V,m} = 12.55 \text{ JK}^{-1} \text{ mol}^{-1})$ at 300 K is compressed adiabatically and reversibly to one fourth of its original volume. What is the final temperature of the gas?

Solution: $\qquad T_1 = 300 \text{ K}; \; V_1 = 4x \text{ dm}^3$

$$T_2 = ? \quad V_2 = x \, dm^2$$

$$\frac{T_2}{T_1} = \left(\frac{V_2}{V_1}\right)^{R/C_V}$$

$$T_2 = 300 \left(\frac{4}{1}\right)^{9.314/12.55} = 752 \, K$$

Problem 5.23: To what pressure must a certain ideal gas ($\gamma = 1.4$) at 373 K and 1 atmosphere pressure be compressed adiabatically in order to raise its temperature to 773 K?

Solution: $\qquad T_1 = 373 \, K; \; P_1 = 1 \, atm$

$$T_2 = 773 \, K; \; P_2 = ?$$

$$\gamma = \frac{C_{P,\,m}}{C_{V,\,m}} = 1.40$$

We know $\qquad\qquad\qquad \dfrac{T_2}{T_1} = \left(\dfrac{P_2}{P_1}\right)^{\frac{\gamma-1}{\gamma}}$

$$\frac{673}{373} = \left(\frac{P_2}{1}\right)^{\frac{1.4-1}{1.4}}$$

or $\qquad\qquad\qquad P_2 = 7.89 \, atm$

Problem 5.24: One mole of an ideal monatomic gas initially at a temperature T_1, pressure P_1 and volume V_1 in a thermally-insulated cylinder closed at one end and fitted with a movable piston at the other end is suddenly compressed by placing a weight on the piston. The gas pressure is raised by $2P$. Prove that the rise in temperature (ΔT) is $\dfrac{2}{5} T_1$ and the change in volume $\Delta V = -\dfrac{3RT_1}{10P_1}$.

Solution: The gas is compressed adiabatically, $Q = 0$, therefore

$$\Delta E = -W$$

$$C_{V,m} \, \Delta T = -P_{ext} \Delta V$$

$$= -2P_1(V_2 - V_1) \qquad\qquad\qquad (\because P_{ext} = 2P_1)$$

$$= -RT_2 + 2RT_1 \qquad\qquad (\because 2P_1 \times V_2 = RT_2 \text{ and } P_1 V_1 = RT_1)$$

$$= -RT_2 + RT_1 + RT_1$$

$$= -R(T_2 - T_1) + RT_1$$

$$= -R\Delta T + RT_1$$

But $C_{V,m} = \dfrac{3}{2} R$ for an ideal monatomic gas therefore

$$\frac{5}{2} R\Delta T = RT_1$$

$$\Delta T = \frac{2}{5} T_1$$

Again, $C_{V,m} \Delta T = -2P_1 \Delta V$

$$C_{V,m} \frac{2}{5} T_1 = 2P_1 \Delta V$$

$$\frac{3}{2} R \frac{2}{5} T_1 = -2P_1 \Delta V$$

or $$\Delta V = -\frac{3RT_1}{10P_1}$$

The negative sign indicates that the final volume is less than the initial volume.

Problem 5.25: One mole of Nitrogen at 300 K and 20 atmospheres expands to 2 atmospheres. Calculate, assuming ideal behaviour, W, Q, ΔE and ΔH if the expansions were (*i*) isothermal and reversible, (*ii*) isothermal and irreversible, (*iii*) adiabatic reversible, and (*iv*) adiabatic irreversible. Also calculate the final volume of the gas in each case. Given $C_{V,m} = 20.816$ JK^{-1} mol^{-1} and $C_{P,m} = 29.13$ JK^{-1}mol^{-1}.

Solution: (*i*) For isothermal reversible expansion, $T_1 = T_2 = 300$ K, hence

$$\Delta E = \Delta H = 0$$

and $$-W = Q = nRT \ln \frac{P_1}{P_2}$$

$$= (1 \text{ mol})(8.314 \text{ JK}^{-1}\text{mol}^{-1})(300 \text{ K}) \times 2.303 \log \frac{20}{2}$$

$$= 5.744 \text{ kJ mol}^{-1}$$

$$V_2 = \frac{P_1 V_1}{P_2} = \frac{(20 \text{ atm})}{(2 \text{ atm})} \times V_1 = 10 V_1$$

$$V_1 = \frac{nRT}{P_1} = \frac{(1 \text{ mol})(0.0821 \text{ dm}^3 \text{ atm K}^{-1}\text{mol}^{-1})(300 \text{ K})}{(20 \text{ atm})}$$

$$= 1.231 \text{ dm}^3\text{mol}^{-1}$$

Therefore, $$V_2 = \frac{P_1 V_1}{P_2} = 12.31 \text{ dm}^3\text{mol}^{-1}$$

(*ii*) Isothermal irreversible expansion

$$\Delta E = \Delta H = 0$$

and $$-W = Q = P_{\text{ext}}\left(V_2 - V_1\right)$$

$$= \left(1.013 \times 10^5 \text{N m}^{-2}\right)\left(12.31 \times 10^{-3} \text{ m}^{-3} \text{ mol}^{-1} - 1.231 \times 10^{-3}\text{m}^3\text{mol}^{-1}\right)$$

$$= 2.245 \text{ kJ mol}^{-1}$$

(*iii*) Adiabatic reversible expansion:

$$Q = 0; \Delta E = W = C_{V,m}\left(T_2 - T_1\right)$$

$$T_2 = T_1 \left(\frac{P_2}{P_1}\right)^{R/C_{P,m}}$$

$$= (300)\left(\frac{2 \text{ atm}}{20 \text{ atm}}\right)\left(\frac{8.314 \text{ JK}^{-1}\text{mol}^{-1}}{29.13 \text{ JK}^{-1}\text{mol}^{-1}}\right)$$

$$= 150.8 \text{ K}$$

Therefore, $$\Delta E = W = \left(20.816 \text{ JK}^{-1}\text{mol}^{-1}\right)(150.8 \text{ K} - 300 \text{ K})$$

$$= -3.106 \text{ kJ mol}^{-1}$$

$$\Delta H = V_{P,m}\left(T_2 - T_1\right) = \left(29.13 \text{JK}^{-1}\text{mol}^{-1}\right)(150.8 \text{ K} - 300 \text{ K})$$

$$= -4.346 \text{ kJ mol}^{-1}$$

$$V_2 = \frac{RT_2}{P_2} = \frac{\left(0.0821 \text{ dm}^3 \text{ atm K}^{-1}\text{mol}^{-1}\right)(150.8 \text{ K})}{(2 \text{ atm})}$$

$$= 6.19 \text{ dm}^3\text{mol}^{-1}$$

(*iv*) Adiabatic irreversible expansion

$$Q = 0; \Delta E = W = C_{V,m}\left(T_2 - T_1\right)$$

$$T_2 = T_1 \frac{C_{V,m} + \left(\dfrac{P_2}{P_1}\right)R}{C_{P,m}}$$

$$= (300 \text{ K}) \left(\frac{20.816 \text{ JK}^{-1}\text{mol}^{-1} + (1/10)(8.314 \text{ JK}^{-1}\text{mol}^{-1})}{(29.13 \text{ JK}^{-1}\text{mol}^{-1})} \right)$$

$$= 198.9 \text{ K}$$

$$\Delta E = W = (20.816 \text{ JK}^{-1}\text{mol}^{-1})(198.9 \text{ K} - 300 \text{ K})$$

$$= -2.105 \text{ kJ mol}^{-1}$$

$$\Delta H = C_{P,m}(T_2 - T_1) = -(29.13 \text{ JK}^{-1}\text{mol}^{-1})(101.1 \text{ K})$$

$$= -3.013 \text{ kJ mol}^{-1}$$

$$V_2 = \frac{RT_2}{P_2} = \frac{(0.0821 \text{ dm}^3 \text{ atm K}^{-1}\text{mol}^{-1})(198.9 \text{ K})}{2}$$

$$= 8.164 \text{ dm}^3\text{mol}^{-1}$$

EXERCISES

1. Define extensive and intensive variables. Classify the following into extensive and intensive properties.
    (i) Energy, (ii) enthalpy, (iii) heat capacity, (iv) specific heat, (v) volume, (vi) vapour pressure, (vii) gas constant (R), (viii) molar mass, (ix) boiling point, (x) viscosity, (xi) surface tension, (xii) dipole moment, (xiii) standard electrode potential, (xiv) dielectric constant, (xv) magnetic susceptibility, (xvi) density, (xvii) critical temperature, (xviii) molar volume, (xix) refractive index, and (xx) melting point.
    Ans. Extensive properties: (i), (ii), (iii), (v) rest are extensive properties.

2. What are state functions? What are their characteristics? Which of the following are state functions?
    (i) Q, (ii) W, (iii) $Q + W$, (iv) $Q - W$, (v) Q_V, (vi) Q_P, (vii) $\dfrac{Q}{W}$, (viii) $\dfrac{Q_{rev}}{T}$, (ix) $\dfrac{\Delta H}{T}$ (x) $E + PV$, (xi) $E - PV$.
    Ans. State functions: (iii), (v), (vi), (vii), (ix), (x).

3. Which of the following processes are reversible?
    (i) Diffusion of a gas into another gas at constant temperature and pressure.
    (ii) Vapourisation of a liquid at its boiling point.
    (iii) Dissolution of sodium chloride in water at room temperature.
    (iv) Neutralisation of an acid by a base.
    (v) Expansion of a gas into vacuum.
    (vi) Expansion of a gas against constant external pressure.
    (vii) Transformation of a solid into its liquid at its melting point.
    Ans. Reversible processes: (ii), (vii).

4. Explain the following statements:
    (i) The internal energy of an isolated system is constant.
    (ii) According to the first law, an isolated metal rod initially at uniform temperature may develop a hot and a cold end.

(*iii*) Q and W are not state functions but become state functions under certain conditions.

(*iv*) Reversible work of expansion for an ideal gas is greater in an isothermal process than in an adiabatic process.

(*v*) Isothermal reversible work of expansion for an ideal gas is greater than that for a real gas between the same initial and final states.

(*vi*) A gas shows cooling effect in adiabatic expansion.

(*vii*) Isothermal free expansion of a gas also has to be adiabatic.

5. State and explain the Euler's theorem of exactness. Test the following functions for their exactness.

(*i*) $dZ = n\dfrac{C_{V,m}}{T} dT + n\dfrac{R}{V} dV$

(*ii*) $d\phi = nC_{V,m} dT + PdV$

(*iii*) $d\phi' = \dfrac{RT}{P} dP - RdT$

(*iv*) $dE = C_{V,m} dT + \dfrac{a}{V^2} dV$

Ans. dZ, $d\phi$ and dE are exact differentials.

6. Show that dP and dV are exact differentials from the relations

(*i*) $PV = RT$, (*ii*) $(P + a/V^2) = RT$ (*iii*) $P(V - b) = RT$. Derive the cyclic rule in each case.

7. The coefficients of thermal expansion (α) and compressibility (k) are defined as

$$\alpha = \frac{1}{V}\left(\frac{\partial V}{\partial T}\right)_P \text{ and } k = -\frac{1}{V}\left(\frac{\partial V}{\partial P}\right)_T$$

Derive their values for (*i*) an ideal gas and (*ii*) for a van der Waals gas

Ans. $\alpha = T^{-1}$, $k = P^{-1}$

$$\alpha = \left[PV - \frac{a}{V} + \frac{2ab}{V^2}\right], \quad k = \frac{V - b}{\left[PV - \dfrac{a}{V} + \dfrac{2ab}{V^2}\right]}$$

8. Show that $\alpha = -\left(\dfrac{1}{\rho}\right)\left(\dfrac{\partial P}{\partial T}\right)_P$, where ρ is the density and α is the coefficient of thermal expansion.

9. Derive the relations:

(*i*) $\left(\dfrac{\partial P}{\partial T}\right)_V = \dfrac{\alpha}{k}$

(*ii*) $\left(\dfrac{\partial \alpha}{\partial P}\right)_T + \left(\dfrac{\partial k}{\partial T}\right)_P = 0$

(*iii*) $\left(\dfrac{\partial E}{\partial V}\right)_T = C_P\left(\dfrac{\partial T}{\partial V}\right)_P - P$

(*iv*) $\left(\dfrac{\partial E}{\partial T}\right)_P = C_P - P\left(\dfrac{\partial V}{\partial T}\right)_P$

(*v*) $\left(\dfrac{\partial T}{\partial V}\right)_E = -\dfrac{a}{C_V V^2}$

(*vi*) $C_V = \left(\dfrac{\partial E}{\partial V}\right)_T\left(\dfrac{\partial V}{\partial T}\right)_E$

10. The molar heat capacity at constant volume ($C_{V,m}$) for a van der Waals gas is given by $C_{V,m} = A + BT$ with

A and B as temperature- independent constants. Obtain an expression that relates the initial and final temperatures to the initial and final volumes in a reversible adiabatic expansion.

Ans. $R\ln\dfrac{V_2-b}{V_1-b} = -A\ln\dfrac{T_2}{T_1} - B(T_2-T_1).$

11. All the gases at relatively low pressures approach the equation of state

$$PV = RT + BP$$

where B is independent of P and V. Prove that

$$\left(\frac{\partial H}{\partial V}\right)_T - \left(\frac{\partial E}{\partial V}\right)_T = -\frac{BRT}{(V-B)^2}$$

12. A house of constant volume V is heated, the air pressure being kept constant at 1 atm. During the heating process, some air escapes out through the keyholes, around doorjams, etc. Assuming that C_P and C_V of air are constants, show that the amount of heat that must be supplied to heat the room from T_1 to T_2, taking into account the continuous ejection of air, is

$$Q = \frac{PVC_P}{R}\ln\frac{T_2}{T_1}$$

13. Show that for an ideal gas undergoing reversible expansion

$$\left(\frac{\partial P}{\partial V}\right)_{\text{isothermal}} = \frac{1}{\gamma}\left(\frac{dP}{dV}\right)_{\text{adiabatic}}$$

14. Calculate Q, W, ΔE and ΔH for each of the following processes for an ideal gas: (*i*) Isothermal reversible expansion; (*ii*) Isothermal irreversible expansion against a constant external pressure; (*iii*) Isothermal free expansion; (*iv*) Adiabatic reversible expansion; (*v*) Adiabatic irreversible expansion; and (*vi*) Adiabatic free expansion.

Ans. (*i*) $-W = Q = nRT\ln\dfrac{V_2}{V_1}$, $\Delta E = \Delta H = 0$

(*ii*) $-W = Q = P_{\text{ext}}(V_2 - V_1)$, $\Delta E = \Delta H = 0$

(*iii*) $-W = Q = \Delta E = \Delta H = 0$

(*iv*) $Q = 0$, $W = \Delta E = nC_{V,m}(T_2 - T_1)$

$\Delta H = nC_{P,m}(T_2 - T_1)$

(*v*) $Q = 0$, $W = \Delta E = nC_{V,m}(T_2 - T_1)$

$\Delta H = nC_{P,m}(T_2 - T_1)$

(*vi*) $Q = -W = \Delta E = \Delta H = 0$

15. Derive the following relations for an ideal gas undergoing adiabatic reversible changes:

(*i*) $PV^\gamma = \text{constant}$, $TV^{R/C_{V,m}} = \text{constant}$, $TP^{-R/C_{P,m}} = \text{constant}$.

Are these relations valid for adiabatic irreversible changes also?

Ans. No.

16. By using the definition $C_V = \left(\dfrac{\partial E}{\partial T} \right)_V$, one often writes

$$dE = C_V dT + \left(\dfrac{\partial E}{\partial V} \right)_T dV$$

as $dE = C_V dT$. This conclusion is not always true. Explain.

17. Using the relation $\left(\dfrac{\partial E}{\partial V} \right)_T = T \left(\dfrac{\partial P}{\partial T} \right)_V - P$ and $\left(\dfrac{\partial H}{\partial P} \right)_T = V - T \left(\dfrac{\partial V}{\partial T} \right)_P$ show that

$$\left(\dfrac{\partial C_V}{\partial V} \right)_T = T \left(\dfrac{\partial^2 P}{\partial T^2} \right)_V \text{ and } \left(\dfrac{\partial C_P}{\partial P} \right)_T = -T \left(\dfrac{\partial^2 V}{\partial T^2} \right)_P$$

Hence prove that C_P and C_V for an ideal gas depend only on the temperature.

18. Considering E as a function of any two of the three variables P, V and T, prove that

(i) $\left(\dfrac{\partial E}{\partial T} \right)_P \left(\dfrac{\partial T}{\partial P} \right)_V = -\left(\dfrac{\partial E}{\partial V} \right)_P \left(\dfrac{\partial V}{\partial P} \right)_T$

(ii) $\left(\dfrac{\partial E}{\partial T} \right)_P \left(\dfrac{\partial T}{\partial P} \right)_V = \left(\dfrac{\partial E}{\partial P} \right)_V \left(\dfrac{\partial P}{\partial V} \right)_E \left(\dfrac{\partial V}{\partial P} \right)_T$

(iii) $\left(\dfrac{\partial E}{\partial T} \right)_P = \left(\dfrac{\partial E}{\partial V} \right)_T \left(\dfrac{\partial V}{\partial T} \right)_P$

(iv) $\left(\dfrac{\partial E}{\partial P} \right)_T = \left(\dfrac{\partial E}{\partial V} \right)_T \left(\dfrac{\partial V}{\partial P} \right)_T$

19. Given the following informations for an ideal gas:

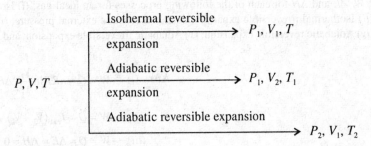

Predict qualitatively whether

(i) $T_2 > T$ or $T_2 = T$ or $T_2 < T$

(ii) $P_2 > P_1$ or $P_2 = P_1$ or $P_2 < P_1$

(iii) $T_1 > T$ or $T_1 = T$ or $T_1 < T$

(iv) $V_2 > V_1$ or $V_2 = V_1$ or $V_2 < V_1$

Ans. (i) $T_2 < T$; (ii) $P_2 < P_1$; (iii) $T_1 < T$; (iv) $V_2 < V_1$.

20. Considering $E = f(V, T)$, one can write

$$dE = \left(\dfrac{\partial E}{\partial V} \right)_T dV + \left(\dfrac{\partial E}{\partial T} \right)_V dT = C_V dT + \left(\dfrac{\partial E}{\partial V} \right)_T dV$$

(since $\left(\dfrac{\partial E}{\partial T} \right)_V = C_V$). On replacing $C_V dT$ by δQ, one can also write

$$dE = \delta Q + \left(\dfrac{\partial E}{\partial V} \right)_T dV$$

But $dE - \delta Q = -PdV$ from the first law. It appears from these considerations that

$$\left(\frac{\partial E}{\partial V}\right)_T = -P$$

This conclusion is obviously not correct. Explain the error in this derivation.

21. What is Joule-Thomson effect? Derive an expression for Joule-Thomson coefficient for an ideal gas and a van der Waals gas.

22. Define, with examples, the following terms:
    (i) System (open, closed and isolated, homogeneous and heterogeneous)
    (ii) Surroundings
    (iii) Boundary
    (iv) Process (isothermal, adiabatic, isobaric, isochoric, reversible, irreversible and cyclic)
    (v) Equilibrium (thermal, mechanical and chemical)
    (vi) Extensive and intensive variables

23. One mole of an ideal gas at 300 K and 30 atm is expanded to double its volume isothermally. Calculate the work of expansion if (a) the expansion were carried out reversibly and (b) irreversibly against a constant opposing pressure of 1.5 atm. **Ans.** (i) −1.72 kJ, (ii) −1.246 kJ

24. A piece of metal of mass 1 kg and volume 1.0×10^{-4} m^3 is immersed in water (density 1.0×10^3 kg m^{-3}) at a certain temperature. calculate the work required in raising the piece of metal upto a height of 0.1 m.
    Ans. 9.712 J.

25. One mole of a linear triatomic gas is heated. When 150 J of heat was absorbed, 41.91 J of work was done by the system on the surroundings. Calculate (a) the change in energy of the system, (b) the change in temperature if (i) the contribution of vibrational degrees of freedom is negligible (ii) the contribution of vibrational degrees of freedom is taken into account. **Ans.** (a) 108.09 J, (b) (i) 5.2 K (ii) 2.0 K.

26. One mole of hydrogen at 300 K occupies a volume of 10 dm^3 in a cylinder fitted with a piston. The gas is expanded isothermally to 20 dm^3. Assuming ideal behaviour for the gas. Calculate $W, Q, \Delta E$ and ΔH if the expansion is carried out (i) reversibly, (ii) irreversibly against an external pressure of 0.1 atm and (iii) against zero external pressure.
    Ans. $\Delta E = \Delta H = 0$ in all the cases;
    (i) $-W = Q = 1732$ J, (ii) $-W = Q = 202.6$ J, (iii) $-W = Q = 0$.

27. For copper, $\alpha = 0.492 \times 10^{-4}$ K^{-1} and $k = 0.70 \times 10^{-6}$ atm^{-1} and the density of the metal is 8.96 kg m^{-3}. Calculate the difference between the heat capacities at constant pressure and at constant volume.
    Ans. $C_{P, m} - C_{V, m} = 0.654$ J mol^{-1} K^{-1}.

28. An ideal gas undergoes a single-stage expansion against a constant external pressure (P_2) from P_1, T, V_1 to P_2, T, V_2.
    (a) What is the magnitude of work done by the system?
    (b) What is the largest mass M which can be raised through a height h in this expansion?
    (c) The system is now restored to its initial state by a single-stage compression. What is the magnitude of work done on the system?
    (d) What is the smallest mass M' which must fall through the height h to restore the system?
    (e) What is the net work done on the system in this cyclic transformation?

$$\textbf{Ans.} \ (a) \ -W = nRT\left(1 - \frac{P_2}{P_1}\right); \ (b) \ M = \frac{nRT}{gh}\left(1 - \frac{P_2}{P_1}\right); \ (c) \ -W' = nRT\left(1 - \frac{P_1}{P_2}\right);$$

$$(d) \ M' = \frac{nRT}{gh}\left(1 - \frac{P_1}{P_2}\right); \ (e) \ -W_{net} = nRT\frac{(P_1 - P_2)^2}{(P_1 P_2)}$$

29. On mole of an ideal gas ($C_{V,\,m}$ = 20.92 Jk^{-1} mol^{-1}) initially at STP is put through the following reversible cycle:

$$A\;(STP) \xrightarrow{\text{Isochoric}} B\;(2\;atm,\;22.4\;dm^3,\;546\;K) \xrightarrow{\text{adiabatic}} C\;(1\;atm,\;V_x,\;273\;K)$$

Isothermal

Calculate W, Q, ΔE, ΔH for each step and for the complete cycle.

Ans. $A \rightarrow B$: $W = 0$, $Q_V = \Delta E = 5.709$ kJ, $\Delta H = 7.995$ kJ;

$B \rightarrow C$: $-W = -\Delta E = -5.709$ kJ,

$Q = 0$, $\Delta H = -7.995$ kJ;

$C \rightarrow A$: $\Delta E = \Delta H = 0$, $-W = Q = -3.959$ kJ;

For the cycle: $\Delta E = \Delta H = 0$,

$$Q = -W = 1.750 \text{ kJ.}$$

30. If μ_{JT} for CO_2 is 1.084 deg atm^{-1} and the heat capacity $C_{P,\,m}$ is 36.69 JK^{-1} mol^{-1},

  (*i*) Calculate the change in enthalpy when 0.05 kg of the gas at 298 K and 1 atm is isothermally compressed to 10 atm; (*ii*) What would be the value for an ideal gas?

Ans. (*i*) –405.85 J, (*ii*) 0.0.

31. Calculate μ_{JT} for N_2 at 298 K and 100 atm. $C_{P,\,m}$ = 29.04 JK^{-1} mol^{-1} and a and b for Nitrogen are 1.41 N m^4 mol^{-2} and 3.92×10^{-5} m^3 mol^{-1}, respectively.

Ans. 0.156×10^{-4} K (Nm^{-2})$^{-1}$

32. Show that the work done by an ideal gas in a reversible adiabatic expansion is given by

$$-W = \frac{P_1 V_1 - P_2 V_2}{\gamma - 1} = C_{V,\,m} T_1 \left[1 - \left(\frac{P_2}{P_1} \right)^{R/C_{P,\,m}} \right]$$

$$= C_{V,\,m} T_1 \left[1 - \left(\frac{V_1}{V_2} \right)^{R/C_{V,\,m}} \right]$$

33. Prove that

$$\left(\frac{\partial C_V}{\partial V} \right)_T = 0 \text{ and } \left(\frac{\partial C_P}{\partial P} \right)_T = 0$$

for an ideal gas.

34. Derive the relations

  (*i*) $C_P - C_V = \left[P + \left(\frac{\partial E}{\partial V} \right)_T \right] \left(\frac{\partial V}{\partial T} \right)_P$

  (*ii*) $C_P - C_V = \left[V - \left(\frac{\partial H}{\partial P} \right)_T \right] \left(\frac{\partial P}{\partial T} \right)_V$

(iii) $C_P - C_V = \left[V + \left(\dfrac{\partial H}{\partial P} \right)_P \left(\dfrac{\partial T}{\partial P} \right)_H \right] \left(\dfrac{\partial P}{\partial T} \right)_V$

(iv) $C_P - C_V = -T \left(\dfrac{\partial V}{\partial T} \right)_P^2 \left(\dfrac{\partial P}{\partial V} \right)_T = \dfrac{TV\alpha^2}{k}$

and show that each of the above formulae simplifies to $C_{P,m} - C_{V,m} = R$ for an ideal gas and

$$C_{P,m} - C_{V,m} = R \left[1 - \frac{2a}{V} \left(\frac{V-b}{a+PV^2} \right) \right]^{-1}$$

for a van der Waals gas.

35. Show that the Joule-Thomson coefficient μ_{JT} is given by

$$\mu_{JT} = \frac{1}{C_P} \left[T \left(\frac{\partial V}{\partial T} \right)_P - V \right] = -\frac{1}{C_P} \left[\left(\frac{\partial E}{\partial V} \right)_T \left(\frac{\partial V}{\partial P} \right)_T + \left(\frac{\partial (PV)}{\partial P} \right)_T \right]$$

For a van der Waals gas prove that the above expression reduces to

$$\mu_{JT} = \frac{1}{C_{P,m}} \left(\frac{2a}{RT} - b \right)$$

36. Prove that

(i) $\left(\dfrac{\partial C_P}{\partial P} \right)_T = -\mu_{JT} \left(\dfrac{\partial C_P}{\partial T} \right)_P - C_P \left(\dfrac{\partial \mu_{JT}}{\partial T} \right)_P$

(ii) $\left(\dfrac{\partial E}{\partial V} \right)_T = 0$, then it follows that $\left(\dfrac{\partial E}{\partial P} \right)_T = 0$

(iii) it does not necessarily follow that if $\left(\dfrac{\partial E}{\partial V} \right)_T = 0$ then $\left(\dfrac{\partial H}{\partial P} \right)_T = 0$.

37. From the equation $\left(\dfrac{\partial E}{\partial V} \right)_T = T \left(\dfrac{\partial P}{\partial T} \right)_V - P$, show that $\left(\dfrac{\partial E}{\partial V} \right)_T = 0$ for an ideal gas and $\left(\dfrac{\delta E}{\partial V} \right)_T = \dfrac{an^2}{V^2}$ for a van der Waals gas.

38. (a) A waterfall falls through a height of 200 m. If there is no other loss of heat, calculate the rise in temperature of water when it reaches the ground.

(b) If the evaporation of water is taken into account, should the height of the fall be increased or decreased to achieve the same rise in temperature.

Ans. (a) 468.45 K, (b) height should be increased.

and show that each of the above equations supplements

CHAPTER 6

Thermochemistry

6.1 INTRODUCTION

Physical and chemical transformations are invariably associated with heat changes. Thermochemistry is the branch of physical chemistry that deals with the heat changes accompanying these transformations. Heat (Q) is either absorbed or evolved in chemical or physical changes. When heat is evolved in a reaction, Q is negative, it is called an *exothermic reaction*. If heat is absorbed by the reacting system, Q has a positive value and the reaction is said to be *endothermic*. The amount of heat evolved or absorbed in a chemical reaction depends on the path of the reaction. It is, therefore, more convenient to express the energy of the system in terms of thermodynamic quantities as they are independent of the path of the reaction.

The subject matter of thermochemistry is based on the first law of thermodynamics. The energy changes in chemical reactions are generally due to breaking up of the existing bonds between the atoms and the formation of new bonds. Thermochemistry, therefore, provides important informations regarding the bond energies.

6.2 ENTHALPY OF A REACTION

It is defined as *the enthalpy change in the transformation of the reactants at a given temperature and pressure into the products at the same temperature and pressure*. When one mole of gaseous hydrogen combines with half a mole of gaseous oxygen at 298 K and 1 atmosphere pressure to form one mole of liquid water at the same temperature and pressure, 285.83 kJ of heat is given out to the surroundings, *i.e.*,

$$H_2(g) + \frac{1}{2}O_2(g) = H_2O(l) \qquad \Delta H = -285.83 \text{ kJ}$$

It is further assumed that the reaction is fast and proceeds to completion with no side products.

Enthalpy of a Reaction at Constant Pressure and at Constant Volume: Enthalpy of a reaction depends upon the conditions under which the reaction is carried out. There are two general conditions under which thermo-chemical measurements are made, namely, (*i*) at constant volume, and (*ii*) at constant pressure. The magnitude of the enthalpy changes in these two conditions are, in general, different. In the first case, the volume of the system is kept constant during the course of the measurement by carrying out the reaction in a closed and rigid container. As there is no change in volume, no work is involved and from the first law of thermodynamics, we have

$$\Delta E = Q_V \qquad \qquad ...(6.1)$$

$$= \text{Enthalpy of the reaction at constant volume}$$

Thus, the enthalpy of the reaction at constant volume is exactly equal to the change in the internal energy ΔE, of the reacting system. In other words, the thermal change that occurs in a chemical reaction is only due to the difference in the sum of the internal energy of the products and the sum of the internal energy of the reactants

$$\Delta E = \sum E_{\text{Products}} - \sum E_{\text{Reactants}} \qquad \qquad ...(6.2)$$

The importance of Eq. (6.1) is that the amount of heat absorbed at constant volume can be identified with the change in the thermodynamic quantity.

At constant pressure, the system is either kept open to the atmosphere or confined within a vessel on which a constant external pressure is exerted. Under these conditions, the volume of the system changes. The thermal change at constant pressure not only involves the change in the internal energy of the system but also the work performed either in expansion or in contraction of the system

$$Q_P = \Delta E - W$$

If W is only pressure-volume work, then

$$Q_P = \Delta E + P\Delta V \qquad \qquad ...(6.3)$$

$$= (\Sigma E_P - \Sigma E_R) + P(V_P - V_R)$$

$$= (\Sigma E_P + PV_P) - (\Sigma E_R + PV_R) \qquad \qquad ...(6.4)$$

where the subscripts P and R refer to the products and the reactants respectively. Since H, *the enthalpy or the heat content* is defined by $H = E + PV$, Eq. (6.4) becomes

$$Q_P = \Sigma H_P - \Sigma H_R$$

$$Q_P = \Delta H \qquad \qquad ...(6.5)$$

It follows therefore that at constant pressure, the heat of the reaction is exactly equal to the enthalpy change, ΔH, of the reacting system.

In Eqs. (6.1) and (6.5), the thermochemical observable quantities $(Q_V$ or $Q_P)$ have been related to the thermodynamic functions $(\Delta E$ or $\Delta H)$.

6.3 RELATION BETWEEN ΔE AND ΔH

According to Eq. (6.3)

$$\Delta H = \Delta E + P\Delta V$$

$$= \Delta E + [PV]_{\text{Products}} - [PV]_{\text{Reactants}} \qquad \qquad ...(6.6)$$

In reactions involving solids or liquids, the volumes of the products and reactants are approximately equal, *i.e.*, ΔV is very small and hence can be neglected. Thus, for solids and liquids, $\Delta H \approx \Delta E$.

For gaseous reactions, however, the situation is different because the volume change that results at constant temperature and pressure is not negligible. If it is assumed that the gases involved in the reaction obey ideal behaviour then product PV may be replaced by nRT.

Hence Eq. (6.6) becomes

$$\Delta H = \Delta E + \left[nRT\right]_{Products} - \left[nRT\right]_{Reactants}$$

$$= \Delta E + RT\left(\left[n\right]_{Products} - \left[n\right]_{Reactants}\right)$$

$$= \Delta E + \Delta nRT \qquad \qquad ...(6.7)$$

where $\Delta n = (n_{products} - n_{Reactants})$, is the difference in the total number of moles of the gaseous products and the total number of moles of the gaseous reactants.

Equation (6.7) can also be written as

$$Q_P = Q_V + \Delta nRT \qquad \qquad ...(6.8)$$

Equation (6.7) can be used in calculating the value of ΔH from ΔE or vice versa. A positive value of ΔH or ΔE shows that heat is absorbed while a negative value of ΔH or ΔE shows that the heat is evolved or given out by the system to the surroundings.

Problem 6.1: For the conversion of a mole of $SO_2(g)$ into $SO_3(g)$ the enthalpy of reaction at constant volume, ΔE, at 298 K is -97.027 kJ. Calculate the enthalpy of the reaction, ΔH, at constant pressure.

Solution: The reaction is

$$SO_2(g) + \frac{1}{2}O_2(g) \rightarrow SO_3(g) \qquad \Delta E = -97.027 \text{ kJ}$$

$$\Delta n = n_{Produts} - n_{Reactants}$$

$$= 1 - \left(1 + \frac{1}{2}\right)$$

$$= -\frac{1}{2}$$

Hence, $\qquad \Delta H = \Delta E + \Delta nRT$

$$= \left(-97.027 \text{ kJ mol}^{-1}\right) + \left(-\frac{1}{2}\right)\left(8.314 \times 10^{-3} \text{kJ K}^{-1}\text{mol}^{-1}\right)(298.17 \text{ K})$$

$$= \left(-97.027 \text{ kJ mol}^{-1}\right) + \left(-1.240 \text{ kJ mol}^{-1}\right)$$

$$= -98.267 \text{ kJ mol}^{-1}$$

6.4 MEASUREMENTS OF ENTHALPY OF REACTIONS

The heat evolved or absorbed by a chemical reaction is measured by the use of a calorimeter known as *adiabatic bomb calorimeter*. It is made up of steel internally enamelled with platinum. A known mass of the substance is placed in a platinum cup inside the calorimeter and is then filled with oxygen at about 20-30 atmospheres. The reaction is started in the calorimeter by heating electrically. The substance on ignition gives a large amount of heat which is determined by the rise in temperature of water around the calorimeter. The product of the rise in temperature and the total heat capacity of the system (i.e., the heat capacity of water and calorimeter) gives the amount of the heat evolved. The heat capacity of the system is predetermined by burning a standard substance (say benzoic acid) of known heat of evolution.

6.5 THERMOCHEMICAL EQUATIONS

The enthalpy of a reaction depends not only on whether the reaction is carried out at constant volume or at pressure, but also on the substances involved, temperature, pressure and the states of aggregations of the substances. In the formation of a mole of carbon dioxide from 1 mole of carbon and 1 mole of oxygen at 298 K, the enthalpy of the reaction is -393.5 kJ mol^{-1}

$$C + O_2 \rightarrow CO_2 \qquad \Delta H = -393.5 \text{ kJ mol}^{-1} \qquad ...(6.9)$$

Equation (6.9) is known as thermochemical equation. If we would have considered 2 moles of carbon dioxide, the enthalpy of reaction would be twice, i.e., -787.0 kJ.

$$2C + 2O_2 \rightarrow 2CO_2 \qquad \Delta H = -787.0 \text{ kJ}$$

It is essential that the thermochemical equations must be balanced and ΔE or ΔH values indicated in the reaction correspond to the amounts or reactants and products given by the equation.

In Eq. (6.9), the physical states of the reactants and products have not been mentioned. This is usually done by adding s, l, g or aq after the substance. As an example, in the formation of a mole of water in liquid or in gaseous forms from its elements, the enthalpies of reaction in the two cases are different.

$$H_2(g) + \frac{1}{2}O_2(g) = H_2O(l) \qquad \Delta H = -285.83 \text{ kJ mol}^{-1}$$

$$H_2(g) + \frac{1}{2}O_2(g) = H_2O(g) \qquad \Delta H = -241.82 \text{ kJ mol}^{-1}$$

These equations are still incomplete until they indicate the temperature and pressure at which the reaction is carried out. The temperature is indicated by a subscript giving the absolute temperature. The equations for the formation of water would then be written as

$$H_2(g) + \frac{1}{2}O_2(g) = H_2O(l) \qquad \Delta H^0_{298} = -285.83 \text{ kJ mol}^{-1}$$

$$H_2(g) + \frac{1}{2}O_2(g) = H_2O(g) \qquad \Delta H^0_{298} = -241.82 \text{ kJ mol}^{-1}$$

The superscript '0' indicates that the pressure is 1 atmosphere.

The difference of the two values gives the enthalpy of vapourization of water at 298 K.

Significance of Thermochemical Equations. In general, for any change in the process, ΔH is given by

$$\Delta H = \Sigma H_{\text{final}} - \Sigma H_{\text{initial}}$$

For a chemical reaction, ΔH is the difference in the heat contents of products and reactants

$$\Delta H = \Sigma H_{\text{Products}} - \Sigma H_{\text{Reactants}}$$

If $\Sigma H_{\text{Products}} > \Sigma H_{\text{Reactants}}$, ΔH will be positive, heat will be absorbed and the reaction will be endothermic. Conversely, if $\Sigma H_{\text{Products}} < \Sigma H_{\text{Reactants}}$, ΔH will be negative, the heat will be evolved or given out and the reaction would be exothermic. In case, $\Sigma H_{\text{Products}} = \Sigma H_{\text{Reactants}}$, $\Delta H = 0$, no heat effects would be observed.

6.6 STANDARD ENTHALPY CHANGES

The enthalpy of a reaction depends on temperature and pressure and therefore for comparison of enthalpies of reactions of different substances a **standard state** is chosen. A convenient standard state for a substance is *the most stable state of aggregation under 1 atmosphere and at the specified temperature, usually at 298 K.* For pure solids, liquids and ideal gases the standard state corresponds to the state of the substances at 1 atm pressure and specified temperature. In cases of the dissolved substances, the standard state of the solute is the concentration required to give unit activity. The standard enthalpy of a reaction at a temperature T and at a pressure of 1 atm is denoted by $\Delta H^0(T)$ and is the value of $\Sigma H_{\text{Products}} - \Sigma H_{\text{Reactants}}$ at the temperature when all the substances (or elements) in the reaction are in their standard states. Since it is not possible to determine the absolute value of enthalpy, it is customary to build the values of standard molar enthalpies of various substances based on the convention that the enthalpy of every element in its standard state is arbitrarily assigned a zero value. For example, the enthalpy of formation of a mole of CO_2 (g) from its elements in the standard state is -393.5 kJ mol^{-1}, *i.e.,*

$$C(\text{graphite}) + O_2(g) = CO_2(g) \qquad\qquad \Delta H^0_{298} = -393.5 \text{ kJ mol}^{-1}$$

ΔH^0_{298} is given by

$$\Delta H^0_{298} = H^0_{CO_2(g)} - \left[H^0_{O_2(g)} + H^0_{C(\text{graphite})} \right]$$

where H^0's are the standard enthalpies per mol.

Since the elements are in their standard states, their heat contents by convention are zero

$$H^0_{C(\text{graphite})} = H^0_{O_2(g)} = 0$$

Hence, under these conditions

$$\Delta H^0_{298} = H^0_{CO_2(g)} = -393.5 \text{ kJ mol}^{-1}$$

Thus the standard enthalpy of any compound is the enthalpy of the reaction by which it is formed from its elements in the standard state.

6.7 VARIOUS TYPES OF ENTHALPY CHANGES

Enthalpy of a reaction is given different names depending upon the types of reaction. Some of these are discussed below.

(i) Enthalpy of Formation

It is defined as *the enthalpy change involved in the formation of a mole of compound from its elements.* If the elements are in their standard states, the enthalpy of formation is called the *standard enthalpy of formation* and is denoted by ΔH_f^0. The standard enthalpy of formation of a mole of $CH_4(g)$ from its elements at 298 K is -74.81 kJ mol^{-1}.

$$C(\text{graphite}) + 2H_2(g) = CH_4(g) \qquad \Delta H_{f, 298}^0 = -74.81 \text{ kJ mol}^{-1}$$

The standard enthalpy of formation of a compound is equal to the enthalpy content of the compound and is related to its stability. A positive value of enthalpy of formation would mean that the compound is less stable than its elements. On the other hand, a negative value implies that the compound would be more stable than its elements. The enthalpy of formation of a compound may be obtained either by direct measurement of ΔH for the reaction or from enthalpies of reactions involving the compound.

The standard enthalpies of formation for a number of compounds at 298 K are given in Table 6.1

Table 6.1 Standard Enthalpies of Formation of Compounds at 298 K

Substance	$\Delta H^0_f (kJ\ mol^{-1})$	Substance	$\Delta H^0_f (kJ\ mol^{-1})$
$H_2O(l)$	-285.8	$Al_2O_3(s)$	-1669.9
$H_2O(g)$	-241.8	$FeS_2(s)$	-178.5
$HCl(g)$	-92.3	$NH_3(g)$	-46.1
$HBr(g)$	-36.4	$NO(g)$	$+90.2$
$HI(g)$	$+26.5$	$NO_2(g)$	$+33.2$
$H_2SO_4(l)$	-811.3	$SO_2(g)$	-296.8
$H_2SO_4(aq)$	-907.5	$H_2S(g)$	-20.6
$CO_2(g)$	-393.3	$CH_4(g)$	-74.8
$CO(g)$	-112.5	$C_2H_6(g)$	-84.6
$NH_4Cl(s)$	-314.5	$C_2H_4(g)$	$+52.3$
$NaCl(s)$	-412.0	$C_2H_2(g)$	$+226.8$
		$C_6H_6(l)$	$+49.0$
		$CH_3OH(l)$	-239.0
		$C_2H_5OH(l)$	-277.0

Problem 6.2: Calculate the enthalpy of formation of $N_2O_5(g)$ on the basis of the following data:

(*i*) $2NO(g) + O_2(g) = 2NO_2(g)$ $\qquad \Delta H^0 = -114.0$ kJ

(*ii*) $4NO_2(g) + O_2(g) = 2N_2O_5(g)$ $\qquad \Delta H^0 = -102.6$ kJ

(*iii*) $N_2(g) + O_2(g) = 2NO(g)$ $\qquad \Delta H^0 = +180.4$ kJ

Solution: The formation of a mole of $N_2O_5(g)$ is as follows

$$N_2(g) + \frac{5}{2}O_2(g) = N_2O_5(g)$$

Multiplying Eq. (*iii*) by 2 and adding to (*ii*), we get

(iv) $2N_2(g) + 3O_2(g) + 4NO_2(g) = 4NO(g) + 2N_2O_5(g)$ $\Delta H^0 = +258.2$ kJ

Multiplying Eq. (i) by 2 and adding it to Eq. (iv) yields

$$2N_2(g) + 5O_2(g) = 2N_2O_5(g)$$ $\Delta H^0 = +30.2$ kJ

or $$N_2(g) + \frac{5}{2}O_2(g) = N_2O_5(g)$$ $\Delta H^0 = +15.1$ kJ mol^{-1}

Problem 6.3: Calculate the enthalpy of combustion of *n*-butane at 298 K from the following reactions:

(i) $C(s) + O_2(g) = CO_2(g)$ $\Delta H^0 = -393.5$ kJ mol^{-1}

(ii) $H_2(g) + \frac{1}{2}O_2(g) = H_2O(l)$ $\Delta H^0 = -285.8$ kJ mol^{-1}

(iii) $4C(s) + 5H_2(g) = C_4H_{10}(g)$ $\Delta H^0 = -126.0$ kJ mol^{-1}

Solution: The combustion of *n*-butane can be represented as

$$C_4H_{10}(g) + \frac{13}{2}O_2(g) = 4CO_2(g) + 5H_2O(l)$$

The enthalpy of combustion for this reaction is given by

$$\Delta H^0 = 4\Delta H^0_{CO_2(g)} + 5\Delta H^0_{H_2O(l)} - \Delta H^0_{C_4H_{10}(g)}$$

$$= \left[(4 \times -393.5) + (5 \times -285.8) - (-126.0) \right] \text{ kJ}$$

$$= -2877 \text{ kJ}$$

(ii) Enthalpy of Combustion

The enthalpy of combustion of a compound or element is *the enthalpy change involved in the complete combustion of a mole of the substance.* Complete combustion in case of organic compounds containing carbon and hydrogen means oxidation of carbon to carbon dioxide and hydrogen to liquid water. The enthalpy of combustion of methane is

$$CH_4(g) + 2O_2(g) = CO_2(g) + 2H_2O(l)$$ $\Delta H^0_{298} = -890.40$ kJ

Enthalpy of combustion may be used to calculate the enthalpy of formation of a compound if the enthalpy of formation of other combustion products are known. In the above example, enthalpy of formation of gaseous methane can be calculated if we know the enthalpies of formation of CO_2 (g) and $H_2O(l)$

$$\Delta H^0_{298} = -890.40 = \Delta H^0_{CO_2(g)} + 2\Delta H^0_{H_2O(l)} - \Delta H^0_{CH_4(g)}$$

$$\Delta H^0_{CH_4(g)} = 890.40 + \Delta H^0_{CO_2(g)} + 2\Delta H^0_{H_2O(l)}$$

$$= 890.40 + (-393.50) + 2(-285.8)$$

$$= -74.70 \text{ kJ mol}^{-1}$$

Enthalpies of combustion are used for determining the calorific values of foods and fuels, estimating the flame temperatures, bond energies and in deciding the constitution of isomeric substances.

(iii) Enthalpy of Hydrogenation

This is the enthalpy change associated when a mole of an unsaturated organic compound is fully hydrogenated. The enthalpies of hydrogenation of ethylene and benzene are represented as

$$CH_2 = CH_2(g) + H_2(g) = CH_3CH_3(g) \qquad \Delta H^0_{298} = -135.5 \text{ kJ mol}^{-1}$$

$$C_6H_6(l) + 3H_2(g) = C_6H_{12}(l) \qquad \Delta H^0_{298} = -238 \text{ kJ mol}^{-1}$$

It is to be noted that the second value is not three times the first value as one may expect due to the presence of three double bonds in benzene and one double bond is ethylene. The enthalpy of hydrogenation of benzene is less by 166.5 kJ mol^{-1} which therefore represents stabilization of benzene due to resonance. This value of 166.5 kJ mol^{-1} is *the resonance energy* of benzene molecule. The π-electrons are completely delocalized throughout the whole benzene ring and give rise to extra stability to the molecule. This method may sometimes be used as the criteria for stabilization of aromatic molecules due to resonance.

(iv) Enthalpy of Neutralization

Enthalpy of neutralization is the enthalpy change when a mole of H_3O^+ ions in dilute solution are completely neutralized by OH^- ions forming undissociated water. The process may be written as

$$H_3O^+(aq) + OH^-(aq) = 2H_2O(l) \qquad \Delta H^0 = -57.32 \text{ kJ mol}^{-1}$$

Dilute solutions should be used to avoid enthalpy changes due to mixing of acid and base. If one mole of a strong monoprotic acid (HCl, HNO$_3$ etc.,) is mixed with 1 mole of a strong base (NaOH, KOH etc.), neutralization takes place as shown above. Since these acids and bases are completely ionized in dilute solutions, the enthalpy change is always −57.32 kJ mol^{-1}.

For a weak acid or a weak base the enthalpy of neutralization is not the same, but less than −57.32 kJ. In these cases, neutralization involves ionization of the acid or the base in addition to the neutralization. The heat required to ionize the weak acid or the weak base is known as the *Enthalpy of ionization*. The enthalpy of ionization of a weak acid can be calculated from the enthalpies of neutralization of strong acid and weak acid by strong bases. For example, in the neutralization of acetic acid by sodium hydroxide, the enthalpy of neutralization is −55.43 kJ mol^{-1}. The enthalpy of ionization will therefore be equal to +1.89 kJ mol^{-1}. This can be seen as follows:

(1) $CH_3COOH(aq) + OH^-(aq) = CH_3COO^-(aq) + H_2O(l) \qquad \Delta H^0 = -55.43 \text{ kJ mol}^{-1}$

(2) $H^+(aq) + OH^-(aq) = H_2O(l) \qquad \Delta H^0 = -57.32 \text{ kJ mol}^{-1}$

(3) $CH_3COOH(aq) = CH_3COO^-(aq) + H^+(aq) \qquad \Delta H^0 = \Delta H^0_{ionization}$

Adding reactions (2) and (3), we get

$$CH_3COOH(aq) + OH^-(aq) = CH_3COO^-(aq) + H_2O(l)$$

and $\qquad \Delta H^0 = -57.32 + \Delta H^0_{ionization}$

But from Eq. (1)

$$CH_3COOH(aq) + OH^-(aq) = CH_3COO^-(aq) + H_2O(l) \qquad \Delta H^0 = -55.43 \text{ kJ mol}^{-1}$$

Hence $\qquad \Delta H^0_{\text{ionization}} = +1.89 \text{ kJ mol}^{-1}$

Table 6.2 gives the enthalpy of neutralization of a few weak acids.

Table 6.2 Enthalpy of Neutralization of a few Weak Acids

Reactions	Enthalpy of Neutralization (kJ mol⁻¹)
$H_2S(aq) + 2NaOH(aq) \rightarrow Na_2S(aq) + 2H_2O(l)$	−15.90
$HCOOH(aq) + NH_3(aq) \rightarrow HCOONH_4(aq)$	−49.78
$HCN(aq) + NaOH(aq) \rightarrow NaCN(aq) + H_2O(l)$	−12.13
$HBO_2(aq) + NaOH(aq) \rightarrow NaBO_2(aq) + H_2O(l)$	−41.84

Problem 6.4: The enthalpy of neutralization of ammonium hydroxide by hydrochloric acid is −51.46 kJ mol⁻¹. Calculate the enthalpy of ionization of ammonium hydroxide.

Solution:

(1) $NH_3(aq) + H^+(aq) = NH_4^+(aq)$ $\qquad\qquad\qquad\qquad \Delta H^0 = -51.46 \text{ kJ mol}^{-1}$

(2) $H^+(aq) + OH^-(aq) = H_2O(l)$ $\qquad\qquad\qquad\qquad \Delta H^0 = -57.32 \text{ kJ mol}^{-1}$

(3) $NH_3(aq) + H_2O(l) = NH_4^+(aq) + OH^-(aq)$ $\qquad\qquad \Delta H^0 = \Delta H^0_{\text{ionization}}$

Adding Eqs. (2) and (3), we get

$$NH_3(aq) + H^+(aq) = NH_4^+(aq) \qquad\qquad \Delta H^0 = -57.32 + \Delta H^0_{\text{ionization}}$$

From Eq. (1)

$$\Delta H^0 = -51.46 \text{ kJ mol}^{-1}$$

Hence $\qquad\qquad \left(-57.32 + \Delta H^0_{\text{ionization}}\right) \text{ kJ mol}^{-1} = -51.46 \text{ kJ mol}^{-1}$

or $\qquad\qquad\qquad \Delta H^0_{\text{ionization}} = +5.86 \text{ kJ mol}^{-1}$

(v) Enthalpy of Solution

The formation of a solution is accompanied by enthalpy changes and depends on the amount of solute as well as solvent taken. The enthalpy of a solution is the *enthalpy change associated when one mole of the solute is dissolved in a specified amount of the solvent*. Consider, for example, the enthalpy changes accompanying the dissolution of HCl(g) in water at 298 K

$$HCl(g) + 25 H_2O(l) = HCl \cdot 25 H_2O \qquad\qquad \Delta H^0 = -72.3 \text{ kJ}$$

$$HCl(g) + 40 H_2O(l) = HCl \cdot 40 H_2O \qquad\qquad \Delta H^0 = -73.18 \text{ kJ}$$

$$HCl(g) + 200H_2O(l) = HCl \cdot 200H_2O \qquad\qquad \Delta H^0 = -74.20 \text{ kJ}$$

$$HCl(g) + \infty H_2O(l) = HCl(aq) \qquad\qquad \Delta H^0 = -75.14 \text{ kJ}$$

where $HCl \cdot 25H_2O$ represents a solution of a mole of HCl (g) in 25 moles of water while HCl (aq) represents that the amount of water is so large that further addition of water produces no heat effects and the corresponding ΔH^0 value is called the enthalpy of solution at infinite dilution. It is the maximum quantity of heat released in the formation of a solution of one mole of HCl (g) in excess of water.

The enthalpy of solution defined above is *the integral enthalpy of solution.* The change in enthalpy when a solution from one specified concentration is diluted to some other specified concentration is called *the integral enthalpy of dilution.*

The differential enthalpy of a solution is defined as *the enthalpy change when one mole of a solute is added to such a large quantity of the solution that its concentration does not change appreciably.* It is also known as the partial molar *enthalpy* of the solution. Likewise, the enthalpy change accompanying the addition of a mole of the solvent to a large volume of the solution without effecting the concentration of the solution is referred to as the *differential enthalpy of dilution or partial molar enthalpy of dilution.*

If ΔH is the enthalpy change when n_2 moles of the solute are added to n_1 moles of the solvent to form a solution, then at constant pressure and temperature, we have

$$\Delta H = f(n_1, n_2)$$

or

$$d(\Delta H) = \left[\frac{\partial(\Delta H)}{\partial n_1}\right]_{P, T, n_2} dn_1 + \left[\frac{\partial(\Delta H)}{\partial n_2}\right]_{P, T, n_1} dn_2$$

$$= \Delta \overline{H}_1 dn_1 + \Delta \overline{H}_2 dn_2$$

where

$$\Delta \overline{H}_1 = \left[\frac{\partial(\Delta H)}{\partial n_1}\right]_{P, T, n_2} \quad \text{and} \quad \Delta \overline{H}_2 = \left[\frac{\partial(\Delta H)}{\partial n_2}\right]_{P, T, n_1}$$

are the partial molar enthalpy of dilution and the partial molar enthalpy of solution respectively.

Direct measurement of differential enthalpy of solution is impracticable and can be obtained by plotting ΔH, the integral enthalpy of solution as a function of concentration (molality). The value of the slope at a given concentration gives the differential enthalpy of solution at that concentration.

For dilute solutions integral and differential enthalpies of solutions are equal while for a concentrated solution, integral enthalpy of the solution approaches a limiting value. The differential enthalpy of a solution in such cases decreases and finally approaches zero for a saturated solution.

Integral enthalpies of solutions, enthalpies of dilutions and enthalpies of reactions in solutions can be evaluated from the enthalpies of formation in solution. In these calculations, the enthalpy of formation of water is neglected if the same number of moles of water appear on both sides of the balanced thermochemical equation.

Table 6.3 gives the integral enthalpies of solutions of some salts at 98 K.

Table 6.3 Integral Enthalpies of Some Salts

Salt	Moles of water per mole of salt	ΔH^0 (kJ mol^{-1})
NH$_4$Cl	200	+16.24
NaCl	200	+5.45
KNO$_3$	200	+35.65
BaCl$_2$	400	−11.30
BaCl$_2$·2H$_2$O	400	+20.60
CuSO$_4$	400	−66.10
CuSO$_4$·5H$_2$O	400	+11.50
MgSO$_4$	400	−87.04
MgSO$_4$·7H$_2$O	400	+99.59
Na$_2$SO$_4$	400	−2.30
NA$_2$SO$_4$·10H$_2$O	400	+79.10

Problem 6.5: Calculate the enthalpy of solution when a mole of HCl (g) dissolves in 100 moles of H$_2$O(l) at 298 K.

Given

$$\Delta H_f^0 (\text{HCl}) = -92.3 \text{ kJ mol}^{-1}$$

and

$$\Delta H_f^0 (\text{HCl} \cdot 100 \text{ H}_2\text{O}) = -168.1 \text{ kJ mol}^{-1}$$

Solution: The process is

$$\text{HCl (g)} + 100 \text{ H}_2\text{O(l)} \rightarrow \text{HCl} \cdot 100 \text{ H}_2\text{O}$$

$$\Delta H^0 = \Delta H_{f(\text{products})}^0 - \Delta H_{f(\text{reactants})}^0$$

$$= \left[(-168.1) - (-92.3) \right] \text{ kJ}$$

$$= (-168.1 + 92.3) \text{ kJ}$$

$$= -75.8 \text{ kJ}$$

In this case since 100 moles of water appear on both sides of the above process, the enthalpy of formation of water is not considered.

(vi) Enthalpies of Formation of Ions in Solution

The enthalpy change in the formation of an ion at unit activity from its elements in aqueous solution is known as the enthalpy of formation of the ion in solution. The absolute value of enthalpy of formation of individual ion in aqueous solution is not possible, but the difference of enthalpy of formation of two ions can be obtained. By convention, the enthalpy of formation of $H^+(aq)$ is arbitrarily taken as zero at 298 K and at unit activity

$$\frac{1}{2}H_2(g) + aq = H^+(aq) + e^- \qquad \Delta H^0_{298} = 0.0 \text{ kJ} \qquad \qquad ...(6.10)$$

With this convention, the enthalpy of formation of other ions can be evaluated. Thus, the enthalpy of formation of $OH^-(aq)$ can be calculated from the following reactions;

(i) $H_2O(l) = H^+(aq) + OH^-(aq) \qquad \Delta H^0 = 57.32 \text{ kJ}$

(ii) $H_2(g) + \frac{1}{2}O_2(g) = H_2O(l) \qquad \Delta H^0 = -285.83 \text{ kJ}$

Adding (i) and (ii), we get

(iii) $H_2(g) + \frac{1}{2}O_2(g) = H^+(aq) + OH^-(aq) \quad \Delta H^0 = -228.51 \text{ kJ}$

Since the enthalpy of formation of H^+ (aq) is equal to zero, hence the enthalpy of formation of $OH^-(aq)$ is obtained by subtracting equation (6.10) from (iii)

$$\frac{1}{2}H_2(g) + \frac{1}{2}O_2(g) + aq + e^- = OH^-(aq) \qquad \Delta H^0 = -228.51 \text{ kJ mol}^{-1}$$

Table 6.4 Enthalpies of Formation of Ions in Solution

Cation	ΔH^0 (kJ mol^{-1})	Anion	ΔH^0 (kJ mol^{-1})
H^+	0.0	OH^-	−229.9
K^+	−251.2	Cl^-	−167.5
Na^+	−329.7	Br^-	−121.0
Li^+	−278.5	I^-	−56.0
Zn^{2+}	−152.4	NO_3^-	−206.6
Mg^{2+}	−461.9	SO_4^{2-}	−907.5
Cu^{2+}	+64.4	HPO_4^{2-}	−1299.0
		PO_4^{3-}	−1284.0

(vii) Enthalpy of Hydration

The enthalpy change when a mole of an anhydrous salt combines with the requisite number of moles of water to form a specified hydrate is known as the enthalpy of hydration. It is obtained from the enthalpies of solutions of hydrous and anhydrous salts. Enthalpy of hydration of copper sulphate can be calculated from the following thermochemical equations

(i)　$CuSO_4 \cdot 5H_2O\,(s) + aq = CuSO_4(aq)$　　　　　　　$\Delta H^0 = 11.72$ kJ

(ii)　$CuSO_4(s) + 5H_2O\,(l) = CuSO_4 \cdot 5H_2O(s)$　　　　　$\Delta H^0 = x$ kJ

(iii)　$CuSO_4(s) + 5\,H_2O\,(l) + aq = CuSO_4(aq)$　　　　　$\Delta H^0 = -66.5$ kJ

From these equations, we get

$$CuSO_4(s) + 5\,H_2O\,(l) + aq = CuSO_4 \cdot 5\,H_2O(s) \qquad \Delta H^0 = -78.22 \text{ kJ}$$

(viii) Enthalpy of Precipitation

Enthalpy change involved in the formation of a mole of precipitate upon mixing dilute solutions of relevant electrolytes is called the enthalpy of precipitation. In the formation of a mole of silver bromide from Ag^+ (aq) and Br^- (aq) the enthalpy change is -17.78 kJ

$$Ag^+ (aq) + Br^- (aq) = AgBr\,(s) \qquad \Delta H^0 = -17.78 \text{ kJ}$$

(ix) Enthalpy of Phase Transition

Enthalpy change in the transformation of a substance from one state to another state is known as the *enthalpy of transition.* It includes transition from solid to liquid (fusion). liquid to vapour (vapourization), solid to vapour (sublimation) and change from one crystalline form to another crystalline form (polymorphic transition). In the transition of sulphur (rhombic) to sulphur (monoclinic), the enthalpy change is 13.14 kJ

$$S_{(rhombic)} = S_{(monoclinic)} \qquad \Delta H^0 = 13.14 \text{ kJ}$$

6.8 HESS'S LAW OF CONSTANT HEAT SUMMATION

The law states that *the total enthalpy change for a reaction is the same whether the reaction takes place in a single step or in several steps.* The thermodynamic aspect of this law is that the enthalpy is a state function, and so depends on the initial and final states of the reacting system, and is independent of the path connecting them. Figure 6.1 shows the transformation of reactants A and B into products C and D by two different ways. In one case, the reaction takes place in one step with ΔH_1 as the enthalpy of reaction, and in the other case, two steps are involved with ΔH_2 and ΔH_3 as the enthalpies of the corresponding reactions.

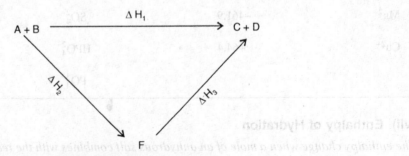

Fig. 6.1 Alternative reaction routes

According to Hess's law

$$\Delta H_1 = \Delta H_2 + \Delta H_3$$

As an example, consider the formation of an aqueous solution of ammonium chloride from gaseous hydrochloric acid and ammonia. This reaction can be carried out in two different ways:

Path I

(i) $HCl(g) + NH_3(g) = NH_4Cl(s)$ $\Delta H^0 = -177.80$ kJ

(ii) $NH_4Cl(s) + aq = NH_4Cl(aq)$ $\Delta H^0 = +16.32$ kJ

Adding (i) and (ii), we get

$HCl(g) + NH_3(g) + aq = NH_4Cl(aq)$ $\Delta H^0 = -161.48$ kJ

Path II

(i) $HCl(g) + aq = HCl(aq)$ $\Delta H^0 = -74.91$ kJ

(ii) $NH_3(g) + aq = NH_3(aq)$ $\Delta H^0 = -35.15$ kJ

(iii) $HCl(aq) + NH_3(aq) = NH_4Cl(aq)$ $\Delta H^0 = -51.42$ kJ

Adding these equations we get

$HCl(g) + NH_3(g) + aq = NH_4Cl(aq)$ $\Delta H^0 = -161.48$ kJ

The thermochemical equations can be treated as simple algebraic equations which can be added, subtracted, multiplied or divided by an integer. With the help of this law, enthalpy changes can be calculated for reactions in which direct experimental measurements are difficult. For example, it is rather difficult to measure the enthalpy change for the partial combustion of carbon (graphite) to carbon monoxide

$$C_{(graphite)} + \frac{1}{2}O_2(g) = CO(g) \qquad\qquad \Delta H_2^0 = ?$$

However, the enthalpy of formation of a mole of carbon dioxide is known from the reaction

$$C_{(graphite)} + O_2(g) = CO_2(g) \qquad\qquad \Delta H_1^0 = -393.5 \text{ kJ}$$

The formation of carbon dioxide can also take place as

$$C_{(graphite)} + \frac{1}{2}O_2(g) = CO(g) \qquad\qquad \Delta H_2^0 = ?$$

$$CO(g) + \frac{1}{2}O_2(g) = CO_2(g) \qquad\qquad \Delta H_3^0 = -280.9 \text{ kJ}$$

Evidently,

$$-280.9 + \Delta H_2^0 = -393.5 \text{ kJ}$$

or $$\Delta H_2^0 = -112.6 \text{ kJ}$$

Problem 6.6: From the following thermochemical reactions, calculate the enthalpy change for the reaction $CH_4(g) + \frac{3}{2}Cl_2(g) = CHCl_3(l) + \frac{3}{2}H_2(g)$

(i) $CHCl_3(l) + \frac{5}{4}O_2(g) = CO_2(g) + \frac{1}{2}H_2O(l) + \frac{3}{2}Cl_2(g)$ $\qquad$ $\Delta H^0 = -373.3$ kJ

(ii) $C_{(graphite)} + 2H_2(g) = CH_4(g)$ $\qquad$ $\Delta H^0 = -74.8$ kJ

(iii) $C_{(graphite)} + O_2(g) = CO_2(g)$ $\qquad$ $\Delta H^0 = -393.5$ kJ

(iv) $H_2(g) + \frac{1}{2}O_2(g) = H_2O(l)$ $\qquad$ $\Delta H^0 = -285.8$ kJ

Solution: On subtracting Eq. (iii) from Eq. (i), we get

(v) $CHCl_3(l) + \frac{1}{4}O_2(g) - C_{(graphite)} = \frac{1}{2}H_2O(l) + \frac{3}{2}Cl_2(g)$ $\qquad$ $\Delta H^0 = +20.2$ kJ

Now adding equation (ii) to equation (v), gives

(vi) $CHCl_3(l) + \frac{1}{4}O_2(g) + 2H_2(g) = CH_4(g) + \frac{1}{2}H_2O(l) + \frac{3}{2}Cl_2(g)$ $\quad$ $\Delta H^0 = -54.6$ kJ

Dividing equation (iv) by 2 and subtracting it from (vi), we get

$CHCl_3(l) + \frac{3}{2}H_2(g) = CH_4(g) + \frac{3}{2}Cl_2(g)$ $\qquad$ $\Delta H^0 = 88.3$ kJ

or $\quad CH_4(g) + \frac{3}{2}Cl_2(g) = CHCl_3(l) + \frac{3}{2}H_2(g)$ $\qquad$ $\Delta H^0 = -88.3$ kJ

Problem 6.7: Calculate the enthalpy of fusion of LiCl (s) at 900 K from the following informations.

(i) $Li(l) + \frac{1}{2}Cl_2(g) = LiCl(l)$ $\qquad$ $\Delta H^0_{900} = -285.8$ kJ

(ii) $Li(l) + \frac{1}{2}Cl_2(g) = LiCl(s)$ $\qquad$ $\Delta H^0_{900} = -405.2$ kJ

Solution: Subtracting (ii) from (i), we get

$LiCl(s) = LiCl(l)$ $\qquad$ $\Delta H^0_{900} = 120.4$ kJ

Problem 6.8: Calculate the enthalpy of the reaction

$C_2H_4(g) + HCl(g) = C_2H_5Cl(g)$

from the following reactions

(i) $2C(s) + \frac{5}{2}H_2(g) + \frac{1}{2}Cl_2(g) = C_2H_5Cl(g)$ $\qquad$ $\Delta H^0 = -112.10$ kJ

(ii) $\frac{1}{2}H_2(g) + \frac{1}{2}Cl_2(g) = HCl(g)$ $\qquad$ $\Delta H^0 = -92.35$ kJ *(iii)* $\quad 2C(s) + 2H_2(g) = C_2H_4(g)$ $\hspace{3cm}$ $\Delta H^0 = +52.30$ kJ

Solution: Adding *(ii)* and *(iii)* yields

$$\frac{5}{2}H_2(g) + 2C(s) + \frac{1}{2}Cl_2(g) = C_2H_4(g) + HCl(g) \hspace{2cm} \Delta H^0 = -40.05 \text{ kJ}$$

Now subtracting equation *(i)* from the above equation, we get

$$C_2H_5Cl(g) = C_2H_4(g) + HCl(g) \hspace{3cm} \Delta H^0 = +72.05 \text{ kJ}$$

or $\quad C_2H_4(g) + HCl(g) = C_2H_5Cl(g)$ $\hspace{3cm}$ $\Delta H^0 = -72.05$ kJ

6.9 BOND ENTHALPIES

In chemical reactions energy is required in breaking bonds between the atoms while energy is released in the formation of bonds between the atoms. Since the measurements are usually carried out at constant pressure, the energy changes are the enthalpy changes associated with the formation or breaking up of bonds. *The amount of enthalpy required to break 1 mole of a particular bond in a given compound and separate the resulting gaseous atoms or radicals from one another is known as the bond dissociation enthalpy.* It depends on the nature of the atoms linked by the bond and the nature of the molecule as a whole. The bond dissociation enthalpy of a hydrogen molecule is 435.9 kJ mol^{-1}.

$$H_2(g) = 2H(g) \hspace{3cm} \Delta H^0 = +435.9 \text{ kJ mol}^{-1}$$

In case of water, the bond dissociation enthalpy of an OH linkage is 497.8 kJ and the enthalpy required to break the O – H bond in the residual OH group is 428.5 kJ.

$$H_2O(g) = H(g) + OH(g) \hspace{3cm} \Delta H^0 = 497.8 \text{ kJ}$$

$$OH(g) = H(g) + O(g) \hspace{3cm} \Delta H^0 = 428.5 \text{ kJ}$$

The average value of the bond dissociation enthalpies of a molecule is known as *the bond enthalpy*. In case of hydrogen and other diatomic molecules the bond enthalpy and bond dissociation enthalpies are equal. However, in water, the bond enthalpy is equal to the average of the two bond dissociation

enthalpies, *i.e.*, $\dfrac{497.8 \text{ kJ} + 428.5 \text{ kJ}}{2} = 463.2$ kJ

The bond dissociation enthalpies for the stepwise dissociation of CH_4 are as

$$CH_4(g) = CH_3(g) + H(g) \hspace{3cm} \Delta H^0 = 427.0 \text{ kJ}$$

$$CH_3(g) = CH_2(g) + H(g) \hspace{3cm} \Delta H^0 = 429.0 \text{ kJ}$$

$$CH_2(g) = CH(g) + H(g) \hspace{3cm} \Delta H^0 = 460.2 \text{ kJ}$$

$$CH(g) = C(g) + H(g) \hspace{3cm} \Delta H^0 = 343.9 \text{ kJ}$$

The enthalpy for each step is different due to the fact that in each case a different dissociating fragment is involved. The C – H bond enthalpy would be one-fourth of the enthalpy required to break a mole of CH_4 and is 415.2 kJ.

The data on the bond enthalpies can be utilized in evaluating the enthalpy of formation of a compound of known structure and the enthalpy of a reaction. The enthalpy of a reaction in the gaseous phase is equal to the sum of the enthalpy required to break all of the bonds in the reactants and the enthalpy released in the formation of all the bonds in the products.

$$\Delta H^0 = \text{(Sum of enthalpies of breaking} \quad + \quad \text{...(Sum of enthalpies of formation}$$
all bonds in the reactants) of all the bonds in the products)

Since bond formation is an exothermic process and is the reverse of bond breaking. The enthalpy of formation of a bond and the bond enthalpy are equal in magnitude but opposite in sign.

The accuracy of calculation of ΔH^0 by using this equation is limited because the strength of a chemical bond varies somewhat depending upon its environment in a given molecule and also that all the reactants and products are gaseous. When other states of matter are involved, the contribution of ΔH^0 of the enthalpies of vaporization or sublimation must be included.

Some experimental values of bond enthalpies are given in Table 6.5.

Table 6.5 Bond Enthalpies in kJ mol^{-1}

H – H	436	H – S	355	C = C	610
Cl – Cl	243	C – C	348	O = O	497
Br – Br	193	N – N	160	N = N	417
I – I	150	O – O	138	C = N	616
C – H	413	C – Cl	328	C ≡ C	812
N – H	390	C – Br	276	N ≡ N	940
O – H	463			C ≡ N	858
				C ≡ O	1070

Problem 6.9: The bond enthalpy of $H_2(g)$ is 436 kJ mol^{-1} and that of $N_2(g)$ is 941.3 kJ mol^{-1}. Calculate the average bond enthalpy of an N – H bond in ammonia. $\Delta H_f^0(NH_3) = -46.0$ kJ mol^{-1}.

Solution: Since

(i) $N_2(g) = 2N(g)$ $\Delta H^0 = 941.3$ kJ mol^{-1}

(ii) $H_2(g) = 2H(g)$ $\Delta H^0 = 436.0$ kJ mol^{-1}

(iii) $\frac{1}{2}N_2(g) + \frac{3}{2}H_2(g) = NH_3(g)$ $\Delta H^0 = -46.0$ kJ mol^{-1}

Multiplying Eq. (i) by $\frac{1}{2}$ and Eq. (ii) by $\frac{3}{2}$ and adding yields

(iv) $\frac{1}{2}N_2(g) + \frac{3}{2}H_2(g) = N(g) + 3H(g)$ $\Delta H^0 = 1124.6$ kJ

Now subtracting Eq. (iii) from (iv), we get

$NH_3(g) = N(g) + 3H(g)$ $\Delta H^0 = 1170.6$ kJ mol^{-1}

The average bond enthalpy is obtained by dividing the above value of ΔH^0 by 3, since there are three N—H bond in NH_3. Hence

$$\Delta H_{N-H} = \frac{1170.6 \text{ kJ}}{3} = 390.2 \text{ kJ mol}^{-1}$$

Problem 6.10: Calculate the bond enthalpy for a C—O bond in methanol from the following data:

(i) $\quad C(s) + 2H_2(g) + \dfrac{1}{2}O_2(g) = CH_2OH(g) \qquad \Delta H^0 = -200.0 \text{ kJ mol}^{-1}$

(ii) $\quad C(s) = C(g) \qquad\qquad\qquad\qquad\qquad\qquad \Delta H^0 = 716.8 \text{ kJ mol}^{-1}$

(iii) $\quad 2H_2(g) = 4H(g) \qquad\qquad\qquad\qquad\qquad \Delta H^0 = 872.0 \text{ kJ mol}^{-1}$

(iv) $\quad \dfrac{1}{2}O_2(g) = O(g) \qquad\qquad\qquad\qquad\quad\;\; \Delta H^0 = 249.0 \text{ kJ mol}^{-1}$

The bond enthalpy for C—H bond is 413 kJ mol^{-1} and for O—H bond it is 463.6 kJ mol^{-1}.
Solution: The enthalpy change for the dissociation of $CH_3OH(g)$ is given

$$CH_3OH(g) = C(g) + 4H(g) + O(g) \qquad \Delta H^0 = ?$$

Adding (ii), (iii) and (iv) gives

$$C(s) + 2H_2(g) + \frac{1}{2}O_2(g) = C(g) + 4H(g) + O(g) \qquad \Delta H^0 = 1837.9 \text{ kJ}$$

Now subtracting Eq. (i) from the above Eq. gives

$$CH_3OH(g) = C(g) + 4H(g) + O(g) \qquad\qquad\qquad \Delta H^0 = 2037.8 \text{ kJ mol}^{-1}$$

Since in methanol, there are three C – H, one C – O and one O – H bonds

Therefore, $\qquad\qquad 2037.8 \text{ kJ} = 3\left(\Delta H^0_{C-H}\right) + 1\left(\Delta H^0_{O-H}\right) + 1\left(\Delta H^0_{C-O}\right)$

$$= 3(415) + (463.6) + \left(\Delta H^0_{C-O}\right)$$

or $\qquad\qquad \left(\Delta H^0_{C-O}\right) = 329.0 \text{ kJ mol}^{-1}$

Problem 6.11: Calculate the enthalpy of formation of methanol, the bond enthalpies (kJ mol^{-1}) are as

$\Delta H^0_{C-H} = 415.0$, $\Delta H^0_{C-O} = 351.5$, $\Delta H^0_{O-H} = 463.0$, $\Delta H^0_{H-H} = 436.0$, $\Delta H^0_{O=O} = 497.0$.

The enthalpy of sublimation $\left(\Delta H^0_S\right)$ of a mole of C(graphite) is 713.0 kJ.

Solution: Methanol is formed from its elements according to the reaction.

$$C_{(graphite)} + \frac{1}{2}O_2(g) + 2H_2(g) = CH_3OH(g)$$

The enthalpy of formation of a mole of methanol is given as

$$\Delta H^0 = \left(2\Delta H^0_{H-H} + \frac{1}{2}\Delta H^0_{O=O} + \Delta H^0_S\right) - \left(3\Delta H^0_{C-H} + \Delta H^0_{C-O} + \Delta H^0_{O-H}\right)$$

$$= \left[\left(2 \times 436.0 + \frac{1}{2} \times 497.0 + 713 \right) - \left(3 \times 415 + 351.5 + 463 \right) \right] kJ$$

$$= (1833.5 - 2059.5) \, kJ$$

$$= -226.0 \, kJ$$

Problem 6.12: Calculate the enthalpy of the reaction

$$C_2H_4(g) + Br_2(g) = C_2H_4Br_2(g)$$

The bond enthalpies $\left(kJ \, mol^{-1} \right)$ are $\Delta H^0_{C-H} = 415.0$, $\Delta H^0_{C=C} = 610.0$, $\Delta H^0_{C-C} = 348.0$,

$\Delta H^0_{C-Br} = 276.0$, $\Delta H^0_{Br-Br} = 193.0$

Solution: The enthalpy of the reaction is given by

$\Delta H^0 =$ (Sum of bond enthalpies of   ...(Sum of bond enthalpies of
         all bonds in the reactants) $^{-}$ all bonds in the products)

$$= \left[4\Delta H^0_{C-H} + \Delta H^0_{C=C} + \Delta H^0_{Br-Br} \right] - \left[4\Delta H^0_{C-H} + 2\Delta H^0_{C-Br} + \Delta H^0_{C-C} \right]$$

$$= \left[\Delta H^0_{C=C} + \Delta H^0_{Br-Br} \right] - \left[\Delta H^0_{C-C} + 2\Delta H^0_{C-Br} \right]$$

$$= (610.0 + 193) \, kJ - (348 + 2 \times 276.0) \, kJ$$

$$= (803.0 - 900.0) \, kJ$$

$$= -97.0 \, kJ$$

Problem 6.13: The enthalpy change for the reaction

$$CH_4(g) + Cl_2(g) = CH_3Cl(g) + HCl(g)$$

is $- 104.6$ kJ. The bond enthalpy of C—H is 83.7 kJ mol^{-1} greater than the bond enthalpy of C-Cl bond. If the bond enthalpies of H—H and H—Cl are almost the same in magnitude, calculate the enthalpy change for the reaction:

$$H_2(g) + Cl_2(g) = 2HCl(g)$$

Solution:

According to the problem, the enthalpy change for the chlorination of methane is

$$4 \Delta H^0_{C-H} + \Delta H^0_{Cl-Cl} - \left(3\Delta H^0_{C-H} + \Delta H^0_{C-Cl} + \Delta H^0_{H-Cl} \right) = -104.6 \, kJ$$

or

$$\Delta H^0_{C-H} + \Delta H^0_{Cl-Cl} - \left(\Delta H^0_{C-Cl} + \Delta H^0_{H-Cl} \right) = -104.6 \, kJ$$

$$\Delta H^0_{Cl-Cl} - \Delta H^0_{H-Cl} = (-104.6 - 83.7) \, kJ = -188.3 \, kJ$$

$$\left(As \; \Delta H^0_{C-H} - \Delta H^0_{C-Cl} = 83.7 \, kJ \right)$$

Adding and subtracting ΔH^0_{H-H} on the left hand side of the above equation, we get

$$\Delta H_{H-H} + \Delta H_{Cl-Cl} - \Delta H_{H-Cl} - \Delta H_{H-H}$$

$$\Delta H^0_{H-H} + \Delta H^0_{Cl-Cl} - 2\Delta H^0_{H-Cl} = -188.3 \text{ kJ} \qquad \left(\because \Delta H_{H-H} \approx \Delta H_{H-Cl}\right)$$

So ΔH^0 for the desired reaction is -188.3 kJ

6.10 TEMPERATURE DEPENDENCE OF ENTHALPIES OF REACTIONS— KIRCHOFF'S EQUATIONS

Enthalpy of a reaction depends upon the temperature. The temperature dependence can be obtained by expressing the enthalpy of the reaction ΔH as

$$\Delta H = \Sigma H_{\text{Products}} - \Sigma H_{\text{Reactants}} \qquad \text{...(6.11)}$$

Differentiating Eq. (6.11) with respect to temperature (T) at constant pressure, we get

$$\left[\frac{d(\Delta H)}{dT}\right]_P = \Sigma \left[\frac{dH_{\text{Products}}}{dT}\right]_P - \Sigma \left[\frac{dH_{\text{Reactants}}}{dT}\right]_P \qquad \text{...(6.12)}$$

Since

$$\left[\frac{dH}{dT}\right]_P = C_P$$

Hence

$$\left[\frac{d(\Delta H)}{dT}\right]_P = \sum C_P(\text{Products}) - \sum C_P(\text{Reactants}) = \Delta C_P \qquad \text{...(6.13)}$$

Similarly, for the enthalpy of the reaction at constant volume, we have

$$\left[\frac{d(\Delta E)}{dT}\right]_V = \Delta C_V \qquad \text{...(6.14)}$$

Eq. (6.13) and (6.14) show that the rate of change of enthalpy of a reaction with temperature is equal to the difference in the heat capacities of the products and reactants. These equations are known as *Kirchhoff's equations*.

Integration of Eq. (6.13) between two temperatures T_1 and T_2 gives

$$\int_{\Delta H_1}^{\Delta H_2} d(\Delta H) = \int_{T_1}^{T_2} \Delta C_P \, dT \qquad \text{...(6.15)}$$

when dT is not too large, ΔC_P may be assumed to be independent of temperature, hence the above equation reduces to

$$\Delta H_2 - \Delta H_1 = \Delta C_P (T_2 - T_1) \qquad \text{...(6.16)}$$

By the use of this equation it is possible to calculate ΔH for reactions at any other temperature if it is known at one temperature and the value of ΔC_P in that temperature range.

However, if ΔC_P is not constant it can be expressed as function of temperature in the form

$$C_P = a + bT + cT^2 + \ldots\ldots \qquad \ldots(6.17)$$

where a, b, c are constants for a given substance and their values are derived from experimental data on heat capacities over a range of temperature. When the heat capacity of products and reactants are so written, we have

$$\Delta C_P = \Delta a + \Delta bT + \Delta cT^2 + \ldots\ldots \qquad \ldots(6.18)$$

where $\Delta a = a_{(Products)} - a_{(Reactants)}$, $\Delta b = b_{(Products)} - b_{(Reactants)}$ and so on.

Integration of Eq. (6.15) after substituting the value of ΔC_P from Eq. (6.18) yields

$$\Delta H_2 - \Delta H_1 = \int_{T_1}^{T_2} \Delta C_P \, dT$$

$$= \int_{T_1}^{T_2} (\Delta a) \Delta T + \int_{T_1}^{T_2} (\Delta b) T \Delta T + \int_{T_1}^{T_2} (\Delta c) T^2 \Delta T + \ldots$$

$$= \Delta a (T_2 - T_1) + \Delta b \left(\frac{T_2^2 - T_1^2}{2} \right) + \Delta c \left(\frac{T_2^3 - T_1^3}{3} \right) + \ldots\ldots \qquad \ldots(6.19)$$

Problem 6.14: The enthalpy of fusion of water at 273 K is 6.0 kJ mol^{-1} at constant pressure of 1 atmosphere. Calculate its value at 263 K.

Given $\qquad\qquad C_{P_{H_2O(l)}} = 74.46$ J mol^{-1} K^{-1}, $C_{P_{H_2O(s)}} = 37.2$ J mol^{-1} K^{-1}.

Solution: If the heat capacities are assumed to be temperature independent then from Eq. (6.16)

$$\Delta H^0 (263 \text{ K}) = \Delta H^0 (273 \text{ K}) + \Delta C_P (T_2 - T_1)$$

$$= \Delta H^0 (273 \text{ K}) + \left[C_{P, H_2O(l)} - C_{P, H_2O(s)} \right](T_2 - T_1)$$

$$= \Delta H^0 (273 \text{ K}) + (74.46 - 37.20)(263 - 273)$$

$$= (6.0 \text{ kJ}) + \left[37.26 \times (-10) \times 10^{-3} \text{ kJ} \right]$$

$$= 5.63 \text{ kJ mol}^{-1}$$

Problem 6.15: For the reaction

$$CO(g) + \frac{1}{2} O_2(g) = CO_2(g)$$

ΔH^0 (298K) = 278.9 kJ mol^{-1}. Find ΔH^0 (1000 K) if the heat capacities in J mol^{-1} K^{-1} are given as

$$C_{P, CO(g)} = 26.86 + 6.97 \times 10^{-3} T - 8.2 \times 10^{-7} T^2$$

$$C_{P,\,CO_2\,(g)} = 26.01 + 43.5 \times 10^{-3}T - 148.0 \times 10^{-7}T^2$$

$$C_{P,\,O_2\,(g)} = 25.70 + 13.0 \times 10^{-3}T - 38.6 \times 10^{-7}T^2$$

Solution: From Eq. (6.19)

(i) $\Delta H^0 (1000\,K) - \Delta H^0(298\,K) = \Delta a(1000 - 298) + \Delta b\dfrac{(1000)^2 - (298)^2}{2} + \Delta c\dfrac{(1000)^3 - (298)^3}{3}$

Here

$$\Delta a = 26.0 - \left(\frac{25.7}{2} + 26.86\right) = -13.7$$

$$\Delta b = 43.5 - \left[\left(\frac{13.0}{2} + 6.97\right)\right] \times 10^{-3} = 30.0 \times 10^{-3}$$

$$\Delta c = -\left[148.0 - \left(\frac{38.6}{2} + 8.20\right)\right] \times 10^{-7} = -120.5 \times 10^{-7}$$

Substituting these values in Eq. (i), we get

$$\Delta H^0(1000\,K) - \Delta H^0(298\,K) = -13.7(702) + 30.0 \times 10^{-3} \times \left[\frac{9.112 \times 10^5}{2}\right]$$

$$-120.5 \times 10^{-7}\left[\frac{7.354 \times 10^7}{3}\right]$$

$$= -9616 + 13668 - 295$$

$$= 3.76\,kJ$$

or

$$\Delta H^0(1000\,K) = 3.76\,kJ + \Delta H^0(298\,K)$$

$$= 3.76 + 278.90$$

$$= 282.66\,kJ\,mol^{-1}$$

6.11 FLAME AND EXPLOSION TEMPERATURES

Maximum Reaction Temperature—Flame Temperature: In the previous sections it has been assumed that reactions take place at constant temperature and the enthalpy of a reaction is simply the heat absorbed by the reactants from the surroundings or evolved to the surroundings. If the reaction occurs at constant pressure under adiabatic conditions, no heat enters or leaves the system, the temperature of the reacting system would change, *i.e.*, products will be at a temperature different from those of the reactants.For reactions, where ΔH is positive, heat is absorbed and the final temperature of the system will fall. On the other hand, the final temperature will rise if heat is evolved during the reaction. The temperature attained in the combustion of hydrocarbons in the presence of excess of air or oxygen is known as *the maximum reaction temperature* or *flame temperature* as the gases at such high temperature burn producing heat and light. The flame temperature can be calculated if the enthalpy of the reaction and the temperature dependence of the heat capacities of the products are known.

Calculations of the Flame Temperature: In calculating the flame temperature, enthalpy of the reaction at a certain temperature say at 298 K is measured. This heat is then used up in heating the products. If ΔH_{298} is the enthalpy of the reaction at 298 K and T_2 the final temperature, then heat required to raise the temperature of the products from 298K to T_2 should be equal in magnitude to the heat of the reaction ΔH_{298} but opposite in sign. The sum, ΔH_{298} and the heat required to raise the temperature, $\Delta H_{\text{heating,}}$ should be zero as ΔH for the whole adiabatic process is zero. If $\Sigma n C_p$ is the heat capacity of the products, then

$$\Delta H_{\text{heating}} = -\Delta H_{298} = \int_{298}^{T_2} \Sigma n C_{P,\,m} dT$$

The calculated flame temperature is generally higher than the observed temperature. The difference may be due to a number of complications. The system may not be truly adiabatic. In combustion excess of air or oxygen is employed. Unreacted air or oxygen has to be heated and consequently a part of the heat would be used up in heating these gases. In calculating the flame temperature, heating of the unreacted gases should also be taken into account. Furthermore at such high temperatures, the products formed might decompose and a part of the heat may be used up in the decomposition of the product molecules.

Maximum Explosion Temperature: If the combustion of hydrocarbons is carried out at constant volume under adiabatic conditions then the maximum temperature attained is known as *the explosion temperature*. The calculations of explosion temperature is similar to the flame temperature except ΔH is replaced by ΔE. The pressure which the reacting system may acquire at the explosion temperature is known as *the maximum explosion pressure*.

Problem 6.16: A mixture of hydrogen gas with the theoretical amount of air at 298 K and a total pressure of 1 atmosphere is exploded in a closed vessel. The mean heat capacities at constant volume for nitrogen and water vapours in the temperature range 298 K to 3000 K are respectively 26.36 JK^{-1} mol^{-1} and 38.91 JK^{-1} mol^{-1}. If the enthalpy of the reaction

$$H_2(g) + \frac{1}{2}O_2(g) = H_2O(g)$$

at constant volume is -240.58 kJ mol^{-1}, calculate the maximum explosion temperature assuming adiabatic conditions.

Solution: We know that

$$\Delta E + \int_{298}^{T_2} \Sigma n C_{V,\,m} dT = 0$$

Since heat capacities are mean values, therefore, we have

$$\Delta E + \Sigma n C_{V,\,m}(T_2 - 298) = 0$$

Now

$$\Delta E = -240.58 \text{ kJ mol}^{-1}$$

$$\Delta n C_{V,\,m} = C_{V,\,m}(H_2O,\,g) + 2\,C_{V,\,m}(N_2,g)$$

$(\because$ 2 moles of N_2 are associated with 1/2 mole of O_2)

$$= (38.91 + 2 \times 26.36)\ JK^{-1}mol^{-1}$$

$$= 91.63\ JK^{-1}mol^{-1}$$

Putting the values of ΔE and $\Sigma n C_{V,\,m}$, we get

$$-240.58 + 91.63 \times 10^{-3}(T_2 - 298) = 0$$

or

$$T = 2924\ K$$

EXERCISES

1. Explain and illustrate the following terms:
    (i) Enthalpy of a reaction   (ii) Enthalpy of formation
    (iii) Standard state and standard molar enthalpy   (iv) Enthalpy of combustion
    (v) Enthalpy of hydrogenation   (vi) Enthalpy of neutralization
    (vii) Enthalpy of ionization   (viii) Integral and differential enthalpies of solutions
    (ix) Integral and differential enthalpies of dilutions
    (x) Enthalpy of hydration   (xi) Enthalpy of formation of ions
    (xii) Enthalpy of phase transition   (xiii) Bond enthalpy and bond dissociation enthalpy
    (xiv) Hess's law of constant heat summation (xv) The maximum flame temperature.

2. Distinguish the terms in the following pairs:
    (i) Exothermic reactions from endothermic reactions
    (ii) Enthalpy of formation from standard enthalpy of formation
    (iii) Integral enthalpy of solution from differential enthalpy of solution
    (iv) Integral enthalpy of dilution from differential Enthalpy of dilution
    (v) Enthalpy of a reaction at constant volume from that at constant pressure
    (vi) Bond enthalpy from bond dissociation enthalpy
    (vii) Enthalpy of dissociation from enthalpy of ionization

3. Explain, giving reasons the following
    (i) For reactions involving condensed phases, i.e., solids and liquids, $\Delta H = \Delta E$.
    (ii) Bond enthalpy and bond dissociation enthalpy of a diatomic molecule are identical.
    (iii) Enthalpy of neutralization of a strong monobasic acid by a strong base is always equal to -57.32 kJ mol^{-1}.
    (iv) The energy required to break an O-H bond in water is 498 kJ mol^{-1} while in hydroxy radical it is 430 kJ mol^{-1}
    (v) The Hess's law of constant heat summation is a direct consequence of the first law of thermodynamics.
    (vi) Differential enthalpy of a solution is identical with the integral enthalpy of solution for every dilute solutions and decreases with increasing concentration and finally becomes zero for the saturated solutions.
    (vii) In stating the ΔH values of chemical reactions, it is presumed that the reactants and products are at the same temperature and pressure.

4. Derive the relations
    (i) $\Delta H = \Delta E + \Delta(PV) = \Delta E + \Delta n_g RT$

(ii) $\left[\dfrac{d(\Delta H)}{dT}\right]_P = \Delta C_P$ and $\left[\dfrac{d(\Delta E)}{dT}\right]_V = \Delta C_V$ (Kirchoff's equation)

(iii) $T = T^0 + \dfrac{\left(-\Delta H_T^0\right)}{\sum C_P(\text{products})}$, where T is the adiabatic flame temperature.

5. (a) Do the products of an exothermic reaction contain more or less energy than the reactants at the same temperature? Explain your answer.

   (b) For each of the following exothermic changes, explain whether the heat evolved at constant pressure is smaller than, larger than, or the same as the heat evolved at constant volume

   (i) $C(s) + O_2(g) = CO_2(g)$

   (ii) $CO(g) + \dfrac{1}{2}O_2(g) = CO_2(g)$

   (iii) $\dfrac{1}{2}H_2(g) + \dfrac{1}{2}Cl_2(g) = HCl(g)$

   (iv) $SO_2(g) + \dfrac{1}{2}O_2(g) = SO_3(g)$

   (v) $PCl_5(g) = PCl_3(g) + Cl_2(g)$

   Ans. (i), (iii) same; (ii), (iv) less; (v) more.

6. (a) Calculate ΔE^0 for the reaction at 298 K

   $$C_6H_6(l) + \dfrac{15}{2}O_2(g) = 6CO_2(g) + 3H_2O(l) \qquad \Delta H^0 = -3267 \text{ kJ}$$

   Ans. $\Delta E^0 = -3263.5$ kJ.

   (b) The standard enthalpy of formation of NO_2 (g), KCl (s), KNO_3 (s) and NOCl (g) are respectively 38.89, -435.97, -492.78 and 52.72 kJ mol^{-1} at 298 K. Calculate ΔE^0 for the reaction.

   Ans. $\Delta E^0 = -69.39$ kJ.

7. From the following thermochemical reactions, calculate the enthalpy change for the reaction $3C_2H_2(g) = C_6H_6(l)$ at 298 K.

   (i) $C_6H_6(l) + \dfrac{15}{2}O_2(g) = 3H_2O(l) + 6CO_2(g) \qquad \Delta H_f^0 = -3267.70$ kJ

   (ii) $C_2H_2(g) + \dfrac{5}{2}O_2(g) = 2CO_2(g) + H_2O(!) \qquad \Delta H^0 = -1299.55$ kJ

8. Given the following informations:

   (i) $H_2(g) + \dfrac{1}{2}O_2(g) = H_2O(l) \qquad \Delta H^0 = -285.84$ kJ

   (ii) $C(s) + O_2(g) = CO_2(g) \qquad \Delta H^0 = -393.51$ kJ

   (iii) $CH_4(g) + 2O_2(g) = CO_2(g) + 2H_2O(l) \qquad \Delta H^0 = -890.35$ kJ

Calculate, at 298 K, the enthalpy change for the reaction

$$CH_4(g) + O_2(g) = C(s) + 2H_2O\,(l)$$

Ans. −496.85 kJ.

9. (a) Calculate the standard enthalpy of hydrogenation for each of the following reactions:

(i) $C_2H_4(g) + H_2(g) = C_2H_6(g)$

(ii) $C_3H_6(g) + H_2(g) = C_3H_8(g)$

(iii) $C_4H_8(g) + H_2(g) = C_4H_{10}(g)$

Given $\Delta H_f^0(C_2H_4(g)) = 52.30$ kJ mol^{-1}, $\Delta H_f^0(C_3H_6(g)) = 20.42$ kJ mol^{-1},

$\Delta H_f^0(C_4H_8(g)) = 1.17$ kJ mol^{-1}, $\Delta H_f^0(C_2H_6(g)) = -84.68$ kJ mol^{-1}, $\Delta H_f^0(C_3H_8(g)) = -103.9$ kJ mol^{-1}

and $\Delta H_f^0(C_4H_{10}(g)) = -124.8$ kJ mol^{-1}

(b) Do these answers suggest that ΔH^0 for any reaction of the type $C_nH_{2n} + H_2 = C_nH_{2n+2}$ might be treated as constant?

Ans. (a) (i) −136.98 kJ, (ii) −124.32 kJ, (iii) −125.97 kJ.
(b) The value of ΔH^0 for the said reaction would be expected to be constant if C—H, C = C and C—C bond enthalpies were same in each of the compounds.

10. Given $C(graphite) + O_2(g) = CO_2(g)$ $\qquad\qquad \Delta H_{298}^0 = -393.51$ kJ

$C(diamond) + O_2(g) = CO_2(g)$ $\qquad\qquad \Delta H_{298}^0 = -395.40$ kJ

Calculate the enthalpy of transition of graphite to diamond. **Ans.** 1.89 kJ.

11. Calculate ΔH^0 and ΔE^0 for the isomerization of $C_2H_5OH(l)$ into $CH_3 - O - CH_3$ (g) from the following data at 298 K:

(i) $C(s) + 3H_2(g) + \dfrac{1}{2}O_2 = C_2H_5OH$ $\qquad\qquad \Delta H^0 = -276.14$ kJ

(ii) $C(s) + O_2(g) = CO_2(g)$ $\qquad\qquad \Delta H^0 = -393.51$ kJ

(iii) $H_2(g) + \dfrac{1}{2}O_2(g) = H_2O\,(l)$ $\qquad\qquad \Delta H^0 = -285.84$ kJ

(iv) $CH_3 - O - CH_3(g) + 3O_2(g) = 2CO_2(g) + 3H_2O(l)$ $\qquad \Delta H^0 = -1456.03$ kJ

Ans. $\Delta H^0 = 87.60$ kJ and $\Delta E^0 = 85.12$ kJ

12. Calculate the enthalpy of the reaction

$$CH_3Cl(g) = C(g) + 3H(g) + Cl(g)$$

The bond enthalpies of C–H and C–Cl bonds are 415.8 kJ mol^{-1} and 326.35 kJ mol^{-1} respectively.

Ans. 1573.75 kJ.

13. Given the standard enthalpy changes for the following reactions:

$$C(\text{graphite}) + 2H_2(g) = CH_4(g) \qquad\qquad \Delta H^0_{298} = -74.75 \text{ kJ mol}^{-1}$$

$$2C(\text{graphite}) + 3H_2(g) = C_2H_6(g) \qquad\qquad \Delta H^0_{298} = -84.50 \text{ kJ mol}^{-1}$$

$$2C(\text{graphite}) + 2H_2(g) = C_2H_4(g) \qquad\qquad \Delta H^0_{298} = 52.60 \text{ kJ mol}^{-1}$$

$$2C(\text{graphite}) + H_2(g) = C_2H_2(g) \qquad\qquad \Delta H^0_{298} = 226.90 \text{ kJ mol}^{-1}$$

$$H_2(g) = 2H(g) \qquad\qquad \Delta H^0_{298} = 435.84 \text{ kJ mol}^{-1}$$

$$C(\text{graphite}) = C(g) \qquad\qquad \Delta H^0_{298} = 716.68 \text{ kJ mol}^{-1}$$

Calculate the bond enthalpies of (*i*) C–H, (*ii*) C–C, (*iii*) C=C and (*iv*) C≡C bonds.

Ans. (*i*) 415.8 kJ mol⁻¹, (*ii*) 347.7 kJ mol⁻¹, (*iii*) 600.7 kJ mol⁻¹, (*iv*) 816.0 kJ mol⁻¹.

14. From the measured enthalpy of the reaction

$$C(\text{graphite}) + \frac{1}{2}Cl_2 + \frac{3}{2}H_2(g) = CH_3Cl(g) \qquad \Delta H^0 = -82.01 \text{ kJ mol}^{-1}$$

calculate the enthalpy of the reaction

$$C(g) + Cl(g) + 3H(g) = CH_3Cl(g)$$

Given that

$$C(\text{graphite}) = C(g) \qquad\qquad \Delta H^0 = 716.68 \text{ kJ mol}^{-1}$$

$$H_2(g) = 2H(g) \qquad\qquad \Delta H^0 = 435.94 \text{ kJ mol}^{-1}$$

$$Cl_2(g) = 2 Cl(g) \qquad\qquad \Delta H^0 = 242.15 \text{ kJ mol}^{-1}$$

Ans. $\Delta H^0 = -1572.68 \text{ kJ mol}^{-1}$

15. The standard enthalpy change for the reaction

$$CH_4(g) + 2O_2(g) = CO_2(g) + 2H_2O(g) \text{ is } -802.24 \text{ kJ}$$

Calculate $\Delta H^0_{C=0}$ if the bond enthalpies (kJ mol⁻¹) of C–H, O–O and O–H are 415.8, 495.04 and 464.4 respectively.

Ans. 798.98 kJ mol⁻¹.

16. Given below are the ΔH^0_f values at 298 K

$$H_2O(l) = -285.84 \text{ kJ}, HCl(aq) = -167.4 \text{ kJ}, NaOH(aq) = -469.6 \text{ kJ}$$

$$NaCl(aq) = -407.0 \text{ kJ}$$

(*i*) What does HCl (aq) signify?

(*ii*) Calculate the standard enthalpy of neutralization of a strong acid by a strong base.

(*iii*) Calculate ΔH^0_f for OH⁻ (aq).

(*iv*) Calculate ΔH^0_f for (a) Na⁺(aq), (b) and Cl⁻(aq).

Ans. (*i*) HCl(aq) signifies a solution of 1 mole of HCl in large excess of water. (*ii*) –55.84 kJ, (*iii*) –230.0 kJ mol⁻¹, (*iv*) (*a*) –239.60 kJ mol⁻¹, (*b*) –167.40 kJ mol⁻¹.

17. From the thermochemical equation

$$Zn(s) + 2H^+(aq) = Zn^{2+}(aq) + H_2(g) \qquad \Delta H^0 = -152.42 \text{ kJ}$$

Calculate the standard enthalpy of formation of Zn^{2+} (aq) ions. **Ans.** -152.42 kJ mol^{-1}.

18. From the data at 298 K

$$\frac{1}{2}H_2(g) + \frac{1}{2}O_2(g) = OH(g) \qquad \Delta H^0 = 42.09 \text{ kJ mol}^{-1}$$

$$H_2(g) + \frac{1}{2}O_2(g) = H_2O(g) \qquad \Delta H^0 = -241.83 \text{ kJ mol}^{-1}$$

$$H_2(g) = 2H(g) \qquad \Delta H^0 = 435.94 \text{ kJ mol}^{-1}$$

$$O_2(g) = 2O(g) \qquad \Delta H^0 = 495.04 \text{ kJ mol}^{-1}$$

Compute ΔH^0 for reactions

(i) $OH(g) = H(g) + O(g)$

(ii) $H_2O(g) = 2H(g) + O(g)$

(iii) $H_2O(g) = H(g) + OH(g)$

Ans. (i) 423.40 kJ, (ii) 925.39 kJ, (iii) 501.89 kJ.

19. Calculate the resonance enthalpy of benzene compared with one Kekulé structure from the following data at 298 K:

(i) $6C(s) + 3H_2(g) = C_6H_6(g) \qquad \Delta H^0 = 82.93$ kJ mol^{-1}

(ii) $C(graphite) = C(g) \qquad \Delta H^0 = 716.68$ kJ mol^{-1}

(iii) $H_2(g) = 2H(g) \qquad \Delta H^0 = 435.94$ kJ mol^{-1}

The bond enthalpies (kJ mol^{-1}) of C–H, C–C and C=C are 415.8, 347.7 and 600.7 respectively.
Ans. Resonance enthalpy of benzene molecule is 174.97 kJ.

20. From the following informations on bond enthalpy data, calculate the enthalpy of formation of gaseous isoprene

$$CH_2 = C - CH = CH_2$$
$$\underset{CH_3}{|}$$

Bond enthalpies of H–H, C–H, C–C, and C=C are 435.94 kJ mol^{-1}, 415.8 kJ mol^{-1}, 347.7 kJ mol^{-1} and 600.7 kJ mol^{-1}, respectively. The enthalpy of sublimation of carbon is 716.68 kJ mol^{-1}. If the enthalpy of formation of gaseous isoprene obtained from the combustion data is 8.79 kJ mol^{-1}, how would you account for the difference in the two values?

Ans. $\Delta H_f^0 = 104.06$ kJ. The difference in the two values (95.27 kJ mol^{-1}) is attributed due to resonance.

21. The enthalpy of formation of HCl (g) at 300 K is -92.30 kJ mol^{-1}. Calculate its value at 400 K. Provide yourself the values of C_P.

Ans. As all the molecules are diatomic and there is no change in the number of moles hence $\Delta C_P = 0$ and $\Delta H_{400}^0 = -92.30$kJ mol^{-1}.

22. Given the following data at 298 K:

(i) $C_6H_5-CH_2-CH_3(l)+3H_2(g)=C_8H_{16}(l)$ $\quad\Delta H^0 = -202.0$ kJ mol^{-1}

(ii) $C_6H_5-CH=CH_2(l)+4H_2(g)=C_8H_{16}(l)$ $\quad\Delta H^0 = -312.3$ kJ mol^{-1}

(iii) $H_2(g)+\dfrac{1}{2}O_2(g)=H_2O(g)$ $\quad\Delta H^0 = -241.83$ kJ mol^{-1}

(iv) $C(graphite)+O_2(g)=CO_2(g)$ $\quad\Delta H^0 = -393.51$ kJ mol^{-1}

(v) $C_8H_{16}(l)+12O_2(g)=8CO_2(g)+8H_2O(g)$ $\quad\Delta H^0 = -5180.0$ kJ mol^{-1}

Calculate (a) the enthalpy of hydrogenation of sytrene to ethylbenzene, (b) the enthalpy of formation of ethyl benzene.

Ans. (a) -110.40 kJ mol^{-1}, (b) 299.3 kJ mol^{-1}.

23. (a) Given the following data at 298 K:

$HCl(g)+10H_2O(l)=HCl.10\,H_2O$ $\quad\Delta H^0 = -69.50$ kJ

$HCl(g)+25H_2O(l)=HCl.25\,H_2O$ $\quad\Delta H^0 = -72.26$ kJ

Calculate the enthalpy change for the process

$$HCl.10H_2O+15\,H_2O(l)=HCl.25\,H_2O$$

Calculate the temperature rise (ΔT) for this dilution assuming that there is no loss of heat to the surroundings and the heat capacity of the more dilute solution is 4.184 J g^{-1} K^{-1}.

Ans.-2.76 kJ, $\Delta T = 1.36$ K.

(b) When 10 g of anhydrous $CuSO_4$ are dissolved in excess of water, 4.184 kJ of heat is evolved. If the same amount of $CuSO_4 \cdot 5H_2O$ (s) is dissolved 460 J of heat is absorbed. Calculate the enthalpy of hydration of $CuSO_4$.

Ans. -77.25 kJ mol^{-1}.

24. The standard enthalpy of formation of CO(g) and H_2O(g) at 298 K are -110.51 kJ mol^{-1} and -241.83 kJ mol^{-1} respectively

Calculate (i) the enthalpy of the following reaction at 298 K:

$$H_2O(g)+C(s)=H_2(g)+CO(g)$$

(ii) If the heat capacity ($C_{P,\,m}$) of all the gases is assumed to be 29.29 JK^{-1} mol^{-1} and $C_{P,\,m}$ (C, s) as 10.46 JK^{-1} mol^{-1}, calculate the enthalpy of the above reaction at 600 K.

Ans. (i) $\Delta H^0 = 131.32$ kJ, (ii) $\Delta H_{600} = 142.62$ kJ.

25. Consider the following process:

$$1 \text{ mol } H_2O \text{ (s, 250 K)} = 1 \text{ mol}\,H_2O \text{ (g, 400 K)}$$

Calculate the enthalpy change required to carry out this process if the enthalpy of vapourization of water is 40.62 kJ mol^{-1} at 373 K and 1 atm and the enthalpy of fusion of ice at 273 K and 1 atm is 5.99 kJ mol^{-1}. The specific heats of ice, liquid water and steam can be taken as 1.925 JK^{-1}g^{-1}, 4.184 JK^{-1} g^{-1} and 1.999 JK^{-1} g^{-1}, respectively.

Ans. 55.93 kJ mol^{-1}.

26. When hydrogen is burnt in oxygen 241.83 kJ of heat is liberated at 298 K. (i) Calculate the temperature upto which water vapours would be heated if this heat does not leave the system. (ii) If the reaction is carried out in air, what would be the final temperature? (Air may be taken as 80% N_2 and 20% O_2 by mole). (iii) Why the temperature in the latter case is lower than in the former?

Given $C_{P,m}(H_2O, g) = 33.63 \text{ JK}^{-1}\text{mol}^{-1}$

$C_{P,m}(N_2, g) = 29.71 \text{ JK}^{-1}\text{mol}^{-1}$

Ans. (*i*) 7486 K, (*ii*) 5283 K, (*iii*) some of the heat is used in heating nitrogen.

27. Calculate the electron affinity of chlorine from the following data at 298 K:

(*i*) $Na(g) = Na^+(g) + e^-$ $\qquad \Delta H^0 = 499.8 \text{ kJ}$

(*ii*) $\frac{1}{2}Cl_2(g) = Cl(g)$ $\qquad \Delta H^0 = 120.9 \text{ kJ}$

(*iii*) $Na(s) = Na(g)$ $\qquad \Delta H^0 = 108.3 \text{ kJ}$

(*iv*) $Na(s) + \frac{1}{2}Cl_2(g) = NaCl(s)$ $\qquad \Delta H^0 = 411.3 \text{ kJ}$

(*v*) $Na^+(g) + Cl^-(g) = NaCl(s)$ $\qquad \Delta H^0 = 975.4 \text{ kJ}$

Ans. −365.3 kJ mol⁻¹.

28. The enthalpy change for the reaction

$$CH_3CHO(g) \rightarrow CH_4(g) + CO(g)$$

at 1 atm and 298 K is −16.736 kJ. Calculate the temperature at which ΔH for the reaction will be zero. $C_{p,m}$ $(CH_4, g) = 37.656 \text{ JK}^{-1} \text{ mol}^{-1}$, $C_{p,m} (CO, g) = 31.38 \text{ JK}^{-1} \text{ mol}^{-1}$ and $C_{p,m} (CH_3CHO, g) = 52.3 \text{ JK}^{-1} \text{ mol}^{-1}$.

Ans. 1298 K.

29. A couple sitting in a warm room on a winter day takes $\frac{1}{2}$ kg of cheese sandwitches (an energy intake of 8130 kJ for both). Supposing that none of the energy is stored in the body, what mass of water would they need to perspire in order to maintain their original temperature. The enthalpy of vapourization of water may be taken as 40.65 kJ mol⁻¹. **Ans.** 3.6 kg.

30. A man weighing 65 kg climbs a tower of 4 m. He wants to keep his energy constant, how much of glucose should be take before climbing. ΔH_{comb} (glucose) −2808 kJ mol⁻¹ and only 30% of this is utilized in useful work. **Ans.** 0.75g

31. Using the data (all values in kJ mol⁻¹ at 298 K) given below, calculate the bond enthalpies of C–C and C–H bonds

$$\Delta H^0(\text{Combustion}), C_2H_6 = -1556.45$$

$$\Delta H^0(\text{Combustion}), C_3H_8 = -2217.52$$

$$\Delta H^0_{C(s) \rightarrow C(g)} = 719.65$$

$$\Delta H^0_{H-H} = 436.00$$

$$\Delta H^0_{f, CO_2(g)} = -393.30$$

$$\Delta H^0_{f, H_2O(l)} = -285.8$$

Ans. $\Delta H^0_{C-C} = 343.1 \text{ kJ mol}^{-1}$ and $\Delta H^0_{C-H} = 414.2 \text{ kJ mol}^{-1}$.

CHAPTER 7

The Second Law of Thermodynamics

7.1 INTRODUCTION

The primary and essential interest of thermodynamics to chemists is to use it as a criterion of feasibility of physical and chemical changes under a given set of conditions. The first law merely sums up our experience regarding the energy changes and states that if a process is to occur then the total energy before and after the transformation is constant. But whether such a process is possible or not, the law gives no information. The two functions E and H introduced in the first law can predict the feasibility of an exothermic process in which ΔE and ΔH decrease. However, there are many endothermic processes in which ΔE and ΔH increase and yet the processes are feasible. Hence, these functions are insufficient in predicting the direction and feasibility of a process under specified conditions. The first law is therefore inadequate, provides no information concerning the feasibility of a process and an additional law is required. The law provides the necessary criterion of feasibility of a process in terms of additional thermodynamic functions and other related expressions.

7.2 SPONTANEOUS PROCESSES

Processes which take place of their own without the external intervention of any kind are known as *spontaneous processes*. All the processes that take place in nature are spontaneous in character, proceed only in one direction and are, therefore, thermodynamically irreversible. They can be reversed only by the aid of an external agency. Let us consider some examples of spontaneous changes to understand their irreversible nature and the conditions which determine their feasibility.

(i) When two metal blocks A and B at temperatures T_A and T_B such that $T_A > T_B$, are brought in contact with each other, heat flows from A to B. The flow of heat is spontaneous and continues until they attain a uniform temperature and a thermal equilibrium is established. The reverse process in which A and B initially at the same temperature attaining a state in which A becomes warmer at the expense of B is never observed. The reverse process is thus non spontaneous.

(ii) Flow of liquids from a higher to a lower level is a spontaneous process; the flow continues until the two levels are equal and a mechanical equilibrium is attained. The reverse process is not observed to occur.

(*iii*) If a vessel containing a gas at higher pressure is connected by means of a valve to another vessel filled with the gas at lower pressure then on opening the valve the gas spontaneously passes from higher pressure to the lower pressure side until the combined system attains a uniform pressure, *i.e.*, a mechanical equilibrium is established. The process of mixing is spontaneous and the reverse change in which the concentration of the gas suddenly becomes greater in one part is never observed.

(*iv*) Two solutions of a solute of different concentrations when brought in contact with each other, diffusion of the solute takes place from higher to lower concentration and ceases when the concentration becomes uniform and a chemical equilibrium is established. The reverse process in which the solute migrates to one part making it more concentrated than the other is not observed and is, consequently, non spontaneous.

(*v*) When a solute such as ammonium chloride is added to water, it dissolves with the absorption of heat. The dissolution is endothermic and spontaneous while the reverse process whereby solid ammonium chloride separates from the solution with the evolution of heat leaving pure water is not observed.

Many examples of spontaneous processes may be mentioned. All these proceed in one direction and are irreversible. The first law would be applicable to the reverse processes but it would provide no indication of whether the change can occur at all or not. Examination of the spontaneous processes reveals that they have a natural tendency to move towards a state of equilibrium. To account for the tendency of the system to change and the direction in which the change can take place, Clausius introduced the function *entropy* (means transformation). The entropy always increases when the change proceeds spontaneously. Since the spontaneous processes occur of their own and pass from a less probable or more ordered state to a more probable or more disordered state, the entropy function is therefore a measure of the probability of a change to occur or the randomness of the system. Furthermore, spontaneous processes tend to move towards the equilibrium state which is therefore a state of maximum probability or maximum randomness.

7.3 STATEMENT OF THE SECOND LAW OF THERMODYNAMICS

The second law is based on our experience and is not derivable from any theory. It is applicable to macroscopic systems and has been stated in various forms. Some of these equivalent forms are:

(*i*) It is impossible to construct a machine working in cycles which will transfer heat from a lower temperature to a higher temperature without the aid of an external agency. Such a machine is called a *perpetual motion machine of the second order.*

(*ii*) Heat can not be completely converted into work without leaving changes either in the system or in the surroundings.

(*iii*) Heat can not pass from a colder to a warmer body.

(*iv*) Entropy increases in irreversible processes.

7.4 CONVERSION OF HEAT INTO WORK

It is a universal experience that all other forms of energy can be converted into heat but the latter has no natural tendency to be transformed into work. Only through the introduction of suitable mechanisms or mechanical devices, usually known as *heat engines*, heat can be converted into work, even then complete conversion of heat into work is impossible. One may, however, quote the instance of isothermal changes involving ideal gases. In these cases, $dT = 0$ and from the first law, heat absorbed is exactly equal to the work performed. But such a transfer of heat into work is accompanied by a change in the state of the system—a change in the volume of the system. However, if one completes a cycle isothermally and reversibly, the system and the surroundings are both restored to their initial states and no net heat is absorbed and consequently, no work is obtained. It is, therefore clear that by an isothermal reversible cycle heat can not be transformed into work. When a gaseous system absorbs heat, a certain amount of work may be obtained from the expansion. If equivalent amount of work is done on the system, it is found that less heat is released during compression indicating incomplete transfer of heat into work in expansion. The impossibility of complete conversion of heat into work suggests that only a part of the heat absorbed by the system can be utilized for obtaining work while the remaining part goes to increase the random motion of the molecules in the system. It is the randomness of the molecules in the system which is responsible for incomplete transfer of heat into work. If the system were completely ordered, then of course, it would have been possible to convert heat completely into work. The entropy function of Clausius is a measure of this randomness and the amount of heat not used up in performing work is obviously proportional to the increase in the entropy function.

Absorption of heat at the same or at a temperature lower than that of the engine and its conversion into work is not possible. However, when heat is absorbed by the engine from a reservoir at higher temperature (known as the source), it is partly converted into work and the remaining portion is given to the reservoir at lower temperature (known as the sink). The fraction of the total heat absorbed converted into work by the system is referred to as the efficiency of the engine. If Q_h is the heat absorbed from the source and Q_c is the amount given to the sink (by convention it is negative) then work produced is given by

$$(-W) = Q_h + Q_c$$

and hence the efficiency of the engine is given as

$$\epsilon = \frac{\text{Work obtained}}{\text{Total heat absorbed}} = \frac{(-W)}{Q_h} = \frac{Q_h + Q_c}{Q_h} = 1 + \frac{Q_c}{Q_h}$$

when $Q_c = 0 \ \epsilon = 1$, i.e., complete conversion of heat into work. Since this is not possible hence the efficiency is always less than unity or heat is only partly converted into work. Furthermore, the efficiency will depend on the mode of operation of the engine. An ideal engine is the one which operates reversibly in cycles so that it comes back to its initial state without involving any work in its own operation. Such an ideal engine was visualized by Carnot which operates in cycles and yields a continuous conversion of a part of heat into work.

7.5 CARNOT CYCLE

The extent to which work can be obtained from heat and its dependence on the temperatures of the source and the sink is given by Carnot cycle. the Carnot heat engine consists of a cylinder fitted with an ideal piston and contains a mole of an ideal gas as the working substance. The engine operates reversibly in cycles between two large heat reservoirs—one at higher temperature (T_2) which acts as the source and other at lower temperature (T_1) that acts as the sink. In a complete cycle, the engine absorbs a certain quantity of heat Q_2 from the source, converts a part of it into work ($-W$) and the rest (Q_1) is transferred to the sink at the lower temperature. The cycle involves four reversible steps—two are performed isothermally and the other two under adiabatic conditions. These isotherms and adiabatics can be represented on a $P - V$ diagram usually known as an *indicator diagram*. The steps involved in the cycle are:

Step I: The cylinder containing the gas is placed in contact with the reservoir at T_2. It absorbs a certain quantity of heat Q_2 and the gas is allowed to expand isothermally and reversibly at the temperature (T_2) of the source. The volume of the gas changes from V_1 to V_2 as indicated by isotherm I in the indicator diagram (Fig. 7.1). Since the absorption of heat takes place isothermally and reversibly and the gas is ideal, there is no change in its energy ($\Delta E = 0$), hence the work obtained is equal to the heat absorbed and is given by

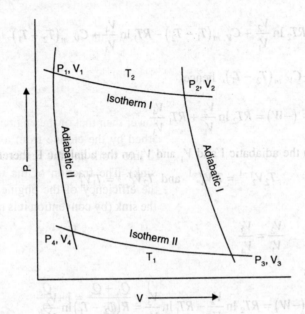

Fig. 7.1 The Carnot cycle

$$Q_2 = -W_1 = RT_2 \ln \frac{V_2}{V_1} \qquad \text{...(7.1)}$$

Step II: The cylinder is removed from the source. It is surrounded by a thermally insulated enclosure and the gas is allowed to expand reversibly and adiabatically from its volume V_2 to V_3 until its temperature drops to T_1, the temperature of the sink. The change is shown by adiabatic I in the diagram. The expansion is adiabatic: no heat enters or leaves the system, hence $Q = 0$ and the adiabatic work of expansion is given as

$$W_2 = C_{V,m}(T_1 - T_2) \qquad \text{...(7.2)}$$

where $C_{V,m}$ is the molar heat capacity of the gas.

Step III: The thermal insulation is removed and the cylinder is kept in contact with the sink at T_1. The gas is compressed isothermally and reversibly at this temperature until its volume changes from V_3 to V_4 as shown by isotherm II in the figure. If Q_1 is the heat given out by the gas to the sink, then the reversible work of compression is given by

$$(-W_3) = Q_1 = RT_1 \ln V_4/V_3 \qquad \text{...(7.3)}$$

Step IV: The cylinder is removed from the sink, surrounded by the thermal insulation and compressed adiabatically and reversibly until its temperature rises to that of the source and the volume decreases from V_4 to V_1 as indicated by adiabatic II in the figure. The work of compression is given by

$$W_4 = C_{V, m}(T_2 - T_1) \qquad \qquad ...(7.4)$$

The system returns to its initial state and the cycle is completed. The net work done by the gas during the complete cycle is given as

$$W = W_1 + W_2 + W_3 + W_4$$

$$= -RT_2 \ln \frac{V_2}{V_1} + C_{V, m}(T_1 - T_2) - RT_1 \ln \frac{V_4}{V_3} + C_{V, m}(T_2 - T_1)$$

But $C_{V, m}(T_1 - T_2) = -C_{V, m}(T_2 - T_1)$, hence

$$(-W) = RT_2 \ln \frac{V_2}{V_1} + RT_1 \frac{V_4}{V_3}$$

Since V_2 and V_3 lie on the adiabatic I and V_1 and V_4 on the adiabatic II therefore,

$$T_2 V_2^{\gamma-1} = T_1 V_3^{\gamma-1} \quad \text{and} \quad T_2 V_1^{\gamma-1} = T_1 V_4^{\gamma-1}$$

Dividing we get

$$\frac{V_2}{V_1} = \frac{V_3}{V_4}$$

Hence, the net work is

$$(-W) = RT_2 \ln \frac{V_2}{V_1} - RT_1 \ln \frac{V_3}{V_4} = R(T_2 - T_1) \ln \frac{V_2}{V_1} \qquad ...(7.5)$$

The efficiency of the engine is thus

$$\epsilon = \frac{(-W)}{Q_2} = \frac{R(T_2 - T_1) \ln \dfrac{V_2}{V_1}}{RT_2 \ln \dfrac{V_2}{V_1}} = \frac{T_2 - T_1}{T_2} = 1 - \frac{T_1}{T_2} \qquad ...(7.6)$$

Equation (7.6) gives the efficiency of any reversible engine working between the temperatures of the source and the sink and it depends only on the temperature difference of the two and is independent of the nature of the working substance. For complete conversion of heat into work ($\epsilon = 1$) either $T_2 = \infty$ or $T_1 = 0$. Both these temperatures can not be realized in actual practice, the obvious conclusion therefore is that heat can not be transformed completely into work or the efficiency of an engine can never be unity.

7.6 CARNOT REFRIGERATOR

In the Carnot cycle all the steps are reversible, it can be operated in the opposite direction where the signs of all the heat and work quantities are reversed. This reverse engine absorbs heat from the lower temperature, some work is done on it by the surroundings and rejects heat at the higher temperature. It thus functions as a refrigerator, that is, it extracts heat from a cold reservoir and passes it to a hot reservoir. The ratio of work done on the engine to the heat absorbed at lower temperature is the *coefficient of performance* of the engine and is given as

$$\frac{W}{Q_1} = \frac{T_2 - T_1}{T_1}$$

$$W = Q_1 \frac{T_2 - T_1}{T_1} \quad ...(7.7)$$

Equation (7.7) represents the minimum amount of work which must be done to remove a quantity of heat Q_1 at T_1 and giving it at higher temperature T_2.

7.7 CARNOT THEOREM

The theorem states that *all reversible engines working between the same two temperatures of the source and the sink are equally efficient.* This important generalisation is the result of the validity of the second law. To prove the theorem, we shall consider two cases as discussed below:

Case I: Let us assume that there are two reversible engines E_r and E_r' both of which operate between the same source and the sink and E_r' being more efficient than E_r. Engine E_r' absorbs a certain quantity of heat (Q_2) from the source at T_2, converts a part of it into work $(-W')$ and gives up the remaining amount $Q_2 - W'$ to the sink at T_1. Engine E_r absorbs the same quantity of heat from the source but being less efficient than E_r', converts a smaller portion into work $(-W)$ and thus transfers a larger amount $(Q_2 + W)$ to the sink. When these reversible engines are coupled the composite system of engines is obtained (Fig. 7.2) in which E_r' operates in the direct manner while E_r in the opposite

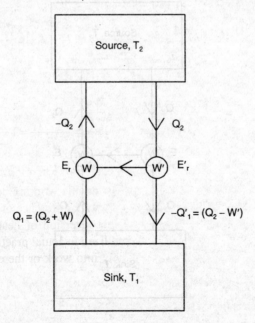

Fig. 7.2 Composite system of two reversible Carnot engines

direction, *i.e.*, it withdraws heat from the sink, some work is being done on it and then gives up heat to the source. E_r thus acts as a refrigerator.

Using the convention that heat absorbed is positive and heat given out as negative and work done by the system as negative and work done on the system as positive, the work and heat changes for each engine and the composite system are as follows:

	Engine E_r' forward	Engine E_r forward	Engine E_r reverse	Composite Engine
Heat transfer at T_2	Q_2	Q_2	$-Q_2$	0
Work involves	$-W'$	$-W$	W	$-W' + W$
Heat transfer at T_1	$-Q_1'$	$-Q_1$	Q_1	$Q_1 - Q_1'$

Since $|W'| > |W|$, hence the composite system is able to convert heat absorbed $(Q_1 - Q_1')$ at the lower temperature completely into work. This is, however, against the second law and therefore the assumption that engine E_r' is more efficient than engine E_r is wrong. We conclude the efficiency of both the engines must be the same, *i.e.*, $\epsilon_r' = \epsilon_r$.

Case II: Let us assume that there are two engines, one is irreversible (E_{ir}) and the other is reversible (E_r) and the efficiency of the irreversible engine is more than that of the reversible one. It means the engines working between the same source and the sink and for the same quantity of heat absorbed from the source, the irreversible engine produces larger magnitude of work $(-W_{ir})$ than the reversible one $(-W_r)$. When the two engines are coupled, the irreversible engine operates in the direct manner because it can not be reversed while the reversible engine operates in the reverse direction and thus acts as a refrigerator (Fig. 7.3). The work and heat changes for the individual and composite engines are as follows:

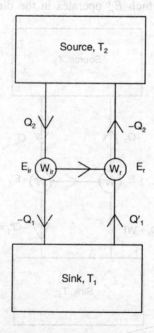

Fig. 7.3 Composite system of an irreversible and a reversible engine

	Irreversible engine E_{ir} forward	Reversible engine E_r forward	Reversible engine reverse	Composite engine
Heat transfer at T_2	Q_2	Q_2	$-Q_2$	0
Work involved	$-W_{ir}$	$-W_r$	W_r	$-W_{ir} + W_r$
Heat transfer at T_1	$-Q_1$	$-Q_1'$	Q_1'	$Q_1' - Q_1$

The composite engine has not withdrawn any heat from the source while the heat withdrawn from the sink has been transformed completely into work. This is, however, contrary to the second law and hence the reversible engine can not be less efficient than the irreversible one. We therefore conclude that the efficiency of any engine must be equal to or less than the efficiency of the reversible engine when both operate between the same two heat reservoirs.

Problem 7.1: A reversible heat engine working between 273 K and 373K absorbs 746J of heat from the source. Calculate (*a*) the work done, (*b*) the heat given to the sink, and (*c*) the efficiency of the engine. What would have been the efficiency if the temperature of the source were 573 K?

Solution: (*a*) Work done in the complete cycle, $-W = 746 \times \dfrac{100}{373}$ J $= 200$ J

(*b*) Heat given to the sink $= 746 - 200 = 546$ J

(*c*) $\epsilon = \dfrac{(-W)}{Q_2} = \dfrac{T_2 - T_1}{T_2} = \dfrac{100}{373} = 0.268$

If the temperature of the source were raised to 573K, the efficiency would be given by $\dfrac{200}{573} = 0.349$.

Problem 7.2: One mole of an ideal monatomic gas is taken as the working substance in a Carnot engine operating between 819 K and 273 K. If in the first reversible isothermal expansion step the volume of gas changes from 0.04 m³ to 0.4 m³, calculate Q, W, ΔE, for the complete cycle. Evaluate ϵ. Would you expect any difference in these quantities if the gas is replaced by a diatomic one?

Solution: $V_1 = 0.04$ m³, $V_2 = 0.4$ m³, $T_h = 819$ K and $T_c = 273$ K. V_3 and V_4 are calculated from the fact that V_2 and V_3 lie on one adiabatic and V_1 and V_4 on the other. Hence, we have

$$\frac{V_2}{V_3} = \left(\frac{T_c}{T_h}\right)^{C_{V,m}/R} \quad \text{and} \quad \frac{V_4}{V_1} = \left(\frac{T_h}{T_c}\right)^{C_{V,m}/R}$$

or

$$V_3 = V_2 \left(\frac{T_h}{T_c}\right)^{C_{V,m}/R} = \left(0.4 \text{ m}^3\right)\left(\frac{819 \text{ K}}{273 \text{ K}}\right)^{3/2} = 2.079 \text{ m}^3$$

and

$$V_4 = V_3 \left(\frac{V_1}{V_2}\right) = \left(2.079 \text{ m}^3\right)\left(\frac{0.04 \text{ m}^3}{0.4 \text{ m}^3}\right) = 0.2079 \text{ m}^3$$

For step I, the expansion is isothermal and reversible,

$$\Delta E_1 = 0 \text{ and } Q_1 = -W_1 = RT_h \ln\left(\frac{V_2}{V_1}\right)$$

$$Q_1 = -W_1 = (1 \text{ mol})(8.314 \text{ JK}^{-1}\text{mol}^{-1})(819 \text{ K})(2.303) \log\frac{0.4}{0.04} = 15.68 \text{ kJ}$$

$$= 15.68 \text{ kJ}$$

For step II, the expansion is adiabatic and reversible, $Q_2 = 0$ hence

$$\Delta E_2 = W_2 = nC_{V,\,m}(T_c - T_h)$$

$$= (1 \text{ mol})\left(\frac{3}{2}\right)(8.314 \text{ JK}^{-1}\text{mol}^{-1})(273 \text{ K} - 819 \text{ K})$$

$$= -6.81 \text{ kJ}$$

For step III, the compression is isothermal and reversible at 273 K hence

$$\Delta E_3 = 0$$

and

$$Q_3 = -W_3 = (1 \text{ mol})(8.314 \text{ JK}^{-1}\text{mol}^{-1})(2.303)(273 \text{ K})\left(\log\frac{0.2079}{2.079}\right)$$

$$= -5.227 \text{ kJ}$$

For step IV, the compression is adiabatic and reversible, $Q_4 = 0$ and

$$\Delta E_4 = W_4 = (1 \text{ mol})(3/2)(8.314 \text{ JK}^{-1}\text{mol}^{-1})(819 \text{ K} - 273 \text{ K})$$

$$= 6.81 \text{ kJ}$$

For the complete cycle

$$\Delta E = 0$$

$$Q = -W = 15.68 \text{ kJ} - 5.227 \text{ kJ} = 10.453 \text{ kJ}$$

and the efficiency

$$= \frac{10.453}{15.68} \times 100 = 67\%$$

When the gas is replaced by the diatomic one ($C_{V,\,m} = 5/2$ R) the volumes V_3 and V_4 are as

$$V_3 = (0.4 \text{ m}^3)\left(\frac{819}{273 \text{ K}}\right)^{5/2R} = 6.232 \text{ m}^3$$

and

$$V_4 = V_3\left(\frac{V_1}{V_2}\right) = (6.232 \text{ m}^3)\left(\frac{0.04 \text{ m}^3}{0.4 \text{ m}^3}\right) = 0.6232 \text{ m}^3$$

The values of Q_1, W_1, Q_3 and W_3 remain unchanged, however, there will be changes in ΔE and W in the second and the fourth steps when the monatomic gas is replaced by the diatomic one.

In the second step,

$$Q_2 = 0$$

$$\Delta E_2 = W_2 = (1 \text{ mol})(5/2)\left(8.314 \text{ J mol}^{-1}\text{K}^{-1}\right)(273 \text{ K} - 819 \text{ K})$$

$$= -11.34 \text{ kJ}$$

In the fourth step

$$\Delta E_4 = W_4 = (1 \text{ mol})(5/2)(8.314 \text{ J mol}^{-1} K^{-1})(819 \text{ K} - 273 \text{ K})$$
$$= 11.34 \text{ kJ}$$

Problem 7.3: How much work must be supplied to a cooling machine working in a room in which the temperature is 298 K in order to prepare 10 kg of ice from water at 273 K? Evaluate the heat given to the surroundings. $\Delta H_{fus, m}$ for water is 6.023 kJ mol^{-1} at 273 K.

Solution: Heat absorbed at 273 K, $Q_c = \left(6.023 \text{ kJ mol}^{-1}\right)\left(\dfrac{10^4}{18} \text{ mol}\right)$

$$= 3.347 \times 10^3 \text{ kJ}$$

This quantity of heat is transferred by the machine from 273 K to 298 K. If W is the work done on the machine then,

$$\frac{W}{Q_c} = \frac{T_h - T_c}{T_c} = \frac{(298 - 273)\text{K}}{273 \text{ K}}$$

$$W = \left(\frac{25 \text{ K}}{273 \text{ K}}\right)\left(3.347 \times 10^3 \text{ kJ}\right)$$

$$= 3.065 \times 10^2 \text{ kJ}$$

Heat transferred to the surroundings at 298 K, $Q_h = Q_c + W =$ Heat absorbed at 293 K + work done on the machine

$$= 3.065 \times 10^2 \text{ kJ} + 3.347 \times 10^3 \text{ kJ}$$

$$= 3.654 \times 10^3 \text{ kJ}$$

Problem 7.4: Two identical metal blocks of constant heat capacities are at the same temperature T_1. A refrigerator operates between these two blocks until one is cooled to the temperature T_2. If the blocks remain at constant pressure and do not undergo any phase changes, show that amount of work needed to do this is given by

$$|W| = C_P\left[\frac{T_1^2}{T_2} + T_2 - 2T_1\right]$$

where C_P is the heat capacity of the metal blocks at constant pressure.

Solution: Heat transferred when the temperature drops from T_1 to T_2 is

$$Q = C_P(T_1 - T_2)$$

If $|W|$ is the work done to effect the change, then

$$\frac{|W|}{Q} = \frac{T_1 - T_2}{T_2}$$

$$|W| = \left(\frac{T_1 - T_2}{T_2}\right) Q = C_P \left(\frac{T_1 - T_2}{T_2}\right) (T_1 - T_2)$$

$$= C_P \left(\frac{T_1^2}{T_2} + T_2 - 2T_1\right)$$

7.8 THE THERMODYNAMIC TEMPERATURE SCALE

With the help of Carnot engine it is possible to define a scale of temperature which is independent of the nature of the working substance. The efficiency of all reversible engines working between the same two temperatures of the source and the sink is a function of the two temperatures only and is independent of nature of the working substance. Therefore, we may write

$$\epsilon = \frac{(-W)}{Q_2} = f(\theta_1, \theta_2)$$

where f is some function of θ_1 and θ_2, the temperatures on any arbitrary scale. But $(-W) = Q_1 + Q_2$, hence

$$\epsilon = 1 + \frac{Q_1}{Q_2} = f(\theta_1, \theta_2)$$

Comparing the absolute values of heat exchanges, we may write

$$\frac{|Q_1|}{|Q_2|} = f(\theta_1, \theta_2) - 1 = F(\theta_1, \theta_2)$$

where F denotes some other function of θ_1 and θ_2. If we have a Carnot engine working successively between any pair of temperatures (θ_1, θ_2), (θ_2, θ_3) and (θ_1, θ_3) and the heat transfer at these temperatures are Q_1, Q_2 and Q_3 respectively, then

$$\frac{|Q_1|}{|Q_2|} = F(\theta_1, \theta_2) \; ; \; \frac{|Q_2|}{|Q_3|} = F(\theta_2, \theta_3); \; \frac{|Q_1|}{|Q_3|} = F(\theta_1, \theta_3)$$

It follows that

$$\frac{|Q_1|}{|Q_3|} = F(\theta_1, \theta_2) . F(\theta_2, \theta_3) = F(\theta_1, \theta_3)$$

In the above equation there is no θ_2 on the right hand side hence the form of F should be such that θ_2 disappears from the left hand side also. Then

$$F(\theta_1, \theta_3) = F(\theta_1, \theta_2) \, F(\theta_2, \theta_3) = \frac{\phi(\theta_1)}{\phi(\theta_2)} . \frac{\phi(\theta_2)}{\phi(\theta_3)}$$

It follows that for any reversible engine

$$\frac{|Q_1|}{|Q_2|} = \frac{\phi(\theta_1)}{\phi(\theta_2)}$$

The function $\phi(\theta)$ was chosen by Kelvin to indicate the temperature of the working substance. Denoting $\phi(\theta)$ by τ, we have

$$\frac{|Q_1|}{|Q_2|} = \frac{\tau_1}{\tau_2}$$

This equation is used to define a new scale of temperature τ, which is called *the thermodynamic* or *Kelvin scale* and is independent of the nature of the working substance. The ratio of any two temperatures on this scale is the same as the ratio of heat absorbed and rejected by a reversible engine working between these two temperatures.

The efficiency ϵ becomes

$$\epsilon = \frac{Q_2 + Q_1}{Q_2} = \frac{T_2 - T_1}{T_2} = \frac{\tau_2 - \tau_1}{\tau_2}$$

The zero on this scale is the temperature at which the efficiency becomes unity, *i.e.*, the engine becomes perfectly efficient and T_1 approaches zero. This is possible only at the absolute zero on the ideal gas scale of temperature. It follows that the kelvin scale and the gas scale, provided the gas is ideal, are really the same.

7.9 MATHEMATICAL FORMULATION OF ENTROPY

From Carnot cycle we have seen that

$$\frac{(-W)}{Q_2} = \frac{Q_2 + Q_1}{Q_2} = \frac{T_2 - T_1}{T_2}$$

or

$$1 + \frac{Q_1}{Q_2} = 1 - \frac{T_1}{T_2}$$

or

$$\frac{Q_2}{T_2} + \frac{Q_1}{T_1} = 0 \qquad \qquad ...(7.8)$$

In the Carnot cycle, heat is exchanged only in the isothermal steps and the sum of $\frac{Q}{T}$ terms for the complete reversible cycle is zero. Since the quantity Q is not a state function but $\frac{Q}{T}$ represents a definite thermodynamic property of the system. It is called the entropy which for an infinitesimally small change in the state of the system is defined as the heat absorbed isothermally and reversibly divided by the temperature at which the absorption of heat takes place, e.g.,

$$dS = \frac{\delta Q_{\text{rev}}}{T} \qquad \qquad ...(7.9)$$

and for a finite change in the state of the system from state A to state B, we may write

$$\Delta S = S_B - S_A = \frac{Q_{\text{rev}}}{T} \qquad \qquad ...(7.10)$$

For the Carnot cycle

$$(\Delta S)_{\text{Carnot cycle}} = \sum \frac{Q_{\text{rev}}}{T} = 0 \qquad \qquad ...(7.11)$$

Any reversible cycle may be visualized as consisting of a large number of Carnot cycles as shown in the Fig. 7.4. Since for each Carnot cycle, the sum of Q_{rev}/T terms is zero, therefore for the whole reversible cycle summation of Q_{rev}/T terms is zero and we write

$$\sum \frac{Q_{\text{rev}}}{T} = \Delta S_{\text{cycle}} = 0 \qquad \qquad ...(7.12)$$

Hence, we may conclude that entropy is a single-valued extensive property of the system. The differential dS is an exact differential and the value of entropy depends only on the state of the system.

For any reversible cycle, the integral $\oint dS$ is zero.

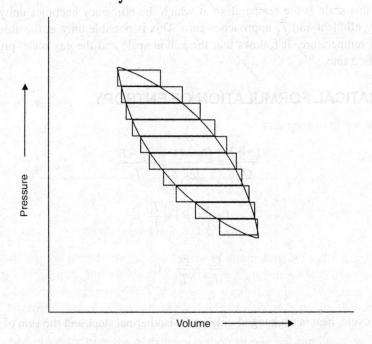

Fig. 7.4 A cyclic process consisting of a number of Carnot cycles

7.10 RELATION BETWEEN ENERGY, ENTHALPY AND ENTROPY— COMBINED FORM OF THE FIRST AND THE SECOND LAW

From the first law for an infinitesimally small change in the state of system, we have

$$\delta Q = dE - \delta W$$

If the process is reversible and the system involves only $P - V$ work then $-\delta W = PdV$ and

$$\delta Q_{\text{rev}} = dE + PdV$$

From the second law

$$\frac{\delta Q_{rev}}{T} = dS$$

Combining these relations we get

$$TdS = dE + PdV \qquad \qquad ...(7.13)$$

Equation (7.13) is the combined form of the first and the second laws of thermodynamics. Also from eq. (5.26)

$$H = E + PV$$

we obtain

$$dH = dE + PdV + VdP$$

Substituting the value of dE from Eq. (7.13), we get

$$dH = TdS - PdV + PdV + VdP$$

$$= TdS + VdP \qquad \qquad ...(7.14)$$

Equation (7.14) gives a relation between enthalpy change and entropy changes.

7.11 ENTROPY CHANGES IN REVERSIBLE (NON-CYCLIC) PROCESSES

In a reversible process, heat absorbed by the system is exactly equal to that lost by the surroundings. Consequently, the entropy increase of the system is equal to the decrease in entropy of the surroundings. If Q_{rev} is the heat absorbed, then

$$\Delta S_{sys} = \frac{Q_{rev}}{T} \text{ and } \Delta S_{surr} = -\frac{Q_{rev}}{T}$$

The total entropy change for the system and the surroundings known as the entropy change of the universe, ΔS_{univ} is

$$\Delta S_{univ} = \Delta S_{sys} + \Delta S_{surr} = 0 \qquad \qquad ...(7.15)$$

Let us now consider the entropy changes for some common reversible processes.

(*a*) **Isothermal Reversible Process:** For an isothermal reversible process which absorbs a certain amount of heat (Q_{rev}), the entropy change of the system is given by

$$\Delta S_{sys} = \frac{Q_{rev}}{T}$$

If the system contains an ideal gas and if its volume changes from V_1 to V_2 during the isothermal reversible absorption of heat, then since $\Delta E = 0$, therefore,

$$Q_{rev} = -W_{rev} = nRT \ln \frac{V_2}{V_1} = nRT \ln \frac{P_1}{P_2} \qquad (\because P_1 V_1 = P_2 V_2)$$

Hence, the entropy increase of the system is given by

$$\Delta S_{sys} = \frac{Q_{rev}}{T} = nR \ln \frac{V_2}{V_1} = nR \ln \frac{P_1}{P_2} \qquad \qquad ...(7.16)$$

Since the surroundings loses an exactly equivalent amount of heat, its entropy decrease is

$$\Delta S_{surr} = -\frac{Q_{rev}}{T}$$

and the entropy change of the universe is

$$\Delta S_{univ} = \Delta S_{sys} + \Delta S_{surr} = 0$$

Entropy as a criterion of reversibility holds only when it is applied to the entropy change of both the system and the surroundings. In the present case of reversible process, the surroundings will lose an equal amount of heat and its entropy will decrease by the same amount.

$$\Delta S_{sys} = -\Delta S_{surr} \text{ and } \Delta S_{sys} + \Delta S_{surr} = 0$$

(b) **Adiabatic Reversible Processes:** In an adiabatic process, the system is thermally isolated from the surroundings, $Q_{rev} = 0$. The entropy change of the surroundings is therefore zero. The process is reversible and the entropy change of the system due to changes in temperature are exactly compensated by those due to changes in volume or pressure of the system. Consequently, ΔS_{sys} is zero and the process is *isoentropic*.

(c) **Reversible Phase Transition:** Transformation of a substance from one phase to another can be carried out reversibly at constant temperature and fixed pressure usually one atmosphere. If Q_{trans} is the heat required for the transformation, then

$$Q_{trans} = \Delta H_{trans}$$

where ΔH_{trans} is the enthalpy change in the phase transition. The change in entropy of the system is given as

$$\Delta S_{trans} = \frac{\Delta H_{trans}}{T_{trans}} \qquad \qquad ...(7.17)$$

Entropy of transition is a general term and is given different names depending on the nature of the phase transition. Thus, we have

Entropy of vapourization, $\qquad \qquad \Delta S_{vap} = \frac{\Delta H_{vap}}{T_b} \qquad \qquad ...(7.18)$

Entropy of fusion, $\qquad \qquad \Delta S_{fus} = \frac{\Delta H_{fus}}{T_f} \qquad \qquad ...(7.19)$

Entropy of sublimation, $\qquad \qquad \Delta S_{sub} = \frac{\Delta H_{sub}}{T_{sub}} \qquad \qquad ...(7.20)$

and entropy of transition corresponding to the transformation of one allotropic form of a substance into another is given by

$$\Delta S_{trans} = \frac{\Delta H_{trans}}{T_{trans}} \qquad \qquad ...(7.21)$$

(d) **Isobaric Reversible Processes Involving Changes in Temperature:** Under isobaric conditions, if the temperature of the system changes from T_1 to T_2 and the absorption of heat takes place reversibly, then the entropy increase of the system is given by

$$\Delta S_{sys} = \sum \frac{(\delta Q_{rev})_P}{T}$$

where $(\delta Q_{rev})_P$ represents an infinitesimally small amount of heat absorbed. At constant pressure $(\delta Q_{rev})_P$ $= dH = C_P dT$ hence ΔS_{sys} is given as

$$\Delta S_{sys} = \sum \frac{C_P dT}{T}$$

If the temperature range is not too large, C_p may be assumed to be constant and independent of temperature and hence integration of the above equation yields

$$\Delta S_{sys} = C_P \ln \frac{T_2}{T_1} = 2.303\, C_P \log \frac{T_2}{T_1} \qquad \qquad ...(7.22)$$

(*e*) **Isochoric Reversible Processes involving Changes in Temperature:** If a system is heated reversibly under isochoric conditions and if it absorbs an infinitesimally small quantity of heat $(\delta Q_{rev})_v$ then the entropy increase of the system is given by

$$\Delta S_{sys} = \sum \frac{(\delta Q_{rev})_V}{T}$$

In isochoric changes, $(\delta Q_{rev})_V = dE = C_V dT$ and the above equation then becomes

$$\Delta S_{sys} = \int_{T_1}^{T_2} \frac{C_V\, dT}{T}$$

If C_V is assumed to be independent of temperature, integration of above equation yields

$$\Delta S_{sys} = C_V \ln \frac{T_2}{T_1} = 2.303\, C_V \log \frac{T_2}{T_1} \qquad \qquad ...(7.23)$$

Problem 7.5: One mole of an ideal gas at 300K expands reversibly and isothermally from $2 \times 10^{-2} m^3$ to $4 \times 10^{-2} m^3$. Calculate the entropy change for the gas. How would you account for the fact that ΔS_{sys} is not zero although the process is reversible?

Solution: For the reversible isothermal process, $\Delta E = 0$, hence the entropy change is given by

$$\Delta S_{sys} = \frac{Q_{rev}}{T} = -\frac{W_{rev}}{T} = nR \ln \frac{V_2}{V_1}$$

$$= (1\ \text{mol})(8.314\ \text{JK}^{-1}\text{mol}^{-1})(2.303)\left(\log \frac{4 \times 10^{-2}}{2 \times 10^{-2}} \right)$$

$$= 5.763\ \text{JK}^{-1}$$

The total entropy change (system and the surroundings) will be zero for a reversible process.

7.12 ENTROPY CHANGES IN IRREVERSIBLE PROCESSES

The entropy is a state function and its value depends only on the state of the system. Consequently, the change in entropy of the system, ΔS_{sys} will be the same for the irreversible process as for the reversible one. To evaluate the entropy change in an irreversible process, a reversible path for the transformation is located between the same initial and final states of the system. We have earlier seen that the entropy change in a reversible process in an isolated system, *i.e.*, system and the surroundings together is zero. In an irreversible isolated system it will be shown here that the entropy change is greater than zero. The magnitude of work produced in a reversible process is greater than that in the irreversible process. For an infinitesimally small change, the first law states that

$$(dE)_{rev} = \delta Q_{rev} + \delta W_{rev} \qquad \qquad ...(7.24)$$

and

$$(dE)_{irr} = \delta Q_{irr} + \delta W_{irr} \qquad \qquad ...(7.25)$$

Since the internal energy is a state function and for a given change in the state of the system $(dE)_{rev} = (dE)_{irr}$. Hence, we have

$$\delta Q_{rev} + \delta W_{rev} = \delta Q_{irr} + \delta W_{irr}$$

Since $|\delta W_{rev}| > |\delta W_{irr}|$ *i.e.*, the reversible process absorbs more heat than the irreversible process for the same change in the state of the system. Further $\delta Q_{rev} = TdS_{sys}$, hence

$$TdS_{sys} > \delta Q_{irr} \qquad \qquad ...(7.26)$$

$$dS_{sys} > \frac{\delta Q_{irr}}{T}$$

or

$$\Delta S_{sys} > \frac{Q_{irr}}{T} \qquad \qquad ...(7.27)$$

The inequality is known as the *Clausius inequality* and is an important relation in any irreversible transformation. The entropy change of the surroundings can be calculated assuming that the heat lost by it occurs reversibly

$$Q_{surr} = -Q_{irr, sys}$$

$$\Delta S_{surr} = \frac{Q_{surr}}{T} = -\frac{Q_{irr, sys}}{T}$$

Hence

$$\Delta S_{sys} + \Delta S_{surr} = \Delta S_{univ} > 0 \qquad \qquad ...(7.28)$$

Combining Eq. (7.28) with Eq. (7.15), we get

$$\Delta S_{univ} \geq 0 \qquad \qquad ...(7.29)$$

For an infinitesimally small change

$$(dS)_{univ} \geq 0 \qquad \qquad ...(7.30)$$

The equality refers to a reversible change while the inequality applies to an irreversible change. Thus, for a spontaneous transformation in isolated systems the essential requirement in terms of entropy is that it must increase. All naturally-occurring processes are attended by an increase in the entropy of the universe and the increase continues until the system attains an equilibrium state where the entropy has a maximum value. The universe is therefore heading for a state of maximum entropy or maximum chaos. Let us calculate the entropy changes in the following irreversible processes:

(*a*) **Entropy Change in Isothermal Irreversible Expansion of an Ideal Gas:** In irreversible isothermal expansion of an ideal gas from an initial volume V_1 to a final volume V_2, the entropy change of the system is always given by

$$\Delta S_{sys} = nR \ln \frac{V_2}{V_1} = nR \ln \frac{P_1}{P_2}$$

The total entropy change of the system and the surroundings however depends on the nature of the expansion. If the expansion occurs in vacuum, *i.e.*, against zero opposing pressure, then no work is done by the system and the expansion is isothermal $\Delta E = 0$, hence

$$Q_{free, exp} = \Delta E - W = 0$$

As no heat is exchanged between the system and the surroundings, the surroundings have been left unchanged and consequently,

$$\Delta S_{surr} = 0$$

The total entropy change of the system and the surroundings is therefore the same as given by Eq. (7.16), *i.e.*,

$$\Delta S_{univ} = \Delta S_{sys} + \Delta S_{surr} = nR \ln \frac{V_2}{V_1} = nR \ln \frac{P_1}{P_2}$$

and is a positive quantity implying an increase of disorder.

When the gas expands against some finite pressure irreversibly, it performs some work the magnitude of which is less than the reversible work of expansion. Since $\Delta E = 0$,

$$Q_{irr} = |W_{irr}| < nRT \ln \frac{V_2}{V_1}$$

or

$$\frac{Q_{irr}}{T} < nR \ln \frac{V_2}{V_1}$$

The entropy change of the gas is still given by the expression

$$\Delta S_{sys} = nR \ln \frac{V_2}{V_1}$$

while the entropy change of the surroundings can be calculated by assuming that Q_{irr} is exchanged reversibly between the system and the surroundings. Thus

$$\Delta S_{surr} = \frac{Q_{surr}}{T} = -\frac{Q_{irr, sys}}{T}$$

The total entropy change is given by

$$\Delta S_{univ} = \Delta S_{sys} + \Delta S_{surr} = nR \ln \frac{V_2}{V_1} + \frac{Q_{surr}}{T}$$

$$= nR \ln \frac{V_2}{V_1} - \frac{Q_{irr, sys}}{T}$$

or

$$\Delta S_{univ} = nR \ln \frac{V_2}{V_1} - \frac{Q_{irr, sys}}{T} > 0 \qquad \qquad ...(7.31)$$

(*b*) **Entropy Changes in Adiabatic Irreversible Expansion of an Ideal Gas:** The entropy change for a reversible adiabatic transformation is zero while for an irreversible process sum of the entropy changes of the system and the surroundings is greater than zero. If the system is thermally insulated from its surroundings, it exchanges no heat with the system and thus suffers no change in entropy, *i.e.*, ΔS_{surr} is zero. From Eq. (7.28) the entropy change of the system in irreversible adiabatic transformations is then given by

$$\left(\Delta S_{sys}\right)_{adia} > 0$$

For irreversible adiabatic expansion of an ideal gas, let us assume that the initial state of the gas is given by $P_1 V_1$ and T_1 and the final state by P_2, V_2 and T_2. The entropy change of the gas between these two states is obtained by assuming the given transformation to be carried out reversibly. Thus, the entropy change of the system is given by

$$\left(\Delta S_{sys}\right)_{adia} = nC_{P,\,m}\ln\frac{T_2}{T_1} + nR\ln\frac{V_2}{V_1} = -nC_{P,\,m}\ln\frac{T_1}{T_2} + nR\ln\frac{V_2}{V_1} \qquad ...(7.32)$$

In expansion, the temperature decreases and volume increases, so the first term on the right side is negative and the second term is positive. When we consider the reversible and irreversible expansions between the same initial and final volumes V_1 and V_2, the final temperature is more in irreversible expansion than in the reversible expansion.

In irreversible expansion $(T_2)_{irr} > (T_2)_{rev}$ it follows that

$$\left(nC_{P,\,m}\ln\frac{T_1}{T_2}\right)_{irr} < \left(nC_{P,\,m}\ln\frac{T_1}{T_2}\right)_{rev}$$

or

$$\left(nC_{P,\,m}\ln\frac{T_1}{T_2}\right)_{irr} < nR\ln\frac{V_2}{V_1}$$

$$nR\ln\frac{V_2}{V_1} - nC_{P,\,m}\ln\frac{T_1}{T_2} > 0$$

Hence, $(\Delta S_{sys})_{adia}$ is a positive quantity.

7.13 VARIATION OF ENTROPY WITH TEMPERATURE AND VOLUME

Change in entropy of a substance with changes in temperature and volume can be evaluated by considering entropy as a function of volume and temperature, *i.e.*, $S = f(V, T)$. For infinitesimal changes, we have

$$dS = \left(\frac{\partial S}{\partial T}\right)_V dT + \left(\frac{\partial S}{\partial V}\right)_T dV \qquad ...(7.33)$$

Considering $E = f(V, T)$ we get

$$dE = \left(\frac{\partial E}{\partial T}\right)_V dT + \left(\frac{\partial E}{\partial V}\right)_T dV$$

$$= nC_{V,m}dT + \left(\frac{\partial E}{\partial V}\right)_T dV$$

Substituting this value of dE in Eq. (7.13), we get

$$dS = \frac{nC_{V,m}}{T}dT + \frac{1}{T}\left[P + \left(\frac{\partial E}{\partial V}\right)_T\right]dV \qquad \text{...(7.34)}$$

Equation (7.34) is general and applicable to all substances solids, liquids and gases. The first term on the right hand side of the equation gives the change in entropy due to changes in temperature and the second expression denotes the contribution to entropy changes due to variation in volume. Comparing Eqs. (7.33) and (7.34) we get

$$\left(\frac{dS}{dT}\right)_V = \frac{nC_{V,m}}{T} \qquad \text{...(7.35)}$$

and

$$\left(\frac{dS}{dV}\right)_T = \frac{1}{T}\left[P + \left(\frac{\partial E}{\partial V}\right)_T\right] \qquad \text{...(7.36)}$$

Since $nC_{V,m}/T$ is a positive quantity, it follows from Eq. (7.35) that entropy increases with increase of temperature in isochoric processes. The total entropy change in such cases is obtained by integrating Eq. (7.35)

$$\Delta S = \int_{T_1}^{T_2} nC_{V,m}\left(\frac{dT}{T}\right)$$

The expression $\frac{1}{T}\left[P + \left(\frac{\partial E}{\partial V}\right)_T\right]$ which denotes the change in entropy from changes in volume in

isothermal processes is usually small and negligible for solids and liquids. For an ideal gas $\left(\frac{\partial E}{\partial V}\right)_T$ is

zero and the expression reduces to

$$\left(\frac{\partial S}{\partial V}\right)_T = \frac{P}{T}$$

and for a mole of an ideal gas $\frac{P}{T} = \frac{R}{V}$ and $\left(\frac{\partial S}{\partial V}\right)_T$ is given by

$$\left(\frac{\partial S}{\partial V}\right)_T = \frac{R}{V}$$

and
$$\Delta S = R \ln \frac{V_2}{V_1} \qquad \qquad ...(7.37(a))$$

For a mole of an ideal gas, Eq. (7.34) reduces to

$$dS = \frac{C_{V,m} dT}{T} + \frac{P}{T} dV = C_{V,m} \frac{dT}{T} + \frac{R}{V} dV \qquad \qquad ...(7.37(b))$$

Integration yields the total change in entropy resulting from simultaneous changes in volume and temperature. The expression is

$$\Delta S = C_{V,m} \ln \frac{T_2}{T_1} + R \ln \frac{V_2}{V_1} \qquad \qquad ...(7.38(a))$$

$$= C_{V,m} \ln \frac{T_2}{T_1} + R \ln \frac{P_1}{P_2} \frac{T_2}{T_1}$$

$$= \left(C_{V,m} + R \right) \ln \frac{T_2}{T_1} + R \ln \frac{P_1}{P_2}$$

$$= C_{P,m} \ln \frac{T_2}{T_1} - R \ln \frac{P_2}{P_1} \qquad \qquad ...(7.38(b))$$

For other substances evaluation of total entropy requires the value of $\left(\frac{\partial E}{\partial V} \right)_T$. This is expressed in terms of easily measurable quantities as indicated in the following treatment.

Equation (7.36) can be rearranged to yield

$$P = T \left(\frac{\partial S}{\partial V} \right)_T - \left(\frac{\partial E}{\partial V} \right)_T \qquad \qquad ...(7.39)$$

Differentiating the above equation with respect to temperature keeping volume constant, we get

$$\left(\frac{\partial P}{\partial T} \right)_V = T \frac{\partial^2 S}{\partial T \partial V} + \left(\frac{\partial S}{\partial V} \right)_T - \frac{\partial^2 E}{\partial T \partial V} \qquad \qquad ...(7.40)$$

Since
$$\left(\frac{dS}{dT} \right)_V = \frac{n C_{V,m}}{T} = \frac{1}{T} \left(\frac{\partial E}{\partial T} \right)_V$$

and differentiating this equation with respect to volume at constant temperature, we obtain

$$\frac{\partial^2 S}{\partial V \partial T} = \frac{1}{T} \frac{\partial^2 E}{\partial V \partial T} \qquad \qquad ...(7.41)$$

Since dS and dE are exact differentials, hence

$$\frac{\partial^2 S}{\partial V \partial T} = \frac{\partial^2 S}{\partial T \partial V} \quad \text{and} \quad \frac{\partial^2 E}{\partial T \partial V} = \frac{\partial^2 E}{\partial V \partial T}$$

Therefore, Eqs. (7.40) and (7.41) yield

$$\left(\frac{\partial S}{\partial V}\right)_T = \left(\frac{\partial P}{\partial T}\right)_V \qquad \ldots(7.42)$$

Thus, the change in entropy with volume at constant temperature can be expressed in terms of $\left(\frac{\partial P}{\partial T}\right)_V$ which can be calculated from the equation of state for the substance. For a mole of an ideal gas

$$\left(\frac{dS}{dV}\right)_T = \left(\frac{dP}{dT}\right)_V = \frac{R}{V}$$

From Eq. (7.36)

$$P + \left(\frac{\partial E}{\partial V}\right)_T = T\left(\frac{\partial S}{\partial V}\right)_T$$

But $\left(\frac{\partial S}{\partial V}\right)_T = \left(\frac{\partial P}{\partial T}\right)_V$, hence

$$P + \left(\frac{\partial E}{\partial V}\right)_T = T\left(\frac{\partial S}{\partial V}\right)_T = T\left(\frac{\partial P}{\partial T}\right)_V$$

and substituting the value of $P + \left(\frac{\partial E}{\partial V}\right)_T$ in Eq. (7.34), we get

$$dS = \frac{nC_{V,\,m}}{T}\,dT + \left(\frac{\partial P}{\partial T}\right)_V dV$$

Integration of the above equation yields

$$\Delta S = nC_{V,\,m}\ln\frac{T_2}{T_1} + \int_{V_1}^{V_2}\left(\frac{\partial P}{\partial T}\right)_V dV \qquad \ldots(7.43)$$

For a mole of van der Waals gas

$$\left(\frac{\partial P}{\partial T}\right)_V = \frac{R}{V-b}$$

and integration of Eq. (7.43) yields

$$\Delta S = C_{V,m}\ln\frac{T_2}{T_1} + R\ln\frac{V_2-b}{V_1-b} \qquad \ldots(7.44)$$

By substituting the value of $\left(\frac{\partial S}{\partial V}\right)_T = \left(\frac{\partial P}{\partial T}\right)_V$ in Eq. (7.36), we get

$$P = T\left(\frac{\partial P}{\partial T}\right)_V - \left(\frac{\partial E}{\partial V}\right)_T \qquad \text{...(7.45)}$$

Equation (7.45) is known as *the thermodynamic equation of state* as it connects the variables, pressure, temperature and volume of the system. It is applicable to all the substances, solids, liquids or gases under all conditions and is a direct consequence of the validity of the first and the second laws of thermodynamics. Equation (7.45) can be used to evaluate the value of $\left(\frac{\partial E}{\partial V}\right)_T$ for any substance. For a mole of an ideal gas

$$PV = RT$$

$$\left(\frac{\partial P}{\partial T}\right)_V = R/V$$

it follows that

$$P = \frac{RT}{V} - \left(\frac{\partial E}{\partial V}\right)_T = P - \left(\frac{\partial E}{\partial V}\right)_T$$

or

$$\left(\frac{\partial E}{\partial V}\right)_T = 0$$

For a mole of van der Waals gas

$$\left(\frac{\partial P}{\partial T}\right)_V = \frac{R}{V - b}$$

Substituting the value of $\left(\frac{\partial P}{\partial T}\right)_V$ in Eq. (7.45), we get

$$P = \frac{RT}{V - b} - \left(\frac{\partial E}{\partial V}\right)_T$$

or

$$-\left(\frac{\partial E}{\partial V}\right)_T = P - \frac{RT}{V - b}$$

$$= -\frac{a}{V^2}$$

Hence,

$$\left(\frac{\partial E}{\partial V}\right)_T = \frac{a}{V^2} \qquad \text{...(7.46)}$$

For *n* moles of the gas we have

$$\left(\frac{\partial E}{\partial V}\right)_T = \frac{an^2}{V^2}$$

7.14 VARIATION OF ENTROPY WITH TEMPERATURE AND PRESSURE

Considering entropy as a function of pressure and temperature, dS can be written as

$$dS = \left(\frac{\partial S}{\partial T}\right)_P dT + \left(\frac{\partial S}{\partial P}\right)_T dP \qquad ...(7.47)$$

Since $E = H - PV$ or $dE = dH - PdV - VdP$. Using this value of dE and putting it in equation,

$dS = \dfrac{dE + PdV}{T}$, we get

$$dS = \frac{dH - PdV - VdP + PdV}{T}$$

$$= \frac{dH}{T} - \frac{V}{T} dP \qquad ...(7.48,$$

Also $H = f(P, T)$ and $dH = \left(\frac{\partial H}{\partial T}\right)_P dT + \left(\frac{\partial H}{\partial P}\right)_T dP$

But $\left(\frac{\partial H}{\partial T}\right)_P = C_p$

Hence, $$dH = C_P dT + \left(\frac{\partial H}{\partial P}\right)_T dT$$

On substituting the above value of dH in Eq. (7.48), we obtain

$$dS = \frac{C_P}{T} dT + \frac{1}{T}\left[\left(\frac{\partial H}{\partial P}\right)_T - V\right] dP \qquad ...(7.49)$$

Equation (7.49) is completely general and applicable to all substances and gives the change in entropy due to simultaneous changes in temperature and pressure of the system. On comparing Eq. (7.47) with Eq. (7.49), we obtain

$$\left(\frac{\partial S}{\partial T}\right)_P = \frac{C_P}{T} \qquad ...(7.50)$$

and $$\left(\frac{\partial S}{\partial P}\right)_T = \frac{1}{T}\left[\left(\frac{\partial H}{\partial P}\right)_T - V\right] \qquad ...(7.51)$$

The derivative $\left(\dfrac{\partial H}{\partial P}\right)_T$ in Eq. (7.51) is zero for an ideal gas while for other substances it has to be expressed in terms of easily-accessible quantities for evaluating the total entropy changes of the system. The procedure adopted is as follows:

At constant temperature, equation $dH = TdS + VdP$ can be rewritten as

$$V = \left(\frac{\partial H}{\partial P}\right)_T - T\left(\frac{\partial S}{\partial P}\right)_T \qquad \ldots(7.52)$$

Differentiating the above equation with respect to temperature at constant volume, we get

$$\left(\frac{\partial V}{\partial T}\right)_P = \frac{\partial^2 H}{\partial T\,\partial P} - T\frac{\partial^2 S}{\partial T\,\partial P} - \left(\frac{\partial S}{\partial P}\right)_T \qquad \ldots(7.53)$$

Also

$$\left(\frac{\partial S}{\partial T}\right)_P = \frac{C_P}{T} = \frac{1}{T}\left(\frac{\partial H}{\partial T}\right)_P$$

and differentiation of the above equation with respect to pressure at constant temperature yields

$$\frac{\partial^2 S}{\partial P\,\partial T} = \frac{1}{T}\frac{\partial^2 H}{\partial P\,\partial T} \qquad \ldots(7.54)$$

Since dS and dH are exact differentials hence

$$\frac{\partial^2 S}{\partial P\,\partial T} = \frac{\partial^2 S}{\partial T\,\partial P} \quad \text{and} \quad \frac{\partial^2 H}{\partial P\,\partial T} = \frac{\partial^2 H}{\partial T\,\partial P}$$

Comparing Eqs. (7.53), and (7.54), we obtain

$$\left(\frac{\partial S}{\partial P}\right)_T = -\left(\frac{\partial V}{\partial T}\right)_P \qquad \ldots(7.55)$$

Since $\left(\dfrac{\partial V}{\partial T}\right)_P$ is positive, the negative sign indicates that entropy decreases with increase of pressure at constant temperature.

Substituting the value of $\left(\dfrac{\partial S}{\partial P}\right)_T = -\left(\dfrac{\partial V}{\partial T}\right)_P$ in Eq. (7.52), we get

$$V = \left(\frac{\partial H}{\partial P}\right)_T + T\left(\frac{\partial V}{\partial T}\right)_P \qquad \ldots(7.56)$$

Equation (7.56) is another form of the thermodynamic equation of state and like Eq. (7.45) is applicable to all substances under different conditions. From Eq. (7.56)

$$\left(\frac{\partial H}{\partial P}\right)_T - V = -T\left(\frac{\partial V}{\partial T}\right)_P$$

Substitution in Eq. (7.49) yields

$$dS = \frac{C_P}{T} dT - \left(\frac{\partial V}{\partial T}\right)_P dP \qquad ...(7.57)$$

If for a substances, the equation of state is available, $\left(\frac{\partial V}{\partial T}\right)_P$ can be calculated and then integrating Eq. (7.57) within specified limits, the total entropy change of the system can be evaluated. The entropy change for a mole of an ideal gas for which $\left(\frac{\partial V}{\partial T}\right)_P = \frac{R}{P}$ is given by

$$\Delta S = C_{P, m} \ln \frac{T_2}{T_1} - R \ln \frac{P_2}{P_1} \qquad ...(7.58)$$

Problem 7.6: One mole of an ideal gas is allowed to expand isothermally from 0.02 m³ to 0.2 m³ at 300 K. Calculate the entropy change for the system, surroundings and universe if the expansion is (a) reversible and (b) irreversible against a constant external pressure of 0.1 atmosphere.

Solution: (a) Reversible expansion—Since the gas expands isothermally ΔE is zero and

$$Q_{rev} = -W = nRT \ln \frac{V_2}{V_1}$$

and

$$\Delta S_{sys} = \frac{Q_{rev}}{T} = nR \ln \frac{V_2}{V_1}$$

$$= (1 \text{ mol})(8.314 \text{ J mol}^{-1}\text{K}^{-1})(2.303) \log \frac{0.20}{0.02}$$

$$= 19.14 \text{ JK}^{-1}$$

The surroundings has lost an exactly equivalent amount of heat and hence its entropy decrease is given by

$$\Delta S_{surr} = \frac{(-Q_{rev})}{T} = -19.14 \text{ JK}^{-1}$$

The entropy change of the universe is given by

$$\Delta S_{univ} = \Delta S_{sys} + \Delta S_{surr} = 0$$

(b) In the irreversible expansion, the entropy change of the system is still the same as in the reversible change, i.e., 19.14 JK⁻¹ but heat lost by the surroundings is given by $-P\Delta V$ and consequently, the entropy change if the transfer was reversible is

$$\Delta S_{surr} = -\frac{Q_{surr}}{T} = -\frac{P\Delta V}{T}$$

$$= -\frac{(0.1 \text{ atm})(0.18 \text{ m}^3)(101325 \text{ Jm}^{-3}\text{atm}^{-1})}{(300 \text{ K})}$$

$$= -6.077 \text{ JK}^{-1}$$

Hence, the entropy change for the universe is given by

$$\Delta S_{univ} = \Delta S_{sys} + \Delta S_{surr}$$
$$= 19.14 - 6.077$$
$$= 12.063 \text{ JK}^{-1}$$

The positive value indicates that the entropy of the universe increases in a real or irreversible process.

Problem 7.7: One mole of an ideal gas, $C_{V, m} = 12.55 \text{ JK}^{-1} \text{ mol}^{-1}$, is transferred from 298 K and 2 atm to 233 K and 0.4 atm. Calculate ΔS for the change in the state of the system.

Solution: Since $C_{V, m} = 12.55 \text{ JK}^{-1} \text{ mol}^{-1}$ and hence $C_{P, m} = 20.864 \text{ JK}^{-1} \text{ mol}^{-1}$. The entropy change is given as

$$\Delta S_{sys} = (1 \text{ mol})(20.864 \text{ JK}^{-1}\text{mol}^{-1})\left(2.303 \log \frac{233}{298}\right)$$

$$-(1 \text{ mol})(8.314 \text{ JK}^{-1}\text{mol}^{-1})\left(2.303 \log \frac{0.4}{2.0}\right)$$

$$= -3.308 + 13.40 = 10.092 \text{ JK}^{-1} \text{ mol}^{-1}$$

Problem 7.8: 1 kg bar of copper at 373 K is placed in 2 kg of water at 273.0 K in an insulated container at 1 atmosphere pressure. Calculate ΔH and ΔS for the system. $C_{P, m}$ values for copper and water are 26.57 $\text{JK}^{-1}\text{mol}^{-1}$ and 77.31 $\text{JK}^{-1}\text{mol}^{-1}$, respectively.

Solution: The process is adiabatic at constant pressure, hence

$$Q_P = \Delta H = 0$$

The entropy changes of copper and water are calculated as follows:

Heat lost by copper = Heat gained by water

If T_f is the final temperature in the system, then

$$\left(\frac{1000}{63.5} \text{mol}\right)(26.57 \text{ JK}^{-1}\text{mol}^{-1})(373 - T_f) = \left(\frac{2000}{18} \text{mol } 77.31 \text{ JK}^{-1}\text{mol}^{-1}\right)(T_f - 273)$$

or
$$T_f = 277.9 \text{ K}$$

For water, the entropy change, ΔS_{water} is given as

$$\Delta S_{water} = \left(\frac{2000}{18} \text{mol}\right)(77.31 \text{ JK}^{-1}\text{mol}^{-1})\left(2.303 \log \frac{277.9}{273.0}\right)$$

$$= 152.4 \text{ JK}^{-1}$$

Entropy change for copper, ΔS_{copper} is

$$\Delta S_{copper} = \left(\frac{1000}{63.5} \text{ mol}\right)\left(26.57 \text{ JK}^{-1}\text{mol}^{-1}\right)\left(2.303 \log \frac{277.9}{373.0}\right)$$

$$= -123.1 \text{ JK}^{-1}$$

Therefore the total entropy change of the system

$$\Delta S = \Delta S_{water} + \Delta S_{copper}$$
$$= 152.4 - 123.1$$
$$= 29.3 \text{ JK}^{-1}$$

Problem 7.9: 2 moles of an ideal monatomic gas ($C_{V,m} = 20.9 \text{ Jmol}^{-1} \text{ K}^{-1}$) are heated from 300 K to 350 K. The volume of the gas changes from 0.02 m^3 to 0.2 m^3. Assuming that the heat capacity remains constant in this temperature range, calculate the entropy change for the system, the surroundings and the universe if the process is carried out (a) reversibly and (b) irreversibly by placing the system in contact with a reservoir at 500 K and allowing the gas to expand against a constant external pressure equal to the final pressure of the gas.

Solution: (a) For the reversible transformation of an ideal gas, the entropy change of the system is given by

$$\Delta S_{sys} = nC_{V,m} \ln\frac{T_2}{T_1} + nR\ln\frac{V_2}{V_1}$$

$$= (2 \text{ mol})\left(20.9 \text{ J mol}^{-1}\text{K}^{-1}\right)(2.303)\log\frac{350}{300}$$

$$+ (2 \text{ mol})\left(8.314 \text{ J mol}^{-1}\text{K}^{-1}\right)(2.303)\log\frac{0.20}{0.02}$$

$$= 6.449 + 38.28 = 44.729 \text{ JK}^{-1}$$

As the process is reversible, the entropy change of the surroundings is

$$\Delta S_{surr} = -44.729 \text{ JK}^{-1}$$

and the entropy change of the universe is

$$\Delta S_{univ} = \Delta S_{sys} + \Delta S_{surr} = 0$$

(b) In the irreversible transformation the entropy change of the system will be the same. Heat lost by the surroundings is

$$Q = \Delta E - W$$
$$\Delta E = -nC_{V,m}(350 - 300), \text{ and } -W = P_{ext}(V_2 - V_1)$$

In the final state
$$T_2 = 350 \text{ K}$$
$$V_2 = 0.2 \text{ m}^3$$

and hence the pressure in given by

$$P_2 = \frac{nRT_2}{V_2} = \frac{(2 \text{ mol})\left(8.314 \text{ J mol}^{-1}\text{K}^{-1}\right)(350 \text{ K})}{\left(0.2 \text{ m}^3\right)}$$

$$= 2.810 \times 10^4 \text{ J m}^{-3}$$

Now $P_{ext} = P_2 = 2.810 \times 10^4$ J m^{-3} and hence the heat lost by the surroundings is

$$-Q = -(2 \text{ mol}) (20.9 \text{ J mol}^{-1}\text{K}^{-1}) (50 \text{ K})$$
$$-(2.8 \times 10^4 \text{ J m}^{-3}) (0.18 \text{ m}^3)$$
$$= -2090 \text{ J} -5048 \text{ J} = -7138 \text{ J}$$

Assuming that this heat is lost reversibly by the surroundings its entropy change is given as

$$\Delta S_{surr} = -\frac{7138}{500 \text{ K}} = -14.276 \text{ JK}^{-1}$$

and the entropy change of the universe is

$$\Delta S_{univ} = \Delta S_{sys} + \Delta S_{surr}$$
$$= 44.729 - 14.276 = 30.453 \text{ J K}^{-1}$$

Problem 7.10: A certain diatomic gas $C_{P,\,m} = 29.3$ J K^{-1} mol^{-1} expands adiabatically from an initial state; $V_1 = 10^{-2}$ m^3, $P_1 = 100$ atm and $T_1 = 400$ K to the final state until the pressure is 1 atm. Calculate the entropy change for the gas if the expansion is (a) reversible and (b) irreversible against a constant external pressure of 1 atm. Assume ideal behaviour for the gas and temperature independence for the heat capacity in this temperature range.

Solution: (a) In the reversible adiabatic transformation the system is always in a state of equilibrium and there is no transfer of heat between the system and the surroundings. Consequently, there is no change in entropy of the system.

(b) The irreversible expansion is spontaneous and is accompanied by a change in entropy of the system. To calculate the entropy change in this case, we first evaluate the number of moles of the gas and then its temperature after expansion.

$$n = \frac{P_1 V_1}{RT_1} = \frac{(100 \text{ atm})(10^{-2} \text{ m}^3)(101325 \text{ Jm}^{-3}\text{atm}^{-1})}{(8.314 \text{ J K}^{-1}\text{mol}^{-1})(400 \text{ K})}$$

$$= 30.45 \text{ mol}$$

The final temperature in a reversible adiabatic expansion as given by Eq. (5.73) in Chapter 5 is

$$T_2 = T_1 \frac{R\dfrac{P_2}{P_1} + C_{V,\,m}}{C_{P,\,m}}$$

$$= (400 \text{ K}) \left[\frac{\left(8.314 \text{ JK}^{-1}\text{mol}^{-1}\right)\left(\dfrac{1}{100}\right) + 20.986 \text{ JK}^{-1}\text{mol}^{-1}}{\left(29.3 \text{ JK}^{-1}\text{mol}^{-1}\right)} \right]$$

$$= 287.7 \text{ K}$$

Now the entropy change for the system as given by Eq. (7.58) is

$$\Delta S_{sys} = nC_{P,\,m} \ln\frac{T_2}{T_1} - nR\ln\frac{P_2}{P_1}$$

$$= (30.45 \text{ mol})(29.3 \text{ J mol}^{-1}\text{K}^{-1})(2.303) \log \frac{287.7}{400.0}$$

$$-(30.45 \text{ mol})(8.314 \text{ J mol}^{-1}\text{K}^{-1})(2.303) \log \frac{1}{100}$$

$$= -501.3 + 1166.0 = 664.7 \text{ JK}^{-1}$$

Problem 7.11: The temperature of an ideal monatomic gas is increased from 273 K to 819 K. Calculate the pressure change in order that the entropy of the gas remains unchanged in the process?

Solution: The entropy change for the system is given by the relation

$$\Delta S_{sys} = nC_{P, m} \ln \frac{T_2}{T_1} - nR \ln \frac{P_2}{P_1}$$

But $\Delta S_{sys} = 0$, hence

$$C_{P, m} \ln \frac{T_2}{T_1} = R \ln \frac{P_2}{P_1}$$

$$\frac{5}{2} R \log \frac{T_2}{T_1} = R \log \frac{P_2}{P_1}$$

$$\frac{5}{2} \log \frac{819 \text{ K}}{273 \text{ K}} = \log \frac{P_2}{P_1}$$

or

$$\frac{P_2}{P_1} = 15.60$$

Therefore, for entropy to remain constant, the pressure of the gas must be increased by 15.60 times its initial value.

Problem 7.12: Two moles of an ideal monatomic gas $\left(C_{P, m} = \frac{5}{2} R \right)$ initially at 1 atmosphere and 300 K are subjected through the following reversible cycle:

(i) Isothermal compression to 2 atmospheres, (ii) isobaric temperature increase to 400 K, (iii) return to the initial state by a different path. Calculate ΔS for each stage and for the whole cycle.

Solution: For stage (i)

$$\Delta S_1 = -nR \ln \frac{P_2}{P_1} = -(2 \text{ mol})(8.314 \text{ JK}^{-1}\text{mol}^{-1})(2.303 \log 2)$$

$$= -11.52 \text{ JK}^{-1}$$

For the stage (ii)

$$\Delta S_2 = nC_{P, m} \ln \frac{T_2}{T_1} = (2 \text{ mol})\left(\frac{5}{2}\right)(8.314 \text{ JK}^{-1}\text{mol}^{-1})\left(2.303 \log \frac{T_2}{T_1} \right)$$

$$= 11.97 \text{ JK}^{-1}$$

For calculating ΔS_3, we know that the total entropy change for the whole reversible cycle is zero, i.e.,

$$\Delta S_{cycle} = \Delta S_1 + \Delta S_2 + \Delta S_3 = 0$$

or

$$-11.52 + 11.97 + \Delta S_3 = 0$$

or

$$\Delta S_3 = -0.45 \text{ JK}^{-1}$$

Problem 7.13: A block of copper with heat capacity C_P and temperature T_1 is brought in contact with another block of copper of same size but at a different temperature T_2. The blocks are allowed to come to the same temperature. Show that (if C_P is regarded as constant)

$$\Delta S = C_P \ln \frac{(T_1 + T_2)^2}{4 T_1 T_2}$$

Solution: Let T be the final temperature and $T_1 > T_2$, then heat gained is $C_P(T - T_2)$ and heat lost is $C_P(T_1 - T)$. At equilibrium

$$C_P(T_1 - T) = C_P(T - T_2)$$

$$T = \frac{T_1 + T_2}{2}$$

The entropy increase of block from T_2 to T is

$$\Delta S_1 = \int_{T_2}^{T} \frac{C_P}{T} dT = C_P \ln \frac{T}{T_2}$$

and entropy decrease of block from T_1 to T is

$$\Delta S_2 = \int_{T_1}^{T} \frac{C_P}{T} dT = C_P \ln \frac{T}{T_1}$$

The total entropy change is

$$\Delta S = \Delta S_1 + \Delta S_2$$

$$= C_P \left[\ln \frac{T}{T_2} + \ln \frac{T}{T_1} \right]$$

$$= C_P \ln \left(\frac{T^2}{T_1 T_2} \right)$$

$$= C_P \ln \frac{(T_1 + T_2)^2}{4 T_1 T_2}$$

$$= C_P \ln\left[\frac{(T_1 - T_2)^2}{4 T_1 T_2} + 1\right]$$

The quantity within the bracket is greater than unity hence, ΔS is positive and the process spontaneous.

7.15 ENTROPY OF MIXING OF IDEAL GASES

Mixing of two or more gases is irreversible and mixing is accompanied by an increase of entropy. We shall derive an expression for the entropy of mixing of ideal and nonreacting gases. Suppose n_A, n_B etc. are the number of moles of ideal gases A, B etc., respectively placed in a vessel in which they are separated by partitions. If V_A, V_B etc., are the volumes of the individual gases, then at constant temperature and pressure the entropies of the gases are given by integrating Eq. [7.37 (b)]

Entropy of gas A is given as

$$S_A = n_A C_{V, m, A} \ln T + n_A R \ln V_A + S_A^0$$

Entropy of gas B is

$$S_B = n_B C_{V, m, B} \ln T + n_B R \ln V_B + S_B^0$$

where S^0s are the integration constants. The total entropy of the system before mixing is thus

$$S_{\text{initial}} = S_A + S_B + \ldots$$

$$= (n_A C_{V, m, A} \ln T + n_A R \ln V_A + S_A^0)$$

$$+ (n_B C_{V, m, B} \ln T + n_B R \ln V_B + S_B^0) + \ldots$$

If the partitions are removed the gases spontaneously mix up and occupy the entire volume of the container which is obviously given by the sum of the individual volumes, *i.e.*,

$$V = V_A + V_B + \ldots$$

The entropies of the gases after mixing are given as

$$S'_A = n_A C_{V, m, A} \ln T + n_A R \ln V + S_A^0$$

$$S'_B = n_B C_{V, m, B} \ln T + n_B R \ln V + S_B^0$$

and the total entropy after mixing is

$$S_{\text{final}} = (n_A C_{V, m, A} \ln T + n_A R \ln V + S_A^0) + \ldots$$

$$+ (n_B C_{V, m, B} \ln T + n_B R \ln V + S_B^0) + \ldots$$

Consequently, the increase in entropy due to mixing is given by

$$\Delta S_{\text{mixing}} = S_{\text{final}} - S_{\text{initial}}$$

$$= (n_A R \ln V - n_A R \ln V_A) + (n_B R \ln V - n_B R \ln V_B) + \ldots$$

$$= \left(-n_A R \ln \frac{V_A}{V} - n_B R \ln \frac{V_B}{V} \ldots\ldots\right)$$

But

$$\frac{V_A}{V} = \frac{n_A}{n_t} = X_A, \quad \frac{V_B}{V} = \frac{n_B}{n_t} = X_B, \ldots\ldots$$

where n_t is the total number of moles in the system and X's are the mole fractions of the individual gases.

Hence

$$\Delta S_{mixing} = -n_A R \ln X_A - n_B R \ln X_B \cdots \cdots$$

$$= -R \Sigma n_i \text{ in } X_i \qquad \qquad ...(7.59)$$

The entropy of mixing per mole of the mixture is obtained by dividing both sides of the above equation by n_i, the total number of moles.

$$\Delta S_{m, mixing} = \frac{\Delta S_{mixing}}{n_t} - R \sum \frac{n_i}{n_t} \ln X_i$$

$$= -R \Sigma X_i \ln X_i \qquad \qquad ...(7.60)$$

Since X_i is always less than unity, its logarithm is negative and therefore the quantity on the right hand side is always positive indicating that mixing is always accompanied by an increase in entropy.

Problem 7.14: The mixing of gases is always accompanied by an increase in entropy. Show that in the formation of a binary mixture of two ideal gases the maximum entropy increase results when $X_1 = X_2 = 0.5$.

Solution: For a binary mixture, the entropy of per mole of the mixture formed is given by

$$\Delta S_{m, mixing} = -R \left[X_1 \ln X_1 + X_2 \ln X_2 \right]$$

$$= -R \left[X_1 \ln X_1 + (1 - X_1) \ln (1 - X_1) \right]$$

For entropy of mixing to be maximum, the first derivative, $\dfrac{\partial \left(\Delta S_{m, mixing} \right)}{\partial X_1}$ should be zero and the second derivative should be negative. Differentiating, $\Delta S_{m, mixing}$ with respect to X_1 and equating it to zero gives

$$\frac{\partial \left(\Delta S_m \right)_{mixing}}{\partial X_1} = -R \left[\ln X_1 + \frac{X_1}{X_1} + \frac{1 - X_1}{1 - X_1} (-1) + (-1) \ln (1 - X_1) \right] = 0$$

or

$$\ln X_1 + 1 - 1 - \ln (1 - X_1) = 0$$

$$\ln \frac{X_1}{1 - X_1} = 0$$

$$X_1 = 1 - X_1$$

$$X_1 = \frac{1}{2}$$

Problem 7.15: One mole of hydrogen and nine moles of nitrogen are mixed at 298 K and 1 atm pressure. Assuming ideal behaviour for the gases, calculate the entropy of mixing per mole of the mixture formed. Would it make any difference if under similar conditions one mole of hydrogen is mixed with nine moles of oxygen?

Solution: For ideal gases, the entropy of mixing per mole of the mixture is given by

$$\Delta S_{m,\text{ mining}} = -R \Sigma X_1 \ln X_1$$

Here $X_{H_2} = 0.1$ and $X_{N_2} = 0.9$

Hence, $\Delta S_{m,\text{ mixing}} = -R \left[0.1 \ln 0.1 + 0.9 \ln 0.9 \right]$

$$= -\left(8.314 \text{ JK}^{-1}\text{mol}^{-1} \right)(2.303)(0.1)\left[\log\frac{1}{10} + 9\log\frac{9}{10} \right]$$

$$= 2.704 \text{ JK}^{-1}\text{mol}^{-1}$$

When hydrogen is mixed with oxygen, the entropy of mixing would remain unchanged provided oxygen also behaves ideally.

7.16 RELATION BETWEEN C_P AND C_V

In Chapter 5 we have proved that

$$C_P - C_V = \left[P + \left(\frac{\partial E}{\partial V} \right)_T \right]\left(\frac{\partial V}{\partial T} \right)_P$$

From thermodynamic equation of state, we have

$$P + \left(\frac{\partial E}{\partial V} \right)_T = T\left(\frac{\partial P}{\partial T} \right)_V$$

Substituting the value of $P + \left(\frac{\partial E}{\partial V} \right)_T$, the difference in the two heat capacities is given as

$$C_P - C_V = T\left(\frac{\partial V}{\partial T} \right)_P\left(\frac{\partial P}{\partial T} \right)_V \qquad \qquad ...(7.61)$$

From cyclic rule we have

$$\left(\frac{\partial P}{\partial T} \right)_V\left(\frac{\partial T}{\partial V} \right)_P\left(\frac{\partial V}{\partial P} \right)_T = -1$$

or

$$\left(\frac{\partial P}{\partial T} \right)_V = -\left(\frac{\partial V}{\partial T} \right)_P\left(\frac{\partial P}{\partial V} \right)_T$$

Substituting the value of $\left(\frac{\partial P}{\partial T} \right)_V$ in Eq. (7.61), we obtain

$$C_P - C_V = -T\left(\frac{\partial V}{\partial T} \right)_P^2\left(\frac{\partial P}{\partial V} \right)_T \qquad \qquad ...(7.62)$$

The derivatives on the right hand side of Eq. (7.62) can be expressed in terms of the coefficient of thermal expansion (α) and the coefficient of compressibility (κ) which are defined as

$$\alpha = \frac{1}{V}\left(\frac{\partial V}{\partial T}\right)_P \text{ and } \kappa = -\frac{1}{V}\left(\frac{\partial V}{\partial P}\right)_T$$

Substitution of these values in Eq. (7.62), yields

$$C_P - C_V = -T(\alpha V)^2\left(\frac{1}{(-\kappa V)}\right) = \frac{T\alpha^2 V}{\kappa} \qquad \qquad ...(7.63)$$

Eq. (7.63) is applicable to solids, liquids or gases. The difference, $C_P - C_V$, can be readily evaluated for any substance from easily accessible quantities. Further α, κ, V^2 and T are all positive, C_P is always greater than C_V.

However, in case of water at 4°C its density is maximum and C_P and C_V are equal. This can be shown with the help of Eq. (7.62). Since density (ρ) is mass per unit volume, i.e.,

$$\rho = \frac{m}{V}$$

At constant pressure

$$\left(\frac{d\rho}{dT}\right)_P = \frac{d}{dT}(m/V) = -\frac{m}{V^2}\left(\frac{dV}{dT}\right)_P$$

For density to be maximum, $\left(\dfrac{dV}{dT}\right)_P$ should be zero. Hence, $C_P = C_V$

For a mole of the van der Waals gas, the difference can be obtained as follows:

The derivative $\left(\dfrac{\partial P}{\partial T}\right)_V$ for a mole of the gas is given by

$$\left(\frac{\partial P}{\partial T}\right)_V = \frac{R}{V-b}$$

To evaluate $\left(\dfrac{\partial V}{\partial T}\right)_P$ for the gas, van der Waals equation for a mole is written as

$$RT = PV - Pb - \frac{ab}{V^2} + \frac{a}{V}$$

Neglecting $\dfrac{ab}{V^2}$ and differentiating the above equation at constant pressure, we get

$$R(dT)_P = P(dV)_P - \frac{a}{V^2}(dV)_P$$

or
$$\left(\frac{\partial V}{\partial T}\right)_P = \frac{R}{P - \dfrac{a}{V^2}}$$

Substituting the values of $\left(\dfrac{\partial P}{\partial T}\right)_V$ and $\left(\dfrac{\partial V}{\partial T}\right)_P$ in Eq. (7.61), we get

$$C_{P,\,m} - C_{V,\,m} = T\left(\frac{R}{V-b}\right)\left(\frac{R}{P - \dfrac{a}{V^2}}\right)$$

$$= \left(\frac{RT}{V-b}\right)\frac{R}{\left(P + \dfrac{a}{V^2}\right) - \dfrac{2a}{V^2}}$$

$$= \left(\frac{RT}{V-b}\right)\frac{R}{\dfrac{RT}{V-b} - \dfrac{2a}{V^2}}$$

$$= \left(\frac{RT}{V-b}\right)\frac{R}{\dfrac{RT}{V-b}\left(1 - \dfrac{2a(V-b)}{RTV^2}\right)}$$

$$= \frac{R}{1 - \dfrac{2a(V-b)}{RTV^2}}$$

$$= R\left[1 - \frac{2a(V-b)}{RTV^2}\right]^{-1}$$

If $b \ll V$, the above equation on expanding reduces to

$$C_{P,\,m} - C_{V,\,m} = R\left(1 + \frac{2a}{RTV}\right)$$

If V is replaced by RT/P, we get

$$C_{P,\,m} - C_{V,\,m} = R\left(1 + \frac{2aP}{R^2T^2}\right) \qquad \ldots(7.64)$$

The difference between $C_{P,\,m}$ and $C_{V,\,m}$ increases as 'a' increases.

7.17 THE THIRD LAW OF THERMODYNAMICS

Variation of entropy of a substance with temperature at constant pressure is given by

$$dS = \frac{C_P}{T} dT$$

Integrating this equation from $T = 0K$ to some temperature T below the melting point of the substance we get

$$S_T - S_0 = \int_0^T \frac{C_P}{T} dT = C_P \, d \ln T \qquad \qquad ...(7.65)$$

where S_0 is the hypothetical value of entropy at absolute zero. Since C_P/T is positive, the entropy at some higher temperature must be greater than that at the absolute zero. In 1913, M. Planck suggested that *entropy of a pure and perfectly crystalline substance is zero at the absolute zero of temperature,* i.e., $S_{\lim T \to 0} = 0$. This known as *the third law of thermodynamics.* Unlike first and second laws, the third law does not lead to the development of any new concept, it merely imposes a limitation on the value of entropy. Eq. (7.65) now becomes

$$S_T = \int_0^T \frac{C_P}{T} dT \qquad \qquad ...(7.66)$$

Knowing the temperature dependence of heat capacity, entropy of a substance at any specified temperature can be calculated using the above equation. In evaluating the absolute value of entropy, contributions to entropy due to phase transformations such as melting, vapourization, sublimation and transition from one allotropic form into other must be taken into account. The entropy of a substance at any temperature above its boiling point is then given as

$$S_T = \int_0^{T_{trans}} \frac{C_P(s_1)}{T} dT + \frac{\Delta H_{trans}}{T_{trans}} + \int_{T_{trans}}^{T_m} \frac{C_P(s_2)}{T} dT + \frac{\Delta H_{fus}}{T_m}$$

$$+ \int_{T_m}^{T_s} \frac{C_P(l)}{T} dT + \frac{\Delta H_{vap}}{T_b} + \int_{T_b}^{T} \frac{C_P(g)}{T} dT \qquad \qquad ...(7.67)$$

Accurate determination of S_T requires that the heat capacity of the substance in its various forms must be accurately determined. However, C_P can not be measured at or around absolute zero. Hence, the heat capacity measurements are first carried out to as low a temperature as possible and C_P value is then obtained by extrapolation using the Debye equation

$$C_V = aT^3$$

Here 'a' is a constant characteristic of the substance. At temperatures in the vicinity of absolute zero, the difference between C_P and C_V is negligible and therefore C_V may be used for C_P in the extrapolation.

The above method of evaluating the entropy of a substance neglects the entropy associated with the nucleus because it is assumed that in ordinary chemical reactions there is no change in the nuclear properties and hence nuclear entropy. Standard entropies of a few substances are given in Table 7.1.

Table 7.1 Absolute Entropies at 298 K and 1 atm

Substance	$S°(JK^{-1} mol^{-1})$	Substance	$S°(JK^{-1} mol^{-1})$
C (graphite)	5.7	HCl (g)	186.6
C (diamond)	2.4	I_2 (s)	116.0
C (g)	198.0	Mg (s)	32.5
CO_2 (g)	213.5	N_2 (g)	191.5
CH_4 (g)	186.3	NH_3 (g)	192.4
C_2H_6 (g)	230.1	NO (g)	210.5
Cl_2 (g)	222.9	NO_2 (g)	240.4
F_2 (g)	202.8	O_2 (g)	205.1
H_2 (g)	130.6	S (rhombic)	31.7
H_2O (l)	70.0	SO_2 (g)	248.2
H_2O (g)	188.8	H_2SO_4 (l)	156.9
Zn (s)	41.9		
ZnO (s)	43.6		

7.18 ENTROPY CHANGE IN A CHEMICAL REACTION AND ITS TEMPERATURE DEPENDENCE

One of the most important applications of the third law is the calculation of entropy changes in chemical reactions. The absolute values of entropies of substances in the standard state of one atmosphere at specified temperature usually 298 K are tabulated. The entropy change for a reaction in the standard state can then be computed from the tabulated data. For a reaction

$$aA + bB + ... = lL + mM + ...$$

occurring in the standard state, the entropy change is given by

$$\Delta S^0 = \left[lS_L^0 + nS_M^0 + ... \right] - \left[aS_A^0 + bS_B^0 + ... \right]$$

$$= \Sigma(S^0)_{Products} - \Sigma(S^0)_{Reactants}$$

In this expression S_M^0 s are the molar entropies of individual species, and a, b, etc., are the stoichiometric coefficients. The entropy at any other temperature can be obtained by differentiating the above equation with respect to temperature keeping pressure constant. The result is

$$\left[\frac{d(\Delta S^0)}{dT} \right]_P = \Sigma \left(\frac{\partial S_{Products}^0}{\partial T} \right)_P - \Sigma \left(\frac{\partial S_{Reactants}^0}{\partial T} \right)_P$$

But

$$\left(\frac{\partial S^0}{\partial T} \right)_P = \frac{C_P}{T}$$

Therefore,
$$\left[\frac{d(\Delta S^0)}{dT}\right]_P = \sum \left(\frac{C_P}{T}\right)_{Products} - \sum \left(\frac{C_P}{T}\right)_{Reactants}$$

Integrating the above equation, we get

$$\Delta S_T^0 - \Delta S_{T_0}^0 = \int_{T_0}^{T} \frac{\Delta C_P}{T} dT \qquad \qquad ...(7.68)$$

Equation (7.68) permits the calculation of entropy change for a reaction at any temperature and is applicable to chemical reactions involving solids, liquids or gases.

Problem 7.16: Using the standard values of entropies from Table 7.1, calculate ΔS^0 for the reaction at 298 K

$$H_2(g) + \frac{1}{2}O_2(g) = H_2O(l)$$

If the enthalpy change for the reaction in the standard state is -285.8 kJ mol^{-1}, what is the entropy change for the surroundings and the universe?

Solution: The standard entropy change for the reaction is

$$\Delta S^0 = S_{H_2O(l)}^0 - \frac{1}{2}S_{O_2(g)}^0 - S_{H_2(g)}^0$$

$$= 69.9 - 102.5 - 130.5 = -163.1 \text{ J mol}^{-1}\text{K}^{-1}$$

The entropy change is negative, however the reaction is spontaneous, it implies that the entropy change of surroundings must be positive and greater than that of the system. Heat lost by the system at constant pressure is gained by the surroundings, *i.e.*,

$$\Delta H_{surr} = -\Delta H_{sys} = Q_P$$

and
$$\Delta S_{surr} = \frac{\Delta H_{surr}}{T} = \frac{-\Delta H_{sys}}{T} = \frac{285.8 \text{ kJ mol}^{-1}}{298}$$

$$= +959.1 \text{ J mol}^{-1} \text{ K}^{-1}$$

Hence,
$$\Delta S_{univ} = \Delta S_{surr} + \Delta S_{sys}$$
$$= -163.1 + 959.1 = +796.0 \text{ JK}^{-1}\text{mol}^{-1}$$

7.19 ENTROPY AND PROBABILITY

Thermodynamic probability is defined as *the total number of ways in which a given system in a specified thermodynamic state can be realised.* The number of such ways and the entropy in spontaneous processes increase. Therefore, a direct relationship exists between entropy and probability. If S is the entropy and W the probability of the system, then

$$S = f(W)$$

The nature of the function is ascertained by considering two systems with entropies S_1 and S_2 and probabilities W_1 and W_2. When the systems are combined, the total entropy (S_{12}) of the resulting system is given by

$$S_{12} = S_1 + S_2$$

Unlike entropies which are additive, probabilities are multiplicative and the probability of the combined system W_{12} is given by

$$W_{12} = W_1 W_2$$
$$S_{12} = S_1 + S_2 = f(W_1, W_2)$$

This condition is obviously satisfied if the function is logarithmic. Therefore, we write

$$S = k \ln W \qquad \qquad ...(7.69)$$

where k is the Boltzmann constant and the relation is known as the *Boltzmann-Planck equation*. From Eq. (7.69) it is clear that at the absolute zero where only one arrangement is possible for a pure perfectly crystalline substance, entropy is zero.

7.20 SOME FUNDAMENTAL RELATIONS BASED ON THE SECOND LAW

(i) $\left(\dfrac{\partial S}{\partial P}\right)_V = \dfrac{\kappa C_V}{\alpha T}$

From the cycle rule, we have

$$\left(\frac{\partial V}{\partial T}\right)_P \left(\frac{\partial T}{\partial P}\right)_V \left(\frac{\partial P}{\partial V}\right)_T = -1 \qquad \qquad ...(a)$$

But $\qquad \alpha = \dfrac{1}{V}\left(\dfrac{\partial V}{\partial T}\right)_P \quad$ and $\quad \kappa = -\dfrac{1}{V}\left(\dfrac{\partial V}{\partial P}\right)_T$

Hence, from Eq. (a)

$$\left(\frac{\partial T}{\partial P}\right)_V = -\frac{1}{\left(\dfrac{\partial V}{\partial T}\right)_P \left(\dfrac{\partial P}{\partial V}\right)_T} = -\frac{1}{(\alpha V)\left(-\dfrac{1}{\kappa V}\right)} = \frac{\kappa}{\alpha}$$

Rewriting the above equation as

$$\left(\frac{\partial T}{\partial S}\right)_V \left(\frac{\partial S}{\partial P}\right)_V = \frac{\kappa}{\alpha}$$

$$\left(\frac{\partial S}{\partial P}\right)_V = \frac{\kappa C_V}{\alpha T} \qquad \left[\because \left(\frac{\partial S}{\partial T}\right)_V = \frac{C_V}{T}\right]$$

(ii) $\left(\dfrac{\partial P}{\partial V}\right)_T \left(\dfrac{\partial T}{\partial P}\right)_S \left(\dfrac{\partial S}{\partial T}\right)_P = -\left(\dfrac{\partial P}{\partial T}\right)_V$

From the cyclic rule

$$\left(\frac{\partial P}{\partial V}\right)_T\left(\frac{\partial V}{\partial T}\right)_P\left(\frac{\partial T}{\partial P}\right)_V = -1$$

Substituting $\left(\dfrac{\partial V}{\partial T}\right)_P = -\left(\dfrac{\partial S}{\partial P}\right)_T$ in the above equation, we get

$$\left(\frac{\partial P}{\partial V}\right)_T\left(\frac{\partial T}{\partial P}\right)_V\left(\frac{-\partial S}{\partial P}\right)_T = -1$$

or $\qquad\qquad \left(\dfrac{\partial P}{\partial V}\right)_T\left(\dfrac{\partial T}{\partial P}\right)_V\left(\dfrac{\partial S}{\partial P}\right)_T = 1 \qquad\qquad\qquad\qquad ...(b)$

Considering entropy as a function of pressure and temperature,

$$dS = \left(\frac{\partial S}{\partial P}\right)_T dP + \left(\frac{\partial S}{\partial T}\right)_P dT$$

If S is constant, $dS = 0$, then

$$\left(\frac{\partial S}{\partial P}\right)_T\left(\frac{\partial P}{\partial T}\right)_S + \left(\frac{\partial S}{\partial T}\right)_P = 0$$

or $\qquad\qquad \left(\dfrac{\partial S}{\partial P}\right)_T = -\left(\dfrac{\partial S}{\partial T}\right)_P\left(\dfrac{\partial T}{\partial P}\right)_S \qquad\qquad\qquad\qquad ...(c)$

Substituting the value of $\left(\dfrac{\partial S}{\partial P}\right)_T$ in Eq. (b) and on rearranging, we get

$$\left(\frac{\partial P}{\partial V}\right)_T\left(\frac{\partial T}{\partial P}\right)_S\left(\frac{\partial S}{\partial T}\right)_P = -\left(\frac{\partial P}{\partial T}\right)_V$$

(iii)
$$\left(\frac{\partial P}{\partial T}\right)_S = \frac{C_P}{T\left(\dfrac{\partial V}{\partial T}\right)_P}$$

Since $\qquad\qquad \left(\dfrac{\partial S}{\partial T}\right)_P = \dfrac{C_P}{T}$

$$\left(\frac{\partial S}{\partial V}\right)_P\left(\frac{\partial V}{\partial T}\right)_P = \frac{C_P}{T} \qquad\qquad\qquad\qquad ...(d)$$

From $dH = VdP + TdS$, we have

$$\left(\frac{\partial S}{\partial V}\right)_P = \left(\frac{\partial P}{\partial T}\right)_S$$

Replacing $\left(\dfrac{\partial S}{\partial V}\right)_P$ by $\left(\dfrac{\partial P}{\partial T}\right)_S$ in Eq. (d), we get

$$\left(\frac{\partial P}{\partial T}\right)_S = \frac{C_P}{T\left(\dfrac{\partial V}{\partial T}\right)_P}$$

(iv) For a mole of the van der Waals gas

$$\left(\frac{\partial V}{\partial T}\right)_S = \frac{-C_V(V-b)}{RT}$$

Considering entropy as a function of volume and temperature

$$S = f(T, V)$$

$$dS = \left(\frac{\partial S}{\partial T}\right)_V dT + \left(\frac{\partial S}{\partial V}\right)_T dV$$

If $dS = 0$, then

$$\left(\frac{\partial S}{\partial V}\right)_T\left(\frac{\partial V}{\partial T}\right)_S = -\left(\frac{\partial S}{\partial T}\right)_V$$

or

$$\left(\frac{\partial V}{\partial T}\right)_S = -\left(\frac{\partial S}{\partial T}\right)_V \frac{1}{\left(\dfrac{\partial S}{\partial V}\right)_T}$$

Since $\left(\dfrac{\partial S}{\partial T}\right)_V = \dfrac{C_V}{T}$, hence

$$\left(\frac{\partial V}{\partial T}\right)_S = -\frac{C_V}{T}\left(\frac{\partial V}{\partial S}\right)_T$$

But from Eq. (7.42), $\left(\dfrac{\partial S}{\partial V}\right)_T = \left(\dfrac{\partial P}{\partial T}\right)_V$

Therefore,

$$\left(\frac{\partial V}{\partial T}\right)_S = -\frac{C_V}{T}\left(\frac{\partial T}{\partial P}\right)_V$$

Now $\left(\dfrac{\partial T}{\partial P}\right)_V$ for a mole of the van der Waals gas is given by

$$\left(\frac{\partial T}{\partial P}\right)_V = \frac{V-b}{R}$$

Substituting the value of $\left(\dfrac{\partial T}{\partial P}\right)_V$ in the above equation, we get

$$\left(\frac{\partial V}{\partial T}\right)_S = -\frac{C_V}{T}\left(\frac{V-b}{R}\right)$$

(v)

$$\left(\frac{\partial S}{\partial V}\right)_P = \frac{C_V}{TV\alpha} + \frac{\alpha}{\kappa}$$

Writing

$$\left(\frac{\partial S}{\partial V}\right)_P = \left(\frac{\partial S}{\partial T}\right)_P\left(\frac{\partial T}{\partial V}\right)_P$$

$$= \frac{C_P}{T}\left(\frac{\partial T}{\partial V}\right)_P$$

But

$$\frac{1}{V}\left(\frac{\partial V}{\partial T}\right)_P = \alpha \text{ or } \alpha V = \left(\frac{\partial V}{\partial T}\right)_P$$

Thus,

$$\left(\frac{\partial S}{\partial V}\right)_P = \frac{C_P}{T\alpha V} \text{ or } C_P = T\alpha V\left(\frac{\partial S}{\partial V}\right)_P$$

Substituting the value of C_P in Eq. (7.63) we get

$$T\alpha V\left(\frac{\partial S}{\partial V}\right)_P = C_V + \frac{TV\alpha^2}{\kappa}$$

$$\left(\frac{\partial S}{\partial V}\right)_P = \frac{C_V}{T\alpha V} + \frac{\alpha}{\kappa}$$

(vi)

$$\left(\frac{\partial P}{\partial V}\right)_S = -\frac{\gamma}{\alpha V}\left(\frac{\partial P}{\partial T}\right)_V \quad \text{for an ideal gas.}$$

If S is considered as a function of pressure and volume

$$S = f(P, V)$$

$$dS = \left(\frac{\partial S}{\partial P}\right)_V dP + \left(\frac{\partial S}{\partial V}\right)_P dV$$

If $dS = 0$, then

$$\left(\frac{\partial S}{\partial P}\right)_V\left(\frac{\partial P}{\partial V}\right)_S + \left(\frac{\partial S}{\partial V}\right)_P = 0$$

$$\left(\frac{\partial P}{\partial V}\right)_S = -\left(\frac{\partial S}{\partial V}\right)_P\left(\frac{\partial P}{\partial S}\right)_V$$

$$= -\left(\frac{\partial S}{\partial T}\right)_P\left(\frac{\partial T}{\partial V}\right)_P \bigg/ \left(\frac{\partial S}{\partial T}\right)_V\left(\frac{\partial T}{\partial P}\right)_V$$

Since
$$\left(\frac{\partial S}{\partial T}\right)_P = \frac{C_P}{T} \text{ and } \left(\frac{\partial S}{\partial T}\right)_V = \frac{C_V}{T}$$

Hence,
$$\left(\frac{\partial P}{\partial V}\right)_S = -C_P \left(\frac{\partial T}{\partial V}\right)_P \Big/ C_V \left(\frac{\partial T}{\partial P}\right)_V$$

$$= -\frac{C_P}{C_V}\left(\frac{\partial T}{\partial V}\right)_P\left(\frac{\partial P}{\partial T}\right)_V$$

But
$$\alpha = \frac{1}{V}\left(\frac{\partial V}{\partial T}\right)_P$$

or
$$\left(\frac{\partial T}{\partial V}\right)_P = \frac{1}{\alpha V}$$

Substitution of $\left(\frac{\partial T}{\partial V}\right)_P$ in the above equation yields

$$\left(\frac{\partial P}{\partial V}\right)_S = -\frac{C_P}{C_V}\frac{1}{\alpha V}\left(\frac{\partial P}{\partial T}\right)_V$$

$$= -\frac{\gamma}{\alpha V}\left(\frac{\partial P}{\partial T}\right)_V$$

(vii) For an ideal gas
$$\left(\frac{\partial P}{\partial V}\right)_S = -\frac{\gamma P}{V}$$

Consider
$$S = f(P, V)$$

$$dS = \left(\frac{\partial S}{\partial P}\right)_V dP + \left(\frac{\partial S}{\partial V}\right)_P dV$$

If $dS = 0$, then
$$\left(\frac{\partial S}{\partial P}\right)_V\left(\frac{\partial P}{\partial V}\right)_S = -\left(\frac{\partial S}{\partial V}\right)_P$$

$$\left(\frac{\partial P}{\partial V}\right)_S = -\left(\frac{\partial S}{\partial V}\right)_P\left(\frac{\partial P}{\partial S}\right)_V$$

$$= -\left(\frac{\partial S}{\partial T}\right)_P\left(\frac{\partial T}{\partial V}\right)_P\left(\frac{\partial P}{\partial T}\right)_V\left(\frac{\partial T}{\partial S}\right)_V$$

$$= -\frac{C_P}{T}\left(\frac{\partial T}{\partial V}\right)_P\frac{T}{C_V}\left(\frac{\partial P}{\partial T}\right)_V$$

$$= -\frac{C_P}{C_V}\frac{R}{V}\frac{P}{R}$$

$$= -\gamma\frac{P}{V}$$

(*viii*) For an ideal gas

$$\left(\frac{\partial E}{\partial V}\right)_S\left(\frac{\partial H}{\partial P}\right)_S = -R\left(\frac{\partial E}{\partial S}\right)_V$$

Since $dE = TdS - PdV$ and $dH = TdS + VdP$

It follows that $\left(\frac{\partial E}{\partial V}\right)_S = -P$ and $\left(\frac{\partial H}{\partial P}\right)_S = V$

The left hand side is thus $-PV$ which is equal to $-RT$. The right hand side is

$$-R\left(\frac{\partial E}{\partial S}\right)_V = -R\left(\frac{\partial E}{\partial T}\right)_V\left(\frac{\partial T}{\partial S}\right)_V$$

$$= -RC_V\frac{T}{C_V}$$

$$= -RT$$

(*ix*) $\mu_J = \dfrac{\beta P - \alpha T}{\beta C_V}$ and for an ideal gas $\mu_J = 0$

Since $E = f(V, T)$

Hence, $dE = C_V dT + \left(\frac{\partial E}{\partial V}\right)_T dV$

For a constant energy process $dE = 0$, and

$$\mu_J = \left(\frac{\partial T}{\partial V}\right)_E = -\frac{1}{C_V}\left(\frac{\partial E}{\partial V}\right)_T$$

But $\left(\frac{\partial E}{\partial V}\right)_T = T\left(\frac{\partial P}{\partial T}\right)_V - P$

$\therefore$

$$\mu_J = -\frac{1}{C_V}\left[T\left(\frac{\partial P}{\partial T}\right)_V - P\right]$$

$$= -\frac{1}{C_V}\left[T\frac{\alpha}{\beta} - P\right]$$

$$= \frac{1}{C_V}\left[\frac{\beta P - \alpha T}{\beta}\right]$$

For ideal gas $\dfrac{\alpha}{\beta} = \dfrac{P}{T}$, hence

$$\mu_J = \frac{1}{C_V}\left[P - P\right] = 0$$

EXERCISES

1. Explain and illustrate the following statements:
   (i) All the spontaneous processes tend to increase the entropy of the universe.
   (ii) The first law of thermodynamics is incapable of predicting the direction of a process.
   (iii) The second law of thermodynamics places a restriction on the first law.
   (iv) Efficiency of a reversible engine is maximum and depends only on the temperatures of the source and the sink.
   (v) In a reversible isothermal expansion of an ideal gas, the heat extracted from the surroundings is completely converted into work, yet it is not a violation of the second law.
   (vi) In an isolated system, entropy change is zero for a reversible process and greater than zero for an irreversible process.
   (vii) Complete conversion of heat into work is impossible without leaving permanent changes elsewhere.
   (viii) Entropy of a substance is maximum in the gaseous state.
   (ix) Entropy change in an irreversible adiabatic process is not zero.
   (x) All the spontaneous processes tend to a state of minimum energy and maximum entropy.

2. Which one in the following pairs will have a higher value of entropy?
   (i) Amorphous glass or crystalline glass.
   (ii) Sulphur rhombic or sulphur monoclinic.
   (iii) $CO_2(g)$ at 298 K, 1 atm or dry ice at 1 atm.
   (iv) A coiled spring or the spring relaxed.
   (v) A full boiled or a half-boiled egg.
   (vi) A metal rod at 1 atm and 298 K or the same at 1 atm and 398 K.
   (vii) A gas in the compressed state or in the expanded state (both at the same temperature).
   (viii) H_2O (l) at 1 atm 373 K or $H_2O(g)$ at 1 atm 373 K.
   (ix) He (g) at 1 atm 298 K or $CH_4(g)$ at 1 atm 298 K.
   (x) 1 mole of hydrogen and 1 mole of oxygen taken separately or a mixture of 1 mole of hydrogen and 1 mole of oxygen (all at the same temperature and pressure).

   Ans. (i) Amorphous glass; (ii) Sulphur monoclinic; (iii) CO_2 (g); (iv) Coiled spring; (v) Full boiled egg, (vi) Rod at 398 K; (vii) Gas in the expanded state; (viii) $H_2O(g)$; (ix) CH_4 (g); (x) Mixture of the two gases.

3. Which of the following substances are expected to have zero value of entropy at 0 K and why?
   (i) Silica glass; (ii) Quartz (crystalline silica); (iii) Sulphur; (iv) Liquid helium; (v) CO; (vi) NO; (vii) Graphite; (viii) Hydrogen; (ix) Ice; (x) Oxygen.

   Ans. Substances with zero entropy—(ii), (iii), (iv), (vii), (x).

4. In the following processes, state whether the entropy of the system increases, decreases or remains unchanged.
   (i) Vapourization of a mole of water into steam at its normal boiling point.
   (ii) Solidification of a mole of liquid at its freezing point.
   (iii) Crystallization of a solute from its saturated solution.

  (iv) Dissolution of a mole of common salt in water at 1 atm 300 K.
  (v) Mixing of two gases (the mixture and the gases separately are at the temperature and pressure).
  (vi) Isothermal reversible expansion of a mole of a gas.
  (vii) Reversible adiabatic expansion of a mole of a gas.
  (viii) Irreversible isothermal compression of a mole of a gas.
  (ix) Mixing of two partially miscible liquids.
  (x) Expansion of a gas into vacuum under isothermal conditions.
  (xi) Neutralization of a strong monobasic acid by a strong base.
  (xii) Separation of a mixture into its constituents.
  (xiii) Isothermal compression of a liquid.
  (xiv) Formation of a compound from its elements in the standard state.
  (xv) Transition of a mole of sulphur rhombic into sulphur monoclinic at its transition temperature.

Ans. Entropy of the system increases in *(i)*, *(iv)*, *(v)*, *(vi)*, *(ix)*, *(x)*, *(xi)*, *(xv)*.
Entropy of the system decreases in *(ii)*, *(iii)*, *(viii)*, *(xii)*, *(xiii)*, *(xiv)*.
Entropy of the system does not change in *(vii)*.

5. For which process(es) given below $\Delta S = \dfrac{\Delta H}{T}$?

   (i) A process for which $\Delta n_g = 0$
   (ii) A cyclic irreversible process.
   (iii) An adiabatic process.
   (iv) An isobaric process.
   (v) An isothermal reversible phase transition.
   (vi) An isothermal reversible process.

Ans. *(v)*.

6. Derive the following relations:

   (i)
   $$\left(\frac{\partial T}{\partial V}\right)_S = -\left(\frac{\partial P}{\partial S}\right)_V$$

   (ii)
   $$\left(\frac{\partial T}{\partial P}\right)_S = \left(\frac{\partial V}{\partial S}\right)_P$$

   (iii)
   $$dS = \frac{C_V}{T}dT + \frac{\alpha}{\kappa}dV$$

   (iv)
   $$\left(\frac{\partial S}{\partial T}\right)_V = \frac{C_V}{T} \text{ and } \left(\frac{\partial S}{\partial T}\right)_P = \frac{C_P}{T}$$

   (v)
   $$dS = \frac{C_P}{T}dT + \left(\frac{\partial S}{\partial P}\right)_T dP = \frac{C_P}{T}dT - V\alpha\, dP$$

   (vi)
   $$\left(\frac{\partial S}{\partial P}\right)_T = -\frac{C_P}{T}\left(\frac{\partial T}{\partial P}\right)_S$$

7. For an ideal gas show that

   (i)
   $$\left(\frac{\partial S}{\partial V}\right)_T = \frac{P}{T} = \frac{R}{V}$$

(ii)

$$\left(\frac{\partial V}{\partial S}\right)_P = \frac{RT}{PC_P}$$

(iii)

$$\left(\frac{\partial E}{\partial V}\right)_T = 0 \text{ and } \left(\frac{\partial H}{\partial P}\right)_T = 0$$

(iv)

$$\left(\frac{\partial T}{\partial V}\right)_E = 0 \text{ and } \left(\frac{\partial T}{\partial P}\right)_H = 0$$

(v)

$$\left(\frac{\partial S}{\partial P}\right)_V = \frac{C_V}{P}$$

8. An imaginary ideal gas heat engine operates on the following cycle: (i) increase in pressure of the gas at constant volume V_2 from P_2 to P_1, (ii) adiabatic expansion from P_1, V_2 to P_2, V_1, (iii) decrease in volume of the gas at constant pressure P_2 from V_1 to V_2. Draw the cycle on a $P - V$ diagram and show that the thermal efficiency is

$$\epsilon = 1 - \gamma \frac{(V_1/V_2) - 1}{(P_1/P_2) - 1}$$

9. A reversible engine operates in a rectangular cycle whose sides are parallel to the $P - V$ axis. The material used in the engine is a monatomic ideal gas. If $P_3 = 3P_1$ and $V_2 = 5V_1$, where P_3 and P_1 are the higher and the lower pressures and V_1 and V_2 the lower and the higher volumes. Calculate the efficiency of the engine.

Ans. $\epsilon = \dfrac{8}{33}$.

10. For a mole of van der Waals gas calculate

(i) $\left(\dfrac{\partial S}{\partial V}\right)_T$, (ii) $\left(\dfrac{\partial E}{\partial V}\right)_T$, (iii) $\left(\dfrac{\partial V}{\partial T}\right)_S$, (iv) $\left(\dfrac{\partial T}{\partial V}\right)_E$, (v) $\left(\dfrac{\partial S}{\partial V}\right)_P$, (vi) $\left(\dfrac{\partial C_V}{\partial V}\right)_T$.

Ans. (i) $\dfrac{R}{V-b}$, (ii) $\dfrac{a}{V^2}$, (iii) $-\dfrac{C_V(V-b)}{RT}$,

(iv) $-\dfrac{a}{C_V V^2}$, (v) $\dfrac{R}{V-b} + \dfrac{C_V}{T}\dfrac{1}{V\alpha}$, (vi) 0.

11. A reversible Carnot machine performs 180 kJ of work per cycle. If 360 kJ of heat per cycle is absorbed at 450 K, calculate (i) the temperature of the sink and (ii) the efficiency of the machine.

Ans. (i) 225 K, (ii) $\epsilon = 0.50$.

12. A Carnot refrigerator removes 50 kJ min^{-1} of heat from a reservoir at 275 K and rejects heat to the hot reservoir at 300 K. Calculate (i) the coefficient of performance and (ii) the heat rejected to the hot reservoir.

Ans. (i) 11.00; (ii) −54.55 kJ min^{-1}.

13. Calculate the entropy increase if 2 moles of He ($C_{V,m} = 12.55$ JK^{-1} mol^{-1}) are heated from 273 K to 546 K at (i) constant volume and (ii) at constant pressure. **Ans.** (i) 17.40 JK^{-1} mol^{-1}, (ii) 36.41 JK^{-1} mol^{-1}.

14. Calculate the entropy change for the following processes:
    (i) H_2O (s, 1 atm, 273 K) → H_2O (1, 1 atm, 273 K)
    (ii) H_2O (1, 1 atm, 273 K) → H_2O (1, 1 atm, 373 K)
    (iii) H_2O (1, 1 atm, 373 K) → H_2O (g, J atm, 373 K).

Given: $\Delta H_{fus,m} = 6.026$ kJ mol^{-1}, $\Delta H_{Vap,m}$ of water = 40.62 kJ mol^{-1} and $C_{P,m}$ of liquid water may be taken as 75.3 JK^{-1} mol^{-1}.

Ans. (*i*) 22.07 JK^{-1} mol^{-1}, (*ii*) 23.50 JK^{-1} mol^{-1}, (*iii*) 108.9 JK^{-1} mol^{-1},

15. A piece of metal weighing 1 kg at 600 K is placed in 2 kg of water at 300 K. If the heat capacity of water is 4.184 JK^{-1}g^{-1} and that of metal 24 JK^{-1}g^{-1}, calculate the final temperature and the entropy change of the system.

Ans. $T = 522.6$ K, $\Delta S_{sys} = 1.33$ kJ K^{-1}.

16. Consider the following processes:

A (1, 1 atm, 300 K) $\rightarrow$ A(g, 1 atm, 300 K) $\rightarrow$ A (g, 1 atm, 600 K) $\rightarrow$ A (g, 2 atm, 600 K).

Given: $\Delta H_{Vap,m\,300} = 43.596$ kJ mol^{-1}, and ($C_{P,m} = 36.0$ JK^{-1} mol^{-1} which may be assumed to be constant in the temperature range 300 – 600 K. Calculate the entropy change for the system. **Ans.** 164.52 JK^{-1} mol^{-1}

17. (*a*) Show that in a binary mixture the entropy change is maximum when $X_1 = X_2 = \dfrac{1}{2}$ and in a ternary

mixture the entropy change is maximum when $X_1 = X_2 = X_3 = 1/3$.
(*b*) Calculate the entropy of mixing at 300 K and 1 atm when
(*i*) 10 moles of He are mixed with 10 moles of Ne.
(*ii*) 10 moles of He are mixed with 20 moles of Ne.
(*iii*) 10 moles of Ne are mixed with 20 moles of an equimolar mixture of He and Ne.

Ans. (*i*) 115.3 JK^{-1} mol^{-1}, (*ii*) 158.8 JK^{-1} mol^{-1}, (*iii*) 43.5 JK^{-1} mol^{-1}.

18. 1 dm^3 of O_2 and 4 dm^3 of H_2 each at 1 atm and 300 K are mixed to form an ideal gas mixture of 3 dm^3 at the same temperature. Calculate the entropy of mixing.

Ans. 1.79×10^{-2} JK^{-1}.

19. Two heat engines are working between three temperatures T_1, T_2 and T_3 as shown in the figure.

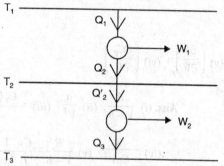

Find the relations between the temperatures T_1, T_2 and T_3 if (*a*) two engines have the same efficiency, (*b*) two engines do the same amount of work.

$$\textbf{Ans.}\ (a)\ T_2^2 = T_1 T_3,\ (b)\ T_2 = \frac{T_1 + T_3}{2}$$

20. Which causes a greater increase in the efficiency of a heat engine—decreasing the temperature of the sink by ΔT or increasing the temperature of the source by ΔT?

Ans. By decreasing the temperature of the sink.

21. A reversible heat engine absorbs 40 kJ of heat at 500 K and performs 10 kJ of work rejecting the remaining amount to the sink at 300 K. Calculate the entropy change for the (*i*) source, (*ii*) sink and (*iii*) universe.

Ans. (*i*) –80.0 JK^{-1}, (*ii*) 100.0 JK^{-1} (*iii*) 20.0 JK^{-1}.

22. A heat engine absorbs 760.0 kJ of heat from a source at 380 K. It rejects (*i*) 650.0 kJ, (*ii*) 560.0 kJ and (*iii*)

504.0 kJ of heat to the sink at 280 K, Calculate $\oint \dfrac{Q}{T}$ for each step and state which of these cases represent

a reversible, an irreversible and an impossible cycle.

Ans. (*i*) –0.3, impossible, (*ii*) 0.0, reversible, (*iii*) 0.8, irreversible.

23. 10 moles of water are heated very slowly establishing reversible conditions from 293 K to 363 K, calculate ΔS_{sys}, ΔS_{surr} and ΔS_{univ}. If the same amount of water is heated by placing water in a hot reservoir at 363 K, calculate ΔS_{sys}, ΔS_{univ} and ΔS_{surr}. $C_{P,m}$ (H_2O, 1) = 75.3 JK^{-1} mol^{-1}.

> **Ans.** $\Delta S_{sys} = -\Delta S_{surr} = 161.3$ JK^{-1}
> $\Delta S_{univ} = 0.0$ JK^{-1}, $\Delta S_{sys} = 161.3$ JK^{-1}
> $\Delta S_{surr} = -144.8$ JK^{-1} $\Delta S_{univ} = 16.5$ JK^{-1}

24. 1 mole of a monatomic ideal gas at 373 K and 2 atm occupies a volume of 15.3 dm^{-3}. The gas is adiabatically compressed against a constant external pressure of 4 atm. (a) Calculate ΔS for the system and the surroundings; (b) If the above process is carried out isothermally and reversibly by placing the cylinder in a bath maintained at 373 K, calculate ΔS for the system and the surroundings.

> **Ans.** (a) $\Delta S_{sys} = 6.05$ JK^{-1}, $\Delta S_{surr} = 0$, $\Delta S_{univ} = 6.05$ JK^{-1}.
> (b) $\Delta S_{sys} = -5.74$ $JK^{-1} = -\Delta S_{surr}$ and $\Delta S_{univ} = 0$.

25. A metal block of mass 7 kg at 873 K is dropped into 30 kg of a liquid at 313 K. If the heat capacity of the metal is 22.59 JK^{-1} g^{-1} and that of liquid is 5.02 JK^{-1} g^{-1} and that no heat is lost to the surroundings, calculate the entropy change of the metal block, the liquid and the total entropy change.

> **Ans.** $\Delta S_{metal} = -59.29$ JK^{-1},
> $\Delta S_{liquid} = 98.14$ JK^{-1},
> $\Delta S_{total} = 38.8$ JK^{-1}.

26. Prove that the compressibility coefficient at constant entropy (adiabatic process) and coefficient of compressibility at constant temperature are related as

$$\left(\frac{\partial V}{\partial P}\right)_T = \gamma \left(\frac{\partial V}{\partial P}\right)_S$$

27. 2 moles of an ideal gas expand isothermally from 4 atm to 1 atm at 300K against a constant external pressure of 1 atm. Calculate (i) ΔS_{sys}, (ii) ΔS_{surr} and (iii) ΔS_{univ}.

> **Ans.** (i) 23.06 JK^{-1}, (ii) –12.47 JK^{-1}, (iii) 10.59 JK^{-1}.

28. 2 moles of an ideal monatomic gas at 300 K and 10 atm pressure is expanded to 20 times its original volume by (i) isothermal reversible path and (ii) adiabatic reversible path. Calculate the entropy change for the system in each case.

> **Ans.** (i) 49.8 JK^{-1}, (ii) 0.0.

29. 10 moles of an ideal monatomic gas ($C_{p,m}$ = 28.314 JK^{-1} mol^{-1}) at 400 K and 10 atm are expanded adiabatically to 2 atm. Calculate the entropy change, ΔS_{sys}, ΔS_{surr} and ΔS_{univ} for each of the following processes:

(i) Expansion is reversible, (ii) expansion is irreversible against a constant external pressure of 2 atm and (iii) expansion is a free expansion.

> **Ans.** (i) $\Delta S_{sys} = -\Delta S_{surr} = \Delta S_{univ} = 0$
> (ii) $\Delta S_{sys} = \Delta S_{univ} = 57.82$ JK^{-1}, $\Delta S_{surr} = 0$
> (iii) $\Delta S_{sys} = \Delta S_{univ} = 133.75$ JK^{-1}, $\Delta S_{surr} = 0$.

Free Energy Functions

8.1 OBJECT OF FREE ENERGY FUNCTIONS

We have seen in Chapter 7 that the concept of entropy is a fundamental consequence of the second law of thermodynamics. An irreversible change is always spontaneous and in an isolated system the entropy must increase and should be maximum at equilibrium. All the natural processes are spontaneous and rarely occur in isolated systems. In selecting entropy as a criterion of spontaneity, one must consider the entropy changes for both the system and the surroundings together. It is always not convenient to do so. Hence, it is desirable to introduce new functions as criteria of spontaneity in which explicit reference to the entropy changes of the surroundings is omitted and the functions automatically include such changes implicitly. These functions are the *Helmholtz free energy* or the *work function* denoted by *A* and the *Gibbs free energy function* or the *Gibbs potential* or the *thermodynamic potential* represented by *G*. They are defined as

$$A = E - TS \qquad \qquad ...(8.1)$$
$$G = H - TS \qquad \qquad ...(8.2)$$

where *E* and *H* are the energy and enthalpy contents of the system, *T* is the temperature and *S* is the entropy of the system. Like *E, H, T* and *S*, the values of *A* and *G* are defined by the state of the system and are independent of the path followed for the change in the state of the system, *i.e.*, both are single-valued thermodynamic functions of the system. *dA* and *dG* are exact differentials and the cyclic integrals

$\oint dA$ and $\oint dG$ are zero. They are extensive properties of the system and depend on the quantity of the matter and the nature of the system.

8.2 RELATION BETWEEN *A* AND *G*

Since $\qquad\qquad H = E + PV$

and from the definition of *G* we have

$$G = H - TS$$
$$= E + PV - TS$$
$$= A + PV \qquad (\because A = E - TS) \qquad ...(8.3)$$

8.3 CHANGES IN *A* AND *G* IN ISOTHERMAL PROCESSES

The change in A for an isothermal process is given by

$$\Delta A = A_2 - A_1$$

$$= \left(E_2 - TS_2\right) - \left(E_1 - TS_1\right)$$

$$= \left(E_2 - E_1\right) - T\left(S_2 - S_1\right) \qquad \qquad ...(8.4)$$

$$= \Delta E - T\Delta S$$

For an infinitesimal change

$$dA = dE - TdS \qquad \qquad ...(8.5)$$

Similarly, the change in Gibbs free energy for isothermal processes is given by

$$\Delta G = G_2 - G_1$$

$$= \left(H_2 - TS_2\right) - \left(H_1 - TS_1\right)$$

$$= \left(H_2 - H_1\right) - T\left(S_2 - S_1\right)$$

$$= \Delta H - T\Delta S \qquad \qquad ...(8.6)$$

and for an infinitesimal change

$$dG = dH - TdS \qquad \qquad ...(8.7)$$

8.4 SIGNIFICANCE OF *A* AND *G*

For a system of fixed composition (closed system), an infinitesimal change in A is given by the total differential of Eq. (8.1),

$$dA = dE - TdS - SdT \qquad \qquad ...(8.8)$$

But from the first and the second laws of thermodynamics, we have

$$dE = TdS + \delta W_{rev}$$

where δW_{rev} represents the *maximum magnitude of reversible work* done by the system and includes both the mechanical and non-mechanical works. Substitution of dE in the above Eq. (8.8) yields

$$dA = TdS - TdS - SdT + \delta W_{rev}$$

$$= -SdT + \delta W_{rev}$$

If the process is isothermal, $dT = 0$, hence

$$\left(dA\right)_T = \delta W_{rev} \qquad \qquad ...(8.9)$$

For a finite change

$$-\left(\Delta A\right)_T = -W_{rev} \qquad \qquad ...(8.10)$$

So A is such a function that *a decrease in its value at constant temperature gives the maximum reversible work done by the system.* Infact, any transformation isothermal or otherwise would always be accompanied by a definite change in the value of *A*. But it is only for an isothermal reversible transformation that this is a measure of maximum reversible work obtainable from the system.

For Gibbs free energy, *dG* is given by

$$dG = dH - TdS - SdT$$

$$= dE + PdV + VdP - TdS - SdT \qquad (\because H = E + PV)$$

But $$dE = TdS + \delta W_{rev}$$

Hence, $$dG = TdS + PdV + VdP - TdS - SdT + \delta W_{rev}$$

$$= PdV + VdP - SdT - PdV + \delta W_{net} \qquad (\because \delta W_{rev} = -PdV + W_{net})$$

$$= VdP - SdT + W_{net} \qquad \qquad ...(8.11)$$

At constant *T* and *P*, *dT* = *dP* = 0

Hence, $$(dG)_{P,T} = \delta W_{net} \qquad \qquad ...(8.12)$$

For a finite change in the state of the system

$$(\Delta G)_{P,T} = -W_{net} \qquad \qquad ...(8.13)$$

Therefore, we see that *a decrease in the value of Gibbs free energy function at constant temperature and pressure is a measure of maximum reversible nonmechanical work done by the system.*

The work term in Eq. (8.10) includes both the mechanical and non-mechanical works. However, if the system does not involve mechanical work, *i.e.*, *P*Δ*V* = 0, then from Eq. (8.10) and (8.13) we get

$$\Delta A = \Delta G \qquad \qquad ...(8.14)$$

Problem 8.1: Calculate the difference between Δ*G* and Δ*A* for the reaction

$$C(s) + \frac{1}{2}O_2(g) = CO(g)$$

at 1 atm and 300 K. Assume ideal behaviour for the gases.

Solution: Since $\Delta G = \Delta H - T\Delta S$ and $\Delta A = \Delta E - T\Delta S$

$\therefore$ $$\Delta G = \Delta E + P\Delta V - T\Delta S$$

$$= \Delta A + P\Delta V$$

or $$\Delta G - \Delta A = P\Delta V = \Delta n_g RT$$

For the given reaction $\Delta n_g = 1 - \frac{1}{2} = \frac{1}{2}$

Hence, $$\Delta G - \Delta A = \frac{1}{2}(mol)\left(8.314 \text{ JK}^{-1}\text{mol}^{-1}\right)(300 \text{ K})$$

$$= 1.247 \text{ kJ}$$

Problem 8.2: It is found that $\Delta H = -2810$ kJ mol^{-1} and $\Delta S = 182.4$ JK^{-1} when glucose is oxidised at 300 K according to the reaction

$$C_6H_2O_6(s) + 6O_2(g) \rightarrow 6CO_2(g) + 6H_2O(l)$$

(*i*) How much of the above energy can be extracted as heat?
(*ii*) How much of it can be extracted as work?

Solution: (*i*) The heat that can be extracted is 2810 kJ mol^{-1}
(*ii*) $\Delta G = \Delta H - T\Delta S$

We have

$$\Delta H = -2810 \text{ kJ mol}^{-1}$$

$$\Delta S = 182.4 \times 10^{-3} \text{ kJ K}^{-1}\text{mol}^{-1}$$

∴

$$\Delta G = (-2810) - (300)\left(182.4 \times 10^{-3}\right) \text{ kJ mol}^{-1}$$

$$= (-2810 - 54.72) \text{ kJ mol}^{-1}$$

$$= -2864.72 \text{ kJ mol}^{-1}$$

Thus, the work that can be extracted from the oxidation of glucose is 2864.72 kJ. If there were no change in volume, no work would result.

8.5 VARIATION OF *A* WITH VOLUME AND TEMPERATURE

Variation of A with Temperature at Constant Volume: For a system of constant composition in which only pressure-volume work is involved, the change in *A* for an infinitesimal reversible transformation is given by

$$dA = dE - TdS - SdT$$

But from the first and the second laws we have

$$\delta Q_{rev} = TdS = dE + PdV$$

Hence,

$$dA = TdS - PdV - TdS - SdT$$

$$= -PdV - SdT \qquad \qquad \qquad ...(8.15)$$

If the process is isochoric, *i.e.*, $dV = 0$

$$(dA)_V = -SdT$$

or

$$\left(\frac{\partial A}{\partial T}\right)_V = -S \qquad \qquad \qquad ...(8.16)$$

Therefore, the rate of change of work function with temperature is a measure of entropy in isochoric processes. Since the entropy of any substance is positive, the minus sign shows that an increase in temperature at constant volume decreases the Helmholtz free energy. The decrease is maximum for gases and least for solids.

Substituting the value of *S* in Eq. (8.1) we get

$$A = E - T\left(-\frac{dA}{dT}\right)_V$$

$$A = E + T\left(\frac{dA}{dT}\right)_V \qquad \qquad ...(8.17)$$

Dividing the above equation by T^2 and on rearranging, we obtain

$$-\frac{A}{T^2} + \frac{1}{T}\left(\frac{dA}{dT}\right)_V = -\frac{E}{T^2}$$

But

$$-\frac{A}{T^2} + \frac{1}{T}\left(\frac{dA}{dT}\right)_V = \frac{d}{dT}(A/T)_V$$

Therefore,

$$\frac{d}{dT}\left(\frac{A}{T}\right)_V = -\frac{E}{T^2} \qquad \qquad ...(8.18)$$

Eq. (8.17) and (8.18) representing the variation of A with temperature at constant volume are known as the *Gibbs-Helmholtz* equations. Other forms, which relate the change of work function with internal energy and the rate of change of work function with temperature at constant volume, are more frequently used. If the system changes from an initial state 1 to a final state 2 isothermally, then from Eq. (8.1), we have

$$A_2 - A_1 = E_2 - E_1 - T(S_2 - S_1)$$

or

$$\Delta A = \Delta E - T\Delta S$$

But

$$\left(\frac{\partial A_1}{\partial T}\right)_V = -S_1 \text{ and } \left(\frac{\partial A_2}{\partial T}\right)_V = -S_2$$

or

$$-(S_2 - S_1) = -\Delta S = \left[\left(\frac{\partial A_2}{\partial T}\right)_V - \left(\frac{\partial A_1}{\partial T}\right)_V\right] = -\left[\frac{\partial(\Delta A)}{\partial T}\right]_V$$

Hence,

$$\Delta A = \Delta E + T\left[\left(\frac{\partial \Delta A}{\partial T}\right)\right]_V \qquad \qquad ...(8.19)$$

Dividing both sides of Eq. (8.19) by T^2 and on rearranging, we get

$$-\frac{\Delta A}{T^2} + \frac{1}{T}\left[\frac{(\partial \Delta A)}{\partial T}\right]_V = -\frac{\Delta E}{T^2}$$

However, the quantity on the left hand side is simply the differential of $\frac{d}{dT}\left(\frac{\Delta A}{T}\right)_V$, hence we have

$$\left[\frac{\partial}{\partial T}\left(\frac{\Delta A}{T}\right)\right]_V = -\frac{\Delta E}{T^2} \qquad \qquad ...(8.20)$$

Change in A with Volume at Constant Temperature: If the process is isothermal, then from Eq. (8.15)

$$(dA)_T = -P(dV)_T$$

$$\left(\frac{\partial A}{\partial V}\right)_T = -P \qquad\qquad ...(8.21)$$

i.e., A decreases with increase in volume and the decrease is equal to the pressure in isothermal processes. If the system consists of an ideal gas P may be replaced by nRT/V and the total change in such cases is obtained by integrating Eq. (8.21)

$$\int_{A_1}^{A_2} dA = -\int_{V_1}^{V_2} P\,dV = -\int_{V_1}^{V_2} \frac{nRT}{V}\,dV$$

$$\Delta A = A_2 - A_1 = -nRT \ln\frac{V_2}{V_1}$$

$$= nRT \ln\frac{V_1}{V_2} \qquad\qquad ...(8.22)$$

$$= nRT \ln\frac{P_2}{P_1} \qquad (\because\ P_1V_1 = P_2V_2) \qquad ...(8.23)$$

8.6 VARIATION OF G WITH TEMPERATURE AND PRESSURE

Variation of G with Temperature at Constant Pressure: If in a closed system only P-V work is involved, W_{net} is zero and from Eq. (8.11), we have

$$dG = -SdT + VdP \qquad\qquad ...(8.24)$$

If the process is isobaric, $dP = 0$, therefore

$$(dG)_P = -S(dT)_P$$

$$\left(\frac{dG}{dT}\right)_P = -S \qquad\qquad ...[8.24\,(a)]$$

Since entropy is always positive, the negative sign indicates that in isobaric transformations G decreases with rise in temperature. Further, the entropy is maximum for gases and minimum for solids. It follows from [8.24 (a)] that the rate of decrease is largest for gases and least for solids.

If we substitute the value of S in Eq. (8.2), we get

$$G = H + T\left(\frac{\partial G}{\partial T}\right)_P \qquad\qquad ...(8.25)$$

Dividing by T^2 gives

$$\frac{G}{T^2} = \frac{H}{T^2} + \frac{1}{T}\left(\frac{\partial G}{\partial T}\right)_P$$

$$\frac{G}{T^2} - \frac{1}{T}\left(\frac{\partial G}{\partial T}\right)_P = \frac{H}{T^2}$$

But the left hand side is simply the differential of $-\left[\dfrac{\partial(G/T)}{\partial T}\right]_P$, hence we have

$$\left[\frac{\partial(G/T)}{\partial T}\right]_P = -\frac{H}{T^2} \qquad \qquad ...(8.26)$$

Equation (8.26) can be expressed in another form. Since $d(1/T) = -1/T^2 dT$, one can replace ∂T in Eq. (8.26) by $-T^2\partial(1/T)$ to get

$$\left[\frac{\partial(G/T)}{\partial(1/T)}\right]_P = H \qquad \qquad ...(8.27)$$

If a system of constant composition changes isothermally from an initial state specified by G_1, H_1 and S_1 to another state specified by G_2, H_2 and S_2, the change in G is given by

$$\Delta G = G_2 - G_1 = \Delta H - T\Delta S$$

But from Eq. [8.24 (a)]

$$-\Delta S = -(S_2 - S_1) = \left(\frac{\partial G_2}{\partial T}\right)_P - \left(\frac{\partial G_1}{\partial T}\right)_P = \left[\frac{\partial(\Delta G)}{\partial T}\right]_P$$

Substituting the value of $-\Delta S$ in the above equation, we get

$$\Delta G = \Delta H + T\left[\frac{\partial(\Delta G)}{\partial T}\right]_P \qquad \qquad ...(8.28)$$

On Dividing Eq. (8.28) by T^2 gives

$$\frac{\Delta G}{T^2} = \frac{\Delta H}{T^2} + \frac{1}{T}\left[\frac{\partial(\Delta G)}{\partial T}\right]_P$$

Since

$$\left[\frac{\partial(\Delta G/T)}{\partial T}\right]_P = \frac{1}{T}\left[\frac{\partial(\Delta G)}{\partial T}\right]_P - \frac{1}{T^2}(\Delta G)$$

Therefore,

$$\frac{\Delta G}{T^2} = \frac{\Delta H}{T^2} + \left[\frac{\partial(\Delta G/T)}{\partial T}\right]_P + \frac{\Delta G}{T^2}$$

$$\left[\frac{\partial(\Delta G/T)}{\partial T}\right]_P = -\frac{\Delta H}{T^2} \qquad ...(8.29)$$

$$\left[\frac{\partial(\Delta G/T)}{\partial(1/T)}\right]_P = \Delta H \qquad ...(8.30)$$

Equations (8.25)–(8.30) are different forms of Gibbs-Helmholtz equation.

Problem 8.3: With the help of Gibbs-Helmholtz equation, find $\Delta G°$ for the reaction at 310 K

$$2\ CO(g) + O_2(g) = 2\ CO_2(g)$$

Given the following data in kJ mol^{-1} at 300 K

For
$$CO(g),\ \Delta H_f^0 = -110.5,\quad \Delta G_f^0 = -137.2$$

For
$$CO_2(g),\ \Delta H_f^0 = -393.5,\quad \Delta G_f^0 = -394.4$$

Assume that $\Delta H°$ values remain unchanged in this temperature range.

Solution: Gibbs-Helmholtz equation is

$$d\left(\Delta G^0/T\right) = -\frac{\Delta H^0}{T^2}\,dT$$

Integrating between T_1 and T_2, we get

$$\left(\frac{\Delta G^0}{T}\right)_{T_2} = \left(\frac{\Delta G^0}{T}\right)_{T_1} + \Delta H^0\left(\frac{T_2 - T_1}{T_1 T_2}\right)$$

For the given reaction, $\Delta H^0 = 2\left(\Delta H_f^0\right)_{CO_2} - 2\left(\Delta H_f^0\right)_{CO_2}$

$$= 2(-393.5 - 110.5)$$

$$= -566\,kJ$$

and
$$\Delta G^0 = 2\left(\Delta G_f^0\right)_{CO_2} - 2\left(\Delta G_f^0\right)_{CO}$$

$$= 2(-394.4 + 137.2)$$

$$= -514.4\ kJ$$

Now
$$\left(\frac{\Delta G^0}{310}\right) = -\frac{514.4}{300.0} + \frac{(-566) \times (10)}{300 \times 310}$$

$$= (-1.715 - 0.0608)\ kJ\ K^{-1}$$

$$= -1.7758 \text{ kJ K}^{-1}$$

$$\therefore \qquad \left(\Delta G^0\right)_{310} = \left(-1.7758 \times 310\right) \text{ kJ}$$

$$= -550.498 \text{ kJ}$$

Variation of G with Pressure in Isothermal Processes: Equation (8.11) under isothermal condition reduces to

$$(dG)_T = V(dP)_T$$

or $$\left(\frac{\partial G}{\partial P}\right)_T = \dot{V} \qquad \qquad ...(8.31)$$

Since the volume of any substance is a positive quantity, eq. (8.31) predicts that increase of pressure increases free energy in isothermal changes. The rate of increase of free energy will be higher for gases and smaller for liquids or solids as molar volumes of gases are larger than those of liquids or solids.

The total free energy change for any substance can be obtained by integrating Eq. (8.31). In case of condensed phases, e.g., solids or liquids, volume is nearly independent of pressure and integration of (8.31) yields

$$\int_{G_1}^{G_2} dG = \int_{P_1}^{P_2} VdP$$

$$\Delta G = V\left(P_2 - P_1\right) \qquad \qquad ...(8.32)$$

To obtain ΔG for gases, V should be known as a function of pressure. In case of an ideal gas,

$V = \dfrac{nRT}{P}$ and Eq. (8.31) becomes

$$dG = \frac{nRT}{P} dP$$

which on integration gives

$$\Delta G = G_2 - G_1 = nRT \ln \frac{P_2}{P_1} \qquad \qquad ...(8.33)$$

$$= nRT \ln \frac{V_1}{V_2} \qquad \qquad ...(8.34)$$

In Eq. (8.33), if $P_1 = 1$ atm and $P_2 = P$, then the change in Gibb's free energy for a mole of an ideal gas is given by

$$\Delta G = G_m - G_m^0 = RT \ln\left(\frac{P}{1 \text{ atm}}\right) \qquad \qquad ...(8.35)$$

where G_m^0 is referred to as the standard molar Gibbs free energy of the substance at 1 atm pressure and specified temperature.

For a van der Waals gas

$$\Delta G = \Delta A + \Delta (PV)$$

Hence,

$$\Delta G = \int_{G_1}^{G_2} dG = -nRT \int_{V_1}^{V_2} \frac{dV}{V - nb} + an^2 \int_{V_1}^{V_2} \frac{dV}{V^2}$$

$$+ nRT \left(\frac{V_2}{V_2 - nb} - \frac{V_1}{V_1 - nb} \right) - an^2 \left(\frac{1}{V_2} - \frac{1}{V_1} \right)$$

$$\Delta G = -nRT \ln \frac{V_2 - nb}{V_1 - nb} - an^2 \left(\frac{1}{V_2} - \frac{1}{V_1} \right)$$

$$+ nRT \left(\frac{V_2}{V_2 - nb} - \frac{V_1}{V_1 - nb} \right) - an^2 \left(\frac{1}{V_2} - \frac{1}{V_1} \right)$$

$$= -nRT \ln \frac{V_2 - nb}{V_1 - nb} - 2an^2 \left(\frac{1}{V_2} - \frac{1}{V_1} \right)$$

$$+ nRT \left(\frac{V_2}{V_2 - nb} - \frac{V_1}{V_1 - nb} \right) \qquad \qquad ...[(8.35\ (a)]$$

Comparison of Eq. (8.33) or (8.34) with Eq. (8.22) or (8.23) shows that $\Delta G = \Delta A$. This equality, however, holds only for isothermal processes involving an ideal gas.

8.7 FUNDAMENTAL EQUATIONS OF THERMODYNAMICS

For a closed system where only mechanical work is involved we have

$$dE = TdS - PdV \qquad \qquad ...(8.36)$$

It is a fundamental equation of thermodynamics. The relation between different thermodynamic functions can be obtained using the definition of the composite functions.

$$H = E + PV$$

$$A = E - TS$$

$$G = H - TS = E + PV - TS$$

On differentiating the above equations, we get

$$dH = dE + PdV + VdP$$

$$dA = dE - TdS - SdT$$

$$dG = dH - TdS - SdT = dE + PdV + VdP - TdS - SdT$$

Replacing dE by $TdS - PdV$ yields

$$dH = TdS - PdV + PdV + VdP = TdS + VdP \qquad ...(8.37)$$

$$dA = TdS - PdV - TdS - SdT = -PdV - SdT \qquad ...(8.38)$$

$$dG = TdS - PdV + PdV + VdP - TdS - SdT = VdP - SdT \qquad ...(8.39)$$

Equations (8.36)-(8.39) are regarded as four fundamental thermodynamic equations for a system of constant composition.

8.8 THE MAXWELL'S RELATIONS

From Eqs. (8.36)–(8.39), four relations extensively used in thermodynamic calculations can be derived. These are known as the Maxwell's relations. From Eq. (8.36), we have

$$\left(\frac{\partial E}{\partial S}\right)_V = T \qquad ...(8.40)$$

and

$$\left(\frac{\partial E}{\partial V}\right)_S = -P \qquad ...(8.41)$$

Differentiating Eq. (8.40) with respect to V at constant S and Eq. (8.41) with respect to S at constant V, we get

$$\frac{\partial^2 E}{\partial V \partial S} = \left(\frac{\partial T}{\partial V}\right)_S \qquad ...(8.42)$$

and

$$\frac{\partial^2 E}{\partial S \partial V} = -\left(\frac{\partial P}{\partial S}\right)_V \qquad ...(8.43)$$

Since dE is an exact differential, hence from Eqs. (8.42) and (8.43), we have

$$\left(\frac{\partial T}{\partial V}\right)_S = -\left(\frac{\partial P}{\partial S}\right)_V \qquad ...(8.44)$$

From Eq. (8.37)

$$\left(\frac{\partial H}{\partial S}\right)_P = T \qquad ...(8.45)$$

and

$$\frac{\partial^2 H}{\partial P \partial S} = \left(\frac{\partial T}{\partial P}\right)_S \qquad ...(8.46)$$

Also

$$\left(\frac{\partial H}{\partial P}\right)_S = V \qquad ...(8.47)$$

and

$$\frac{\partial^2 H}{\partial S \partial P} = \left(\frac{\partial V}{\partial S}\right)_P \qquad ...(8.48)$$

Hence,

$$\left(\frac{\partial T}{\partial P}\right)_S = \left(\frac{\partial V}{\partial S}\right)_P \qquad ...(8.49)$$

Again, from Eq. (8.38)

$$\left(\frac{\partial A}{\partial T}\right)_V = -S \qquad ...(8.50)$$

and

$$\left(\frac{\partial^2 A}{\partial V \partial T}\right) = -\left(\frac{\partial S}{\partial V}\right)_T \qquad ...(8.51)$$

Again

$$\left(\frac{\partial A}{\partial V}\right)_T = -P \qquad ...(8.52)$$

and

$$\frac{\partial^2 A}{\partial T \partial V} = -\left(\frac{\partial P}{\partial T}\right)_V \qquad ...(8.53)$$

As dA is an exact differential, hence

$$\left(\frac{\partial S}{\partial V}\right)_T = \left(\frac{\partial P}{\partial T}\right)_V \qquad ...(8.54)$$

Lastly, from Eq. (8.39)

$$\left(\frac{\partial G}{\partial P}\right)_T = V \qquad ...(8.55)$$

and

$$\frac{\partial^2 G}{\partial T \partial P} = \left(\frac{\partial V}{\partial T}\right)_P \qquad ...(8.56)$$

Also

$$\left(\frac{\partial G}{\partial T}\right)_P = -S \qquad ...(8.57)$$

hence

$$\frac{\partial^2 G}{\partial P \partial T} = -\left(\frac{\partial S}{\partial P}\right)_T \qquad ...(8.58)$$

From Eqs. (8.56) and (8.58), we get

$$\left(\frac{\partial V}{\partial T}\right)_P = -\left(\frac{\partial S}{\partial P}\right)_T \qquad ...(8.59)$$

Relations (8.44), (8.49), (8.54) and (8.59) are collectively known as *the four Maxwell's relations*. From Eqs. (8.40) and (8.45),

$$\left(\frac{\partial E}{\partial S}\right)_V = T = \left(\frac{\partial H}{\partial S}\right)_P \qquad \qquad ...(8.60)$$

and from Eqs. (8.41) and (8.52)

$$\left(\frac{\partial E}{\partial V}\right)_S = -P = \left(\frac{\partial A}{\partial V}\right)_T \qquad \qquad ...(8.61)$$

Comparison of Eqs. (8.47) and (8.55) yields

$$\left(\frac{\partial H}{\partial P}\right)_S = V = \left(\frac{\partial G}{\partial P}\right)_T \qquad \qquad ...(8.62)$$

and Eqs. (8.50) and (8.57) give

$$\left(\frac{\partial A}{\partial T}\right)_V = -S = \left(\frac{\partial G}{\partial T}\right)_P \qquad \qquad ...(8.63)$$

8.9 CRITERIA OF SPONTANEITY AND THERMODYNAMIC EQUILIBRIA

A system is said to be in a state of equilibrium if its observable properties do not change with time, i.e., $dP = dV = dT = 0$. A reversible process remains effectively in a state of equilibrium during the transformation. The condition of reversibility is therefore a condition of thermodynamic equilibrium. For a reversible process

$$\delta Q_{rev} = TdS = dE - \delta W$$

and for an irreversible process

$$\delta Q_{irr} = (dE - \delta W)_{irr} < TdS$$

Combining these two relations, we get

$$dE - \delta W \le TdS$$

$$TdS - dE + \delta W \ge 0 \qquad \qquad ...(8.64)$$

where the equality implies a reversible transformation or an equilibrium state and the inequality refers to an irreversible change. Since all the irreversible changes are spontaneous, it means the inequality gives the condition for a process to occur. In Eq. (8.64) δW includes both the mechanical and non-mechanical works. If the system involves only P-V work then Eq. (8.64) becomes

$$TdS - dE - PdV \ge 0 \qquad \qquad ...(8.65)$$

    Criteria of Spontaneity in Terms of Entropy: Imposing the restrictions that the energy of the system remains constant (isodynamic process, $dE = 0$) and that no mechanical work is done (isochoric change $dV = 0$), then Eq. (8.65) reduces to

$$(TdS)_{E, V} \ge 0 \qquad \qquad ...(8.66)$$

The entropy change for an *isodynamic* and *isochoric process* in an isolated system must be positive or entropy should increase if the process is to occur spontaneously. All the processes that occur in nature are spontaneous and are accompanied by a net increase in the entropy. The entropy of the universe is, therefore, increasing continuously. These processes tend to go ultimately to a state of equilibrium where the entropy attains its maximum value. Any attempt to change the state of the system at equilibrium under these conditions will decrease its value.

Criteria of Spontaneity in Terms of Energy: In Eq. (8.65) if we put $dV = dS = 0$, then

$$(-dE)_{V,\ S} \geq 0$$

$$(dE)_{V,\ S} \leq 0 \qquad \qquad ...(8.67)$$

Thus, for an irreversible or spontaneous process, internal energy of the system must decrease at constant volume and constant entropy. Consequently, E has its minimum value at equilibrium.

Criteria of Spontaneity in Terms of Work Function: Replacing dE by $dA + TdS + SdT$ in Eq. (8.65), we get

$$TdS - dA - TdS - SdT - PdV \geq 0$$

$$-dA - SdT - PdV \geq 0$$

On imposing the conditions of constant volume and constant temperature gives

$$(-dA)_{T,\ V} \geq 0$$

or
$$(dA)_{T,\ V} \leq 0$$

Thus, in an irreversible process at constant T and V, the work function A decreases and will have the minimum value at equilibrium.

Criteria of Spontaneity in Terms of Gibbs Free Energy Function:

Since
$$dG = dH - TdS - SdT$$

$$dG = dE + PdV + VdP - TdS - SdT$$

or
$$dE = dG + SdT + TdS - PdV - VdP$$

Substituting the value of dE in Eq. (8.65), we obtain

$$TdS - dG - SdT - TdS + PdV + VdP - PdV \geq 0$$

$$-dG - SdT + VdP \geq 0$$

When the temperature and pressure are constant

$$(-dG)_{T,\ P} \geq 0$$

or
$$(dG)_{T,\ P} \leq 0 \qquad \qquad ...(8.69)$$

Hence, for an irreversible process at constant P and T in which only P-V work is done, the Gibbs free energy must decrease and should attain a minimum value at equilibrium.

Criteria of Spontaneity in Terms of Enthalpy:

Since
$$dH = dE + PdV + VdP$$

$$dE = dH - PdV - VdP$$

Substituting of this value of dE in (8.65) gives

$$TdS - dH + PdV + VdP - PdV \geq 0$$

$$TdS - dH + VdP \geq 0$$

$$(-dH)_{S,P} \geq 0$$

or
$$(dH)_{S,P} \leq 0 \qquad \qquad ...(8.70)$$

Thus, in an irreversible process at constant S and P, enthalpy must decrease and should attain a minimum value at equilibrium.

The conditions for reversibility and irreversibility for process involving only mechanical work (P-V work) are summarised in Table 8.1.

Table 8.1 Criteria for Reversible and Irreversible Processes Involving only P-V Work

For reversible process	For irreversible process
$(dS)_{E,V} = 0$	$(dS)_{E,V} > 0$
$(dE)_{V,S} = 0$	$(dE)_{V,S} < 0$
$(dA)_{T,V} = 0$	$(dA)_{T,V} < 0$
$(dG)_{P,T} = 0$	$(dG)_{P,T} < 0$
$(dH)_{S,P} = 0$	$(dH)_{S,P} < 0$

8.10 RELATION BETWEEN ΔG SYSTEM AND ΔS UNIVERSE

For isothermal and isobaric processes $(\Delta G)_{sys}$ accounts for the entropy changes of the system and surroundings. If $(\Delta G)_{sys}$ is negative ΔS_{univ} is positive and vice-versa. This can be shown as follows:

For isothermal and isobaric systems, the change in Gibbs free energy is given by

$$\Delta G_{sys} = \Delta H_{sys} - T\Delta S_{sys}$$

where ΔH_{sys} and ΔS_{sys} are the enthalpy and entropy changes of the system respectively. Since pressure is constant, the system absorbs heat (Q_P) from the surroundings. The entropy of the system increases while that of the surroundings decreases. If the heat transfer had taken place reversibly between the system and the surroundings then

$$\Delta S_{surr} = -\frac{Q_P}{T} = -\frac{\Delta H_{sys}}{T}$$

or
$$\Delta H_{sys} = -T\Delta S_{surr}$$

Hence, we have

$$\Delta G_{sys} = -T\Delta S_{surr} - T\Delta S_{sys}$$

$$= -T\left(\Delta S_{surr} + \Delta S_{sys}\right)$$

$$= -T(\Delta S)_{univ} \qquad \qquad ...(8.70a)$$

For spontaneous processes $(\Delta S)_{univ}$ is positive hence $(\Delta G)_{sys}$ must be negative while for nonspontaneous processes $(\Delta G)_{sys} > 0$ and $(\Delta S)_{univ} < 0$, and for a reversible process $(\Delta G)_{sys} = -T\Delta S_{univ} = 0$.

8.11 DRIVING FORCES OF REACTIONS

For natural or irreversible processes at constant temperature and pressure, ΔG must be negative. Any transformation is feasible only if it is accompanied by a free energy decrease under these conditions. Thus, ΔG is a measure of driving force in any reaction or transformation. Since $\Delta G = \Delta H - T\Delta S$, it implies that a decrease in ΔH and increase in ΔS favour in making ΔG negative. Following cases may be helpful in deciding about the spontaneity of any process/reaction:

(i) When $\Delta H < 0$ and $T\Delta S > 0$: For such reactions, ΔG will always be negative and the change will always be spontaneous.

(ii) When $\Delta H < 0$ and $\Delta S < 0$: In such cases, $\Delta G < 0$ only if $|\Delta H| > T\Delta S$. The reactions should be strongly exothermic to overcome the entropy decrease. At higher temperatures where $|T\Delta S| > \Delta H$, $\Delta G > 0$ and the change will no longer be spontaneous.

(iii) When $\Delta H > 0$ and $\Delta S > 0$: Under these conditions $\Delta G < 0$ only if $T\Delta S > \Delta H$. These reactions are nonspontaneous at lower temperatures but spontaneous at higher temperatures.

(iv) When $\Delta H > 0$ and $\Delta S < 0$: The net result in such cases is that ΔG is always positive and the change is always forbidden.

These conclusions may be summarised in the following table:

ΔH	ΔS	ΔG	Conclusion
–	+	–	Always spontaneous
+	–	+	Always nonspontaneous
+	+	+ at low T	Nonspontaneous
		– at high T	Spontaneous
–	–	– at low T	Spontaneous
		+ at high T	Nonspontaneous

Problem 8.4: For the reaction

$$n\text{-}C_4H_{10}(g) = \text{iso-}C_4H_{10}(g)$$

at 298 K, enthalpies and entropies of formation of n-butane and iso-butane are as

	$\Delta H_f^0 \left(kJ\ mol^{-1} \right)$	$\Delta S_f^0 \left(JK\ mol^{-1} \right)$
n-butane	–124.7	–365.8
iso-butane	–131.6	–381.1

State whether the isomerisation is spontaneous or not.

Solution: For the given reaction the enthalpy and entropy changes are

$$\Delta H^0 = (-131.6) - (-124.7) \text{ kJ mol}^{-1} = -6.9 \text{ kJ mol}^{-1}$$

$$\Delta S^0 = (-381.1) - (-365.8) \text{ JK}^{-1} \text{ mol}^{-1} = -15.3 \text{ JK}^{-1} \text{ mol}^{-1}$$

Hence

$$\Delta G^0 = \Delta H^0 - T\Delta S^0$$

$$= -6.9 - (298)(-15.3 \times 10^{-3}) \text{ kJ mol}^{-1}$$

$$= -2.4 \text{ kJ mol}^{-1}$$

Since $\Delta G^\circ < 0$, the reaction is spontaneous.

Problem 8.5: The entropy and enthalpy changes for the reaction

$$CO(g) + H_2O(g) = CO_2(g) + H_2(g)$$

at 300 K and 1 atm pressure are respectively -42.4 JK^{-1} and -41.2 kJ. Calculate (*i*) the free energy change, ΔG for the reaction, (*ii*) predict if the reaction is feasible and (*iii*) the temperature at which the reaction will go in the opposite direction.

Solution: The free energy change for the reaction is given by

$$\Delta G = \Delta H - T\Delta S = (-41.20 + 300 \times 42.4) \text{ kJ}$$

$$= (-41.20 + 12.72) \text{ kJ}$$

$$= -28.48 \text{ kJ}$$

Since $\Delta G < 0$, the reaction is spontaneous, it will go in the opposite direction as soon as ΔG starts changing its sign. So the minimum temperature at which ΔG becomes zero can be calculated as

$$\Delta G = \Delta H - T\Delta S = 0$$

or

$$T = \frac{\Delta H}{\Delta S} = \frac{41.2 \times 10^3}{42.4} = 971.7 \text{ K}$$

8.12 FUNDAMENTAL THERMODYNAMIC EQUATIONS FOR OPEN SYSTEMS-PARTIAL MOLAR QUANTITIES

So far we have formulated equations for closed systems, *i.e.*, where the composition of the system remains unchanged. However, in an open system, the composition of the system changes by adding substances to the system or by taking them out from the system or by a chemical reaction. In such cases, the state of the system must involve another variable, viz., the composition of the system. So any extensive thermodynamic property, X may be written as

$$X = f(T, P, n_1, n_2, \ldots\ldots, n_i)$$

where n_i is the number of moles of substance i. Since dX is an exact differential, therefore we may write

$$dX = \left(\frac{\partial X}{\partial P}\right)_{T, n_1, n_2, \ldots} dP + \left(\frac{\partial X}{\partial T}\right)_{P, n_1, n_2, \ldots} dT + \left(\frac{\partial X}{\partial n_1}\right)_{T, P, n_2, \ldots} dn_1 + \left(\frac{\partial X}{\partial n_2}\right)_{T, P, n_1, \ldots} dn_2 + \cdots \qquad \ldots(8.71)$$

The term $\left(\dfrac{\partial X}{\partial n_1}\right)_{T,P,n_2,\dots}$ is called the *partial molar property* of the first component when all the variables except the mole number of component 1 are unchanged and is denoted by $\overline{X}_1$. It may be defined as *the increase in X per mole of component 1 when an infinitesimal amount of it is added to the system keeping temperature, pressure and all other compositions constant.*

If a system undergoes a change in the composition of the components at constant temperature and pressure, then

$$(dX)_{T,P} = \left(\frac{\partial X}{\partial n_1}\right)_{T,P,n_2,\dots} dn_1 + \left(\frac{\partial X}{\partial n_2}\right)_{T,P,n_1,\dots} dn_2 + \dots \dots \qquad \dots(8.72)$$

If the extensive thermodynamic property is G then Eq. (8.71) becomes

$$dG = \left(\frac{\partial G}{\partial P}\right)_{T,n_i} dP + \left(\frac{\partial G}{\partial T}\right)_{P,n_i} dT + \sum_{i=1}^{k} \left(\frac{\partial G}{\partial n_i}\right)_{T,P,n_j} dn_i \qquad \dots(8.73)$$

where $j \neq k$, which means that in the derivatives in the summation, the number of moles of all the components except the one are kept constant. Also, at constant P and T Eq. (8.73) becomes

$$(dG)_{T,P} = \sum_{i=1}^{k} \left(\frac{\partial G}{\partial n_i}\right)_{T,P,n_i} dn_i$$

$$(dG)_{T,P} = \sum_{i=1}^{k} \overline{G}_i \, dn_i \qquad \dots(8.74)$$

From Eq. [(8.24 (*a*)] and (8.31) for closed systems

$$\left(\frac{\partial G}{\partial T}\right)_{P,n_i} = -S$$

and

$$\left(\frac{\partial G}{\partial P}\right)_{T,n_i} = V$$

Hence, Eq. (8.73) becomes

$$dG = VdP - SdT + \sum_{i=1}^{k} \left(\frac{\partial G}{\partial n_i}\right)_{T,P,n_i} dn_i \qquad \dots(8.75)$$

Now, we define

$$\mu_i = \left(\frac{\partial G}{\partial n_i}\right)_{T,P,n_j} \qquad \dots(8.76)$$

Therefore, Eq. (8.75) can be written as

$$dG = VdP - SdT + \sum_{i=1}^{k} \mu_i \, dn_i \qquad \qquad ...(8.77)$$

Since E, H and A can be defined in terms of G as

$$E = G - PV + TS$$

$$H = G + TS$$

$$A = G - PV$$

Differentiating these equations, we get

$$dE = dG - PdV - VdP + TdS + SdT$$

$$dH = dG + TdS + SdT$$

$$dA = dG - PdV - VdP$$

Substituting the value of dG from Eq. (8.77) in the above equations, we get

$$dE = TdS - PdV + \sum_{i=1}^{k} \mu_i \, dn_i \qquad \qquad ...(8.78)$$

$$dH = VdP + TdS + \sum_{i=1}^{k} \mu_i \, dn_i \qquad \qquad ...(8.79)$$

$$dA = -SdT - VdP + \sum_{i=1}^{k} \mu_i \, dn_i \qquad \qquad ...(8.80)$$

Eq. (8.77)–(8.80) are the fundamental equations for open systems.

Chemical Potential: The quantity μ_i defined as

$$\mu_i = \left(\frac{\partial G}{\partial n_i} \right)_{T, P, n_j}$$

is known as the *chemical potential* of the (ith) component and is obviously *the increase in G per mole that results when a small amount dn_i moles are added to the system keeping temperature, pressure and all other compositions constant.* The amount added is so small that its addition practically does not alter the composition of the system. It is an intensive property of the system and must have the same value throughout the system at equilibrium. In case, where the chemical potential of a substance is not uniform throughout the system, matter will flow spontaneously from a region of higher chemical potential to a region of lower chemical potential until its value is uniform throughout the system.

From Eqs. (8.77), (8.78), (8.79) and (8.80), we have

$$\mu_i = \left(\frac{\partial G}{\partial n_i} \right)_{P, T, n_j} = \left(\frac{\partial E}{\partial n_i} \right)_{S, V, n_j} = \left(\frac{\partial H}{\partial n_i} \right)_{S, P, n_j} = \left(\frac{\partial A}{\partial n_i} \right)_{T, V, n_j}$$

Another name of $\left(\dfrac{\partial G}{\partial n_i}\right)_{P,\,T,\,n_j}$ is the partial molar Gibbs free energy.

The other partial molar thermodynamic quantities are defined as

$$\overline{E}_i = \left(\frac{\partial E}{\partial n_i}\right)_{T,\,P,\,n_j} \quad ; \quad \overline{H}_i = \left(\frac{\partial H}{\partial n_i}\right)_{T,\,P,\,n_j}$$

$$\overline{A}_i = \left(\frac{\partial A}{\partial n_i}\right)_{T,\,P,\,n_j} \quad ; \quad \overline{V}_i = \left(\frac{\partial V}{\partial n_i}\right)_{T,\,P,\,n_j}$$

$$\overline{S}_i = \left(\frac{\partial S}{\partial n_i}\right)_{T,\,P,\,n_j}$$

If we differentiate the defining equations for H, A and G with respect to n_i keeping P, T and n_j constant and using the above definition, we obtain

$$\overline{H}_i = \overline{E}_i + P\overline{V}_i$$

$$\overline{A}_i = \overline{E}_i - T\overline{S}_i$$

$$\overline{G}_i = \mu_i = \overline{H}_i - T\overline{S}_i$$

Variation of Chemical Potential with Temperature and Pressure: Differentiating Eq. (8.76) with respect to T gives

$$\left(\frac{\partial \mu_i}{\partial T}\right)_{P,\,n_j} = \frac{\partial}{\partial T}\left(\frac{\partial G}{\partial n_i}\right)_{T,\,P,\,n_j} = \frac{\partial}{\partial n_i}\left(\frac{\partial G}{\partial T}\right)_{P,\,n_j} = -\left(\frac{\partial S}{\partial n_i}\right)_{T,\,P,\,n_j} = -\overline{S}_i$$

This equation suggests that when temperature is changed at constant pressure and composition, the differential change in μ_i is equal to the partial molar entropy of component 'i'.

Since entropy is always positive, therefore the chemical potential of a substance decreases with rise of temperature at constant pressure and composition.

Now differentiating Eq. (8.76) with respect to P, we get

$$\left(\frac{d\mu_i}{dP}\right)_{T,\,n_j} = \frac{\partial}{\partial P}\left(\frac{\partial G}{\partial n_i}\right)_{T,\,P,\,n_j} = \frac{\partial}{\partial n_i}\left(\frac{\partial G}{\partial P}\right)_{T,\,n_j} = \left(\frac{\partial V}{\partial n_i}\right)_{T,\,P,\,n_j} = \overline{V}_i$$

In other words at constant temperature and composition, the differential change in μ_i with pressure is equal to the partial molar volume of the component.

As $\overline{V}_i$ for any substance is positive and so the chemical potential increases with pressure at constant temperature and composition.

Integrating Eq. (8.77) at constant temperature and pressure gives

$$G = \Sigma\, n_i\, \mu_i \qquad\qquad ...(8.81)$$

Differentiation of the above equation with respect to temperature at constant pressure and composition yields

$$\left(\frac{\partial G}{\partial T}\right)_{P,\, n_i} = \sum n_i \left(\frac{\partial \mu_i}{\partial T}\right)_{P,\, n_i}$$

But

$$\left(\frac{\partial G}{\partial T}\right)_{P,\, n_i} = -S$$

and

$$\left(\frac{\partial \mu_i}{\partial T}\right)_{P,\, n_i} = -S_i$$

Hence,

$$S = \sum n_i \overline{S}_i, \qquad\qquad\qquad ...(8.82)$$

Similarly, it can be shown that any intensive property $\overline{V}_i$, $\overline{H}_i$, $\overline{A}_i$ or $\overline{E}_i$, etc. is related to the corresponding extensive property by the relation

$$V = \sum n_i\, \overline{V}_i, \; H = \sum \overline{n}_i\, \overline{H}_i, \; A = \sum n_i\, \overline{A}_i \text{ and } E = \sum n_i\, \overline{E}_i$$

Chemical potential of an ideal gas:

Since

$$\left(\frac{\partial \mu_i}{\partial P}\right)_{T,\, n_j} = V_m$$

or

$$d\mu_i = V_m dP$$

$$= \frac{RT}{P} dP \left(\because V_m = \frac{RT}{P} \text{ for a mole of an ideal gas} \right)$$

Integrating this equation within limits gives

$$\int_{\mu_i^0}^{\mu_i} d\mu_i = RT \int_{P_i^0}^{P_i} \frac{dP}{P}$$

$$\mu_i - \mu_i^0 = RT \ln\left(P_i/P_i^0\right)$$

$$\mu_i = \mu_i^0 + RT \ln P_i \qquad\qquad\qquad ...(8.83)$$

where μ_i^0 and P_i^0 are the chemical potential and standard pressure in the standard state, *i.e.*, at 1 atmosphere pressure and the specified temperature.

In a mixture of ideal gases, chemical potential of the ith component is given by

$$\mu_i = \mu_i^0 + RT \ln p_i \qquad\qquad\qquad ...(8.84)$$

where p_i is the partial pressure of the ith component of the mixture. μ_i^0 is the chemical potential of the ith component in the standard state. Since $p_i = X_i P$, where X_i is the mole fraction of the ith component in the mixture and P is the total pressure, therefore, Eq. (8.84) becomes

$$\mu_i = \mu_i^0 + RT \ln(X_i P)$$

$$= \mu_i^0 + RT \ln P + RT \ln X_i \qquad \qquad ...(8.85)$$

The first two terms in Eq. (8.85) represent the chemical potential of the pure ith component under pressure P, so Eq. (8.85) reduces to

$$\mu_i = \mu_{i(\text{pure})} + RT \ln X_i \qquad \qquad ...(8.86)$$

Since X_i is always less than one, $RT \ln X_i$ will be a negative quantity and therefore the chemical potential of any gas in the mixture will always be less than that of the pure component under the same total pressure.

8.13 PARTIAL MOLAR QUANTITIES IN A MIXTURE OF IDEAL GASES

In a mixture of ideal gases, the various partial molar quantities can be evaluated using relation (8.85)

$$\mu_i = \mu_i^0 + RT \ln P + RT \ln X_i$$

Differentiation with respect to temperature at constant pressure and composition gives

$$\left(\frac{\partial \mu_i}{\partial T} \right)_{P, n_i} = \left(\frac{\partial \mu_i^0}{\partial T} \right)_{P, n_i} + R \ln P + R \ln X_i$$

But
$$\left(\frac{\partial \mu_i}{\partial T} \right)_{P, n_i} = -\bar{S}_i, \text{ so we have}$$

$$-\bar{S}_i = -\bar{S}_i^0 + R \ln P + R \ln X_i$$

$$\bar{S}_i = \bar{S}_{i(\text{pure})} - R \ln X_i \qquad \qquad ...(8.87)$$

Similarly differentiation of μ_i with respect to pressure at constant temperature and composition gives

$$\left(\frac{\partial \mu_i}{\partial P} \right)_{T, n_i} = \frac{RT}{P}$$

But
$$\left(\frac{\partial \mu_i}{\partial P} \right)_{T, n_i} = V_i$$

Therefore,
$$V_i = \frac{RT}{P}$$

But $\dfrac{RT}{P}$ for an ideal gas mixture is $\dfrac{V}{n}$. Hence

$$V_i = \frac{V}{n} = \text{average molar volume}$$

Thus, partial molar volume of a component of an ideal gas mixture is simply the average molar volume.

8.14 THERMODYNAMICS OF MIXING OF IDEAL GASES

Mixing of ideal gases is a spontaneous process and is accompanied by a decrease in Gibbs free energy. The equations derived in the previous section may be readily applied to calculate the changes in thermodynamic properties on mixing.

Gibb's free energy of mixing (ΔG_{mix}): If a number of ideal components 1, 2, 3 etc., with mole number n_1, n_2, n_3, ... etc., are mixed at constant temperature (T) and pressure (P), then the total Gibb's free energy before mixing is

$$G_{initial} = n_1\mu_1^* + n_2\mu_2^* + n_3\mu_3^* + \ldots = \sum n_i\mu_i^* \qquad \ldots(8.88)$$

where μ_i^* is the chemical potential of pure ith component. The total Gibb's free energy after mixing of these components is given by

$$G_{final} = \mu_i n_1 + n_2\mu_2 + \ldots = \Sigma n_i \mu_i \qquad \ldots(8.89)$$

The chemical potential μ_i of the ith component in the mixture is given by

$$\mu_i = \mu_i^* + RT \ln X_i$$

where X_i is the mole fraction of ith component in the mixture. The free energy of mixing is given by $\Delta G_{mix} = G_{final} - G_{initial}$. On inserting the values of G_{final} and $G_{initial}$, we obtain

$$\Delta G_{mix} = \sum_i n_i\mu_i - \sum_i n_i \mu_i^* = \sum_i n_i\left(\mu_i - \mu_i^*\right)$$

But $\mu_i - \mu_i^* = RT \ln X_i$, hence, we get

$$\Delta G_{mix} = \sum_i n_i RT \ln X_i$$

$$= RT\left(n_1 \ln X_1 + n_2 \ln X_2 + \ldots\right) \qquad \ldots(8.90)$$

Equation (8.90) can be put in a slightly more convenient form by substituting $n_i = X_i n$, where n is the total number of moles in the mixture.

Thus,

$$\Delta G_{mix} = nRT \sum_i X_i \ln X_1 \qquad \ldots(8.91)$$

and free energy of mixing per mole of the mixture is given by

$$\Delta G_{mix,\,m} = \frac{\Delta G_{mix}}{n} = RT \sum_i X_i \ln X_i \ldots \qquad \ldots(8.92)$$

From the above Eqs. (8.91) and (8.92), it is clear that Gibb's free energy of mixing is negative, because X_i is always less than one and $\ln X_i$ is negative. So mixing is a spontaneous process.

Entropy of Mixing (ΔS_{mix}): We know that

$$\left(-\frac{dG}{dT}\right)_P = -S$$

So differentiation of Eq. (8.91) with respect to T at constant pressure and composition yields

$$\Delta S_{mix} = -\left[\frac{d(\Delta G_{mix})}{dT}\right]_{P_1, n_i} = -nR\sum_i X_i \ln X_i \qquad \ldots(8.93)$$

or entropy of mixing per mole is

$$\Delta S_{mix, m} = \frac{\Delta S_{mix}}{n} = -R\sum_i X_i \ln X_i \qquad \ldots(8.94)$$

Enthalpy of mixing (ΔH_{mix}): This can be calculated from the relation $\Delta G_{mix} = \Delta H_{mix} - T\Delta S_{mix}$. Using the values of Gibb's free energy and entropy of mixing from Eqs. (8.92) and (8.94) we obtain

$$nRT\sum_i X_i \ln X_i = \Delta H_{mix} + nRT\sum_i X_i \ln X_i$$

which gives $\qquad \qquad \Delta H_{mix} = 0$

Thus, the enthalpy of mixing of ideal components is zero, *i.e.*, no heat effects are associated with the formation of an ideal mixture.

Volume of Mixing (ΔV_{mix}): The volume of mixing can be obtained by differentiating the Gibb's free energy of mixing Eqn. 8.91 with respect to pressure at constant temperature and composition

$$\Delta V_{mix} = \left[\frac{d(\Delta G_{mix})}{dP}\right]_{T_1, n_i} \qquad \ldots(8.95)$$

But Eq. (8.92) shows that Gibb's free energy of mixing is independent of pressure, so the derivative in Eqn. (8.95) is zero; hence

$$\Delta V_{mix} = 0$$

Ideal mixing is not accompanied by a volume change.

In a binary ideal mixture, it is found that the greatest decrease in ΔG_{mix} results when $X_1 = X_2 = \dfrac{1}{2}$.

Similarly, for a ternary mixture, maximum free energy decrease is obtained when $X_1 = X_2 = X_3 = 1/3$.

Problem 8.6: Show that ΔG_{mix} is minimum for a binary mixture if $X_1 = X_2 = \dfrac{1}{2}$.

Solution: The free energy of mixing is given as

$$\Delta G_{mix} = nRT\left[X_1 \ln X_1 + X_2 \ln X_2\right]$$

$$= nRT\left[X_1 \ln X_1 + (1 - X_1)\ln(1 - X_1)\right]$$

For ΔG_{mix} to be minimum, $\left[\dfrac{d(\Delta G_{mix})}{dX_1}\right]_{P,T}$ should be zero.

Therefore, on differentiating the above equation, we get

$$\left[\frac{d(\Delta G_{mix})}{dX_1}\right]_{P,T} = X_1\frac{1}{X_1} + \ln X_1 + \frac{1-X_1}{1-X_1}(-1) + \ln(1-X_1)(-1) = 0$$

$$= 1 + \ln X_1 - 1 - \ln(1-X_1) = 0$$

or
$$X_1 = 1 - X_1$$

or
$$X_1 = \frac{1}{2}$$

Hence, ΔG_{mix} is minimum for a binary mixture if $X_1 = X_2 = 1/2$.

Problem 8.7: What should be the maximum positive value of enthalpy of mixing of two non-ideal components at 300 K so that mixing is possible.

Solution: For an ideal solution

$$\Delta H_{mix} = 0$$

So,
$$\Delta G_{mix} = -T\Delta S_{mix}$$

For a binary solution the entropy of mixing is maximum if the mole fractions of two components are equal, *i.e.*, $X_1 = X_2 = \dfrac{1}{2}$. Hence, the entropy of mixing per mole of mixture is given by

$$\Delta S_{mix,\,m} = -nR\left(X_1 \ln X_1 + X_2 \ln X_2\right)$$

$$= \left(8.314 \text{ JK}^{-1}\text{mol}^{-1}\right)\left[\frac{1}{2}\ln\frac{1}{2} + \frac{1}{2}\ln\frac{1}{2}\right]$$

$$= 5.76 \text{ JK}^{-1}\text{mol}^{-1}$$

Also
$$\Delta G_{mix,\,m} = -T\Delta S_{mix}$$

$$= -(300 \text{ K})\left(5.76 \text{ JK}^{-1}\text{mol}^{-1}\right)$$

$$= -1728 \text{ J mol}^{-1}$$

For spontaneous mixing $\Delta G_{mix,\,m} < 0$. Hence,

$$\Delta G_{mix,\,m} = \Delta H_{mix,\,m} - T\Delta S_{mix,\,m}$$

So, ΔG_{mix} can vary from 0 to -1728 J mol^{-1} for spontaneous mixing. If ΔH_{mix} is more positive than 1728 J mol^{-1}, $\Delta G_{mix,\,m}$ will be positive and mixing would not be spontaneous. Therefore, maximum positive value of $\Delta H_{mix,\,m}$ is 1728 J mol^{-1}.

8.15 GIBBS DUHEM EQUATION

From Eq. (8.77)

$$dG = VdP - SdT + \sum_{i=1}^{k} \mu_i \, dn_i$$

At constant temperature and pressure, the above equation reduces to

$$(dG)_{P,T} = \sum_{i=1}^{k} \mu_i \, dn_i \qquad \qquad ...(8.96)$$

Since G is given by

$$G = \sum_{i=1}^{k} n_i \, \mu_i$$

Differentiating the above equation at constant T and P yields

$$(dG)_{P,T} = \sum_{i=1}^{k} \mu_i \, dn_i + \sum_{i=1}^{k} d\mu_i n_i \qquad \qquad ...(8.97)$$

On comparing Eqs. (8.96) and (8.97)

$$\sum_{i=1}^{k} \mu_i \, dn_i = \sum_{i=1}^{k} \mu_i \, dn_i + \sum_{i=1}^{k} n_i d\mu_i$$

$$\sum_{i=1}^{k} n_i d\mu_i = 0 \qquad \qquad ...(8.98)$$

Equation (8.98) is known as the *Gibbs-Duhem equation*. It relates the change in chemical potential with composition and shows that chemical potentials do not vary independently but in a related manner. For a system having only two components, 1 and 2, Eq. (8.98) becomes

$$n_1 d\mu_1 + n_2 d\mu_2 = 0$$

or

$$d\mu_2 = -\frac{n_1}{n_2} d\mu_1 \qquad \qquad ...(8.99)$$

Thus, $d\mu_2$ can be calculated if the change in chemical potential of component 1 is known.

8.16 THE CLAPEYRON EQUATION

For a pure substance present in two phases 1 and 2 at a pressure P and temperature T, the condition of equilibrium is

$$G_{m,2} = G_{m,1}$$

or

$$\Delta G = 0 \qquad \qquad ...(8.100)$$

where $G_{m, 2}$ and $G_{m, 1}$ are the free energies per mole in phase 2 and 1, respectively. The relation between variables of the system at equilibrium can be obtained from thermodynamic considerations. If the pressure of the system is changed to $P + dP$ and temperature to $T + dT$, the value G_m will change to $G_m + dG_m$. The condition of equilibrium at $T + dT$ and $P + dP$ is given by

$$G_{m,1} + dG_{m, 1} = G_{m, 2} + dG_{m, 2}$$

But

$$G_{m, 1} = G_{m, 2}$$

Hence

$$dG_{m,1} = dG_{m,2}$$

From Eq. (8.24), we have

$$dG_{m, 1} = V_{m, 1} dP - S_{m,1} dT$$

and

$$dG_{m, 2} = V_{m, 2} dP - S_{m, 2} dT$$

Therefore,

$$V_{m,1} dP - S_{m, 1} dT = V_{m, 2} dP - S_{m, 2} dT$$

$$\left(S_{m, 2} - S_{m, 1}\right) dT = \left(V_{m, 2} - V_{m, 1}\right) dP$$

$$\frac{dT}{dP} = \frac{\left(V_{m, 2} - V_{m, 1}\right)}{\left(S_{m, 2} - S_{m, 1}\right)}$$

$$\frac{dT}{dP} = \frac{\Delta V_m}{\Delta S_m} \qquad \qquad ...(8.101)$$

where ΔS_m and ΔV_m are the changes per mole in entropy and volume when the substance is transferred from phase 1 to 2.

Equation (8.101) is known as *the Clapeyron equation* and holds for the equilibrium between two phases of a substance. It relates quantitatively the variation of equilibrium pressure with temperature. We shall apply Clapeyron equation to (*i*) liquid-vapour equilibrium or vapourisation, (*ii*) solid-vapour equilibrium or sublimation, and (*iii*) solid-liquid equilibrium or fusion.

(*i*) **Liquid-Vapour Equilibrium:** Since the molar entropy and molar volume of a gas are higher than those for the liquid, therefore, ΔS_m and ΔV_m are always positive for liquid-vapour transformation and the quantity dP/dT will be positive. A rise in temperature increases the equilibrium vapour pressure of the liquid.

(*ii*) **Solid-Vapour Equilibrium:** For solid-vapour transformation

$$\Delta S_m = S_{m, g} - S_{m, s}$$

$$= \frac{\Delta H_{sub, m}}{T} = \text{positive} \qquad \left(\because S_{m, g} > S_{m, s}\right)$$

Since

$$\Delta V_m = V_{m, g} - V_{m,s} = \text{positive} \qquad \left(\because V_{m, g} > V_{m, s}\right)$$

Therefore, $$\frac{dP}{dT} = \text{positive}$$

Increase in temperature increases the equilibrium vapour pressure of the solid. Further

$$\Delta H_{\text{sub}, m} = \Delta H_{\text{fus}, m} + \Delta H_{\text{vap}, m}$$

or $$\Delta H_{m, \text{sub}} > \Delta H_{m, \text{vap}}$$

It follows

$$\left(\frac{dP}{dT}\right)_{s \to g} > \left(\frac{dP}{dT}\right)_{l \to g}$$

i.e., at the temperature where all the three phases of a substance are in equilibrium, the slope of vapour pressure versus temperature plot for solid-vapour equilibrium is larger than that for the liquid-vapour equilibrium.

(*iii*) **Solid-Liquid Equilibrium:** In this case

$$\Delta S_m = S_{m, l} - S_{m, s} = \frac{\Delta H_{\text{fus}, m}}{T} = \text{positive}$$

For most of the substances

$$\Delta V_m = V_{m, l} - V_{m, s} = \text{positive}$$

and dP/dT in such cases will be a positive quantity and increase in pressure will raise the melting point of the substance. For water, however, ΔV_m is negative so increase of pressure will lower its freezing point.

8.17 CLAUSIUS-CLAPEYRON EQUATION

In the solid-vapour or liquid-vapour equilibrium if $V_{m, l}$ or $V_{m, s}$ can be neglected in comparison to $V_{m, g}$, then $V_{m, g} - V_{m, l} \approx V_{m, g}$ or $V_{m, g} - V_{m, s} \approx V_{m, g}$ and the Clapeyron Equation (8.101) becomes

$$\frac{dP}{dT} = \frac{\Delta S_m}{\Delta V_m} = \frac{\Delta H_{\text{vap}, m}}{T V_{m, g}} \qquad \qquad ...(8.102)$$

$$\left(\because \Delta S_m = \frac{\Delta H_{\text{vap}, m}}{T} \right)$$

If the vapours are assumed to behave ideally, then $V_{m, g}$ can be replaced by $\dfrac{RT}{P}$ and we have

$$\frac{dP}{dT} = \frac{\Delta H_{\text{vap}, m} P}{T \cdot RT}$$

$$\frac{dP}{P} = \frac{\Delta H_{\text{vap}, m}}{RT^2} dT$$

For small temperature variations, $\Delta H_{vap, m}$ may be assumed to be constant. Integration of the above equation then yields

$$\ln \frac{P_2}{P_1} = \frac{\Delta H_{vap,m}}{RT_1 T_2}(T_2 - T_1) \qquad \qquad ...(8.103)$$

Problem 8.8: One mole of an ideal gas expands isothermally and reversibly from 5 dm³ to 10 dm³ at 300 K. Calculate Q, W, ΔE, ΔH, ΔG and ΔA. What would be the magnitudes of these quantities if the gas expanded into a vacuum?

   Solution: For both processes

$$\Delta E = \Delta H = 0$$

and

$$\Delta A = \Delta G = -RT \ln \frac{10}{5} = -1729 \text{ J mol}^{-1}$$

When the expansion is isothermal and reversible

$$Q = -W = 1729 \text{ J mol}^{-1}$$

For expansion into vacuum

$$-W = Q = 0 \text{ and } \Delta G = \Delta A$$

Problem 8.9: The boiling point of water is 373 K at 1 atmosphere pressure. Calculate W, Q, ΔE, ΔH, ΔG, ΔA and ΔS, when a mole of steam is compressed isothermally and reversibly. The latent heat of vapourisation of water is 40.67 kJ mol⁻¹.

   Solution:

$$-W = P\Delta V = P(V_{m, l} - V_{m,g}) = -PV_{m, g} = -RT$$

$$= -(8.314 \text{ J K}^{-1}\text{mol}^{-1})(373 \text{ K})$$

$$= -3100 \text{ J mol}^{-1}$$

or

$$W = 3.100 \text{ kJ mol}^{-1}$$

$$Q_P = \Delta H = -40.67 \text{ kJ mol}^{-1}$$

$$\Delta E = \Delta H - P\Delta V = (-40.67 + 3.1) \text{ kJ mol}^{-1}$$

$$= -37.57 \text{ kJ mol}^{-1}$$

$$\Delta G = \int V \, dP = 0$$

$$\Delta A = W$$

$$= 3.1 \text{ kJ mol}^{-1}$$

$$\Delta S = \frac{Q_{rev}}{T}$$

$$= -\frac{40.67 \text{ kJ mol}^{-1}}{373 \text{ K}}$$

$$= -109 \text{ JK}^{-1}\text{mol}^{-1}$$

Problem 8.10: Deduce the thermodynamic equations of state

(i) $\left(\dfrac{\partial E}{\partial V}\right)_T = T\left(\dfrac{\partial P}{\partial T}\right)_V - P$ and (ii) $\left(\dfrac{\partial H}{\partial P}\right)_T = V - T\left(\dfrac{\partial V}{\partial T}\right)_P$

Solution: (i) From the first and the second laws we have

$$dE = TdS - PdV$$

$$\left(\frac{\partial E}{\partial V}\right)_T = T\left(\frac{\partial S}{\partial V}\right)_T - P \qquad \qquad \ldots(i)$$

But from Maxwell's relation (8.54), we have

$$\left(\frac{\partial S}{\partial V}\right)_T = \left(\frac{\partial P}{\partial T}\right)_V$$

Substituting the value of $\left(\dfrac{\partial S}{\partial V}\right)_T$ in Eq. (i), we get

$$\left(\frac{\partial E}{\partial V}\right)_T = T\left(\frac{\partial P}{\partial T}\right)_V - P$$

(ii) From the relation $dH = VdP + TdS$, we have

$$\left(\frac{\partial H}{\partial P}\right)_T = T\left(\frac{\partial S}{\partial P}\right)_T + V$$

But $\left(\dfrac{\partial S}{\partial P}\right)_T = -\left(\dfrac{\partial V}{\partial T}\right)_P$ (vide Maxwell's relation (8.59))

Hence, we have $\left(\dfrac{\partial H}{\partial P}\right)_T = V - T\left(\dfrac{\partial V}{\partial T}\right)_P$

Problem 8.11: Express the value of $(\partial V/\partial S)_P$ for an ideal gas in terms of P, T and C_p.
Solution: From the Maxwell's relation (8.49)

$$\left(\frac{\partial V}{\partial S}\right)_P = \left(\frac{\partial T}{\partial P}\right)_S$$

Considering entropy as a function of P and T, then from cyclic rule we have

$$\left(\frac{\partial S}{\partial P}\right)_T\left(\frac{\partial P}{\partial T}\right)_S\left(\frac{\partial T}{\partial S}\right)_P = -1$$

$$\left(\frac{\partial T}{\partial P}\right)_S = -\left(\frac{\partial S}{\partial P}\right)_T\left(\frac{\partial T}{\partial S}\right)_P$$

But

$$\left(\frac{\partial S}{\partial P}\right)_T = -\left(\frac{\partial V}{\partial T}\right)_P \ \left[cf \text{ relation } (8.59)\right]$$

and

$$\left(\frac{\partial S}{\partial T}\right)_P = \frac{C_P}{T}$$

Hence,

$$\left(\frac{\partial V}{\partial S}\right)_P = \left(\frac{\partial T}{\partial P}\right)_S = \frac{T}{C_P}\left(\frac{\partial V}{\partial T}\right)_P = \frac{RT}{C_P P}$$

Problem 8.12: Evaluate ΔG and ΔA for the reversible isothermal expansion of a mole of the gas having an equation of state $PV = RT(1 + B/V)$ from an initial volume V_1 to a final volume V_2 where V_1 and V_2 are the molar volume of the gas in the two states.

Solution: We know that

$$dG = VdP - SdT$$

For isothermal processes, $dT = 0$

Hence

$$dG = VdP$$

From the equation of state

$$P = \frac{RT}{V} + \frac{BRT}{V^2}$$

$$dP = -\left(\frac{RT}{V^2} + \frac{2BRT}{V^3}\right)dV$$

Therefore,

$$dG = VdP$$

$$= -\frac{RT}{V}dV - \frac{2BRT}{V^2}dV$$

Integrating, we get

$$\Delta G = -\int_{V_1}^{V_2}\frac{RT}{V}dV - \int_{V_1}^{V_2}2\frac{BRT\,dV}{V^2}$$

$$= -RT\ln\frac{V_2}{V_1} + 2BRT\left(\frac{1}{V_2} - \frac{1}{V_1}\right)$$

Now
$$(dA)_T = -PdV$$

or
$$\Delta A = \int_{V_1}^{V_2} -PdV$$

$$= \int_{V_1}^{V_2} -\frac{RT}{V}dV - \int_{V_1}^{V_2} \frac{BRT}{V^2}dV$$

$$= -RT\ln\frac{V_2}{V_1} + BRT\left(\frac{1}{V_2} - \frac{1}{V_1}\right)$$

EXERCISES

1. Show that
   (i) for an isothermal expansion of an ideal gas

   $$\Delta A = \Delta G = nRT\ln\frac{V_1}{V_2}.$$

   (ii) for a system, decrease in the Helmholtz free energy function ($-\Delta A$) at constant temperature and volume represents the maximum amount of work obtainable from the system.
   (iii) decrease in the Gibbs free energy function ($-\Delta G$) at constant temperature and pressure represents the net non-mechanical work that can be obtained from the system.
   (iv) free energy change of a system under suitable conditions accounts automatically for the entropy changes of the system and the surroundings.
   (v) $\Delta G = \Delta A$ for an isothermal expansion of an ideal gas.

2. For each of the following processes state which of the quantities ΔE, ΔH, ΔS, ΔG or ΔA are equal to zero.
   (a) An ideal gas is taken around a Carnot cycle.
   (b) H_2 and O_2 react to form H_2O in a thermally-isolated bomb.
   (c) A non-ideal gas is adiabatically expanded through a throttling valve.
   (d) Liquid water is vapourised at 373 K and 1 atm pressure.
   (e) An ideal gas expands reversibly and adiabatically.

   Ans. (a) All, (b) ΔE, (c) ΔH, (d) ΔG, (e) ΔS.

3. Derive the relations:
   (i) $$\left(\frac{\partial T}{\partial V}\right)_S = -\frac{T}{C_V}\left(\frac{\partial P}{\partial T}\right)_V$$

   (ii) $$\left(\frac{\partial T}{\partial P}\right)_S = \frac{T}{C_P}\left(\frac{\partial V}{\partial T}\right)_P$$

   (iii) $$\left(\frac{\partial V}{\partial T}\right)_S = \left(\frac{\partial V}{\partial P}\right)_T\left(\frac{\partial T}{\partial V}\right)_P\left[\frac{C_P}{T} + \left(\frac{\partial V}{\partial T}\right)_P^2\left(\frac{\partial P}{\partial V}\right)_T\right]$$

(iv) $\left(\dfrac{\partial H}{\partial T}\right)_S = \dfrac{VC_P}{T}\left(\dfrac{\partial T}{\partial V}\right)_P$

(v) $\left(\dfrac{\partial E}{\partial T}\right)_S = -\dfrac{PC_V}{T}\left(\dfrac{\partial T}{\partial P}\right)_V$

(vi) $\left(\dfrac{\partial A}{\partial T}\right)_S = \left(\dfrac{\partial E}{\partial T}\right)_S - S = -P\left(\dfrac{\partial V}{\partial P}\right)_T\left(\dfrac{\partial T}{\partial V}\right)_P\left[\dfrac{C_P}{T}+\left(\dfrac{\partial V}{\partial T}\right)_P^2\left(\dfrac{\partial P}{\partial V}\right)_T\right] - S$

(vii) $\left(\dfrac{\partial G}{\partial T}\right)_S = \left(\dfrac{\partial H}{\partial T}\right)_S - S = \dfrac{VC_P}{T}\left(\dfrac{\partial T}{\partial V}\right)_P - S$

4. Derive the Maxwell's relations:

(i) $\left(\dfrac{\partial P}{\partial S}\right)_V = -\left(\dfrac{\partial T}{\partial V}\right)_S$

(ii) $\left(\dfrac{\partial V}{\partial S}\right)_P = \left(\dfrac{\partial T}{\partial P}\right)_S$

(iii) $\left(\dfrac{\partial V}{\partial S}\right)_T = \left(\dfrac{\partial T}{\partial P}\right)_V$

(iv) $\left(\dfrac{\partial P}{\partial S}\right)_T = -\left(\dfrac{\partial T}{\partial V}\right)_P$

5. Using the Maxwell's relations prove that

$$\left(\dfrac{\partial C_V}{\partial V}\right)_T = T\left(\dfrac{\partial^2 P}{\partial T^2}\right) = T\dfrac{\partial}{\partial T}\left[\left(\dfrac{\alpha}{k}\right)\right]_V$$

$$\left(\dfrac{\partial C_P}{\partial P}\right)_T = -T\left(\dfrac{\partial^2 V}{\partial T^2}\right)_P = -T\left[\dfrac{\partial}{\partial T}(\alpha V)\right]_P$$

6. Starting from the relations $dE = TdS - PdV$ and $dH = TdS + VdP$, derive the thermodynamic equations of state $\left(\dfrac{dE}{\partial V}\right)_T = T\left(\dfrac{\partial P}{\partial T}\right)_V - P$ and $\left(\dfrac{\partial H}{\partial P}\right) = V - T\left(\dfrac{\partial V}{\partial T}\right)_P$. (Hint: Make use of the Maxwell's relations).

7. Derive the following relations:

(i) $(dE)_{S,V} \le 0$, (ii) $(dH)_{S,P} \le 0$, (iii) $(dG)_{P,T} \le 0$,

(iv) $(dA)_{T,V} \le 0$, (v) $(dS)_{E,V} \ge 0$.

8. Consider the following
(i) $A, (l, 1\text{ atm}, 263\text{ K}) = A (s, 1\text{ atm}, 263\text{ K})$
(ii) $A, (l, 1\text{ atm}, 269\text{ K}) = A (s, 1\text{ atm}, 269\text{ K})$
(iii) $A, (l, 1\text{ atm}, 273\text{ K}) = A (g, 1\text{ atm}, 273\text{ K})$

If 269 K is the fusion temperature, which of the above processes is spontaneous and why? Which of the phases would be stable?

Ans. Process (*i*) is spontaneous and solid is the more stable phase.

9. Calculate the value of $\Delta G - \Delta A$ at 300 K for each of the following reaction:

     (*i*) $\quad H_2O(g) = H_2O(g) + \dfrac{1}{2}O_2(g)$ (*ii*) $\quad CO_2(g) + H_2(g) = CO(g) + H_2O(g)$

     (*iii*) $\quad PCl_5(g) = PCl_3(g) + Cl_2(g)$ (*iv*) $\quad C_6H_6(g) + \dfrac{7}{2}O_2(g) = 6CO_2(g) + 3H_2O(g)$

     (*v*) $\quad N_2(g) + 3H_2(g) = 2NH_3(g)$

Ans. (*i*) 1.247 kJ, (*ii*) 0, 0 kJ, (*iii*) 2.494 kJ (*iv*) 11.22 kJ, (*v*) –4.99 kJ.

10. Derive the following forms of the Gibbs-Helmholtz equation:

     (*i*) $\quad G = H + T\left(\dfrac{\partial G}{\partial T}\right)_P$ (*ii*) $\quad \left[\dfrac{\partial(G/T)}{\partial T}\right]_P = -\dfrac{H}{T^2}$

     (*iii*) $\quad \left[\dfrac{\partial(G/T)}{\partial(1/T)}\right]_P = H$ (*iv*) $\quad \Delta G = \Delta H + T\left[\dfrac{\partial(\Delta G)}{\partial T}\right]_P$

     (*v*) $\quad \left[\dfrac{\partial(\Delta G/T)}{\partial T}\right]_P = -\dfrac{\Delta H}{T^2}$ (*vi*) $\quad \left[\dfrac{\partial(\Delta G/T)}{\partial(1/T)}\right]_P = \Delta H$

11. Derive the corresponding relations for the Helmholtz free energy function A.

     Show that

     (*i*) $\quad \left(\dfrac{\partial E}{\partial V}\right)_T = -\left[\dfrac{\partial(P/T)}{\partial(1/T)}\right]_V$ (*ii*) $\quad \left(\dfrac{\partial H}{\partial P}\right)_T = \left[\dfrac{\partial(V/T)}{\partial(1/T)}\right]_P$

12. Calculate ΔG and ΔA when 4 moles of an ideal gas are expanded isothermally and reversibly from 5 atm to 1 atm at 323 K.   **Ans.** $\Delta G = \Delta A = -17.30$ kJ.

13. Calculate the value of Gibbs free energy over and above that in the standard state for a mole of an ideal gas at 298 K and 400 mm Hg.   **Ans.** $\Delta G = G - G^0 = -1.58$ kJ.

14. 1 mole of O_2 at 1 atm and 298 K is heated to 400 K at constant volume. Calculate the value of ΔA for the above process if $S^0 (O_2) = 205.03$ EU and $C_{V,\,m} = 21.13$ JK^{-1} mol^{-1}. Assume C_V to be temperature independent.   **Ans.** 21.25 kJ.

15. 1 mole of CO_2 at 1 atm and 298 K is heated to 400 K at constant pressure. Calculate ΔH, ΔG for the process if $S^0 (CO_2) = 213.64$ EU and $C_{P,\,m} (CO_2) = 37.49$ JK^{-1} mol^{-1}. Assume $C_{P,\,m}$ to be temperature independent.   **Ans.** $\Delta H = 3.82$ kJ, $\Delta G = -22.39$ kJ, $\Delta S = 10.96$ JK^{-1}.

16. Liquid butyl methacrylate (molar mass 1.42×10^{-1} kg mol^{-1}) has a density of 0.886 kg dm^{-3} at 300 K. Calculate the change in ΔG for the isothermal compression of a mole of the liquid from 1 atm to 20 atm.   **Ans.** $\Delta G = 308.79$ J mol^{-1}.

17. Saturated vapour pressure of supercooled CO_2 at 214 K is 3495 torr and that of solid CO_2 at the same temperature is 3294.6 torr. What is the change in ΔG when a mole of supercooled CO_2 solidifies at the above temperature. The vapours of CO_2 may be assumed to behave ideally.   **Ans.** $\Delta G = -105.4$ J mol^{-1}.

18. Enthalpy of vapourization of a certain liquid is 24.914 kJ mol^{-1} and entropy of vapourisation is 94.684 EU. Calculate the temperature at which both the phases coexist.   **Ans.** 263.15 K.

19. Calculate ΔA and ΔG for the following reversible processes:

    (i) $AB\,(l,\,349.75\ \text{K},\,1\ \text{atm}) \longrightarrow AB\,(g,\,349.75\ \text{K},\,1\ \text{atm})$

    (ii) $AB\,(g,\,349.75\ \text{K},\,1\ \text{atm}) \longrightarrow AB\,(g,\,349.75\ \text{K},\,100\ \text{torr})$

    Ans. (i) $\Delta G = 0$, $\Delta A = -2.9$ kJ mol^{-1}. (ii) $\Delta G = \Delta A = -5.9$ kJ mol^{-1}.

20. Using the results of the previous problem, calculate ΔA and ΔG for the process
    $AB\,(l,\,349.75\ \text{K},\,1\ \text{atm}) = AB\,(g,\,349.75\ \text{K},\,100\ \text{torr})$.

    Ans. $\Delta A = -8.8$ kJ mol^{-1}, $\Delta G = -5.9$ kJ mol^{-1}.

21. For the reaction

$$H_2S\,(g) + \frac{3}{2}O_2(g) = H_2O\,(l) + SO_2(g)$$

    ΔH is -562.589 kJ and ΔS is -194.743 EU at 298 K.

    Show that the reaction is nonspontaneous and calculate the minimum temperature at which the reaction will be reversed.   **Ans.** 2889 K.

22. For the reaction,

$$CO\,(g) + H_2O\,(g) = CO_2\,(g) + H_2\,(g)$$

    at 298 K and 1 atm the standard enthalpy and entropy changes are -41.19 kJ and -42.4 EU; respectively. Indicate whether the reaction is feasible or not. Calculate the temperature at which the reaction will go in the reverse direction assuming that ΔH and ΔS are independent of temperature.

    Ans. $\Delta G_{298} = -28.55$ kJ, reaction is feasible and $T = 971.5$ K.

23. Assuming that He and N$_2$ form an ideal gaseous mixture, calculate ΔE, ΔH, ΔV, ΔG, ΔA and ΔS of mixing when 5 moles of He and 3 moles N$_2$ are mixed at 298 K. If the total entropy of the two gases before mixing is 2000 EU, calculate the total entropy of the mixture.

    Ans. $\Delta H = \Delta E = \Delta V = 0$, $\Delta G = \Delta A = -1.639$ kJ mol^{-1}, $\Delta S_{mix} = 44$ EU;

    Total entropy after mixing is 2044 EU.

24. Calculate ΔG and ΔA for the isothermal reversible expansion of a mole of an ideal gas from 100 atm to 20 atm at 298 K. If the same expansion were carried out against a constant external pressure of 1 atm, how would ΔG and ΔA change.

    Ans. $\Delta G = \Delta A = -3.988$ kJ mol^{-1}. In the irreversible expansion ΔG and ΔA would be the same as for the reversible expansion.

25. The partial molar volumes of ethanol and water in a solution containing 5.0 moles of water and 1.05 moles of ethanol are 11.839×10^{-3} dm^3 and 55.10×10^{-3} dm^3, respectively. Indicate whether the solution is ideal or non-ideal.

    $d_{ETOH} = 0.7893$ kg dm^{-3}.   **Ans.** Non-ideal, $\Delta V_{excess} = -0.68 \times 10^{-3}$ dm^3 mol^{-1}.

26. Calculate ΔH, ΔS and ΔG for the vapourisation of a mole of liquid water at 363 K and 383 K. The enthalpy of vapourisation of water at 373 K is 40.62 kJ mol^{-1} and $C_{P,\,m}$ (H$_2$O, l) = 75.31 JK^{-1} mol^{-1} and

    $C_{P,\,m}$ (H$_2$O, g) = 37.06 JK^{-1} mol^{-1}.   **Ans.** $\Delta H_{363} = 41.1$ kJ mol^{-1}, $\Delta S_{363} = 107.62$ EU.

    $\Delta G_{363} = 1.1$ kJ mol^{-1}, $\Delta H_{383} = 40.14$ kJ mol^{-1},

    $\Delta S_{383} = 110.24$ EU, $\Delta G_{383} = 1.07$ kJ mol^{-1}.

27. 10 moles of water at 298 K are mixed with 10 moles of water at 328 K. Calculate (*a*) the final temperature of the system, (*b*) ΔS and (*c*) ΔG for the process. Given $S^0_{298,\,m}(H_2O,1) = 69.95\,EU$, $C_{P,\,m}(H_2O,1)$ $= 75.31\,JK^{-1}\,mol^{-1}$, $C_{P,m}$ value of water may be assumed to be independent of temperature in the range 298 K to 328 K. **Ans.** (*a*) 313 K, (*b*) $\Delta S = 1.57$ EU, (*c*) $\Delta G = -17.9$ J.

28. 1 dm^3 of an ideal gas at 300 K and 15 atm pressure is allowed to expand isothermally and reversibly to a volume of 10 m^3. Calculate W, ΔE, ΔH, ΔA, and ΔS for the process. How would these quantities change if the expansion were (*i*) irreversible against an external pressure of 2 atm and (*iii*) a free expansion?

    Ans. $-W = 3.497$ kJ, $\Delta E = \Delta H = 0$, $\Delta G = \Delta A = -3.497$ kJ, $\Delta S = 11.66$ EU;

    (*i*) $-W = 1.893$ kJ, $\Delta E = \Delta H = 0$, $\Delta G = \Delta A = -3.497$ kJ; $\Delta S = 11.66$ EU.

    (*ii*) $-W = \Delta E = \Delta H = 0$, $\Delta G = \Delta A = -3.497$ kJ, $\Delta S = 11.66$ EU.

29. 1 mole of an ideal gas ($C_{V,\,m} = 30\,JK^{-1}\,mol^{-1}$) initially at 300 K and 1 atm is heated at constant pressure until the final volume is doubled. Calculate (*i*) Q (*ii*) W (*iii*) ΔE, (*iv*) ΔH, (*v*) ΔG and (*vi*) ΔS for the process.

    Ans. (*i*) (*iv*) = 9.0 kJ mol^{-1}, (*ii*) 2.49 kJ mol^{-1}, (*iii*) 6.51 kJ mol^{-1}, (*v*) -48.5 kJ mol^{-1}, (*vi*) = 28.1 EU.

30. The enthalpy and free energy of formation of silver chloride from its elements under normal conditions are -126.78 kJ mol^{-1} and -110.04 kJ mol^{-1}, respectively at 291 K. What is the entropy change for the reaction? Calculate the change in free energy for a 10° rise of temperature, assuming the rate of change of ΔG with temperature, *i.e.*, $\left[\dfrac{d(\Delta G)}{dT}\right]_P$ to remain constant. **Ans.** $\Delta S = -57.52$ EU; 575.2 Jmol^{-1}.

CHAPTER

9

Chemical Equilibrium

9.1 INTRODUCTION

It is a well established fact that many reactions do not go to completion even if favourable conditions are maintained. Reactions proceed to some extent and then apparently stop often leaving considerable amounts of unreacted reactants. When such a stage is reached in the course of a reaction that no further reaction is apparent, it is said to have attained a state of equilibrium at that temperature and the observable properties of the system do not change with time. It is obvious that the reaction can proceed in either way and the composition of the system at equilibrium is fixed. At equilibrium the reaction proceeds in both directions at equal rates so that the rate of formation of the products is exactly equal to the rate of disappearance of the reactants. Under these conditions no perceptible transformation can be observed in the system and it appears that the reaction comes to rest. However, in reality, both the forward and the reverse reactions are occurring at equal rates all the time. The equilibrium is thus *dynamic* in nature.

At the equilibrium state, if there is a change in the physical state, the equilibrium is called *physical equilibrium*. If it involves a change in the chemical species, then the equilibrium is referred to as *chemical equilibrium*. In this chapter we shall discuss the matter relating to chemical equilibrium.

9.2 REVERSIBLE REACTIONS

Consider a reaction between gaseous hydrogen and iodine in a closed vessel at 723K. Hydrogen and iodine react to give hydrogen iodide

$$H_2(g) + I_2(g) \rightarrow 2HI(g)$$

On the other hand, pure hydrogen iodide when heated at the same temperature, it decomposes to give hydrogen and iodine

$$2HI(g) \rightarrow H_2(g) + I_2(g)$$

It follows that in a mixture of three gases, H_2, I_2 and HI, both the above reactions take place and neither of them will reach a state of completion. There are several other reactions of similar type. They are said to be reversible reactions under experimental conditions and are written by two half arrows pointing in opposite directions instead of a single arrow. These two half arrows indicate that the reaction proceeds in both the forward and the reverse directions, *i.e.,*

$$H_2(g) + I_2(g) \rightleftharpoons 2HI(g)$$

or $$2HI\ (g) \rightleftharpoons H_2\ (g) + I_2\ (g)$$

The extent of reversibility of a reaction depends on the nature of the reaction and the experimental conditions of temperature, pressure and the concentration of the substances.

It has been observed that all the reversible reactions reach a state of chemical equilibrium, *i.e.*, a state in which no further change in the composition of the reaction mixture takes place until and unless some external disturbance such as a change in temperature, pressure or the addition or removal of the substances involved in the reaction, is imposed.

9.3 THE LAW OF MASS ACTION

This law was the result of a series of studies made on reaction rates and states that *at constant temperature, the rate of a chemical reaction is proportional to the product of the active masses of the reacting substances.* The term active mass is a thermodynamic quantity and is defined as $a = fC$ where a is the active mass, f is activity coefficient and C is the molar concentration. For ordinary systems like gases at low pressures or dilute solutions which do not deviate appreciably from ideal behaviour, $f = 1$ and hence $a = C$, *i.e.,* the active mass may be replaced by molar concentration.

Mathematical Formulation of the Law of Chemical Equilibrium (Kinetic Approach): Consider a simple reversible reaction occurring in a homogeneous system at a given temperature. Let one mole of A react with one mole of B to produce one mole each of L and M as indicated by the reaction.

$$A + B \rightleftharpoons L + M$$

According to the law of mass action, the rate of the forward reaction will be proportional to the molar concentration of A and B, *i.e.,* rate of the forward reaction $\alpha[A]\ [B]$

$$= k_1\ [A]\ [B]$$

where k_1 is a proportionality constant and depends on temperature and nature of the reactants. The concentration of the reactants would diminish with the progress of the reaction and hence the rate would decrease with time.

When the reaction is reversible, rate of the reverse reaction would be proportional to the molar concentration of L and M. Hence, the rate of the reverse reaction $\alpha[L][M]$

$$= k_2\ [L][M]$$

where k_2 is a constant of proportionality.

In the equilibrium state the two rates in opposite directions should be equal, *i.e.,*

$$k_1\ [A][B] = k_2\ [L][M]$$

or $$\frac{[L][M]}{[A][B]} = \frac{k_1}{k_2} = K_C\ (\text{constant}) \qquad ...(9.1)$$

The constant K_C is called the *equilibrium constant* of the reaction and is defined as *the ratio of the products of the molar concentration of products to that of the reactants at equilibrium.*

In the foregoing treatment, the stoichiometric coefficients of reactants and products are unity. Let us now consider a more general reaction of the type

$$aA + bB + \cdots\cdots \rightleftharpoons lL + mM + \cdots\cdots$$

where a, b,... represent the stoichiometric coefficients of the reactants A, B,....... and l, m... are the stoichiometric coefficients of products L, M, ...*etc.*

On applying the law of mass action, the rate of such a reaction is proportional to the concentration of each species raised to a power equal to its stoichiometric coefficient in the reaction. It follows, therefore, that at equilibrium

$$k_1 [A]^a [B]^b \cdots = k_2 [L]^l [M]^m \cdots$$

or

$$\frac{[L]^l [M]^m \cdots}{[A]^a [B]^b \cdots} = \frac{k_1}{k_2} = K_C \qquad \qquad ...(9.2)$$

The value of K_C is independent of the molar concentration of the reactants and products but depends only on temperature. K_C is dimensionless, if there is no net change in the number of moles in a reaction.

Gaseous Reactions: In case of reactions involving ideal gases, it is sometimes more convenient to express the concentration of the gases in terms of their partial pressures at any given temperature.

If p_A, p_B, p_L and p_M etc., are the partial pressures of the gaseous species in the reaction considered previously, then the equilibrium constant K_P may be expressed as

$$K_P = \frac{p_L^l \, p_M^m \cdots}{p_A^a \, p_B^b \cdots} \qquad \qquad ...(9.3)$$

If the concentrations are expressed in terms of mole fractions, then the equilibrium constant K_x, for the reaction is given as

$$K_X = \frac{(X_L)^l (X_M)^m \cdots}{(X_A)^a (X_B)^b \cdots} \qquad \qquad ...(9.4)$$

9.4 RELATIONSHIP BETWEEN K_C, K_P AND K_X

For a gaseous reaction the equilibrium constant K_P is represented by equation (9.3). However, for such a reaction K_C may not be the same. It is, therefore, desirable to derive a relationship between these two constants at a given temperature. If the participants behave ideally, then the pressure of the ith component in the mixture is given by

$$p_i = \left(\frac{n_i}{V} \right) RT$$

where n_i is the number of moles of the gas occupying a volume V.

Since $\dfrac{n_i}{V} = C_i =$ the molar concentration, therefore,

$$p_i = C_i \, RT$$

Substituting the values of partial pressures of various participants in Eq. (9.3), we get

$$K_P = \frac{(C_L RT)^l (C_M RT)^m \cdots}{(C_A RT)^a (C_B RT)^b \cdots}$$

$$= \frac{(C_L)^l (C_M)^m \cdots}{(C_A)^a (C_B)^b \cdots} (RT)^{(l+m+\cdots)-(a+b+\cdots)}$$

$$= \frac{(C_L)^l (C_M)^m \cdots}{(C_A)^a (C_B)^b \cdots} (RT)^{\Delta v}$$ ...(9.5)

where $\Delta v = [(l + m + \cdots) - (a + b + \cdots)]$ is equal to the difference in the number of moles of products and reactants during the reaction. Furthermore, Δv may be positive, negative or zero.

Since $$K_C = \frac{(C_L)^l (C_M)^m \cdots}{(C_A)^a (C_B)^b \cdots}$$

therefore, Eq. (9.5) reduces to

$$K_P = K_C (RT)^{\Delta v}$$ ...(9.6)

Equation (9.6) represents the relationship between K_P and K_C. When Δv is positive, *i.e.*, the number of moles of reactants are less than those of the product, K_P is greater than K_C. When Δv is negative, *i.e.*, the number of moles of reactants are more than those of the products; K_P is less than K_C. When $\Delta v = 0$, *i.e.*, the number of moles of reactants and products are equal, Eq. (9.6) becomes $K_P = K_C$. The relation between K_P and K_X can be derived as follows.

Since the mole fraction of an ith component of a gaseous mixture is given by $X_i = p_i / P$ or

$$p_i = X_i P$$

where P is the total pressure of the gaseous mixture.

Substituting the values of the partial pressures in Eq. (9.3), we get

$$K_P = \frac{(X_L P)^l (X_M P)^m \cdots}{(X_A P)^a (X_B P)^b \cdots}$$

$$= \frac{(X_L)^l (X_M)^m \cdots}{(X_A)^a (X_B)^b \cdots} P^{(l+m+\cdots)-(a+b+\cdots)}$$

$$K_P = \frac{(X_L)^l (X_M)^m \cdots}{(X_A)^a (X_B)^b \cdots} P^{\Delta v}$$

$$= K_X P^{\Delta v}$$ ...(9.7)

Since K_P is independent of pressure, it is evident from Eq. (9.7) that K_X is a function of pressure except when $\Delta v = 0$ and is constant only with respect to changes in $X's$ at constant temperature and pressure. Equations (9.6) and (9.7) may be used for comparing K_C and K_X values

$$K_C (RT)^{\Delta v} = K_X (P)^{\Delta v}$$

$$K_C = K_X \left(\frac{P}{RT} \right)^{\Delta v}$$ ...(9.8)

$$= K_X\left(\frac{n}{V}\right)^{\Delta v} \qquad \qquad ...(9.9)$$

$$= K_X(C)^{\Delta v} \qquad \qquad ...(9.9(a))$$

The equilibrium constant K_P or K_C defined so far has units if $\Delta v \neq 0$. But in subsequent sections we will define a dimensionless equilibrium constant in all our discussions.

9.5 THERMODYNAMICS OF CHEMICAL REACTIONS

A general reaction of the type

$$aA + bB + \cdots \rightarrow lL + mM + \cdots$$

occurring in a closed system can be represented as

$$\Sigma_i \, v_i A_i = 0 \qquad \qquad ...(9.10)$$

where v_i represents the stoichiometric coefficients and A_i represents the chemical formulae of the participating substances. In Eq. (9.10), v_i are positive for products and negative for reactants.

If the Gibbs free energy decreases as the reaction advances, then the reaction proceeds spontaneously in the forward direction. The advance of the reaction and the decrease in Gibbs free energy continue until the free energy of the system reaches a minimum value. At this stage, the system attains a state of equilibrium. However, if the Gibbs free energy of the system increases with the advance of the reaction in the forward direction, then the reaction will go spontaneously with the decrease in the Gibbs free energy in the opposite direction; again the mixture will reach a minimum value of Gibbs free energy at equilibrium.

The change in Gibbs free energy of the reaction at constant temperature and pressure at any instant during the course of the reaction is given by

$$(dG)_{P,T} = \sum_i \mu_i dn_i \qquad \qquad ...(9.11)$$

When a reaction occurs, the change in the number of moles of various reactants and products are related through stoichiometric coefficients of the balanced chemical equation. If the system initially contains n_i^0 moles of i, then its number of moles (n_i) at any time during the course of the reaction is

$$n_i = n_i^0 + v_i \xi \qquad \qquad ...(9.12)$$

where ξ (pronounced as x_i) is the extent of reaction or the degree of advancement of the reaction and is expressed in moles.

Since n_i^0 is constant, therefore the change in n_i can be obtained by differentiating Eq. (9.12) as

$$dn_i = v_i d\xi \qquad \qquad ...(9.12a)$$

Combining equation 9.11 and 9.12 (a), we set

$$(dG)_{P,T} = \sum_i \mu_i \, v_i \, d\xi$$

or

$$\left(\frac{dG}{\partial \xi}\right)_{P,T} = \sum_i \mu_i \, v_i \qquad \qquad ...(9.13)$$

The quantity, $\left(\dfrac{dG}{\partial \xi}\right)_{P,\,T}$ is the rate of change of Gibbs free energy of the mixture with the advance-

ment ξ of the reaction. The term on the right hand side of the Eq. (9.13) is the free energy change $(\Delta G)_{P,\,T}$ of the reaction at constant temperature and pressure. Thus

$$(\Delta G)_{P,\,T} = \left(\frac{\partial G}{\partial \xi}\right)_{P,\,T} = \sum_i \mu_i \, \nu_i \qquad \qquad ...(9.14)$$

The decrease in the free energy of a reaction is defined as the chemical affinity, A_f

$$A_f = -(\Delta G)_{T,\,P} = -\left(\frac{\partial G}{\partial \xi}\right)_{P,\,T} \qquad \qquad ...(9.15)$$

If the derivative $\left(\dfrac{dG}{\partial \xi}\right)_{P,\,T}$ is negative, the free energy of the mixture decreases as the reaction

progresses in the direction indicated by the arrow, implying it to be spontaneous. On the other hand, if

$\left(\dfrac{dG}{\partial \xi}\right)_{P,\,T}$ is positive, the reaction would be nonspontaneous in the indicated direction. If $\left(\dfrac{dG}{\partial \xi}\right)_{P,\,T}$ is

zero, G has a minimum value and the reaction would be at equilibrium. Hence

$$\left(\frac{\partial G}{\partial \xi}\right)_{P,\,T} = (\Delta G)_{P,\,T} = \sum \nu_i \, \mu_i = 0 \qquad \qquad ...(9.16)$$

for a reaction at equilibrium. Variation of G with ξ in a homogeneous reaction is shown in Fig. (9.1).

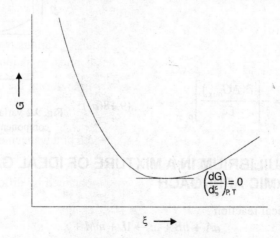

Fig. 9.1 Variation of G with ξ

The minimum in the curve shows the equilibrium state where $\left(\dfrac{dG}{\partial \xi}\right)_{P,\,T} = 0$ and G is minimum. Equation

(9.16) in a general expression which is applicable to any reversible chemical reaction under equilibrium conditions at constant temperature and pressure. The equation simply means that the sum of the chemical potentials of the products and reactants is equal to zero at equilibrium. The Gibbs free energy at any stage is given by

$$G = \sum n_i \mu_i$$

Adding and subtracting μ_i^0 on the right hand side of the above equation yields

$$G = \sum_i n_i \left(\mu_i^0 + \mu_i - \mu_i^0 \right)$$

$$= \sum_i n_i \mu_i^0 + \sum_i n_i \left(\mu_i - \mu_i^0 \right) \qquad ...(9.17)$$

The first term on the right side of Eq. (9.17) is the total free energy of the pure components (G_{pure}) and the second term is the Gibbs free energy of mixing (ΔG_{mix}). Therefore, we have

$$G = G_{\text{pure}} + \Delta G_{\text{mix}} \qquad ...(9.18)$$

Since ΔG_{mix} is negative, it follows that the total Gibbs free energy is always less than the free energy of the pure components. ΔG_{mix} contributes greatly in making the free energy of the system more negative.

Dependence of G, G_{pure} and ΔG_{mix} on ξ is shown in Fig. 9.2. If we differentiate G in Eq. (9.18) with respect to ξ at constant T and P, we get

$$\left(\frac{\partial G}{\partial \xi} \right)_{P,T} = \left(\frac{\partial G_{\text{pure}}}{\partial \xi} \right)_{P,T} + \left[\frac{\partial (\Delta G_{\text{mix}})}{\partial \xi} \right]_{P,T}$$

At equilibrium

$$\left(\frac{\partial G}{\partial \xi} \right)_{P,T} = 0$$

so

$$\left(\frac{\partial G_{\text{pure}}}{\partial \xi} \right)_{P,T} = -\left[\frac{\partial (\Delta G_{\text{mix}})}{\partial \xi} \right]_{P,T} \qquad ...(9.18(a))$$

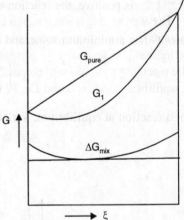

Fig. 9.2 Variation of G with ξ for the pure component and equilibrium mixture

9.6 CHEMICAL EQUILIBRIUM IN A MIXTURE OF IDEAL GASES THERMODYNAMIC APPROACH

Consider a general chemical reaction

$$aA + bB + ... \rightarrow lL + mM + ...$$

involving ideal gases. The chemical potential of each species in the mixture is given by $\mu_i = \mu_i^0 + RT \ln$

$\dfrac{p_i}{p^0}$. The free energy change (ΔG) at constant temperature and pressure is given by

$$(\Delta G)_{P,T} = \left(\frac{\partial G}{\partial \xi}\right)_{P,T} = (l\mu_L + m\mu_M + ...) - (a\mu_A + b\mu_B + ...) \qquad ...(9.19)$$

Substituting the value of chemical potentials of various species in Eq. (9.19), we get

$$(\Delta G)_{P,T} = (l\mu_L^0 + m\mu_m^0 + ...) - (a\mu_A^0 + b\mu_B^0 + ...) + RT \ln \frac{\left(p_L/p^0\right)^l \left(p_m/p^0\right)^m ...}{\left(p_A/p^0\right)^a \left(p_B/p^0\right)^b ...}$$

$$= (\Delta G^0) + RT \ln Q_P \qquad ...(9.20)$$

where $\Delta G^0 = (l\mu_L^0 + m\mu_M^0 + \cdots) - (a\mu_A^0 + b\mu_B^0 + \cdots)$ is the standard free energy of the reaction when all the reactants and products are in the standard state, *i.e.*, at 1 atm and specified temperature. The argument of logarithm (Q_p) is called proper quotient of pressure and is given by

$$Q_P = \frac{\left(p_L/p^0\right)^l \left(p_m/p^0\right)^m ...}{\left(p_A/p^0\right)^a \left(p_B/p^0\right)^b ...} \qquad ...(9.21)$$

The sign of ΔG is determined by the sign and magnitude of $\ln Q_p$ and ΔG^0. If one starts with all reactants and very little products $\ln Q_p$ will be negative hence ΔG will be negative and infinitely large and increase the tendency for products to form. On the other hand, if we have mainly products and very little reactants, then ΔG will be positive and infinitely large, formation of reactants will be spontaneous. At equilibrium, $\Delta G = 0$ and Eq. (9.20) becomes

$$\Delta G^0 + RT \left[\ln \frac{\left(p_L/p^0\right)^l \left(p_m/p^0\right)^m ...}{\left(p_A/p^0\right)^a \left(p_B/p^0\right)^b ...} \right]_{eq} = 0$$

$$\frac{\Delta G^0}{RT} = - \left[\ln \frac{\left(p_L/p^0\right)^l \left(p_m/p^0\right)^m ...}{\left(p_A/p^0\right)^a \left(p_B/p^0\right)^b ...} \right]_{eq}$$

Therefore

$$e^{-\frac{\Delta G^0}{RT}} = \left[\frac{\left(p_L/p^0\right)^l \left(p_m/p^0\right)^m ...}{\left(p_A/p^0\right)^a \left(p_B/p^0\right)^b ...} \right]_{eq} = K_P \qquad ...(9.22)$$

where the subscript 'eq' indicates the equilibrium partial pressures of reactants and products. Since $\frac{\Delta G^0}{RT}$ is a function of temperature only hence the right hand side of the above equation is constant and is called the equilibrium constant for the reaction and depends on temperature only.

$$\Delta G^0 = -RT \ln K_p \qquad \qquad ...(9.23)$$

The equilibrium constant K_p defined in this way is a pure number because the standard pressure (p^0) is taken at 1 atm (101.325 kPa) and if the partial pressures of various species are also expressed in atmospheres, then $\left(p_i/p^0\right)$ will be a dimensionless quantity. The numerical value of K_p will depend on the choice of p^0. The equilibrium constant may also be expressed in terms of molar concentrations of the species. In order to define a dimensionless equilibrium constant, we introduce the standard concentration C^0 (usually expressed in mol dm^{-3} or mol L^{-1}) for each of the species. Thus

$$K_C = \frac{\left(C_L/C^0\right)^l \left(C_M/C^0\right)^m \cdots}{\left(C_A/C^0\right)^a \left(C_B/C^0\right)^b \cdots} \qquad \qquad ...(9.24)$$

Since $p_i/p^0 = \dfrac{C_i RT}{p^0}$, dividing and multiplying by standard concentration C^0, we get

$$\frac{p_i}{p^0} = \frac{C_i}{C^0}\left(\frac{C_0 RT}{p^0}\right)$$

The relation between K_p and K_C is obtained by substituting the value of (p_i/p^0) in Eq. (9.22). So we have

$$K_p = \frac{\left(\dfrac{p_L}{p^0}\right)^l \left(\dfrac{p_M}{p^0}\right)^m \cdots}{\left(\dfrac{p_A}{p^0}\right)^a \left(\dfrac{p_B}{p^0}\right)^b \cdots} = \frac{\left(\dfrac{C_L}{C^0}\dfrac{C^0 RT}{p^0}\right)^l \left(\dfrac{C_M}{C^0}\dfrac{C^0 RT}{p^0}\right)^m \cdots}{\left(\dfrac{C_A}{C^0}\dfrac{C^0 RT}{p^0}\right)^a \left(\dfrac{C_B}{C^0}\dfrac{C^0 RT}{p^0}\right)^b \cdots} = \frac{\left(\dfrac{C_L}{C^0}\right)^l \left(\dfrac{C_M}{C^0}\right)^m \cdots}{\left(\dfrac{C_A}{C^0}\right)^a \left(\dfrac{C_B}{C^0}\right)^b \cdots}\left(\dfrac{C^0 RT}{p^0}\right)^{(l+m+\cdots)-(a+b+\cdots)}$$

or
$$= K_C \left(\frac{C^0 RT}{p^0}\right)^{\Delta\nu}$$

where $\Delta\nu = (l + m + \cdots) - (a + b + \cdots)$ $\qquad \qquad ...(9.25)$

Like K_p, K_C is also a function of temperature only. In Eq. (9.25), if $C^0 = 1$ mol $dm^{-3} = 10^3$ mol m^{-3} and $p^0 = 101.325$ kPa, then $\dfrac{C^0 RT}{p^0}$ at 298.15 K is 24.46. One can also calculate ΔG^0 from the value of K_C using the relation

$$\Delta G^\circ = -RT \ln K_c \qquad \qquad ...(9.26)$$

But the value of ΔG^0 calculated from the above equation would be different from that obtained by using Eq. (9.23) and have different interpretation.

The relation between K_p and K_X is obtained by using the relation

$$p_i/p^0 = x_i\left(p/p^0\right)$$

where p is the total pressure of the system.

$$K_P = \frac{X_L^l \, X_M^m \cdots}{X_A^a \, X_B^b \cdots} \left(p/p^0\right)^{\Delta \nu}$$

$$= K_X \left(p/p^0\right)^{\Delta \nu} \qquad \qquad \text{...(9.27)}$$

Since K_P is independent of pressure, K_X will depend on pressure unless $\Delta \nu$ is zero.

From Eqs. (9.25) and (9.27), we see that

$$K_P = K_C \left(\frac{C^0 RT}{p^0}\right)^{\Delta \nu} = K_X \left(p/p^0\right)^{\Delta \nu} \qquad \qquad \text{...(9.28)}$$

If we remember that $C^0 = 1$ mol dm^{-3} and $p^0 = 1$ atm, then the above relationships can be expressed as

$$K_p = K_C \left(RT\right)^{\Delta \nu} = K_X (p)^{\Delta \nu}$$

which are identical with those derived in section (9.4) but K_P and K_C are now taken as unitless and their values will depend on the choice of standard pressure and standard concentration respectively.

Problem 9.1: At 298 K and 1 atm the equilibrium constant (K_p) for the reaction $2H_2(g) + O_2(g) = 2H_2O(g)$ is 1.122×10^{40}. Calculate at 298 K (*i*) ΔG° and (*ii*) ΔG for the reaction $2H_2(g, 1 \text{ atm}) + O_2 (g, 2 \text{ atm}) = 2H_2O (g, 10 \text{ atm})$.

Solution: (*i*) Since the standard free energy change is given by the relation $\Delta G^\circ = -RT \ln K_p$
Hence $\qquad \Delta G^\circ = -(8.314 \, JK^{-1} \text{ mol}^{-1})(298 \text{ K})(2.303 \log 1.122 \times 10^{40})$
$\qquad \qquad \quad = -228.6 \, kJ \text{ mol}^{-1}$

(*ii*) In this case

$$\Delta G = \Delta G^0 + RT \ln \frac{\left(p_{H_2O}/p^0\right)^2}{\left(p_{O_2}/p^0\right)\left(p_{H_2}/p^0\right)^2}$$

As p°, the standard pressure, is 1 atm so

$$\Delta G = \Delta G^0 + RT \ln \frac{(10)^2}{(1)^2 (2)}$$

$$= -228.6 \, kJ \text{ mol}^{-1} + (8.314)(298)(2.303) \log 50$$

$$= -228.60 \, kJ \text{ mol}^{-1} + 9.7 \, kJ \text{ mol}^{-1}$$

$$= -218.9 \, kJ \text{ mol}^{-1}$$

Problem 9.2: At a total pressure of 2 atmospheres and 673 K the equilibrium constant for the reaction

$$N_2(g) + 3H_2 (g) \rightleftharpoons 2NH_3 (g)$$

$K_p = 1.64 \times 10^{-4}$. Calculate K_C and K_X.

Solution: Since $K_P = K_C \left(\dfrac{C^0 RT}{p^0} \right)^{\Delta v}$

Here

$$\Delta v = 2 - 4 = -2$$

$$R = 0.0821 \text{ dm}^3 \text{ atm K}^{-1} \text{ mol}^{-1}$$

$$T = 673 \text{ K}$$

$$C^0 = 1 \text{ mol dm}^{-3} \text{ and}$$

$$P^0 = 1 \text{ atm, then}$$

$$K_C = \frac{K_P}{(RT)^{\Delta v}}$$

$$= \frac{1.64 \times 10^{-4}}{(0.0821 \times 673)^{-2}}$$

$$= 0.50$$

Further

$$K_P = K_X (P)^{\Delta v} \text{ or}$$

$$K_X = \frac{K_P}{(P)^{\Delta v}}$$

$$= \frac{1.64 \times 10^{-4}}{(2)^{-2}}$$

$$= 1.64 \times 10^{-4} \times 4$$

$$= 6.56 \times 10^{-4}$$

9.7 EQUILIBRIUM CONSTANT AND THE FORM OF EQUATION

The numerical value of the equilibrium constant depends on the way the chemical equation is written.

(i) Thus the reaction, $H_2(g) + I_2(g) \rightleftharpoons 2HI(g)$ can also be written as $\dfrac{1}{2} H_2(g) + \dfrac{1}{2} I_2(g) \rightleftharpoons HI(g)$.

The corresponding expressions for the equilibrium constants are given as

$$K_P = \frac{\left(p_{HI}/p^0 \right)^2}{\left(p_{H_2}/p^0 \right)\left(p_{I_2}/p^0 \right)} \text{ and } K_p' = \frac{\left(p_{HI}/p^0 \right)}{\left(p_{H_2}/p^0 \right)^{1/2} \left(p_{I_2}/p^0 \right)^{1/2}}$$

So

$$K_P = \left(K_P' \right)^2 \qquad \qquad ...(9.29)$$

(ii) If a reaction is reversed, then the equilibrium constant for the reversed reaction will be equal to the reciprocal of the equilibrium constant for the original reaction. Thus for the reaction

$$2HI(g) \rightleftharpoons H_2(g) + I_2(g)$$

$$K_P'' = \frac{\left(p_{H_2}/p^0\right)\left(p_{I_2}/p^0\right)}{\left(p_{HI}/p^0\right)^2} = \frac{1}{\cdot K_P} \qquad \qquad ...(9.29(a))$$

(*iii*) If two chemical equations are added to get a new chemical equation, then the equilibrium constant for the new reaction is obtained by multiplying the equilibrium constants of the original reactions. For example, the reaction

$$2NO(g) + 2H_2(g) \rightleftharpoons N_2(g) + 2H_2O(g)$$

can be obtained from the reactions

$$2NO(g) \rightleftharpoons N_2(g) + O_2(g)$$

$$2H_2(g) + O_2(g) \rightleftharpoons 2H_2O(g)$$

The equilibrium constants for these respective reactions are

$$K_P = \frac{\left(p_{N_2}/p^0\right)\left(p_{H_2O}/p^0\right)^2}{\left(p_{NO}/p^0\right)^2\left(p_{H_2}/p^0\right)^2}, \quad K_P' = \frac{\left(p_{N_2}/p^0\right)\left(p_{O_2}/p^0\right)}{\left(p_{NO}/p^0\right)^2}$$

and

$$K_P'' = \frac{\left(p_{H_2O}/p^0\right)^2}{\left(p_{H_2}/p^0\right)^2\left(p_{O_2}/p^0\right)}$$

Thus

$$K_P = K_P' \, K_P''$$

Problem 9.3: The equilibrium constant K_P for the reaction

$$N_2O_4(g) \rightleftharpoons 2NO_2(g)$$

at 1 atm pressure and 298 K is 0.141. Calculate the equilibrium constant for the following reactions:

(*i*) $\dfrac{1}{2} N_2O_4(g) \rightleftharpoons NO_2(g)$

(*ii*) $2NO_2(g) \rightleftharpoons N_2O_4(g)$

(*iii*) $NO_2(g) \rightleftharpoons \dfrac{1}{2} N_2O_4(g)$

Solution: For the reaction

$$N_2O_4(g) \rightleftharpoons 2NO_2(g)$$

$$K_P = \frac{\left(p_{NO_2}/p^0\right)^2}{\left(p_{N_2O_4}/p^0\right)} = 0.141$$

(*i*) For the reaction $$\frac{1}{2} N_2O_4 (g) \rightleftharpoons NO_2(g)$$

$$K_P' = \frac{\left(p_{NO_2}/p^0\right)}{\left(p_{N_2O_4}/p^0\right)^{1/2}} = (K_P)^{1/2} = (0.141)^{1/2} = 3.76 \times 10^{-2}$$

(*ii*) For the reaction $$2NO_2(g) \rightleftharpoons N_2O_4(g)$$

$$K_P'' = \frac{\left(p_{N_2O_4}/p^0\right)}{\left(p_{NO_2}/p^0\right)^2} = \frac{1}{K_P} = \frac{1}{0.141} = 7.092$$

(*iii*) For the reaction $$NO_2(g) \rightleftharpoons \frac{1}{2} N_2O_4(g)$$

$$K_P''' = \frac{\left(p_{N_2O_4}/p^0\right)^{1/2}}{\left(p_{NO_2}/p^0\right)} = \left(K_p''\right)^{1/2} = (7.092)^{1/2} = 2.663$$

9.8 THE LECHATELIER'S PRINCIPLE

This principle elucidates the behaviour of a system at equilibrium, if it is subjected to changes in parameters like pressure, temperature or concentration. According to this principle *"if a system at equilibrium is disturbed by changing the variables such as pressure, temperature or concentration then the system will tend to adjust itself so as to minimise the effect of that change as far as possible".*

(*i*) **Effect of Change of Pressure:** The effect of change of pressure is relatively small on equilibrium state of reactions which involve solids or liquids. However, in reactions involving gases, a small change in pressure has a significant effect on the state of equilibrium. Consider a gaseous reaction

$$N_2(g) + 3H_2(g) \rightleftharpoons 2NH_3(g)$$

The forward reaction is favoured by a decrease in the volume of the reaction mixture. In this case there is a decrease in volume from four to two volumes. If the pressure is increased on the system, the

volume will decrease (since $P \propto \dfrac{1}{V}$) and therefore, according to the LeChatelier's principle, the reac-

tion will move in that direction which favours the decrease in volume. In other words, the formation of ammonia will be favoured at high pressures. It is for this reason that in the Haber's process for the synthesis of ammonia, a high pressure is maintained.

Now consider the dissociation of gaseous phosphorous pentachloride

$$PCl_5(g) \rightleftharpoons PCl_3 (g) + Cl_2(g)$$

This reaction is accompanied by an increase in volume of the reaction. According to the LeChatelier's principle, high pressure will favour the reverse reaction, *i.e.*, the dissociation of PCl_5 will be suppressed at high pressures. Such reactions should, therefore, be studied at low pressures.

(*ii*) **Effect of Change of Concentration:** If the concentration of one of the components at equilibrium is increased, then according to this principle, the equilibrium will shift in such a way so as to decrease the concentration of that substance. On the other hand, a decrease in the concentration of the substance would cause the production of more of that substance.

(*iii*) **Effect of Change of Temperature:** A change in temperature results in a change in the equilibrium state of the reaction. In the reaction

$$N_2(g) + 3H_2(g) \rightleftharpoons 2NH_3(g) + \text{Heat}$$

a large amount of heat is evolved, *i.e.*, the reaction is exothermic. On increasing the temperature, the equilibrium shifts in the reverse direction and thus favours the dissociation of ammonia. In order to obtain high yield of ammonia the reaction should be carried out at low temperatures. However, at these temperatures the rate of formation of ammonia is exceedingly low and therefore, optimum conditions of temperature and pressure are maintained for the synthesis of ammonia. Similarly, consider the formation of gaseous nitric oxide.

$$N_2(g) + O_2(g) \rightleftharpoons 2NO(g) - \text{Heat}$$

It is an endothermic reaction, the forward reaction will be favoured at high temperature. Thus in general, one can say that the exothermic reactions should be carried out at low temperatures and the endothermic reactions at high temperatures to obtain the maximum yield of the products.

9.9 THERMODYNAMIC TREATMENT OF LE CHATELIER'S PRINCIPLE

In the previous section we have given a qualitative aspect of the Le Chatelier's principle. Thermodynamic considerations may be employed to show how a change in temperature or pressure affects the equilibrium value of advancement ξ_e of a reaction. The Gibbs free energy change (ΔG) of a reaction depends on temperature, pressure and the extent of reaction (ξ), *i.e.*,

$$\Delta G = f(P, T, \xi)$$

The total differential can be written as

$$d(\Delta G) = \left[\frac{\partial(\Delta G)}{\partial P}\right]_{T,\xi} dP + \left[\frac{\partial(\Delta G)}{\partial T}\right]_{P,\xi} dT + \left(\frac{\partial(\Delta G)}{\partial \xi}\right)_{P,T} d\xi \qquad ...(9.30)$$

But
$$\Delta G = \left(\frac{\partial G}{\partial \xi}\right)_{P,T}; \quad \left[\frac{\partial(\Delta G)}{\partial P}\right]_{T,\xi} = \Delta V \text{ and } \left[\frac{\partial(\Delta G)}{\partial T}\right]_{P,\xi} = -\Delta S$$

So
$$d(\Delta G) = d\left(\frac{\partial G}{\partial \xi}\right)_{P,T} = \Delta V\, dP - \Delta S\, dT + G''$$

where
$$G'' = \left[\frac{\partial(\Delta G)}{\partial \xi}\right]_{P,T} = \frac{\partial^2 G}{\partial \xi^2}. \qquad ...(9.31)$$

If we consider the variations in P, T and ξ in such a way that the reaction is still at equilibrium, then

$\frac{\partial G}{\partial \xi} = 0$ and hence $d(\Delta G) = 0$. So

$$\Delta V(dP)_{eq} - \Delta S(dT)_{eq} + G_e''(d\xi)_{eq} = 0 \qquad ...(9.32)$$

In equation (9.32) G_e'' is the equilibrium value of G''. Since G is minimum at equilibrium; therefore G_e'' must be positive.

At constant pressure, $dP = 0$ and Eq. (9.32) reduces to

$$\left(\frac{\partial \xi_e}{\partial T}\right)_P = \frac{\Delta H}{TG_e''} \qquad \left(\because \Delta S = \frac{\Delta H}{T}\right) \qquad ...(9.33)$$

while at constant temperature, $dT = 0$, Eq. (9.32) gives

$$\left(\frac{\partial \xi_e}{\partial T}\right)_T = -\frac{\Delta V}{G_e''} \qquad ...(9.34)$$

Equations (9.33) and (9.34) describe the dependence of the advancement of the reaction at equilibrium on temperature and pressure respectively. They are the quantitative statements for the Le Chatelier principle. Since G_e'' is positive, the sign of $\left(\frac{\partial \xi_e}{\partial T}\right)_P$ in Eq. (9.33) depends on the sign of ΔH. If ΔH is positive (endothermic reaction), then $\left(\frac{\partial \xi_e}{\partial T}\right)_P$ is positive, so increase in temperature increases the advancement at equilibrium. For exothermic reaction, ΔH is negative and thus $\left(\frac{\partial \xi_e}{dT}\right)_P$ is negative; increase in temperature decreases the advancement at equilibrium.

Similarly the sign of $\left(\frac{d\xi_e}{dT}\right)_T$ depends on the sign of ΔV. If ΔV is negative, the reaction proceeds with a decrease in volume, $\left(\frac{d\xi_e}{dP}\right)_T$ is positive. Increase in pressure increases equilibrium advancement. Conversely if ΔV is positive $\left(\frac{d\xi_e}{dP}\right)_T$ is negative, increase of pressure decreases the equilibrium advancement.

9.10 TYPES OF EQUILIBRIA AND APPLICATION OF THE LAW OF CHEMICAL EQUILIBRIUM TO THE CALCULATIONS OF EQUILIBRIUM CONSTANT

There are two types of chemical equilibria, viz., (i) homogeneous equilibria, in which all the reactants and products are in the same phase and (ii) heterogeneous equilibria, where the reactants and the products are present in two or more phases. Let us consider some examples involving these equilibria.

(i) Homogeneous Reactions in Gaseous Systems

The gaseous reactions are broadly classified into two categories:

Type I: Such types of gaseous reactions which involve no change in the number of moles, *i.e.*, the total number of reactant and product molecules are equal, $\Delta v = 0$. Some examples are

$$H_2(g) + I_2(g) \rightleftharpoons 2HI(g)$$

$$N_2(g) + O_2(g) \rightleftharpoons 2NO(g)$$

$$H_2(g) + CO_2(g) \rightleftharpoons H_2O(g) + CO(g)$$

The hydrogen iodine equilibrium: Let a moles of hydrogen and b moles of iodine be heated in a vessel of volume V and let $2x$ be the moles of hydroiodic acid formed at equilibrium

$$H_2(g) + I_2(g) \rightleftharpoons 2HI(g)$$

$\dfrac{a}{V}$	$\dfrac{b}{V}$	0	Initial concentrations
$\dfrac{a-x}{V}$	$\dfrac{b-x}{V}$	$\dfrac{2x}{V}$	Equilibrium concentrations

If the standard concentration $C^0 = 1$ mol dm^{-3}, then the equilibrium constant for the reaction is given as

$$K_C = \frac{C_{HI}^2}{C_{H_2} \times C_{I_2}}$$

Substituting the values of the various concentration terms in the above equation, we get

$$K_C = \frac{\left(\dfrac{2x}{V}\right)^2}{\left(\dfrac{a-x}{V}\right)\left(\dfrac{b-x}{V}\right)}$$

$$= \frac{4x^2}{(a-x)(b-x)} \qquad \qquad ...(i)$$

It should be noted that the volume V does not appear in the above equation. This is true of all reactions in which the number of moles of reactants and products are equal, *i.e.*, $\Delta v = 0$. Thus, the change in pressure or volume has no effect on the equilibrium constant.

The equilibrium constant can be expressed in terms of partial pressures of the reactants and products.

$$H_2 + I_2 \rightleftharpoons 2\,HI$$

a	b	0	Initial moles
$a - x$	$b - x$	$2x$	Moles at equilibrium

Total number of moles at equilibrium = $a - x + b - x + 2x = a + b$. If P is the total equilibrium pressure of the system, then partial pressure of H_2, $\left(p_{H_2}\right) = \dfrac{\text{number of moles of } H_2}{\text{total number of moles}} \times P$

$$= \frac{a-x}{a+b}P$$

partial pressure of I_2, $\left(p_{I_2}\right)$ $\qquad = \dfrac{b-x}{a+b}P$

and the partial pressure of HI, $\left(p_{HI}\right)$ $\qquad = \dfrac{2x}{a+b}P$

Hence, $\qquad\qquad\qquad K_P = \dfrac{\left(p_{HI}/p^0\right)^2}{\left(p_{H_2}/p^0\right)\left(p_{I_2}/p^0\right)}$

If $p^0 = 1$ atm, then $\qquad\qquad K_P = \dfrac{\left(p_{HI}\right)^2}{\left(p_{H_2}\right)\left(p_{I_2}\right)}$

$$= \frac{\left(\dfrac{2x}{a+b}P\right)^2}{\left(\dfrac{a-x}{a+b}P\right)\left(\dfrac{b-x}{a+b}P\right)}$$

$$= \frac{4x^2}{(a-x)(b-x)} \qquad\qquad\qquad\qquad ...(ii)$$

Since Eq. (i) and (ii) are identical, hence

$$K_P = K_C$$

Determination of equilibrium constant requires the equilibrium concentrations or partial pressures of the reactants and the products. The equilibrium concentrations are determined without affecting the equilibrium state. Measurements of physical quantities like density, refractive index, light absorption, electrical conductivity etc., may be employed for evaluating the equilibrium concentrations. In these cases the equilibrium state is not affected. Chemical methods, when employed for the analysis of the reaction mixture should ensure that the reaction is completely stopped at equilibrium. This is done by sudden chilling of the reaction mixture to a temperature where reaction rate is negligible.

Problem 9.4: A mixture of hydrogen and iodine in the mole ratio of 1 : 2 is heated at 730 K in a 1dm^3 vessel until equilibrium is attained. Assuming the equilibrium constant for the reaction: H_2 (g) + I_2 (g) $\rightleftharpoons$ 2HI (g) to be 50 at 730 K, calculate the moles of HI formed at equilibrium.

Solution: Let the number of moles of H_2 be 1 and that of I_2 be 2. The equilibrium constant for the reaction is given by

$$K_C = \frac{\left(C_{HI}/C^0\right)^2}{\left(C_{H_2}/C^0\right)\left(C_{I_2}/C^0\right)} = \frac{C_{HI}^2}{C_{H_2} C_{I_2}} \qquad \left(\because \ C^0 = 1 \, \text{mol dm}^{-3}\right)$$

If $2x$ is the number of moles of HI formed at equilibrium, then

$$C_{H_2} = (1 - x), \ C_{I_2} = (2 - x) \qquad \qquad \left(\because V = 1 \, \text{dm}^3\right)$$

Hence

$$K_C = \frac{(2x)^2}{(1 - x)(2 - x)} = \frac{4x^2}{2 - 3x + x^2} = 50$$

Solving for x we get

$$x = 0.913 \text{ or } 2.33.$$

Since x can not be more than 2, hence $x = 0.913$. Therefore moles of HI formed at equilibrium are 1.826.

Water gas equilibrium: This reaction is also of type I, *i.e.*, $\Delta v = 0$. Let a moles of hydrogen and b moles of carbon dioxide react to give x moles each of water and carbon monoxide at equilibrium.

$$H_2 (g) + CO_2 (g) \rightleftharpoons H_2O(g) + CO(g)$$

Initial moles	a	b	0	0
Moles at equilibrium	$a - x$	$b - x$	x	x

Let V be the volume of the vessel in which the reaction takes place. Then the concentration of various species at equilibrium are

$$C_{H_2} = \frac{a - x}{V}; \ C_{CO_2} = \frac{b - x}{V}$$

$$C_{H_2O} = C_{CO} = \frac{x}{V}$$

The equilibrium constant for this reaction is given by

$$K_C = \frac{C_{H_2O} C_{CO}}{C_{H_2} C_{CO_2}} \qquad \left(\because \ C^0 = 1 \, \text{mol dm}^{-3}\right)$$

$$= \frac{\left(\dfrac{x}{V}\right)\left(\dfrac{x}{V}\right)}{\left(\dfrac{a - x}{V}\right)\left(\dfrac{b - x}{V}\right)}$$

$$= \frac{x^2}{(a - x)(b - x)}$$

Again, the equilibrium constant K_C, is independent of pressure or volume.

The equilibrium constant in terms of partial pressures can be calculated as follows:

The total number of moles at equilibrium $= a - x + b - x + x + x = a + b$. If P is the total equilibrium pressure, then the partial pressures of various species are given as

$$p_{CO_2} = \frac{a - x}{a + b} P \; ; \quad p_{H_2} = \frac{b - x}{a + b} P$$

$$p_{CO} = p_{H_2O} = \frac{x}{a + b} P$$

The equilibrium constant K_P is written as

$$K_P = \frac{p_{CO} p_{H_2O}}{p_{CO_2} p_{H_2}} \quad \left(\text{If } p^0 = 1 \text{ atm}\right)$$

$$= \frac{\left(\dfrac{x}{a + b} P\right)\left(\dfrac{x}{a + b} P\right)}{\left(\dfrac{a - x}{a + b} P\right)\left(\dfrac{b - x}{a + b} P\right)}$$

$$= \frac{x^2}{(a - x)(b - x)}$$

This shows that $K_P = K_C$.

Characteristics of gaseous reactions of type I

(*i*) K_P and K_C are equal.

(*ii*) *Effect of addition of a reaction product to the equilibrium mixture:* The addition of a reaction product to the equilibrium mixture disturbs the equilibrium state and the reverse reaction predominates which decreases the concentration of the other reaction products and increases the concentration of the reactants.

(*iii*) *Effect of addition of an inert gas:* In reactions where $K_P = K_C$, the addition of an inert gas at constant pressure or at constant volume will not affect the equilibrium state of the reaction.

Type II: Gaseous reactions of such types are those in which the number of moles of reactants differ from the number of moles of products, *i.e.*, $\Delta v \neq 0$.

Some examples are

$$N_2O_4(g) \rightleftharpoons 2NO_2(g)$$

$$PCl_5(g) \rightleftharpoons PCl_3(g) + Cl_2(g)$$

$$N_2(g) + 3H_2(g) \rightleftharpoons 2NH_3(g)$$

$$2SO_2(g) + O_2(g) \rightleftharpoons 2SO_3(g)$$

For all these reactions $K_P \neq K_C$

(*a*) **Dissociation of Nitrogen tetroxide:** Nitrogen tetroxide dissociates according to the reaction

$$N_2O_4(g) \rightleftharpoons 2NO_2(g)$$

If we start with 1 mole of the gas and assume α to be the degree of dissociation, then the number of moles of NO_2 and N_2O_4 are 2α and $1 - \alpha$ respectively. The total number of moles will be $1 + \alpha$. The mole fractions and partial pressure are given as

$$X_{N_2O_4} = \frac{1-\alpha}{1+\alpha}, \quad X_{NO_2} = \frac{2\alpha}{1+\alpha}$$

and

$$P_{N_2O_4} = \frac{1-\alpha}{1+\alpha} P \text{ and } P_{NO_2} = \frac{2\alpha}{1+\alpha} \cdot P$$

where P is the total pressure of the system. Hence, the equilibrium constant K_p is given by

$$K_P = \frac{\left(p_{NO_2}/p^0\right)^2}{\left(p_{N_2O_4}/p^0\right)}$$

If p° is taken as 1 atm, then

$$K_P = \frac{p_{NO_2}^2}{p_{N_2O_4}} = \frac{\left(\dfrac{2\alpha}{1+\alpha} P\right)^2}{\left(\dfrac{1-\alpha}{1+\alpha} P\right)} = \frac{4\alpha^2}{1-\alpha^2} P \quad \text{...(9.35)}$$

From which it can be shown that

$$\alpha = \left(\frac{K_p}{K_p + 4P}\right)^{1/2} \qquad \text{...(9.36)}$$

It is clear that as $P \to 0$, $\alpha \to 1$, while as $P \to \infty$, $\alpha \to 0$. This is in accordance with the Le Chatelier principle.

At moderately high pressure, $K_p \ll 4P$ and $\alpha = \frac{1}{2} K_p^{1/2} P^{-\frac{1}{2}}$. The degree of dissociation can be calculated from the determination of the density of partially dissociated gas. As the gas dissociates more molecules are produced and the density of the gas mixture changes. Since temperature and total pressure are constant, the volume of the system increases with increase in the number moles of the gas. For ideal behaviour, it follows that the density of mixture is inversely proportional to the number of moles of the gas mixture. The ratio of the density (ρ_0) of the undissociated gas to the density (ρ_1) of the partially dissociated gas is given by the expression

$$\frac{\rho_0}{\rho_1} = 1 + \alpha$$

from which

$$\alpha = \frac{\rho_0 - \rho_1}{\rho_0}$$

Since molar mass is proportional to the density of the gas, so the above expression for α can be written as

$$\alpha = \frac{M_0 - M_1}{M_0} \qquad \qquad ...(9.37)$$

olar mass before dissociation and M_1 is the average molar mass of the gaseous mixture.

(b) **Dissociation of PCl_5 :** Consider the reaction

$$PCl_5(g) \rightleftharpoons PCl_3(g) + Cl_2(g)$$

Let us start with a moles of PCl_5 and let α be the degree of dissociation at equilibrium. If V is the volume of the vessel in which the reaction takes place, then the concentration of the various species at equilibrium are

$$C_{PCl_5} = \frac{a(1-\alpha)}{V}$$

$$C_{PCl_3} = C_{Cl_2} = \frac{a\alpha}{V}$$

If the standard concentration is 1 mol dm^{-3}, then the equilibrium constant (K_C) of the reaction is given by

$$K_C = \frac{C_{PCl_3} C_{Cl_2}}{C_{PCl_5}}$$

$$= \frac{\left(\dfrac{a\alpha}{V}\right)\left(\dfrac{a\alpha}{V}\right)}{\dfrac{a(1-\alpha)}{V}}$$

$$= \frac{a\alpha^2}{V(1-\alpha)} \qquad \qquad ...(9.38)$$

Thus the increase of V must proportionately increase $\dfrac{\alpha^2}{1-\alpha}$ in order to keep K_C constant. Hence, the increase in volume increases the degree of dissociation.

If $\alpha \ll 1$, Eq. (9.38) reduces to

$$K_C = \frac{a\alpha^2}{V}$$

or

$$\alpha = \sqrt{\frac{V K_C}{a}}$$

Since a and K_C are constant, therefore,

$$\alpha \propto \sqrt{V} \qquad ...(9.39)$$

$$\alpha \propto \sqrt{\frac{1}{P}}$$

i.e., the degree of dissociation varies inversely as the square root of pressure.

Calculation of K_p: The equilibrium constant K_p for the reaction in terms of partial pressure can be calculated as follows:

$$PCl_5(g) \rightleftharpoons PCl_3(g) + Cl_2(g)$$

a	0	0	Initial moles
$a(1-\alpha)$	$a\alpha$	$a\alpha$	Moles at equilibrium

Total number of moles at equilibrium $= a(1 - \alpha + \alpha + \alpha) = a(1 + \alpha)$. The partial pressure of PCl_5

at equilibrium, $p_{PCl_5} = \dfrac{a(1-\alpha)}{a(1+\alpha)}P = \dfrac{1-\alpha}{1+\alpha}P$ where P is the total pressure of the system. Similarly the

partial pressure of PCl_3 at equilibrium, $p_{PCl_3} = \dfrac{a\alpha}{a(1+\alpha)}P = \dfrac{\alpha}{1+\alpha}P$

The partial pressure of Cl_2 at equilibrium, $p_{Cl_2} = \dfrac{a\alpha}{a(1+\alpha)}P = \dfrac{\alpha}{1+\alpha}P$

If $p° = 1$ atm, then

$$K_P = \frac{p_{PCl_3}\, p_{Cl_2}}{p_{PCl_5}}$$

$$= \frac{\left(\dfrac{\alpha}{1+\alpha}P\right)\left(\dfrac{\alpha}{1+\alpha}P\right)}{\left(\dfrac{1-\alpha}{1+\alpha}P\right)}$$

$$= \frac{\alpha^2}{(1-\alpha)(1+\alpha)}P$$

$$= \frac{\alpha^2}{1-\alpha^2}P \qquad ...(9.40)$$

Therefore, a decrease in pressure increases α in agreement with the LeChatelier's principle.

(c) **Synthesis of Ammonia:** The equilibrium

$$N_2(g) + 3H_2(g) \rightleftharpoons 2NH_3(g)$$

has been extensively studied by Haber, Larson and Dodge. Ammonia is obtained by combination of one mole of nitrogen and three moles of hydrogen. Suppose there are 1 mole of nitrogen and 3 moles of hydrogen present initially in a vessel of volume V. Let x moles of the former be converted into ammonia at equilibrium. Then the concentrations of the various species at equilibrium are:

$$C_{N_2} = \frac{1-x}{V}; \ C_{H_2} = \frac{3-3x}{V}$$

and

$$C_{NH_3} = \frac{2x}{V}$$

If the standard concentration, $C^0 = 1$ mol dm^{-3}, then the equilibrium constant K_C is given by

$$K_C = \frac{C_{NH_3}^2}{C_{N_2} C_{H_2}^3}$$

$$= \frac{\left(\dfrac{2x}{V}\right)^2}{\left(\dfrac{1-x}{V}\right)\left(\dfrac{3-3x}{V}\right)^3}$$

$$= \frac{4x^2 V^2}{27(1-x)^4} \qquad \qquad \dots(9.41)$$

Hence, decrease of V would increase the value of x, $i.e.$, the formation of ammonia.

Calculation of K_p : In the formation of ammonia, the number of moles of various species at equilibrium are

$$\text{number of moles of N}_2 = 1 - x$$
$$\text{number of moles of H}_2 = 3 - 3x$$
$$\text{number of moles of NH}_3 = 2x$$

Therefore, the total number of moles at equilibrium $= 1 - x + 3 - 3x + 2x = 4 - 2x$

If P is the total pressure at equilibrium, then the partial pressure of various species are

$$p_{N_2} = \frac{1-x}{4-2x}P \ ; \ p_{H_2} = \frac{3-3x}{4-2x}P$$

$$P_{NH_3} = \frac{2x}{4-2x}P$$

Hence,

$$K_P = \frac{\left(p_{NH_3}\right)^2}{\left(p_{N_2}\right)\left(p_{H_2}\right)^3} \qquad \qquad \left(\text{If } p^0 = 1 \text{ atm}\right)$$

$$= \frac{\left(\dfrac{2x}{4-2x}P\right)^2}{\left(\dfrac{1-x}{4-2x}P\right)\left(\dfrac{3-3x}{4-2x}P\right)^3}$$

$$= \frac{4x^2(4-2x)^2}{27(1-x)^4 P^2} \quad \ldots(9.42)$$

If $x \ll 1$, Eq. (9.42) reduces to

$$K_P = \frac{64x^2}{27 P^2} \quad \ldots(9.43)$$

or

$$x^2 = \frac{27}{64} K_P P^2$$

or

$$x \propto P \text{ (Since } K_P \text{ is constant at constant temperature)}$$

It is thus clear that the formation of ammonia is directly proportional to the total pressure P. This means at higher pressures the yield of ammonia would be better. This result is in agreement with that expected from Le Chatelier's principle.

Characteristics of gaseous reactions of type II

(i) K_P and K_C are not equal.

(ii) Effect of addition of a product of the dissociation at constant pressure or at constant volume will favour the reverse reaction and, therefore it will suppress the formation of the products. Thus the addition of PCl_3 or Cl_2 will decrease the degree of dissociation of PCl_5.

(iii) *Effect of addition of an inert gas:* At constant volume, the various concentration terms involved are not changed. Hence, the equilibrium will not be affected. However, at constant pressure, the addition of an inert gas will increase the volume of the system and thus decrease the concentrations and the partial pressures of the species involved. Therefore, according to LeChatelier's principle, the equilibrium will shift in that direction in which the concentrations of the species increase, *i.e.*, the degree of dissociation should increase. In other words, the formation of products will be favoured.

In reactions where Δv is negative, addition of an inert gas at constant pressure will favour the reverse reaction, *i.e.*, the formation of the reactants will be favoured.

Problem 9.5: K_P for the reaction $PCl_3 (g) + Cl_2 (g) \rightleftharpoons PCl_5 (g)$ is 2.93 at 400 K. A mixture containing 1 mole of PCl_3 and 2 moles of Cl_2 is allowed to attain equilibrium at 400 K and 1 atmospheric pressure. Calculate the amount of PCl_5 formed at equilibrium.

Solution:

$$PCl_3 (g) + Cl_2 (g) \rightleftharpoons PCl_5 (g)$$

| 1.0 | 2.0 | 0.0 | Initial conc. (mol dm^{-3}) |
| $1-x$ | $2-x$ | x | Equilibrium conc. (mol dm^{-3}) |

Total number of moles at equilibrium $= 1 - x + 2 - x + x = 3 - x$

$$\text{Partial pressure of } PCl_3, \ p_{PCl_3} = \frac{1-x}{3-x} P$$

$$\text{Partial pressure of } Cl_2, \ p_{Cl2} = \frac{2-x}{3-x}P$$

$$\text{Partial pressure of } PCl_5, \ p_{PCl_5} = \frac{x}{3-x}P$$

The equilibrium constant K_P, for the reaction is given as

$$K_P = \frac{p_{PCl_5}}{p_{PCl_3} \ p_{Cl_2}} \qquad\qquad \left(\because p^0 \doteq 1 \text{ atm}\right)$$

$$= \frac{\left(\dfrac{xP}{3-x}\right)}{\left(\dfrac{1-x}{3-x}P\right)\left(\dfrac{2-x}{3-x}P\right)}$$

Since $P = 1$ atmosphere

Therefore,

$$K_P = \frac{\left(\dfrac{x}{3-x}\right)}{\left(\dfrac{1-x}{3-x}\right)\left(\dfrac{2-x}{3-x}\right)} = 2.93$$

Solving for x, we get

$$x = 0.63 \text{ mol dm}^{-3}$$

Problem 9.6: Compute the equilibrium constant K_p for the reaction

$$3O_2(g) \rightleftharpoons 2O_3(g)$$

at 298 K. Assuming that the advancement at equilibrium ξ_e, is very much less than unity, show that $\xi_e = \frac{3}{2}\sqrt{K_P P}$. Initially only 3 moles of O_2 are present.

Solution: The conditions at equilibrium are

$$3O_2(g) \rightleftharpoons 2O_3(g)$$

$$3(1-\xi_e) \quad 2\xi_e$$

Total moles at equilibrium $= 3(1-\xi_e) + 2\xi_e = 3 - \xi_e$ and the partial pressures are

$$p_{O_2} = \frac{3(1-\xi_e)}{3-\xi_e}P, \ p_{O_3} = \frac{2\xi_e}{3-\xi_e}P$$

If the standard pressure $p^0 = 1$ atm, then

$$K_P = \frac{p_{O_3}^2}{p_{O_2}^3} = \frac{\left(\dfrac{2\xi_e}{3-\xi_e}P\right)^2}{\left(\dfrac{3(1-\xi_e)}{3-\xi_e}P\right)^3} = \frac{4\xi_e^2(3-\xi_e)}{27(1-\xi_e)^3 P}$$

If $\xi_e \ll 1$, then

$$K_P = \frac{4\xi_e^2}{9P} \quad \text{or} \quad \xi_e = \frac{3}{2}\sqrt{K_P P}$$

Problem 9.7: One mole of N_2O_4 is confined in a vessel at 298 K under a pressure of 1 atm. When the equilibrium is attained, N_2O_4 is found to be 16.6% dissociated into NO_2. (a) Calculate the equilibrium constant for the dissociation of N_2O_4 into NO_2. (b) 5 moles of argon are introduced (i) at constant volume, and (ii) at constant pressure. What would be the degree of dissociation in each case?

Solution: (a) The dissociation of N_2O_4 takes place as

$$N_2O_4(g) \rightleftharpoons 2NO_2(g)$$

Initially   1.0   0
At equilibrium   1 − 0.166   2 × 0.166

Total number of moles at equilibrium = 0.834 + 0.332 = 1.166

$$K_P = \frac{p_{NO_2}^2}{p_{N_2O_4}} \qquad \left(\because p^0 = 1 \text{ atm}\right)$$

Partial pressure of $p_{NO_2} = \dfrac{0.332}{1.166}$ since $P = 1$ atm.

Partial pressure of $p_{N_2O_4} = \dfrac{0.836}{1.166}$

Therefore

$$K_P = \left(\frac{0.332}{1.166} \times 1\right)^2 \bigg/ \left(\frac{0.834}{1.166} \times 1\right)$$

$$= 0.113$$

(b) (i) At constant volume, addition of argon does not cause any change in the dissociation of N_2O_4 as the partial pressures of N_2O_4 and NO_2 remain unchanged.

(ii) However, at constant pressure, addition of argon, decreases the partial pressures of N_2O_4 and NO_2. The dissociation would increase and the extent of dissociation can be calculated as

Total number of moles = $5 + 2\alpha + 1 - \alpha = 6 + \alpha$

where α is the degree of dissociation after adding 5 moles of argon. The partial pressures are

$$p_{N_2O_4} = \frac{1-\alpha}{6+\alpha} \cdot p \text{ and } p_{NO_2} = \frac{2\alpha}{6+\alpha} \cdot p$$

So
$$K_P = 0.113 = \frac{4\alpha^2}{(1-\alpha)(6+\alpha)}$$

or
$$\alpha = 0.351$$

Problem 9.8: The equilibrium constant K_P for the reaction

$$N_2O_4(g) \rightleftharpoons 2NO_2(g)$$

is 0.174 at 300 K. Calculate the apparent molar mass of an equilibrium mixture of N_2O_4 and NO_2 formed by the dissociation of pure N_2O_4 at a total pressure of 2 atm at this temperature.

Solution:
$$N_2O_4(g) \rightleftharpoons 2NO_2(g)$$
$$1-\alpha \qquad 2\alpha \qquad \text{moles at equilibrium}$$

Total number of moles at equilibrium = $(1 - \alpha + 2\alpha) = (1 + \alpha)$

$$p_{N_2O_4} = \frac{1-\alpha}{1+\alpha} \times 2 \text{ and } p_{NO_2} = \frac{2\alpha}{1+\alpha} \times 2$$

If the standard pressure p° is taken as 1 atm, then

$$K_p = \frac{p_{NO_2}^2}{p_{N_2O_4}} = \frac{4(2\alpha/1+\alpha)^2}{\left(\dfrac{1-\alpha}{1+\alpha} \times 2\right)} = 2\left[\frac{4\alpha^2}{1-\alpha^2}\right]$$

Or
$$\frac{8\alpha^2}{1-\alpha^2} = 0.174$$

On solving we get, $\alpha = 0.146$

If M_1 is the apparent molar mass of the equilibrium mixture and M_0 is the molar mass of pure N_2O_4, then

$$\alpha = \frac{M_0 - M_1}{M_0}$$

$$0.146 = \frac{92 - M_1}{M_0}$$

or
$$M_1 = 78.58 \text{ g mol}^{-1}$$

Problem 9.9: In the reaction $XY_2 \rightleftharpoons X + 2Y$ at 300 K, all the three substances are ideal gases. A 10.0 dm^3 vessel contains, initially, 0.40 mole of XY_2. A catalyst for dissociation is then introduced. When equilibrium is attained, the pressure of the mixture is 1.20 atm. Calculate the equilibrium constant for the reaction.

Solution: $\qquad XY_2 \rightleftharpoons X + 2Y$

$\qquad\qquad\quad 0.4 - x \quad x \quad 2x$

where x moles of XY_2 have decomposed at equilibrium.

Total number of moles at equilibrium $n_t = 0.4 - x + x + 2x = 0.4 + 2x$

Since the substances are ideal in behaviour, therefore

$$(0.4 + 2x) = \frac{PV}{RT} = \frac{(1.2 \text{ atm})(10.0 \text{ dm}^3)}{(0.0821 \text{ atm dm}^3 \text{ mol}^{-1}\text{K}^{-1})(300 \text{ K})}$$

$$= 0.487$$

or $\qquad\qquad\qquad\qquad x = 0.044$

If the standard pressure is assumed to be 1.0 atm, then

$$K_P = \frac{p_X p_Y^2}{p_{XY_2}} = \left(\frac{0.044}{0.356}\right)\left(\frac{0.088}{0.487}\right)^2 (1.2)^2$$

$$= 5.8 \times 10^{-3}$$

Problem 9.10: At 523 K, PCl_5 is 80% dissociated at a pressure of 1 atm. What is the percentage dissociation at equilibrium after sufficient nitrogen has been added at constant pressure to produce a nitrogen partial pressure of 0.9 atm? The total pressure is kept at 1 atm.

Solution: PCl_5 dissociates as

$$PCl_5(g) \rightleftharpoons PCl_3(g) + Cl_2(g)$$

Initially if PCl_5 is mole, then at equilibrium moles of PCl_5, PCl_3 and Cl_2 are 0.2, 0.8 and 0.8 respectively. Hence the partial pressures are

$$p_{Cl_2} = p_{PCl_3} = \frac{0.8 \times 1}{1.8} \text{ and } p_{PCl_5} = \frac{0.2 \times 1}{1.8}$$

If the standard pressure is taken as 1 atm, then the equilibrium constant K_P is given as

$$K_P = \frac{p_{PCl_3} \, p_{Cl_2}}{p_{PCl_5}} = \frac{(0.8/1.8)^2}{(0.2/1.8)} = 1.78$$

Let the degree of dissociation of PCl_5 in the presence of nitrogen be α', then the total number of moles (n_t) in the system are

$$n_t = n_{N_2} + n_{Cl_2} + n_{PCl_3} + n_{PCl_5}$$

$$= n_{N_2} + \alpha' + \alpha' + (1 - \alpha')$$

$$= 1 + \alpha' + n_{N_2}$$

Since the partial pressure of nitrogen is 0.9 atm, so its mole fraction is 0.9 ($\because$ total pressure is 1 atm). The number of moles of nitrogen is given as

$$n_{N_2} = 0.9\, n_t$$

So the total number of moles, $n_t = 1 + \alpha' + 0.9\, n_t$

$$0.1 n_t = 1 + \alpha'$$

$$n_t = 10(1 + \alpha')$$

Now the partial pressures are

$$p_{Cl_2} = p_{PCl_3} = \frac{\alpha'}{10(1 + \alpha')}$$

$$p_{PCl_5} = \frac{1 - \alpha'}{10(1 + \alpha')}$$

So $\qquad K_p = \dfrac{p_{Cl_2}\, p_{PCl_3}}{p_{PCl_5}}\ $ or $\ 1.78 = \dfrac{(\alpha')^2}{10(1 - \alpha')^2}$

Hence $\qquad \alpha' = 0.973$

The percentage dissociation is 97.3.

Problem 9.11: At 480 K and a total pressure of 1 atmosphere, a mixture consisting of nitrogen and hydrogen in the mole ratio of 1 : 3 contains 16% of ammonia at equilibrium. Calculate K_p for the reaction.

Solution: The reaction can be written as

$$N_2(g) + 3H_2(g) \rightleftharpoons 2NH_3(g)$$

| 1 | 3 | 0 | Initial moles |
| $1 - x$ | $3 - 3x$ | $2x$ | Moles at equilibrium |

Total number of moles $= 1 - x + 3 - 3x + 2x$

$$= 4 - 2x$$

$$= 2(2 - x)$$

Partial pressure of N_2 at equilibrium, $p_{N_2} = \dfrac{1 - x}{2(2 - x)} \times 1$

Partial pressure of H_2 at equilibrium, $p_{H_2} = \dfrac{3(1 - x)}{2(1 - x)} \times 1$

Partial pressure of NH_3 at equilibrium, $p_{NH_3} = \dfrac{2x}{2(2 - x)} \times 1$

If the standard pressure, $p^\circ = 1$ atm then K_p is given by

$$K_P = \frac{4x^2 4(2-x)^2}{27(1-x)^4}$$

For ammonia in equilibrium mixture, we have

$$\frac{2x}{2(2-x)} = 0.16$$

$$x = 0.276$$

Hence

$$K_p = 0.544$$

(ii) Homogeneous Equilibrium in Liquid Systems

One of the most common examples of a homogeneous liquid systems is the esterification of acetic acid by ethanol, *i.e.*,

$$CH_3COOH(l) + C_2H_5OH(l) \rightleftharpoons CH_3COOC_2H_5(l) + H_2O(l)$$

Let the initial concentration of ethanol and acid be a and b moles respectively and x be the moles of ethyl acetate formed at equilibrium in a system of volume V. Then at equilibrium

$$[C_2H_5OH] = \frac{a-x}{V} \; ; \; [CH_3COOH] = \frac{b-x}{V}$$

$$[CH_3COOC_2H_5] = \frac{x}{V} \text{ and } [H_2O] = \frac{x}{V}$$

The equilibrium constant of the reaction is given as

$$K_C = \frac{[CH_3COOC_2H_5][H_2O]}{[C_2H_5OH][CH_3COOH]}$$

$$= \frac{\left(\dfrac{x}{V}\right)\left(\dfrac{x}{V}\right)}{\left(\dfrac{a-x}{V}\right)\left(\dfrac{b-x}{V}\right)}$$

$$= \frac{x^2}{(a-x)(b-x)} \qquad \qquad ...(9.44)$$

The equilibrium constant is, therefore, independent of the volume of the system.

In the derivation of the above equation it should be kept in mind that the concentrations of the various species are not high and the solution obeys Raoult's law and Henry's law. In case the solution is not dilute, it is advisable to use the activities.

Problem 9.12. At 298 K, 1 mole of acetic acid is mixed with 1 mole of ethanol in a vessel of volume V dm³. At equilibrium 0.667 moles of acetic acid have reacted. Calculate (*i*) K_C. (*ii*) How much ester would be formed when 0.5 mole of ethanol is added to 1.0 mole of acetic acid under similar conditions?

Solution:

(i) $CH_3COOH(l) + C_2H_5OH(l) \rightleftharpoons CH_3COOC_2H_5(l) + H_2O(l)$

$$K_C = \frac{[CH_3COOC_2H_5][H_2O]}{[CH_3COOH][C_2H_5OH]}$$

$$= \frac{\left(\dfrac{0.667}{V}\right)\left(\dfrac{0.667}{V}\right)}{\left(\dfrac{0.333}{V}\right)\left(\dfrac{0.333}{V}\right)}$$

$$= 4.0$$

(ii) $CH_3COH(l) + C_2H_5OH(l) \rightleftharpoons CH_3COOC_2H_5(l) + H_2O(l)$

$$\dfrac{1.0}{V} \qquad \dfrac{0.5}{V} \qquad\qquad 0 \qquad\qquad 0 \qquad \text{Initial concentrations}$$

$$\dfrac{(1-x)}{V} \qquad \dfrac{(0.5-x)}{V} \qquad \dfrac{x}{V} \qquad \dfrac{x}{V} \qquad \text{Equilibrium concentrations}$$

$$K_C = \frac{\left(\dfrac{x}{V}\right)\left(\dfrac{x}{V}\right)}{\left(\dfrac{1.0-x}{V}\right)\left(\dfrac{0.5-x}{V}\right)}$$

or

$$4.0 = \frac{x^2}{(1.0-x)(0.5-x)}$$

$$x = 1.575 \text{ mol or } 0.425 \text{ mol}$$

Since the first value is not possible as the maximum amount can not exceed 0.5 mole, therefore, the amount of ester formed at equilibrium is 0.425 mole.

9.11 HETEROGENEOUS EQUILIBRIA

(a) Equilibria Between Ideal Gases and Condensed Phases

So far we have dealt with homogeneous equilibria. If, in addition to gases, a chemical reaction involved one or more pure liquids or solids, the expression for the equilibrium constant is slightly different. For pure solids or pure immiscible liquids, the chemical potentials are constants and the free energy change for a reaction like

$$CaCO_3(s) \rightleftharpoons CaO(s) + CO_2(g)$$

is given by

$$\Delta G = \left(\frac{\partial G}{\partial \xi}\right)_{P,\, T} = \mu_{CaO} + \mu_{CO_2} - \mu_{CaCO_3}$$

At equilibrium
$$\left(\frac{\partial G}{\partial \xi}\right)_{P,\,T} = 0$$

Hence
$$\mu_{CaO} + \mu_{CO_2} = \mu_{CaCO_3}$$

Under ordinary condition, the chemical potentials of solid components is taken equal to the chemical potentials of pure substances

$$\mu_{CaO} = \mu^0_{CaO} \text{ and } \mu_{CaCO_3} = \mu^0_{CaCO_3}$$

Therefore,
$$\Delta G = \left(\mu^0_{CaO} + \mu^0_{CO_2} - \mu^0_{CaCO_3}\right) + RT \ln\left(p_{CO_2}/p^0\right)$$

$$= \Delta G^0 + RT \ln\left(p_{CO_2}/p^0\right)$$

where ΔG^0 is the standard free energy of reaction.
At equilibrium $\Delta G = 0$, hence

$$\Delta G^0 = -RT \ln\left(p_{CO_2}/p^0\right) = -RT \ln K_P$$

or
$$K_P = \left(p_{CO_2}/p^0\right) \qquad \qquad ...(9.45)$$

when
$$p^0 = 1 \text{ atm},$$

then
$$K_P = p_{CO_2}$$

The equilibrium constant, K_P for such reactions contains only the partial pressures of the gaseous constituents and does not include terms for the concentration of either pure solids or liquids. However, ΔG^0, the standard free energy of the reaction contains the standard Gibbs energies of all the reactants and products.

(b) Dissociation of Ammonium Carbamate

On heating ammonium carbamate dissociates into ammonia and carbon dioxide as

$$NH_2COONH_4 (s) \rightleftharpoons 2NH_3 (g) + CO_2 (g) \qquad \qquad ...(3)$$

If $p^0 = 1$ atm, then equilibrium constant K_P is given as

$$K_P = p^2_{NH_3} p_{CO_2}$$

where p_{NH_3} and p_{CO_2} are the partial pressures of ammonia and carbon-dioxide respectively.

Problem 9.13: Solid NH_4HS is placed in a flask containing ammonia at a pressure of 1.50 atmospheres. What are the partial pressures of ammonia and H_2S when equilibrium is attained? ($K_p = 0.11$).

Solution: Because some ammonia is already present in the flask, therefore the partial pressures of ammonia and hydrogen sulphide will not be equal when equilibrium is attained. The equilibrium can be written as

$$NH_4HS(s) \rightleftharpoons NH_3 (g) + H_2S(g)$$

$$p_{NH_3} = 1.50 + p_{H_2S}$$

and
$$K_P = p_{NH_3} p_{H_2S} \qquad\qquad (\because p^0 = 1 \text{ atm})$$

$$0.11 = \left(1.50 + p_{H_2S}\right)\left(p_{H_2S}\right)$$

or
$$p_{H_2S} = 0.06 \text{ atm or } -1.56 \text{ atm}$$

Out of these two values, 0.06 atmosphere is correct.

Hence
$$p_{NH_3} = 1.50 + 0.06 = 1.56 \text{ atm}$$

Problem 9.14: At a certain temperature, K_p for the dissociation of solid calcium carbonate is 4.0×10^{-2} atm and for the reaction $C(s) + CO_2(g) \rightleftharpoons 2CO(g)$ it is 2.0 atm respectively. Calculate the pressure of CO at this temperature when solid carbon, CaO and $CaCO_3$ are mixed and allowed to attain equilibrium.

Solution:

$$CaCO_3(s) \rightleftharpoons CaO(s) + CO_2(g) \qquad\qquad ...(i)$$

$$C(s) + CO_2(g) \rightleftharpoons 2CO(g) \qquad\qquad ...(ii)$$

K_p for reaction (i) is given as

$$K_P = p_{CO_2} \qquad\qquad (\because p^0 = 1 \text{ atm})$$

and K_P' for reaction (ii) is given by

$$K_P' = \frac{p_{CO}^2}{p_{CO_2}}$$

or
$$K_P K_P' = \frac{p_{CO_2} \, p_{CO}^2}{p_{CO_2}} = p_{CO}^2$$

which gives

$$p_{CO} = \sqrt{K_P K_P'}$$

$$= \sqrt{\left(4.0 \times 10^{-2}\right)(2.0)}$$

$$= 0.28 \text{ atm}$$

9.12 EFFECT OF TEMPERATURE ON CHEMICAL EQUILIBRIUM

The equilibrium constant varies with temperature. The Le Chatelier principle gives only a qualitative idea of the shift of equilibrium when the temperature is changed. However, a quantitative expression for the variation of equilibrium constant with temperature can be derived thermodynamically as follows: From Eq. (9.23), we have

or

$$\Delta G^0 = -RT \ln K_P$$

$$\ln K_P = -\frac{\Delta G^0}{RT} \qquad \qquad ...(9.46)$$

On differentiation Eq. (9.46) with respect to T at constant pressure we get

$$\frac{d \ln K_P}{dT} = -\frac{1}{R} \left[\frac{d\left(\Delta G^0 / T\right)}{dT} \right]_P \qquad \qquad ...(9.47)$$

Since

$$\left[\frac{d\left(\Delta G^0 / T\right)}{dT} \right]_P = -\frac{\Delta H^0}{T^2}$$

therefore, Eq. (9.47) becomes

or

$$\frac{d \ln K_P}{dT} = -\frac{1}{R} \left(\frac{-\Delta H^0}{T^2} \right)$$

$$\frac{d \ln K_P}{dT} = \frac{\Delta H^0}{RT^2} \qquad \qquad ...(9.48)$$

If the equilibrium constant is expressed in terms of K_C, then

$$K_C = K_p \left(\frac{C^0 RT}{p^0} \right)^{-\Delta v}$$

$$\ln K_C = \ln K_p - \Delta v \ln \left(\frac{C^0 RT}{p^0} \right)$$

$$\frac{d \ln K_C}{dT} = \frac{d \ln K_P}{dT} - \frac{\Delta v}{T}$$

But

$$\frac{d \ln K_p}{dT} = \frac{\Delta H^0}{RT^2}$$

Hence

$$\frac{d \ln K_C}{dT} = \frac{\Delta H^0 - \Delta v RT}{RT^2} = \frac{\Delta E^0}{RT^2} \qquad \qquad ...(9.49)$$

$$\left(\because H = E + PV = E + vRT \text{ for an ideal gas so } \Delta H^0 - \Delta v RT = \Delta E^0 \right)$$

Equations (9.48) and (9.49) are of fundamental importance and represent the variation of equilibrium constant with temperature. Equation (9.48) is generally known as the *van't Hoff' equation.*

In order to integrate the equations (9.48) or (9.49), ΔH^0 or ΔE^0 must be known as a function of temperature. Assuming ΔH^0 to be constant over a small range of temperature, integration of Eq. (9.48) yields

$$\int_{K_{P_1}}^{K_{P_2}} d\ln K_P = \int_{T_1}^{T_2} \frac{\Delta H^0}{RT^2} dT$$

$$\left[\ln K_P \right]_{K_{P_1}}^{K_{P_2}} = \frac{\Delta H^0}{R}\left[-\frac{1}{T} \right]_{T_1}^{T_2}$$

$$\ln \frac{K_{P_2}}{K_{P_1}} = \frac{\Delta H^0}{R}\left[-\frac{1}{T_2} + \frac{1}{T_1} \right]$$

$$= \frac{\Delta H^0}{R}\left[\frac{T_2 - T_1}{T_1 T_2} \right]$$

$$\log \frac{K_{P_2}}{K_{P_1}} = \frac{\Delta H^0}{2.303R}\left[\frac{T_2 - T_1}{T_1 T_2} \right] \qquad ...(9.50)$$

Equation (9.50) helps in calculating K_{P_2} at T_2 provided the enthalpy of the reaction at constant pressure ΔH^0, K_{P_1} and T_1 are known. Alternatively, ΔH^0 can be determined if K_P is known at two temperatures.

Integrating Eq. (9.48) without using limits gives

$$\int d\ln K_P = \int \frac{\Delta H^0}{RT^2} dT$$

$$\ln K_P = -\frac{\Delta H^0}{RT} + \text{constant}$$

or
$$\log_{10} K_P = -\frac{\Delta H^0}{2.303\, RT} + \text{constant} \qquad ...(9.51)$$

The value of the constant can be calculated for any reaction by substituting a known value of K_P at a given temperature. Equation (9.51) shows that a plot of $\log_{10} K_P$ versus $\frac{1}{T}$ should give a straight line with slope $= -\frac{\Delta H^0}{2.303\,R}$. From the slope, value of ΔH^0 can be calculated, *i.e.,*

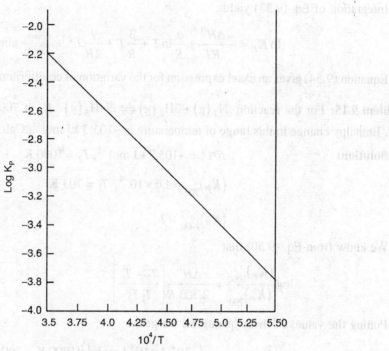

Fig. 9.3 Plot of log K_P against $1/T$

$$\Delta H^0 = -2.303\,R \times \text{slope}$$

$$= -20.947 \times \text{slope} \quad (\because \quad R = 8.314\ \text{JK}^{-1}\text{mol}^{-1})$$

Figure 9.3 shows the plot of $\log_{10} K_P$ against $1/T$ for the reaction $N_2(g) + O_2(g) \rightleftharpoons 2NO(g)$. The enthalpy of the reaction ΔH^0 in the range of $1900 - 2600$ K can be calculated from the slope of the line as follows:

$$\Delta H^0 = -\text{slope} \times 4.576$$

$$= -(-9510)(4.576)$$

$$= 43.500\ \text{k cal mol}^{-1}$$

$$= 183.00\ \text{kJ mol}^{-1}$$

In the derivation of Eq. (9.51) it has been assumed that ΔH^0 is constant. However, ΔH^0 often varies considerably with temperature and can be expressed as a function of temperature as

$$\Delta H^0 = \Delta H_0^0 + \alpha T + \beta T^2 + \gamma T^3 + \ldots\ldots\ldots \qquad \ldots(9.52)$$

where α, β, γ, ... etc., are determined by the heat capacities of the substances involved in the reaction. Putting the value of ΔH^0 in Eq. (9.48), we get

$$\frac{d\ln K_P}{dT} = \frac{\Delta H_0^0}{RT^2} + \frac{\alpha}{RT} + \frac{\beta}{R} + \frac{\gamma}{R}T + \ldots\ldots \qquad \ldots(9.53)$$

Integration of Eq. (9.53) yields

$$\ln K_P = -\frac{\Delta H^0}{RT} + \frac{\alpha}{R}\ln T + \frac{\beta}{R}T + \frac{\gamma}{2R}T^2 + \ldots\ldots + \text{const.} \qquad \ldots(9.54)$$

Equation (9.54) gives an exact expression for the variation of equilibrium constant with temperature.

Problem 9.15: For the reaction $N_2(g) + 3H_2(g) \rightleftharpoons 2NH_3(g)$, K_P at 700 K was found to be 1.6×10^{-4}. Enthalpy change in this range of temperature is -105.3 kJ mol^{-1}. Calculate K_P at 1000 K.

Solution: $\Delta H^0 = -105.3$ kJ mol^{-1}, $T_2 = 1000$ K

$$(K_P)_{700} = 1.6 \times 10^{-4}, \quad T_1 = 703 \text{ K}$$

$$(K_P)_{1000} = ?$$

We know from Eq. (9.50) that

$$\log\frac{(K_P)_{1000}}{(K_P)_{700}} = \frac{\Delta H^0}{2.303\,R}\left[\frac{T_2 - T_1}{T_1 T_2}\right]$$

Putting the values of these quantities, we get

$$\log\frac{(K_P)_{1000}}{1.6 \times 10^{-1}} = \frac{\left(-105.3 \times 10^3 \text{ J mol}^{-1}\right)(1000 \text{ K} - 700 \text{ K})}{\left(2.303 \times 8.314 \text{ JK}^{-1}\text{mol}^{-1}\right)(1000 \text{ K})(700 \text{ K})}$$

$$= -2.356$$

or $\log(K_P)_{1000} = -2.356 + \log\left(1.6 \times 10^{-4}\right)$

or $(K_P)_{1000} = 7.049 \times 10^{-7}$

9.13 PRESSURE DEPENDENCE OF EQUILIBRIUM CONSTANT

The equilibrium constant, K_P is related to standard free energy change ΔG^0 by the relation
$$\Delta G^0 = -RT \ln K_P$$

Since ΔG^0 is the free energy change of the reaction when the reactants and products are in the standard state, i.e., at 1 atmosphere and its value depends on temperature only. Hence K_P also depends on temperature only and is independent of pressure of the reacting system. Like K_P, K_C is also independent of pressure. However, K_X depends on pressure as shown by the following considerations:

$$K_P = K_X\left(p/p^0\right)^{\Delta v}$$

or $\ln K_X = \ln K_p - \Delta v \ln\left(p/p^0\right)$

Differentiating with respect to P at constant T, we get

$$\left(\frac{d\ln K_X}{dP}\right)_T = \left(\frac{d\ln K_P}{dP}\right)_T - \frac{\Delta v \times \left(1/p^0\right)}{\left(p/p^0\right)}$$

Since,
$$\left(\frac{d\ln K_P}{dP}\right)_T = 0,$$

Therefore,
$$\left(\frac{d\ln K_X}{dP}\right)_T = -\frac{\Delta v}{(p)} \qquad ...(9.55)$$

If $\Delta v = 0$, K_X is independent of pressure, but depends on pressure, if $\Delta v \neq 0$ for a reaction.

Problem 9.16: When NH_4Cl is heated, the vapour pressure at 700 K is 6.0 atm. At 732 K the vapour pressure rises to 11.0 atm. What are the equilibrium constants for the dissociation at these temperatures. Also calculate ΔH^0 and ΔS^0 at 700 K.

Solution: Ammonium chloride dissociates as

$$NH_4Cl(s) \rightleftharpoons HCl(g) + NH_3(g)$$

$$p = p_{NH_3} + p_{HCl} = 6.0 \text{ atm}$$

But
$$p_{NH_3} = p_{HCl}$$

So
$$p_{NH_3} = p_{HCl} = 3 \text{ atm}$$

Now
$$K_P = p_{NH_3}\, p_{HCl} \qquad \left(\because p^0 = 1 \text{ atm}\right)$$

$$= (3)^2 = 9.0$$

Since
$$\Delta G^0 = -RT \ln K_P$$

$$= -(8.314)(700)(2.303)\log 9.0$$

$$= -12.8 \text{ kJ mol}^{-1}$$

At 732 K

$$p_{NH_3} = p_{HCl} = 5.5 \text{ atm}$$

So
$$K_P \text{ at 732 K is } p_{NH_3}p_{HCl} = (5.5)^2 = 30.25$$

Now
$$\log\frac{K_{P,\,732}}{K_{P,\,700}} = \frac{\Delta H^0(32)}{(8.314)(2.303)(700)(732)}$$

Hence,
$$\Delta H^0 = 161.42 \text{ kJ mol}^{-1}$$

Therefore
$$\Delta G^0 \text{ at 700 K} = \Delta H^0 - T\Delta S^0$$

From which
$$\Delta S^0 = 248.9 \text{ JK}^{-1}\text{mol}^{-1}$$

9.14 COUPLED REACTIONS

There are many reactions which would be useful to produce a desirable product but have positive values of $\Delta G°$. Such reactions can be made to proceed spontaneously (making $\Delta G°$ negative) by coupling them with other reactions which have larger negative $\Delta G°$ values. For example, the reaction

$$TiO_2(s) + 2Cl_2(g) = TiCl_4(l) + O_2(g)$$

is nonspontaneous $\left(\Delta G_{298}^0 = 152.3 \text{ kJ mol}^{-1}\right)$. It could be made spontaneous by coupling it with another reaction which has a $\Delta G°$ value more negative than 152.3 kJ mol^{-1} and consumes a product of the above reaction. Thus the reaction

$$C(s) + O_2(g) = CO_2(g), \quad \Delta G_{298}^0 = -394.4 \text{ kJ mol}^{-1}$$

can be coupled with the above reaction. For the composite reaction

$$TiO_2(s) + C(s) + 2Cl_2(g) = TiCl_4(l) + CO_2(g)$$

$\Delta G°$ value would be -242.1 kJ mol^{-1} and so it would proceed spontaneously.

Coupled reactions are important in biological systems where vital functions in an organ often depend on reactions which have positive value of $\Delta G°$. These reactions are coupled with metabolic reactions which have large negative $\Delta G°$ values.

EXERCISES

1. Write down the expressions for K_P and K_C for the following reactions:

    (i) $N_2O_4(g) \rightleftharpoons 2NO_2(g)$

    (ii) $PCl_5(g) \rightleftharpoons PCl_3(g) + Cl_2(g)$

    (iii) $4HCl(g) + O_2(g) \rightleftharpoons 2Cl_2(g) + 2H_2O(g)$

    (iv) $2SO_2(g) + O_2(g) \rightleftharpoons 2SO_3(g)$

    How are K_P and K_C related in each case?

2. Two moles of ammonia gas are introduced into a previously evacuated 1.0 dm^3 vessel in which it partially dissociates at high temperature. At equilibrium 1.0 mole of ammonia remains. The equilibrium constant K_C for the dissociation is $\dfrac{27}{16}, \dfrac{27}{8}, \dfrac{27}{4}$. Select the correct answer.   **Ans.** $\dfrac{27}{16}$.

3. Periodic analysis of a mixture at equilibrium shows that the concentrations of reactants and products remain unchanged. This indicates that (i) the chemical reaction has ceased or (ii) the reaction has not ceased but the two opposing reactions—forward and backward, proceed at equal rates. Select the correct answer.

    Ans. (ii) is correct.

4. For the reaction,

    $$CH_4(g) + 2O_2(g) \rightleftharpoons CO_2(g) + 2H_2O(l) + 1770.8 \text{ kJ}$$

    state which of the following statements are true and which are false:
    (i) As written, the reaction is exothermic.
    (ii) At equilibrium, the concentrations of CO_2 (g) and H_2O (l) are equal.

(*iii*) From the thermochemical equation, we can conclude that the point of equilibrium is to the right.

(*iv*) The equilibrium constant for the reaction is given by $K_P = \dfrac{[CO_2]}{[CH_4][O_2]}$.

(*v*) If the equilibrium constant has a large value, the point of equilibrium for the reaction will be far to the right.

(*vi*) The equilibrium constant K_P has the units of $(concentration)^{-2}$.

(*vii*) A decrease in total pressure will shift the equilibrium to the right.

(*viii*) An increase in temperature will shift the equilibrium to the right.

(*ix*) Addition of a catalyst will cause the shift to the left.

(*x*) Addition of CH_4 (g) or O_2 (g) at equilibrium will cause a shift to the right.

Ans. True: (*i*), (*v*), (*x*); rest false.

5. The reaction N_2 (g) + $3H_2$ (g) $\rightleftharpoons$ $2NH_3$ is exothermic. For a suitable yield of ammonia which of the following conditions would be satisfactory? (*i*) Low temperature and low pressure, (*ii*) low temperature and high pressure, (*iii*) high temperature and low pressure, (*iv*) high temperature and high pressure, and (*v*) none of these. **Ans. (*ii*) is correct.**

6. Which of the following equilibria are not affected by pressure changes and why?

(*i*) $PCl_5(g) \rightleftharpoons PCl_3(g) + Cl_2(g)$

(*ii*) $N_2(g) + O_2(g) \rightleftharpoons 2NO(g)$

(*iii*) $2O_3(g) \rightleftharpoons 3O_2(g)$

(*iv*) $H_2(g) + I_2(g) \rightleftharpoons 2HI(g)$

(*v*) $2NO_2(g) \rightleftharpoons N_2O_4(g)$ **Ans. (*ii*) and (*iv*).**

7. For the reaction

$$CO_2(g) + H_2(g) \rightleftharpoons CO(g) + H_2O(g)$$

the equilibrium constant at 1000 K is 0.53.

(*i*) Write the expression for the equilibrium constant K_C.

(*ii*) Is a gaseous mixture containing 0.20 mole of CO, 0.25 mole of H_2O, 0.42 mole of CO_2 and 0.33 mole of H_2 in a 1 dm^3 vessel at equilibrium ?

(*iii*) If a mixture at equilibrium in a 1 dm^3 vessel contains 0.25 mole of CO, 0.5 mole of CO_2 and 0.6 mole of H_2, how many moles of H_2O are there in the vessel ?

(*iv*) Suppose that 1.0 mole of H_2 and 1.0 mole of CO_2 are mixed in a 1 dm^3 vessel. How many moles of CO and H_2O will be produced when equilibrium is reached ?

(*v*) 0.5 mole of an inert gas is added to the equilibrium mixture in (*iv*) at (*a*) constant volume and (*b*) at constant pressure. Predict the equilibrium concentrations of CO_2 and H_2O.

Ans. (*i*) $K_C = \dfrac{[H_2O][CO]}{[CO_2][H_2]}$. (*ii*) No, (*iii*) 0.636 mole,

(*iv*) 0.42 mole of each, (*v*) (*a*) and (*b*) 0.42 mole of each.

8. For the reaction $A + B \rightleftharpoons C + D$, will the addition of C to the system change the value of equilibrium constant K? Will the addition of D change the ratio $\dfrac{[C][D]}{[A][B]}$ at equilibrium? If K_P or K_C for the reaction are

independent of pressure changes in the system and volume of the system is reduced by one half, will the partial pressures of any reactants or products change ?

Ans. K does not change, the ratio remains constant and partial pressures of each component would be doubled.

9.   The reaction A (g) $+ B$ (g) $\rightleftharpoons C$ (g) is in equilibrium in a 1 dm^3 container. An inert gas is introduced into the container and the volume is allowed to expand so that the initial pressure of the system is maintained. Does the expansion place a stress on the system? How can the stress be relieved ?

Ans. Yes, some C (g) must decompose to yield A (g) and B (g).

10. For the reaction AB (g) $\rightleftharpoons A$ (g) $+ B$ (g) the equilibrium constant is 5.0×10^{-5} mol dm^{-3} at a certain temperature. A solution which is 1.0×10^{-4} molar in AB is allowed to equilibrate at the same temperatures, calculate the equilibrium concentrations of AB (g), A (g) and B (g).

Ans. $[A] = [B] = 5 \times 10^{-5}$ mol dm^{-3}, $[AB] = 0.5 \times 10^{-4}$ mol dm^{-3}.

11. At 1750 K, 1 mole of Br$_2$ (g) enclosed in a 1 dm^3 vessel was found to be 1% dissociated. Calculate K_C and K_P for the dissociation of Br$_2$ gas at 1750 K.   **Ans.** 4×10^{-4}, 5.75×10^{-2}.

12. 2.50 moles of COCl$_2$ (g) were introduced into a 2 dm^3 vessel at 273 K and heated to 350 K where the equilibrium $COCl_2(g) \rightleftharpoons CO(g) + Cl_2(g)$ is established. Calculate the equilibrium concentration of each species and the percentage dissociation of COCl$_2$ (g) The equilibrium constant K_C or the reaction at 350 K is 0.19.

Ans. $[CO] = [Cl_2] = 0.402$ mol dm^{-3}, $[COCl_2] = 0.85$ mol dm^{-3}, percentage dissociation = 28.

13. A mixture of N$_2$ and H$_2$ in the stoichiometric proportion (1 : 3) was heated to a temperature of 700 K at constant pressure of 30 atm. At equilibrium the pressure of N$_2$ was found to be 4.0 atm. Calculate the individual partial pressures, K_P and K_C for the reaction: N$_2$(g) $+ 3$H$_2$ $\rightleftharpoons 2$NH$_3$ (g).

Ans. $p_{N_2} = 4.0$ atm, $p_{H_2} = 12.0$ atm, $p_{NH_3} = 14$ atm, $K_P = 0.028$, $K_C = 11.80$.

14. The equilibrium constant for the reaction,

$$SO_2(g) + \frac{1}{2}O_2(g) \rightleftharpoons SO_3(g)$$

at 1000 K is 1.85. What is the ratio of P_{SO_3}/P_{SO_2} (a) when the partial pressure of oxygen at equilibrium is 0.3 atm? (b) when the partial pressure of oxygen at equilibrium is 0.6 atm? Predict the effect of addition of an inert gas at constant volume on the equilibrium.

Ans. (a) 1.01, (b) 1.44, no effect if the gases behave ideally.

15. At 300 K, K_P for the reactions, $SO_2(g) + \frac{1}{2}O_2(g) \rightleftharpoons SO_3(g)$ is 1.7×10^{12}. Calculate K_P and K_C for the reaction $2SO_3(g) \rightleftharpoons 2SO_2(g) + O_2(g)$ at 300 K.   **Ans.** $K_P = 3.5 \times 10^{-23}$ $K_C = 1.4 \times 10^{-26}$

16. NOCl (g) is put into a 1 dm^3 vessel and then heated so that it partially decomposes according to the reaction 2 NOCl (g) $\rightleftharpoons$ 2 NO (g) + Cl$_2$ (g). When equilibrium is reached, NOCl (g) was found to be 0.10 mol dm^{-3}. More NOCl (g) was introduced into the vessel and when equilibrium was re-established NOCl was 0.8 mol dm^{-3}. How had the concentration of NO and Cl$_2$ changed ?

Ans. Concentration of each has been quadrupled.

17. Ammonium hydrosulphide decomposes according to the reaction,

$$NH_4HS(s) \rightleftharpoons NH_3(g) + H_2S(g)$$

The equilibrium constant K_p for the reaction is 12.0 at a certain temperature. Some solid NH_4HS is placed in a vessel containing 1.0 atm of NH_3 (g) at the same temperature. What is pressure of NH_3 (g) at equilibrium ?
Ans. 3 atm.

18. At 525 K, PCl_5 (g) is 80% dissociated at a pressure of 1 atm. Calculate K_p for the dissociation reaction. Sufficient quantity of an inert gas at constant pressure is introduced into the above reaction mixture to produce an inert gas partial pressure of 0.9 atm. What is the degree of dissociation (α) of PCl_5 (g) when equilibrium is re-established ? **Ans.** $K_p = 1.78$, $\alpha = 97.3\%$.

19. The equilibrium constant for the isomerisation of *n*-butane to isobutane at 300 K is 2.54. Calculate the percentage isomerisation of *n*-butane into isobutane. **Ans.** 71.7%.

20. For the reaction A (g) + B (g) $\rightleftharpoons$ AB (g) the equilibrium constant is 1.446. Under what total pressure must an equimolar gaseous mixture of A and B be placed to produce a 40% conversion into AB (g) ?
Ans. 0.063 atm.

21. K_p for the dissociation of PCl_5 at 250°C is 1.78. Calculate the degree of dissociation when 0.1 mole is placed in a 3 dm^3 vessel containing Cl_2 at 0.5 atm. **Ans.** 0.574.

22. $COCl_2$ (g) is introduced into a 2 dm^3 vessel and then heated so that it dissociates as $COCl_2(g) \rightleftharpoons CO(g) + Cl_2(g)$. When equilibrium was reached, $COCl_2$ concentration was 0.4 mol dm^{-3}. More $COCl_2$ (g) was then introduced and when the equilibrium was re-established $COCl_2$ was 1.6 mol dm^{-3}. How had [CO] changed ? **Ans.** [CO] is doubled.

23. NH_3 is formed from 1 mole of N_2 and 3 moles of H_2. Under equilibrium conditions at 400°C and 10 atm pressure, 3.85 mole per cent NH_3 is formed (*i*) Calculate K_p.
(*ii*) What would be the total pressure of the system if 5 mole percent NH_3 is to be obtained.
Ans. (*i*) $K_p = 1.64 \times 10^{-4}$ (*ii*) $P = 13.3$ atm.

24. K_p for the reaction at 40°C, $LiCl.3NH_3(s) \rightleftharpoons LiCl.NH_3(s) + 2NH_3(g)$ is 9.0. How many moles of NH_3 must be added at this temperature to 5 dm^3 vessel containing 0.1 mole of $LiCl.3NH_3$ in order to completely convert the solid into $LiCl. 3 NH_3$ (s). **Ans.** 0.78 moles.

25. At 1105 K, the value of K_p for the reaction

$$SO_2(g) + \frac{1}{2}O_2(g) = SO_3(g)$$

is 0.63. Calculate (*i*) the standard free energy change for the reaction at 1105 K and (*ii*) the free energy change at 1105 K for the reaction

$$SO_2\left(1 \text{ atm}\right) + \frac{1}{2}O_2\left(25 \text{ atm}\right) = SO_3\left(2 \text{ atm}\right)$$

What is the significance of the signs of the answers in (*i*) and (*ii*).
Ans. (*i*) $\Delta G° = 4.245$ kJ mol^{-1} (*ii*) $\Delta G = -4.174$ kJ mol^{-1}

Reaction in (*i*) is nonspontaneous while in (*ii*) it is spontaneous.

26. Calculate the partial pressure of oxygen over CuO and Cu at 298 K in the reaction,

$$2 \text{ CuO (s)} \rightarrow 2 \text{ Cu(s)} + O_2(g)$$

Given that $\Delta G^0_{f, CuO} = -127.2$ kJ mol^{-1} **Ans.** $P_{O_2} = 5.094 \times 10^{-23}$ atm.

27. For the reaction A (g) + $2B$ (g) = C (g) + D (g), K_C is 2.0×10^5. If 1 mole of A and 3 moles of B react in a 1L container, calculate the conc. of A at equilibrium. **Ans.** $|A| = 5 \times 10^{-6}$ mol L^{-1}.

28. The following equilibria are established on mixing NO and NO_2:

 (i) $2NO_2 \rightleftharpoons N_2O_4$ $K_P = 6.8$

 (ii) $NO + NO_2 \rightleftharpoons N_2O_3$

 If NO and NO_2 are mixed in the mole ratio 1:2, calculate the equilibrium partial pressure of NO and equilibrium constant K_P for the formation of N_2O_3. Given the final pressure as 5.05 atm and the equilibrium pressure of N_2O_4 as 1.7 atm.   **Ans.** 1.05 atm, $K_P = 3.43$.

29. For the reaction, $CO (g) + 2H_2 (g) = CH_3OH (g)$ hydrogen is introduced into a 5L flask at 327°C containing 0.2 mol of CO and a catalyst until the equilibrium is attained. At this stage 0.1 mole of CH_3OH (g) is formed and the total pressure of the system was 4.92 atm. Calculate K_P for the reaction.   **Ans.** 277.78.

30. A container of volume V liter contains an equilibrium mixture that consists of 2 moles of each PCl_5, PCl_3 and Cl_2 (all gases). The pressure is 3 atm and temperature T K. A certain mass of Cl_2 (g) is now introduced keeping the pressure and temperature constant until the volume is 2 V litres. Calculate the number of moles of chlorine that were added and K_P for the reaction

$$PCl_5(g) \rightleftharpoons PCl_3(g) + Cl_2(g).$$

Ans. $K_P = 1$ and moles of chlorine = 6.67.

Solutions

10.1 INTRODUCTION

A solution is defined as *a mixture of two or more nonreacting substances whose composition may be varied between certain limits*. A mixture may be homogeneous or heterogeneous. A homogeneous mixture is a single phase system whose constituents can not be separated from each other by mechanical means and has the same composition throughout. Such a homogeneous mixture is called a true solution, *e.g.*, a solution of common salt in water. A heterogeneous mixture, on the other hand, can be readily separated from each other by simple mechanical devices. Such a heterogeneous mixture is called a coarse mixture, *e.g.*, a mixture of salt and sugar. Besides these, there are solutions which appear homogeneous to the naked eye but are heterogeneous. Their heterogeneity can be revealed through a microscope or an ultramicroscope. Such solutions are called colloidal solutions. Milk is an example under this category of solutions.

In solutions, there is no fixed ratio as such in which the constituents are mixed. It is in this respect that a solution differs from a compound in which the constituents are present in a fixed ratio.

The constituents of a solution are generally referred to as the *solute* and the *solvent*. A solute is frequently a substance that dissolves and a solvent is one in which dissolution takes place. The solvent is generally present in large amount in comparison to the solute. Thus, for a solution of a solid or gas in a liquid, where liquid is in large excess over the solid or gas, is termed as the solvent and the solid or gas being the solute.

If a solution contains, at a given temperature as much solute as can be dissolved, the solution is said to be *saturated*. If the quantity of the solute is less than this amount, it is known as *an unsaturated solution*. On the other hand, if the quantity of the solute dissolved is more than the saturation value, the solution is said to be *supersaturated*.

10.2 TYPES OF SOLUTIONS

Although solutions with many components can be prepared, but in this chapter we shall confine our attention to solutions containing only two components. Such solutions are called *binary solutions*. Since the solvent and solute may be either gas, liquid or solid, the different types of possible binary solutions are given below in Table 10.1.

Table 10.1 Possible Types of Binary Solutions

S.No.	Solute	Solvent	Examples
1	Gas	Gas	Mixture of gases or vapours
2	Gas	Liquid	Carbon dioxide in water
3	Gas	Solid	Hydrogen in palladium; nitrogen in titanium
4	Liquid	Gas	Vapourization of a liquid into a gas
5	Liquid	Liquid	Alcohol in water
6	Liquid	Solid	Mercury in gold; liquid benzene in solid iodine
7	Solid	Gas	Sublimation of a solid into a gas
8	Solid	Liquid	Salt in water; sugar in water
9	Solid	Solid	Copper in gold; zinc in copper

Of all these types, the most significant types of solutions which will be discussed are solutions of

(*i*) gases in liquids,

(*ii*) liquids in liquids, and

(*iii*) solids in liquids.

10.3 MEASURES OF COMPOSITION (CONCENTRATION UNITS)

The relative amounts of the solute and solvent present in a solution can be expressed in a number of ways. Consider a binary solution of two components. Let W_1, W_2 be the masses, n_1 and n_2 the number of moles and V_1 and V_2 the volumes in dm^3 of solvent 1 and solute 2 respectively. The various units commonly employed to express the composition of the solutions are:

(*i*) **Mass Per cent:** The mass per cent of solvent in a solution is given by

$$\text{Mass per cent of solvent} = \frac{W_1}{W_1 + W_2} \times 100$$

(*ii*) **Volume Per cent:** Volume per cent of solvent in a solution is given by

$$\text{Volume per cent of solvent} = \frac{V_1}{V_1 + V_2} \times 100$$

(*iii*) **Molarity (*M*):** This is the most common concentration unit. The molarity of a solution is *the number of moles per dm^3 of the solution* at a given temperature. Thus,

$$\text{Molarity, } M = \frac{\text{Number of moles of the solute}}{\text{Volume in } dm^3 \text{ of the solution}}$$

Sometimes the term formality is used for solutions of ionic compounds. Formality of a solution is *the number of formula weight dissolved in one dm^3 of the solution*. It is usually denoted by *F*.

(*iv*) **Molality (*m*):** The molality of a solution is defined as *the number of moles of solute per kilogram of the solvent (mol kg^{-1})*. Thus, one molal (1 *m*) aqueous solution of sodium chloride is obtained by dissolving 58.5 g of NaCl in 1 kg of water. Molarity and molality are identical in cases where the density of the solution is equal to that of the solvent.

$$\text{Molality, } m = \frac{\text{Number of moles of solute}}{\text{kg of solvent}}$$

$$= \frac{n_2}{W_1}$$

where W_1 is the mass of the solvent.

(v) **Normality (N):** The normality of a solution is defined as *the number of gram equivalents of the solute dissolved per dm^3 of the solution*

$$\text{Normality, } N = \frac{\text{Number of gram equivalents of the solute}}{\text{Volume in dm}^3 \text{ of the solution}}$$

$$= \frac{\text{Strength in gram of solute per dm}^3}{\text{Equivalent weight of solute}}$$

(vi) **Mole Fraction (X):** The mole fraction of any component in a solution is given by *the ratio of the number of moles of the component to the total number of moles of all the components present in the solution.* For a solution consisting of two components 1 and 2 the mole fractions of components 1 and 2 in the solution are given by

$$X_1 = \frac{\text{Number of moles of component 1}}{\text{Total number of moles}} = \frac{n_1}{n_1 + n_2}$$

and

$$X_2 = \frac{\text{Number of moles of component 2}}{\text{Total number of moles}} = \frac{n_2}{n_1 + n_2}$$

In general,

$$X_i = \frac{n_i}{\sum_i n_i}$$

The mole fractions are such that

$$X_1 + X_2 = 1$$

or

$$\sum_i X_i = 1$$

If we write the number of moles in terms of masses and molar masses, then

$$X_1 = \frac{\dfrac{W_1}{M_1}}{\dfrac{W_1}{M_1} + \dfrac{W_2}{M_2}}$$

and
$$X_2 = \frac{\dfrac{W_2}{M_2}}{\dfrac{W_1}{M_1} + \dfrac{W_2}{M_2}}$$

where M_1 and M_2 are the molar masses of the components 1 and 2.

The relationship between molality of component 2 and its mole fraction X_2 for a solution of two components in which the solvent 1 has a molar mass M_1 is given by

$$X_2 = \frac{m}{\dfrac{1000}{M_1} + m}$$

or
$$X_2 = \frac{mM_1}{1000 + mM_1}$$

In case of dilute solutions, $mM_1 \ll 1000$, hence

$$X_2 = \frac{mM_1}{1000}$$

This shows that the mole fraction is proportional to the molality (m) of the solution.

The relation between molarity and mole fraction can be derived as follows:

$$X_2 = \frac{n_2}{n_1 + n_2}$$

where n_1 and n_2 are the number of moles of the components in a dm^3 of the solution. If C_1 and C_2 are the molar concentrations then we have

$$X_2 = \frac{C_2}{C_1 + C_2}$$

Again if $d(\text{g cm}^{-3})$ is the density of the solution, then the mass of the solution is $1000d$ and the mass of the solute is C_2M_2. Therefore, the mass of the solvent is $(1000d - C_2M_2)$ and its number of moles would be

$$\frac{(1000d - C_2M_2)}{M_1}$$

Hence,
$$X_2 = \frac{C_2}{C_2 + \left(\dfrac{1000d - C_2M_2}{M_1}\right)}$$

$$= \frac{M_1C_2}{C_2M_1 + 1000d - C_2M_2}$$

$$= \frac{C_2 M_1}{1000d + C_2 (M_1 - M_2)}$$

For dilute solutions, the density of solution is not very much different from that of the pure solvent, and $1000\,d \gg C_2(M_1 - M_2)$ so that

$$X_2 \approx \frac{M_1 C_2}{1000\,d}$$

Since the density of the solution varies with temperature, therefore the molarity C_2 changes with temperature. However, the mole fractions and molality are temperature independent.

Problem 10.1: An aqueous solution containing 10.0 g of sodium hydroxide and 90.0 g of water had a density of 1.12 kg dm^{-3}. Find (a) mass per cent of sodium hydroxide, (b) molality, (c) mole fraction of sodium hydroxide, (d) molarity, and (e) normality.

Solution:

(a) Mass per cent of NaOH $= \dfrac{\text{Mass of NaOH}}{\text{Total mass}} \times 100$

$$= \frac{10}{(10 + 90)} \times 100 = 10.0$$

(b) Number of moles of NaOH $= \dfrac{\text{Mass of NaOH}}{\text{Molar mass of NaOH}}$

$$= \frac{10}{40} = 0.25$$

Number of moles of water $= \dfrac{90}{18} = 5.0$

Therefore, Molality or $m = \dfrac{0.25 \times 1000}{90} = 2.78$ m

(c) $X_{\text{NaOH}} = \dfrac{\text{Number of moles of NaOH}}{\text{Total number of moles}}$

$$= \frac{0.25}{5 + 0.25}$$

$$= 0.0476$$

(d) Volume of the solution V, corresponding to 100×10^{-3} kg of solution is

$$V = \frac{100 \times 10^{-3}\,\text{kg}}{1.12\,\text{kg dm}^{-3}}$$

$$= 89.3 \times 10^{-3} \, \text{dm}^3$$

Hence,   Molarity or $M = \dfrac{0.25 \, (\text{moles})}{89.3 \times 10^{-3} (\text{dm}^3)}$

$$= 2.8$$

(e) The normality of the solution is equal to its molarity.

Problem 10.2: 105 ml of pure water at 4°C is saturated with ammonia gas giving a solution of density 0.9g per ml containing 30% ammonia by mass. Calculate the volume of the solution formed and the volume of ammonia used at 278 K and 770 torr.

Solution: Since water is at 4°C therefore its density is 1 g per ml.

Mass of ammonia corresponding to 105 g of water $= \dfrac{105 \times 30}{70}$

$$= 45 \, \text{g}$$

and the number of moles of ammonia $= \dfrac{45}{17}$

Hence the volume of ammonia corresponding $\dfrac{45}{17}$ moles

$$= \dfrac{45}{17} \times \dfrac{0.084 \times 278 \times 760}{770}$$

$$= 59.6 \, \text{L}$$

The total mass of the solution $= (105 + 45)g = 150 \, \text{g}$

Hence volume of the solution $= \dfrac{\text{Mass}}{\text{density}}$

$$= \dfrac{150 \, \text{g}}{0.9 \, \text{g ml}^{-1}}$$

$$= 166.67 \, \text{ml}$$

10.4 THERMODYNAMIC FUNCTIONS OF MIXING

Since solution formation is a spontaneous process and therefore it is associated with a decrease in the value of Gibbs free energy, G. This change in G has been calculated and given by the expression (Eq. 8.91).

$$\Delta G_{\text{mix}} = nRT \sum_i X_i \ln X_i$$

The entropy of mixing (ΔS_{mix}) has been calculated as given by Eq. (8.94)

$$\Delta S_{\text{mix}} = -nR \sum_i X_i \ln X_i \quad \text{and is positive.}$$

For ideal components, the enthalpy of mixing (ΔH_{mix}) and the volume of mixing (ΔV_{mix}) are both zero.

10.5 SOLUTIONS OF GASES IN LIQUIDS–HENRY'S LAW

Gases dissolve in liquids to form true solutions. Such solutions are examples of two component systems. The solubility of a gas depends on (a) the temperature of the solution, (b) the pressure of the gas over the solution, (c) the nature of the gas, and (d) the nature of the solvent. Substances which have similar chemical characteristics are readily soluble in each other than the substances which have different chemical characteristics.

The solubility of different gases in the same solvent (say water) varies considerably. It has been observed that gases like nitrogen, oxygen etc., dissolve to a small extent than gases like ammonia, sulphur dioxide, hydrogen chloride etc. The solubility of latter gases is due to the chemical interactions of gases with water to form ammonium hydroxide, sulphurous acid respectively.

$$NH_3 + H_2O \rightleftharpoons NH_4^+ + OH^-$$

$$SO_2 + H_2O \rightleftharpoons H_2SO_3$$

$$HCl + H_2O \rightleftharpoons H_3O^+ + Cl^-$$

The solubility of a gas is usually determined by measuring the volume rather than the mass that dissolves. It is frequently expressed in terms of Bunsen absorption coefficient (α) which is defined as *the volume of the gas at STP (273 K and 1 atm pressure) dissolved by unit volume of the solvent at the given temperature under a partial pressure of 1 atmosphere of the gas.* If V_0 is the volume of the gas that dissolves reduced to STP, V is the volume of solvent and p the partial pressure of the gas in atmosphere, then the absorption coefficient α, is given by

$$\alpha = \frac{V_0}{V_p}$$

Table 10.2 shows the Bunsen absorption coefficient (α) for some of the gases at 298 K in different solvents.

Table 10.2 Bunsen Absorption Coefficient of Gases at 298 K

Solvent	He	H_2	N_2	O_2	CO	CO_2
Water	0.0087	0.0019	0.0014	0.0028	0.0025	0.088
Ethanol	0.0282	0.0820	0.1320	0.1450	0.1750	3.00
Benzene	0.0180	0.0658	0.1050	0.1630	0.1550	—
Acetone	0.0320	0.0660	0.1300	0.2070	0.1990	6.50

Effect of Temperature on Solubility: Gases generally dissolve in a liquid with the evolution of heat. Hence, LeChatelier's principle predicts that an increase in temperature will result in a decrease in the solubility of the gas. It is for this reason that gases are readily expelled from solutions by boiling. However, there are certain gases such as hydrogen and inert gases in non-aqueous solvents where the solubility increases with increase in temperature. At constant pressure variation of solubility with temperature is given by

$$\frac{d \ln s}{dT} = \frac{\Delta H}{RT^2}$$

where s is the solubility in mol dm^{-3} of the gas in the solvent and ΔH, the enthalpy of the solution. If ΔH is regarded as temperature independent then integration of the above equation within limits gives

$$\ln \frac{s_2}{s_1} = \frac{\Delta H}{RT_1 T_2}(T_2 - T_1)$$

where s_2 and s_1 are the solubilities at T_2 and T_1 respectively.

Effect of Pressure on Solubility—Henry's Law: LeChatelier's principle predicts that with the increase of pressure the solubility of a gas should increase. Consider a system at equilibrium, containing a gas in contact with its solution in a given solvent. On increasing the pressure, the volume of the gas will be reduced and hence an increase in solubility will result from an increase of pressure.

Henry's law states *that the mass of a gas dissolved by a unit volume of a solvent at constant temperature is directly proportional to the pressure of the gas with which it is in equilibrium.* If X_2 is the mole fraction of the gas dissolved by unit volume of the solvent at equilibrium pressure P, then

$$X_2 \propto P$$

or

$$X_2 = K_H' P$$

or

$$P = K_H X_2 \qquad \qquad ...(i)$$

where K_H is a proportionality constant known as Henry's law constant and has the dimensions of pressure. The magnitude of K_H depends on the nature of the gas, solvent and the units of pressure.

Equation (i) is an equation of a straight line passing through the origin. Thus, a plot of solubility of the gas against the equilibrium pressure at a given temperature gives a straight line passing through the origin (Fig. 10.1). This shows the validity of Henry's law.

It has been found that Henry's law is obeyed by dilute solutions of gases that do not react with the solvent.

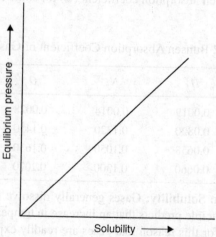

Fig. 10.1 Variation of solubility of a gas with pressure

Henry's law may be stated in another form also. The mass of the gas (m) dissolved per unit volume of the solvent is proportional to its concentration in solution (C_2), whereas the pressure P of the gas is given by $P = C_1RT$ (C_1 being its concentration in the gas phase). Hence

$$K'_H = \frac{m}{P} = \frac{k'C_2}{C_1RT}$$

At constant temperature,

$$\frac{C_2}{C_1} = K_1 \text{ (constant)}$$

or

$$\frac{\text{Concentration of the gas in liquid phase}}{\text{Concentration of the gas in gaseous phase}} = K_1$$

In other words, the concentrations in the gaseous and liquid phases bear a constant ratio to one another at constant temperature.

Again, if we consider the volume of the gas dissolved instead of mass or concentration, we have

$$PV = \frac{m}{M}RT$$

or

$$m = \frac{MPV}{RT}$$

$$= kPV \left(k = \frac{M}{RT} \right)$$

where V is the volume of the gas dissolved per unit volume of the solvent, M is the molar mass of the gas. Hence

$$K'_H = \frac{m}{P} = \frac{kPV}{P}$$

$$V = \frac{K'_H}{k} = \text{constant}$$

Hence the Henry's law may also be stated as the volume of the gas dissolved by a solvent at a given temperature and is independent of pressure.

When several gases are simultaneously dissolved in a solvent, equation (i) is valid independently for each gas, P being the partial pressure of the gas considered. The Henry's law constant K_H would be different for different gases.

Limitations of Henry's law: Henry's law is valid only for an ideal gas. For real gases the law holds if

(i) the pressure is low, at high pressure the law becomes less exact and the proportionality constant shows a considerable variation;

(ii) the temperature is not too low;

(iii) the dissolved gas neither reacts with the solvent nor dissociates or associates in the solvent; and

(iv) the solubility of the gas is low.

For example, Henry's law is not obeyed in case of solubility of HCl or NH_3 gas in water due to the chemical reactions, whereas it is obeyed by these gases in benzene as solvent.

Problem 10.3: 1 kg of water under a nitrogen pressure of 1 atmosphere dissolves 2×10^{-5} kg of nitrogen at 293 K. Calculate Henry's law constant.

Solution:

$$P = K_H X_2$$

$$X_2 = \frac{n_2}{n_1 + n_2}$$

$$= \frac{\dfrac{2 \times 10^{-5}}{28 \times 10^{-3}}}{\dfrac{2 \times 10^{-5}}{28 \times 10^{-3}} + \dfrac{1}{18 \times 10^{-3}}}$$

$$= 1.29 \times 10^{-5}$$

Therefore,

$$K_H = \frac{P}{X_2} \qquad \qquad (\because P = 1 \text{ atm})$$

$$= \frac{1}{1.29 \times 10^{-5}} \text{ atm}$$

$$= 7.7 \times 10^6 \text{ atm}$$

Problem 10.4: Calculate the amount of oxygen (0.20 atm) dissolved in 1 kg of water at 293 K. The Henry's law constant for oxygen is 4.58×10^4 atmosphere at 293 K.

Solution: Since

$$X_2 = \frac{P}{K_H}$$

$$= \frac{0.2}{4.58 \times 10^4} = 4.35 \times 10^{-6}$$

Now

$$X_2 = \frac{n_2}{n_1 + n_2}$$

$$= \frac{1}{18 \times 10^{-3}} + n_2 = 4.37 \times 10^{-6}$$

or

$$n_2 = 2.43 \times 10^{-4}$$

Hence the amount of oxygen dissolved

$$= 2.43 \times 10^{-4} \times 32 \times 10^{-3}$$

$$= 7.77 \times 10^{-6} \text{ kg}$$

10.6 IDEAL SOLUTIONS—RAOULTS LAW

As the concept of an ideal gas has been used in the study of many thermodynamic properties, it would be helpful to find out some similar concept in case of solutions. *An ideal solution* is defined as *the one in which there is complete uniformity in cohesive forces*. The solute-solute, solvent-solvent and solute-solvent interactions are identical. Thus, if there are two components A and B forming an ideal solution, then the intermolecular forces between A—A, A—B and B—B are essentially equal.

Characteristics of an Ideal Solution: An ideal solution possesses the following characteristics:

(*i*) When two pure substances mix to form an ideal solution, there is no evolution or absorption of heat, *i.e.*, the heat of mixing (ΔH_{mixing}) is zero.

(*ii*) The total volume of an ideal solution will be equal to the sum of the volumes of the components mixed, *i.e.*, the volume of mixing (ΔV_{mixing}) is zero.

(*iii*) The ideal solution must obey Raoult's law and Henry's law over the whole range of concentration.

Raoult's Law: An important property in the theory of solutions is the vapour pressure of a component above solution. The partial vapour pressure is a measure of the tendency of molecules of the components to escape from solution into the vapour phase. If we have an ideal solution containing volatile components 1 and 2, then the tendency of molecules 1 or 2 to escape is the same whether it is surrounded entirely by 1 molecules or by 2 molecules or partly by both 1 and 2. The vapours present above the solution (due to the escaping tendency) are in equilibrium and exert definite vapour pressures. In an ideal solution, therefore, each component exerts its equilibrium vapour pressure and the total vapour pressure is the sum of the individual vapour pressure of the components according to Dalton's law of partial pressure. If p_1 and p_2 are the partial pressures of two components 1 and 2, then the total pressure P is equal to $p_1 + p_2$. It is found experimentally that the vapour pressure of the individual components of an ideal solution can be easily determined by *Raoult's law*. This law states *that at a given temperature the vapour pressure of any volatile component of a solution is directly proportional to its mole fraction in the solution*. If p_s is the vapour pressure of the solution and X_1 its mole fraction in the solution, then

$$p_s \propto X_1$$

or

$$p_s = \text{Const.} \, X_1$$

The value of the constant can be obtained using initial conditions. If $X_1 = 1$ (pure component), $p_s = \text{constant} = p^0 = $ vapour pressure of the pure component. So we have

$$p_s = p^0 X_1 \qquad \qquad ...(10.1)$$

For a binary solution of two volatile components 1 and 2, we have

$$p_1 = p_1^0 \, X_1 \qquad \qquad ...(10.2(a))$$

and

$$p_2 = p_2^0 \, X_2 \qquad \qquad ...(10.2(b))$$

where X_1 and X_2 are the mole fractions of 1 and 2 in the solution. An ideal solution obeys Raoult's law over the whole range of concentration.

The total vapour pressure P of the solution is given by

$$P = p_1 + p_2$$

$$= p_1^0 \, X_1 + p_2^0 \, X_2 \qquad \qquad (10.3)$$

Since

$$X_1 + X_2 = 1$$

or $$X_1 = 1 - X_2$$

Therefore, Eq. (10.3) can be written as

$$P = p_1^0(1 - X_2) + p_2^0 X_2$$

$$= p_1^0 + X_2(p_2^0 - p_1^0) \qquad ...(10.4)$$

The relations (10.3 – 10.4) are such that if p_1, p_2 and P are plotted against mole fraction of either of the components in the solution, say X_2 at a given temperature, straight lines will result. These plots are shown in Fig. 10.2.

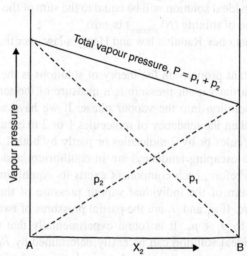

Fig. 10.2 Total and partial vapour pressures of ideal solutions

In Fig. 10.2, the dotted lines represent the plots of Eq. (10.2) for the partial pressures of 1 and 2. These lines pass through the origin indicating that both components are behaving ideally. When $X_2 = 1$, *i.e.*, only pure component 2 is present, $P = p_2^0$ whereas, if $X_2 = 0$, *i.e.*, pure component 1 is present, $P = p_1^0$. The solid line indicates the total vapour pressure of the ideal solution. At any concentration, the total pressure is the sum of the partial pressures of two components.

Raoult's law may be regarded as a special case of Henry's law. From Eq. (*i*), we have

$$p_2 = K_H X_2$$

In case when Henry's law is applicable over the whole range of concentration, that is, from an infinitely dilute solution ($X_2 \to 0$, pure solvent) to the liquid solute ($X_2 \to 1$, pure solute), then p_2 would become the vapour pressure of the pure solute. Hence

$$p_2^0 = K_H$$

Substituting this value of K_H in the above equation, we get

$$p_2 = p_2^0 X_2$$

This expression is identical with the Raoult's law Eq. (10.3) for a volatile solute. All systems which obey Raoult's law must satisfy Henry's law, but the reverse will only be true if Henry's law applies over the whole range of concentration.

Problem 10.5: Two liquids A and B form an ideal solution. At 300 K, the vapour pressure of the solution containing 1 mole of A and 3 moles of B is 550 mm Hg. At the same temperature, if one more mole of B is added to this solution, the vapour pressure of the solution is increased by 10 mm Hg. Determine p_A^0 and p_B^0.

Solution: Vapour pressure of solution of 1 mole of A + 3 moles of B = 550 mm Hg
Vapour pressure of solution of 1 mole of A + 4 moles of B = 560 mm Hg

Let the vapour pressure of component A be p_A^0 and that of B be p_B^0.
Therefore,

$$p_A^0 X_A + p_B^0 X_B = 550$$

$$= \frac{1}{4} p_A^0 + \frac{3}{4} p_B^0 = 550$$

Similarly

$$\frac{1}{5} p_A^0 + \frac{4}{5} p_B^0 = 560$$

On solving, we get

$$p_A^0 = 400 \text{ mm Hg}$$

and

$$p_B^0 = 600 \text{ mm Hg}$$

10.7 GIBBS–DUHEM–MARGULES EQUATION

This equation gives information regarding the variation of partial vapour pressures and the composition of various components in a solution. The Gibbs-Duhem equation for a binary solution is written as

$$n_1 d\mu_1 + n_2 d\mu_2 = 0$$

Dividing this equation by the total number of moles of the solution, i.e. $(n_1 + n_2)$, we get

$$\frac{n_1}{n_1 + n_2} d\mu_1 + \frac{n_2}{n_1 + n_2} d\mu_2 = 0$$

$$X_1 d\mu_1 + X_2 d\mu_2 = 0 \qquad \text{...(10.5)}$$

where X_1 and X_2 are the mole fractions of 1 and 2 respectively in the solution.

The chemical potential of a component (behaving ideally) is expressed as

$$\mu_i = \mu_i^0 + RT \ln p_i \qquad \text{...(10.6)}$$

Differentiation of this equation yields

$$d\mu_i = RTd \ln p_i \qquad \text{...(10.7)}$$

Putting the value of $d\mu$ in Eq. (10.5) gives

$$X_1 RT(d \ln p_1) + X_2 RT(d \ln p_2) = 0$$
$$RT(X_1 d \ln p_1 + X_2 d \ln p_2) = 0$$
$$X_1 d \ln p_1 + X_2 d \ln p_2 = 0$$

or

$$\frac{X_1 d \ln p_1}{dX_1} + \frac{X_2 d \ln p_2}{dX_1} = 0 \qquad ...(10.8)$$

Since $X_1 + X_2 = 1$, so $dX_1 = -dX_2$, therefore Eq. (10.8) becomes

$$\frac{X_1 d \ln p_1}{dX_1} - \frac{X_2 d \ln p_2}{dX_2} = 0$$

$$\frac{d \ln p_1}{dX_1/X_1} - \frac{d \ln p_2}{dX_2/X_2} = 0$$

or $$\frac{d \ln p_1}{d \ln X_1} = \frac{d \ln p_2}{d \ln X_2} \qquad ...(10.9)$$

or $$\frac{X_1}{p_1} \frac{dp_1}{dX_1} = \frac{X_2}{p_2} \frac{dp_2}{dX_2} \qquad ...(10.10)$$

Eqs. (10.9) and (10.10) are known as Duhem-Margules equation. These equations are valid whether the vapour phase behaves ideally or non-ideally. This equation shows that if in component 1 there is an increase in the mole fraction (dX_1), it will cause an increase in the partial pressure (dp_1) of the component 1, and will also bring a change in the partial pressure of the other component.

Let X_1 be the mole fraction of component 1 in the liquid phase and Y_1 be the mole fraction in the vapour phase, then in a binary system, Dalton's law of partial pressure gives

$$p_1 = Y_1 P$$

and $$p_2 = Y_2 P = (1 - Y_1) P$$

Substituting these values in Eq. (10.10), we get

$$\frac{X_1}{Y_1 P} \left(\frac{dp_1}{dX_1} \right) = \frac{X_2}{Y_2 P} \left(\frac{dp_2}{dX_2} \right)$$

Since $$dX_1 = -dX_2$$

Therefore $$\frac{X_1}{Y_1 P} \left(\frac{dp_1}{dX_1} \right) = -\frac{X_2}{Y_2 P} \left(\frac{dp_2}{dX_1} \right)$$

or $$\frac{X_1}{Y_1} \left(\frac{dp_1}{dX_1} \right) = -\frac{X_2}{Y_2} \left(\frac{dp_2}{dX_1} \right)$$

$$\frac{dp_1}{dX_1} = -\frac{Y_1 X_2}{X_1 Y_2} \left(\frac{dp_2}{dX_1} \right)$$

$$\left(\frac{dp_2}{dX_1} \right) = -\frac{X_1 Y_2}{Y_1 X_2} \left(\frac{dp_1}{dX_1} \right) \qquad ...(10.11)$$

Since

$$P = p_1 + p_2$$

Hence

$$\frac{dP}{dX_1} = \frac{dp_1}{dX_1} + \frac{dp_2}{dX_1} \qquad ...(10.12)$$

Substituting the value of $\left(\dfrac{dp_2}{dX_1}\right)$ from Eq. (10.11) into Eq. (10.12), we get

$$\frac{dP}{dX_1} = \frac{dp_1}{dX_1}\left[1 - \frac{X_1 Y_2}{Y_1 X_2}\right] \qquad ...(10.13)$$

This equation gives the change in total pressure with the change in the composition.

Since $\dfrac{dP}{dX_1}$ is positive and therefore the right hand side of Eq. (10.13) will also be positive. Since

$\dfrac{dp_1}{dX_1}$ is always positive, therefore $\left(1 - \dfrac{X_1 Y_2}{Y_1 X_2}\right)$ should also be positive, *i.e.*

$$\frac{X_1 Y_2}{Y_1 X_2} < 1$$

or

$$\frac{X_1(1 - Y_1)}{Y_1(1 - X_1)} < 1$$

Hence

$$Y_1 > X_1 \qquad ...(10.14)$$

This is known as Konovalov's law. This states that a saturated vapour in equilibrium with a binary liquid mixture is richer in that component whose addition to the liquid mixture increases the vapour pressure. In other words, the vapour phase is richer in that component which is more volatile.

For liquid pairs having either a maximum or minimum boiling points are called azeotropes. Azeotropic solutions distill unchanged in composition implying same composition of liquid and vapour phase. At

minimum or maximum point $\dfrac{dP}{dX_1} = 0$, hence Eq. (10.13) may be written as

$$\frac{dP}{dX_1} = 0 = \frac{dp_1}{dX_1}\left[1 - \frac{X_1 Y_2}{X_2 Y_1}\right]$$

Since $\dfrac{dp_1}{dX_1}$ is not zero, therefore

$$1 - \frac{X_1 Y_2}{X_2 Y_1} = 0$$

or

$$X_1 Y_2 = X_2 Y_1 = X_1(1 - Y_1) = (1 - X_1)Y_1$$

Hence

$$X_1 = Y_1 \text{ and } X_2 = Y_2 \qquad ...(10.15)$$

That is the mole fraction of each component in liquid phase (X_1) is equal to its mole fraction in vapour phase (Y_1). This is known as second law of Konovalov.

Vapour Pressure-Composition Diagram for Ideal Solutions: Equation (10.4) gives a relationship between the total pressure and the mole fraction of the components of the solution. It is also easy to find out the relation between the composition of vapour above a solution and the composition of the solution. Suppose Y_2 is the mole fraction of B in the vapour phase and X_2 its mole fraction in the solution, then according to Dalton's law of partial pressure

$$Y_2 = \frac{p_2}{P} = \frac{p_2}{p_1 + p_2}$$

$$= \frac{p_2^0 X_2}{p_1^0 X_1 + p_2^0 X_2}$$

$$= \frac{p_2^0 X_2}{p_1^0 + X_2\left(p_2^0 - p_1^0\right)} \qquad \qquad ...(10.16)$$

Since p_1^0 and p_2^0 are constants and known quantities, hence Y_2 can be calculated for different values of X_2. Furthermore, from Eq. (10.16) it is clear that X_2 and Y_2 are not identical except when $p_1^0 = p_2^0$.

From Eq. (10.16)

$$X_2 = \frac{Y_2\, p_1^0}{p_2^0 + Y_2\left(p_1^0 - p_2^0\right)}$$

Substituting this value of X_2 in Eq. (10.4) and rearranging, we get

$$\frac{1}{P} = \frac{1}{p_1^0} + Y_2\left(\frac{1}{p_2^0} - \frac{1}{p_1^0}\right)$$

$$= \frac{1}{p_1^0}(1 - Y_2) + \frac{Y_2}{p_2^0} \qquad \qquad ...(10.17)$$

$$= \frac{Y_1}{p_1^0} + \frac{Y_2}{p_2^0} \qquad (\because 1 - Y_2 = Y_1) \qquad \qquad ...(10.18)$$

Relations (10.17) or (10.18) give the dependence of the total pressure on the composition of the vapour phase. A plot of P versus Y_2 from Eq. (10.17) or (10.18) will not be a straight line.

The ratio of mole fraction of component 2 in vapour phase to its mole fraction in solution is obtained as

$$Y_2 = \frac{p_2}{p_1 + p_2}$$

$$= \frac{p_2^0 X_2}{p_1^0 X_1 + p_2^0 X_2}$$

or

$$\frac{Y_2}{X_2} = \frac{p_2^0}{p_1^0 X_1 + p_2^0 X_2}$$

$$= \frac{1}{X_2 + \dfrac{p_1^0}{p_2^0} X_1}$$ ...(10.19)

It is clear from the above equation that if $p_2^0 > p_1^0$, *i.e.*, component 2 is more volatile than compo-

nent 1, the ratio $\dfrac{Y_2}{X_2}$ would be greater than 1. In other words, the vapour is richer in more volatile component 2 than the solution.

With the help of Eq. (10.16), vapour pressure composition diagram can be constructed by plotting P versus X_2 or Y_2 for solutions obeying Raoult's law. This is shown in Fig. 10.3. It is found that the vapour composition curve always lies below the liquid composition curve. The liquid is stable at higher pressure while the vapours exist at lower pressure. Hence, the liquid composition curve lies above the vapour composition curve.

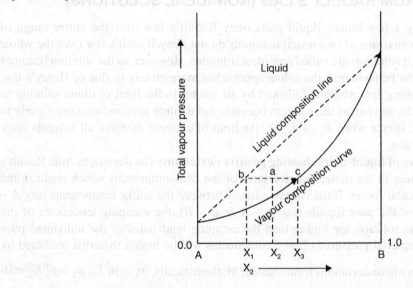

Fig. 10.3 Liquid and vapour composition curves for ideal solution

The points lying just above the liquid composition curve correspond to the lowest pressure at which liquid can exist by itself and vapour appears if the points lie on the curve. Liquid can not be present alone below the liquid composition curve. Similarly, vapours can not exist alone above the vapour composition curve. The points lying between the curves represent the state of the system where liquid and vapour coexist in equilibrium. For example, point a in the liquid-vapour region is made up of liquid having a composition X_1, and vapour having a composition X_3. This has been obtained by drawing a horizontal line bac known as a 'tie-line', because it connects the compositions of the liquid and vapour phases in equilibrium.

We can calculate the relative amounts of liquid and vapours required to yield an overall composition corresponding to a. Let n_v and n_l be the total number of moles of both the components 1 and 2 in vapour and liquid phases respectively. Then from material balance, we have,

$$X_2(n_l + n_v) = X_1 n_l + X_3 n_v$$

$$\frac{n_l}{n_v} = \frac{X_3 - X_2}{X_2 - X_1} = \frac{ac}{ab} \qquad \qquad ...(10.20)$$

This expression is known as the *lever rule,* point a being the fulcrum of the lever. The ratio of the number of moles of liquid to the number of moles of vapour is given by the ratio of the lengths of the line segments connecting a to c and b. If a lies very close to c, then ac is very small and $n_l \ll n_v$, the system consists mainly of vapours. Similarly, when a lies very close to b, $n_l \gg n_v$; the system consists mainly of liquid. This law is applicable to any two compositions of two phases in equilibrium connected by a tie-line in a phase diagram of a two component system.

Only a few pairs of liquids have been found to obey Raoult's law over the entire range of concentration. A few examples are benzene-toluene, n-hexane-n-heptane, benzene-ether, chlorobenzene-bromobenzene etc.

10.8 DEVIATIONS FROM RAOULT'S LAW (NON-IDEAL SOLUTIONS)

As stated previously, only a few binary liquid pairs obey Raoult's law over the entire range of concentration. Most of the mixtures of two miscible liquids do not obey Raoult's law over the whole range of concentration. Such solutions are called non-ideal solutions. However, as the solution becomes more dilute, $X_2 \rightarrow 0$, *i.e.*, the behaviour of the solute approaches more closely to that of Henry's law. Thus, Henry's law is a limiting law which is followed by all solutes in the limit of dilute solution as $X_2 \rightarrow 0$. The behaviour of the solvent, as the solution becomes more dilute approaches more closely to that given by Raoult's law. Hence when $X_1 \rightarrow 1$, *i.e.*, the limit of extreme dilution, all solvents obey Raoult's law as a limiting case.

Vapour pressure curves of liquid-pairs showing positive deviations: The deviations from Raoult's law are due to the differences in the molecular structures of the two components which result in the difference in the intermolecular forces. If the cohesive forces between the unlike components (say $A - B$) are weaker than those of the pure liquids (say $A - A$ or $B - B$), the escaping tendencies of the components A and B in the solution are higher than the escaping tendencies of the individual pure components. Therefore the partial pressures of pure components will be higher than that predicted by

Raoult's law. This leads to positive deviations from ideality. Mathematically, $p_1 > p_1^0 X_1$, $p_2 > p_2^0 X_2$ and

$p > p_1^0 X_1 + p_2^0 X_2$ This is shown in the vapour pressure versus composition diagram in Fig. 10.4. In the figure, dotted lines represent the ideal behaviour while the solid lines represent the actual vapour pressure for each component and the solution. Systems exhibiting positive deviations from Raoult's law are water-dioxane, acetone-ether, benzene-chlorohexane, acetone-carbon sulphide etc. In such systems there would be an increase in volume on mixing and also an absorption of heat on mixing.

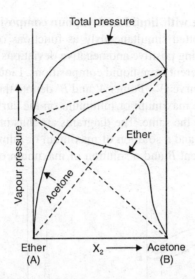

Fig. 10.4 The vapour pressure diagram for ether-acetone system

Vapour pressure curves of liquid pairs showing negative deviation: If the attractive forces between the unlike molecules in solution (A---B) are stronger than those between the like molecules (A–A and B–B) in pure liquids, then the escaping tendency of a component from the solution would be less than it would be from the pure liquid. Therefore, the partial pressure of both the components will be less than that predicted by Raoult's law. This amounts to a negative deviation from Raoult's law. This is shown in Fig. 10.5. Few examples of liquid pairs which exhibit negative deviations from ideality are chloroform-acetone, methanol-acetone, pyridine-acetic acid etc. When acetone and chloroform are mixed they form hydrogen bonds with each other. As a result, the intermolecular attractions between acetone and chloroform becomes stronger. The tendency of the molecules to escape from the solution decreases and hence the vapour pressure also shows a decrease in its value. In such systems there would be a contraction in volume and evolution of heat on mixing.

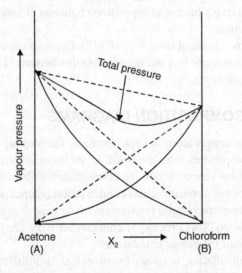

Fig. 10.5 The vapour pressure diagram for chloroform-acetone system

Vapour pressure variation with liquid and vapour composition: In Fig. 10.6 (*a*) and (*b*), the vapour pressures have been plotted simultaneously as functions of liquid compositions and vapour compositions for solutions showing positive and negative deviations from Raoult's law. At equilibrium, the vapour compositions are different from liquid compositions. Liquid composition curve (*L*) is always above the vapour composition curve (*V*). Points A' and B' denote the vapour pressures of pure components and point *O* represents the maximum or minimum on the curve. At point *O*, the composition of the vapour and liquid phases are the same. The diagrams are thus made up of two portions, namely (*i*) one between pure component *A* and a solution of maximum or minimum vapour pressure and, (*ii*) the other between the pure component *B* and a solution of maximum or minimum vapour pressure.

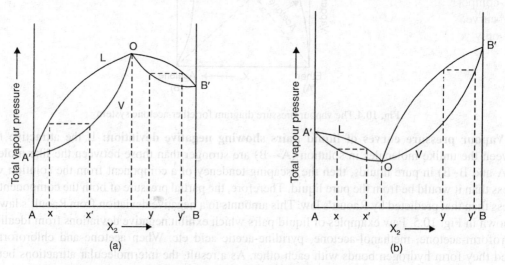

Fig. 10.6 Vapour pressure diagrams for liquid pairs showing (*a*) positive deviations and (*b*) negative deviations from Raoult's law

In Fig. 10.6 (*a*), mixtures having compositions between *A* and *O* will have vapours richer in *B* than the solution. But for liquid mixtures having compositions between *O* and *B* will have vapours richer in *A* as compared to that in solution.

Similar findings can also be obtained from Fig. 10.6(*b*). Liquid mixtures between *A* and *O* will have vapours poorer in *B* than the solution. But the liquid mixtures between *O* and *B* will be richer in *B* in the vapour state than the solution.

10.9 TEMPERATURE COMPOSITION DIAGRAMS

In all the above diagrams, the temperature is kept constant. The vapour above the solution is always richer in the more volatile components than the solution. At constant temperature, if such a vapour is removed and condensed, the new vapour above the condensate will be considerably richer in the more volatile constituent. If this process of removal and condensation is repeated several times, it is possible to obtain a concentration of the more volatile constituent in the vapour and the concentration of the less volatile constituent in the solution. This process of concentrating the constituents of a solution in steps or stages is known as *isothermal fractional distillation*.

In practice, this type of distillation is rather inconvenient and difficult to carry out. It is for this reason that the distillation is conducted at constant pressure, usually at 1 atmospheric pressure.

According to Raoult's law, different concentrations of solutions have different vapour pressures, hence the solutions of different concentrations will boil at different temperatures. Solutions whose components have low vapour pressures will boil at higher temperatures than solutions in which the components have high vapour pressures. This is due to the fact that external pressure is attained at a lower temperature in case of volatile components. Thus, the solution with a high vapour pressure starts boiling at a lower temperature.

From the above arguments it is possible to construct the boiling point-composition diagrams corresponding to the three general types of vapour pressure-composition curves already discussed.

Case I: Boiling Point Composition Diagrams for Ideal Liquid Pairs: Fig. 10.7 shows a boiling point-composition curve for an ideal solution. Comparing Fig. 10.7 with Fig. 10.3, it is noted that the liquid curve is below the vapour curve. This is due to the fact that at constant pressure above the boiling point only vapours will exist.

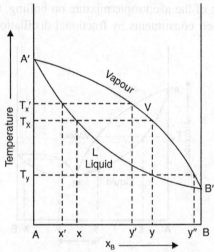

Fig. 10.7 Boiling point-composition diagram for a binary solution showing ideal behaviour

In Fig. 10.7, $A'LB'$ is the boiling point-liquid composition curve and $A'VB'$ represents the boiling point-vapour composition curve. Suppose we heat a solution of composition X, on heating the vapour pressure of the system will increase until it reaches a constant value equal to the external pressure. At this stage the liquid begins to boil. The temperature T_X therefore corresponds to the boiling point of the solution of composition x. At T_X, the vapours in equilibrium with the liquid will have the composition Y which is richer in the more volatile component B than X. If the vapour corresponding to y is condensed, a liquid will result which will boil at a temperature $T_Y (T_Y < T_X)$. The composition of the vapours in equilibrium with this condensate is given by Y''. It is again richer in B than the original vapour. If this process of condensing and redistilling is repeated a number of times, ultimately vapours containing pure B can be obtained.

The initial residue left after the removal of the vapours will be richer in the less volatile component A, as X'. The residue corresponding to X' will boil at a temperature $T_X' (T_X' > T_X)$. The corresponding composition of the vapours in equilibrium with solution of composition X' is given by Y'. These vapours are again richer in B and the residual liquid richer in A. In this manner, if the vapour at one boiling point is condensed and redistilled at a higher temperature and the process is repeated again and again, the residue becomes richer and richer in A than the original solution until pure A is obtained.

In case of ideal liquid pairs, complete separation of two liquids is possible by fractional distillation.

Case II: Boiling Point Composition Diagrams for Nonideal Liquid Pairs Azeotropic Mixtures:
(a) Boiling point-composition diagrams exhibiting positive deviation: In this type of liquid pairs, the vapour pressure composition curves show positive deviations from ideality [Fig. 10.6(a)]. The boiling point-composition diagram, however, passes through a minimum where the liquid and vapour phases have the same composition as shown in Fig. 10.8. If a mixture of composition (say x) is heated, the solution will boil at a temperature T_X. The vapours in equilibrium with the solution have the composition y and will be richer in B than the residue. By repeating the process several times as discussed in case I, a stage is reached when the residual solution contains only pure component A and the distillate corresponding to the composition at the minimum point M in Fig. 10.8. At this point, the composition of the liquid and the vapour phases is the same. A mixture with composition corresponding to a minimum on the boiling point diagram is called an *azeotropic mixture*. Evidently, the azeotropic mixture will have a boiling point lower than the boiling point of any other mixtures of A and B. Since there is no change in the composition of the azeotropic mixture on boiling, therefore such mixtures can not be completely separated into their constituents by fractional distillation as discussed in section 10.7.

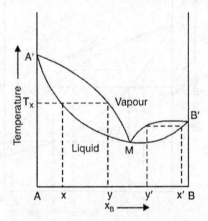

Fig. 10.8 Boiling point composition diagram for a binary solution showing positive deviation

On the other hand, if a solution of composition x' between B and M is heated, the vapours coming off with composition y' will be richer in A than the residue. On repeated distillation the composition of residue will tend towards pure B while the distillate will yield an azeotropic mixture corresponding to M. In other words, by fractional distillation any mixture of this type can be separated only into one pure component and the azeotropic mixture. It is not possible to separate them completely into pure components by fractional distillation. Table 10.3 shows some liquid pairs of this type.

Table 10.3 Binary Liquid Mixtures Showing Positive Deviation (Minimum Boiling Point)

Component		Minimum boiling	Composition
A	*B*	*point (C)*	*(mass % of B)*
Water	Ethanol	78.1	95.6
Water	n-propanol	88.0	72.0
Benzene	Acetic acid	80.1	2.0
Water	Pyridine	92.0	52.0
Carbondisulphide	Ethyl acetate	46.0	3.0

(b) **Boiling point composition diagrams exhibiting negative deviation:** In these types of liquid pairs, the vapour pressure composition curve shows a minimum [Fig. 10.6(*b*)], *i.e.*, a negative deviation. Consequently, the boiling point composition diagram would show a maximum (Fig. 10.9). At a certain composition corresponding to the maximum point *M* on the boiling point diagram, there is an azeotropic mixture boiling at a fixed temperature unchanged in composition. From reasonings analogous to those described previously, repeated distillation of a solution of composition *x* between *AM* would yield pure component *A* in the final distillate and an azeotropic mixture in the residue. There will be no pure component *B*. Similarly, repeated distillation of mixtures having composition between *M* and *B* would give pure component *B* in the final distillate and an azeotropic mixture in the residue. There will be no pure component *A*.

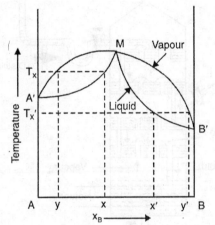

Fig. 10.9 Boiling point composition diagram for a binary solution showing negative deviation

Some binary mixtures with maximum boiling point are given in Table 10.4.

Table 10.4 Binary Liquid Mixtures Showing Negative Deviation (Maximum Boiling Point)

Component		Maximum boiling point (°C)	Composition (mass % of B)
A	B		
Water	Hydrochloric acid	108.5	20.2
Water	Nitric acid	120.5	68.0
Chloroform	Acetone	64.7	20.0
Water	Formic acid	107.0	77.0

The fact that an azeotrope although distills unchanged in its composition at a definite temperature suggests that it may be a true chemical compound. However, this is not true as its composition depends on pressure. When the azeotrope is distilled under changed pressure, its composition also changes indicating that it is a mixture and not a chemical compound.

10.10 THE FRACTIONATING COLUMNS

From the boiling point composition diagram of Fig. 10.7, one can see that if a small amount of vapour is removed from a solution of composition X, the vapour would have a composition higher in the more volatile component than the original solution. The process of separating the two components by collecting fractions from a simple distillation and then by redistilling these fractions is tedious, laborious and time consuming. To overcome this difficulty, a fractionating column is generally used. A fractionating column is a distillation apparatus in which many distillations occur continuously. A general and most common fractionating column used is bubble-cap column shown in Fig. 10.10.

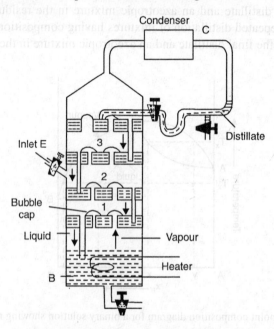

Fig. 10.10 Bubble-cap fractionating column

It consists of a series of bubble-cap plates attached to a boiler (B) having a heating coil at the bottom and to a condenser (C) at the top. Each plate in the column is essentially a single distillation apparatus. The mixture to be distilled is admitted through E and boiled in the boiler by the heating coil. On boiling, the vapours move upward through the caps to the plates where they come in contact with the liquid. This liquid is somewhat cooler than that in the boiler so that a partial condensation takes place. The vapours that leave plate 1 are, therefore, richer in more volatile component than the vapours from the boiler. Again, when these vapours reach plate 2, they come in contact with the descending (or refluxing) cooler liquid so that again partial condensation takes place. The vapours which move up further will be richer in the more volatile component than the vapours in plate 1. A similar enrichment will take place at each plate so that the ascending vapours become richer in the more volatile component and the descending (or refluxing) liquid becomes richer in less volatile component. In this way, less volatile component can be taken off from the boiler and the more volatile component can be drawn off in pure form by condensing the vapours at the top of the column.

The efficiency of distilling column is measured by the number of each equilibrium stages that it attains. Each stage is called a *theoretical plate*. In a well designed bubble-cap column, each unit acts as one theoretical plate.

Complete separation of two liquids by fractional distillation is possible only in cases of ideal liquid pairs.

10.11 PARTIALLY MISCIBLE LIQUIDS

Type I. Systems Having Upper Critical Solution Temperature: There are certain liquid pairs which are partially miscible. For example, if a small quantity of phenol is added to water at ordinary temperature, it will dissolve in water completely. As the amount of phenol is increased, a stage is reached when no more phenol dissolves and two liquid layers are formed. The upper layer is a saturated solution of phenol in water while the lower layer is a saturated solution of water in phenol. These two solutions in equilibrium with each other are called *conjugate solutions.*

At constant temperature, composition of the layers although different from each other, remains constant as long as two phases are present. Addition of small amount of phenol or water merely changes the relative volumes of the two layers and not their composition. As the temperature is raised, mutual solubility of the two liquid increases, until at a certain temperature the two liquids become completely miscible. This temperature is known as the *mutual solubility temperature (MST).*

Variation of mutual solubility of water in phenol is shown in Fig. 10.11. In the figure *AB* represents the solubility curve of phenol in water. It gives the percentage of phenol dissolved in water at different temperatures. As the temperature is raised, the solubility increases. On the other hand, when small amounts of water is added to phenol, it dissolves. If the amount of water is increased, the limit of saturation is reached and water forms a separate layer. The solubility curve of water in phenol is given by *CB.*

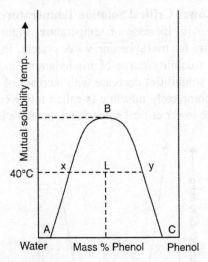

Fig. 10.11 Mutual solubility of water phenol system at various temperature

At a temperature (say 40°C), point *x* represents the composition of phenol in water and point *y* represents the composition of water in phenol. Thus at points *x* and *y*, completely miscible and homogeneous solutions will result. Between *x* and *y* all mixtures yield two layers of compositions *x* and *y*, while a point on the left of *x* or on the right of *y* will correspond to a homogeneous solution. *ABC* is thus a boundary between homogeneous and heterogeneous conditions of the system. Any point lying on the dome-shaped area represents the existence of two liquid phases and the area outside the dome corresponds to a single layer. The temperature (66°C) corresponding to the maximum in the curve (point *B*, having composition 33% phenol by mass) at and above which the two liquids become completely miscible in all proportions is called the *upper consolute temperature or upper critical solution temperature (CST).*

At this temperature the two compositions become identical and two layers merge into a single layer.

If L represents a system of two layers whose relative composition is given by X and Y respectively, the relative masses of two layers are given by the lever rule as

$$\frac{\text{Mass of phenol layer}}{\text{Mass of water layer}} = \frac{\text{distance } LY}{\text{distance } LX}$$

Other liquid pairs having upper critical solution temperature are given in Table 10.5.

Table 10.5 Partially Miscible Liquid Pairs with an Upper Critical Solution Temperature

Component		Critical solution temperature
A	B	(°C)
Aniline	Hexane	59.6
Water	Aniline	167.0
Carbon disulphide	Methanol	40.5
Cyclohexane	Methanol	49.0

Type II. Systems Having Lower Critical Solution Temperature: There are liquid pairs in which the mutual solubility decreases with increase of temperature. Figure 10.12 shows the variation of mutual solubility with temperature for triethylamine-water system. In this case the shape of the curve is reverse of type I. AB is the solubility curve of triethylamine in water and CB that of water in triethylamine. In both cases, the solubilities decrease with increase of temperature. The temperature at which the two liquids become completely miscible is called lower critical solution temperature. The composition corresponding to the lower critical solution temperature is 50% by mass of triethylamine.

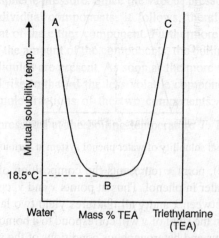

Fig. 10.12 Solubility of triethylamine in water at various temperature

As in the previous case, any point within the curve ABC corresponds to heterogeneity of the system while any point outside ABC shows a homogeneous phase.

Other liquid pairs which have lower critical solution temperature are given in Table 10.6.

Table 10.6 Partially Miscible Liquid Pairs Showing a Lower Critical Solution Temperature

Component		Critical solution temperature
A	B	(°C)
Water	Diethylamine	43.0
Water	Methylpiperidine	48.0

Type III. Systems Having Both Upper and Lower Critical Solution Temperatures: There are cases where mutual solubility curve is closed one having both an upper critical solution temperature and a lower critical solution temperature. Nicotine-water system is an example of this type. Figure 10.13 shows the variations of mutual solubility with temperature for this system. Within the enclosed area, the liquids are partially miscible while outside the enclosed area, they are completely miscible. The upper critical solution temperature is 208°C and lower critical solution temperature is 60.8°C. The composition corresponding to these two temperatures is the same, *i.e.,* 32% by mass of nicotine.

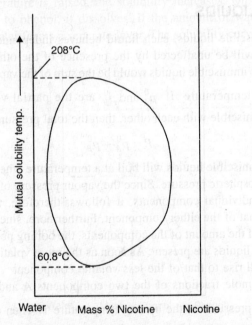

Fig. 10.13 Solubility of nicotine in water at several temperatures

It has been observed that pressure has a marked effect on this system. On applying external pressure to the system, the upper and lower critical solution temperatures approach each other and at a certain pressure the two liquids become completely miscible.

Other systems of this type are given in Table 10.7.

Effect of Foreign Substances (Impurities) on Critical Solution Temperature: The impurities have a marked effect on the critical solution temperature. If an impurity is soluble in one of the two liquids, the critical solution temperature of the system increases. For example, a concentration of 0.1 M naphthalene per dm^3 of water raises the critical solution temperature of phenol-water system by 20°C. This increase in temperature is due to the salting out of water. When the added substance dissolves in both the liquids, the critical solution temperature is lowered due to negative salting out effect, This can be seen by adding succinic acid to phenol-water system. It has been seen that the CST varies directly with the amount of the impurity added.

Table 10.7 Partially Miscible Liquid Pairs Having Lower and Upper Critical Solution Temperature

System	Upper critical solution temperature (°C)	Lower critical solution temperature (°C)
Ethylmethyl ketone-water	133.0	−6.0
Glycerol-m-toluidine	120.0	7.0
β-picoline-water	153.0	49.0

The critical solution temperature is so sensitive to the traces of impurities that it may be used as a criterion of purity of the substance.

10.12 IMMISCIBLE LIQUIDS

In a mixture of two immiscible liquids, each liquid behaves independently of the other. Hence the properties of each liquid will be unaffected by the presence of the other. Consequently, the vapour pressure of a mixture of two immiscible liquids would be the sum of the vapour pressures of the individual pure components at that temperature. If p_A^0 and p_B^0 are the partial vapour pressures of the pure components which are immiscible with each other, then the total pressure P is given by

$$P = p_A^0 + p_B^0$$

The mixture of two immiscible liquids will boil at a temperature when the total vapour pressure of the mixture equals the atmospheric pressure. Since the vapour pressure of the mixture is the sum of the vapour pressures of the individual components, it follows, therefore, that the boiling point of the mixture will be less than that of the either component. Furthermore, since the total vapour pressure is constant and independent of the amount of the components, the boiling point of the mixture will remain constant as long as the two liquids are present. As soon as the more volatile component is boiled away, the boiling temperature will rise to that of the less volatile component.

Let X_1 and X_2 be the mole fractions of the two components A and B in the vapour phase and p_A^0 and p_B^0 be their partial pressures at the boiling temperature T. Then according to Dalton's law of partial pressure

$$p_A^0 = X_1 P$$

and

$$p_B^0 = X_2 P$$

where P is the total pressure.

Taking the ratio of these equations we get

$$\frac{p_A^0}{p_B^0} = \frac{X_1}{X_2}$$

...(10.21)

Since
$$X_1 = \frac{n_1}{n_1 + n_2}$$

and
$$X_2 = \frac{n_2}{n_1 + n_2}$$

where n_1 and n_2 are the number of moles of A and B in the vapour phase. Substituting X_1 and X_2 in Eq. (10.21) yields

$$\frac{p_A^0}{p_B^0} = \frac{\dfrac{n_1}{n_1 + n_2}}{\dfrac{n_2}{n_1 + n_2}}$$

$$= \frac{n_1}{n_2} \qquad \qquad ...(10.22)$$

Since at a given temperature, p_A^0 and p_B^0 are constants, so $\dfrac{n_1}{n_2}$ is also constant as long as both the liquids are present.

Further
$$n_1 = \frac{W_1}{M_1} \quad \text{and} \quad n_2 = \frac{W_2}{M_2}$$

where W's and M's correspond to the masses and molar masses of the respective components. Eq. (10.22) then becomes

$$\frac{p_A^0}{p_B^0} = \frac{W_1/M_1}{W_2/M_2} = \frac{W_1 M_2}{W_2 M_1}$$

or
$$\frac{W_1}{W_2} = \frac{p_A^0 M_1}{p_B^0 M_2} \qquad \qquad ...(10.23)$$

Thus the masses of the two distillate depend upon the molar masses and the vapour pressures of the pure components. Eq. (10.23) can be applied to steam distillation of liquids.

The process of steam distillation is quite useful and is generally applied to immiscible liquids which have either high boiling points or decompose before their normal boiling points are reached. The liquid to be steam distilled should have fairly high volatility near the boiling point of water. In the laboratory, steam is generally passed through the liquid to be steam distilled (see Fig. 10.14). When the temperature is raised high enough to make $p_A^0 + p_B^0 = 760$ mm Hg; the mixture distills with a composition given by Eq. (10.23).

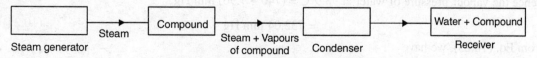

Fig. 10.14 Block diagram for steam distillation

Consider, for example, the purification of iodobenzene. It has a boiling point 180°C. When iodobenzene is heated with water with which it is immiscible by passing steam into it, it boils below the boiling point of water. The distillation takes place at 98°C. At this temperature, $p^0_{H_2O} = 712$ mm Hg and $p^0_{iodobenzene} = 48$ mm Hg; so that the total pressure is equal to $(712 + 48) = 760$ mm Hg. iodobenzene which distills is given by Eq. (10.23), *i.e.*,

$$\frac{W_{iodobenzene}}{W_{H_2O}} = \frac{48 \times 204}{18 \times 712} \approx \frac{7}{9}$$

Hence, out of 16 g of distillate, 7 g would be iodobenzene. Though the vapour pressure of iodobenzene is much lower, but its high molar mass (204 g mol^{-1}) counterbalances so as to make the relative yield appreciably large,

Water is mainly used as a carrier of vapours in distillation due to its easy availability, fairly low boiling point and low molar mass.

Problem 10.6: An immiscible liquid A when steam distilled with water gave a distillate 0.200 dm^3 of which contained 0.0572 dm^3 of A. The observed boiling point for the distillation was 98.2°C and the atmospheric pressure was 758 mm Hg. The vapour pressure of water at 98.2°C was 712 mm Hg. The relative density of liquid was found to be 1.83. Calculate the molar mass of the unknown liquid.

Solution: Vapour pressure due to $A = 758 - 712 = 46$ mm Hg

Volume of A in the distillate = 0.0572 dm^3

Volume of water in the distillate = $(0.2 - 0.0572)$ dm^3

$$= 0.1428 \text{ dm}^3$$

If the density of water is assumed to be 1 kg dm^{-3}, then mass of water = 1.428×10^{-1} kg and mass of $A = 0.0572 \times 1.83 = 1.047 \times 10^{-1}$ kg. Now using Eq. (10.23), we get

$$\frac{1.047 \times 10^{-1}}{1.428 \times 10^{-1}} = \frac{M_A \times 46}{18 \times 712 \times 10^{-3}}$$

or

$$M_A = \frac{18 \times 712 \times 104.7}{142.8 \times 46 \times 10^{-3}}$$

$$= 0.204 \text{ kg mol}^{-1}$$

Problem 10.7: A mixture of quinoline and water boils at 98.9°C under a pressure of 740 mm Hg. The distillate contains 7.79×10^{-2} kg of quinoline and 1 kg of water. The vapour pressure of quinoline at 98.9°C is 7.96 mm Hg. Calculate the molar mass of quinoline.

Solution: Vapour pressure of quinoline = 7.96 mm Hg

Total vapour pressure = 740 mm Hg

Hence the vapour pressure of water at 98.9°C = $(740 - 7.96)$ mm Hg

$$= 732.04 \text{ mm Hg}$$

From Eq. (10.23), we have

$$\frac{7.79 \times 10^{-2}}{1.00} = \frac{M \times 7.96}{732.04 \times 18 \times 10^{-3}}$$

or

$$M = \frac{7.79 \times 10^{-2} \times 732.04 \times 18 \times 10^{-3}}{1.00 \times 7.96}$$

$$= 129 \times 10^{-3} \, \text{kg mol}^{-1}$$

10.13 SOLUTIONS OF SOLIDS IN LIQUIDS

When a solid (solute) is dissolved in a liquid solvent at a given temperature, the dissolution continues until the solution attains a certain maximum concentration. The solution is then said to be saturated at that temperature. At this temperature the maximum quantity of solute that can be dissolved by the solvent is its solubility. Solubility of a given substance is usually defined as the amount of the solid that dissolves in 100 g of solvent at a given temperature to give a saturated solution. On the other hand, molar solubility is defined as the maximum number of moles of the solute dissolved per dm^3 of the solution at a given temperature. In a saturated solution, the dissolved solute and undissolved solute are in equilibrium with each other. The chemical potential of the pure solid and the chemical potential of the dissolved solute will be the same.

The solubility of a substance depends on (a) nature of the solute, (b) the nature of the solvent, (c) temperature, and (d) pressure. Pressure has little effect on the solubility unless gases are involved.

(a) **Nature of the Solute:** Variation in the solubility of different solutes in the same solvent may be explained due to changes in the solute-solvent interactions.

(b) **Nature of the Solvent:** A useful generalization is that "like dissolves like". Polar solvents like water etc., readily dissolve ionic or electrovalent compounds whereas nonpolar solvents dissolve covalent compounds. Thus, sodium chloride is soluble in water but insoluble in nonpolar solvents like benzene. The solubility of NaCl in water is due to electrostatic attractions between the dipoles of water and Na^+ and Cl^- ions. The interionic forces are weakened by water molecules and the ions become free to move in solution.

(c) **Effect of Temperature:** Temperature has a marked effect on the solubility of a solute in a solvent. The solubility may increase or decrease with increase of temperature. The direction in which solubility of a solute in a given solvent changes with temperature depends on the enthalpy of the solution. If the solute dissolves with the evolution of heat solubility decreases with increase of temperature. On the other hand, if the solute dissolves with the absorption of heat, solubility increases with rise in temperature. This is in accordance with the LeChatelier's principle.

10.14 THE SOLUBILITY CURVES

The curve indicating the variation of solubility of a solute with temperature is known as the *solubility curve*. These curves are generally of two types, viz., (a) continuous solubility curves and (b) discontinuous solubility curves.

(a) **Continuous Solubility Curves:** In these cases solubility shows a continuous variation with temperature as shown in Fig. 10.15 (a) and (b). Solubility of most of the salts such as lead nitrate, potassium chlorate, potassium nitrate etc., in water increases with rise in temperature (Fig. 10.15 (*a*)). In case of certain calcium salts of organic acids the solubility decreases with increase of temperature (Fig. 10.15 (*a*)).

(*b*) **Discontinuous Solubility Curves:** Here the solubility curve is not continuous but shows breaks (Fig. 10.15 (*c*), (*d*) and (*e*)). A break in the curve indicates that two solid phases are in equilibrium with the saturated solution. The temperature corresponding to the break in the solubility curve is known as the *transition temperature* as at this temperature one solid form changes into another solid form. The solubility curve of ferrous sulphate (Fig. 10.15 (*c*)) shows a break at 61.8°C. At this temperature the heptahydrate changes into tetrahydrate. The solubility of heptahydrate increases while that of the tetrahydrate decreases with the rise in temperature.

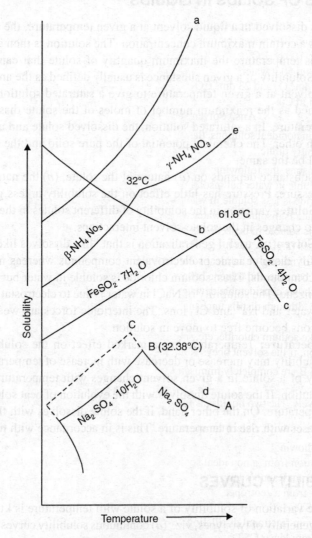

Fig. 10.15 Solubility Curves

The solubility curve of sodium sulphate (Fig. 10.15 (*d*)) shows a sharp break at 32.38°C. At this point (32.38°C), there is an equilibrium between the solid decahydrate, $Na_2SO_4 \cdot 10\ H_2O$ and anhydrous Na_2SO_4. Below this temperature only sodium sulphate decahydrate, $Na_2SO_4 \cdot 10\ H_2O$ exists while above this temperature anhydrous sodium sulphate is the stable form. The curve AB can be followed backwards a short distance by seeding the saturated solution with heptahydrate. The metastable curve BC is obtained.

Ammonium nitrate is an example of a polymorphic change. From the solubility curve (Fig. 10.15(e)), it is clear that a distinct break occurs at 32°C, the transition temperature of β-rhombic ammonium nitrate. Below this temperature, β-form is stable while above 32°C γ-form is stable and at 32°C both the forms are in equilibrium with the saturated solution.

EXERCISES

1. Name the solvent and the solute in the following solutions:
    (*i*) 90% ethanol and 10% water (by mass),
    (*ii*) 50 g H_2SO_4 in 100 g H_2O,
    (*iii*) 50 g ethanol and 50 g water,
    (*iv*) 75 dm^3 H_2, 2 dm^3 O_2 and 23 dm^3 CO_2,
    (*v*) 10 mole % Ni in Cu.
    Ans. Solvents: (*i*) ethanol, (*ii*) water (*iii*) an arbitrary choice, (*iv*) H_2, (*v*) Cu.

2. Explain why even in nonideal solutions, the vapour pressure of the solvent is given by Raoult's law when the solution is sufficiently dilute.

3. Explain, giving reasons, the following:
    (*i*) Sucrose is soluble in water but insoluble in benzene.
    (*ii*) Lithium chloride is less soluble in water than caesium chloride.
    (*iii*) Barium sulphate is insoluble in water while calcium sulphate is highly soluble.
    (*iv*) Naphthalene is soluble in benzene but insoluble in water.
    (*v*) Dissolved gases (*e.g.,* N_2 or O_2 etc.,) from water can be removed by boiling.
    (*vi*) The enthalpy of mixing of an ideal solution is zero.
    (*vii*) A solution of benzene and toluene behaves nearly ideal while that of ethanol and water or chloroform and acetone shows considerable deviations from ideality.
    (*viii*) An azeotrope although distills unchanged in composition at a given pressure, yet it is not a chemical compound.
    (*ix*) Impurities, like sodium chloride, etc., raise the mutual solubility temperature of phenol-water system.
    (*x*) In any solution, if the solvent obeys Roult's law, the solute obeys the Henry's law.

4. Two liquids A and B are completely immiscible with each other. Their normal boiling points are T_A and T_B $(T_A > T_B)$ respectively. The two liquids taken together will boil at (*i*) T_A or (*ii*) T_B or (*iii*) $\dfrac{T_A + T_B}{2}$ or (*iv*) less than T_B or (*v*) none of these. Select the most appropriate answer.   **Ans.** (*iv*) is the correct answer.

5. Distinguish the following:
    (*i*) An ideal solution from a non ideal solution.
    (*ii*) Henry's law from Raoult's law.
    (*iii*) An azeotrope from a zeotrope.
    (*iv*) MST from CST.
    (*v*) Distillation from fractional distillation.
    (*vi*) Upper CST from lower CST.

6. Show that while the total vapour pressure in a binary ideal solution is a linear function of mole fraction of either of the components in the liquid, the reciprocal of the total pressure is a linear function of the mole fraction of either of the components in the vapour.

7. If P_1^0 is the vapour pressure of the solvent and K_H the Heɪry's law constant for the solute, write the expression for the total pressure (P_t) over the solution as a function of X, the mole fraction of the solute in the solution. Assume ideal solution.   **Ans.** $P_t = P_1^0 + K_H X - P_1^0 X.$

8. A solution of 20.0% ethanol by mass in water has a density of 0.966 kg dm^{-3}. Calculate (i) the mole fraction, (ii) the molality and (iii) the molarity of ethanol in this solution.
    Ans. (i) $X_{ethanol} = 0.891$, (ii) $m = 5.43$ mol kg^{-1}, (iii) 4.19 mol dm^{-3}.

9. Determine the molarity of concentrated HCl solution that is 37% by mass HCl. The solvent is water and the density of the solution is 1.19 kg dm^{-3}.   **Ans.** 12.1 M.

10. A solution of acetic acid containing 80.8 g (mol. mass 60 g mol^{-1}) per dm^3 has a density of 1.0097 kg dm^{-3}. Calculate (i) the mass per cent, (ii) mole fraction, (iii) molarity and (iv) molality of acetic acid in this solution.
    Ans. (i) 8%, (ii) 0.025, (iii) 1.34 and (iv) 1.45.

11. (a) State and explain Henry's law. What are the limitations of the law ?
    (b) The Henry's law constant for CO_2 in water at 298 K is 1.64×10^3 atm. Calculate (i) the solubility of CO_2 AT 298 K and 1 atm and (ii) the Bunsen absorption coefficient for CO_2.
    Ans. (i) 3.38×10^{-2} mol dm^{-3}, (ii) 0.757.

12. The Henry's law constant for argon in water is 2.17×10^4 atm at 273 K and 3.97×10^4 atm at 303 K. Calculate the standard enthalpy of solution of argon in water.   **Ans.** −13.96 kJ mol^{-1}.

13. If the Henry's law constants for H_2 and 5.34×10^7 torr in water and 2.75×10^6 torr in benzene at 298 K and 1 atm pressure, how many times more soluble is H_2 in benzene than in water ?   **Ans.** 19.4.

14. The vapour pressures of $CHCl_3$ and CCl_4 at 298 K are 199.1 and 114.5 mm Hg respectively. Assuming ideal solution, calculate (i) the total vapour pressure and (ii) the mass per cent of $CHCl_3$ in the vapour in equilibrium with a liquid mixture containing 1 mole of each liquid.   **Ans.** (i) 156.8 mm Hg, (ii) 57.4%.

15. Two liquids A and B form a nearly ideal solution. The vapour pressure of A is 44.5 mm Hg and that of B is 88.7 mm Hg at 298 K. (a) Calculate the mole fractions of A and B in a solution obtained by mixing 0.1 kg of each. (b) Calculate the partial pressures and the total vapour pressure (P_t) of the solution. (c) Calculate the mole fraction of A in the vapour phase. Molar masses of A and B are 46 and 32 g mol^{-1} respectively.
    Ans. (a) $X_A = 0.41$, $X_B = 0.59$; (b) $p_A = 18.25$ $p_B = 52.32$ mm Hg and $P_t = 70.57$ mm Hg; (c) 0.259.

16. At 353 K, the vapour pressures of pure benzene and toluene are 753 mm Hg and 290 mm Hg respectively. (a) Calculate the vapour pressure of each above a solution at 353 K containing 0.1 kg of each liquid. (b) Calculate the applied pressure at which this solution will boil at 353 K. (c) What is the composition of the vapour that will first distill over at this temperature?
    Ans. (a) $p_{C_6H_6} = 406$ mm Hg, $p_{C_6H_5CH_3} = 133$ mm Hg (b) 539 mm Hg; (c) 0.76.

17. 60 g of phenol is mixed with 40 g of water at 303 K. How many g of each liquid phase will be formed ? The relative proportion of water and phenol layers is 10 : 51.   **Ans.** 16.4 g, 83.6 g Phenol.

18. Phenol-water system separates into two liquid phases at a temperature of 333 K; the first phase contains 16.8% by weight of phenol, the second 44.9% by mass of water. If the system contains 0.09 kg water and 0.06 kg phenol, what is the mass of each phase.
    Ans. 0.0586 kg water layer and 0.0914 kg phenol layer.

19. The boiling point of the immiscible liquid system naphthalene-water is 371 K under a pressure of 733 mm Hg. The vapour pressure of water at 371 K is 707 mm Hg. Calculate the mass per cent of naphthalene in the distillate.   **Ans.** 20.7%.

20. Aniline-water mixture boils at 371.4 K and 1 atm. At this temperature vapour pressure of aniline is 42 mm Hg. If the mass ratio of aniline to water in the distillate is 0.13, calculate the molar mass of aniline.
    Ans. 93 g mol^{-1}.

21. Chlorobenzene (mol. mass $0.112 \text{ kg mol}^{-1}$) is steam distilled at 734 mm Hg and 363 K. The vapour pressure of chlorobenzene and water at 363 K are 208 and 526 mm Hg respectively. Calculate the mass of steam required to distill 0.5 kg chlorobenzene. **Ans.** 0.203 kg.

22. Construct the vapour pressure-composition and boiling point-composition plots for binary liquid pairs showing (*i*) ideal behaviour and (*ii*) nonideal behaviour. Why liquid pairs showing nonideal behaviour cannot be separated completely into the pure components by fractional distillation ?

23. What are azeotropes? How do they differ from zeotropes? Is an azeotrope a mixture or chemical compound? Explain. How the individual components can be recovered from an azeotrope ?

24. What is fractional distillation ? Why it is not convenient to carry out isothermal fractional distillation? Describe the fractional distillation at constant pressure of binary liquid mixtures showing ideal behaviour and nonideal behaviour (showing both positive and negative deviations from ideality).

25. Explain the terms: Mutual solubility temperature (MST), critical solution temperature (CST), conjugate solutions, and tie-line as applied to the solubilities of partially miscible liquids. Discuss the variation of mutual solubility of phenol-water system.

26. State and explain (*i*) Henry's law and (*ii*) Raoult's law. Under what conditions are they obeyed by solutions ? When can they be applied to the same solution ? Comment on the statement that Henry's law applies to the solute and Raoult's law to the solvent in a solution.

27. What type of liquid pairs are steam distilled ? Why steam is advantageous in this kind of distillation? How steam distillation is useful in evaluating the molar masses of liquids ?

Dilute Solutions—
Colligative Properties

11.1 INTRODUCTION

A colligative property of a system is one which depends only on the number of particles present in solution and not in any way on the nature of the particles. The various colligative properties which we shall consider in this chapter are (*a*) vapour pressure lowering of the solvent; (*b*) boiling point elevation of the solution; (*c*) freezing point depression of the solution and (*d*) osmotic pressure of the solution.

Solutions may be divided into two categories, viz., (*i*) solutions of nonelectrolytes where the dissolved solute persists in the same form as it exists in the solid form, *i.e.*, it does not show any tendency to undergo association or dissociation, and (*ii*) solutions of electrolytes which undergo either association or dissociation in solution yielding smaller or larger number of particles respectively. Consequently, the colligative properties will show an enhanced value in dissociation and a lower value in association. We shall first discuss these properties for solutions of nonvolatile nonelectrolytic solutes. Furthermore, it is assumed that the solutions are dilute, *i.e.*, the interactions between the solute-solvent particles are negligibly small and the solutions behave ideally.

Colligative properties have been extensively used in the determination of molar masses of dissolved substances which are nonvolatile.

11.2 LOWERING OF VAPOUR PRESSURE OF SOLVENT

Whenever a non volatile substance is dissolved in a solvent, the vapour pressure of the solvent is lowered. The lowering of the vapour pressure can be readily understood in terms of the Raoult's law. Consider a solution obtained from a non-volatile solute dissolved in a solvent. Let X_1 and X_2 be the mole fractions of the solvent and solute and P^0 and P_s be the vapour pressures of the pure solvent and the solution respectively. Then according to Raoult's law

$$P_s = P^0 X_1 \qquad \qquad ...(11.1)$$

Since X_1 is always less than unity, hence P_s is less then P^0, *i.e.*, the vapour pressure of the solution is less than that of pure solvent. Thus, the addition of a non electrolytic solute to the solvent tends to lower the vapour pressure of the pure solvent. Therefore, the lowering in vapour pressure, ΔP, is given as

$$\Delta P = P^0 - P_s$$
$$= P^0 - P^0 X_1$$
$$= P^0 (1 - X_1)$$
$$= P^0 X_2 \qquad \qquad ...(11.2)$$

The above equation can be written as

$$\frac{\Delta P}{P^0} = \frac{P^0 - P_s}{P^0} = X_2 \qquad \qquad ...(11.3)$$

The quantity $\left(\dfrac{P^0 - P_s}{P^0} \right)$ is known as the *relative lowering of vapour pressure* and is independent

of the nature of the solute or solvent. However, it depends only on the mole fraction of the solute and is independent of the temperature at which it is measured. Equation (11.3) can now be written as

$$\frac{P^0 - P_s}{P^0} = X_2 = \frac{n_2}{n_1 + n_2} \qquad \qquad ...(11.4)$$

where n_1 and n_2 are the number of moles of solvent and solute respectively. For a dilute solution $n_1 \gg n_2$, hence

$$\frac{P^0 - P_s}{P^0} \approx \frac{n_2}{n_1} \qquad \qquad ...(11.5)$$

For a definite quantity of a solvent, n_1 and P^0 are both constants, therefore

$$\frac{\Delta P}{P^0} \propto n_2 \qquad \qquad ...(11.6)$$

Equation (11.6) shows that the relative lowering of vapour pressure of a solvent is directly proportional to the number of moles of the solute. In other words, the relative lowering of vapour pressure of the solvent depends on the concentration of the solute only.

Equation (11.5) can be used in determining the molar mass of the solute provided the vapour pressures of the pure solvent and the solution are known. Since

$$n_2 = \frac{W_2}{M_2} \text{ and } n_1 = \frac{W_1}{M_1}$$

where W_1 and W_2 are the masses of the solvent and the solute and M_1 and M_2 their molar masses respectively. Putting these values of n_1 and n_2 in Eq. (11.5), we get

$$\frac{P^0 - P_s}{P^0} = \frac{W_2/M_2}{W_1/M_1}$$

$$= \frac{W_2 M_1}{W_1 M_2}$$

or
$$M_2 = \left(\frac{P^0}{P^0 - P_s} \right)\left(\frac{W_2}{W_1} \right) M_1 \qquad \qquad ...(11.7)$$

If all the quantities on the right hand side of Eq. (11.7) are known, M_2, the molar mass of the solute can be calculated.

11.3 EXPERIMENTAL MEASUREMENT OF VAPOUR PRESSURE LOWERING

The lowering of vapour pressure can be determined generally by two methods, viz., (a) static method, and (b) dynamic method.

(a) **Static Method:** In this method a differential manometer consisting of a U-tube containing a liquid of low volatility and low density, e.g., n-butyl phthalate or β-bromo naphthalene is commonly used (Fig. 11.1). One arm of the U-tube is attached to a bulb containing solution and the other to the pure solvent. The taps T_1 and T_2 are opened and the air inside the apparatus is removed by connecting it to a vacuum pump. The difference in levels of the liquid in the two limbs of the manometer is read off with the help of a moving telescope. This gives the difference between the vapour pressures of the pure solvent and the solution, $(P^0 - P_s)$.

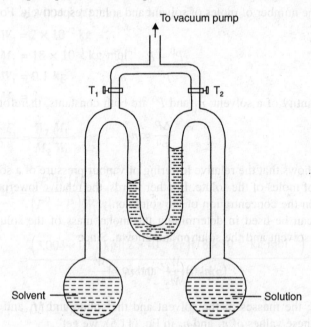

Fig. 11.1 Differential Manometer

(b) **Dynamic Method:** Dynamic methods have been more extensively used and are easier to handle. In the Ostwald and Walker's method a stream of dry air is first passed through a series of bulbs containing the solution and then through the pure solvent (Fig. 11.2). As it passes through the solution, it becomes saturated upto the vapour pressure of the solution. The actual loss of vapours from the bulb is obtained by weighing them before and after the air has been passed through them. The loss in mass of solution is proportional to the vapour pressure of the solution. The loss in mass of solution $\Delta W_1 \propto P_s$.

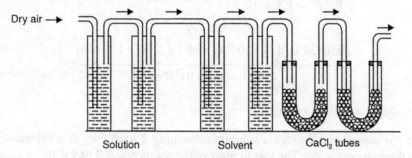

Fig. 11.2 Ostwald and Walker's apparatus

The air (already saturated with vapours of the solvent upto pressure P_s) is next passed through another series of bulbs previously weighed and containing the pure solvent. Since the vapour pressure of the pure solvent P^0 is greater than P_s, air will further take up some more vapours from pure solvent until it is further saturated upto a pressure P^0. The bulbs are weighed again to obtain the loss in mass ΔW_2 which is required to saturate air from pressure P_s to P^0. Therefore,

$$\Delta W_2 \propto P^0 - P_s$$

Finally, the air is passed through a set of weighed U-tubes containing an absorbent for the vapours of the solvent, e.g., anhydrous $CaCl_2$ is used if water is the solvent. The increase in mass of the U-tube is determined. It gives the total loss $\Delta W_1 + \Delta W_2$. This loss in mass is the measure of the vapour pressure required to saturate air upto pressure P^0. Therefore

$$\frac{P^0 - P_s}{P^0} = \frac{\Delta W_2}{\Delta W_1 + \Delta W_2} = \frac{\text{Loss in mass of the solvent}}{\text{Gain in the mass of } CaCl_2 \text{ tube}}$$

Problem 11.1: The vapour pressure of water at 293 K is 17.540 mm Hg and the vapour pressure of a solution of 0.10824 kg of a nonvolatile solute in 1 kg of water at the same temperature is 17.354 mm Hg. Calculate the molar mass of the solute.

Solution:

Here

$$P^0 - 17.540 \text{ mm Hg} = \frac{1.013 \times 10^5 \times 17.54}{760} \text{ Nm}^{-2} = 2.337 \times 10^3 \text{Nm}^{-2}$$

$$P_s = 17.354 \text{ mm} = \frac{1.013 \times 10^5 \times 17.354}{760} \text{ N m}^{-2} = 2.313 \times 10^3 \text{Nm}^{-2}$$

$$W_2 = 0.10824 \text{ kg}$$

$$M_2 = ?$$

$$W_1 = 1 \text{ kg}$$

$$M_1 = 18 \times 10^{-3} \text{ kg mol}^{-1}$$

We know $\quad \dfrac{P^0 - P_s}{P^0} = \dfrac{W_2 M_1}{M_2 W_1}$

or
$$M_2 = \frac{W_2 \times M_1 \times P^0}{W_1 \left(P^0 - P_s\right)}$$

$$= \frac{(0.10824 \text{ kg})\left(18 \times 10^{-3} \text{ kg mol}^{-1}\right)\left(2.337 \times 10^3 \text{ N m}^{-2}\right)}{(1 \text{ kg})\left(0.024 \times 10^3 \text{ N m}^{-2}\right)}$$

$$= 0.1837 \text{ kg mol}^{-1}$$

Problem 11.2: Air was passed through a solution containing 2×10^{-2} kg of a substance in 0.1 kg of water and then through pure water. The loss in mass of the solution was 2.945×10^{-3} kg and that of pure water was 5.9×10^{-5} kg. Calculate the molar mass of the substance.

Solution: Here $(P^0 - P_S) \propto$ Loss in mass of pure water

$$P \propto \text{Loss in mass of solution}$$

Therefore,
$$P^0 - P_S \propto 5.9 \times 10^{-5} \text{ kg}$$
$$P \propto 2.945 \times 10^{-3} \text{ kg}$$
$$P^0 \propto (5.9 \times 10^{-5} + 2.945 \times 10^{-3}) \text{ kg}$$
$$\propto 3.004 \times 10^{-3} \text{ kg}$$
$$W_2 = 2 \times 10^{-2} \text{ kg}$$
$$M_1 = 18 \times 10^{-3} \text{ kg mol}^{-1}$$
$$W_1 = 0.1 \text{ kg}$$
$$M_2 = ?$$

Since
$$\frac{P^0 - P_s}{P^0} = \frac{W_2 M_1}{M_2 W_1}$$

or
$$M_2 = \frac{P^0 W_2 M_1}{\left(P^0 - P_s\right) W_1}$$

$$= \frac{\left(3.004 \times 10^{-3} \text{ kg}\right)\left(2 \times 10^{-2} \text{ kg}\right)\left(18 \times 10^{-3} \text{ kg mol}^{-1}\right)}{\left(5.9 \times 10^{-5} \text{ kg}\right)(0.1 \text{ kg})}$$

$$= 0.183 \text{ kg mol}^{-1}$$

Problem 11.3: In Ostwald-Walker experiment, air was blown through a solution containing a certain amount of solute ($M = 0.2785$ kg mol^{-1}) in 15×10^{-2} kg of water and then through pure water. The loss in mass of water was found to be 8.27×10^{-5} kg while the mass of water absorbed in sulphuric acid tube was 3.317×10^{-3} kg. Calculate the amount of the solute.

Solution:
$$P^0 \propto \text{Mass of water absorbed by sulphuric acid}$$
$$P^0 - P_S \propto \text{Loss in mass of water}$$
$$P^0 \propto 3.317 \times 10^{-3} \text{ kg}$$

$$P^0 - P_s \propto 8.27 \times 10^{-5} \text{ kg}$$

$$M_2 = 0.2785 \text{ kg mol}^{-1}$$

$$W_2 = ?$$

$$M_1 = 18 \times 10^{-3} \text{ kg mol}^{-1}$$

$$W_1 = 15 \times 10^{-2} \text{ kg}$$

We know $\quad \dfrac{P^0 - P_s}{P^0} = \dfrac{W_2 \, M_1}{M_2 \, W_1}$

or $\qquad W_2 = \dfrac{\left(P^0 - P_s\right) M_2 \, W_1}{P^0 M_1}$

$$W_2 = \frac{\left(8.27 \times 10^{-5}\,\text{kg}\right)\left(0.2785 \text{ kg mol}^{-1}\right)\left(15 \times 10^{-2}\,\text{kg}\right)}{\left(3.317 \times 10^{-3}\,\text{kg}\right)\left(18 \times 10^{-3}\,\text{kg mol}^{-1}\right)}$$

$$= 5.7 \times 10^{-2} \text{ kg}$$

11.4 ELEVATION OF BOILING POINT OF A SOLUTION

Boiling point of a solution is the temperature at which the vapour pressure of the liquid is equal to the external pressure, usually one atmospheric pressure. The addition of a nonvolatile solute to the solvent lowers its vapour pressure and thereby elevates the boiling point of the solution. The difference between the boiling point of the solution and the pure solvent is known as the *elevation of boiling point* of the solution. The elevation of boiling point of the solution depends on the nature of the solvent and the concentration of the solute. Boiling point elevation can be readily understood in terms of the lowering of vapour pressure. Figure 11.3 shows the variation of vapour pressure with temperature of pure solvent (curve *AB*) and solution (curve *CD*). Since the vapour pressure of the solution is lower than that of the

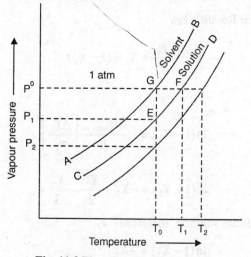

Fig. 11.3 Elevation of boiling points

pure solvent, the vapour pressure temperature curve for the solution thus lies below the curve for the pure solvent.

Let T_0 be the boiling point of the pure solvent at one atmospheric pressure. At this temperature, the solution has lower vapour pressure than one atmosphere and hence it will not boil. With increase of temperature, say to T_1, the vapour pressure of the solution rises to one atmosphere and the solution boils. This means that the solution has a higher boiling point than that of the pure solvent. Thus $T_1 - T_0 = \Delta T_b$, represents the elevation in the boiling point of solution. Points G and E represent the vapour pressures of pure solvent and solution respectively at the same temperature, T_0. The lowering in vapour pressure is given by

$$P^0 - P_1 = \Delta P = GE$$

Since points E and F lie on the vapour pressure curve of the solution at temperature T_0 and T_1, then from Clausius Clapeyron equation we have

$$\ln \frac{P^0}{P_1} = \frac{\Delta H_{vap,\, m}}{R} \left[\frac{1}{T_0} - \frac{1}{T_1} \right]$$

$$= \frac{\Delta H_{vap,\, m}}{R} \left[\frac{T_1 - T_0}{T_1 T_0} \right] \qquad \qquad ...(11.8)$$

where P_1 is the vapour pressure of the solution at temperature T_0 while P^0 is the vapour pressure at T_1, $\Delta H_{vap,\, m}$ is the enthalpy of vapourization per mole of the solvent. For a dilute solution, T_0 and T_1 are not very different and therefore, $T_0 T_1 \approx T_0^2$, and hence Eq. (11.8) reduces to

$$\ln \frac{P^0}{P_1} = \frac{\Delta H_{vap,\, m}}{R} \left[\frac{\Delta T_b}{T_0^2} \right]$$

$$\ln \frac{P_1}{P^0} = -\frac{\Delta H_{vap,\, m}}{R} \left[\frac{\Delta T_b}{T_0^2} \right] \qquad \qquad ...(11.9)$$

Furthermore, according to the Raoult's law

$$\frac{P_1}{P^0} = X_1 = \left(1 - X_2 \right)$$

hence Eq. (11.9) becomes

$$\ln \left(1 - X_2 \right) = -\frac{\Delta H_{vap,\, m}}{R} \left[\frac{\Delta T_b}{T_0^2} \right] \qquad \qquad ...(11.10)$$

Now $$\ln \left(1 - X_2 \right) = -X_2 + \frac{X_2^2}{2} - \frac{X_2^3}{3} + ...$$

and X_2 is small in case of a dilute solution, therefore

$$\ln \left(1 - X_2 \right) \approx -X_2$$

Hence Eq. (11.10) becomes

$$-X_2 = -\frac{\Delta H_{vap,\,m}}{R}\left[\frac{\Delta T_b}{T_0^2}\right]$$

or

$$\Delta T_b = \frac{RT_0^2 X_2}{\Delta H_{vap,\,m}} \qquad\qquad ...(11.11)$$

THERMODYNAMIC DERIVATION OF BOILING POINT ELEVATION OF SOLUTIONS

The Chemical potential (μ_l) of the solvent in a dilute solution of a non-volatile solute (behaving as an ideal solution) is given by

$$\mu_l = \mu_l^0 + RT \ln X_1$$

where the subscript 'l' refers to the liquid phase and X_1 is the mole fraction of the solvent and μ_l^0 is the chemical potential of pure solvent. At the boiling point of the solution where the equilibrium exists with vapour at a pressure of 1 atm

$$\mu_l = \mu_v^0$$

where μ_v^0 is the chemical potential of pure vapour. Thus, at the boiling point of the solution one can write

$$\mu_v^0 = \mu_l = \mu_l^0 + RT \ln X_1$$

On rearranging, we get,

$$RT \ln X_1 = \mu_v^0 - \mu_l^0$$

$$\ln X_1 = \ln(1 - X_2) = \mu_v^0 - \mu_l^0 = \frac{\Delta G_{vap,\,m}}{RT} \qquad\qquad ...(11.12)$$

Here $\Delta G_{vap,\,m}^0$ is the molar Gibbs free energy of vapourization of pure solvent and X_2 is the mole fraction of the solute in the solution. Since

$$\Delta G_{vap,\,m} = \Delta H_{vap,m} - T\Delta S_{vap,\,m}$$

Therefore, Eq. (11.12) becomes

$$\ln(1 - X_2) = \frac{\Delta H_{vap,\,m}}{RT} - \frac{\Delta S_{vap,\,m}}{R} \qquad\qquad ...(11.13)$$

When $X_2 = 0$, $T = T_b$ = boiling point of the pure solvent and from Eq. (11.13), we have

$$\frac{\Delta H_{vap,\,m}}{RT_b} = \frac{\Delta S_{vap,\,m}}{R} \qquad\qquad ...(11.14)$$

Comparison of Eq. (11.13) and (11.14) yields

$$\ln(1 - X_2) = \frac{\Delta H_{vap,\,m}}{R}\left[\frac{1}{T} - \frac{1}{T_b}\right]$$

Since, the solution is very dilute $X_2 \ll 1$, therefore $\ln(1 - X_2)$ can be written as

$$\ln(1 - X_2) \approx -X_2$$

and hence we obtain

$$-X_2 = \frac{\Delta H_{vap,\,m}}{R}\left[\frac{1}{T} - \frac{1}{T_b}\right] = -\frac{\Delta H_{vap,\,m}}{R}\left[\frac{1}{T_b} - \frac{1}{T}\right]$$

or

$$X_2 = \frac{\Delta H_{vap,\,m}}{RT\,T_b}(T - T_b)$$

$$= \frac{\Delta H_{vap,\,m}}{RT_b^2}\Delta T_b \qquad\qquad (\because T \approx T_b)$$

where ΔT_b is the elevation in the boiling point of the solution

or

$$\Delta T_b = \frac{RT_b^2 X_2}{\Delta H_{vap,\,m}} \qquad\qquad\qquad ...(11.15)$$

Equations (11.11) or (11.15) give the elevation of boiling point of a solution in terms of the molar enthalpy of vapourization of the solvent, the boiling point of the solvent, and mole fraction of the solute in solution. Since T_0 and ΔH_{vap} are constant for a given solvent, therefore the elevation of boiling point of the solution is directly proportional to the mole fraction of the solute and is independent of the nature of the solute.

Again,

$$X_2 = \frac{n_2}{n_1 + n_2} \approx \frac{n_2}{n_1} \qquad\qquad \text{(for a dilute solution)}$$

$$= \frac{W_2/M_2}{W_1/M_1}$$

$$= \frac{W_2 M_1}{W_1 M_2}$$

Substituting this value of X_2 in Eq. (11.15), we get

$$\Delta T_b = \left(\frac{RT_0^2}{\Delta H_{vap,\,m}}\right)\left(\frac{W_2 M_1}{W_1 M_2}\right) \qquad\qquad ...(11.16)$$

Since the molality m of the solution is given as

$$m = \frac{1000\,W_2}{W_1 M_2} \qquad\qquad\qquad ...(11.17)$$

Therefore Eq. (11.16) becomes

$$\Delta T_b = \frac{RT_0^2 \, mM_1}{\Delta H_{vap, m} 1000}$$

$$= \frac{RT_0^2 m}{\Delta H_{vap, m} \, n_1} \qquad ...(11.18)$$

where $n_1 (= 1000/M_1)$ is the number of moles of solvent in 1000 g of solvent. For any solvent, the

quantity $\dfrac{RT_0^2 \, M_1}{1000 \, \Delta H_{vap, m}}$ is constant and is equal to K_b, known as the *molal boiling point elevation* or

molal ebullioscopic constant

$$K_b = \frac{RT_0^2}{\Delta H_{vap, m} n_1} = \frac{RT_0^2 M_1}{\Delta H_{vap, m} 1000} \qquad ...(11.19)$$

Hence Eq. (11.18) becomes,

$$\Delta T_b = K_b m \qquad ...(11.20)$$

It is clear from this equation that the elevation in boiling point of a solution is directly proportional to the molality of the solution.

For a solution, where $m = 1$, $\Delta T_b = K_b$, *i.e.,* the molal elevation constant is therefore defined as *the elevation in boiling point of a solution of unit molality.*

Equation (11.20) can be verified in three ways (*i*) the elevation of boiling point should be proportional to the molality of the solution, (*ii*) the proportionality constant K_b should be independent of the nature of the solute, and (*iii*) the value of K_b obtained from experiments and the one predicted by Eq. (11.19) should be in agreement.

For water, $\Delta H_{vap, m} = 40670$ J mol^{-1}, $T_0 = 373.16$ K, $M_1 = 18$ g mol^{-1} and hence the value of K_b from Eq. (11.19)

$$K_b = \frac{RT_0^2 M_1}{1000 \, \Delta H_{vap, m}}$$

$$= \frac{\left(8.314 \text{ JK}^{-1}\text{mol}^{-1}\right)\left(373.16 \text{ K}\right)^2 \left(18 \text{ g mol}^{-1}\right)}{\left(1000 \text{ g kg}^{-1}\right)\left(40670 \text{ J mol}^{-1}\right)}$$

$$= 0.513 \text{ kg mol}^{-1} \text{ K or } 0.513 \text{ K}/\left(\text{mol kg}^{-1}\right)$$

Some results comparing the values of K_b obtained from Eq. (11.19) and those obtained from measurements of the boiling point elevation using Eq. (11.20) are shown in Table 11.1. The results are in good agreement.

Table 11.1 Molal Boiling Point Elevation Constant at 1 Atmospheric Pressure

Solvent	Boiling Point (K)	K_b(Obs) $\Delta T_b/m$	ΔT_b (Calculated)
Water	373.0	0.51	0.51
Ethanol	351.4	1.22	1.20
Benzene	353.1	2.54	2.61
Chloroform	334.3	3.63	3.77
Carbon tetrachloride	349.8	5.00	5.05

Molar Mass Determination from Boiling Point Elevation

From Eq. (11.20), it is possible to calculate the molar mass of the solute as

$$\Delta T_b = K_b m$$

$$= K_b \frac{1000 \ W_2}{W_1 M_2}$$

or

$$M_2 = \frac{1000 \ W_2 K_b}{W_1 \Delta T_b} \qquad \qquad ...(11.21)$$

This equation permits us to calculate the molar mass of the solute since W_1, the mass of the solvent, W_2, the mass of the solute, ΔT_b, the elevation of boiling point and K_b the ebullioscopic constant are known.

11.5 EXPERIMENTAL MEASUREMENT OF BOILING POINT ELEVATION

In determining the elevation of boiling point of a solution, sufficient precaution is needed to avoid superheating. The following two methods are generally used for determining the boiling point elevation of solutions:

(*a*) **Landsberger's Method:** In this method the solution is heated by passing through it the vapours of the pure solvent. This is done to avoid superheating. The apparatus used is shown in Fig. 10.4. It

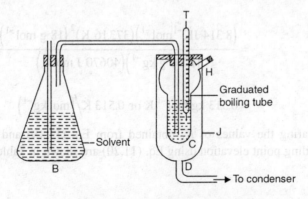

Fig. 11.4 Landsberger's apparatus

consists of a boiling flask B in which the pure solvent is boiled. It is connected by a delivery tube to a graduated boiling tube C which also contains a small amount of the solvent. The tube C is fitted with a Beckmann thermometer T which can be read off with an accuracy of 0.01°C. The middle portion of C is blown into a bulb with a hole H through which the solute can be added to the solvent. The tube is surrounded by an outer jacket J. End D is connected to a condenser to condense the outgoing vapours.

To start with, a known volume (about 5–6 ml) of the pure solvent is taken in the boiling tube. Vapours of pure solvent from the boiling flask B are passed through it until the liquid starts boiling. When the temperature attains a constant value the reading of the thermometer is recorded. This gives the boiling point of the solvent. Now a weighed amount of solute under investigation is introduced into the boiling tube. Vapours of the solvent are again passed and their passage is continued until the solution boils and the temperature is again recorded. This temperature is the boiling point of the solution. The volume of the solution is noted at this stage. Knowing the density of the solvent, its mass can be calculated. From the masses of the solute and the solvent, the boiling point elevation can be calculated. To calculate the molar mass of the solute, Eq. (11.21) can be used.

(*b*) **Cottrell's Method:** In the above method superheating is not completely eliminated and it is difficult to know the composition of the solution corresponding to the boiling point. These sources of errors have been minimized in the Cottrell's method. The form of the apparatus used is shown in Fig. 11.5. A is a wide glass tube in which a known amount of the pure solvent is taken. A sensitive thermometer (T) is inserted in the tube such that the bulb of the thermometer is at some distance above the liquid surface. The tube is provided with a side tube D which is connected to a water condenser. Vapours of the solvent get condensed in it and flow back into solution. Inside the tube an inverted funnel shaped tube B with bifurcated stem is placed. The liquid is heated slowly; the vapours along with a stream of boiling liquid move up the stem of the funnel and are discharged on the bulb of the thermometer. The bulb of the thermometer is in contact with a layer of boiling solvent in equilibrium with its vapours and the temperature recorded is the actual boiling point of the solution.

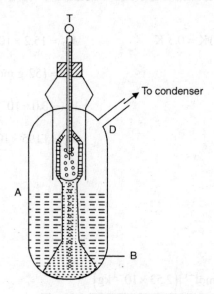

Fig. 11.5 Cottrell's apparatus

A weighed amount of the solute is then introduced and the boiling point of the solution determined as before. The difference in two boiling points gives the boiling point elevation of the solution.

Problem 11.4: The boiling point of chloroform was raised by 0.325 K when 5.141×10^{-4} kg of anthracene was dissolved in 3.5×10^{-2} kg of chloroform. Calculate the molar mass of the solute (molal elevation constant for chloroform is 3.9).

Solution: Here,

$$\Delta T_b = 0.325 \text{ K} \qquad\qquad W_1 = 3.5 \times 10^{-2} \text{ kg}$$

$$K_b = 3.9 \text{ K kg mol}^{-1} \qquad\qquad W_2 = 5.141 \times 10^{-4} \text{ kg}$$

$$M_2 = ?$$

We know,
$$\Delta T_b = K_b \frac{W_2 \times 1000}{M_2 W_1}$$

or
$$M_2 = \frac{K_b W_2 \times 1000}{\Delta T_b W_1}$$

$$M_2 = \frac{\left(3.9 \text{ K kg mol}^{-1}\right)\left(5.141 \times 10^{-4} \text{ kg}\right)\left(1000 \text{ g kg}^{-1}\right)}{\left(0.325 \text{ K}\right)\left(3.5 \times 10^{-2} \text{ kg}\right)}$$

$$= 176.3 \text{ g mol}^{-1}$$

$$= 0.1763 \text{ kg mol}^{-1}$$

Problem 11.5: A solution of 3.0×10^{-4} kg of camphor $(C_{10}H_{16}O)$ in 2.53×10^{-2} kg of chloroform boils at 334.3 K. Boiling point of chloroform is 334.0 K. Calculate $\Delta H_{vap,m}$ and K_b for chloroform.

Solution: Here,

$$\Delta T_b = (334.3 - 334.0) \text{ K} = 0.3 \text{ K} \qquad\qquad M_2 = 15.2 \times 10^{-2} \text{ kg mol}^{-1}$$

$$= 152 \text{ g mol}^{-1}$$

$$W_1 = 2.53 \times 10^{-2} \text{ kg} \qquad\qquad\qquad W_2 = 3.0 \times 10^{-4} \text{ kg}$$

$$K_b = ? \qquad\qquad\qquad\qquad\qquad M_1 = 1.195 \times 10^{-1} \text{ kg mol}^{-1}$$

Since
$$\Delta T_b = K_b \frac{W_2 \times 1000}{M_2 \times W_1}$$

or
$$K_b = \frac{\Delta T_b M_2 W_1}{W_2 \times 1000}$$

$$= \frac{\left(0.3 \text{ K}\right)\left(152 \text{ g mol}^{-1}\right)\left(2.53 \times 10^{-2} \text{ kg}\right)}{\left(3 \times 10^{-4} \text{ kg}\right)\left(1000 \text{ g kg}^{-1}\right)}$$

$$= 3.83 \text{ K kg mol}^{-1}$$

Now, $$K_b = \frac{RT_0^2 M_1}{1 \text{ kg } \Delta H_{vap,m}}$$

or $$\Delta H_{vap,m} = \frac{RT_0^2 M_1}{K_b 1000}$$

$$= \frac{\left(8.314 \text{ JK}^{-1}\text{mol}^{-1}\right)\left(334 \text{ K}\right)^2\left(119.5 \text{ g mol}^{-1}\right)}{\left(3.83 \text{ K kg mol}^{-1}\right)\left(1000 \text{ g kg}^{-1}\right)}$$

$$= 14500 \text{ J mol}^{-1}$$

$$= 14.5 \text{ kJ mol}^{-1}$$

11.6 DEPRESSION OF FREEZING POINT OF SOLUTIONS

The freezing point of a liquid is the temperature at which the solid phase begins to separate out from the liquid. At this temperature solid and liquid phases are in equilibrium and have equal vapour pressures.

A solution freezes at a temperature lower than that of the pure solvent. This is due to the lowering of the vapour pressure of a solution as a result of addition of a small amount of nonvolatile solute. Figure 11.6 shows the vapour pressure as a function of temperature for the solution and the pure solvent. CA is the sublimation curve of the solid solvent and AB represents the vapour pressure curve of the pure liquid solvent. These two curves intersect at point A, where the vapour pressures of the solid solvent and liquid solvent are equal. The temperature T_0, corresponding to this vapour pressure P^0 is the freezing point of the pure solvent.

The vapour pressure curve of the solution of a nonvolatile solute will be lower than that of the pure solvent and is represented by DE. This curve intersects the sublimation curve at point E, where the solution will have the same vapour pressure as the pure solid solvent. Hence T_1 is the freezing point of the solution and is lower than T_0.

The depression of freezing point of the solution is given by $\Delta T_f = T_0 - T_1$. The magnitude of ΔT_f depends on the nature of the solvent and the amount of the solute. Let P^0 be the vapour pressure of the solid and pure solvent at temperature T_0 and P_1 the vapour pressure of the solution at temperature T_1. Since points A and E lie on the same vapour pressure curve, they must both be related by Clausius-Clapeyron equation.

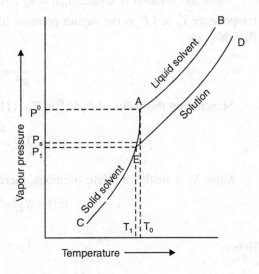

Fig. 11.6 Depression of freezing point of a solvent

$$\ln \frac{P^0}{P_1} = -\frac{\Delta H_{sub,m}}{R}\left[\frac{1}{T_0} - \frac{1}{T_1}\right]$$

$$= -\frac{\Delta H_{\text{sub}, m}}{R}\left[\frac{T_1 - T_0}{T_0 T_1}\right]$$

or
$$\ln\frac{P_0}{P_1} = \frac{\Delta H_{\text{sub}, m}}{R}\left[\frac{T_0 - T_1}{T_0 T_1}\right] \qquad \qquad ...(11.22)$$

Again for solution, P_s is the vapour pressure at temperature T_0 and P_1 is the vapour pressure at temperature T_1, therefore,

$$\ln\frac{P_s}{P_1} = -\frac{\Delta H_{\text{vap}, m}}{R}\left[\frac{T_1 - T_0}{T_0 T_1}\right] = \frac{\Delta H_{\text{vap}, m}}{R}\left[\frac{T_0 - T_1}{T_0 T_1}\right] \qquad \qquad ...(11.23)$$

On subtracting (11.23) from (11.22), we get

$$\ln P^0 - \ln P_s = \frac{\left(\Delta H_{\text{sub}, m} - \Delta H_{\text{vap}, m}\right)\left(T_0 - T_1\right)}{R T_0 T_1} \qquad \qquad ...(11.24)$$

But $\Delta H_{\text{sub}, m} - \Delta H_{\text{vap}, m} = \Delta H_{\text{fus}, m}$ the molar enthalpy of fusion of solvent. Hence Eq. (11.24) becomes

$$\ln\frac{P^0}{P_s} = \frac{\Delta H_{\text{fus}, m}\Delta T_f}{R T_0 T_1}$$

or
$$\ln\frac{P_s}{P^0} = -\frac{\Delta H_{\text{fus}, m}\Delta T_f}{R T_0 T_1} \qquad \qquad ...(11.25)$$

Since the solution is dilute, $T_0 T_1 \approx T_0^2$. Again P^0 is the vapour pressure of the pure solvent at temperature T_0 and P_s is the vapour pressure of the solution at the same temperature. Therefore, from Raoult's law

$$\frac{P_s}{P^0} = X_1 = \left(1 - X_2\right)$$

Substituting this value of P_s/P^0 in Eq. (11.25), we get

$$\ln\left(1 - X_2\right) = -\frac{\Delta H_{\text{fus}, m}\,\Delta T_f}{R T_0^2}$$

Since X_2 is small for dilute solutions, therefore

$$\ln\left(1 - X_2\right) = -X_2$$

Hence
$$-X_2 = -\frac{\Delta H_{\text{fus}, m}}{R}\frac{\Delta T_f}{T_0^2}$$

or
$$\Delta T_f = \frac{R T_0^2 X_2}{\Delta H_{\text{fus}, m}} \qquad \qquad ...(11.26)$$

THERMODYNAMIC DERIVATION OF DEPRESSION OF FREEZING POINT OF SOLUTIONS

When a solution freezes, pure solid solvent and the solution with solute present at a mole fraction X_1 are in equilibrium. The chemical potentials of the solvent must be the same in both phases, viz., solid and liquid phases

$$\mu^0(s) = \mu(l)$$

The chemical potential of the solvent in the solution is given by

$$\mu(l) \doteq \mu^0(l) + RT \ln X_1$$

where X_1 is the mole fraction of the solvent in the solution.

On rearranging, we get

$$\frac{\mu^0(l) - \mu(s)}{RT} = -\ln X_1$$

$$= -\ln(1 - X_2)$$

or

$$-\ln(1 - X_2) = \frac{\Delta G_{\text{fus, } m}}{RT}$$

$$= \frac{\Delta H_{\text{fus, } m} - T\Delta S_{\text{fus, } m}}{RT}$$

$$= \frac{\Delta H_{\text{fus, } m}}{RT} - \frac{\Delta S_{\text{fus, } m}}{R} \qquad \ldots(11.27)$$

when $X_2 = 0$, the freezing point is that of pure liquid, T_f

and

$$\ln(1) = \frac{\Delta H_{\text{fus, } m}}{RT_f} - \frac{\Delta S_{\text{fus, } m}}{R}$$

$$0 = \frac{\Delta H_{\text{fus, } m}}{RT_f} - \frac{\Delta S_{\text{fus, } m}}{R} \qquad \ldots(11.28)$$

On subtracting Eq. (11.28) from Eq. (11.27), we get

$$-\ln(1 - X_2) = \frac{\Delta H_{\text{fus, } m}}{R}\left[\frac{1}{T} - \frac{1}{T_f}\right]$$

Since X_2 is small ($X_2 \ll 1$) therefore $\ln(1 - X_2)$ can be written as $\ln(1 - X_2) \approx -X_2$, so

$$X_2 = \frac{\Delta H_{\text{fus, } m}}{R}\left[\frac{1}{T} - \frac{1}{T_f}\right]$$

$$= \frac{\Delta H_{\text{fus, } m}}{R}\left[\frac{T_f - T}{T_f T}\right]$$

$$= \frac{\Delta H_{fus,m}}{RT_f^2} \Delta T_f \qquad \left(\because \quad T_f \approx T \right) \qquad ...(11.29)$$

where ΔT_f is the depression in the freezing point of the solvent.

Further,

$$X_2 \approx \frac{n_2}{n_1} = \frac{W_2 M_1}{M_2 W_1}$$

and

$$m(\text{molarity}) = \frac{1000 \ W_2}{W_1 M_2}$$

hence Eq. (11.26) or Eq. (11.29) reduces to

$$\Delta T_f = \frac{RT_0^2 \ mM_1}{\Delta H_{fus, m} \ 1000}$$

$$= \frac{RT_0^2 \ m}{\Delta H_{fus, m} \ n_1}$$

$$= K_f m \qquad\qquad\qquad ...(11.30)$$

where

$$K_t = \frac{RT_0^2}{\Delta H_{fus, m} n_1} = \frac{RT_0^2}{\Delta H_{fus, m}} \ \frac{M_1}{1000} \qquad ...(11.31)$$

and is known as the *molal freezing point constant* or *cryoscopic constant* of a solvent.

When $m = 1$, $K_f = \Delta T_f$. The molal depression constant can thus be defined as the *depression in the freezing point of solutions of unit molality*. Equation (11.30) is analogous to Eq. (11.20). Since K_f is constant for a given solvent, therefore the depression in freezing point of a solution is dependent only on the concentration of the solute and not on the nature of the solute. It is for this reason the depression of freezing point is a colligative property.

For water $T_0 = 273.16$ K, $M_1 = 1.8 \times 10^{-2}$ kg mol^{-1}, $\Delta H_{fus,m} = 6031$ J mol^{-1}, K_f can be calculated from Eq. (11.31) as

$$K_f = \frac{\left(8.314 \ \text{JK}^{-1}\text{mol}^{-1}\right)\left(273.16 \ \text{K}\right)^2 \left(18 \ \text{g mol}^{-1}\right)}{\left(1000 \ \text{g kg}^{-1}\right)\left(6031 \ \text{J mol}^{-1}\right)}$$

$$= 1.857 \ \text{K kg mol}^{-1}$$

Determination of Molar mass from Freezing Point Depression

From Eq. (11.30), it is possible to calculate the molar mass of the solute as

$$\Delta T_f = K_f m$$

$$= K_f \left(\frac{1000 \ W_2}{W_1 M_2} \right)$$

or

$$M_2 = \frac{1000 \, W_2 \, K_f}{W_1 \Delta T_f}$$ ...(11.32)

Hence, to calculate the molar mass of the solute, K_f for the solvent must be known. The value of K_f is obtained either from Eq. (11.30) using a dilute solution or computed from equation (11.31). Different solvents have their specific molal freezing point constants, some of which are given in Table 11.2.

Table 11.2 Molal Freezing Point Constants

Solvent	Freezing point (K)	K_f	Solvent	Freezing point(K)	K_f
Water	273.16	1.86	Cyclohexane	279.66	20.2
Benzene	278.66	5.10	Naphthalene	353.36	7.0
Acetic acid	289.66	3.90	Camphor	–	40.0
Nitrobenzene	278.76	6.90			

11.7 EXPERIMENTAL DETERMINATION OF FREEZING POINT DEPRESSION

(*i*) **Beckmann's Method:** The apparatus (Fig. 11.7) consists of a wide glass tube *A* containing the solvent and is provided with a side arm *B* through which a weighed quantity of the solute can be introduced. The tube is fitted with a cork through which a Beckmann thermometer *T* and a stirrer are introduced. Tube *A* is surrounded by an outer air jacket *C* which prevents rapid cooling of the solvent. The entire assembly is then kept in a freezing mixture giving a temperature of about 5°C below the freezing point of the solvent.

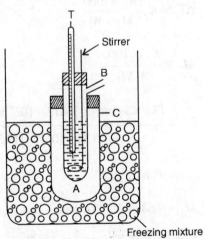

Fig. 11.7 Beckmann's freezing point apparatus

A known mass of the solvent is taken in tube *A* and is stirred slowly; the temperature decreases steadily. The temperature falls below the freezing point of the solvent due to unavoidable supercooling.

But as the crystallization starts the temperature rises rapidly and then attains a constant value for sometimes and is recorded. This gives the freezing point of the solvent. The tube A is then removed, warmed slightly to melt the solid and a weighed quantity of the solute is added to the solvent through the side tube B. It is dissolved by stirring and the freezing point of the solution is determined in the same manner as for the solvent. The difference of the two readings gives the depression of the freezing point of the solution.

(*ii*) **Rast's Method:** The method has been developed by Rast and uses camphor as the solvent. From Table 11.2, it is clear that the molal depression constant for camphor ($K_f = 40$) is nearly twenty times higher than that for water ($K_f = 1.86$). Thus, a molal solution in water will show a lowering of 1.86°C, while in camphor it will show a lowering of about 40°C in the freezing point of the solvent. Even for dilute solutions, the freezing point lowering is considerable and the temperature can be recorded with sufficient accuracy using an ordinary thermometer.

The melting point of the pure camphor is first determined in the usual manner. A known mass of the solute is mixed with a known mass of camphor (about 10 to 15 times that of the solute) and the mixture is melted to form a homogeneous solution. The mixture is cooled, powdered and its melting point is determined. This is the melting point of the solution. From the difference in the two readings, the depression in the freezing point is calculated.

Rast's method is applicable only in cases where the solute is miscible with camphor.

Problem 11.6: The lowering of freezing point of benzene was 2.33 K when 4.12×10^{-4} kg of a solute of unknown molar mass was dissolved in 9.31×10^{-3} kg of benzene. Calculate the molar mass of the solute. Molal depression constant for benzene is 5.1 K kg mol^{-1}.

Solution: Here,

$$\Delta T_f = 2.33 \text{ K} \qquad\qquad K_f = 5.1 \text{ K kg mol}^{-1}$$
$$M_2 = ? \qquad\qquad W_1 = 9.31 \times 10^{-3} \text{kg}$$
$$W_2 = 4.12 \times 10^{-4} \text{ kg}$$

We know,

$$\Delta T_f = K_f \frac{W_2 \times 1000}{M_2 \times W_1}$$

or

$$M_2 = \frac{K_f W_2 1000}{W_1 \Delta T_2}$$

$$= \frac{\left(5.1 \text{ K kg mol}^{-1}\right)\left(4.12 \times 10^{-4} \text{ kg}\right)\left(1000 \text{ g kg}^{-1}\right)}{\left(9.31 \times 10^{-3} \text{kg}\right)(2.33 \text{ K})}$$

$$= 96.87 \text{ g mol}^{-1}$$

$$M_2 = 9.687 \times 10^{-2} \text{ kg mol}^{-1}$$

Problem 11.7: A brass sample composed of 20% zinc and 80% copper by mass melts at 1268 K. Pure copper melts at 1357 K. What is the molal freezing point constant for copper ? (Atomic mass of zinc is 65 g mol^{-1}).

Solution:

$$\Delta T_f = (1357 - 1268) \text{ K} = 89 \text{ K}, \qquad W_1 = 8.0 \times 10^{-2} \text{ kg}$$

$$M_2 = 6.5 \times 10^{-2} \text{ kg mol}^{-1}, \qquad W_2 = 2.0 \times 10^{-2} \text{ kg}$$
$$= 65 \text{ g mol}^{-1}$$

Since
$$\Delta T_f = K_f \frac{W_2 \times 1000}{M_2 \times W_1}$$

or
$$K_f = \frac{\Delta T_f W_1 \times M_2}{W_2 \times 1000}$$

$$= \frac{(89 \text{ K})(8.0 \times 10^{-2} \text{ kg})(65 \text{ g mol}^{-1})}{(2.0 \times 10^{-2} \text{ kg})(1000 \text{ g kg}^{-1})}$$

$$= 23.14 \text{ K kg mol}^{-1}$$

Problem 11.8: There are two solutions of a certain non-volatile solute X in a solvent Y. The molalities of these solutions are m_1 and m_2. If K_f and K_b for the solvent are 1.8 and 0.9 (K kg mol^{-1}), then for equal values ΔT_f for m_1 and ΔT_b for m_2, calculate the ratio of m_1 and m_2.

Solution:
$$\Delta T_f = 1.8 \ m_1$$
and
$$\Delta T_b = 0.9 \ m_2$$
But
$$\Delta T_f = \Delta T_b, \text{ hence}$$
$$1.8 \ m_1 = 0.9 \ m_2$$

or
$$\frac{m_1}{m_2} = \frac{1}{2}$$

Problem 11.9: Calculate the mass of ice that will separate out on cooling a solution containing 50 g $(CH_2OH)_2$ in 200 g of water to $-9.3°C$. K_f for water is 1.86 K kg mol^{-1}.

    Solution: Molar mass of $(CH_2OH)_2 = 62$ g mol^{-1}

$$\text{molality of the solution, } m = \frac{50 \times 1000}{62 \times W_1}$$

where W_1 is the mass of the solvent.

Therefore
$$\Delta T_f = K_f m$$

$$= \frac{50 \times 1000}{62 \times W_1} \times 1.86$$

Since
$$\Delta T_f = \left[0 - (-9.3) \right]°C = 9.3°C$$

Hence
$$W_1 = \frac{1.86 \times 50 \times 1000}{9.3 \times 62} \text{ g}$$

$$= 161.29 \text{ g}$$

So the mass ice separated on cooling $= (200 - 161.29)$ g

$$= 38.71 \text{ g.}$$

11.8 OSMOSIS AND OSMOTIC PRESSURE

Abbe' Nollet in 1748 observed an important colligative property known as osmotic pressure. He observed that when a solution is separated from a pure solvent by *a semipermeable membrane,* (which allows through it the flow of solvent molecules only), there is spontaneous flow of solvent into the solution. This phenomenon of spontaneous flow of a solvent through a semi permeable membrane into a solution or from a dilute solution to a concentrated one is termed as *osmosis.* By applying a certain pressure to the solution, osmosis can be prevented. *The minimum pressure required to prevent osmosis is known as the osmotic pressure.* Osmotic pressure of a solution is a colligative property and at a given temperature its magnitude depends only on the concentration of the solute. The nature of the membrane used in osmosis depends on the nature of the solvent and solute. Some common membranes include animal membranes, cellulose and a film of cupric ferrocyanide, $Cu_2[Fe(CN)_6]$ etc.

Osmosis differs from diffusion in the following respects:

Osmosis	*Diffusion*
1. There is a flow of solvent into the solution through a semipermeable membrane.	1. There is a flow of both the solvent and the solute and no semipermeable membrane is required.
2. Solvent flows from the solution of lower concentration to solution of higher concentration.	2. Solution flows from higher concentration to lower concentration until an equilibrium in concentration is achieved.

Osmosis can be easily understood with the help of an apparatus shown in Fig. 11.8. A semipermeable membrane (SPM) of pig bladder is tied over the end of a thistle funnel. It is then filled with a solution of sugar and is dipped into a beaker containing water (solvent). Due to osmosis, water will pass through the membrane and the level of sugar solution will rise until the hydrostatic pressure of the liquid column equalizes the osmotic pressure of the solution. This hydrostatic pressure of the liquid column is a measure of osmotic pressure and is equal to hdg where h is the height upto which the solution level rises in the funnel and d is the density of the solution.

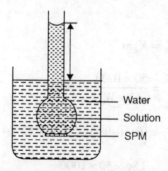

Fig. 11.8 Osmosis through a semipermeable membrane

Another example may be given to illustrate the phenomenon of osmosis and osmotic pressure. Chamber A, open at one end, is fitted with a movable piston at the other end (Fig. 11.9). The chamber is divided by a semipermeable membrane into two compartments. The left compartment is filled with the solution and the right one with the pure solvent. Solvent will pass through the semipermeable membrane into the solution compartment due to osmosis and will push the piston upward. The upward movement of the piston can be prevented by applying pressure on the piston to keep it in the original position. The mechanical pressure that must be applied on the solution side in order to prevent osmosis is the osmotic pressure of the solution. It is denoted by π. If the solvent in the above experiment is replaced by a solution of different concentration, osmosis will still occur from dilute solution towards concentrated solution. If the solutions have same concentration, no osmosis will occur and the solutions are said to be *isotonic*.

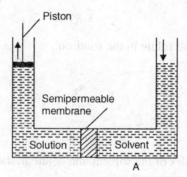

Fig. 11.9 Osmotic pressure of solutions

11.9 THERMODYNAMIC DERIVATION OF OSMOTIC PRESSURE OF A SOLUTION

When a solution separated from the pure solvent by a semipermeable membrane is at equilibrium, the chemical potential of the solvent must be the same on both sides of the membrane. If $\mu_A^0(P)$ is the chemical potential of pure solvent and $\mu_A(P + \pi, X_1)$ the chemical potential of the solvent in the solution at a given temperature the equilibrium condition is

$$\mu_A^0(P) = \mu_A(P + \pi, X_1)$$

For ideal solution
$$\mu_A(P + \pi, X_1) = \mu_A^0(P + \pi) + RT \ln X_1$$

So
$$\mu_A^0(P) = \mu_A^0(P + \pi) + RT \ln X_1 \qquad \text{...(11.33)}$$

The chemical potential of the solvent under a pressure of $P + \pi$ is now expressed in terms of the chemical potential under a pressure P. From the fundamental equation at constant temperature, we have

$$d\mu_A^0 = V_A^0 dP$$

Integrating, we get
$$\int \mu_A^0(P + \pi, X_1) - \mu_A^0(P) = \int_P^{P+\pi} V_A^0 dP \qquad \text{...(11.34)}$$

Hence from Eq. (11.33), we obtain

$$\int_{P}^{P+\pi} V_A^0 dP + RT \ln X_1 = 0 \qquad \qquad ...(11.35)$$

In Eq. (11.35), V_A^0 is the molar volume of the pure solvent. If the solvent is incompressible, then V_A^0 is independent of pressure. Then from Eq. (11.35), we get

$$V_A^0 \pi = -RT \ln X_1 = -RT \ln(1 - X_2)$$

$$= RTX_2 \qquad \qquad \left(\because \ln(1 - X_2) \right) \approx X_2$$

where X_2 is the mole fraction of the solute in the solution.

For dilute solutions

$$X_2 = \frac{n_2}{n_1} \qquad \qquad \left(\text{As } n_1 \gg n_2 \right)$$

Hence

$$\pi V_A^0 = n_2 RT \qquad \qquad ...(11.36)$$

n_1 and n_2 being the number of moles of the solvent and solute in the solution respectively.

Equation (11.36) can also be expressed as

$$\pi = \left(\frac{n_2}{V_A^0} \right) RT$$

$$= CRT \qquad \qquad ...(11.37)$$

where $C \left(= \dfrac{n_2}{V_A^0} \right)$ is the molar concentration of the solute in the solution.

11.10 MEASUREMENT OF OSMOTIC PRESSURE

Osmotic pressure is generally measured by the following methods:

(a) **Pfeffer's Method:** The apparatus used by Pfeffer is shown in Fig. 11.10. It consists of a porous pot A. An artificial membrane of copper ferrocyanide is deposited into the pores of the porous pot by filling the cell with a 3% solution of $K_4[Fe(CN)_6]$ and then placing it in a 3% solution of copper sulphate for few hours. Diffusion of Cu^{2+} and $[Fe(CN)_6]^{4-}$ ions leads to a deposit of a jelly like precipitate of copper ferrocyanide in the pores of the porous pot. After deposition of $Cu_2[Fe(CN)_6]$, the cell is thoroughly washed with water and filled with the solution whose osmotic pressure is to be measured. The cell is attached to a mercury manometer through a wide glass tube B. The pot is then placed in the solvent bath at a constant temperature. Solvent enters the pot and the osmotic pressure is noted from the readings of the manometer.

(b) **Morse and Frazer's Method:** They followed essentially the same technique except that the membrane was prepared electrolytically. In their preparation of the semipermeable membrane,

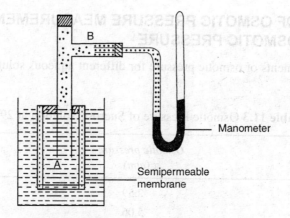

Fig. 11.10 Measurement of osmotic pressure

they took copper sulphate solution inside the clean porous pot and placed the pot partly immersed in potassium ferrocyanide solution. On passing an electric current, Cu^{2+} and $[Fe(CN)_6]^{4-}$ ions move towards oppositely charged electrodes. These ions when meet each other in the pores of the porous wall, form a deposit of copper ferrocyanide. The membrane so obtained was found to be capable of withstanding fairly high pressures.

(c) **Berkeley and Hartley's Method:** In the above methods used for measuring the osmotic pressure, concentration of the solution changes due to osmosis and hence concentration at equilibrium is different from the initial concentration. This difficulty is overcome in the method developed by Berkeley and Hartley. In their technique the osmosis is prevented by applying a pressure to the solution and the magnitude of this applied pressure gives the osmotic pressure of the solution. The apparatus used is shown in Fig. 11.11. An inner jacket containing the membrane (electrolytically deposited $Cu_2[Fe(CN)_6]$) is filled with the pure solvent. One end of this tube is attached to a capillary indicator C and the other end to a reservoir through a stopcock S. The jacket is surrounded by a vessel containing solution whose osmotic pressure is to be determined. Due to osmosis, level of the solvent in the capillary indicator C falls, a pressure is simultaneously applied to the solution from the piston D such that the level of the solvent in the capillary indicator C remains at its initial position. The pressure is the osmotic pressure of the solution.

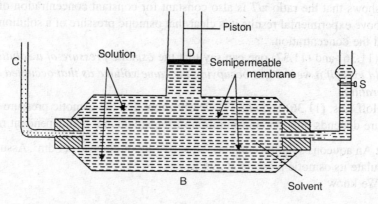

Fig. 11.11 Measurement of osmotic pressure (Berkeley and Hartley)

11.11 RESULTS OF OSMOTIC PRESSURE MEASUREMENTS AND THE LAWS OF OSMOTIC PRESSURE

Results of the measurements of osmotic pressure for different aqueous solutions of sucrose at 293 K are given in Table 11.3.

Table 11.3 Osmotic Pressure of Sucrose Solution at 293 K

Concentration (mol dm^{-3})	Osmotic pressure π (atm)	π/m (atm mol^{-1}dm^3)
0.1	2.59	25.9
0.2	5.06	25.3
0.4	10.14	25.3
0.6	15.39	25.6
0.8	20.91	26.1
1.0	26.61	26.6

The above table clearly shows that the ratio π/m is approximately constant at constant temperature.

Table 11.4 shows the variation of osmotic pressure of 1% sucrose solution at different temperatures.

Table 11.4 Osmotic Pressure of 1% Sucrose Solution

Temperature (K)	Osmotic pressure π (atm)	π/T ($\times 10$) (atm K^{-1})
273	7.085	2.594
283	7.335	2.591
293	7.605	2.595
298	7.729	2.594

This table shows that the ratio π/T is also constant for constant concentration of the solution.

From the above experimental results it is clear that osmotic pressure of a solution depends both on temperature and the concentration.

From Eqs. (11.36) and (11.37) one can say that the *osmotic pressure of a solution is equal to the pressure it would exert if it were a gas occupying the same volume as that occupied by the solution at the same temperature.*

The van't Hoff Eqs. (11.36) and (11.37) clearly show that the osmotic pressure of a solution at a given temperature depends only on concentration of the solute and is independent of its nature.

Problem 11.10: An aqueous solution contains 2.0×10^{-2} kg of glucose per dm^3. Assuming the solution to be ideal, calculate its osmotic pressure at 298 K.

Solution: We know

$$\pi = \frac{n}{V} RT$$

where n is the number of moles of solute in V dm^3 of the solution.

Therefore
$$n = \frac{2.0 \times 10^{-2}\,\text{kg}}{1.80 \times 10^{-1}\,\text{kg mol}^{-1}} = \frac{1}{9}\,\text{mol}$$

Hence
$$\pi = \left(\frac{1}{9}\,\text{mol}\right)\frac{\left(0.0821\,\text{atm dm}^3\,\text{K}^{-1}\,\text{mol}^{-1}\right)(298\,\text{K})}{\left(1\,\text{dm}^3\right)}$$

$$= 2.718\,\text{atm}$$

Problem 11.11: Calculate the osmotic pressure of an aqueous solution containing 1g each of sucrose and glucose per dm^3 at 300 K. If this pressure were measured and it were not known that the solute was a mixture, what molar mass would be expected?

Solution: We know that
$$\pi = CRT$$

Here
$$C = C_1 + C_2$$

where
$$C_1 = \frac{1}{342}$$

$$C_2 = \frac{1}{180}$$

Therefore
$$C = \left(\frac{1}{180} + \frac{1}{342}\right)RT$$

$$= 2.17\,\text{atm}$$

Again,
$$\pi = \frac{2}{M}RT$$

$$M = \frac{2 \times RT}{\pi} = \frac{2 \times 0.0821 \times 300}{2.17}$$

$$= 2.36 \times 10^{-1}\,\text{kg mol}^{-1}$$

The molar mass would be average molar mass depending upon their concentrations.

Problem 11.12: A 5.13% solution of cane sugar is isotonic with a 0.9% solution of an unknown solute. Calculate the molar mass of the solute.

Solution: For cane sugar solution
$$W = 5.13\,\text{g}, \ M = 342\,\text{g mol}^{-1} \text{ and } V = 0.1\,\text{dm}^3$$

$$\pi = \frac{5.13\,RT}{342 \times 0.1}$$

For the unknown solute
$$W = 0.9\,\text{g}, \ M = ? \text{ and } V = 0.1\,\text{dm}^3$$

$$\pi = \frac{0.9 \, RT}{M \times 0.1}$$

Since the solutions are isotonic, hence

$$\frac{0.9 \, RT}{M \times 0.1} = \frac{5.13 \times RT}{342 \times 0.1}$$

or

$$M = \frac{0.9 \times 342}{5.13} = 60 \text{ g mol}^-$$

11.12 RELATIONSHIP BETWEEN DIFFERENT COLLIGATIVE PROPERTIES

The expressions of colligative properties, viz, the relative lowering of vapour pressure, the elevation of boiling point, the depression of freezing point and osmotic pressure are expressed in a common term, mole fraction of the solute *i.e.*,

$$X_2 = \frac{P^0 - P_s}{P^0} = \frac{\Delta H_{\text{vap},\, m} \Delta T_b}{RT_0^2} = \frac{\Delta H_{\text{fus},\, m} \Delta T_f}{RT_0^2} = \frac{\pi \overline{V}_A}{RT} \qquad \qquad ...(11.38)$$

Equation (11.38) can be used to find the value of a colligative property if the value of any other colligative property is known.

11.13 ABNORMAL COLLIGATIVE PROPERTIES OF SOLUTIONS

In the derivation of colligative properties, it has been assumed that the molecular form of the solute remains unchanged in solution. Furthermore the solutions are dilute and behave ideally. In such cases, experimental value of the colligative property is in agreement with the theoretically calculated value. However, there are certain substances like solutions of salts, acids or bases in water or acetic acid in benzene where the experimental value differs considerably from the calculated value. Such solutions are said to be *abnormal solutions*. The abnormalities observed in such solutions are of two types: (*i*) dissociation of solute molecules, and (*ii*) association of the solute molecules.

Association leads to a decrease in the number of solute particles and hence the colligative properties will show lower values. In case of dissociation, the number of solute particles increases and consequently, the colligative properties will show abnormally enhanced values.

In order to account for the abnormal behaviour of such solutions, van't Hoff introduced a factor "*i*" which is called *the van't Hoff factor* and is defined as *the ratio of the experimental value of a colligative property to the calculated value of that property, i.e.*,

$$i = \frac{\text{Experimental value of the colligative property}}{\text{Calculated value of the property when the solution behaves ideally}}$$

Since the colligative property is proportional to number of solute particles in solution, hence

$$i = \frac{\text{Actual number of solute particles present in solution}}{\text{Number of solute particles in solution if it behaves ideally}}$$

or, we may write

$$i = \frac{(\Delta T_b)_{obs}}{(\Delta T_b)_{cal}} = \frac{(\Delta T_f)_{obs}}{(\Delta T_f)_{cal}} = \frac{(\Delta P/P^0)_{obs}}{(\Delta P/P^0)_{cal}} = \frac{\pi_{obs}}{\pi_{cal}} = \frac{M_{cal}}{M_{obs}} \qquad \text{...(11.39)}$$

where M is the molar mass of the solute and ΔT_b, ΔT_f, $\Delta P/P^0$ and π are the boiling point elevation, freezing point depression, relative lowering of vapour pressure and the osmotic pressure of the solution respectively. The subscripts 'obs' and 'cal' refer to the experimental and calculated values of the colligative properties.

(*i*) **Dissociation of Solute:** Consider an electrolyte A_xB_y which partly dissociates in solution yielding x ions of A^{y+} and y ions of B^{x-} and if α is the degree of dissociation, *i.e.,* the fraction of the total number of molecules which dissociates and C the initial concentration of the solute, then the dissociation equilibrium in solution can be represented as

$$A_xB_y \rightleftharpoons xA^{y+} + yB^{x-}$$

Initial concentration $\qquad\qquad\qquad C \qquad 0 \qquad 0$

Concentration at equilibrium $\qquad\quad C(1-\alpha) \quad Cx\alpha \quad Cy\alpha$

The total number of moles at equilibrium $= Cx\alpha + Cy\alpha + C(1-\alpha)$

$$= C[1 - \alpha + x\alpha + y\alpha]$$
$$= C[1 + \alpha(x + y - 1)]$$

Hence $\qquad\qquad\qquad\qquad i = \dfrac{C[1 + \alpha(x + y - 1)]}{C}$

and the degree of dissociation α is given by

$$\alpha = \frac{i-1}{(x+y-1)} \qquad\qquad \text{...(11.40)}$$

Equation (11.40) is applicable to any colligative property and provides an important method for calculating the degree of dissociation of a solute. If $\alpha = 1$, *i.e.,* the dissociation is complete, $i = x + y$, the observed colligative property will be $(x + y)$ times the calculated value. On the other hand, when no dissociation occurs, $\alpha = 0$ and $i = 1$, the calculated and observed values will be equal.

(*ii*) **Association of Solute:** Consider the association of a solute A into its associated form $(A)_n$ according to the reaction

$$nA \rightleftharpoons (A)_n$$

where n is the number of molecules of solute which combine to form an associated species. If C is the initial concentration and α the degree of association of the solute, at equilibrium the number of moles of the undissociated solute is $C(1 - \alpha)$ and that of associated form is $\dfrac{C\alpha}{n}$. The total number of moles in solution is given by

$$C(1-\alpha) + \frac{C\alpha}{n}$$

or
$$C\left(1-\alpha+\frac{\alpha}{n}\right)$$

Hence the van't Hoff factor,

$$i = \frac{C\left(1-\alpha+\frac{\alpha}{n}\right)}{C}$$

$$= 1-\alpha+\frac{\alpha}{n}$$

$$= \left[1+\left(\frac{1}{n}-1\right)\alpha\right]$$

or
$$\alpha = \frac{i-1}{\frac{1}{n}-1} \qquad\qquad ...(11.41)$$

If association is complete, i.e., $\alpha = 1$, $i = 1/n$, the observed value of a colligative property is $1/n$ times the calculated value and if $\alpha = 0$, no association occurs in solution, i.e., $i = 1$ and the observed and calculated values will be equal.

Problem 11.13: A solution of 1.0×10^{-2} kg of sodium chloride in 1000 g of water freezes at $-0.604°C$. The molal depression constant K_f of water is (1.85 K kg mol^{-1}). Calculate the degree of dissociation of sodium chloride.

Solution:

$$\left(\Delta T_f\right)_{cal} = K_f \frac{W_2 \times 1000}{W_1 M_2}$$

$$= \frac{\left(1.85 \text{ deg kg mol}^{-1}\right)\left(1\times 10^{-2}\text{ kg}\right)\left(1000\text{ g kg}^{-1}\right)}{\left(1.00\text{ kg}\right)\left(58.5\text{ g mol}^{-1}\right)}$$

$$= 0.316°C$$

$$\left(\Delta T_f\right)_{obs} = 0.0 - (-0.604) = 0.604°C$$

van't Hoff factor,
$$i = \frac{\left(\Delta T_f\right)_{obs}}{\left(\Delta T_f\right)_{cal}}$$

$$= \frac{0.604}{0.316} = 1.91$$

Sodium chloride dissociates as $\qquad$ $NaCl \rightleftharpoons Na^+ + Cl^-$

Number of moles initially	1	0	0

Number of moles after dissociation $\qquad 1 - \alpha \qquad \alpha \qquad \alpha$

Total number of moles after dissociation $= 1 - \alpha + \alpha + \alpha = 1 + \alpha$

$$i = \frac{\text{Number of moles after dissociation}}{\text{Number of moles initially present}} = \frac{1 + \alpha}{1}$$

Therefore, $\qquad \dfrac{1 + \alpha}{1} = 1.91$

or $\qquad \alpha = 0.91$ or 91%

The degree of dissociation $= 91\%$

Problem 11.14: A solution containing 3.0×10^{-4} kg of benzoic acid ($M = 1.22 \times 10^{-1}$ kg mol^{-1}) in 2.0×10^{-3} kg of benzene freezes at $0.317°C$ below the freezing point of the solvent. Calculate (*i*) the degree of association assuming that the acid exists as dimer in benzene, and (*ii*) the apparent molar mass of the acid exists as dimer in benzene, and (*ii*) the apparent molar mass of the acid; K_f for benzene is 5.1.

Solution:

(*i*) $\qquad \left(\Delta T_f\right)_{cal} = K_f \dfrac{W_2 \times 1000}{M_2 W_1}$

$$= \frac{\left(5.1 \text{ deg kg mol}^{-1}\right)\left(3 \times 10^{-4} \text{ kg}\right)\left(1000 \text{ g kg}^{-1}\right)}{\left(122 \text{ g mol}^{-1}\right)\left(2.0 \times 10^{-2} \text{ kg}\right)}$$

$$= 0.627°C$$

The observed value of $\Delta T_f = 0.317°C$.

Hence van't Hoff factor i is given as

$$i = \frac{\left(\Delta T_f\right)_{obs}}{\left(\Delta T_f\right)_{cal}}$$

$$= 0.506$$

From Eq. (11.41), α is given by

$$\alpha = \frac{i - 1}{\dfrac{1}{n} - 1}$$

$$= \frac{0.506 - 1}{\dfrac{1}{2} - 1} = 98.8\%$$

(*ii*) Since

$$i = \frac{(M)_{cal}}{(M)_{obs}}$$

$$0.506 = \frac{122}{(M)_{obs}}$$

or

$$(M)_{obs} = \frac{122}{0.506} = 241 \text{ g mol}^{-1}$$

Problem 11.15: The freezing point of a solution of 1g of an organic acid, RCOOH in 100 g of water was found to be −0.168°C and 0.2 g of the acid could be neutralized by 15.1 ml of 0.1 Na_2CO_3 solution. Calculate the degree of dissociation of the acid. $K_f = 1.86 \ K$ kg mol^{-1}.

Solution: Number of equivalent of the acid $= \dfrac{0.2}{\text{Eq. wt.}}$

This must be equal to the number of equivalent of Na_2CO_3 ($= 1.51 \times 10^{-2} \times 0.1$)

Therefore equivalent weight of the acid $= \dfrac{0.2 \times 10^2}{1.51 \times 0.1}$

$$= 132.45 \text{ g eq}^{-1}$$

Since the acid is monoprotic, its eq. wt. is the same as its molecular weight. Now the observed molality m_{obs} as given by the freezing point depression is

$$m_{obs} = \frac{\Delta T_f}{K_f} = \frac{0.168}{1.86} = 0.090$$

But the molality (m_{cal}) if the acid were not dissociating is

$$m_{cal} = \frac{\dfrac{1}{132.45}}{100} \times 1000$$

$$= 0.0755$$

Therefore

$$i = \frac{m_{obs}}{m_{cal}}$$

$$= \frac{0.09}{0.0755} = 1.196$$

But $i = 1 + \alpha$ where α is the degree of dissociation.

Hence $\alpha = 0.196$ or 19.6%

EXERCISES

1. Explain, giving reasons, the following:
    (*i*) Addition of a nonvolatile solute lowers the freezing point and elevates the boiling point of a solvent.

(ii) Relative lowering of vapour pressure of a solvent depends only on the amount of the solute and is independent of its nature.

(iii) Molar mass of sodium chloride in aqueous solutions as determined by the use of colligative properties is approximately one-half of the expected value.

(iv) Equimolar solutions of sucrose and sodium chloride in water are not isotonic.

(v) A salt solution fails to quench thirst.

(vi) Salt solution is used for gargling by patients suffering from bad throat.

2. State whether the following statements are true or false:

(i) K_f or K_b are characteristic of the solvent only and do not depend on the nature of solute.

(ii) Osmosis is a special case of diffusion.

(iii) Equimolar aqueous solutions of urea and sodium chloride are isotonic solutions.

(iv) The molal freezing point constant of a solvent is the freezing point depression of a 1 molal solution.

(v) Abnormal colligative properties are shown by solutions where the solutes undergo either dissociation or association.

Ans. True statements: (i), (ii), (iv) and (v)

3. Given the following aqueous solutions at 300 K (i) 1 M sucrose, (ii) 1 M NaCl, (iii) 1 M $BaCl_2$, and (iv) 1 M Phenol.

The electrolytes are completely ionized while phenol is fully dimerized. Which solution would show highest value of the colligative property ? Explain.

Ans. 1 M $BaCl_2$ solution.

4. A dilute solution contains m moles of a solute A in 1 kg of a solvent with a boiling point elevation constant K_b. The solute dimerizes in solution in accordance with the reaction, $2A \rightleftharpoons A_2$, with equilibrium constant K. Show that

$$K = \frac{K_b\left(K_b m - \Delta T_b\right)}{\left(2\Delta T_b - K_b m\right)^2}$$

where ΔT_b is the boiling point elevation in a solution of molality m in A.

5. An electrolyte, $A_x B_y$, undergoes dissociation in a solution as

$$A_x B_y \rightarrow xA^{y+} + yB^{x-}$$

Show that the degree of dissociation α, is given by

$$\alpha = \frac{i-1}{n-1}$$

where 'i' is the van't Hoff factor and n is the total number of ions produced by a molecule of $A_x B_y$ in solution.

6. At 300 K, 10 g of a nonvolatile solute in 100 g of benzene lowers the vapour pressure of benzene by 8.8 torr. If the vapour pressure of benzene at 300 K is 121.8 torr, calculate the molar mass of the solute.

Ans. 101 g mol⁻¹.

7. The vapour pressure of water at 313 K is 55.32 torr. Calculate the amount of a nonvolatile solute (molar mass 342 g mol⁻¹) that must be dissolved in 175 g of water at 313 K to lower the vapour to 53.95 torr.

Ans. 84.5 g.

8. 0.25 g of a solute in 96.8 g of CCl_4(K_b = 5.03 K kg mol⁻¹) showed an elevation of 0.055°C. Calculate the molar mass of the solute. If the solute contained 10.13% carbon and 89.87% chlorine, what is the molecular formula of the compound ?

Ans. 236.1 g mol⁻¹, C_2Cl_6.

9. What should be the value of the molal boiling point constant of a solvent if 0.5 g of a solute (molar mass 100g mol⁻¹) in 25 g of the solvent elevates the boiling point by 1°C ?

Ans. K_b should be 5.

10. A solution containing 0.5126 g of naphthalene (mol. mass 128 g mol^{-1}) in 50 g of CCl$_4$ yields a boiling point elevation of 0.402°C. 0.6216 g of an unknown solute in the same mass of solvent gives a boiling point elevation of 0.647°C. Calculate the molar mass of the unknown solute.

Ans. 96.7 g mol^{-1}.

11. An organic compound contains 68% C, 10% H and the rest oxygen. A solution of 0.032 g of the compound in 0.722 g of cyclohexane had a freezing point of 6.39°C less than that of the solvent. Calculate the molar mass and molecular formula of the compound.

Ans. 144 g mol^{-1}C$_8$H$_{16}$O$_2$

12. A solution containing 2.43 of sulphur in 100 g of naphthalene (m. pt 80.1°C) had a freezing point depression of 0.64°C. The latent heat of fusion of naphthalene is 19.4 kJ mol^{-1}. What is the molar mass and molecular formula of sulphur in the solution ?

Ans. 264 g mol^{-1}, S$_8$.

13. What is the physical significance of molal freezing point constant K_f? Calculate K_f for CCl$_4$ on the basis that $\Delta H_{f, m}$ = 2.5 kJ mol^{-1}, T_f = 250.3 K and molar mass of CCl$_4$ is 153.8 g mol^{-1}.

Ans. K_f = 32 K kg mol^{-1}.

14. (a) Define molal depression constant. Derive an expression relating the freezing point depression of a solution with the mole fraction of the dissolved solute. Discuss the utility of the expression in determining the molar mass of a nonvolatile solute.

(b) Calculate the amount of sucrose that must be added to 4 kg of water to yield a solution that will freeze at −3.72°C. **Ans. 2.74 kg.**

15. A solution (1 : 1 mole ratio) of two liquids A and B is cooled. Which one will freeze first ? Given

	Molar mass (g mol^{-1})	K_f	T_f(°C)
A	109	12.1	7
B	78	5.0	7

Assume the solutions to be ideal.

Ans. B will freeze first.

16. 0.020 kg of urea is dissolved in 0.250 kg of water. Calculate under standard pressure the freezing point (T_f) and boiling point (T_b) of the solution. K_f and K_b for water are 1.86 and 0.52 respectively.

Ans. T_f = −2.48°C and T_b = 100.69°C.

17. A solution contains 1.0% glycerol (mol. mass 92 g mol^{-1}) and 99% water by mass. The vapour pressure of pure water at 298 K is 23.756 mm Hg. Assuming glycerol to be nonvolatile and the solution has the same density as pure water, calculate (i) the vapour pressure of the solution at 298 K, (ii) the freezing point of the solution, (iii) the boiling point of the solution at 1 atm pressure, (iv) the osmotic pressure of the solution at 298 K. **Ans. (i) 23.709 mm Hg. (ii) −0.20°C (iii) 100.056°C, (iv) 2.66 atm.**

18. Explain the terms osmosis, osmotic pressure and isotonic solutions. How is osmotic pressure determined experimentally ? A solution of 0.4 g of a polymer in 1 dm^3 of an aqueous solution has an osmotic pressure of 3.74 torr at 300 K. Calculate the molar mass of the polymer. **Ans. 2 kg mol^{-1}.**

19. Calculate at 300 K, the osmotic pressure of a solution containing 1 g of glucose and 1 g of sucrose in 1 kg of water at 298 K. If this pressure was measured and it were not known that the solute was a mixture, what molar mass would have been calculated ? Would it be mass average or number average molar mass ?

Ans. 0.2095 atm; 235.1 g mol^{-1}, number average molar mass.

20. Calculate the osmotic pressure at 300 K of a 0.5% solution of sucrose in water. If the density of the solution is 1.017 kg dm^{-3}, find the height of a column of the solution which would just balance this osmotic pressure ? **Ans. 0.36 atm, 368.9 cm of the solution.**

21. A tube of 1 cm^2 cross-sectional area is closed at one end with a semipermeable membrane, 0.90 g of glucose (molar mass 180 g mol^{-1}) is placed inside the tube and it is then just kept dipped into pure water at 300 K. Calculate the height of the liquid inside the tube when equilibrium is reached. What is the osmotic pressure and molality of the solution ? The density of the solution is 1 kg dm^{-3} and g = 9.81 m s^{-2}.

Ans. Height = 356.6 cm, π = 0.345 atm m = 0.014.

22. At 300 K, two solutions of glucose in water of concentrations 0.01 M and 0.001 M are separated by a semipermeable membrane. On what solution the pressure need to be applied to prevent osmosis ? Calculate the magnitude of the applied pressure. **Ans.** 0.2216 atm.

23. Two open beakers A and B are placed side by side in a closed container. Beaker A initially contains 0.1 mole of naphthalene in 100 g of benzene and beaker B initially contains 10 g of an unknown solute dissolved in 100 g of benzene. The beakers are allowed to stand in the container until equilibrium is attained. Beaker A is then removed and weighed, it is found to have lost 8 g. Calculate the molar mass of the solute in B. Also state the approximation used in the calculations.

24. Under what conditions abnormal molar masses of solutes are obtained from measurements of colligative properties. How is van't Hoff factor 'i' related to the degree of association and dissociation of a solute.

25. 1.15 g of NaCl in 500g of water (K_b = 0.514 K kg mol^{-1}) elevates the boiling point of water by 0.0514°C. Calculate (i) the apparent molality (ii) the apparent molar mass, (iii) the van't Hoff factor, 'i', and (iv) the degree of dissociation (α) of the salt. **Ans.** (i) 0.10, (ii) 30.2 g mol^{-1}, (iii) 1.94, and (iv) 94%.

26. A certain amount of solute in 100 g of benzene lowers its freezing point by 1.28°C. The same mass of the solute in 100 g of water lowers the freezing point by 1.395°C. If the solute has its normal molar mass in benzene and is completely dissociated in water, into how many ions does a molecule of the solute dissociate when placed in water ? **Ans.** 3 ions.

27. A 0.25 molal aqueous solution of tetraminocobaltic chloride Co(NH$_3$)$_4$Cl$_3$ freezes at –0.93°C. Determine the number of ions produced per formula unit of the compound. **Ans.** 2 ions.

28. At 283 K, the osmotic pressure of a solution of urea is 500 mm Hg. When the solution is diluted and the temperature is raised to 298 K, the osmotic pressure is found to be 105.3 mm Hg. Determine the extent of dilution. **Ans.** 5 times.

29. 1.0 m aqueous solution of hydrofluoric acid (HF) has a freezing point of –1.91°C. Calculate the degree of ionization of HF in the solution. What is the ionization constant of the acid ? **Ans.** 3%, 9.2 × 10^{-3}.

30. The freezing point of a normal human blood is –0.58°C. Calculate the osmotic pressure of the blood. Assume that the density of blood is approximately 1 kg dm^{-3}. **Ans.** 7.9 atm.

CHAPTER
12

Phase Equilibria
–The Phase Rule

12.1 INTRODUCTION

The phase rule is an important and a versatile tool in the study of heterogeneous equilibria. It relates the conditions which must be specified to describe the state of a system at equilibrium. The phase rule was deduced from thermodynamic considerations by Willard Gibbs in 1876 and is an elegant generalization concerning the heterogeneous equilibria. The rule is stated in terms of the number of *phases* (*P*), *the number of components* (*C*) *and the degrees of freedom* (*F*) of a heterogeneous system. Mathematically, it is expressed as

$$P + F = C + 2$$

The numeral 2 on the right hand side accounts for the effect of pressure and temperature.

Before we proceed to derive and apply this rule, let us define and explain the terms *P*, *F* and *C*.

12.2 DEFINITIONS OF VARIOUS TERMS

Phase: A phase is defined as *the part of a system which is homogeneous throughout and is separated from other homogeneous parts of the system by means of a definite boundary. A phase is physically distinct and mechanically separable part of the system.* A system consisting of a gas or gaseous mixture always constitutes a single phase. In the case of liquids, depending upon their mutual solubility, one or more phases can arise. Water and ethanol system always gives one phase while water and carbon tetrachloride yield two phases separated by a definite boundary. Partially miscible liquids like water-phenol can have one or two phases depending upon their mutual solubility. In liquids, the number of phases is equal to the number of liquid layers in the system.

A system containing a liquid and its vapours in equilibrium has two phases, viz., the liquid phase and the vapour phase. Each phase is separated from the other by a definite boundary. Similarly, ice-liquid water-water vapours constitute a system containing three phases. Dispersion of a pure solid in another solid is a one phase system if the solids are completely miscible with each other and two phases if they do not form a solid solution. For example, an alloy of two metals is a two phase system if the metals are immiscible, but a single phase if they are completely miscible. In the decomposition of calcium carbonate into its dissociated products, calcium oxide and carbon dioxide, there are two solid phases and one gas phase present at equilibrium. It is, therefore, a three phase system.

Components: The composition of a system can be described in terms of species present in the system. The number of components of a system is *the minimum number of independent constituents necessary to define the composition of all the phases present in the system.*

In water system, for example, the phases that are present are ice, liquid water and water vapours. The composition of each phase can be expressed by a single component, water (H_2O). Hence it is a one component system. Similarly, in the sulphur system there are four phases, viz., rhombic sulphur, monoclinic sulphur, liquid and sulphur vapours. Each phase can be regarded as being made up of sulphur only and is, therefore, a one component system. An aqueous common salt solution will be a two component system since there are two independent chemical substances which determine the composition of the solution, viz., H_2O and NaCl. In the salt-water system, *e.g.*, ferric chloride-water, the various phases that exist are: anhydrous Fe_2Cl_6, $Fe_2Cl_6 \cdot 4H_2O$, $Fe_2Cl_6 \cdot 5H_2O$, $Fe_2Cl_6 \cdot 7H_2O$, $Fe_2Cl_6 \cdot 12H_2O$, solution of ferric chloride in water, ice and water vapours. However, the composition of some of these phases may be expressed in terms of only one of these constituents (Fe_2Cl_6) or water, whereas the composition of others may be stated in terms of two independent components (Fe_2Cl_6 and H_2O). Since these two components are the smallest number by means of which the composition of all the phases can be described and hence it is a two component system.

The situation is slightly different when a chemical equilibrium exists between the species in the system. In such cases each equilibrium step places a restriction on the freedom and the variance of the system is reduced by the number of independent equilibria. For example, in the system

$$CaCO_3(s) \rightleftharpoons CaO(s) + CO_2(g)$$

The equilibrium between the three species CaO, $CaCO_3$ and CO_2 places a restriction on the number of components and only two are sufficient in terms of which the composition of each phase can be expressed. If CaO and CO_2 are chosen as the two components, then the composition of various phases can be described as follows:

Phase	Composition
$CaCO_3$	$CaO + CO_2$
CaO	$CaO + 0CO_2$
CO_2	$0CaO + CO_2$

If the two components chosen are $CaCO_3$ and CO_2, then the composition of the phases CaO, $CaCO_3$ and CO_2 would be given as

Phase	Composition
$CaCO_3$	$CaCO_3 + 0CO_2$
CaO	$CaCO_3 - CO_2$
CO_2	$0CaCO_3 + CO_2$

In terms of $CaCO_3$ and CaO as the components, the composition of each phase can be expressed as

Phase	Composition
$CaCO_3$	$CaCO_3 + 0CaO$
CaO	$0CaCO_3 + CaO$
CO_2	$CaCO_3 - CaO$

In the case of liquid water, a large number of species H_2O, $(H_2O)_2$, $(H_2O)_3$, ...$(H_2O)_n$ may be visualized. The equilibria between these species are established and there are $(n-1)$ such independent equilibria. Consequently, only one component H_2O, is sufficient to describe the composition of each species.

In the dissociation of ammonium chloride: $NH_4Cl(s) \rightleftharpoons NH_3(g)+HCl(g)$, the equilibrium between these three species places a restriction and the minimum number of components is two. However, if it is assumed that $p_{HCl} = p_{NH_3}$, an additional restriction is imposed and the number of components is one.

In the absence of a catalyst, a mixture of $H_2O(g)$, $H_2(g)$ and $O_2(g)$ at room temperature is a three component system. At higher temperature or in the presence of a catalyst the reaction

$$H_2(g) + \frac{1}{2}O_2(g) \rightleftharpoons H_2O(g)$$

proceeds and the number of components would be decreased by one. Furthermore, if it is assumed that $p_{H_2} = 2p_{O_2}$, the number of components of the system is one.

In general, the number of components (C) in a system is obtained by subtracting from the total number of constituents (C') the number of restrictions (m), i.e.,

Number of components, $C = C' - m$

Degrees of Freedom: The degree of freedom or variance of a system is defined as *the smallest number of independent variables such as pressure, temperature and concentration that must be specified in order to describe completely the state of the system.* Let us consider a gaseous system. To describe completely the state of such a system only two of the three variables are essential as the third one is automatically known from the equation of state. These could be P and V, or T and V, or T and P. The system is thus said to be *bivariant*. In other words, there are two degrees of freedom or the variance, $F = 2$.

For a system involving a liquid in equilibrium with its vapours only one variable, say temperature, is required to specify the state of the system. Once temperature is fixed, its vapour pressure is automatically fixed. In general, when two phases are present in equilibrium, only one of the variables is sufficient to define the state of the system completely. Systems which have only one degree of freedom $(F = 1)$ are called *univariant* or *monovariant* systems.

When three phases of a substance are in equilibrium, there is no freedom to choose either the pressure or the temperature as variant. The system is *invariant* or *nonvariant*; there are no degrees of freedom; $F = 0$. For a one component system, in general, if there are P phases present then the degrees of freedom is given by

$$F = 3 - P$$

12.3 DERIVATION OF THE PHASE RULE

Consider a system in equilibrium containing P phases and C components. The composition of each phase can be specified if the amount of each component is known. All we need here is to describe the mole fraction of each component. If C is the number of components required to describe the composition of a phase, then the total number of composition variables for P phases are PC. Besides these, there are two more variables, temperature and pressure, which have to be considered. The total number of independent variables is $PC + 2$.

In each phase there is a relationship between the mole fractions

$$X_1 + X_2 + X_3 + \ldots \ldots + X_c = 1$$

$$\sum_i X_i = 1 \qquad \qquad ...(12.1)$$

From Eq. (12.1) the mole fraction of any component in a phase can be calculated if the mole fractions of all other components are known. For each phase there is one such equation and for P phases there are P equations similar to Eq. (12.1). Therefore the total number of independent variables to be specified are

$$CP + 2 - P$$

or

$$P(C - 1) + 2$$

When a heterogeneous system is in equilibrium at a constant temperature and pressure, the chemical potential of a particular component must be the same in all the phases in which it appears. For a one-component system having two phases α and β, the equality of chemical potential implies

$$\mu(\alpha) = \mu(\beta)$$

Hence there is one equilibrium relation that gives the distribution of the component between two phases. Similarly in a one component system having three phases α, β and γ, we have

$$\mu(\alpha) = \mu(\beta) = \mu(\gamma)$$

Thus two additional equilibrium relations between the variables exist. In general, for each component in P phases, $(P - 1)$ relations are possible. Since there are C components, the total number of these equations are $C(P - 1)$.

Therefore the degrees of freedom or the number of independent variables F is given by

F = Total number of variables – Total number of relations among the variables

$$= PC + 2 - P - C(P - 1)$$

$$= C - P + 2$$

or

$$F + P = C + 2 \qquad \qquad ...(12.2)$$

Equation (12.2) is the phase rule given by Willard Gibbs, the fundamental relation controlling the equilibria in heterogeneous systems.

It can be seen from Eq. (12.2) that for a system of given number of components, greater the number of phases smaller will be the number of degrees of freedom. For example, in case of a one component system like water, the maximum number of phases that can coexist at equilibrium is three. For this equilibrium the degree of freedom ($F = 1 + 2 - 3$) is zero. In general, for a system of given number of components where the number of phases is maximum the degree of freedom is zero. However, for a system with a given number of phases, larger the number of components greater will be the number of degrees of freedom such as temperature, pressure and concentration which must be specified to describe completely the state of the system. Thus if to a one-component-one phase system like liquid water some salt is added to form an unsaturated solution, the number of degrees of freedom increases from two to three.

The phase rule does not depend upon the nature or the amount of the substances present in the system at equilibrium. It takes into account the effect of variables like temperature, pressure and composition; effects of other variables such as electric, magnetic, gravitational, surface forces etc., are not taken into account. The phase rule does not tell us anything concerning the composition of the matter. It merely states that systems having the same degrees of freedom behave alike thermodynamically. The phase rule is an important generalization and enables us to classify equilibria and study the more complex heterogeneous systems.

Problem 12.1: Write down the number of components, number of phases and evaluate the degrees of freedom for the following equilibria:

(i) $N_2O_4 (g) \rightleftharpoons 2NO_2(g)$;

(ii) $NH_4Cl(s) \rightleftharpoons NH_3(g) + HCl(g)$ when (a) $p_{NH_3} \neq p_{HCl}$

and (b) $p_{NH_3} = p_{HCl}$;

(iii) Pure partly frozen acetic acid;

(iv) Solid carbon in equilibrium with gaseous CO, CO_2 and O_2 at 100°C;

(v) A dilute solution of sulphuric acid in water;

(vi) An aqueous solution saturated with respect to both sodium chloride and potassium chloride and in equilibrium with the vapour phase;

(vii) An aqueous solution of a mixture of sodium chloride and potassium bromide and in equilibrium with the vapour phase;

(viii) A liquid at its critical point;

(ix) A binary azeotrope;

(x) A mixture of nitrogen, hydrogen and ammonia at temperatures at which the equilibrium $N_2(g)$ $+ 3H_2(g) \rightleftharpoons 2NH_3(g)$ is readily established.

(xi) Reduction of $Fe_2O_3(s)$ by CO in the presence of (a) air and (b) oxygen alone.

Solution:

(i) Number of components, C = Total number of components—The relations between them
$$= 2 - 1 = 1$$

Number of phases = 1

Hence the degree of freedom, $\quad F = C + 2 - P = 1 + 2 - 1 = 2$

(ii) (a) Number of components, $\quad C = 3 - 1 = 2$

$$P = 2$$

$$F = 2 + 2 - 2 = 2$$

(b) Number of components is reduced by one because $p_{HCl} = p_{NH_3}$

or $\quad\quad\quad\quad\quad\quad\quad\quad\quad\quad C = 3 - 2 = 1$

$$P = 2$$

$$F = 1 + 2 - 2 = 1$$

(iii) The system is $\quad\quad CH_3COOH(s) \rightleftharpoons CH_3COOH (l)$

$$C = 1$$

$$P = 2$$

$$F = 1$$

(iv) The different equilibria are

$$C(s) + O_2(g) \rightleftharpoons CO_2(g)$$

$$C(s) + \frac{1}{2}O_2(g) \rightleftharpoons CO(g)$$

Hence $\quad\quad\quad\quad\quad\quad\quad C = 4 - 2 = 2$

$$P = 2$$
$$F = 2$$

(v) The ionization equilibria in aqueous sulphuric acid solution are

$$H_2SO_4 + H_2O \rightleftharpoons H_3O^+ + HSO_4^-$$
$$HSO_4^- + H_2O \rightleftharpoons H_3O^+ + SO_4^{2-}$$

There are five different species in the solution. In addition to these two relations between these species, the solution is electrically neutral. Hence the number of components, $C = 5 - 3 = 2$. Number of phases, $P = 1$ and the degrees of freedom $F = 3$.

(vi) The total number of chemical species are seven [NaCl(s), KCl(s), K^+(aq), Na^+(aq), Cl^-(aq), H_2O(l) and H_2O(g)]. In addition to the condition of electroneutrality the following three equilibria exist between the components:

(a)
$$NaCl(s) \overset{H_2O}{\rightleftharpoons} Na^+(aq) + Cl^-(aq)$$

(b)
$$KCl(s) \overset{H_2O}{\rightleftharpoons} K^+(aq) + Cl^-(aq)$$

(c)
$$H_2O(l) \rightleftharpoons H_2O(g)$$

Therefore the number of components, $C = 7 - 4 = 3$

$P = 4$ (two solid phases, one liquid phase and one gas phase)

$$F = 1$$

(vii) The different chemical species are NaCl(s), KBr(s), KCl(s), NaBr(s), K^+(aq), Na^+(aq), Cl^-(aq), Br^-(aq), H_2O(l), H_2O(g). The following five independent equilibria may be visualized:

(a)
$$NaCl(s) \overset{H_2O}{\rightleftharpoons} Na^+(aq) + Cl^-(aq)$$

(b)
$$KBr(s) \overset{H_2O}{\rightleftharpoons} K^+(aq) + Br^-(aq)$$

(c)
$$NaBr(s) \overset{H_2O}{\rightleftharpoons} Na^+(aq) + Br^-(aq)$$

(d)
$$NaCl + KBr \rightleftharpoons NaBr + KCl$$

(e)
$$H_2O(l) \rightleftharpoons H_2O(g)$$

Including the condition of electroneutrality, there are six relations between the different species. The number of components is thus $10-6 = 4$ and the number of phases is six. Hence the degree of freedom is zero.

(viii) At the critical point the liquid phase is indistinguishable from its vapour phase and it would place a restriction on the variance of the system. Thus at the critical point of a liquid

$$C = 1$$
$$P = 2$$

and
$$F = 1 + 2 - 2 - 1 = 0$$

The critical point of a liquid is invariant.

(ix) In a binary azeotrope, the compositions of the liquid and the vapour phases are the same and hence a restriction on the variance of the system. Thus

$$C = 2$$
$$P = 2$$

and one restriction due to identical composition of the liquid and vapour phase, therefore, the degree of freedom F is given by

$$F = 2 + 2 - 2 - 1 = 1$$

(x) There are three chemical species and one equilibrium condition

$$N_2(g) + 3H_2(g) \rightleftharpoons 2NH_3(g)$$

hence the number of components is two. The number of phases is 1 and hence the degree of freedom is 3.

(xi) (a) Here in the presence of air (containing mainly nitrogen and oxygen), the different species which could exist are $FeO(s)$, $Fe_2O_3(s)$, $Fe(s)$, $CO(g)$, $CO_2(g)$, $N_2(g)$ and $O_2(g)$. The total number of phases are four and the following reactions may occur:

$$Fe_2O_3(s) + CO(g) \rightleftharpoons 2FeO(s) + CO_2(g)$$

$$FeO(s) + CO(g) \rightleftharpoons Fe(s) + CO_2(g)$$

$$CO(g) + \frac{1}{2}O_2(g) \rightleftharpoons CO_2(g)$$

Since the number of components are $7 - 3 = 4$ and the degree of freedom F is

$$4 + 2 - 4 = 2$$

(b) If the reduction were carried out in the presence of oxygen, the number of components is given by $6 - 3 = 3$ and the degree of freedom is $3 + 2 - 4 = 1$.

12.4 STABILITY OF PHASES

At constant temperature and pressure the thermodynamic requirement for equilibrium between phases is the equality of chemical potential of a component in all the phases. The phase with the lowest value of chemical potential is the most stable phase. For a one component system the molar Gibbs free energy is equal to its chemical potential. For a one component system, we have

$$d\left(\frac{G}{n}\right) = d\mu = -S_m dT + V_m dP$$

Hence

$$\left(\frac{\partial \mu}{\partial T}\right)_P = -S_m \qquad \qquad ...(12.3)$$

and

$$\left(\frac{\partial \mu}{\partial P}\right)_T = V_m \qquad \qquad ...(12.4)$$

The entropy of a substance is always positive and is highest for gases and least for solids and therefore the slopes (μ vs T plots) are negative. The slope is more negative for the gas than for liquid and more negative for the liquid than for the solid. The negative sign in Eq. (12.3) indicates that the chemical potential decreases with increase in temperature at constant pressure, and the decrease is largest for gases and smallest for solids. A plot of chemical potential versus temperature for the three phases solid-liquid-vapour of a pure component is shown in Fig. (12.1 (a)). If two or three phases of a single component have the same chemical potential, they will co-exist at equilibrium, as at the melting point or the triple point. Above the boiling point, T_b, gas is the stable phase and has the lowest value of chemical potential. At the boiling point (T_b) the liquid and its vapour coexist and have the same value of chemical potential.

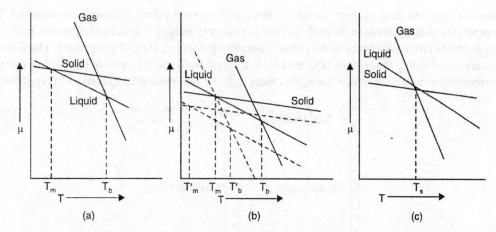

Fig. 12.1 (*a*) Temperature dependence of chemical potential of solid, liquid and gas phases at constant pressure.
　　　　(*b*) Pressure-dependence of chemical potential and its effects on melting and boiling points. The dashed
　　　　　　lines are for lower pressure.
　　　　(*c*) μ versus *T* plot for a substance that sublimes.

Below T_b the liquid is the stable phase. At the melting point (T_m), solid and liquid are in equilibrium and have the same value of chemical potential. Below the melting point, solid has the lowest chemical potential and is the stable phase. Between T_m and T_b liquid is the stable phase.

Effect of Pressure on the Stability of Phases: Since molar volume is always positive and Eq. (12.4) shows that the chemical potential decreases with the decrease of pressure at constant temperature. Furthermore, the molar volumes of gases are much larger than the molar volumes of either liquids or solids. Equation (12.4) predicts that the decrease in pressure lowers the chemical potential of gases to a larger extent than those of solids or liquids. This decrease in chemical potential lowers both the boiling point (from T_b to T'_b) and generally the melting point from T_m to T'_m as shown in Fig. 12.1(*b*). However, relatively large effect on the boiling point is due to the large difference in the molar volumes of the gas and the liquid. As a result the range of temperature over which the liquid is the stable phase has been considerably reduced. If the pressure is reduced to a sufficiently low value, the curve for the chemical potential of the gas will intercept the solid curve below the melting point of the substance (Fig. 12.1 (*c*)). The temperature T_s at which solid-gas coexist in equilibrium is *the sublimation temperature* of the solid. At this temperature, the solid will sublime instead of melting.

12.5 PHASE DIAGRAMS

A diagram giving the conditions of equilibrium between various phases of a substance is called a *phase diagram*. Such diagrams can be constructed from a knowledge of the relative stability of various phases of a substance present in different regions of pressure and temperature (Fig. 12.2). Along the boundary between any two phases solid-liquid, liquid-vapour or solid-vapour are in equilibrium and have equal chemical potentials. *e.g.*, $\mu_l(P, T) = \mu_g(P, T)$; $\mu_l(P, T) = \mu_s(P, T)$ and $\mu_s(P, T) = \mu_g(P, T)$. By solving these equations for P as a function of T, we obtain equations of the boundary lines between various phases. The shape of the phase diagram depends on the slope of the boundary lines between the various phases. The effect of changes in temperature or in pressure or composition on the change of phases in a system can be easily predicted and understood with the help of such a graphical representations. When there are only two variables such as temperature and pressure or temperature and composition, rectangular coordinates are used. In case of three variables, three-dimensional phase diagrams are required. The phase diagrams show at a glance the properties of the substances; melting points, boiling points, transition points, triple points etc. Every point in the phase diagram represents a state of the system. The lines on the phase diagram dividing the regions labelled as solid, liquid and vapour represent two phases existing in equilibrium while the points where three lines meet indicate that three phases coexist in equilibrium.

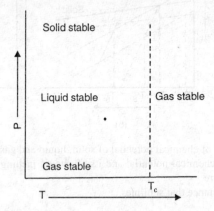

Fig. 12.2 Regions of stability of different phases on a P-T diagram

12.6 ONE-COMPONENT SYSTEM

In a one-component system, $C = 1$. Therefore, the phase rule becomes
$$F = 1 - P + 2 = 3 - P$$

When only one phase is present $F = 2$, the system is bivariant and two independent variables have to be specified to describe the state of the system. The two variables are pressure and temperature. A single phase is therefore represented by an area on a pressure-temperature graph.

When two phases solid-liquid, liquid-vapour or solid-vapour are in equilibrium then $F = 1$, the system is univariant which means that only one of the two variables such as temperature or pressure is sufficient to describe the system adequately. If we select temperature as a variable the pressure can not be changed without changing the state of the system. Alternatively, if pressure is selected as the variable then temperature is fixed and the equilibria between any two of the three phases occur at definite well-defined temperatures. On a pressure temperature graph these two-phase equilibria are indicated by lines.

When three phases (solid, liquid and vapour) are in equilibrium then $F = 0$, *i.e.,* the system is nonvariant or invariant. Three phases can coexist only at a definite temperature and pressure. None of the variables can be changed without changing the number of phases existing at equilibrium. The state of a nonvariant system on a pressure temperature diagram is indicated by a point called *the triple point.* However, if the solid exists in two modifications, one may visualize a situation where four phases (two solids, one liquid and one vapour) may coexist. But from the phase rule $F = -1$ which is meaningless implying that such a system involving one component does not exist.

The phase diagram for system having only one component can be drawn using the Clausius-Clapeyron Eq. (8.91), *i.e.,*

$$\frac{dP}{dT} = \frac{\Delta S_m}{\Delta V_m}$$

For solid-vapour or liquid-vapour equilibrium, dp/dT is always positive for all the substances as ΔS_m and ΔV_m both are positive for such equilibria. Hence the lines indicating these equilibria in a pressure-temperature diagram will have positive slopes, *i.e.*, the lines will slope away from the pressure axis. Furthermore, the slope (dP/dT) of the line representing solid-vapour equilibrium is larger than the slope of the line representing liquid-vapour equilibrium, hence the former would be steeper than the latter. For solid-liquid equilibrium, dP/dT for most of the substances is positive except for water where it is negative. Therefore the line indicating solid-liquid equilibrium will have a positive slope, *i.e.*, the line will slope away from the pressure axis. For water the line indicating solid-liquid equilibrium will slope towards the pressure axis.

The general shape of the phase diagram for a one component system is shown in Fig. 12.3.

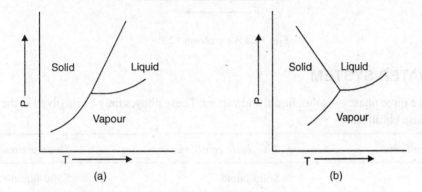

Fig. 12.3 Phase diagram for a one-component system.
(*a*) Molar volume of solid is less than the molar volume of liquid, and
(*b*) Molar volume of solid is greater than that of the liquid.

Problem 12.2: A certain substance X exists in two solid modifications X_1 and X_2 as well as liquid and vapour under one atmospheric pressure. X_1 is stable at lower temperature while X_2 at higher temperature and the transition from X_1 to X_2 is accompanied by increase in molar volume. Both X_1 and X_2 are denser than the liquid phase. If no metastable equilibria are observed, draw a pressure-temperature phase diagram for the system. Label each area of the diagram.

Solution: For the transition
$$X_1(s) \rightarrow X_2(s)$$

$$\frac{dP}{dT} = \frac{S_{X_2,m} - S_{X_1,m}}{V_{X_2,m} - V_{X_1,m}}$$

But
$$S_{X_2,m} > S_{X_1,m}$$

and
$$V_{X_2,m} > V_{X_1,m}$$

Hence dP/dT is a positive quantity, *i.e.*, the line representing the equilibrium between X_1 and X_2 will slope away from the pressure axis. Again for the $X_1(s) \rightarrow$ liquid and $X_2(s) \rightarrow$ liquid transformations both ΔS and ΔV are positive therefore, dP/dT for both the transitions are positive implying that the lines indicating the equilibria $X_1(s) \rightleftharpoons$ liquid and $X_2(s) \rightleftharpoons$ liquid will slope away from the pressure axis. The required phase diagram is shown in Fig. 12.4.

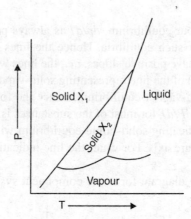

Fig. 12.4 For problem 12.2

12.7 THE WATER SYSTEM

In water there are three phases—solid, liquid and vapour. These phases may be involved in the following seven stable phase equilibria:

One-phase equilibria	Two-phase equilibria	Three-phase equilibria
Solid	Solid-liquid	Solid-liquid-vapour
Liquid	Solid-vapour	
Vapour	Liquid-vapour	

The phases and the equilibria between them are depicted in Fig. 12.5 on a *P-T* diagram. It consists of three curves *OA, OB* and *OC* each indicating the equilibrium between two phases. These curves divide the diagram into three parts: *AOB, BOC* and *AOC* respectively where vapour, liquid and solid phases exist.

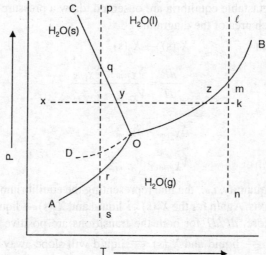

Fig. 12.5 Phase diagram for water

The discussion of the diagram involves the study of the areas, curves and points. This is done as follows:

The Areas: The solid phase is enclosed by the lines *OA* and *OC* (area *AOC*), liquid phase by *OB* (area *BOC*) and *OC* while the vapour phase by *OA* and *OB* (area *AOB*). For all these phases the degree of freedom is

$$F = C + 2 - P$$
$$= 1 + 2 - 1$$
$$= 2$$

Hence these one-phase equilibria are bivariant and both temperature and pressure must be specified to define the state of the system.

The Curves: The two-phase equilibria are indicated by the curves *OA*, *OB* and *OC*. The degree of freedom for these systems is

$$F = C + 2 - P$$
$$= 1 + 2 - 2$$
$$= 1$$

These are, therefore, uni-or monovariant systems, *i.e.,* only one variable is sufficient to specify the state of the system.

Curve OB: Curve OB separates the liquid region from the vapour region and therefore represents the equilibrium between the liquid and vapour at different temperatures. This is known as the vapour pressure curve of water. The vapour pressure increases with rise of temperature. For any given temperature on the curve there is only one value of the vapour pressure and vice-versa. Just above the curve, liquid is the stable phase while below it vapour is the stable phase. If we start from a point *l* within the liquid phase and lower the pressure at constant temperature, the vapour phase appears at *m* and both the liquid and the vapour exist in equilibrium at *m*. On further lowering the pressure to *n*, the liquid phase disappears and only the vapour phase remains. The curve *OB* extends up to the critical point of water (647 K and 220 atmospheres). At this point the liquid and vapour phases are no longer distinguishable from each other.

Curve OA: The curve *OA* represents the variation of vapour pressure of the solid with temperature. Along this curve solid and vapour are in equilibrium. This curve is known as the vapour pressure curve or the sublimation curve of ice. The curve separates the region of solid from the region of vapour. The curve *OA* starts from point *O* and should extend up to the absolute zero of temperature. Again, it can be seen that for each temperature there is one pressure and similarly for each pressure there is one temperature at which both the phases coexist.

Curve OC: This curve represents the equilibrium between the solid and liquid and is the freezing point curve of ice. The curve indicates the influence of pressure on the melting point of ice. The curve starts from *O* and extends to very high values of pressure. The slope of the curve is negative implying that the melting point is lowered by the increase of pressure or ice melts with a decrease in volume.

Metastable Curve OD: It is sometimes possible to cool liquid water below the point *O* without solidification, as is shown by the dotted curve *OD*. The liquid below the freezing point is in the supercooled state. This state is not quite stable and is usually known as a metastable state. The metastable state is spontaneously converted into stable state by the addition of a small amount of stable phase. For example, the addition of a small amount of ice to the supercooled liquid will result in the solidification of water. Thus the curve OD represents water and vapour phase in metastable equilibrium. The curve *OD* is a continuation of curve *BO*. Since the curve *OD* lies above the curve OA, the vapour pressure of the metastable supercooled water is higher than the vapour pressure of the stable solid phase at the same temperature. This is universally true and shows that the former will spontaneously pass into the latter.

The Point O: It will be seen from the figure that the three curves *OA, OB* and *OC* meet at one point *O*. This is called the triple point; at this point all the three phases ice, water and vapour coexist in equilibrium. The temperature and pressure corresponding to this equilibrium are 0.0075°C and 4.58 mm of mercury respectively. Since three phases are present, hence the system has no degree of freedom at the triple point. If either the temperature or the pressure or both are changed, the three phases would no longer coexist and at least one of them would disappear. The phase that disappears depends on how the change is accomplished. For example, along *OB* solid would not exist, along *OA* liquid would not exist while along *OC* vapour would not exist and under these conditions the system changes from nonvariant to univariant.

Effect of changes of temperature and pressure on the phase equilibrium: Let us consider the effect of temperature at constant pressure on a system initially at *x* in Fig. 12.5. When it is heated at constant pressure, the increase of temperature shifts the system along *xy*. At *y* fusion takes place and the liquid phase is in equilibrium with the solid phase. The bivariant system reduces to a monovariant system. On further heating ice simply melts at constant temperature and when it is completely converted into liquid water, the system again becomes bivariant. The temperature begins to rise along *yz*. At *z* vapourization begins and the vapour is in equilibrium with the liquid phase. The system again becomes monovariant and the temperature will remain constant until all the liquid is converted into vapours. Further increase of temperature merely increases the temperature of the vapours. The phase changes occurring at constant pressure are shown in a temperature-time graph (Fig. 12.6).

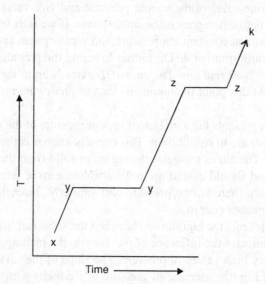

Fig. 12.6 Effect of changes in temperature on phase transitions at constant pressure

The effect of changes in pressure can similarly be studied at constant temperature. The system initially at *p* contains liquid. By decreasing the pressure, the state *q* is reached where the solid phase appears and is in equilibrium with the liquid phase. At this point isothermal and isobaric transformation

---

* Pure water freezes at 0.0023°C and at 1 atmosphere pressure. Hence the experimental value of triple point is 0.0075°C + 0.0023°C = 0.0098°C.

of the liquid into solid results. After all the liquid has been converted into ice, pressure drops along qr and at r the vapour phase appears. The vapour is in equilibrium with the solid. When the pressure is sufficiently lowered, the solid phase disappears and only the vapour phase remains between rs. The pressure-time plot (Fig. 12.7) shows the phase transitions that result when the pressure is varied at constant temperature.

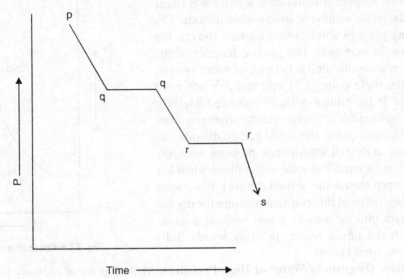

Fig. 12.7 Pressure-time plot at constant temperature for water system

Table 12.1. summarizes the salient features of water system.

Table 12.1 Salient Features of Water System

Phase Equilibria	Degrees of Freedom	Location in the Phase Diagram
One-phase equilibria		
Water vapour	2	Area below the curve AOB
Liquid water	2	Area between OC and OB
Ice	2	Area on the left of the curve AOC
Two-phase equilibria		
Fusion: $H_2O(s) \rightleftharpoons H_2O(l)$	1	Along the curve OC
Vapourization: $H_2O(l) \rightleftharpoons H_2O(g)$	1	Along the curve OB
Sublimation: $H_2O(s) \rightleftharpoons H_2O(g)$	1	Along the curve OA
Three-phase equilibrium		At the triple point O (0.0075°C
$H_2O(s) \rightleftharpoons H_2O(l) \rightleftharpoons H_2O(g)$	0	and 4.58 mm Hg)

12.8 CARBON DIOXIDE SYSTEM

Figure 12.8 is the phase diagram for carbon dioxide. The curve OC is the freezing point curve of liquid carbon dioxide. Along this curve solid and liquid phases are in equilibrium and the curve slopes away from the pressure axis. This is due to the fact that the molar volume of liquid carbon dioxide is larger than the molar volume of solid carbon dioxide. The melting point of solid carbon dioxide rises as the pressure is increased. The general features of the diagram are quite similar to those of water system. O is the triple point (5.11 atm and $T = -56.6°C$) while P is the critical point (73 atm and 31.1°C). From the diagram, it is clear that the triple point lies above 1 atmosphere, the liquid carbon dioxide can not exist at normal atmospheric pressure whatever is the temperature. The solid will sublime when left in the open (hence the normal dry ice). If we raise the temperature at this constant pressure the dry ice will pass into the vapour phase without passing through the liquid phase. In other words, sublimations would occur.

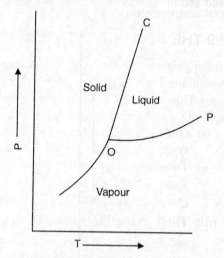

Fig. 12.8 Phase diagram for carbon dioxide

Phase Diagram of Water at High Pressures: Melting point of ordinary ice (I) is lowered by the increase of pressure. It falls to about −22°C at a pressure of 2040 atm (Fig. 12.9). Further increase of pressure results in the transformation of ice (I) into a new modification ice (III). Its melting point is

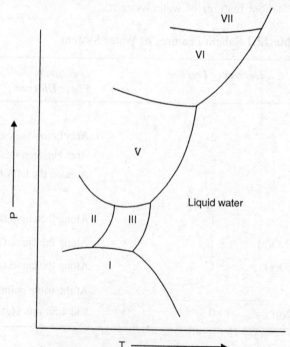

Fig. 12.9 Phase diagram for water at high pressures

raised by the increase of pressure. In addition to these two modifications, existence of four other forms of ice have been confirmed. These are stable at high pressures and are designated as ice (II), ice (V), ice (VI) and ice (VII). These different forms of ice differ in their crystal structures and physical properties. Existence of ice (IV), however, has not been confirmed. In the diagram there are six triple points. Forms III, V, VI and VII are denser than water. At high pressure the melting point of ice is considerably raised and in fact ice (VII) melts at 190°C at a pressure of 40,000 atm.

12.9 THE SULPHUR SYSTEM

Sulphur exists in the two allotropic forms, namely rhombic (S_r) and monoclinic (S_m). The transition temperature is 95.6°C below which rhombic form is stable while above it monoclinic is the stable variety. However, at 95.6°C both these forms are in equilibrium. These two solids along with the liquid sulphur (S_l) and sulphur vapour (S_v) give rise to the following phase equilibria:

  (i) **One-Phase Equilibria:** There are four such equilibria, S_r, S_m, S_l and S_v. These are bivariant systems $(F = C - P + 2 = 1 - 1 + 2 = 2)$ and each phase is represented by an area in the diagram.

 (ii) **Two-Phase Equilibria:** Six such two-phase equilibria are possible for this system. These are $S_r \rightleftharpoons S_m$, $S_r \rightleftharpoons S_l$, $S_r \rightleftharpoons S_v$, $S_m \rightleftharpoons S_l$, $S_l \rightleftharpoons S_v$ and $S_m \rightleftharpoons S_v$ and are monovariant $(F = C - P + 2 = 1 - 2 + 2 = 1)$ systems. These equilibria are represented by lines in the diagram.

(iii) **Three-Phase Equilibria:** Three such stable equilibria are $S_r \rightleftharpoons S_m \rightleftharpoons S_l$, $S_r \rightleftharpoons S_m \rightleftharpoons S_v$ and $S_m \rightleftharpoons S_l \rightleftharpoons S_v$. In addition to these stable equilibria there is one metastable equilibrium involving $S_r \rightleftharpoons S_l \rightleftharpoons S_v$ These systems are nonvariant $(F = C - P + 2 = 1 - 3 + 2 = 0)$. In the diagram these are represented by triple points.

 (iv) The possibility of a four-phase equilibrium $(S_r \rightleftharpoons S_m \rightleftharpoons S_l \rightleftharpoons S_v)$ is ruled out as the degree of freedom would be negative $(F = C - P + 2 = 1 - 4 + 2 = -1)$ for such a system.

The phase diagram for sulphur system is shown in Fig. 12.10. It consists of the following parts:

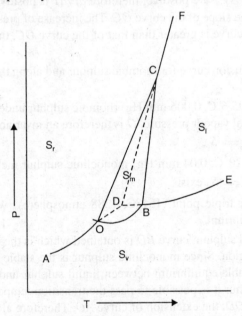

Fig. 12.10 Phase diagram for sulphur system.

The areas: In the figure there are four distinct areas. On the left of *AOCF* is the region where only rhombic sulphur is present.

Similarly, in the area enclosed by curve *EB, BC* and *CF* liquid sulphur is the stable phase. In the area below *AOBE* only sulphur vapour (S_v) is present. Lastly, in the area *OBC* bounded by the curve *OB, OC* and *BC*, monoclinic sulphur (S_m) exists.

Curve OA: OA is the sublimation curve of rhombic sulphur and shows the change of vapour pressure of rhombic sulphur with changes in temperature. Rhombic sulphur and sulphur vapour ($S_r \rightleftharpoons S_v$) are in equilibrium along the curve.

Curve OB: It is the sublimation curve of monoclinic sulphur and shows the variation of vapour pressure of monoclinic sulphur with temperature. Monoclinic sulphur is in equilibrium with sulphur vapours along *OB*.

Curve BE: BE is the vapour pressure curve of liquid sulphur and shows the variation of vapour pressure of liquid sulphur with temperature. Liquid sulphur and sulphur vapours exist along this curve.

Curve OC: Curve *OC* is the transition curve for rhombic sulphur and indicates the effect of pressure on the transition temperature. Sulphur rhombic and sulphur monoclinic are in equilibrium along this curve. The system is monovariant. Since monoclinic sulphur is stable at higher temperatures it has therefore higher molar entropy than the rhombic form and the transformation of rhombic into monoclinic is accompanied by an increase in volume. Hence both ΔS_m and ΔV_m are positive. It, therefore, follows from the Clausius-Clapeyron equation that dP/dT is always positive, and therefore the slope of the line is positive. Increase of pressure will thus cause an increase in the transition temperatures of rhombic sulphur.

Curve BC: Curve *BC* indicates the variation of melting point of monoclinic sulphur with pressure and is the fusion curve for monoclinic sulphur. At any point on the curve *BC*, monoclinic and liquid sulphur are in equilibrium forming a univariant system. In the transformation from monoclinic to liquid sulphur both the ΔS_m and ΔV_m are positive; therefore dP/dT is positive. Hence the slope of the line is positive but greater than the slope of the curve *OC*. The increase of pressure will raise the melting point of S_m. As the slope of the curve is greater than that of the curve *OC*, the two curves, therefore, meet at point *C*.

Curve CF: CF is the fusion curve for rhombic sulphur and along this curve it is in equilibrium with the liquid phase.

Point O: At point *O* (95.6°C, 0.006 mm Hg) rhombic sulphur undergoes a transition to monoclinic sulphur and both have equal vapour pressure. *O* is therefore an invariant (triple) point corresponding to the equilibrium $S_r \rightleftharpoons S_m \rightleftharpoons S_v$.

Point B: At point *B*(120°C, 0.04 mm Hg) monoclinic sulphur melts and is the triple point where the equilibrium $S_m \rightleftharpoons S_l \rightleftharpoons S_v$ exists.

Point C: C is another triple point (151°C, 1288 atmospheres) where rhombic, monoclinic and liquid sulphur are in equilibrium.

By supercooling liquid sulphur, curve *BD* is obtained which is the continuation of the curve *EB* in the monoclinic sulphur region. Since monoclinic sulphur is the stable phase in this region, curve *BD* thus represents the metastable equilibrium between liquid sulphur and sulphur vapours. Similarly by superheating rhombic sulphur it is possible to pass the transition temperature without changing it into monoclinic sulphur along *OD*, the extension of curve *AO*. Therefore along *OD* the metastable equilibrium $S_r \rightleftharpoons S_v$ exists. The two curves *BD* and *OD* intersect at point *D*(115°C, 0.03 mm Hg) representing the melting point of the metastable rhombic sulphur. This is the metastable triple point where S_r, S_l and S_v are in equilibrium. Along the line DC the metastable equilibrium $S_r \rightleftharpoons S_l$ exists.

Table 12.2 summarizes the salient features of the sulphur system.

Table 12.2 Salient Features of Sulphur System

Phase Equilibria	Degrees of Freedom	Location in the Phase Diagram
One-phase equilibria		
Sulphur rhombic (S_r)		Area on the left of the curve $AOCF$
Sulphur monoclinic (S_m)	2	Area enclosed by the curves OB, OC and BC
Sulphur liquid (S_l)		Area on the right of curve $FCBE$
Sulphur vapour (S_v)		Area below the curve $AOBE$
Two-phase equilibria		
$S_r \rightleftharpoons S_v$		Along the curve AO
$S_m \rightleftharpoons S_v$		Along the curve OB
$S_l \rightleftharpoons S_v$	1	Along the curve BE
$S_r \rightleftharpoons S_m$		Along the curve OC
$S_m \rightleftharpoons S_l$		Along the curve BC
$S_r \rightleftharpoons S_l$		Along the curve CF
Three-phase equilibria		
$S_r \rightleftharpoons S_m \rightleftharpoons S_v$		At the triple point O (95.6°C, 0.006 mm Hg)
$S_m \rightleftharpoons S_l \rightleftharpoons S_v$	0	At the triple point B (120°C, 0.04 mm Hg)
$S_m \rightleftharpoons S_r \rightleftharpoons S_l$		At the triple point C (151°C, 1288 atmospheres)
$S_r \rightleftharpoons S_l \rightleftharpoons S_v$ (metastable)		At the metastable triple point D (115°C, 0.03 mm Hg)

12.10 TWO-COMPONENT SYSTEMS

For a two-component system, $C = 2$, the phase rule can be written as

$$F = C - P + 2$$
$$= 2 - P + 2$$
$$= 4 - P$$

For a system having one phase, the number of degrees of freedom would be three. This means that three variables, temperature, pressure and composition must be specified in order to describe a two component system completely. In order to represent such a system graphically three coordinates (such as temperature, pressure and composition) at right angles to each other are necessary, This obviously requires a three-dimensional figure which is rather difficult to construct. It is, therefore, customary to represent such systems by any two of the three variables, keeping the third constant. In this way one can represent the various relations in two component systems.

In a two component system the various possible phase equilibria are liquid $\rightleftharpoons$ vapour, solid $\rightleftharpoons$ liquid, liquid $\rightleftharpoons$ liquid, solid $\rightleftharpoons$ vapour and solid $\rightleftharpoons$ solid. Here we shall confine our attention to solid $\rightleftharpoons$ liquid equilibria. Such equilibria are generally characterised by the absence of the vapour phase and are relatively unaffected by changes in pressure. Such systems are often called *condensed systems* and are studied at constant pressure, usually one atmosphere. With this restriction of constant pressure, the phase rule then reduces to

$$F = C - P + 1$$

This is known as *the reduced phase rule*.

For the two component system, we have

$$F = 2 - P + 1$$
$$= 3 - P$$

The variables are temperature and composition and the solid $\rightleftharpoons$ liquid equilibria are therefore represented on a temperature-composition diagram.

Solid-Liquid Equilibria–Construction of Phase Diagrams

To determine the equilibrium conditions for solid-liquid systems, it is necessary to determine the composition of the mixture at different temperatures. This is generally done by (*i*) experimental techniques which include (*a*) the thermal analysis method, and (*b*) the solubility or saturation method, and (*ii*) theoretical considerations.

(*i*) Experimental Techniques

(*a*) *Thermal analysis method:* in this technique a mixture of two components of known composition is heated until a homogeneous melt or liquid phase is obtained. To avoid oxidation, it is desirable to carry out heating in an inert atmosphere. The melt is then cooled at a slow rate. During cooling, the melt is thoroughly stirred to avoid supercooling. The temperature of the melt is recorded at regular intervals by a standardized thermocouple till it completely solidifies. The process is repeated for other mixtures covering the entire range of composition (0 – 100%). Temperature-time plots called *cooling curves* for each composition are then constructed as shown in Fig. 12.11. From such diagrams, it is possible to detect the various transformations and phase transitions that occur during cooling.

When a melt containing only the pure component (say *A*) is cooled slowly, a cooling curve as shown in Fig. 12.11(*i*) is obtained. The figure reveals that the slope of the curve is constant up to *b* and represents the cooling of the melt. At *b*, the cooling curve becomes parallel to the time axis, *i.e.,* the temperature remains constant. The horizontal portion in the cooling curve, known as *the halt,* is due to the heat evolved when the liquid solidifies. When solidification is complete the curve *cd* is obtained which represents the progressive cooling of the pure solid.

When a melt of two components (say *A* and *B*) is cooled slowly, a typical cooling curve of the type shown in Fig. 12.11 (*ii*) is obtained. Portion *ef* of the curve denotes normal cooling of the melt. At *f*

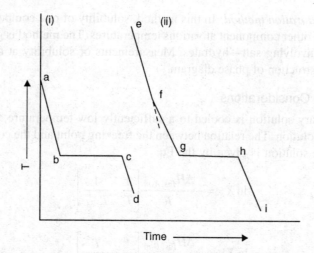

Fig. 12.11 Cooling curves for a binary system with a eutectic point. (*i*) Pure component, (*ii*) a mixture of two components.

there is a change in the slope of the curve (break in the cooling curve) as one of components begins to crystallize out from the melt and a one-phase system changes into a two-phase system. The system becomes univariant ($F = 3 - 2 = 1$). On further cooling more and more of the pure component separates out. At g, the second component also begins to crystallize from the melt and three phases are in equilibrium and the system becomes invariant ($F = 3 - 3 = 0$). The temperature remains constant as indicated by the flat horizontal portion (halt) gh in the cooling curve. Finally when solidification is complete, the system regains a degree of freedom, the temperature drops and the portion hi of the curve shows uniform cooling of the solid mass.

The experiment is repeated for different compositions of A and B and the temperatures of the breaks and the halts for each cooling curve are recorded and are plotted as functions of compositions when a diagram of the type (Fig. 12.12) is obtained. In this diagram curve $A'OB'$ is known as the *liquidus curve*. Above this curve only the liquid phase exists. $A'XOYB'$ is the *solidus curve*, below XOY only the solid phase is present. Between the curves $A'OB'$ and XOY both the solid and the liquid phases are in equilibrium. At O three phases coexist and is known as *the eutectic point*. The composition corresponding to this point has the lowest melting point.

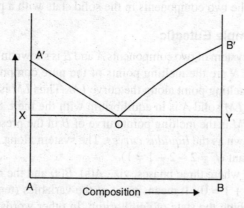

Fig. 12.12 Phase diagram for a binary system with a eutectic point

(b) *Solubility or saturation method:* In this method, solubility of one component is determined in the presence of other component at various temperatures. The method is generally employed in the equilibria involving salt—hydrates. Measurements of solubility at different temperatures lead to the construction of phase diagram.

(ii) From Theoretical Considerations

When an ideal binary solution is cooled to a sufficiently low temperature, it freezes and a solid separates out from the solution. The relation between the freezing point and the composition (expressed in mole fraction) of the solution is given by the Eq.

$$\ln X_A = -\frac{\Delta H_{fus, A, m}}{R}\left[\frac{1}{T} - \frac{1}{T_{o, A}}\right] \qquad ...(12.3)$$

and

$$\ln X_B = -\frac{\Delta H_{fus, B, m}}{R}\left[\frac{1}{T} - \frac{T}{T_{o, B}}\right] \qquad ...(12.4)$$

where $T_{o, A}$ and $T_{o, B}$ are the freezing points of the pure components A, B and $\Delta H_{fus, m}$'s are the molar enthalpies of fusion of A and B respectively. It is apparent from the above equations that plots of freezing point of the solution against mole fractions X_A and X_B yield two curves intersecting at the eutectic point.

12.11 CLASSIFICATION OF TWO COMPONENT SOLID-LIQUID EQUILIBRIA

Based on the miscibility of the two components in the molten state and the nature of the solid phases that separate out during cooling, the solid-liquid equilibria are divided into the following classes:

- (i) Only the pure components crystallize from the melt
- (ii) The two components form compound(s) with congruent melting point(s)
- (iii) The two components form compound(s) with incongruent melting point(s)
- (iv) The components are completely miscible in the solid state yielding a complete series of solid solutions
- (v) Partial miscibility of the two components in the solid state with a eutectic
- (vi) Partial miscibility of the two components in the solid state with a peritectic.

Type I–Systems with a Simple Eutectic

A general phase diagram for a system of two components A and B is shown in Fig. 12.13(a). Temperatures corresponding to points L and N are the melting points of the pure components A and B respectively. Addition of B to A lowers its melting point along the curve LM. Thus LM is the melting point curve for A in the presence of B. Along LM solid A is in equilibrium with the melt. Similarly addition of A to B lowers its melting point and NM is the melting point curve of B in the presence of varying amounts of A. Curves LM and NM are known as the *liquidus curves*. The system along LM and NM has two phases and is consequently monovariant ($F = 2 - 2 + 1 = 1$).

The two curves meet at M where three phases, viz., $A(s)$, $B(s)$ and the melt are in equilibrium. The system is invariant ($F = 2 - 3 + 1 = 0$). It means none of the variables (temperature and composition) can be changed without disturbing the state of equilibrium. In other words if temperature or composition is changed, one of the phases will disappear. On lowering the temperature, melt disappears and the whole mass solidifies, while increase of temperature melts the solid. The composition corresponding to *M* has the lowest melting point and is the lowest temperature at which the melt can exist in equilibrium with both the solids *A* and *B*. Point *M* is known as the *eutectic point* and the composition *X* is the *eutectic composition* while the temperature T_{eu} is *eutectic temperature*. The eutectic mixture has a definite composition and a sharp melting point, *i.e.*, it melts giving a liquid of the same composition. In this respect it resembles a compound. However, it is not a compound for the components are not present in stoichiometric proportions and the mixture is heterogeneous as revealed under a microscope. The heterogeneity of the eutectic mixture differentiates it from a true solid solution.

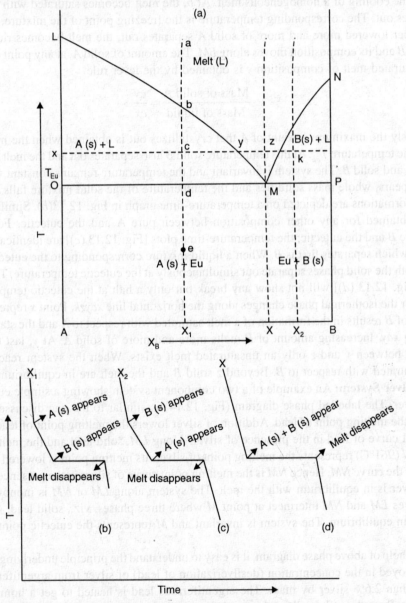

Fig. 12.13 (*a*) Phase diagram for a binary system with a eutectic point, (*b*), (*c*) and (*d*) are cooling curves for different compositions: X_1, X_2, and X

Above the liquidus curve LMN only the unsaturated homogeneous melt is present. As only one phase is present, the system is bivariant. Both the temperature and composition should be specified to define the state of the system. Below the line OMP (solidus curve) only the solid phases exist. In the areas between the liquidus and solidus curves two phases, solid and liquid are present. In the region LOM, we have solid A and the melt while in the region MNP solid B is in equilibrium with the melt. The systems in these areas are univariant.

Let us consider the phase changes that result when a melt corresponding to an overall composition X_1 is cooled from point a to e along the constant composition line $acde$ (known as *an isopleth*) · ab represents the cooling of a homogeneous melt. At b, the melt becomes saturated with respect to A and it crystallizes out. The corresponding temperature is the freezing point of the mixture. As the temperature is further lowered more and more of solid A separates out, the melt becomes richer in the other component B and its composition moves along bM. The amount of solid A, at any point c, in equilibrium with the saturated melt of composition y is obtained by the lever rule

$$\frac{\text{Mass of solid A}}{\text{Mass of liquid}} = \frac{cy}{cx}$$

Obviously the maximum amount of A that crystallizes out is obtained when the melt is cooled up to the eutectic temperature T_{eu}. At this temperature solid B also separates out and the melt is in equilibrium with solid A and solid B. The system is invariant and the temperature remains constant. When the liquid phase disappears, whole mass solidifies and the temperature of the solid mixture falls along de. These phase transformations are depicted on a temperature-time graph in Fig. 12.13(b). Similar types of plots would be obtained for any other composition between pure A and the eutectic. For compositions between pure B and the eutectic; the temperature-time plots [Fig. 12.13 (c)] are identical except that the component which separates first is B. When a liquid mixture corresponding to the eutectic composition is cooled, both the solid phases separate out simultaneously at the eutectic temperature. The temperature-time plot [Fig. 12.13 (d)] will not show any break but only a halt at the eutectic temperature.

Consider the isothermal phase changes along the horizontal line $xcyzk$. Point x represents pure solid A. Addition of B results in the formation of a melt saturated with respect to A and the state of the system moves along xcy. Increasing amount of B melts more and more of solid A. At y, last trace of solid A remains and between y and z only an unsaturated melt exists. When the system reaches z, the melt becomes saturated with respect to B. Beyond z solid B and the melt are in equilibrium along zk.

Lead-Silver System: An example of a two component system showing a simple eutectic is that of lead and silver. The labelled phase diagram (Fig. 12.14) is similar to the one discussed earlier. Point $L(327°C)$ is the melting point of lead. Addition of silver lowers the melting point of lead and LM is the melting point curve of lead in the presence of silver. Along LM, solid lead and the melt are in equilibrium. Point N (961°C) represents the melting point of silver. Its melting point is lowered by the addition of lead along the curve NM. Hence NM is the melting point curve of silver in the presence of lead. Along NM solid silver is in equilibrium with the melt. The system along LM or NM is monovariant.

The curves LM and NM intermeet at point M where three phases, viz., solid lead, solid silver and the melt are in equilibrium. The system is invariant and M represents the eutectic point (303°C, 2.6% Ag by mass).

With the help of above phase diagram, it is easy to understand the principle underlying the Pattinson's process employed in the concentration (desilverization of lead) of silver from argentiferrous lead containing less than 2.6% silver by mass. The argentiferrous lead is heated to get a homogeneous melt represented by the point a. It is allowed to cool when solid lead begins to separate out from point b. As the temperature is lowered more and more of lead separates out and the melt becomes richer in silver and its composition moves along the curve *bM*. In this way a maximum concentration of silver (2.6% by mass) in the melt can be obtained.

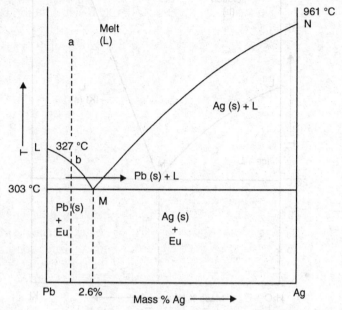

Fig. 12.14 Phase diagram for lead-silver system

Salt-water systems with simple eutectic: A typical example of a two component system involving a salt and water is that of KI-H_2O. The labelled phase diagram is shown in Fig. 12.15.

$L(0°C)$ is the freezing point of water and is lowered by the addition of salt. *LM* is, therefore, the freezing point of water in the presence of potassium iodide. Along *LM* ice separates out from the solution and the system is monovariant. *NM* is the solubility curve of potassium iodide. Since the melting point of salt is much higher than the critical temperature of water and hence cannot be realized in this phase diagram. From the slope of the curve it is apparent that the solubility of potassium iodide increases with the rise of temperature.

At *M* where the curves *LM* and *NM* meet, three phases (ice, solid potassium iodide and solution) are in equilibrium and the system is invariant, Hence *M* is the eutectic point (–23°C, 52% KI by mass). In case of systems involving salt and water, the eutectic point is known as the *cryohydric point*. The temperature at *M* is the *cryohydric temperature* and the solution of composition *M* is the *cryohydric solution*. For such systems the lowest temperature that can be attained is the cryohydric temperature and is characteristic of each system.

The invariance of the system at the cryohydric point permits salt-ice mixtures to be used as constant temperature bath. Addition of a salt such as potassium iodide to ice at 0°C results in the melting of some ice and dissolution of salt. As melting of ice and formation of salt solution involve absorption of heat, hence lowering of temperature takes place. If sufficient amount of potassium iodide has been added, the temperature will fall up to the cryohydric temperature, –23°C. At this point three phases—ice, solid salt and the saturated solution are in equilibrium and the temperature remains constant. Mixtures of salts and ice are used for obtaining low temperatures. Some systems with simple eutectic are given in Table 12.3.

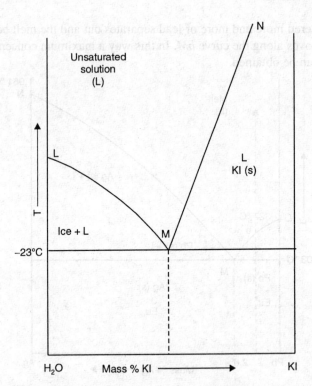

Fig. 12.15 Phase diagram for potassium iodide-water system

Table 12.3 Some Common Systems with Eutectic Temperature and Eutectic Composition

Components		Eutectic Temperature	Eutectic Composition
A	B	(°C)	(mass % of A)
Bi (273°C)	Cd (323°C)	140.0	60.0
Zn (419°C)	Cd (323°C)	270.0	67.0
Au (1064°C)	Tl(302°C)	131.0	27.0
KCl	Ice	−10.7	20.0
NH₄NO₃	Ice	−18.0	43.0
NH₄Cl	Ice	−15.4	19.7
Na₂SO₄	Ice	−1.3	4.7

Problem 12.3: The system Pb (m. pt. 327°C) and Sb (m. pt. 631 °C) exhibits a simple eutectic at 86% Pb (by mass) and 246°C. Breaks in the cooling curves in thermal analysis were found for the following compositions:

T(°C)	550	500	400	300	296
Mass % Pb	30	44	66	80	96

Draw a tentative phase diagram for the system and label it. Calculate the amount of antimony that crystallizes out from 20 kg of a melt containing 35% Pb by mass after cooling it to a temperature of 400 °C. How much is the maximum amount of *Sb* that can be recovered from this melt?

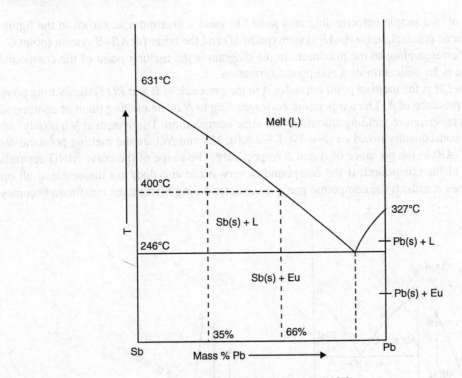

Fig. 12.16 For problem 12.3

Solution: The tentative phase diagram is shown in the Fig. 12.16. At 400 °C, the composition of the melt is 66% by mass of Pb.

Hence from the lever rule

$$\frac{\text{Mass of solid Sb}}{\text{Mass of melt}} = \frac{66-35}{35-0} = \frac{31}{35}$$

But the total mass is 20 kg, therefore,

$$\frac{\text{Mass of solid Sb}}{20 - \text{mass of solid Sb}} = \frac{31}{35}$$

or mass of solid antimony = 9.4 kg.

The maximum amount of solid antimony is obtained when it is cooled up to the eutectic temperature (86 mass% Pb). The mass of solid Sb at the eutectic temperature is given by

$$\frac{\text{Mass of solid Sb}}{20 - \text{mass of solid Sb}} = \frac{86-35}{35}$$

or mass of solid Sb = 11.4 kg.

Type II: Formation of Compound(s) with Congruent Melting Point(s)

A compound is said to have a congruent melting point if it melts to give a liquid having the same composition as that of the solid compound.

Let *A* and *B* be the two components and *AB* the congruently melting compound formed by them. The labelled phase diagram for this system is shown in Fig. 12.17 (*a*). The diagram may be regarded as a combination of two simple eutectic diagrams joined to yield a maximum as shown in the figure. There are two eutectic points; one for $A-AB$ system (point M) and the other for $AB-B$ system (point O). The temperature corresponding to the maximum in the diagram is the melting point of the compound and its appearance is an indication of a compound formation.

In the diagram LM is the melting point curve for A in the presence of B and PO is the melting point curve for B in the presence of A. The temperature corresponding to N is the melting point of compound AB. It melts at this temperature yielding a liquid of the same composition. The system at N has only one component and is consequently invariant ($F = 1 + 1 - 2 = 0$). MN and NO are the melting point curves for the compound (AB) in the presence of A and B respectively. The shape of the curve MNO depends upon the stability of the compound. If the compound is very stable and does not dissociate at all on melting, a sharp apex results. If the compound partly dissociates during melting the maximum becomes broader.

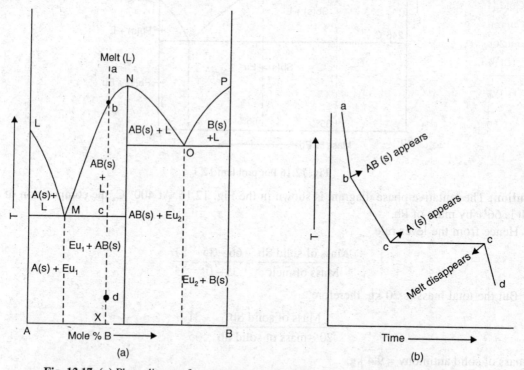

Fig. 12.17. (*a*) Phase diagram for a two component system with a congruent melting point
(*b*) A typical cooling curve

Let us now consider the phase transformations that result when *a* melts with an overall composition (say X) is cooled (Fig. 12:17 (*b*)). *ab* represents the normal cooling of the melt. At *b* the melt becomes saturated with respect to AB and it crystallizes out. The amount of solid AB goes on increasing as the temperature is lowered and the melt becoming progressively richer in A. Between *b* and *c* the relative amounts of solid AB and melt are obtained by the lever rule. At the eutectic point solid A also separates out from the melt and three phases, viz., solid AB, solid A and the melt are in equilibrium. As the temperature drops below the eutectic point the whole mass solidifies without further change of composition. On the other hand, if the overall composition of the melt were between pure AB and the eutectic O, the cooling curve would be identical with a difference that solid B would separate out at the eutectic point O.

Some examples of systems showing the formation of a congruent melting compound are given in Table 12.4.

Table 12.4 Two Components with Congruent Melting Compounds

| Components | | Compound | Melting point of |
A	B		the Compound (°C)
Aluminium (657°C)	Magnesium (650°C)	Al_3Mg_4	463.0
Magnesium (650°C)	Silicon (1420°C)	Mg_2Si	1102.0
Mercury (–39°C)	Thallium (303°C)	Tl_2Hg_5	15.0
Gold (1064°C)	Tin (232°C)	AuSn	425.0
Cuprous chloride (424°C)	Ferric chloride (298°C)	$CuCl·FeCl_3$	320.0
Benzophenone (48°C)	Diphenylamine (53°C)	AB	40.2
Urea (132°C)	Phenol (43°C)	AB_2	61.0

A typical phase diagram for the system tin-magnesium is shown in Fig. 12.18.

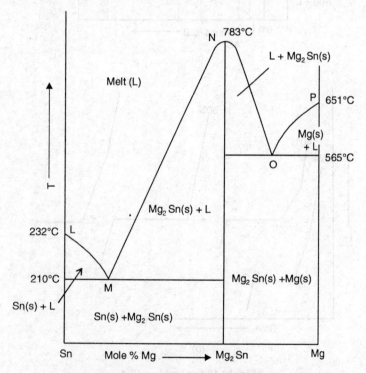

Fig. 12.18 Phase diagram of tin-magnesium system

Problem 12.4: For the system A (at. mass 209, m.pt. 308°C) and B (at. mass 24, m.pt. 652°C), a compound is formed corresponding to 19% by mass of B. The compound melts at 710°C yielding a liquid having the same composition. There are two eutectics (*i*) at 271°C and 9% by mass of B and, (*ii*) at 550°C and 50% by mass of B. Draw a tentative phase diagram for the system, label each area, deduce the formula of the compound and draw cooling curves for melts with overall composition, 15%, 40%, 50% and 80% by mass of B.

Solution: Since the compound on melting yields a liquid having the same composition, therefore it is a congruently melting compound and its formula can be deduced by calculating the ratio of the relative number of atoms of A and B in the compound, *i.e.,*

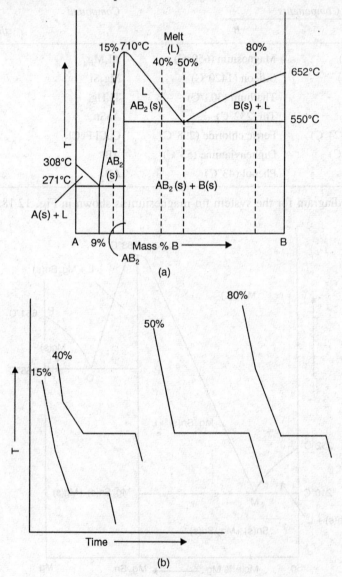

Fig. 12.19 For problem 12.4

$$A:B = \frac{\dfrac{81}{209}}{\dfrac{19}{24}} = \frac{81}{209} \times \frac{24}{19} = \frac{1}{2}$$

The compound is AB_2.

The tentative phase diagram and the cooling curves are shown in Figs. 12.19 (a) and (b) respectively.

Problem 12.5: Two components A (m. pt. 0°C) and B (m. pt. –25°C) form two compounds X and Y melting congruently. X melts at –49.6°C and contains 40 mole per cent B while Y melts at –40°C and contains 60 mole per cent B. There are three eutectic points at –51.2°C, 28 mole % B; –63.5°C, 48 mole % B and –49.4°C, 66 mole % B. Deduce the formulae of the compounds and draw a tentative phase diagram consistent with the given data.

Solution: If n_A and n_B are the number of moles of A and B in the compounds, then the mole ratio of A

and B in $X = \dfrac{n_A}{n_B} = \dfrac{60}{40} = \dfrac{3}{2}$. Therefore, X is $A_3 B_2$.

Mole ratio of A and B in $Y = \dfrac{n_A}{n_B} = \dfrac{40}{60} = \dfrac{2}{3}$

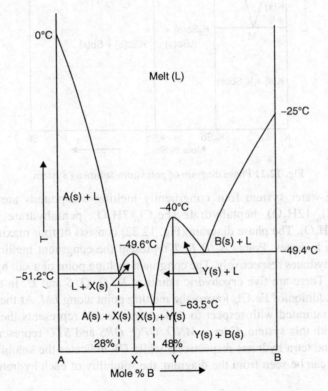

Fig. 12.20 For problem 12.5

Hence Y is $A_2 B_3$

The phase diagram is shown in Fig. 12.20.

Systems having a number of congruently melting compounds: If two components form several different chemical compounds which do not decompose upto their melting points, the phase diagram shows as many maxima as the number of compounds formed. The phase diagram may be looked upon as the combination of a number of diagrams for the two component system. The compounds differ in their stability. In the phase diagram (Fig. 12.21) for K-Sb system, two compounds K_3Sb and KSb are formed; the former is more stable than the latter.

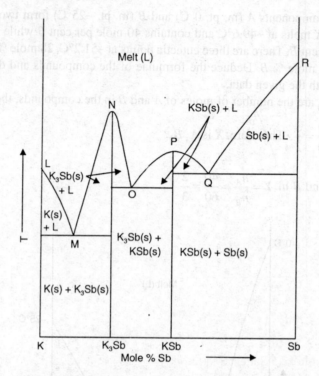

Fig. 12.21 Phase diagram of potassium-antimony system

In ferric chloride-water system four congruently melting compounds are formed. These are dodecahydrate ($Fe_2Cl_6 \cdot 12H_2O$), heptahydrate ($Fe_2Cl_6 \cdot 7H_2O$), pentahydrate ($Fe_2Cl_6 \cdot 5H_2O$) and tetrahydrate ($Fe_2Cl_6 \cdot 4H_2O$). The phase diagram (Fig. 12.22) consists of four maxima corresponding to the formation of these hydrates. Points *N, P, R, T* represent the congruent melting points of dodeca, hepta, penta and tetra hydrates respectively. The congruent melting point of a salt hydrate is also known as the *dystectic point*. There are five cryohydric points at *M, O, Q, S* and *U*. In the diagram *L* is the melting point of ice. Addition of Fe_2Cl_6 lowers the melting point along *LM*. At the cryohydric point *M* the solution becomes saturated with respect to dodecahydrate and represents the lowest temperature that can be attained with this system. Curves *MNO, OPQ, QRS* and *STU* represent the solubilities of dodeca, hepta, penta and tetra hydrates respectively while *UV* indicates the solubility characteristic of the anhydrous salt. As can be seen from the diagram, the solubility of each hydrate increases with rise of temperature.

The relevant data such as the melting points of the hydrates, temperature and composition at each cryohydric point and the phases existing at the cryohydric points are summarized in Table 12.5.

Let us consider the phase changes that result when an unsaturated solution represented by point *k* is concentrated isothermally by adding anhydrous ferric chloride along *ku*. At first a saturated solution of dodecahydrate results at *l*. At *m* the whole mass solidifies to form dodecahydrate which melts when more of ferric chloride is added. Dodecahydrate disappear beyond *n* and between *n* and *o* an unsaturated solution exists. The solution becomes saturated with respect to heptahydrate at *o*. Further addition of ferric chloride increases the amount of solid heptahydrate in the solution and at *p* the whole solution

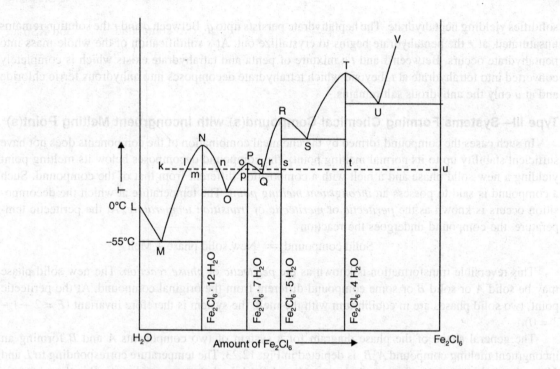

Fig. 12.22 Phase diagram of ferric chloride-water system

Table 12.5 Salient Features of Ferric Chloride-Water System

	Point	Temperature (°C)	Phases in equilibrium	Moles of Fe_2Cl_6 per 100 moles of water
Freezing point of water	L	0.0	Ice and Water	0.0
Eutectic	M	−55.0	Ice, $Fe_2Cl_6 \cdot 12H_2O(s)$, solution	3.10
Congruent m.pt.	N	37.0	$Fe_2Cl_6 \cdot 12H_2O(s)$, solution	8.33 (1:12)
Eutectic	O	27.4	$Fe_2Cl_6 \cdot 12H_2O(s)$, $Fe_2Cl_6 \cdot 7H_2O(s)$, solution	12.20
Congruent m.pt.	P	32.5	$Fe_2Cl_6 \cdot 7H_2O(s)$, solution	14.25 (1:7)
Eutectic	Q	30.0	$Fe_2Cl_6 \cdot 7H_2O(s)$, $Fe_2Cl_6 \cdot 5H_2O(s)$, solution	15.10
Congruent m.pt.	R	56.0	$Fe_2Cl_6 \cdot 5H_2O(s)$, solution	20.00 (1:5)
Eutectic	S	55.0	$Fe_2Cl_6 \cdot 5H_2O(s)$, $Fe_2Cl_6 \cdot 4H_2O(s)$, solution	20.40
Congruent m.pt.	T	73.5	$Fe_2Cl_6 \cdot 4H_2O(s)$, solution	25.00 (1:4)
Eutectic	U	66.0	$Fe_2Cl_6 \cdot 4H_2O(s)$, $Fe_2Cl_6(s)$, solution	29.90

solidifies yielding heptahydrate. The heptahydrate persists upto q. Between q and r the solution remains unsaturated, at r the pentahydrate begins to crystallize out. At s solidification of the whole mass into pentahydrate occurs. Between s and t a mixture of penta and tatrahydrate exists which is completely converted into tetrahydrate at t, beyond which tetrahydrate decomposes into anhydrous ferric chloride and at u only the anhydrous salt remains.

Type III—Systems Forming Chemical Compound(s) with Incongruent Melting Point(s)

In such cases the compound formed by the chemical combination of the components does not have sufficient stability up to its normal melting point. The compound decomposes below its melting point yielding a new solid phase and a melt with a composition different from that of the compound. Such a compound is said to possess an *incongruent melting point*. The temperature at which the decomposition occurs is known as the *peritectic* or *meritectic* or *transition temperature*. At the peritectic temperature, the compound undergoes the reaction

$$\text{Solid compound} \rightleftharpoons \text{New solid phase + Melt}$$

This reversible transformation is known as the *peritectic* or *phase reaction*. The new solid phase may be solid A or solid B or some compound different from the original compound. At the peritectic point, two solid phases are in equilibrium with the melt, the system is therefore invariant ($F = 2 + 1 - 3 = 0$).

The general shape of the phase diagram for a system of two components A and B forming an incongruent melting compound A_xB_y is depicted in Fig. 12.23. The temperature corresponding to L and M are the melting points of pure components A and B while that corresponding to P is the peritectic temperature where the compound A_xB_y decomposes yielding solid A and a melt of composition $O \cdot LO$ is the melting point curve of A in the presence of increasing amount of B. MN is the melting point curve for B in the presence of A. ON is the melting point curve for the compound when B is added to it. The

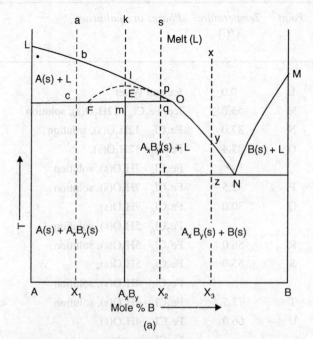

Fig. 12.23 (*a*) Phase diagram of a two component system with an incongruent melting point

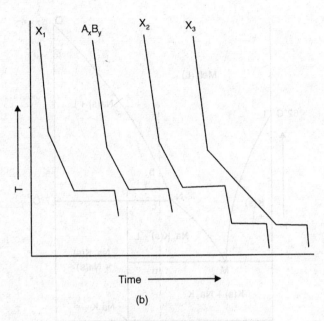

Fig. 12.23 (*b*) Cooling curve

dashed curve *OEF* would result if the compound were congruently melting. There is one eutectic at *N* where solid A_xB_y and solid *B* are in equilibrium with the melt.

Let us consider the behaviour of the system when a melt of composition X_1 is cooled from point *a*. At *b* solid *A* begins to separate out from the melt. The cooling curve (Fig. 12.23 (*b*)) shows a break at *b*. The proportion of solid *A* increases on cooling, the melt becomes richer in *B* and its composition moves along *bO*. At *c* the peritectic reaction: $A(s) + L \rightleftharpoons A_xB_y(s)$ sets in and the system becomes invariant, temperature remains constant and consequently, a halt is observed in the cooling curve. The melt solidifies into solid *A* and solid A_xB_y when the temperature drops below the peritectic point.

If the melt corresponding to the composition of the compound A_xB_y is cooled from point *k*, solid *A* begins to crystallize out from the melt at *l*. The amount of *B* increases in the melt and its composition moves along *lO*. At *m* the peritectic reaction sets in and the solid compound and solid *A* are in equilibrium with the melt. The temperature remains constant. Below the peritectic temperature the whole mass solidifies into pure solid compound A_xB_y. The various phase changes are shown in the cooling curve (Fig. 12.23(*b*)).

When a melt corresponding to X_2 is cooled from point *s*, solid *A* begins to separate at *p*; the cooling curve shows a break at this point (Fig. 12.23 (*b*)). At the peritectic point a halt is observed in the cooling curve indicating the coexistence of three phases, viz. solid A_xB_y, solid *A* and the melt. Further lowering of temperature results in the disappearance of solid *A* while solid A_xB_y and the melt coexist between *q* and *r*. At *r* solid *B* also crystallizes out and again three phases, solid A_xB_y, solid *B* and the melt are in equilibrium. The cooling curve shows a second halt at *r*. Below the eutectic temperature the melt disappears and only the eutectic mixture of A_xB_y and *B* remain.

Now if the melt of composition X_3 is cooled from *x*, the solid compound A_xB_y starts crystallizing out at *y* and a break is observed in the cooling curve (Fig. 12.23 (*b*)). At the eutectic temperature solid *B* also separates out, three phases coexist and a halt is observed in the cooling curve. Below the eutectic temperature the whole mass solidifies to yield solid a mixture of A_xB_y and solid *A*.

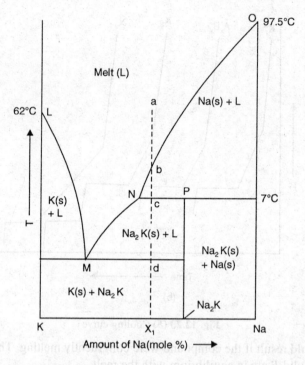

Fig. 12.24 Phase diagram for the system sodium-potassium

The system of sodium-potassium is a typical example of systems showing an incongruent melting compound. The alloy Na_2K is a definite compound formed on mixing sodium (m. pt. 97.5°C) and potassium (m. pt. 62°C) in the appropriate proportions. The labelled phase diagram for the system is shown in Fig. 12.24. There is one eutectic point at M and the incongruent melting compound Na_2K decomposes at the peritectic temperature (7°C) to yield solid sodium and a melt richer in potassium of composition N.

When a melt of composition X_1 is cooled from a, solid sodium begins to crystallize out and the melt gets richer in potassium until point c is reached where the peritectic reaction occurs. The temperature remains constant until solid sodium disappears. The cooling curve will show a halt at this temperature. Between c and d, a two-phase mixture of Na_2K and melt exists. At d the melt becomes saturated with respect to potassium and a three phase system results. The cooling curve at this point shows a second halt. The whole mass solidifies into an intimate mixture of Na_2K and Na below the eutectic temperature.

Sodium Chloride-Water System

The phase diagram for the system is shown in Fig. 12.25. L represents the melting point of ice. Addition of sodium chloride lowers the melting point and LM is the melting point curve of ice in the presence of sodium chloride. Ice and saturated solution are in equilibrium along LM and the system is univariant. At point $M(-21°C)$, a new solid phase $NaCl \cdot 2H_2O$ separates out from the solution. M is the eutectic or cryohydric point where three phases, viz., ice, incongruent melting compound ($NaCl \cdot 2H_2O$) and the solution are in equilibrium and the system is invariant. Below $-21°C$ only ice and $NaCl \cdot 2H_2O$ exist. On further addition of sodium chloride, the freezing point rises along MN which is the solubility curve of dihydrate. Point $N(0.15°C)$ is the peritectic point where the dihydrate changes into anhydrous sodium chloride and solution. NO is the solubility curve for anhydrous sodium chloride.

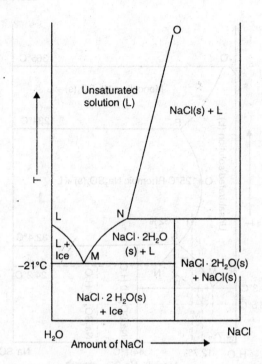

Fig. 12.25 Phase diagram for the system sodium chloride-water

Sodium Sulphate-Water System

Anhydrous sodium sulphate exists in two allotropic forms. Rhombic variety is stable below 234°C while monoclinic is stable above 234°C. $Na_2SO_4 - H_2O$ system forms two incongruent melting compounds, viz., decahydrate ($Na_2SO_4 \cdot 10H_2O$) and metastable heptahydrate ($Na_2SO_4 \cdot 7H_2O$). The labelled phase diagram is shown in Fig. 12.26. *L* is the melting point of ice. It is lowered by the addition of sodium sulphate. *LM* is the melting point curve of ice that results when increasing amount of anhydrous sodium sulphate is added to ice. The system is univariant ($F = 2 + 1 - 2 = 1$) along *LM*. At the eutectic or cryohydric point $M(-1.3°C, 4.7\% Na_2SO_4)$ the solution becomes saturated with respect to decahydrate and three phases (ice, solid $Na_2SO_4 \cdot 10H_2O$ and saturated solution) are in equilibrium and the system becomes invariant. The cryohydric temperature −1.3°C is evidently the lowest temperature that can be attained with $Na_2SO_4 - H_2O$ system. With the further addition of sodium sulphate ice disappears and the curve *MN* results. Along this curve solid decahydrate and the solution are in equilibrium, and is therefore the solubility curve for decahydrate. The solubility of decahydrate increases with rise of temperature as is apparent from the curve. At *N* decahydrate undergoes peritectic change yielding anhydrous rhombic sodium sulphate, *i.e.*,

$$Na_2SO_4 \cdot 10H_2O(s) \rightleftharpoons Na_2SO_4(s) + \text{Solution}$$

Thus $N(32.4°C, 32\% Na_2SO_4)$ is the incongruent melting point of decahydrate and at this point decahydrate and anhydrous sodium sulphate are in equilibrium with the solution. Above the peritectic temperature rhombic sodium sulphate exists in equilibrium with the solution and the curve *NOP* is obtained. The curve shows that the solubility of anhydrous rhombic form first decreases slightly with rise of temperature, passes through a minimum at *O* (125°C) and then increases with rise of temperature up to point *P* (234°C). This type of solubility behaviour is known as *retrograde solubility*. At *P* the

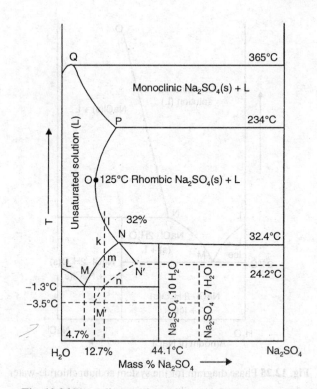

Fig. 12.26 Phase diagram for sodium sulphate-water system

transition of rhombic into monoclinic form results and the system again has three phases, viz., rhombic, monoclinic forms of sodium sulphate and the saturated solution. PQ is the solubility curve for monoclinic sodium sulphate. The solubility decreases with temperature upto Q (365°C) which is the critical temperature of the solution.

When an unsaturated solution of composition k is heated, anhydrous rhombic variety crystallizes at l, if it is cooled, the decahydrate separates out at m. However, it is possible to prevent crystallization of decahydrate by supercooling the solution to a temperature below m, when the metastable heptahydrate crystallizes out at n. The dashed curve $M'N'$ is the solubility curve for the heptahydrate. The peritectic point of the heptahydrate is 24.2°C where it yields anhydrous rhombic sodium sulphate and the solution. M' is the cryohydric point (−3.5°C, 12.7% Na_2SO_4) where ice, heptahydrate and the saturated solution coexist. The solubility curve for heptahydrate lies in the region where decahydrate and saturated solution exist; hence the equilibrium between heptahydrate and its saturated solution is metastable. The system has a spontaneous tendency to yield crystals of decahydrate.

Incongruent melting compounds are formed by systems: gold-antimony ($AuSb_2$), gold-lead (Au_2Pb, $AuPb_2$), picric acid-benzene (AB), acetamide salicylic acid (AB), calcium fluoride-calcium chloride (AB), potassium sulphate-cadmium sulphate (AB_3, AB_2), etc.

Problem 12.6: For the system A (m.pt. 1525°C) and B(m.pt. 1560°C), an incongruent melting compound is formed at 40 mole % B. It decomposes at 1320°C yielding a melt containing 65 mole % B. There is a eutectic at 80 mole % B and 1230°C. Construct the phase diagram, label all the areas and draw cooling curves for melt having 30 mole %, 50 mole % and 90 mole % B.

Solution: Mole % B in the compound = 40

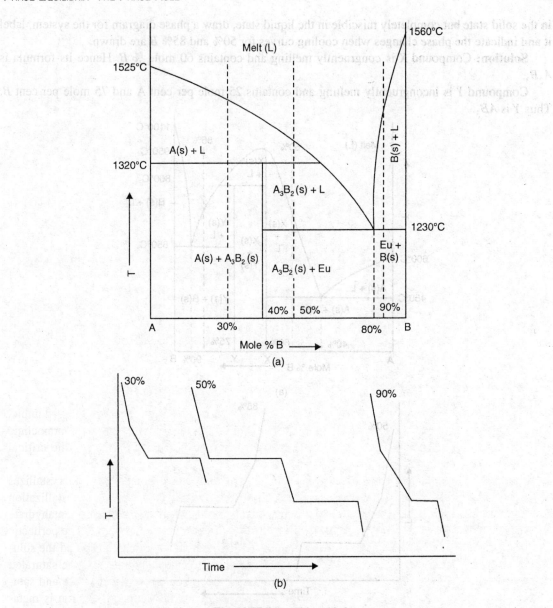

Fig. 12.27 For problem 12.6

Mole % A in the compound = 60

Hence the formula of the compound = A_3B_2

The labelled phase diagram and the cooling curves corresponding to the given compositions are given in Fig. 12.27 (a) and (b) respectively.

Problem 12.7: Two components A (m.pt. 600°C) and B (m.pt. 1100°C) form two compounds X and Y. X contains 60% B (by mole) and melts sharply (950°C) giving a melt of the same composition while Y contains 75% B (by mole) and decomposes at 800°C giving X and a melt having 80 mole per cent B. There are two eutectic points (450°C, 40% B and 650°C, 90% B). Assuming that the solids are immiscible in the solid state but completely miscible in the liquid state, draw a phase diagram for the system, label it and indicate the phase changes when cooling curves for 50% and 85% B are drawn.

Solution: Compound X is congruently melting and contains 60 mole % B. Hence its formula is A_2B_3.

Compound Y is incongruently melting and contains 25 mole per cent A and 75 mole per cent B. Thus Y is AB_3.

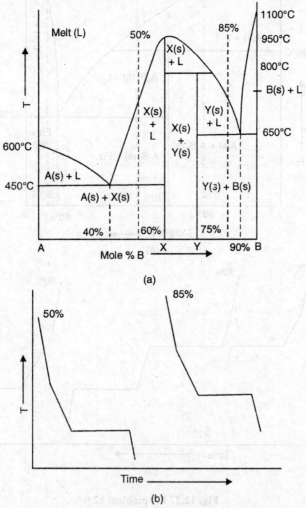

Fig. 12.28 For problem 12.7

It is a system in which both congruent and incongruent melting compounds are formed. The tentative phase diagram for the system is shown in Fig. 12.28 (a). The phase changes when melts containing 50% and 85% B are cooled are shown in Fig. 12.28 (b).

Type IV—Complete Miscibility in the Solid State

The system that we have considered so far consisted of components which were immiscible in the solid state. When crystal lattices of the two components are identical, they are capable of yielding a series of homogeneous *solid solutions*. A solid solution can have any composition and in this respect differs from a solid compound where the components combine in a definite and fixed ratio. In a solid solution, atoms of one constituent enter the crystal lattice of the other and are uniformly distributed throughout the entire lattice. This uniform distribution of components distinguishes a solid solution from a solid mixture which is heterogeneous and each component retains its characteristic crystal structure.

The system of copper and nickel is a well known example where there is complete miscibility in the liquid and solid states. The phase diagram for the system is depicted in Fig. 12.29 (a). The upper curve is the liquidus curve while the lower one is the solidus curve.

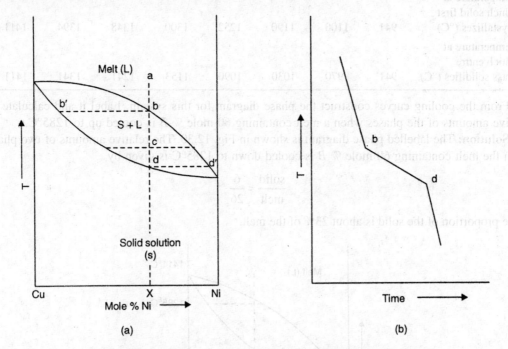

Fig. 12.29 (a) Phase diagram of copper-nickel system (b) Cooling curve

When a melt of composition X is cooled from point a, at b a solid solution of composition b′ begins to crystallize out from the melt. Lowering of temperature separates more and more of solid solution and between b and d two phases, solid solution and the melt exist. At d the solid solution is in equilibrium with a melt of composition d′. Below d, the entire mass solidifies yielding a homogeneous solid solution of copper and nickel. Since the maximum number of phases in equilibrium is two the system never becomes invariant and hence the cooling curves will not show a halt, instead only two breaks will be observed (Fig. 12.29 (b)).

The phase diagram is helpful in discussing the principle underlying *fractional crystallization*. For systems which have phase diagrams of the type given above, complete separation of constituents by fractional crystallization is possible. The melt becomes richer in the component having lower melting point while the solid solution is enriched in the component having higher melting point.

Completely miscible systems are known where the liquidus and the solidus curves show *maxima* or *minima*. The shapes of the phase diagrams are similar to the liquid-vapour curves in systems which form azeotropes. The composition corresponding to the maximum or minimum possesses a sharp melting point. By fractional crystallization complete separation of these components into pure components is not possible. In either case a maximum or minimum melting solid solution results.

Systems which form solid solutions are gold-silver, gold-platinum, cobalt-nickel, naphthalene-β-naphthol, silver chloride-sodium chloride etc.

Problem 12.8: The following data were obtained when liquid mixtures of two components A and B were cooled slowly:

Mole % B	0	15	30	45	60	75	90	100
Temperature at which solid first crystallizes (°C)	941	1100	1190	1252	1300	1348	1394	1411
Temperature at which entire mass solidifies (°C)	941	970	1030	1090	1153	1241	1341	1411

From the cooling curves construct the phase diagram for this system. Label it and calculate the relative amounts of the phases when a melt containing 60 mole % B is cooled up to 1285°C.

Solution: The labelled phase diagram is shown in Fig. 12.30. The relative amounts of two phases when the melt containing 60 mole % B is cooled down to 1285°C is given by

$$\frac{\text{solid}}{\text{melt}} = \frac{6}{26}$$

or the proportion of the solid is about 23% of the melt.

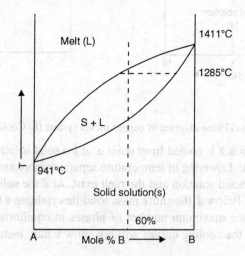

Fig. 12.30 For problem 12.8

Types V and VI—Partial Miscibility in the Solid State—System with a Eutectic or a Peritectic Point

When two components A and B are partially miscible in the solid state, two solid solutions are formed. One is the solid solution of B in A (S_1) and the other is the solid solution of A in B (S_2). The phase diagram in such systems may show either a eutectic or a peritectic point (Fig. 12.31 (a) and 12.32)).

In the Fig. 12.31 (a), The area labelled as S_1 is the region where a homogeneous solid solution of B in A exists. Similarly in the region marked S_2 the solid solution of A in B exists. The solid solutions

S_1 and S_2 are in equilibrium in the area *AOPB*. *M* is the eutectic point where these solid solutions are in equilibrium with the melt.

If a melt of composition X_1 is cooled from point *a*, solid solution S_1 separates out at *b*. As the temperature is lowered, the composition of the solid solution and the melt changes. At *c* the solid solution is in equilibrium with melt of composition *c'*. When the temperature drops below *c*, the entire mass solidifies to yield solid solution S_1. Between *c* and *d* uniform cooling of a homogeneous solid results and at *d* another solid solution S_2 appears. The proportion of solid S_2 increases as the temperature is further lowered. The cooling curve will show three breaks at *b*, *c* and *d*.

Cooling a melt of composition X_2 from *k* first yields a solid solution S_1 at *l*. At *m* the melt has the eutectic composition *M* and is saturated with respect to both S_1 and S_2. The system is invariant. Below the eutectic temperature the melt disappears and a solid mixture of S_1 and S_2 results. The relative amounts of the two solids change as the temperature is lowered. The phase changes are shown in Fig. 12.31(*b*).

The behaviour of the system on cooling a melt having composition between *M* and *P* such as X_3 is almost identical with that of X_2 except solid solution S_2 separates first. Similarly a melt with composition X_4 lying between *P* and pure *B* first yields a saturated solution of S_2 at *t* which solidifies completely below *u*. Between *u* and *v* only the solid solution S_2 is present. Finally, it changes into a mixture of S_1 and S_2 below *v*.

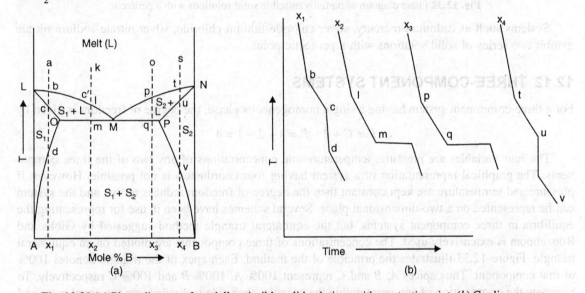

Fig. 12.31 (*a*) Phase diagram of partially miscible solid solutions with a eutectic point. (*b*) Cooling curves

Phase diagram of the type discussed above have been obtained with systems like iron-chromium, tin-cadmium, gold-nickel, naphthalene monochloro acetic acid etc.

The phase diagram for the system where one of the solid solutions is unstable above a certain temperature shows a peritectic point (Fig. 12.32). In the diagram solid solution S_2 is unstable above the peritectic temperature. The system is invariant along the line *MNO* where S_1, S_2 and the melt of composition *O* are in equilibrium. Cooling a melt of composition lying between *MN* yields solid solution S_1 at *b* and at the peritectic point solid solution S_2 also separates. Below the peritectic temperature the melt disappears yielding a solid mixture of S_1 and S_2. If the composition is between *N* and *O*, cooling the melt from *k* first separates S_1 at *l* which disappears below the peritectic temperature. Solid solution

S_2 and the melt remain between m and n. Below n the melt solidifies to yield a homogeneous solid solution S_2 which changes into S_1 and S_2 below s.

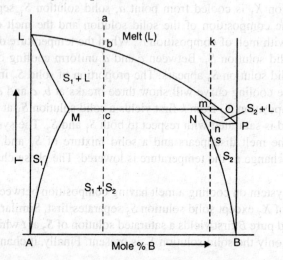

Fig. 12.32 Phase diagram of partially miscible solid solutions with a peritectic

Systems such as cadmium-mercury, silver chloride-lithium chloride, silver nitrate-sodium nitrate exhibit two series of solid solutions with a peritectic point.

12.12 THREE-COMPONENT SYSTEMS

For a three-component system having a single homogeneous phase, the degree of freedom is given by

$$F = C + 2 - P = 3 + 2 - 1 = 4$$

The four variables are pressure, temperature and concentrations of any two of the three components. The graphical representation of a system having four coordinates is not possible. However, if pressure and temperature are kept constant then the degree of freedom reduces to two and the system can be represented on a two-dimensional plane. Several schemes have been in use for representing the equilibria in three component systems, but the equilateral triangle method suggested by Gibbs and Roozeboom is extensively used. The concentrations of three components are plotted on an equilateral triangle. Figure 12.33 illustrates the principle of the method. Each apex of the triangle denotes 100% of that component. Thus apices A, B and C represent 100% A, 100% B and 100% C respectively. To represent the composition of any point within the triangle, each side is divided into ten equal parts and then lines parallel to each side are drawn as shown in the figure. Lines parallel to AB represent the various compositions of C. Along AB, C is 0% while along ab, C will be 10%. Similarly lines parallel to BC represent different compositions of A. It is 0% along BC and 10% along xy. The composition of B is given by lines parallel to AC. It is 0% along AC and 10% along kl.

For representing the composition of any point (say O) within the triangle two methods are generally employed. These are known as the *perpendicular and parallel methods*. In the first scheme, perpendiculars are drawn from the desired point on to the three sides. The length of the perpendicular on to a given side of the triangle represents the percentage composition of the component present at the vertex opposite to that side. Thus the perpendicular length OQ represents 20% A, OP 20% B while OR

60% C. The sum of the perpendicular lengths is equal to the height of the triangle which is taken as 100%.

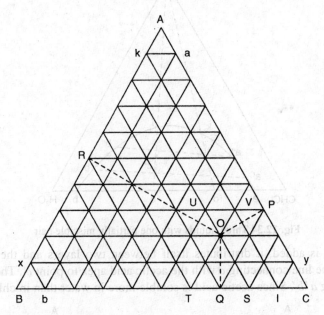

Fig. 12.33 Graphical representation of a three-component system

In the parallel method, the composition of point O is obtained as follows: Line SU representing 20% B is drawn parallel to AC and another line TV representing 60% C is drawn parallel to AB. Point of intersection of these lines is the required point O having 20% A.

We shall now briefly discuss only two systems, viz., (i) three partially miscible liquid components, and (ii) two solid components and a liquid.

(i) Three Partially Miscible Liquid Components

These are further classified into three groups depending upon the miscibility of the liquids:

(a) Systems having one pair of partially miscible liquids
(b) Systems having two pairs of partially miscible liquids
(c) Systems having three pairs of partially miscible liquids

(a) Systems Having One Pair of Partially Miscible Liquids: $CHCl_3$–H_2O–HAc is an example of such a system. $CHCl_3$ and H_2O are partially miscible while acetic acid is completely miscible with both the components. The phase diagram is shown in Fig. 12.34. The area enclosed by the curve $aklb$ indicates two phases while outside it only a single homogeneous phase is present. The curve $aklb$ is known as the *binodal curve*. Point a represents a saturated solution of water in $CHCl_3$ while b denotes the saturated solution of $CHCl_3$ in water. These points represent the conjugate solutions in the absence of acetic acid. If the overall composition of the system is given by a point the relative masses of the two layers are given by the lever rule

$$\frac{\text{Mass of water rich layer}}{\text{Mass of } CHCl_3 \text{ rich layer}} = \frac{ac}{bc}$$

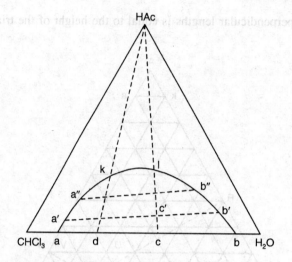

Fig. 12.34 Three liquids with one partially miscible pair

When acetic acid is added, it distributes itself between two layers and the composition of the system moves along the line connecting c with the acetic acid apex to point c'. The composition of the solution changes along $a'b'$. Since acetic acid is soluble more in water than in chloroform, the tie-line

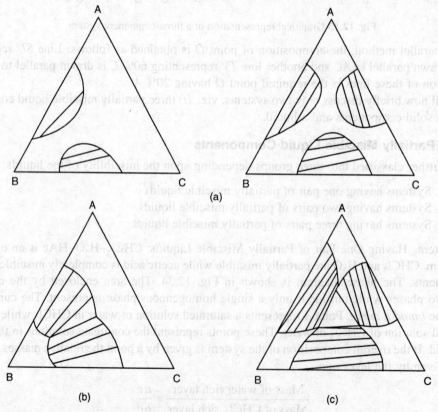

Fig. 12.35 (*a*) Liquids with two and three partially miscible pairs; (*b*) and (*c*) the binodal curves intersect

$a'b'$ is not parallel to ab. Further addition of acetic acid shifts the composition along c-HAc line. The proportion of water rich layer increases at the expense of chloroform rich layer. At l last trace of chloroform rich layer remains, beyond which a homogeneous solution results.

From the above discussions, it is clear that complete miscibility beyond l is not brought by coalescence of the two layers into one but rather by the disappearance of the $CHCl_3$–layer. However, if the starting composition corresponded to d then complete miscibility at k results by merging of the two layers into one. At this point the compositions of two layers become identical, the boundary between them vanishes and a homogeneous solution is formed. This point is known as *the plait point*.

Systems (*b*) and (*c*) Having Two and Three Partially Miscible Liquids: The phase diagrams for such systems are shown in Fig. 12.35 (*a*).

For each pair, a binodal curve is obtained at sufficiently high temperature. However at lower temperatures where the solubility of each component is low, the binodal curves may intersect each other and one gets bands in the two phase regions (Fig. 12.35(*b*)). In systems where three immiscible pairs are formed, a three-phase region results (Fig. 12.35 (*c*)).

(ii) Systems Composed of Two Solids and a Liquid

Depending upon the nature of the solid phases, such systems are classified into the following classes:

- (*i*) Crystallization of pure components
- (*ii*) Formation of a binary compound
- (*iii*) Formation of a ternary compound
- (*iv*) Formation of a complete series of solid solution
- (*v*) Partial miscibility in the solid state

We shall discuss systems in which only the pure components crystallize out. The simplest example being that of water and two salts B and C having an ion in common, *e.g.*, H_2O–$(NH_4)_2SO_4$–NH_4Cl. The phase diagram is shown in Fig. 12.36. Each salt influences the solubility of the other. K and L represent the solubility of B and C respectively in water. Solubility of B is lowered by the addition of C along KM. Similarly addition of B lowers the solubility of C along LM. Point M represents the state of the solution when it becomes saturated with respect to both B and C. At this point three phases coexist and is therefore *the isothermal invariant point*.

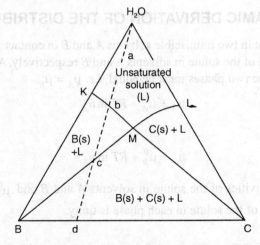

Fig. 12.36 Crystallization of only the pure components from the solution

If an unsaturated solution at *a* is isothermally evaporated, at *b* pure solid *B* crystallizes out from the solution and its amount increases as we move down along *bc*. The amount of *C* increases in the mother liquor along *b M* and at *c* the solution of composition *M* results and solid *C* also separates out. In the region between *c* and *d*, solid *B* and *C* are in equilibrium with a saturated solution of composition *M*. At *d*, water disappears and a solid mixture of *B* and *C* results.

12.13 THE NERNST DISTRIBUTION LAW

When a solute at constant temperature is added into two immiscible solvents in contact with each other, the solute gets distributed between the two solvents with different equilibrium concentrations. For example, when iodine is added to water and carbon tetrachloride, it distributes in such a way that at equilibrium the ratio of the concentrations of iodine in the two solvents is constant at any given temperature. If C_A and C_B are the concentrations of iodine in water and carbon tetrachloride, then

$$\frac{C_A}{C_B} = K_D$$

...(12.5)

The constant K_D is called *the distribution* or *partition coefficient* of the solute between the two solvents at the given temperature. The value of K_D depends on the nature of the solute and the solvent pair. Equation (12.5) is the mathematical form of the Nernst distribution law. This law states that at *constant temperature, when different quantities of a solute are allowed to distribute between two immiscible solvents in contact with each other then at equilibrium the ratio of the concentration of the solute in two layers is constant.* This law holds for ideal solutions. However, if the amount of the solute added is sufficiently small, then the distribution coefficient is relatively independent of the concentration. **Conditions for the Applicability of the Distribution Law:** The essential preconditions for the validity of the distribution law are:

(*i*) The same molecular species should be present in both solvents

(*ii*) The solution should be dilute

(*iii*) The two solvents should be immiscible. The mutual solubility of the two solvents should not be affected by the solute.

12.14 THERMODYNAMIC DERIVATION OF THE DISTRIBUTION LAW

Suppose a solute *X* is present in two immiscible solvents *A* and *B* in contact with each other. Let μ_A and μ_B be the chemical potential of the solute in solvents *A* and *B* respectively. At equilibrium the chemical potentials of the solute in the two phases must be equal, *i.e.* $\mu_A = \mu_B$.

Now

$$\mu_A = \mu_A^0 + RT \ln a_A$$

and

$$\mu_B = \mu_B^0 + RT \ln a_B$$

where a_A and a_B are the activities of the solute in solvents *A* and *B* and μ_A^0 and μ_B^0 are the chemical potentials when the activity of the solute in each phase is unity.

Therefore,

$$\mu_A^0 + RT \ln a_A = \mu_B^0 + RT \ln a_B$$

$$RT \ln \frac{a_A}{a_B} = \mu_B^0 - \mu_A^0$$

At constant temperature, μ_A^0 and μ_B^0 are constant. Therefore,

$$\frac{a_A}{a_B} = \text{constant} \qquad \text{...(12.6)}$$

For dilute solutions the activities may be replaced by the molar concentrations, hence, Eq. (12.6) reduces to

$$\frac{C_A}{C_B} = \text{constant} \qquad \text{...(12.7)}$$

This is the Nernst distribution law.

12.15 LIMITATIONS OF THE NERNST DISTRIBUTION LAW

The law is valid only when the molecular state of the solute is the same in both the solvents. If the solute undergoes dissociation or association in any one of the solvents, then in such cases the distribution law as given by Eq. (12.7) no longer holds good. Thus, if the solute remains unchanged in one of the solvents and undergoes partial dissociation in the other solvent, the ratio of the total concentrations in two solvents will not be constant. In such cases the ratio of the concentrations of the undissociated solute molecules in two solvents would be constant. For example, benzoic acid essentially remains as monomer in water whereas in nonpolar solvents like benzene it partly associates to form dimers, $(C_6H_5COOH)_2$. The distribution coefficient for such a system is given by the ratio of the total concentration of benzoic acid in water and the concentration of the unassociated benzoic acid in benzene. The distribution law can be applied in such cases with some modifications. This is done as follows:

Dissociation of Solute in one of the Solvents: Consider a solute X which dissolves in solvent A without any change and dissociates in solvent B to species Y and Z (Fig. 12.37). Let C_A be the concentration

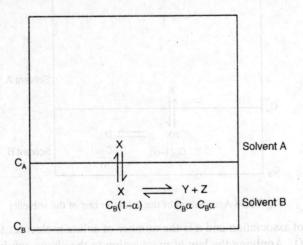

Fig. 12.37 Dissociation of solute in one of the solvents

of the solute in solvent A and C_B its total concentration in solvent B. If α is the degree of dissociation of the solute X in solvent B, then the equilibrium concentrations of the species in solvent B are given as:

$$X \rightleftharpoons Y + Z$$
$$C_B(1-\alpha) \quad \alpha C_B \quad \alpha C_B$$

In such a case, the ratio of the concentrations of the undissociated species in the two solvents would be constant, *i.e.*

$$\frac{C_A}{C_B(1-\alpha)} = \text{constant} \qquad ...(12.8)$$

Similarly, if the solute dissociates in both the solvents, then the distribution law becomes

$$\frac{C_A(1-\alpha_A)}{C_B(1-\alpha_B)} = \text{constant} \qquad ...(12.9)$$

where α_A and α_B are the degrees of dissociation of the solute in solvent A and B respectively.

Association of the Solute in one of the Solvents: Suppose there is no change in the molecular state of the solute X in solvent A, but it undergoes association in solvent B yielding an associated species $(X)_n$ (Fig. 12.38). Let C_A be the concentration of the solute in solvent A and C_B its total concentration in solvent B. The equilibrium between the associated and the unassociated solute molecules in solvent B is given as

$$nX \rightleftharpoons (X)_n$$
$$C_B(1-\alpha) \quad C_B\left(\frac{\alpha}{n}\right)$$

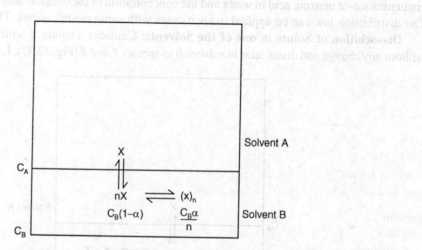

Fig. 12.38 Association of the solute in one of the solvents

where α is the degree of association and n is the number of solute molecules that combines to form an associated molecule $(X)_n$. Applying the law of mass action to the above equilibrium, we get

$$K = \frac{C_B\left(\dfrac{\alpha}{n}\right)}{\left[C_B(1-\alpha)\right]^n}$$

or

$$\left[C_B(1-\alpha)\right]^n = \left(\frac{\alpha C_B}{nK}\right)$$

$$C_B(1-\alpha) = \left(\frac{\alpha C_B}{nK}\right)^{1/n} \qquad ...(12.10)$$

Hence the distribution constant is given as

$$K_D = \frac{C_A}{C_B(1-\alpha)}$$

$$= \frac{C_A}{\left[\dfrac{C_B\alpha}{nK}\right]^{1/n}}$$

$$= \frac{C_A}{C_B^{1/n}}\left(\frac{nK}{\alpha}\right)^{1/n} \qquad ...(12.11)$$

Since K and α are constant and dependent on temperature only, hence at constant temperature, the quantity nK/α is constant and equation (12.11) becomes

$$K_D = \text{constant}\,\frac{C_A}{C_B^{1/n}}$$

or

$$K_D' = \frac{C_A}{C_B^{1/n}} \qquad ...(12.12)$$

or

$$\log C_A = \log K_D' + \frac{1}{n}\log C_B \qquad ...(12.13)$$

From Eq. (12.13), it is clear that a plot of $\log C_A$ versus $\log C_B$ will give a straight line with slope equal to $1/n$ and the intercept equal to $\log K_D'$. Hence the value of n and K_D' can be calculated.

Problem 12.9: The distribution constant of a certain solid X between two immiscible solvents A and B is 8 at 298 K. If the solubility of the solid in solvent A is 4.2 mol dm^{-3}, what is its solubility in B?

Solution: The distribution constant, K_D is given by

$$K_D = \frac{(X)_A}{(X)_B} = 8$$

The solubility of X in B is given by

$$(X)_B = \frac{(X)_A}{K_D}$$

$$= \frac{4.2}{8}$$

$$= 0.525 \text{ mol dm}^{-3}$$

Problem 12.10: In the distribution of iodine between carbon disulphide and water, the following results were obtained:

Concentration of iodine in water (g dm^{-3})	0.1	0.161	0.314	0.423
Concentration of iodine in carbon disulphide (g dm^{-3})	41	66	129	174.

Calculate the distribution constant of iodine between carbon disulphide and water. What could be predicted regarding the molecular state of iodine in these solvents?

Solution: The ratio of the concentration of iodine in carbon disulphide and water from the above results are:

(1) $\dfrac{41}{0.1} = 410.0$ (2) $\dfrac{66}{0.161} = 409.3$

(3) $\dfrac{129}{0.314} = 410.8$ (4) $\dfrac{174}{0.423} = 411.1$

These values are constant and hence the distribution constant is approximately 410. The constancy of the ratio indicates that iodine dissolves in both the solvents without any change in its molecular state.

Problem 12.11: Benzoic acid was distributed between water and benzene at 298 K and the following results were obtained:

Concentration of acid in water C_W (g eq dm^{-3}) $\times$ 100	1.5	1.95	2.98
Concentration of acid in benzene C_B (g eq dm^{-3}) $\times$ 10	2.42	4.1	9.07

Predict the molecular complexity of the acid in benzene if its ionization in water is neglected.

Solution: $\dfrac{C_W}{C_B}$ values are 6.2×10^{-2}, 4.7×10^{-2} and 3.2×10^{-2}.

The variation in the ratio indicates that distribution constant is not given by C_W / C_B. However, if we calculate $C_W / \sqrt{C_B}$, we find a reasonably constant value 3.048×10^{-2}, 3.038×10^{-2} and 3.035×10^{-2}). The constancy of $C_W / \sqrt{C_B}$ shows that the acid exists as dimer in benzene layer. We can also conclude from the slope $\left(\dfrac{1}{2}\right)$ of the graph obtained by plotting $\log C_W$ versus $\log C_B$ that dimerization of the acid occurs in benzene layer.

Problem 12.12: At 298 K, an aqueous solution of an acid containing 0.18 mol dm^{-3} of the solution is in equilibrium with an ethereal solution containing 0.36 mol dm^{-3}. Assuming that the acid has its normal molar mass in both the layers, calculate the distribution constant of the acid between ether and water. What is the concentration of an ethereal solution of the acid which is in equilibrium with an aqueous solution containing 0.28 mol dm^{-3} at 298 K?

Solution: The distribution constant of the acid between ether and water is given by

$$K_D = \frac{C_{ether}}{C_{water}}$$

$$= \frac{0.36}{0.18} = 2.0$$

In the second case, concentration of acid in water layer is 0.28 mol dm^{-3}, hence the concentration in ether layer is

$$C_{ether} = K_D \, C_{water}$$

$$= (2)(0.28) = 0.56 \text{ mol dm}^{-3}$$

12.16 APPLICATIONS OF THE DISTRIBUTION LAW

Some of the important applications of the distribution law are:

(*i*) **Molecular Complexity of the Solute:** From the distribution experiments, the molecular state of a solute in solvents can be ascertained. If the ratio of the concentrations of the solute in both the solvents is constant, then the solute dissolves without any change in its state of aggregation in both the solvents. However, if the ratio (C_A/C_B) is not constant but Eq. (12.8) or (12.9) gives a constant value, then it is concluded that the solute undergoes dissociation in solvent B or in both the solvents A and B. In case Eq. (12.12) holds good, the solute is associated into dimeric molecules in solvent B.

(*ii*) **Determination of the Equilibrium Constant:** The distribution law is successfully and conveniently used in determining the equilibrium constant for the reactions where one of the reactants or products is soluble in two immiscible solvents. For example, in the determination of the equilibrium constant of the reaction

$$I_2 + KI \rightleftharpoons KI_3$$

or

$$I_2 + I^- \rightleftharpoons I_3^-$$

an aqueous solution of potassium iodide of known concentration (say x mole dm^{-3}) is taken, some iodine is added so that the complex tri-iodide is formed. To this solution, some non-aqueous solvent like CCl_4 is added and the solution is shaken vigorously until equilibrium is established. On standing, the mixture separates into two layers. The concentration of iodine is determined in both the layers by titrating it against standard hypo solution. Let y and z be the total concentrations of iodine in water and in carbon tetrachloride respectively and K_D the distribution coefficient of iodine between water and carbon terachloride (determined separately at the same temperature), then

$$K_D = \frac{C_{\text{water}}}{C_{\text{CCl}_4}},$$

or $C_{\text{water}} = K_D \times C_{\text{CCl}_4} = K_D \times z$

Since the concentration of iodine in aqueous layer is the sum of the concentration of free iodine

and the concentration of I_3^-. Therefore, the concentration of I_3^- in aqueous layer $= y - K_D z$.

Concentration of free KI in aqueous layer $= x - y + K_D z$

Hence the equilibrium constant of the reaction: $y_2 + KI \Rightarrow KI_3$ is

$$K = \frac{[KI_3]}{[I_2][KI]}$$

$$= \frac{y - K_D z}{(K_D z)(x - y + K_D z)}$$

(*iii*) **Determination of the Hydrolysis Constant and the Degree of Hydrolysis:** When one of the products of hydrolysis of a salt is soluble in an immiscible solvent like benzene, while the salt and the other components are not soluble in it, the distribution experiment can be employed in evaluating the hydrolysis constant. For example, aniline hydrochloride undergoes hydrolysis yielding aniline and hydrochloric acid. If its aqueous solution is shaken with benzene, aniline gets distributed between water and benzene whereas the salt and acid are insoluble in benzene. Let x be the initial concentration of the salt and y be the concentration of aniline in benzene layer. If K_D is the distribution coefficient of aniline between water and benzene

$$K_D = \frac{C_{\text{water}}}{C_{\text{Benzene}}}$$

or $C_{\text{water}} = K_D \times C_{\text{Benzene}} = K_D y$

The concentration of acid in water must be equal to the concentration of aniline in water and benzene, *i.e.*,

$$[HCl] = K_D y + y$$

Hence the concentration of unhydrolysed salt $= x - (K_D y + y)$. Therefore,

$$K_h = \frac{[\text{Acid}][\text{Aniline}]}{[\text{Aniline hydrochloride}]}$$

$$= \frac{(K_D y)(K_D y + y)}{[x - (K_D y + y)]}$$

(*iv*) **Solvent Extraction:** One of the most common uses of the distribution principle is in the extraction of a solute from a solution by another immiscible solvent. This method is generally employed both in the laboratory and in industry. In the laboratory, the solute is generally extracted from an aqueous solution with the help of suitable organic solvents such as benzene, ether, chloroform, etc. These are known as the extracting solvents. The extracting solvent should meet the following requirements:

(a) It should be completely immiscible with the original solvent.

(b) The solute should be more soluble in the extracting solvent.

(c) The extracting solvent should be volatile so that the solute can be recovered from it by warming the solution on a water bath.

On shaking the solution containing the solute with a suitable extracting solvent, two layers are formed. The layers are separated and the non-aqueous layer is distilled to obtain the solute. The extraction with the extracting solvent can be carried out in two different ways: (a) by using the entire volume of the extracting solvent in one lot, or (b) by using the extracting solvent in fractional quantities and repeating the process of extraction a number of times. It can be shown that the stepwise extraction is more advantageous than the single step extraction.

When solute does not associate, dissociate or react with the solvent, one can calculate the amount of the solute that can be extracted from the solution. Let V_0 be the volume of the solution containing W g of the solute and V_1 be the volume of the extracting solvent used in each step. Let W_1 be the amount in g of the solute that remains unextracted in the original solvent after the first stage of extraction, then

the concentration of the solute in the extracting solvent $= \dfrac{W - W_1}{V_1}$ and the concentration of the solute

in the original solvent $= \dfrac{W_1}{V_0}$.

Therefore, the distribution coefficient,

$$K_D = \frac{C_{\text{original solvent}}}{C_{\text{extracting solvent}}}$$

$$= \frac{\dfrac{W_1}{V_0}}{\dfrac{W - W_1}{V_1}} = \frac{W_1 V_1}{V_0 (W - W_1)}$$

or $$W_1 = \frac{K_D V_0 W}{V_1 + K_D V_0} \qquad \qquad ...(12.14)$$

In the second extraction, again the same volume V_1 of the solvent is used and if the amount of the solute left in the solution is W_2, then the amount extracted is $(W_1 - W_2)$ and

$$K_D = \frac{W_2 / V_0}{(W_1 - W_2) / V_1}$$

or $$W_2 = W_1 \times \frac{K_D V_0}{V_1 + K_D V_0}$$

$$= W \left(\frac{K_D V_0}{V_1 + K_D V_0} \right) \left(\frac{K_D V_0}{V_1 + K_D V_0} \right)$$

$$= W\left(\frac{K_D V_0}{V_1 + K_D V_0}\right)^2 \qquad \qquad ...(12.15)$$

If the process of extraction is carried out n times, then at the end of nth extraction the amount of solute that still remains unextracted is given by

$$W_n = W\left(\frac{K_D V_0}{V_1 + K_D V_0}\right)^n \qquad \qquad ...(12.16)$$

On the other hand, if all the volume nV_1 of the extracting solvent is used in one lot, the amount of the solute W_n' still unextracted will be given by

$$W_n' = W\left(\frac{K_D V_0}{nV_1 + W_D V_0}\right)$$

$$= W\left(\frac{1}{1 + \dfrac{nV_1}{K_D V_0}}\right) \qquad \qquad ...(12.17)$$

It can be shown mathematically that the multistep extraction is more advantageous than the single step extraction, *i.e.*, $W_n < W_n'$. Equation (12.16) can be rewritten as

$$W_n = W\left(\frac{1}{1 + \dfrac{V_1}{K_D V_0}}\right)^n$$

Let

$$\frac{V_1}{K_D V_0} = y,$$

then

$$W_n = W\left(\frac{1}{1 + y}\right)^n$$

Expanding this in the power series, we get

$$W_n = W\left[\frac{1}{1 + ny + \dfrac{n(n-1)^2}{2}y^2 + ...}\right] \qquad \qquad ...(12.18)$$

Similarly, Eq. (12.17) can be written as

$$W_n' = W\left(\frac{1}{1 + ny}\right) \qquad \qquad ...(12.19)$$

It is obvious that the denominator of Eq. (12.18) is greater than that of Eq. (12.19). Therefore, W_n is less than W_n'; hence the multistep extraction will always be better than the single step extraction.

Problem 12.13: The solubility of methyl amine at 298 K in water is 8.49 times higher than in chloroform. Calculate the percentage of the base that remains in 1000 ml of chloroform if it is extracted (*i*) four times, each with 200 ml of water, (*ii*) twice with 400 ml of water, and (*iii*) once with 800 ml of water.

Solution: (*i*) Let the initial amount of the base in chloroform be 100 g and x_4 be the amount that still remains in it after the fourth stage of extraction. From Eq. (12.16), we have

$$x_4 = 100 \left(\frac{K_D V_0}{V_1 + K_D V_0} \right)^4$$

In this problem $K_D = \dfrac{1}{8.49}$, $V_0 = 1000$ ml and $V_1 = 200$ ml. Therefore, the amount x_4 unextracted is given by

$$x_4 = 100 \left(\frac{\dfrac{1}{8.49} \times 1}{\dfrac{1}{8.49} \times 1 + 0.2} \right)^4 = 1.89 \text{ g or } 1.89\%$$

(*ii*) When the extraction is carried out in two steps, the amount x_2 unextracted is given by

$$x_2 = 100 \left(\frac{\dfrac{1}{8.49} \times 1}{\dfrac{1}{8.49} \times 1 + 0.4} \right)^2 = 5.17 \text{ g or } 5.17\%$$

(*iii*) In the single step extraction the amount unextracted x_1 is given as

$$x_1 = 100 \left(\frac{\dfrac{1}{8.49} \times 1}{\dfrac{1}{8.49} \times 1 + 0.8} \right) = 14.6 \text{ g or } 14.6\%$$

Problem 12.14: The distribution constant of iodine between carbon tetrachloride and water is given by the ratio of molarities $\dfrac{C_{CCl_4}}{C_{H_2O}} = 85$. How many ml of carbon tetrachloride are required for 95% of the iodine to be extracted from 100 ml of aqueous solution in one-step?

Solution: When 95% of iodine is extracted 5% still remains unextracted. If V be the volume of carbon tetrachloride, then we have

$$5 = 100 \left(\frac{\dfrac{1}{85} \times 0.1}{\dfrac{1}{85} \times 0.1 + V} \right)$$

$$= 22.35 \text{ ml}$$

Problem 12.15: The solubility of a solute is three times as high in ether as in water. Compare the amounts extracted from 100 ml of the aqueous solution by (a) 100 ml of ether in one-step, and (b) two successive extractions each with 50 ml of ether.

Solution: (a) Let the initial amount of solute be W g and the amount extracted by ether in single step extraction be x g.

Then
$$\frac{3}{1} = \frac{x/100}{\dfrac{W-x}{100}}$$

$$x = \frac{3}{4} W \text{ or } 75\% \text{ of the initial amount is extracted.}$$

(b) If x' is the amount left in the two-step extraction, then it is given by

$$x' = W \left(\frac{K_D \times 0.10}{K_D \times 0.10 + 0.05} \right)^2$$

$$= \frac{4}{25} W \text{ or } 84\% \text{ is extracted}$$

EXERCISES

1. Select the correct statements from the following:
   (i) Systems with lower chemical potentials are more stable than those with higher chemical potentials.
   (ii) For a one-component system, the maximum number of phases that can exist in equilibrium is three.
   (iii) A system can have negative degrees of freedom.
   (iv) The number of phases in a system depends on the amount of the various substances present at equilibrium.
   (v) The phase rule, $P + F = C + 2$, is valid even if some of the components may not be present in all the phases.
   (vi) Information regarding the structure of matter can be obtained from studies of phase equilibria.
   (vii) The cryohydric point of $NaCl–H_2O$ system is $-21°C$. A temperature of $-30°C$ can be obtained by adding a large amount of NaCl to ice.
   (viii) An invariant system has no degree of freedom.
   (ix) For a two-component system, a maximum in the phase diagram corresponds to the formation of a definite compound.
   (x) A eutectic is identical with a solid solution.
   (xi) The stable allotropic modification of a substance has a higher melting point than the unstable or less stable form.

   Ans. Correct statements: (i), (ii), (v), (viii), (ix), (xi).

2. Distinguish the following:
   (a) A stable equilibrium from an unstable equilibrium.
   (b) A eutectic point from a peritectic point.
   (c) A eutectic from a solid solution.
   (d) A solid solution from a compound.
   (e) A eutectic from a compound.
   (f) A congruent melting compound from an incongruent melting compound.

3. Explain, giving reasons, the following:
   (i) For the solid $\rightleftharpoons$ liquid, slope of P versus T plot is negative for water and positive for other substances.
   (ii) NaCl-KCl-H_2O is a three-component system while NaCl–KBr–H_2O is a four-component system.
   (iii) The system, NH_4Cl (s) $\rightleftharpoons$ NH_3 (g) + HCl (g), is a one-component system if $P_{NH_3} = P_{HCl}$ and two-component system if $P_{NH_3} \neq P_{HCl}$.
   (iv) A eutectic mixture has a definite composition and a sharp melting point yet it is not a compound.
   (v) The lowest temperature attained in a system of salt and ice is the cryohydric temperature.
   (vi) In water, a large number of molecular species like H_2O, $(H_2O)_2$, $(H_2O)_3$... exist yet the number of components is only one.
   (vii) Though tritium and deuterium usually occur with natural hydrogen yet hydrogen is regarded as a one-component.

4. In the examples given below calculate for each; the number of phases, the number of components and the degrees of freedom.
   (i) H_2O (s) $\rightleftharpoons$ H_2O(l) $\rightleftharpoons$ H_2O (g)
   (ii) A mixture of N_2, O_2 and NO in which the equilibrium
   $$N_2(g) + O_2(g) \rightleftharpoons 2\,NO\,(g)$$
   is established.
   (iii) S (r) $\rightleftharpoons$ S (m) $\rightleftharpoons$ S (l) $\rightleftharpoons$ S (g)
   (iv) $CaCO_3$ (s) $\rightleftharpoons$ CaO (s) + CO_2 (g)
   (v) A eutectic mixture in a binary system.
   (vi) C (s) in equilibrium with CO (g), CO_2 (g) and O_2 (g) at 1 atm 298 K.
   (vii) PCl_5 (g) $\rightleftharpoons$ PCl_3 (g) + Cl_2 (g) when

   (a) $p_{PCl_3} = p_{PCl_2}$ and $p_{PCl_3} \neq p_{PCl_2}$.

   (viii) I_2(s) $\rightleftharpoons$ I_2($CHCl_3$) $\rightleftharpoons$ I_2(H_2O)
   (ix) $Na_2SO_4 \cdot 10H_2O$(s) $\rightleftharpoons$ Na_2SO_4(s) + $10H_2O$ (g)
   (x) $H_3PO_4 + H_2O \rightleftharpoons H_2PO_4^- + H_3O^+$, $H_2PO_4^- + H_2O \rightleftharpoons HPO_4^{2-} + H_3O^+$

   and $HPO_4^{2-} + H_2O \rightleftharpoons PO_4^{3-} + H_3O^+$.

   Ans. (i) $P = 3$, $C = 1$, $F = 0$; (ii) $P = 1$, $C = 2$, $F = 3$; (iii) $P = 4$, $C = 1$, $F = -1$;
   (iv) $P = 3$, $C = 2$, $F = 1$; (v) $P = 2$, $C = 2$, $F = 2$; (vi) $P = 2$, $C = 2$, $F = 2$;
   (vii) (a) $P = 1$, $C = 1$, $F = 2$; (b) $P = 1$, $C = 2$, $F = 3$;
   (viii) $P = 3$, $C = 3$, $F = 2$; (ix) $P = 3$, $C = 2$, $F = 1$;
   (x) $P = 1$, $C = 2$, $F = 3$.

5. Explain the terms: phase, number of components and the degrees of freedom. Derive the phase rule, $P + F = C + 2$.

6. Sketch a plot of chemical potential against temperature for the solid, liquid and gaseous forms of a substance. Why do all the three curves slope downhill with increasing temperature? Which curve slopes downhill most steeply? Explain. Indicate the melting point of the solid and boiling point of the liquid in this plot. What thermodynamic criterion would you use to locate the boiling and melting points?

7. An element exists in three solid allotropic modification A, B, and C. At the triple point $S_{B,m} > S_{C,m} > S_{A,m}$, and $V_{C,m} > V_{A,m} > V_{B,m}$ where S_m and V_m are the molar entropy and molar volume respectively. Sketch a suitable P–T diagram on the basis of the given information. Label each area, line and point.

8. (a) What is the maximum number of phases that can be in equilibrium at constant temperature and pressure in one, two and three-component systems?

   (b) Draw a phase diagram representing schematically each of following:

   (i) A temperature-composition phase diagram for a binary system A-B having a single eutectic, a single peritectic with no solid solutions.

   (ii) A temperature-composition phase diagram for a binary system A-B having a congruent melting compound AB and no solid solutions.

   (iii) A temperature-composition phase diagram for a binary system A-B having a liquid phase and two partially miscible solid phases. There is no vapour phase.

   (iv) A temperature-composition phase diagram for a binary system A-B forming a complete series of solid solution.

   Ans. (a) 3, 4, 5.

9. Suppose four distinct phases were observed in a laboratory specimen of a binary alloy. Is such an observation possible? Explain your answer.

10. Mr. A claims to have discovered a new element x which exists in two solid modifications x_1 and x_2. Mr. A then studies its phase diagram and claims to have the following equilibria $x_1(s) \rightleftharpoons x_2(s) \rightleftharpoons x(l) \rightleftharpoons x(g)$. Do you agree with the claims of Mr. A? Explain.

11. A certain substance has two triple points, one for solid α-liquid-vapour, and other at much higher pressure for solid β-solid α-liquid. Whenever α and liquid are in equilibrium, α is more dense phase, whenever β and liquid are in equilibrium, β is the more dense phase, and when α and β are in equilibrium, β is the more dense phase, and the system absorbs heat from the surrounding during the transition $\beta \rightarrow \alpha$.

   Sketch the phase diagram on a P–T plane indicating in each region the phase which is stable.

12. Enthalpies of fusion of two metals A and B are 2.5 kJ mol^{-1} and 4.0 kJ mol^{-1} and their fusion temperatures are 800 K and 945 K respectively. Suppose they form an ideal solution and are immiscible in the solid state, construct the tentative phase diagram. Determine the eutectic composition and eutectic temperature (T_{eu}).

   Ans. $X_B = 0.412$, $T_{eu} = 331$ K.

13. In the one-component phase diagram, generally, the slope of the line representing the equilibrium solid $\rightleftharpoons$ vapour is more than that of the line representing the liquid $\rightleftharpoons$ vapour equilibrium. Explain.

14. Draw the phase diagram for a one-component system X from the following data. X exists in two solid modifications X_1 and X_2 which are denser than the liquid. The transition temperature of X_1 and X_2 increases with the increase of pressure. X_1 is stable at lower pressures and temperatures. Label the diagram.

15. Construct the phase diagram from the following data of a two-component system A and B miscible in the liquid state only:

Mass % B	0.0	10	25	35	45	55	65	80	92	100
Freezing point (°C)	119	112	99	90	78	83	95	108	113	115

Calculate the composition at the eutectic point and also determine the eutectic temperature. Label the diagram and also draw cooling curves for melts with compositions 40% and 80% B (by mass). Indicate the phases separating during cooling of the melts.

Ans. $T_{eu} = 74°C$, $[B]_{eu} = 48\%$ by mass.

16. The following data on cooling curves have been obtained for the lead-antimony system:

Temperature (°C)	631	550	550	400	300	327
Mass % Pb	0	30	44	66	80	100

Construct the phase diagram and label the areas.

(a) How many kg of Sb crystallizes from 20 kg of Pb-Sb melt containing 35% by mass of Pb after cooling to a temperature of 400°C? (a) What is the maximum mass in kg of pure Sb that can be obtained from this melt?

17. Construct the phase diagram for Zn-Mg system from the following data: M.pt. of Zn = 419°C, m.pt. of Mg = 651°C. A congruently compound Mg_xZn_y at 15% by mass of Mg melts at 599°C. The lowest freezing point of Zn observed in 368°C for composition containing 3.3% Mg by mass and that for Mg at 347°C for a composition containing 49% by mass of Mg. Determine the molecular formula of the compound, label all the areas and draw cooling curves for melts having 8%, 15% and 49% by mass of Mg.

Ans. $Mg\ Zn_2$.

18. Thermal analysis of melts containing Mg and Si resulted in the following data:

Mass % of Mg	0	15	30	43	55	63	80	97	100
Temp. of first break in the cooling curve (°C)	–	1290	1250	–	1070	–	1000	–	–
Temp. of the halt in the cooling curve (°C)	1420	950	950	950	950	1102	640	640	651

Construct the phase diagram from the above data for Mg–Si system. Indicate the formula of the compound, if any. Label the phases. Answer the following questions with reference to the phase diagram.

   (*a*) What is approximately the solubility of Mg in the melt at 1100°C?

   (*b*) What is the approximate melting point of the melt containing 20% by mass of Mg?

   (*c*) What is the m.pt. of the compound?

   (*d*) Is the compound congruent or incongruent melting?

   (*e*) What happens when a melt containing 50% by mass of Mg is cooled to 800°C?

   (*f*) 20 kg of a melt containing 20% by mass of Mg is cooled to 1100°C. Calculate the amount of solid silicon separated from the melt on cooling.

   (*g*) What is the maximum amount of solid silicon that can be separated from 20 kg of the melt containing 20% by mass of Mg?

Ans. Mg_2Si; (*a*) 33% by mass of Mg; (*b*)1230°C; (*c*) 1102°C; (*d*) Congruently melting; (*e*) Compound Mg_2Si separates at 1030°C and complete solidification takes place at 950°C; (*f*) 7.88 kg (*g*) 10.7 kg.

19. For the system *A*(m. pt. –22.7°C) and *B* (m.pt. 11.8°C), a compound ($A_x B_y$) is formed at 50 mole% of *B*. The compound melts at 45°C giving a liquid of the same composition as the compound. *A* and *B* are completely miscible in the molten state but are immiscible in the solid state. What is the formula of the compound? How many eutectic points are there is the phase diagram? Is the compound congruently or incongruently melting?

Ans. *AB*; 2; Congruently melting.

20. Draw a tentative temperature composition phase diagram for a binary system *A-B* having a congruent melting compound (A_3B) and an incongruent melting compound (AB_3). *A* and *B* are completely miscible in molten state but immiscible in the solid state. Label all the areas in the diagram. How many eutectics are there in the diagram. Name the phases (*i*) at the peritectic point and (*ii*) at the eutectic points.

Ans. Two eutectic points; (*i*) AB_3(s), *B*(s) and melt; (*ii*) *A*(s), A_3B(s) and melt; A_3B(s), AB_3(s) and melt.

21. The melting point of mercury is –39°C and that of thallium is 303°C. The compound formed Tl_2Hg_5 has a melting point of 15°C. 8% by mass of Tl lowers the melting point of mercury to the minimum –60°C. The eutectic temperature of Tl and the compound Tl_2Hg_5 is –0.4°C and the corresponding composition of the eutectic mixture is 41% (by mass of Tl). Sketch a phase diagram for the system of Hg and Tl and label all the areas. Determine the maximum amount of Tl obtainable from 10 kg of Tl amalgam containing 80% by mass of Tl.

Ans. 6.6 kg.

22. Metals *A* and *B* form compounds AB_3 and A_2B_3. Solids *A*, *B*, AB_3 and A_2B_3 are immiscible with each other but are completely miscible in the molten state. *A* and *B* melt at 600°C and 1100°C respectively. Compound A_2B_3 melts congruently at 900°C and gives a simple eutectic with *A* at 450°C. Compound AB_3 decomposes at 800°C to give the other compound and a melt. There is a eutectic at 650°C. Draw a phase diagram

consistent with this information and label all the areas. Sketch cooling curves for melts of composition 90% and 30% by mass of A and label the phases appearing or disappearing at each break and halt.

23. Bismuth and cadmium are used to form an alloy containing 70% by mass of Cd. The m.pt. of Bi and Cd are 270°C and 320°C respectively. The metals form no solid solutions or compounds with each other but form a eutectic at 140°C corresponding to 40% by mass of cadmium. Assuming that the liquid lines are straight lines calculate.

   (i) the temperature at which the alloy begins to crystallize out from the melt,

   (ii) the proportion of solid in the alloy at 175°C,

   (iii) the proportion of the solid in the alloy at 20°C, and

   (iv) the density of alloy at 20°C, given that the densities of Bi and Cd are 9.8 kg dm^{-3} and 8.6 kg dm^{-2} at 20°C.

   Ans. (i) 230°C, (ii) 37.5% by mass of Cd, (iii) 50% by mass of Cd, (iv)8.93 kg dm^{-3}.

24. The following data have been obtained by cooling solutions of magnesium and nickel:

Ni, mass%	0	10	28	38	54.7	60	75	83	88	100
Break in the cooling curve (°C)	–	608	–	770	–	1050	1120	–	–	–
Halt in the cooling curve (°C)	651	510	510	510	770	770	770	1180	1080	1450

   Plot the phase diagram, deduce the formula, if any, of the compound(s) formed indicating whether they are congruent or incongruent melting compounds. State the variance(s) for each area and eutectic/peritectic.

   Ans. Mg$_2$Ni-incongruent melting compound MgNi$_2$-congruent melting compound. In the single phase (liquid) region $F = 2$, in the two phase regions $F = 1$ and at the eutectic and peritectic point $F = 0$.

25. Sketch qualitatively the phase diagram of the system of three liquid A-B-C in which the pairs A-B and A-C are completely miscible while B and C are partly miscible with each other at a given temperature and pressure. As component A is added, they become more and more miscible until the system becomes a homogeneous phase. Discuss this three component liquid system and give one example of such a system.

26. Construct the isothermal equilibrium diagram for a ternary system composed of water and two salts having a common ion which does not form a compound. Explain how this diagram is helpful in understanding the principle of isothermal fractional crystallization.

27. Explain the following terms:

   (i) Phase, (ii) number of components, (iii) degrees of freedom, (iv) eutectic point, (v) congruent melting point, (vi) incongruent or peritectic point (vii) solid solution, (viii) breaks and halts in the cooling curves.

28. What are the conditions under which the formula $P + F = C + 2$ is valid? How is the rule modified in reacting systems?

29. Draw phase diagrams for (a) water, (b) CO$_2$ and (c) sulphur systems. Label the diagrams. Discuss the phase changes when rhombic sulphur at 0.03 mm Hg and 96°C is heated at constant pressure up to 140°C.

30. Describe the applications of phase rule in (i) the desilverization of lead and (ii) purification of metals.

31. State the distribution law. How the law is helpful in ascertaining the molecular complexity of the dissolved solute? Explain why multistep extraction is more economical than the single extraction?

32. In the distribution of iodine between water and carbon tetrachloride at 298 K, the following results were obtained:

[I$_2$] is water layer (mol dm^{-3}) × 10^4	2.35	4.69	7.03	9.30
[I$_2$] is CCl$_4$ layer (mol dm^{-3}) × 10^2	2.00	4.00	6.00	8.00

Show that these results obey the distribution law, $[I_2]_{CCl_4}/[I_2]_{H_2O}$. Evaluate the distribution coefficient of iodine between CCl_4 and water.

Ans. 85.5.

33. In the distribution of a weak organic acid (HA) between water and benzene at 298 K, the following results were obtained:

| [HA] in water (g/dm³) | 1.50 | 1.95 | 2.89 |
| [HA] in benzene (g/dm³) | 14.20 | 41.20 | 96.50 |

Assuming that the acid is not ionized in water and shows normal molar mass in water, ascertain its molecular complexity in benzene.

Ans. HA exists as dimer in benzene.

34. If the value of the distribution constant is 410.0 for the distribution of I_2 between water and CS_2, find the fraction of I_2 remaining in water layer after an amount of CS_2 equal to that of water has been allowed to equilibriate with the aqueous phase.

Ans. 2.43×10^{-3}.

35. The solubility of methylamine at 298 K in water is 8.49 times greater than in chloroform. What percentage of methylamine remains in 1 dm³ of chloroform solution of methylamine if it is extracted (*i*) four times, always with 0.2 dm³ of water, (*ii*) twice with 0.4 dm³ of water?

Ans. (*i*) 1.89%, (*ii*) 5.17%.

CHAPTER

13

Electrolytic Conduction

13.1 ELECTRICAL CONDUCTORS

Substances which allow the flow of current are called electrical conductors. The conductors are broadly classified into two categories (*i*) metallic conductors or electronic conductors, and (*ii*) electrolytic conductors.

(*i*) **Metallic Conductors or Electronic Conductors:** In these the conduction of electricity is due to the movement of free electrons from a higher negative potential to a lower one without producing chemical changes. Examples of such conductors are metals, alloys, graphite, certain solid salts like CuS, CdS etc.

(*ii*) **Electrolytic Conductors:** In electrolytic conductors, flow of current is due to the movement or migration of ions towards oppositely charged electrodes and is accompanied by the chemical changes at electrodes. Molten salts, aqueous solutions of salts, acids and bases are examples of electrolytic conductors.

Distinction between Electronic and Electrolytic Conductions

(*i*) In electronic conduction, electrons flow from negative to the positive end while in electrolytic conduction charged species (ions) move towards oppositely charged electrodes.

(*ii*) In electronic conduction no change in form or composition of the conductor occurs while in electrolytic conduction new products are formed at electrodes due to transport of ions from one part of the system to another.

(*iii*) In metallic conduction, conductance decreases with rise in temperature due to the resistance offered to the moving electrons by vibration of atoms or ions composing the conductor. Metallic conduction becomes specially pronounced at low temperature, *e.g.*, 3-4 K. Under these conditions the resistance of many conductors becomes exceedingly low and practically no resistance is offered to the flow of the electrons. The conductors become super conducting.

Electrolytic conduction, on the other hand, increases with rise in temperature due to (*a*) increase in the mobility of the ions and (*b*) increase in the degree of ionization of the electrolytes.

13.2 ELECTROLYSIS

Chemical changes at the electrodes due to the passage of electric current are called *electrolysis*. When the current passes through an electrolytic solution, ions migrate and electrons are gained or lost by ions at the electrode surface. Electrode that is positively charged has deficit of electrons is called anode and the other negatively charged has excess of electrons is called cathode. The electrons are drawn from one electrode and supplied to the other either by a dynamo or by the chemical reactions of a battery. The removal of electrons is termed as oxidation and it occurs at the anode while the addition of electrons is known as reduction and it occurs at the cathode.

In classifying the electrode reactions it is convenient to distinguish two types of electrodes, viz., *inert electrodes* and *reacting electrodes*. Inert electrodes do not participate in chemical reactions. They merely help in the transfer of electrons to and from the solution. Pt, Au, etc., are examples of inert electrodes. Reacting electrodes enter chemically into the electrode reactions. A reacting electrode generally consists of a metal which contributes metal ions to the solution or accepts the metal ions from the solution. The products of electrolysis depend on the types of electrodes used. For example, if copper electrodes are used in the electrolysis of an aqueous solution of $CuCl_2$, copper goes into solution as Cu^{2+} ions at the anode while Cu^{2+} ions are discharged at the cathode. The processes are:

at anode: $Cu \rightarrow Cu^{2+} + 2e^-$

at cathode: $Cu^{2+} + 2e^- \rightarrow Cu$

With Pt electrodes, Cl^- and OH^- ions are discharged at the anode while H^+ ions at the cathode. The changes are

at anode: $Cl^- \rightarrow Cl + e^-$
                         $Cl + Cl \rightarrow Cl_2$

at anode: $OH^- \rightarrow OH + e^-$
                         $OH + OH \rightarrow H_2O + \frac{1}{2}O_2$

at cathode: $H^+ + e^- \rightarrow H$
                         $H + H \rightarrow H_2$

When several ions are competing for the transfer of electrons, the products formed depend upon the concentration of ions and the energy required for discharging the ions. If there are no easily reducible or oxidizable ions in solutions, H^+ and OH^- ions from water are discharged. The discharge of an ion depends upon the *deposition potential—the potential at which an ion is deposited.*

Electrolysis of an aqueous solution of sodium chloride may now be considered to emphasize the fact that the products of electrolysis depend on the electrodes used. With Pt electrodes the reactions are

at cathode: $H^+ + e^- \rightarrow H$
                         $H + H \rightarrow H_2$

at anode: $Cl^- \rightarrow Cl + e^-$
                         $Cl + Cl \rightarrow Cl_2$

Discharge of Na^+ ions does not occur at the cathode as long as H^+ ions are present. This is because the discharge potential of H^+ ions on Pt cathode is less than that of Na^+ ions and hence H^+ ions are discharged preferentially over Na^+ ions. Na^+ ions simply conduct the current in solution. Similarly Cl^- ions due to their lower discharge potential are discharged preferentially over OH^- ions. If the electrolysis were carried out using mercury cathode, Na^+ ions are discharged in preference over H^+ ions as H^+ ions have higher discharge potential over Na^+ ions on mercury. With silver electrodes hydrogen would be produced at the cathode but AgCl will form at the anode

at cathode: $H^+ + e^- \rightarrow H$
                         $H + H \rightarrow H_2$

at anode: $Ag + Cl^- \rightarrow AgCl + e^-$

In the above examples, the ions discharged are always those having lower discharge potentials.

Electrolysis of an aqueous solution of sodium hydroxide liberates H_2 at the cathode, O_2 at the anode and Na^+ ions are not discharged. Na^+ and OH^- ions present in solution carry the current while H^+ and OH^- ions from water are discharged. Sodium hydroxide simply provides the conducting medium. The reactions are

at cathode: $\qquad\qquad\qquad H^+ + e^- \rightarrow H$

$\qquad\qquad\qquad\qquad\qquad\quad H + H \rightarrow H_2$

at anode: $\qquad\qquad\qquad\quad OH^- \rightarrow OH + e^-$

$\qquad\qquad\qquad\quad OH + OH \rightarrow H_2O + \dfrac{1}{2}O_2$

Similarly in the electrolysis of aqueous sulphuric acid, H_2 appears at the cathode and O_2 at the anode. SO_4^{2-} ions are not discharged. Sulphuric acid provides the conducting medium.

Some typical electrolytic reactions are given below:

Electrolyte	Electrode	Cathode reaction	Anode reaction
Water	Pt	$2H^+ + 2e^- \rightarrow H_2$	$2OH^- \rightarrow H_2O + \dfrac{1}{2}O_2 + 2e^-$
Silver nitrate	Ag	$Ag^+ + e^- \rightarrow Ag$	$Ag \rightarrow Ag^+ + e^-$
	Pt	$Ag^+ + e^- \rightarrow Ag$	$2OH^- \rightarrow H_2O + \dfrac{1}{2}O_2 + 2e^-$
Copper chloride	Pt	$Cu^{2+} + 2e^- \rightarrow Cu$	$\left[\begin{array}{l} 2Cl^- \rightarrow Cl_2 + 2e^- \\ 2OH^- \rightarrow H_2O + \dfrac{1}{2}O_2 + 2e^- \end{array}\right.$
	Cu	$Cu^{2+} + 2e^- \rightarrow Cu$	$Cu \rightarrow Cu^{2+} + 2e^-$
Sodium chloride	Pt	$2H^+ + 2e^- \rightarrow H_2$	$2Cl^- \rightarrow Cl_2 + 2e^-$
	Hg	$2Na^+ + 2e^- \rightarrow 2Na$	$2Cl^- \rightarrow Cl_2 + 2e^-$

13.3 FARADAY'S LAWS OF ELECTROLYSIS

Faraday studied a quantitative relationship between the quantity of electricity passed through an electrolyte and the amount of electrolysis occurred at the electrodes. His results may be expressed in two simple and fundamental laws of electrolysis.

First Law: The amount of any substance deposited or liberated at an electrode is directly proportional to the quantity of electricity passed through the electrolyte. If W is the mass of the substance deposited or liberated and Q the quantity of electricity passed, then mathematically,

$$W \propto Q$$

Since Q is the product of the current and time, $Q = It$, therefore,

$$W \propto It$$

$$W = ZIt \qquad\qquad\qquad ...(13.1)$$

where Z is a proportionality constant and is called the electrochemical equivalent. If in the above equation, $I = 1$ ampere and $t = 1$ second, then

$$W = Z \qquad \qquad ...(13.2)$$

Hence, the electrochemical equivalent of a substance is defined as the mass of the substance deposited by the passage of a current of one ampere for 1 second (1 coulomb).

Second Law: If the same quantity of electricity is passed through different electrolytes, the amounts of different substances deposited or dissolved are proportional to their chemical equivalent masses.

To illustrate this, consider two solutions of $AgNO_3$ and $CuSO_4$ in series and the same quantity of electricity be passed through them. After sometime the cathodes are weighed. It will be seen that

$$\frac{\text{Mass of silver deposited}}{\text{Mass of copper deposited}} = \frac{\text{Equivalent mass of silver}}{\text{Equivalent mass of copper}}$$

$$= \frac{107.87}{31.80} \qquad \qquad ...(13.3)$$

Since the amount of deposition is proportional to the chemical equivalent, it follows that the same quantity of electricity would be required to produce 1g equivalent of any substance by electrolysis. This quantity of electricity which can liberate 1g equivalent of any substance is called 1 faraday of electricity, F and its value is 96485 coulombs equiv^{-1}.

If E_1 and E_2 be the chemical equivalents of two substances with electrochemical equivalents Z_1 and Z_2, then

$$\frac{E_1}{E_2} = \frac{Z_1}{Z_2} \qquad \qquad ...(13.4)$$

i.e., the electrochemical equivalents are proportional to the chemical equivalents of the substances.

Since 1 faraday liberates 1 g equivalent of the substance, it follows that electrochemical equivalent, by definition, would be equal to the equivalent mass divided by F, i.e.,

$$Z = \frac{\text{Equivalent mass}}{F} = \frac{\text{Equivalent mass}}{96485}$$

For silver its value is

$$\frac{107.87}{96485} = 0.001118 \text{ g}$$

Significance of the Second Law: Since 1 g equivalent mass of any ion requires one faraday of electricity, it follows that the amount of charge carried by one gram equivalent of any ion is one faraday. If n is the valency of the ion, then its one g ion contains n g equivalents and, therefore, carries n faradays, i.e., nF coulombs of electricity. Since one gram ion of a substance contains N_A ions (6.023×10^{23}), therefore, the charge carried by any ion is equal to nF/N_A coulombs. For a univalent ion $n = 1$, therefore, the unit of electric charge is $96485/(6.023 \times 10^{23}) = 1.602 \times 10^{-19}$ coulomb.

Problem 13.1: A current of 0.1 ampere is passed through an aqueous copper sulphate solution for 15 minutes using platinum electrodes. Calculate (i) the amount of copper deposited at the cathode, (ii) number of copper atoms deposited, and (iii) the volume of oxygen liberated at the anode at STP.

Solution: (i) Amount of copper deposited

$$= \frac{(15 \times 60 \text{ s}) \, (1 \text{ ampere}) \left(63.54/2 \text{ g equiv}^{-1}\right)}{\left(96845 \text{ ampere-second equiv}^{-1}\right)}$$

$$= 0.02963 \text{ g}$$

(*ii*) Number of atoms deposited

$$= \frac{(0.02963 \text{ g}) \left(6.023 \times 10^{23} \text{ atom mol}^{-1}\right)}{\left(63.54 \text{ g mol}^{-1}\right)}$$

$$= 2.808 \times 10^{20}$$

(*iii*) Amount of oxygen liberated

$$= \frac{(15 \times 60s)(0.1 \text{ ampere})\left(8 \text{ g equiv}^{-1}\right)}{\left(96485 \text{ ampere-second equiv}^{-1}\right)}$$

$$= 7.459 \times 10^{-3}\text{g}$$

Therefore, the volume of oxygen liberated at *STP* is

$$= \frac{\left(7.459 \times 10^{-3}\text{ g}\right)\left(0.0821 \text{ L atm K}^{-1} \text{ mol}^{-1}\right)(298 \text{ K})}{\left(32 \text{ g mol}^{-1}\right)(1 \text{ atm})}$$

$$= 0.05703 \text{ L}$$

$$= 0.05703 \text{ dm}^3$$

Problem 13.2: In a cell containing a solution of silver nitrate, a certain amount of current was passed for 3 hours. The amount of silver deposited was found to be 60.8 g. Calculate the current strength.

Solution:

Since

$$W = ItZ$$

$$I = \frac{W}{tZ} = \frac{W \times F}{t \times \text{equivalent mass}}$$

$$= \frac{(60.8 \text{ g})\left(96485 \text{ coulomb equiv}^{-1}\right)}{(3 \times 60 \times 60s)\left(107.87 \text{ g equiv}^{-1}\right)}$$

$$= 5.036 \text{ coulomb s}^{-1}$$

$$= 5.036 \text{ ampere}$$

Problem 13.3: A current of 1.7 ampere is passed through 300 ml of 0.16 M ZnSO$_4$ solution for 230s with a current efficiency of 90%. Calculate the molarity of the solution after deposition of Zn. Assume that the volume of the solution remains constant.

Solution:

Quantity of electricity passed

$$= 1.7 \text{ ampere} \times 230 \times \frac{90}{100} \times \text{second}$$

$$= 351.9 \text{ C}$$

Moles of zinc deposited

$$= \frac{351.9 \times 0.5}{96500}$$

$$= 0.0018$$

Moles of zinc before electrolysis $= \dfrac{300 \times 0.16}{1000}$

$= 0.048$

Hence moles of zinc left in the solution $= 0.048 - 0.0018$

$= 0.0462$

Therefore the molarity of the solution $= \dfrac{0.0462 \times 1000}{300}$

$= 0.154 \text{ M}$

13.4 CONDUCTANCE OF ELECTROLYTES

Solutions, like metallic conductors, obey Ohm's law which relates the *EMF* applied to a conductor and the strength of the current flowing through it. Ohm's law states that *the current strength (I) is directly proportional to the applied EMF (E), and inversely proportional to the resistance (R) of the conductor.* Thus

$$I = \frac{E}{R} \qquad \qquad \qquad ...(13.5)$$

where E is the voltage in volts, I the current in ampere and R the resistance in ohms*.

Equation (13.5) can be written as

$$\text{Ampere} = \frac{\text{Volt}}{\text{Ohm}}$$

The resistance of any uniform conductor varies directly as its length (*l* metre) and inversely to its area of cross section (*A* metre^2), so that

$$R \propto \frac{l}{A}$$

or $$R = \rho \frac{l}{A} \qquad \qquad \qquad ...(13.6)$$

where ρ (rho) is a constant for the given conductor and is called *the specific resistance or resistivity*. Its units are ohm m.

If in the above equation $l = 1$ m and $A = 1$ m^2, then $R = \rho$. Hence the specific resistance is the resistance of a conductor of unit length and unit area of cross section. In other words, specific resistance is the resistance of a metre cube of the material.

---

*In SI system, the units of current, potential (*EMF*) and resistance are ampere, volt and ohm respectively. The ampere is defined as the invariable current of such strength which deposits 0.001118 g of silver in one second when passed through an aqueous solution of silver nitrate. Quantity of electricity passing through a conductor is the product of current strength and time and is called coulomb. The coulomb is the quantity of electricity carried by a current of 1 ampere in 1 second. A volt is defined as the difference in potential required to send a current of 1 ampere through a resistance of 1 ohm. An ohm (W) is defined as the resistance at 0°C of a column of mercury of uniform cross section 106.3 cm long and containing 14.4521 g of mercury.

The specific conductance or conductivity of any conductor is defined as the reciprocal of specific resistance. It is represented by κ (kappa).

Since

$$\kappa = \frac{1}{\rho}$$

Eq. (13.6) becomes

$$R = \frac{1}{\kappa} \frac{l}{A} \qquad \qquad ...(13.7)$$

or

$$\kappa = \frac{1}{R} \frac{l}{A} \qquad \qquad ...(13.8)$$

Since the resistance is measured in ohm (Ω), the units of κ are ohm^{-1} m^{-1} (Ω^{-1} m^{-1}) or siemen m^{-1}. Ω^{-1} or reciprocal ohm is sometimes called mho.

The conductance L is defined as the reciprocal of the resistance, so that Eq. (13.8) becomes

$$L = \frac{1}{R} = \kappa \frac{A}{l} \ \text{ohm}^{-1} \qquad \qquad ...(13.9)$$

Now if $l = 1$ m and $A = 1$ m^2, then

$$L = \kappa$$

Hence the specific conductance κ is *the conductance of a material of a unit length and unit area of cross section.* Alternatively, the specific conductance is the conductance of a one metre cube of the material. For electrolytic solutions, the specific conductance is the conductance of a 1 metre cube of the solution.

13.5 EQUIVALENT CONDUCTANCE AND MOLAR CONDUCTANCE

Although, the specific conductance is a property of the conducting medium, in dealing with solutions of electrolytes, a quantity of greater significance is *the equivalent conductance,* Λ. The equivalent conductance of an electrolyte is defined as *the conductance of a volume of solution containing one gram equivalent of the electrolyte placed between two parallel electrodes 1 metre apart,* Λ is measured from the specific conductance. If C is the concentration of a solution in gram equivalent per m^3, then the volume containing one equivalent of the electrolyte is $1/C$ m^3. If κ is the specific conductance (in ohm^{-1} m^{-1}), then the equivalent conductance is given as

$$\Lambda = \kappa V = \frac{\kappa}{C} \ \text{ohm}^{-1} \text{m}^2 \text{equiv}^{-1} \qquad \qquad ...(13.10)$$

However, if C is expressed in g equivalent per litre, then the volume containing 1 g equivalent is $1000/C$ cm^3. If κ is the conductance of a centimetre cube of the solution, then the conductance of $1000/C$ cm^3 of the solution will be

$$\Lambda = \kappa V = \frac{1000\kappa}{C} \ \text{ohm}^{-1} \text{cm}^2 \text{equiv}^{-1} \qquad \qquad ...(13.11)$$

However, the term molar conductance (Λ_m) is often used in place of equivalent conductance. It is defined as the conductivity per unit molar concentration and is expressed as

$$\Lambda_m = \frac{\kappa}{C} \qquad\qquad ...(13.12)$$

where C is the concentration of the electrolyte in mol m^{-3}. It is usually expressed in siemen centimetre squared per mole (Scm^2 mol^{-1}) is CGS units. In *SI* units it is expressed as S m^2 mol^{-1}.

The molar conductivity of an electrolyte would be independent of concentration if κ were proportional to the concentration of the electrolyte. However, in practice, the molar conductivity is found to vary with concentration.

Problem 13.4: A cell with electrodes that are 2×10^{-4} m^2 in area and 0.1 m apart is filled with 0.1×10^3 mol m^{-3} aqueous solution of NaCl. The molar conductance is 106.7×10^{-4} S mol^{-1} m^2 at 298 K. If the applied *EMF* across the electrodes is 50 volts, calculate the current in ampere flowing through the cell.

Solution: From Eq. (13.10)

$$\Lambda = \frac{\kappa}{C}$$

or

$$\kappa = \Lambda C$$
$$= (0.1 \times 10^3 \text{ mol m}^{-3}) (106.7 \times 10^{-4} \text{ S mol}^{-1}\text{m}^2)$$
$$= 1.067 \text{ S m}^{-1}$$

From Eq. (13.7)

$$R = \frac{1}{\kappa} \frac{l}{A}$$

$$= \frac{(0.1 \text{ m})}{\left(1.067 \text{ S m}^{-1}\right)\left(2 \times 10^{-4}\text{m}^2\right)}$$

$$= 468.6 \text{ ohm}$$

Hence

$$I = \frac{E}{R} = \frac{50 \text{ V}}{468.6 \text{ ohm}}$$

$$= 0.1067 \text{ ampere}$$

13.6 MEASUREMENT OF CONDUCTANCE

Measurement of conductance of a solution amounts to the determination of the resistance of the solution and use of Eq. (13.9). The familiar Wheatstone bridge is generally employed to measure resistance of the solution. The arrangement of the apparatus is shown in Fig. 13.1. C is a cell containing the electrolyte (solution of which the resistance is to be measured) and R_s is a resistance box by which the resistance can be changed. S is a source of alternating current. Direct current cannot be used as it causes polarization and thereby changes the resistance of the solution. G is a current detecting device. AB is a uniform slide wire across which moves a contact point X. To balance the bridge, the contact point X is moved along the resistance wire AB until no current is detected. When this condition is reached, the resistances in the arms of the bridge are related by

$$\frac{R_c}{R_s} = \frac{AX}{XB}$$

where R_c is the resistance of the cell and R_s is the standard resistance. The above relation holds provided the resistance of the various leads are negligible. The resistance R_s should be of such a magnitude that the bridge is balanced almost at the mid point of AB. With electrolytes at low concentrations, it is difficult to obtain a sharp balance point unless the capacity of the cell C is compensated by a variable condenser connected across R_s as shown in the figure. Since the resistance R_s is known and the ratio $\frac{AX}{XB}$ can be measured, the resistance of the cell can be calculated.

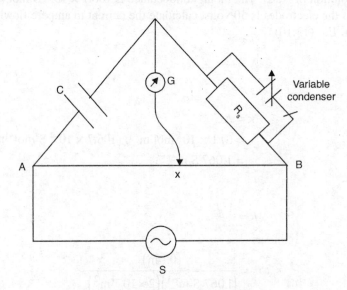

Fig. 13.1 Measurement of conductance

Kohlrausch used a small induction coil as a source of alternating current. This does not give pure alternating current and so does not eliminate polarization completely. Various types of sources for alternating current have been recommended, but a valve oscillator giving a frequency of about 1000 cycles per second is generally used. Since a current of this frequency is within the reach of the human ear, the galvanometer can be replaced by a set of earphones. At the null point, the sound should be minimum. A preferred indicator over the earphones is the cathode ray oscilloscope.

Various types of cells have been designed and are in use for the measurement of conductance of a solution. These are made of pyrex glass fitted with electrodes of platinum or gold. To overcome the imperfections in the current and the other effects at the electrodes, these are coated with a layer of finely divided platinum black. This is achieved by electrolysing a 3% solution of chloroplatinic acid containing a little of lead acetate. The distance between the electrodes is determined by the conductance of the solution to be measured. For highly conducting solutions, the electrodes are widely spaced whereas for low conducting solutions the electrodes are mounted near each other. In Fig. 13.2 are shown some cells commonly employed in the laboratory for conductance measurements.

Conductance Water: For conductance measurement, specially pure water known as conductance water is used. Conductance water for most of the conductivity measurements is obtained by double distillation of distilled water containing a small amount of potassium permanganate and potassium hydroxide. It has a specific conductance of 0.8×10^{-4} S m^{-1} at 298 K mainly due to dissolved carbon dioxide from the air. Sometimes this is known as "equilibrium water". Purest water absolutely free from air is known 'as ultra pure water' and is required only for most accurate work. It has a specific conductance of 5.8×10^{-6} S m^{-1} at 298 K. For accurate measurements conductance of water should be subtracted from the conductance of solution.

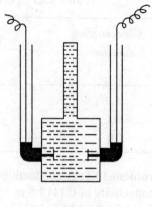

Cell Constant: According to Eq. (13.9), the specific conductance of any electrolytic conductor is given by

$$\kappa = L\left(\frac{l}{A}\right)$$

$$= \frac{1}{R}\left(\frac{l}{A}\right) \qquad \qquad ...(13.13)$$

where l may be taken as the distance between the electrodes in the conductance cell and A is the area of cross section of each electrodes. For a given cell, l and A are constant, and the quantity (l/A) is called the *cell constant*. Equation (13.13) thus reduces to

$$\kappa = \frac{1}{R} \text{ (cell constant)}$$

$$= \text{(conductance)} \times \text{(cell constant)}$$

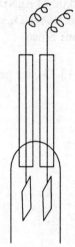

To obtain the value of the cell constant, it is necessary to determine l and A directly. Instead, it is measured by a solution of known specific conductance. Potassium chloride solutions are invariably used for this purpose, since their conductances have been measured with sufficient accuracy in cells of known dimensions. A given solution of potassium chloride of specific conductance κ' is placed in the cell and its resistance R' is measured.

Fig. 13.2 Cells for measurement of conductance

The cell constant is then equal to $\kappa'R'$. If the resistance of the unknown solution is R then its specific conductance is given by

$$\kappa = \frac{\text{cell constant}}{\text{resistance}}$$

The molar conductance is then obtained with the help of Eq. (13.12)

$$\Lambda_m = \frac{\kappa}{C}$$

Table 13.1 shows the specific conductance of 0.01 N, 0.1 N and 1.0 N aqueous potassium chloride solutions at several temperatures.

Table 13.1 Specific Conductance of Aqueous Potassium Chloride Solutions

Concentration	Specific conductance (Sm^{-1})		
mol. dm^{-3}	273 K	291 K	298 K
1.0	6.5170	9.7840	11.1900
0.1	0.7140	1.1166	1.2890
0.0	0.0774	0.1221	0.1413

Problem 13.5: A conductivity cell was filled with 0.01 M KCl which was known to have a specific conductivity of 0.1413 S m^{-1} at 298 K. Its measured resistance at 298 K was 94.3 ohms. When the cell filled with 0.02 M $AgNO_3$ its resistance was 50.3 ohms. Calculate (i) the cell constant, (ii) the specific conductance of $AgNO_3$ solution.

Solution: Since
$$\kappa = 0.1413 \text{ S m}^{-1}$$
$$R = 94.3 \text{ ohm}$$

Using Eq. (13.13), we get

(i)
$$\kappa = \frac{1}{R}\left(\frac{l}{A}\right)$$

or
$$\left(\frac{l}{A}\right) = \text{cell constant} = \kappa R$$

$$= (0.1413 \text{ S m}^{-1}) (94.3 \text{ ohm})$$
$$= 13.32 \text{ m}^{-1}$$

(ii) Now
$$R = 50.3 \text{ ohm}$$

$$\frac{l}{A} = 13.32 \text{ m}^{-1}$$

Therefore
$$\kappa = \frac{1}{R}\left(\frac{l}{A}\right)$$

$$= \frac{\left(13.32 \text{ m}^{-1}\right)}{(59.3 \text{ ohm})}$$

$$= 2.648 \times 10^{-1} \text{ S m}^{-1}$$

Problem 13.6: A conductance cell was calibrated by filling it with a 0.02 M solution of potassium chloride ($\kappa = 0.2768$ S m^{-1}) and measuring the resistance at 298 K, which was found to be 457.3 ohm. The cell was then filled with a calcium chloride solution containing 0.555 g of $CaCl_2$ per litre. The measured resistance was 1050 ohm. Calculate (a) the cell constant for the cell, (b) the conductivity of the $CaCl_2$ solution, and (c) the molar conductivity of $CaCl_2$ at this concentration.

Solution: (a) The cell constant is given as

$$\left(\frac{l}{A}\right) = \kappa R$$

$$= (0.2768 \text{ S m}^{-1}) \ (457.3 \text{ ohm})$$
$$= 126.6 \text{ m}^{-1}$$

(b) Now,

$$\frac{l}{A} = 126.6 \text{ m}^{-1}, \quad R = 1050 \text{ ohm}$$

Therefore the conductivity of $CaCl_2$ solution is

$$\kappa = \frac{1}{R}\left(\frac{l}{A}\right)$$

$$= \frac{\left(126.6 \text{ m}^{-1}\right)}{(1050 \text{ ohm})}$$

$$= 0.1206 \text{ S m}^{-1}$$
$$= 0.001206 \text{ S cm}^{-1}$$

(c) The concentration of $CaCl_2$ solution is $\dfrac{0.555}{111.0}$ mol dm^{-3}

$$= 0.005 \text{ mol dm}^{-3}$$
$$= 5 \text{ mol m}^{-3}$$

Therefore, the molar conductance $= \dfrac{\kappa}{C}$

$$= \frac{\left(0.1206 \text{ S m}^{-1}\right)}{\left(5 \text{ mol m}^{-3}\right)}$$

$$= 0.0241 \text{ mol}^{-1} \text{ S m}^2$$

Problem 13.7: The resistance of a conductivity cell was 702 ohm when filled with 0.1 N KCl solution ($\kappa = 0.14807$ S m^{-1}) and 6920 ohm when filled with 0.01 N acetic acid solution. Calculate the cell constant and Λ_m for the acid solution.

Solution: The cell constant is given as

$$\left(\frac{l}{A}\right) = \kappa R$$

$$= (0.14807 \text{ S m}^{-1}) \ (702 \text{ ohm})$$
$$= 98.9 \text{ m}^{-1}$$
$$= 0.989 \text{ cm}^{-1}$$

The conductivity of acetic acid, $\kappa = \dfrac{1}{R}\left(\dfrac{l}{A}\right)$

$$= \frac{1}{(6920 \text{ ohm})}\left(98.9 \text{ m}^{-1}\right)$$

$$= 1.429 \times 10^{-2} \text{ S m}^{-1}$$

$$= 1.429 \times 10^{-4} \text{ S cm}^{-1}$$

Now $C = 0.01 \text{ M} = 0.01 \text{ mol dm}^{-3}$

$$= 0.01 \times 10^3 \text{ mol m}^{-3} \qquad \left(\begin{array}{l} \because 10 \text{ dm} = 1 \text{ m} \\ \text{or } 1 \text{ dm}^3 = \dfrac{1 \text{ m}^2}{10^3} \\ \qquad\quad = 10^{-3} \text{ m}^3 \end{array}\right)$$

Therefore,

$$\Lambda_m = \frac{\kappa}{C}$$

$$= \frac{\left(1.429 \times 10^{-2} \text{ S m}^{-1}\right)}{\left(0.01 \times 10^3 \text{ mol m}^{-3}\right)}$$

$$= 1.429 \times 10^{-3} \text{ mol}^{-1} \text{ S m}^2$$

13.7 VARIATION OF CONDUCTANCE WITH CONCENTRATION

We have already noted that the specific conductance of an ionic solution increases with increasing concentration. For strong electrolytes, the increase in specific conductance with increase of concentration is sharp. However, for weak electrolytes, the increase in specific conductance is more gradual. In both cases the increase in the conductance with concentration is due to an increase in the number of ions per unit volume of the solution. For strong electrolytes, which are completely ionized, the increase in specific conductance is almost proportional to the concentration. In weak electrolytes, however, the increase in specific conductance is not large due to the low ionization of the electrolytes, and consequently the specific conductance does not go up so rapidly as in the case of strong electrolytes.

Table 13.2 shows the variation of molar conductance of a number of electrolytes at various concentrations at 298 K. It is observed that in contrast to the specific conductance, the molar conductance, Λ_m invariably increases with decreasing concentration for both weak and strong electrolytes.

The above results are depicted in Fig. 13.3 in which the molar conductance, Λ_m, of electrolytes at a constant temperature is plotted against $\sqrt{C}$. It may be seen from the figure that two different types of behaviours are exhibited. The electrolytes which show a linear plot (almost straight lines) are classified as strong or true electrolytes, e.g, salts like KCl, NaCl or acids such as HCl, H_2SO_4 etc. The electrolytes which seem to approach the dilute solution limit almost tangentially are classified as weak or potential electrolytes, *e.g.*, ammonia, organic fatty acids etc. It is however, impossible to draw a sharp line of demarcation between the two categories as many substances are known to exhibit intermediate behaviour, *e.g.*, nickel sulphate. Such electrolytes are sometimes called moderately strong electrolytes.

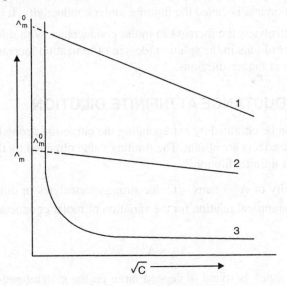

Fig. 13.3 Variation of molar conductance with concentration. (1) Strong electrolytes. (2) Moderately strong electrolytes. (3) Weak electrolytes.

Table 13.2 Molar Conductance of Electrolytes in Aqueous Solution at 298 K (10^4 Sm^2 mol^{-1})

Mol dm^{-3}	KCl	NaCl	HCl	$AgNO_3$	CH_3COOH	CH_2COONa
1.0	111.9	89.9	332.8	–	–	49.1
0.1	129.0	106.7	391.3	109.1	5.2	72.8
0.05	133.4	111.1	399.1	115.7	7.4	76.9
0.01	141.3	118.5	412.0	124.8	16.3	83.8
0.005	143.5	120.6	415.8	127.2	22.9	85.7
0.001	146.9	123.7	421.4	130.5	49.2	88.5
0.0005	147.8	124.5	422.7	131.4	67.7	89.2

The conductance of a solution depends on the number of ions and the speed with which the ions move in solution. In case of strong electrolytes the number of ions is the same at all dilutions (since strong electrolytes are completely ionized) and the variation of molar conductance with dilution is therefore due to the change in the speed of ion with dilution. In a concentrated solution of such electrolytes, the interionic effects among the oppositely charged ions would be quite appreciable. The ions may also form some ion-pairs of the type A^+B^- which would not contribute to the conductance. These interionic forces considerably lower the speed of the ions and hence the conductivity of the solution. As the dilution is increased the interionic effects decrease with the result that the ions will move more freely and independently of their co-ions and thus increase the molar conductance with dilution. At infinite dilution where the ionization is complete, and the ions are quite far apart, the interionic effects are almost absent and each ion moves completely independent of its co-ions and hence the molar conductivity increases with dilution. The molar conductance then approaches a limiting value at infinite dilution and is called the limiting molar conductivity. It is denoted by Λ_m^0 or Λ_m^∞.

In case of weak electrolytes, the increase in molar conductance with dilution is mainly due to (a) an increase in the number of ions in the solution (degree of ionization increases with dilution), and (b) smaller interionic effects at higher dilutions.

13.8 MOLAR CONDUCTANCE AT INFINITE DILUTION

An important relation can be obtained by extrapolating the curve for strong electrolytes (Fig. 13.3) to $C \to 0$ where all interionic effects are absent. The limiting value obtained by this extrapolation is called the molar conductance at infinite dilution''.

Observing the linearity of Λ_m versus $\sqrt{C}$ for strong electrolytes in dilute solutions, Kohlrausch suggested the following empirical relation for the variation of molar conductance of strong electrolytes with dilution

$$\Lambda_m = \Lambda_m^0 - b\sqrt{C} \qquad \qquad ...(13.14)$$

where b is a coefficient which is found to depend more on the stoichiometry of the electrolyte, i.e., whether it is of the form MA or M_2A than on its specific identity and Λ_m^0 is the molar conductance of the electrolyte at infinite dilution. The validity of this equation may be seen from the plot for strong electrolytes like HCl, KCl etc. To obtain Λ_m^0 of such electrolytes the curve is extrapolated to $C \to 0$ and the intercept so obtained gives the value of Λ_m^0. The same method cannot be used for obtaining Λ_m^0 for weak electrolytes because of the steep increase in Λ_m at high dilutions.

13.9 KOHLRAUSCH LAW OF INDEPENDENT MIGRATION OF IONS

The law states that *at infinite dilution, where ionization of all electrolytes is complete and where all interionic effects are absent, each ion migrates independently of its co-ion, and contributes a definite share to the total molar conductance of the electrolyte.* In other words, Λ_m^0 for any electrolyte should be the sum of the contributions of the molar conductances of the individual ions. If the molar conductance of a cation at infinite dilution is λ_+^0 and that for the anion it is λ_-^0, then according to the above law

$$\Lambda_m^0 = v_+\lambda_+^0 + v_-\lambda_-^0 \qquad \qquad ...(13.15)$$

where v_+ and v_- are the number of cations and anions per formula unit of the electrolyte, e.g., $v_+ = v_- = 1$ for HCl, NaCl etc. and $v_+ = 1$ and $v_- = 2$ for $MgCl_2$, $BaCl_2$ etc.

Kohlrausch law suggests that at the infinite dilution the conductance of an electrolyte, KCl for example, depends on independent contributions from K^+ and Cl^- ions. The independence of these contributions is seen from the difference between Λ_m^0 values of electrolytes containing a common ion

(Table 13.3). For example, when salts of potassium and lithium with a common anion are taken, the difference between $\lambda^0_{K^+}$ and $\lambda^0_{Li^+}$ is constant. The same is also true for salts with a common cation, *i.e.*, $\lambda^0_{Cl^-} - \lambda^0_{NO_3^-}$ would be constant.

Table 13.3: Kohlrausch Law of Independent Migration of Ions (Values at 298 K)

Electrolyte	$\Lambda^0_m \times 10^4$ $S\ cm^2\ mol^{-1}$	Difference $\lambda^0_{K^+} - \lambda^0_{Li^+}$	Electrolyte	$\Lambda^0_m \times 10^4$ $S\ cm^2\ mol^{-1}$	Difference $\lambda^0_{Cl^-} - \lambda^0_{NO_3^-}$
KCl	149.86		LiCl	115.03	
LiCl	115.03	34.83	LiNO₃	110.10	4.93
KNO₃	144.96		KCl	149.86	
LiNO₃	110.10	34.86	KNO₃	144.96	4.90
KOH	271.50		HCl	426.16	
LiOH	236.70	34.80	HNO₃	421.30	4.86

The table shows that these differences are independent of the other ionic species present. It should be noted that Kohlrausch law gives no way of finding the contributions of the individual ions. These values are obtained from transference number measurements.

In case of weak electrolytes, Λ^0_m cannot be obtained directly. In fact, the law of independent migration of ions is used for calculating the limiting molar conductance Λ^0_m for weak electrolytes. Thus in calculating Λ^0_m for acetic acid the molar conductance for three strong electrolytes, namely, HCl, NaCl and NaAc should be known. Therefore, one can write

$$\Lambda^0_{m,\ HAc} = \Lambda^0_{m,\ HCl} + \Lambda^0_{m,\ NaAc} - \Lambda^0_{m,\ NaCl} \qquad \qquad ...(13.16)$$

$$= \lambda^0_{Na^+} + \lambda^0_{Ac^-} + \lambda^0_{H^+} + \lambda^0_{Cl^-} - \lambda^0_{Na^+} - \lambda^0_{Cl^-}$$

$$= \lambda^0_{H^+} + \lambda^0_{Ac^-}$$

Since the quantities on the right hand side of Eq. (13.16) are experimentally determined and are known, hence $\Lambda^0_{m,\ HAc}$ can be calculated.

Values of some ionic conductivities at infinite dilutions at 298 K are given in Table 13.4.

Table 13.4: Ionic Conductivities at Infinite Dilution at 298 K

Cation	Conductance × 10^4 $(Sm^2\ mol^{-1})$	Anion	Conductance × 10^4 $(Sm^2\ mol^{-1})$
H^+	349.8	OH^-	197.6
Li^+	38.7	Cl^-	76.3
Na^+	50.1	Br^-	78.4
K^+	73.5	I^-	76.8
Ag^+	61.9	NO_3^-	71.4
NH_4^+	73.4	CH_3COO^-	40.9
$\frac{1}{2}Mg^{2+}$	53.1	$\frac{1}{2}SO_4^{2-}$	79.8
$\frac{1}{2}Ca^{2+}$	59.5	ClO_4^-	68.0
$\frac{1}{2}Cu^{2+}$	54.0		
$\frac{1}{2}Ba^{2+}$	63.6		
$\frac{1}{3}La^{3+}$	68.0		

* For NaCl, 1 equivalent is 1 mole whereas for $CaCl_2$, 1 equivalent is 1/2 mole; 1 mole of $CaCl_2$ gives 1 mole of Ca^{2+} ions each having a charge of +2 and 2 moles of Cl^- ions each having a charge of −1 unit. For an ion with multiple charge, we write $\frac{1}{2}Mg^{2+}$, $\frac{1}{2}SO_4^{2-}$ etc., to remind that conductance of 1 equivalent and not of 1 mole. Thus, for Na_2SO_4 we write

$$\Lambda^0_{m\ Na_2SO_4} = 2\lambda^0_{Na^+} + \lambda^0_{SO_4^{2-}}$$

Problem 13.8: The molar conductivities at infinite dilution of KCl, KNO_3 and $AgNO_3$ at 298 K are 0.01499 S m^2 mol^{-1}, 0.01450 Sm^2 mol^{-1} and 0.01334 S m^2 mol^{-1} respectively. What is the molar conductivity of AgCl at infinite dilution at this temperature?

 Solution: Since $\qquad \Lambda^0_{m,AgCl} = \Lambda^0_{m,AgNO_3} + \Lambda^0_{m,KCl} - \Lambda^0_{m,KNO_3}$

$$= (0.01334 + 0.01499 - 0.01450)\ S\ m^2\ mol^{-1}$$

$$= 0.01383\ S\ m^2\ mol^{-1}$$

Problem 13.9: The molar conductances of aqueous sodium acetate, hydrochloric acid and sodium chloride at infinite dilution are 0.0091 Sm^2 mol^{-1}, 0.0425 Sm^2 mol^{-1} and 0.01281 Sm^2 mol^{-1} respectively. Calculate the molar conductance of acetic acid at infinite dilution.

$$\Lambda^0_{m,HAc} = \Lambda^0_{m,NaAc} + \Lambda^0_{m,HCl} - \Lambda^0_{m,\,NaCl}$$

$$= (0.0091 + 0.0425 - 0.01281)\,Sm^2\,mol^{-1}$$

$$= 0.03879\,Sm^2\,mol^{-1}$$

Problem 13.10: Calculate the molar conductance of aqueous $BaSO_4$ solution at infinite dilution.

Given $\Lambda^0_{m,\,Ba(NO_3)_2} = 270.08 \times 10^{-4}\,Sm^2\,mol^{-1}$; $\Lambda^0_{m,H_2SO_4} = 859.20 \times 10^{-4}\,Sm^2\,mol^{-1}$

and $\qquad \Lambda^0_{HNO_3} = 421.24 \times 10^{-4}\,Sm^2\,mol^{-1}$.

Solution: The molar conductance of $BaSO_4$ is given as

$$\Lambda^0_{m,BaSO_4} = \Lambda^0_{m,\,Ba(NO_3)_2} + \Lambda^0_{m,H_2SO_4} - 2\Lambda^0_{m,HNO_3}$$

$$= \left(270.08 \times 10^{-4} + 859.2 \times 10^{-4} - 842.48 \times 10^{-4}\right)\,Sm^2\,mol^{-1}$$

$$= 286.80\,sm^2\,mol^{-1}$$

13.10 THE CONDUCTANCE RATIO

The molar conductance of a weak electrolyte falls off more rapidly with increasing concentration than predicted by equation (13.10). It has been stated previously that the conductance of a solution depends on the number of ions and their speeds. If it is assumed that the speed does not vary appreciably with dilution then the increase in conductivity with dilution is mainly due to the formation of more ions in solution. At infinite dilution, the electrolyte is completely ionized and all the ions take part in conducting the current. At appreciable concentration, only a fraction of the electrolyte is ionized and the degree of ionization α, of the electrolyte is given as

$$K_a = \frac{C\alpha^2}{(1-\alpha)}$$

where C is the concentration of the electrolyte. On solving the above quadratic equation for α, we get

$$\alpha = \frac{K_a}{2C}\left\{\left(1 + \frac{4C}{K_a}\right)^{1/2} - 1\right\} \qquad\qquad ...(13.17)$$

If the molar conductivity of the hypothetical fully ionised electrolyte is Λ'_m, then since only a fraction α is actually present as ions in the actual solution, the measure of molar conductivity Λ_m is given by

$$\Lambda_m = \alpha \cdot \Lambda'_m$$

When the concentration of ions in solution is very low, one can take Λ'_m by its limiting value, $\left(\Lambda^0_m\right)$ and therefore the above equation can be written as

$$\Lambda_m = \alpha \, \Lambda_m^0$$

or

$$\alpha = \frac{\Lambda_m}{\Lambda_m^0}$$

However, such an explanation cannot be applied to strong electrolytes and in such cases the quan-

tity $\dfrac{\Lambda_m}{\Lambda_m^0}$ is termed as the *conductance ratio*.

13.11 EFFECT OF OTHER FACTORS ON CONDUCTANCE

(*a*) **Effect of Temperature and Pressure:** The conductance of all electrolytes increases with increasing temperature. The variation of molar conductance at infinite dilution with temperature is given by an empirical equation

$$\Lambda_{m,\,t}^0 = \Lambda_{m,25}^0 = \left[1 + x(t - 25)\right] \qquad \qquad ...(13.18)$$

where $\Lambda_{m,\,t}^0$ and $\Lambda_{m,25}^0$ are the values of molar conductances at $t\,^\circ C$ and $25^\circ C$ respectively, and x is a constant for each electrolyte. For salts x is about 0.022 to 0.025 and for acids and bases it is usually 0.016 to 0.019. It means that molar conductance increases approximately by 2% for every one degree rise in temperature. For strong electrolytes, even at appreciable concentration, Eq. (13.18) holds good, whereas in case of weak electrolytes, the variation of Λ_m with temperature is not so regular. The rise in conductance with temperature is due to the decrease in the viscosity of the solution, increase in the speed of ions and an increase in the degree of ionization in case of weak electrolytes.

The molar conductance increases slightly with increase in pressure. The effect is mainly through changes in the viscosity of the medium which decreases by an increase in pressure. Consequently, the molar conductance of the solution will increase with rise in pressure.

(*b*) **Effect of Solvent:** In solvents of low dielectric constants, having small ionizing effect on the electrolytes, the electrostatic forces between oppositely charged ions would be appreciable and molar conductance will have small value. However, solvents with high dielectric constants yield more conducting solutions.

(*c*) **Viscosity of the Medium:** The dependence of conductance on viscosity of the medium is given by *Walden's rule*, according to which the molar conductance of an electrolyte is inversely proportional to the viscosity of the medium, *i.e.*,

$$\Lambda_m^0 \, \eta_0 = \text{constant}$$

where Λ_m^0 is the molar conductance at infinite dilution and η_0 is coefficient of viscosity of the solvent. If ions are not solvated, *i.e.*, they have the same size in all the solvents, then it follows from Walden rule that $\Lambda_m^0 \, \eta_0$ should be constant and independent of the nature of the solvent. This is true only for ions like tetra-alkyl ammonium cations which are not solvated. Ions where extensive solvation occurs, effective radii of the ions will not be constant and Walden rule will not be obeyed.

(*d*) **Effect of High Voltages and High Frequencies:** An increase in molar conductance is observed when conductance measurements are carried out at high voltages (2000 volt cm^{-1}). This influence of high voltage on conductance is known as the Wien effect. At such high voltages, the ions move quite fast in solution and are practically free from the influence of oppositely charged ions. The conductance, therefore, increases and approaches a limiting value for infinite dilution. The Wien effect provides one of the strongest evidences for the existence of an ionic atmosphere.

Molar conductance increases when the frequency of the alternating current is increased. At sufficiently high frequency of the alternating current, the retardation of ionic speed is considerably lowered and the conductance shows an enhanced value. This influence of frequency on the molar conductance is known as Debye-Falkenhagen effect and can be explained better in terms of interionic attraction theory.

13.12 THE INTERIONIC ATTRACTION THEORY

To account for the variation of molar conductance Λ_m with concentration in case of strong electrolytes which exist in the form of ions even in solid state, Debye and Hückel in 1923 proposed the interionic attraction theory.

The basic principle of this theory is that as a result of electrostatic attraction between oppositely charged ions, each ion in solution is surrounded by an *ionic atmosphere* of opposite charge. The ionic atmosphere is spherically and symmetrically distributed in the absence of an external applied electric field (Fig. 13.4 (*a*)). When a potential is applied across the solution, ions move towards oppositely charged electrodes. In the movement of ions, say a cation, moving towards the cathode and the negative ionic atmosphere towards the anode, the ionic atmosphere of oppositely charged ions does not have time to adjust itself to remain spherically symmetrical around the cation. It thus lags behind, and consequently, the motion of the cation is retarded by the ionic atmosphere, for the negative charges behind would be greater than those in front of the central ion Fig. 13.4 (*b*). The force that retards will be in a direction opposite to that of the motion of the central ion. This drag on the moving ion is known as *the asymmetry effect* or *relaxation effect* because it arises from the lack of symmetry in the ionic atmosphere of a moving ion.

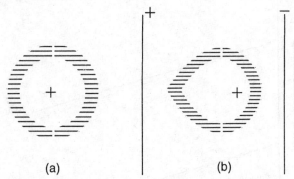

Fig. 13.4 Ionic atmosphere. (*a*) Field off. (*b*) Field on

Another factor that retards the motion of the ions arises from the tendency of the ionic atmosphere associated with the solvent molecules to move in a direction opposite to that of the ion. Cations thus have to move through a medium moving with the negative ions towards the anode. Similarly, anions have to move through solvent carrying cations in the opposite direction. The moving ions are thus forced to swim upstream against the flow of the solvent. This effect slows down the speed of the ion and is called *the electrophoretic effect*. The frictional forces of the medium which are determined by the

Stokes' law also oppose the migration of ions. When a potential is applied, these retarding forces are balanced by the electric field and the ions move with the steady velocity.

Debye and Hückel showed that these retarding effects on an ion produce a decrease in molar conductance and depend on its concentration. For a uni-univalent electrolyte, such as KCl, the following equation was derived by Debye and Hückel:

$$\Lambda_m = \Lambda_m^0 - \left[\frac{82.4}{(\varepsilon T)^{1/2} \eta} + \frac{8.20 \times 10^5 \, \Lambda_m^0}{(\varepsilon T)^{3/2}} \right] \sqrt{C} \qquad ...(13.19)$$

where ε is the dielectric constant, T is the temperature in degree absolute and η is the coefficient of viscocity of the medium. The above equation can be reduced to

$$\Lambda_m = \Lambda_m^0 - \left[A + B\Lambda_m^0 \right] \sqrt{C} \qquad ...(13.20)$$

where A and B are constants depending on the temperature and the nature of the solvent. Since the quantity in bracket is constant, Eq. (13.20) is identical in form with Eq. (13.14) proposed by Kohlrausch on empirical grounds. Table 13.5 gives the values of A and B at 298 K for a few solvents.

Table 13.5 Values of A and B at 298 K

Solvent	A	B
Water	60.2	0.229
Methanol	151.1	0.923
Ethanol	89.7	1.330
Acetonitrile	22.9	0.716

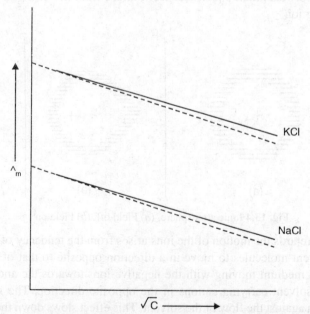

Fig. 13.5 Experimental (solid line) and theoretical (dashed lines) molar conductances

The validity of Eq. (13.20) is tested by plotting the experimental value of Λ_m against $\sqrt{C}$. Λ_m^0 obtained by extrapolation is then compared with the limiting value predicted by the equation. Some comparisons between theory and experiments are shown in Fig. 13.5. The agreement is usually good at very low concentration, however, in more concentrated solutions, the conductivity is higher than that predicted by Eq. (13.20).

13.13 ACTIVITIES AND ACTIVITY COEFFICIENT OF STRONG ELECTROLYTES

The chemical potential of a strong, completely dissociated electrolyte MX is equal to the sum of the chemical potentials of the cation and anion

$$\mu_{MX} = \mu_{M^+} + \mu_{X^-}$$

Since

$$\mu = \mu^0 + RT \ln a$$

Therefore

$$\mu_{MX}^0 + RT \ln a_{MX} = \mu_{M^+}^0 + RT \ln a_{M^+} + \mu_{X^-}^0 + RT \ln a_{X^-} \qquad ...(13.21)$$

where μ_{MX}^0, $\mu_{M^+}^0$ and $\mu_{X^-}^0$ are the chemical potentials of MX, M^+(cation) and X^-(anion) in the standard state. Further

$$\mu_{MX}^0 = \mu_{M^+}^0 + \mu_{X^-}^0$$

then Eq. (13.21) yields

$$\ln a_{MX} = \ln a_{M^+} + \ln a_{X^-}$$

or

$$a_{MX} = \left(a_{M^+}\right)\left(a_{X^-}\right) \qquad ...(13.22)$$

The activity of a substance is usually given as the product of the concentration of the substance and activity coefficient (γ). If the concentration is expressed in molality (m), then the activities of the cation and anion is given as

$$a_{M^+} = m\gamma_+ \text{ and}$$

$$a_{X^-} = m\gamma_-$$

Then

$$a_{MX} = \left(m\gamma_+\right)\left(m\gamma_-\right)$$

$$= m^2\gamma_\pm^2 \qquad ...(13.23)$$

where $\gamma_\pm$ is the mean ionic activity coefficient for the electrolyte having univalent cation and univalent anion, i.e., for 1-1 electrolyte

$$\gamma_\pm = \left(\gamma_+\gamma_-\right)^{1/2}$$

The mean ionic activity coefficient is important and can be determined experimentally whereas individual ionic activity coefficient can not be determined. In dilute solution, when the concentration of MX $\rightarrow 0$, $\gamma_\pm$ approaches unity. For an electrolyte with polyvalent ions,

$$M_x X_y \rightleftharpoons xM^{y+} + yX^{x-}$$

where y^+ and x^- are the charges on the cation and anion respectively. The activity of the electrolyte is expressed as

$$a = \left(a_+^x\right)\left(a_-^y\right) \qquad \qquad ...(13.24)$$

If n is the total number of ions furnished by a single unit of $M_x X_y$, then

$$n = x + y$$

The mean activity of the electrolyte is given as

$$a_\pm = \left(a_+^x \cdot a_-^y\right)^{1/x+y} = \left(a_+^x a_-^y\right)^{1/n}$$

The activity of the ion is related to its concentration through the relation

$$a_+ = m_+ \gamma_+$$

$$a_- = m_- \gamma_-$$

Substituting these values in Eq. (13.24), we get

$$a = \left[\left(m_+\gamma_+\right)^x \left(m_-\gamma_-\right)^y\right]$$

$$= \left[\left(m_+^x \cdot m_-^y\right)\left(\gamma_+^x \cdot \gamma_-^y\right)\right]$$

The mean activity is given as

$$a_\pm = a^{1/n} = \left(m_+^x \cdot m_-^y\right)^{1/n} \left(\gamma_+^x \cdot \gamma_-^y\right)^{1/n} \qquad \qquad ...(13.24\ (a))$$

The quantity $\left(\gamma_+^x \cdot \gamma_-^y\right)^{1/n}$ is the mean activity coefficient $(\gamma_\pm)$ and $\left(m_+^x \cdot m_-^y\right)^{1/n}$ is the mean molality $(m_\pm)$ of the electrolyte. Hence from Eq. (13.24 (a)), we have

$$a_\pm = m_\pm \gamma_\pm$$

The mean ionic molality of a 1-1 electrolyte like NaCl is equal to m. The mean ionic molality for a 2-1 electrolyte like $CaCl_2$ is $\sqrt[3]{4m^3} = 4^{1/3} m$, for a 2-2 electrolyte like $CuSO_4$ is equal to m; for a 3-1 electrolyte like $LaCl_3$ it is $27^{1/4}$ m.

13.14 IONIC STRENGTH

Lewis and Randall introduced the concept of ionic strength to explain the non-ideal behaviour of ionic solutions in terms of interionic effects. Electrolytes having ions with multiple charge have larger effect on activity coefficient of ions than electrolytes containing only singly charged ions. The ionic strength I is a characteristic of the solution and is expressed as

$$I = \frac{1}{2} \sum_i m_i z_i^2 \qquad \qquad ...(13.25)$$

where z_i is the charge of an ion (positive for cations and negative for anions) and m_i its molality. The sum extends over all the ions present in the solution. For solution consisting of two types of ions at molalities m_+ and m_-

$$I = \frac{1}{2}\left[m_+ z_+^2 + m_- z_-^2\right] \qquad ...(13.26)$$

The ionic strength emphasizes the charge of the ions because the charge numbers occur as their squares. The ionic strength for 1-1 electrolytes like KCl, NaCl etc. is equal to its molality (m). The ionic strength for a 1-2 electrolyte is 3 m and for a 2-2 electrolyte it is 4 m.

13.15 THE DEBYE-HÜCKEL LIMITING LAW

Debye and Hückel were able to calculate the ratio of activity to the concentration of an ion in a dilute solution. The basic principle used is that the attractive forces between an ion and its surrounding ionic atmosphere reduces the activity coefficient of the electrolyte. The difference between actual and ideal free energy changes is a measure of the activity coefficient of the particular ion in a given solution. The energy and therefore chemical potential of any given central ion is lowered as a result of its electrostatic attraction with its ionic atmosphere. This concept of Debye and Hückel leads to calculate the activity coefficient at a very low concentration by the relation

$$\log \gamma_\pm = -A z_+ z_- I^{1/2} \qquad ...(13.27)$$

where A is 0.509 for an aqueous solution at 298K and I is the ionic strength of the solution.

It is a limiting law at low concentration in the same way as the ideal gas law is a limiting law at low pressure. Figure 13.6 shows the plot of $\log \gamma_\pm$ versus $\sqrt{I}$ in which solid curves are the experimental data and dashed lines are the values predicted by limiting law, Eq. 13.27. The plots show a good agreement at low concentration (molalities) indicating evidence in support of the model. However, the deviation is large at high concentration (molalities).

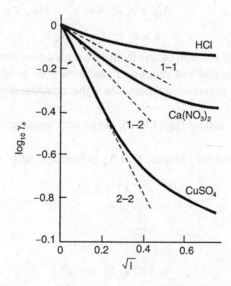

Fig. 13.6 Plot of $\log \gamma_\pm$ versus $\sqrt{I}$ for different electrolytes

13.16 ABSOLUTE VELOCITIES OF IONS OR IONIC MOBILITIES

The velocity of an ion in a solution depends on the nature of the ions, concentration of the solution, temperature and the applied potential gradient (volt cm^{-1}). *The velocity with which an ion moves under a potential gradient of 1 volt per cm in a solution is known as its ionic mobility.*

$$\text{Ionic mobility} = \frac{\text{Velocity of the ion}}{\text{Field strength}}$$

In CGS units it is expressed in $cm^2 s^{-1} V^{-1}$ while in SI units it is expressed in $m^2 s^{-1} V^{-1}$. The limiting value of ionic mobility is obtained for infinitely dilute solutions as the interionic effects are almost absent for such solutions. The ionic mobilities are proportional to the ionic conductivities.

The ionic conductivity at infinite dilution depends upon the charge and velocity of the ion. If v_+ and v_- are the number of cations of charge $Z_+ e$ and anions of charge $Z_- e$ in a solution of an electrolyte, then the molar conductance of cation is given by

$$v_+ \lambda_+^0 = k_1 \, v_+ \, z_+ \, e^- u_+ \qquad \qquad ...(13.28)$$

and the contribution of the anion is

$$v_- \lambda_-^0 = k_1 \, v_- z_- \, e^- u_- \qquad \qquad ...(13.29)$$

where u_+ and u_- are the ionic mobilities and k_1 the proportionality constant. The total conductance of the electrolytic solution is then the sum of these ionic conductances, *i.e.*,

$$\Lambda_m^0 = v_+ \lambda_+^0 + v_- \lambda_-^0$$

$$= k_1 v_+ \, z_+ \, e^- \, u_+ + k_1 \, v_- \, z_- \, e^- u_-$$

For eletroneutrality, we have

$$v_+ z_+ = v_- z_-$$

Hence

$$\Lambda_m^0 = v_+ \lambda_+^0 + v_- \lambda_-^0 = k(u_+ + u_-) \qquad \qquad (13.29)$$

where

$$k = k_1 \, v_+ \, z_+ \, e^- = k_1 \, v_- z_- \, e^-.$$

If we now consider a dilute solution of an electrolyte with a concentration of C moles being placed in a cube of 1 m side with electrodes of cross sectional area 1 m^2 at opposite faces and if an *EMF* of 1 volt is applied, *i.e.*, a unit potential gradient; then the conductance of 1 m cube is the specific conductance (κ) by definition, and by Eq. (13.12), the molar conductance is $\dfrac{\kappa}{C}$ m^2 S mol^{-1}. Since the solution is sufficiently dilute, we may assume that Λ_m is identical with Λ_m^0, then Eq. (13.29) becomes

$$\Lambda_m^0 = v_+ \lambda_+^0 + v_- \lambda_-^0$$

$$= \frac{k}{C}$$

$$\kappa = C\left(v_+ \lambda_+^0 + v_- \lambda_-^0\right) \qquad \qquad ...(13.30)$$

The current flowing through a solution is given by Ohm's law

$$I = \frac{E}{R}$$

$$I = \frac{1}{R}(E = 1V)$$

$$= L$$

$$= \kappa \text{ (here } L = \kappa)$$

From Eq. (13.30) the number of coulombs passing per unit time, *i.e.*, the quantity of charge is given by

$$I = \kappa$$

$$= C\left(v_+\lambda_+^0 + v_-\lambda_-^0\right) \qquad \qquad ...(13.31)$$

Now in one second, under a potential gradient of 1 V m^{-1}, all cations within a distance of u_+ m will pass across a given plane towards the cathode while all anions within a distance of u_- m will move in the opposite direction towards the anode. If the plane has an area of 1 m^2, all the cations in a volume u_+ m^3 and anions in u_- m^3 will move in the opposite directions in one second. The total number of moles of ions transported by the current to the two electrodes in 1 second would be

$$Cu_+ + Cu_- = C\left(u_+ + u_-\right) \qquad \qquad ...(13.32)$$

Since each mole carries 1 faraday of electricity, the total quantity of electricity per second is given by $CF(u_+ + u_-)$ coulombs. But from Eq. (13.31), we have seen that the quantity of electricity is given by $C\left(v_+\lambda_+^0 + v_-\lambda_-^0\right)$ coulombs per second. Hence we have

$$CF\left(u_+ + u_-\right) = C\left(v_+\lambda_+^0 + v_-\lambda_-^0\right)$$

or

$$F\left(u_+ + u_-\right) = v_+\lambda_+^0 + v_-\lambda_-^0 \qquad \qquad ...(13.33)$$

But from Eq. (13.29), $v_+\lambda_+^0 = ku_+$ and $v_-\lambda_-^0 = ku_-$, hence we have

$$u_+ = v_+\frac{\lambda_+^0}{F} \qquad \qquad ...(13.34)$$

and

$$u_- = v_-\frac{\lambda_-^0}{F} \qquad \qquad ...(13.35)$$

The ionic mobility in a molar solution at infinite dilution is thus obtained by dividing the molar conductance of the ion by the faraday, *i.e.*, 96485 coulombs. The values obtained are for infinitely dilute solutions and are the limiting mobilities. For appreciable concentrations they are slightly less. Values of ionic mobilities for some common ion are given in Table 13.6.

From the Table 13.6, one may notice that smaller ions of alkali metals and halogen families have lower mobilities. Ions with smaller radii having high electric field are more extensively hydrated by water molecules than larger ions. The hydrated ion, therefore, moves more slowly than a less hydrated or an unhydrated ion.

Table 13.6 Mobilities of Ions in Aqueous Solution at 298 K

Cation	$u_+ \times 10^8$ $(m^2\,V^{-1}\,s^{-1})$	Anion	$u_- \times 10^8$ $(m^2V^{-1}\,s^{-1})$
H^+	36.30	OH^-	20.50
Li^+	4.01	F^-	5.70
Na^+	5.20	Cl^-	7.90
K^+	7.62	Br^-	8.13
Ag^+	6.41	I^-	7.95
NH_4^+	7.60	NO_3^-	7.4
Ca^{2+}	6.16	SO_4^{2-}	8.27
Ba^{2+}	6.60	CO_3^{2-}	7.46
		CH_3COO^-	4.23

Experimental Measurement of Ionic Mobility: Moving boundary method is employed for measuring directly the mobility of an ion in solution. In this method the velocity of a boundary between electrolytic solutions is measured. A tube (Fig. 13.7) of uniform cross-sectional area is filled up to the mark AA' with say a solution of $CdCl_2$ and then a solution of 0.1 M potassium chloride is layered over it in such a manner that a sharp boundary between the junction of two solutions results. A current is passed through the solution. K^+ ions move towards the cathode. These are followed by the slow moving Cd^{2+} ions and the boundary moves. If dx is the distance up to which the boundary moves in time dt and E the field strength, then the ionic mobility is given by

$$u_{K^+} = \frac{dx/dt}{E} \qquad ...(13.36)$$

Problem 13.11: The conductivities of Li^+, Na^+ and K^+ are 38.7 S cm^2 mol^{-1}, 50.1 S cm^2 mol^{-1} and 73.5 S cm^2 mol^{-1} respectively. Calculate their mobilities.

Solution: Since $\quad u_{Li^+} = \dfrac{\lambda^0_{Li^+}}{F}$

$$= \frac{\left(38.7\ \text{S cm}^2\ \text{mol}^{-1}\right)}{\left(96485\ \text{coulombs mol}^{-1}\right)}$$

$$= \frac{38.7\ \text{S cm}^2}{(96845\ \text{ampere s})}$$

$$= 4.0 \times 10^{-4}\ \frac{\text{cm}^2\text{s}^{-1}}{\text{ampere}}$$

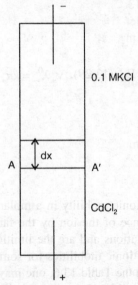

Fig. 13.7 Determination of ionic mobility with moving boundary method

$$= 4.0 \times 10^{-4} \, cm^2 V^{-1} s^{-1}$$

$$= 4.0 \times 10^{-8} \, m^2 V^{-1} s^{-1}$$

Similarly

$$u_{Na^+} = \frac{\lambda^0_{Na^+}}{F}$$

$$= \frac{\left(50.1 \, cm^2 \, mol^{-1}\right)}{\left(96485 \, coulombs \, mol^{-1}\right)}$$

$$= 5.2 \times 10^{-4} \, cm^2 V^{-1} s^{-1}$$

$$= 5.2 \times 10^{-8} \, m^2 V^{-1} s^{-1}$$

and

$$u_{K^+} = \frac{\lambda^0_{K^+}}{F}$$

$$= \frac{\left(73.5 \, S \, cm^2 \, mol^{-1}\right)}{\left(96485 \, coulombs \, mol^{-1}\right)}$$

$$= 7.6 \times 10^{-4} \, cm^2 V^{-1} s^{-1}$$

$$= 7.6 \times 10^{-8} \, m^2 V^{-1} s^{-1}$$

Problem 13.12: In a moving boundary experiment with 0.1 M KCl, the boundary moved 0.04 m in 4000 s when a current of 6×10^{-3} ampere was used. If the cross-sectional area of the tube was $0.3 \times 10^{-4} \, m^2$, and $\kappa = 1.0 \, S \, m^{-1}$ at 298 K. Calculate the mobility of K^+ ions.

Solution: The field strength is given by $= \dfrac{\left(6 \times 10^{-3} \, ampere\right)}{\left(0.3 \times 10^{-4} \, m^2\right)\left(1.0 \, Sm^{-1}\right)}$

$$= 2 \times 10^2 \, V \, m^{-1}$$

The ionic mobility of K^+ ion is

$$u_{K^+} = \frac{0.04 \, m}{\left(4000 \, s\right)\left(2 \times 10^2 \, V \, m^{-1}\right)}$$

$$= 5 \times 10^{-8} \, m^2 V^{-1} s^{-1}$$

Mobilities of Hydrogen and Hydroxyl Ions: Table 13.6 reveals that hydrogen and hydroxyl ions have exceptionally high ionic mobilities in hydroxylic solvents like water and alcohols. In water, hydrogen ion is strongly hydrated forming hydronium ion, H_3O^+, which is able to transfer a proton to the neighbouring hydrogen bonded water molecules by re-arrangement of the hydrogen bonds.

$$H-\overset{+}{\underset{|}{O}}-H \cdots O-H \cdots O-H \rightarrow H-O \cdots H-O \cdots H-O \cdots H-O^+ -H$$
$$\quad\;\; | \qquad\quad | \qquad\quad | \qquad\qquad\;\; | \qquad\quad | \qquad\quad | \qquad\quad |$$
$$\quad\;\; H \qquad\quad H \qquad\quad H \qquad\qquad H \qquad\quad H \qquad\quad H \qquad\qquad H$$

The net result is that the proton is transferred from one end of the series to the other end without actually migrating through the solution. For the transfer of another hydrogen ion from left to right, the process is followed by the molecular rotation of water molecules

$$H-O \rightarrow O-H$$
$$\quad | \qquad\quad |$$
$$\quad H \qquad\quad H$$

Similarly, the high mobility of hydroxyl ion in water is assumed to be due to a proton transfer between the hydroxyl ion and water molecules

$$O^- H-O \cdots H-O \cdots H-O \rightarrow O-H \cdots O-H \cdots O-HO^-$$
$$\quad\;\; | \qquad\quad | \qquad\quad | \qquad\quad | \qquad\quad | \qquad\qquad | \qquad\quad | \qquad\quad |$$
$$\quad\;\; H \qquad\quad H \qquad\quad H \qquad\quad H \qquad\quad H \qquad\qquad H \qquad\quad H \qquad\quad H$$

13.17 TRANSFERENCE (OR TRANSPORT) NUMBER

Fraction of the total current which is transported through a solution by the migration of cations and anions is not necessarily the same. For example, in a dilute solution of nitric acid, the nitrate ion carries only 0.16 of the total current, while the hydrogen ion carries the remaining fraction, *i.e.*, 0.84. Thus the hydrogen ions transport the larger fraction of the current because in solution they move faster than the nitrate ions. If both ions in a solution move with the same speed, each would transport the same amount of current in any given time. However, when speeds of the two ions are different, the faster ion will carry the larger fraction of the total current in any given time. The transport number (fraction of the total current carried) of the ions is thus directly proportional to their absolute velocities.

The fraction of the total current carried by an ionic species is called its transference or transport number. The transport number of the cation is denoted by t_+ and that of an anion by t_-.

Thus
$$t_+ = \frac{u_+}{u_+ + u_-} \qquad\qquad ...(13.37)$$

and
$$t_- = \frac{u_-}{u_+ + u_-} \qquad\qquad ...(13.38)$$

where u_+ and u_- are the velocities of the cations and anions respectively.

On dividing Eq. (13.37) by Eq. (13.38), we get

$$\frac{t_+}{t_-} = \frac{u_+}{u_-} \qquad\qquad ...(13.39)$$

No matter what the ratio between t_+ and t_- may be, the sum of two transference numbers will be equal to one, *i.e.*,

$$t_+ + t_- = 1 \qquad\qquad ...(13.40)$$

Migration of Ions: The fact that in electrolysis ions move with different speeds causes different changes in concentration around the electrodes. To understand the nature of these changes and their dependence on the ionic speed, consider a cell shown as in Fig. 13.8. The cell is divided into three compartments, namely anode, central and cathode by two imaginary partitions. Suppose that at the commencement of electrolysis the anode and cathode compartments contain equal number of cations and anions (say 7), as shown in Fig. 13.8 (I). Now suppose that on applying a potential, the cations only are able to move and that in given time, two of these cations move towards the cathode. The condition attained will then be as shown in Fig. 13.8 (II). At each electrode there are two ions unpaired and they must be discharged at the respective electrodes. The concentration of the anode compartment has decreased by two equivalents while that of cathode compartment remains unchanged as shown in Fig. 13.8 (III).

Now suppose that both the cations and anions move with the same speed. If 6 faradays of electricity is passed through the solution, 6 equivalents of cations and 6 equivalents of anions will be deposited at the respective electrodes. This is shown in Fig. 13.8 (IV). When these changes are taking place at the electrodes, ions migrate in the solution. As the ions are moving with the same speeds, 3 faradays of current will be carried by the cations and 3 faradays by the anions. Thus, 3 equivalents of cations will migrate from anode to cathode compartment and 3 equivalents of anions from anode to cathode compartment as shown in Fig. 13.8 (V). When these migrations are summed up, the final changes at the respective electrodes are shown in Fig. 13.8 (VI). The concentration in both the anode and cathode compartments has decreased equally. However, the concentration of the central compartment remains unchanged.

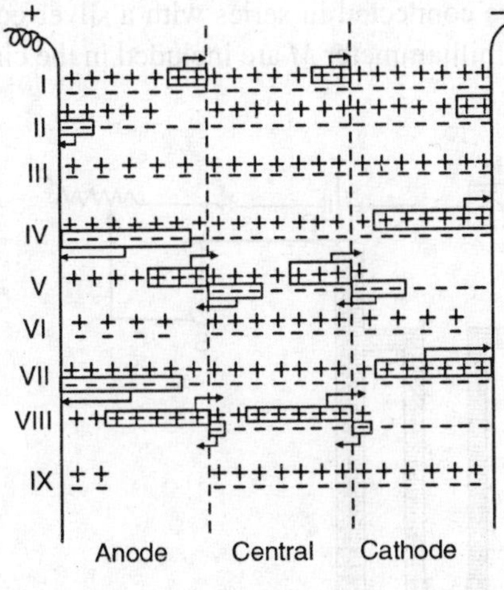

Fig. 13.8 Concentration changes due to migration of ions

Finally, suppose that the cations and anions move with different speeds so that in a given time 5 cations move towards the cathode and one anion towards the anode. In other words, the ionic speeds are in the ratio of 5:1. The quantity of electricity that passes through the solution is again 6 faradays. As before, 6 equivalents of ions will be deposited at each electrode as shown in Fig. 13.8 (VII). Of the 6 faradays, 5 faradays will be carried by the cations and only 1 faraday by the anions. Thus, 5 equivalents of the cations and one equivalent of the anions will migrate (Fig. 13.8 (VIII)). The final state after migration is given in Fig. 13.8 (IX). It is clear from the figure that there is no change in the concentration of the central compartment. However, the concentration of the cathode compartment has decreased by 1 equivalent and that of the anode compartment by 5 equivalents.

From the above considerations it is apparent that the amount of electrolyte lost from each compartment is proportional to the speed of the ions migrating away from it, namely,

$$\frac{\text{Loss in cation equivalents at anode due to migration}}{\text{Loss in anion equivalents at cathode due to migration}} = \frac{t_+}{t_-} = \frac{u_+}{u_-}$$

Since, $t_+ + t_- = 1$, the above expression can be written as

$$\frac{\text{Loss in cation equivalents at anode due to migration}}{\text{Total current passed}} = \frac{t_+}{1} = t_+$$

and similarly,

$$\frac{\text{Loss in anion equivalents at cathode due to migration}}{\text{Total current passed}} = \frac{t_-}{1} = t_-$$

13.17 DETERMINATION OF TRANSFERENCE NUMBERS

Transference numbers are generally determined by two methods:

(a) Hittorf method, and (b) the moving boundary method.

(a) **Hittorf Method:** This method is based on the fact that concentration changes occur around the electrodes due to the migration of ions. The apparatus used for the determination of transference number by Hittorf's method is shown in Fig. 13.9. The apparatus consists of a transport cell C and the electrodes are connected in series with a silver coulometer S. A variable resistance (R), a battery B and a milliammeter M are included in the circuit for the adjustment of the current to any desired value.

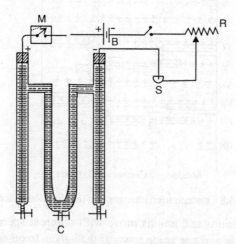

Fig. 13.9 Transference number determination by Hittorf's method

The cell is filled with the electrolyte to be investigated. The anode and cathode are fitted firmly. If the electrolyte is silver nitrate, then the silver electrodes may be used. A current of about 10-20 milliamperes is usually passed and the solution is electroysed for sufficiently long time to give an appreciable change in concentration around the electrodes. After the electrolysis, solutions are withdrawn from the electrode compartments, weighed and analysed. The quantity of current passed through the electrolyte is obtained from the increase in the mass of the cathode in the coulometer. There should be no change in the concentration of the solution of the central compartment.

Calculations: Let us assume that a solution of silver nitrate is electrolysed using silver electrodes. Suppose the mass of the solution collected from the anode compartment after electrolysis = a g.

On analysis it has been found to contain b g of silver nitrate. The mass of water in the collected anolyte = $(a - b)$ g.

If c g of anode solution contains d g of $AgNO_3$ before electrolysis then the mass of water = $(c - d)$g.

Therefore, mass of $AgNO_3$ in $(a - b)$ g of water $= \dfrac{d \times (a - b)}{(c - d)} g = x\, g\, (\text{say})$

In determining the transference number of silver ions in silver nitrate solution using silver electrodes, the nitrate ions attack the silver anode bringing silver ions in the anode compartment. Thus the concentration of the anode compartment increases. The increase of $AgNO_3$ in anolyte during electrolysis will be = $(b - x)$ g.

Let W g be the mass of silver deposited on the cathode in the coulometer. This must be the mass of silver deposited on the cathode or silver dissolved from the anode of the transport cell. This is converted into the mass of $AgNO_3$ which would be equal to $\left(\dfrac{W \times 170}{108}\right) = y\, g.$ This would have been the increase in the mass of $AgNO_3$ after electrolysis if no migration of silver ions had occurred during electrolysis away from the anode.

Loss in mass of $AgNO_3$ from anolyte due to migration of Ag^+ ions = $y - (b - x)$ g.

Transference number of Ag^+ ions,

$$t_{Ag^+} = \frac{\text{Loss of equivalents of } AgNO_3 \text{ from anolyte due to migration of } Ag^+ \text{ ions}}{\text{Total equivalents of electrolytic action on the anode}}$$

$$= \frac{y - (b - x) \div 170}{y \div 170}$$

$$= \frac{y - (b - x)}{y}$$

where 170 g is the gram equivalent mass of $AgNO_3$.

If the electrolysis of $AgNO_3$ was carried out with electrodes like Pt or Au, which are not attacked, then the calculations of the transference numbers are as follows: Suppose a g of $AgNO_3$ solution after electrolysis contains b g of $AgNO_3$, then $(a - b)$ g of water contains b g of $AgNO_3$. If c g of $AgNO_3$ solution before electrolysis contains d g of $AgNO_3$, then $(c - d)$ g of water contains d g of $AgNO_3$.

Therefore $(a - b)$ g of water will contain $\dfrac{d}{(c - d)} \times (a - b)g$ of $AgNO_3$. Let it be x g. If w g be the mass of $AgNO_3$ deposited in the coulometer, then the loss in the anode compartment is $(x - b)$ g. Therefore, the transference number is given as

$$t_+ = \frac{x - b}{w}$$

13.19 MOVING BOUNDARY METHOD

This is one of the most accurate methods used for the determination of transport number. In this method the motion of a boundary between two ionic solutions having a common ion is observed as the current flows.

Let MX be the salt placed into a tube with known uniform bore and occupy the upper part of the tube (Fig. 13.10). This solution is generally called the leading solution. The other solution having a common anion NX occupies the lower part of the tube. The solution of NX is called the indicator solution. The two electrolytes form a sharp boundary between them. The indicator solution (NX) should be denser than the leading solution (MX). The two electrolytes are so chosen that the mobility of the M^+ ion must be greater than that of N^+ ion. When a current I is passed through the cell for a time t, the boundary will move. N^+ ions will neither be able to overtake M^+ ions nor lag behind it and therefore the boundary between the electrolytes will be preserved. Let the boundary move from XX to YY (distance of x) and therefore all the M^+ ions in the volume between XX and YY must have passed through YY. Let C be the concentration of the electrolyte. If the area of cross-section of the tube is A, then $xA = V$, where V is the volume of the column of electrolyte between the boundaries before and after the experiment. Hence, the number of moles of electrolyte in this volume is equal to VC. Each mole of cation M^+ carries a charge Z_+F. Thus the charge carried by VC moles of the cation is $VC Z_+F$. The total quantity of charge supplied is It. Hence

$$t_+ = \frac{\text{Charge carried by the cation}}{\text{Total charge}}$$

$$= \frac{VCZ_+F}{It} = \frac{x \cdot A \cdot CZ_+F}{It} = \frac{xACF}{It} \quad (\because Z_+ = 1 \text{ in the present case.}) \qquad \ldots(13.41)$$

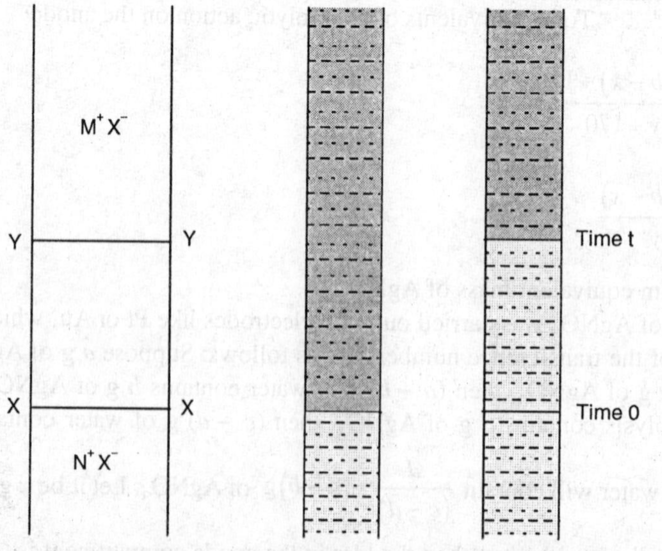

Fig. 13.10 Moving boundary method for the measurement of transport number

The results obtained by moving boundary method are more accurate. Experimentally it is easier to handle. The difficulties are experienced in establishing sharp boundaries, excessive heating by the flow of current and necessity of avoiding convection currents. However, once the boundary is established the flow of current sharpens the boundary, making this only a minor difficulty.

Table 13.7 gives the transference numbers of ions for some electrolytes in aqueous solution.

The relationship between the transference number and the ionic conductance can be derived by using the relations given by Eq. (13.34) and (13.35), i.e.,

$$t_+ = \frac{u_+}{u_+ + u_-} = \frac{\lambda_+^0}{\lambda_+^0 + \lambda_-^0} = \frac{\lambda_+^0}{\Lambda_m^0} \qquad \qquad ...(13.42)$$

Similarly,

$$t_- = \frac{\lambda_-^0}{\Lambda_m^0} \qquad \qquad ...(13.43)$$

Table 13.7 Transference Number of Cations at 298 K

Electrolyte	Concentration in mole per dm^2					
	0.01	0.02	0.05	0.1	0.2	0.5
HCl	0.825	0.827	0.829	0.831	0.834	–
KCl	0.490	0.490	0.490	0.490	0.489	0.489
NaCl	0.392	0.390	0.388	0.385	0.382	–
HNO_3	0.839	0.840	0.843	–	–	–
H_2SO_4	–	–	0.822	0.822	0.820	0.815
$AgNO_3$	0.465	0.465	0.466	0.468	–	–
NaOH	0.202	–	0.189	0.182	0.175	0.170
$CuSO_4$ (291 K)	–	0.375	0.375	0.373	0.361	0.327
CdI_2 (291 K)	0.444	0.442	0.396	0.296	0.127	0.003

It is, therefore, possible to evaluate the limiting transference numbers of the ions from the conductances at infinite dilution.

Problem 13.13: A solution of hydrochloric acid is electrolysed in a transport cell using platinum electrodes. 20.175 g of the cathode solution contained 0.175 g of Cl^- ion before electrolysis and 18.466 g of the cathode solution contained 0.146 g Cl^- ion after electrolysis. A silver coulometer connected in series had a deposit of 0.2508 g Ag. Calculate the transport number of Cl^- and H^+ ions.

Solution: After electrolysis, 18.466 g of the cathode solution contained 0.146 g of Cl^- ions

∴   Mass of water = (18.466 – 0.146) g

                 = 18.320 g

Before electrolysis, 20.175 g of the cathode solution contained 0.175 g of Cl^- ions

∴   Mass of water = (20.175 – 0.175) g

                 = 20.0 g

Now mass of Cl^- ions before electrolysis in 18.32 g of water

$$= \frac{18.32 \times 0.175}{20.0} \, g = 0.1603 \, g$$

Loss of Cl^- ions in the cathode $= (0.1603 - 0.146) = 0.0143 \, g$

0.2508 of Ag deposited in the coulometer is equivalent to $\dfrac{0.2508 \times 35.5}{108.0} \, g \, Cl^-$

Hence transport number of Cl^- ion

$$t_{Cl^-} = \frac{\text{Loss of anion equivalent in cathode}}{\text{Equivalent of current passed}}$$

$$= \frac{0.0143}{0.2508 \times 35.5/108.0} = 0.17$$

and the transport number of hydrogen ions, $t_{H^+} = 1 - 0.17 = 0.83$

Problem 13.14: In the determination of the transport number of Ag^+ ions in a Hittorf's cell, it has been found that before the experiment 6.156 g of $AgNO_3$ solution required 13.28 ml of N/50 potassium thiocyanate solution and after the electrolysis 11.69 g of anode solution required 34.74 ml of thiocyanate solution. Silver deposited in a Ag-coulometer in series when converted into silver nitrate required 18.08 ml of thiocyanate solution. Calculate the transport number of the silver ions.

   Solution: 1 ml of N/10 potassium thiocyanate = 0.010766 g Ag = 0.01699 g $AgNO_3$
   Before electrolysis 13.28 ml of N/50 thicyanate solution will contain

$$= \frac{0.01699 \times 13.28}{5} \, g \, AgNO_3 = 0.04516 \, g \, AgNO_3$$

Mass of water $= 6.156 - 00.04516 = 6.11084 \, g$

Hence mass of $AgNO_3$ per g of water $= \dfrac{0.04516}{6.11084} = 0.00739 \, g$

After electrolysis 11.69 g of anode solution will contain $= \dfrac{34.74 \times 0.01699}{5} \, g \, AgNO_3$

$$= 0.118 \, g \, AgNO_3$$

Mass of water after electrolysis $= (11.69 - 0.0118) \, g = 11.5720 \, g$

Hence mass of silver nitrate before electrolysis in 11.5720 g of water

$$= 11.5722 \times 0.00739 = 0.08563 \, g$$

Increase in silver nitrate concentration in the anode

$$= (0.118 - 0.08563) \, g = 0.03237 \, g$$

But the actual increase in silver nitrate as shown by the coulometer $= 0.06146 \, g$

Thus the fall in anode concentration due to migration

$$= 0.06146 - 0.03237 = 0.02909 \, g \, AgNO_3$$

Hence $t_{Ag^+} = \dfrac{\text{Loss due to migration}}{\text{Total equiv passed}} = \dfrac{0.02909}{0.06146} = 0.4733$

and $t_{NO_3^-} = 1 - 0.4733 = 0.5267.$

Problem 13.15: A solution of $AgNO_3$ was electrolysed between Ag electrodes. 10 g of anode solution contained 17.88 mg of $AgNO_3$ before electrolysis while 20.09 g of the anode solution contained 62.27 mg of $AgNO_3$ after electrolysis. A silver coulometer connected in series had a deposit 0.002982 equivalent of $AgNO_3$. Calculate the transport number of NO_3^- ion.

Solution:

After electrolysis 20.09 g of anode solution contained 0.06227 g $AgNO_3$

Mass of water = (20.09 − 0.06227) g = 20.02773 g

Hence 20.02773 g of water is associated with 0.06277 g $AgNO_3$

or $\quad\quad\quad$ 0.06227/170 = 0.0003664 eqiv of $AgNO_3$

10 g of solution before electrolysis contained 0.01788 g $AgNO_3$

$\therefore \quad\quad$ Mass of water = (10.00 − 0.01788) g = 9.98212 g

Mass of silver nitrate associated with 20.02773 g of water before electrolysis

$$= \dfrac{0.01788 \times 20.02773}{9.98212} \text{ g } AgNO_3$$

$$= 0.03588 \text{ g } AgNO_3$$

$$= \dfrac{0.03588}{170} \text{ eqiv. of } AgNO_3$$

$$= 0.0002111 \text{ eqiv. } AgNO_3$$

Hence the increase of $AgNO_3$ in anode chamber = 0.0003664 − 0.0002111

$$= 0.0001553 \text{ eqiv of } AgNO_3$$

But the actual increase as given by the coulometer = 0.0002982 eqiv $AgNO_3$

Hence loss due to migration = 0.0002982 − 0.0001553

$$= 0.0001429 \text{ eqiv } AgNO_3$$

and the transport number of silver ions

$$= \dfrac{\text{Loss due to migration}}{\text{Total equivalents passed}}$$

$$= \dfrac{0.01429}{0.0002982} = 0.4792$$

$\therefore \quad$ transport number of NO_3^- ions $\quad = 1 - 0.4792 = 0.5208$

Problems 13.16: In the determination of the transport number of K^+ and Cl^- ions, electrolysis of KCl solution was carried out using inert electrodes. It was found that 117.51 g of cathode solution contained 0.6658 g of KCl after electrolysis and 0.8722 g of KCl before electrolysis. A silver coulometer in series showed a deposit of 0.005688 equiv of Cl^- ions.

Solution: After electrolysis mass of water = (117.51 − 0.6658) g

$$= 116.8442 \text{ g}$$

Before electrolysis mass of water = (117.51 − 0.8722) g = 116.6378 g

Hence mass of KCl before electrolysis in 116.8442 g of water

$$= \frac{116.8442}{116.6378} \times 0.8722 = 0.8736 \text{ g}$$

Now initial amount of KCl = 0.8736 g or 0.01172 equiv of KCl and the amount after electrolysis = 0.6658 g or 0.00893 equiv of KCl. Hence the transport number of the K^+ ions $= \dfrac{0.01172 - 0.00893}{0.005688} = 0.49$

and

$$t_{Cl^-} = 1 - 0.49 = 0.51$$

13.20 ABNORMAL TRANSFERENCE NUMBER

Transference numbers vary with the concentration of the solution and with temperature. Table 13.7 shows that the transference number of cadmium ion decreases with increasing CdI_2 concentration and at higher concentration, it is actually negative. In other words, Cd^{2+} ions migrate towards the anode. To explain this anomalous behaviour of Cd^{2+} ions, Hittorf (1859) postulated that in fairly concentrated solution a complex anion of the type, CdI_4^{2-} is formed, and its concentration increases with the total concentration of cadmium iodide in solution. If it is assumed that ionization occurs as

$$2CdI_2 \rightleftharpoons Cd_2I_4 \rightleftharpoons Cd^{2+} + CdI_4^{2-}$$

then cadmium in the form of Cd^{2+} ions migrate out of the anode compartment while it is simultaneously replaced by CdI_4^{2-} ions. If both Cd^{2+} and CdI_4^{2-} ions are present in equal amounts and have the same mobility, the decrease in concentration of the anode compartment may be almost negligible. Thus the transference number of Cd^{2+} ions will be apparently zero. In dilute solutions, the complex anion dissociates into simple ions and normal transference number is obtained.

13.21 SOME APPLICATIONS OF CONDUCTANCE MEASUREMENTS

There are a number of direct applications of conductance measurements to chemical problems. It is used to obtain information concerning the behaviour of the electrolytes. A discussion of some of these applications is given below:

(*i*) **Determination of Solubility and Solubility Products of Sparingly Soluble Salts:** The solubilities of sparingly soluble salts such as barium sulphate, silver chloride, lead sulphate etc., can be determined by conductance measurements. Consider a sparingly soluble salt *MX*, in contact with its saturated solution, the equilibrium may be represented as

$$MX \text{ (solid)} \rightleftharpoons M^+(\text{aq}) + X^- \text{ (aq)}$$

and the solubility product is given by

$$K_{sp} = [M^+] [X^-]$$

Let κ_s be the specific conductance of the saturated solution of the salt and k_0 be the specific conductance of pure water in which the salt is sparingly soluble. Then the specific conductance of the salt alone is given as

$$\kappa_{salt} = \kappa_s - k_0$$

The conductivity per unit molar concentration is then given as

$$\Lambda_m = \frac{\kappa_{salt}}{C}$$

where C is the concentration of the salt in mole per m³ and hence the solubility. This solution may be regarded as infinitely dilute and hence the molar conductance would be Λ_m^0, i.e.,

$$\Lambda_m^0 = \frac{\kappa_{salt}}{C}$$

or,

$$C = \frac{\kappa_{salt}}{\Lambda_m^0}$$

Since the value of Λ_m^0 can be obtained as the sum of the ionic conductances

$$\Lambda_m^0 = v_+ \lambda_+^0 + v_- \lambda_-^0$$

hence

$$C = \frac{\kappa_{salt}}{v_+ \lambda_+^0 + v_- \lambda_-^0} \qquad ...(13.44)$$

The specific conductance (κ_s) of a saturated solution of silver chloride in water at 298 K is 3.41×10^{-4} Sm⁻¹, and if 1.60×10^{-4} Sm⁻¹ is subtracted for the conductance of water, then $\kappa_{salt} = 1.81 \times 10^{-4}$ Sm⁻¹. Also, Λ_m^0 for silver chloride is given as $\lambda_{Ag^+}^0 + \lambda_{Cl^-}^0 = (76.2 \times 10^{-4} + 61.9 \times 10^{-4})$ Smol m² = 138.2×10^{-4} Smol m².

Hence,

$$C = \frac{\left(1.81 \times 10^{-4} \text{ S m}^{-1}\right)}{\left(138.2 \times 10^{-4} \text{S mol}^{-1}\text{m}^2\right)}$$

$$= \frac{1.81}{138.2} \text{mol m}^{-3}$$

$$= 1.31 \times 10^{-2} \text{ mol m}^{-3}$$

$$= 1.31 \times 10^{-5} \text{ mol dm}^{-3}$$

The solubility product is then calculated as

$$K_{sp} = [Ag^+] [Cl^-]$$

$$= (1.31 \times 10^{-5}) (1.31 \times 10^{-5})$$

$$= 1.72 \times 10^{-10}$$

Problem 13.17: The conductivity of a saturated solution of a sparingly soluble salt MX in water at 298 K is 1.887×10^{-4} S m^{-1}. The molar conductivity of MX at infinite dilution at this temperature is 138.3×10^{-4} S m^2 mol^{-1}. Calculate the solubility and the solubility product of MX at this temperature.

Solution: Let s be the solubility of the salt, then

$$\Lambda_m^0 = \frac{\kappa}{s}$$

or

$$s = \frac{\kappa}{\Lambda_m^0}$$

$$= \frac{\left(1.887 \times 10^{-4} \text{ S m}^{-1}\right)}{\left(138.3 \times 10^{-4} \text{ S m}^2 \text{mol}^{-1}\right)}$$

$$= 1.34 \times 10^{-2} \text{ mol m}^{-3}$$

$$= 1.34 \times 10^{-5} \text{ mol dm}^{-3}$$

Therefore,

$$\text{Solubility product} = (1.34 \times 10^{-5})^2$$

$$= 1.796 \times 10^{-10}$$

Problem 13.18: The specific conductance of a saturated aqueous solution of barium sulphate at 298 K is 1.84×10^{-3} S m^{-1} and that of water is 1.60×10^{-4} S m^{-1}. The ionic conductivities at infinite dilution of Ba^{2+} and SO_4^{2-} ions at 298 K are 63.6×10^{-4} S m^2 mol^{-1} and 79.8×10^{-4} S m^2 mol^{-1} respectively. Calculate the solubility and solubility product of barium sulphate at 298 K.

Solution: Let s be the solubility of the salt, then

$$\Lambda_m^0 = \frac{\kappa}{s}$$

or

$$s = \frac{\kappa}{\Lambda_m^0} = \frac{\kappa}{\lambda_{m, Ba^{2+}}^0 + \lambda_{m, SO_4^{2-}}^0}$$

where k is the specific conductance of the salt.

Specific conductance due to $BaSO_4 = (1.84 \times 10^{-3} - 1.60 \times 10^{-4})$ S m^{-1}

$$= 1.68 \times 10^{-3} \text{ S m}^{-1}$$

$$= \frac{\left(1.68 \times 10^{-3} \text{S m}^{-1}\right)}{\left(63.6 \times 10^{-4} + 79.8 \times 10^{-4} \text{S m}^2 \text{ mol}^{-1}\right)}$$

$$= \frac{1.68 \times 10^{-3} \text{ S m}^{-1}}{143.4 \times 10^{-4} \text{ S m}^2 \text{mol}^{-1}}$$

$$= 0.1171 \text{ mol m}^{-3}$$

$$= 1.171 \times 10^{-4} \text{ mol dm}^{-3}$$

Therefore, the solubility product $= (1.171 \times 10^{-4})(1.171 \times 10^{-4})$

$$= 1.370 \times 10^{-8}$$

(ii) **Degree of Ionization and Ionization Constant of Weak Electrolytes:** A weak electrolyte like acetic acid is partially ionized at appreciable concentration and completely ionized only at infinite dilution. If Λ_m and Λ_m^0 are the molar conductances at the given concentration and at infinite dilution, then the degree of ionization is given as

$$\alpha = \frac{\Lambda_m}{\Lambda_m^0}$$

The ions in solution are in equilibrium with the unionized molecules and the ionization constant is given by

$$K_a = \frac{\left[H_3O^+\right]\left[Ac^-\right]}{\left[HAc\right]}$$

Knowing the value of α, we can calculate the value of ionization constant.

Problem 13.19: The resistance of a 0.02 mol dm^{-3} solution of acetic acid in a cell (cell constant = 0.2063 cm^{-1}) was found to be 888 Ω. What is the degree of ionization of the acid at this concentration? (Given Λ_m^0 for acetic acid = 387.9 × 10^{-4} S mol^{-1} m^2).

Solution: Since

$$\kappa = \frac{1}{R} \times \text{cell constant}$$

$$= \frac{0.2063 \text{ cm}^{-1}}{888 \ \Omega}$$

$$= 2.324 \times 10^{-4} \text{ S cm}^{-1}$$

$$= 2.324 \times 10^{-2} \text{ S m}^{-1}$$

$$C = 0.02 \text{ mol dm}^{-3}$$

$$= 0.02 \times 10^3 \text{ mol m}^{-3}$$

Therefore,

$$\Lambda_m = \frac{\kappa}{C} = \frac{\left(2.324 \times 10^{-2} \text{ S m}^{-1}\right)}{0.02 \times 10^3 \text{ mol m}^{-3}}$$

$$= 1.162 \times 10^{-3} \text{ S mol}^{-1} \text{ m}^2$$

Given
$$\Lambda_m^0 = 387.9 \times 10^{-4} \text{ S mol}^{-1} \text{m}^2$$

$$\alpha = \frac{\Lambda_m}{\Lambda_m^0}$$

$$= \frac{1.162 \times 10^{-2} \text{ S mol}^{-1} \text{m}^2}{387.9 \times 10^{-4} \text{ Smol}^{-1} \text{m}^2}$$

$$= 0.03$$

(iii) **Determination of Ionic Product of Water:** An important application of conductance measurement is the determination of ionic product of water. Since water is a weak electrolyte and ionizes as

$$2\text{H}_2\text{O} \rightleftharpoons \text{H}_3\text{O}^+ + \text{OH}^-$$

and the ionic product of water
$$K_w = [\text{H}_3\text{O}^+] [\text{OH}^-]$$

In pure water,
$$[\text{H}_3\text{O}^+] = [\text{OH}^-] = (K_w)^{1/2}$$

At 298 K, the specific conductance of a pure sample of distilled water is 5.8×10^{-6} S m^{-1}. The density of water at 298 K is 0.997 kg dm^{-3}. Therefore, molar concentration of water

$$C = \frac{\left(0.997 \text{ kg dm}^{-3}\right)}{\left(18 \times 10^{-3} \text{kg mol}^{-1}\right)}$$

$$= 55.3 \text{ mol dm}^{-3}$$

$$= 55.3 \times 10^3 \text{ mol m}^{-3}$$

Now, the equivalent conductance, Λ_m, is equal to

$$\Lambda_m = \frac{\kappa}{C}$$

where C is the concentration in mol m^{-3}.

Since
$$\kappa = 5.8 \times 10^{-6} \text{ S m}^{-1}$$

Therefore,
$$\Lambda = \frac{\left(5.8 \times 10^{-6} \text{ Sm}^{-1}\right)}{\left(55.3 \times 10^{-3} \text{mol m}^{-3}\right)}$$

$$= 1.05 \times 10^{-10} \text{ S mol}^{-1} \text{m}^2$$

The molar conductance of water at infinite dilution in given by Kohlrausch law as the sum of the molar conductances of hydrogen and hydroxyl ions, or

$$\Lambda_{m,\text{H}_2\text{O}}^0 = \lambda_{m,\text{H}_3\text{O}^+}^0 + \lambda_{m,\text{OH}^-}^0$$

$$= (349.8 \times 10^{-4} + 198.0 \times 10^{-4}) \text{ S mol}^{-1} \text{m}^2$$

$$= 547.8 \times 10^{-4} \text{ S mol}^{-1} \text{m}^2$$

Hence, the degree of ionization of water is

$$\alpha = \frac{\Lambda_m}{\Lambda_m^0} = \frac{1.05 \times 10^{-10}\, Smol^{-1}m^2}{547.8 \times 10^{-4}\, Smol^{-1}m^2}$$

$$= 1.9 \times 10^{-9}$$

The hydrogen and hydroxyl ion concentrations are equal and each is equal to $C\alpha = (55.3\ mol\ dm^{-3}) \times (1.9 \times 10^{-9}) = 105.07 \times 10^{-9}\ mol\ dm^{-3}$

$$= 1.05 \times 10^{-7}\ mol\ dm^{-3}$$

Therefore, $K_w = [H_3O^+][OH^-]$

$$= (1.05 \times 10^{-7})\,(1.05 \times 10^{-7})$$

$$= 1.1 \times 10^{-14}$$

(*iv*) **Degree of Hydrolysis and Hydrolysis Constant:** The molar conductance of an aqueous solution of a salt of strong acid and weak base like aniline hydrochloride is partly due to HCl formed as a result of hydrolysis and partly due to the unhydrolysed salt.

The conductance of aniline formed may be neglected as it is a very weak base and exists completely in the unionized form. If the concentration of the salt be 1 mol dm^{-3} and α_h its degree of hydrolysis then the concentrations of the various species at equilibrium are

$$C_6H_5N^+H_3Cl^- \xrightarrow{\ H_2O\ } C_6H_5NH_2 + H^+Cl^-$$

| 1 | 0 | 0 | $\rightarrow$ Initial concentration |
| $1 - \alpha_h$ | α_h | α_h | $\rightarrow$ Concentration at equilibrium |

The molar conductance of the salt solution is, therefore, equal to the conductance of $(1 - \alpha_h)$ mole of the unhydrolysed salt and α_h mole of the acid formed due to hydrolysis, *i.e.*,

$$\Lambda_m = (1 - \alpha_h)\Lambda_{m,c} + \alpha_h\Lambda_{m,\ HCl}$$

where Λ_m is molar conductance of the salt solution, $\Lambda_{m,c}$ is the molar conductance of the unhydrolysed salt at the given concentration and $\Lambda_{m,\ HCl}$ is the molar conductance of hydrochloric acid. From Eq. (13.45), we get

$$\alpha_h = \frac{\Lambda_m - \Lambda_{m,c}}{\Lambda_{m,\ HCl} - \Lambda_{m,c}} \qquad\qquad ...(13.46)$$

In order to calculate α_h, we must know Λ_m, $\Lambda_{m,c}$ and $\Lambda_{m,\ HCl}$. The value of Λ_m is obtained directly from the conductance measurements of the salt solution at the given concentration. $\Lambda_{m,c}$ for the unhydrolysed salt is obtained by measuring the molar conductance of the salt solution in presence of excess of the base. Under these conditions the hydrolysis of the salt is virtually suppressed and the conductance of the salt solution can be taken as $\Lambda_{m,c}$. $\Lambda_{m,\ HCl}$ is generally taken as the molar conductance of HCl at infinite dilution as its concentration is very small.

(*v*) **Conductometric Titrations:** The conductance of a solution depends largely on the number of ions and their mobilities. The variation in conductance of a solution during titration is employed in determining the end point of a titration. Consider the titration of a strong acid by a strong base, say HCl by NaOH. When the base is added, the reaction

$$H^+ + Cl^- + Na^+ + OH^- \rightarrow Na^+ + Cl^- + H_2O$$

occurs. For each mole of hydroxyl ions added, one mole of hydrogen ions is removed. The concentration of hydrogen ions decreases during the titration. The molar conductance of hydrogen ion at infinite dilution is 349.8×10^{-4} S m^2 mol^{-1} and that of sodium ion is 50.1×10^{-4} S m^2 mol^{-1}. Thus, more conducting hydrogen ions are being replaced by less conducting sodium ions. Consequently, the conductivity of the solution decreases. This continues until the equivalence point is reached where all the hydrogen ions from the acid are removed by the hydroxyl ions from the added base. At this point the conductivity is due to sodium and chloride ions. Further addition of the base introduces excess of

fairly high conducting hydroxyl ions ($\lambda^0_{OH^-} = 197.6 \times 10^{-4}$ S m^2 mol^{-1}) and these cause the conductivity

to increase rapidly. Hence, in the titration of a strong acid by a strong base, the conductivity has a minimum value at the equivalence point. The plot of conductivity versus volume of alkali added yields a V-shaped curve Fig. 13.11 (a). Portion AB of the curve represents the variation in conductivity of a mixture of sodium chloride and hydrochloric acid while BC indicates the conductivity of excess of base and sodium chloride. Slope of BC is less than that of AB because hydroxyl ions are less conducting than hydrogen ions. At B neither the hydrogen ions nor the hydroxyl ions are in excess and hence it is the end point or the equivalence point.

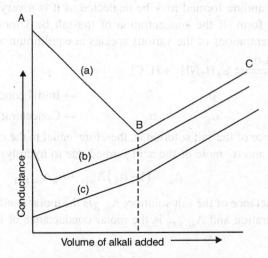

Fig. 13.11 Conductometric acid-base titration

When a moderately weak acid such as acetic acid ($K_a \cong 10^{-5}$) is titrated by a strong base like NaOH the conductivity in the initial stages is low and decreases owing to the common ion effect in suppressing the ionization of the acid. With further addition of the base up to the equivalence point, the conductivity gradually increases because of the increase in the concentration of the salt formed. After the equivalence point, a rapid increase in conductivity results due to the excess of hydroxyl ions. The titration curve obtained in such cases is shown in Fig. 13.11 (b).

In the titration of very weak acids, such as phenols (K_a) lying in the range ($10^{-5} - 10^{-8}$) by sodium hydroxide, the conductivity of the original solution is very low and it rises from the beginning of the neutralization and increases rapidly after the equivalence point. The titration curve is shown in Fig. 13.11 (c).

Conductometric Titration of Salts: Titration of salts of weak acids or weak bases can be carried out by conductivity measurements. When a strong acid is added to a salt of a weak acid, the anion of the weak acid is replaced by that of the stronger one and the weak acid itself is liberated in the unionized form. Similarly the addition of a strong base to salt of a weak base replaces the cation and liberates the weakly ionized base. Thus in the titration of sodium acetate by hydrochloric acid

$$H^+ + Cl^- + Na^+ + Ac^- \rightarrow Na^+ + Cl^- + HAc$$

less conducting acetate ions ($\lambda^0_{AC^-} = 40.9 \times 10^{-4}$ S m^2 mol^{-1}) are replaced by more conducting chloride ions ($\lambda^0_{Cl^-} = 76.34 \times 10^{-4}$ S m^2 mol^{-1}). Hence the conductivity of the solution increases gradually up to the equivalence point. When all the acetate ions are replaced, excess of hydrogen ions cause a sharp increase in the conductivity Fig. 13.12 (a).

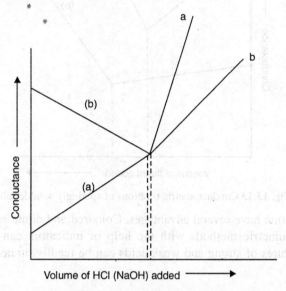

Fig. 13.12 Conductometric titration of NaAc (NH₄Cl)

Similarly, in the titration of ammonium chloride by sodium hydroxide

$$NH_4^+Cl^- + Na^+OH^- \rightarrow NH_3 + Na^+Cl^- + H_2O(l)$$

more conducting ammonium ions are replaced by less conducting sodium ions and hence the initial conductivity falls. After the equivalence point due to excess of hydroxyl ions the conductivity rises rapidly as shown in Fig. 13.12 (b).

Precipitation Titrations: Precipitation titrations can be followed by conductivity measurements. In the titration of potassium chloride by silver nitrate

$$K^+Cl^- + Ag^+NO_3^- \rightarrow K^+NO_3^- + AgCl$$

the chloride ions are replaced by nitrate ions. The conductivity of chloride ion is 76.34×10^{-4} S m^2 mol^{-1} while that of nitrate ion is 71.44×10^{-4} S m^2 mol^{-1}. Since there is not much difference in the conductivity of Cl$^-$ ions and NO$_3^-$ ions therefore conductivity decreases only slightly and increases rapidly after the equivalence point due to excess of silver nitrate as shown in Fig. 13.13 (b).

If both the products are sparingly soluble salts as in titration of magnesium sulphate by barium hydroxide

$$MgSO_4 + Ba(OH)_2 \rightarrow Mg(OH)_2 + BaSO_4$$

the conductivity falls until the equivalence point is reached and then increases due to excess of barium hydroxide. The titration curve is given in Fig. 13.13 (a).

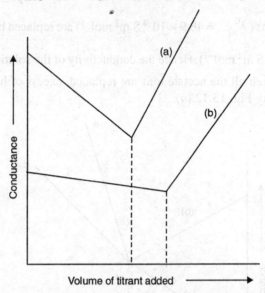

Fig. 13.13 Conductometric titrations of sparingly soluble salts

Conductometric titration have several advantages. Coloured and dilute solutions which cannot be titrated by ordinary volumetric methods with the help of indicators can be successfully titrated conductometrically. Mixtures of strong and weak acids can be readily titrated.

EXERCISES

1. Explain, giving reasons, the following:
    (i) In the electrolysis of aqueous sodium chloride solution using Pt electrodes Na^+ ions are not discharged at the cathode.
    (ii) Specific conductance decreases while equivalent conductance increases with dilution.
    (iii) Metallic conductance decreases while electrolytic conductance increases with rise in temperature.
    (iv) A *DC* current cannot be used for conductance measurements.
    (v) H^+ and OH^- ions in aqueous media have exceptionally high ionic conductances.
    (vi) Transport number of Cd^{2+} ions in concentrated solutions of CdI_2 is negative.
    (vii) Conductance increases with increasing field strength and frequency of the alternating current.
    (viii) Molar conductance values for alkali metal cations are in the order $Rb^+ > K^+ > Na^+ > Li^+$.
    (ix) Transport number of Cl^- ion in aqueous 0.1 M HCl solution is lower than that in aqueous 0.1 M NaCl solution under identical conditions.
    (x) Molar conductance of NaI at infinite dilution in acetone is more than that in water.

2. At the same temperature and concentration which one in the following pairs will have higher molar conductance:
    (1) LiCl or NaCl.
    (2) Acetic acid or monochloroacetic acid.
    (3) Cl^- ion in HCl or in NaCl

(4) NaF or NaCl

(5) Na_2SO_4 or $NaHSO_4$

3.   State and explain the Faraday's Laws of electrolysis. What is the significance of these laws?

4.   Define the term: Cell constant, conductance, specific conductance, and molar conductance. How are equivalent and molar conductances related to the specific conductance of the solution? For the following electrolytes derive the relationships between equivalent conductance (Λ) and molar conductance (μ).

(i) KCl, (ii) K_2SO_4, (iii) $CrCl_3$, (iv) $Al_2(SO_4)_3$, and (v) $K_4Fe(CN)_6$.

Ans. (i) $\Lambda = \mu$, (ii) $2\Lambda = \mu$, (iii) $3\Lambda = \mu$,

(iv) $6\Lambda = \mu$, (v) $4\Lambda = \mu$.

5.   What is cell constant? How is the conductance of an electrolyte determined? Why an alternating current is used in conductance measurements? Why are the Pt electrodes coated with Pt black?

6.   Explain the variation of specific and molar conductances with dilution. State Kohlrausch law of independent ionic migration. How is the law helpful in evaluating the molar conductance of weak electrolytes at infinite dilution?

7.   What are the various factors affecting the conductance of a solution? How do you account for the increase in conductance of solutions at high field strength and at high frequency? Why is the Walden's rule not obeyed by ions with smaller sizes?

8.   Define ionic mobility. Discuss the factors affecting ionic mobility. How is it determined experimentally? Why H^+ and OH^- ions have exceptionally high ionic mobilities in aqueous media? Derive the relationship between ionic mobility and ionic conductance.

9.   What is the transport number of an ion? How is it related to (i) ionic mobility and (ii) ionic conductance? Describe (a) the Hittorf's method and (b) the moving boundary method employed in determining the transport number of an ion.

10. What is meant by abnormal transport number of an ion? Under what conditions an aqueous solution of CdI_2 shows negative transport number for Cd^{2+} ions?

11. How are the following determined experimentally from conductance measurements?

(i) Degree of ionization and ionization constant of a weak electrolyte.

(ii) Degree of ionization and ionic product of water.

(iii) Solubility and solubility product of a sparingly soluble salt.

(iv) Degree of hydrolysis and hydrolysis constant of a hydrolysable salt.

12. Discuss the principle underlying the conductometric titrations. What are the advantages of conductometric titrations over the ordinary titrations? Sketch schematically the titration curves for the following titrations:

(i) A strong acid by a strong base.

(ii) A strong acid by a weak base.

(iii) A weak acid by a strong base.

(iv) A mixture of a strong acid (HCl) and a weak acid (HAc) by a strong base.

(v) A solution of NaCl by a solution of $AgNO_3$.

(vi) A solution of $MgSO_4$ by a solution of $Ba(OH)_2$.

(vii) A solution containing a mixture of NaCl and NaI by a solution of $AgNO_3$.

13. How many grams of Na and Cl_2 would be produced if a current of 25 amperes is passed for 8 hr into a solution of molten sodium chloride?   **Ans.** 172 g Na, 265 g Cl_2.

14. How long would it take to deposit 25 g of Cr from a solution of $CrCl_3$ by a current of 2.75 amperes? (at. mass of Cr is 52 g mol^{-1}).   **Ans.** 14 hr.

15. Specific conductance of water is 7.6×10^{-3} S dm^{-1} at 300 K and that of a 0.1 mol dm^{-3} aqueous potassium chloride solution is 1.1639×10^{-1} S dm^{-1}. A cell had a resistance of 33.21 Ω when filled with 0.1 mol dm^{-3} potassium chloride solution and 735.3 Ω when filled with 0.1 mol dm^{-3} acetic acid solution. Calculate

(*i*) the cell constant, (*ii*) the specific conductance of a 0.1 mol dm^{-3} acetic acid solution, (*iii*) the equivalent and molar conductances of 0.1 mol dm^{-3} acetic acid solution.

Ans. (*i*) 3.616 dm^{-1}, (*ii*) 4.919 × 10^{-3} S dm^{-1}
(*iii*) each is 4.919 S mol^{-1} dm^2.

16. When a certain conductance cell was filled with 0.20 mol dm^{-3} aqueous potassium chloride solution, its conductivity was 0.2768 S m^{-1} and had a resistance of 82.4 Ω at 300 K. When it was filled with 0.0025 mol dm^{-3} aqueous potassium sulphate solution it had a resistance of 325.0 Ω. Calculate (*i*) the cell constant, (*ii*) the conductivity and (*iii*) the equivalent and molar conductances of potassium sulphate solution.

Ans. (*i*) 22.81 m^{-1}, (*ii*) 6.997 × 10^{-2} S m^{-1}, (*iii*) equivalent conductance 1.399 × 10^{-2} S m^2 eq^{-1}, molar conductance 2.798 × 10^{-2} S m^{2}mol^{-1}.

17. At 300 K, the molar conductance at infinite dilution of KCl, KNO$_3$ and AgNO$_3$ are 149.9 × 10^{-4} S m^2 mol^{-1}, 145.0 × 10^{-4} S m^2 mol^{-1} and 133.4 × 10^{-4} S m^2 mol^{-1} respectively. Calculate the molar conductance of AgCl at infinite dilution. If the conductivity of a saturated solution of AgCl at 300 K is 1.887 × 10^{-4} S m^{-1}, calculate the solubility and solubility product of AgCl?

Ans. 138.3 × 10^{-4} S m^2 mol^{-1}, 1.34 × 10^{-5} mol dm^{-3}, 1.8 × 10^{-10}.

18. Assuming that water is completely ionized, calculate its limiting molar conductance at 300 K. Given:

$$\Lambda^0_{HCl} = 26 \times 10^{-4}\, S\, m^2 mol^{-1}, \Lambda^0_{NaOH} = 247.8 \times 10^{-4}\, S m^2 mol^{-1}$$

and $$\Lambda^0_{NaCl} = 126.45 \times 10^{-4}\, S m^2 mol^{-1}.$$ Ans. 547.8 × 10^{-4} S m^2 mol^{-1}.

19. Calculate the equivalent and molar conductance of

     COONa
     |

(*i*)   COOK   and (*ii*) K$_2$SO$_4$ Al$_2$(SO$_4$)$_3$ · 24H$_2$O. Given that

$$\lambda^0_{1/2\, O^{2-}_x} = 74.1 \times 10^{-4}\, S m^2 eq^{-1}, \lambda^0_{K^+} = 73.5 \times 10^{-4}\, S m^2 eq^{-1},$$

$$\lambda^0_{Na} = 50.1 \times 10^{-4}\, S m^2 eq^{-1}, \lambda^0_{1/2\, SO^{2-}_4} = 79.8 \times 10^{-4}\, S m^2 eq^{-1},$$

$$\lambda^0_{\frac{1}{3}\, Al^{3+}} = 63.0 \times 10^{-4}\, S m^2 eq^{-1}.$$

Ans. (*i*) 135.90 × 10^{-4} S m^2 eq^{-1},
271.80 × 10^{-4} S m^2 mol^{-1};
(*ii*) 145.425 × 10^{-4} S m^2 eq^{-1},
1163.4 × 10^{-4} S m^2 mol^{-1}.

20. The specific conductance of a 0.01 mol dm^{-3} aqueous acetic acid solution at 298 K was 1.65 × 10^{-3} S m^{-1}. The molar conductance of acetic acid at infinite dilution was 390.7 × 10^{-4} S m^2 mol^{-1}. Calculate the degree of ionization (α) and the ionization constant (K$_a$) of the acid.

Ans. α = 0.422, K$_a$ = 1.86 × 10^{-5}.

21. Calculate the ionic mobilities of H$^+$ and SO$_4^{2-}$ ions at infinite dilution. Given

$$\lambda^0_{H^+} = 349.8 \times 10^{-4}\, S m^2 mol^{-1} \text{ and}$$

$$\lambda^0_{SO_4^{2-}} = 159.6 \times 10^{-4}\, S m^2 mol^{-1}.$$

Ans. u_{H^+} = 3.625 × 10^7 m^{2}V^{-1}s^{-1},
$u_{SO_4^{2-}}$ = 8.27 × 10^{-8} m^{2}V^{-1}s^{-1}

22. At infinite dilution, the ionic mobilities of Cd^{2+} and Cl^- ions are 6.16×10^{-8} $m^2V^{-1}s^{-1}$ and 7.91×10^{-s} $m^2V^{-1}s^{-1}$ respectively. Calculate the equivalent and molar conductances of the salt at infinite dilution.

Ans. 136.77×10^{-4} m^2 S eq^{-1} and 273.54×10^{-4} m^2 S mol^{-1}.

23. In the determination of transport number by Hittorf's method, a certain current was passed through an aqueous solution of an electrolyte MA, M^+ is discharged at the cathode while A^- at the anode. Calculate the net loss of MA in the anode and cathode compartments for each faraday of electricity passed.

Ans. t_- g eq of MA in the cathode and t_+ g eq of MA in the anode.

24. In the determination of transport number Ag^+ ions in a Hittorf's cell using Ag electrodes and $AgNO_3$ solution, it was found that 0.2157 g of Ag was present in 24.96 g of water in the anode compartment before electrolysis. After electrolysis, 0.28 g of Ag was present in 27.8538 g of solution. A copper coulometer connected in series showed a deposit of 0.014 g of copper. Calculate t_{Ag^+}. **Ans.** 0.44.

25. In the determination of transport number by using a Hittorf's cell, it was found that the normality of $AgNO_3$ solution before and after electrolysis was 4.88×10^{-2} N and 5.60×10^{-2} N respectively. The same amount of curent deposited 0.01307 g of copper in a copper coulometer. Calculate t_{Ag^+} and t_{Cl^-}.

Ans. $t_{Ag^+} = 0.473$

$t_{Cl^-} = 0.527$.

26. Using Ag – AgCl electrodes, a solution of HCl was electrolysed in a Hittorf's cell. Initially the solution contained 0.3856×10^{-3}g HCl per g of water while after passing a current of 2 mA for 3 hr, the cathode solution contained 0.0267 g HCl per 51.7436 g of the solution. Calculate t_{H^+}. **Ans.** 0.83.

27. A 2.0 molal solution of $FeCl_3$ was electrolysed between Pt electrodes. The cathode compartment contained 50.0 g of water and was 1.575 molal in $FeCl_3$ and 0.50 molal in $FeCl_2$. Calculate the transport number of Cl^- ions. **Ans.** 0.55.

28. A 0.2% solution of NaOH was electrolysed using the Pt electrodes in a Hittorf's cell. A current of 20 mA was passed for 1/2 hr. After electrolysis 25.64 g of the cathode solution contained 0.056 g NaOH. Calculate t_{Na^+}. **Ans.** 0.21.

29. The molar conductance of 0.05 M aqueous HCl solution is 399.09×10^{-4} S m^2 mol^{-1} and the transport number of hydrogen ion at this concentration is 0.829. Calculate the molar ionic conductances of H^+ and Cl^- ions.

Ans. $\lambda_{H^+} = 330.85 \times 10^{-4}$ Sm^2mol^{-1}

$\lambda_{Cl^-} = 38.24 \times 10^{-4}$ Sm^2mol^{-1}

30. In a moving boundary experiment for the determination of transport number of H^+ ion, a current of 25 mA was passed for 1C min. It was found that the boundary moved a distance of 9.1 cm. If the radius of the tube was 0.3 cm, calculate t_{H^+}

Ans. 0.829.

31. In a moving boundary experiment carried out with 0.1 mol dm^{-3} solution of HCl at 300 K($\kappa = 2.24$ Sm^{-1}) sodium ions are caused to follow the H^+ ions. When a current of 3 mA was passed through the solution, the boundary moved a distance of 3.08 cm in 1 hr. If the cross-sectional area of the tube were 0.3 cm^2, calculate (i) the mobility of H^+ ions, (ii) t_{H^+} and (iii) the mobility of Cl^- ions.

Ans. (i) $36.3 \times 10^{-8}m^2$ V^{-1}s^{-1},

(ii) 0.826, and (iii) 7.64×10^{-8} m^2 V^{-1}s^{-1}

32. The equivalent ionic conductances of Na^+ and O_x^{2-} ions at infinite dilution are 50.1×10^{-4} S m^2 eq^{-1} and 74.1×10^{-4} S m^2 eq^{-1} respectively. Calculate the transport numbers of Na^+ and O_x^{2-} ions in an infinitely dilute solution of sodium oxalate. If a Na^+ ion is replaced by a K^+ ion $\left(\lambda_{K^+}^0 = 73.5 \times 10^{-4} \, S \, m^2 eq^{-1}\right)$ how the transport number of Na^+ and O_x^{2-} ions are affected?

Ans. In sodium oxalate,

$$t_{Na^+} = 0.4024, \, t_{O_x^{2-}} = 0.5976.$$

In potassium sodium oxalate,

$$t_{Na^+} = 0.184, \, t_{O_x^{2-}} = 0.545.$$

33. The equivalent ionic conductances of H^+ and Cl^- ions at infinite dilution are 349.8×10^{-4} S m^2 eq^{-1} and 76.3×10^{-4} S m^2 eq^{-1} respectively. Calculate t_{H^+} and t_{Cl^-} at infinite dilution. An infinitely dilute equimolar solution of HCl and NaCl is prepared. How are the transport numbers of H^+ and Cl^- ions modified in the mixture?

Ans. $t_{H^+} = 0.82$ in HCl;

$$t_{H^+} = 0.632, \, t_{Cl^-} = 0.277 \text{ in the mixture.}$$

34. At 291 K, specific conductance of an aqueous saturated solution of CaF_2 was 3.86×13^{-3} S m^{-1} and that of pure water used in the preparation of the solution was 1.5×10^{-4} S m^{-1}. The equivalent conductance of Ca^{2+} and F^- ions are 51.0×10^{-4} S m^2 eq^{-1} and 47.0×10^{-4} S m^2 eq^{-1} respectively. Calculate the solubility and solubility product of the salt.

Ans. 2.895×10^{-4} mol dm^{-3}, 2.71×10^{-11}

Ionic Equilibria

14.1 THE ARRHENIUS THEORY OF ELECTROLYTIC DISSOCIATION

Prior to the development of the theory of Arrhenius in 1887, a number of suggestions were made to explain the conduction of electricity of solutions of electrolytes. van't Hoff studies of osmotic pressures of dilute solutions of electrolytes showed large deviations from his osmotic pressure equation, $\Pi = CRT$. In order to explain the behaviour of electrolytes in solutions Arrhenius put forward the theory of electrolytic dissociation of electrolytes into cations and anions in aqueous solutions.

The number of these ions may or may not be same, but the total positive and negative charges are equal so that the resulting electrolyte solution is electrically neutral. The extent of dissociation is different for different electrolytes. It depends on the concentration of the electrolyte, temperature and the nature of the electrolyte. At extreme dilutions, all the electrolytes are almost completely ionized. The fraction of the total number of molecules ionized, called the degree of ionization (α), is equal to the actual number of ions in solution divided by the total number of ions that would form if the electrolyte were completely ionized. Thus

$$\alpha = \frac{\text{number of molecules dissociated or ionised}}{\text{total number of molecules}}$$

Calculations of the degree of ionization for various electrolytes in aqueous solutions show that practically all salts, strong acids and bases are highly ionized in water. These are known as *strong* or *true electrolytes*. Aqueous solutions of these electrolytes are therefore good conductors of electricity. On the other hand, there are many substances whose aqueous solutions are poor conductors of electricity. These include many organic acids and bases (such as acetic acid, benzoic acid, methylamine, aniline, etc.), inorganic acids and bases (such as carbonic acid, hydrocyanic acid, ammonium hydroxide, hydrazine, etc.). These are called *potential* or *weak electrolytes*. This division into strong and weak electrolytes is a qualitative one. There are some electrolytes such as $BaCl_2$ etc., which exhibit an intermediate behaviour.

Factors Controlling the Degree of Dissociation: The degree of ionization depends on the following factors:

(i) *Nature of the electrolyte:* Weak electrolytes are only partly ionized and, therefore, their degree of ionization is low. Strong electrolytes which are almost completely ionized have high degree of ionization.

(ii) *Nature of the solvent:* The nature of the solvent plays an important role in the dissociation of electrolytes. Generally, solvents with high dielectric constant and with high solvating power such as water ionize the electrolytes to greater extent than the solvents with low dielectric constant such as benzene. This is due to the fact that solvents having high dielectric constant considerably reduce the forces of attractions between oppositely charged ions and hence enhance ionization.

(iii) *Concentration of the electrolyte:* Dissociation of the electrolyte increases with the increase in dilution.

(iv) *Temperature:* Dissociation is an endothermic process and hence increases with the increase in temperature.

(v) *Presence of other electrolytes:* Presence of common ions tend to reduce the degree of ionization (common ion effect).

EVIDENCES IN FAVOUR OF ARRHENIUS THEORY

(i) *Ionic reactions:* Evidence for the existence of ions in aqueous solution is provided by the reactions of salts in inorganic chemistry. For example, when an aqueous solution of a metal halide is mixed with a solution of silver nitrate a precipitate of silver halide is obtained. The reaction, according to ionic theory is,

$$Ag^+ + X^- \rightarrow AgX$$

This reaction clearly shows the existence of ions in solutions.

(ii) *Enthalpy of neutralization of acids and bases*: Enthalpy of neutralization of a strong acid by a strong base in dilute solution is 57.3 kJ. As strong acids and bases are almost completely ionized, the neutralization is merely a reaction between hydrogen ions from the acid and hydroxyl ions from the base to form water.

$$H^+ (aq) + OH^- (aq) \rightarrow H_2O (l) \quad \Delta H = 57.3 \text{ kJ mol}^{-1}$$

However, when either the acid or the base is weak, the value is comparatively less and its difference from the above value is the enthalpy of ionization of the weak acid or the weak base.

(iii) *Colour of certain compounds and their solutions:* It is well known that solution of electrolytes with a common ion show similar physical and chemical properties. For example, solutions of copper sulphate, copper chloride are all blue due to the common cupric Cu^{2+} ions. Similarly, solutions of sodium and potassium chromates are yellow due to chromates ions.

(iv) *Ions present in solid salts:* X-ray diffraction studies of solid salts have shown that they are built up of ions and not of neutral molecules. Sodium chloride, for example, does not contain neutral NaCl units but is built up in such a way that each Na^+ ion is surrounded by six Cl^- ions and vice versa.

(v) *Colligative properties:* The colligative properties like osmotic pressure, elevation of the boiling point, depression of the freezing point, and relative lowering of vapour pressure depend upon the number of particles in solution. When an electrolyte in solution undergoes ionization the number of particles increases causing an increase in the value of the colligative property. The freezing point depression for a one molal solution of a nonvolatile nonelectrolyte in water is 1.86°C, whereas a one molal aqueous solution of sodium chloride under similar conditions would show a freezing point depression of approximately twice the above value *i.e.*, 3.72°C.

(vi) *Electrolytic conductance:* Conduction of electricity in solution is due to the presence of ions. The fact that electrolytes obey Ohm's law proves that the current passed is used in overcoming resistance of the solution and no part is used in ionizing the molecules.

Limitations of the Arrhenius Theory: Arrhenius theory is satisfactory for weak electrolytes. However, when applied to strong electrolytes many anomalies and inconsistencies have been observed which seriously question the validity of some of the postulates of Arrhenius theory. Some of the important discrepancies are:

(i) The degree of dissociation obtained from the conductivity measurements and from colligative properties are in good agreement for weak electrolytes. But for strong electrolytes the agreement is very poor.

(ii) The Ostwald dilution law is obeyed by weak electrolytes but not at all by strong electrolytes.

(iii) Arrhenius theory assumes the existence of ions but does not take into account the electrostatic attractions between ions. The effect produced by the interionic attractions is quite small in solutions of weak electrolytes where the number of ions is not large. But in case of strong electrolytes in concentrated solutions the number of ions is large consequently the effect of interionic attractions would be quite pronounced. The effect is more significant for electrolytes having higher valencies of ions.

These points conclude that Arrhenius theory is essentially valid for weak electrolytes but does not describe the behaviour of strong electrolytes which are completely ionized even at moderate concentrations and the degree of ionization calculated for strong electrolytes merely gives an indication of the interionic-attractions operating in such solutions.

14.2 THE OSTWALD DILUTION LAW

Arrhenius theory of electrolytic dissociation assumes a dynamic equilibrium between the ions and unionized molecules. Ostwald, therefore, applied the law of mass action to such a system. Consider a simple binary electrolyte AB which ionizes according to the equation

$$AB \rightleftharpoons A^+ + B^-$$

where A^+ and B^- are ions of the electrolyte and AB is the unionized electrolyte. Applying the law of mass action, we get

$$K_a = \frac{[A^+][B^-]}{[AB]} \qquad \text{...(14.1)}$$

Let α be the degree of ionization and C the total concentration of the electrolyte in moles/litre. At equilibrium, the concentrations of various species would be

$$[A^+] = C\alpha$$
$$[B^-] = C\alpha$$
$$[AB] = C(1 - \alpha)$$

On substituting these values in Eq. (14.1), we get

$$K_a = \frac{(C\alpha)(C\alpha)}{C(1-\alpha)}$$

$$K_a = \frac{C\alpha^2}{(1-\alpha)} \qquad \text{...(14.2)}$$

Equation (14.2) is the mathematical representation of the Ostwald's dilution law. The equilibrium constant, K_a is called the dissociation or ionization constant of the electrolyte. It is constant at a given temperature.

For a weak electrolyte, the value of α is very small as compared to unity, $i.e., 1 - \alpha \cong 1$. Hence Eq. (14.2) reduces to

$$K_a = C\alpha^2$$

or

$$\alpha = \sqrt{\frac{K_a}{C}} \qquad \qquad ...(14.3)$$

which shows that the degree of dissociation is inversely proportional to the square root of the concentration.

The degree of ionization at different dilutions can be determined by conductance measurements, using the equation $\alpha = \Lambda/\Lambda^0$, where Λ and Λ^0 are the equivalent conductances at the given and infinite dilution respectively. Substituting this value of α in Eq. (14.2), we get

$$K_a = \frac{C\left(\dfrac{\Lambda}{\Lambda^0}\right)^2}{\left(1 - \dfrac{\Lambda}{\Lambda^0}\right)}$$

$$K_a = \frac{C\Lambda^2}{\Lambda^0\left(\Lambda^0 - \Lambda\right)}$$

or,

$$K_a = \frac{\Lambda^2}{V\Lambda^0\left(\Lambda^0 - \Lambda\right)}$$

where $V\left(= \dfrac{1}{C}\right)$ is the dilution.

This law was found to hold good in cases of weak electrolytes such as acetic acid, ammonium hydroxide, etc. as the value of K_a was found to be fairly constant. Table 14.1 shows the results for acetic acid obtained at 298 K.

Table 14.1. Dissociation Constant of Acetic Acid in Aqueous Solution at 298 K ($\Lambda^0 = 390.71 \times 10^{-4}$ S m^2 equiv.$^{-1}$)

Concentration (C) mol dm^{-3}	Λ (S m^2 equiv^{-1}) $\times 10^4$	$\alpha = \dfrac{\Lambda}{\Lambda^0}$	$K_a = \dfrac{C\alpha^2}{(1-\alpha)}$
0.505	2.211	0.0057	1.65×10^{-5}
0.186	3.804	0.0098	1.81×10^{-5}
0.093	5.360	0.0138	1.80×10^{-5}
0.040	8.390	0.0216	1.92×10^{-5}
0.0158	13.030	0.0336	1.85×10^{-5}

Table 14.1 shows that the value of K_a at different concentrations is almost constant. However, the law fails completely when applied to strong electrolytes like HCl, NaOH, etc.

14.3 ACIDS AND BASES

Arrhenius Concept: According to Arrhenius, an acid is any substance that can increase the concentration of hydrogen ions in aqueous solution. A base is a substance that increases the hydroxyl ion concentration in water. The hydrogen ions in water are produced through the ionization of the acid while the hydroxyl ions are produced from the ionization of the base

$$HCl + H_2O \longrightarrow H_3O^+ + Cl^-$$

$$NaOH \xrightarrow{H_2O} Na^+ + OH^-$$

The hydrogen ions in aqueous solutions are extensively hydrated forming a hydrated proton, H_3O^+, called *hydronium* or *hydrooxonium ion*. The properties which are characteristic of the Arrhenius acids are those of H^+ (aq) and similarly the properties which are characteristic of the Arrhenius bases are due to OH^- (aq)

$$H^+(aq) + HCO_3^-(aq) \longrightarrow H_2O(l) + CO_2(g)$$

$$OH^-(aq) + NH_4^+(aq) \longrightarrow NH_3(aq) + H_2O(l)$$

This definition of acids and bases is restricted because it limits the discussion of acid-base phenomenon in aqueous solutions only.

Brønsted-Lowry Concept of Acids and Bases: A major improvement over the Arrhenius concept of acids and bases was suggested independently by the Danish chemist, J.N. Brønsted and the British chemist T.M. Lowry in 1923. According to them an acid is a substance that is able to donate a proton, (*i.e.*, a hydrogen ion H^+) to some other substance. A base, on the other hand, is defined as a substance that is able to accept a proton from an acid. An acid is thus a *proton donor* and a base is a *proton acceptor*. According to this definition, there must be a relationship between the acid and the base. For example, when HCl is added to water the reaction

$$HCl + H_2O \rightarrow H_3O^+ + Cl^-$$

shows HCl acting as a proton donor (Brønsted acid) and H_2O acting as a proton acceptor (Brønsted base). The reverse of the above reaction is also an acid base reaction in the Brønsted-Lowry concept with hydronium ion serving as an acid by giving up its proton, and with chloride ion functioning as a base by accepting it. Thus, we might view our reaction as an equilibrium where we have two acids and bases

$$\underset{\text{acid}}{HCl} + \underset{\text{base}}{H_2O} \rightleftharpoons \underset{\text{acid}}{H_3O^+} + \underset{\text{base}}{Cl^-}$$

When a proton donor HX gives up a proton it forms a species X^-, which can pick up a proton to regenerate HX. In other words, when an acid loses a proton the residue has the tendency to accept the proton and hence will act as a base. Thus, every Brønsted acid is coupled with a related Brønsted base. When the acid HCl reacts it yields the base Cl^-. These two substances are related to one another by the loss or gain of a single proton. These two together constitute *conjugate acid-base pair*. In general, we say that every acid has its conjugate base and every base has its conjugate acid. In the above reaction there are two conjugate acid-base pairs, namely, HCl/Cl^- and H_3O^+-H_2O. We say that Cl^- is the conjugate base of the acid HCl and HCl is the conjugate acid of the base Cl^-, similarly H_2O is the conjugate base of H_3O^+ and H_3O^+ is the conjugate acid of H_2O. In general, we can represent any Brønsted-Lowry acid-base reaction as

$$\text{acid I} + \text{base II} \rightleftharpoons \text{acid II} + \text{base I}$$

where acid I and base I represent one conjugate pair and acid II and base II the other. Some examples of conjugate acid-base pairs are given below:

Acid I		Base II		Acid II		Base I
HCl	+	H_2O	$\rightleftharpoons$	H_3O^+	+	Cl^-
HNO_3	+	H_2O	$\rightleftharpoons$	H_3O^+	+	NO_3^-
CH_3COOH	+	H_2O	$\rightleftharpoons$	H_3O^+	+	CH_3COO^-
H_2O	+	NH_3	$\rightleftharpoons$	NH_4^+	+	OH^-
H_2SO_4	+	H_2O	$\rightleftharpoons$	H_3O^+	+	HSO_4^-
HSO_4^-	+	H_2O	$\rightleftharpoons$	H_3O^+	+	SO_4^{2-}
H_2CO_3	+	H_2O	$\rightleftharpoons$	H_3O^+	+	HCO_3^-
H_2O	+	H_2O	$\rightleftharpoons$	H_3O^+	+	OH^-
NH_3	+	NH_3	$\rightleftharpoons$	NH_4^+	+	NH_2^-

All these conjugate acid-base pairs differ by a single proton. In the above examples, we notice that there are many molecules or ions which can behave as acids in one instance and can function as bases in the other. Such substances which can serve in either capacity depending on the conditions are said to be *amphiprotic*. H_2O, NH_3, HSO_4^- are such substances in the above examples.

Relative Strengths of Acids and Bases: The strength of an acid is determined by its tendency to give up a proton and the strength of a base is determined by its tendency to accept a proton. A strong acid has a strong tendency to donate H^+ and a strong base has a strong tendency to accept H^+. Aqueous solutions of acids like $HClO_4$, HCl, H_2SO_4, HNO_3, etc., are essentially completely ionized, *i.e.*, the reactions in which they donate protons to water proceed to almost completion. These acids are, therefore, relatively strong. However, water solutions of acids like acetic acid, formic acid, hydrocyanic acid, etc., are partially ionized; they tend to donate protons to water only to a limited extent. Such acids are relatively weak. Between these two extremes we have moderately strong acids.

Any Brønsted Lowry acid-base reaction can be viewed as two opposing or competing reactions between acids and bases. For example, the reaction of HCl with water

$$HCl + H_2O \rightleftharpoons H_3O^+ + Cl^-$$

proceeds to virtual completion. In other words, the equilibrium lies far to the right and the reverse occurs to a very small extent. Thus H_2O has a much stronger affinity for a proton than does a chloride ion. We express this relative ability to pick up a proton by putting two arrows of unequal lengths and by saying that water is a strong base than chloride ion. We can also speak of the relative strengths of two acids, HCl and H_3O^+. Of the two acids, HCl is better able to donate its proton than H_3O^+ and hence is a stronger acid.

The position of equilibrium in an acid-base reaction tells us the relative strengths of the acids and bases involved. Hydrogen chloride is a strong acid in water because the equilibrium lies far to the right. However, with HF there is little tendency to transfer the proton to H_2O and is thus a weak acid.

Ionisation of a weak acid such as acetic acid

$$HAc + H_2O \rightleftharpoons H_3O^+ + Ac^-$$

occurs to a limited extent, *i.e.*, the equilibrium lies far to the left. It is therefore a weaker acid than H_3O^+ and its conjugate base CH_3COO^- is a stronger base than water. Again, stronger acid H_3O^+ has a weaker conjugate base H_2O and a stronger base CH_3COO^- has a weaker conjugate acid CH_3COOH. In general, where a Brønsted-Lowry reaction proceeds very far towards completion, both strong acid and strong base produce weak acid and weak base.

Strong acid [HA] + strong base [B⁻] $\rightleftharpoons$ *weak base [A⁻] + weak acid [HB]*.

A generalisation is that a strong acid has a weak conjugate base. For example, the strong acid HCl has Cl^- ion as its weak conjugate base while an amide ion NH_2^- is a strong base having NH_3 as its weak conjugate acid.

In the Brønsted-Lowry concept, the classification of acids is done according to their ability to donate protons to a specified base. All strong acids are completely ionized in water forming H_3O^+ which is the strongest acid that can exist in water. Thus in water, the strengths of all acids (*e.g.*, HCl, HNO_3, $HClO_4$, etc.) stronger than H_3O^+ are reduced to the same level of H_3O^+, *i.e.*, these acids appear to be of equal strength in water which is acting as the base. This effect on the strength of an acid by a solvent is called the *leveling effect*. Similarly, all bases stronger than OH^- (oxide ion O^{2-}, amide ion NH_2^-, hydride ion H^- etc.) reacts completely with water to give OH^- ions. Therefore with water as a solvent, the base strengths of these bases are reduced to the same level of OH^- ion. In other words, it is impossible to differentiate their base strengths. Hence the relative strengths of acids stronger than H_3O^+ cannot be measured in water. One can measure the acid strengths in such cases by using a solvent that does not produce a leveling effect. For example, there is an appreciable difference between the extent to which the reactions

$$HCl + HC_2H_3O_2 \rightleftharpoons H_2C_2H_3O_2^+ + Cl^-$$

$$HNO_3 + HC_2H_3O_2 \rightleftharpoons H_2C_2H_3O_2^+ + NO_3^-$$

$$HClO_4 + HC_2H_3O_2 \rightleftharpoons H_2C_2H_3O_2^+ + ClO_4^-$$

proceed in acetic acid. In fact, we find that the strengths of these three acids increasing in the order $HNO_3 < HCl < HClO_4$. For these substances water is a leveling solvent while acetic acid serves as a differentiating solvent.

Table 14.2 shows the relative strengths of acid-base pairs as judged from the position of equilibrium in acid-base reactions.

Table 14.2. Relative Strengths of Acid-Base Pairs

	Conjugate acid	*Conjugate base*	
Strongest	$HClO_4$	ClO_4^-	Weakest
	H_2SO_4	HSO_4^-	
	HCl	Cl^-	
	H_3O^+	H_2O	
	HF	F^-	
	$HC_2H_3O_2$	$C_2H_3O_2^-$	
	H_2S	HS^-	
	NH_4^+	NH_3	
	HCO_3^-	CO_3^{2-}	
	H_2O	OH^-	
Weakest	NH_3	NH_2^-	Strongest

Lewis Concept of Acids and Bases: In the Brønsted-Lowry concept of acids and bases, the stress has been laid on the proton, and acid-base reactions are regarded as proton transfer reactions. G.N. Lewis proposed a new theory of acids and bases even broader in scope than that of Brønsted and Lowry. In this concept the emphasis has been put on the electron pair transfer and the covalent bond formation. According to him, an acid is any species that acts as *an electron pair acceptor* and a base any species that acts as *an electron pair donor*. The acid is, therefore, known as an electrophile while the base as a nucleophile. An acid base reaction is the sharing of an electron pair provided by the base to the acid. For example, in the reaction

$$H^+ + \underset{\text{base}}{:\overset{\displaystyle N}{\underset{\displaystyle H}{N:}\,H}} \longrightarrow \left[H\overset{\displaystyle N}{\underset{\displaystyle H}{:N:}\,H} \right]^+$$

the Lewis acid H^+ accepts a lone pair of electrons donated by the Lewis base NH_3. The generality of the Lewis definition can be seen from the fact that it covers very diverse reactions such as

$$H\!:\!\overset{\displaystyle H}{\underset{\displaystyle H}{N}}\!: + \; B\!:\!\overset{\displaystyle :F:}{\underset{\displaystyle :F:}{F}}\!: \longrightarrow H\!:\!\overset{\displaystyle H}{\underset{\displaystyle H}{N}}\!:\!B\!:\!\overset{\displaystyle :F:}{\underset{\displaystyle :F:}{F}}\!:$$

and

$$: \overset{..}{\underset{..}{Cl}} : \qquad \left[\begin{array}{c} : \overset{..}{\underset{..}{Cl}} : \\ \end{array}\right]^{-}$$

$$: \overset{..}{\underset{..}{Cl}} : Al \ + : \overset{..}{\underset{..}{Cl}} :^{-} \longrightarrow \left[: \overset{..}{\underset{..}{Cl}} : Al : \overset{..}{\underset{..}{Cl}} :\right]^{-}$$

$$: \overset{..}{\underset{..}{Cl}} : \qquad : \overset{..}{\underset{..}{Cl}} :$$

Lewis definition considerably extends the number of substances that can be classified as acids. A Lewis acid must have vacant orbitals capable of receiving the electron pair of the base. The proton is just a single example of a Lewis acid.

Lewis acid can be classified into the following categories:

(i) *Simple Cations:* All cations are potential Lewis acids, although their strengths as acids vary within wide limits. Thus, K^+ is a weak Lewis acid while Al^{3+} is a powerful Lewis acid. Typical acid-base reactions involving cations are

$$Al^{3+} + 6 : O \overset{H}{\underset{H}{<}} \longrightarrow \left[Al(H_2O)_6\right]^{3+}$$

$$Cu^{2+} + 4 : NH_3 \longrightarrow \left[Cu(NH_3)_4\right]^{2+}$$

$$Li^+ + : O \overset{CH_3}{\underset{H}{<}} \longrightarrow \left[Li \leftarrow O \overset{CH_3}{\underset{H}{<}}\right]^{+}$$

$$Fe^{3+} + 6 : CN^- \longrightarrow \left[Fe(CN)_6\right]^{3-}$$

An increase in the charge density of cations increases the capacity to accept the pair of electrons and therefore increases the acid character.

(ii) *Compound in which the Central Atom has an Incomplete Octet:* Typical examples of such Lewis acids are BF_3, BCl_3, $AlCl_3$, $FeBr_2$, etc. and some of the reactions of these acids with bases are

$$: \overset{\overset{..}{F}:}{\underset{\underset{..}{F}:}{\overset{|}{\underset{|}{B}}}} \ : F - \ + : O \overset{OC_2H_5}{\underset{OC_2H_5}{<}} \longrightarrow \overset{F}{\underset{F}{\overset{|}{\underset{|}{F - B}}}} \leftarrow O(OC_2H_5)_2$$

$$: F - \overset{..}{Be} - \overset{..}{F} : + 2F^- \longrightarrow \left[\overset{F}{\underset{F}{\overset{|}{\underset{|}{F - Be - F}}}}\right]^{2-}$$

The strengths of such acids will increase with an increase in the nuclear charge, increase in the number and relative electronegativity of the atoms attached to the central atom.

(iii) *Compounds in which the Octet of the Central Atom can be Expanded:* $SiCl_4$ or SiF_4 acts as a Lewis acid. Si with its vacant d ortibals can accept electron pairs by expanding its octet. This is shown by the action of SiF_4 with F^- to form fluosilicate ion.

$$
\begin{array}{c}
F \\
| \\
F-Si-F \\
| \\
F
\end{array}
+ 2F^- \longrightarrow
\left[
\begin{array}{ccc}
F & & F \\
 & \vee & \\
F & - \ Si \ - & F \\
 & \wedge & \\
F & & F
\end{array}
\right]^{2-}
$$

Similarly, compounds like $SnCl_4$, $TiCl_4$, PCl_3, SF_4, etc. act as Lewis acids due to the vacant d orbitals of the central atoms. In CCl_4 or CF_4 carbon with no available d orbitals cannot act as Lewis acid.

(iv) *Molecules with a Multiple Bond Between Atoms of Dissimilar Electronegativities:* Examples of such substances are CO_2, SO_2, etc. In CO_2, oxygen atoms are more electronegative than the carbon atom. As a result, the electron density due to the π electrons is displaced away from the carbon atom towards the oxygen atoms. The carbon atom is electron deficient and can accept electron pair from a Lewis base. The reaction of CO_2 and SO_2 with hydroxyl ions can be represented as

$$
\overset{..}{O}=C^{\delta+}=\overset{..}{\underset{..}{O}}{}^{-\delta} +
\left[
\overset{..}{\underset{..}{O}}-H
\right]^-
=
\left[
\begin{array}{c}
\overset{..}{O} \\
\| \\
C-\overset{..}{\underset{..}{O}}-H \\
| \\
\overset{..}{\underset{..}{O}}{\vdots}
\end{array}
\right]^-
$$

$$
\begin{array}{c}
\overset{..}{O} \\
\| \\
\overset{\delta+}{S} \\
\| \\
\underset{..\ \delta-}{\overset{..}{O}}
\end{array}
+
\left[
\overset{..}{\underset{..}{O}}-H
\right]^-
=
\left[
\begin{array}{c}
O \\
\| \\
S-\overset{..}{\underset{..}{O}}-H \\
| \\
\overset{..}{\underset{..}{O}}{\vdots}
\end{array}
\right]^-
$$

Similarly, Lewis bases can be classified into three categories:

(i) All the anions are Lewis bases; they are electron rich and have greater ability to donate an electron pair. Greater the charge density on the anion greater will be the ability to donate an electron pair and therefore stronger it will act as a base.

(ii) Molecules in which an atom has one or two unshared pairs of electron is a Lewis base, *e.g.,* ammonia.

(iii) Molecules with carbon-carbon double bonds are Lewis bases. The base character in these cases is due to the easy availability of the π electrons.

Some other Concepts of acids and bases

According to Cady and Elsey (1928) an acid is a substance which increases the concentration of positive ions characteristic of the solvent and base is a substance which increases the concentration of negative ions characteristic of the solvent. For example, all ammonium (NH_4^+) salts in liquid ammonia will behave as acids, since they all provide NH_4^+ ions and thus increase the concentration of positive ions which are characteristic of the solvent liquid NH_3. Similarly all soluble amides will behave as bases, as they all increase the concentration of NH_2^- ions characteristic of the solvent liquid NH_3.

The Lux-Flood defined acids as oxides which accept oxygen and bases as oxides which donate oxygen.

The Usanovich defined an acid as any species capable of giving cations, combining with anions or electrons or neutralizing a base to give a salt. In other words, an acid is a cation, a cation donor, an electron pair acceptor. Similarly, a base is defined as any species capable of giving anions or electrons, combining with cation or neutralizing an acid to give a salt.

It is thus obvious that this concept of acid and base includes all the previous acid base definitions. It also includes many reactions such as oxidation-reduction reactions involving the transfer of electrons.

Hard and soft acids and bases: A hard acid, like a hard base, is difficult to polarise. A cationic hard acid such as H^+, Be^{2+}, Al^{3+}, etc. are generally small in size, having high positive charge and a noble gas configuration. Soft acids and bases are larger in size and are readily polarisable, have low positive charge and do not have a noble gas configuration *e.g.* Cu^+, Hg^{2+}, Ag^+, Tl^+ etc.

14.4 ACID-BASE STRENGTH AND STRUCTURE

The correlation between molecular structure and acid-base strength is complex and involves many factors. Polar molecules with a hydrogen atom situated at the positive end of the dipole are acids, in such molecules electrons are withdrawn from hydrogen atom thereby facilitating its release as a proton. the strongest acid is one where the hydrogen atoms are in electron deficient surroundings. The strongest base would be an anion with a large negative charge on an atom of low electronegativity. We shall discuss here some of the more important factors which determine the acid-base character.

(*i*) **Acidity, Basicity and Charge:** Other factors (size, electronegativity, etc.), being equal, acidity increases with positive charge and basicity with negative charge. $\left[Fe(H_2O)_6\right]^{3+}$ is a stronger acid than $\left[Fe(H_2O)_6\right]^{2+}$ and HPO_4^{2-} is a stronger base than $H_2PO_4^-$. Similarly in the series H_3O^+, H_2O, OH^- and O^{2-}; H_3O^+ would be expected to be a powerful acid while O^{2-} will be a strong base.

$$\xrightarrow{\hspace{5cm}} \text{Increasing acid character}$$
$$O^{2-} < OH^- < H_2O < H_3O^+$$

(*ii*) **Acidity, Basicity and Relative Electronegativities:** In an acid HA, the more strongly A withdraws the bonding electron pair from H, the more stronger would be the acid or the acidity of HA should increase with increasing electronegativity of *A*. In a horizontal period of elements in the periodic table electronegativity increases with atomic number. We would therefore predict that acid character of the hydrides should vary in the order

Order of increasing acidity

$$LiH < BeH_2 < CH_4 < NH_3 < H_2O < HF$$

Many acids and bases are compounds in which the basic centre is an oxygen or a nitrogen atom to which hydrogen is attached. Such acids and bases may be regarded as derivatives of H_2O and NH_3. For any derivative of H_2O or NH_3, YOH or YNH_2, the acid and base strengths can vary widely in either direction from those of parent compounds depending on the electronegativity of Y. If Y is less electronegative than hydrogen then Y will increase the electron pair availability at oxygen or nitrogen atom and will decrease electron pair withdrawal from hydrogen bonded to oxygen or nitrogen atom. Consequently, YOH or YNH_2 will be more basic or less acidic than its parent compound H_2O or NH_3. On the other hand, if Y is more electronegative than hydrogen then Y will decrease the electron availability at oxygen or nitrogen atom and will increase electron withdrawal from the hydrogen linked to oxygen or nitrogen atoms. The compound YOH or YNH_2 will therefore be less basic or more acidic than its parent compound.

If Y = Na, YOH is NaOH — a strong base; and YNH_2 is $NaNH_2$ — a strong base.

In case, Y = Cl, YOH is HOCl — more acidic than water; and YNH_2 is $ClNH_2$ — less basic than ammonia. If Y = R, YOH is ROH — less acidic than water and YNH_2 is RNH_2 — more basic than ammonia.

As an example of the effect of an increase in the electronegativity of Y in increasing acidity and decreasing basicity in YOH, consider a series of compounds in which all the central atoms to which OH groups are attached belong to the same family and exhibit the same oxidation state. Acidity increases with increasing electronegativity. Hence in the series we predict:

$$\overline{HOCl > HOBr > HOI} \rightarrow \text{Decreasing order of acidity}$$

$$\overline{HClO_3 > HBrO_3 > HIO_3} \rightarrow \text{Decreasing order of acidity}$$

$$\overline{HClO_4 > HBrO_4 > HIO_4} \rightarrow \text{Decreasing order of acidity}$$

$$\overline{HNO_3 > H_3PO_4 > H_3AsO_4 > HSb(OH)_6 > HBiO_3} \rightarrow \text{Decreasing order of acidity}$$

For compounds containing OH group attached to the central atom, acidity increases with an increase in the number of electronegative atoms attached to the central atom. This is indicated by the series

$$\overline{HOCl < HClO_2 < HClO_2 < HClO_4} \rightarrow \text{Increasing order of acidity}$$

In a horizontal period electronegativity as well as oxidation state increases and consequently, acidity of hydroxides increases from left to right in a period.

$\rightarrow$ Increasing order of acidity

$$\overline{NaOH < Mg(OH)_2 < Al(OH)_3^{\cdot} < Si(OH)_4 < H_3PO_4 < H_2SO_4 < HClO_4}$$

(iii) **Acidity, Basicity and Ion Size:** In a group, the atomic size increases from top to bottom. The charge dispersal is greater in larger ions or in molecules with larger central atom. For halide ions, ionic size increases from F^- to I^-. It means that the charge dispersal increases, charge density decreases and the basic character of these ions decreases from F^- to I^-. Hence in HF, hydrogen will be strongly bonded to fluorine while in HI it will be held less firmly to iodine and the removal of hydrogen as a proton is easier from HI than from HF. HI would therefore be a stronger acid than HF. For the series we have

$$\overline{} \rightarrow \text{Decreasing order of electronegativity}$$
$$F^- > Cl^- > Br^- > I^-$$

$$\overline{} \rightarrow \text{Increasing order of size and charge dispersal and decreasing order of basicity of anions.}$$

$$\underline{HF < HCl < HBr < HI} \rightarrow \text{Increasing order of acidity}$$

Similarly, for the series

$$\overline{\phantom{H_2O < H_2S < H_2Se < H_2Te}} \rightarrow \text{Increasing order of acidity}$$
$$H_2O < H_2S < H_2Se < H_2Te$$

$$\overline{\phantom{NH_3 < PH_3 < AsH_3 < SbH_3}} \rightarrow \text{Increasing order of acidity}$$
$$NH_3 < PH_3 < AsH_3 < SbH_3$$

(*iv*) **Acidity, Basicity and Resonance:** Due to resonance the positive or the negative charge is effectively dispersed. In such cases, resonance may have a pronounced influence on acidity or basicity of a compound. Delocalisation of electron density stabilises the base and thus decreases its tendency to accept proton and weakens the base character. CH_3COOH is a stronger

acid than water because the conjugate base $CH_3 - \overset{\displaystyle |}{\underset{\displaystyle O_-}{C}} = O$ is stabilised by resonance. Phenol is

a stronger acid than water because the phenolate anion is stabilised by resonance. In the anions ClO_4^-, ClO_3^-, ClO_2^- and ClO^- the negative charge is stabilised due to resonance more effectively in ClO_4^- and hence it would act as a weak base. Consequently, its conjugate acid $HClO_4$ will be a stronger acid in the series. Thus we have

Increasing order of charge dispersal

$$\overline{} \rightarrow$$

$$\left[Cl \overset{..}{-} O\right]^- < \left[\begin{matrix} Cl \overset{..}{-} O \\ | \\ O \end{matrix}\right]^- < \left[O \overset{..}{-} \overset{..}{\underset{|}{Cl}} \overset{..}{-} O\right]^- < \left[O \overset{..}{-} \overset{\overset{\displaystyle O}{\displaystyle \|}}{\underset{|}{Cl}} \overset{..}{-} O\right]^-$$

$$\overline{} \rightarrow \text{Decreasing order of basicity}$$
$$\overline{HOCl < HClO_2 < HClO_3 < HClO_4} \rightarrow \text{Increasing order of acidity}$$

Similarly, in the ions F^- and $HSiF_6^-$ charge dispersal is more in the latter, it is thus a weak base and its conjugate acid H_2SiF_6 would be stronger than HF.

(*v*) **Acidity, Basicity and Type of Bonding in the Molecule:** Acid base character also depends on the kind of orbitals used in bond formation. An *s* orbital is spherically symmetrical while *p* or *sp* hybridised orbitals have directional characteristics and the charge density is localised along the axis of these orbitals. We can illustrate this by comparing the acid characters of CH_4, $CH_2 = CH_2$ and $CH \equiv CH$. The orbitals involved in bonding in these compounds are sp^3, sp^2 and sp hybrid orbitals respectively. The s character in CH_4 is 25% while in $CH \equiv CH$ it is 50%. Thus $CH \equiv CH$ would be expected to be a weaker base (or stronger acid) in comparison to CH_4.

The base character of NH_3 and PH_3 can also be explained in terms of the orbitals that house the lone pair of electrons. In NH_3, nitrogen atom uses sp^3 hybrid orbitals while in PH_3 the lone pair is in the s orbital. The electron density on phosphorus atom is less due to the spherical symmetry of s orbital while on nitrogen atom it is more because of the directional character of the sp^3 hybridised orbitals. PH_3 is therefore less basic than NH_3.

14.5 IONIZATION OF WEAK ACIDS AND WEAK BASES

Weak acids or weak bases are incompletely ionized in water and the unionised molecules exist in equilibrium with the ions in solution. In the case of a weak acid like HA, the equilibrium may be represented as

$$HA + H_2O \rightleftharpoons H_3O^+ + A^-$$

The equilibrium constant of this ionization is given by

$$K = \frac{a_{H_3O^+} a_{A^-}}{a_{HA} a_{H_2O}} \qquad ...(14.4)$$

where *a*'s are the activities of the respective species.

The activity is defined as the product of the concentration, C (in moles per litre) and the activity coefficient γ

$$a = \gamma C$$

For dilute solutions, the activity coefficient γ is equal to unity and hence the activity is equal to concentration. Equation (14.4) then becomes

$$K = \frac{\left[H_3O^+\right]\left[A^-\right]}{[HA][H_2O]} \qquad ...(14.5)$$

Since the concentration of water remains almost constant and can be amalgamated with K, Eq. (14.5) becomes

$$K_a = K[H_2O] = \frac{\left[H_3O^+\right]\left[A^-\right]}{[HA]} \qquad ...(14.6)$$

where K_a is the *ionization constant* for the acid. If α is the degree of ionization and C the initial concentration of the acid, then

$$[HA] = C(1 - \alpha)$$

$$\left[H_3O^+\right] = \left[A^-\right] = C\alpha$$

Substituting these values in Eq. (14.6), we get

$$K_a = \frac{C\alpha^2}{(1-\alpha)} \qquad \qquad ...(14.7)$$

For a weak acid, $\alpha \ll 1$, therefore, Eq. (14.7) reduces to

$$K_a = C\alpha^2$$

or

$$\alpha = \sqrt{K_a/C} \qquad \qquad ...(14.8)$$

Hence

$$\left[H_3O^+\right] = C\alpha = C\sqrt{K_a/C} = \sqrt{K_aC} \qquad \qquad ...(14.9)$$

For calculating exact value of $[H_3O^+]$, Eq. (14.7) should be used.

However, for acids where $\alpha \ll 1$, Eq. (14.9) can be used. The ionization constant, K_b for a weak base which ionizes according to the reaction

$$BOH \underset{}{\overset{H_2O}{\rightleftharpoons}} B^+ + OH^-$$

is given by

$$K_b = \frac{\left[B^+\right]\left[OH^-\right]}{\left[BOH\right]}$$

If α is the degree of ionization of the base and C its initial concentration, K_b is given by

$$K_b = \frac{\left[B^+\right]\left[OH^-\right]}{\left[BOH\right]} = \frac{C\alpha^2}{1-\alpha} \qquad \qquad ...(14.10)$$

If $\alpha \ll 1$,

$$K_b = C\alpha^2$$

or

$$\alpha = \sqrt{K_b/C}$$

Hence,

$$\left[OH^-\right] = C\alpha = \sqrt{K_bC} \qquad \qquad ...(14.11)$$

Since α is a measure of acid or base strength, Eq. (14.8) or (14.11) can be used for comparing strengths of weak acids or weak bases in aqueous solutions.

If at a given concentration, α_1 is the degree of ionization of one acid and α_2 that of another acid at the same concentration, then from Eq. (14.8), the ratio of acid strengths is given by

$$\frac{(\text{strength of acid})_1}{(\text{strength of acid})_2} = \frac{\alpha_1}{\alpha_2} = \sqrt{\frac{K_{a_1}}{K_{a_2}}}$$

14.6 EXACT TREATMENT OF IONIZATION EQUILIBRIA OF A WEAK MONOPROTIC ACID

The two equilibria in solution are ionization of the acid and ionization of water. The corresponding ionization constant and ionic product of water are given as

$$HA + H_2O \rightleftharpoons H_3O^+ + A^-$$

$$K_a = \frac{\left[H_3O^+\right]\left[A^-\right]}{\left[HA\right]} \qquad \qquad ...(14.12)$$

and

$$H_2O + H_2O \rightleftharpoons H_3O^+ + OH^-$$

$$K_w = \left[H_3O^+\right]\left[OH^-\right] \qquad \qquad ...(14.13)$$

The mass balance for the acid requires

$$\left[HA\right]_0 = \left[HA\right] + \left[A^-\right] \qquad \qquad ...(14.14)$$

where $[HA]_0$ is the initial concentration of the acid while $[HA]$ and $[A^-]$ are the concentrations of the unionized and ionized forms of the acid in solution. From the charge balance for the solution, we have

$$\left[H_3O^+\right] = \left[A^-\right] + \left[OH^-\right]$$

Since

$$\left[OH^-\right] = \frac{K_w}{\left[H_3O^+\right]}$$

therefore,

$$\left[H_3O^+\right] = \left[A^-\right] + \frac{K_w}{\left[H_3O^+\right]}$$

or,

$$\left[A^-\right] = \left[H_3O^+\right] - \frac{K_w}{\left[H_3O^+\right]} \qquad \qquad ...(14.15)$$

Similarly $[HA]$ from Eq. (14.14) is given by

$$\left[HA\right] = \left[HA\right]_0 - \left[A^-\right] \qquad \qquad ...(14.16)$$

Substituting the value of $[A^-]$ from Eq. (14.15), gives

$$\left[HA\right] = \left[HA\right]_0 - \left[H_3O^+\right] + \frac{K_w}{\left[H_3O^+\right]}$$

Putting the values of concentrations of $[HA]$ and $[A^-]$ in equation (14.12) yields

$$K_a = \frac{[H_3O^+]\left\{[H_3O^+] - \dfrac{K_w}{[H_3O^+]}\right\}}{[HA]_0 - [H_3O^+] + \dfrac{K_w}{[H_3O^+]}}$$

$$= \frac{[H_3O^+]\left\{[H_3O^+]^2 - K_w\right\}}{[H_3O^+][HA]_0 - [H_3O^+]^2 + K_w} \qquad ...(14.17)$$

From this equation one can calculate the exact concentration of $[H_3O^+]$ ions in the solution. The concentrations of other species, viz., $[A^-]$, $[HA]$ and $[OH^-]$ can then be obtained. Since (14.17) is cubic in $[H_3O^+]$ and is difficult to solve, one can therefore solve this equation for $[H_3O^+]$ under different conditions.

Case I: When $[H_3O^+] > 10^{-6}M$; hydronium ions contributed by water are negligible in comparison to those contributed by the acid, i.e.,

$[OH^-] = \dfrac{K_w}{[H_3O^+]}$ can be neglected. Hence equation (14.17) reduces to

$$K_a = \frac{[H_3O^+]^2}{[HA]_0 - [H_3O^+]}$$

This is a quadratic equation in $[H_3O^+]$ which on solving gives

$$[H_3O^+] = \frac{-K_a \pm \sqrt{K_a^2 + 4Ka(HA)_0}}{2} \qquad ...(14.18)$$

This equation gives two values of $[H_3O^+]$, only the positive value is to be considered.

Case II: When the ionization constant of the acid is small and ionizes only to a limited extent, i.e.,

$$[HA]_0 >> [H_3O^+]$$

and

$$K_a[HA]_0 = [H_3O^+]^2$$

so

$$[H_3O^+] = \sqrt{K_a(HA)_0}$$

Ionization of a Weak Monoacidic Base

The exact concentration of hydroxyl ions in an aqueous solution of a base BOH can be obtained in the same manner as done above.

$$BOH \overset{H_2O}{\rightleftharpoons} B^+ + OH^-$$

$$K_b = \frac{[B^+][OH^-]}{[BOH]} \qquad \qquad ...(14.19)$$

and
$$H_2O + H_2O \rightleftharpoons H_3O^+ + OH^-$$

$$K_w = [H_3O^+][OH^-] \qquad \qquad ...(14.20)$$

The material balance requires

$$[BOH]_0 = [BOH] + [B^+] \qquad \qquad ...(14.21)$$

While the charge balance gives

$$[OH^-] = [B^+] + [H_3O^+] \qquad \qquad ...(14.22)$$

From charge balance Eq. (14.22), we get

$$[B^+] = [OH^-] - [H_3O^+]$$

$$= [OH^-] - \frac{K_w}{[OH^-]} \qquad \qquad ...(14.23)$$

From Eq. (14.23) and (14.21), we have

$$[BOH] = [BOH]_0 - [OH^-] + \frac{K_w}{[OH^-]}$$

Substituting the values of $[B^+]$ and $[BOH]$ in Eq. (14.19), we get

$$K_b = \frac{\left\{ [OH^-] - \dfrac{K_w}{[OH^-]} \right\} [OH^-]}{[BOH]_0 - [OH^-] + \dfrac{K_w}{[OH^-]}}$$

Once the $[OH^-]$ is known, the concentration of the other species viz, $[B^+]$, $[BOH]$ and $[H_3O^+]$ can be calculated in the solution.

Problem 14.1: Calculate the degree of ionization and the hydrogen ion concentration of a 10^{-3} M acetic acid solution at 298 K ($K_a = 1.85 \times 10^{-5}$).

   Solution: $C = 10^{-3}$ M and $K_a = 1.85 \times 10^{-5}$

   If α is the degree of ionization of the acid then from Eq. (14.7)

$$K_a = \frac{\left(10^{-3}\alpha^2\right)}{(1-\alpha)} = 1.85 \times 10^{-5}$$

On solving it for α, we get

$$\alpha = 0.127 \text{ or } 12.7\%$$

and

$$\left[H_3O^+\right] = C\alpha = 10^{-3} \times 0.127 \text{ M}$$

$$= 1.27 \times 10^{-4} \text{ M}$$

Problem 14.2: What is the concentration of acetic acid which can be added to 0.5 M formic acid solution so that the percentage dissociation of both is equal?

$$K_a \text{ (HA}_c) = 1.8 \times 10^{-5}, K_a \text{ (HCOOH)} = 2.4 \times 10^{-4}$$

Solution: Since percentage dissociation is the same, so $[H_3O^+]$ from acetic acid and formic acid will be the same. Now

and

$$\left[H_3O^+\right]_{HA} = \sqrt{C_{HAc} K_a(HAc)}$$

$$\left[H_3O^+\right]_{HCOOH} = \sqrt{C_{HCOOH} K_a(HCOOH)}$$

or

$$C_{HAc} = \frac{C_{HCOOH} K_a(HCOOH)}{K_a(HAc)} = \frac{0.5 \times 2.4 \times 10^{-4}}{1.8 \times 10^{-5}} = \frac{20}{3} \text{ M}$$

Problem 14.3: Calculate the degree of ionization and the hydroxyl ion concentration in 0.2 M NH_3 solution ($K_b = 1.85 \times 10^{-5}$ at 298 K).

Solution:

$$NH_3 + H_2O \rightleftharpoons NH_4^+ + OH^-$$

$$K_a = \frac{\left[NH_4^+\right]\left[OH^-\right]}{\left[NH_3\right]} = 1.85 \times 10^{-5}$$

If α is the degree of ionization, then at equilibrium

$$\left[NH_4^+\right] = \left[OH^-\right] = 0.2\,\alpha$$

and

$$\left[NH_3\right] = 0.2(1-\alpha)$$

Therefore

$$K_b = \frac{(0.2\,\alpha)^2}{0.2(1-\alpha)} = 1.85 \times 10^{-5}$$

or

$$\alpha = 0.962 \times 10^{-2}$$

Hence

$$\left[OH^-\right] = 0.2\alpha = 1.924 \times 10^{-3} \text{ M}$$

Problem 14.4: Compare the acidity of 0.1 M HCNO with that of 0.1 M HCN. $K_{HCNO} = 1.2 \times 10^{-4}$ and $K_{HCN} = 4.0 \times 10^{-10}$ at 298 K.

Solution: Since the acidities are directly proportional to the square root of the ionization constants therefore,

$$\frac{\text{acidity of HCNO}}{\text{acidity of HCN}} = \sqrt{\frac{1.2 \times 10^{-4}}{4 \times 10^{-10}}} = 550$$

The solution of HCNO is 550 times more acidic than the solution of HCN.

14.7 MULTISTAGE IONIC EQUILIBRIA

Ionization of Polybasic or Polyprotic acids: Polybasic or polyprotic acids are those which can furnish more than one proton per molecule. Some of the common examples are H_2SO_4, $H_2C_2O_4$, H_2CO_3, H_2SO_3, H_3PO_4 etc. Polyprotic acids ionize in a stepwise manner and there is an ionization constant for each step which is indicated by adding subscripts to K_a. For a dibasic acid H_2A, first and second stages of ionization can be represented by the equilibria

$$H_2A + H_2O \rightleftharpoons H_3O^+ + HA^- \; ; K_{a_1} = \frac{\left[H_3O^+\right]\left[HA^-\right]}{\left[H_2A\right]}$$

$$HA^- + H_2O \rightleftharpoons H_3O^+ + A^{2-} \; ; K_{a_2} = \frac{\left[H_3O^+\right]\left[A^{2-}\right]}{\left[HA^-\right]}$$

where K_{a_1} and K_{a_2} are the ionization constants of the successive steps. These ionization constants give a measure of the extent to which each ionization step has proceeded. Primary ionization is stronger than the secondary ionization because a proton is released more readily by an acid molecule rather than by a uninegative ion. If $K_{a_1} \gg K_{a_2}$ the second ionization would be very small and will be appreciable only at high dilutions. In such cases a dibasic acid may behave so far as ionization is concerned as a monobasic acid.

For a dibasic acid, if the difference between (K_{a_1}) and (K_{a_2}) is large $\left(\dfrac{K_{a_1}}{K_{a_2}} > 10^4\right)$, the solution behaves like a mixture of two acids with ionization constants K_{a_1} and K_{a_2} respectively. However, if $\dfrac{K_{a_1}}{K_{a_2}} < 10^4$ (e.g. carbonic acid $K_{a_1} = 4.2 \times 10^{-7}$ and $K_{a_2} = 4.8 \times 10^{-11}$), only the first stage will show a point of inflexion in the neutralization curve. The second stage of ionization $\left(K_{a_2}\right)$ is very weak and will not exhibit any point of inflexion in the titration curve.

In case of H_2SO_4, primary ionization is essentially complete and the secondary ionization occurs only to a limited extent.

$$H_2SO_4 + H_2O \rightleftharpoons H_3O^+ + HSO_4^-$$

$$HSO_4^- + H_2O \rightleftharpoons H_3O^+ + SO_4^{2-} ; K_{a_2} = 1.26 \times 10^{-2}$$

Carbonic acid, H_2CO_3, undergoes ionization in two steps; both the ionization constants are weak.

$$H_2CO_3 + H_2O \rightleftharpoons HCO_3^- + H_3O^+ ; K_{a_1} = 4.2 \times 10^{-7}$$

$$HCO_3^- + H_2O \rightleftharpoons H_3O^+ + CO_3^{2-} ; K_{a_2} = 4.8 \times 10^{-11}$$

Let us now consider the ionization of a tribasic acid such as H_3PO_4 in a 0.1 M solution. The concentration of H_3O^+, $H_2PO_4^-$, HPO_4^{2-}, PO_4^{3-} and H_3PO_4 resulting from the ionization can be calculated as follows:

The ionization of H_3PO_4 takes place in three steps as represented by the equilibria

I $\qquad\qquad H_3PO_4 + H_2O \rightleftharpoons H_3O^+ + H_2PO_4^-$

$$K_{a_1} = \frac{[H_3O^+][H_2PO_4^-]}{[H_3PO_4]} = 7.1 \times 10^{-3}$$

II $\qquad\qquad H_2PO_4^- + H_2O \rightleftharpoons H_3O^+ + HPO_4^{2-}$

$$K_{a_2} = \frac{[H_3O^+][HPO_4^{2-}]}{[H_2PO_4^-]} = 6.3 \times 10^{-8}$$

III $\qquad\qquad HPO_4^{2-} + H_2O \rightleftharpoons H_3O^+ + PO_4^{3-}$

$$K_{a_3} = \frac{[H_3O^+][PO_4^{3-}]}{[HPO_4^{2-}]} = 4.2 \times 10^{-13}$$

Low values of K_{a_2} and K_{a_3} indicate that the second and the third ionizations are low and consequently, $[HPO_4^{2-}]$ and $[PO_4^{3-}]$ are exceedingly small. It follows, therefore, that the primary ionization is of importance and to a good approximation $[H_3O^+]$ and $[H_2PO_4^-]$ are equal *i.e.*,

$$[H_3O^+] = [H_2PO_4^-] \text{ and } [H_3PO_4] \cong 0.1 \text{ M}$$

Therefore,

$$K_{a_1} = \frac{[H_3O^+][H_2PO_4^-]}{0.1} = 7.1 \times 10^{-3}$$

or

$$[H_3O^+]^2 = 7.1 \times 10^{-3} \times 0.1$$

$$\left[H_3O^+\right] = 2.64 \times 10^{-2}\,M$$

Similarly, $\left[HPO_4^{2-}\right]$ can be calculated from

$$K_{a_2} = \frac{\left[H_3O^+\right]\left[HPO_4^{2-}\right]}{\left[H_2PO_4^-\right]}$$

But

$$\left[H_2PO_4^-\right] = \left[H_3O^+\right]$$

Hence

$$\left[HPO_4^{2-}\right] = K_{a_2} = 6.3 \times 10^{-8}\,M$$

On substituting these values in the equilibrium expression for the ionization

$$K_{a_3} = \frac{\left[H_3O^+\right]\left[PO_4^{3-}\right]}{\left[HPO_4^{2-}\right]}$$

we get,

$$\left[PO_4^{3-}\right] = \frac{\left[K_{a_3}\right]\left[HPO_4^{2-}\right]}{\left[H_3O^+\right]}$$

$$= \frac{\left(4.2 \times 10^{-13}\right)\left(6.3 \times 10^{-8}\right)}{\left(2.64 \times 10^{-2}\right)}$$

$$= 1.1 \times 10^{-19}\,M$$

Similarly, the ionization of polyacidic bases can take place in stages. Their ionization equilibria are treated in the same manner as illustrated for polybasic acids.

Exact Treatment of Ionization

Equilibria for a diprotic acid: A diprotic acid ionizes in two stages according to the equilibrium

$$H_2A + H_2O \rightleftharpoons H_3O^+ + HA^-$$

$$K_{a_1} = \frac{\left[H_3O^+\right]\left[HA^-\right]}{\left[H_2A\right]} \qquad \qquad ...(14.24)$$

$$HA^- + H_2O \rightleftharpoons H_3O^+ + A^{2-}$$

$$K_{a_2} = \frac{\left[H_3O^+\right]\left[A^{2-}\right]}{\left[HA^-\right]} \qquad \qquad ...(14.25)$$

$$H_2O + H_2O \rightleftharpoons H_3O^+ + OH^-$$

$$K_w = \left[H_3O^+\right]\left[OH^-\right] \qquad ...(14.26)$$

Material balance condition gives

$$\left[H_2A\right]_0 = \left[H_2A\right] + \left[HA^-\right] + \left[A^{2-}\right] \qquad ...(14.27)$$

and the charge balance condition gives

$$\left[H_3O^+\right] = \left[HA^-\right] + 2\left[A^{2-}\right] + \left[OH^-\right] \qquad ...(14.28)$$

Since A^{2-} carries two units of negative charge so it is multiplied by a factor of two.
Using equation (14.24), (14.25) and (14.26) Eq. (14.28) becomes

$$\left[H_3O^+\right] = \frac{K_{a_1}\left[H_2A\right]}{\left[H_3O^+\right]} + \frac{2K_{a_1}K_{a_2}\left[H_2A\right]}{\left[H_3O^+\right]^2} + \frac{K_w}{\left[H_3O^+\right]} \qquad ...(14.29)$$

From equation (14.27), the concentration of $[H_2A]$ can be expressed in terms of $[H_2A]_0$ as

$$\left[H_2A\right] = \left[H_2A\right]_0 - \frac{K_{a_1}\left[H_2A\right]}{\left[H_3O^+\right]} - \frac{2K_{a_1}K_{a_2}\left[H_2A\right]}{\left[H_3O^+\right]^2}$$

$$\left[H_2A\right] = \frac{\left[H_2A\right]_0}{1 + \dfrac{K_{a_1}}{\left[H_3O^+\right]} + \dfrac{2K_{a_1}K_{a_2}}{\left[H_3O^+\right]^2}}$$

Substituting the value of $[H_2A]$ in equation (14.29), we get

$$\left[H_3O^+\right] = \frac{K_{a_1}}{\left[H_3O^+\right]}\left\{\frac{\left[H_2A\right]_0}{1 + \dfrac{K_{a_1}}{\left[H_3O^+\right]} + \dfrac{2K_{a_1}K_{a_2}}{\left[H_3O^+\right]^2}}\right\}\left\{1 + \frac{2K_{a_2}}{\left[H_3O^+\right]}\right\} + \frac{K_w}{\left[H_3O^+\right]} \qquad ...(14.30)$$

The solution of this equation for $[H_3O^+]$ is cumbersome and it is therefore desirable to use it under different conditions as discussed below.

First approximation: When ionization of water is neglected: This is the case when $[H_3O^+]$ is greater than or equal to 10^{-6} M.

Thus the last term $\dfrac{K_w}{\left[H_3O^+\right]}$ is negligible in comparison to $[H_3O^+]$. The equation (14.30) thus reduces to

$$\left[H_3O^+\right] = \left\{\frac{\left[H_2A\right]_0 K_{a_1}}{\left(H_3O^+\right) + K_{a_1} + \dfrac{2K_{a_1}K_{a_2}}{\left[H_3O^+\right]}}\right\}\left\{1 + \frac{2K_{a_2}}{\left[H_3O^+\right]}\right\} \qquad ...(14.31)$$

Second approximation. When $K_{a_1} \gg K_{a_2}$. In such cases, one assumes that most of $[H_3O^+]$ ions are contributed by the first stage of the ionization and only a negligible amount is contributed from the second stage of ionization. In such a case both the terms $\dfrac{2K_{a_1}K_{a_2}}{[H_3O^+]}$ and $\dfrac{2K_{a_2}}{[H_3O^+]}$ can be neglected.

The equation (14.31) simplifies to

$$\left[H_3O^+\right] = \frac{[H_2A]_0 \, K_{a_1}}{\left[H_3O^+\right] + K_{a_1}}$$

or rearranging $$K_{a_1} = \frac{\left[H_3O^+\right]^2}{[H_2A]_0 - \left[H_3O^+\right]}$$ ...(14.31(a))

which is the same expression as derived for a monoprotic acid.

Problem 14.5: Calculate $[HS^-]$ and $[S^{2-}]$ in a 0.1 M aqueous solution of H_2S.

Given $K_{a_1} = 9.1 \times 10^{-8}$ and $K_{a_2} = 1.2 \times 10^{-15}$ at 298 K.

Solution: Two stage ionization of H_2S takes place as

$$H_2S + H_2O \rightleftharpoons H_3O^+ + HS^- \; ; \; K_{a_1} = \frac{\left[H_3O^+\right]\left[HS^-\right]}{[H_2S]} = 9.1 \times 10^{-8} \qquad \ldots(i)$$

$$HS^- + H_2O \rightleftharpoons H_3O^+ + S^{2-} \; ; \; K_{a_2} = \frac{\left[H_3O^+\right]\left[S^{2-}\right]}{[HS^-]} = 1.2 \times 10^{-15} \qquad \ldots(ii)$$

Since $K_{a_1} \gg K_{a_2}$, it follows that only the primary ionization is of significance and $[H_3O^+] =$ $[HS^-]$ and $H_2S = 0.1$ M. Substituting these values in equation (i), we get

$$\left[H_3O^+\right] = \left[HS^{-1}\right] = \sqrt{K_{a_1}[H_2S]} = \sqrt{9.1 \times 10^{-8} \times 0.1}$$

$$= 9.5 \times 10^{-5} \, M$$

Both the equations (i) and (ii) must be satisfied simultaneously. On substituting these values for $[H_3O^+]$ and $[HS^-]$ in equation (ii), we get,

$$\left[S^{2-}\right] = \frac{K_{a_2}\left[HS^-\right]}{\left[H_3O^+\right]} = \frac{(1.2 \times 10^{-15})(9.5 \times 10^{-5})}{(9.5 \times 10^{-5})}$$

$$= 1.2 \times 10^{-15} \, M$$

Problem 14.6: What would be the $[H_3O^+]$ of a 0.36 M H_2SO_4? K_{a_2} is 1.26×10^{-2} at 298 K.

Solution: H_2SO_4 is a strong acid so 0.36 M H_2SO_4 will produce 0.36 M H_3O^+ and 0.36 M HSO_4^- ions. Let x be the number of moles/litre of HSO_4^- ionized. It produces x moles/litres of H_3O^+ ions and x moles/litre of SO_4^{2-} ions, therefore

$$\left[HSO_4^-\right] = (0.36 - x)$$

$$\left[H_3O^+\right] = (x + 0.36) \text{ and } \left(SO_4^{2-}\right) = x$$

Now,

$$K_{a_2} = \frac{\left[H_3O^+\right]\left[SO_4^{2-}\right]}{\left[HSO_4^-\right]} = \frac{(0.36 + x)(x)}{(0.36 - x)} = 1.26 \times 10^{-2}$$

Solving this equation for x, we get

$$x = 0.0118 \text{ M}.$$

Hence

$$\left[H_3O^+\right] = (0.36 + 0.0118) = 0.3718 \text{ M}$$

14.8 IONIZATION OF WATER

Water is the most commonly used solvent in the study of ionic equilibria. It is a weak electrolyte and ionizes to a small extent. Water can act both as an acid and as a base, *i.e.*, it acts as an ampholyte. The ionization can be represented as

$$H_2O + H_2O \rightleftharpoons H_3O^+ + OH^-$$

On applying the law of mass action to the above ionization equilibrium, we write

$$K = \frac{\left[H_3O^+\right]\left[OH^-\right]}{\left[H_2O\right]^2}$$

where K is the equilibrium constant for the ionization of water. Since the ionization takes place to a very small extent, the concentration of water remains practically same, therefore $[H_2O]^2$ can be included with the equilibrium constant K. Hence, we get

$$K\left[H_2O\right]^2 = K_w = \left[H_3O^+\right]\left[OH^-\right] \qquad \qquad ...(14.32)$$

The left side of this expression is the product of two constants which is also a constant denoted by K_w. The quantity K_w is known as the *ionic product of water* and has a value of 10^{-14} at 298 K. This equilibrium is always present in any aqueous solution and Eq. (14.32) must always be satisfied regardless of other equilibria taking place in aqueous solutions.

For pure water or neutral aqueous solutions $[H_3O^+] = [OH^-]$, therefore $[H_3O^+] = [OH^-] = 10^{-7}$ M at 298 K. Hence when the concentrations of H_2O^+ and OH^- ions are equal to 10^{-7} M, as in case of pure water, the solution is said to be neutral. When $[H_3O^+]$ is greater than 10^{-7} M, the solution is acidic and when it is less than 10^{-7} M, the solution is alkaline. However, it may be remembered that there are always some OH^- ions present in an acidic solution just as there are always some H_3O^+ ions present even if the solution is basic. At all times, Eq. (14.32) is obeyed if the solution is at equilibrium.

Ionization of water always contributes to the $[H_3O^+]$ and $[OH^-]$ ions. But in the presence of acids or bases the ionization is suppressed and in such cases the contribution of water to H_3O^+ and OH^- ions may be neglected. In any solution the product of $[H_3O^+]$ and $[OH^-]$ is always constant and equal to K_w. In a 0.02 M HCl solution the contribution of OH^- ions from water at 298 K will be approximately given by

$$[OH^-] = \frac{K_w}{[H_3O^+]} = \frac{10^{-14}}{2 \times 10^{-2}} = 5 \times 10^{-13} M$$

Similarly in a 0.01 M NaOH solution, $[H_3O^+]$ from water would be given by

$$[H_3O^+] = \frac{K_w}{10^{-2}} = 10^{-12} M$$

In either case the contribution made by water to the hydrogen and hydroxyl ions is negligibly small in comparison to the hydrogen or hydroxyl ions furnished by the added acid or the base. In calculating the $[H_3O^+]$ or $[OH^-]$ ions of a solution, ionization of water should be taken into account when $[H_3O^+]$ and $[OH^-]$ ions furnished by the added acid or the base are comparable with those produced by water.

Ionization of water is an endothermic process. It increases with increase in temperature and therefore K_w increases with rise in temperature. Values of K_w at various temperatures are given in Table 14.3.

Table 14.3 Ionic product of Water at Various Temperatures

Temperature (K)	$K_w \times 10^{14}$	Temperature (K)	$K_w \times 10^{14}$
273	0.12	303	1.47
283	0.29	313	2.92
293	0.68	323	5.47
298	1.01	333	9.61

14.9 pH AND pH-SCALE

The hydrogen or hydroxyl ion concentration in dilute solutions are often small. H_3O^+ and OH^- ions enter into many equilibria in addition to the ionization of water. It is therefore necessary to specify the concentrations of aqueous solutions. These concentrations may range from high values to very small values. The concentration of these ions in mole per litre or in equivalent per litre are often expressed as negative power of 10. To express the concentration of hydrogen ions in a more compact and convenient way without involving negative exponent, S.P.L. Sorenson introduced the pH scale. On this scale, pH of any solution is defined as

$$pH = -\log_{10} a_{H_3O^+}$$

For dilute solutions, activity may be replaced by molar concentration and pH is given by

$$pH = -\log_{10}\left[H_3O^+\right] = \log_{10}\frac{1}{\left[H_3O^+\right]}$$

or
$$\left[H_3O^+\right] = 10^{-pH}$$

The quantity pH is thus defined as *the negative logarithm (to the base 10) of the hydrogen ion concentration or is equal to the logarithm of the reciprocal of the hydrogen ion concentration of a solution.*

Similarly, the hydroxyl ion concentration of a solution can be expressed on a pOH scale as

$$pOH = -\log_{10} a_{OH^-}$$

or
$$pOH = -\log_{10}\left[OH^-\right] = \log_{10} 1/\left[OH^-\right]$$

For a 0.01 M HCl solution, $[H_3O^+] = 10^{-2}$ M and pH = 2.0; for a 0.01 M NaOH solution, $[OH^-] = 10^{-2}$ M and pOH = 2.0 and pH = 12.0. The ionic product of water K_w is

$$K_w = \left[H_3O^+\right]\left[OH^-\right]$$

Taking logarithm of both sides gives

$$\log K_w = \log\left[H_3O^+\right] + \log\left[OH^-\right]$$

or
$$-\log K_w = -\log\left[H_3O^+\right] - \log\left[OH^-\right]$$

or
$$pK_w = pH + pOH \qquad\qquad \left(\because -\log K_w = pK_w\right)$$

at 298 K,
$$K_w = 10^{-14}$$

therefore
$$pK_w = 14 = pH + pOH \qquad\qquad\qquad ...(14.33)$$

From Eq. (14.33) it follows that the sum of pH and pOH for any aqueous solution is constant and at 298 K it is equal to 14.0. When pH of a solution increases pOH decreases and vice versa. In a neutral solution, $[H_3O^+] = [OH^-] = 10^{-7}$ M and pH = pOH = 7.0. In an acidic solution, $[H_3O^+] > 10^{-7}$ M and the pH is less than 7.0. In an alkaline solution, $[H_3O^+] < 10^{-7}$ M and the pH is greater than 7.0.

As K_w increases with increase of temperature the pH value of a solution would, therefore, be expected to decrease with rise in temperature.

A relationship between H_3O^+, pH, OH^- and pOH for aqueous solutions at 298 K is shown below.

$\left[H_3O^+\right]$	10^0		10^{-7}		10^{-14}
pH	0		7		14

$\left[OH^-\right]$	10^{-14}		10^{-7}		10^0
pOH	14		7		0

Problem 14.7: Calculate the pH of (*i*) 1.3×10^{-4} M HCl, (*ii*) 3.0×10^{-3} M, HNO_3 and (*iii*) 1.0×10^{-3} M NaOH aqueous solutions at 298 K.

Solution: (*i*)
$$[H_3O^+] = 1.3 \times 10^{-4} \text{ M}$$
$$pH = -\log [H_3O^+]$$
$$= -\log [1.3 \times 10^{-4}) = -(0.114 - 4)$$
$$= 3.886$$

(*ii*)
$$[H_3O^+] = 3.0 \times 10^{-3} \text{ M}$$
$$pH = -\log (3.0 \times 10^{-3}) = 2.523$$

(*iii*)
$$\left[H_3O^+\right] = \frac{K_w}{\left[OH^-\right]} = \frac{10^{-14}}{10^{-3}} = 10^{-11} \text{M and pH} = 11.0$$

Problem 14.8: Calculate the hydrogen ion concentration for solutions having pH values (*i*) 3.0, (*ii*) 4.5, and (*iii*) 9.6.

Solution:
$$pH = -\log [H_3O^+]$$

(*i*)
$$3.0 = -\log [H_3O^+]$$
$$[H_3O^+] = 10^{-3} \text{ M}$$

(*ii*)
$$4.5 = -\log [H_3O^+]$$
$$\log [H_3O^+] = -4.5 = \overline{5}.5$$
$$[H_3O^+] = \text{antilog } (\overline{5}.5) = 3.162 \times 10^{-5} \text{ M}$$

(*iii*)
$$9.6 = -\log [H_3O^+]$$

or
$$\log [H_3O^+] = -9.6 = \overline{10}.4$$

or
$$[H_3O^+] = \text{antilog } [\overline{10}.4]$$
$$= 2.512 \times 10^{-10} \text{ M}$$

Problem 14.9: Calculate the pH of a 10^{-8} M HCl aqueous solution at 298 K (K_w is 10^{-14}).

Solution: The hydrogen ions contributed by HCl are small and are comparable with those produced by water. Therefore, ionization of water should be taken into consideration. If x is the hydrogen or hydroxyl ion concentration produced by water then the total $[H_3O^+]$ is equal to hydrogen ions from HCl plus hydrogen ions from water, *i.e.*,

$$\left[H_3O^+\right] = \left(10^{-8} + x\right)$$

and
$$\left[OH^-\right] = x$$

Now
$$K_w = \left[H_3O^+\right]\left[OH^-\right] = x\left(10^{-8} + x\right)$$

or
$$x^2 + 10^{-8} x = 10^{-14}$$

Solving for x gives

$$x = 9.525 \times 10^{-8} \text{M}$$

Hence the total
$$[H_3O^+] = (9.525 \times 10^{-8}) + 10^{-8} \text{ M}$$

$$= 10.525 \times 10^{-8} \text{ M}$$
$$= 1.0525 \times 10^{-7} \text{ M}$$

Therefore

$$pH = -\log [H_3O^+]$$
$$= -\log (1.5025 \times 10^{-7})$$
$$= -0.0215 + 7.0$$
$$= 6.9785$$

Problem 14.10: An aqueous solution has a pH of 6.5 at 313 K. Will it be acidic, neutral or alkaline? The ionic product of water at 313 K is 2.92×10^{-14}.

    Solution: $\qquad\qquad K_w = 2.92 \times 10^{-14} = [H_3O^+] [OH^-]$

The neutral solution at 313 K would have a pH given by

$$pH = -\log [H_3O^+]$$
$$= \frac{1}{2} \log K_w$$
$$= 6.787$$

Thus the neutral solution at 313 K has a pH value of 6.787. Hence the aqueous solution of pH 6.5 would be acidic.

Problem 14.11: An aqueous solution contains 10% ammonia by mass and has a density of 0.99 g cm^{-3}. Calculate the pH and pOH of the solution. K_a for NH_4^+ is 5.0×10^{-10} and K_w for water is 1.0×10^{-14} at 298 K.

    Solution: Volume of 100 g solution $\quad = \dfrac{\text{Mass}}{\text{density}} = \dfrac{100}{0.99}$

$$= 101.01 \text{ ml}$$

Moles of ammonia in 10g $\qquad\qquad = \dfrac{10}{17}$

Hence molar concentration of NH_3 is $\dfrac{10}{17} \times \dfrac{1000}{101.01} = 8.24 \text{ M}$

Now K_b for ammonia is given by

$$K_b = \frac{K_w}{K_a} = \frac{1.0 \times 10^{-14}}{5 \times 10^{-10}} = 2 \times 10^{-5}$$

Now the ionization of ammonia takes place as

$$NH_3 + H_2O \rightleftharpoons NH_4^+ + OH^-$$

If x moles of ammonia ionize, then $\left[NH_4^+ \right] = \left[OH^- \right] = x$

and $\qquad\qquad\qquad\qquad\qquad [NH_3] = 8.24 - x$

Hence

$$K_b = \frac{\left[NH_4^+\right]\left[OH^-\right]}{\left[NH_3\right]} = \frac{x^2}{8.24 - x}$$

which gives

$$x = \left[OH^-\right] = 1.28 \times 10^{-2} \text{ or pOH} = 1.89$$

and

$$pH = 12.11$$

14.10 COMMON ION EFFECT

Consider the ionization of a weak acid, HA in water

$$HA + H_2O \rightleftharpoons H_3O^+ + A^-$$

The equilibrium is shifted to the left, *i.e.*, the ionization is suppressed when H_3O^+ ions (in the form of strong acid such as HCl) or A^- (in the form of a salt, $Na^+ A^-$) are added to the solution. This effect is referred to as *the common ion effect;* it results when an electrolyte having an ion in common with the acid *HA* is added to its aqueous solution. Thus to an aqueous solution of acetic acid, addition of acetate ions from sodium acetate would result in the suppression of the ionization of acetic acid. Similarly, when hydrogen ions are added in the form of hydrochloric acid, ionization of acetic acid would again be suppressed. Addition of any other electrolyte like potassium chloride having no ion in common with those produced by the weak acid, will affect the ionization of the acid only through changes in the ionic strength of the medium.

In a mixture of weak acid and its salt, the concentration of the H_3O^+ ions is determined almost entirely by the concentration of the salt. Similarly, in a mixture of strong and weak acids the $[H_3O^+]$ is determined by the concentration of the strong acid only. Likewise, ionization of weak bases are suppressed by either the hydroxyl ions or by a salt having a common cation.

Common ion effect provides a valuable method for controlling the concentration of ions furnished by a weak electrolyte. Thus in qualitative mixture analysis, dilute hydrochloric acid is added before precipitating the cations of second group. In the presence of dilute hydrochloric acid ionization of H_2S is suppressed, $[S^{2-}]$ is lowered but it is still sufficient to precipitate sulphides of the second group. Similarly in the third group, the role of ammonium chloride is to control the concentration of hydroxyl ions produced by the ionization of ammonium hydroxide.

Problem 14.12: A solution is 0.2 molar each with respect to acetic acid and sodium acetate. Calculate the pH of the solution. $K_a = 1.85 \times 10^{-5}$ at 298 K.

Solution: If x is the concentration of hydrogen ions furnished by the acid then the concentration of unionised acid = $(0.2 - x)$ moles/litre and that of the salt $(0.2 + x)$ moles/litre.
Hence,

$$K_a = 1.85 \times 10^{-5} = \frac{(0.2 - x)(x)}{(0.2 + x)}$$

If $x << 0.2$, then

$$\frac{0.2x}{0.2} = 1.85 \times 10^{-5}$$

or $$x = 1.85 \times 10^{-5}\,\text{M}$$

and $$pH = -\log\left[1.85 \times 10^{-5}\right] = 4.73$$

Problem 14.13: Calculate the sulphide ion concentrations in water for (*i*) a 0.1 M solution of H₂S, and (*ii*) a solution 0.1 M with respect to both hydrochloric acid and H₂S. K_{a_1} and K_{a_2} are 9.1×10^{-8} and 1.2×10^{-15} respectively at 298 K.

Solution: (*i*) The ionization of H₂S takes place in two steps,

$$H_2S + H_2O \rightleftharpoons H_3O^+ + HS^-\,;\; K_{a_1} = \frac{\left[H_3O^+\right]\left[HS^-\right]}{\left[H_2S\right]} = 9.1 \times 10^{-8} \qquad ...(i)$$

$$HS^- + H_2O \rightleftharpoons H_3O^+ + S^{2-}\,;\; K_{a_2} = \frac{\left[H_3O^+\right]\left[S^{3-}\right]}{\left[HS^-\right]} = 1.2 \times 10^{-15} \qquad ...(ii)$$

Multiplying (*i*) and (*ii*), we get,

$$K_{a_1} K_{a_2} = \frac{\left[H_3O^+\right]\left[S^{2-}\right]}{\left[H_2S\right]} = 1.1 \times 10^{-22}$$

or, $$\left[S^{2-}\right] = \frac{\left[H_2S\right]\left[1.1 \times 10^{-22}\right]}{\left[H_3O^+\right]^2} \qquad ...(iii)$$

As H₂S is a very weak acid and [H₂S] may be taken as approximately equal to 0.1 M. Furthermore, the second ionization is extremely small and does not contribute significantly to the [H₃O⁺] and hence we have

$$\left[H_3O^+\right] = \left[HS^-\right]$$

or $$9.1 \times 10^{-8} = \frac{\left[H_3O^+\right]^2}{\left[H_2S\right]}$$

But $$\left[H_2S\right] = 0.1\,\text{M}$$

Hence, $$\left[H_3O^+\right]^2 = 0.1 \times 9.1 \times 10^{-8} = 9.1 \times 10^{-9}$$

or $$\left[H_3O^+\right] = 9.5 \times 10^{-5}\,\text{M}$$

Substituting the value of $\left[H_3O^+\right]$ in Eq. (*ii*) we get

$$\left[S^{2-}\right] = \frac{\left[1.1 \times 10^{-22}\right]\left[0.1\right]}{9.5 \times 10^{-5}} = 1.2 \times 10^{-14}\,\text{M}$$

(*ii*) When $[H_3O^+] = 0.1$ M, all the hydrogen ions are contributed mainly by HCl

$$[S^{2-}] = \frac{[1.1 \times 10^{-22}][0.1]}{(0.1)^2} = 1.1 \times 10^{-20} \, M$$

Thus, in the presence of 0.1 M HCl, $[S^{2-}]$ is reduced from 1.2×10^{-14} M to 1.1×10^{-20} M

14.11 BUFFER SOLUTIONS

These are solutions which resist changes in their pH values when small amount of acids or bases are added to them. This resistance to change in the pH value of a solution is known as the buffer action. Buffer solutions usually consist of

  (*i*) a mixture of a weak acid and its salt (acidic buffer) such as acetic acid and sodium acetate and
  (*ii*) a mixture of a weak base and its salt (alkaline buffer) like ammonium hydroxide and ammonium chloride.

Let us explain how a buffer solution acts and maintains its pH constant. In an acidic buffer, like acetic acid and sodium acetate, ionization of the weak acid is suppressed by the salt and the solution contains a large amount of unionized acetic acid (CH_3COOH), a large amount of acetate ions (CH_3COO^-) and a small amount of H_3O^+ ions. If a strong acid (HCl) is added to such a mixture the equilibrium is disturbed; H_3O^+ ions added would combine with the acetate ions forming unionized acetic acid according to the neutralization reaction

$$H_3O^+ + CH_3COO^- \rightleftharpoons CH_3COOH + H_2O$$

Thus, acetate ions of the mixture neutralize the added acid and thereby pH of the buffer is almost maintained constant.

However, addition of hydroxyl ions in the form of a strong base (NaOH) neutralizes the acid forming salt and water.

$$OH^- + CH_3COOH \rightleftharpoons CH_3COO^- + H_2O$$

The pH of the solution remains very close to its original value. Similarly, addition of a strong acid or a strong base to an alkaline buffer (NH$_3$ and NH$_4$Cl) causes the following reactions:

$$NH_3 + NH_4Cl \xrightarrow[H_2O^+]{+ \text{ acid}} NH_3 + H_3O^+ \rightarrow NH_4^+ + H_2O$$

$$\downarrow \text{base OH}^-$$

$$NH_4^+ + OH^-$$

The added acid is neutralized by the base (NH_3) while the added base (OH^-) is neutralized by the salt (NH_4Cl) and consequently there is no change in pH of the buffer. Buffer solutions are thus considered to possess reserved acidity or reserved alkalinity. In acetic acid sodium acetate buffer the reserved acidity is due to acetic acid and reserved alkalinity is due to the presence of the salt, sodium acetate.

Addition of acids or bases to pure water or to aqueous solutions of NaCl causes considerable changes in the pH values. Water and NaCl solutions are therefore, highly unbuffered.

Relation between pH of a Buffer and the Concentration of the Components of the Buffer: pH of a buffer depends on the concentration of the buffer components. Consider a buffer containing a weak acid, *HA* and its salt Na$^+$A$^-$, ionization of the weak acid may be represented as

$$HA + H_2O \rightleftharpoons H_3O^+ + A^-$$

The ionization constant K_a is given by

$$K_a = \frac{[H_3O^+][A^-]}{[HA]}$$

or

$$[H_3O^+] = K_a \frac{[HA]}{[A^-]} \qquad \qquad ...(14.34)$$

If the initial concentration of the acid is C_a and that of the salt C_s, the concentration of the unionized acid is $C_a - [H_3O^+]$. The solution is electrically neutral hence $[A^-] = C_s + [H_3O^+]$ (the salt is completely ionized). Substituting these values in Eq. (14.34), we get

$$[H_3O^+] = K_a \frac{C_a - [H_3O^+]}{C_s + [H_3O^+]} \qquad \qquad ...(14.35)$$

This is a quadratic equation in H_3O^+ and may be solved in the usual manner. It can, however, be simplified by making some valid approximations. In a mixture of weak acid and its salt, ionization of the acid is suppressed by the salt and, therefore, $[H_3O^+]$ may be taken as negligibly small in comparison to C_a and C_s. This simplifies Eq. (14.35) to give

$$[H_3O^+] = K_a \frac{C_a}{C_s}$$

or

$$[H_3O^+] = K_a \frac{[acid]}{[salt]}$$

or

$$pH = pK_a + \log \frac{[salt]}{[acid]} \qquad \qquad ...(14.36)$$

This is known as *the Henderson equation* and enables us to work out the proportions of $\frac{[salt]}{[acid]}$ required to yield a specified pH value with a given weak acid. Similarly, for a mixture of a weak base and its salt

$$[OH^-] = K_b \frac{[base]}{[salt]}$$

or

$$pOH = pK_b + \log \frac{[salt]}{[base]} \qquad \qquad ...(14.37)$$

where K_b is the ionization constant of the base.

Let us now confine our attention to the case in which the concentrations of the acid and its salt are equal, *i.e.*, [salt] = [acid]; Eq. (14.36) reduces to

$$pH = pK_a$$

The pH of a half neutralized solution of a weak acid is equal to the pK_a value of the acid. For acetic acid, K_a is 1.85×10^{-5} at 298 K, $pK_a = 4.73$; a half neutralized solution of acetic acid will have a pH of 4.73.

Buffer Capacity, β: The extent of buffer action depends on the concentration of the buffer components. The buffer capacity, β, is defined as *the number of moles of acid or base added per litre of the buffer required to cause a unit change in pH*.

$$\text{Buffer capacity, } \beta = \frac{dx}{dpH} = \frac{\text{Number of moles of acid or base added per litre of the buffer}}{\text{Change in pH}}$$

Addition of a base raises the pH of the buffer while addition of an acid lowers its pH value. Larger the amount of acid or base required to produce a unit change in pH, greater will be the buffer capacity. Solutions having high concentrations of both the components will have high buffer capacity. For a given total concentration, the solution containing equal concentrations of acid and its salt will have maximum buffer capacity.

Let us consider a weak acid containing 'a' moles/litre to which 'b' moles/litre of the base is added. The salt formed will have concentration of b moles/litre and the concentration of the weak acid will be $(a - b)$ moles/litre. This mixture will behave as an acidic buffer. Using Henderson equation, we have

$$pH = pK_a + \log\frac{[\text{Salt}]}{[\text{Acid}]}$$

$$= pK_a + \log\frac{b}{a - b}$$

on differentiating this equation with respect to b we get,

$$\left(\frac{\partial pH}{\partial b}\right) = \left[\frac{a-b}{b}\right]\left[\frac{a-b+b}{(a-b)^2}\right]$$

$$= \frac{a}{b(a-b)}$$

Therefore, the buffer capacity β is given by

$$\beta = \frac{\partial b}{\partial pH} = \frac{b(a-b)}{a}$$

For a solution to have maximum buffer capacity, the first derivative of β with respect to b should be equal to zero, *i.e.*,

$$\frac{\partial \beta}{\partial b} = 1 - \frac{2b}{a} = 0$$

or

$$b = \frac{a}{2}$$

The buffer solution will have maximum buffer capacity when the acid is half-neutralized or when the concentration of the salt and acid are equal in the solution.

Other mixtures of salt and acid also possess considerable buffer capacity, but it decreases as the ratio of acid changes in either direction.

In a quarter-neutralized solution of an acid,

$$[acid] = 3[salt]$$

and

$$pH = pK_a + \log(1/3)$$
$$= pK_a - 0.48$$

For a three quarter neutralized acid [salt] = 3 [acid] and
$$pH = pK_a + 0.48$$

It is generally accepted that the buffer is effective within the range 1 acid to 10 salt or vice versa. The approximate pH range of an acidic buffer is

$$pH = pK_a \pm 1 \qquad \qquad ...(14.38a)$$

and for an alkaline buffer it is

$$pOH = pK_b \pm 1 \qquad \qquad ...(14.38b)$$

To prepare a buffer solution of a given pH value it is necessary to choose an acid (or base) with its pK value as far as possible close to the required pH (or pOH) for the buffer capacity to be appreciable in that range. The actual ratio of acid to salt concentration can then be calculated from the Henderson Eq. (14.36) or (14.37). A list of few buffers and their effective ranges are given in Table 14.4.

Each buffer is generally applicable over a limited range. By making suitable mixtures of acids and acid salts it is possible to prepare "universal buffer mixtures". Additions of various predetermined amounts of alkali to the buffer mixtures, buffer solutions of any desired pH value ranging from 2 to 12 may be obtained. An example is a mixture of phosphoric acid, acetic acid and boric acid.

Table 14.4 Buffer Mixtures

Buffer mixture	pH range	Buffer mixture	pH range
Phthalic acid and hydrogen phthalate	2.2–3.8	Boric acid and borax	6.8–9.2
Potassium acid phthalate and potassium phthalate	4.0–6.2	Borax and sodium hydroxide	9.2–11.0
Sodium dihydrogen phosphate and disodium hydrogen phosphate	5.9–8.0	Disodium hydrogen phosphate and sodium hydroxide	11.0–12.0

Applications of Buffer Solutions: Buffers are important in analytical chemistry and in general laboratory work. Biochemical reactions in particular require maintenance of definite pH values. Blood, milk and various animal fluids are highly buffered with bicarbonate ions and carbonic acid and with proteins. Normal human blood has a pH of about 7.4. Ordinarily variations are very small and an increase or decrease of as much as 0.4 pH unit is likely to be fatal and show pathological conditions such as diabetic, coma, etc. Catalytic activity of an enzyme is maximum at a particular pH value. In the industrial field, buffers are used in the fermentation of alcohol where the pH of the solution is maintained around 6. Similarly they are used in electroplating, tanning of leather and manufacture of sugar where a constant pH of the medium is essential. For proper productivity of crops pH control of the soil is essential. To an acidic soil limestone is added while sulphur is added to a soil that is alkaline.

Problem 14.14: (*i*) Calculate the pH of a buffer solution containing 0.2 M acetic acid and 0.02 M sodium acetate. (*ii*) What will be the change in pH when 1 ml of 1 N HCl is added to 1 litre of this buffer? (*iii*) Compare the pH change when the same amount of acid is added to 1 litre of water ($pK_a = 4.73$).

Solution: (*i*) $[CH_3COOH] = 0.2$ M, $[CH_3COO^-] = 0.02$ M. Using the Henderson equation

$$pH = pK_a + \log\frac{[salt]}{[acid]} = 4.73 - 1.0 = 3.73$$

(*ii*) When HCl is added it reacts with the salt forming acetic acid

$$H_3O^+ + CH_3COO^- \rightleftharpoons CH_3COOH + H_2O$$

Hence acetic acid concentration increases and that of the salt decreases. Acetic acid formed by the addition of HCl is 0.001 M (neglecting the small volume change of the solution). The total acetic acid concentration is $(0.02 + 0.001) = 0.201$ M and the salt concentration is $(0.02 - 0.001) = 0.019$ M. The pH value of the solution is given by

$$pH = pK_a + \log\frac{[0.019]}{[0.201]} = 3.71$$

Therefore, the change in pH = $3.73 - 3.71 = 0.02$

(*iii*) When HCl is added to one litre of water, $[H_3O^+] = 10^{-3}$ M and pH = 3.0.

Problem 14.15. Calculate the volume of 0.1 N HCl that should be added to 500 ml of 0.1 M sodium acetate solution to prepare a buffer of pH 5.0. pKa for acetic acid is 4.74.

Solution: Let the volume of 0.1 N HCl added be V mL.

So moles of HCl in V ml = 0.1 V

and moles of sodium acetate in 500 ml $= \dfrac{0.1 \times 500}{1000} = 0.05 = 5 \times 10^{-2}$

When HCl is added, acetic acid will form and sodium acetate concentration will decrease. Moles of acetic acid formed will be equal to moles of HCl added *i.e.*, $V \times 10^{-4}$

and   moles of salt left $= 5 \times 10^{-2} - 10^{-4} V$

Now using Henderson equation, we have

$$pH = 5.0 = 4.74 + \log\left(\frac{5 \times 10^{-2} - 10^{-4} V}{10^{-4} V}\right)$$

which on solving gives $V = 177.3$ ml.

Problem 14.16: 20 ml of 0.2 M Sodium hydroxide solution was added to 50 ml of 0.2 M acetic acid solution to give 70 ml of the solution. What is pH of the resulting solution? Calculate the additional volume of 0.2 M sodium hydroxide solution required to make the pH of the solution equal to 4.74. K_a (HAc) $= 1.8 \times 10^{-5}$.

Solution: Addition of sodium hydroxide will decrease the concentration of acetic acid and the mixture of sodium acetate and remaining acetic acid will act as buffer. The concentration of the salt formed is

$$\frac{20 \times 0.2}{70} M = \frac{0.4}{7} M$$

and the concentration of acetic acid remaining will be

$$\frac{50 \times 0.2}{70} - \frac{20 \times 0.2}{70} = \frac{1}{7} - \frac{0.4}{7} = \frac{0.6}{7} M$$

From Henderson equation: $\qquad pH = pK_a + \log \dfrac{[Salt]}{[Acid]}$, we have

$$= 4.74 + \log \left(\frac{0.4/7}{0.6/7} \right)$$

$$= 4.74 + \log \frac{4}{6} = 4.56$$

For the second part of the problem, let V (ml) be the additional volume of base added, then the number of moles of the base added is $\dfrac{0.2V}{1000}$. The base will react with the acid and hence the salt concentration will increase while that of acid will decrease proportionately.

$$\text{Now total moles of salt} = \frac{0.2V}{1000} + \frac{0.4 \times 70}{1000 \times 7}$$

$$\text{and the moles of acid remaining} = \frac{0.6}{7} \times \frac{70}{1000} - \frac{0.2V}{1000}$$

Since the resulting pH $= pK_a$, the moles of acid and the salt will be equal

$$\frac{0.2V}{1000} + \frac{0.4 \times 70}{1000 \times 7} = \frac{0.6 \times 70}{7 \times 1000} - \frac{0.2V}{1000}$$

which gives V as 5 ml.

14.12 SALT HYDROLYSIS

A Brønsted acid when neutralized by a Brønsted base in aqueous solution results in the formation of a salt and water. If both the acid and alkali are strong, the solution will be neutral, pH of the solution would be 7 at room temperature. When a strong acid like HCl is neutralized by a weak base like NH_3, the solution will not be neutral but acidic, pH would be less than 7. Again, when a weak acid such as acetic acid is neutralized by a strong base, the resulting solution will be alkaline, pH would be greater than 7. In case when both the acid and the alkali are weak the resulting solution may be acidic or alkaline depending upon their relative strengths.

The acidity or alkalinity of solutions in these cases is due to the tendency of the ions of the salt formed to react with water. It is a process opposite to that of neutralization and is known as hydrolysis. It may be defined as *an interaction between an ion or ions of a salt with water resulting in the formation of (i) a weak acid or a weak base or (ii) both a weak acid and a weak base.*

Consider the reaction of an anion A^- with water

$$A^- + H_2O \rightleftharpoons HA + OH^-$$

Anion A^- will not be hydrolysed if its conjugate acid HA is stronger than H_3O^+ ion as the above equilibrium in that case will be far more to the left. Thus, Cl^- which is the conjugate base of HCl is too weak a base to accept a proton from water and is not hydrolysed. On the other hand, anion A^- will be partially hydrolysed if its conjugate acid HA is weaker than H_3O^+ ion but stronger than water. For example, the acetate ion which is the conjugate base of acetic acid is sufficiently basic to accept protons from water. When the equilibrium is established excess OH^- ions would be present in the solution making it alkaline. Anion A^- will be completely hydrolysed if its conjugate acid is weaker than water as the above equilibrium in that case will lie far to the right. For example, NH_2^- ion is a strong base even stronger than OH^- ion. It will be completely hydrolysed as its conjugate acid NH_3 is a weaker acid than water.

Similarly, for the reaction of a cation, B^+ with water

$$B^+ + H_2O \rightleftharpoons BOH + H^+$$

the cation B^+ will be completely hydrolysed if its conjugate base BOH is too weak a base to accept protons from water. As the equilibrium would lie far to the right and the solution will be acidic. For example, PH_4^+ ion is completely hydrolysed as its conjugate base PH_3 is a very weak base and has practically no tendency to accept protons. On the other hand, a cation like NH_4^+ which has a conjugate base NH_3 will be partly hydrolysed. However, if the cation has a conjugate base stronger than water or OH^- ion it will not be hydrolysed. Thus, Na^+ ions will not be hydrolysed to any extent as the equilibrium in that case will lie far to the left in the above reaction.

There are four distinct groups of hydrolytic behaviour of various salts. These are

- (*a*) Salts of strong acids and strong bases
- (*b*) Salts of strong acids and weak bases
- (*c*) Salts of weak acids and strong bases
- (*d*) Salts of weak acids and weak bases

(*a*) **Salts of Strong Acids and Strong Bases:** The salt of a strong acid and a strong base does not undergo hydrolysis and the solution of such a salt is neutral and the pH of the solution will be 7, at 298 K.

(*b*) **Salts of Strong Acids and Weak Bases:** The hydrolysis of any salt of strong acid and a weak base is due to the hydrolysis of the cation of the weak base. The hydrolysis of the cation can be represented as

$$B^+ + 2H_2O \rightleftharpoons BOH + H_3O^+$$

or

$$NH_4^+ + H_2O \rightleftharpoons NH_3 + H_3O^+$$

Applying the law of mass action to the above equilibrium, the equilibrium constant is given by

$$K = \frac{[BOH][H_3O^+]}{[B^+][H_2O]^2}$$

or
$$K_h = K[H_2O]^2 = \frac{[BOH][H_3O^+]}{[B^+]} \qquad ...(14.39)$$

The concentration of water may be taken as constant and may be amalgamated with the equilibrium constant K. The quantity, K_h is called the hydrolysis constant or hydrolytic constant and determines the extent to which the cation B^+ is hydrolysed. It may also be regarded as the ionization constant K_a for the NH_4^+ ion as it is donating a proton to water in the hydrolytic reaction.

Let us derive a relation between the pH of the solution and the concentration of the salt. If C is the initial concentration of the salt and α the degree of hydrolysis, then

$$[BOH] = C\alpha; \; [H_3O^+] = C\alpha$$

$$[B^+] = C(1-\alpha)$$

Substituting these values in Eq. (14.39), we get

$$K_h = \frac{(C\alpha)(C\alpha)}{C(1-\alpha)} = \frac{C\alpha^2}{1-\alpha} \qquad ...(14.40)$$

The degree of hydrolysis α, can be calculated if K_h is known. When $\alpha \ll 1$, Eq. (14.40) reduces to

$$K_h = C\alpha^2$$

or
$$\alpha = \sqrt{K_h/C} \qquad ...(14.41)$$

Equation (14.39) can be rewritten as

$$K_h = \frac{[BOH][H_3O^+][OH^-]}{[B^+][OH^-]} = \frac{K_w}{K_b} \qquad ...(14.42)$$

where $K_b = \dfrac{[B^+][OH^-]}{[BOH]}$ is the ionization constant of the weak base BOH and

$K_w = [H_3O^+][OH^-]$.

The hydrogen ion concentration is given by

$$[H_3O^+] = C\alpha$$

$$= C\sqrt{\frac{K_h}{C}}$$

$$= \sqrt{K_h C}$$

$$= \sqrt{\frac{K_w}{K_b} C} \qquad \qquad ...(14.43)$$

Taking logarithm of Eq. (14.43), we get

$$\log\left[H_3O^+\right] = \frac{1}{2}\left[\log K_w - \log K_b + \log C\right]$$

or $\qquad\qquad$ $$pH = \frac{1}{2}\left[pK_w - pK_b - \log C\right] \qquad ...(14.44)$$

In order to calculate the pH in such cases, we must know K_w, K_b and the concentration of the salt. The general rule that the degree of hydrolysis increases with dilution and with decreasing strength of the base (eqn. 14.41) for the salt of the weak base and strong acid. It is evident from (Eq. (14.44) that the pH of the solution must be less than 1/2 pK_w, i.e., less than 7.0 at 298 K. In other words, aqueous solutions of salts of the type under consideration will be acidic.

Problem 14.17: Calculate the hydrolytic constant, the degree of hydrolysis and pH of a 0.02 M aqueous NH_4Cl solution.

Solution: $\qquad\qquad$ $$K_h = \frac{K_w}{K_b} = \frac{10^{-14}}{1.85 \times 10^{-5}} = 5.4 \times 10^{-10}$$

The degree of hydrolysis, α $\qquad\qquad$ $$= \sqrt{\frac{K_h}{C}} = \sqrt{\frac{K_w}{K_b C}}$$

$$= \sqrt{\frac{10^{-14}}{1.85 \times 10^{-5} \times 0.02}} = 5 \times 10^{-3}$$

The pH of the solution is given by

$$pH = \frac{1}{2}\left[pK_w - pK_b - \log C\right]$$

$$= \frac{1}{2}\left[(14) - (4.73) - \log\left(2 \times 10^{-2}\right)\right]$$

$$= 5.48$$

(c) **Salts of Weak Acids and Strong Bases:** When salt of a weak acid and a strong base like sodium acetate or sodium cyanide, etc., undergoes hydrolysis the resulting solution is alkaline.

The hydrolysis of acetate ion may be written as

$$CH_3COO^- + H_2O \rightleftharpoons CH_3COOH + OH^-$$

In general, hydrolysis of a salt BA of a weak acid HA and a strong base BOH is due to the hydrolysis of the anion of the salt according to the reaction

$$A^- + H_2O \rightleftharpoons HA + OH^-$$

The equation for this hydrolysis equilibrium is written as

$$K = \frac{[HA][OH^-]}{[A^-][H_2O]}$$

$$K_h = K[H_2O] = \frac{[HA][OH^-]}{[A^-]} \qquad \text{...(14.45)}$$

where K_h is the hydrolytic constant. It may be looked as K_b for the anion A^- as it is extracting a proton from water and thus acting as base.

If C is the initial salt concentration and α the degree of hydrolysis of the salt, then

$$[OH^-] = [HA] = C\alpha$$

and

$$[A^-] = C(1-\alpha)$$

Substituting these values in Eq. (14.45), we get

$$K_h = \frac{[C\alpha][C\alpha]}{C(1-\alpha)} = \frac{C\alpha^2}{(1-\alpha)} \qquad \text{...(14.46)}$$

If $\alpha \ll 1$, Eq. (14.46) reduces to

$$K_h = C\alpha^2$$

or

$$\alpha = \sqrt{\frac{K_h}{C}} \qquad \text{...(14.47)}$$

Thus the degree of hydrolysis of the salt is proportional to the square root of the hydrolysis constant and inversely proportional to the square root of the concentration.

Rewriting Eq. (14.45)

$$K_h = \frac{[HA][OH^-]}{[A^-]} = \frac{[HA][OH^-][H_3O^+]}{[H_3O^+][A^-]} = \frac{K_w}{K_a}$$

Therefore, the degree of hydrolysis, α, from Eq. (14.47) is given by

$$\alpha = \sqrt{\frac{K_w}{K_a C}} \qquad \text{...(14.48)}$$

Since,

$$[OH^-] = C\alpha = \sqrt{\frac{K_w C}{K_a}}$$

Therefore,

$$[H_3O^+] = \frac{K_w}{[OH^-]} = \sqrt{\frac{K_w K_a}{C}} \qquad \text{...(14.49)}$$

Taking logarithm of Eq. (14.49), we get

$$\log\left[H_3O^+\right] = \frac{1}{2}\left[\log K_w + \log K_a - \log C\right]$$

or

$$pH = \frac{1}{2}\left[pK_w + pK_a + \log C\right] \qquad \qquad ...(14.50)$$

It follows from the Eq. (14.50) that the pH of the solution is more than 7.0 *i.e.*, the solution is alkaline. Furthermore, pH of the solution increases with the increasing salt concentration.

Problem 14.18: Calculate the hydrolytic constant, the degree of hydrolysis and the pH of an aqueous 0.01 M sodium acetate solution (K_a is 1.85×10^{-5} at 298 K).

Solution: pH of the solution is given by

$$pH = \frac{1}{2}\left[pK_w + pK_a + \log C\right]$$

$$= \frac{1}{2}\left[(14) + (4.73) + \log\left(10^{-2}\right)\right]$$

$$= 7.0 + 2.365 - 1 = 8.365$$

The hydrolytic constant

$$K_h = \frac{K_w}{K_a} = \frac{10^{-14}}{1.85 \times 10^{-5}} = 5.45 \times 10^{-10}$$

and the degree of hydrolysis,

$$\alpha = \sqrt{\frac{K_h}{C}}$$

$$= \sqrt{\frac{5.45 \times 10^{-10}}{10^{-2}}}$$

$$= 2.34 \times 10^{-4}$$

(*d*) **Salts of Weak Acids and Weak Bases:** When the salt of a weak acid and a weak base like ammonium acetate is added to water both the ammonium and the acetate ions undergo hydrolysis as

$$CH_3COONH_4 + H_2O \rightleftharpoons CH_3COOH + NH_3 + H_2O$$

or

$$CH_3COO^- + NH_4^+ + H_2O \rightleftharpoons CH_3COOH + NH_3 + H_2O$$

The products of hydrolysis are weak acid and weak base and would be almost unionized. In general, the salt *BA* is hydrolysed as

$$B^+ + A^- + H_2O \rightleftharpoons BOH + HA$$

The hydrolytic constant for this is given by

$$K_h = \frac{[BOH][HA]}{[B^+][A^-]} \qquad \qquad ...(14.51)$$

$$= \frac{[BOH][HA]\left[H_3O^+\right]\left[OH^-\right]}{\left[B^+\right]\left[OH^-\right]\left[H_3O^+\right]\left[A^-\right]}$$

$$= \frac{K_w}{K_a K_b} \qquad\qquad\qquad \text{...(14.52)}$$

where $K_a = \dfrac{\left[H_3O^+\right]\left[A^-\right]}{[HA]}$; $K_b = \dfrac{\left[B^+\right]\left[OH^-\right]}{[BOH]}$ and $K_w = \left[H_3O^+\right]\left[OH^-\right]$.

In order to calculate the pH of the salt solution, let us assume that C be the initial concentration of the salt and α the degree of hydrolysis, then

$$[BOH] = [HA] = C\alpha$$

$$\left[B^+\right] = \left[A^-\right] = C(1-\alpha)$$

Substituting these values of Eq. (14.51), we get

$$K_h = \frac{[C\alpha][C\alpha]}{[C(1-\alpha)][C(1-\alpha)]} = \frac{\alpha^2}{(1-\alpha)^2}$$

or

$$\sqrt{K_h} = \frac{\alpha}{1-\alpha} \qquad\qquad\qquad \text{...(14.53)}$$

Furthermore, for a weak acid

$$K_a = \frac{\left[H_3O^+\right]\left[A^-\right]}{[HA]}$$

or

$$\left[H_3O^+\right] = K_a \frac{[HA]}{\left[A^-\right]}$$

$$= K_a \frac{C\alpha}{C(1-\alpha)}$$

$$= K_a \frac{\alpha}{1-\alpha}$$

$$= K_a \sqrt{K_h}$$

$$= K_a \sqrt{\frac{K_w}{K_a K_b}}$$

$$= \sqrt{\frac{K_a K_w}{K_b}} \qquad \qquad ...(14.54)$$

Taking logarithm of Eq. (14.54), we get

$$\log\left[H_3O^+\right] = \frac{1}{2}\left[\log K_w + \log K_a - \log K_b\right]$$

or
$$pH = \frac{1}{2}\left[pK_w + pK_a - pK_b\right] \qquad \qquad ...(14.55)$$

pH of the salt solution will depend on the pK values of the acid and the base. If $pK_a < pK_b$, then according to Eq. (14.55), pH of the solution will be less than $1/2\, pK_w$ and consequently, the solution will be acidic. In case $pK_a > pK_b$, pH of the solution will be more than $1/2\, pK_w$ and hence the solution will be alkaline. However, when $pK_a = pK_b$, pH of the solution will be equal to $1/2\, pK_w$ and the solution will be neutral. It is apparent from Eq. (14.55) that pH of the solution is independent of the salt concentration.

Problem 14.19: Calculate the pH of a 0.1 M ammonium acetate solution $K_a = 1.85 \times 10^{-5}$; $K_b = 1.85 \times 10^{-5}$ at 298 K.

Solution:
$$pH = \frac{1}{2}\left[pK_w + pK_a - pK_b\right]$$

$$= \frac{1}{2}\left[(14) + (4.73) - (4.73)\right] = 7.0$$

Hence the solution of ammonium acetate would be neutral.

14.13 THEORY OF ACID-BASE INDICATORS

In the acid-alkali titrations, the equivalence point is detected by the use of substances called acid-base indicators which change their colour at or near the equivalence point. An acid base indicator is *a weak organic acid or a base which possesses one colour in acid solutions and an entirely different colour in alkaline solution*. The actual colour that it produces in solution depends on the pH of the solution. The change in colour of the indicator is not sudden and abrupt but takes place in a small pH range. This pH range is called the "*colour change interval*" of the indicator. Let us examine briefly how the acid-base indicators work.

(*i*) **Ostwald Theory:** The first attempt in the theory of indicators was made by Ostwald. The acid-base indicators are regarded as weak organic acids or bases. The unionized form of the acid indicator HIn or the basic indicator InOH had one colour and the corresponding ionized form had another colour. The ionizing equilibrium in aqueous solutions may be written as

$$HIn + H_2O \rightleftharpoons H_3O^+ + In^-$$

and
$$InOH \overset{H_2O}{\rightleftharpoons} OH^- + In^+$$

Let us apply the law of mass action to the ionization equilibrium of an acid indicator HIn. The ionization constant of the indicator is given by

$$K_{ind} = \frac{[H_3O^+][In^-]}{[HIn]}$$

or

$$[H_3O^+] = K_{ind} \frac{[HIn]}{[In^-]}$$

$$[H_3O^+] = K_{ind} \frac{[\text{unionized form}]}{[\text{ionized form}]} \quad ...(14.56)$$

In acid solution presence of excess of H_3O^+ ions will suppress the ionization of the acid indicator and $[In^-]$ will be small. The colour will therefore be mainly due to the unionized form HIn. On the other hand, in alkaline solutions the ionization equilibrium is shifted to the right increasing the concentration of ionized form In^-. Hence in alkaline medium the indicator will exist mainly in the ionized form and the colour of the ionized form becomes apparent.

The actual colour of the indicator depends on the ratio of the concentration of the ionized and unionized forms, and is thus directly related to the hydrogen ion concentration of the medium. Equation (14.56) may be rewritten as

$$pH = pK_{ind} + \log \frac{[In^-]}{[HIn]} \quad ...(14.57)$$

For a base indicator, an exactly analogous expression may be deduced and can be written as

$$pOH = pK_{ind} + \log \frac{In^+}{InOH} \quad ...(14.58)$$

At any given pH of the solution, both forms of the indicators will be present. It is important to realise that the human eye has a limited ability to detect either of the two colours when one of the two predominates. In general, when $\frac{[HIn]}{[In^-]} = 10$, Eq. (14.57) reduces to

$$pH = pK_{ind} - 1$$

and the colour of the solution will appear to be due to the unionized form. On the other hand, when the ratio of $\frac{[In^-]}{[HIn]} = 10$, Eq. (14.57) reduces to

$$pH = pK_{ind} + 1$$

and the colour in alkaline solution will be due to In^-. The colour change interval is accordingly given by

$$pH = pK_{ind} \pm 1 \quad ...(14.59)$$

and extends over approximately two pH units one above and one below the pK value of the indicator. Within this range, the indicator changes its colour from one form to another. The change will be gradual as it depends on the logarithm of the ratio of the concentration of the two coloured forms (unionized and ionized forms). When the pH of the solution is equal to the ionization constant of the indicator, pK_{ind}, the ratio $\left[\dfrac{HIn}{In^-}\right]$ becomes unity and the indicator will have a colour due to an equimolar mixture of the acid and base forms. This is sometimes called as the "*middle tint*" of the indicator. This applies strictly if the two colours are of equal intensity.

(*ii*) **Quinonoid Theory:** The colour in most of the naturally occurring organic compounds has been attributed to be due to the presence of quinonoid structure.

Quinonoid structure
(coloured)

A theory called *quinonoid theory* based on this observation was put forward to explain the change in colour of indicators with pH. According to this theory, the colour changes are believed to be due to structural changes including the production of the quinonoid and resonating forms. This may be illustrated by reference to phenolphthalein where (*I*) represents the structure of phenolphthalein which in the presence of dilute alkalis changes to structure (*II*). This triphenyl carbinol structure (*II*) undergoes typical loss of water, then yields a red resonating dianion (III). If phenolphthalein is treated with excess of concentrated alcoholic alkalis the red colour first produced disappears owing to the formation of carbinol form (*IV*).

Similarly, the two forms of methyl orange are:

**Methyl orange in presence of alkalis
(Non quinonoid structure—yellow)**

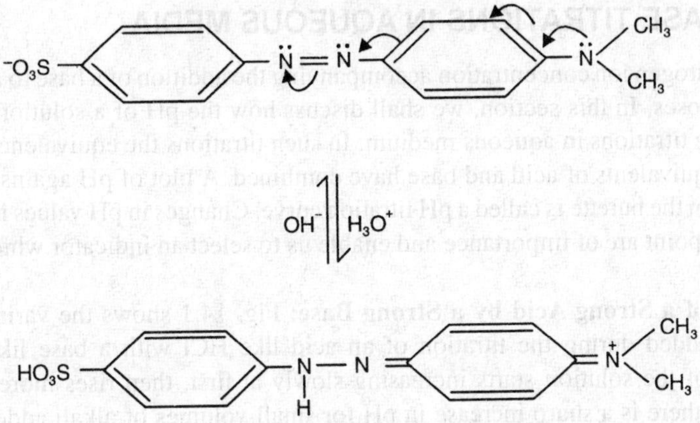

^-O_3S ——— $\ddot{N} = \ddot{N}$ ——— $\ddot{N}$ $\begin{smallmatrix} CH_3 \\ CH_3 \end{smallmatrix}$

OH^- H_3O^+

HO_3S ——— $\overset{H}{\underset{}{N}}-N$ ——— $\overset{+}{N}$ $\begin{smallmatrix} CH_3 \\ CH_3 \end{smallmatrix}$

**Methyl orange in presence of acids
(Quinonoid structure—red)**

Table 14.5 contains a selected list of some indicators along with their colour change intervals.

Table 14.5 Some Indicators and Their Characteristic pH Ranges

Indicator	pH range	Colour in	
		acidic solution	alkaline solution
Cresol red	0.2–1.8	Red	Yellow
m–cresol purple	1.2–2.8	Red	Yellow
Methyl orange	3.1–4.4	Red	Orange
Methyl red	4.2–6.3	Red	Yellow
Phenol red	6.8–8.4	Yellow	Red
Cresol red	7.2–8.8	Yellow	Red
Thymol blue	8.0–9.6	Yellow	Blue
Phenolphthalein	8.3–10.0	Colourless	Red
Alizarin yellow	10.1–12.1	Yellow	Orange red

By suitably mixing certain indicators the colour change may be made to extend over a considerable pH range. Such a mixture is known as "*universal indicator*". These are mostly employed for determining the approximate pH of solutions. One such indicator is a mixture of methyl red, methyl orange, bromothymol blue and phenolphthalein. It covers a pH range of 3-11 and gives colour changes at different pH values as shown below.

pH	3	4	5	6	7	8	9	10	11
Colour	Red	Orange	Orange	Yellow	Yellowish green	Greenish blue	Blue	Violet	Reddish violet

14.14 ACID-BASE TITRATIONS IN AQUEOUS MEDIA

The changes in hydrogen ion concentration accompanying the addition of a base to an acid are important for analytical purposes. In this section, we shall discuss how the pH of a solution changes during the course of acid-base titrations in aqueous medium. In such titrations the equivalence point occurs when equal number of equivalents of acid and base have combined. A plot of pH against the volume of base (or acid) added from the burette is called a pH titration curve. Changes in pH values in the neighbourhood of the equivalence point are of importance and enable us to select an indicator which will give the least titration error.

(*a*) **Titration of a Strong Acid by a Strong Base:** Fig. 14.1 shows the variation of pH with the volume of alkali added during the titration of an acid like HCl with a base like NaOH. It will be observed that pH of the solution starts increasing slowly at first, then rises more rapidly until at the equivalence point, there is a sharp increase in pH for small volumes of alkali added. After the equivalence point, increase in pH is small on addition of excess alkali.

Let us consider the titration of 100 ml of 1N HCl by 1N NaOH solution. The initial pH is zero and at the end point it is seven.

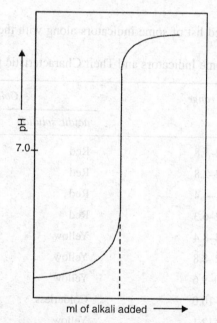

Fig. 14.1 Titration of 1.0 M hydrochloric acid with 1.0 M sodium hydroxide

The pH of the solution throughout the titration can be computed by calculating $[H_3O^+]$ present in the solution each time after a certain quantity of NaOH is added to the HCl solution. For example, the number of moles per litre of H_3O^+ ions present when 90 ml of 1.0N NaOH solution have been added can be calculated as

$$\frac{\left(1.0 \text{ mol L}^{-1}\right)}{(190 \text{ ml})}(10 \text{ ml}) = 5.26 \times 10^{-2} \text{mol L}^{-1}$$

and the pH is 1.3.

The concentration of H_3O^+ ions and pH values during the course of titration are summarized in Table 14.6.

From the table 14.6 it is apparent that between 99.9 ml to 100.1 ml of alkali added, pH of the solution rises sharply from 3.3 to 10.7. Hence any indicator with an effective range between pH 3.0 and 10.5 may be used. Consequently, both phenolphthalein (pH range 8.3–10.0) and methyl orange (pH range 3.1–4.4) may be used. If the solutions are dilute to 0.01N, change in pH and the equivalence point are less sharp and the range is limited to pH 5.5–8.5. Indicators such as methyl red, bromothymol blue will be satisfactory.

Table 14.6: pH During the Titration of 100 ml of 1N HCl with 1N NaOH Solution

Volume of alkali added (ml)	$[H_3O^+]$, mole/litre	pH
0.0	1.0	0.00
50.0	3.33×10^{-1}	0.48
75.0	1.43×10^{-1}	0.94
90.0	5.26×10^{-2}	1.30
98.0	1.01×10^{-2}	2.00
99.0	5.03×10^{-2}	2.30
99.9	5.01×10^{-4}	3.30
100.0	1.00×10^{-7}	7.00
100.1	1.995×10^{-11}	10.70
100.2	1.00×10^{-11}	11.00
100.5	3.98×10^{-12}	11.40

(*b*) **Titration of a Weak Acid by a Strong Base:** Consider the titration of 100 ml of 0.1N CH_3COOH by 0.1N NaOH solution. The initial pH of the solution is not one as the acid is only partly ionized. Initially when acetic acid is the only species present, pH of the solution can be calculated from Eq. (14.9).

When alkali is added to the acid solution, sodium acetate is formed and the mixture of acetic acid and sodium acetate acts as a buffer. The pH values up to the equivalence point can be calculated using Henderson Eq. (14.36).

$$pH = pK_a + \log \frac{[\text{salt}]}{[\text{acid}]}$$

For each addition, concentrations of the salt and the acid may be calculated. For example, when 25 ml of 0.1N NaOH have been added to 100 ml of 0.1N acetic acid solution, concentrations of the salt formed and acetic acid are

$$\left[CH_3COO^-\right] = \frac{(25 \text{ ml})}{(125 \text{ ml})}\left(0.1 \text{ mol L}^{-1}\right) = 2 \times 10^{-2} \text{ mol L}^{-1}$$

and $\quad [CH_3COOH] = \dfrac{(75\ ml)}{(125\ ml)}\left(0.1\ mol\ L^{-1}\right) = 6 \times 10^{-2}\ mol\ L^{-1}$

$$pH = 4.74 + \log\left(\dfrac{2 \times 10^{-2}}{6 \times 10^{-2}}\right)$$

$$= 4.30$$

Therefore, the pH is 4.3. When half of the acid has been neutralized, salt and acid concentrations are equal and the pH is equal to pK_a (4.73). The pH at the equivalence point will not be seven due to hydrolysis of CH_3COO^- ions. The pH value at the equivalence point can be calculated considering the hydrolysis of CH_3COO^- ions using Eq. (14.50).

$$pH = \dfrac{1}{2}\left[pK_w + pK_a + \log C\right]$$

$$= \dfrac{1}{2}\left[(14) + (4.73) + (\overline{2}.699)\right]$$

$$= 8.72$$

After the equivalence point excess of OH^- ions will suppress the hydrolysis of the anion and pH is then solely dependent on the concentration of OH^- ions provided by the added NaOH. The titration curve has been given in Fig. 14.2 and the pH values at different stages of titration are given in Table 14.7.

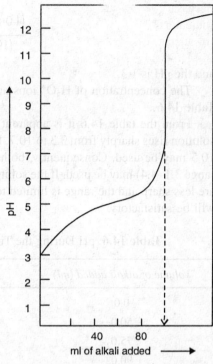

Fig. 14.2 Titration of 100 ml of 0.1N acetic acid with 0.1 N sodium hydroxide

Table 14.7 pH During the Titration of 100 ml of 0.1N Acetic Acid by 0.1N NaOH Solution

Volume of alkali added (ml)	$[H_3O^+]$, mole/litre	pH
0.0	1.260×10^{-2}	2.90
25.0	5.012×10^{-5}	4.30
50.0	1.800×10^{-5}	4.73
90.0	1.995×10^{-6}	5.70
99.0	1.995×10^{-7}	6.70
99.9	1.995×10^{-8}	7.70
100.0	1.995×10^{-9}	8.70
100.1	1.995×10^{-10}	9.70
100.2	1.000×10^{-10}	10.00
101.0	1.995×10^{-11}	10.70

The equivalence point lies at a pH of about 8.7 and sharp pH changes are observed near the end point where the pH increases from 7.7 to 9.7 by the addition of a small amount of alkali. It is, therefore, necessary to use an indicator with a pH range slightly on alkaline side. Hence the commonly used indicators are phenolphthalein or thymol blue. Any indicator changing its colour below pH 8 will be unsatisfactory. Comparing the plot in Fig. 14.2 with that in Fig. 14.1, we see that in this case the change in pH near the equivalence point is less sharp. For weaker acids like HCN, etc., pH changes near the equivalence point become still less pronounced.

(c) **Titration of a Weak Base by a Strong Acid:** Consider the titration of 100 ml of 0.1N NH_3 solution by 0.1N HCl solution. When no acid is added the pH value is calculated using Eq. (14.11). Addition of HCl produces the salt, NH_4Cl and the mixture of NH_3 and NH_4Cl acts as a buffer and its pH value up to the equivalence point can be calculated using the Henderson Eq. (14.37)

$$pOH = pK_b + \log\frac{[\text{salt}]}{[\text{base}]}$$

At the equivalence point the solution contains the salt and the pH of the solution is determined by the hydrolysis of NH_4^+ ions using Eq. (14.44).

$$pH = \frac{1}{2}\left[pK_w - pK_b - \log C\right]$$

$$= \frac{1}{2}\left[(14) - (4.73) - (\overline{2}.699)\right] = 5.29$$

Thus the pH at the equivalence point is 5.29. Beyond the equivalence point addition of HCl suppresses the hydrolysis of the salt and the pH is controlled by excess of H_3O^+ ions from HCl. The pH values at different stages of titration are given in Table 14.8 and the titration curve in Fig. 14.3. The

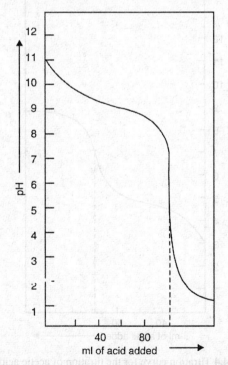

Fig. 14.3 Titration of 100 ml of 0.1N ammonium hydroxide solution with 0.1 N hydrochloric acid

equivalence point is at pH 5.3. It is therefore, necessary to use an indicator with a pH range slightly on the acidic side. Methyl orange, methyl red, bromophenol blue, or bromocresol green, etc. are usually employed.

Table 14.8: pH during the Titration of 100 ml of 0.1N NH_3 by 0.1N HCl solution

Volume of HCl added (ml)	$[H_3O^+]$, mole/litre	pH
0.0	7.90×10^{-12}	11.1
25.0	1.59×10^{-10}	9.8
50.0	5.01×10^{-10}	9.3
90.0	5.01×10^{-9}	8.3
99.0	5.01×10^{-9}	7.3
99.9	5.01×10^{-7}	6.3
100.0	5.01×10^{-6}	5.3
100.2	1.00×10^{-4}	4.0
100.5	2.50×10^{-4}	3.6

(*d*) **Titration of a Weak Acid by a Weak Base:** The titration curve for a weak acid say, acetic acid, by a weak base like NH_3 is shown in Fig. 14.4.

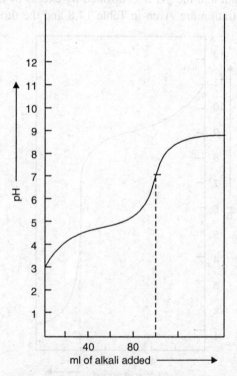

Fig. 14.4 Titration curve for the titration of acetic acid
with ammonium hydroxide

The pH at the equivalence point is calculated by using Eq. 14.55

$$pH = \frac{1}{2}\left[pK_w + pK_a - pK_b\right]$$

$$= \frac{1}{2}\left[(14) + (4.74) - (4.74)\right]$$

$$= 7.0$$

The main features of the titration curve is that the pH changes during the entire course of the titration are gradual. Hence no sharp end point can be obtained with the commonly employed indicators. However, a mixed indicator which shows a sharp colour change over a limited pH range may sometimes be used. In the titration of ammonium hydroxide by acetic acid, neutral red methylene blue indicator may be occasionally used. Such titrations are usually avoided.

14.15 SOLUBILITY PRODUCT

In a saturated solution of a sparingly soluble salt, a dynamic equilibrium exists between the insoluble salt and its dissociated ions. For example, a salt like AgCl when added to water, a small amount of it goes into the solution yielding Ag^+ and Cl^- ions and the rest remains as excess solid. Solid AgCl is thus in equilibrium with Ag^+ and Cl^- ions. The equilibrium may be represented as

$$AgCl(solid) \rightleftharpoons Ag^+(aq) + Cl^-(aq)$$

for which we can write

$$K = \frac{a_{Ag^+} \, a_{Cl^-}}{a_{AgCl}}$$

The activity of pure solid AgCl may be taken as unity and hence we can write

$$K_{sp} = \left[a_{Ag^+}\right]\left[a_{Cl^-}\right] \qquad \qquad ...(14.60)$$

where K_{sp} is known as *the solubility product of* AgCl and is defined as *the product of the activities of the ions in a saturated solution of a sparingly soluble salt*. Since the salt is sparingly soluble and the solution is dilute and hence the activities of the ions may be replaced by the corresponding concentration terms. Equation (14.60) can then be written as

$$K_{sp} = \left[Ag^+\right]\left[Cl^-\right]$$

Solubility product is dependent on temperature and is nearly independent of the concentration of various other ions provided the solution is dilute. In the case of an insoluble salt such as CaF_2, the stoichiometric coefficients in the dissociation equilibrium are not equal to unity

$$CaF_2(s) \rightleftharpoons Ca^{2+}(aq) + 2F^-(aq)$$

The K_{sp} for CaF_2 is then given by

$$K_{sp} = \left[Ca^{2+}\right]\left[F^-\right]^2$$

Hence the solubility product constant is equal to the product of the concentration of the ions present in a saturated solution each raised to a power equal to its stoichiometric coefficient in the balanced chemical equation.

In general, for a salt of the type A_xB_y which in solution yields A^{y+} and B^{x-} ions according to the equilibrium

$$A_xB_y\,(s) \rightleftharpoons xA^{y+} + yB^{x-}$$

The solubility product is given by

$$K_{sp} = \left[A^{y+}\right]^x \left[B^{x-}\right]^y$$

A saturated solution exists only when the ionic product is equal to or greater than K_{sp}. When the ionic product is less than K_{sp}, the solution is unsaturated because more of the salt can be dissolved in order to raise the concentrations of the ions to the point where the ionic product equals K_{sp}. When the ionic product exceeds K_{sp}, a supersaturated solution exists and hence the precipitation will occur. Consequently, the value of the ionic product in a solution tells us whether precipitation will occur or not. We can summarise as

Ionic product $< K_{sp}$ ⎫
Ionic product $= K_{sp}$ ⎬   no precipitation will occur
Ionic product $> K_{sp}$ ⎭

Ionic product $> K_{sp}$ precipitation will occur

14.16 RELATION BETWEEN SOLUBILITY AND SOLUBILITY PRODUCT

For a salt like AgCl, if S is the solubility expressed in mole/litre then the $[Ag^+]$ and $[Cl^-]$ ions are each equal to S. Hence the solubility product K_{sp} is given by

$$K_{sp} = \left[Ag^+\right]\left[Cl^-\right] = S^2$$

or

$$S = \sqrt{K_{sp}}$$

For CaF_2

$$\left[Ca^{2+}\right] = S \text{ and } \left[F^-\right] = 2S$$

and

$$K_{sp} = [S][2S]^2 = 4S^3$$

or

$$S = \sqrt[3]{\frac{K_{sp}}{4}}$$

In general, for a salt like A_xB_y if S is the solubility then

$$\left[A^{y+}\right] = xS \text{ and } \left[B^{x-}\right] = yS$$

hence

$$K_{sp} = \left[xS\right]^x\left[yS\right]^y$$

$$= x^x y^y S^{x+y}$$

or
$$S = \left[\frac{K_{sp}}{x^x y^y} \right]^{\frac{1}{x+y}} \qquad ...(14.61)$$

Determination of Solubility Product

Solubility product of a salt can be determined from the measurement of solubility. Solubilities of sparingly soluble salts can be measured from conductance, potentiometric or colorimetric measurements. Solubility products of some sparingly soluble salts are given in Table 14.9.

Applications of Solubility Product

(i) *Determination of solubilities of sparingly soluble salts:* Knowing solubility product, the solubility of a salt can be calculated using Eq. (14.61).

(ii) *Fractional precipitation:* To an aqueous solution of KI and KCl when a solution of silver nitrate is added, precipitation of AgI and AgCl will take place. From solubility product principle, one can predict which salt will precipitate first and how much of the first salt would be precipitated out when the second starts precipitating. The solubility product of AgI is 1.5×10^{-16} and that of AgCl is 1.56×10^{-10}. It is evident that AgI is less soluble and will precipitate first and AgCl will precipitate only when

the $[Ag^+]$ is greater than $\dfrac{1.56 \times 10^{-10}}{Cl^-}$

i.e.,
$$\left[Ag^+ \right] > \frac{K_{sp,\ AgCl}}{\left[Cl^- \right]} > \frac{1.56 \times 10^{-10}}{\left[Cl^- \right]}$$

and both the salts will precipitate simultaneously when

$$\frac{\left[I^- \right]}{\left[Cl^- \right]} = \frac{K_{sp,\ AgI}}{K_{sp,\ AgCl}} = \frac{1.5 \times 10^{-16}}{1.56 \times 10^{-10}} = 9.8 \times 10^{-7}$$

Table 14.9 Solubility Product for Some Sparingly Soluble Salts at 298 K

Salt	K_{sp}	Salt	K_{sp}
PbCl$_2$	1.6×10^{-5}	Fe(OH)$_3$	4.5×10^{-27}
Hg$_2$Cl$_2$	2.0×10^{-18}	Al(OH)$_3$	2.0×10^{-33}
AgCl	1.6×10^{-10}	Mn(OH)$_2$	4.5×10^{-14}
AgBr	5.0×10^{-18}	Mg(OH)$_2$	1.2×10^{-11}
AgI	1.5×10^{-16}	BaSO$_4$	1.5×10^{-9}
CuS	8.6×10^{-36}	PbSO$_4$	1.7×10^{-8}
CdS	3.6×10^{-28}	SrSO$_4$	2.5×10^{-7}
AgS	1.6×10^{-54}	Ag$_2$CrO$_4$	9.0×10^{-12}
PbS	7.0×10^{-27}	PbCrO$_4$	1.8×10^{-14}
CoS	3.0×10^{-26}	PbC$_2$O$_4$	2.7×10^{-11}
NiS	2.0×10^{-21}		
ZnS	1.2×10^{-23}		

Hence AgCl will start precipitating out when the $[I^-]$ is approximately one millionth part of $[Cl^-]$, or the precipitation of I^- ion as AgI will be almost complete.

(*iii*) *In qualitative analysis:* Classification of cations into six groups in salt analysis is based on the principle of solubility product. In the first group solubility products of chlorides of Hg_2^{2+} Pb^{2+} and Ag^+ are sufficiently low, hence they are precipitated out as their chlorides. Chlorides of common metals are highly soluble and they are therefore not precipitated. In group II, cations are precipitated as sulphides by passing H_2S gas through their solutions containing dilute HCl (0.2–0.3 N). In such a solution ionization of H_2S is suppressed by HCl, the concentration of sulphide ions is greatly reduced and only the sulphides of second group having low solubility products are precipitated out. Sulphides of Zn group are not precipitated because of their comparatively higher solubility products. These are, therefore, precipitated by H_2S in alkaline medium.

Similarly, in the third group, addition of NH_4Cl suppresses the ionization of ammonia; lowers the $[OH^-]$ to a sufficiently low value. It is still enough to exceed the solubility product of hydroxides of Al, Fe and Cr but not those of the subsequent groups.

(*iv*) *Purification of NaCl and salting out of soaps:* Sodium chloride from aqueous solution is precipitated by passing HCl gas through it. HCl increases the $[Cl^-]$ in the solution. Ionic product of $[Na^+]$ $[Cl^-]$ exceeds the solubility product of NaCl which precipitates out in the pure form.

The same principle is used in the precipitation of soaps. Soaps are sodium or potassium salts of higher fatty acids. Addition of NaCl increases the $[Na^+]$ and hence the ionic product exceeds the solubility product of the soap which is separated out.

Problem 14.20: Solubility product of Ag_2CrO_4 is 9.0×10^{-12} at 298 K. Calculate the solubility of Ag_2CrO_4.

Solution: Let S be the solubility of the salt, then $\left[CrO_4^{2-}\right] = S$ and $[Ag^+] = 2S$ (as 1 mole of Ag_2CrO_4 furnishes 2 moles of Ag^+ ions in the solution).

Hence

$$K_{sp} = \left[Ag^+\right]^2 \left[CrO_4^{2-}\right] = (2S)^2 \times (S) = 9 \times 10^{-12}$$

$$2^2 S^3 = 9 \times 10^{-12}$$

or

$$S = 1.3 \times 10^{-4} \, \text{mol dm}^{-3}$$

Problem 14.21: Calculate the solubility of $Mg(OH)_2$ in (*i*) pure water, (*ii*) 0.01 M NaOH, and (*iii*) 0.01 M $Ba(OH)_2$. K_{sp} for $Mg(OH)_2$ is 1.2×10^{-11}.

Solution: (*i*) Let S be the solubility of $Mg(OH)_2$ in water then

$$\left[Mg^{2+}\right] = S, \left[OH^-\right] = 2S$$

Hence

$$K_{sp} = \left[Mg^{2+}\right]\left[OH^-\right]^2 = (S)(2S)^2 = 1.2 \times 10^{-11}$$

or

$$S = 1.442 \times 10^{-4} \, \text{mol dm}^{-3}$$

(*ii*) Solubility of $Mg(OH)_2$ will decrease in presence of NaOH due to common ion effect. If S' is the solubility in presence of 0.01 M NaOH, then

$$[Mg^{2+}] = S'; [OH^-] = 0.01 + 2S' \text{ and}$$

$$[Mg^{2+}][OH^-]^2 = (S')(0.01 + 2S')^2 = 1.2 \times 10^{-11}$$

Neglecting $2S'$ in comparison to 0.01, we get

$$S' \times 10^{-4} = 1.2 \times 10^{-11}$$

or

$$S' = 1.2 \times 10^{-7} \text{ mol dm}^{-3}$$

(iii) If S'' be the solubility of $Mg(OH)_2$ in 0.01 M $Ba(OH)_2$, then

$$[Mg^{2+}] = S'', [OH^-] = 0.02 + 2S''$$

Hence

$$[Mg^{2+}][OH^-]^2 = [S''][0.02 + 2S'']^2 = 1.2 \times 10^{-11}$$

Neglecting $2S''$ in comparison to 0.02, we get

$$S'' = \frac{1.2 \times 10^{-11}}{4 \times 10^{-4}} = 3 \times 10^{-8} \text{ mol dm}^{-3}$$

Problem 14.22: The solubility product of AgCl is 1.56×10^{-10} at 298 K. Calculate the solubility of AgCl in (i) pure water, (ii) a solution 0.1 M with respect to NaCl, and (iii) a solution 0.1 M with respect to $AgNO_3$.

Solution: (i) Let S be the solubility of the salt in water, then

$$[Ag^+] = [Cl^-] = S \text{ and}$$

$$K_{sp} = [Ag^+][Cl^-] = [S][S] = 1.56 \times 10^{-10}$$

or

$$[S] = \sqrt{1.56 \times 10^{-10}} = 1.25 \times 10^{-5} \text{ mol dm}^{-3}$$

(ii) The solubility of AgCl will be lowered by the presence of either Cl^- or Ag^+ ions due to common ion effect. Let S' be the solubility of the salt in presence of 0.1M NaCl, then the total $[Cl^-] = S' + 0.1$ and $[Ag^+] = S'$. Hence, we have

$$K_{sp} = 1.56 \times 10^{-10} = [Ag^+][Cl^-] = [0.1 + S'][S']$$

Since S' is very small we can neglect S' in comparison to 0.1.

Then

$$0.1 \times S' = 1.56 \times 10^{-10}$$

or

$$S' = 1.56 \times 10^{-9} \text{ mol dm}^{-3}$$

(iii) If S'' is the solubility of AgCl in the presence of 0.1 M $AgNO_3$, then $[Ag^+] = 0.1 + S''$ and $[Cl^-] = S''$ and

$$K_{sp} = 1.56 \times 10^{-10} = [Ag^+][Cl^-] = [0.1 + S''][S''] = 0.1 \times S'' \qquad [\because S'' << 0.1]$$

Therefore,

$$S'' = \frac{1.56 \times 10^{-10}}{(0.1)} = 1.56 \times 10^{-9} \, \text{mol dm}^{-3}$$

The solubility of AgCl is considerably reduced in 0.1M $AgNO_3$ or in 0.1M NaCl solution due to common ion effect.

Problem 14.23: 100 ml of 0.004M $Ba(NO_3)_2$ solution is mixed with 400 ml of 0.05M Na_2SO_4. Will a precipitate of $BaSO_4$ form? K_{sp} for $BaSO_4$ is 1.5×10^{-9}.

Solution: The total volume of the solution after mixing is 500 ml. The molar concentrations of Ba^{2+} and SO_4^{2-} ions in the final solution are given by

$$\left[Ba^{2+}\right] = \frac{\left(0.004 \, \text{mol dm}^{-3}\right)(100 \, \text{ml})}{(500 \, \text{ml})} = 8.0 \times 10^{-4} \, \text{mol dm}^{-3}$$

$$\left[SO_4^{2-}\right] = \frac{\left(0.05 \, \text{mol dm}^{-3}\right)(400 \, \text{ml})}{(500 \, \text{ml})} = 4.0 \times 10^{-2} \, \text{mol dm}^{-3}$$

The product of ionic concentrations in the final solution is therefore

$$\left[Ba^{2+}\right]\left[SO_4^{2-}\right] = \left(8 \times 10^{-4}\right)\left(4 \times 10^{-2}\right) = 3.2 \times 10^{-5}$$

As the ionic product exceeds the solubility product 1.5×10^{-9} therefore a precipitate of $BaSO_4$ will be formed.

Problem 14.24: 500 ml of a saturated solution of $Ca(OH)_2$ is mixed with 500 ml of 0.4 M sodium hydroxide solution. How many milligrams of $Ca(OH)_2$ would be precipitated out? K_{sp} of $Ca(OH)_2$ is 4.42×10^{-5}.

Solution: For the saturated solution of $Ca(OH)_2$, we have

$$Ca(OH)_2\,(s) \rightleftharpoons Ca^{2+} + 2OH^-$$

If S is the solubility of $Ca(OH)_2$ then

$$\{Ca^{2+}\} = S \text{ and } [OH^-] = 2S$$

So

$$4.42 \times 10^{-5} = [S][2S]^2 \text{ or } S = 2.227 \times 10^{-2} \, M$$

When 500 ml of 0.4 M sodium hydroxide solution is added, the total volume of the solution is 1L and $[OH^-] = 0.2$ M. If S' is the solubility of $Ca(OH)_2$ then

$$[S'] = [Ca^{2+}] = \frac{4.42 \times 10^{-5}}{[OH^-]^2} = \frac{4.42 \times 10^{-5}}{(0.2)^2} = 1.105 \times 10^{-3} \, M$$

Hence the moles of Ca $(OH)_2$ precipitated per litre are

$$\left(22.27 \times 10^{-3} - 1.105 \times 10^{-3}\right) = 21.165 \times 10^{-3}$$

or

$$= 1.0582 \times 10^{-2} \text{ moles from 500 ml}$$

Therefore, milligrams of $Ca(OH)_2$ precipitated from 500 ml solution

$$= 1.0582 \times 10^{-2} \times 74 \times 10^3$$
$$= 783 \text{ mg}$$

Problem 14.25: Calculate the solubility of AgBr and AgSCN when present together in a solution saturated with respect to both the salt at 298 K. K_{sp} (AgBr) $= 5.0 \times 10^{-13}$ and K_{sp} (AgSCN) $= 10 \times 10^{-12}$

Solution: The two equilibria are

$$AgBr(s) \rightleftharpoons Ag^+ + Br^-, K_{sp}(AgBr) = [Ag^+][Br^-] = 5.0 \times 10^{-13} \qquad ...(i)$$

$$AgSCN(s) \rightleftharpoons Ag^+ + SCN^-, K_{sp}(AgSCN) = [Ag^+][SCN^-] = 1.0 \times 10^{-12} \quad ...(ii)$$

Dividing, (ii) by (i) we get

$$\frac{[SCN^-]}{[Br^-]} = \frac{1.0 \times 10^{-12}}{5 \times 10^{-13}} = 2$$

From charge balance, we have

$$[Ag^+] = [Br^-] + [SCN^-]$$

or

$$\frac{[Ag^+]}{[Br^-]} = \frac{[SCN^-]}{[Br^-]} + 1$$

$$= 2 + 1 = 3$$

So

$$[Ag^+] = 3[Br^-]$$

Substituting the value of $[Ag^+]$ in equation (i), yields

or

$$[3 Br^-][Br^-] = 5.0 \times 10^{-13}$$

$$[Br^-] = \sqrt{\frac{5}{3} \times 10^{-13}} = 4.1 \times 10^{-7} M = \text{Solubility of AgBr}$$

Also

$$[SCN^-] = 2[Br^-] = 8.2 \times 10^{-7} M = \text{Solubility of AgSCN}$$

Problem 14.26: The solubility product of $Ag_2C_2O_4$ at 298 K is 1.29×10^{-11}. A solution of $K_2C_2O_4$ containing 0.152 moles in 500 ml water is treated with excess of Ag_2CO_3 till the following equilibrium is reached

$$Ag_2CO_3(s) + K_2C_2O_4 \rightleftharpoons Ag_2C_2O_4(s) + K_2CO_3$$

At equilibrium, the solution contains 0.0358 mole of K_2CO_3. Assuming the degree of dissociation of K_2CO_3 and $K_2C_2O_4$ to be equal. Calculate K_{sp} (Ag_2CO_3).

Solution: Initial concentration of $K_2C_2O_4 = 0.152 \times 2 = 0.304$ M

and that of Ag_2CO_3 at equilibrium $= 0.0358 \times 2 = 0.0716$ M

As 1 mole of Ag_2CO_3 reacts with one mole of $K_2C_2O_4$ to form 1 mole of K_2CO_3 and 1 mole of $Ag_2C_2O_4$, so the number of moles of $K_2C_2O_4$ left unreacted = $(0.304 - 0.0716) = 0.2324$

From the solubility product of $Ag_2C_2O_4$, we have

$$\left|Ag^+\right|^2\left[C_2O_4^{2-}\right] = 1.29 \times 10^{-11}$$

As $\left[C_2O_4^{2-}\right] = 0.2324$, so $\left[Ag^+\right]^2 = \dfrac{1.29 \times 10^{-11}}{0.2324}$

And for the solubility product of Ag_2CO_3, we have

$$K_{sp}(Ag_2CO_3) = \left[Ag^+\right]^2\left[CO_3^{2-}\right]$$

$$= \frac{1.29 \times 10^{-11}}{0.2324} \times 0.0716 = 3.97 \times 10^{-12}$$

Problem 14.27: A solution is 0.05 M with respect to $MgCl_2$ and 0.05 M with respect to ammonia. Calculate the concentration of NH_4Cl required to prevent formation of Mg $(OH)_2$ from this solution. K_{sp}(Mg $(OH)_2$) is 9.0×10^{-12} and K_b (NH_3) is 1.8×10^{-5}.

Solution:

$$K_{sp}Mg(OH)_2 = \left[Mg^{2+}\right]\left[OH^-\right]^2 = 9.0 \times 10^{-12}$$

So $$\left[OH^-\right]^2 = \frac{9.0 \times 10^{-12}}{\left[Mg^{2+}\right]} = \frac{9.0 \times 10^{-12}}{5 \times 10^{-2}}$$

or $$\left[OH^-\right] = 1.342 \times 10^{-5}\,M$$

Ammonium chloride will suppress ionization of ammonia

$$NH_3 + H_2O \rightleftharpoons NH_4^+ + OH^-$$

and $$K_b = \frac{\left[NH_4^+\right]\left[OH^-\right]}{\left[NH_3\right]} = \frac{\left[NH_4^+\right]\left[1.342 \times 10^{-5}\right]}{0.05 - \left[NH_4^+\right]}$$

Assuming $0.05 \gg \left[NH_4^+\right]$, we have

$$1.8 \times 10^{-5} = \frac{\left[NH_4^+\right]\left[1.342 \times 10^{-5}\right]}{5.0 \times 10^{-2}}$$

Hence $$\left[NH_4^+\right] = \frac{1.8 \times 10^{-5} \times 5.0 \times 10^{-2}}{1.342 \times 10^{-5}}$$

$$= 6.71 \times 10^{-2}\,M$$

14.17 COMPLEX IONS

A complex ion is formed by the combination of a simple metal ion with either other ions of opposite charges or with molecules. The substances that combine with the metal ion are called *ligands*. For example, when NH_3 is added to an aqueous solution of copper sulphate, a white precipitate of $Cu(OH)_2$ is first formed which dissolves on adding excess of NH_3 forming a complex ion, $Cu(NH_3)_4^{2+}$

$$Cu^{2+} + 4NH_3 \rightleftharpoons Cu(NH_3)_4^{2+}$$

The complex ion behaves as a weak electrolyte and dissociates to a small extent according to the reaction

$$Cu(NH_3)_4^{2+} \rightleftharpoons Cu^{2+} + 4NH_3$$

The equilibrium constant for the reaction is the ionization constant for the complex ion and is referred to *as the instability constant, K_{ins}*, for the complex ion

$$K_{ins} = \frac{\left[Cu^{2+}\right]\left[NH_3\right]^4}{\left[Cu(NH_3)_4^{2+}\right]}$$

The reciprocal of K_{ins} is known as *the stability constant* for the complex ion and is defined as

$$K_{stab} = \frac{1}{K_{ins}} = \frac{\left[Cu(NH_3)_4^{2+}\right]}{\left[Cu^{2+}\right]\left[NH_3\right]^4}$$

and is the association constant for the reaction. The stability of a complex ion is expressed in terms of K_{ins}. Smaller the value of K_{ins} greater will be the stability of the complex ion.

Complex ion formation is used in analytical chemistry for the separation of ions in solutions. Thus, when KCN is added to a solution of copper and cadmium ions, both form complexes with CN^- ions; cadmium complex, $Cd(CN)_4^{2-}$, is less stable and is precipitated by H_2S while copper complex, $Cu(CN)_4^{2-}$, remains in solution.

Complex formation in a solution of an insoluble salt reduces the concentration of the free metal ion. In such cases the solubility of the insoluble salt increases with the formation of complex ion. Solubility of AgCl in ammonia can be explained due to the formation of $Ag(NH_3)_2^+$ ion according to the following reactions

$$AgCl(s) \rightleftharpoons Ag^+ + Cl^- ; K_{sp} = \left[Ag^+\right]\left[Cl^-\right]$$

$$Ag^+ + 2NH_3 \rightleftharpoons Ag(NH_3)_2^+ ; K_{stab} = \frac{\left[Ag(NH_3)_2^+\right]}{\left[Ag^+\right]\left[NH_3\right]^2}$$

Formation of $Ag(NH_3)_2^+$ in the second reaction upsets the first equilibrium thereby causing it to shift to the right. As a result, some of the solid AgCl dissolves. The overall reaction can be obtained by adding together the two equilibrium reactions

$$AgCl(s) + 2NH_3 \rightleftharpoons Ag(NH_3)_2^+ + Cl^-$$

The equilibrium constant for the reaction is

$$K_{eq} = \frac{\left[Ag(NH_3)_2^+\right]\left[Cl^-\right]}{\left[NH_3\right]^2}$$

$$= \frac{\left[Ag^+\right]\left[Cl^-\right]\left[Ag(NH_3)_2^+\right]}{\left[NH_3\right]^2\left[Ag^+\right]}$$

$$= K_{sp}K_{stab}$$

From this the solubility of AgCl in NH_3 can be obtained.

Problem 14.28: Calculate the solubility of Zn (OH)$_2$ in 1M NH_3 at 298 K. Given $K_{ins} = 6.1 \times 10^{-11}$ and $K_{sp} = 4.5 \times 10^{-17}$

Solution: The overall equilibrium reaction is

$$Zn(OH)_2 + 4NH_3 \rightleftharpoons Zn(NH_3)_4^{2+} + 2OH^-$$

for which the equilibrium constant is given by

$$K_{eq} = \frac{\left[Zn(NH_3)_4^{2+}\right]\left[OH^-\right]^2}{\left[NH_3\right]^4}$$

If x be the solubility of Zn (OH)$_2$ in 1M NH_3 then the concentration of various species at equilibrium are

$$[NH_3] = 1 - 4x \; ; [OH^-] = 2x \text{ and } \left[Zn(NH_3)_4^{2+}\right] = x$$

Substituting these values in the expression for equilibrium constant, we have

$$K_{eq} = \frac{(x)(2x)^2}{(1-4x)^4} = \frac{4.5 \times 10^{-17}}{6.1 \times 10^{-11}}$$

Since $4x \ll 1$, hence we can write

$$(x)(2x)^2 = \frac{4.5}{6.1} \times 10^{-6}$$

Solving for x, we obtain　　　　　　$x = 5.75 \times 10^{-3} \text{ mol dm}^{-3}$

EXERCISES

1. Explain, giving reasons, the following:
   (*i*) Water acts both as an acid and as a base.
   (*ii*) pH of an aqueous 10^{-2} M acetic acid solution is not 2.0.
   (*iii*) pH of a 10^{-7} M HCl aqueous solution is not 7.0.
   (*iv*) A mixture of sodium acetate and acetic acid resists changes in its pH value on adding acids or bases.
   (*v*) An aqueous solution of sodium carbonate is alkaline, copper sulphate is acidic and that of ammonium acetate is neutral.
   (*vi*) pH of water at 298 K is 7.0, at other temperatures it may be more or less than 7.0.
   (*vii*) Phenolphthalein is not a suitable indicator for the titration of HCl against aqueous ammonia.
   (*viii*) Methyl orange is used as an indicator in the titration of a strong acid versus weak base.
   (*ix*) AgCl is less soluble in silver nitrate solution than in pure water.
   (*x*) H_2S is passed through an acidified solution to precipitate cations of the second group whereas in the fourth group it is passed through an alkaline solution.
   (*xi*) Al $(OH)_3$ is precipitated by NH_3 and NH_4Cl while $Zn(OH)_2$ is not precipitated by these reagents.
   (*xii*) Although perchloric acid is stronger than sulphuric acid yet in water they appear equally strong.
   (*xiii*) Addition of solid NH_4Cl to a beaker containing solid $Mg(OH)_2$ in contact with water causes $Mg(OH)_2$ to dissolve.

2. Identify the Brϕnsted acids and bases in the following equations:

$$H_2SO_4 + Cl^- \rightleftharpoons HCl + HSO_4^-$$

$$C_6H_5OH + OH^- \rightleftharpoons C_6H_5O^- + H_2O$$

$$HClO_4 + HSO_4^- \rightleftharpoons H_2SO_4 + ClO_4^-$$

$$HSO_4^- + CH_3COOH \rightleftharpoons H_2SO_4 + CH_3COO^-$$

$$HS^- + OH^- \rightleftharpoons S^{2-} + H_2O$$

$$H_2O^+ + HCO_3^- \rightleftharpoons H_2CO_3 + H_2O$$

$$H_2O^+ + CN^- \rightleftharpoons HCN + H_2O$$

   Also name the stronger acid and the stronger base in each case.

3. (*a*) Which is the stronger acid in each of the following pairs and why?

   K^+, Cs^+; HCl, HI ; HSO_4^-, SO_4^{2-}; H_2O, H_2S ; C_6H_5OH, C_2H_5OH ; and H_2CO_3, H_2SO_4.

   (*b*) Which is the stronger base in each case of the following pairs and why?

   OH^-, CH_3COO^-; OH^-, Cl^-; OH^-, NH_2^- ; CH_3^-, NH_2^- ; Cl^-, CH_3COO^- and NH_3, CH_3NH_2.

4. What are the conjugate acids and bases of the following?

   $H_2PO_4^-, HPO_4^{2-}, H_2O, HS^-, HCO_3^-, C_2H_5OH, Al(OH)(H_2O)_5^{2+}, HSO_3^-$ and NH_4^+.

5. (*a*) Arrange each of the following sets in order of increasing basicity:

   (*i*) NH_3, PH_3, AsH_3; (*ii*) $NH_3, NH_2^-, CH_3^-, OH^-$;

   (*iii*) Cl^-, HS^-, PH_2^-; (*iv*) $HSO_4^-, HSO_3^-, SO_4^{2-}$;

    (*v*) H_2O, OH^-, O^{2-}.

    (*b*)   Arrange each of the following sets in order of decreasing acidity:

       (*i*)   HF, HCl, HBr, HI ;   (*ii*) H_2SO_4, H_2SO_3, HSO_4^- ;

       (*iii*) CH_3Cl, CH_2Cl_2, $CHCl_3$;   (*iv*) H_2O, H_2S, H_2Te ;

       (*v*) H_3AsO_4, H_3AsO_3, $H_2AsO_4^-$;   (*vi*) C_2H_2, C_2H_4, C_2H_6.

6.   Name the Lewis acids and bases in the following reactions:

       (*i*) $Ag^+ + Cl^- = AgCl$ (*ii*) $Cu^+ + 4NH_3 = Cu(NH_3)_4^{2+}$

       (*iii*) $(CH_3)_3N + BF_3 = (CH_3)_3NBF_3$ (*iv*) $AlCl_3 + Cl^- = AlCl_4^-$

       (*v*) $SnCl_4 + 2Cl^- = SnCl_4^{2-}$

7.   Write the following reactions in order of increasing tendency to proceed from left to right.

       (*i*) $NH_3 + H_2O \rightleftharpoons NH_4^+ + OH^-$ (*ii*) $HClO_4 + NH_2^- \rightleftharpoons NH_3 + ClO_4^-$

       (*iii*) $H_2O + NO_3^- \rightleftharpoons HNO_3 + OH^-$ (*iv*) $NH_3 + Cl^- \rightleftharpoons NH_2^- + HCl$

       (*v*) $HCl + OCl^- \rightleftharpoons HOCl + Cl^-$ (*vi*) $HNO_3 + F^- \rightleftharpoons HF + NO_3^-$

       (*vii*) $HF + CH_3COO^- \rightleftharpoons F^- + CH_3COOH$

8.   Indicate whether the following would be expected to serve as either a Lewis acid or a base:

       (*i*) $AlCl_3$,   (*ii*) OH^- (*iii*) NO^+

       (*iv*) H_2O (*v*) Fe^{2+} (*vi*) SbF_5,

       (*vii*) SiF_4,   (*viii*) BF_3 (*ix*) CO_2

       (*x*) $(CH_3)_2O$.

9.   Liquid HCN can act both an acid and as a base according to the reaction

$$HCN + HCN \rightleftharpoons H_2CN^+ + CN^-$$

    (*a*)   Would HCN be considered as an acid or a base in this solvent?

    (*b*) H_2SO_4 is an acid in HCN. Write the equation for the ionization of H_2SO_4 in this solvent.

    (*c*) $(CH_3)_2N$ is a base in HCN. Write the equation for the reaction of $(CH_3)_3N$ with the solvent.

    (*d*)   What is the ionic equation for the neutralization of H_2SO_4 by $(CH_3)_3N$ in liquid HCN?

10.   (*a*)   State and explain the Ostwald's dilution law. Why the law is not applicable in cases of strong electrolytes?

    (*b*)   The ionization constant of a weak base is 1.8×10^{-5}. Calculate the concentration of hydroxyl ions in a 0.1 M solution.   **Ans.** 1.3×10^{-2} M.

11.   (*a*)   How are acids and bases defined in (*i*) Brønsted-Lowry's concept, and (*ii*) Lewis concept?

    (*b*)   Name the strongest acid and the base that can exist in (*i*) liquid NH_3, (*ii*) H_2O, (*iii*) CH_3OH and (*iv*) H_2SO_4.

    (*c*)   What is meant by the leveling effect of a solvent?

12.   (*a*)   Define pH and pOH of a solution.

    (*b*)   Calculate the pH and pOH of the following aqueous solutions:

       (*i*) 0.001 M HCl, (*ii*) 0.001 M KOH, (*iii*) 10^{-8} M NaOH and (*iv*) 10^{-7} M HCl.

13.   (*a*)   What is meant by the ionic product of water? In what way is it different from the ionization constant of water? Does it vary with temperature?

(b) What is the pH of a neutral aqueous solution at 323 K? At 323 K, K_w is 5.35×10^{-14}.

(c) An aqueous solution has a pH of 6.8 at 323 K. Will it be acidic, neutral or alkaline?

Ans. (b) 6.64, (c) alkaline.

14. (a) What are buffer solutions? How do they react? When is buffer capacity of a buffer maximum? Derive an expression relating the pH of a buffer with the concentration of its components.

(b) Explain how the following act as buffers:

(i) $NaHCO_3$, (ii) NaH_2PO_4, (iii) Na_2HPO_4 and (iv) CH_3COONH_4.

(c) Calculate the pH of a buffer solution made by adding 0.35 mole of acetic acid and 0.225 mole of sodium acetate to enough water to make 0.4 dm^2 solution. $K_a = 1.85 \times 10^{-5}$.   **Ans.** (c) 4.54.

15. Define the terms hydrolytic constant and the degree of hydrolysis of a salt. What type of ions are hydrolysed by water? Derive an expression for the pH of an aqueous solution of (i) NH_4Cl, (ii CH_3COONa and (iii) CH_3COONH_4.

16. (a) What are the acid base-indicators? Why only small amounts of indicators are used? How do they change their colour with changes in hydrogen ion concentration of the solution? What is meant by the colour change interval of an indicator?

(b) Which indicators would be suitable in the titration of

(i) H_2SO_4 versus Na_2CO_3, (ii) CH_3COOH versus $NaOH$ and (iii) NH_3 versus HCl? Give reasons for your answers.

(c) An acid indicator, HIn, has $K_{in} = 1.4 \times 10^{-8}$. Calculate its pH range. Name an acid and a base which can be titrated using this indicator.

17. (a) Define solubility product. Write expressions for the solubility products of (i) Ag_2CrO_4, (ii) Cu_2S, (iii) CaF_2, (iv) $Al(OH)_3$, (v) $Zn_3(PO_4)_2$ and (vi)$Fe_3(PO_4)_2$.

(b) Discuss some of the applications of solubility product in qualitative and quantitative analysis.

18. Write short notes on the following:

(a) Common ion effect;

(b) Buffer capacity;

(c) Drawbacks in the Arrhenius theory of electrolytic dissociation and

(d) Complex ions.

19. (a) At 298 K, the degree of ionization of water has been found to be 1.8×10^{-9}. Calculate the ionization constant and ionic product of water at this temperature.

(b) How is the degree of ionization of water affected in the presence of 10^{-7} N HCl (assuming complete ionization of the acid)? What is the total $[H_3O^+]$?   **Ans.** (a) $K = 1.8 \times 10^{-16}$, $K_w = 1.0 \times 10^{-14}$

(b) Lowered in the presence of HCl; $[H_3O^+] = 1.6 \times 10^{-7}$ M.

20. (a) Why do we generally ignore H_3O^+ ions contributed by the ionization of water when we calculate $[H_3O^+]$ in solutions containing an acid. Under what conditions do we have to consider the $[H_3O^+]$ from the ionization of water? Why does pH + pOH = pK_w?

(b) A sample of an orange juice has a pH of 3.8. What is its $[H_3O^+]$ and $[OH^-]$?

Ans. (b) $[H_3O^+] = 1.6 \times 10^{-4}$ M, $[OH^-] = 6.3 \times 10^{-11}$ M.

21. Calculate at 298 K the $[H_3O^+]$ and $[OH^-]$ for solutions having pH values

(i) 2.0, (ii) 0.903, (iii) 12.38 and (iv) 11.92.

Ans. (i) $\left[H_3O^+\right] = 1.0 \times 10^{-2}$ M, $\left[OH^-\right] = 1.0 \times 10^{-12}$ M; (ii) $\left[H_3O^+\right] = 0.125$ M, $\left[OH^-\right] = 8.0 \times 10^{-14}$ M;

(iii) $\left[H_3O^+\right] = 4.2 \times 10^{-13}$ M, $\left[OH^-\right] = 2.4 \times 10^{-2}$ M; (iv) $\left[H_3O^+\right] = 1.2 \times 10^{-12}$ M, $\left[OH^-\right] = 8.4 \times 10^{-3}$ M.

22. Calculate $[H_3O^+]$, $[Ac^-]$ and $[HAc]$ for 0.001 M acetic acid solution. K_a is 1.85×10^{-5} at 298 K.

Ans. $[H_3O^+] = [Ac^-] = 1.36 \times 10^{-4}$ M and $[HAc] = 8.64 \times 10^{-4}$ M.

23. At 298 K, pH of a 0.1 M weak acid is found to be 5.37. Calculate the ioisation constant of the acid.

Ans. $K_a = 1.8 \times 10^{-10}$.

24. What is the pH of an aqueous solution made by diluting 0.1 mole of HCl and 0.5 mole of sodium acetate to 1 dm^3?   **Ans. 5.35**

25. Calculate the pH of a solution made by adding 0.001 mole of sodium hydroxide to 100 ml of 0.5 M acetic acid and 0.5 M sodium acetate solution.   **Ans. 4.75**

26. How many grams of HCl gas would have to be dissolved in 0.5 dm^3 of 1.0 M CH$_3$COONa to give a solution having a pH of 4.74?   **Ans. 9.1 g**

27. What must be the ratio of [NH$_3$] to $\left[\text{NH}_4^+\right]$ to have a buffer of pH 10.0?   **Ans. 5.6.**

28. Calculate of change in pH if 0.1 mole of HCl is added to 1.0 dm^3 of a solution containing 0.45 mole of formic acid and 0.55 mole of sodium formate. $K_a = 1.8 \times 10^{-4}$.   **Ans. −0.17 pH unit.**

29. A solution is prepared by mixing one mole of HA_1 with one mole of HA_2 and diluting it to a total volume of 1 dm^3 with water. Both HA_1 and HA_2 are weak acids which ionize according to the following schemes:

$$HA_1 + H_2O \rightleftharpoons H_3O^+ + A_1^-, \quad K_{a_1} = 2.0 \times 10^{-6}$$

$$HA_2 + H_2O \rightleftharpoons H_3O^+ + A_2^-, \quad K_{a_2} = 2.0 \times 10^{-6}$$

Assume that the concentration of each ionized acid is much less than the initial concentration of acid for all calculations.

(a) When the above solution is at equilibrium, what will be the value of $\left[A_1^-\right], \left[A_2^-\right]$ and $\left[H_3O^+\right]$? and [H$_3$O$^+$]? How does the presence of HA_2 affect the ionization of HA_1?

Ans. (a) $\left[A_1^-\right] = \left[A_2^-\right] = 1.0 \times 10^{-3}$ M. $\left[H_3O^+\right] = 2.0 \times 10^{-3}$ M

30. Predict whether the aqueous solutions of the following will be acidic, neutral or alkaline.
    (i) KCl   (ii) HCOONa,
    (iii) NH$_4$NO$_3$ (iv) C$_6$H$_5$N$^+$H$_3$Cl$^-$ and
    (v) CH$_3$COONH$_4$.

    If each solution were 0.1 M, which one would be most acidic? Which one would be most alkaline?
    Ans. (i) Neutral, (ii) alkaline, (iii) acidic, (iv) acidic, (v) neutral,
    (iv) most acidic and (ii) most alkaline.

31. (a) Show that the degree of ionization of a weak electrolyte HX which ionizes according to the equation

$$HX \rightleftharpoons H^+ + X^-$$

is given by

$$\alpha = \frac{K_a}{2C}\left[-1 + \sqrt{1 + \frac{4C}{K_a}}\right]$$

where K_a is the ionization constant and C the initial molarity of HX.

(b) If C is much greater than K_a, to what does the expression in (a) simplify?

32. Calculate at 298 K the equilibrium constant for the reaction

$$CN^- + HAc \rightleftharpoons HCN + Ac^-$$

The ionization constants of acetic acid and hydrocyanic acid are 1.8×10^{-5} and 4.9×10^{-10} respectively.
                                                                                       Ans. 3.6 × 10^{-4}

33. (a) Show that

$$\left[H_3O^+\right] = \sqrt{K_h C}$$

in a solution containing a salt of a weak base and strong acid and

$$[OH^-] = \sqrt{K_h C}$$

in a solution containing a salt of a strong base and a weak acid.

(b) pH value of 0.1 M solution of three sodium salts, NaX, NaY and NaZ are respectively 7.0, 9.0 and 11.0. Arrange the acids, HX, HY and HZ in order of increasing strength. Where possible, calculate the ionization constant of the acids.

34. A buffer solution containing 1 M acetic acid and 1 M sodium acetate has a pH of 4.73.

    (i) What is the pH of the solution after 0.01 mole of HCl has been added to 1 litre of the buffer?

    (ii) What is the pH of the solution after the addition of 0.01 mole per litre of NaOH, $pK_a = 4.73$.

    Ans. (i) 4.72 and (ii) 4.74.

35. To what volume must 1 dm^3 of 0.5 M weak acid ($pK_a = 4.73$) solution be diluted in order to (i) double the pH and (ii) double the pOH? **Ans.** (i) 3.37×10^3 dm^3, (ii) 4.0 dm^3.

36. Calculate [H$_3$O$^+$] and the pH of a 0.5 M solution of NH$_4$Br at 298 K. K_b for ammonia is 1.84×10^{-5} M.

    Ans. 2.7×10^{-5}; 4.8.

37. For the indicator thymol blue, the pH value is 2.0 when half of it is in the unionized form. Calculate the percentage of the indicator in the unionized form in a solution that is 4.0×10^{-3} M with respect to H$_3$O$^+$ ion.

38. (a) Write the expression for K_{inst} for the complexions

    (i) $Fe(CN)_6^{4-}$,   (ii) $Cu(NH_3)_4^{2+}$,

    (iii) SiF_6^{2-}, and   (iv) $AlCl_4^-$.

    (b) Solubility of Ag$_2$CrO$_4$ in water is 0.024 dm^{-3} at 298 K. Calculate the solubility product of the salt.

    Ans. 9.0×10^{-13}.

39. Calculate the solubility of PbI$_2$ in (i) pure water, (ii) 0.04 molar KI, and (iii) 0.04 molar Pb (NO$_2$)$_2$ at 298 K. K_{sp} of PbI$_2$ is 7.1×10^{-5}.

40. K_{sp} for PbBr$_2$ is 9.0×10^{-6}. Calculate its solubility in (a) water, (b) 0.5 M NaBr and (c) 0.25 M Pb (NO$_2$)$_2$.

    Ans. (a) 1.34×10^{-2} mol dm^{-3};

    (b) 4.0×10^{-5} mol dm^{-3};

    (c) 3.0×10^{-3} mol dm^{-3}.

41. The solubility of CaF$_2$ in water is 2.04×10^{-4} mol dm^{-3} at 298 K. Calculate (i) the solubility product and (ii) the solubility in 0.01 molar NaF solution. **Ans.** (i) 3.4×10^{-11}, (ii) 3.4×10^{-7} mol dm^{-3}.

42. How many moles of NH$_4$Cl (s) must be added to 1.0 dm^3 of water to dissolve 0.1 mole of solid Mg (OH)$_2$? K_{sp} of Mg (OH)$_2$ is 1.2×10^{-11} and K_b of NH$_4$OH is 1.8×10^{-5}. **Ans.** 0.52 mole.

43. Which will precipitate first when Na$_2$CrO$_4$ (s) is gradually added to a solution containing 0.1 M Pb^{2+} and 0.1 M Ba^{2+}? What will be the concentration of the ions precipitated first when the other ion just begins to form a precipitate?

    K_{sp} of PbCrO$_4$ and BaCrO$_4$ are 1.8×10^{-14} and 2.4×10^{-10} respectively.

    Ans. PbCrO$_4$ will precipitate first and [Pb^{2+}] = 7.5×10^{-7} M.

44. 1.75 g of solid NaOH are added to 0.25 dm^3 of a 0.1 M NiCl$_2$ solution. What is the mass of Ni(OH)$_2$ formed? What will be the pH of final solution?

    $$K_{sp} \text{ of Ni (OH)}_2 \text{ is } 1.6 \times 10^{-14}$$

    Ans. 2.0 g Ni(OH)$_2$, pH = 8.0.

45. A 3.0×10^{-2} M solution of $\left[Ag(NH_3)_2\right]NO_3$ is prepared by dissolving the solid in water. If K_{inst} of the complex ion is 6.2×10^{-8}, what is $[Ag^+]$ and $[NH_3]$ in the solution at equilibrium? What fraction of the complex ion has dissociated. Assume that NH_3 does not dissociate as a base.

$$\textbf{Ans. } \left[Ag^+\right] = 7.7 \times 10^{-4} \text{M}. \quad \left[NH_3\right] = 1.54 \times 10^{-3} \text{M}$$

46. Excess AgCl (s) is treated with a 0.1 M solution of NH_3. The reaction

$$AgCl(s) + 2NH_3 \rightleftharpoons Ag(NH_3)_2^+ + Cl^-$$

takes place. What are the equilibrium concentrations of NH_3, $Ag(NH_3)_2^+$, Cl^- and Ag^+ ?

$$\textbf{Ans. } \left[NH_3\right] = 0.09 \text{M}, \left[Ag(NH_3)_2^+\right] = \left[Cl^-\right] = 4.9 \times 10^{-9} \text{M}$$

$$\left[Ag^+\right] = 3.7 \times 10^{-9} \text{M}.$$

Electrochemical Cells

15.1 INTRODUCTION

A cell is an electrochemical device for the conversion of electrical energy into chemical energy or vice-versa. It consists of two electrodes dipping into an ionic solution and connected by an external metallic conductor. The chemical reactions that occur on the surface of an electrode is a transfer of charge, usually in the form of electrons to or from neutral molecules or ions. An electrode can act as a *source* of electrons or as a *sink* for electrons.

The electrochemical cells may be divided into two classes: (*a*) Galvanic cells such as a dry cell or a lead storage battery etc., where the chemical energy is converted into electrical energy, and (*b*) electrolytic cells where the electrical energy from an external source is used to bring about a physical or a chemical change. Charging of a lead storage battery or electrolytic purification of metals are examples where electrical energy brings about the chemical changes.

A typical example of a galvanic cell is that of a Daniell cell (Fig. 15.1). In this a zinc rod is dipped into a solution containing Zn^{2+} ions and a copper electrode immersed in a solution of Cu^{2+} ions. The two solutions are separated by a porous diaphragm (D) which allows electrical contact but prevents

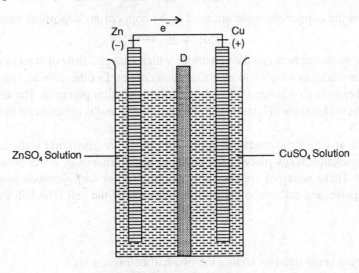

Zn
(−)

Cu
(+)

e

D

ZnSO₄ Solution ——

—— CuSO₄ Solution

Fig. 15.1 The Daniell cell

intermixing of electrolytes. The two half cells Zn | Zn^{2+} and Cu | Cu^{2+} constitute the cell which is represented as Zn | Zn^{2+} || Cu^{2+} | Cu. The single vertical line denotes the phase boundary and double vertical lines indicate that the liquid junction potential has been eliminated. At each electrode the metal atoms have a tendency to pass into solution as metal ions. Each time an ion leaves the electrode surface, two electrons are left on the electrode surface making it negatively charged. This process of dissolution does not continue indefinitely as the negative charge on the electrode surface renders further dissolution of the metal difficult. Soon a dynamic equilibrium is established at each electrode

$$Zn \rightleftharpoons Zn^{2+} + 2e^- \qquad \qquad ...(15.1)$$

and $$Cu \rightleftharpoons Cu^{2+} + 2e^- \qquad \qquad ...(15.2)$$

At the same time, metal cations from the solution tend to withdraw electrons from the electrode surface and get deposited as metal atoms on electrode. This process decreases the availability of electrons on the electrode surface and thus leaves the electrode surface positively charged. The deposition of cations from the solution again does not proceed indefinitely and ultimately a dynamic equilibrium is set up at each electrode

$$Zn^{2+} + 2e^- \rightleftharpoons Zn$$

and $$Cu^{2+} + 2e^- \rightleftharpoons Cu$$

The electrode surface may acquire a net positive or negative charge depending on whether the rate of deposition or dissolution predominates. However, in either case a charge separation results across the metal–solution interface. The potential difference that exists across the metal–solution interface is known as *the electrode potential*. For a given electrode, the potential depends on the concentration (activity) of the ions in solution. If the ions in solution are at unit activity the electrode potential is termed as *the standard electrode potential*.

The two electrodes in the above set up are at different potentials and when they are connected externally by a metallic conductor a current flows. The zinc atoms give up electrons to the copper electrode to form zinc ions,

$$Zn \rightleftharpoons Zn^{2+} + 2e^-$$

These electrons at the copper electrode are used up by copper ions depositing metallic copper.

$$Cu^{2+} + 2e^- \rightleftharpoons Cu$$

The difference of potential between the electrodes which causes a flow of current is due to the fact that zinc has a greater tendency to give up electrons than copper. In other words, electrons will flow from electrode of higher oxidation potential to one of lower oxidation potential. The difference of potential between these electrodes is *the electromotive force of the cell* and is abbreviated as emf and is expressed in volts.

The electrode at which the oxidation occurs (electrons are given off) is the anode while the electrode at which reduction takes place is the cathode; anode (being at lower potential) to cathode (at higher potential). These reactions are known as *the half cell* or *half electrode reactions*. In a galvanic cell anode is negative and cathode is the positive terminal of the cell. The half cell reactions are

at anode: $$Zn \rightleftharpoons Zn^{2+} + 2e^-$$

at cathode: $$Cu^{2+} + 2e^- \rightleftharpoons Cu$$

The overall reaction is obtained by adding the two half cell reactions,

$$Zn + Cu^{2+} \rightleftharpoons Zn^{2+} + Cu \qquad \qquad ...(15.3)$$

15.2 REVERSIBLE AND IRREVERSIBLE CELLS

An electrochemical cell may be *reversible or irreversible*. The reactions in a reversible cell are always in a state of equilibrium and only infinitesimally small currents are drawn from it. A reversible cell should satisfy the following conditions. When the cell is connected to an external source of emf (driving force) exactly equal to that of the cell (opposing force), no chemical reaction should occur within the cell. If the driving force is decreased by an infinitesimally small amount, then the current should flow from the cell to the external source. On the other hand, when the driving force is increased by the same amount, the same current should flow through the cell in the opposite direction. The chemical changes which occur in the cell due to the current produced should be exactly reversed. When these conditions are not satisfied, the cell is said to be irreversible.

A familiar example of a reversible cell is the Daniell cell. When the two electrodes are connected to an external source of emf infinitesimally smaller than the cell emf, the current flows from the zinc electrode to the copper electrode and the net cell reaction is

$$Zn + Cu^{2+} \rightleftharpoons Cu + Zn^{2+}$$

This process continues as the external opposing emf is infinitesimally smaller than that of the cell. However, if the external emf becomes infinitesimally greater than that of the cell, the current flows in the opposite direction and the cell reaction is reversed. When the external emf becomes exactly equal to that of the cell, no current flows and the cell reaction ceases.

On the other hand, a cell consisting of zinc and copper electrodes dipped into a solution of sulphuric acid is irreversible. The cell when connected to an external source of emf slightly smaller than that of the cell, zinc dissolves in sulphuric acid forming zinc sulphate with the evolution of hydrogen. The cell reaction is

$$Zn + H_2SO_4 \rightarrow ZnSO_4 + H_2$$

If the emf of the external source is slightly greater than that of the cell, copper goes into solution, hydrogen is liberated at the other electrode and the reaction

$$Cu + H_2SO_4 \rightarrow CuSO_4 + H_2$$

takes place. It is clear from the above reactions that the cell is not reversible, in each case different sets of products are formed.

15.3 MEASUREMENT OF EMF OF CELLS

The potential difference that causes a flow of current from electrode of higher oxidation potential to another of lower potential is known as the electromotive force of the cell. The emf of a cell is measured by the use of potentiometer. For accurate values of emf, measurements must be made under conditions that no appreciable current is drawn from the cell. When some current is drawn from the cell, reaction products are formed at the electrode surfaces which cause concentration changes of the electrolyte around the electrodes. This polarization of the electrodes changes the emf of the cell. Hence potential measuring devices like potentiometers which require only small currents are suitable for accurate measurements and other instruments like voltmeter, etc., which draw appreciable currents from the cell are unsuitable for emf measurements.

Figure 15.2 gives a basic circuit diagram for a potentiometer. AB is the slide wire of uniform cross-sectional area having high resistance. A cell C, usually a storage battery of constant emf larger than the emf of the cell to be measured, is connected in series with the resistance across the terminal of the resistance wire AB. The cell X of unknown emf is connected to A with poles in the same direction as the cell C. The other terminal of the cell is connected through the galvanometer G to the sliding wire by a double pole-double throw (DPDT) key. The position of the terminal is moved along the sliding wire and the rheostat is adjusted until at O no current flows through the galvanometer. At this point the potential difference between A and O just balances the emf E_X of the cell X. Next the standard cell S with emf E_S is connected to the sliding wire by means of DPDT. The null point O' on the slide wire is again determined. The fall in potential along AO is exactly compensated by the emf of the standard cell, E_S. Since the cross-sectional area of the wire is uniform, we have

$$\frac{E_X}{E_S} = \frac{\text{Drop of potential from A to O}}{\text{Drop of potential from A to O'}} = \frac{\text{length AO}}{\text{length AO'}}$$

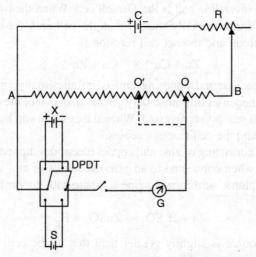

Fig. 15.2 Basic circuit diagram for emf measurement

Thus E_X can be calculated. If the resistance wire is calibrated with the standard cell, the unknown emf can be directly read from the reading of the resistance wire.

The standard cell should be capable of giving a constant and reproducible emf. The most widely used standard cell is a Weston cell (Fig. 15.3). The positive electrode consists of mercury covered with a paste of mercury–mercurous sulphate and the negative electrode is a 12.5% cadmium amalgam. A saturated solution of cadmium sulphate $\left(CdSO_4 \cdot \frac{8}{3}H_2O \right)$ is placed over the electrodes. The cell reactions when it operates spontaneously are

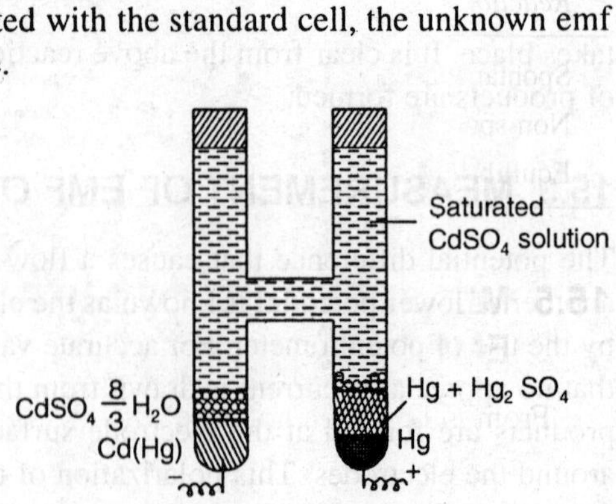

Fig. 15.3 Weston standard cell

Anode reaction: $\quad Cd(Hg) \rightleftharpoons Cd^{2+} + Hg + 2e^-$

$$Hg_2SO_4 + 2e^- \rightleftharpoons 2Hg + SO_4^{2-}$$

Cathode reaction: $\dfrac{}{Cd(Hg) + Hg_2SO_4 \rightleftharpoons Cd^{2+} + 3Hg + SO_4^{2-}}$

The emf of a standard cadmium cell at 298 K is 1.01832 V and varies only slightly with temperature, the temperature coefficient $\left(\dfrac{dE}{dT}\right)_P$ being -0.00005 V K^{-1}.

15.4 FREE ENERGY AND EMF OF A CELL REACTION

In a reversible electrochemical cell if an infinitesimal amount of current is drawn from or allowed to pass the cell, the reversible electrical work at constant temperature and pressure is maximum and is equal to the product of the voltage and the quantity of electricity. If in a cell n equivalents of reactants are converted into the products, then the quantity of electricity that flows through the cell is nF, where F is the faraday constant and is equal to 96485 coulombs per equivalent. If this amount of charge is transported, through the cell of emf E volts, the amount of electrical work done by the cell is nEF.

The work done by the cell is at the expense of the free energy decrease resulting from the cell reaction. Furthermore, the electrical work is maximum only when the cell operates reversibly and the decrease in Gibbs free energy is equal to the electrical work done by the cell. Hence we have

Gibbs free energy decrease = Electrical work obtainable from the cell

i.e.,
$$(-\Delta G)_{P,\,T} = nEF \qquad \qquad \text{...(15.4)}$$

The cell reaction can proceed spontaneously only if $(\Delta G)_{P,\,T} < 0$ or from equation (15.4), $E > 0$. Under these conditions, the cell can act as a source of electrical energy. However, a positive value of $(\Delta G)_{P,\,T}$ refers to a non-spontaneous change and E will be negative, the cell will not operate spontaneously. A zero value of $(\Delta G)_{P,\,T}$ or E shows that the cell is in a state of equilibrium.

The criteria of spontaneity of a cell reaction in terms of ΔG or E are given in Table 15.1.

Table 15.1 Criteria of Spontaneity in Terms of ΔG and E

Reaction	Magnitude of ΔG	Magnitude of E
Spontaneous	$\Delta G < 0$	$E > 0$
Non-spontaneous	$\Delta G > 0$	$E < 0$
Equilibrium	$\Delta G = 0$	$E = 0$

15.5 MEASUREMENT OF ENTROPY AND ENTHALPY CHANGES FROM EMF DATA

From Gibbs-Helmholtz Eq. (8.28) we have

$$\Delta G = \Delta H + T \left[\frac{\partial (\Delta G)}{\partial T} \right]_P \qquad \qquad \text{...(15.5)}$$

From Eq. (15.4), $\Delta G = -nEF$ and differentiating ΔG with respect to temperature at constant pressure yields

$$\left[\frac{d(\Delta G)}{\partial T} \right]_P = -nF \left(\frac{\partial E}{\partial T} \right)_P \qquad \qquad \text{...(15.6)}$$

The quantity $\left(\dfrac{\partial E}{\partial T}\right)_P$ is the temperature coefficient of the cell. Substituting the value of $\left[\dfrac{\partial(\Delta G)}{\partial T}\right]_P$ in Eq. (15.5), we get

$$\Delta G = \Delta H - nFT\left(\frac{\partial E}{\partial T}\right)_P \qquad \qquad ...(15.7)$$

Also

$$\Delta G = \Delta H - T\Delta S \qquad \qquad ...(15.8)$$

Hence from Eqs. (15.7) and (15.8), we obtain

$$\Delta S = nF\left(\frac{\partial E}{\partial T}\right)_P \qquad \qquad ...(15.9)$$

Equation (15.9) can be used for calculating the entropy changes for the cell reaction in terms of the temperature coefficient of the cell emf. Equation (15.7) can also be written as

$$-nFE = \Delta H - nFT\left(\frac{\partial E}{\partial T}\right)_P$$

or

$$\Delta H = nF\left[T\left(\frac{\partial E}{\partial T}\right)_P - E\right] \qquad \qquad ...(15.10)$$

From Eq. (15.10), the enthalpy change for cell reaction can be determined from the measurements of cell emf and the temperature coefficient of the emf.

At constant pressure the enthalpy change, when the cell operates, must be equal to $[Q + (-W)]$, where Q is the heat absorbed when the cell is in operation and $(-W)$ is the electrical work obtained from the cell,

$$\Delta H = Q + (-W)$$

or

$$Q = \Delta H + W$$

But

$$W = -\Delta G = nEF \qquad \qquad \text{(cf. equation 15.4)}$$

therefore,

$$Q = \Delta H + nEF \qquad \qquad ...(15.10(a))$$

Substituting the value of ΔH from Eq. (15.7) in Eq. (15.10(a)), we get

$$Q = -nEF + nFT\left(\frac{\partial E}{\partial T}\right)_P + nEF$$

$$= nFT\left(\frac{\partial E}{\partial T}\right)_P$$

The sign of $\left(\dfrac{\partial E}{\partial T}\right)_P$ will determine the value of Q.

Case I: When $\left(\dfrac{\partial E}{\partial T}\right)_P$ is positive, the heat is absorbed when the cell operates and, therefore, the electrical energy is greater than the decrease in the enthalpy of the cell reaction. This is the case with a few galvanic cells.

Case II: When $\left(\dfrac{\partial E}{\partial T}\right)_P$ is zero, no heat is absorbed or evolved during the cell operation (Q = 0).
Thus the whole of the chemical energy is available as electrical energy. This is an example of Daniell cell.

Case III: When $\left(\dfrac{\partial E}{\partial T}\right)_P$ is negative. The heat is evolved during the operation of the cell (Q = –ve).
This would result in electrical energy lesser than the decrease in the enthalpy of the reaction. This is the case in most of the galvanic cells.

Problem 15.1: The emf of a standard cadmium cell is 1.01832 V at 298 K. The temperature coefficient of the cell is -5.0×10^{-5} V K^{-1}. Calculate ΔG, ΔH and ΔS for the cell reaction.

Solution: $\Delta G = -nEF$

$\qquad\qquad = -(2 \text{ equiv mol}^{-1}) \times (96485 \text{ coulombs equiv}^{-1}) \times (1.01832 \text{ V})$

$\qquad\qquad = -196.508 \text{ kJ mol}^{-1}$

$$\Delta S = nF\left(\frac{\partial E}{\partial T}\right)_P$$

$\qquad\qquad = (2 \text{ equiv mol}^{-1})(96485 \text{ coulombs equiv}^{-1})(-5 \times 10^{-5} \text{ VK}^{-1})$

$\qquad\qquad = -9.65 \text{ JK}^{-1} \text{ mol}^{-1}$

$\qquad \Delta H = -196.508 - 2.876 = -199.384 \text{ kJ mol}^{-1}$

15.6 THERMODYNAMICS OF ELECTRODE AND CELL POTENTIALS— NERNST EQUATION

The electrode potential and the emf of a cell depend on the nature of the electrode, temperature and the activities of the ions in solution. The variation of electrode and cell potentials with the activities of ions in solution can be obtained from thermodynamic considerations. For a general reaction such as

$$aA + bB + ... \rightleftharpoons lL + mM + ...$$

occurring in the cell, the Gibbs free energy change is given by the equation

$$\Delta G = \Delta G^0 + RT \ln \frac{a_L^l \, a_M^m \cdots}{a_A^a \, a_B^b \cdots} \qquad \qquad ...(15.11)$$

where a's represent the activities of the reactants and products under a given set of conditions and ΔG^0 refers to the free energy change for the reaction in the standard state, *i.e.*, when the activities of the reactants and products are all unity. On substituting the value of $\Delta G = -nEF$ and $\Delta G^0 = -nE^0F$ in Eq. (15.11), we get

$$-nEF = -nE^0F + RT \ln \frac{a_L^l \, a_M^m \cdots}{a_A^a \, a_B^b \cdots}$$

or
$$E = E^0 - \frac{RT}{nF} \ln \frac{a_L^l \, a_M^m \cdots}{a_A^a \, a_B^b \cdots} \qquad \qquad ...(15.12)$$

Equation (15.12) is known as the Nernst equation and gives the dependence of the electrode or cell potential in terms of the activities of the reactants and products. The quantity E^0 is known as the *standard emf of the cell* and is the cell potential when the activities are all unity ($E = E^0$ as the logarithmic term vanishes). At a given temperature E^0 is constant and characteristic of the electrode or the cell. At 298 K, Eq. (15.12) reduces to

$$E = E^0 - \frac{(8.314)(298)(2.303)}{n(96485)} \log \frac{a_L^l \, a_M^m \cdots}{a_A^a \, a_B^b \cdots}$$

$$E = E^0 - \frac{0.0591}{n} \log \frac{a_L^l \, a_M^m \cdots}{a_A^a \, a_B^b \cdots} \qquad \qquad ...(15.13)$$

When the activities of the reactants and products correspond to those of the equilibrium state, $E = E^0$ and Eq. (15.13) becomes

$$E^0 = \frac{RT}{nF} \ln K = \frac{0.0591}{n} \log K \qquad \qquad ...(15.14)$$

where K is the equilibrium constant for the electrode or the cell reaction and hence Eq. (15.13) can also be written as

$$E = \frac{0.0591}{n} \left[\log K - \log \frac{a_L^l \, a_M^m \cdots}{a_A^a \, a_B^b \cdots} \right] \qquad \qquad ...(15.15)$$

15.7 STANDARD ELECTRODE POTENTIAL—ITS MEASUREMENT

Absolute value of a single electrode potential cannot be measured. However, one can assign numerical values to the electrode potentials relative to a reference or standard electrode. The potential of the reference electrode is arbitrarily assigned a zero value and the potentials of all other electrodes are then referred to it. The reference electrode so chosen is *the standard hydrogen electrode* abbreviated as SHE. An SHE is shown in Fig. 15.4. A small platinum sheet coated with platinum black is placed in a solution where the hydrogen ion activity is unity. The electrode is partly immersed in the solution and is partly exposed to an atmosphere of hydrogen gas. Pure hydrogen gas at 1 atmosphere is continuously bubbled through the solution. The equilibrium between hydrogen molecules and the hydrogen ions in solution is established and the electrode behaves as if it were a metallic electrode and is reversible with respect to the hydrogen ions; its potential is controlled by the activity of the hydrogen ions in the solution. It is represented as $Pt \mid H_2 \, (P = 1 \text{ atm}) \mid H^+ \, (a = 1)$ and the electrode reaction is

$$H^+ \, (a = 1) + e^- \rightleftharpoons \frac{1}{2} H_2 \, (P = 1 \text{ atm})$$

The potential of the electrode as given by the Nernst Eq. (15.12) is

$$E = E^0 - \frac{RT}{F} \ln \frac{P_{H_2}^{1/2}}{a_{H^+}} \qquad \qquad ...(15.16)$$

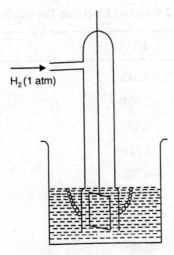

Fig. 15.4 The hydrogen electrode

The potential of the electrode, when $a_{H^+} = 1$ and pressure of hydrogen gas is 1 atmosphere, is the standard potential of the hydrogen electrode and is arbitrarily assigned a zero value at all temperatures. The standard electrode potential of any other electrode is then obtained by combining the electrode with the SHE. Since the standard potential of the hydrogen electrode is zero, the measured potential is the standard electrode potential of the other electrode. The standard electrode potential is assigned a positive value if this electrode is more positive with respect to SHE and a negative value if it is more negative than the SHE.

IUPAC has laid down the following rules regarding the sign convention of electrode potential:

(1) All electrode reactions are written as reduction reactions.
(2) All reactions that produce better reducing agents than hydrogen are given a negative reduction potential value.

An arrangement of electrode systems (Table 15.2) in order of increasing standard electrode potential (reduction potential) is known as the electrochemical series. The magnitude of the standard electrode potential is a measure of the tendency for reduction to occur. The reduced form of a half cell higher up in the series has a greater tendency to donate electrons and get oxidised than the reduced form of the half cell which is below it in the series. Similarly, the oxidised form of the half cell lower in the series has a greater tendency to accept electrons and be reduced than the oxidised form of the half cell which is above it in the series. For example, in the system Zn^{2+} | Zn and Cu^{2+} | Cu, zinc is higher up in the series. Therefore zinc has a greater tendency to donate electrons than copper and zinc ions have smaller tendency to accept electrons than copper ions. Thus two electrodes when combined to form a cell, the electrode having a higher standard electrode potential will favour reduction: $M^+ (a = 1) + e^- \rightleftharpoons M$ and will act as the positive electrode. The other electrode with a lower value of standard electrode potential will favour oxidation $M' \rightleftharpoons M'^+ (a = 1) + e^-$ and constitutes the negative terminal of the cell. The overall cell reaction will be

$$M^+ (a = 1) + M' \rightleftharpoons M'^+ (a = 1) + M$$

Table 15.2 Standard Electrode Potentials at 298 K

Electrode	$E^0(V)$	Electrode Reaction
$Li^+ \mid Li$	−3.045	$Li^+ + e^- \rightleftharpoons Li$
$K^+ \mid K$	−2.925	$K^+ + e^- \rightleftharpoons K$
$Ca^{2+} \mid Ca$	−2.870	$Ca^{2+} + 2e^- \rightleftharpoons Ca$
$Na^+ \mid Na$	−2.714	$Na^+ + e^- \rightleftharpoons Na$
$Zn^{2+} \mid Zn$	−0.762	$Zn^{2+} + 2e^- \rightleftharpoons Zn$
$Fe^{2+} \mid Fe$	−0.441	$Fe^{2+} + 2e^- \rightleftharpoons Fe$
$Cr^{3+}, Cr^{2+} \mid Pt$	−0.410	$Cr^{3+} + e^- \rightleftharpoons Cr^{2+}$
$Cd^{2+} \mid Cd$	−0.403	$Cd^{2+} + 2e^- \rightleftharpoons Cd$
$Tl^+ \mid Tl$	−0.336	$Tl^+ + e^- \rightleftharpoons Tl$
$Co^{2+} \mid Co$	−0.277	$Co^{2+} + 2e^- \rightleftharpoons Co$
$Ni^{2+} \mid Ni$	−0.250	$Ni^{2+} + 2e^- \rightleftharpoons Ni$
$I^- \mid AgI \mid Ag$	−0.152	$AgI + e^- \rightleftharpoons Ag + I^-$
$Sn^{2+} \mid Sn$	−0.140	$Sn^{2+} + 2e^- \rightleftharpoons Sn$
$Pb^{2+} \mid Pb$	−0.126	$Pb^{2+} + 2e^- \rightleftharpoons Pb$
$H^+ \mid H_2 \mid Pt$	0.000	$H^+ + e^- \rightleftharpoons \frac{1}{2} H_2$
$Br^- \mid AgBr \mid Ag$	+0.095	$AgBr + e^- \rightleftharpoons Ag + Br^-$
$Sn^{4+}, Sn^{2+} \mid Pt$	+0.150	$Sn^{4+} + 2e^- \rightleftharpoons Sn^{2+}$
$Cl^- \mid AgCl \mid Ag$	+0.2225	$AgCl + e^- \rightleftharpoons Ag + Cl^-$
$Cu^{2+} \mid Cu$	+0.337	$Cu^{2+} + 2e^- \rightleftharpoons Cu$
$I^- \mid I_2 \mid Pt$	+0.5355	$I_2 + 2e^- \rightleftharpoons 2I^-$
$SO_4^{2-} \mid Hg_2SO_4 \mid Pt$	+0.614	$Hg_2SO_4 + 2e^- \rightleftharpoons 2Hg + SO_4^{2-}$
$Fe^{3+}, Fe^{2+} \mid Pt$	+0.771	$Fe^{3+} + e^- \rightleftharpoons Fe^{2+}$
$Ag^+ \mid Ag$	+0.799	$Ag^+ + e^- \rightleftharpoons Ag$
$Br^- \mid Br_2 \mid Pt$	+1.0652	$Br_2 + 2e^- \rightleftharpoons 2Br^-$
$Cl^- \mid Cl_2 \mid Pt$	+1.3595	$Cl_2 + 2e^- \rightleftharpoons 2Cl^-$
$Ce^{4+}, Ce^{3+} \mid Pt$	+1.61	$Ce^{4+} + e^- \rightleftharpoons Ce^{3+}$
$Co^{3+}, Co^{2+} \mid Pt$	+1.82	$Co^{3+} + e^- \rightleftharpoons Co^{2+}$

15.8 REPRESENTATION OF ELECTROCHEMICAL CELLS AND CELL REACTIONS FROM SINGLE ELECTRODE POTENTIALS

(a) **Cell construction from cell reaction:** From a given chemical reaction, one can write down the steps involved in the construction of a cell as follows:

(i) Write the balanced ionic equation from the given chemical reaction.

(ii) Separate this ionic equation into two parts; one in which oxidation takes place and the other in which reduction occurs. Balance both equations using electrons. Sometimes H^+, OH^- and H_2O may be added to either side of the equation for proper balancing.

(iii) The electrode at which reduction ($M^+ + e^- \rightarrow M$) occurs must appear on the right and the electrode at which oxidation occurs ($M \rightarrow M^+ + e^-$) must appear on the left hand side of the cell.

(iv) The electrodes are shown at the extreme right and left positions. These electrodes are separated from the corresponding electrolytes by means of single vertical lines. In case of gas electrodes and many redox systems, inert electrodes such as Pt wire or carbon rod are used for electrical contact.

(v) A single vertical line indicates a phase boundary and two vertical lines indicate that the solutions are connected by a salt bridge eliminating the liquid junction potential. A dotted line shows a porous barrier.

(vi) The concentration of the electrolyte, the pressure of the gas and the physical state of the electrodes are usually represented with parentheses.

Using the above steps, let us construct a cell for the reaction

$$Zn + CuSO_4 \rightarrow ZnSO_4 + Cu$$

Let us assume that the concentration of $ZnSO_4$ and $CuSO_4$ are C_1 and C_2 respectively.

Step I: The balanced ionic equation is

$$Zn + Cu^{2+} \rightarrow Zn^{2+} + Cu$$

Step II: Oxidation, at the left electrode (anode): $Zn \rightarrow Zn^{2+} + 2e^-$

Reduction, at the right electrode (cathode): $Cu^{2+} + 2e^- \rightarrow Cu$

Step III:	Left hand side	Right hand side
	Zn, Zn^{2+}	Cu^{2+}, Cu
Step IV:	Zn ∣ $ZnSO_4$	$CuSO_4$ ∣ Cu
Step V:	Zn ∣ $ZnSO_4$ ∥ $CuSO_4$ ∣ Cu	
Step VI:	Zn ∣ $ZnSO_4$ (C_1) ∥ $CuSO_4$ (C_2) ∣ Cu	

(b) **Steps for writing the cell reaction for a given galvanic cell:**

The various steps involved in writing the cell reactions are:

(i) Write the half-cell reaction corresponding to oxidation taking place at anode (left electrode): $M \rightleftharpoons M^+ + e^-$

$$E_{anode} = E^0_{anode} - \frac{RT}{F} \ln \frac{a_M}{a_{M^+}}$$

(ii) Similarly, write the half-cell reaction for the reduction taking place at cathode (right electrode): $M'^+ + e^- \rightarrow M'$

$$E_{\text{cathode}} = E_{\text{cathode}}^0 - \frac{RT}{F} \ln \frac{a_{M'}}{a_{M'^+}}$$

(*iii*) Combine the above two half-cell reactions so that the number of electrons released at the anode should be equal to the number of electrons used at the cathode

$$M + M'^+ \rightleftharpoons M^+ + M'$$

(*c*) **Calculation of emf of the cell:** Once the steps involved in the cell reactions are written, the emf of the cell is obtained by subtracting the electrode potential of the anode (left hand electrode) from the electrode potential of the cathode (right hand electrode), *i.e.*,

$$E_{\text{cell}} = E_R - E_L$$

$$= \left(E_R^0 - \frac{RT}{F} \ln \frac{a_{M'}}{a_{M'^+}} \right) - \left(E_L^0 - \frac{RT}{F} \ln \frac{a_M}{a_{M^+}} \right)$$

$$= E_R^0 - E_L^0 - \frac{RT}{F} \ln \frac{a_{M'}\, a_{M^+}}{a_{M'^+} + a_M}$$

$$= E_R^0 - E_L^0 - \frac{RT}{F} \ln \frac{a_{M^+}}{a_{M'^+}} \quad (\because a_M = a_{M'} = 1) \qquad ...(15.17)$$

Both the electrode potentials are reduction potentials.

In the standard state, the activity of each species is unity, hence Eq. (15.17) gives the standard potential of the cell as

$$E_{\text{cell}}^0 = E_R^0 - E_L^0 \qquad ...(15.18)$$

For the above cell, emf $\left(E_{\text{cell}} \right)$ is positive if E_R is greater than E_L. The cell reaction is spontaneous and the electrons flow through the external circuit from the left hand electrode to the right hand electrode. Conversely, if E_{cell} is negative, the cell as denoted will not operate spontaneously, instead the cell reaction would now occur in the opposite direction, viz, from right. However, if the concentrations of the electrolytes are so adjusted that E_{cell} is zero, then there is no tendency for the cell reaction to occur from left to right or vice versa. The cell is in a state of equilibrium.

Problem 15.2: What is the cell reaction and the cell emf at 298 K of the cell

$$\text{Zn} \mid \text{Zn}^{2+} (a = 1) \parallel \text{Pb}^{2+} (a = 1) \mid \text{Pb}?$$

Given $E_{\text{Zn}^{2+}/\text{Zn}}^0 = -0.762$ V and $E_{\text{Pb}^{2+}/\text{Pb}}^0 = -0.126$ V. Calculate ΔG^0 for the cell reaction. Will zinc precipitate lead from a solution in which the activity of lead ions is unity?

Solution: The cell reaction is

Left hand electrode, oxidation: $\text{Zn} \rightleftharpoons \text{Zn}^{2+} (a = 1) + 2e^-$; $E_{\text{Zn}^{2+}|\text{Zn}}^0 = -0.762$ V

Right hand electrode, reduction: $\text{Pb}^{2+} (a = 1) + 2e^- \rightleftharpoons \text{Pb}$; $E_{\text{Pb}^{2+}|\text{Pb}}^0 = -0.126$ V

Overall cell reaction: $\text{Zn} + \text{Pb}^{2+} (a = 1) \rightleftharpoons \text{Zn}^{2+} (a = 1) + \text{Pb}$

$$E^0_{cell} = E^0_R - E^0_L$$

$$= -0.126 + 0.762$$

$$= +0.636 \text{ V}$$

Now

$$\Delta G^0 = -nE^0F$$

$$= -(2 \text{ equiv mol}^{-1})(96485 \text{ coulombs equiv}^{-1})(0.636 \text{ V})$$

$$= -122.7 \text{ kJ mol}^{-1}$$

Since E^0_{cell} is positive and ΔG^0 is negative, the cell reaction is spontaneous, *i.e.*, zinc will precipitate lead ions from a solution where their activities are unity.

Problem 15.3: Write down the cell for which the overall reaction is

$$Cd + Cu^{2+} (a = 1) \rightleftharpoons Cd^{2+} (a = 1) + Cu$$

If $E^0_{Cd^{2+}|Cd} = -0.403 \text{ V}$ and $E^0_{Cu^{2+}|Cu} = 0.337 \text{ V}$ at 298 K, calculate the cell emf.

Solution: From the overall cell reaction it is clear that Cd is oxidized to Cd^{2+} and Cu^{2+} ions are reduced to metallic copper. Hence the half cell reactions are

Oxidation at the left electrode: $Cd \rightleftharpoons Cd^{2+} (a = 1) + 2e^-$; $E^0_{Cu^{2+}|Cu} = -0.403 \text{ V}$

Reduction at the right electrode: $Cu^{2+} (a = 1) + 2e^- \rightleftharpoons Cu$; $E^0_{Cu^{2+}|Cu} = +0.337 \text{ V}$

Hence the cell is

$$Cd \mid Cd^{2+} (a = 1) \parallel Cu^{2+} (a = 1) \mid Cu$$

and

$$E^0_{cell} = E^0_R - E^0_L = 0.337 - (-0.403)$$

$$= 0.740 \text{ V}$$

Problem 15.4: Will $Ce^{3+} (a = 1)$ ions reduce chlorine to $Cl^- (a = 1)$ ions at 298 K according to the reaction

$$Ce^{3+} (a = 1) + \frac{1}{2}Cl_2 (P = 1 \text{ atm}) \rightleftharpoons Ce^{4+} (a = 1) + Cl^- (a = 1)?$$

Given that

$$E^0_{Ce^{4+}|Ce^{3+}|Pt} = 1.82 \text{ V}$$

and

$$E^0_{Cl^-|Cl_2|Pt} = 1.3595 \text{ V}$$

Solution: According to the above reaction, the left hand electrode is

$$Pt \mid Ce^{3+} (a = 1), Ce^{4+} (a = 1)$$

where the reaction

$$Ce^{3+} (a = 1) \rightleftharpoons Ce^{4+} (a = 1) + e^-$$

occurs. The right hand electrode is $Cl^- (a = 1) \mid Cl_2 \mid (P = 1 \text{ atm}) Pt$. Hence the reaction

$$\frac{1}{2}Cl_2 (P = 1 \text{ atm}) + e^- \rightleftharpoons Cl^- (a = 1)$$

takes place at this electrode. The cell that corresponds to the above reaction is therefore

$$\text{Pt} \mid \text{Ce}^{3+} \ (a = 1), \ \text{Ce}^{4+} \ (a = 1) \| \ \text{Cl}^- \ (a = 1) \mid \text{Cl}_2 \ (1 \text{ atm}) \mid \text{Pt}$$

Consequently, E^0_{cell} will be

$$E^0_R - E^0_L = 1.3595 - 1.82 = -0.4605 \text{ V}$$

and the free energy change for the cell reaction is

$$\Delta G^0 = -(1)\,(-0.4605)\,(96485)$$
$$= 44.44 \text{ kJ mol}^{-1}$$

The negative value of E^0_{cell} and the positive value of ΔG^0 indicate that Ce^{3+} ions will not reduce chlorine to chloride ion. It is the reverse reaction which will proceed spontaneously, *i.e.*, chloride ions will reduce Ce^{4+} ions into Ce^{3+}. For this the cell should be written as

$$\text{Pt} \mid \text{Cl}_2 \ (P = 1 \text{ atm}) \mid \text{Cl}^- \ (a = 1) \| \ \text{Ce}^{4+} \ (a = 1) \ \text{Ce}^{3+} \ (a = 1) \mid \text{Pt}.$$

Problem 15.5: Calculate the potential of the following cell at 298 K

$$\text{Zn} \mid \text{Zn}^{2+} \ (a = 0.1) \| \ \text{Cu}^{2+} \ (a = 0.01) \mid \text{Cu}$$

$$E^0_{\text{Zn}^{2+}|\text{Zn}} = -0.762 \text{ V}$$

and

$$E^0_{\text{Cu}^{2+}|\text{Cu}} = +0.337 \text{ V}$$

Compare the free energy change for this cell with the free energy of the cell in the standard state.
Solution: The overall cell reaction is

$$\text{Zn} + \text{Cu}^{2+} \ (a = 0.01) \rightleftharpoons \text{Zn}^{2+} \ (a = 0.1) + \text{Cu}$$

and the cell potential as given by Nernst equation is

$$E_{cell} = E^0_{cell} - \frac{RT}{2F} \ln \frac{a_{\text{Zn}^{2+}} \ a_{\text{Cu}}}{a_{\text{Zn}} \ a_{\text{Cu}^{2+}}}$$

$$= E^0_{cell} - \frac{RT}{2F} \ln \frac{a_{\text{Zn}^{2+}}}{a_{\text{Cu}^{2+}}} \qquad \text{(Since activity of a pure metal is unity)}$$

Now

$$E^0_{cell} = 0.337 - (-0.762) = 1.099 \text{ V}$$

Hence

$$E_{cell} = 1.099 - \frac{0.0591}{2} \log \frac{0.1}{0.01}$$

$$= 1.099 - \frac{0.0591}{2} \log 10$$

$$= 1.099 - 0.02956$$

$$= 1.0694 \text{ V}$$

The free energy change ΔG is given by

$$\Delta G = -(2 \text{ equiv mol}^{-1})\,(1.0694 \text{ V})\,(96485 \text{ coulombs equiv}^{-1})$$
$$= -206.4 \text{ kJ mol}^{-1}$$

The standard free energy change

$$\Delta G° = -(2 \text{ equiv mol}^{-1}) (1.099 \text{ V}) (96485 \text{ coulombs equiv}^{-1})$$
$$= -212.1 \text{ kJ mol}^{-1}$$

The free energy change for the cell is less negative than that in the standard state because the activity of the product is greater than the activity of the reactant.

Problem 15.6: At 298 K, calculate the change in the electrode potential of the hydrogen electrode if the pressure of hydrogen gas is increased from 1 atm to 5 atm. Would you expect the electrode at 5 atm to be more or less positive than at 1 atm?

Solution: If the hydrogen ion activity remains constant, the change in electrode potential from Nernst equation is given by

$$\Delta E = E(5 \text{ atm}) - E(1 \text{ atm})$$

$$= -0.0591 \log \frac{(5)^{1/2}}{a_{H^+}} + 0.0591 \log \frac{(1)^{1/2}}{a_{H^+}}$$

$$= -0.0591 \log (5)^{1/2}$$

$$= -0.0591 \times \frac{1}{2} \log 5$$

$$= -0.0204 \text{ V}$$

The electrode potential decreases by 0.0204 V for a five-times increase in the pressure of the gas. With increase of pressure the equilibrium

$$H^+ \left(a_{H^+}\right) + e^- \rightleftharpoons \frac{1}{2} H_2 (P)$$

shifts to the left. Hence the electrode would be more negative at 5 atm than at 1 atm.

Problem 15.7: The standard emf of the Daniell cell is 1.1 V. Calculate the equilibrium constant for the reaction at 298 K.

Solution: From Eq. (15.14),

$$E_{cell}^0 = \frac{RT}{2F} \ln K$$

At 298 K

$$E_{cell}^0 = \frac{0.0591}{2} \log K$$

$$\log K = \frac{1.1 \times 2}{0.0591} = 37.28$$

or

$$K = 1.905 \times 10^{37}$$

The large value of the equilibrium constant shows that the reaction

$$Zn + Cu^{2+} \rightleftharpoons Zn^{2+} + Cu$$

is quantitative and at equilibrium the amount of copper ions in solution would be negligible.

Problem 15.8: The standard electrode potentials for the reactions

(i) $Fe^{2+} + 2e^- \rightleftharpoons Fe$

(ii) $Fe^{3+} + e^- \rightleftharpoons Fe^{2+}$

are respectively −0.441 V and +0.771 V. Calculate the standard electrode potential for the reaction

(iii) $Fe^{3+} + 3e^- \rightleftharpoons Fe$

Solution: The electrode potential is an intensive property. When we add up the potentials of two half cells to obtain the potential of the cell, the half cell reactions are written so that the number of electrons involved in each half cell reaction is the same. In reactions where the number of electrons are not equal we cannot just add up the electrode potentials instead we add the free energy changes for the various reactions. Thus in the above problem, reaction (iii) can be obtained by adding reactions (i) and (ii). Hence free energy change $\left(\Delta G_3^0\right)$ for reaction (iii) is equal to the sum of the free energy changes for the reactions (i) and (ii). If these are ΔG_1^0 and ΔG_2^0, then

$$\Delta G_3^0 = \Delta G_1^0 + \Delta G_2^0$$

But

$$\Delta G_1^0 = (-2)(-0.441)F; \quad \Delta G_2^0 = (-1)(+0.771)F; \quad \Delta G_3^0 = -(3)E^0 F$$

where E^0 is the standard electrode potential for reaction (iii), hence,

$$-3E^0 F = 0.882F - 0.771 \ F$$

$$-3E^0 = 0.111 \text{ or } E^0 = -0.037 \text{ V}$$

Problem 15.9: For the cell

$$Al \mid Al^{3+} (a) \parallel Sn^{4+} (a), Sn^{2+} (a) \mid Pt$$

the standard electrode potentials at 298 K are

$$E^0_{Al^{3+}|Al} = -1.66 \text{ V}; \quad E^0_{Sn^{4+}, Sn^{2+}|Pt} = +0.15 \text{ V}$$

Write the cell reaction. Calculate (a) the cell emf when the activities are all 0.1 and 1.0, (b) ΔG^0 for the cell reaction, and (c) the equilibrium constant for the reaction.

Solution: (a) The half cell reactions are:

At the left electrode: $Al \rightleftharpoons Al^{3+} + 3e^-$

At the right electrode: $Sn^{4+} + 2e^- \rightleftharpoons Sn^{2+}$

Overall cell reaction: $2Al + 3Sn^{4+} \rightleftharpoons 3Sn^{2+} + 2Al^{3+}$

The cell emf when all the activities are 0.1 is given by

$$E = E^0 - \frac{RT}{6F} \ln \frac{\left(a^2_{Al^{3+}}\right)\left(a^3_{Sn^{2+}}\right)}{\left(a^3_{Sn^{4+}}\right)}$$

$$= 1.81 - \frac{0.0591}{6} \log \frac{(0.1)^2 (0.1)^3}{(0.1)^3}$$

$$= 1.81 + \frac{0.0591 \times 2}{6}$$

$$= 1.83 \text{ V}$$

The cell emf when the activities are all unity is

$$E = E^0 = 1.81 \text{ V}$$

(b) The free energy change for the cell in the standard state is

$$\Delta G^0 = -(6 \text{ equiv mol}^{-1}) \ (1.81 \text{ V}) \ (96485 \text{ coulombs equiv}^{-1})$$

$$= -1048 \text{ kJ mol}^{-1}$$

(c) The equilibrium constant is given as

$$\log K = \frac{nE^0}{0.0591} = \frac{6 \times 1.81}{0.059} = 186$$

or

$$K = 10^{186}$$

Problem 15.10: The standard electrode potential for $Hg_2^{2+} \, | \, Hg$ and $Hg^{2+} \, | \, Hg$ are 0.799 V and 0.855 V respectively. Calculate at 298K the equilibrium constant for the reaction $Hg^{2+} + Hg \rightleftharpoons Hg_2^{2+}$

Solution: (a) $Hg^{2+} + 2e^- \rightleftharpoons Hg; \quad E^0 = 0.855$ V and

(b) $Hg_2^{2+} + 2e^- \rightleftharpoons 2Hg; \quad E^0 = 0.799$ V

The desired reaction can be obtained by subtracting reaction (b) from reaction (a), i.e.,

$$Hg^{2+} + Hg = Hg_2^{2+} \text{ and } E^0 = 0.056 \text{ V}$$

Now

$$\Delta G^0 = -RT \ln K = -nE^0 F$$

or

$$\log K = \frac{(0.056) \times (2)(96485)}{2.303 \times 8.314 \times 298}$$

or

$$K = 78.34$$

Problem 15.11: If the standard half cell potentials are 1.45 V for $ClO_3^- \, | \, Cl^- | Pt$ and 1.47 V for $ClO_3^- \, | \, Cl_2 | Pt$ calculate E^0 for the half cell $Pt \, | \, Cl_2 \, | \, Cl^-$.

Solution: The standard electrode potential for $Pt \, | \, Cl_2 \, | \, Cl^-$ can be calculated as

(1) $2ClO_3^- + 12H^+ + 12e^- \rightleftharpoons 2Cl^- + 6H_2O; \ \Delta G_1^0 = -(12)(1.45)(F)$

(2) $2ClO_3^- + 12H^+ + 10e^- \rightleftharpoons Cl_2 + 6H_2O; \ \Delta G_2^0 = -(10)(1.47)F$

Subtracting reaction (2) from (1), we get

$$Cl_2 + 2e \rightleftharpoons 2Cl^-; \Delta G_3^0 = -(2)E^0 F$$

$$= \Delta G_1^0 - \Delta G_2^0$$

$$= -17.4F + 14.70F$$

$$= -2.7\ F$$

or $E^0 = +1.35$ V

Problem 15.12: The solubility product of CuCl at 298 K is 2.29×10^{-7} and standard electrode for the half cell $Cl^- (a = 1) | CuCl(s) | Cu$ is 0.129 V. Calculate the standard electrode potential of the couple $Cu^+ | Cu$.

Solution: The solubility product is 2.29×10^{-7} at 298 K. Hence E^0 for the reaction

$$CuCl(s) \rightleftharpoons Cu^+ + Cl^-$$

is given by

$$E^0 = 0.0591 \log K_{sp} = 0.0591 \log (2.29 \times 10^{-7}) = -0.393 \text{ V}$$

Now   (i) $CuCl \rightleftharpoons Cu^+ + Cl^-$; $E^0 = -0.393$ V

(ii) $CuCl + e^- \rightleftharpoons Cu + Cl^-$; $E^0 = +0.129$ V

Subtracting Eq. (i) from Eq. (ii) we get

$$CuCl + e^- - CuCl = Cu + Cl^- - Cu^+ - Cl^-$$

$$Cu^+ + e^- = Cu \ ; \ E^0 = 0.522 \text{ V}$$

15.9 TYPES OF ELECTRODES

In an electrochemical cell, there are two electrodes, positive and negative. Each electrode constitutes a half cell or a single electrode. Although a number of electrodes are possible but the more important of these electrodes are grouped into the following types:

(i) Metal–metal ion electrodes, (ii) Metal–metal insoluble salt electrodes, (iii) Metal–amalgam electrodes, (iv) Gas–ion electrodes, (v) Oxidation–reduction or redox electrodes.

We shall denote these electrodes as right hand ones, i.e., the electrode reactions would correspond to reductions.

(i) **Metal–Metal Ion Electrodes:** These electrodes consist of a pure metal (M) in equilibrium with a solution of its cation (M^{n+}). For example, a silver rod immersed in a solution of Ag^+ ions or copper rod in a solution of Cu^{2+} ions. The electrode is represented as $M^{n+} (a) | M$ and the electrode reaction can be written as

$$M^{n+} (a) + ne^- \rightleftharpoons M$$

Since the electrode is reversible to the metal cation, its electrode potential can be expressed as

$$E_{M^{n+}|M} = E^0_{M^{n+}|M} - \frac{RT}{nF} \ln \frac{a_M}{a_{M^{n+}}}$$

$$= E^0_{M^{n+}|M} + \frac{RT}{nF} \ln a_{M^{n+}} \quad (\because a_M = 1) \qquad \qquad ...(15.19)$$

and depends on the activity of the metal ion in the solution.

(ii) **Metal–Metal Insoluble Salt Electrodes:** Such electrodes are important and are frequently used in electrochemical works. These consist of a metal (M) covered by a layer of sparingly soluble salt

(*MX*) immersed in a solution containing a common anion (*X⁻*). Examples of such electrodes are mercury-mercurous chloride in contact with the solution of potassium chloride or mercury-mercurous sulphate in contact with a solution of potassium sulphate or a silver wire coated with silver chloride immersed in potassium chloride solution. These electrodes are represented as

$$X^-(a) \mid MX \mid M$$

The overall electrode reaction is

$$MX + e^- \rightleftharpoons M + X^-(a)$$

and the electrode potential is given by

$$E_{X^- \mid MX \mid M} = E^0_{X^- \mid MX \mid M} - \frac{RT}{F} \ln a_{X^-} \qquad ...(15.20)$$

Since E^0 for the electrode is constant, therefore, the electrode potential is controlled by the activity of the anion only. Hence the electrode is reversible to the concn. of anion of the sparingly soluble salt, X^-.

(*iii*) **Metal–Amalgam Electrodes:** Sometimes when the metal is highly reactive, it is more convenient to use the metal in the form of amalgams. The activity of the metal is lowered by dilution with mercury. These electrodes are generally set up by placing the metal-amalgam in contact with a solution of metal ion. These electrodes are represented as

$$M^{n+}(a) \mid M\,(Hg)$$

and the electrode reaction is

$$M^{n+}(a) + ne^- \rightleftharpoons M\,(Hg)$$

The electrode potential is given by

$$E_{M^{n+} \mid M(Hg)} = E^0_{M^{n+} \mid M} - \frac{RT}{nF} \ln \frac{a_{M(Hg)}}{a_{M^{n+}}} \qquad ...(15.21)$$

and depends on the activity of the metal cation in the solution and the activity of metal in the amalgam. When $a_{M(Hg)}$ and $a_{M^{n+}}$ are both unity, the electrode potential is the standard electrode potential of the metal. Since the activity of the metal in the amalgam is not unity, Eq. (15.21) can be written as

$$E_{M^{n+} \mid M(Hg)} = E^0_{M^{n+} \mid M} - \frac{RT}{nF} \ln a_{M(Hg)} + \frac{RT}{nF} \ln a_{M^{n+}}$$

$$= E^0_{amalgam} + \frac{RT}{nF} \ln a_{M^{n+}} \qquad ...(15.22)$$

From Eqs. (15.19) and (15.22), the difference in the potential ΔE of the metal and metal amalgam electrodes is given as

$$\Delta E = E_{M^{n+} \mid M} - E_{M^{n+} \mid M(Hg)}$$

$$= E^0_{M^{n+} \mid M} + \frac{RT}{nF} \ln a_{M^{n+}} - E^0_{amalgam} - \frac{RT}{nF} \ln a_{M^{n+}}$$

$$= E^0_{M^{n+} \mid M} - E^0_{amalgam} \qquad ...(15.23)$$

Hence knowing the difference in potential ΔE and E^0_{amalgam}, $E^0_{M^{n+}|M}$ can be evaluated.

(*iv*) **Gas-Ion Electrodes:** A gas electrode consists of an inert metal, usually gold or platinum, immersed in a solution containing ions to which the gas is reversible. A current of pure gas is continuously bubbled through the solution. The inert metal electrode does not participate in the electrode reaction but simply helps in making electrical contact. The gas (X_2) electrode is denoted as

$$X^-(a)/X_2\,(P = x\ \text{atm})/\text{Pt}$$

The electrode reaction can be written as

$$X_2(P) + 2e^- \rightleftharpoons 2X^-(a)$$

The electrode potential is given by

$$E = E^0_{X^-|X_2|\text{Pt}} - \frac{RT}{2F} \ln \frac{a^2_{X^-}}{P_{X_2}} \qquad \qquad ...(15.24)$$

The potential depends both on the pressure of the gas and the activity of X^- ions in solution.

(*v*) **Oxidation–Reduction or Redox Electrodes:** These are electrodes in which the emf arises from the presence of ions of a substance in two different oxidation states. The electrodes are nonreactive with solution and are just carriers of electrons. These electrodes are set up by dipping an inert metal like gold or platinum into a solution containing ions in two different oxidation states of the substance. For example, a platinum wire immersed in a solution of ferrous and ferric ions or stannous and stannic ions constitutes a redox electrode. These electrodes are represented as

$$\text{Pt} \mid M^{n_1+}\left(a_1\right),\ M^{n_2+}\left(a_2\right)$$

and the electrode reaction is

$$M^{n_1+}\left(a_1\right) + ne^- \rightleftharpoons M^{n_2+}\left(a_2\right)$$

where M^{n_1+} is the higher oxidation state and M^{n_2+} is the lower oxidation state. The electrode potential is given by the expression

$$E = E^0_{M^{n_1+},\ M^{n_2+}|\text{Pt}} - \frac{RT}{nF} \ln \frac{a_2}{a_1} \qquad \qquad ...(15.25)$$

and depends on the activities of both the ions in the solution.

15.10 OTHER REFERENCE ELECTRODES

(i) Calomel Electrode

Since a standard hydrogen electrode is difficult to prepare and maintain, it is usually replaced by other reference electrodes which are known as secondary reference electrodes. These are convenient to handle and are prepared easily. The potentials of these electrodes are determined accurately with respect to the SHE. One such common reference electrode is the calomel electrode. It consists of (Fig. 15.5) mercury at the bottom over which a paste of mercury-mercurous chloride is placed. A solution of potassium chloride is then placed over the paste. A platinum wire helps in making the electrical contact. If potassium chloride solution is saturated, the electrode is known as saturated calomel electrode (SCE) and if the solution of potassium chloride is 1N, the electrode is known as normal calomel electrode (NCE) while for 0.1N potassium chloride solution the electrode is referred to as a decinormal calomel electrode (DNCE). The electrode reaction when the cell acts as cathode is

$$\frac{1}{2}Hg_2Cl_2(s) + e^- \rightleftharpoons Hg + Cl^-\left(a_{Cl^-}\right)$$

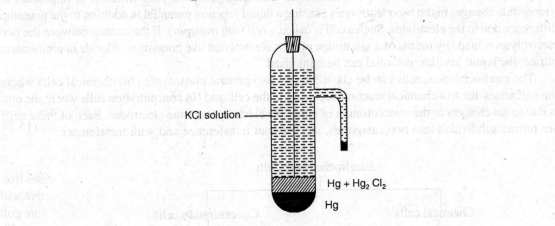

KCl solution

$Hg + Hg_2\,Cl_2$

Hg

Fig. 15.5 The calomel electrode

and its potential is given by

$$E = E^0_{Cl^- \mid Hg_2Cl_2 \mid Pt} - \frac{RT}{F}\ln a_{Cl^-} \qquad \qquad ...(15.26)$$

The potential depends on the activity of the chloride ions and decreases as the activity of the chloride ions increases. The potentials (reduction) of the calomel electrodes on the hydrogen scale at 298 K are given as

0.1 N KCl	0.3338 V
1.0 N KCl	0.2800 V
Saturated KCl	0.2415 V

To obtain the potential of any other electrode on the hydrogen scale, it is combined with the calomel electrode and the emf of the resulting cell is measured. Knowing the cell emf and the electrode potential of the calomel electrode, the potential of the other electrode can be evaluated.

(ii) Silver-Silver Chloride Electrode

This is another widely used reference electrode. Silver chloride is deposited electrolytically on a silver or platinum wire and it is then immersed in a solution containing chloride ions. The electrode is reproducible and its standard electrode potential with respect to the SHE is 0.2224 V at 298 K. The electrode is represented as

$$Ag \mid AgCl \mid Cl^-\left(a_{Cl^-}\right)$$

and the electrode reaction is

$$AgCl + e^- \rightleftharpoons Ag + Cl^-\left(a_{Cl^-}\right)$$

The electrode is reversible with respect to the chloride ions.

15.11 CLASSIFICATION OF ELECTROCHEMICAL CELLS

An electrochemical cell has two suitable half cells. If the electrodes of the half cells are immersed in the same electrolyte so that there is no liquid junction, the cell is known as a *cell without transport*. If the electrolytes of the half cells are different or same but at different concentrations, then on bringing them in contact, ions of the electrolytes migrate across the liquid junction. This diffusion of ions leads to irreversible changes in the two electrolytes causing a liquid junction potential in addition to the potential difference due to the electrodes. Such a cell is called a *cell with transport*. If the contact between the two electrolytes is made by means of a salt bridge of inert electrolytes like potassium chloride or ammonium nitrate, the liquid junction potential can be minimised.

The electrochemical cells can be classified into two general classes, *viz.*, (*a*) chemical cells where the emf arises due to a chemical reaction occurring in the cell, and (*b*) concentration cells where the emf is due to the changes in the concentration of either the electrolytes or the electrodes. Each of these cells are further subdivided into two categories, *viz.*, without transference and with transference.

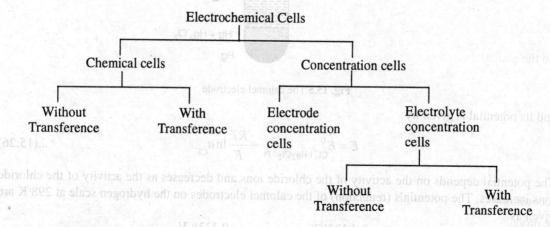

15.12 CHEMICAL CELLS

(i) Chemical Cells without Transference

A chemical cell without transference can be constructed using two electrodes and an electrolyte such that one of the electrodes is reversible with respect to the cation of the electrolyte and the other with respect to its anion. A typical example of such a cell is

$$Pt \mid H_2 \, (P \text{ atm}) \mid HCl \, (a = x) \mid AgCl(s) \mid Ag$$

It consists of a hydrogen electrode on the left hand side and Ag | AgCl electrode on the right, dipping directly in hydrochloric acid giving a cell with no liquid junction. In the cell, the hydrogen electrode is negative and reversible with respect to hydrogen ions whereas the Ag | AgCl electrode is positive and reversible with respect to chloride ions.

On the left electrode, oxidation occurs

$$\frac{1}{2} H_2 \, (P \text{ atm}) \rightleftharpoons H^+ \, (x) + e^-$$

and

$$E_L = E_L^0 - \frac{RT}{F} \ln \frac{P_{H_2}^{1/2}}{a_{H^+}}$$

$$= -\frac{RT}{F} \ln \frac{P_{H_2}^{1/2}}{a_{H^+}}$$

On the right electrode, reduction takes place

$$AgCl + e^- \rightleftharpoons Ag + Cl^-(x)$$

and

$$E_R = E_{Ag|AgCl|Cl^-}^0 - \frac{RT}{F} \ln a_{Cl^-}$$

The net cell reaction is

$$\frac{1}{2} H_2 (P \text{ atm}) + AgCl \rightleftharpoons Ag + Cl^-(x) + H^+(x)$$

and the emf of the cell is given as

$$E = E_R - E_L = E_{Ag|AgCl|Cl^-}^0 - \frac{RT}{F} \ln a_{Cl^-} - \frac{RT}{F} \ln \frac{a_{H^+}}{P_{H_2}^{1/2}}$$

$$= E_{Ag|AgCl|Cl^-}^0 - \frac{RT}{F} \ln \frac{a_{H^+} \cdot a_{Cl^-}}{P_{H_2}^{1/2}} \qquad ...(15.27)$$

According to Eq. (15.27), emf of the cell does not depend on the activity of the individual ions, but on the product $a_{H^+} \cdot a_{Cl^-}$. As there is no measurable quantity which depends on the individual ion activity, hence we write $a_{H^+} \cdot a_{Cl^-} = a_{HCl}$. Equation (15.27), therefore, becomes

$$E = E_{Ag|AgCl|Cl^-}^0 - \frac{RT}{F} \ln \frac{a_{HCl}}{P_{H_2}^{1/2}} \qquad ...(15.28)$$

The cell reaction indicates that the cell emf results from a chemical reaction, namely, the reduction of silver chloride by hydrogen gas to solid silver and hydrochloric acid. Furthermore, the emf of the cell as given by Eq. (15.28) depends upon the activity of hydrochloric acid and the pressure of hydrogen gas. If the pressure of the gas is 1 atm, Eq. (15.28) becomes

$$E = E_{Ag|AgCl|Cl^-}^0 - \frac{RT}{F} \ln a_{HCl} \qquad ...(15.29)$$

Such cells are extensively used in the determination of the activity coefficients of various electrolytes as discussed later.

Some other examples of chemical cells without transference are

$$Cd \,|\, CdSO_4 \,|\, Hg_2SO_4 \,|\, Hg$$

$$Pt \,|\, H_2 \,|\, H_2SO_4 \,|\, Hg_2SO_4 \,|\, Hg$$

and the chemical reactions that occur in these cells are

$$Cd + Hg_2SO_4 \rightleftharpoons 2Hg + CdSO_4$$

$$H_2 + Hg_2SO_4 \rightleftharpoons 2Hg + H_2SO_4$$

(ii) Chemical Cells with Transference

Some of the cells of these types are

$$Zn \mid Zn^{2+}\left(a_{Zn^{2+}}\right) \vdots Cu^{2+}\left(a_{Cu^{2+}}\right) \mid Cu$$

$$Hg \mid Hg_2Cl_2 \mid Cl^-\left(a_{Cl^-}\right) \vdots Cu^{2+}\left(a_{Cu^{2+}}\right) \mid Cu$$

$$H_2 \mid Pt \mid H_3O^+\left(a_{H_3O^+}\right) \vdots Cl^-\left(a_{Cl^-}\right) \mid Hg_2Cl_2 \mid Hg$$

The dotted vertical lines indicate liquid-liquid contact between the electrolytes. The emf in these cells arises due to the chemical changes occurring within the cells. However, when the two electrolytes of different concentrations, different ions or both are brought in contact with each other, a potential develops across the liquid junction. This potential arises due to a difference in the concentration of the ions across the boundary. The ions diffuse from the concentrated solution towards the dilute solution tending to equalize the concentration. The faster moving ion moves ahead of the slower moving ion and the dilute solution always acquires the charge of the faster moving ions. This difference in the mobilities of two ions causes a charge separation at the junction leading to the development of the liquid junction potential. If the mobilities of two ions of an electrolyte are equal no net charge separation would be expected and consequently no liquid junction potential will develop in such cases. The liquid junction potential (E_j) must be taken into account for the accurate measurement of the cell emf which is given by

$$E_{cell} = E_R - E_L \pm E_j \qquad \qquad ...(15.30)$$

In most of the cases measurement of E_j is difficult and in such cases it is advisable to minimise or practically eliminate E_j through the use of a salt bridge of potassium chloride or ammonium nitrate. A hot aqueous solution of potassium chloride (or ammonium nitrate) and agar is filled in a U-shaped delivery tube and the tube is then cooled when a semi-solid mass sets in the tube. This tube is then employed for making electrical contacts between two electrolytes. The role of electrolytes like potassium chloride etc., in eliminating E_j is probably due to the fact that the mobilities of K^+ and Cl^- ions are almost equal and the E_j values between the solutions and the bridge are almost counter-balanced.

When the liquid junction potentials are eliminated, the cell may be represented as

$$Zn \mid Zn^{2+}\left(a_{Zn^{2+}}\right) \mid\mid Cu^{2+}\left(a_{Cu^{2+}}\right) \mid Cu$$

$$Hg \mid Hg_2Cl_2 \mid Cl^-\left(a_{Cl^-}\right) \mid\mid Cu\left(a_{Cu^{2+}}\right) \mid Cu$$

$$Pt \mid H_2 \mid H_3O^+\left(a_{H_3O^+}\right) \mid\mid Cl^-\left(a_{Cl^-}\right) \mid Hg_2Cl_2 \mid Hg$$

The cell emf is then given by

$$E_{cell} = E_R - E_L$$

and the treatment is similar to the one discussed earlier for chemical cells without transference.

15.13 CONCENTRATION CELLS

(i) Electrode Concentration Cells

An electrode concentration cell consists of two identical electrodes of different concentrations dipped in a common electrolyte containing ions of the electrode material. A simple electrode concentration cell is obtained when two hydrogen electrodes at different pressures are placed in the same solution of hydrochloric acid. The electrode with a higher pressure of the gas forms the anode and the other with a lower pressure of the gas forms the cathode. The cell may be denoted as

$$\text{Pt} \mid \text{H}_2 \, (P_1) \mid \text{HCl} \, (a) \mid \text{H}_2 \, (P_2) \mid \text{Pt}; \, P_1 > P_2$$

The oxidation reaction at the left electrode is

$$\frac{1}{2}\text{H}_2(P_1) \rightarrow \text{H}^+(a) + e^-$$

$$E_\text{L} = -\frac{RT}{F}\ln\frac{P_1^{1/2}}{a_{\text{H}^+}}$$

and at the right electrode reduction occurs

$$\text{H}^+(a) + e^- \rightarrow \frac{1}{2}\text{H}_2(P_2)$$

$$E_\text{R} = -\frac{RT}{F}\ln\frac{P_2^{1/2}}{a_{\text{H}^+}}$$

The overall change is

$$\frac{1}{2}\text{H}_2(P_1) \rightarrow \frac{1}{2}\text{H}_2(P_2) \qquad \qquad ...(15.31)$$

and the cell emf is

$$E = E_\text{R} - E_\text{L} = -\frac{RT}{F}\ln\left(\frac{P_2}{P_1}\right)^{1/2}$$

$$= \frac{RT}{2F}\ln\frac{P_1}{P_2} \qquad \qquad ...(15.32)$$

Equation (15.32) shows that the cell reaction involves a transfer of hydrogen gas from higher pressure P_1 to lower pressure P_2. The emf of the cell depends only on the pressure of hydrogen gas at each electrode and is independent of the activity of hydrogen ions in the solution. Further, since $P_1 > P_2$, the cell emf is positive and it will operate spontaneously until P_1 and P_2 become equal. When $P_1 = P_2$, $E_\text{cell} = 0$ and the cell ceases to operate.

Another commonly employed electrode consists of two amalgam electrodes at different activities in contact with a solution of an electrolyte containing ions of the metal dissolved in the amalgam, e.g.,

$$\text{Cd} - \text{Hg}(a_1) \mid \text{CdSO}_4(a) \mid \text{Cd} - \text{Hg}(a_2) \,; \qquad a_1 > a_2$$

The reactions are

at the left electrode:
$$Cd - Hg(a_1) \rightarrow Cd^{2+}(a) + 2e^-$$

and
$$E_L = E_L^0 - \frac{RT}{2F} \ln \frac{a_1}{a_{Cd^{2+}}}$$

at the right electrode:
$$Cd^{2+}(a) + 2e^- \rightarrow Cd - Hg(a_2)$$

and
$$E_R = E_R^0 - \frac{RT}{2F} \ln \frac{a_2}{a_{Cd^{2+}}}$$

The overall change is

$$Cd - Hg(a_1) \longrightarrow Cd - Hg(a_2) \qquad \qquad ...(15.33)$$

and the cell emf is

$$E_{cell} = E_R - E_L$$

$$= -\frac{RT}{2F} \ln \frac{a_2}{a_1}$$

$$= \frac{RT}{2F} \ln \frac{a_1}{a_2} \qquad \qquad ...(15.34)$$

The cell emf results from the transfer of cadmium from amalgam of higher activity (a_1) to an amalgam of lower activity (a_2). If the amalgams are assumed to be ideal solutions, the activities may be replaced by concentrations.

Problem 15.13: For the electrode concentration cell
$$Zn\,(X_1) - Hg\,|\,ZnSO_4\,|\,Zn\,(X_2) - Hg$$

E at 298 K is 0.0594 V. X_1 and X_2, the mole fractions of Zn in Hg, are respectively 3×10^{-2} and 3×10^{-4}. Calculate the ratio of the activity coefficients of Zn (on mole fraction basis) in the two amalgams.

Solution: The emf of the cell is given by

$$E = \frac{RT}{2F}\left[\ln \frac{X_1}{X_2} + \ln \frac{\gamma_1}{\gamma_2} \right]$$

or
$$0.0594 = \frac{0.0591}{2}\left[\log \frac{3 \times 10^{-2}}{3 \times 10^{-4}} + \log \frac{\gamma_1}{\gamma_2} \right]$$

or
$$\log \frac{\gamma_1}{\gamma_2} = \frac{2(0.0594 - 0.0591)}{0.0591}$$

$$= 0.01015$$

or
$$\frac{\gamma_1}{\gamma_2} = 1.023$$

(ii) Electrolyte Concentration Cells without Transference

An electrolyte concentration cell without transference is set up by combining two chemical cells without transference which differ in their electrolyte concentrations. The following is an example of such a cell:

$$\text{Ag} \mid \text{AgCl} \mid \text{HCl} (a_2) \mid \text{H}_2 (1 \text{ atm}) \mid \text{Pt} \mid \text{HCl} (a_1) \mid \text{AgCl} \mid \text{Ag} : a_2 > a_1.$$

The anode is dipped in hydrochloric acid solution of higher activity (a_2). The overall reaction occurring in the left cell is

$$\text{Ag} + \text{H}^+\text{Cl}^- (a_2) \rightleftharpoons \frac{1}{2}\text{H}_2 + \text{AgCl}$$

and the emf of this cell is given by

$$E_L = E_L^0 - \frac{RT}{F} \ln a_2$$

Similarly, the reaction on the right cell is

$$\frac{1}{2}\text{H}_2 + \text{AgCl} \longrightarrow \text{Ag} + \text{HCl}(a_1)$$

and its emf is given as

$$E_R = E_R^0 - \frac{RT}{F} \ln a_1$$

When these two cells are connected so as to oppose each other, the complete cell reaction that occurs is

$$\text{HCl}(a_2) \longrightarrow \text{HCl}(a_1) \qquad \qquad ...(15.35)$$

The total emf of the cell is given by the difference of two emf's, E_R and E_L.

$$E = E_R - E_L$$

$$= \left(E_R^0 - \frac{RT}{F} \ln a_1 \right) - \left(E_L^0 - \frac{RT}{F} \ln a_2 \right) \qquad \qquad ...(15.36)$$

$$= \frac{RT}{F} \ln \frac{a_2}{a_1} \left(\because E_R^0 = -E_L^0 \right)$$

Thus the overall change in the cell is the transfer of hydrochloric acid from activity a_2 to a_1. However, there is no direct transfer of electrolyte from left to right. Hydrochloric acid is removed from left side by the reaction

$$\text{HCl} + \text{Ag} \longrightarrow \text{AgCl} + \frac{1}{2}\text{H}_2$$

and is added to the right side by the reverse reaction. When $a_2 = a_1$, the cell will cease to operate and the cell emf will be zero.

Cells of such type may be used to obtain the ratio of activity coefficients of an electrolyte at two different concentrations.

(iii) Electrolyte Concentration Cells with Transference

These cells consist of two identical electrodes immersed in two solutions of the same electrolyte at different concentrations. The electrodes should be reversible to one of the ions of the electrolyte. The two electrolytes are somehow prevented from mechanical mixing by means of a porous diaphragm as in the case of a Daniell cell. A simple concentration cell with liquid junction potential is

$$Pt \,|\, H_2 \,(1 \text{ atm}) \,|\, HCl\,(a_1) : HCl\,(a_2) \,|\, H_2\,(1 \text{ atm}) \,|\, Pt; \quad a_1 < a_2 \qquad (A)$$

The emf of the cell is composed of two single electrode potentials plus the liquid junction potential. Various reactions that occur in the cell are

Anode reaction :
$$\frac{1}{2}H_2\,(1 \text{ atm}) \longrightarrow H^+(a_1) + e^-$$

Cathode reaction :
$$H^+(a_2) + e^- \longrightarrow \frac{1}{2}H_2\,(1 \text{ atm})$$

Net electrode reaction :
$$H^+(a_2) \longrightarrow H^+(a_1) \qquad \qquad ...(15.37)$$

The emf of the cell corresponds to sum of all the reactions occurring in the cell, *i.e.*, the electrode reactions and the migration of ions across the liquid junction.

If 1 faraday of electricity is passed through the cell, 1 mol of hydrogen ions will be produced at the left electrode and 1 mol of hydrogen ions will be discharged at the right electrode. In the solution, current is carried by H^+ and Cl^- ions. As H^+ ions are discharged at the right electrode, H^+ ions in solution move from left to right and at the same time Cl^- ions move from right to left. If t_{H^+} and t_{Cl^-} are the transference numbers of H^+ and Cl^- ions then for each faraday of electricity passed through the solution t_{H^+} mol of H^+ ions must cross the junction from left to right and $t_{Cl^-} = \left(1 - t_{H^+}\right)$ mol of Cl^- ions should migrate from right to left. Thus the changes that occur in addition to the electrode reactions are:

$$t_{H^+}H^+(a_1) \longrightarrow t_{H^+}H^+(a_2) \qquad \qquad ...(15.38)$$

$$\left(1 - t_{H^+}\right)Cl^-(a_2) \longrightarrow \left(1 - t_{H^+}\right)Cl^-(a_1) \qquad \qquad ...(15.39)$$

The total cell reaction is given by the sum of the Eqs. (15.37), (15.38) and (15.39), *e.g.*,

$$H^+(a_2) + t_{H^+}H^+(a_1) + \left(1 - t_{H^+}\right)Cl^-(a_2) = H^+(a_1) + t_{H^+}H^+(a_2) + \left(1 - t_{H^+}\right)Cl^-(a_1)$$

$$H^+(a_2)\left[1 - t_{H^+}\right] + \left(1 - t_{H^+}\right)Cl^-(a_2) = H^+(a_1)\left[1 - t_{H^+}\right] + \left[1 - t_{H^+}\right]Cl^-(a_1)$$

$$\left[1 - t_{H^+}\right]\left[H^+(a_2) + Cl^-(a_2)\right] = \left[1 - t_{H^+}\right]\left[H^+(a_1) + Cl^-(a_1)\right]$$

But $1 - t_{H^+} = t_{Cl^-}$, therefore

$$t_{Cl^-}\left[H^+(a_2) + Cl^-(a_2)\right] = t_{Cl^-}\left[H^+(a_1) + Cl^-(a_1)\right]$$

$$t_{Cl^-}HCl(a_2) = t_{Cl^-}HCl(a_1) \qquad \qquad ...(15.40)$$

This equation shows that for 1 faraday of electricity passed through the cell with transference, t_{Cl^-} mol of HCl are transferred from solution of higher activity (a_2) to solution of lower activity (a_1). The emf of the cell is given as

$$E = -\frac{RT}{F} \ln \frac{(a_1)^{t_{Cl^-}}}{(a_2)^{t_{Cl^-}}}$$

$$= -t_{Cl^-} \frac{RT}{F} \ln \frac{a_1}{a_2}$$

$$= t_{Cl^-} \frac{RT}{F} \ln \frac{a_2}{a_1} \qquad \qquad ...(15.41)$$

The expression for cell emf depends on whether the electrodes are reversible to the cation or to the anion of the electrolyte. In the above cell, the electrodes are reversible to the cation (H^+), the transference number of the anion appears in the equation for the emf of the cell. Consider a cell

$$\text{Ag | AgCl | HCl } (a_1) : \text{HCl}(a_2) \text{ | AgCl | Ag; } a_1 > a_2 \qquad \qquad (B)$$

in which the electrodes are reversible to the anion, Cl^-. The emf of the cell involves the transference number of the cation t_{H^+} as can be shown below:

The electrode reactions are

Anode reaction: $\qquad \text{Ag} + Cl^-(a_1) \rightarrow \text{AgCl} + e^-$

Cathode reaction: $\qquad \text{AgCl} + e^- \rightarrow \text{Ag} + Cl^-(a_2)$

Net electrode reaction: $\quad Cl^-(a_1) \rightarrow Cl^-(a_2) \qquad \qquad ...(15.42)$

In the solution Cl^- ions migrate from right to left while the hydrogen ions move in the reverse direction, i.e., from left to right across the liquid junction. When one faraday of electricity is passed 1 mol of Cl^- ions are consumed at the left electrode and 1 mol of Cl^- ions are produced at the right electrode. If t_{H^+} and t_{Cl^-} are the transference numbers of the cation and anion then t_{H^+} mol of H^+ ions will migrate from left to right while t_{Cl^-} mol of the Cl^- ions will migrate in the opposite direction. The changes across the liquid junction are

$$t_{H^+} H^+(a_1) \longrightarrow t_{H^+} H^+(a_2) \qquad \qquad ...(15.43)$$

$$t_{Cl^-} Cl^-(a_2) \longrightarrow t_{Cl^-} Cl^-(a_1) \qquad \qquad ...(15.44)$$

The net transfer of electrolyte from higher to lower activity is given by the sum of Eqs. (15.42), (15.43) and (15.44).

$$Cl^-(a_1) + t_{Cl^-} Cl(a_2) + t_{H^+} H^+(a_1) = Cl^-(a_2) + t_{H^+} H^+(a_2) + t_{Cl^-} Cl^-(a_1)$$

$$Cl^-(a_1) + t_{H^+} H^+(a_1) - t_{Cl^-} Cl^-(a_1) = Cl^-(a_2) + t_{H^+} H^+(a_2) - t_{Cl^-} Cl^-(a_2)$$

$$\left[1 - t_{Cl^-} \right] Cl^-(a_1) + t_{H^+} H^+(a_1) = \left[1 - t_{Cl^-} \right] Cl^-(a_2) + t_{H^+} H^+(a_2)$$

$$t_{H^+} Cl^-(a_1) + t_{H^+} H^+(a_1) = t_{H^+} Cl^-(a_2) + t_{H^+} H^+(a_2)$$

$$t_{H^+} HCl(a_1) = t_{H^+} HCl(a_2) \qquad \qquad ...(15.45)$$

Thus for the passage of each faraday the overall change in the cell is the transfer of t_{H^+} mol of hydrochloric acid from activity a_1 to a_2. The emf of the cell is given by

$$E = -t_{H^+} \frac{RT}{F} \ln \frac{a_2}{a_1}$$

$$= t_{H^+} \frac{RT}{F} \ln \frac{a_1}{a_2} \qquad \qquad ...(15.46)$$

and it involves the transference number of the cation. In general, the emf of electrolyte concentration cells with transference involves the transference number of the ion other than the one to which the electrodes are reversible.

In terms of the mean activity of ions (defined as $a_{H^+} \cdot a_{Cl^-} = a_\pm^2$), Eq. (15.46) can be written as

$$E = t_{H^+} \frac{RT}{F} \ln \frac{(a_\pm^2)_1}{(a_\pm^2)_2}$$

$$= 2t_{H^+} \frac{RT}{F} \ln \frac{(a_\pm)_1}{(a_\pm)_2} \qquad \qquad ...(15.47)$$

Further, $a_\pm = m\gamma_\pm$ where m is the molality and $\gamma_\pm$ is the mean activity coefficient of the electrolyte. Substituting the value of $a_\pm$ in Eq. (15.47) we get

$$E = 2t_{H^+} \frac{RT}{F} \ln \frac{(m\gamma_\pm)_1}{(m\gamma_\pm)_2}$$

$$= 2t_{H^+} \frac{RT}{F} \ln \frac{m_1}{m_2} + 2t_{H^+} \frac{RT}{F} \ln \frac{(\gamma_\pm)_1}{(\gamma_\pm)_2} \qquad ...(15.48)$$

Knowing the values of molalities, m_1 and m_2, the measurement of emf permits the calculation of the ratio of mean activity coefficients of electrolyte at these two concentrations.

Problem 15.14: The emf of the concentration cell

Pb | PbSO$_4$ | CuSO$_4$ ($a_\pm = 0.022$) : CuSO$_4$ ($a_\pm = 0.0064$) | PbSO$_4$ | Pb

is 0.0118 V at 298 K. Calculate the transference number of the copper ions.

Solution: The cell is a concentration cell with transference where the electrodes are reversible to the anion, therefore its emf is given by

$$E = 2t_+ \frac{RT}{2F} \ln \frac{(a_\pm)_1}{(a_\pm)_2}$$

$$= 2t_+ \frac{RT}{2F} \ln \frac{0.022}{0.0064}$$

$$t_+ = \frac{0.0118}{0.0591} \log \frac{0.022}{0.0064}$$

$$= 0.37$$

15.14 MAGNITUDE OF LIQUID JUNCTION POTENTIAL

In cell B (p. 649), if there were no migration of ions across the liquid junction, *i.e.*, the cell would operate as an electrolyte concentration cell without transference, then the overall change would be simply the sum of the electrode reactions, *viz.*,

$$Cl^-(a_1) \to Cl^-(a_2)$$

The potential of this concentration cell without transference is given by

$$E_{\text{wot}} = -\frac{RT}{F} \ln \frac{(a_\pm)_2}{(a_\pm)_1} = \frac{RT}{F} \ln \frac{(a_\pm)_1}{(a_\pm)_2} \qquad \qquad \ldots (15.49)$$

If we subtract Eq. (15.49) from Eq. (15.47), we get the magnitude of liquid junction potential, E_j

$$E_j = E_{\text{wt}} - E_{\text{wot}} = 2t_{H^+} \frac{RT}{F} \ln \frac{(a_\pm)_1}{(a_\pm)_2} - \frac{RT}{F} \ln \frac{(a_\pm)_1}{(a_\pm)_2}$$

$$= \left(2t_{H^+} - 1\right) \frac{RT}{F} \ln \frac{(a_\pm)_1}{(a_\pm)_2}$$

$$= \left(2t_{H^+} - t_{H^+} - t_{Cl^-}\right) \frac{RT}{F} \ln \frac{(a_\pm)_1}{(a_\pm)_2} \qquad \left(\because t_{H^+} + t_{Cl^-} = 1\right)$$

$$= \left(t_{H^+} - t_{Cl^-}\right) \frac{RT}{F} \ln \frac{(a_\pm)_1}{(a_\pm)_2} \qquad \qquad \ldots (15.50)$$

Equation (15.50) shows that the value of E_j depends on (*i*) the activities of ions in the two solutions constituting the liquid junction and (*ii*) the difference in the transference numbers of the two ions of the electrolyte. As can be seen from Eq. (15.50), E_j vanishes if $t_+ = t_-$. It is precisely due to this fact that electrolytes like potassium chloride etc., with almost identical values of the transference numbers are used in the preparation of salt bridge. If $t_+ > t_-$, *i.e.*, cation is faster moving ion, E_j is positive and it adds to the cell potential. If $t_+ < t_-$ (anion is faster moving ion), E_j is negative; it opposes the emf of the cell. The relation (15.50) is correct only if the electrolytes are binary, *i.e.*, they produce only two ions in the solution.

On dividing Eq. (15.47) by Eq. (15.49) we obtain

$$\frac{E_{\text{wt}}}{E_{\text{wot}}} = 2t_{H^+}$$

or,

$$E_{\text{wt}} = 2t_{H^+} E_{\text{wot}} \qquad \qquad (15.51)$$

Hence by measuring the emf of the cells with and without transference one can calculate the transference number of the ions of the electrolytes. Similar considerations would apply to cells with transference where the electrodes are reversible to the cation of the electrolyte.

Problem 15.15: The emf of cell with transference

$$Ag \mid AgCl \mid HCl \; (a_\pm = 0.01751) \; \vdots \; HCl \; (a_\pm = 0.009048) \mid AgCl \mid Ag$$

at 298 K is 0.02802 V. The corresponding cell without transference has an emf of 0.01696 V. Calculate the transference number of hydrogen ion and the liquid junction potential.

Solution: Since the electrodes are reversible with respect to the anion,

hence

$$E_{wt} = 2t_+ \frac{RT}{F} \ln \frac{0.01751}{0.009048}$$

and

$$E_{wot} = \frac{RT}{F} \ln \frac{0.01751}{0.009048}$$

Therefore

$$\frac{E_{wt}}{E_{wot}} = 2t_{H^+}$$

or

$$t_{H^+} = \frac{0.02802}{2 \times 0.01696} = 0.82$$

Also

$$E_j = \left(2t_{H^+} - 1\right) \frac{RT}{F} \ln \frac{0.01751}{0.009048}$$

$$= (1.64 - 1)(0.0591) \log \frac{17510}{9048}$$

$$= 0.011 \text{ V}$$

Problem 15.16: A concentration cell having two electrodes of a metal X, one dipping into an $M/2$ solution of one of its salts and the other into an $M/20$ solution of the same salt, has an emf of 0.028 V at 298 K; Assuming that the mean activity coefficients of ions are unity and there is no liquid junction potential, calculate the valency of X.

Solution: The emf of the concentration cell assuming that there is no liquid junction potential is given by

$$E = \frac{RT}{nF} \ln \frac{a_2}{a_1}; \; a_2 > a_1$$

where a_2 and a_1 are the mean activities and n is the valency of the metal. If the activity coefficients are unity then activities may be replaced by molarities and we have

$$E = \frac{RT}{nF} \ln \frac{(1/2)}{(1/20)}$$

At 298 K

$$0.028 = \frac{0.0591}{n} \log \frac{20}{2}$$

$$n = \frac{0.0591}{0.028} \cong 2$$

15.15 APPLICATIONS OF EMF MEASUREMENTS

(i) Determination of Standard Electrode Potential, E^0

The method of evaluating the standard electrode potential of an electrode may be illustrated by taking a specific case of silver-silver chloride electrode. The half electrode is combined with a hydrogen electrode to yield a cell

$$Pt \mid H_2 \, (1 \, atm) \mid HCl \, (m) \mid AgCl \mid Ag$$

The electrode reactions of this cell are

Left electrode:
$$\frac{1}{2} H_2 \, (1 \, atm) \rightleftharpoons H^+ \left(a_{H^+} \right) + e^-$$

$$E_L = -\frac{RT}{F} \ln \frac{1}{a_{H^+}}$$

Right electrode:
$$AgCl + e^- \rightleftharpoons Ag + Cl^- \left(a_{Cl^-} \right)$$

$$E_R = E^0_{Cl^- \mid AgCl \mid Ag} - \frac{RT}{F} \ln a_{Cl^-}$$

Overall cell reaction:
$$AgCl + \frac{1}{2} H_2 \, (1 \, atm) \rightleftharpoons Ag + H^+ \left(a_{H^+} \right) + Cl^- \left(a_{Cl^-} \right).$$

The emf of the cell is

$$E = E_R - E_L = E^0_{Cl^- \mid AgCl \mid Ag} - \frac{RT}{F} \ln a_{H^+} a_{Cl^-} \qquad ...(15.52)$$

In terms of $a_\pm$, the mean activity of hydrochloric acid, Eq. (15.52) can be written as

$$E = E^0_{Cl^- \mid AgCl \mid Ag} - \frac{2RT}{F} \ln a_\pm \qquad \left(\because a_{H^+} a_{Cl^-} = a_\pm^2 \right)$$

Since $\qquad a_\pm = m \gamma_\pm$

Therefore, the above equation becomes

$$E = E^0_{Cl^- \mid AgCl \mid Ag} - \frac{2RT}{F} \ln m - \frac{2RT}{F} \ln \gamma_\pm$$

$$E + \frac{2RT}{F} \ln m = E^0_{Cl^- \mid AgCl \mid Ag} - \frac{2RT}{F} \ln \gamma_\pm$$

At 298 K

$$E + 0.118 \log m = E^0_{Cl^-|AgCl|Ag} - 0.118 \log \gamma_\pm \qquad \qquad ...(15.53)$$

From Debye-Hückel limiting law, $\log \gamma_\pm = -0.509(m)^{1/2}$ for a 1 : 1 electrolyte and therefore Eq. (15.53) becomes

$$E + 0.118 \log m = E^0_{Cl^-|AgCl|Ag} + 0.059 \, (m)^{1/2} \qquad \qquad ...(15.54)$$

By measuring emf of the cell at different molalities of hydrochloric acid, the quantity on the left is calculated and is then plotted as a function of $\sqrt{m}$ and extrapolated to $m = 0$. The intercept on the y-axis gives the value of the standard electrode potential of silver-silver chloride electrode (Fig. 15.6).

(ii) Determination of Activities and Activity Coefficients from Emf Measurements

Measurement of cell emf is a powerful technique in the evaluation of activities and activity coefficients. E^0 value for the cell is first accurately obtained by extrapolation as was done in the previous section. The mean activity $(a_\pm)$ or the mean activity coefficient $(\gamma_\pm)$ at any other concentration of the electrolyte can then be calculated by measuring the emf of the cell at that concentration.

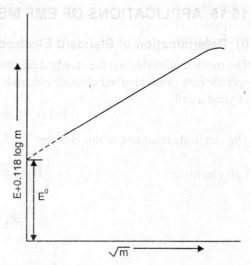

Fig. 15.6 Determination of E^0 by extrapolation

(iii) Determination of Equilibrium Constant from Standard Electrode Potentials

The relation between the standard free energy change and the equilibrium constant of a reaction is given by

$$\Delta G^0 = -RT \ln K$$

But the standard free energy change is related to the standard electrode potential by the expression

$$\Delta G^0 = -nE^0F$$

Hence

$$E^0 = \frac{RT}{nF} \ln K$$

At 298 K

$$E^0 = \frac{0.0591}{n} \log K$$

Therefore measurement of E^0 enables the determination of the equilibrium constant for the electrode reaction.

(iv) Determination of Solubility Products

In case of a sparingly soluble salt such as AgI, its saturated solution in water is so dilute that it is completely ionized as

$$AgI \, (s) \rightleftharpoons Ag^+ + I^-$$

The solubility product constant K_{sp} is equal to the product of the activities of two ions and is written as

$$K_{sp} = a_{Ag^+} a_{I^-}$$

When the solution is dilute the activity coefficients of the ions are unity and the activities may be replaced by the concentrations. The concentration of the ions can be estimated by measuring the concentration of one of the ions by a reversible electrode. A cell is set up whose overall reaction corresponds to reaction (C) and its potential is measured by combining it with a reference electrode. Inspection of reaction (C) reveals that the cell should be a combination of a Ag | AgI electrode with a silver electrode

$$Ag \,|\, Ag^+ \,||\, I^-(aq) \,|\, AgI(s) \,|\, Ag$$

The electrode reactions are:

At left electrode: $\qquad Ag \rightleftharpoons Ag^+ + e^-; \; E_L^0 = 0.799 \text{ V}$

At right electrode: $\quad AgI + e^- \rightleftharpoons Ag + I^-; \; E_R^0 = -0.152 \text{ V}$

The overall reaction: $\quad AgI \rightleftharpoons Ag^+ + I^-; \; \left(E_R^0 - E_L^0\right) = -0.951 \text{ V}$

But we know that

$$\Delta G^0 = -nE^0 F = -RT \ln K_{sp}$$

or $\qquad\qquad E^0 = \dfrac{RT}{nF} \ln K_{sp} = \dfrac{2.303 \, RT}{nF} \log K_{sp}$

$$= \dfrac{0.0591}{n} \log K_{sp} \qquad\qquad ...(15.55)$$

Since the number of electrons in the present case is one and substituting the value of E^0 in Eq. (15.55), we get

$$\log K_{sp} = \dfrac{E^0}{0.0591} = \dfrac{-0.951}{0.0591} = -16.71$$

or $\qquad\qquad K_{sp} = 1.95 \times 10^{-17}$

Problem 15.17: The solubility of AgBr at 298 K is 1.19×10^{-6} mol dm^{-3}. What is the standard emf of the cell Ag | Ag$^+(a)$ || Br$^-(a_1)$ | AgBr | Ag?

Solution: Solubility of AgBr = 1.19×10^{-6} mol dm^{-3}. Hence the solubility product K_{sp} of the salt is

$$K_{sp} = C_{Ag^+} C_{Br^-} = \left(1.19 \times 10^{-6}\right)^2 = 1.416 \times 10^{-12}$$

Now $\qquad E^0 = +0.0591 \log K_{sp} = 0.0591 \log \left(1.416 \times 10^{-12}\right) = -0.07 \text{ V}$

Problem 15.18: The standard electrode potential of Pb | Pb^{2+} is -0.126 V while the standard electrode potential of the cell

$$\text{Pt} \mid \text{H}_2 \mid \text{H}_2\text{SO}_4 \, (a=1) \mid \text{PbSO}_4 \mid \text{Pb}$$

is -0.351 V. Calculate the solubility product of PbSO_4 at 298 K.

Solution: Given that

$$\text{PbSO}_4 + 2e^- \rightleftharpoons \text{Pb} + \text{SO}_4^{2-}; \qquad E^0 = -0.351 \text{ V}$$

and

$$\text{Pb} \rightleftharpoons \text{Pb}^{2+} + 2e^-; \qquad E^0 = -0.126 \text{ V}$$

Adding

$$\text{PbSO}_4 \rightleftharpoons \text{Pb}^{2+} + \text{SO}_4^{2-}; \qquad E^0 = -0.225 \text{ V}$$

Now

$$\log K_{sp} = \frac{2E^0 F}{RT} = \frac{-2 \times 0.225}{0.0591}$$

or

$$K_{sp} = 2.455 \times 10^{-3}$$

Determination of pH

The pH of a solution can be conveniently measured from emf measurements. In principle, the activity of hydrogen ions or the concentration of hydrogen ions in a solution can be determined by setting a cell in which one of the electrodes is reversible to hydrogen ions. The electrode is dipped in the solution of unknown pH. The other electrode is a reference electrode such as an SHE or an SCE or any other reference electrode. The liquid junction potential can be eliminated either by using a salt bridge or by dipping the reference electrode directly into the solution.

The following electrodes are commonly used in the measurement of pH values of solutions.

(a) **Hydrogen Electrode:** A cell of the type

$$\text{Pt} \mid \text{H}_2 \, (1 \text{ atm}) \mid \text{H}^+ \left(a_{\text{H}^+}\right) \mid\mid \text{H}^+ (a=1) \mid \text{H}_2 \, (1 \text{ atm}) \mid \text{Pt}$$

is set up. The net cell reaction is

$$\text{H}^+ (a=1) \rightleftharpoons \text{H}^+ \left(a_{\text{H}^+}\right)$$

and the emf of the cell is given as

$$E = -\frac{RT}{F} \ln a_{\text{H}^+}$$

By definition $\text{pH} = -\log_{10} a_{\text{H}^+}$, hence the above equation becomes

$$E = \left(\frac{2.303 \, RT}{F}\right) \text{pH}$$

$$E = 0.0591 \, \text{pH} \qquad\qquad ...(15.56)$$

The emf of the cell is linearly dependent on the pH value of the solution.

When the SHE is replaced by reference calomel electrodes then the cell would be

$$\text{Pt} \mid \text{H}_2 \, (1 \text{ atm}) \mid \text{H}^+ \left(a_{\text{H}^+}\right) \mid\mid \text{Cl}^- \left(a_{\text{Cl}^-}\right) \mid \text{Hg}_2\text{Cl}_2 \mid \text{Hg}$$

The reaction at the left electrode is

$$\frac{1}{2}\text{H}_2 \, (P=1 \text{ atm}) \rightleftharpoons \text{H}^+ \left(a_{\text{H}^+}\right) + e^-$$

and its potential is given by

$$E_L = \frac{RT}{F} \ln a_{H^+}$$

The emf of the cell is given by

$$E = E_R - E_L$$

$$= E_{ref} - E_L$$

$$= E_{ref} - 0.0591 \log a_{H^+}$$

$$= E_{ref} + 0.0591 \, pH$$

or

$$pH = \frac{E - E_{ref}}{0.0591} \qquad \qquad ...(15.57)$$

Hence by measuring the emf of the cell obtained by combining the hydrogen electrode with a reference electrode of known potential, the pH of the solution can be evaluated.

The principal difficulties in using a hydrogen electrode is that the platinum is easily poisoned by the adsorption of impurities from the solution. This adsorption creates difficulties in establishing the equilibrium between hydrogen and hydrogen ions at the electrode surface, hence the electrode does not behave reversibly. Also, presence of oxidants in the solution hinders the establishment of the equilibrium and thus alters the potential of the electrode.

Problem 15.19: The emf of a cell measured by means of a hydrogen electrode against a saturated calomel electrode at 298 K is 0.4188 V. If the pressure of the hydrogen gas was maintained at 1 atm, calculate (*i*) the pH of the unknown solution and (*ii*) the hydrogen ion activity in the solution.

Solution: (*i*) The pH of the solution at 298 K is given by

$$pH = \frac{E - 0.2415}{0.0591}$$

$$= \frac{0.4188 - 0.2415}{0.0591} = 3.0$$

(*ii*)

$$-\log a_{H^+} = 3.0$$

$$a_{H^+} = 10^{-3} \, mol \, dm^{-3}$$

(*b*) **Quinhydrone Electrode:** It is another commonly employed electrode for pH measurements Quinhydrone is a 1 : 1 molecular compound of quinone (Q) and hydroquinone (H$_2$Q).

It is sparingly soluble in acid solution and decomposes to yield quinone and hydroquinone. To measure the pH of an unknown solution it is saturated with quinhydrone and an inert electrode of gold or platinum is dipped into the solution. The electrode is then combined with a reference electrode such as an SCE to form the cell

Pt I Solution of unknown pH ‖ SCE

(saturated with quinhydrone)

The reaction at the left electrode

$$H_2Q \rightleftharpoons 2H^+ + Q + 2e^-$$

and its potential is given by

$$E_L = E_L^0 - \frac{RT}{2F} \ln \frac{a_{H_2Q}}{a_Q} + \frac{RT}{F} \ln a_{H^+} \qquad \text{...(15.58)}$$

where E_L^{0} of the quinhydrone electrode is +0.699 V at 298 K. The electrode potential depends on the activities of Q, H_2Q and hydrogen ions. Since the concentration of Q and H_2Q are equal, $a_{H_2Q} \, / \, a_Q$ may approximately be assumed to be unity and under these conditions Eq. (15.58) becomes

$$E_L = E_L^0 + \frac{RT}{F} \ln a_{H^+} = E_L^0 - 0.0591 \, \text{pH} \qquad \text{...(15.59)}$$

Equation (15.59) shows that the electrode potential depends only on the activity of H^+ ions or pH of the solution. The cell emf is given by

$$E = E_{ref} - E_L = E_{ref} - E_L^0 + 0.0591 \, \text{pH}$$

$$E = 0.2415 - 0.699 + 0.0591 \, \text{pH}$$

$$E = -0.4575 + 0.0591 \, \text{pH}$$

$$\text{pH} = \frac{E + 0.4575}{0.0591} \qquad \text{...(15.60)}$$

If the pH of the solution is greater than seven, the electrode acts as the cathode and the cell should be represented as

SCE ‖ Unknown solution I Pt

(saturated with quinhydrone)

The emf of the cell is given by

$$E = E_R^0 - 0.0591 \, \text{pH} - E_{ref}$$

$$= 0.699 - 0.0591 \, \text{pH} - 0.2415$$

$$= 0.4575 - 0.0591 \, \text{pH}$$

or

$$\text{pH} = \frac{0.4575 - E}{0.0591} \qquad \text{...(15.61)}$$

The electrode is not satisfactory for solutions having pH values more than 8. Under these conditions hydroquinone is readily oxidised and also undergoes partial ionization.

(c) **Glass Electrode:** It is the universally employed electrode for pH measurement. It was introduced by F. Fritz and K. Klemensiewicz who showed that when two solutions of unknown pH values are separated by a glass membrane made of low melting and high conductivity glass, an exchange of hydrogen ions between the solutions and glass takes place. Due to this exchange a potential develops across the membrane. The magnitude of this potential depends on the difference in the pH values of the two solutions. If the pH of one of the solutions is maintained constant and the other is varied the potential of the electrode obeys the equation

$$E_G = E_G^0 - \frac{RT}{F} \ln a_{H^+}$$

At 298 K it becomes

$$E_G = E_G^0 + 0.0591 \text{ pH} \qquad \qquad ...(15.62)$$

where E_G^0 is a constant characteristic of each glass electrode and its value depends on the particular arrangement employed. Equation (15.62) suggests that the glass electrode can be conveniently employed for the determination of pH values of solutions.

The assembly of glass electrode (Fig. 15.7) consists of a thin glass bulb filled with 0.1 N HCl and a silver wire coated with silver chloride is immersed in it. The bulb is then placed in the solution of unknown pH and is combined with a reference electrode yielding the cell

$$\text{Ag | AgCl | 0.1 N HCl | Glass | Solution (pH = } x) \text{ || SCE}$$

The emf of the cell at 298 K is given as

$$E = E_R - E_L = E_{ref} - E_G^0 - 0.0591 \text{ pH} \qquad \qquad ...(15.63)$$

Thus the cell emf is a linear function of the pH of the solution in which the glass electrode is dipped.

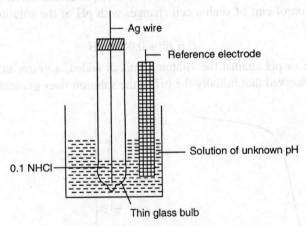

Fig. 15.7 The glass electrode

To measure the pH of an unknown solution, E_G^0 is first measured by dipping the glass electrode in a series of solutions of known pH values. Once E_G^0 for a particular arrangement is determined the electrode is then placed in the solution of unknown pH, the emf of the cell is measured and using Eq. (15.63) its pH can be calculated.

For the measurement of emf of the glass electrode ordinary potentiometers cannot be used because of high resistance of glass. However, vacuum tube voltmeter or quadrant electrometer which requires very little currents for their operations is used.

Glass electrode is the most convenient and nearest approach to a universal pH electrode. It is not affected by oxidising or reducing agents or by impurities in the solution. In strongly alkaline solution, ordinary glass is attacked by alkali and electrode made of special quality glass should be used.

15.16 POTENTIOMETRIC TITRATIONS

The potential of an electrode depends on the concentration of the ions to which it is reversible. The changes in the concentration of the ions in a titration can be followed through the measurement of the electrode potential. Such titrations where the measurements of electrode potentials are made with the addition of a titrant are called potentiometric titrations. It is seen that the change in the emf is maximum at the equivalence point and hence it can be identified. The potentiometric titrations are generally of three types: (*i*) acid-base neutralisation titrations; (*ii*) oxidation-reduction (redox) titrations; and (*iii*) precipitation titrations.

Potentiometric titrations have a number of advantages over the ordinary titrations using indicators. Indicators cannot be used in coloured solutions while potentiometric titrations can be successfully carried out in such cases. In the ordinary acid-base titration, *a priori* information concerning the relative strengths of acids and bases is required before selecting the indicators. But, no such information is needed in potentiometric titrations.

Acid–Base Neutralization Titrations

In the acid-base titration (HCl versus NaOH), emf of the solution is measured by immersing in the solution an electrode reversible to the hydrogen ions. This electrode is then coupled with a suitable reference electrode to form a cell. When alkali is added, pH of the solution changes and as shown previously the variation of emf of such a cell changes with pH of the solution in accordance with the equation

$$E = E^0 + 0.0591 \text{ pH}$$

If we now plot E or pH against the volume of alkali added, a graph as shown in Fig. 15.8(*a*) is obtained. It will be observed that initially the pH of the solution rises gradually and then more rapidly

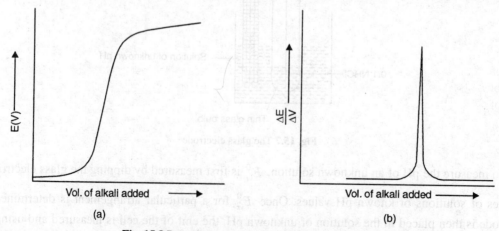

Fig. 15.8 Potentiometric titration of an acid with a base

at the equivalence point. After the equivalence point, again, pH of the solution increases slightly on the addition of excess alkali. However, if we plot the slope of the curve ($\Delta E/\Delta V$) instead of emf of the cell versus the volume of alkali added, a maximum would be observed at the end point (Fig. 15.8 (b)).

Oxidation–Reduction Titrations

The oxidation-reduction titrations are carried out potentiometrically in the same manner as the acid-base neutralization titrations. However, the electrode reversible to hydrogen ions is replaced by an inert metal such as a platinum wire which is immersed in a solution containing both the oxidised and the reduced form of the same substance. This electrode acts as an oxidation-reduction electrode and is coupled with a suitable reference electrode.

Suppose that a platinum electrode is dipped in a solution containing both Fe^{3+} and Fe^{2+} ions. The electrode reaction is

$$Fe^{3+} + e^- \rightleftharpoons Fe^{2+}$$

The potential of the electrode is given by

$$E = E^0_{Fe^{3+}|Fe^{2+}} - \frac{RT}{F} \ln \frac{\left[Fe^{2+}\right]}{\left[Fe^{3+}\right]}$$

$$= E^0_{Fe^{3+}|Fe^{2+}} + 0.0591 \log \frac{\left[Fe^{3+}\right]}{\left[Fe^{2+}\right]} \qquad ...(15.64)$$

As the ratio $[Fe^{3+}]/[Fe^{2+}]$ changes, the emf of the electrode changes till an equilibrium is reached.

Let us now consider a reaction

$$Fe^{2+} + Ce^{4+} \rightarrow Fe^{3+} + Ce^{3+}$$

where ceric ions are added to ferrous ions to carry out the titration of Fe^{2+} ions. The progress of the reaction is observed by measuring the emf of the cell. The cell can be discussed in terms of two half reactions

$$Fe^{3+} + e^- \rightleftharpoons Fe^{2+} ; E^0_{Fe^{3+}|Fe^{2+}} = 0.77 \text{ V}$$

$$Ce^{4+} + e^- \rightleftharpoons Ce^{3+} ; E^0_{Ce^{4+}|Ce^{3+}} = 1.61 \text{ V}$$

Before the addition of Ce^{4+} ions, the solution contains mostly Fe^{2+} ions and only a small amount of Fe^{3+} ions. The potential of the electrode is controlled by the Fe^{3+}/Fe^{2+} couple. However, when a small amount of Ce^{4+} ions is added to the solution, only a small amount of Fe^{2+} ions is oxidised to Fe^{3+} ions.

If the $\dfrac{\left[Fe^{3+}\right]}{\left[Fe^{2+}\right]} = \dfrac{1}{100}$, the electrode potential at 298 K is given by

$$E = E^0_{Fe^{3+}|Fe^{2+}} + 0.0591 \log \frac{1}{100}$$

$$= E^0_{Fe^{3+}|Fe^{2+}} - 0.1182$$

Further addition of Ce^{4+} ions changes the ratio $\dfrac{[Fe^{3+}]}{[Fe^{2+}]}$ and hence the electrode potential. When enough

of Ce^{4+} ions have been added so that these dominate the solution, the potential of the electrode is now controlled mainly by Ce^{4+}/Ce^{3+} couple. Since the potential of the electrode can take only one value and, therefore, the potential of these systems must be equal and at any stage of the titration up to the equivalence point we may write

$$E = E^0_{Fe^{3+}|Fe^{2+}} + \frac{RT}{F} \ln \frac{[Fe^{3+}]}{[Fe^{2+}]}$$

$$= E^0_{Ce^{4+}|Ce^{3+}} + \frac{RT}{F} \ln \frac{[Ce^{4+}]}{[Ce^{3+}]}$$

At the equivalence point we have $[Fe^{2+}] = [Ce^{4+}]$ and $[Fe^{3+}] = [Ce^{3+}]$ and the electrode potential is given by

$$E_{eq} = E^0_{Fe^{3+}|Fe^{2+}} + \frac{RT}{F} \ln \frac{[Fe^{3+}]}{[Fe^{2+}]}$$

$$= E^0_{Ce^{4+}|Ce^{3+}} + \frac{RT}{F} \ln \frac{[Ce^{4+}]}{[Ce^{3+}]}$$

where E_{eq} is the electrode potential at the equivalence point. Adding these equations and substituting the above equalities, we get

$$2 E_{eq} = E^0_{Fe^{3+}|Fe^{2+}} + E^0_{Ce^{4+}|Ce^{3+}} + \frac{RT}{F} \ln(1)$$

$$E_{eq} = \frac{E^0_{Fe^{3+}|Fe^{2+}} + E^0_{Ce^{4+}|Ce^{3+}}}{2} \qquad \qquad ...(15.65)$$

Beyond the equivalence point $[Fe^{2+}] \cong 0$, and the potential of the electrode is now controlled only by the $Ce^{4+}|Ce^{3+}$ couple. At the equivalence point, the potential of the electrode changes very rapidly from the region of $E^0_{Fe^{3+}|Fe^{2+}}$ to the region of $E^0_{Ce^{4+}|Ce^{3+}}$.

Redox indicators: *A redox indicator is a compound which can be reversibly oxidised or reduced and the two respective forms possess different colours.* With the help of these indicators, redox titrations can be carried out in a manner similar to the acid-base titrations using indicators. Let us denote the oxidised and the reduced forms of an indicator as Ox and Red and write the redox reaction as

$$Ox + ne^- \rightleftharpoons Red$$

and the potential of the redox system is given by the equation

$$E = E^0_{Ox|Red} + \frac{RT}{nF} \ln \frac{a_{Ox}}{a_{Red}}$$

Replacing the activities by the concentration terms, we get

$$E = E^0_{Ox|Red} + \frac{RT}{nF} \ln \frac{[Ox]}{[Red]} \qquad ...(15.66)$$

where E^0 is the standard electrode potential of the redox indicator.

If a few drops of the indicator are added to a redox system, the concentration of the oxidised and the reduced forms of the indicator will depend on the potential of the system. The colour of the solution will depend on the relative amounts of the oxidised and the reduced forms of the indicator. When the potential of the system changes it affects the ratio $\frac{[Ox]}{[Red]}$. If we assume that $\frac{[Ox]}{[Red]} = \frac{1}{10}$, *i.e.*, the colour is mainly due to the reduced form, then at 298 K

$$E = E^0_{Ox|Red} - \frac{0.0591}{n}$$

However, if $\frac{[Ox]}{[Red]} = \frac{10}{1}$, then the colour would be mainly due to the oxidised form and

$$E = E^0_{Ox|Red} + \frac{0.0591}{n}$$

Consequently, the potential range in which the indicator changes its colour is

$$E = E^0_{Ox|Red} \pm \frac{0.0591}{n} \qquad ...(15.67)$$

We have seen in the redox titrations that there are sharp changes in the potential of the system around the equivalence point. Hence a satisfactory redox indicator is one where its colour change interval lies within the limit of the sharp change of potential. In the titration of Fe^{2+} ions by $Cr_2O_7^{2-}$ ions in acid solution using diphenyl amine ($E^0 = 0.76$ V) as the redox indicator, the potential range in which the indicator changes its colour is approximately 0.73 V – 0.79 V. Below 0.73 V, the colour is due to the reduced form of diphenylamine which is colourless while above 0.79 V the colour will be due to the oxidised form which is blue-violet. However, the potential of the system at the equivalence point is

$1/7 \left[E^0_{Fe^{3+}|Fe^{2+}} + 6 E^0_{Cr_2O_7^{2-}|Cr^{3+}} \right]$, *i.e.*, 1.25 V and the sharp change of potential around the equivalence point extends from approximately 0.94 V to 1.30 V. But the colour change interval of diphenylamine does not lie within this range and hence may be regarded as unsatisfactory. However, addition of phosphoric acid or fluoride ions to the solution causes the formation of stable complexes of the type $[Fe(PO_4)_2]^{3-}$ or $[FeF_6]^{3-}$; thus lowering the concentration of ferric ions and consequently the potential at which the colour change begins. The colour change interval of potential is now within the range in which sharp changes in the potential of the system $Fe^{3+}|Fe^{2+}$ takes place.

Precipitation Titrations

In precipitation titration, an ion from the solution is precipitated out by the addition of a titrant. The changes in the concentration of the ion during the course of the titration can be followed by measuring the potential of an electrode reversible to the ion. In the titration of silver nitrate solution by sodium chloride, a silver wire is dipped in silver nitrate solution. When sodium chloride solution is added, AgCl is formed and we have a silver-silver chloride electrode. It is combined with a reference electrode like SCE and the emf of the cell

$$Ag \mid AgCl \mid Cl^- \parallel SCE$$

is given by

$$E = E_{SCE} - E^0_{Cl^- \mid AgCl \mid Ag} - \frac{RT}{F} \ln a_{Cl^-}$$

But the activity of chloride ions is controlled by the solubility product of silver chloride through the relation

$$K_{sp} = a_{Ag^+} a_{Cl^-}$$

Hence the cell emf can be written as

$$E = E_{SCE} - E^0_{Cl^- \mid AgCl \mid Ag} - \frac{RT}{F} \ln K_{sp} + \frac{RT}{F} \ln a_{Ag^+}$$

At 298 K

$$E = \text{Const} + 0.0591 \log a_{Ag^+} \qquad \qquad ...(15.68)$$

Thus, as the activity of silver ions decreases the potential of the cell decreases. The decrease is, however, small in the initial stages of the titration. At the equivalence point silver ion concentration is very small due to slight solubility of silver chloride, the potential therefore changes rapidly. Excess of chloride ions after the equivalence point do not affect significantly the concentration of silver ions and hence the potential of the electrode changes rather slowly.

EXERCISES

1. Explain, giving reasons, the following:
    (i) Maximum electrical work is obtained from a cell when it operates reversibly.
    (ii) The standard electrode potential of hydrogen electrode is taken as zero at all temperatures.
    (iii) Use of KCl or NH_4NO_3 in agar bridge minimises the liquid junction potential.
    (iv) Quinhydrone electrode is not suitable for pH measurements in strongly alkaline solutions.
    (v) Copper is not able to displace H^+ ions from acid solutions.

2. Distinguish the following:
    (i) A reversible cell from an irreversible cell.
    (ii) Standard electrode potential from the electrode potential.
    (iii) An electrode concentration cell from an electrolyte concentration cell.
    (iv) A cell with transport from a cell without transport.
    (v) A galvanic cell from an electrolyte cell.

3. Write the half cell reactions and the overall cell reactions for the following cells:
    (i) $Pt \mid Hg \mid Hg_2Cl_2 \mid HCl \, (a = 1) \mid H_2 \, (p = 1 \text{ atm}) \mid Pt$
    (ii) $Pb \mid PbSO_4 \mid H_2SO_4 \, (a = 1) \mid PbSO_4 \mid PbO_2 \mid Pt$
    (iii) $Pt \mid H_2 \, (p = 1 \text{ atm}) \mid HCl \, (a = 1) \mid AgCl \mid Ag$
    (iv) $Zn \mid ZnO_2^{2-} \, (a = 1), \, OH^- \, (a = 1) \mid HgO \mid Hg$

4. From the following cell reactions, represent the cells, calculate the standard emf (E^0) of the cell in each case and indicate whether the cell so represented would operate spontaneously or non-spontaneously.

665

(i) $2Li + Mn^{2+} (a = 1) \rightarrow 2Li^+ (a = 1) + Mn$,

$E^0_{Li^+|Li} = -3.05$ V and $E^0_{Mn^{2+}|Mn} = -1.03$ V

(ii) $Pb + H_2SO_4 (a = 1) + 2AgCl \rightarrow PbSO_4 + 2HCl (a = 1) + 2Ag$,

$E^0_{SO_4^{2-}|PbSO_4|Pb} = -0.36$ V and $E^0_{Cl^-|AgCl|Ag} = 0.222$ V

(iii) $Cl_2 (p = 1 \text{ atm}) + 2F^- (a = 1) = F_2 (p = 1 \text{ atm}) + 2Cl^- (a = 1)$,

$E^0_{Cl^-|Cl_2|Pt} = +1.36$ V and $E^0_{F^-|F_2|Pt} = 2.87$ V

(iv) $Sn + Cu^{2+} (a = 1) \rightarrow Sn^{2+} (a = 1) + Cu$,

$E^0_{Cu^{2+}|Cu} = 0.34$ V and $E^0_{Sn^{2+}|Sn} = -0.15$ V

(v) $2Al + 3Br_2 (p = 1 \text{ atm}) \rightarrow 2Al^{3+} (a = 1) + 6Br^- (a = 1)$

$E^0_{Al^{3+}|Al} = -1.67$ V and $E^0_{Br^-|Br_2|Pt} = 1.09$ V

Ans. (i) $Li \mid Li^+ (a = 1) \parallel Mn^{2+} (a = 1) \mid Mn$, $E^0 = 2.02$ V, spontaneous.
(ii) $Pb \mid PbSO_4 \mid H_2SO_4 (a = 1) \parallel HCl (a = 1) \mid AgCl \mid Ag$,
$E^0 = 0.58$ V, spontaneous.
(iii) $Pt \mid F_2 (p = 1 \text{ atm}) \mid F^-(a = 1) \parallel Cl^- (a = 1) \mid Cl_2 (p = 1 \text{ atm}) \mid Pt$,
$E^0 = -1.51$ V, non-spontaneous.
(iv) $Sn \mid Sn^{2+} (a = 1) \parallel Cu^{2+} (a = 1) \mid Cu$, $E^0 = 0.48$ V, spontaneous.
(v) $Al \mid Al^{3+} (a = 1) \parallel Br^- (a = 1) \mid Br_2 (p = 1 \text{ atm}) \mid Pt$
$E^0 = 2.76$ V, spontaneous.

5. For the reaction

$$Fe^{2+}(a = 1) + \frac{1}{2}I_2 \longrightarrow Fe^{3+}(a = 1) + I^-(a = 1)$$

(i) Write down the cell, (ii) calculate its standard emf, and (iii) indicate whether the cell reaction as represented by the above equation is spontaneous or not.

$$E^0_{Fe^{3+}, Fe^{2+}|Pt} = 0.771 \text{ V and } E^0_{I^-|I_2|Pt} = 0.535 \text{ V}$$

Ans. (i) The cell is $Pt \mid Fe^{3+} (a = 1), Fe^{2+} (a = 1) \parallel I^- (a = 1) \mid I_2 \mid Pt$.
(ii) $E^0 = -.236$ V, (iii) non-spontaneous.

6. Will Fe reduce Fe^{3+} ions to Fe^{2+} ions? Given $E^0_{Fe^{2+}|Fe} = -0.441$ V and $E^0_{Fe^{3+}, Fe^{2+}|Pt} = 0.771$ V.

Ans. Yes, because the standard emf of the reaction $Fe + 2Fe^{3+} \rightarrow 3Fe^{2+}$ is 1.212 V.

7. For the cell, $Sn \mid SnCl_2 (0.5 \text{ M}) \mid AgCl \mid Ag$, $E^0 = 0.363$ V at 298 K. Calculate E.

Ans. 0.434 V.

8. For the cell $Cu \mid CuCl_2 (0.5 \text{ M}) \mid Cl_2 (1.5 \text{ atm}) \mid Pt$, $E^0_{Cu^{2+}|Cu} = 0.377$ V and $E^0_{Pt|Cl_2|Cl^-} = 1.3595$ V at 298 K.

Calculate (i) E^0, ΔG^0 and ΔG for the cell reaction, (ii) the equilibrium constant (K) for the reaction, (iii) if the operation of the above cell is spontaneous, (iv) of the two oxidising agents Cu^{2+} ions and Cl_2 which is a stronger oxidising agent and which is a stronger reducing agent, Cu or Cl^- ions?

Ans. (i) $E^0 = 1.0225$ V, $E = 1.0368$ V; $\Delta G^0 = -197.3$ kJ, $\Delta G = -200.1$ kJ; (ii) $K = 3.715 \times 10^{34}$,
(iii) Yes, spontaneous; (iv) Cl_2 is a stronger oxidising agent; Cu is a stronger reducing agent.

9. For the cell, $Zn \mid ZnCl_2 (a = 0.5) \mid AgCl \mid Ag$
(a) Write the cell reaction at 298 K; (b) Calculate E^0, E, ΔG, ΔG^0 and the equilibrium constant K for the

cell reaction as written (a); (c) What difference would it make in the values in (b) if the reaction is written as

$$\frac{1}{2}Zn + AgCl = \frac{1}{2}ZnCl_2 + Ag, \quad E^0_{Zn^{2+}|Zn} = -0.763 \text{ V}, E^0_{Cl^-|AgCl|Ag} = 0.222 \text{ V}$$

Ans. (a) $Zn + 2AgCl = ZnCl_2 + 2Ag$; (b) $E^0 = 0.985$ V, $E = 0.994$ V, $\Delta G^0 = -109.1$ kJ; $\Delta G = -191.4$ kJ, $K = 2.089 \times 10^{23}$; (c) E^0 and E remain unchanged; ΔG and ΔG^0 are halved and $K = 4.571 \times 10^{16}$.

10. The standard electrode potentials of the Zn and Cu electrodes at 298 K are given as

$$Zn^{2+} | 2e^- \rightarrow Zn; \qquad E^0 = -0.763 \text{ V}$$
$$Ni^{2+} + 2e^- \rightarrow Ni; \qquad E^0 = -0.25 \text{ V}$$

(a) What will be the electrode polarities when Ni electrode is coupled with a standard hydrogen electrode to form a galvanic cell?

(b) Of the substances Zn, Zn^{2+}, Ni, Ni^{2+} which is the (i) strongest reducing agent, and (ii) the strongest oxidising agent?

(c) Will a noticeable reaction occur when metallic Ni is placed in 1 M solution of Zn^{2+} ions?

(d) Zn^{2+} ions form a complex with OH^- ions $Zn(OH)_4^{2-}$. If OH^- ions are added to the Zn half cell, would its electrode potential as written above increase or decrease? Justify your answer.

(e) If Zn and Ni half cells are coupled together to form a galvanic cell, which electrode would be negative? What would be the cell emf?

Ans. (a) Ni electrode would be negative;
(b) (i) Zn strongest reducing agent;
(ii) Ni^{2+} ions the strongest oxidising agent;
(c) Not appreciable;
(d) The electrode potential would increase;
(e) Zn electrode negative and $E^0_{cell} = 0.513$ V.

11. For the cell $Ag | AgCl | Cl^-(a = 1) | Cl_2 | Pt$, E^0_{cell} at 1000 K is 0.8401 V. If $a_{Ag^+} = 1$ and $p_{Cl_2} = 0.4305$ atm, calculate emf of the cell. Does the emf of the cell depend on the Cl^- ion concentration? Evaluate the equilibrium constant K for the cell reaction.

Ans. $E_{cell} = 0.8293$ V, independent of Cl^- ion concentration; $K = 1.66 \times 10^{14}$.

12. Calculate E^0, ΔG^0 and the equilibrium constant K for the reaction $Cr^{2+} + 2e^- \rightarrow Cr$ at 298 K. Given

$$Cr^{2+} + 3e^- = Cr, \qquad E^0 = 0.50 \text{ V}$$
$$Cr^{3+} + e^- = Cr^{2+}, \qquad E^0 = -0.41 \text{ V}$$

Ans. $E^0 = 0.955$ V; $\Delta G^0 = -184.3$ kJ; $K = 1.202 \times 10^{32}$.

13. The standard electrode potentials for the system $Zn^{2+} | Zn$ and $Cu^{2+} | Cu$ are respectively -0.763 V and 0.337 V. What should be the concentration of Cu^{2+} ions in a solution containing 0.1 M Zn^{2+} ions such that both the metals can be deposited simultaneously? **Ans.** 10^{-38} M.

14. The standard electrode potentials for the system $Cu^{2+} | Cu$ and $Cu^+ | Cu$ at 298 K are 0.337 V and 0.521 V respectively.

(a) Calculate (i) the standard emf for the reaction $Cu^{2+} + e^- \rightarrow Cu^+$, (ii) the standard free energy change for the above reaction, (iii) the equilibrium constant (K) for the above reaction.

(b) Is it easy to oxidise Cu to Cu^{2+} ions or Cu to Cu^+ ions?

(c) If excess of copper is added to 0.2 M Cu^{2+} ions in solution, calculate the concentration of Cu^+ ions.

Ans. (a) (i) 0.153 V; (ii) $\Delta G^0 = -14.765$ kJ; (iii) $K = 2.587$;

(b) Easy to oxidise Cu to Cu^{2+} ions than Cu to Cu^+ ions;

(c) 3.31×10^{-3} mol dm^{-3}.

15. Under what conditions the following formulae are valid?

(i) $E = 0$ for a cell, (ii) $E^0 = 0$ for a cell, (iii) $t_+ = \dfrac{E_{wt}}{2E_{wot}}$, (iv) $\Delta H = -nF\left[E - T\left(\dfrac{dE}{dT}\right)_P\right]$.

Ans. (i) Cell at equilibrium; (ii) Equilibrium constant is unity; (iii) E_{wt} emf of the cell reversible to anion and E_{wot} emf of the same cell without transport; (iv) Reversible cell.

16. The standard reduction potentials for the reactions:

$$Sn^{2+} + 2e^- \rightarrow Sn$$

$$Sn^{4+} + 2e^- \rightarrow Sn^{2+}$$

are -0.136 V and 0.15 V respectively. (a) Calculate (i) E^0 for the reaction $Sn^{4+} + 4e^- \rightarrow Sn$ and (ii) ΔG^0 for the reaction. (b) Which oxidation is easier $Sn \rightarrow Sn^{2+}$ or $Sn \rightarrow Sn^{4+}$.

Ans. (a) (i) 0.006 V; (ii) $\Delta G^0 = -2.702$ kJ; (b) $Sn \rightarrow Sn^{2+}$ is easier than $Sn \rightarrow Sn^{4+}$.

17. The standard free energy change for the reaction

$$H_2(g, 1 \text{ atm}) + \frac{1}{2}O_2(g, 1 \text{ atm}) = H_2O(l)$$

is -237.19 kJ mol^{-1} at 298 K. (a) Write the electrode reactions if the reaction is to occur in a galvanic cell. (b) Calculate the standard electrode potentials for the electrodes (i) Pt $|$ O_2 $|$ OH^- ($a = 1$) and (ii) Pt $|$ O_2 $|$ H^+ ($a = 1$), (iii) Pt $|$ H_2 $|$ OH^- ($a = 1$). Given

$$H_2O \rightleftharpoons H^+ + OH^-, \quad E^0 = -0.8277 \text{ V}.$$

Ans. (a) Anode reaction: $H_2 + 2OH^- = 2H_2O + 2e^-$.

Cathode reaction: $\dfrac{1}{2}O_2 + H_2O + 2e^- = 2OH^-$,

(b) (i) 0.041 V; (ii) 1.229 V; (iii) -0.8277 V.

18. The standard electrode potential for the reaction

$O_2 + 4H^+ + 2e \rightarrow 2H_2O(l)$ is 1.23 V in 0.1 N acid solution.

Calculate the potential of this couple in aqueous solution having pH = 14.0. **Ans.** 0.462 V.

19. The standard hydrogen electrode is described as one where $a_{H^+} = 1$, $P_{H2} = 1$ atm and $E^0 = 0.0$ V.

If the standard electrode be considered as

$$a_{OH^-} = a_{H^+} = 10^{-7},$$

calculate the standard electrode potential of hydrogen electrode under these conditions at 298 K.

Ans. -0.4137 V.

20. The standard electrode potential for the reaction

$$NO_3^- + 4H^+ + 3e^- \longrightarrow NO(g) + 2H_2O(l)$$

at 298 K is 0.96 V. (a) What will be its value at pH = 7.0?

(b) Will NO_3^- ions at pH = 0 be able to oxidise Cl_2 to ClO_4^- if E^0 for the reaction

$$ClO_4^- + 8H^+ + 7e^- \longrightarrow \frac{1}{2}Cl_2 + 4H_2O \text{ at 298 K is 1.38 V.} \qquad \textbf{Ans.} \text{ (a) 0.408 V; (b) No.}$$

21. Given the following reaction scheme in acidic medium (E^0 values in volts at 298 K).

$$MnO_4^- \xrightarrow{0.564} MnO_4^{2-} \xrightarrow{2.26} MnO_2 \xrightarrow{0.95} Mn^{3+} \xrightarrow{1.51} Mn^{2+} \xrightarrow{-1.18} Mn$$

Calculate (i) E^0 for $MnO_4^- \longrightarrow Mn^{2+}$; (ii) Which is the better oxidising agent in acidic media, MnO_4^- or MnO_4^{2-} when the final product in each case is Mn^{2+}?

Ans. (i) 1.51 V; (ii) MnO_4^{2-} is a better oxidising agent.

22. Will O_2 oxidise Au to $Au(CN)_2^-$ in the presence of CN^- and OH^- ions? Give reasons in support of your answer. Given the reactions

$$Au + 2CN^- = Au(CN)_2^- + e^-, \quad E^0 = 0.60 \text{ V}$$
$$O_2 + 2H_2O + 4e^- = 4\,OH^-, \quad E^0 = 0.401 \text{ V}$$

Ans. Yes, CN^- ions form a stable complex $Au(CN)_2^-$

23. For the cell Cd | $CdSO_4$ ($a = 1$) | Hg_2SO_4 | Hg at 318 K, calculate ΔG, ΔS and ΔH. The cell emf is given by $E(V) = 0.6708 - 1.02 \times 10^{-4} (t - 25) - 2.4 \times 10^{-6} (t - 25)^2$, where t is temperature in °C.

Ans. $\Delta G = -128.86$ kJ, $\Delta S =$ JK^{-1}, $\Delta H = 141.01$ kJ.

24. The solubility product of CuCl at 298 is 2.29×10^{-7}. Calculate the standard electrode potential of the half cell Cl^- | CuCl | Cu. Given

$$E^0_{Cu^+|Cu} = 0.522 \text{ V}.$$

Ans. 0.129 V

25. Calculate solubility product of $Fe(OH)_3$. Given

$$Fe(OH)_3 + 3e^- \rightarrow Fe + 3OH^-; \quad E^0 = -0.77 \text{ V}$$
$$Fe^{3+} + 3e^- \rightarrow Fe \qquad\qquad E^0 = -0.036 \text{ V}$$

Ans. 1.82×10^{-37}.

26. Consider the following cell at 298 K.

$$\text{Ag | AgCl | HCl (0.01 M) | } H_2 \text{ } (p = 1.5 \text{ atm}) \text{ | Pt}$$

The standard electrode potential for the silver-silver chloride electrode is 0.2225 V. (a) Write the electrode reactions; (b) Calculate E_{cell} (i) assuming activity coefficients to be unity, (ii) taking $\gamma_\pm$ for HCl as 0.9865 and $\gamma_{H2} = 1$.

Ans. (a) $Ag + HCl(0.01 \text{ M}) = AgCl + \dfrac{1}{2}H_2$; (b) (i) 0.4539, (ii) 0.5132 V.

27. For the electrode concentration cell

$$\text{Cd} - \text{Hg } (C_1) \text{ | } Cd^{2+} \text{ } (a = 1) \text{ | Cd} - \text{Hg } (C_2)$$

the cell emf at 298 K is 0.0591 V. (i) Write the cell reaction and (ii) calculate the ratio (C_1/C_2) of Cd in the amalgams. It may be assumed that the amalgams behave as ideal solutions.

Ans. (i) $Cd - Hg(C_1) \rightarrow Cd - Hg(C_2)$
(ii) $C_1/C_2 = 10^2$.

28. Consider the cell without transport at 298 K

$$\text{Pt | } H_2 \text{ | HCl (0.01 m) | AgCl} - \text{Ag} - \text{AgCl/HCl (0.1 m) | } H_2 \text{ | Pt}$$

Write the electrode and the overall cell reactions. Calculate the emf of cell assuming activity coefficients of each ion to be unity.

Ans. $E_{cell} = 0.0591$ V.

29. The emf of the following concentration cell is 0.0284 V at 298 K.

$$Cu \mid CuSO_4(0.001 \text{ M}) : CuSO_4 (0.01 \text{ M}) \mid Cu$$

The activity of Cu^{2+} ion in 0.01 M solution is 0.00404 and in 0.001 M solution it is 0.00069. Calculate the transport number of the Cu^{2+} ions. **Ans.** 0.374

30. The emf of the cell with transference

$$Ag \mid AgCl \mid HCl \, (a_\pm = 0.01751) : HCl \, (a_\pm = 0.009048) \mid AgCl \mid Ag \text{ at 298 K is } 0.02807 \text{ V}.$$ The corresponding cell without transference has an emf of 0.01696 V. Calculate the transference number of H^+ and the value of liquid junction potential. **Ans.** 0.825, 0.01106 V.

31. E^0 for the half cell $Pt \mid H_2 \, (p = 1 \text{ atm}) \mid OH^- \left(a_{OH^-} = 1\right)$ is -0.8277 V at 298 K. Find the ionic product of water at 298 K. **Ans.** $K_w = 1.0 \times 10^{-14}$.

32. E^0 for the concentration cell

$$Pt \mid H_2 \, (p = 1 \text{ atm}) \mid H^+\left(a_{H^+} = x\right) \mid\mid H^+\left(a_{H^+} = 0.1\right) \mid H_2 \, (p = 1 \text{ atm}) \mid Pt$$

at 298 K is 0.1182 V. Calculate pH of the unknown solution. **Ans.** pH =3.0.

33. A hydrogen electrode and a normal calomel electrode had a voltage of 0.435 V when placed in a certain solution at 298 K. Calculate pH and a_{H^+} of the solution. **Ans.** pH = 2.597, $a_{H^+} = 2.513 \times 10^{-3}$.

34. Calculate the stability constant for the complex formed in the reaction

$$Cu^{2+} + 4NH_3 = Cu(NH_3)_4^{2+}$$

Given $\qquad\qquad Cu^{2+} + 2e^- = Cu, \qquad E^0 = 0.337 \text{ V}$

$$Cu(NH_3)_4^{2+} + 2e^- = Cu + 4NH_3, \quad E^0 = -0.12 \text{ V} \qquad \textbf{Ans. } 2.92 \times 10^{15}.$$

35. In the redox couple, $Ox + ne^- \rightleftharpoons Red$, with $a_{ox} = a_{red} = 1$, what must be the value of E^0 of the couple if the oxidant is to liberate oxygen by the half cell reaction

$$O_2(g) + 2H_2O + 2e^- \rightarrow 4OH^-, \qquad E^0 = 0.401 \text{ V}$$

(a) from a basic solution, $a_{OH^-} = 1$, (b) from an acid solution $a_{H^+} = 1$, (c) from water pH = 7? (d) Is oxygen a better oxidising agent in acidic or alkaline solutions? **Ans.** (a) > 0.401 V; (b) >1.220 V; (c) > 0.815 V; (d) Acid solutions.

36. Consider a redox couple, $Ox + ne^- \rightleftharpoons Red$, with the oxidised and the reduced species at unit activity.

(a) What must be the value of E^0 if the couple is to liberate hydrogen from (i) acid solution, $a_{H^+} = 1$,

(ii) water, pH = 7.0? (b) Is hydrogen a better reducing agent in acidic or alkaline solutions? Explain.
Ans. (a) (i) < 0.0 V; (ii) < 0.414 V; (b) Hydrogen is a better reducing agent in alkaline solutions.

37. What is a galvanic cell? When does it operate spontaneously? How does a galvanic cell differ from an electrolytic cell? What is the source of energy in a galvanic cell? Calculate the electrical energy obtainable from a Daniell's cell (emf = 1.1 V).

38. Explain clearly what is meant by electrode potential, standard electrode potential and emf of a cell. How are single electrode potentials and cell potentials measured? Can the absolute value of an electrode potential be determined?

39. What is a reversible cell? What are its requirements? Give examples of such cells. Does the operation of a reversible cell yield maximum electrical work?

40. What is an electrochemical series? What are its uses? Explain why Zn liberates hydrogen from acid solution while Cu does not.

41. What is a standard cell? What are its criteria? Describe a Weston cadmium cell.

42. Derive Nernst equation relating the emf of a cell with the concentrations of the reactants and products of the reaction. What is the emf of the cell at equilibrium?

43. What is a reference electrode? Describe *SHE*, *SCE* and Ag-AgCl electrodes.

44. What types of electrodes are used for pH measurements?

     Describe the use of (*i*) *SHE*, (*ii*) Quinhydrone electrode, and (*iii*) Glass electrode in pH measurements.

45. How is the cell emf used in calculating ΔG, ΔG^0, ΔH, ΔS and K for the cell reaction?

46. What are concentration cells? Derive an expression for the emf of an electrolyte concentration cell with transport cell? What is the value of E^0_{cell} in these cases? How are such cells used in calculating activity coefficients of ions?

47. What is liquid junction potential? How can it be minimized? Is it possible to reduce it to zero?

48. A solution of Fe^{2+} ions is usually contaminated by Fe^{3+} ions which are usually formed by atmospheric oxidation of Fe^{2+} ions. Suppose a solution of Fe^{2+} ions is to be kept pure and free from Fe^{3+} ions, which procedure from the following would you recommend?

     (*i*) Add Ag^+ ions; (*ii*) Add Zn^{2+} ions; (*iii*) Add Ag; (*iv*) Add Zn and; (*v*) Add Fe.
     Given

$$E^0_{Fe^{2+}|Fe} = -0.44 \text{ V},$$

$$E^0_{Fe^{3+},\ Fe^{2+}|Pt} = 0.77 \text{ V},$$

$$E^0_{Ag^+|Ag} = 0.80 \text{ V}$$

and

$$E^0_{Zn^{2+}|Zn} = -0.76 \text{ V}.$$

Assume that the ions are at unit activity.

Chemical Kinetics

16.1 INTRODUCTION

Chemical kinetics is the branch of physical chemistry which deals with a study of the rate of chemical reactions. Such studies enable us to elucidate the mechanism by which a reaction occurs. In chemical equilibria, only the initial and final states of the chemical reactions were considered. Furthermore, the energy relations between the reactants and products are governed by the laws of thermodynamics, but no attempt is made to indicate the intermediate stages of the reaction. In chemical equilibrium the rate at which the equilibrium is attained does not appear. In chemical kinetics the rate of the reaction is followed and time as a variable is introduced.

There are many reactions for which the kinetic studies are not possible. Many ionic and explosive reactions occur instantaneously and in such cases it is not easy to measure their rates. Special techniques have been devised to study their kinetics. On the other hand, there are reactions which are so slow that it is difficult to observe appreciable changes in concentrations at room temperature even after months or years. Between these two extremes are reactions for which it is easy to determine their rates. The gaseous reactions like decomposition of HI or N_2O_5, the reactions in liquid phase like the hydrolysis of ester etc., come under this category.

Experimentally, it is found that the rate of a chemical reaction is dependent on factors like temperature, pressure and the concentration of the reacting species. The presence of a catalyst can increase or decrease the rate of a reaction by many powers of ten.

From the kinetic stand point, the reactions are classified into two groups, *viz.*, (*a*) homogeneous reactions which occur in one phase only; it may be a gaseous phase or a liquid phase, and (*b*) heterogeneous reactions which take place in two or more phases, *e.g.*, gaseous reactions taking place on the surface of a solid catalyst or on the walls of the container.

16.2 RATE OF A REACTION

Rate, speed or *velocity* of a reaction has the same meaning in chemical kinetics. The rate of a reaction at any instant during the course of the reaction is defined as *the rate at which the concentrations of the reacting species change with time and is represented by dC/dt* where *C* is the concentration of the reacting substance at any time *t*. The average rate of a reaction during a finite time interval, Δt is given by $\Delta C/\Delta t$. In case of reactants, concentrations decrease with time and, therefore, a negative sign is put before dC/dt, i.e., $-dC/dt$. On the other hand, the concentrations of the products increase with time and consequently the rate is written as dC/dt.

Consider, for example, the reaction

$$N_2(g) + O_2(g) \rightarrow 2NO(g)$$

The rate of this reaction may be expressed in terms of the changes in concentration of any one of the participants with time.

Thus the rate of disappearance of N_2 is $-\dfrac{d[N_2]}{dt}$

Similarly, the rate of disappearance of O_2 is $-\dfrac{d[O_2]}{dt}$

and the rate of formation of NO is $\dfrac{d[NO]}{dt}$

These expressions of the rate are related to one another through the stoichiometry of the reaction.

Since one mole each of N_2 and O_2 react to produce 2 moles of NO, which means that the N_2 and O_2 disappear at the same rate but NO appears at twice this rate, i.e., the rate of formation of NO is equal to two times the rate of consumption of N_2 or O_2. Mathematically,

$$-2\frac{d[N_2]}{dt} = -2\frac{d[O_2]}{dt} = \frac{d[NO]}{dt}$$

or

$$-\frac{d[N_2]}{dt} = -\frac{d[O_2]}{dt} = \frac{1}{2}\frac{d[NO]}{dt}$$

In general, for a reaction of the type

$$aA + bB + ... \rightarrow lL + mM + ...$$

the rate of the reaction is given by

$$-\frac{1}{a}\frac{d[A]}{dt} = -\frac{1}{b}\frac{d[B]}{dt} = ... = \frac{1}{l}\frac{d[L]}{dt} = \frac{1}{m}\frac{d[M]}{dt} = ...$$

where a, b, l, m, etc., are the stoichiometric coefficients.

The variation in concentration of the reactants and products with time is shown in Fig. 16.1. In the initial stages of the reaction, the rate of disappearance of the reactants is large and decreases as the reaction proceeds and finally approaches a limiting value. In other words, the reaction never proceeds to completion. Similarly, the rate of appearance of the products is large in the initial stages of the reaction and ultimately attains a limiting value. The rate of the reaction at any instant during the course of the reaction is equal to the slope of the concentration time curve at that instant.

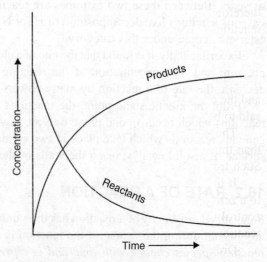

Fig. 16.1 Plot of the concentration versus time for the reactants and products of a reaction

Units of Rate: The rate has the units of concentration divided by time. If the concentration is expressed in mol/dm^3 and the time in seconds, then the rate is given in mol/dm^3/s or mol dm^{-3} s^{-1}.

16.3 ORDER OF A REACTION

The order of a reaction is defined as *the sum of powers of the concentration terms in the rate equation.* These powers are not the stoichiometric coefficients as they appear in the balanced chemical equation but must be determined through experiments. Consider the following reactions:

$$A \rightarrow \text{Products} \qquad \qquad ...(16.1)$$

$$\left. \begin{array}{l} A + B \rightarrow \text{Products} \\ A + A \rightarrow \text{Products} \end{array} \right] \qquad ...(16.2)$$

$$\left. \begin{array}{l} A + 2B \rightarrow \text{Products} \\ 2A + B \rightarrow \text{Products} \end{array} \right] \qquad ...(16.3)$$

According to the law of mass action, the rate of reaction (16.1) is proportional to the concentration of A, i.e.,

$$-\frac{d[A]}{dt} = k[A]$$

where the proportionality constant k is known as *the rate constant or the specific reaction rate and is numerically equal to the rate of the reaction when the reactant concentration is unity.* The value of rate constant depends only on temperature and is independent of the concentrations. The expression which gives the dependence of rate upon concentration of reacting substances is known as the *rate law.* Since the rate depends on the first power of the concentration therefore, the reaction is said to be a *first order* reaction. The rate of reaction (16.2) is given by $k [A] [B]$ or $k [A]^2$ and is said to be a *second order* reaction. Similarly the rate of reaction (16.3) is given by $k[A] [B]^2$ or $k[A]^2 [B]$ and the reaction is, therefore, of *third order.* In general, if several reactants A, B, C etc., are involved then the rate of the reaction is given by

$$-\frac{d[C]}{dt} = k[A]^a [B]^b [C]^c \, ...$$

and the order of the reaction would be given by the sum of the exponents, $(a+b+c+...)$. The reaction is said to be of ath order with respect to A, bth order with respect to B, etc.

Though theoretically reactions of higher orders are possible, but it is doubtful if reactions higher than third order exist. However, there are reactions in which the order is fractional, i.e., 1/2, 3/4, etc. Such fractional orders indicate the complex nature of the reactions.

If the reaction rate is independent of the concentration of the reacting species, the reaction is said to a *zero order* reaction. In such reactions, factors other than the concentration of the reacting species control the rate of the reaction. Some heterogeneous or surface reactions are examples of zero order reactions.

Order of a reaction is an experimental quantity and can change depending upon the experimental conditions under which the reaction is investigated.

Problem 16.1: For the reaction

$$2NO\,(g) + 2H_2\,(g) \rightarrow N_2\,(g) + 2H_2O\,(g)$$

the overall rate can be expressed in any one of the following ways:

$$\frac{d[H_2O]}{dt} = k[NO]^2[H_2]$$

$$\frac{d[N_2]}{dt} = k_1[NO]^2[H_2]$$

$$-\frac{d[NO]}{dt} = k_1'[NO]^2[H_2]$$

$$-\frac{d[H_2]}{dt} = k_1''[NO]^2[H_2]$$

How are the rate constants k_1, k_1' and k_1'' related to k?

Solution: From the stoichiometry, we have

$$-\frac{1}{2}\frac{d[NO]}{dt} = -\frac{1}{2}\frac{d[H_2]}{dt} = \frac{d[N_2]}{dt} = \frac{1}{2}\frac{d[H_2O]}{dt}$$

Therefore, $k = k_1' = k_1''$

and $k = k_1' = k_1'' = 2k_1$

16.4 MOLECULARITY OF A REACTION

Most of the chemical reactions proceed through a series of intermediate steps. These steps are known as *the elementary steps*. Investigation of these steps constitute the mechanism of the reaction. In the discussion of the mechanism we refer to *the molecularity* of a step. The molecularity of a reaction is defined as *the number of reactant molecules which take part in an elementary reaction*. The reactions are said to be *unimolecular, bimolecular* or *trimolecular* depending upon whether one, two or three molecules are involved in a chemical reaction. The order and molecularity of a reaction are generally different and the distinction between the two should be clearly understood.

In Eq. (16.1), the order of the reaction is one and the molecularity is also one. Such reactions are generally known as unimolecular or monomolecular reactions. Reactions represented by Eq. (16.2) have order and molecularity of two. Such reactions are generally referred to as bimolecular reactions. Similarly, reactions given by Eq. (16.3) are of order three and of molecularity three. These are called trimolecular reactions.

The reaction between hydrogen and iodine

$$H_2 + I_2 \rightarrow 2HI$$

is a second order reaction because the rate of formation of hydrogen iodide is proportional to the concentrations of both hydrogen and iodine. The reaction involves two molecules and is, therefore, called a bimolecular reaction. For elementary reactions, as stated above, order and molecularity are identical. For others they are different. For example, the inversion of cane sugar in the presence of a mineral acid represented as

$$C_{12}H_{22}O_{11} + H_2O \xrightarrow{\;H_3O^+\;} C_6H_{12}O_6 + C_6H_{12}O_6$$

Cane sugar   Water   Glucose   Fructose

involves two reactant molecules, *viz.*, sugar and water and is a bimolecular reaction. In presence of excess water, the order of the reaction is found to be one—indicating that the order and molecularity of the reaction are different. Such a reaction is generally referred to as a *pseudo unimolecular reaction.*

The molecularity of a reaction must be an **integral** value and is applied to individual elementary reactions. If a reaction proceeds through several steps, each step (elementary reaction) has its own molecularity and order which are identical. In such cases, it is meaningless to talk of the molecularity of the overall reaction and there is no correlation between the order and molecularity or between stoichiometric representation and the molecularity. For example, the decomposition of nitrogen pentoxide represented stoichiometrically as

$$2\,N_2O_5 \rightarrow 4\,NO_2 + O_2$$

involves two molecules of N_2O_5 and is a first order reaction. The various steps suggested in the mechanism are as follows:

(*i*) $N_2O_5 \rightarrow NO_2 + NO_3$

(*ii*) $NO_2 + NO_3 \rightarrow NO_2 + O_2 + NO$

(*iii*) $NO_2 + NO_3 \rightarrow N_2O_5$

(*iv*) $NO + N_2O_5 \rightarrow 3\,NO_2$

In this scheme three steps are bimolecular and one unimolecular. The slowest step controls the overall rate of decomposition of N_2O_5.

Order is an empirical quantity and is obtained from the rate law; molecularity of steps refers to the mechanism of the reaction.

16.5 FIRST ORDER REACTIONS

Consider a reaction

$$A \rightarrow \text{Products}$$

Let a mol dm^{-3} be the initial concentration of A. If after time t, x mol dm^{-3} of A decompose, the remaining concentration of A is $(a-x)$. The rate of formation of the product at any instant is dx/dt.

For a first order reaction, the rate is proportional to the instantaneous concentration of A, so that

$$-\frac{d(a-x)}{dt} = \frac{dx}{dt} \propto (a-x)$$

or

$$\frac{dx}{dt} = k(a-x)$$

or

$$\frac{dx}{a-x} = k\,dt \qquad\qquad\qquad ...(16.4)$$

where k is the proportionality constant called the first order rate constant. Its unit is $(\text{time})^{-1}$ as can be deduced from Eq. (16.4).

Integration of Eq. (16.4) gives

$$\int \frac{dx}{a-x} = \int k\,dt$$

$$-\ln(a-x) = kt + I \qquad \qquad ...(16.5)$$

where I is the constant of integration and its value is obtained from the initial conditions of the reaction. Initially, when $t = 0$, $x = 0$, putting these values in Eq. (16.5), we get

$$I = -\ln a$$

and hence Eq. (16.5) becomes

$$-\ln(a-x) = kt - \ln a$$

$$\ln \frac{a}{a-x} = kt \qquad \qquad ...(16.6)$$

$$x = a(1 - e^{-kt})$$

or

$$[A]_t = [A]_0\, e^{-kT} \qquad \qquad ...(16.6(a))$$

where $[A]_0$ is the initial concentration of the reactants and $[A]_t$ its value after time t. It is clear from this expression that the quantity of reacting material falls off exponentially, and theoretically the reaction is complete, i.e., $[A]_t = 0$, only when t is infinite. In other words, the reaction is never 100% complete. The rate at which the curve (Fig. 16.1) approaches time axis depends on the value of k. If the value of k is large, the curve will approach the time axis in a shorter time than for a smaller value of k.

Equation (16.6) can be rewritten as

$$k = \frac{1}{t}\ln \frac{a}{a-x}$$

or

$$k = \frac{2.303}{t}\log \frac{a}{a-x} \qquad \qquad ...(16.7)$$

$$k = \frac{2.303}{t}\log \frac{[A]_0}{[A]_t}$$

This equation is known as the integrated rate equation for a reaction of the first order. For such a reaction, insertion of the values for a and $(a - x)$ corresponding to different time t during the course of the reaction should give a constant value of k.

If $\log\left(\dfrac{a}{a-x}\right)$ is plotted against t, a straight line passing through the origin is obtained; the slope of which is $k/2.303$ (Fig. 16.2).

Even when the initial concentration a is not known but the concentrations at two different time intervals t_1 and t_2 are known, the rate equation can be derived. This can be done by integrating Eq. (16.4) between limits x_1 to x_2 and t_1 to t_2, i.e.,

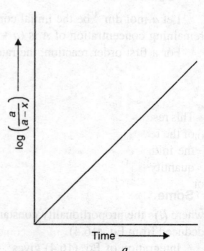

Fig. 16.2 Plot of $\log\dfrac{a}{a-x}$ versus t

$$\int_{x_1}^{x_2} \frac{dx}{a-x} = \int_{t_1}^{t_2} k\, dt$$

$$\left[-\ln(a-x)\right]_{x_1}^{x_2} = \left[kt\right]_{t_1}^{t_2}$$

$$\ln\frac{(a-x_1)}{(a-x_2)} = k(t_2 - t_1)$$

$$k = \frac{1}{t_2 - t_1}\ln\frac{(a-x_1)}{(a-x_2)}$$

$$k = \frac{2.303}{(t_2 - t_1)}\log\frac{(a-x_1)}{(a-x_2)} \qquad \qquad ...(16.8)$$

$$= \frac{2.303}{\Delta t}\log\frac{[A]_1}{[A]_2}$$

where $[A]_1$ and $[A]_2$ are the concentrations of the reactant at two instants differing by Δt.

Half-Life Period of First Order Reactions

The time required when half of the reactant is converted into the products is called half-life period of a reaction. It is denoted by $t_{1/2}$.

Mathematically, when

$$x = \frac{a}{2}; \quad t = t_{1/2}$$

Putting these values in Eq. (16.7), we get

$$k = \frac{2.303}{t_{1/2}}\log\frac{a}{a-a/2}$$

$$t_{1/2} = \frac{0.693}{k} \qquad \qquad ...(16.9)$$

This result shows that for a first order reaction the half-life period is independent of the initial concentration of the reactant. This means that for a given first order reaction, half-life period is the same, whatever be the initial concentration. This simple relation represented by Eq. (16.9) makes the half-life a useful quantity for first order reactions.

Some Characteristics of the First Order Reaction

(i) In a first order reaction, $[A]_t = [A]_0\, e^{-kt}$, it means the reaction never proceeds to completion because $[A]_t$ would become zero only at infinite time t.

(*ii*) A plot of $\log\left(\dfrac{a}{a-x}\right)$ versus t would give a straight line passing through the origin with a slope

= $k/2.303$, from which the rate constant can be calculated.

(*iii*) The half-life period is constant for the given reaction and is independent of the initial concentration of the reactant.

Some Examples of the First Order Reaction

(*i*) The thermal decomposition of nitrogen pentoxide in gaseous phase is a first order reaction and the products are oxygen, nitrogen dioxide and nitrogen tetroxide. The overall reaction is represented as

$$\overset{\shortmid}{N}_2O_5 \rightleftharpoons N_2O_4 + \frac{1}{2}O_2$$
$$\updownarrow$$
$$2NO_2$$

(*ii*) *Hydrolysis of an ester in the presence of a mineral acid:* The hydrolysis of an ester is usually catalysed by an acid. The reaction is represented as

$$CH_3COOC_2H_5 + H_2O \xrightarrow{H_3O^+} CH_3COOH + C_2H_5OH$$

The rate of this reaction is determined only by the concentration of the ester as water is present in large excess and its concentration is assumed to be constant. Hence this is a first order reaction. The kinetics of the reaction is studied in the laboratory by titrating a known volume of the ester containing HCl against standard alkali. The amount of alkali used is equivalent to the amount of acetic acid obtained by the ester hydrolysis and the total amount of HCl added. When $t = 0$, i.e., at the start of the reaction, volume of alkali used is equivalent to the HCl added. Let it be V_0. If V_t is the volume of alkali used after time t, then $(V_t - V_0)$ is the volume required to neutralize acetic acid formed by the hydrolysis of ester in time t. This quantity $(V_t - V_0)$ is thus proportional to x in the rate equation for first order reaction. When the reaction is complete, i.e., at $t = \infty$, let V_∞ be the volume of alkali used. This corresponds to the amount of acetic acid obtained by complete hydrolysis of the ester and the amount of the HCl initially added. Thus, $(V_\infty - V_0)$ is proportional to a, the initial concentration of the ester. Since the concentration of the ester at any time t is proportional to $(a - x)$ and this can be obtained as

$$(a - x) \propto (V_\infty - V_0) - (V_t - V_0)$$
$$= V_\infty - V_t$$

Hence the equation for the first order reaction becomes

$$k = \frac{2.303}{t} \log \frac{V_\infty - V_0}{V_\infty - V_t}$$

(*iii*) The inversion of cane sugar in the presence of dilute mineral acids is a first order reaction and is represented as

$$C_{12}H_{22}O_{11} \xrightarrow{H_3O^+} C_6H_{12}O_6 + C_6H_{12}O_6$$

The progress of this reaction has been followed by measuring the change in the angle of rotation at various intervals of time. Let α_0, α_t and α_∞ represent the angles of rotation when $t = 0$ (at the start of the reaction), after time t and at the completion of the reaction respectively. Then evidently, $a \propto (\alpha_0 - \alpha_\infty)$

and $(a - x) \propto (\alpha_t - \alpha_\infty)$. Hence the rate equation becomes

$$k = \frac{2.303}{t} \log \frac{\alpha_0 - \alpha_\infty}{\alpha_t - \alpha_\infty}$$

Problem 16.2: From the following data at a certain temperature show that the decomposition of hydrogen peroxide in aqueous solution is a first order reaction.

Time (in seconds)	0	300	600	900	1200
KMnO$_4$ solution (ml)	22.8	17.7	13.8	10.6	8.2

Solution: For the first order reaction

$$k = \frac{2.303}{t} \log \frac{a}{a - x}$$

Here $a \propto 22.8$ ml, the initial concentration of H_2O_2

At $t = 300$ s, $(a - x) \propto 17.7$ ml

Substituting these values in the above equation, we get

$$k = \frac{2.303}{300} \log \frac{22.8}{17.7} = 8.445 \times 10^{-4} \text{ s}^{-1}$$

At $t = 600$ s, $(a - x) \propto 13.8$ ml

$$k = \frac{2.303}{600} \log \frac{22.8}{13.8} = 8.37 \times 10^{-4} \text{ s}^{-1}$$

At $t = 900$ s, $(a - x) \propto 10.6$ ml

$$k = \frac{2.303}{900} \log \frac{22.8}{10.6} = 8.51 \times 10^{-4} \text{ s}^{-1}$$

At $t = 1200$ s, $(a - x) \propto 8.2$ ml

$$k = \frac{2.303}{1200} \log \frac{22.8}{8.2} = 8.52 \times 10^{-4} \text{ s}^{-1}$$

The constant value of k shows that the reaction is of first order.

Problem 16.3: From the following data at 298 K on the hydrolysis of ethyl acetate in the presence of hydrochloric acid, show that it is a first order reaction.

Time (minutes)	0	25	40	60	∞
Vol. of alkali used (ml)	19.2	24.2	26.6	29.5	42.1

Solution: For a first order reaction

$$k = \frac{2.303}{t} \log \frac{V_\infty - V_0}{V_\infty - V_t}$$

where V_0, V_t and V_∞ represent the volumes of alkali used at the start of the reaction after time t and at the completion of the reaction, respectively.

The value of k calculated at different intervals of time is as follows:

$$t = 25 \text{ minutes, } k = \frac{2.303}{25} \log \frac{(42.1 - 19.2)}{(42.1 - 24.2)} = 9.847 \times 10^{-1} \text{ (minute)}^{-1}$$

$$t = 40 \text{ minutes}, \ k = \frac{2.303}{40} \log \frac{(42.1 - 19.2)}{(42.1 - 26.6)} = 9.76 \times 10^{-1} (\text{minute})^{-1}$$

$$t = 60 \text{ minutes}, \ k = \frac{2.303}{60} \log \frac{(42.1 - 19.2)}{(42.1 - 29.5)} = 9.99 \times 10^{-1} (\text{minute})^{-1}$$

A constant value of k shows that the hydrolysis of ethyl acetate is a first order reaction.

Problem 16.4: The optical rotation of sucrose in 0.9 N HCl at 300 K at various intervals of time is given below:

Time (minutes)	0	15	30	45	60	∞
Rotation (degree)	+32.4	+28.8	+25.5	+22.4	+19.4	−11.0

Show that the reaction is of first order.

Solution: For a first order reaction

$$k = \frac{2.303}{t} \log \frac{\alpha_0 - \alpha_\infty}{\alpha_t - \alpha_\infty}$$

where α_0, α_t and α_∞ represent the optical rotations at the start of reaction after time t and at the completion of the reaction respectively.

In this case

$$\alpha_0 - \alpha_\infty = 32.4 - (-11.0) = +43.4$$

At $t = 15$ minutes, $k = \dfrac{2.303}{15} \log \dfrac{32.4 - (-11.0)}{28.8 - (-11.0)} = 5.7 \times 10^{-3} \text{min}^{-1}$

At $t = 30$ minutes, $k = \dfrac{2.303}{30} \log \dfrac{43.4}{36.5} = 5.77 \times 10^{-3} \text{min}^{-1}$

At $t = 45$ minutes, $k = \dfrac{2.303}{45} \log \dfrac{43.4}{35.5} = 5.82 \times 10^{-3} \text{min}^{-1}$

At $t = 60$ minutes, $k = \dfrac{2.303}{60} \log \dfrac{43.4}{30.4} = 5.92 \times 10^{-3} \text{min}^{-1}$

The constancy of k indicates that the inversion of sucrose is a first order reaction.

16.6 SECOND ORDER REACTIONS

The reaction

$$A + A \rightarrow \text{Product(s)}$$

follows a second order kinetics if the rate is proportional to the square of the concentration of A, i.e.,

$$-\frac{d[A]}{dt} = k[A]^2 \qquad\qquad ...(16.10)$$

However, if the reaction is

$$A + B \rightarrow \text{Product(s)}$$

the rate is proportional to the product of the concentration of each reactant

$$-\frac{d[A]}{dt} = -\frac{d[B]}{dt} = \frac{dx}{dt} = k[A][B] \qquad \text{...(16.11)}$$

where dx/dt is the rate of disappearance of A or B or appearance of the products. From Eq. (16.10)

$$\frac{dx}{dt} = k(a-x)^2 \qquad \text{...(16.12)}$$

and from Eq. (16.11)

$$\frac{dx}{dt} = k(a-x)(b-x) \qquad \text{...(16.13)}$$

In these equations a and b are the initial concentrations of A and B in mol dm^{-3} respectively. In Eq. (16.13) if $a = b$, i.e., when the concentration of two reacting species are same, then the rate is given by Eq. (16.12). Integrating this equation we get

$$\int \frac{dx}{(a-x)^2} = \int k \, dt$$

$$\frac{1}{(a-x)} = kt + I \qquad \text{...(16.14)}$$

where I is the constant of integration and its value can be obtained by applying the initial conditions, i.e., when $t = 0$, $x = 0$

$$I = 1/a$$

Putting the value of integration constant in Eq. (16.14), we get

$$\frac{1}{a-x} = kt + \frac{1}{a}$$

$$k = \frac{x}{at(a-x)} \qquad \text{...(16.15)}$$

From Eq. (16.15), it is clear that k has the units of (time)$^{-1}$ (concentration)$^{-1}$. A plot of $x/a(a-x)$ versus t should be a straight line passing through the origin with slope equal to k (Fig. 16.3).

Equation (16.10) when integrated between the limits $[A]_0$ and $[A]_t$, we get

$$-\int_{[A]_0}^{[A]_t} \frac{dA}{A^2} = \int_0^t k \, dt$$

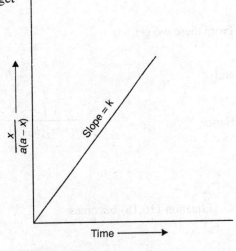

Fig. 16.3 Plot of $\dfrac{x}{a(a-x)}$ versus t

$$\frac{1}{[A]_t} - \frac{1}{[A]_0} = kt$$

This expression rearranges to

$$[A]_t = \frac{[A]_0}{1 + kt[A]_0}$$ ...(16.15a)

When the concentrations of the reacting species are different, *i.e.*, $a \neq b$, then the rate is given by Eq. (16.13)

$$\frac{dx}{dt} = k(a-x)(b-x)$$

Separating the variables, we get

$$\frac{dx}{(a-x)(b-x)} = k\,dt$$ ...(16.16)

The expression $\dfrac{1}{(a-x)(b-x)}$ can be resolved into partial fractions as

$$\frac{1}{(a-x)(b-x)} = \frac{A}{a-x} + \frac{B}{b-x}$$

$$\frac{1}{(a-x)(b-x)} = \frac{A(b-x) + B(a-x)}{(a-x)(b-x)}$$

$$1 = A(b-x) + B(a-x)$$

$$1 = Ab + Ba$$

and

$$-A - B = 0$$

From these we get

$$A = \frac{1}{b-a}$$

and

$$B = \frac{1}{a-b}$$

Hence

$$\frac{1}{(a-x)(b-x)} = \frac{1}{(b-a)(a-x)} + \frac{1}{(a-b)(b-x)}$$

$$= \frac{1}{(a-b)}\left[\frac{1}{(b-x)} - \frac{1}{(a-x)}\right]$$

Equation (16.16) becomes

$$\frac{1}{(a-b)}\left[\frac{1}{(b-x)} - \frac{1}{(a-x)}\right]dx = kdt$$

On integrating this equation, we get

$$\frac{1}{(a-b)}\left[\int \frac{dx}{(b-x)} - \int \frac{dx}{(a-x)}\right] = \int k \, dt$$

$$\frac{1}{(a-b)}\left[-\ln(b-x) + \ln(a-x)\right] = kt + I \qquad ...(16.17)$$

Again, when $t = 0$, $x = 0$, and therefore

$$\frac{1}{(a-b)}\left[\ln\left(\frac{a}{b}\right)\right] = I$$

Putting the value of I in Eq. (16.17), we obtain

$$\frac{1}{(a-b)}\left[-\ln(b-x) + \ln(a-x)\right] = kt + \frac{1}{(a-b)}\left[\ln\left(\frac{a}{b}\right)\right]$$

or

$$kt = \frac{1}{(a-b)}\ln\frac{b(a-x)}{a(b-x)}$$

or

$$k = \frac{2.303}{(a-b)t}\log\frac{b(a-x)}{a(b-x)} \qquad ...(16.18)$$

or

$$t = \frac{2.303}{k(a-b)}\log\frac{b(a-x)}{a(b-x)} \qquad ...(16.19)$$

$$t = \frac{2.303}{k\{[A]_0 - [B]_0\}}\log\frac{[B]_0[A]_t}{[A]_0[B]_t}$$

where $[A]_0$ and $[B]_0$ are the initial concentrations of A and B ($t = 0$) and $[A]_t$ and $[B]_t$ are the concentrations of A and B at any time t.

The equation (16.19) shows that the plot of $\log\left\{\dfrac{b(a-x)}{a(b-x)}\right\}$

versus t for such a reaction would be a straight line passing through the origin and the slope of the line is equal to

$\dfrac{k(a-b)}{2.303}$ (Fig. 16.4). From its slope the rate constant k can

be obtained.

In the reaction $A + B \to$ Products, if the concentration of one of the reactants is taken in large excess, the reaction

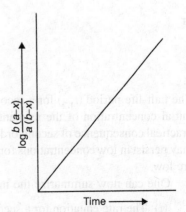

Fig. 16.4 Plot of $\log \dfrac{b(a-x)}{a(b-x)}$ versus t

then becomes kinetically of first order. This can be shown as follows:

Let b be the excess concentration, i.e., $b >> a$ or x, so that

$$a - b \approx -b \text{ and } b - x \approx b$$

Therefore Eq. (16.18) reduces to

$$k = \frac{2.303}{-bt} \log \frac{b(a-x)}{ab}$$

$$= -\frac{2.303}{bt} \log \frac{(a-x)}{(a)}$$

$$= \frac{2.303}{bt} \log \frac{a}{a-x}$$

Since B is the reactant present in excess, so its concentration b may be taken as almost constant and hence the above equation is equivalent to that for a first order reaction (Eq. 16.7).

Half-Life Period for a Second Order Reaction

The half-life period for a second order reaction in which the reactants are identical or different but have equal initial concentration can be calculated using Eq. (16.15). However, the half-life period cannot be calculated for reactions where concentrations of A and B are different as both A and B will have different times for half conversion.

Thus in equation

$$k = \frac{x}{ta(a-x)}$$

when $t = t_{1/2}$, $x = a/2$, we get

$$k = \frac{a/2}{t_{1/2}\, a(a-a/2)}$$

or

$$t_{1/2} = \frac{1}{ka} \qquad \qquad ...(16.20a)$$

$$t_{1/2} \propto \frac{1}{a} \qquad \qquad ...(16.20b)$$

The half-life period ($t_{1/2}$) for a second order reaction is inversely proportional to the first power of the initial concentration of the reactant. Knowing $t_{1/2}$ and a, k is readily calculated from Eq. (16.20). A practical consequence of second order reaction is that the species which decay by second order reactions may persist in low concentrations for long time because their half-lives are long when their concentrations are low.

One can now summarize the main characteristics for the second order reaction as follows:

(*i*) The rate equation for a second order reaction is given by

$$k = \frac{x}{at(a-x)}$$

or
$$k = \frac{2.303}{t(a-b)} \log \frac{b(a-x)}{a(b-x)}$$

(*ii*) The plot of $\frac{x}{a(a-x)}$ or $\log\left\{\frac{b(a-x)}{a(b-x)}\right\}$ versus *t* would give a straight line passing through the

origin with a slope $= k$ or $\frac{k(a-b)}{2.303}$.

(*iii*) The half-life period varies inversely as the initial concentration of the reactant.

Some Examples of Second Order Reactions

(*i*) The saponification of an ester is an example of a second order reaction.

$$CH_3COOC_2H_5 + OH^- \rightarrow CH_3COO^- + C_2H_5OH$$

A reaction mixture is prepared by mixing known quantity of the ester with a known volume of alkali. Let *a* and *b* be the initial concentrations of the ester and OH^- ions respectively. At frequent time intervals, a portion of the reaction mixture is removed, chilled and titrated against a standard acid. The decrease in the concentration of OH^- ions in the reaction mixture is a measure of the extent of the reaction. If *x* is the decrease in the concentration of OH^- ions at any time *t*, then $(b - x)$ gives the concentration of OH^- ions remaining unreacted. Similarly $(a - x)$ gives the amount of the ester which remains unreacted at time *t*. The rate constant can then be calculated by using the expression (16.19).

(*ii*) Decomposition of HI

$$2HI \rightarrow H_2 + I_2$$

which follows the rate law

$$-\frac{d[HI]}{dt} = k[HI]^2$$

is a second order reaction.

(*iii*) Conversion of ozone into oxygen at 373 K

$$2O_3 \rightarrow 3O_2$$

(*iv*) Thermal decomposition of chlorine monoxide at 473 K

$$2Cl_2O \rightarrow 2Cl_2 + O_2$$

(*v*) Thermal decomposition of acetaldehyde

$$CH_3CHO \rightarrow CH_4 + CO$$

Problem 16.5: The following table gives the kinetic data for the reaction between $Na_2S_2O_3$ and CH_3I at 298 K, the concentration being expressed in arbitrary units.

Time (min)	0	4.75	10	20	35	55
$Na_2S_2O_3$	35.35	30.5	27.0	23.2	20.3	18.6
CH_3I	18.25	13.4	9.9	6.1	3.2	1.5

Show that the reaction follows a second order kinetics and calculate the mean specific rate constant.

Solution: For a second order reaction

$$k = \frac{2.303}{t\left(C_{0(A)} - C_{0(B)}\right)} \log \frac{C_A C_{0(B)}}{C_B C_{0(A)}}$$

where $C_0(A)$, $C_0(B)$ are the initial concentrations of A and B, and C_A and C_B are the concentrations of A and B after time t respectively.

$$t = 4.75 \text{ minutes, } k = \frac{2.303}{(4.75)(35.35 - 18.25)} \log \frac{(30.5)(18.25)}{(13.4)(35.35)}$$

$$= 1.98 \times 10^{-3} \text{min}^{-1}\text{conc.}^{-1}$$

$$t = 10 \text{ minutes, } k = \frac{2.303}{(10)(35.35 - 18.25)} \log \frac{(27.0)(18.25)}{(9.9)(35.35)}$$

$$= 1.99 \times 10^{-3} \text{min}^{-1}\text{conc.}^{-1}$$

$$t = 20 \text{ minutes, } k = \frac{2.303}{(20)(35.35 - 18.25)} \log \frac{(23.2)(18.25)}{(6.1)(35.35)}$$

$$= 1.97 \times 10^{-3} \text{min}^{-1}\text{conc.}^{-1}$$

$$t = 35 \text{ minutes, } k = \frac{2.303}{(35)(35.35 - 18.25)} \log \frac{(20.3)(18.25)}{(3.2)(35.35)}$$

$$= 1.98 \times 10^{-3} \text{min}^{-1}\text{conc.}^{-1}$$

$$t = 55 \text{ minutes, } k = \frac{2.303}{(55)(35.35 - 18.25)} \log \frac{(18.6)(18.25)}{(1.5)(35.35)}$$

$$= 1.97 \times 10^{-3} \text{min}^{-1}\text{conc.}^{-1}$$

The constant value of k shows that it is a second order reaction
    The mean specific rate constant is

$$= \frac{(1.98 + 1.99 + 1.97 + 1.98 + 1.97) \times 10^{-3}}{5}$$

$$= 1.98 \times 10^{-3} \text{min}^{-1} \text{conc}^{-1}$$

Problem 16.6: At a certain temperature ethyl acetate on saponification gave the following results:

t (min)	0	5	25	55	120	∞
ml of 0.1 N acetic acid used to titrate 10 ml of unreacted alkali	16	10.2	4.3	2.3	1.1	0

Show that it is a second order reaction. How much fraction of the ester will be decomposed in 40 minutes?

Solution: For a second order reaction.

$$k = \frac{x}{at(a-x)}$$

Here $a \propto 16.0$ ml

when $t = 5$ min

$(a-x) \propto 10.2$ ml

and $x = a - (a-x) \propto (16.0 - 10.2) \propto 5.8$ ml

In order to express the results in terms of dm^3 mol^{-1} min^{-1} units it is necessary to divide the value of k determined by using values by N/V, where N is the normality of the acid used and V (ml) the volume of the reaction for each titration.

$$k = \frac{(5.8)(10)}{(16.0)(5.0)(10.2)(0.1)} = 7.03 \times 10^{-1} min^{-1} dm^3 mol^{-1}$$

when $t = 25$ min

$(a-x) \propto 4.3$ and $x = a - (a-x) \propto (16.0 - 4.3) \propto 11.7$

$$k = \frac{(11.7)(10)}{(16.0)(25.0)(4.3)(0.1)} = 6.8 \times 10^{-1} min^{-1} dm^3 mol^{-1}$$

when $t = 55$ min

$(a-x) \propto 2.3$ and $x = a - (a-x) \propto (16.0 - 2.3) \propto 13.7$

$$k = \frac{(13.7)(10)}{(16.0)(55.0)(2.3)(0.1)} = 6.75 \times 10^{-1} min^{-1} dm^3 mol^{-1}$$

when $t = 120$ min

$(a-x) \propto 1.1$ and $x = a - (a-x) \propto (16.0 - 1.1) \propto 14.9$

$$k = \frac{(14.9)(10)}{(16.0)(120.0)(1.1)(0.1)} = 7.04 \times 10^{-1} min^{-1} dm^3 mol^{-1}$$

Since the value of k is approximately constant the reaction is therefore of second order. The average value of $k = 6.9 \times 10^{-1}$ min^{-1} dm^3 mol^{-1}.

Let after 40 minutes x be the amount of ester decomposed out of 1 mole ($a = 1$), then

$$k = \frac{x}{at(a-x)} = \frac{x}{(1)(40.0)(1-x)} = 6.9 \times 10^{-1} mol^{-1} dm^3 min^{-1}$$

Solving for x, we get

$$x = 0.965$$

Hence the fraction of ester decomposed in 40 minutes is 96.50%.

16.7 THIRD ORDER REACTIONS

The simplest case of a third order reaction is

$$3A \rightarrow \text{Product(s)}$$

The rate of such a reaction is given by

$$\frac{dx}{dt} = k(a-x)^3 \qquad \qquad ...(16.21)$$

where a is the initial concentration of the reactants.

On integration Eq. (16.21) gives

$$\int \frac{dx}{(a-x)^3} = \int k \, dt$$

$$\frac{1}{2(a-x)^2} = kt + I \qquad \qquad ...(16.22)$$

where I is the integration constant and its value is obtained when $t = 0$, $x = 0$ and hence

$$I = \frac{1}{2a^2}$$

Putting the value of I in Eq. (16.22), we get

$$\frac{1}{2(a-x)^2} = kt + \frac{1}{2a^2}$$

$$kt = \frac{1}{2}\left[\frac{1}{(a-x)^2} - \frac{1}{a^2} \right]$$

$$k = \frac{x(2a-x)}{2t\,a^2(a-x)^2} \qquad \qquad ...(16.23)$$

The half-life period $(t_{1/2})$ for such a reaction is given by

$$t_{1/2} = \frac{\dfrac{a}{2}\left(2a - \dfrac{a}{2}\right)}{2ka^2\left(a - \dfrac{a}{2}\right)^2}$$

$$t_{1/2} = \frac{3}{2\,ka^2} \qquad \qquad ...(16.24)$$

The half-life period $(t_{1/2})$ is thus inversely proportional to the square of the initial concentration of the reactants.

In case of a reaction of the type

$$A + B + C \rightarrow \text{Product(s)}$$

the rate equation can be written as

$$\frac{dx}{dt} = k(a-x)(b-x)(c-x)$$

Integration of this equation gives

$$k = \frac{1}{2t} \frac{(b-c)\ln\dfrac{a-x}{a} + (c-a)\ln\dfrac{b-x}{b} + (a-b)\ln\dfrac{c-x}{c}}{(a-b)(b-c)(c-a)}$$

In the case of a reaction where two of the reactants are identical or have the same initial concentration

$$2A + B \rightarrow \text{Products(s)}$$

the rate of the reaction can be represented as

$$\frac{dx}{dt} = k(a-2x)^2(b-x)$$

which on integration gives

$$kt = \frac{1}{(2b+a)} \frac{2x}{a(a-2x)} + \frac{1}{(2b-a)}\ln\frac{b(a-2x)}{a(b-x)}$$

Some Examples of Third Order Reactions

There are not many reactions showing the third order kinetics. A few examples are

    (i) $2NO\,(g) + O_2\,(g) \rightarrow 2NO_2\,(g)$

   (ii) $2NO\,(g) + Cl_2\,(g) \rightarrow 2NOCl\,(g)$

16.8 GENERAL EXPRESSION FOR THE RATE OF A REACTION

Reactions in which only one reactant is involved may be represented as

$$nA \rightarrow \text{Product(s)}$$

The rate equation of such reactions is given as

$$\frac{dx}{dt} = k(a-x)^n \qquad \qquad ...(16.25)$$

Integration of Eq. (16.25) gives

$$\int_0^x \frac{dx}{(a-x)^n} = \int_0^t k\,dt$$

$$\frac{1}{(n-1)}\left[\frac{1}{(a-x)^{n-1}} - \frac{1}{a^{n-1}}\right] = kt \qquad \qquad ...(16.26)$$

This equation holds for all values of n except for $n = 1$. When $n = 1$, $(n - 1) = 0$, the equation becomes indeterminate.

The half-life period $(t_{1/2})$ for a reaction of nth order is given by

$$t_{1/2} = \frac{2^{n-1} - 1}{(n-1)a^{n-1}k}$$

or

$$t_{1/2} \propto \frac{1}{a^{n-1}}$$ ...(16.27)

16.9 ZERO ORDER REACTIONS

A number of reactions are known in which the rate of a reaction is independent of the concentration of the reacting substances. In such cases some factor(s) other than the concentration of the reacting substance controls the rate of the reaction. The rate of the reaction is constant and is given by

$$-\frac{d[A]}{dt} = \frac{dx}{dt} = k$$

or

$$x = kt$$

The decomposition of NH_3 on a number of metal surfaces such as gold and molybdenum are examples of zero order reactions. The metals act as catalysts for the decomposition reaction.

16.10 DETERMINATION OF THE ORDER OF A REACTION

The complications in a reaction often lead to erroneous value of the order of a reaction. It is, therefore, desirable to determine the order of a reaction in the initial stages of the reaction when only a small amount of the reaction has occurred and the complications are minimum.

Various methods used to determine the order of a reaction are given below.

(i) Using the Appropriate Rate Equations

In this method concentrations of the reactants after various intervals of time are determined by analysis. The data is substituted in different integrated rate equations given by (16.7), (16.15), etc. The equation which gives a constant value of k indicates the order of the reaction. For simple homogeneous reactions, this method of hit and trial is quite satisfactory and often used. But for complex reactions, this method may lead to erroneous conclusions.

(ii) Method of Half-Life Period

It has been seen previously that the time at which half of the reactant disappears is the half-life period $(t_{1/2})$. Equation (16.9) shows that for a first order reaction this value is constant and is independent of the initial concentration of the reactant. For a second order reaction [Eq. (16.20)], $t_{1/2}$ is inversely proportional to the initial concentration of the reactant. In general, for a reaction of nth order, $t_{1/2}$ is given by Eq. (16.27), i.e.,

$$t_{1/2} \propto \frac{1}{a^{n-1}}$$

where a is the initial concentration of the reactant and n is the order of the reaction.

Suppose two different experiments are carried out with initial concentrations as a_1 and a_2, then their half-life periods $(t_{1/2})_1$ and $(t_{1/2})_2$ would be related as

$$\frac{(t_{1/2})_1}{(t_{1/2})_2} = \left(\frac{a_2}{a_1}\right)^{n-1}$$

$$(n-1) \log \left(\frac{a_2}{a_1}\right) = \log \frac{(t_{1/2})_1}{(t_{1/2})_2}$$

or

$$n = 1 + \frac{\log \dfrac{(t_{1/2})_1}{(t_{1/2})_2}}{\log \left(\dfrac{a_2}{a_1}\right)}$$

Hence n can be evaluated.

(iii) The Differential Method

This method was suggested by van't Hoff and therefore it is sometimes called as van't Hoff's method. According to this method the rate of a reaction of nth order is proportional to the nth power of concentration

$$-\frac{d[A]}{dt} = k[A]^n$$

where [A] is the concentration at any instant. In two experiments with initial concentrations $[A]_1$ and $[A]_2$

$$-\frac{d[A]_1}{dt} = k[A]_1^n$$

$$-\frac{d[A]_2}{dt} = k[A]_2^n$$

Taking logarithms, we get

$$\log \left(-\frac{d[A]_1}{dt}\right) = \log k + n \log[A]_1$$

and

$$\log \left(-\frac{d[A]_2}{dt}\right) = \log k + n \log[A]_2$$

On subtracting, we have

$$n = \frac{\log\left(-\dfrac{d[A]_1}{dt}\right) - \log\left(-\dfrac{d[A]_2}{dt}\right)}{\log[A]_1 - \log[A]_2}$$

An approximate method used to determine $-\dfrac{d[A]}{dt}$ is as follows: The rate of change in A over an

appreciable time interval, *i.e.*, $-\dfrac{\Delta A}{\Delta t}$ is measured and assumed to be $-\dfrac{d[A]}{dt}$ corresponding to the mean value of A in the interval considered.

A better method is to plot concentration versus time for two experiments with different initial

concentrations. The slope $\left(-\dfrac{dA}{dt}\right)$ at a given time interval is measured by drawing tangents. Using

these values of slopes $\left(-\dfrac{dA}{dt}\right)$ in the above equation, n is determined.

(iv) By Changing the Concentration of the Reactants by a Known Factor

This method can be used to evaluate the order of a reaction when more than one reactants are involved. For example, the rate of the reaction, $A + B \rightarrow$ Product(s), is given by

$$\left(-\frac{dA}{dt}\right) = k[A]^a[B]^b$$

where a and b are the orders with respect to A and B and the total order is $(a + b)$. If in two experiments, $[B]$ is kept constant and $[A]$ is doubled then the ratio of the two rates is given by

$$\frac{\left(-\dfrac{dA}{dt}\right)_{\text{Exp I}}}{\left(-\dfrac{dA}{dt}\right)_{\text{Exp II}}} = \frac{k[A]^a[B]^b}{k[2A]^a[B]^b} = \frac{1}{2^a}$$

from which a can be calculated.

Next, in the second set of experiments, if $[B]$ is doubled while $[A]$ is maintained constant, b may be calculated. Hence the total order of the reaction $(a+b)$ would be known.

In the above method the rates should be compared in the initial stages of the reactions where the complications would be minimum.

(v) The Isolation Method

This method introduced by Ostwald in 1902 is used to determine the order of a reaction by taking all the reactants except one in excess. The reaction rate then depends on the reactant present in lesser amount. Suppose a reaction is of ath order with respect to A and bth order with respect to B. If a large excess of B is used so that its concentration throughout the reaction virtually remains constant, then the rate of the reaction will be given by

$$-\frac{d[A]}{dt} = k[A]^a[B]^b$$

$$= k'[A]^a$$

where $\qquad\qquad k' = k[B]^b$

Thus, the order of the reaction a may be determined by any one of the methods described above. The value of b can similarly be obtained by using a large excess of the reactant A. Care should be taken while using this method, for if the reaction is a complex one excess of some component may alter the mechanism of the reaction and in consequence, a wrong result may be obtained.

Problem 16.7: In the reduction of nitric oxide 50% of the reaction was completed in 140 seconds when initial pressure was 258 mm Hg and in 224 seconds when initial pressure was 202 mm Hg. Find the order of the reaction.

Solution: Since we know

$$\frac{(t_{1/2})_2}{(t_{1/2})_1} = \left(\frac{a_1}{a_2}\right)^{n-1}$$

where $(t_{1/2})_1$ and $(t_{1/2})_2$ are the half-life periods of a reaction, a_1 and a_2 the initial concentrations and n is the order of the reaction.

The above equation can be written as

$$n = 1 + \frac{\log\dfrac{(t_{1/2})_2}{(t_{1/2})_1}}{\log\left(\dfrac{a_1}{a_2}\right)}$$

Substituting the various values, we get

$$n = 1 + \frac{\log(224/140)}{\log(258/202)}$$

$$= 1 + \left(\frac{0.2041}{0.1062}\right)$$

$$= 1 + 2$$

$$= 3$$

Hence the order of the reaction is three.

Problem 16.8: In a particular reaction the time required to complete half of the reaction was found to increase nine times when the initial concentration of the reactant was reduced to one-third. What is the order of the reaction?

Solution: Let a be the initial concentration of the reactant and $t_{1/2}$ the half-life period of the reaction. When the concentration of the reactant reduces to one-third, *i.e.*, $a/3$, the half-life period $(t_{1/2})_2$ becomes $9\,(t_{1/2})_1$.

Thus

$$\frac{(t_{1/2})_2}{(t_{1/2})_1} = \left(\frac{a_1}{a_2}\right)^{n-1}$$

or

$$n = 1 + \frac{\log\dfrac{(t_{1/2})_2}{(t_{1/2})_1}}{\log\left(\dfrac{a_1}{a_2}\right)} = 1 + \frac{\log(9)}{\log\left(a\,\dfrac{3}{a}\right)}$$

$$= 1 + \frac{0.9542}{0.4771} = 3$$

Hence the order of the reaction is 3.

Problem 16.9: For the reaction

$$F_2 + 2\,ClO_2 = 2\,FClO_2$$

the following data have been obtained at 260 K:

$-\dfrac{d[F_2]}{dt} \times 10^3$ (mol dm^{-3} s^{-1})	Reactant concentration, mol dm^{-3}	
	$[F_2]$	$[ClO_2]$
1.2	0.10	0.01
4.8	0.10	0.04
2.4	0.20	0.01

Determine the overall order of the reaction. Calculate the rate constant and the rate of formation of $[FClO_2]$ at the instant when $[F_2] = 0.01$ mol dm^{-3} and $[ClO_2] = 0.02$ mol dm^{-3} at 260 K.

Solution: When $[F_2]$ is kept constant and the concentration of ClO_2 is quadrupled, the rate is also quadrupled. Hence the rate of the reaction is proportional to $[ClO_2]$. Again when $[ClO_2]$ is kept constant and $[F_2]$ is doubled, the rate is also doubled indicating that the rate is proportional to $[F_2]$. The rate equation is therefore

$$\text{Rate} = -\frac{d[F_2]}{dt} = k[F_2][ClO_2]$$

and the overall order of the reaction is 2.

From the above equation

$$k = \frac{-\dfrac{d[F_2]}{dt}}{[F_2][ClO_2]} = \frac{1.2 \times 10^{-3}}{0.1 \times 0.01} = 1.2 \; dm^3 mol^{-1} s^{-1}$$

The rate of disappearance of F_2 is given as

$$-\frac{d[F_2]}{dt} = k[F_2][ClO_2]$$

Since

$$[F_2] = 0.01 \text{ mol dm}^{-3}$$

$$[ClO_2] = 0.02 \text{ mol dm}^{-3}$$

Therefore

$$-\frac{d[F_2]}{dt} = 1.2 \times 0.01 \times 0.02$$

$$= 2.4 \times 10^{-4} \text{ mol dm}^{-3} \text{ s}^{-1}$$

From the stoichiometry of the reaction it is clear that the rate at which $FClO_2$ appears is twice the rate at which F_2 disappears. Hence the rate of formation of $FClO_2$ is twice the above value, i.e.,

$$4.8 \times 10^{-4} \text{ mol dm}^{-3} \text{ s}^{-1}$$

16.11 COMPLICATIONS IN REACTION KINETICS

There are many reactions which are accompanied by side reactions in addition to the main reaction. Such reactions do not take place in a single stage but occur in a number of well defined steps. In these cases the rate law is inconsistent with the stoichiometric equation for the reaction. The usual types of complications are:

(*i*) Reversible or opposing reactions;
(*ii*) Consecutive reactions;
(*iii*) Parallel reactions.

Reversible or Opposing Reactions

So far in the formulation of the rate equations it is assumed that the reactions proceed in one direction only. If the products formed react to produce the reactants back, the reaction is said to be *an opposing* or *a reversible* reaction. In such instances, the rate of the reverse reaction increases as more and more of the products are formed and eventually the two rates, *viz.*, forward and reverse become equal; the overall rate is then zero. A well known example is the hydrolysis of ethyl acetate in aqueous solution

$$CH_3COOC_2H_5 + H_2O \underset{}{\overset{H_2O^+}{\rightleftharpoons}} CH_3COOH + C_2H_5OH$$

In order to deduce the rate equation in such a case, the rate of the reversible reaction must be taken into account. Consider a simple reversible first order reaction

$$A \underset{k_{-1}}{\overset{k_1}{\rightleftharpoons}} B$$

Initial concentration	a	0
Concentration after time, t	$(a-x)$	x

Let k_1 be the first order rate constant in the forward direction and k_{-1} the rate constant in the reverse direction. The rates of the reactions are given as

$$\left(\frac{dx}{dt}\right)_{forward} = k_1\left(a-x\right)$$

and

$$\left(\frac{dx}{dt}\right)_{reverse} = k_{-1}x$$

Thus, the net rate of the reaction in the forward direction is

$$\left(\frac{dx}{dt}\right) = \left(\frac{dx}{dt}\right)_{forward} - \left(\frac{dx}{dt}\right)_{reverse}$$

$$= k_1\left(a-x\right) - k_{-1}\left(x\right) \qquad \qquad ...(16.28)$$

Equation (16.28) involves two constants, and hence another relation between k_1 and k_{-1} is required before the rate constants can be evaluated. For obtaining this relation we use the fact that at equilibrium $dx/dt = 0$ and $x = x_e$, the equilibrium concentration of B.

Hence

$$\left(\frac{dx}{dt}\right)_{forward} = \left(\frac{dx}{dt}\right)_{reverse} = k_1\left(a-x_e\right) - k_{-1}\left(x_e\right) = 0$$

$$k_{-1} = \frac{k_1\left(a-x_e\right)}{x_e} \qquad \qquad ...(16.29)$$

Substituting the value of k_{-1} in equation (16.28), we get

$$\frac{dx}{dt} = k_1\frac{a}{x_e}\left[x_e - x\right] \qquad \qquad ...(16.30)$$

Integration of equation (16.30) between the limits, $t = 0$, $x = 0$ and at $t = t$, $x = x_e$, gives

$$\ln\frac{x_e}{x_e - x} = \frac{tk_1 a}{x_e} \qquad \qquad ...(16.31)$$

From the above equation the rate constant k_1 can be evaluated provided x_e is known.

However, an alternative equation is often used in reversible reactions. From Eq. (16.29), it can be shown that

$$k_1 + k_{-1} = \frac{ak_1}{x_e}$$

Hence, Eq. (16.31) may be written as

$$k_1 + k_{-1} = \frac{1}{t}\ln\frac{x_e}{x_e - x} \qquad \qquad ...(16.31(a))$$

The above equation is an expression for the first order reaction where the initial concentration is being replaced by x_e, the equilibrium concentration. Thus, a reversible first order reaction may be treated as if it were a simple first order reaction.

In the above derivation it has been assumed that the initial concentration of the product is zero. If this is not the case then the rate Eq. (16.28) becomes

$$\frac{dx}{dt} = k_1 (a - x) - k_{-1} (b + x) \qquad \text{...(16.32)}$$

where b is the initial concentration of the product.

At equilibrium, since $\dfrac{dx}{dt} = 0$

$\therefore$
$$k_1 (a - x_e) = k_{-1} (b + x_e)$$

or
$$k_{-1} = k_1 \frac{(a - x_e)}{(b + x_e)} \qquad \text{...(16.33)}$$

The net rate of reaction $\dfrac{dx}{dt}$ can be expressed as (16.31(a))

$$\frac{dx}{dt} = k_1 (a - x) - k_1 \frac{(a - x_e)(b + x)}{(b + x_e)}$$

$$= k_1 \frac{(a + b)(x_e - x)}{(b + x_e)}$$

or
$$k_1 dt = \frac{(b + x_e)}{(a + b)} \left\{ \frac{dx}{(x_e - x)} \right\} \qquad \text{...(16.34)}$$

Integration of expression (16.34) gives

$$k_1 t + I = \frac{(b + x_e)}{(a + b)} \left[-\ln(x_e - x) \right] \qquad \text{...(16.35)}$$

At $t = 0$, $x = 0$, then

$$I = \left(\frac{b + x_e}{a + b} \right)(-\ln x_e)$$

Substituting the value of I in the expression (16.35), we get

$$k_1 t + \left(\frac{b + x_e}{a + b} \right)(-\ln x_e) = \left(\frac{b + x_e}{a + b} \right)\left[-\ln(x_e - x) \right]$$

or
$$k_1 = \frac{1}{t} \left(\frac{b + x_e}{a + b} \right) \ln\left(\frac{x_e}{x_e - x} \right) \qquad \text{...(16.36)}$$

Eq. (16.33) gives
$$x_e = \left(\frac{k_1 a - k_{-1} b}{k_1 + k_{-1}} \right)$$

Substituting this value of x_e in equation (16.36) gives

$$\left(k_1 + k_{-1}\right) = \frac{1}{t}\ln\frac{x_e}{x_e - x}$$

This equation is similar to one obtained for a case in which no B was present initially.

Consecutive Reactions

These are reactions which proceed from reactants to products through one or more intermediate steps. Consider a simple first order consecutive reaction scheme

$$A \xrightarrow{k_1} B \xrightarrow{k_1'} C$$

Initial concentration	a	0	0
Concentration after time t	x	y	z

In the above reaction each stage has its own rate constant given by k_1 and k_1' as shown. The overall rate of the reaction will depend upon the relative magnitudes of these rate constants. If $k_1 \gg k_1'$ —conversion of B to C is a slow step and will determine the rate of formation of the products. On the other hand, if $k_1' \gg k_1$—formation of B from A will control the overall rate of the reaction. However, if the two rate constants are of comparable magnitudes, the overall rate of the reaction will depend on both the rate constants and the problem becomes more complicated.

The rate of disappearance of A, $\quad -\dfrac{d[A]}{dt} = -\dfrac{dx}{dt} = k_1 x$ ...(16.37)

The rate of formation of B, $\quad \dfrac{d[B]}{dt} = \dfrac{dy}{dt} = k_1 x - k_1' y$ ...(16.38)

The rate of formation of C, $\quad \dfrac{d[C]}{dt} = \dfrac{dz}{dt} = k_1' y$ ...(16.39)

Equation (16.37) on integration in the limits $x = a$, $t = 0$ and $x = x$ to $t = t$, gives

$$k_1 t = \ln\frac{a}{x}$$

or $\qquad\qquad\qquad\qquad x = a e^{-k_1 t}$ ...(16.40)

The concentration of A decreases exponentially with time as happens in any first order reaction. Substituting this value of x in equation (16.38) gives

$$\frac{dy}{dt} = k_1 a e^{-k_1 t} - k_1' y$$

This is a linear first order differential equation whose solution is

$$y = \frac{k_1 a}{k_1' - k_1}\left[e^{-k_1 t} - e^{-k_1' t}\right]$$ ...(16.41)

During the reaction there is no change in the number of moles, *i.e.,*

$$x + y + z = a$$

or

$$z = a - (x + y)$$

$$= a - \frac{ak_1}{k_1' - k_1}\left[e^{-k_1 t} - e^{-k_1' t}\right] - ae^{-k_1 t}$$

$$z = \frac{a}{k_1' - k_1}\left[\left(k_1' - k_1' e^{-k_1 t}\right) - \left(k_1 - k_1 e^{-k_1' t}\right)\right] \qquad ...(16.42)$$

In Fig. 16.5, the concentrations of x, y and z are plotted as functions of time. It is clear from the figure that the concentration of A decreases exponentially while that of C increases gradually to the value of a when all A has changed into C. The concentration of the intermediate B rises to a maximum value and then falls off asymptotically to zero.

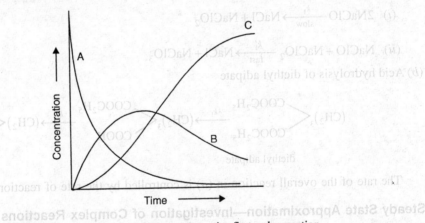

Fig. 16.5 Concentration changes in a consecutive first order reaction

If $k_1' \gg k_1$ in equation (16.41), then $e^{-k_1' t}$ is much less than $e^{-k_1 t}$ and the equation (16.41) reduces

to

$$y = \frac{ak_1}{k_1' - k_1}e^{-k_1 t}$$

Since

$$x = ae^{-k_1 t}$$

hence

$$\frac{y}{x} = \frac{k_1}{k_1' - k_1}$$

i.e., the ratio of the amounts of B and A formed in a definite interval of time after the start of the reaction becomes constant. The amounts of A and B falls to the same extent. Such a state is called the transient equilibrium. If $k_1' \gg k_1$ then

$$\frac{y}{x} = \frac{k_1}{k_1'}$$

For a first order reaction

$$\frac{x}{y} = \frac{\left(t_{1/2}\right)_B}{\left(t_{1/2}\right)_A}$$

This equation is called secular equilibrium.

The formation of C therefore involves only the smaller rate constant k_1' and is, therefore, the rate determining step. Similarly, when $k_1' \gg k_1$, Eq. (16.42) reduces to

$$z \approx a\left(1 - e^{-k_1 t}\right)$$

which again involves the rate constant of the slower step.

Examples of Consecutive Reactions

(a) Decomposition of sodium hypochlorite takes place in two steps as

(i) $2NaClO \xrightarrow[\text{slow}]{k_1} NaCl + NaClO_2$

(ii) $NaClO + NaClO_2 \xrightarrow[\text{fast}]{k_1'} NaCl + NaClO_3$

(b) Acid hydrolysis of diethyl adipate

$$(CH_2)_3 \!\! \begin{array}{c} COOC_2H_5 \\ \\ COOC_2H_5 \end{array} \xrightarrow{k_1} (CH_2)_3 \!\! \begin{array}{c} COOC_2H_5 \\ \\ COOH \end{array} \xrightarrow{k_1'} (CH_2) \!\! \begin{array}{c} COOH \\ \\ COOH \end{array}$$

diethyl adipate   adipic acid

The rate of the overall reaction in (a) is controlled by the rate of reaction (i).

Steady State Approximation—Investigation of Complex Reactions

In the preceding section we have seen that the concentration of the intermediate B grows up to a certain small and fixed value. At this stage the rates of formation of the intermediate and its disappearance are equal, i.e.

$$\frac{d[B]}{dt} = 0$$

This fact of constant concentration of an unstable intermediate species is called *the principle of steady state approximation*.

From equation (16.41), we have

$$y = \frac{k_1 a}{k_1' - k_1}\left[e^{-k_1 t} - e^{-k_1' t}\right]$$

From the principle of steady state,

$$\frac{dy}{dt} = a\frac{k_1}{k_1' - k_1}\left[-k_1 e^{-k_1 t} + k_1' e^{-k_1' t}\right] = 0$$

therefore,

$$k_1' e^{-k_1' t} = k_1 e^{-k_1 t}$$

$$\frac{k_1}{k_1'} = \frac{e^{-k_1' t}}{e^{-k_1 t}}$$

Replacing t by t_{max}, we have

or

$$\ln \frac{k_1}{k_1'} = \left(k_1 - k_1'\right) t_{max}$$

or

$$t_{max} = \frac{1}{\left(k_1 - k_1'\right)} \ln \frac{k_1}{k_1'} \qquad \qquad ...(16.43)$$

The maximum concentration of B (y_{max}) is given by

$$y_{max} = a \left[\frac{k_1'}{k_1}\right]^{\frac{k_1'}{k_1 - k_1'}} \qquad \qquad ...(16.44)$$

The maximum amount of the intermediate B depends not on the absolute values of the rate constants k_1

and k_1' but only on the ratio $\frac{k_1'}{k_1}$.

By the use of this principle it is possible to obtain the overall rate equation of complex reactions. As an example, consider the reaction

$$2NO + 2H_2 \xrightarrow{k} N_2 + 2H_2O$$

The overall rate equation is given by $k\,[NO]^2\,[H_2]$

The following mechanism may be proposed:

$$NO + NO \underset{k_{-1}}{\overset{k_1}{\rightleftharpoons}} N_2O_2 \qquad \qquad ...(i)$$

$$N_2O_2 + H_2 \xrightarrow{k_2} N_2O + H_2O \qquad \qquad ...(ii)$$

$$N_2O + H_2 \xrightarrow{k_3} N_2 + H_2O \qquad \qquad ...(iii)$$

The rate equations for the intermediates N_2O_2 and N_2O are

$$\frac{d[N_2O_2]}{dt} = k_1 [NO]^2 - k_{-1} [N_2O_2] - k_2 [N_2O_2][H_2] \qquad \qquad ...(iv)$$

and

$$\frac{d[N_2O]}{dt} = k_2 [N_2O_2][H_2] - k_3 [N_2O][H_2] \qquad \qquad ...(v)$$

Using the steady state approximation, we get

$$k_1[NO]^2 = k_{-1}[N_2O_2] + k_2[N_2O_2][H_2]$$

or,

$$[N_2O_2] = \frac{k_1[NO]^2}{k_{-1} + k_2[H_2]}$$

and

$$k_2[N_2O_2][H_2] - k_3[N_2O][H_2] = 0$$

or

$$[N_2O] = \frac{k_2[N_2O_2]}{k_3}$$

Substituting the value of $[N_2O_2]$ in the above equation, we get

$$[N_2O] = \frac{k_2 k_1[NO]^2}{k_3\left(k_{-1} + k_2[H_2]\right)}$$

The overall rate of the reaction can be expressed as

$$\frac{d[N_2]}{dt} = k_3[N_2O][H_2]$$

$$= k_3\left(\frac{k_2}{k_3}\right)\frac{k_1[NO]^2[H_2]}{k_{-1} + k_2[H_2]}$$

$$= \frac{k_2 k_1[NO]^2[H_2]}{k_{-1} + k_2[H_2]}$$

If $k_{-1} \gg k_2$, then $k_2[H_2]$ can be neglected, and the rate becomes

$$\frac{d[N_2]}{dt} = \frac{k_2 k_1[NO]^2[H_2]}{k_{-1}}$$

which is similar to the observed rate equation $k[NO]^2[H_2]$.

Problem 16.10: For the reaction

$$2NO + Cl_2 = 2NOCl$$

following mechanism has been proposed:

$$NO + Cl_2 \underset{k_{-1}}{\overset{k_1}{\rightleftharpoons}} NOCl_2$$

$$NO + NOCl_2 \overset{k_2}{\longrightarrow} 2NOCl$$

Show that the overall rate of the reaction is given by $k[NO]^2[Cl_2]$ assuming that $k_2[NO] \ll k_{-1}$.

Show that the overall rate of the reaction is given by $k[NO]^2[Cl_2]$ assuming that $k_2[NO] \ll k_{-1}$.

Solution: Applying the steady state approximation to the concentration of $NOCl_2$, we have

$$\frac{d[NOCl_2]}{dt} = 0 = k_1[NO][Cl_2] - k_{-1}[NOCl_2] - k_2[NO][NOCl_2]$$

or
$$[NOCl_2] = \frac{k_1[NO][Cl_2]}{k_{-1} + k_2[NO]}$$

The overall rate of the reaction is given as

$$\frac{d[NOCl]}{dt} = k_2[NO][NOCl_2]$$

Substituting the value of $[NOCl_2]$ in the above equation, we get

$$\frac{d[NOCl]}{dt} = \frac{k_1 k_2[NO][NO][Cl_2]}{k_{-1} + k_2[NO]}$$

If $k_2[NO] \ll k_{-1}$

$$\frac{d[NOCl]}{dt} = \frac{k_1 k_2}{k_{-1}}[NO]^2[Cl_2]$$

$$= k[NO]^2[Cl_2]$$

where
$$k = \frac{k_1 k_2}{k_{-1}}$$

Problem 16.11: For the thermal decomposition of O_3 following mechanism has been suggested:

(i) $O_3 \underset{k_{-1}}{\overset{k_1}{\rightleftharpoons}} O_2 + O$

(ii) $O_3 + O \xrightarrow{k_2} 2O_2$

Assuming that $k_{-1}[O_2] \gg k_2[O_3]$, show that the rate of the overall reaction is

$$-\frac{d[O_3]}{dt} = \frac{k[O_3]^2}{[O_2]}.$$

What could be concluded from the appearance of $\frac{1}{[O_2]}$ in the rate equation?

Solution: Applying steady state approximation to the intermediate O atom, we get

$$\frac{d[O]}{dt} = k_1[O_3] - k_{-1}[O_2][O] - k_2[O][O_3] = 0$$

$$[O][k_{-1}[O_2] + k_2[O_3]] = k_1[O_3]$$

$$[O] = \frac{k_1[O_3]}{k_{-1}[O_2] + k_2[O_3]}$$

The rate of decomposition of O_3 is given by

$$-\frac{d[O_3]}{dt} = k_1[O_3] - k_{-1}[O_2][O] + k_2[O_3][O]$$

$$= k_1[O_3] + [k_2[O_3] - k_{-1}[O_2]][O]$$

Substituting the value of [O] in the above equation, we get

$$-\frac{d[O_3]}{dt} = k_1[O_3] + [k_2[O_3] - k_{-1}[O_2]]\left[\frac{k_1[O_3]}{k_{-1}[O_2] + k_2[O_3]}\right]$$

$$= \frac{k_{-1}k_1[O_3][O_2] + k_1k_2[O_3]^2 + k_1k_2[O_3]^2 - k_1k_{-1}[O_3][O_2]}{k_{-1}[O_2] + k_2[O_3]}$$

$$= \frac{2k_1k_2[O_3]^2}{k_{-1}[O_2] + k_2[O_3]}$$

If $k_{-1}[O_2] \gg k_2[O_3]$, i.e., step (ii) is slow, we get

$$-\frac{d[O_3]}{dt} = \frac{2k_1k_2[O_3]^2}{k_{-1}[O_2]} = k\frac{[O_3]^2}{[O_2]}$$

The appearance of $\dfrac{1}{[O_2]}$ in the rate equation suggests that the reaction is of order −1 with respect to O_2 or it retards the rate of the reaction.

Parallel Reactions

These are reactions in which the reacting molecules react or decompose in more than one ways yielding different sets of products. The reaction yielding maximum amount of the product is known as the main or major reaction and the other reactions are referred to as the *side* or *parallel reactions*. To calculate the overall rate constant in such cases, the rate of the side reactions should be taken into account. Consider a reaction

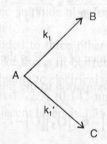

The rates of these two processes are given as

$$\frac{d[B]}{dt} = k_1[A] \qquad \qquad ...(16.45)$$

and

$$\frac{d[C]}{dt} = k_1'[A] \qquad \qquad ...(16.46)$$

The overall rate of disappearance of A is given by

$$-\frac{d[A]}{dt} = k_1[A] + k_1'[A]$$

$$= [k_1 + k_1'][A] \qquad \qquad ...(16.47)$$

The ratio of the two rates is given as

$$\frac{\dfrac{d[B]}{dt}}{\dfrac{d[C]}{dt}} = \frac{k_1}{k_1'} \qquad \qquad ...(16.48)$$

With the help of Eqs. (16.47) and (16.48), the rate constants for individual steps can be calculated. Some examples of parallel reactions:

(*i*) Nitration of phenol

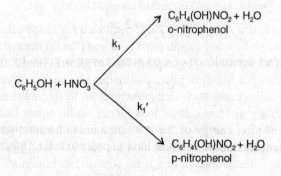

(*ii*) Dehydration of ethanol

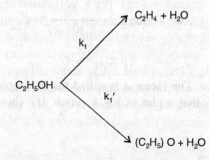

Rate Equation for Autocatalytic Reactions

In some cases, the product of the reaction is able to accelerate the rate of a reaction. Such reactions are called *autocatalytic* reactions. Oxidation of oxalic acid by $KMnO_4$ in acidic medium is catalysed by Mn^{2+} ions. The reaction rate increases with time. The rate equation in such cases involves the concentration of the product which catalyses the reaction. Thus for the reaction

$$A \rightarrow B + C$$

in which the product B catalyses the reaction, the rate equation is given by

$$\frac{dx}{dt} = k(a - x)(x)$$

where x is the amount of A decomposed at any instant and a is its initial concentration. Similarly, for the reaction

$$A + B \rightarrow C + D$$

in which C catalyses the reaction, the expression for the rate is given as

$$\frac{dx}{dt} = kx(a - x)(b - x)$$

where a and b being the initial concentrations of A and B.

16.12 EFFECT OF TEMPERATURE ON REACTION RATES

It has been found that an increase in temperature generally increases the rate of a reaction. In majority of cases it has been seen that the rate of a reaction increases by a factor of 2 or 3 for every 10°C rise in temperature. This is empirically given by the relation

$$\frac{k_{t+10}}{k_t} \approx 2 \text{ or } 3$$

However, a more correct dependence of k on temperature is given by Arrhenius equation

$$\frac{d \ln k}{dT} = \frac{E_a}{RT^2} \qquad \qquad ...(16.49)$$

where E_a is called *the activation energy* of the reaction and is characteristic of the reaction. It is the threshold energy that the reactant molecules must have in order to react. Integration of Eq. (16.49) yields

$$\ln k = -\frac{E_a}{RT} + I \qquad \qquad ...(16.50)$$

$$\log k = -\frac{E_a}{2.303 \, RT} + I' \qquad \qquad ...(16.51)$$

$$k = Ae^{-E_a/RT} \qquad \qquad ...(16.52)$$

where I is the integration constant. The factor A is called the pre-exponential factor or the frequency factor. Equation (16.51) suggests that a plot of log k versus $1/T$ should be a straight line for many reactions as shown in Fig. 16.6.

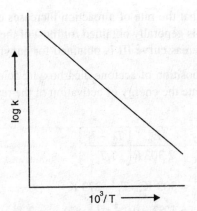

Fig. 16.6 Plot of log k versus $1/T$

The slope of the plot is equal to $-\dfrac{E}{2.303\,R}$ and the intercept equal to I'. From the slope of this plot the activation energy can be evaluated. However, if we integrate Eq. (16.49) between the limits $k = k_1$ at $T = T_1$ and $k = k_2$ at $T = T_2$, then

$$\ln\frac{k_2}{k_1} = \frac{E_a}{R}\left[-\frac{1}{T}\right]_{T_1}^{T_2}$$

$$= \frac{E_a}{R}\left[\frac{1}{T_1} - \frac{1}{T_2}\right]$$

$$= \frac{E_a}{R}\left[\frac{T_2 - T_1}{T_1\,T_2}\right]$$

or

$$\log\frac{k_2}{k_1} = \frac{E_a}{2.303\,R}\left[\frac{T_2 - T_1}{T_1\,T_2}\right] \qquad \text{...(16.53)}$$

From this equation it is evident that the activation energy, E_a, can be obtained from the value of the rate constants at two different temperatures.

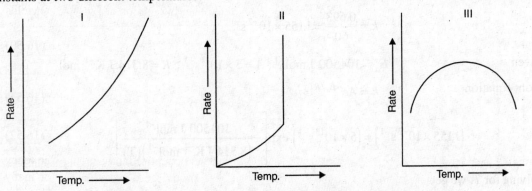

Fig. 16.7 Various types of curves showing variation of the rate with temperature

Arrhenius equation shows that the rate of a reaction increases exponentially with rise in temperature (Fig. 16.7). Curve of type *I* is generally obtained for most of the reactions. For explosive reactions, curve of type II is obtained whereas curve III is obtained for enzyme catalysed reactions.

Problem 16.12: For the decomposition of acetone dicarboxylic acid, $k = 2.46 \times 10^{-5}$ s^{-1} at 273 K and 1.63×10^{-3} s^{-1} at 303 K. Calculate the energy of activation of the reaction.

Solution: Since

$$\log \frac{k_2}{k_1} = \frac{E_a}{2.303\,R}\left[\frac{T_2 - T_1}{T_1 T_2}\right]$$

Here

$$T_2 = 303 \text{ K}; \quad T_1 = 273 \text{ K}$$

and

$$(k)_{303} = 1.63 \times 10^{-3}\,\text{s}^{-1}; \quad (k)_{273} = 2.46 \times 10^{-5}\,\text{s}^{-1}$$

$$R = 8.314 \text{ JK}^{-1}\,\text{mol}^{-1}$$

Hence

$$\log \frac{1.63 \times 10^{-3}}{2.46 \times 10^{-5}} = \frac{E_a}{(2.303)(8.314)}\frac{(30)}{(273 \times 303)}$$

or

$$E_a = \frac{(2.303)(8.314)(273 \times 303)}{30}\log \frac{1.63 \times 10^{-3}}{2.46 \times 10^{-5}}$$

$$= 96510 \text{ J mol}^{-1} = 96.51 \text{ kJ mol}^{-1}$$

Problem 16.13: If a first order reaction has an activation energy of 104 500 J mol^{-1} and the pre-exponential factor A in the Arrhenius equation has a value of 5.0×10^{13} s^{-1}, at what temperature will the reaction have a half-life of (*i*) 1 minute and (*ii*) 30 days?

Solution: (*i*) For a first order reaction

$$t_{1/2} = \frac{0.693}{k}$$

or

$$k = \frac{0.693}{t_{1/2}}$$

Since

$$t_{1/2} = 60\,\text{s}$$

$$k = \frac{0.693}{60} = 1.155 \times 10^{-2}\,\text{s}^{-1}$$

Given

$$E_a = 104500 \text{ J mol}^{-1}; \quad A = 5 \times 10^{13}\,\text{s}^{-1}; \quad R = 8.314 \text{ J K}^{-1}\,\text{mol}^{-1}$$

From equation

$$k = A e^{-E_a/RT}$$

$$\left(1.155 \times 10^{-2}\,\text{s}^{-1}\right) = \left(5 \times 10^{13}\,\text{s}^{-1}\right)\exp\left[-\frac{104500 \text{ J mol}^{-1}}{\left(8.314 \text{ J K}^{-1}\,\text{mol}^{-1}\right)(T)}\right]$$

Solving for T, we get

$$T = 348 \text{ K or } 75°\text{C}$$

(*ii*) Now $\qquad t_{1/2} = 30$ days $= (30 \times 24 \times 60 \times 60)$ s

Therefore $\qquad k = \dfrac{0.693}{(30 \times 24 \times 60 \times 60)} = 2.67 \times 10^{-4}\,\text{s}^{-1}$

Again from equation $\qquad k = Ae^{-E_a/RT}$

$$2.67 \times 10^{-4} = 5 \times 10^{13} \exp - \left[\frac{104500}{8.314 \times T} \right]$$

Solving for T, we get $\qquad T = 268$ K or $-5°$C

16.13 THE ENERGY OF ACTIVATION

In Arrhenius equation appearance of E_a suggests that molecules must acquire a certain amount of energy before they could undergo chemical reactions. This means that before the chemical reaction to occur the molecules must be activated, *i.e.*, they must be raised to a higher energy state. *The minimum energy which the reacting molecules must possess before the reaction to occur is known as the energy of activation.* According to the concept of activation, the transformation of the reactants into the products does not take place directly. The reacting molecules, however, must acquire sufficient energy to cross an activation energy barrier. This idea may be made clear with the help of a schematic diagram as shown in Fig. 16.8 for the reaction $A \rightarrow B$. Let E_A represent the average energy of the reactants and E_B those of the products. Even if E_A is greater than E_B, the reactants A will not be directly converted into the products B. The reacting molecules must first attain the minimum energy E_a, for the reaction to occur. Molecules at C having energy E_a, are said to be in an activated state. The excess energy $(E_a - E_A)$, which the reactant molecules must absorb in order to become activated and react, is the energy of activation E_1 for the forward direction, *i.e.*, $A \rightarrow C$.

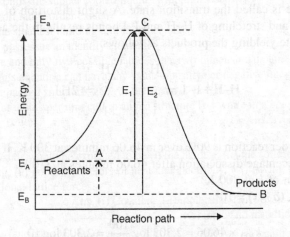

Fig. 16.8 Energy of activation

Energy of activation = Energy of the activated state − Energy of the reactants

$$E_1 = E_a - E_A$$

When the activated complex decomposes into the products, energy (E_2) is given out. This can be taken as the energy of activation of the process $B \rightarrow C$, *i.e.*,

$$E_2 = E_a - E_B$$

Thus, the difference ΔE, between E_A and E_B is given as

$$\Delta E = E_1 - E_2$$
$$= (E_a - E_A) - (E_a - E_B)$$
$$= E_B - E_A$$

ΔE is simply the difference in energy between the products and reactants and is known as the enthalpy of the reaction at constant volume. This means that when the activated complex decomposes into the products, it gives out an energy E_2 which is equal to the energy absorbed by the reactant molecules from A to C plus the enthalpy of reaction. If $E_2 > E_1$, the reaction is evidently exothermic, whereas if $E_2 < E_1$, the reaction is endothermic.

We will now apply the idea of activation energy to the reaction

$$H-H + I-I \rightleftharpoons 2HI$$

When two molecules (H_2 and I_2) are far apart and the total energy of the system is equal to the potential energies of H_2 and I_2, this part of the reaction is represented by the horizontal portion of the curve in Fig. 16.8. As the molecules approach each other, H–H and I–I bonds begin to stretch and HI bond begins to form. The energy starts increasing and is represented by the rising portion of the curve. HI bond formation increases and that of H–H and I–I bonds breakage increases, a point is reached when the energy is maximum (point C). At this point the activated complex of the type shown below is formed:

$$\text{H} \cdots\cdots \text{H}$$
$$\vdots \qquad\quad \vdots$$
$$\text{I} \cdots\cdots \text{I}$$

The point C in the curve is called the transition state. A slight distortion of the bond in the form of compression of HI bond and stretching of H–H and I–I bonds results in the activated complex to pass through the transition state yielding the products as follows:

$$\text{H-H} + \text{I-I} \rightleftharpoons \begin{array}{c} \text{H} \cdots\cdots \text{H} \\ \vdots \qquad\quad \vdots \\ \text{I} \cdots\cdots \text{I} \end{array} \rightleftharpoons 2\text{HI}$$

Problem 16.14: A first order reaction is 90% over in 46.06 minutes at 300 K. If E_a, the activation energy is 93 kJ, calculate the percentage dissociation after 46.06 minutes at 310 K.

Solution: Calculation of k at 300 K

$$a = 100, (a - x) = 10$$

Hence

$$k_{300} \times 46.06 = 2.303 \log \frac{100}{10} = 2.303 \log 10$$

$$k_{300} = 5.0 \times 10^{-2} \, \text{min}^{-1}$$

Now

$$\log \frac{k_{310}}{k_{300}} = \frac{93000 \times 10}{2.303 \times 300 \times 310 \times 8.314} = 0.5222$$

or

Now at 310 K,

$$k_{310} = 1.664 \text{ min}^{-1}$$
$$a = 100, (a-x) = ?$$

Using the equation

$$\left(1.664 \text{ min}^{-1}\right)(46.06 \text{ min}) = 2.303 \log \frac{100}{a-x}$$

gives $(a-x)$, the amount that is undissociated as

$$a - x = 4.68 \times 10^{-2} = 0.0468$$

∴ The amount dissociated = $100 - 0.0468 = 99.95\%$

16.14 COLLISION THEORY OF REACTION RATES

The collision theory attempts to account for the observed kinetics of reactions in terms of kinetic molecular theory. This theory has been found to be satisfactory for gaseous reactions and postulates that the reacting molecules must collide. If collision is the only requirement for a reaction to occur then the rate of the reaction should be proportional to the number of collisions between the reacting molecules. In order to explain this discrepancy, it is assumed that molecules are activated and only those molecules possessing energy equal to or greater than the activation energy are able to form the products. Furthermore, in many cases it is assumed that molecules must be properly oriented so that rearrangement of atoms can occur with minimum expenditure of energy and time.

Thus, in collision theory the essential requirements for reactions to occur are:

(*i*) Collisions between the reactant molecules
(*ii*) Activation of molecules and
(*iii*) Proper orientation of the reacting molecules at the time of collision.

For a bimolecular gaseous reaction

$$A + A \xrightarrow{k} \text{Product(s)}$$

the rate of the reaction is given by

$$-\frac{d[A]}{dt} = k[A]^2$$

If the concentration of A is 1 mol dm^{-3}, we get

$$-\frac{d[A]}{dt} = k \qquad \qquad ...(16.54)$$

According to the collision theory the rate of the reaction is given by

$$-\frac{d[A]}{dt} = k = Z_{11}q \qquad \qquad ...(16.55)$$

where Z_{11} is the number of collisions between the reacting molecules per second per dm^3 and q is the fraction of the total number of molecules which are activated. The values of Z_{11} and q can be calculated from the kinetic theory of gases. Z_{11} is given by (Eq. 2.47).

$$Z_{11} = \frac{1}{2} \sqrt{2} \pi \sigma^2 (n')^2 C_{av} \qquad \qquad ...(16.56)$$

and
$$q = \frac{n^*}{n'} = e^{-E_a/RT} \qquad \qquad ...(16.57)$$

where σ is the collision diameter and C_{av} the average velocity of the molecules in dm per second, n^* the number of molecules per dm^3 having energy equal to or more than the activation energy E_a and n' is the total number of molecules per dm^3. Substituting the value of C_{av} in Eq. (16.56), we get

$$Z_{11} = \frac{1}{2} \sqrt{2} \, \pi \sigma^2 (n')^2 \sqrt{\frac{8RT}{\pi M}}$$

$$= 2\sigma^2 (n')^2 \sqrt{\frac{\pi RT}{M}} \qquad \qquad ...(16.58)$$

The number of collisions per second between two unlike molecules 1 and 2 is given by

$$Z_{12} = n'_1 n'_2 \left(\frac{\sigma_1 + \sigma_2}{2} \right)^2 \sqrt{\frac{8\pi kT}{\mu}} \qquad \qquad ...(16.59)$$

where n_1' and n_2' are the number of molecules per dm^3 of reactants 1 and 2, σ_1 and σ_2 are the collision diameters of the molecules 1 and 2 and μ is reduced mass given by

$$\frac{1}{\mu} = \frac{1}{m_1} + \frac{1}{m_2}$$

Hence the expression for the rate of a reaction involving identical molecules is given by

$$\text{Rate} = qZ_{11} = 2\sigma^2 (n')^2 \sqrt{\frac{\pi RT}{M}} \, e^{-E_a/RT} \qquad \qquad ...(16.60)$$

and for different reactant molecules

$$\text{Rate} = qZ_{12} = n'_1 n'_2 \left(\frac{\sigma_1 + \sigma_2}{2} \right)^2 \sqrt{\frac{8\pi KT}{\mu}} \, e^{-E_a/RT} \qquad \qquad ...(16.61)$$

Comparison of Eq. (16.60) with Eq. (16.52) shows that the pre-exponential factor A in the Arrhenius equation is equal to Z_{11}.

The results predicted by Eqs. (16.60) and (16.61) can be compared with the experimental values of the rate constants.

We can take the example of dissociation of a mole of HI per dm^3 at 556 K. The value of activation energy for this reaction has been found to be 185.0 kJ, the collision diameter for HI is 3.5×10^{-9} dm, the molar mass is 1.28×10^{-1} kg mol^{-1} and the number of molecules per dm^3 is 6.023×10^{23}. Substituting these values in Eq. (16.58), we obtain

$$Z_{11} = 2\sigma^2 (n')^2 \sqrt{\frac{\pi RT}{M}}$$

$$= 2 \times \left(3.5 \times 10^{-9}\,\text{dm}\right)^2 \left(6.023 \times 10^{23}\,\text{dm}^{-3}\right)^2 \times \left(\frac{3.14 \times 8.314 \times 10^2\,\text{kg dm}^2\text{s}^{-2}\,\text{K}^{-1}\text{mol}^{-1} \times 556\,\text{K}}{1.28 \times 10^{-1}\,\text{kg mol}^{-1}}\right)^{1/2}$$

$$= 2.99 \times 10^{34}\,\text{s}^{-1}\text{dm}^{-3}$$

The number of colliding molecules per second per dm^3 is twice the value of Z_{11}, *i.e.*, 5.98×10^{34}.

The fraction of the total number of molecules, q, is given by

$$q = e^{-E_a/RT}$$

$$= \exp\left[-\frac{185 \times 10^3}{8.314 \times 556}\right] = 5.2 \times 10^{-18}$$

Hence

$$k = q\,Z_{11}$$

$$= 5.98 \times 10^{34} \times 5.2 \times 10^{-18}$$

$$= 3.12 \times 10^{17}\ \text{molecules/dm}^3/\text{sec}$$

If this value is divided by Avogadro constant, we get the rate constant in units of $\text{mol}^{-1}\text{dm}^3\,\text{s}^{-1}$.
Therefore,
$$k = 5.2 \times 10^{-7}\ \text{mol}^{-1}\ \text{dm}^3\ \text{s}^{-1}$$

The experimental value of k has been found to be $3.5 \times 10^{-7}\ \text{mol}^{-1}\text{dm}^3\ \text{s}^{-1}$.

The agreement between these two values is quite satisfactory indicating the validity of the theory. However, the agreement between the calculated and the observed values has been found to hold only for simple bimolecular gaseous reactions and in solutions where the reacting molecules are simple. For reaction involving complex molecules, the experimental rates are quite different from the calculated values. In order to account for the observed discrepancy it is further postulated that the molecules must be properly oriented at the time of the collision and an additional term is introduced in the expression for the rate of the reaction, *i.e.*,

$$k = P\,Z_{11}\,e^{-Ea/RT} \qquad\qquad ...(16.62)$$

where P is referred to as the probability or steric factor and is related to the geometry of the molecule. It is a measure of the deviation from the calculated value. It can have values ranging from unity to about 10^{-9} for slow reactions.

16.15 THE TRANSITION STATE THEORY OR THE THEORY OF ABSOLUTE REACTION RATES

The collision theory of reaction rates suffers from the following drawbacks: (*i*) It is difficult to calculate the steric factor from molecular geometry for complex molecules; (*ii*) the theory is applicable essentially to gaseous reactions. An alternate theory called absolute reaction rate theory or frequently known as transition state theory of reaction rates has been developed by Eyring in 1935. This theory attempts to treat the reaction rates from thermodynamic considerations. It is assumed that an equilibrium is established between the reactants and the activated complex. The activated complex is treated formally as a molecule in spite of its transitory existence and the laws of thermodynamics can be applied to it. As stated previously that all the reactions proceed through an activated or transition state which has energy higher than the reactants or the products. The rate of reaction depends upon two factors, *viz.*, (*i*) the concentration of the transition state species and (ii) the rate at which the activated complex decomposes. Consider a simple bimolecular reaction between molecules A and B as

$$A + B \rightleftharpoons [AB^{\ddagger}] \xrightarrow{k_2} \text{Products}$$

The rate of such a reaction = [Concentration of the activated complex molecule] × [Frequency of decomposition of the activated complex into the products]

In order to calculate the concentration of the activated complex it is assumed that the complex is in equilibrium with the reactant molecules. Hence the equilibrium constant $K_{eq}^{\ddagger}$ is given as

$$K_{eq}^{\ddagger} = \frac{[AB^{\ddagger}]}{[A][B]}$$

or
$$[AB^{\ddagger}] = K_{eq}^{\ddagger}[A][B] \qquad \qquad ...(16.63)$$

The activated complex is an aggregate of atoms and is assumed to be similar to an ordinary molecule except that it breaks up into products at a special vibration at which it is unstable. The frequency of such a vibration is something like the rate at which the activated complex decomposes. If ν is the frequency of such a vibration, then the rate of decomposition of the activated complex is given as

$$-\frac{d[A]}{dt} = -\frac{d[B]}{dt} = k_2[A][B]$$

$$= [AB^{\ddagger}]\nu = K_{eq}^{\ddagger}[A][B]\nu \qquad \qquad ...(16.64)$$

Since an activated complex is an unstable species and is held together by loose bonds, therefore the vibration of low frequency will decompose the activated complex. The average energy of such a vibrational degree of freedom is given by kT (where k is the Boltzmann constant and is equal to R/N where N is the Avogadro constant). The energy E of this vibration is given by Planck's expression, $E = h\nu$.

From these expressions, the frequency is calculated as

$$\nu = \frac{E}{h} = \frac{kT}{h} = \frac{RT}{N_A h}$$

Substituting this value of ν in Eq. (16.64), we get

$$k_2[A][B] = K_{eq}^{\ddagger}[A][B]\frac{RT}{N_A h}$$

or
$$k_2 = K_{eq}^{\ddagger}\frac{RT}{N_A h} \qquad \qquad ...(16.65)$$

Thermodynamic Aspects: The result given by expression (16.65) is of importance when the equilibrium constant is interpreted thermodynamically by introducing the terms, free energy of activation, $\Delta G^{\ddagger}$, the enthalpy of activation, $\Delta H^{\ddagger}$ and the entropy of activation, $\Delta S^{\ddagger}$. These quantities represent the difference between the values of the respective thermodynamic functions between the activated complex and the reactants, all substances being in their standard states, *i.e.*, activity being unity.

Since we have

$$\Delta G^{\ddagger} = -RT \ln K_{eq}^{\ddagger}$$

or

$$\ln K_{eq}^{\ddagger} = -\Delta G^{\ddagger}/RT \qquad \text{...(16.66)}$$

and

$$\Delta G^{\ddagger} = \Delta H^{\ddagger} - T\Delta S^{\ddagger} \qquad \text{...(16.67)}$$

Putting the value of $\Delta G^{\ddagger}$ in Eq. (16.66), we get

$$\ln K_{eq}^{\ddagger} = -\frac{\Delta H^{\ddagger} - T\Delta S^{\ddagger}}{RT}$$

or

$$K_{eq}^{\ddagger} = \exp\left(-\frac{\Delta H^{\ddagger}}{RT}\right)\exp\left(\frac{\Delta S^{\ddagger}}{R}\right) \qquad \text{...(16.68)}$$

Substituting this value of $K_{eq}^{\ddagger}$ in Eq. (16.65) gives

$$k_2 = \frac{RT}{N_A h}\left[\exp\left(-\frac{\Delta H^{\ddagger}}{RT}\right)\exp\left(\frac{\Delta S^{\ddagger}}{R}\right)\right] \qquad \text{...(16.69)}$$

Equation (16.69) can be expressed in a form which involves the experimental activation energy E_a, instead of enthalpy of activation $\Delta H^{\ddagger}$. The variation of $K_{eq}^{\ddagger}$ with temperature is given by

$$\frac{d \ln K_{eq}^{\ddagger}}{dT} = \frac{\Delta E^{\ddagger}}{RT^2} \qquad \text{...(16.70)}$$

where $\Delta E^{\ddagger}$ represents the increase in energy when the reactants go from the initial state to the activated state. Taking logarithm of Eq. (16.65), we get

$$\ln k_2 = \ln T + \ln K_{eq}^{\ddagger} + \ln\frac{R}{N_A h} \qquad \text{...(16.71)}$$

Differentiating the above equation with respect to temperature, we obtain

$$\frac{d \ln k_2}{dT} = \frac{1}{T} + \frac{d \ln K_{eq}^{\ddagger}}{dT} \qquad \text{...(16.72)}$$

Substituting the value $\dfrac{d \ln}{aT} K_{eq}^{\ddagger}$ from Eq. (16.70), we get

$$\frac{d \ln k_2}{dT} = \frac{1}{T} + \frac{\Delta E^{\ddagger}}{RT^2}$$

$$= \frac{RT + \Delta E^{\ddagger}}{RT^2} \qquad ...(16.73)$$

Comparison of Eq. (16.73) with (16.49) leads to

$$E_a = \Delta E^{\ddagger} + RT$$

Since

$$\Delta E^{\ddagger} = \Delta H^{\ddagger} - P\Delta V^{\ddagger}$$

Therefore

$$E_a = \Delta H^{\ddagger} + RT - P\Delta V^{\ddagger} \qquad ...(16.74)$$

For ideal gases, Eq. (16.74) reduces to

$$E_a = \Delta H^{\ddagger} + RT - \Delta n^{\ddagger} RT \quad (\because P\Delta V^{\ddagger} = \Delta n^{\ddagger} RT) \qquad ...(16.75)$$

where $\Delta V^{\ddagger}$ is the change in volume and $\Delta n^{\ddagger}$ is the change in number of molecules in passing from the initial state to the activated state. For a unimolecular reaction, there is no change in the number of molecules as the activated complex is formed. Therefore, $\Delta V^{\ddagger}$ is zero and Eq. (16.74) reduces to

$$E_a = \Delta H^{\ddagger} + RT \qquad ...(16.76)$$

and the rate Eq. (16.69) becomes

$$k_2 = \frac{RT}{N_A h} \exp\left(\frac{\Delta S^{\ddagger}}{R}\right) \exp\left(-\frac{E_a - RT}{RT}\right)$$

$$= \frac{RT}{N_A h} \exp\left(\frac{\Delta S^{\ddagger}}{R}\right) \exp\left(-\frac{E_a}{RT}\right) e \qquad ...(16.77)$$

For a bimolecular reaction $\Delta n^{\ddagger} = -1$ and Eq. (16.75) becomes

$$E_a = \Delta H^{\ddagger} + 2 RT \qquad ...(16.78)$$

The rate Eq. (16.69) now becomes

$$k_2 = \frac{RT}{N_A h} \exp\left(\frac{\Delta S^{\ddagger}}{R}\right) \exp\left(-\frac{E_a - 2RT}{RT}\right)$$

$$= \frac{RT}{N_A h} e^2 \exp\left(\frac{\Delta S^{\ddagger}}{R}\right) \exp\left(-\frac{E_a}{RT}\right) \qquad ...(16.79)$$

The entropy of activation can be calculated from the experimental values of rate constant and activation energy. It has been found that the difference between $\Delta H^{\ddagger}$ and E_a is small and in fact, for reactions in solutions and for unimolecular reactions $\Delta H^{\ddagger} \approx E_a$. In other cases involving gases, an additional term $\Delta n^{\ddagger} RT$ has been included. Hence without much error, we may write

$$k_2 = \frac{RT}{N_A h} \exp\left(\frac{\Delta S^{\ddagger}}{R}\right) \exp\left(-\frac{E_a}{RT}\right) \qquad ...(16.80)$$

$$= \frac{RT}{N_A h} \exp\left(\frac{\Delta S^{\ddagger}}{R}\right) \exp\left(-\frac{\Delta H^{\ddagger}}{RT}\right) \qquad ...(16.81)$$

This expression resembles the Arrhenius equation except that $\Delta H^{\ddagger}$ appears instead of E_a. The quantity $\Delta H^{\ddagger}$ is often called the enthalpy of activation. A comparison of Eq. (16.81) with Eq. (16.52) shows that the pre-exponential factor A is related to the entropy of activation as

$$A = \frac{RT}{N_A h} \exp\left(\frac{\Delta S^{\ddagger}}{R}\right) \qquad \qquad ...(16.82)$$

An exact calculation of A needs the evaluation of $\Delta S^{\ddagger}$. A negative value of $\Delta S^{\ddagger}$ means that the activated complex is more ordered than the reactants. A more negative value of $\Delta S^{\ddagger}$ indicates that A will have smaller value which means the reaction will be slower. A positive value of activation entropy $\Delta S^{\ddagger}$ means that the entropy of the complex is greater than the entropy of the reactants. A loosely bound complex has a higher entropy than a tightly bound one. More often there is a decrease in entropy in passing through the activated complex. The steric (probability) factor used in the collision theory is more or less analogous to the entropy of activation in transition state theory. It should be noted that the quantity $RT/N_o h$ does not depend on the nature of the reactant or activated complex and, therefore, will be same for all reactions at the same temperature.

From the collision theory, $k_2 = P Z_{11} \exp(-E_a /RT)$, i.e., the activation energy determines k_2, while in transition state theory it is determined by the free energy of activation, $\Delta G^{\ddagger}$. For slower reactions, a higher value of $\Delta G^{\ddagger}$ will be observed at a given temperature. Since

$$k_2 = P Z_{11} \exp\left(-\frac{E_a}{RT}\right) \qquad \qquad \text{(from collision theory)} \quad ...(16.83)$$

and

$$k_2 = \frac{RT}{N_A h} \exp\left(\frac{\Delta S^{\ddagger}}{R}\right) \exp\left(-\frac{\Delta H^{\ddagger}}{RT}\right) \qquad \text{(from transition state theory)} \quad ...(16.84)$$

Hence the orientation factor P is related to $\Delta S^{\ddagger}$, i.e., the entropy of activation. The steric (probability) factor A in the Arrhenius equation is equal to Z_{11} of the collision theory and is equal to $\dfrac{RT}{N_A h} \exp\left(\dfrac{\Delta S^{\ddagger}}{R}\right)$

For simple molecules these values are identical. For more complex reactant molecules where the collision theory fails the transition state theory still gives satisfactory value of A.

Problem 16.15: For the hydrolysis of sulphamic acid, $k_2 = 1.16 \times 10^{-3}$ mol^{-1} dm^3 s^{-1} at 363 K, while $E_a = 127490$ J mol^{-1}.
From these data find (a) $\Delta G^{\ddagger}$, (b) $\Delta H^{\ddagger}$, and (c) $\Delta S^{\ddagger}$ of the reaction at 363 K.

Solution: We know from Eq. (16.65)

$$k_2 = \frac{RT}{N_A h} K_{eq}^{\ddagger}$$

$$K_{eq}^{\ddagger} = \frac{k_2 N_A h}{RT}$$

$$= \frac{(1.16 \times 10^{-3} \text{mol}^{-1}\text{dm}^3\text{s}^{-1})(6.023 \times 10^{23} \text{mol}^{-1})(6.626 \times 10^{-34} \text{ J s})}{(8.314 \text{ J K}^{-1}\text{mol}^{-1})(363 \text{ K})}$$

$$= 1.534 \times 10^{-16} \, \text{mol}^{-1} \text{dm}^3$$

Now $\Delta G^{\ddagger} = -RT \ln K^{\ddagger} = -2.303 \, RT \log K^{\ddagger}$

$$= -(2.303)(8.314 \, \text{J K}^{-1} \text{mol}^{-1})(363 \, \text{K}) \log(1.534 \times 10^{-16})$$

$$= 109900 \, \text{J mol}^{-1} = 109.9 \, \text{kJ mol}^{-1}$$

Since we know

$$E_a = \Delta H^{\ddagger} + RT$$

$$\Delta H^{\ddagger} = E_a - RT = (127490 \, \text{J mol}^{-1}) - (8.314 \, \text{JK}^{-1} \, \text{mol}^{-1})(363 \, \text{K})$$

$$= 124473 \, \text{J mol}^{-1} = 124.473 \, \text{kJ mol}^{-1}$$

Again, $\Delta G^{\ddagger} = \Delta H^{\ddagger} - T \Delta S^{\ddagger}$

$$\Delta S^{\ddagger} = \frac{\Delta H^{\ddagger} - \Delta G^{\ddagger}}{T}$$

$$= \frac{(124473 - 109900)}{363}$$

$$= 40.14 \, \text{J mol}^{-1} \text{K}^{-1}$$

Problem 16.16: Calculate $\Delta H^{\ddagger}$, $\Delta G^{\ddagger}$ and $\Delta S^{\ddagger}$ for second order reaction

$$2NO_2(g) \rightarrow 2NO(g) + O_2(g)$$

at 500 K. Given $A = 2.0 \times 10^9 \, \text{s}^{-1}$ and the energy of activation = 111 kJ mol^{-1}.

    Solution: For a bimolecular reaction

$$E_a = \Delta H^{\ddagger} + 2 \, RT$$

or $\Delta H^{\ddagger} = E_a - 2 \, RT$

$$= (111 \, \text{kJ mol}^{-1}) - (2)(8.314 \, \text{JK}^{-1} \, \text{mol}^{-1})(500 \, \text{K})$$

$$= 102.7 \, \text{kJ mol}^{-1}$$

From Eq. (16.82), we have

$$A = \frac{RT}{N_A h} \exp\left(\frac{\Delta S^{\ddagger}}{R}\right)$$

$$\exp\left(\frac{\Delta S^{\ddagger}}{R}\right) = \frac{ANh}{RT}$$

or $\Delta S^{\ddagger} = R \ln\left(\dfrac{AN_A h}{RT}\right)$

$$= 2.303 \, R \log\left(\frac{Ah}{kT}\right) \qquad \left(\because k = \frac{R}{N_A}\right)$$

$$= 2.303\left(8.314 \ JK^{-1} \ mol^{-1}\right)\log\frac{\left(2.0\times10^{9}\,s^{-1}\right)\left(6.626\times10^{-34}\ Js\right)}{\left(1.38\times10^{-23}\ JK^{-1}\right)\left(500\ K\right)}$$

$$= -71.17 \ JK^{-1} \ mol^{-1}$$

Since $\qquad \Delta G^{\ddagger} = \Delta H^{\ddagger} - T\Delta S^{\ddagger}$

Therefore, $\qquad \Delta G^{\ddagger} = (102.7 \ kJ \ mol^{-1}) - (500 \ K)\,(-71.17 \ JK^{-1} \ mol^{-1})$

$$= 138.3 \ kJ \ mol^{-1}$$

16.16 THEORY OF UNIMOLECULAR REACTIONS

The collision theory and the absolute reaction rate theory satisfactorily account for the bimolecular reactions. However, a number of unimolecular gaseous reactions have been studied, which were found to be of first order as, for example, the decomposition of N_2O_5

$$N_2O_5(g) \rightarrow NO_2(g) + NO_3(g)$$

If the energy of activation of these first order reactions is believed to come from bimolecular collisions then the question that arises is how these reactions occur. To investigate the kinetics of such reactions, Lindemann in 1922 proposed that the behaviour of unimolecular reactions can be explained on the basis of bimolecular collisions. It is postulated that when the reactant molecules are activated by collisions with other molecules there may be a time lag before decomposition of the activated molecules. In other words, the activated molecules do not decompose immediately into products but remain in the activated state for a finite time. During this time-lag, the energized molecules may lose their extra energy in a second bimolecular collision or it may be deactivated to ordinary molecules. Consequently, the rate of the reaction will not be proportional to all the molecules activated but only to those which remain active. The process of activation or deactivation by collisions may be represented by the following mechanism:

$$A + A \xrightarrow{\ k_1\ } A + A^* \qquad\qquad \text{(activation)}$$

$$A + A^* \xrightarrow{\ k_2\ } A + A \qquad\qquad \text{(deactivation)}$$

$$A^* \xrightarrow{\ k_3\ } \text{Products} \qquad\qquad \text{(decomposition)}$$

where A is an inactive molecule and A^* the activated molecule. The rate at which A will disappear is proportional to the concentration of A^*, viz.,

$$-\frac{d[A]}{dt} = k_3\left[A^*\right] = k_1\left[A\right]^2 - k_2\left[A\right]\left[A^*\right] \qquad\qquad ...(16.85)$$

Since $[A^*]$ is not known and it is necessary to obtain it in terms of $[A]$ this can be done with the help of steady state principle. According to this, it is assumed that in the steady state the concentration of the intermediate (activated complex) is small and does not change with time, i.e., the rate of formation and the rate of decomposition of the intermediate are equal, i.e.,

$$k_1[A]^2 - k_2 \, [A] \, [A^*] - k_3 \, [A^*] = 0$$

$$k_1[A]^2 - k_2 \, [A] \, [A^*] = k_3 \, [A^*]$$

$$[A^*] = \frac{k_1 [A]^2}{k_2 [A] + k_3}$$

Hence

$$-\frac{d[A]}{dt} = \frac{k_3 k_1 [A]^2}{k_3 + k_2 [A]}$$

...(16.86)

Equation (16.86) predicts two limiting possibilities.

Case I: When $k_2 [A] \gg k_3$, Eq. (16.86) reduces to

$$-\frac{d[A]}{dt} = \frac{k_1 k_3}{k_2}[A]$$

which is a first order rate equation. This corresponds to a situation in which the concentration of A is high enough to produce appreciable deactivation of A^* by collisions with A so that the rate of deactivation $k_2[A] [A^*]$ is appreciably large in comparison to the rate of decomposition, $k_3[A^*]$.

Case II: When $k_3 \gg k_2 [A]$, *i.e.*, rate of decomposition is large as compared to the rate deactivation, Eq. (16.86) becomes

$$-\frac{d[A]}{dt} = k_1 [A]^2$$

In such cases the reaction should be of second order. This situation corresponds to low concentration of A where the rate of activation becomes slow and hence the rate controlling.

In a gaseous reaction as the pressure of the system is decreased, the deactivation, $k_2[A][A^*]$, decreases. At low pressure, therefore, the conditions for the first order kinetics fail and $k_2[A]$ is no longer greater than k_3. Thus the first order kinetics is replaced by the second order kinetics.

EXERCISES

1. Suggest whether the following statements are true or false:

    (*i*) The dimensions of k for a first order reaction is (time)$^{-1}$ while that for a second order it is (time)$^{-1}$ (concentration)$^{-1}$.

    (*ii*) The rate of a zero order reaction is controlled by factors other than the concentrations of the reactants.

    (*iii*) Stoichiometry of a reaction tells nothing about the order of a reaction unless it is known that the reaction is an elementary reaction.

    (*iv*) The exponents of concentrations terms in the rate law are the stoichiometric coefficients of reactants in the balanced chemical equation.

    (*v*) In a second order bimolecular reaction, if the concentration of one of the reactants is taken in excess then the reaction becomes kinetically of the first order.

    (*vi*) Order and molecularity of a reaction are always identical.

    (*vii*) In a first order reaction, doubling the initial concentration of the reactant quadruples the rate.

    (*viii*) Increase in temperature invariably increases the rate of a reaction by increasing the fraction of the energized molecules.

    (*ix*) For a zero order reaction, the rate and rate constant are identical.

    (*x*) In a bimolecular gaseous reaction every collision between the reacting molecules leads to chemical reaction.

    (*xi*) Half-life period for a zero order reaction is directly proportional to the initial concentration of the reactant.

Ans. True statements: (*i*), (*ii*), (*iii*), (*v*), (*viii*), (*ix*) and (*xi*).

2. Explain, giving reasons, the following:

   (*i*) In the determination of the order of a reaction, it is always advisable to investigate it in the initial stages of the reaction.

   (*ii*) Reactions of third and higher orders are usually not very common.

   (*iii*) Order of a reaction cannot be predicted from the overall stoichiometry of the reaction.

   (*iv*) Increase of temperature invariably increases the rate of reaction.

   (*v*) The overall kinetics of a reaction involving several steps is controlled by the kinetics of the slowest step.

   (*vi*) In the steady state, the concentration of the reactive intermediate though small remains the same for an appreciable time.

   (*vii*) Higher the activation energy of a reaction slower is the rate of the reaction.

3. Rewrite the following sentences selecting the appropriate word(s) given in brackets:

   (*i*) For the gas phase reaction $CCl_3CHO + NO \rightarrow$ Products, the rate equation is $k[CCl_3CHO][NO]$. The reaction is (first/second/third) order and the units of k are sec/sec^{-1}/dm^3 mol^{-1} sec^{-1}/dm^6 mol^{-2} sec^{-1}).

   (*ii*) Collision theory states that a chemical reaction occurs with (every collision/only energetic collisions) and the rate is (directly/inversely) proportional to the number of collisions per second.

   (*iii*) For the system ($A \rightarrow B$), the reaction is exothermic. The activation energy will be (more/less) for the forward reaction than for the reverse reaction. Potential energy of the activated complex is (smaller/greater) for the forward reaction than for the reverse reaction.

   Ans. (*i*) second, dm^3 mol^{-1} sec^{-1}; (*ii*) only energetic collisions, directly; (*iii*) less, none, as the potential energy of the complex is the same for the reaction in either direction.

4. Discuss the following reactions with respect to order, catalysts, etc.:

   (*i*) $2A \rightarrow$ Products; $-\dfrac{d[A]}{dt} = k[A]$

   (*ii*) $2A + B \rightarrow C$; $\dfrac{d[C]}{dt} = k[A][B]$

   (*iii*) $2A + B \rightarrow 2C + D + B$; $\dfrac{-d[A]}{dt} = k[A][C]$

   (*iv*) $2A + B \rightarrow 2C$; $\dfrac{d[C]}{dt} = k[A][C]^{-1/2}$

5. Predict the overall order of a reaction for which half-life period and units of k (*a*) do not depend on concentration, (*b*) depend inversely on the concentration.

   Ans. (*a*) first order reaction, $t_{1/2} = \dfrac{0.693}{k}$ and units of k are sec^{-1},

   (*b*) second order, $t_{1/2} = \dfrac{1}{Ck}$ and units of k are conc^{-1} sec^{-1}.

6. The rate constant for a certain gaseous reaction is 3×10^{-2} mol^{-1} dm^3 s^{-1} at 293 K. Express it in units of mol^{-1} cm^3 s^{-1}, molecule^{-1} cm^3 s^{-1} and atm^{-1} s^{-1}.

   Ans. 30 mol^{-1} cm^3 s^{-1}, 4.9×10^{-23} molecule^{-1} cm^3 s^{-1}, 1.34×10^{-3} atm^{-1} s^{-1}.

7. For the reaction, $A \rightarrow B$, the rate law is

$$-\frac{d[A]}{dt} = k[A]^{1/2}$$

(i) Integrate the rate equation.

(ii) How would a plot of $[A]^{1/2}$ against t vary?

(iii) Derive an expression for the half-life period in terms of k and $[A]_0$.

(iv) What are the units of k?

Ans. (i) $2\left[(A_0)^{1/2} - (A)^{1/2}\right] = kt$, (ii) plot of $[A]^{1/2}$ versus t would be linear,

(iii) $t_{1/2} = \dfrac{0.586[A]^{1/2}}{k}$, (iv) $(\text{mol dm}^{-3})^{1/2} \text{ s}^{-1}$.

8. From the following rate laws write the corresponding stoichiometric equations. The initial concentrations are written as a, b, c and x represents the concentration units of A that have reacted.

(i) $\dfrac{dx}{dt} = k(a-x)(b-x)$

(ii) $\dfrac{dx}{dt} = k(a-x)(b-x)(c-x)$

(iii) $\dfrac{dx}{dt} = k(a-x)(b-2x)$

(iv) $\dfrac{dx}{dt} = kb(a-x)$

(v) $\dfrac{dx}{dt} = k(a-x)(b+x)$

(vi) $\dfrac{dx}{dt} = k_1(a-x) - k_{-1}(x)$

Ans. (i) $A + B \rightarrow$ Products, (ii) $A + B + C \rightarrow$ Products, (iii) $A + 2B \rightarrow$ Products, (iv) $A + B \rightarrow$ Products (B is in excess or acting as a catalyst),

(v) $A + B \rightarrow$ Products (B is acting as an autocatalyst), (vi) $A \underset{k_{-1}}{\overset{k_1}{\rightleftharpoons}} B$.

9. For the reaction, $2\text{NaI }(aq) + \text{Br}_2 (g) \rightarrow 2\text{NaBr }(aq) + \text{I}_2 (g)$, discuss qualitatively the effect on the reaction rate of

(i) lowering the temperature,

(ii) replacing $\text{Br}_2 (g)$ by $\text{Cl}_2 (g)$ or $\text{F}_2 (g)$,

(iii) adding some solid sodium iodide,

(iv) mixing $\text{Br}_2 (g)$ with some inert gas like argon,

(v) adding some iodine gas in the initial reaction mixture.

Ans. (i) decreases, (ii) increases, (iii) increases, (iv) decreases, (v) decreases.

10. For the reaction, $2A + B_2 \rightarrow 2AB$, it is found that doubling the initial concentration of both the reactants increases the initial rate by a factor of eight, but on doubling the concentration of B_2 alone the rate is doubled. What is the order of the reaction with respect to A and B_2?

Ans. Order is 3 and the rate $= k[A]^2[B_2]$.

11. For the reaction, $2A \rightarrow 4B + C$, the rate of the reaction can be expressed as

$$-\frac{d[A]}{dt} = k[A]$$

$$\frac{d[B]}{dt} = k'[A]$$

$$\frac{d[C]}{dt} = k''[C]$$

How are k' and k'' related to k? **Ans.** $k' = 2k$ and $k'' = \dfrac{k}{2}$.

12. The rate of the reaction, $aA + bB + cC \rightarrow$ Products, is given by the relation, rate $= k\,[A]^a[B]^b[C]^c$.
    From the following data determine the order of the reaction and calculate the rate constant for the reaction:

Rate $(\text{mol dm}^{-3}\,\text{s}^{-1}) \times 10^5$	$[A]_0$ (mol dm^{-3})	$[B]$ (mol dm^{-3})	$[C]$ (mol dm^{-3})
5.0	0.010	0.005	0.010
5.0	0.010	0.005	0.015
2.5	0.010	0.010	0.010
15.0	0.020	0.005	0.010

Ans. $a = 3/2$, $b = -1$, $c = 0$ and
$k = 2.5 \times 10^{-4}\ (\text{mol dm}^{-3})^{-1/2}\ \text{s}^{-1}$.

13. The half-life for a given reaction was doubled when the initial concentration was doubled. Evaluate the order of the reaction. **Ans.** zero order.

14. The isotope $_{19}K^{42}$ has a $t_{1/2}$ of 12 hours. What fraction of the initial concentration of $_{19}K^{42}$ remains after 60 hours? **Ans.** 1/32.

15. On the top of a certain mountain the atmospheric pressure is 0.7 atm and pure water boils at 363 K. A climber finds that it takes 300 minutes to boil an egg as against 3 minutes at 373 K.
    (i) What is the ratio of the rate constants k_{273}/k_{363}?
    (ii) Assuming the Arrhenius frequency factor A to be the same, calculate the activation energy for the reaction that occurs when egg is boiled.
    Ans. (i) $k_{273}/k_{363} = 100$, (ii) 997.68 kJ mol^{-1}.

16. The rate of hydrolysis of ethyl acetate catalysed by hydrochloric acid obeys rate law, rate $= \dfrac{d[\text{ester}]}{dt} = k$
    [ester] [HCl] where $k = 0.1$ mol^{-1} dm^3 h^{-1} at 298 K. Neglecting any back reaction, calculate the time required for half of the ester to be hydrolysed if the initial concentrations of the ester and hydrochloric acid are 0.02 mol dm^{-3}, respectively. **Ans.** $t_{1/2} = 693$ h.

17. A solution of X is mixed with an equal volume of a solution of Y containing the same number of moles and the reaction $X + Y \rightarrow Z$ occurs. At the end of 1 hour 75% of X has reacted. How much of X will be left unreacted at the end of 2 hours if the reaction is (i) first order in X and zero order in Y, (ii) first order in both X and Y, (iii) zero order in both X and Y.
    Ans. (i) 6.25%, (ii) 14.3%, (iii) 0%.

18. Thermal decomposition of stilbine SbH_3 on glass takes place according to the reaction $2SbH_3 (g) \rightarrow 2Sb (s)$ $+ 3H_2 (g)$. At 630 K, variation of total pressure with time is given by the following data:

Time (h)	0	4.33	16.0	25.5	37.66	447.5
Total pressure (mm Hg)	392	403	436.5	453.5	480.5	488.5

Ascertain the order of the reaction and calculate the value of the rate constant, k.

Ans. First order and $k = 1.52 \times 10^{-2}$ h^{-1}.

19. Calculate k_f and k_r from the following data for the given reaction:

$$A \underset{k_r}{\overset{k_f}{\rightleftharpoons}} B$$

t (min)	0	10	100
A (mol dm^{-3})	0.15	0.142	0.102

The equilibrium concentration of A is 0.086 mol dm^{-3}.

Ans. $k_f = 5.6 \times 10^{-3}$ s^{-1}, $k_r = 7.8 \times 10^{-3}$ s^{-1}

20. The half-life period of a reaction of nth order is given by

$$t_{1/2} = \frac{2^{n-1} - 1}{(n-1)k a^{n-1}}$$

where k is the rate constant of the reaction and a is the initial concentration of the reactant. Show that the

half-life period $t_{1/2}$ is related to temperature by the equation $\ln t_{1/2} = \ln A' + \dfrac{E_a}{RT}$ where A' is equal to

$\dfrac{2^{n-1} - 1}{A(n-1)a^{n-1}}$ and A is the pre-exponential factor in the Arrhenius equation and E_a is the activation energy.

21. Benzene diazonium chloride decomposes according to the reaction, $C_6H_5N_2Cl \rightarrow C_6H_5Cl + N_2$. Kinetics of this reaction was followed by measuring the pressure of nitrogen gas evolved at different time intervals. From the following data investigate the order of the reaction and evaluate the rate constant.

t (min)	0	4.0	12.0	20.0	34.0	50.0
Pressure (mm Hg)	0	2.20	5.90	9.01	13.10	16.30

Ans. First order, $k = 2.56 \times 10^{-2}$ min^{-1}.

22. The rate constant for a certain reaction is found to be trippled when the temperature is increased from 288 K to 323 K. If the enthalpy of the reaction is 50 kJ mol^{-1}, calculate the activation energy of the reaction.

Ans. 24.28 kJ mol^{-1}.

23. Given the following second order reactions occurring at a certain temperature (T_1)

(i) $A + B \xrightarrow{k_1}$ Products and

(ii) $C + D \xrightarrow{k_2}$ Products.

The activation energy for reaction (i) is E_{a1} and for (ii) it is E_{a2} such that $E_{a1} > E_{a2}$. If the temperature of both the systems is increased from T_1 to T_2, choose the correct relation from the following:

(a) $\dfrac{k_1(T_2)}{k_1(T_1)} = \dfrac{k_2(T_2)}{k_2(T_1)}$ (b) $\dfrac{k_1(T_2)}{k_1(T_1)} > \dfrac{k_2(T_2)}{k_2(T_1)}$,   (c) $\dfrac{k_1(T_2)}{k_1(T_1)} < \dfrac{k_2(T_2)}{k_2(T_1)}$

Ans. (b).

24. Suppose there are two first order reactions with half-life periods $t_{1/2}$ (1) and $t_{1/2}$ (2) and rate constants k_1 and k_2 such that k_2 is twice that of k_1. How are the two half life periods related to each other?

Ans. $t_{1/2}$ (1) = $2t_{1/2}$ (2).

25. For a certain reversible first order reaction $A \underset{k_{-1}}{\overset{k_1}{\rightleftharpoons}} B$, the Arrhenius equation for the forward and reverse

reactions are: $k_1\left(s^{-1}\right) = 10^{11} \exp\left(\dfrac{-260 \text{ kJ mol}^{-1}}{RT}\right)$ and $k_{-1} = 10^{11} \exp\left(\dfrac{-220 \text{ kJ mol}^{-1}}{RT}\right)$. Calculate the tem-

perature at which both the rate constants are equal.

Ans. 696.1 K.

26. Show that for a first order reaction, the time required for 99.9% completion of the reaction is 10 times the time for 50.0% completion.

27. In a reaction, all the reactants have initial concentration a. Show that the half-life is given by

$$t_{1/2} = \frac{2^{n-1} - 1}{a^{n-1} k(n-1)}$$

where n is the order of the reaction and k is the rate constant.

28. A zero order reaction is 50% complete in 20 minutes. What percentage would be completed at the end of 30 minutes? In how many minutes would the concentration be reduced to zero?

Ans. 75%, 40 min.

29. The activation energy of a certain uncatalysed reaction at 300 K is 76 kJ mol^{-1}. The activation energy is lowered to 57 kJ mol^{-1} by the use of a catalyst. By what factor is the rate of the catalysed reaction increased?

Ans. 2,000 times the rate of uncatalysed reaction.

30. Define the following terms:
    (*i*) Reaction rate;
    (*ii*) Order of a reaction;
    (*iii*) Molecularity of a reaction step;
    (*iv*) Rate constant;
    (*v*) Activation energy;
    (*vi*) Activated complex;
    (*vii*) Frequency factor.

31. Explain why the hydrolysis of an ester in the presence of a dilute acid follows first order kinetics while that in the presence of dilute alkali it follows a second order kinetics.

32. (*a*) Comment on the statement that ionic reactions are fast while the molecular reactions are very slow.
    (*b*) Discuss the effect of temperature on reaction rates.
    (*c*) How is the activation energy of a reaction calculated?

33. Discuss the collision theory for reaction rates. On the basis of this theory show that temperature changes will have significant effect on reaction rates. How could it be applied to unimolecular and bimolecular reactions?

34. Discuss the theory of absolute reaction rate. How is this theory considered superior to the collision theory?

35. The experimental rate for the reaction

$$2NO + 2H_2 \rightarrow N_2 + 2H_2O$$

can be expressed in the form, rate = $k[NO]^2 [H_2]$. The following three schemes for the reaction have been suggested. Which one of these fits into the rate equation? Use steady state approximation:

A: (i) $NO + H_2 \underset{k_{-2}}{\overset{k_2}{\rightleftharpoons}} NOH_2$

     (ii) $NOH_2 + NO \xrightarrow{k_2'} N_2 + H_2O_2$

     (iii) $H_2O_2 + H_2 \xrightarrow{k_2''} 2H_2O$

B: (i) $NO + H_2 \underset{k_{-2}}{\overset{k_2}{\rightleftharpoons}} NOH_2$

     (ii) $H_2 + NOH_2 \xrightarrow{k_2'} H_2O + NH_2$

     (iii) $NH_2 + NO \xrightarrow{k_2''} N_2 + H_2O$

C: (i) $NO + NO \underset{k_{-2}}{\overset{k_2}{\rightleftharpoons}} N_2O_2$

     (ii) $H_2 + N_2O_2 \xrightarrow{k_2'} H_2O + N_2O$

     (iii) $N_2O + H_2 \xrightarrow{k_2''} N_2 + H_2O$

Ans. Schemes *A* and *C*.

36.   The following mechanism has been suggested for the decomposition of O_3.

     (i) $O_3 \underset{k_{-1}}{\overset{k_1}{\rightleftharpoons}} O_2 + O$

     (ii) $O_3 + O \xrightarrow{k_2} 2O_2$

     (a)   Assuming $k_{-1}[O_2] > k_2[O_3]$, show that the rate of the overall reaction is $-\dfrac{d[O_2]}{dt} = \dfrac{k[O_3]^2}{[O_2]}$.

     (b)   What could be concluded from the appearance of $\dfrac{1}{[O_2]}$ in the rate equation?

Ans. The appearance of $\dfrac{1}{[O_2]}$ in the rate equation suggests that the reaction

is of -1 order with respect to O_2 and it retards the decomposition of O_3.

Adsorption and Adsorption Isotherms

17.1 ADSORPTION

Molecules on the surface of a liquid experience a strong inward pull due to which the liquid surface has a tendency to contract and exhibit the property of surface tension. This phenomenon arises due to the unbalance or unsaturation of molecular forces on the surface. Similarly, the surface of a solid does not have all its forces satisfied by union with other molecules or ions. Gases or dissolved substances, on coming in contact with liquid or solid surfaces, are retained by them. This phenomenon of accumulation of a substance on the surface of a solid or liquid is called *adsorption*. The reverse of adsorption is called *desorption*. The substance adsorbed on the surface is called *adsorbate* while the substance to which it is attached is called *adsorbent*. Adsorption is a surface phenomenon and at a given temperature and pressure depends upon the surface area of the adsorbent. Larger the surface area greater will be the extent of adsorption. Solids in the finely divided state, where the surface area is large, are good adsorbents. Adsorption is an exothermic process and increases with the decrease of temperature.

Adsorption should be differentiated from absorption. In *absorption* the substance is not only retained on the surface but passes through the surface into the bulk of a solid or liquid. Thus, hydrogen gas is absorbed by metallic palladium whereas acetic acid is adsorbed from its solution by charcoal. Sometimes the word *sorption* is used to include both adsorption and absorption.

17.2 TYPES OF ADSORPTION

Depending upon the nature of the forces holding the gas molecules to the solid surface, adsorption can be of the following two types, *viz.*,

    (*i*) physical adsorption or van der Waals' adsorption; and
    (*ii*) chemical adsorption or activated adsorption or chemisorption.

All gases have a tendency to be adsorbed on the surface of a solid and these gas molecules are held by physical or van der Waals' forces. But when valence forces come into play to hold the molecules on the surface, chemisorption occurs.

Distinction between Physical Adsorption and Chemisorption: The main distinguishing characteristics of the two kinds of adsorption are summarised in the following table.

Physical adsorption	Chemisorption
1. It is characterised by low enthalpy of adsorption of the order of 20 kJ mol^{-1} of the adsorbate. The adsorption equilibrium is reversible and is established rapidly. There is a van der Waals' interaction between the adsorbate and adsorbent.	1. It is accompanied by high enthalpy of adsorption of the order of 80–200 kJ mol^{-1}. The attachment of the adsorbate on the adsorbent is stronger, *i.e.*, the adsorbate firmly sticks to the surface of the adsorbent. The equilibrium is established slowly and irreversibly. The high enthalpy of adsorption indicates that adsorption consists of a combination of gas molecules with the surface to form a chemical compound usually with a covalent bond.
2. Adsorption is more pronounced at temperatures below the boiling point of the adsorbate.	2. Chemisorption usually occurs at high temperatures.
3. In physical adsorption no appreciable amount of activation energy is involved.	3. An activation energy may be involved in chemisorption.
4. Physical adsorption is usually multilayer.	4. Chemisorption is mainly unilayer or monolayer.
5. Physical adsorption is more a function of adsorbate than the adsorbent.	5. Chemisorption is characteristic of both the adsorbate and the adsorbent.
6. The extent of physical adsorption increases with increase of pressure of the adsorbate and ultimately attains a limiting value.	6. Chemisorption decreases with the increase of pressure of the adsorbate.

17.3 ADSORPTION ISOTHERMS

The extent of adsorption on a surface generally depends on the nature of the adsorbent and the molecules of the adsorbate and is a function of its pressure or concentration and temperature. A plot between the amount of the adsorbate substance adsorbed and the pressure or concentration of the adsorbate at constant temperature called *an adsorption isotherm.* In adsorption of gases on solid surfaces five general types of isotherms have been observed (Fig. 17.1).

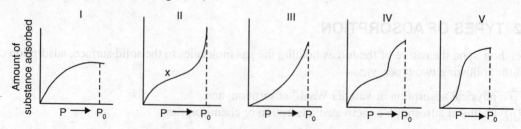

Fig. 17.1 Five types of adsorption isotherms

Type I isotherm is obtained in case of chemisorption while all other isotherms have been observed in physical adsorption. In chemisorption (Type I) the amount of the gas adsorbed per unit mass of the adsorbent increases linearly with pressure in the initial stages and then more slowly attaining a limiting value as the surface becomes fully covered by the gas molecules. Variation of the amount of adsorption per unit area or per unit mass of the adsorbent with pressure is often represented empirically by an equation of the type

$$y = \frac{x}{m} = k(P)^n \qquad \qquad ...(17.1)$$

where x is the mass of the gas adsorbed and m is the mass of the adsorbent so that x/m denotes the mass of the gas adsorbed per unit mass of adsorbent, P is the equilibrium pressure of the gas, k and n are the empirical constants depending upon the nature of the solid, gas and temperature. A plot of x/m versus P is shown in Fig. 17.2 (a).

Taking logarithm of both sides of Eq. (17.1), we get

$$\log y = \log k + n \log P$$

Equation (17.1) is known as the *Freundlich isotherm* and was used in measuring the extent of adsorption. A plot of log y versus log P would give a straight line with slope equal to n and the ordinate intercept equal to log k [Fig. 17.2 (b)]. However, the experimental data show deviations from linearity specially at low temperatures. The isotherm is applicable only in the limiting case of low concentration. Table 17.1 shows the adsorption of different acids on charcoal. The values of n determined by Freundlich from the slope of the curves are given in the table.

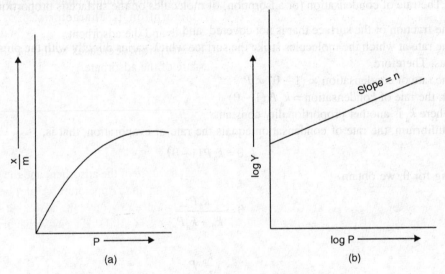

Fig. 17.2 Freundlich adsorption isotherm

Table 17.1 Adsorption of Acids on Charcoal at 298 K

Adsorbate	n	Adsorbate	n
Acetic acid	0.425	Succinic acid	0.243
Propionic acid	0.394	Benzoic acid	0.338
Butyric acid	0.301		

Langmuir Isotherm: The first quantitative theory of adsorption was given by Langmuir in 1916. The various assumptions of the theory are:

(*i*) The solid surface is homogeneous and has a fixed number of adsorption sites.

(*ii*) Each site cannot adsorb more than one molecule, *i.e.*, the adsorption of molecules is confined to a monomolecular layer. The ability of a molecule to adsorb on one site does not affect the occupation of neighbouring sites.

(*iii*) The adsorbed gas behaves ideally in the vapour phase.

(*iv*) Adsorption is considered as an equilibrium between condensation of the adsorbate molecules on the adsorbent and their desorption from it. In other words, the rates of condensation and desorption eventually become equal at equilibrium.

(*v*) There is no interaction between the adsorbed molecules.

These postulates can be formulated mathematically as follow:

Let θ be the fraction of the total surface occupied by gas molecules at any instant. The rate of evaporation of the molecules from the surface is proportional to the fraction of the surface, θ, occupied by the molecules, *i.e.*,

the rate of evaporation $\propto \theta$

$$= k_d\, \theta$$

where k_d is proportionality constant. The fraction of the surface that is bare and available for adsorption is $(1 - \theta)$. The rate of condensation (or adsorption) of molecules on the surface is proportional to

(*i*) the fraction of the surface that is not covered, and

(*ii*) the rate at which the molecules strike the surface which varies directly with the pressure of the gas. Therefore,

the rate of condensation $\propto (1 - \theta) \propto P$

or, the rate of condensation $= k_a P (1 - \theta)$

where k_a is another proportionality constant.

At equilibrium, the rate of condensation equals the rate of evaporation, that is,

$$k_d \theta = k_a P (1 - \theta)$$

Solving for θ, we obtain

$$\theta = \frac{k_a P}{k_d + k_a P}$$

$$= \frac{\dfrac{k_a}{k_d} P}{1 + \dfrac{k_a}{k_d} P}$$

$$= \frac{bP}{1 + bP}$$

where $b = \dfrac{k_a}{k_d}$ and is called the adsorption coefficient.

The mass of the gas adsorbed per unit area or per unit mass of the adsorbent y, will obviously be proportional to the fraction of surface covered and hence

$$y = \frac{x}{m} = k\theta \qquad \qquad ...(17.2)$$

$$= k\frac{bP}{1 + bP}$$

or

$$y = \frac{x}{m} = \frac{aP}{1 + bP} \qquad \qquad ...(17.3)$$

where the constant $a = kb$.

Equation (17.3) relates the amount of gas adsorbed to the pressure of the gas at constant temperature and is known as the *Langmuir adsorption isotherm*.

Equation (17.3) can be rewritten as

$$\frac{P}{y} = \frac{P}{aP/(1 + bP)}$$

$$= \frac{1}{a} + \frac{b}{a}P \qquad \qquad ...(17.4)$$

Equation (17.4) suggests that a plot of $\dfrac{P}{y}$ $\left(\text{or } \dfrac{P}{x/m} \right)$ versus P should give a straight line with

intercept equal to $1/a$ and slope equal to b/a. Hence a and b in Eq. (17.3) can be evaluated. Values of these constants have been found to be characteristics of the system under consideration. Fig. 17.3 shows the adsorption of some gases on silica. The straight lines indicate the validity of the Langmuir adsorption isotherm.

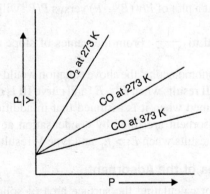

Fig. 17.3 Adsorption of various gases on silica

Two limiting cases of Langmuir adsorption isotherm are of interest. These are

Case I: When $bP \ll 1$, *i.e.*, when the pressure of the gas is very low, Eq. (17.3) reduces to

$$y = aP$$

or

$$y \propto P$$

This shows that the adsorption is directly proportional to the pressure of the gas.

Case II: When $bP \gg 1$, *i.e.*, pressure is very large or the whole of the surface is covered, then Eq. (17.3)

becomes $y = \dfrac{a}{b}$, that is, the adsorption reaches at its limiting value. This corresponds to the latter portion of the isotherm [Fig. 17.2 (a)].

However, in the intermediate pressure range the amount of adsorption will follow a relation
$$y = kP^n$$
where n lies between 1 and 0. This is the Freundlich isotherm as stated earlier.

B.E.T. Isotherm

Deviations from the Langmuir adsorption isotherm occur when adsorption is multilayer or adsorbate and adsorbent react chemically or when the surface is not uniform. Brunauer, Emmett and Teller extended the Langmuir approach and proposed a theory for multilayer adsorption. In this theory it is assumed that molecules of adsorbate after the formation of a monomolecular layer may condense on it. There is a dynamic equilibrium between the adsorbate molecules in successive layers. Enthalpy of adsorption in each layer except the first layer is the same and forces which cause condensation are responsible for holding the molecules in the successive layers. By the use of these assumptions, they derived an equation generally known as BET equation which is given by

$$\frac{P}{v\left(P^0 - P\right)} = \frac{1}{V_m C} + \left(\frac{C-1}{V_m C}\right)\frac{P}{P^0} \qquad \qquad ...(17.5)$$

where v is the volume of the gas adsorbed under pressure P, P^0 is the saturated vapour pressure of the gas at the same temperature, V_m is the volume of the gas adsorbed corresponding to the formation of a

mono-molecular layer and C is a constant for the given adsorbate and is given by $C = \exp\left[\dfrac{E_1 - E_L}{RT}\right]$ in

which E_1 is the enthalpy of adsorption in the first layer and E_L is the enthalpy of liquefaction of the gas. From the Eq. (17.5) it is clear that a plot of $P/v\,(P^0 - P)$ versus P/P^0 will yield a straight line with a slope

$(C - 1)/V_m C$ and intercept equal to $\dfrac{1}{V_m C}$. From the values of slope and intercept, V_m and C can be

calculated. If the adsorption is monomolecular, the above equation would reduce to the Langmuir isotherm. In Fig. 17.1 adsorption isotherm II results when $E_1 > E_L$ and curve III is obtained when $E_L > E_1$. Isotherm of types IV and V can be explained when it is assumed that in addition to multilayer adsorption, the pores and capillaries of the adsorbent are filled by condensation at pressures much lower than the saturation pressure P^0. Type IV results when $E_1 > E_L$ and type V results if $E_L > E_1$.

Calculations of Surface Area of the Adsorbent

BET isotherm is used widely for calculating the surface area of solid catalysts and adsorbents. The method consists in determining the volume of the gas required to form a monomolecular layer. The volume (V_m) corresponding to point X (isotherm II, Fig. 17.1) represents formation of a monomolecular layer reduced to STP. The number of moles of the gas adsorbed at STP is given by $P^0 V_m / RT_0$. If β is the surface area occupied by a single gas molecule then the total surface area S covered by all the molecules of the adsorbed gas is given by

$$S = \frac{P^0 V_m}{RT_0} N_A \beta \quad (N_A \text{ being the Avogadro constant}).$$

The value of β, *i.e.*, area per adsorbed molecule is obtained from its density at its boiling point

$$\beta = \left(\frac{M}{N_A d}\right)^{2/3}$$

where M is the molar mass of the gas adsorbed and d is the density of the liquefied gas.

The surface area calculated in this way is generally satisfactory in spite of a large number of approximations.

17.4 GIBBS ADSORPTION EQUATION

A dissolved solute may increase or decrease the surface tension of the solvent. Solutes which increase the surface tension of liquids are said to possess negative surface activity. On the other hand, solutes which decrease the surface tension of liquids are known to have positive surface activity. Gibbs derived a relationship between the amount of adsorption and the variation in surface tension of the solvent with concentration. The equation is usually known as the *Gibbs adsorption equation* and may be written as

$$\Gamma = -\frac{Cd\gamma}{RTdC} \qquad \ldots(17.6)$$

where Γ is known as the *surface excess* and represents the moles of the solute retained per unit area of the surface, C is the concentration of the solution and $d\gamma/dC$ denotes the variation in surface tension with concentration.

When $d\gamma/dC$ is negative, Γ is positive meaning thereby a positive adsorption. It means the solute would tend to accumulate on the surface. In case $d\gamma/dC$ is positive and Γ is negative, a negative adsorption would result. This is sometimes called desorption. Substances like soaps, sulphonic acids and sulphonates, alcohols and detergents, etc., lower the surface tension of water. These substances are called surface active agents. However, strong electrolytes and amino benzoic acid in water increase the surface tension.

17.5 APPLICATIONS OF ADSORPTION

Adsorption finds a large number of applications both in laboratory and industry. Some of the important applications are:

(*i*) A large number of industrial processes like synthesis of ammonia, manufacture of sulphuric acid, synthetic petrol, alcohols, etc. are catalysed reactions where the reactants are adsorbed on the surface of solid catalysts.

(*ii*) Chromatography, a powerful and versatile technique used in separating and analysing minute quantities of various components from a mixture, is based on adsorption. In column chromatography, a mixture containing the components is poured into a column that contains a finely divided adsorbent usually aluminium oxide, silica gel, etc. As the mixture passes down, the more adsorbed constituents are readily retained or adsorbed in the upper layer of the column, while the weaker adsorbed constituents are retained in the lower portion of the column. On pouring down the solvent, weakly adsorbed components are washed out first followed by strongly adsorbed components. These are collected separately and are analysed.

(*iii*) Softening of hard by ion exchangers is based on adsorption of cations.

(*iv*) Removal of colouring materials from various types of solutions by charcoal is another example of adsorption.

(*v*) Surface active agents are widely used in washing, paints, lubricants, etc.

(*vi*) Most of the drugs function through adsorption on body tissues and germs.

(*vii*) Dyeing of fabrics with the help of mordants, tanning of leather, electroplating etc. are examples where adsorption finds immense applications.

EXERCISES

1. Explain the following:

    (*a*) Adsorption is an exothermic process.

    (*b*) Physical adsorption is multilayer while chemical adsorption is usually monolayer.

    (*c*) Adsorption is accompanied by a decrease in enthalpy and entropy of the system.

    (*d*) Easily liquefiable gases are adsorbed to a larger extent than those difficult to liquefy.

    (*e*) Adsorption is a surface phenomenon.

2. Distinguish the following:

    (*i*) Adsorption from absorption.

    (*ii*) Adsorbate from adsorbent.

    (*iii*) Physical adsorption from chemical adsorption.

    (*iv*) Adsorption from desorption.

3. Select the correct statement from the following:

    (*i*) The binding between the adsorbate and adsorbent is stronger in chemisorption and weaker in physical adsorption.

    (*ii*) Adsorption decreases surface energy.

    (*iii*) Adsorption is an irreversible process.

    (*iv*) Adsorption increases with rise in temperature.

    (*v*) At equilibrium, the rate of adsorption on the surface is equal to the rate of desorption from the surface.

    (*vi*) Adsorption arises due to unsaturation of valence forces of atoms or molecules on the surface.

    (*vii*) Adsorption always leads to a decrease in enthalpy and entropy of the system.

    (*viii*) Surface excesses could be positive or negative.

    Ans. True statement: (*i*), (*ii*), (*v*), (*vi*), (*vii*), (*viii*).

4. Which one of the following gases would be expected to be more strongly adsorbed on charcoal at room temperature? (*i*) O_2, (*ii*) CO_2, and (*iii*) NH_3. Give reasons.

5. It is found that air containing gasoline vapours when passed through a bed of activated carbon, the gasoline vapours are removed from the air and the temperature of the carbon bed rises. Account for this phenomenon.

6. Explain and illustrate the following:

    (*i*) Adsorption; (*ii*) Absorption; (*iii*) Freundlich adsorption isotherm; (*iv*) Surface excess; (*v*) Gibbs adsorption equation and (*vi*) BET isotherm.

7. Explain the term adsorption. Distinguish it from absorption. How does adsorption depend on (*i*) temperature, (*ii*) concentration of the adsorbate and nature of the adsorbate and adsorbent? Why adsorption of a gas on a solid surface is accompanied by a decrease in enthalpy and entropy of the system?

8. Derive an expression for Langmuir unimolecular adsorption isotherm. Under what conditions does it reduce to Freundlich adsorption isotherm? What are the limitations of Langmuir's theory of adsorption?

9. Discuss the application of adsorption in industry and in everyday life.

10. It was found that 0.106 mg of an adsorbate covered 5.0×10^{-2} m^2 of a solid surface. If the molar mass of the adsorbate was 0.284 kg mol^{-1}, calculate the molecular area of the adsorbate.

Ans. 2.2×10^{-19} m^2.

11. The volume of nitrogen gas at 1 atm and 273 K required to cover a sample of silica gel with a monomolecular layer is 0.129 dm^3 per gram of the gel. Calculate the surface area of the gel if each nitrogen molecule occupied 16.2×10^{-20} m^2.

Ans. 560.0 m^2 g^{-1}.

12. The following data have been obtained with the adsorption of nitrogen on active charcoal at 273 K at a series of pressures:

p (mm Hg)	3.93	12.98	22.94	34.01	56.23
v (ml g^{-1})	0.987	3.04	5.08	7.04	10.31

Verify the Langmuir isotherm and determine the values of the constants a and b.

Ans. $a = 0.036$ dm^3 g^{-1}, $b = 7.1 \times 10^{-3}$ mm^{-1}.

Catalysis

18.1 INTRODUCTION

A catalyst is a substance that increases the rate of a chemical reaction without itself being used up and can be recovered unchanged chemically at the end of a chemical reaction. A catalyst provides an alternative path, usually of lower activation energy (Fig. 18.1) for the reaction to proceed at an accelerated rate. Let E_a be the activation energy of the catalysed reaction and E'_a the activation energy for the same reaction in the absence of the catalyst. One can see from Fig. 18.1 that E'_a is larger than E_a. The same is true for the reverse reaction also. Consider, for example, the formation of oxygen by heating potassium chlorate. The reaction is very slow and takes place as follows:

$$2\,KClO_3 \xrightarrow{\text{Heating}} 2\,KCl + 3O_2$$

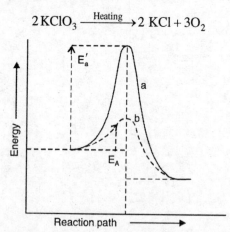

Fig. 18.1 Activation energy for (*a*) uncatalysed (*b*) catalysed reactions

A small addition of manganese dioxide to potassium chlorate accelerates the rate of the reaction and can be recovered unchanged at the end of the reaction. Thus, manganese dioxide acts as catalyst.

Various other examples of catalysts are:

(*i*) In the manufacture of ammonia by Haber's process, iron acts as a catalyst.

$$N_2 + 3H_2 \xrightarrow{\text{Fe}} 2NH_3$$

(*ii*) In contact process for the manufacture of sulphuric acid, platinum acts as a catalyst.

$$2SO_2 + O_2 \xrightarrow{\text{Pt}} 2SO_3$$

(*iii*) Combination of hydrogen and chlorine takes place in the presence of water vapours.

$$H_2 + Cl_2 \xrightarrow{\text{H}_2\text{O}} 2HCl$$

In these examples, the catalysts accelerate the rate of a chemical reaction and are, therefore, sometimes termed as *positive catalysts*. On the other hand, there are substances which when added to a chemical reaction retard its reaction rate and are thus called *negative catalysts or inhibitors*. Some common examples of negative catalysts are:

(*i*) Auto oxidation of benzaldehyde is strongly inhibited by traces of some sulphur compounds.

(*ii*) Decomposition of H_2O_2 is retarded by the presence of a small quantity of sulphuric acid.

(*iii*) Oxidation of chloroform is retarded by traces of alcohols.

18.2 CHARACTERISTICS OF CATALYSTS

(*i*) A catalyst remains chemically unaffected at the end of a chemical reaction. The catalyst does not undergo any chemical change, although there may be a change in its physical state such as the particle size or change in the colour of the catalyst etc.

(*ii*) Small quantity of a catalyst is usually required to bring about a reaction. A very small amount of a catalyst is sufficient for reactants to combine together. This is because the catalyst is not used up in the reaction. Thus 10^{-4} g of molybdic acid is sufficient for the oxidation of HI by H_2O_2. However, sometimes in many homogeneous catalytic processes, the rate of a catalytic reaction is proportional to the concentration of the catalyst. For example, in the inversion of cane sugar hydrochloric acid acts as a catalyst.

(*iii*) Presence of a catalyst does not affect the position of equilibrium in a reversible reaction. This is true when a small amount of the catalyst is used. The catalyst helps in attaining the equilibrium more quickly by increasing the rates of both the forward and the reverse reactions to the same extent. It cannot change the relative amounts of the reactants and products at equilibrium. If, however, the catalyst is present in large amount, the same is not true. Some instances are known where the equilibrium constant changes. For example hydrolysis of ethyl acetate in the presence of varying amounts of HCl, which acts as a catalyst, changes the value of equilibrium constant.

(*iv*) A catalyst does not initiate a reaction but only increases or decreases its speed. Generally, a catalyst speeds up the reaction which is already occurring slowly in its absence. However, this is not true in all reactions. Many reactions are known to occur only in the presence of a catalyst.

(*v*) The action of a catalyst is specific. A catalyst can catalyse only a specific reaction and cannot be used for every reaction. For example, manganese dioxide can catalyse the decomposition of potassium chlorate but not potassium nitrate or other substances. Change of a catalyst also changes the nature of the reaction, e.g.,

$$HCOOH \begin{cases} \xrightarrow{\text{Cu or ZnO}} H_2 + CO_2 \\ \\ \xrightarrow{\text{Al}_2\text{O}_3 \text{ or TiO}_2} H_2O + CO \end{cases}$$

$$CO + H_2 \begin{array}{c} \xrightarrow{\text{Ni}} CH_4 + H_2O \\ \\ \xrightarrow{\text{ZnO}} CH_3OH \end{array}$$

(*vi*) A catalyst has an optimum temperature at which the action of the catalyst is maximum.

(*vii*) A catalyst is poisoned by the presence of traces of certain substances which destroy the catalytic activity and are called *catalytic poisons*. Some of the catalytic poisons are arsenious oxide, carbon monoxide, hydrogen cyanide etc.

(*viii*) The activity of a catalyst is enhanced by the presence of a substance called *promoter*. For example, in the synthesis of ammonia by Haber's process, molybdenum is used as a promoter to the catalyst iron.

18.3 TYPES OF CATALYSIS

There are generally two types of catalysis: (*a*) homogeneous catalysis and (*b*) heterogeneous catalysis.

Homogeneous Catalysis

In homogeneous catalysis, the catalyst is present in the same phase as the reacting substances. Many homogeneous catalysed reactions have been studied in the gas and liquid phases. Some common examples of such catalysis in gas phase are:

(*i*) In the lead chamber process for the manufacture of sulphuric acid, nitric oxide gas catalyses the oxidation of sulphur dioxide.

$$2SO_2 + O_2 \xrightarrow{\text{NO}} 2SO_3$$

(*ii*) Decomposition of acetaldehyde is catalysed by iodine vapours.

$$CH_3CHO \xrightarrow[\text{vapours}]{I_2} CH_4 + CO$$

(*iii*) Nitric oxide acts as a catalyst in the combination of carbon monoxide and oxygen

$$2CO + O_2 \xrightarrow{\text{NO}} 2CO_2$$

Examples of homogeneous catalysis in liquid phase: Important examples of homogeneous catalysis in liquid phase are acid-base catalysis. The most common acid catalyst in water is the hydronium ion and the most common base catalyst is the hydroxyl ion. If an acid catalyses a reaction, the reaction is said to be the subject of acid catalysis. Inversion of cane sugar and hydrolysis of esters are some examples of acid catalysed reactions. However, it was shown that different acids have different catalytic activity; hydrochloric acid has a greater activity than acetic acid. So it is evident that the actual catalysts are H^+ (or H_3O^+) ions. The rates of reaction are found to be proportional to the concentration of H_3O^+ ions and the concentration of the reacting molecules or ions.

$$C_{12}H_{22}O_{11} + H_2O \xrightarrow{H_3O^+} C_6H_{12}O_6 + C_6H_{12}O_6$$

$$CH_3COOC_2H_5 + H_2O \xrightarrow{H_3O^+} CH_3COOH + C_2H_5OH$$

Such reactions which are catalysed by certain acids (or H_3O^+ ions only) are said to be *specific acid catalysis*. Similarly, there are reactions which are catalysed by OH^- ions only and hence are said to be *specific hydroxyl ion catalysis*. Conversion of acetone into diacetonyl alcohol or the decomposition of nitroso-triacetoneamine are examples of hydroxyl ion catalysis.

$$CH_3COCH_3 + CH_3COCH_3 \xrightarrow{OH^-} CH_3COCH_2C(CH_3)_2 OH$$

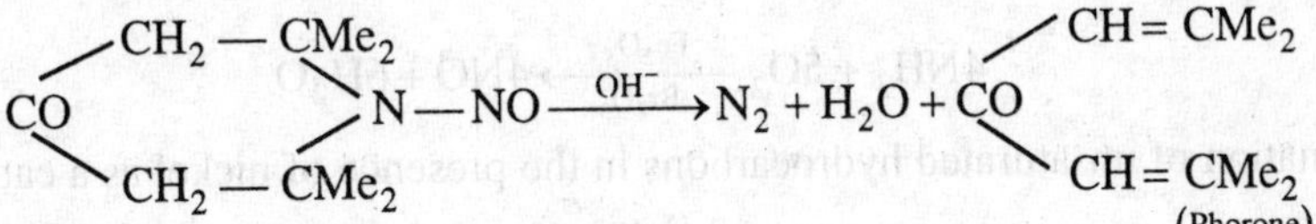

There are many reactions in which both H_3O^+ ions and OH^- ions simultaneously act as catalysts, probably along with water. The mechanism of hydrolysis of ester can be expressed as follows:

(*i*) With H⁺ ions as catalyst

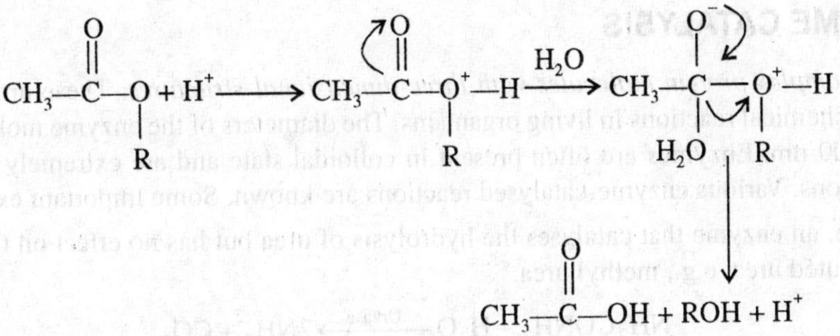

(*ii*) With hydroxyl ions as catalyst

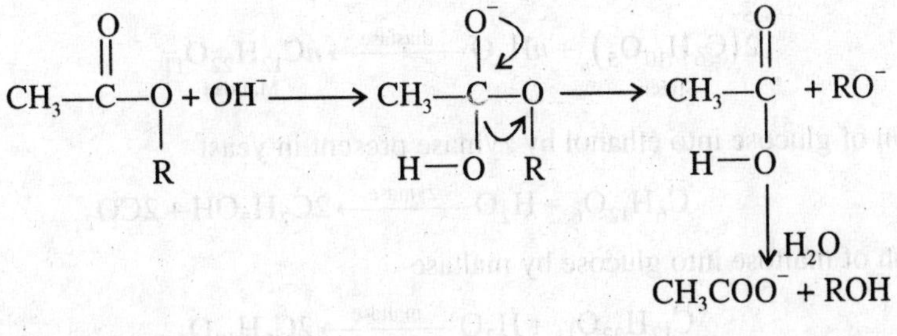

Heterogeneous Catalysis

In heterogeneous catalysed reactions the catalyst is present in a different phase from the reactants. In a number of cases, the catalyst is the solid phase and the reactants are gaseous in most cases or liquids in others. The catalysts which are commonly used are metals like platinum, nickel, copper and iron and certain metal oxides such as ferric oxide, zinc oxide, molybdenum oxide etc. Some important examples of heterogeneous catalysis are:

(*i*) In contact process for the manufacture of sulphuric acid, sulphur dioxide is directly oxidized into sulphur trioxide by atmospheric oxygen in the presence of platinum as catalyst.

$$2SO_2 + O_2 \xrightarrow{Pt} 2SO_3$$

(ii) Haber's process for the manufacture of ammonia in which nitrogen and hydrogen in the ratio of 1 : 3 are passed over heated iron which contains a promoter (molybdenum).

$$N_2 + 3H_2 \xrightarrow{Fe} 2NH_3$$

(iii) The oxidation of ammonia to nitric oxide and finally to nitric acid in the presence of a mixture of ferric oxide and bismuth oxide.

$$4NH_3 + 5O_2 \xrightarrow[Bi_2O_3]{Fe_2O_3} 4NO + 6H_2O$$

(iv) Hydrogenation of unsaturated hydrocarbons in the presence of nickel as a catalyst.

$$-R-CH=CH-R' + H_2 \xrightarrow{Ni} R-CH_2-CH_2-R'$$

(v) Oxidation of HCl by oxygen in the presence of $CuCl_2$ as catalyst.

$$4HCl + O_2 \xrightarrow{CuCl_2} 2H_2O + 2Cl_2$$

18.4 ENZYME CATALYSIS

Enzymes are complex protein molecules with three-dimensional structures. These are responsible for catalysing the chemical reactions in living organisms. The diameters of the enzyme molecules fall in the range of 10–100 nm. Enzymes are often present in colloidal state and are extremely specific in their catalytic functions. Various enzyme-catalysed reactions are known. Some important examples are:

(i) Urease, an enzyme that catalyses the hydrolysis of urea but has no effect on the hydrolysis of substituted urea, e.g., methyl urea.

$$NH_2CONH_2 + H_2O \xrightarrow{Urease} 2NH_3 + CO_2$$

(ii) Peptide, glycyl-L-glutamyl-L-tyrosine is hydrolysed by an enzyme known as pepsin.

(iii) Hydrolysis of starch into maltose by diastase

$$2\underset{\text{Starch}}{(C_6H_{10}O_5)_n} + nH_2O \xrightarrow{\text{diastase}} n\underset{\text{Maltose}}{C_{12}H_{22}O_{11}}$$

(iv) Conversion of glucose into ethanol by zymase present in yeast

$$C_6H_{12}O_6 + H_2O \xrightarrow{\text{zymase}} 2C_2H_5OH + 2CO_2$$

(v) Conversion of maltose into glucose by maltase

$$C_{12}H_{22}O_{11} + H_2O \xrightarrow{\text{maltase}} 2C_6H_{12}O_6$$

(vi) Oxidation of alcohol to acetic acid by micoderma aceti

$$C_2H_5OH + O_2 \xrightarrow[\text{aceti}]{\text{micoderma}} CH_3COOH + H_2O$$

Almost all enzymes fall into one of the two classes, the *hydrolytic enzymes* and the *oxidation-reduction enzymes*. The hydrolytic enzymes appear to be complex acid-base catalysis which accelerate the ionic reactions mainly due to the transfer of hydrogen ions. The oxidation-reduction enzymes catalyse electron transfer perhaps through the formation of an intermediate radical.

Mechanism of Enzyme Reactions

The mechanism of an enzyme reaction was proposed by Michaelis and Menten and can be represented in the following manner : Let E represent the enzyme and S the substrate it acts on, then the overall reaction is

$$E + S \underset{k_{-1}}{\overset{k_1}{\rightleftharpoons}} [ES] \overset{k_2}{\longrightarrow} E + P$$

It is to be noted that in the formation of the product P, the enzyme does not undergo any change. The rate of formation of the product depends on the concentration of the enzyme. In the above scheme ES denotes the intermediate between the enzyme and the substrate which decomposes into the product with a first order rate constant k_2. The rate of formation of the product is given by

$$\frac{d[P]}{dt} = k_2 [ES] \qquad \qquad ...(18.1)$$

In order to solve the Eq. (18.1) it is necessary to know the concentration of ES. This can be calculated through the steady-state principle (see Chapter 16).

$$\frac{d[ES]}{dt} = k_1 [E][S] - k_{-1}[ES] - k_2[ES] = 0$$

or

$$[ES] = \frac{k_1 [E][S]}{k_{-1} + k_2}$$

$$= \frac{[E][S]}{\dfrac{k_2 + k_{-1}}{k_1}}$$

$$= \frac{[E][S]}{K_m} \qquad \qquad ...(18.2)$$

where $K_m = \dfrac{k_2 + k_1}{k_1}$ and is often referred to as *Michaelis constant*.

In this equation, the quantities $[E]$ and $[S]$ are the concentrations of free enzyme and free substrate. If $[E]_0$ and $[S]_0$ are the initial concentrations of the enzyme and the substrate respectively, then we can write

$$[E]_0 = [E] + [ES]$$

or

$$[E] = [E]_0 - [ES]$$

and

$$[S]_0 = [S] + [ES]$$

Since only a little enzyme is added, hence $[ES]$ is very small in comparison to $[S]$ $[ES] << S]$, therefore,

$$[S]_0 \cong [S]$$

Substituting the value of $[E]$ in Eq. (18.2), we get

$$[ES] = \frac{\{[E]_0 - [ES]\}[S]}{K_m}$$

$$[S + K_m][ES] = [E]_0[S]$$

$$[ES] = \frac{[E]_0[S]}{[S] + K_m}$$

Consequently, the rate of formation of products is

$$\frac{d[P]}{dt} = k_2[ES]$$

$$= \frac{k_2[E]_0[S]}{K_m + [S]} \qquad \text{...(18.3)}$$

According to Eq. (18.3), if $[S] << K_m$, then the rate of enzymolysis varies linearly with the enzyme and substrate concentrations, i.e., the reaction will be first order in E and S. However, if $[S] >> K_m$

$$\frac{d[P]}{dt} = \frac{k_2[E]_0[S]}{[S]}$$

$$= k_2[E]_0 \qquad \text{...(18.4)}$$

the rate of the reaction will be independent of substrate concentration and will be first order in E.

A plot of $\dfrac{d[P]}{dt}$ versus $[S]$ for constant enzyme concentration yields a curve (Fig. 18.2) from which it is possible to calculate the value of k_2 and K_m. Further, when the rate is half the maximum value

$$\frac{d[P]}{dt} = \frac{k_2[E]_0}{2} = \frac{k_2[E]_0[S]}{K_m + [S]}$$

or
$$K_m + [S] = 2[S]$$

$$[S] = K_m$$

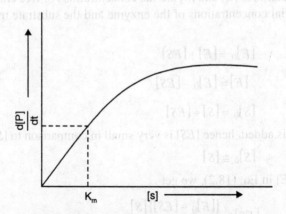

Fig. 18.2 Plot of Michaelis-Menten equation

Rates of enzyme-catalysed reactions are slowed down by compounds which are structurally related to the substrate. These compounds combine with the active sites of the enzyme and thus cause inhibition. In cases where the substrate and the inhibitor compete for the active sites, the rate may be increased by taking larger concentrations of substrate.

An enzyme reaction has an optimum pH value at which the catalytic activity of the enzyme is maximum. The rate of the reaction decreases as the pH is raised or lowered from the optimum value. At extreme pH they are irreversibly denatured.

Rate versus temperature graph for an enzyme-catalysed reaction as given in Fig. 16.7 (*iii*) in Chapter 16 shows that rate is maximum at a certain temperature. Above this temperature the enzyme is denatured and hence the rate decreases.

18.5 THEORY OF CATALYSIS

As stated earlier, the essential requirement for a reaction to occur is that the reacting molecules must acquire sufficient energy. In case a catalyst is added to the reaction, the energy required to activate the molecules is less than in the absence of a catalyst. Due to lower activation energy more molecules will take part in the reaction and hence the rate of the catalysed reaction would increase. The action of a catalyst can be explained by two different mechanisms, *viz.*, (*a*) intermediate compound formation theory, and (*b*) adsorption theory.

Intermediate Compound Formation Theory

In this theory essentially two steps are involved

  (*i*) Combination of the catalyst with one or more of the reactants forming intermediate compound; and

  (*ii*) Decomposition of the intermediate compound or its combination with other reactants yielding the product and the catalyst back. Consider a reaction between the reactants A and B giving the product, *viz.*,

$$A + B \rightarrow AB$$

This reaction is very slow and is catalysed by the presence of a catalyst X. The reaction will therefore proceed as

$$A + X \rightarrow AX \quad \text{(Intermediate compound)}$$

$$AX + B \rightarrow AB + X$$

The formation of an intermediate compound AX is an easy reaction and needs low energy of activation thereby accelerating the rate of the chemical reaction.

Some examples of intermediate compound formation

  (*i*) In lead chamber process for the manufacture of sulphuric acid, the catalyst NO first forms an intermediate compound with oxygen

$$2NO + \frac{1}{2}O_2 \rightarrow 2NO_2 \left(\text{Intermediate compound}\right)$$

and then

$$NO_2 + SO_2 \rightarrow SO_3 + NO$$

(*ii*) In the preparation of diethyl ether from ethanol using concentrated H_2SO_4, $C_2H_5HSO_4$ is first formed as an intermediate.

$$C_2H_5OH + H_2SO_4 \rightarrow C_2H_5HSO_4 + H_2O$$

$$C_2H_5HSO_4 + C_2H_5OH \rightarrow C_2H_5 - O - C_2H_5 + H_2SO_4$$

(*iii*) The formation of water by combination of hydrogen and oxygen in presence of copper as a catalyst is as follows :

$$2Cu + \frac{1}{2}O_2 \rightarrow Cu_2O$$

$$Cu_2O + H_2 \rightarrow H_2O + 2Cu$$

Limitations of intermediate compound formation theory: This theory does not explain the cases of heterogeneous catalysis in general and more specifically the deactivation by a catalytic poison and the activation by a promoter.

Adsorption Theory

A large number of gaseous reactions take place in the presence of solid catalysts. The surface of the catalyst has certain active centres due to the unsaturation of valencies. Appreciable quantities of the reactant molecules are adsorbed or retained by solid surfaces at these active centres and the reactions occur at the surface of the solid. For this reason this type of catalysis is sometimes referred to as the contact catalysis. The adsorbed molecules form some sort of an activated complex on the surface which then decomposes forming the products. The products are ultimately desorbed from the surface. A catalytic reaction involves the following steps:

(*i*) Diffusion of the reactants from the bulk on to the surface.
(*ii*) Adsorption of the reactants on the surface of the catalyst.
(*iii*) Activation of the adsorbed reactants leading to a reaction in the adsorbed phase.
(*iv*) Desorption of the products from the surface of the catalyst.
(*v*) Diffusion of the products away from the surface of the catalyst.

Any one of these steps may be slowest and consequently the rate determining but generally step (*iii*) is the rate controlling step.

Due to adsorption the concentration of the reactants tends to increase on the surface of the catalyst and according to the law of mass action, the rate of the reaction will increase. Furthermore, adsorption being an exothermic process, the heat evolved during adsorption is utilized in the activation of the surface reaction. Adsorption may also lead to proper orientation of the reacting molecules, partial loosening of the bonds in the adsorbed state and thus requiring only small energy to form the activated complex.

Adsorption theory can explain the enhanced catalytic action of a catalyst in the finely divided state. It is due to the larger surface area available for adsorption and also the formation of more active centres.

$$
\begin{array}{ccc}
| & | & \\
-Ni - Ni - & & -Ni - \quad -Ni - \\
| & | & \longrightarrow \quad | \quad + \quad | \\
-Ni - Ni - & & -Ni - \quad -Ni - \\
| & | & | \quad\quad |
\end{array}
$$

Action of promoters which enhance the catalytic activity can also be explained in terms of this theory. A promoter generally increases the number of active centres by the adsorption on the surface of a catalyst. Similarly, poisoning of a catalyst results due to the adsorption of the catalytic poisons on the surface and thereby reducing the number of active centres on the surface of a catalyst.

18.6 AUTOCATALYSIS

Sometimes a product of the reaction may catalyse the reaction. Such substances are called autocatalysts. In the oxidation of oxalate ions by permanganate ions in acidic medium manganous ions produced in the reaction catalyse the reaction

$$C_2O_4^{2-} \rightarrow 2CO_2 + 2e] \times 5$$

$$MnO_4^- + 8H^+ + 5e \rightarrow Mn^{2+} + 4H_2O] \times 2$$

$$5C_2O_4^{2-} + 2MnO_4^- + 16H^+ \rightarrow 10CO_2 + 2Mn^{2+} + 8H_2O$$

18.7 INHIBITION AND POISONING

For the enhancement of the reaction rate, the reactants must be adsorbed more or less to the same extent. If one of the reactants is more strongly adsorbed than the other or if a product is adsorbed to a greater extent than the reactants, then the active centres on the surface of the catalyst will not be available completely for the reaction and the reaction rate decreases. Such a condition is called inhibition of the catalyst. One of the reactants or products which gets strongly adsorbed and thereby decreases the reaction rate is called the inhibitors.

Sometimes the reaction could be inhibited by a foreign molecule that does not take part in a reaction. This is called catalytic poisoning. This phenomenon can be explained by the fact that the active centres of the catalyst constitute only a small fraction of the total surface sites on a catalyst and the meagre amount of poison could occupy these positions. This prevents the occupation of reactant molecules.

EXERCISES

1. What is meant by catalysis? Discuss the general characteristics of a catalyst.

2. Differentiate between homogeneous and heterogeneous catalysis. Explain the following on the basis of heterogeneous catalysis :

    (*i*) active centres, (*ii*) specificity of a catalyst, (*iii*) the action of catalytic poisons, (*iv*) the action of promoters, (*v*) the activity of a finely divided catalyst.

3. Select the correct statements from the following for a catalysed reaction :

    (*i*) The use of a catalyst provides an alternate path of lower activation energy.

    (*ii*) The catalyst does not change the position of equilibrium.

    (*iii*) The equilibrium position is attained earlier.

    (*iv*) An enzyme has an optimum temperature at which its catalytic action is maximum.

    (*v*) The use of a catalyst changes the rate constant of the reaction.

    (*vi*) The catalyst remains unchanged at the end of the reaction. It may, however, undergo a change in its physical state. **Ans.** True statements : (*i*), (*ii*), (*iv*), (*vi*).

4. Explain and illustrate the following:

   (*i*) Negative catalysts; (*ii*) Catalytic poisons; (*iii*) Promoters; (*iv*) Autocatalysis; (*v*) Active centres ; (*vi*) Acid-base catalysis; and (*vii*) Enzyme catalysis.

5. Illustrate the intermediate compound formation and adsorption theories of catalysis. How are these helpful in explaining the characteristics of catalysed reactions ?

6. What is meant by acid-base catalysis ? Explain, giving examples, the theories of acid-base catalysis.

7. What is meant by enzyme catalysis ? Why are they highly specific in their actions ? How do you account for the fact that an enzyme reaction has an optimum pH at which its activity is maximum ? Discuss in detail the mechanism of enzyme catalysed reactions.

8. Explain, with examples, the function of catalytic promoters and poisons in a chemical reaction.

9. When oxalic acid is added to an acidified solution of potassium permanganate no appreciable decolourization occurs for a comparatively long period of time, but once decolourization occurs it proceeds rapidly. Explain.

10. Hydrolysis of methyl trichloroacetate to trichloroacetic acid and methanol is catalysed by H_3O^+ ions. Should the time required to convert a given quantity of the ester to products, in a given quantity of water at a given pH, be different in buffered and unbuffered solutions ? If so, in which solution should the time be shorter ? Explain briefly.

Colloidal State

19.1 INTRODUCTION

An ordinary solution consists of a solvent and solute(s). The particles of the solute are usually normal molecules or ions. For example, when sugar or common salt is added to water a true solution is formed. On the other hand, when substances like sand, powdered glass etc. are added to water, they settle down. Such solutions are called *coarse suspensions*. Between these two extremes of true solutions and coarse suspensions exist systems called *colloidal solutions* having properties in between them. A colloidal solution, therefore, consists of solute particles which are larger than the normal molecules but not large enough to be seen by a microscope. However, there is no sharp line of demarcation between the true solution and the colloidal solution on one hand, and between colloidal solution and the coarse suspension on the other. In a colloidal solution the particle size lies in the range 1 mμ to 1 μ (0.001 to 1 mμ). Thus, the essential difference between the solutions, colloids and coarse suspensions lies in their relative particle size. A colloidal solution cannot always be distinguished from a true solution with the naked eye. The particles of a colloidal solution can pass through an ordinary filter paper. A colloidal solution is defined as *a heterogeneous system consisting of two phases (i) a dispersed phase which consists of the colloidal particles, and (ii) a dispersion medium, the solvent*. For example, the dispersion of As_2S_3, gold or oil in water forms a colloidal solution.

Table 19.1 Distinguishing characteristics of Colloids, Suspensions and Solutions

Properties	Suspension	Colloid	Solution
1. Particle size	> 1μ	1 mμ – 1μ	< 1 mμ
2. Separation			
(i) Ordinary filtration	Possible	Not Possible	Not possible
(ii) Ultrafiltration	Possible	Possible	Not possible
3. Settling	Settles under gravity	Settles on centrifugation	Does not settle
4. Appearance	Opaque	Generally clear	Clear
5. Diffusion	Not possible	Diffuses slowly	Diffuses rapidly
6. Brownian motion	Shows	Shows	Not observable
7. Tyndall effect	Shows	Shows	Not observable

Some of the distinguishing characteristics of solution, colloid and suspension are given in Table 19.1.

19.2 CLASSIFICATION OF COLLOIDS

For the classification of colloids a number of criteria have been employed. These are:

(*i*) **Classification Based on the State of Aggregation of the Dispersed Phase and the Dispersion Medium:** On the basis of this, eight different classes of colloids are possible and are shown in Table 19.2. Colloidal solutions are generally known as sols. We shall mainly deal with the colloidal systems in which the dispersed phase is a solid and the dispersion medium a liquid. If the dispersion medium is water they are called hydrosols or aquasols.

Table 19.2 Classification of Colloidal Solutions

Dispersion medium	Dispersed phase	Name	Some examples
Gas	Liquid	Aerosol	Clouds, mist
	Solid	Aerosol	Smoke, haze
Liquid	Gas	Foam	Froath, whipped cream
	Liquid	Emulsion	Milk (fats in water),
	Solid	Sols	dispersion of oil in water
			AgCl, As$_2$S$_3$ in water
Solid	Gas	Solid foam	Pumice stone, ice cream, cake
	Liquid	Gels	Jellies, curd, cheese
	Solid	Solid sols	Gems, ruby glass

(*ii*) **Classification Based on the Affinity of the Two Phases:** On the basis of affinity between the dispersed phase and the dispersion medium, there are two classes of colloids, viz., *lyophobic*

Table 19.3 Distinguishing characteristics of Lyophobic and Lyophilic Sols

Lyophobic sols	Lyophilic sols
1. Small quantities of electrolytes bring about their precipitation.	1. These are stable and are not affected by small amounts of electrolytes.
2. Lyophobic sol particles contain electric charges and hence migrate towards the electrode in an electric field.	2. The particles may or may not migrate in an electric field depending upon the pH of the medium.
3. Viscosity of a lyophobic sol is almost equal to that of the dispersion medium.	3. Lyophilic sols have high viscosities.
4. Surface tension is similar to that of the dispersion medium.	4. Surface tension is lower than that of the dispersion medium.
5. Lyophobic sol particles are easily detected under an ultramicroscope.	5. The particles cannot be readily detected by the ultramicroscope.
6. These can be prepared by indirect methods.	6. These are prepared generally by simple solution methods.

(*solvent hating*) and *lyophilic* (*solvent loving*). Because of the poor interactions between the dispersed phase and the dispersion medium, lyophobic sols are less stable, precipitate out easily and are obtained with difficulty, hence these are irreversible in character, e.g., gold, As_2S_3 in water etc. Lyophilic sols are easily formed and are, therefore, reversible, e.g., gums, starch, etc. Other essential differences between the two types of sols are given in Table 19.3.

19.3 PREPARATION OF COLLOIDAL SOLUTIONS

Many substances such as gelatin, starch and other high molar mass polymers when warmed with a suitable dispersion medium go into the solution forming a colloidal solution. Such sols are stable, reversible and are called lyophilic sols. Lyophobic sols, on the other hand, are unstable, irreversible and therefore have to be prepared by special methods yielding particles of the appropriate size. Two methods are generally used for their preparations: (*a*) Condensation or aggregation method in which the particles present in the true solutions as ions or molecules are allowed to grow in size to particles of colloidal dimensions. (*b*) Dispersion method in which the bigger particles are disintegrated into particles of colloidal dimensions which remain in the dispersion medium.

Condensation Method

The substance which is to be dispersed in the dispersion medium is obtained by chemical reactions or sometimes by the physical changes under controlled conditions of temperature and concentration. The various methods employed are:

By reduction

This method is generally used for the preparation of metal sols and is of historical interest as the earliest known gold sols were prepared by this method. The method involves the reduction of soluble salts of metals by reducing agents such as hydrogen, formaldehyde, hydrazine, hydrogen peroxide, tannin etc. A silver sol may be prepared by passing a current of pure hydrogen through a saturated solution of silver oxide at 50–60°C. A gold sol may be prepared by the reduction of chloroauric acid ($HAuCl_4$) solution containing a small amount of K_2CO_3 by formaldehyde or hydrazine.

By oxidation

Sulphur sols are easily obtained by the oxidation of aqueous hydrogen sulphide solution by sulphur dioxide, nitric acid or bromine water.

$$2H_2S + SO_2 \rightarrow 2H_2O + 3S$$

$$H_2S \xrightarrow[HNO_3]{[o]} H_2O + S$$

By double decomposition

A silver chloride sol can be obtained by mixing dilute solutions of $AgNO_3$ and KCl in nearly equivalent amounts. The precipitated AgCl is stabilised by the excess of Ag^+ or Cl^- ions.

Aqueous arsenious sulphide sol is obtained by passing H_2S through a dilute solution of arsenious oxide

$$As_2O_3 + 3H_2S \rightarrow As_2S_3 + 3H_2O$$

By hydrolysis

This method is used to obtain sols of oxides or hydroxides of weakly electropositive metals like iron, aluminium, etc. A solution of ferric oxide is prepared by adding a small quantity of ferric chloride to boiling water when ferric hydroxide and hydrochloric acid are produced. Small quantities of ferric ions and hydrogen ions stabilise the sol. Similarly, sols of hydroxides of tin, iron, chromium, bismuth etc., can be obtained by hydrolysis of their chlorides or nitrates.

By exchange of solvent

This method is based on the principle that if a substance A is insoluble in one solvent, say X, but soluble in other solvent, say Y, then the colloidal solution of that substance is prepared by dissolving the substance A in Y and then pouring the solution into an excess of solvent X. This method is used in preparing sulphur or phosphorus sols by first dissolving them in alcohol (in which these are soluble) and then pouring their alcoholic solutions into water. Such sols are usually unstable and are stabilised by the addition of some stabilisers.

Dispersion Method

Various methods used in dispersion are:

Mechanical disintegration

Many substances can be disintegrated into particles of colloidal size in a "colloid mill" consisting of two steel discs each rotating in opposite direction at a speed of about 7000 rpm. The dispersion medium along with the dispersed substance and a protective agent is allowed to pass through the mill when a colloidal solution results.

Peptization

The process of dispersing a precipitate into a colloidal solution by adding small quantity of electrolyte is called *peptization*. For example, freshly precipitated $Fe(OH)_3$ can be peptized by a dilute solution of ferric chloride.

$$\underset{\text{ppt}}{Fe(OH)_3} + Fe^{3+} \rightarrow \underset{\text{sol}}{Fe(OH)_3\, Fe^{3+}}$$

Precipitates of many sulphides can be dispersed by passing H_2S through water in which they are suspended.

Bredig's arc method

This method is employed in preparing colloidal solutions of metals like Au, Pt, Ag, etc. It consists in striking an electric arc between the electrodes of metal in water (Fig. 19.1). The heat of the arc evaporates

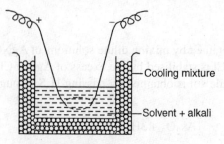

Fig. 19.1 Bredig's arc method

the metal and the vapours are condensed in water. Traces of alkali metal hydroxide are necessary to stabilise the colloidal solution. This method was improved by passing an alternating current by T. Svedberg who succeeded in obtaining organosols, hydrosols of metals and nonmetals.

19.4 PURIFICATION OF COLLOIDAL SOLUTIONS

The sols prepared by any one of the methods mentioned above contain some soluble impurities and excess of electrolytes. It is, therefore, necessary to remove these impurities and to reduce the concentration of the electrolytes to obtain pure sols. The most commonly employed techniques are (*a*) dialysis, and (*b*) ultrafiltration.

Dialysis: In this method the sol to be purified is taken in a parchment paper or cellophane bag which is suspended in a container of distilled water as shown in Fig. 19.2. On standing, the dissolved ions in the sol pass through the cellophane wall due to diffusion and are carried by the solvent. From time to time the container is refilled with pure water. In certain sols such as Al_2O_3 hydrosol, the dispersed phase is too small to be retained by the cellophane paper and so the dialysis is carried out at somewhat higher temperature. The particles thereby grow in sizes and dialysis becomes fast. This is known as *hot dialysis*.

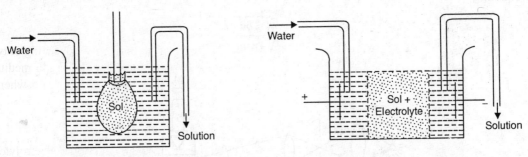

Fig. 19.2 Dialysis   **Fig. 19.3** Electrodialysis

To hasten the process of purification, dialysis is carried out by applying an electric field. This process is then called *electrodialysis* and is shown in Fig. 19.3. The colloidal solution is placed between two dialysing membranes and pure water is filled in the outer compartment surrounding the colloidal solution. On passing an electric current, the ionic impurities migrate out of the colloidal solution, cations move towards cathode and anions towards anode. For effective separation, a continuous supply of water should be maintained (Fig. 19.3).

Ultrafiltration: This method is similar to simple filtration with the exception that a filter paper treated with collodion and hardened by formaldehyde is used. This helps in reducing the pore size of the filter paper which will allow the passage of the electrolytes and medium but not the colloidal particles.

19.5 PROPERTIES OF COLLOIDS

Colour

Colloidal solutions are invariably coloured. The colour of the sol depends on the size and the shape of the colloidal particles.

Optical Properties

An important characteristic of colloids is the scattering of light. If a beam of light is passed through a medium which is optically clear, that is, it contains no particles of appreciably large size than the molecules of true solutions, it is difficult to detect the path of the light. But when light is passed through a colloidal system in which the particle size is large, the rays are scattered. This phenomenon of scattering of light by particles was studied by Tyndall and is generally known as the *Tyndall effect*. If a beam of light is passed through a colloidal solution in a dark room, solution becomes luminescent when viewed through a microscope at right angle to the path of the incident light. Tyndall observed the scattered beam to be polarised and the intensity of the same to be dependent on the position of observer, nature of the system, the wavelength of light used etc.

Quantitative study of the Tyndall effect and other kinetic properties (like Brownian motion etc.) have been rendered possible with the help of ultramicroscope introduced by Zsigmondy in 1903. The arrangement of the system is shown in Fig. 19.4. A strong beam of light is passed through a cell containing colloidal solution and is viewed through a microscope. Zsigmondy showed that if the colloidal particles are seen from a direction at right angles to the incident light, the colloidal particles appear as bright spots against a dark background. The radius of the particles can be calculated by using the equation

$$r = \sqrt[3]{\frac{3bv}{4\pi nd}}$$

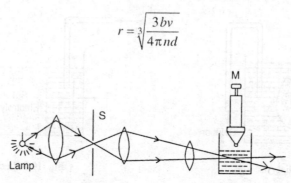

Fig. 19.4 An ultramicroscope

It is assumed that the colloidal particles are spherical in nature and the density of the substance in the colloidal state is the same as that in the dry state. In the above equation, b denotes the number of grams of the substance per dm^3 in the colloidal solution, n is the number of particles observed in a field of view of volume v dm^3 and d is the density of the dry substance.

Kinetic Property—Brownian Movement

Robert Brown (1927), a botanist, discovered that pollen grains when suspended in a liquid and observed under a microscope exhibit ceaseless chaotic and random motions. Such motion of the particles is called Brownian motion. It is to be noted that Brownian movement is due to constant molecular impacts from the medium on all sides of the dispersed particles. Furthermore, Brownian motion becomes less and less vigorous with increase in the size of the suspended particles and also with the increase in the viscosity of the medium. It would increase with rise in temperature.

Electrical Properties

(*i*) **Charge on colloidal particles:** Colloidal particles always carry some charge, otherwise the colloidal system would be unstable. The charge on the colloidal particles is of the same type in a colloidal solution and may be either positive or negative. The charge on particles may be due to

(a) *Preferential adsorption of ions:* The charge on the colloidal particles in some cases results from adsorption of either positive or negative ions from the medium in which they are prepared. Generally, a preference for those ions which are common with one of the ions composing colloidal particles is observed. Thus when $FeCl_3$ is added to hot water and dialysed, $Fe(OH)_3$ colloidal particles so formed adsorb Fe^{3+} ions and a positively charged sol is obtained. But when $Fe(OH)_3$ sol is prepared from $FeCl_3$ solution containing excess of alkali, the colloidal particles adsorb OH^- ions and, therefore, a negatively charged sol is obtained.

Similarly, if a dilute solution of a silver salt is added to excess of dilute KI solution, a negatively charged sol of AgI is obtained. On the other hand, if a dilute solution of iodide is added to an excess of silver salt solution, a positively charged sol results. The stability and the negative charge of the sol in presence of excess of iodide can be explained by the adsorption of iodide ions on the surface of each silver iodide particle.

(b) *Due to the presence of acidic and basic groups:* The charge in case of proteins, amino acids, polypeptides etc., can be explained due to the presence of acidic (such as —COOH, or phenolic—OH) and basic (such as —NH_2, >NH or ≥N) groups in the molecule. In acid solution, the molecules will have positive charge due to the protonation of the basic groups, while in alkaline solution the molecules will be negatively charged due to ionisation of the acidic groups as shown in the following scheme:

$$R \cdots CH \cdots COO^- \xleftarrow{OH^-} R \cdots CH \cdots COOH \xrightarrow{H_3O^+} R \cdots CH \cdots COOH$$
$$\underset{NH_2}{|} \qquad\qquad \underset{NH_2}{|} \qquad\qquad \underset{NH_3^+}{|}$$

Negative charge in alkaline	Protein molecule	Positive charge in acidic
medium		medium

It is clear that the charge in such cases is a function of pH of the medium. The pH at which the net charge on the molecule is zero is called the *isoelectric point*. The molecules at the isoelectric point exist as *zwitter ions*. A lyophilic colloid has minimum stability at this pH.

(c) *Due to ionisation of molecules adsorbed on the surface:* Colloidal particles such as As_2S_3 can be represented by $(As_2S_3)_m(H_3AsS_4)_n(H_3AsS_4)$, where m and n are large numbers. The negative charge on As_2S_3 may be assumed to be due to the ionisation of the arsenic acid molecules on the surface, e.g.,

$(As_2S_3)_m (H_3AsS_4)_n (H_2AsS_4)^- H^+$.

(d) *Due to the dissociation of the surface molecules:* In case of soaps, the charge on the particles is due to ionisation of the molecule, e.g., $C_{15}H_{31}COO^-Na^+$.

(ii) *Electrophoresis:* Colloidal particles are charged and when placed in an electric field, these particles migrate either towards the cathode or anode depending upon their charges. This phenomenon of migration of colloidal particles in an electric field is called *electrophoresis* or *cataphoresis*. The speed of colloidal particles when the applied field strength is 1 volt m^{-1} is known as *the electrophoretic* or *cataphoretic mobility*. The electrophoretic mobility depends upon the molecular size of the colloidal particles. The difference in the electrophoretic mobility is used in the separation of mixtures. On the other hand, if the colloidal particles are prevented from moving then the dispersion medium moves in the electric field, the phenomenon is known as *electroosmosis*.

The apparatus used for electrophoresis is shown in Fig. 19.5. It consists of a U-tube containing a hydrosol covered by a pure dispersion medium, e.g., ferric hydroxide sol and water in which the electrodes are dipped and connected to a source of EMF. On applying a high potential, the boundary between the colloid and water begins to move towards the cathode. The potential gradient is known from the applied EMF and the dimensions of the apparatus. Hence the velocity of the particles under a potential of 1 volt m^{-1} can be calculated.

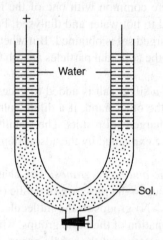

Fig. 19.5 Electrophoresis

In electroosmosis, the sol particles are enclosed between diaphragms DD' (Fig. 19.6), so that the motion of the colloidal particles is prevented and movement of the dispersion medium is observed. The rate at which the dispersion medium moves is a measure of the electroosmosis.

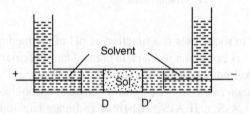

Fig. 19.6 Electroosmosis

19.6 PRECIPITATION OF COLLOIDS

Traces of electrolytes are essential for the stability of a sol while the addition of a comparatively large amounts of electrolytes makes the sol unstable; the colloidal particles grow in size and are precipitated out. This phenomenon of precipitation or coagulation of the sol particles is known as *flocculation* and was observed by T. Graham in 1861. The amount of electrolytes required to precipitate a given sol depends on the nature of both the sol and the electrolyte. For a given sol the precipitating power of an electrolyte is determined by two factors, namely,

  (*i*) coagulation of the sol is effective by ions carrying a charge opposite to that of the colloidal particles, and

  (*ii*) the precipitating power increases considerably with increasing valency of the coagulating ion.

These generalisations are often known as *Hardy-Schultze rule*.

The minimum concentration of an electrolyte which is able to bring about the flocculation of a sol is called its flocculation value. It is generally expressed in *millimoles of electrolyte per dm³ of the sol.* Table 19.4 shows the flocculation values for a positively charged sol and a negatively charged sol.

Table 19.4 Effect of Ions on Coagulation of Various Sols

Fe_2O_3 (positive) sol			As_2S_3 (negative) sol		
Electrolyte	*Anion valency*	*Minimum concentration (millimoles per dm³)*	*Electrolyte*	*Cation valency*	*Minimum concentration (millimoles per dm³)*
KCl	1	103	NaCl	1	51
KBr	1	138	KCl	1	50
KNO_3	1	131	KNO_3	1	50
K_2CrO_4	2	0.325	$CaCl_2$	2	0.65
K_2SO_4	2	0.219	$BaCl_2$	2	0.69
$K_3Fe(CN)_6$	3	0.096	$ZnCl_2$	2	0.68
			$AlCl_3$	3	0.093

It is clear from the table that on increasing the valency of the precipitating ion the flocculation value decreases. The precipitating effect of a trivalent ion is about 600 to 1000 times more than that of a monovalent ion.

Precipitation of colloids can also be brought about by prolonged dialysis, electrophoresis and mixing two colloids of opposite charges in equivalent proportions.

19.7 PROTECTIVE ACTION OF COLLOIDS

When a lyophilic sol is added to a lyophobic sol, the latter becomes more stable and less sensitive towards the electrolytes. In other words, a lyophobic sol is prevented from precipitation. The lyophilic sol thus plays a protective role, usually by forming an adsorbed layer completely covering the particles

Table 19.5 Gold Numbers and their Reciprocals of Certain Lyophilic Sols

Protective colloid	Gold Number	Reciprocal Gold Number
Gelatin	0.005–0.01	200–100
Haemoglobin	0.03–0.07	33–14
Albumin	0.1–0.2	10–5
Dextrin	6–20	0.17–0.05
Sodium oleate	0.4–1.0	2.5–1.0
Potato starch	25	0.04

of the lyophobic sol, so that it virtually behaves like a lyophilic sol. The protective capacity of various lyophilic colloids are expressed by Zsigmondy in terms of *gold number*. It is defined as *the mass in milligrams of a dry lyophilic sol which when added to 10 ml of a standard gel sol to just prevent its coagulation (i.e., the change of colour from red to blue) on the addition of 1 ml of a 10 percent solution of sodium chloride*. The change in colour indicates the initiation of a flocculation. Smaller the gold number greater is the protective action of a lyophilic colloid. Gelatin, agar, albumin, etc., have low gold numbers and thus have high protective powers. Values of gold numbers and their reciprocals for a few lyophilic colloids are given in Table 19.5.

The protective action of a lyophilic sol on a lyophobic colloid against coagulation is not clearly understood but it is reasonably certain that the particles of the two sols are associated or united in some manner.

19.8 EMULSIONS

An emulsion is a dispersed system in which both the dispersed phase and the dispersion medium are liquids. Milk is a naturally occurring emulsion in which the particles (or globules) of liquid fats are dispersed in water. The size of the particles approximately lies in the range from 0.1–1 μ or more in diameter and so are larger than those found in sols. Emulsions are generally prepared by vigorously shaking the two liquids. Their stability is poor and can separate out on standing for some time. To avoid this, it is necessary to add small amounts of substances called *emulsifying agents* or *emulsifiers*. The function of the emulsifying agent is to reduce the interfacial tension between the two liquids forming the emulsion. Soaps of different types, long chain sulphonic acids, gelatin, albumin, etc., are some examples of emulsifying agents.

Emulsions are broadly classified into two types, namely, (*i*) emulsions of oil in water, in which the dispersed phase in an oil while water is the dispersion medium, and (*ii*) emulsions of water in oil in which water is dispersed in oil. Here the term oil designates any liquid immiscible with water. The type of emulsion that results on vigorous mixing of two liquids depends (*a*) on the relative proportions of the two, the one in excess acts as *the outer phase* and the other in lesser proportion as *the inner phase* or *dispersoid*; (*b*) on the nature of the emulsifying agent used. The phase in which emulsifier is more soluble forms the outer phase. Thus, when sodium oleate is added as an emulsifier an oil in water emulsion results. But the addition of water insoluble emulsifier like calcium oleate forms water in oil type of emulsion; (*c*) on the relative magnitude of the surface tension of the two liquids. Generally, the liquid with higher surface tension forms the inner phase due to its greater tendency to form spherical drops.

Emulsions have characteristic properties similar to those of lyophobic colloids. They show Tyndall effect and Brownian motion provided the particles are not too large. Globules carry electrical charges and thus show electrophoretic motion under an electric field. The emulsions can be coagulated by electrolytes; particularly those containing polyvalent cations. Emulsions may also be broken (or converted) into two separate layers by heating, freezing, centrifuging etc. This process is sometimes referred to as demulsification. The conversion of cream into butter by churning is an example of breaking of an emulsion of fats in water.

19.9 GELS

Generally, coagulation of a lyophilic sol yields a precipitate, more or less a semisolid, known as a gel. The process by which it is formed is called *gelation*. For example, gels of agar-agar, gelatin and other similar substances are generally prepared by cooling a not too dilute dispersion of these substances in hot water. On cooling, the particles in the sol associate to form chains which then interlock in the form of a loose framework wherein the sorbed molecules of the medium are accommodated.

Gels are characterised by (*i*) high viscosity, and (*ii*) swelling if placed in the dispersion medium. This phenomenon of swelling is known as *imbibition*. Gels, on standing, give out small quantities of liquid (e.g., water) which accumulates on the surface. This is known as *syneresis* or *weeping*.

Gels are broadly divided into two types, *viz.*, elastic and rigid (nonelastic) gels. An elastic gel, say gum, on partial dehydration leads to the formation of an elastic solid from which the gel can be easily obtained by the addition of water. A nonelastic or rigid gel, such as silica, on dehydration gives a glassy powder which loses the elasticity. The sol cannot be obtained by adding water. Such gels like ferric phosphate, ferric oxide, etc., when vigorously agitated lose their semisolid gel character and acquire the behaviour of sol. They can again set to a gel on standing. This reversible phenomenon of gel-sol transformation is called *thixotropy*. Sometimes thixotropic gels are obtained by adding electrolytes within certain limits to ordinary sols.

19.10 PROTEIN SOLS

The sols of proteins are of special biological importance and their studies present some interesting features. Solutions of lyophilic colloids like gelatin molecules show the phenomenon of electrophoresis, but the direction of movement of the charged particles depends on the pH of the medium. In an acidic medium, the protein molecule acquires a positive charge and thus moves towards the cathode, whereas in an alkaline medium the protein acquires a negative charge and, therefore, moves towards the anode. At an intermediate pH of the solution, the sol does not exhibit any movement in the electric field. The pH at which the particles are uncharged and do not show any movement under the influence of an applied electric field is called *the isoelectric point*. At the isoelectric point the net charge on the molecule is zero, *i.e.*, it contains equal number of positive and negative charges. The molecule at the isoelectric point exists as a zwitter ion of the type

$$R-CH_2-CH-COO^-$$
$$|$$
$$N^+H_3$$

Gelatin has an isoelectric point at pH 4.7. The isoelectric point of different proteins are different. The mobility of a protein at a definite pH and ionic strength is a useful identifying characteristic. Proteins are least soluble at the isoelectric point and therefore have the greatest tendency to coagulate at the isoelectric point.

19.11 APPLICATIONS OF COLLOIDS

(*i*) *Purification of Industrial Smoke:* Cottrell precipitator is used for the purification of industrial smoke. Extremely fine dust, carbon and other particles suspended in air can be removed by subjecting polluted air to a strong electric field. A high voltage is passed over plates kept hanging in the precipitator. The suspended charged particles are attracted towards oppositely charged electrodes and are thus discharged. The air pollution could thus be minimised. This method has been successfully used in purifying gases from dusts, in removing dust of cement plant etc.

(*ii*) In drilling deep wells or tubewells, a colloidal solution is used to prevent the rock chips cut by the drill from forming a compact mass.

   (*iii*) Tanning of leather utilises the colloidal properties. It is a coagulative hardening of leather surface by chemicals.

   (*iv*) Colloidal medicines are easily adsorbed by the body tissues from their dispersion medium.

    (*v*) In purification of water, addition of alums precipitates colloidal particles.

   (*vi*) Formation of river deltas is due to the clay particles in river water which are precipitated by saline seawater. This forms good soil for cultivation.

  (*vii*) The disposal of sewage water by passing it into tank fitted with metallic electrodes at high voltage. The suspended particles which are charged move towards oppositely charged electrodes, get discharged and are precipitated out.

EXERCISES

1. Distinguish the following:
    (*i*) A dispersed phase from a dispersion medium.
    (*ii*) A lyophobic colloid from a lyophilic colloid.
    (*iii*) A colloidal solution from a true solution.
    (*iv*) A colloidal solution from a suspension.
    (*v*) Coagulation from peptization.
    (*vi*) Electrophoresis from electroosmosis.
    (*vii*) An ion from a zwitter ion.

2. Explain, giving reasons, the following:
    (*i*) Lyophilic colloids are more stable than lyophobic colloids.
    (*ii*) Precipitation of a lyophilic colloid is easier at its isoelectric point.
    (*iii*) Aluminium sulphate is more effective for coagulating turbid water than sodium sulphate.
    (*iv*) A colloidal solution of AgI is positively charged when prepared from a solution containing excess of Ag^+ ions and negatively charged when prepared from a solution containing excess of I^- ions.
    (*v*) Charge on colloidal particles is a must for their stability.
    (*vi*) In an amino acid, the molecules do not migrate to either of the electrodes at the isoelectric point.
    (*vii*) Tyndall effect is not shown by suspensions.
    (*viii*) A molecule of protein is negatively charged in alkaline medium while positively charged below its isoelectric point.
    (*ix*) The sky looks blue.
    (*x*) Alum is used in the town water supply.
    (*xi*) Arsenius sulphide sol is negatively charged.
    (*xii*) Lyophilic colloids like protein, etc. have least stability at the isoelectric point.

3. Select the correct statements from the following:
    (*i*) Precipitation of a lyophobic colloid is easier than a lyophilic colloid.
    (*ii*) Brownian movement arises due to the continual bombardment of the colloidal particles by the molecules of the dispersion medium.
    (*iii*) Coagulating effect of an ion is proportional to its valence.
    (*iv*) Larger the value of the gold number greater the protective power of the colloid.
    (*v*) The molecule of a protein is uncharged at its isoelectric point.
    (*vi*) Lyophobic colloids are reversible in character.
    (*vii*) Particles of a suspension do not show Tyndall effect.
    (*viii*) Brownian movement is slowed down at higher temperature.
    (*ix*) Mutual precipitation of colloids takes place when two colloids of opposite charges are mixed in equivalent proportion.
    (*x*) In electroosmosis, both the dispersed phase and the dispersion medium move.

4. Complete the following sentences:
    (*i*) Freshly precipitated ferric hydroxide can be peptized by ....
    (*ii*) A colloidal suspension of graphite in water is known as ....
    (*iii*) Aqueous emulsions are obtained by dispersing oil in ....
    (*iv*) Rise in temperature favours .... of emulsions.
    (*v*) A lyophobic colloid is protected from precipitation by ....
    (*vi*) Prolonged passage of an electric current through a colloidal solution causes its ....

5. How are colloidal solutions distinguished from (*i*) true solutions and (*ii*) suspensions? How are they classified? Why are lyophilic colloids more stable than lyophobic colloids?

6. What are the various methods available for preparing the colloidal solutions? How are colloidal solutions purified?

7. Suggest methods for preparing colloidal solutions of the following in water:
    (*i*) a colloidal solution of gold,
    (*ii*) a colloidal solution of sulphur,
    (*iii*) a colloidal solution of AgCl,
    (*iv*) a colloidal solution of $Fe(OH)_3$,
    (*v*) a colloidal solution of gelatin,
    (*vi*) a colloidal solution of As_2S_3.

8. You are given a colloidal solution of gold in water containing some stabilizer. Explain what happens when:
    (*i*) it is allowed to stand for a couple of months,
    (*ii*) it is heated for some time,
    (*iii*) it is mixed with an electrolyte,
    (*iv*) a beam of light is passed through it,
    (*v*) an electric current is passed through it.

9. Explain and illustrate the terms:
    (*i*) Lyophobic and lyophilic colloids; (*ii*) Dialysis; (*iii*) Peptisation; (*iv*) Coagulation; (*v*) Tyndall effect; (*vi*) Brownian movement; (*vii*) Electrophoresis; (*viii*) Electroosmosis; (*ix*) Hardy-Schultze law; (*x*) Gold number; (*xi*) Emulsions; (*xii*) Emulsifiers; (*xiii*) Flocculation value; (*xiv*) Isoelectric point.

10. Discuss the origin of charge on colloidal particles. How would you determine the charge on a colloid? Describe briefly the electrical properties of colloids.

11. Describe the use of (*i*) dialysis, (*ii*) hot dialysis, (*iii*) electrodialysis and (*iv*) ultrafiltration in the purification of colloidal solutions.

12. What are emulsions? How are they prepared? What is the role of an emulsifier?

13. What are protective colloids? What is meant by gold number? Discuss how a lyophilic colloid protects a lyophilic colloid.

14. Describe a method for the preparation of a metal sol. Explain why it remains stable for a considerable period.

15. For a given solution the minimum amounts required for coagulation were found to be 0.5 mol per dm^3 of KCl, 0.033 mol per dm^3 of K_2SO_4 and 0.0069 mol per dm^3 of $BaCl_2$. What is the sign of charge on the colloidal particles? State the rule which these results illustrate.

16. How can aerial pollution by colloidal particles of smoke be prevented? Explain the principle of the method.

17. What do you understand by (*i*) electrophoresis and (*ii*) electroosmosis and (*iii*) electrophoretic mobility. How can electrophoresis be used in the separation of colloidal particles of different molar masses?

CHAPTER

20

Atomic Structure-I

20.1 INTRODUCTION

Dalton's atomic theory is generally regarded as the modern attempt to explain the reactivity of elements. According to this theory

(*i*) every atom is composed of indivisible particles called atom;

(*ii*) atoms of one element are all alike and have the same mass;

(*iii*) atoms are indestructible and can combine together to form compounds in definite ratio of whole number.

However, the concept of indestructibility of atom has been discarded by the discovery of various fundamental particles like electron, proton, neutron etc.

Faraday made an extensive study of the decomposition of solutions of salts, acids and bases by the passage of electric current. From these results he stated his laws of electrolysis. It was soon realised that in solution current is carried by the charged particles of matter called ions. It was observed that 1 g equivalent of any ion carries the same amount of current, *viz.*, one faraday (96485 coulombs). The number of g equivalents in 1 g ion is equal to the valency of the ion. If n is the valency of the ion under consideration then the charge carried by 1 g ion is nF. Since the number of ions in 1 g ion of any substance is the same, *i.e.*, the Avogadro number (N_A), a single ion would therefore carry a charge equal to nF/N_A. Since n is an integer, therefore the current carried by a single ion is a multiple of the fundamental quantity F/N_A which implies that electricity like matter is atomic and F/N_A is the unit of electric charge and was named as *electron* by Stoney. Faraday's experiment on electrolysis thus proved that electrons are the fundamental constituents of matter.

20.2 CONDUCTION OF ELECTRICITY THROUGH GASES

It has been known for a long time that air and other gases are poor conductors of electricity under ordinary conditions. However, when the pressure is reduced and a high potential is applied conduction occurs more readily and various luminous effects are observed. A typical apparatus to study these phenomena is shown in Fig. 20.1. It consists of a pyrex glass tube fitted with two electrodes at two ends and there is a side tube connected to a vacuum pump. When the pressure is gradually decreased, say to 1 mm of mercury, and a high potential is applied, the tube is seen to be filled up with a reddish glow in case of air. On further reducing the pressure to about 0.1 mm Hg, the glow becomes less intense around the cathode detaching itself leaving a space between it and the electrode. This dark space is known as Crookes dark space. When the pressure is still lowered to about 0.01 mm Hg, the Crookes dark space extends and fills up the entire tube. At this stage a stream of rays, named as *cathode rays*, are emitted from the cathode. These rays are independent of the gas present in the cathode tube and the material of the cathode indicating that they are common constituents of matter. These rays produce fluorescence on the opposite wall of the tube.

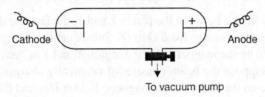

Cathode   Anode

To vacuum pump

Fig. 20.1 Electric discharge tube

Properties of the Cathode Rays: Some of the important characteristics of the cathode rays are as follows:

(*i*) Cathode rays travel in straight lines. This is confirmed by the shadow formed when an object is placed in their path.

(*ii*) Cathode rays have a penetrating power and can pass through very thin metal foils.

(*iii*) These rays possess a considerable amount of momentum and can rotate a small paddle wheel placed in their path.

(*iv*) Cathode rays are deflected from their original path by magnetic and electric fields suggesting that they are electrically charged. Perrin (1895) and J.J. Thomson (1897) were able to show that cathode rays consist of negatively charged particles.

These negatively charged particles which were emitted by the cathode with a high velocity were called electrons. The study of conduction through gases at low pressures established that electrons are the fundamental particles of all types of matter.

It was observed by Goldstein that if the cathode is perforated another kind of rays are emitted from the anode. These rays move towards the cathode, pass through it and appear on the opposite side. They are called *canal rays* or *positive rays*. Unlike cathode rays, they are not identical in all cases and in this respect differ from the cathode rays. Their charge and mass depend on the nature of the gas present in the discharge tube. For example, charge to mass ratio for positive rays obtained from hydrogen and neon are not the same. whereas the charge to mass ratio of electron is the same irrespective of the nature of the gas in the discharge tube.

20.3 DETERMINATION OF e/m OF CATHODE RAYS

Thomson devised a method for the determination of the ratio of charge to mass of the cathode rays. The method is based on the principle that the cathode rays are deflected by magnetic and electric fields. The apparatus used by Thomson is shown in Fig. 20.2. It consists of a cathode C which emits cathode rays. These rays are allowed to pass through a narrow slit of anode A. Most of the cathode rays strike the anode, but some of them pass through a hole in it with a velocity v and hit the fluorescent screen at point O.

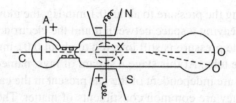

Fig. 20.2 J.J. Thomson's apparatus for the determination of *e/m*

On applying an electric field E between the plates X and Y, the rays are deflected from their original path such that the fluorescent spot moves from O to O'. Subsequently, a magnetic field H, perpendicular to the electric field is applied by the magnet NS in the region X and Y in such a way that the beam comes to its original position O. Suppose the beam consists of negatively charged particles each with charge e and mass m, then the force on the beam due to magnetic field is Hev and this is equal to the centrifugal force mv^2/r where r is the radius of curvature of the path of the cathode rays when deflected by a magnetic field H. Hence,

$$Hev = \frac{mv^2}{r}$$

$$\frac{e}{m} = \frac{v}{Hr} \qquad \qquad ...(20.1)$$

In this equation r and H are known but the value of v is unknown and is calculated as follows:

If E be the strength of the electric field, then the force due to electric field is Ee. Since the electric and magnetic fields are acting simultaneously in opposite directions and are equal, therefore,

$$Hev = Ee$$

$$v = \frac{E}{H} \qquad \qquad ...(20.2)$$

It is thus possible to determine the velocity of the particle from the ratio of the strengths of two fields. Substituting this value of v in equation (20.1) gives

$$\frac{e}{m} = \frac{E}{H^2 r} \qquad \qquad ...(20.3)$$

The value of *e/m* obtained by J.J. Thomson was 1.76×10^8 *emu/g*. The accepted value of *e/m* for an electron is 1.76×10^{11} coulombs per kg.

The value of *e/m* was found to be independent of the electrode material and the gas used in the discharge tube. The constancy of *e/m* value under different conditions suggests that the electrons are universal constituents of all matters.

20.4 DETERMINATION OF THE CHARGE ON THE ELECTRON

R.A. Millikan in 1909 had used droplets of oil in a cloud chamber to determine the charge of the electron. The essential parts of his apparatus are illustrated in Fig. 20.3. It consists of a vessel A placed in a thermostat. Inside A are two metal plates P' and P separated by a certain distance. The upper plate is connected to a known high potential (5,000 ~ 10,000 volts) and the lower plate being earthed. Oil drops could be introduced through the upper plate having a hole O with the help of an atomizer B. The vessel is provided with two windows W_1 and W_2 on the opposite walls in the same line as the parallel plates. The gas is ionized by passing a beam of X-ray through window W_2 between the two plates. A telescope is fitted at the other window W_1 for observing the movement of the drop. The space between the two plates is illuminated by a powerful source of light L.

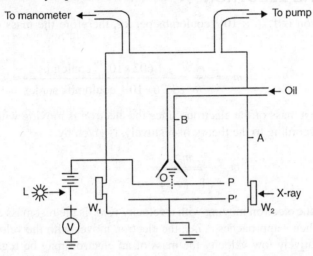

Fig. 20.3 Millikan's apparatus for determination of charge of electron

A drop of oil, usually positively charged due to friction, is introduced through hole O between the space of two parallel plates. The hole is then closed and air is ionized by exposure to X rays. The droplet after entering moves downward towards P'. As the drop reaches almost to P', the electric field is applied by charging the upper plate P so that the drop now begins to move upward towards P. When the droplet reaches near P the field is switched off and the droplet again moves towards the lower plate. Thus the droplet can be made to rise or fall many times.

It has been found that the time taken by the drop when it falls under the influence of gravity alone is constant. But when it moves under the influence of an applied field the time taken on different journeys varies considerably due to the fact that the drop captures different number of ions.

If v_1 be the velocity of the drop under gravity and v_2 be its velocity when the electric field of strength X acts in opposition to gravity, then

$$\frac{v_1}{v_2} = \frac{mg}{Xe - mg}$$

$$e = \frac{mg}{X v_1}(v_1 + v_2) \qquad \qquad ...(20.4)$$

where m is the mass of the oil drop and e the charge it carries. Knowing the time taken by the oil droplet to travel the actual distance, the values of v_1 and v_2 are determined and hence the charge e of the electron can be calculated from equation (20.4). The value of v_1, *i.e.*, the velocity under the influence of gravity of the spherical drop can be calculated from the Stokes' law which states that

$$v_1 = \frac{2gr^2 d}{9\eta} \qquad \qquad ...(20.5)$$

where r is the radius of the spherical drop, g is the acceleration due to gravity, d the density of the drop and η the viscosity of air. By this experiment, Millikan was able to determine the value of e as $(4.775 \pm 0.005) \times 10^{-10}$ esu. The most widely accepted value of e is 4.802×10^{10} esu or 1.602×10^{-19} coulombs.

20.5 MASS OF THE ELECTRON

Since e/m for an electron is 1.76×10^{11} coulombs per kg, therefore the mass of the electron can be calculated as

$$m_e = \frac{e}{e/m} = \frac{1.602 \times 10^{-19} \text{ coulombs}}{1.76 \times 10^{11} \text{ coulombs per kg}} = 9.109 \times 10^{-31} \text{ kg}$$

This is, however, the rest mass of the electron. Since the electron is moving with high speed, then the mass of the electron, according to the theory of relatively, is given by

$$m = \frac{m_0}{\sqrt{1 - (v/c)^2}} \qquad\qquad ...(20.6)$$

where m is the mass of the electron moving with a velocity v, m_0 is the rest mass of the electron and c is the velocity of light. When v approaches c, $i.e.$, the electron moves with the velocity of light, m would become infinite. At relatively low velocity the mass of an electron may be regarded as constant and almost equal to its rest mass.

It is perhaps more informative to calculate the ratio of the mass of an electron to that of an average mass of hydrogen atom (m_H). Since

$$m_H = \frac{1.008 \text{ g}}{6.023 \times 10^{23}} = 1.673 \times 10^{-24} \text{ g} = 1.673 \times 10^{-27} \text{ kg}$$

Hence the ratio is given by

$$\frac{m_e}{m_H} = \frac{9.109 \times 10^{-31} \text{ kg}}{1.673 \times 10^{-27} \text{ kg}} = \frac{1}{1837}$$

This result, that the mass of an electron is very small compared with the mass of hydrogen atom as a whole, led Thomson to formulate the first modern theory of atom.

20.6 THOMSON MODEL OF THE ATOM

The first attempt to account the fact that electrons are constituent parts of the atom was made by J.J. Thomson. He proposed a model of atom as consisting of a uniform sphere of positive charge in which electrons are embedded to confer on it electrical neutrality (Fig. 20.4). This model was satisfactory to the extent that the electrostatic forces of repulsion among the electrons could be balanced by the attractive forces between the positively charged mass and the electrons to give an electrostatically stable system. However, the model fails to explain the results of ionization and scattering experiments and is, therefore, discarded.

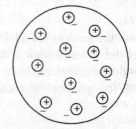

Fig. 20.4 Thomson atomic model

20.7 RUTHERFORD MODEL OF THE ATOM

In 1910, Geiger and Marsden at the instance of Rutherford studied the scattering of α-particles by passing them through the thin gold foils (Fig. 20.5). When α-particles, which are the nuclei of helium atoms (He_2^4), are passed through a thin gold foil, most of them passed through the metal foil with little or no deviations. However, a small proportion of the α-particles were scattered through large angles and even bounced back, i.e., deflected through 180°. The number of α-particles which were strongly deflected was not large, but this number increased with the metal foil of heavier atomic masses. Rutherford showed that this observation was not consistent with the model of atom as was suggested by Thomson.

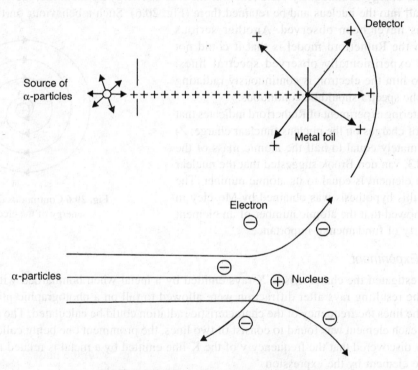

Fig. 20.5 Scattering of α-particles by gold foil

To explain these results, Rutherford suggested that large scattering occurs due to the repulsion between the positive charge on α-particles and the positive charges on the atoms of the metal foil. He further argued that scattering at very large angles is due to the collision that occurs between the α-particles and the positively charged centre where the whole mass of the atom is concentrated. This massive part of the atom was called *nucleus* of the atom.

To explain relatively small deflections or even no deflection of most of the α-particles, Rutherford suggested that the electrons which have a negligible mass would not appreciably effect the motion of the fast moving α-particles. The α-particles will, therefore, pass through the metal foil without causing significant scattering.

From these considerations Rutherford proposed that the atom is composed of (*i*) a positively charged nucleus where the whole mass of the atom is concentrated, and (*ii*) around the nucleus at a relatively large distance are extranuclear electrons equal to the number of net positive charge on the nucleus. These electrons are constantly moving around the nucleus in different orbits. To support the fact that the electrons do not fall into the nucleus as a result of electrostatic attraction, Rutherford postulated the rapid rotation of the electrons about the nucleus quite analogous to the solar system. The centrifugal force arising from this motion balances the electrostatic attraction between the nucleus and the extra-nuclear electrons. The electrons, therefore, do not fall into the nucleus.

Drawbacks of Rutherford Model of Atom

The most fundamental objection arises from the electromagnetic theory of radiation which predicts that when a charged body moves in a circular path, it should radiate energy continuously, *i.e.*, the collapse of the atom. Since the electron is a negatively charged particle revolving around the nucleus, it should radiate energy continuously. As a result of the loss of energy by radiation, the electron should eventually fall into the nucleus and be retained there (Fig. 20.6). Such a behaviour on the part of the electron has never been observed. Another serious drawback in the Rutherford model is that it could not explain the experimentally observed spectral lines. According to him the electron is continuously radiating energy and the spectra should be continuous.

The scattering experiment of Rutherford indicates that the number of charges on the nucleus (nuclear charge, Z) was approximately equal to half the atomic mass of the atom. In 1913, van den Brook suggested that the nuclear charge of an element is equal to its atomic number. The evidence to this hypothesis was obtained by Moseley in 1913 who showed that the atomic number of an element was a property of fundamental importance.

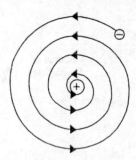

Fig. 20.6 Continuous decrease in energy of the electron

Moseley's Experiment

Moseley investigated the characteristic X-rays emitted by a metal when bombarded with high-speed electrons. The resulting rays after diffraction were allowed to fall on a photographic plate. From the position of the lines the frequency of the characteristic radiation could be calculated. The characteristic spectrum of each element was found to consist of two lines, the prominent one being called the K-line.

Moseley discovered that the frequency v of the K-line emitted by a metal is related to the nuclear charge of the element by the expression

$$\sqrt{v} = a(Z - b) \qquad ...(20.7)$$

where a is a proportionality constant and b is another constant which is same for all the lines in a given series.

A plot of $\sqrt{v}$ versus Z gives a straight line showing the validity of equation (20.7). This is shown in Fig. 20.7. However, no such relationship was obtained when the frequency was plotted against atomic mass. Moseley therefore concluded that *the atomic number* is closely related to the properties of the element. Thus atomic number represents the magnitude of the positive charge on the nucleus.

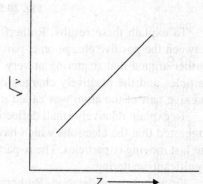

Fig. 20.7 Variation of X-ray frequency with atomic number

Later in 1920, Chadwick made the direct determination of the nuclear charge of the elements copper, silver and platinum by measuring the exact angle of scattering of α-particles. From these Chadwick confirmed that the nuclear charge is equal to the atomic number. In an atom the number of electrons present is equal to the number of positive charge present in the nucleus.

Atomic number = Number of positive charge present in nucleus
= Number of extranuclear electrons.

20.8 DIMENSION OF THE NUCLEUS

As seen above, the Rutherford scattering experiment of α-particles is due to their interaction with the nucleus. The charge on the nucleus is $+Ze$, and that of an α-particle carrying two units of positive charge is $2e$. The repulsive forces, according the Coulomb's law, is $2Ze^2/r^2$ where r is the distance of the α-particle from the nucleus. The corresponding potential energy is equal to $2Ze^2/r$. The kinetic energy of the α-particle is given as $1/2 \, mv^2$. Supposing, as a rough approximation, that the α-particle commences to reverse its direction when its kinetic energy is equal to its potential energy due to repulsion, *i.e.*,

$$\frac{1}{2}mv^2 = \frac{2\,Ze^2}{r}$$

$$r = \frac{4\,Ze^2}{mv^2}$$

where r may be taken as the effective radius of the nucleus. The mass of the α-particle is four times the mass of a hydrogen atom and is $4 \times 1.673 \times 10^{-27}$ kg, the velocity v of the α-particles is approximately 2×10^7 ms^{-1}. Taking the electronic charge as 1.602×10^{-19} C and $Z = 79$ for gold, then

$$r = \frac{(4)\times(79)\left(1.602\times10^{-19}\,\text{C}\right)^2}{\left(4\times1.673\times10^{-27}\,\text{kg}\right)\left(2\times10^7\,\text{ms}^{-1}\right)^2\left(1.1126\times10^{-10}\,\text{C}^2\text{N}^{-1}\text{m}^{-2}\right)}$$

$$= 2.721 \times 10^{-14} \text{ m}$$

Other similar calculations done involving the smallest distance of approach between an atomic nucleus and an α-particle indicate that all the nuclei have sizes of the order of 10^{-14} to 10^{-15} m. Since the radius of an atom has been found from other measurements to be about 10^{-10} m, it is thus clear that most of the space in an atom is empty.

20.9 THE NUCLEUS

The atom is electrically neutral and the electrons contribute only a very small fraction of the total mass. Hence the entire mass of the atom is concentrated in the nucleus. For example, in hydrogen atom there is one extra-nuclear electron revolving around the nucleus having a unit positive charge (a proton). The mass of the proton has been found to be very nearly equal to that of the hydrogen atom. The next element, helium, has the atomic number two (two units of positive charge) and atomic mass 4. It is therefore four times heavier than the hydrogen atom, *i.e.*, its nucleus must be four times heavy as a proton. But its nucleus contains only 2 protons accounting for two units of mass and two units of charge. The rest must be attributed due to some other particles. This led to the inevitable conclusion that the nucleus must contain some other massive uncharged particles. These particles were called neutrons by Chadwick. He confirmed their independent existence by bombarding boron or beryllium by α-particles when a highly penetrating radiation was emitted not previously encountered. The radiations consisted of particles having a mass almost equal to that of a proton but no charge.

Thus, if there are Z protons in a nucleus of atomic mass A, then $(A - Z)$ would be the number of neutrons in the nucleus. In oxygen, for example, the atomic number is 8 and atomic mass 16; it contains eight protons and eight neutrons.

The next question that arises is how in the small nucleus the protons and neutrons are held together. Normally the protons repel each other due to similar charges. In order to overcome this difficulty Yukawa in 1935 suggested the existence of new type of particles called *mesons* carrying a unit positive or negative charge but having a mass of about 200 times that of an electron. Their average life is about 10^{-6} second. In the nucleus the protons and neutrons are held together by exchange forces. These forces are effective only at extremely short distances and can overcome the long range electrostatic repulsions. Due to exchange forces there is a continuous exchange between the proton-neutron, neutron-neutron through the sharing of a meson. A proton releases a positive meson and would become neutron whereas a neutron would give a negative meson to become a proton as indicated below

$$p \rightarrow n + \pi^+ \qquad\qquad p + \pi^- \rightarrow n$$

$$n \rightarrow p + \pi^- \qquad\qquad n + \pi^+ \rightarrow p$$

There may be exchanges even through uncharged meson (π^0) between neutron-neutron or proton-proton as

$$n + \pi^0 \rightleftharpoons n$$

$$p + \pi^0 \rightleftharpoons p$$

20.10 LIGHT AS ELECTROMAGNETIC WAVE

Solids when heated emit radiations in the form of wave. It is characterised by the properties such as frequency, wavelength and wavenumber. These properties can be understood by considering a wave propagating in one dimension (Fig. 20.8).

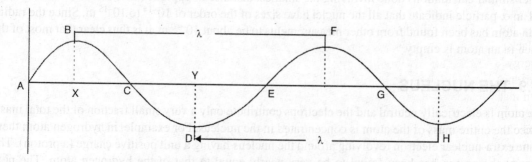

Fig. 20.8 Propagation of electromagnetic wave in one dimension

Wavelength (λ): It is the distance between two successive crests or troughs. The length BF or DH is equal to wavelength and is expressed in SI units as metre (m).

Frequency (ν): It is the number of waves per second. It is denoted by ν (nu) and its unit is Hertz (Hz).

Wavelength and frequency are related as

$$\lambda = \frac{c}{\nu}$$

where c is the velocity of light. In vacuum $c = 2.998 \times 10^8 \text{ ms}^{-1}$.

Wave number ($\overline{\nu}$). The reciprocal of wavelength is the wavenumber. It is related to frequency and wavelength as

$$\overline{\nu} = \frac{1}{\lambda} = \frac{\nu}{c}$$

The SI unit of wavenumber is m^{-1}.

Amplitude: The peak height XB or trough depth YD is called amplitude of the wave.

20.11 ORIGIN OF QUANTUM THEORY

The wave nature of light successfully explained many phenomena, *e.g.*, diffraction, interference, etc. But some of the other observable properties such as emission of electrons from metal (photoelectric effect), and Compton effect could not be explained from the wave nature. Therefore, a different theory had to be given to explain these facts.

Black Body Radiation

When radiation falls on an object, a part of it is reflected, a part is absorbed and the remaining part is transmitted. This is due to the fact that no object is a perfect absorber. In contrast to this, we may visualise a *black body* which completely absorbs all the radiations that incidents on it and retains all the radiant energy that strikes it. For experimental purposes, a black body is generally a blackened metallic surface, a hollow sphere, blackened on the inside with a hole. All the radiations that enter through the hole will be absorbed completely by successive reflections inside the enclosure. Such a material is called a black body and a good approximation to it is a pin-hole in a container.

A black body is not only a perfect absorber of radiant energy, but also an idealised radiator. In other words, when the black body is heated, it radiated the maximum amount of energy. The radiation emerging from the hole will also be very nearly equal to that of the black body. It has been shown that the energy which radiates is dependent on the temperature of the enclosure and is independent of the nature of the interior material. The black body radiation was studied by O. Lummer and E. Pringsheim (1897-99). The curves representing the distribution of radiation from a black body at different temperatures are shown in Fig. 20.9.

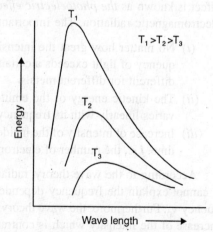

Fig. 20.9 Spectral distribution of radiation from a black body at various temperatures

The shape of the curve could not be explained on the basis of classical electromagnetic theory in which it was assumed that the body radiates energy continuously. Furthermore, in this theory, the intensity of radiation should increase continuously without limit as the frequency increases and it should be proportional to the square of the frequency of radiation. However, the experimental observations are contrary to the classical view. For each temperature there is a maximum in the curve corresponding to a particular wavelength, indicating the maximum radiation of energy. This wavelength is called λ_{max} value of that temperature. At higher temperatures, the position of the maximum in the curve shifts towards shorter wavelength and becomes more pronounced. To explain the distribution of black body radiation as a function of frequency or wavelength of radiation, Max Planck in 1900 resolved this discrepancy by postulating the revolutionary assumption that *the black body radiates energy not continuously but discontinuously in the form of energy packets called quanta,* given by

$$\varepsilon = h\nu \qquad \qquad ...(20.8)$$

and the energy (E_n) can only have integral values of a quantum, *i.e.,*

$$E_n = nh\nu \qquad \qquad [20.8\ (a)]$$

where ε is the quantum of energy radiated, ν is the frequency of radiation emitted or absorbed and h is a constant called Planck's constant having a value of 6.26×10^{-27} ergs sec or 6.26×10^{-34} J s, and n is a positive integer. On the basis of this equation, Planck obtained an expression which correctly gives the distribution of energy in black body radiation. Equation (20.8) is the fundamental relation of the quantum theory of radiation.

Planck's theory of quantized radiation of black body led Einstein to a generalisation of the quantum theory. Einstein stated that all radiations absorbed or emitted by a body must be in quanta, their magnitude depends on the frequency according to equation (20.8) or multiple thereof.

20.12 THE PHOTOELECTRIC EFFECT

The first important application of the quantum theory of radiation was the explanation of the photoelectric effect by Einstein in 1905. This interpretation put the quantum theory on a sound footing.

When a beam of light falls on a clean metal surface in vacuum, the surface emits electrons. This effect is known as *the photoelectric effect* and cannot be explained on the basis of classical theory of electromagnetic radiation. The important observations made are:

(*i*) No matter how great the intensity of light is, electrons would not be emitted unless the frequency of light exceeds a certain critical value, ν_0, known as the threshold frequency. This is different for different metals.

(*ii*) The kinetic energy of the emitted electron is independent of the incident light intensity but varies linearly with its frequency.

(*iii*) Increase of intensity of the incident radiation increases the number of electrons emitted per unit time, *i.e.*, the number of electrons emitted depends on the number of photons.

According to the wave theory, radiant energy is independent of the frequency of radiation; hence it cannot explain the frequency dependence of kinetic energy and the existence of the threshold frequency ν_0. Furthermore, the wave theory predicted that the energy of electrons should increase with the increase of the intensity which is contrary to the experimental fact.

Einstein pointed out that the photoelectric effect could be explained if light consisted of discrete particles or photons of energy $h\nu$. When a photon of frequency ν strikes the metal surface, it knocks out the electrons. In doing so, a certain amount of energy is used up in extricating the electron from the metal. This energy is called the work function of the metal surface. The remaining energy, which will be the difference between the energy $h\nu'$ imparted by the incident photon and the energy used up at the surface W, would be given as kinetic energy to the emitted electron. Hence, we have

$$hv = W + \frac{1}{2}mv^2 \qquad \qquad ...(20.9)$$

It is apparent from this equation that W accounts for the threshold frequency by the relation $W = hv_0$. Thus equation (20.9) reduces to

$$hv = hv_0 + \frac{1}{2}mv^2$$

$$\frac{1}{2}mv^2 = hv - hv_0 \qquad ...(20.10)$$

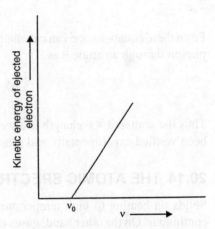

From the equation (20.10) it is clear that if the energy of the incident photon is less than the energy required by an electron to escape from the surface, no emission can take place regardless of the intensity of the incident light, *i.e.*, the number of photons that strike the surface per second.

Now, if the kinetic energy of the ejected electrons is plotted as a function of frequency, a straight line with slope equal to Planck's constant h and intercept equal to hv_0 is obtained. This is shown in Fig. 20.10.

This clearly proves the correctness of Einstein's theory of photoelectric emission and incidentally gives a proof in favour of the quantum theory.

Fig. 20.10 Variation of energy with frequency of incident light

20.13 THE COMPTON EFFECT

When light of a short wavelength strikes on an electron, it is scattered and its frequency is shifted towards lower value. This shift of frequency is independent of the frequency v of the incident radiation. This behaviour is called *the Compton effect* and is shown in Fig. 20.11. This effect can be explained on the basis of a collision between a photon of energy hv and momentum hv/c with an electron of mass m_0.

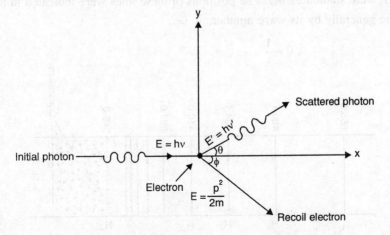

Fig. 20.11 Impact of a photon on a free electron

Following the impact, energy of the photon is reduced to $h\nu'$ and its momentum is reduced to $h\nu'/c$ at an angle θ to the x-axis. During collision the electron gains energy. If mc^2 be its total energy and mv be its total momentum directed at an angle ϕ to the x-axis, then from the conservation of energy and momentum, we have

$$h\nu - h\nu' = mc^2 - m_0 c^2 \qquad \text{...(20.11a)}$$

$$\frac{h\nu}{c} = \frac{h\nu'}{c}\cos\theta + mv\cos\phi \quad \text{(for the x-component)} \qquad \text{...(20.11b)}$$

$$0 = h\nu'\sin\theta - mv\sin\theta \quad \text{(for the y-component)} \qquad \text{...(20.11c)}$$

From these equations one can calculate the change in wavelength of the original photon and the scattered photon through an angle θ as

$$\Delta\lambda = \lambda' - \lambda = \frac{h}{m_0 c}(1 - \cos\theta) \qquad \text{...(20.12)}$$

Thus the scattered wavelength is always greater than the incident wavelength. The above equation has been verified experimentally and provides a convincing evidence to the quantum nature of radiation.

20.14 THE ATOMIC SPECTRA

Solids on heating to high temperatures emit radiations continuously and the spectra so obtained is continuous. On the other hand, gases or vapours under identical conditions yield spectra having a series of lines called *the line spectra*. The spectral lines occupy definite positions and thus correspond to definite wavelength or frequency. The line spectra are obtained with atoms and is often known as the *atomic spectra*. However, the spectra produced by gaseous molecules consists of often closely spaced lines and is generally known as the *band spectra*. Here we shall be mainly concentrating on the atomic spectra from which information concerning the extranuclear electrons can be obtained.

Of all the elements, hydrogen atom has the simplest spectra. Figure 20.12 shows the part of the hydrogen spectra in the visible region where it consists of a large number of lines out of which the four H_α, H_β, H_γ and H_δ were studied earlier. The positions of these lines were indicated in terms of wavelength (λ) or more generally by its wave number, $\bar{\nu}$ *i.e.*,

$$\bar{\nu} = \frac{1}{\lambda}$$

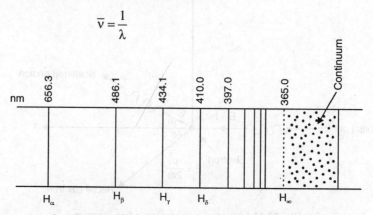

Fig. 20.12 Balmer series of lines in the spectrum of atomic hydrogen

In 1885, Balmer showed that the frequencies of some of the observed spectral lines of the hydrogen atom, now known as the *Balmer series*, could be expressed by an empirical relation

$$\bar{\nu} = \frac{1}{\lambda} = R_z \left[\frac{1}{2^2} - \frac{1}{n^2} \right] \qquad \ldots(20.13)$$

where R_z is a constant called the Rydberg constant and has a value 1.09678×10^7 m^{-1}, and n is an integer having values equal to 3, 4, 5, ... It should be noted from equation (20.13) that n cannot have values less than 2 as $\bar{\nu}$ would then become a negative number which is meaningless. Also, n cannot have a value of 2 since $\bar{\nu}$ then becomes zero. It would be seen that the spacings between the lines decreases as the frequency increases. At very high frequencies, the spectral lines converge to give a continuous spectrum or continuum. As n increases, the corresponding value of $\bar{\nu}$ becomes large. When n is large enough it causes $\bar{\nu}$ to increase very slightly. As n approaches infinity, $\bar{\nu}$ attains a limiting value equal to $1/4 \, R_z$.

In 1908, Ritz discovered *the principle of combination* and proposed a more general formula which, for hydrogen, takes the form

$$\bar{\nu} = R_z \left[\frac{1}{n_2^2} - \frac{1}{n_1^2} \right] \qquad \ldots(20.14)$$

where both n_1 and n_2 are integers such that $n_1 > n_2$. By assigning suitable values to n_1 and n_2, as shown in Table 20.1, one can evaluate the values of $\bar{\nu}$ which correspond to the values allowed for the spectral line.

Table 20.1 Spectral Series Observed in Atomic Hydrogen

Series	n_2	n_1	Spectral region
Lyman	1	2, 3, 4, ...	Ultraviolet
Balmer	2	3, 4, 5, ...	Visible
Paschen	3	4, 5, 6, ...	Near-infrared
Brackett	4	5, 6, 7, ...	Far-infrared
Pfund	5	6, 7, 8, ...	Far-infrared

It is important to note that every line in the spectrum can be represented as a difference of two terms, R_z/n_1^2 and R_z/n_2^2. The spectra of other atoms are more complicated, but it is possible to represent the lines in the spectra as difference between the two terms.

20.15 BOHR'S THEORY OF THE HYDROGEN ATOM

To overcome the difficulties in the Rutherford model of the atom, Neils Bohr in 1913 successfully developed a model for hydrogen atom on the basis of quantum theory. Bohr, like Rutherford, considered the atom as consisting of a positively charged nucleus with electron revolving around it. However, where Rutherford placed no restrictions on the movement of the electron, Bohr placed certain restrictions on the motion of the electron to explain and interpret the spectrum of hydrogen and hydrogen-like atoms. His postulates are:

(*i*) Electrons can move around the nucleus only in certain definite orbits. These orbits do not radiate energy and are called *stationary orbits*. The number of such permissible orbits is determined by the quantum condition that the angular momentum of the orbital electron is an integral multiple of $h/2\pi$. Mathematically, one can write

$$mvr = \frac{nh}{2\pi} \tag{20.15}$$

where m is the mass of the electron moving around the nucleus with velocity v in a circular path of radius r and n is an integer.

(*ii*) During the emission or absorption of radiant energy the Planck's equation $E = h\nu$ is obeyed. That is, when an electron jumps from an orbit of energy E_2 to another orbit of energy E_1, then the difference of this energy is emitted or absorbed in the form of radiation of a definite frequency ν in accordance with the equation

$$\Delta E = E_2 - E_1 = h\nu \tag{20.16}$$

On the basis of these postulates Bohr calculated the radii and energies of the stationary orbits in hydrogen or hydrogen-like atoms.

Consider an electron of mass m revolving around the nucleus of charge $+Ze$ (where Z is the atomic number or the effective charge of the nucleus; for hydrogen, $Z = 1$) with a velocity v in an orbit of radius r as shown in Fig. 20.13. The electrostatic attraction between the nucleus and the electron is

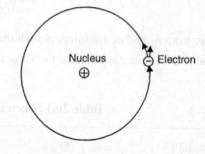

Fig. 20.13 Electron revolving in a circular orbit about a fixed nucleus of charge $+Ze$

given by the Coulomb's law as $\dfrac{-Ze^2}{4\pi\varepsilon_0 r^2}$. Here ε_0 is

the permittivity of a vacuum and is equal to $8.854 \times 10^{-12}\ C^2\ N^{-1}\ m^{-2}$. This force is opposed by the outward centrifugal force of the electron, mv^2/r. As long as the electron moves in a stationary orbit it is necessary that these two forces must be equal and opposite, *i.e.*,

$$\frac{Ze^2}{4\pi\varepsilon_0 r^2} = \frac{mv^2}{r} \tag{20.17a}$$

$$r = \frac{Ze^2}{4\pi\varepsilon_0 mv^2} \tag{20.17b}$$

According to the first postulate of Bohr,

$$mvr = \frac{nh}{2\pi}$$

$$v = \frac{nh}{2\pi mr}$$

Substituting the value of v in equation (20.17b), we get,

$$r = \frac{\varepsilon_0 n^2 h^2}{\pi m e^2 Z} \qquad \qquad \qquad ...(20.18)$$

For hydrogen, the charge on the nucleus $Z = 1$ and if $n = 1$, then $r = a_0$, the radius of the first Bohr orbit

$$a_0 = \frac{\varepsilon_0 h^2}{\pi m e^2}$$

Substituting the values of the constants, we obtain

$$a_0 = \frac{\left(6.626 \times 10^{-34}\, Js\right)^2 \left(8.854 \times 10^{-12}\, C^2 N^{-1} m^{-2}\right)}{(3.1416)\left(9.109 \times 10^{-31}\, kg\right)\left(1.602 \times 10^{-19}\, C\right)^2}$$

$$= 5.292 \times 10^{-11}\ m$$

$$= 0.0529\ nm$$

If $n = 2$, the radius of second Bohr orbit is $n^2 \times 0.0529$ nm

$$= 2^2 \times 0.0529\ nm$$

$$= 0.2116\ nm$$

So, we can infer that the radius of a particular orbit in hydrogen atom is proportional to the square of 'n'

Now the total energy E of the electron in its orbit in a hydrogen atom ($Z = 1$) is given by the sum of its kinetic and potential energies. Hence

$$\text{Total energy, } E = \text{K.E.} + \text{P.E.}$$

The kinetic energy of an electron in an orbit moving with a velocity v is given by $1/2\ mv^2$. The potential energy of the electron is defined as the work necessary to take the electron to infinity from its equilibrium distance r with respect to the nucleus. Since the coulombic force between the electron and the nucleus is $\dfrac{-Ze^2}{4\pi\varepsilon_0 r^2}$, therefore, the potential energy is calculated as follows:

$$\text{P.E.} = \int_r^\infty \frac{-Ze^2}{4\pi\varepsilon_0 r^2}\, dr$$

$$= \frac{-Ze^2}{4\pi\varepsilon_0} \int_r^\infty \frac{dr}{r^2}$$

$$= \frac{-Ze^2}{4\pi\varepsilon_0} \left| -\frac{1}{r} \right|_r^\infty$$

$$= -\frac{Ze^2}{4\pi\varepsilon_0 r}$$

The negative sign indicates that work must be done on the electron to remove it to infinity.

Therefore, the total energy E is given as

$$E = \frac{1}{2}mv^2 - \frac{Ze^2}{4\pi\varepsilon_0 r} \qquad \qquad ...(20.19)$$

Since $\dfrac{1}{2}mv^2 = \dfrac{Ze^2}{8\pi\varepsilon_0 r}$ from equation 20.17 (a), hence equation (20.19) becomes

$$E = \frac{Ze^2}{8\pi\varepsilon_0 r} - \frac{Ze^2}{4\pi\varepsilon_0 r}$$

$$= -\frac{Ze^2}{8\pi\varepsilon_0 r} \qquad \qquad ...(20.20)$$

On substituting the value of r from equation (20.18) in equation (20.20) yields

$$E_n = -\frac{Z^2 e^4 m}{8\varepsilon_0^2 n^2 h^2} \qquad \qquad ...(20.21)$$

Equation (20.21) thus gives the total energy of a single electron moving around the nucleus. The equation involves constants and an integer having values 1, 2, 3, ...

Now according to Bohr's second postulate, that when the electron jumps from n_2th orbit of energy E_{n_2} to the n_1th orbit of energy E_{n_1} such that $n_2 > n_1$, then the difference in energy, ΔE, should be emitted as a quantum of energy $h\nu$, i.e.,

$$\Delta E = E_{n_2} - E_{n_1} = \left[-\frac{Z^2 e^4 m}{8\varepsilon_0^2 n_2^2 h^2} \right] - \left[-\frac{Z^2 e^4 m}{8\varepsilon_0^2 n_1^2 h^2} \right]$$

$$\Delta E = h\nu = \frac{Z^2 e^4 m}{8\varepsilon_0^2 h^2} \left[\frac{1}{n_1^2} - \frac{1}{n_2^2} \right]$$

or

$$\nu = \frac{Z^2 e^4 m}{8\varepsilon_0^2 h^3} \left[\frac{1}{n_1^2} - \frac{1}{n_2^2} \right] \qquad \qquad ...(20.22)$$

The wave number $\bar{\nu}$ is given as

$$\bar{\nu} = \frac{\nu}{c} = \frac{Z^2 e^4 m}{8\varepsilon_0^2 c h^3} \left[\frac{1}{n_1^2} - \frac{1}{n_2^2} \right] \qquad \qquad ...(20.23)$$

$$\bar{\nu} = R_z \left[\frac{1}{n_1^2} - \frac{1}{n_2^2} \right] \qquad \qquad ...(20.24)$$

where
$$R_z = \frac{Z^2 e^4 m}{8\varepsilon_0^2 ch^3}$$
...(20.25)

and is generally known as the *Rydberg's constant* and its value, 1.09768×10^7 m^{-1}, can be obtained by substituting the values of the constants. The calculated value agrees nicely with the experimental value and may thus be regarded as a triumph for Bohr theory. This principal result of Bohr predicts the quantum numbers n_1 and n_2. The Bohr theory provides an explanation of the atomic spectra of hydrogen. The different series of spectral lines can be obtained by varying the values of n_2 and n_1 in equation (20.24).

20.16 REFINEMENTS TO BOHR THEORY

In the above derivation it has been tacitly assumed that the nucleus is fixed at the centre of the orbit. In fact, the nucleus (mass M) and the electron (mass m) are rotating about their common centres of mass. It is, therefore, necessary to replace the mass m by the reduced mass μ given by

$$\frac{1}{\mu} = \frac{1}{m} + \frac{1}{M}$$

or
$$\mu = \frac{mM}{m+M} = \frac{m}{1+\dfrac{m}{M}}$$

and equation (20.23) becomes

$$\bar{v} = \frac{Z^2 e^4 \mu}{8\varepsilon_0^2 ch^3}\left[\frac{1}{n_1^2} - \frac{1}{n_2^2}\right]$$

$$= \frac{Z^2 e^4}{8\varepsilon_0^2 ch^3}\frac{m}{1+\dfrac{m}{M}}\left[\frac{1}{n_1^2} - \frac{1}{n_2^2}\right]$$
...(20.26)

Equation (20.21) can also be written as

$$E_n = -\frac{Z^2 e^4}{8\varepsilon_0^2 n^2 h^2}\frac{m}{1+\dfrac{m}{M}}$$
...(20.27)

Equation (20.27) now correctly describes the energy of a moving electron. The more accurate value of the Rydberg constant R_z will, therefore, be

$$\bar{R}_z = \frac{Z^2 e^4}{8\varepsilon_0^2 ch^3}\frac{m}{1+\dfrac{m}{M}}$$
...(20.28)

Evidently, value of Rydberg constant will slightly vary from atom to atom depending upon the nuclear mass. Equation (20.28) has been derived for an atomic system in which one electron is revolving around the nucleus. It, therefore, represents not only the spectra of hydrogen atom but also hydrogen-like systems such as He^+, Li^{2+}, Be^{3+}, etc.

Bohr model of an atom provides explanation for the absorption and emission of spectral lines in atomic hydrogen in terms of energy levels. In the lowest energy state, $n_1 = 1$, the electron occupies the lowest stable state called the ground state of the atom. On absorption of energy, the electron is raised to some higher energy levels. The excited atom emits energy in the form of radiation when the electron returns to the lower energy levels producing a series of spectral lines. These lines result from the transition of electron from one energy state to another as shown in Fig. 20.14.

The lines in the Lyman series result when the electron jumps from $n_2 = 2$, 3, ... to $n_1 = 1$. In the Balmer series the transition occurs from $n_2 = 3$, 4, ... to $n_1 = 2$. Likewise, Paschen, Brackett and Pfund series result when the electron jumps from higher energy level to $n_1 = 3$, 4 and 5 respectively.

In Fig. 20.14, the separation of energy levels goes on decreasing with the increasing value of n. For sufficiently high value of n, the lines converge to a limit when the electron is completely free from the influence of the nucleus. The observed spectrum would then show a continuum, *i.e.*, a region of continuous absorption or emission of radiation without any line structure. This is due to the fact that the electron no longer obeys the quantised condition and may absorb continuously the ordinary kinetic energy of translation, corresponding to its speed in the free space, $1/2\ mv^2$.

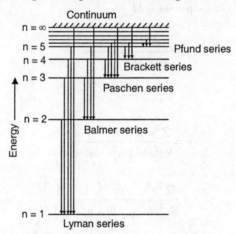

Fig. 20.14 Energy levels of hydrogen atom

20.17 IONIZATION POTENTIAL

The amount of energy required to remove an electron from a gaseous atom in its ground state to an infinite distance resulting in the formation of positive ion is called the ionization potential. It is measured in electron volts or joules. For hydrogen atom the process is

$$H(g) \rightarrow H^+(g) + e^-$$

The ionization potential can be calculated as

$$I.P. = E_f - E_1 = \frac{Z^2 e^4 m}{8\varepsilon_0^2 h^2} \frac{1}{1 + \dfrac{m}{M}} \left[\frac{1}{n_\infty^2} - \frac{1}{1^2} \right]$$

$$= -\frac{Z^2 e^4 m}{8\varepsilon_0^2 h^2}\frac{1}{1+\dfrac{m}{M}}$$

$$= -R_z ch \qquad\qquad \left(\because 1 >> \frac{m}{M}\right)$$

$$= -\left(1.09678\times10^7\,\mathrm{m}^{-1}\right)\left(3\times10^8\,\mathrm{ms}^{-1}\right)\left(6.626\times10^{-34}\,\mathrm{J\,s}\right)$$

$$= -21.81\times10^{-19}\,\mathrm{J}$$

$$= -13.62\,\mathrm{eV}$$

Thus, the ionization potential of hydrogen atom is 13.62 eV. If, however, the electron absorbs energy more than this value, then the difference would increase the kinetic energy of the freed electron. In both the cases the positively charged ion results and the atom is said to be ionized. On the other hand, if the energy absorbed is less than this value (13.62 eV), the electron will be excited to one of the permitted higher energy levels. In this case, the atom is not ionized, it is excited and the excited electron then comes to the normal state by emitting energy either in one step or in a number of steps.

If an atom contains more than one electrons, there will be first, second, third, etc. ionization potentials corresponding to the removal of first, second, third, etc. electrons from the ground state of the atom. These successive ionization potentials will increase as the electron has to be removed from a positively charged species.

20.18 LIMITATIONS OF BOHR THEORY

Bohr theory as outlined above, though explains well the positions of the lines in the hydrogen spectra, but does not account for their fine structures, i.e., the appearance of a set of closely spaced lines as observed with spectroscopes of high resolving power. The obvious explanation is that the electronic energy levels associated with any Bohr quantum number (n) actually consists of a series of sublevels each with its own quantum number. The energy values of these sublevels are quite close to each other.

Another serious objection to the Bohr model is that it enables us to locate both the position and momentum of the orbital electron simultaneously. This is, however, contrary to *the uncertainty principle* (see later). Bohr's theory also fails to explain the intensity of the spectral lines. Keeping these drawbacks in view, Sommerfeld in 1915 extended the Bohr theory.

20.19 SOMMERFELD THEORY

According to Sommerfeld (i) the electron revolves around the nucleus in an elliptical orbit with the nucleus situated at one of the two foci. Circle is a special case of an ellipse in which the major and minor axes are equal. Since the motion of the particle in an ellipse has two degrees of freedom, hence two quantum numbers are necessary to represent the motion of the electron.

(ii) Only those elliptical orbits are permitted which satisfy the following conditions:

$$p_\phi = k\frac{h}{2\pi} \qquad\qquad ...(20.29a)$$

and
$$p_r = n_r \frac{h}{2\pi}$$
...(20.29b)

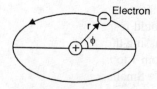

Fig. 20.15 Elliptical orbit of the electron

where p_ϕ and p_r are the angular and the radial momenta of the electron with coordinates ϕ and r, h is the Planck's constant, k and n_r are two positive integers called the azimuthal and radial quantum numbers respectively (Fig. 20.15).

The combination of two momenta in equation (20.27) yields

$$E_n = -\frac{Z^2 e^4}{8\varepsilon_0^2 h^2 (n_r + k)^2} \frac{m}{1 + \frac{m}{M}}$$
...(20.30)

Since n_r and k are integers, it follows that their sum may be put equal to n, also an integer. Therefore, equation (20.30) may be written as

$$E_n = -\frac{Z^2 e^4}{8\varepsilon_0^2 h^2 n^2} \frac{m}{1 + \frac{m}{M}}$$
...(20.31)

Equation (20.31) is identical with equation (20.27) derived for circular orbits. The number n is now called the principal quantum number, and there are several possible values of k for each value of n. It can be shown that the ratio of n to k is the same as the ratio of the major to minor axis of an elliptical orbit.

$$\frac{n}{k} = \frac{\text{length of major axis}}{\text{length of minor axis}}$$

The principal quantum number n thus determines the major axis of the elliptical orbit and k the azimuthal quantum number determines the minor axis or the eccentricity of the elliptical orbit. For the orbit closest to the nucleus $n = 1$ and the orbit is circular. For the next orbit $n = 2$, both circular and elliptical

Table 20.2 Eccentricity of Elliptical Orbit for Different Values of n and k

n	k	Major axis	Minor axis
1	1	a	a
2	1	4a	2a
	2	4a	4a
3	3	9a	9a
	2	9a	6a
	1	9a	3a
4	4	16a	16a
	3	16a	12a
	2	16a	8a
	1	16a	4a

orbits are possible. When $n = 3$ ($k = 3$), the orbit is circular and a series of orbits of different eccentricities would result for $k = (n - 1)$, $(n - 2) \ldots l$. When k is zero, the elliptical orbit reduces to a straight line passing through the nucleus of the atom. It may be stated that there are n possible values for k ranging from 1 to n. This is shown in Table 20.2 where a is the diameter of the first Bohr orbit.

Smaller the value of k for any value of n, greater would be the eccentricity of the elliptical orbit and more deeply does it penetrate into the core of the atom. The Bohr-Sommerfeld orbit for different values of n and k are shown in Fig. 20.16.

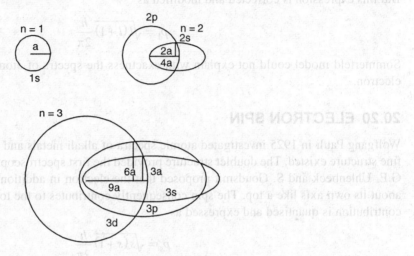

Fig. 20.16 Permitted electronic orbits of hydrogen atom

Let the electron jump from $n = 3$ to $n = 2$ to produce a spectral line in the Balmer series (Fig. 20.17). According to Bohr's model a spectral line would result only one way, but in terms of Sommerfeld model a line results in more than one ways.

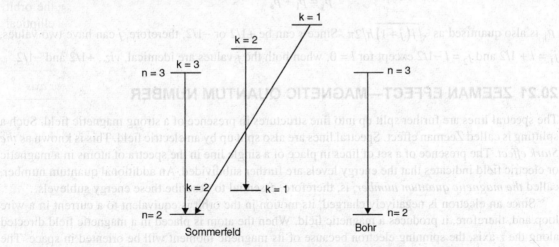

Fig. 20.17 Comparison of Sommerfeld and Bohr schemes

Sommerfeld theory though gives the correct total values of n of possible azimuthal quantum num-. bers but the actual values are incorrect. Sommerfeld suggested the value of azimuthal quantum number from n to l, but the quantum theory suggested the values of azimuthal quantum from 0 to $(n-1)$. Thus for $n = 4$, the azimuthal quantum number may have the values 3, 2, 1 and 0. The new azimuthal quantum number is denoted by l and is related to k by $l = k - l$. Sommerfeld originally expressed the orbital angular momentum as

$$p = k\frac{h}{2\pi}$$

But this expression is corrected and modified as

$$p_1 = \sqrt{l(l+1)}\frac{h}{2\pi}$$

Sommerfeld model could not explain with exactness the spectra of atoms containing more than one electron.

20.20 ELECTRON SPIN

Wolfgang Pauli in 1925 investigated atomic spectra of alkali metals and showed that a doublet in the fine structure existed. The doublet structure provided the first spectroscopic evidence for electron spin. G.E. Uhlenbeck and S. Goudsmit proposed that the electron in addition to its orbital motion rotates about its own axis like a top. The spin consequently contributes to the total angular momentum. This contribution is quantised and expressed as

$$p_s = \sqrt{s(s+1)}\frac{h}{2\pi}$$

where s is *the spin quantum number* having only two possible values, *viz.*, +1/2 or −1/2. The total angular momentum is given as the vector sum of the orbital angular momentum p_1 and the spin angular momentum p_s, *i.e.*,

$$\vec{p}_j = \vec{p}_1 + \vec{p}_s$$

$\vec{p}_j$ is also quantised as $\sqrt{j(j+1)}\,h/2\pi$. Since s can be +1/2 or −1/2, therefore, j can have two values, $j_1 = l + 1/2$ and $j_2 = l - 1/2$ except for $l = 0$, when both the j values are identical, *viz.*, +1/2 and −1/2.

20.21 ZEEMAN EFFECT—MAGNETIC QUANTUM NUMBER

The spectral lines are further split up into fine structures in presence of a strong magnetic field. Such a splitting is called Zeeman effect. Spectral lines are also split up by an electric field. This is known as *the Stark effect*. The presence of a set of lines in place of a single line in the spectra of atoms in a magnetic or electric field indicates that the energy levels are further subdivided. An additional quantum number, called *the magnetic quantum number*, is, therefore, essential to describe these energy sublevels.

Since an electron is negatively charged, its motion in the orbit is equivalent to a current in a wire loop and, therefore, it produces a magnetic field. When the atom is placed in a magnetic field directed along the z-axis, the spinning electron because of its magnetic moment will be oriented in space. The space orientation is quantised and is due to the interaction between the applied magnetic field and the magnetic field of the rotating and spinning electron. If the angular momentum of the electron is represented by a vector with a length proportional to the magnitude of the angular momentum and orientation perpendicular to the plane of rotation (Fig. 20.18), then the z-component of the vector will have a

magnitude proportional to $m_1 \dfrac{h}{2\pi}$. It means that orientation of the plane of rotation takes only certain

discrete values. Here m_1 is called the magnetic quantum number and can take values from $-l$ to $+l$ including zero. Thus, in general, there are $(2l + 1)$ possible values of m.

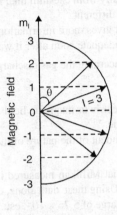

Fig. 20.18 Possible orientations for angular momentum vector

20.22 THE FOUR QUANTUM NUMBERS

The state of an electron in an atom can be adequately described by the four quantum numbers discussed above. These are summarised below:

(i) *Principal Quantum Number* (*n*): It represents the principal energy level to which the electron belongs. It can have only integer values

$$n = 1, 2, 3, \ldots$$

(ii) *Azimuthal Quantum Number* (*l*): This determines the energy associated with the angular momentum of the electron and will never exceed the total energy as determined by the principal quantum number, *n*. It gives the possible sublevels within the major energy level. The azimuthal quantum number accounts for the appearance of a group of closely spaced spectral lines in the spectra of hydrogen and hydrogen-like atoms. For each value of *n* there may be *n* integral values of *l* ranging from 0 to *n* − 1. Each value may therefore be looked upon as the sublevels of the major level. The different sublevels are designated as *s, p, d, f,* ... etc. for *l* corresponding to 0, 1, 2, 3, etc. respectively.

(iii) *Magnetic Quantum Number* (*m*): It determines the different quantised space orientations of the angular momentum of the electron. It accounts for the further splitting of each sublevel into finer levels differing slightly from each other in energy. For each value of *l*, there are $2l + 1$ values of *m* ranging from −*l* to + *l* including zero, *i.e.*,

$$m = 0, \pm 1, \pm 2, \ldots \pm l$$

(iv) *Spin Quantum Number* (*s*): It accounts for the spin of the electron about its own axis. For each set of values of *n, l* and *m* there are only two possible values of *s, viz., s* = 1/2 and *s* = −1/2.

EXERCISES

1. Explain, giving reasons, the following:
   (*i*) For the cathode rays, e/m is independent of the nature of the gas and the material of the electrode in the discharge tube.
   (*ii*) The energy emitted by a black body is not continuous but discontinuous.
   (*iii*) Light can eject electrons more easily from caesium than from sodium.
   (*iv*) Spectrum of each type of atom is different.
   (*v*) The atomic number of an element gives more information regarding its atomic structure.
   (*vi*) Bohr's theory was found to be inadequate soon after it was widely acclaimed.

2. Which of the following statements concerning the gas discharge tube are correct?
   (*i*) Canal rays are positive ions.
   (*ii*) Canal rays are electrons.
   (*iii*) Canal rays are not deflected by electric or magnetic fields.
   (*iv*) Canal rays travel towards the anode.
   (*v*) Nature of the canal rays is independent of the nature of the gas in the discharge tube.
   Ans. Statement (*i*) is correct.

3. Some values of the charges (in esu) that Millikan measured in his oil drop experiment are: 4.32×10^{-9}, 3.84×10^{-9}, 2.88×10^{-9}, 9.60×10^{-10}. Using these data alone, calculate how many electrons are attached to an oil drop for which he measured a charge of 5.76×10^{-9} esu.
   Ans. 12

4. Describe how the discoveries of cathode rays, positive rays and X-rays have contributed to the knowledge of the structure of atom.

5. Describe Millikan's method for the determination of charge on an electron.

6. Describe the Rutherford experiment that led him to discover that atoms contain a very small and massive nucleus. What were the drawbacks in the Rutherford atomic model? How were they overcome by Bohr's atomic model?

7. (*a*) Show that the ratio of the mass of the electron to that of the hydrogen atom is 1/1837.
   (*b*) Calculate e/m for the He$^+$ ion and compare it with that for the electron.
   Ans. 4.87×10^7 coulomb kg^{-1}.

8. What is meant by atomic number of an element? On what experimental basis have atomic numbers been assigned to elements?

9. An atom is known to absorb and emit energy equal to 6.0×10^{-18} J. At what wavelength and wave number would you find an emission or absorption line in its spectrum? **Ans.** 33 nm, 3.0×10^7 m^{-1}.

10. What is photoelectric effect? How did it help in putting quantum theory on a strong footing? Light of wavelength 400 nm strikes a certain metal which has a photoelectric work function of 3.13 eV. Calculate
    (*i*) the energy of the photon,
    (*ii*) the kinetic energy of the most energetic electron in eV,
    (*iii*) velocity of the ejected electrons, and
    (*iv*) the stopping potential.
    Ans. (*i*) 3.1 eV, (*ii*) 0.97 eV, (*iii*) 5.85×10^3 ms^{-1}, (*iv*) 0.97 V.

11. When light of 450 nm wavelength impinges on a clean surface of metallic sodium electrons with maximum energy of 0.4 eV are ejected. What is the maximum wavelength of light which will eject electrons from metallic sodium? What is the binding energy of an electron to a sodium crystal?
    Ans. 1880 nm, 0.66 eV.

12. (*a*) What is Compton effect? What is its significance?
    (*b*) A monochromatic X-ray beam of wavelength 0.0558 nm is scattered through an angle of 46°. What is the wavelength of the scattered beam? **Ans.** 0.0565 nm.

13. What is meant by quantization of energy and quantization of angular momentum? How these concepts have been helpful in explaining the existence of different lines in hydrogen spectrum?

14. What is the impact of Bohr's theory of hydrogen atom in understanding the structure of matter? What modifications were suggested by Sommerfeld?

15. Explain the statement that hydrogen is the simplest atom and should have the simplest spectrum of all the neutral atoms. Calculate the energy of the hydrogen atom when the principal quantum number is (i) 1, and (ii) 3. What does the negative sign signify?

Ans. (i) -21.79×10^{-19} J atom.
(ii) -2.421×10^{-19} J atom.

16. Calculate the velocity of an electron which has been accelerated by a potential difference of 1.0 V. The rest mass of the electron is 9.105×10^{-31} kg. **Ans.** 5.65×10^5 ms^{-1}.

17. If the energy of the electron of the He$^+$ ion could assume any value, what type of emission spectrum would you predict for the He$^+$ ion? How much work is required to remove the electron in the hydrogen atom from the energy level, $n = 3$ to infinity? **Ans.** 145.021 kJ mol^{-1}.

18. When applying the Ritz combination principle

$$\bar{v} = Z^2 R_z \left[\frac{1}{n_1^2} - \frac{1}{n_2^2} \right]$$

in each of the following cases what values would you substitute for n_1 and n_2?

(i) The calculation of $\bar{v}$ for the absorption line produced by the complete ionisation of a hydrogen atom from the ground state.

(ii) The calculation of $\bar{v}$ for the absorption line in the Paschen series produced by the transfer of an electron in a hydrogen atom from the lowest possible level for this series ($n_1 = 3$) to the third from the lowest possible level in the same series. **Ans.** (i) $n_1 = 1, n_2 = \infty$, (ii) $n_1 = 3, n_2 = 5$.

19. Calculate the wavelength of the first spectral line in the Balmer series of He$^+$ ion. The value of Rydberg constant for He$^+$ ion is 1.09722×10^7 m^{-1}. **Ans.** 164.1 nm.

20. If the electron of the hydrogen atom has been excited to a level corresponding to 10.2 eV, what is the wavelength of the line emitted when the atom returns to its ground state? **Ans.** 121.8 nm.

21. The line of the highest wavelength of a particular series in the atomic spectrum of hydrogen is at 656.3 nm. What is the series? Given that

$$R_z = 1.09678 \times 10^7 \text{ m}^{-1}.$$

22. Calculate the energy required to shift the electron of the hydrogen atom from the first Bohr orbit to the fifth Bohr orbit. What is the wave length (λ) of the line emitted when the electron returns to the ground state? Given that

$$R_z = 1.09678 \times 10^7 \text{ m}^{-1}.$$

Ans. 20.9 kJ, $\lambda = 95$ nm.

23. The wavelength of a certain line in the Balmer series is observed at 487.6 nm. To what value of n_2 does it correspond? **Ans.** 4.

24. Calculate the wavelengths of the spectral lines emitted by the lowest energy transitions for the Lyman, Balmer and Paschen series in the hydrogen atom. Calculate the energy of each transition in (i) ergs (ii) eV.

Ans. Lyman, $\lambda = 122.0$ nm, $E = 1.64 \times 10^{-11}$ erg = 10.2 eV
Balmer, $\lambda = 658.0$ nm, $E = 3.03 \times 10^{-12}$ erg = 1.89 eV
Paschen, $\lambda = 1880$ nm, $E = 1.06 \times 10^{-13}$ erg = 0.66 eV.

25. A particle strikes a normal hydrogen atom exciting the electron to its 6th energy level ($n = 6$); this electron then drops to its second energy level ($n = 2$). What is the energy of the photon?

Ans. 4.84×10^{19} J per atom.

26. If an electron falls through an electric potential difference of 1.0 V, it acquires an energy of one electron volt. If the electron is to have a wavelength of 0.1 nm, what potential difference must it pass through?

Ans. 150 V.

27. The ionization potential of hydrogen atom is 13.6 eV. Calculate the ionization potential of He$^+$, that is, the energy for the process

$$He^+ \longrightarrow He^{2+} + e^-$$

Ans. 54.4 eV.

28. Calculate the radii of the 5th and 6th Bohr orbits.

Ans. 1.325 nm, 1.91 nm.

29. In what region the spectral line resulting from the electronic transition from fifth to the tenth electronic level in the hydrogen atom would fall?

Ans. I.R.

30. Derive an expression for the kinetic energy and the total energy of an electron in a Bohr's orbit. The ionization potential of hydrogen is 13.6 eV. To which quantum level does the electron jump from the lowest level if it is given an energy corresponding to 99% of the ionization potential?

Ans. $n_2 = 10$.

31. What would be the temperature through which atomic hydrogen at 298 K would have to be raised to excite the electron from $n = 1$ to $n = 2$ assuming that the translational energy of hydrogen atom is converted into electronic energy? Comment on the value.

32. What was the necessity of introducing second, third and fourth quantum numbers? State the name, symbol, meaning and permissible values of each of the four quantum numbers for the electron with the highest energy in sodium atom.

33. Describe briefly the following:
   (*i*) Canal rays;
   (*ii*) Photoelectric effect;
   (*iii*) Compton effect;
   (*iv*) Black body radiation;
   (*v*) Stationary states;
   (*vi*) Ritz combination principle;
   (*vii*) Quantum numbers;
   (*viii*) Ionization potential; and
   (*ix*) Rutherford nuclear model of atom.

CHAPTER

CHAPTER
21

Atomic Structure-II

21.1 PARTICLES AND WAVES

Bohr theory though successfully explained the spectra of hydrogen and hydrogen-like atoms, but could not explain the spectra of helium and other more complex atoms. It was in early 1920's that the conflict between the wave and particle nature of light arose. The conflict was due to the fact that certain phenomena like reflection, diffraction and scattering of electromagnetic radiation could be explained on the basis of wave nature of light, whereas the black body radiation, the photoelectric effect etc. could be explained by assuming the corpuscular nature of light. It, therefore, seemed necessary to set up a new mechanics which would resolve the wave–particle conflict and would account for many experimental facts regarding the behaviour of systems of atomic size. In 1926, a new approach called *wave* or *quantum mechanics* was developed independently by Heisenberg and Schrödinger. Heisenberg's approach is referred to as *matrix mechanics* and Schrödinger's approach is referred to as *wave mechanics*. Although the two methods appear to be different but can be shown to be mathematically equivalent.

The first step in the development was taken by L. de Broglie in 1924. According to de Broglie, *every material particle is associated with a wave*. He proposed a relation between the momentum and wavelength of a particle in motion. According to the quantum theory of radiation, the energy of a photon is equal to $h\nu$

$$E = h\nu$$

where ν is the frequency of the radiation and h the Planck's constant.

Since $\nu = \dfrac{c}{\lambda}$, where λ is the wavelength of radiation and c the velocity of light, then

$$E = h\nu = \frac{hc}{\lambda} \qquad \qquad ...(21.1)$$

Now from the theory of relativity,

$$E = mc^2$$

where m is the mass of the photon. Combining this with Eq. (21.1), we get

$$mc^2 = \frac{ch}{\lambda}$$

$$mc = \frac{h}{\lambda}$$

or, momentum
$$p = \frac{h}{\lambda}$$

$$\lambda = \frac{h}{p} \qquad ...(21.2)$$

This is the fundamental equation of de Broglie's theory and gives the wavelength λ of the matter wave associated with material particles. The above relation is applicable to any particle having a mass m and moving with a velocity v and can be written as

$$\lambda = \frac{h}{mv} \qquad ...(21.3)$$

The wavelength λ associated with any material particle is inversely proportional to both, the mass and the velocity. The validity of this hypothesis was verified experimentally by Davidson and Germer (1927) and by G.P. Thomson (1928). They observed that electrons are diffracted by nickel crystals in a manner similar to the diffraction of X-rays supporting de Broglie's postulate of matter wave.

From Eq. (21.3) it is obvious that h/mv is negligible for relatively large objects, while with sub-atomic particles this quantity is no longer so small as to be negligible. Thus, the particle aspect of the matter is predominant in describing the properties of relatively large objects whereas the wave character is more important in enunciating the characteristic of subatomic particles. In order to visualise the wavelength associated with a relatively large object, consider a base ball having a mass of 0.3 kg moving with a velocity of 2×10^1 ms^{-1}. From de Broglie's equation the wavelength of the associated wave is

$$\lambda = \frac{\left(6.626 \times 10^{-34}\, \text{kg m}^2\, \text{s}^{-1}\right)}{(0.3\, \text{kg})\left(2 \times 10^1\, \text{m s}^{-1}\right)} = 1.104 \times 10^{-34}\, \text{m}$$

This shows that the wavelength is too small to be observed. On the other hand, the wavelength associated with an electron with a rest mass of 9.109×10^{-31} kg moving with the same velocity is

$$\lambda = \frac{\left(6.626 \times 10^{-34}\, \text{kg m}^2\, \text{s}^{-1}\right)}{\left(9.109 \times 10^{-31}\, \text{kg}\right)\left(2 \times 10^1\, \text{m s}^{-1}\right)} = 3.6 \times 10^{-5}\, \text{m}$$

This is a fairly large value and can be measured.

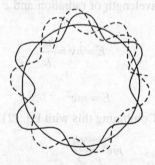

Fig. 21.1 A stationary de Broglie electron wave around the nucleus. The solid line represents a stationary wave and the dotted line shows a wave of somewhat different wavelength which is destroyed by interference.

Let us use the idea of de Broglie to see how the wave-like nature of electron gives rise to stable orbit. For electron moving around a nucleus in a circular path two possible electron waves of different wavelengths are possible as shown in Fig. 21.1. In one case, the circumference of the electron orbit is an integral multiple of wavelength. This is shown as solid line. In the second case, the wave is destroyed by interference as the circumference of the electron orbit is not a whole number multiple of wavelength and hence will not exist. This is shown by dotted lines. Therefore the necessary condition for a stable orbit of radius r is

$$2\pi r = n\lambda \qquad \qquad ...(21.4)$$

The wave satisfying the condition represented by Eq. (21.4) is called a stationary or standing wave. Thus a wave associated with an electron in a stable orbit should give rise to a stationary state of given energy corresponding to the wavelength of the standing wave.

Substituting the value of λ from Eq. (21.3) in Eq. (21.4) gives

$$2\pi r = \frac{nh}{mv}$$

or

$$mvr = \frac{nh}{2\pi}$$

which is simply the original Bohr condition (Eq. 20.15) for a stable orbit. Hence, the idea that electrons have wave-like properties confirms Bohr postulate of quantization of energy.

21.2 THE HEISENBERG UNCERTAINTY PRINCIPLE

According to classical mechanics, one can determine precisely both the position and the momentum of a body at any point in space. However, with sub-atomic particles, *it is not possible to determine accurately the position and the momentum simultaneously.* This means experiments that are designed to measure momentum or velocity of the particle accurately would make the measurement of the position of the particle less precise. Similarly, momentum or velocity will be less precise if the position of the particle is accurately determined. This uncertainty of either the position or of momentum is evidently not a matter of imperfection of experimental technique but is due to the interaction of the system with the measuring technique. This uncertainty therefore represents a fundamental limit of nature. This is the famous Heisenberg's principle of uncertainty and holds for a pair of any two *canonically conjugate quantities.* Heisenberg in 1927 showed that the product of the uncertainty in the position of body Δx, and the uncertainty in the momentum, Δp_x along the x-direction, is equal to or greater than the Planck's constant

$$(\Delta x)(\Delta p_x) \geq h \qquad \qquad ...(21.5)$$

or more correctly,

$$(\Delta x)(\Delta p_x) \geq \frac{h}{4\pi} \qquad \qquad ...(21.6)$$

Similarly we can write,

$$(\Delta y)(\Delta p_y) \geq \frac{h}{4\pi}$$

and

$$(\Delta z)(\Delta p_z) \geq \frac{h}{4\pi}$$

Consequently, as the position of the particle is defined exactly, *i.e.*, Δx is made exceedingly small, Δp_x correspondingly becomes very large. Similarly, if an attempt is made to define Δp_x exactly it will lead to a large uncertainty in x, *i.e.*, Δx would be very large. Thus, if we use light to locate the position of an electron, we cannot locate the electron more accurately than $\pm\lambda$, the wavelength of light used. Naturally, we would try to make λ as small as possible and so in principle locate electron to any required degree of accuracy. But can we determine the momentum of the electron at the same instant when we determine its position? The answer to this question is no, for in determining the position of the electron we inevitably change its momentum by an unknown amount. The value of the momentum will thus be made uncertain. The shorter the wavelength used the more is the uncertainty in momentum.

As an example, suppose we wish to locate the electron within 0.005 nm (or 5×10^{-10} cm). According to uncertainty principle, any such measurement of the electron position would have associated with it an uncertainty in momentum given by

$$\Delta p_x = \frac{h}{4\pi\Delta x} = \frac{\left(6.626 \times 10^{-34}\, \text{kg m}^2\text{s}^{-1}\right)}{(4\pi)\left(5 \times 10^{-12}\, \text{m}\right)}$$

$$= 1.05 \times 10^{-23}\, \text{kg ms}^{-1}$$

Since the mass of the electron is 9.109×10^{-31} kg, the uncertainty in the electron velocity is given as

$$\Delta v = \frac{p_x}{m} = \frac{1.05 \times 10^{-23}\, \text{kg ms}^{-1}}{9.109 \times 10^{-31}\, \text{kg}} = 1.16 \times 10^{7}\, \text{ms}^{-1}$$

Thus the uncertainty in the electron velocity would be nearly as large as the velocity of light, or as great as or even greater than what we might expect the actual electron velocity to be. In short, we say that the velocity of the electron is uncertain.

21.3 THE SCHRÖDINGER EQUATION

Schrödinger argued that if an electron has wave-like properties, then it must be described by a wave function. The wave function is represented by ψ (psi) and denotes the amplitude of the wave at a given point.

If the electron is considered as a wave which moves in one direction, say x-direction only, then

$$\frac{d^2\psi}{dx^2} = -\frac{4\pi^2\psi}{\lambda^2}$$

or

$$\frac{d^2\psi}{dx^2} + \frac{4\pi^2\psi}{\lambda^2} = 0 \qquad \qquad ...(21.7)$$

This equation is applicable to all particles including electrons and protons.

Since
$$\lambda = \frac{h}{mv} \qquad \qquad \text{[de Broglie equation (21.2)]}$$

Therefore equation (21.7) becomes

$$\frac{d^2\psi}{dx^2} + \frac{4\pi^2 m^2 v^2}{h^2}\psi = 0 \qquad \qquad ...(21.8)$$

The total energy E of a moving particle is made up of kinetic energy and potential energy (V), i.e.,

$$E = K.E. + P.E.$$

or

$$K.E. = E - P.E.$$
$$= E - V$$

The kinetic energy of a particle of mass m moving with velocity v is given by

$$K.E. = \frac{1}{2}mv^2$$

So,

$$\frac{1}{2}mv^2 = E - V$$

or,

$$v^2 = \frac{2}{m}(E - V)$$

Substituting the value of v^2 in equation (21.8) yields

$$\frac{d^2\psi}{dx^2} + \frac{8\pi^2 m}{h^2}(E - V)\psi = 0 \qquad \qquad ...(21.9)$$

Equation (21.9) is the well-known Schrödinger equation in one-dimension. In three-dimension it may be written as

$$\frac{d^2\psi}{dx^2} + \frac{d^2\psi}{dy^2} + \frac{d^2\psi}{dz^2} + \frac{8\pi^2 m}{h^2}(E - V)\psi = 0$$

Alternatively, it can also be written as

$$\nabla^2\psi + \frac{8\pi^2 m}{h^2}(E - V)\psi = 0 \qquad \qquad ...(21.10)$$

where

$$\nabla^2 = \frac{\partial^2}{\partial x^2} + \frac{\partial^2}{\partial y^2} + \frac{\partial^2}{\partial z^2}$$

and ∇ is known as Laplacian operator.

Equation (21.10) is customarily written in the following form

$$\left[\frac{-h^2}{8\pi^2 m}\nabla^2 + V\right]\psi = E\psi \qquad \qquad ...(21.11)$$

Defining the Hamiltonian operator H as

$$H = \left(-\frac{h^2}{8\pi^2 m}\nabla^2 + V\right)$$

equation (21.11) becomes

$$H\psi = E\psi \qquad \qquad ...(21.12)$$

which is the abbreviated form of Schrödinger equation.

Interpretation of Ψ and Ψ^2

Schrödinger's equation is a second order differential equation and therefore has a large number of solutions. However, only a few values of Ψ have physical significance. These are values of Ψ which correspond to certain definite or discrete values of total energy called *eigenvalues*. The corresponding wave function is referred to as *an eigenfunction* or *a characteristic function*. The wave function Ψ is a state function and as such has no physical significance except that it represents the amplitude of the wave.

For any particular physical situation under consideration, ψ must be finite, single-valued and continuous; then only the wave function is said to be well-behaved.

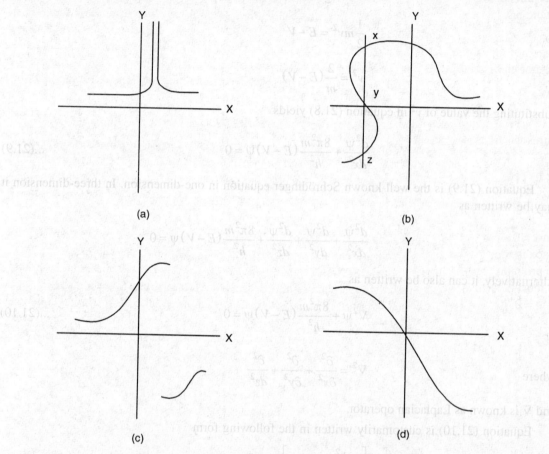

Fig. 21.2 The wave function ψ (a) not finite, (b) not single valued, (c) not continuous and (d) single valued

In Fig. 21.2 (a) the wave function shown is not well-behaved because it is not finite. Similarly, the wave function shown in 21.2 (b) is not single valued for a particular value of x. It has three values of ψ at points x, y and z. Similarly, the wave function shown in Fig. 21.2 (c) is not continuous. The wave function shown in Fig. 21.2 (d) is single valued, finite and continuous. Hence it is a well-balanced wave function.

Since we presume that ψ^2 is proportional to the probability of finding an electron in a given region of space and not equal to the probability, the wavefunction ψ has to be multiplied by a constant N so that its square becomes

$$\langle N^2 \psi^2 \rangle = N^2 \psi^2$$

When an electron is confined in a particular region of space $d\tau$, the probability of locating the electron in this region can be obtained by integration. The integral has to be equal to unity. Thus

$$\int N^2 \psi^2 d\tau = N^2 \int \psi^2 d\tau = 1$$

Here N is called the normalization constant and it ensures that the probability of finding the electron is equal to unity and not just proportional to it.

Concept of ψ: Sometimes ψ is a complex function. Therefore, the probability of finding the particle has to be a real quantity. However, the above normalization condition given as

$$N^2 \int \psi \psi \, d\tau = 1$$

does not yield real values. In these cases, the normalization condition is given by

$$N^2 \int \psi \psi^* \, d\tau = 1$$

where ψ^* is a complex conjugate of ψ and is obtained by replacing i (square root of -1) in ψ by $-i$. This ensures $\psi \psi^*$ is a real number.

21.4 THE PARTICLE IN A BOX

The simplest application of the Schrödinger equation is the problem of a particle moving in a box. Since the particle travels along X-axis and its movement is restricted between the walls of the box, *i.e.*, from $x = 0$ and $x = a$ (Fig. 21.3). For these values of x, the particle is free and the potential energy inside the box is zero. However, beyond this region, the potential energy increases to infinity and there will be zero probability of finding the particle. It follows therefore that ψ^2 must be zero for $x < 0$ and $x > a$; so also must be the ψ. To avoid discontinuity, we take $\psi = 0$ at walls also. Mathematically, it can be stated that $\psi = 0$, if $x \leq 0$ and $x \geq a$.

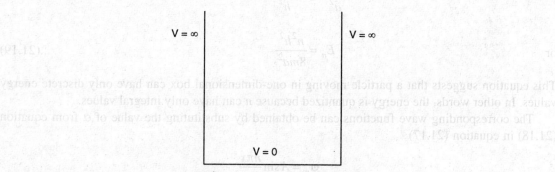

Fig. 21.3 One-dimensional potential box

Since the potential energy inside the box is zero, *i.e.*, $V = 0$, the Schrödinger equation (21.9) reduces to

$$\frac{d^2 \psi}{dx^2} = -\frac{8\pi^2 m}{h^2} E \psi \qquad \qquad ...(21.13)$$

The general solution of this differential equation is

$$\psi = A \sin \alpha x + B \cos \alpha x \qquad \qquad ...(21.14)$$

where

$$\alpha^2 = \frac{8\pi^2 mE}{h^2} \qquad \qquad ...(21.15)$$

To satisfy the condition that $\psi = 0$ at $x = 0$, equation (21.14) becomes

$$A \sin \alpha \cdot 0 + B \cos \alpha \cdot 0 = 0$$

$$A \cdot 0 + B = 0$$

or

$$B = 0$$

Putting $B = 0$ in equation (21.14), we get

$$\psi = A \sin \alpha x \qquad \qquad ...(21.16)$$

When $x = a$, we can write the above equation as

$$\psi = A \sin \alpha a \qquad \qquad ...(21.17)$$

The right hand side of equation (21.17) can be zero only when either $A = 0$ or $\sin \alpha a = 0$. If $A = 0$, then ψ will be zero at all points in the box which is impossible, therefore

$$\sin \alpha a = 0$$

This is valid only when αa is any integral multiple of $n\pi$, i.e.,

$$\alpha a = n\pi$$

$$\alpha = \frac{n\pi}{a} \qquad \qquad ...(21.18)$$

Substituting the value of α from equation (21.18) in equation (21.15), we get

$$\frac{n^2\pi^2}{a^2} = \frac{8\pi^2 mE_n}{h^2}$$

or

$$E_n = \frac{n^2 h^2}{8ma^2} \qquad \qquad ...(21.19)$$

This equation suggests that a particle moving in one-dimensional box can have only discrete energy values. In other words, the energy is quantized because n can have only integral values.

The corresponding wave functions can be obtained by substituting the value of α from equation (21.18) in equation (21.17)

$$\psi_n = A \sin \frac{n\pi x}{a}$$

It is important to note that values of E_n decreases as the value of a increases (Eq. 21.19). Further-more, the integer n is a quantum number indicating the number of nodes in the wave. When $n = 1$, the number of nodes is equal to zero, i.e., there are no nodes. When $n = 2$, the number of nodes = 1, and this node is in the centre of the box. For $n = 3$, there are two nodes and so on. This is shown in Fig. 21.4 (a). The probability distribution function ψ^2 is shown in Fig. 21.4 (b).

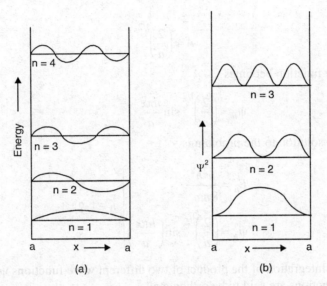

Fig. 21.4 (a) Plot of energy versus x. (b) Plot of probability distribution function against x

The value of energy is directly proportional to n^2 and this rises rapidly as the number of nodes increases. The lowest energy level ($n = 1$) is

$$E_1 = \frac{h^2}{8ma^2}$$

Thus the particle will have this minimum energy which is sometimes called *the zero point energy*. The next higher energy level ($n = 2$) is given by

$$E_2 = \left(\frac{4h^2}{8ma^2}\right)$$

it is four times higher than the minimum energy. Similarly, for $n = 3$ or $n = 4$ the energy will be 9 or 16 times more than the minimum value.

The value of constant A can be evaluated by using the fact that $\psi^2(x)\,dx$, the probability of finding the particle between $x = 0$ and $x = a$ is unity. Such a condition is called *the normalization* of the wave function.

$$\int_0^a \psi^2(x)\,dx = 1 \qquad \qquad ...(21.20)$$

Substituting the value of $\psi(x)$ in Eq. (21.20) yields

$$A^2 \int_0^a \sin^2\left(\frac{n\pi x}{a}\right)dx = 1$$

$$A^2 \frac{a}{2} = 1 \qquad \qquad \left(\because \int_0^a \sin\frac{n\pi x}{a}\,dx = \frac{a}{2}\right)$$

$$A = \left(\frac{2}{a}\right)^{1/2}$$

Therefore, the wave function becomes

$$\psi_n = \left(\frac{2}{a}\right)^{1/2} \sin\frac{n\pi x}{a} \qquad \qquad ...(21.21)$$

Hence the complete solution to the problem is

$$\left.\begin{array}{c} E_n = \dfrac{n^2 h^2}{8ma^2} \\[4mm] \psi_n = \left(\dfrac{2}{a}\right)^{1/2} \sin\left(\dfrac{n\pi x}{a}\right) \end{array}\right\} \; n = 1, 2, ...$$

and

However, when the integration of the product of two different wave functions $\psi(x)$ and $\psi^*(x)$ is equal to zero, the wave functions are said to be orthogonal

$$\int_0^a \psi(x)\psi^*(x)\, dx = 0$$

For the motion of the particle in three-dimension, the allowed energy levels are

$$E = \frac{n_x^2 h^2}{8ma^2} + \frac{n_y^2 h^2}{8mb^2} + \frac{n_z^2 h^2}{8mc^2} \qquad \qquad ...(21.22)$$

where a, b and c are the lengths of the sides of the box in x, y and z directions respectively. The energy thus depends on the sum of the squares of the three quantum numbers. If the lengths of two edges of a box are in the ratio of integers, several distinct combinations of the three quantum numbers give rise to the same energy level. Such an energy level is said to be degenerate. It can be shown that for a cubical box of side a the energy level corresponding to three different independent states having quantum numbers (2, 1, 1) (1, 2, 1) and (1, 1, 2) have equal energy viz.,

$$E = \frac{6h^2}{8m}$$

This level is, therefore, called a *threefold degenerate or a triply degenerate state.*

21.5 THE HYDROGEN ATOM

The simplest atomic systems are those containing a nucleus of charge $+Ze$ and one electron of mass m and charge $-e$. The Schrödinger equation may be solved exactly for these hydrogen-like atoms. The treatment of the hydrogen atom is too complicated and tedious, so only the results are given.

Since the hydrogen atom consists of an electron and a proton of charge $+e$, the potential energy of this system is given by

$$V = -\frac{e^2}{4\pi\varepsilon_0 r}$$

The Schrödinger equation can then be written as

$$\cdot \frac{\partial^2 \psi}{\partial x^2} + \frac{\partial^2 \psi}{\partial y^2} + \frac{\partial^2 \psi}{\partial z^2} + \frac{8\pi^2 m}{h^2}\left[E + \frac{e^2}{(4\pi\varepsilon_0)r}\right]\psi = 0 \qquad \text{...(21.23)}$$

This equation can be solved by transforming the Cartesian coordinates to spherical coordinates r, θ, ϕ using the following relations

$$x = r\sin\theta\cos\phi$$
$$y = r\sin\theta\sin\phi$$
$$z = r\cos\theta$$

as shown in Fig. 21.5. The equation after transformation takes the form

$$\frac{1}{r^2}\frac{\partial}{\partial r}\left(r^2\frac{\partial \psi}{dr}\right) + \frac{1}{r^2\sin\theta}\cdot\frac{\partial}{\partial\theta}\left(\sin\theta\frac{\partial\psi}{\partial\theta}\right) + \frac{1}{r^2\sin^2\theta}\frac{\partial^2\psi}{\partial\phi^2} + \frac{8\pi^2 m}{h^2}\left(E + \frac{e^2}{r(4\pi\varepsilon_0)}\right)\psi = 0 \qquad \text{...(21.24)}$$

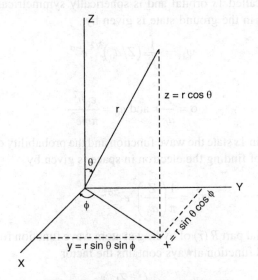

Fig. 21.5 Spherical polar coordinates

The wave equation in this form can be written as a product of three functions, the first of which depends only on r, the second only on θ, and the third only on ϕ.

$$\psi(r, \theta, \phi) = R(r)\Theta(\theta)\Phi(\phi) \qquad \text{...(21.25)}$$

When we substitute the value of ψ from Eq. (21.25) in Eq. (21.24) and solve it, three ordinary differential equations result. Each one of these differential equations on solving by imposing the boundary conditions leads to the emergence of three quantum numbers. These must be integers.

   (i) n, the principal quantum number arises from the freedom of the electron to vary its distance from the nucleus and have values 1, 2, 3, ...
   (ii) l, the azimuthal quantum number and takes the integral values from 0 to $(n-1)$.
   (iii) m, the magnetic quantum number having the integral values from $-l$ to $+l$, including zero; thus giving a total of $(2l + 1)$ values.

The eigenvalues for the energy of hydrogen or hydrogen-like atoms is given by

$$E_n = -\frac{Z^2 m e^4}{8\varepsilon_0^2 n^2 h^2}, \qquad n = 1, 2, 3, \ldots$$

If $Z = 1$, the above equation gives energy of a hydrogen atom with respect to a proton and an electron separated by an infinite distance. Thus the energies of various states of hydrogen atom are inversely proportional to the square of the principal quantum number, n. The energy is negative because the electron in a hydrogen-like atom has less energy than when it is free.

The wave function ψ for electrons in atoms and molecules is called *atomic orbital*. The shape and orientation of an atomic orbital is mainly determined by l and m and is independent of n.

The total wave functions, for hydrogen-like atom, is the product of the radial function $R(r)$ and the two angular wave functions $\Theta(\theta)$ and $\Phi(\phi)$. The expression for the radial and angular components for $n = 1$ to $n = 3$ are given in Table 21.1.

For the ground state, the orbital depends only on the radial coordinate (r) and is independent of θ and ϕ. In other words, for the ground state $n = 1$ and the other two quantum numbers, l and m are equal to zero. Such an orbital is called $1s$ orbital and is spherically symmetrical in shape. The normalised wave function for $1s$ orbital in the ground state is given by

$$\psi_{1s} = \frac{1}{\sqrt{\pi}} (Z/a_0)^{3/2} e^{-\sigma} \qquad \qquad \ldots(21.26)$$

where

$$\sigma = \frac{Z}{a_0} r \text{ and } a_0 = \frac{\varepsilon_0 h^2}{\pi m e^2}$$

Equation (21.26) shows that in $1s$ state the wave function and the probability distribution are independent of θ and ϕ. The probability of finding the electron in space is given by

$$\psi_{1s}^2 = \frac{1}{\pi} \left(\frac{Z}{a_0} \right)^3 e^{-2\sigma}$$

In Fig. 21.6 (a), a plot of radial part $R(r)$ of hydrogen atom wave function for $1s$ and $2s$ orbitals is made as a function of r. The radial function always contains the factor

$$\exp\left(-\frac{Zr}{na_0} \right)$$

where n is the principal quantum number. As the effective nuclear charge (Z) increases, the radial wave function falls off more rapidly with increasing r indicating that the electron is attracted more closely to the higher positively charged nucleus. The curve shows that $R(r)$ is maximum at $r = 0$, *i.e.*, at the nucleus itself.

The probability of finding the electron in the region between two spheres of radii r and $r + dr$ is given by $(4\pi r^2 dr) \psi^2$, where $4\pi r^2 dr$ is the volume of the spherical shell and ψ^2 is constant. The function $4\pi r^2 \psi^2$ is called *the radial distribution function*, $D(r)$. A plot of radial distribution function $D(r)$, versus r/a_0 for $1s$ and $2s$ electrons is shown in Fig. 21.6 (b). The curve shows a maximum at $r = a_0$, the radius of the first Bohr orbit. It is seen that though the electron density is maximum at $r = 0$, the probability of finding the electron in a spherical shell near the nucleus is very small and decreases for both shorter and larger values than a_0. There is a fundamental difference between the Bohr atom and

Table 21.1 Real Hydrogen-like Wave Functions

Orbital designation	n	l	m_l	R	θΦ	Total wave functions
1s	1	0	0	$2\left(\dfrac{Z}{a_0}\right)^{3/2}e^{-\sigma}$	$\left(\dfrac{1}{4\pi}\right)^{1/2}$	$\psi_{1s}=\dfrac{1}{\sqrt{\pi}}\left(\dfrac{Z}{a_0}\right)^{3/2}e^{-\sigma}$
2s	2	0	0	$\dfrac{1}{2\sqrt{2}}\left(\dfrac{Z}{a_0}\right)^{3/2}(2-\sigma)e^{-\sigma/2}$	$\left(\dfrac{1}{4\pi}\right)^{1/2}$	$\psi_{2s}=\dfrac{1}{4\sqrt{2\pi}}\left(\dfrac{Z}{a_0}\right)^{3/2}(2-\sigma)e^{-\sigma/2}$
2p$_z$	2	1	0	$\dfrac{1}{2\sqrt{6}}\left(\dfrac{Z}{a_0}\right)^{3/2}\sigma e^{-\sigma/2}$	$\sqrt{\dfrac{3}{4\pi}}\cos\theta$	$\psi_{2p_z}=\dfrac{1}{4\sqrt{2\pi}}\left(\dfrac{Z}{a_0}\right)^{3/2}\sigma e^{-\sigma/2}\cos\theta$
2p$_x$	2	1	+1	$\dfrac{1}{2\sqrt{6}}\left(\dfrac{Z}{a_0}\right)^{3/2}\sigma e^{-\sigma/2}$	$\left(\dfrac{3}{4\pi}\right)^{1/2}\sin\theta\cos\phi$	$\psi_{2p_x}=\dfrac{1}{4\sqrt{2\pi}}\left(\dfrac{Z}{a_0}\right)^{3/2}\sigma e^{-\sigma/2}\sin\theta\cos\phi$
2p$_y$	2	1	-1	$\dfrac{1}{2\sqrt{6}}\left(\dfrac{Z}{a_0}\right)^{3/2}\sigma e^{-\sigma/2}$	$\left(\dfrac{3}{4}\right)^{1/2}\sin\theta\sin\phi$	$\psi_{2p_y}=\dfrac{1}{4\sqrt{2\pi}}\left(\dfrac{Z}{a_0}\right)^{3/2}\sigma e^{-\sigma/2}\sin\theta\sin\phi$
3s	3	0	0	$\dfrac{2}{81\sqrt{3\pi}}\left(\dfrac{Z}{a_0}\right)^{3/2}(27-18\sigma+2\sigma^2)e^{-\sigma/3}$	$\left(\dfrac{1}{4\pi}\right)^{1/2}$	$\psi_{3s}=\dfrac{1}{81\sqrt{3\pi}}\left(\dfrac{Z}{a_0}\right)^{3/2}(27-18\sigma+2\sigma^2)e^{-\sigma/3}$

the quantum mechanical atom. In Bohr model of atom the electron always revolves in an orbit at a fixed distance from the nucleus whereas in the wave mechanical approach the electron is mostly located at this point, but there is a definite probability of finding it somewhere else also.

For $n = 2$, $l = 0$ or 1. When $n = 2$ and $l = 0$, the orbital is the 2s orbital. The wave function for such an orbital is given as

$$\psi_{2s} = \frac{1}{4\sqrt{2\pi}} \left(\frac{Z}{a_0}\right)^{3/2} (2 - \sigma) \exp\left(-\frac{\sigma}{2}\right) \qquad \ldots(21.27)$$

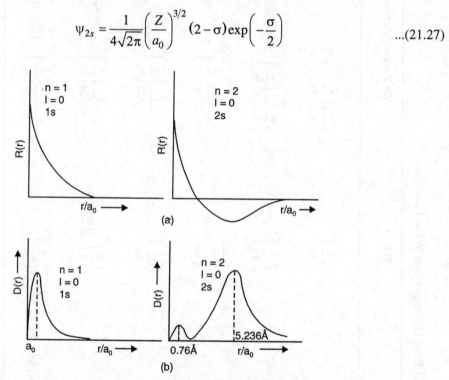

Fig. 21.6 (a) The variation of density, (b) probability density for finding the electron at a distance between r and $r + dr$

A plot of the radial distribution function against r for such an orbital gives two peaks as shown in Fig. 21.6 (b). The main peak corresponds to a distance $r = 5.2\ a_0$ and the subsidiary peak at $r = 0.8\ a_0$. This means that 2s electron is most likely to occur at a distance $5.2\ a_0$ from the nucleus for most of the time. However, there is a lesser probability of finding it at $r = 0.8\ a_0$. These facts show that as the distance of the electron from the nucleus increases more delocalization of the electron takes place and the electrostatic attraction between the electron and the nucleus decreases.

21.6 ANGULAR DEPENDENCE OF THE WAVE FUNCTION AND SHAPES OF THE ORBITALS

The shapes of atomic orbitals depend on the angles θ and ϕ which in other words determine the geometry or the spatial distribution of the orbitals. The angular dependence is represented by spherical polar coordinates θ and ϕ. For 1s orbital, the angular dependence part is just $\dfrac{1}{\sqrt{4\pi}}$, which means that the *s*-orbital is independent of the angle θ and φ. Therefore the angular portion of the wave function is constant. Hence the *s* orbital is spherically symmetrical (Fig. 21.7).

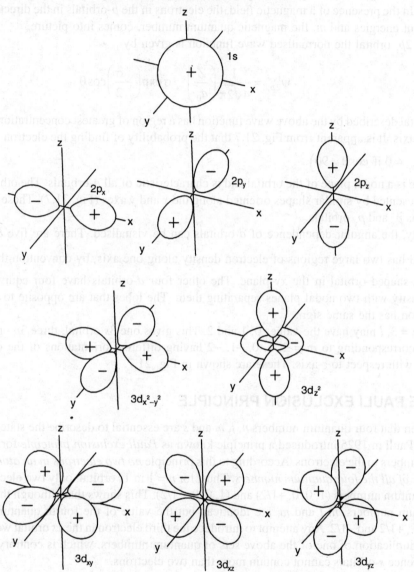

Fig. 21.7 Shapes of *s, p* and *d*-orbitals

The orientation of the *p* orbitals can be calculated by considering the magnitude and signs of trigonometric functions. For $2p_z$ orbital, the θΦ term contains cos θ which according to the relation given in equation (21.27) implies that this orbital is directed along the z-direction. Similarly, for $2p_y$ orbital, the wave function contains sin θ sin φ term indicating that the orbital points to the y-direction. The wave function for $2p_x$ orbital contains sin θ cos φ term and hence will direct towards x-direction. In the same way, we can conclude that the 2s and 3s orbitals are spherically symmetrical as they do not have θ and φ terms in their angular functions. We can similarly interpret the directional characteristics of 3p and 3d orbitals. In the absence of electric and magnetic field electrons in p_x, p_y and p_z orbitals all have the same energy, which depends on the value of n. Hence the three p-orbitals are termed as triply degenerate. In the presence of a magnetic field, the electrons in the p-orbitals in the direction of the field have different energies and m, the magnetic quantum number, comes into picture.

For the $2p_z$ orbital the normalised wave function is given by

$$\psi_{2p_z} = \frac{1}{4\sqrt{2\pi}} \left(\frac{Z}{a_0}\right)^{3/2} \sigma \exp\left(-\frac{\sigma}{2}\right) \cos\theta \qquad \ldots(21.28)$$

The $2p_z$ orbital described by the above wave function has a region of greatest concentration or probability along the z-axis. It is apparent from Fig. 21.7 that the probability of finding the electron in the xy plane is zero $\left(\psi_{2p_z} = 0 \text{ if } \cos\theta = 90\right)$.

The xy plane is a nodal plane of the orbital and is characteristic of all p-orbitals. The other two orbitals may be represented by similar shapes oriented along the x and y axes (Fig. 21.7). These are, therefore, referred to as p_x and p_y orbitals.

Similarly, the angular dependence of d orbitals can be visualised. There are five d orbitals. The $3d_{z^2}$ orbital has two large regions of electron density along one axis, by convention the z-axis and a small donut-shaped orbital in the xy plane. The other four d-orbitals have four equivalent lobes of electron density with two nodal planes separating them. The lobes that are opposite to each other the wave function has the same sign.

When $n = 3$, l may have the values 0, 1 and 2. This gives one 3s orbital, three 3p orbitals and five 3d orbitals corresponding to $m = 2, 1, 0, -1, -2$ having different orientations of the orbital angular momentum with respect to z-axis. These are shown in Fig. 21.7.

21.7 THE PAULI EXCLUSION PRINCIPLE

We have seen that four quantum numbers n, l, m and s are essential to describe the state of an electron in an atom. Pauli in 1925 introduced a principle known as *Pauli exclusion principle* for assigning quantum numbers to the electrons. According to this principle *no two electrons in an atom can have the same values of all the four quantum numbers*. Thus, for $n = 1$ in 1s orbital, only two electrons can exist with the quantum numbers $(1, 0, 0, +1/2)$ and $(1, 0, 0, -1/2)$. This shows that although the values of the three quantum numbers, n, l and m, are identical, but the value of the fourth quantum number s is different, *i.e.*, $+1/2$ and $-1/2$. Any attempt to introduce the third electron in the 1s orbital would inevitably lead to the duplication of one of the above sets of quantum numbers, which is contrary to the Pauli's principle. Hence s-orbitals cannot contain more than two electrons.

The maximum number of electrons for each principal quantum number is given by $2n^2$. This would give the maximum number of electrons in successive shells as 2, 8, 18, 32 and 50. Bohr and Bury suggested that the maximum number of electrons in an outer-most shell is 8 and then a new shell is started. This is shown in Table 21.2.

21.8 THE AUFBAU PRINCIPLE AND PERIODIC TABLE

The distribution of electrons in an atom in the periodic table is done from the combined use of Pauli exclusion principle, Bohr-Bury postulate and the spectroscopic studies. The electronic configuration of elements is obtained by putting electrons successively in orbitals (energy sublevels) in order of increasing

Table 21.2 Assignment of Electrons in Shells

Principal quantum number n	Energy level (shell)	Azimuthal quantum number l	Energy sublevels (sublevels)	Magnetic quantum number m	Spin quantum number	Number of energy states	Total number of electron
1	K	0	s	0	+1/2, −1/2	2	2
2	L	0	s	0	+1/2, −1/2	2	
		1	p	+1, 0, −1	+1/2, −1/2	6	8
3	M	0	s	0	+1/2, −1/2	2	
		1	p	1, 0, −1	+1/2, −1/2	6	18
		2	d	2, 1, 0, −1, −2	+1/2, −1/2	10	
4	N	0	s	0	+1/2, −1/2	2	
		1	p	1, 0, −1	+1/2, −1/2	6	32
		2	d	2, 1, 0, −1, −2	+1/2, −1/2	10	
		3	f	3, 2, 1, 0, −1, −2, −3	+1/2, −1/2	14	

energy. The electrons will enter first the sublevels of lowest energy. The relative energies of the sublevels are shown in Fig. 21.8. These are 1s < 2s < 2p < 3s < 3p < 4s < 3d < 4p < 5s < 4d < 5p < 6s < 4f < 5d < 6p < 7s. As stated above, each sublevel holds only two electrons governed by Pauli exclusion principle.

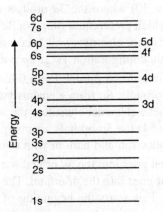

Fig. 21.8 Relative energy levels for the subshells

The hydrogen atom has only one electron and will occupy the 1s level. The electronic configuration can be written as $1s^1$. The next element helium ($Z = 2$) has two electrons, and both of these occupy the 1s level and have opposite spins. The resulting electronic configuration is thus written as $1s^2$.

Lithium ($Z = 3$) has three electrons, two of which are in 1s level and the third one will go into the 2s level ($n = 2$, $l = 0$). As stated previously, the 2s level electron is at about a distance of $5a_0$ (where a_0 is the radius of the first Bohr orbit) from the nucleus and is partly shielded from +3 unit of charge of the nucleus by the two inner electrons. Thus the electronic configuration of lithium is $1s^2\ 2s^1$ and it is easier to remove the outer 2s electron producing an ion having the electronic structure of helium. Berrylium ($Z = 4$), the next element, has two electrons in 1s and two electrons in 2s orbitals having the electronic configuration $1s^2\ 2s^2$. It is obvious from this that K-shell is completed and s-subgroup of L-shell is also filled up. In boron ($Z = 5$), the fifth electron will go into the p-orbital of L-shell. The next electron in case of C ($Z = 6$) can go into the p-orbital in the following manner:

↑↓				↑	↓			↑	↑	
$2p_x$	$2p_y$	$2p_z$		$2p_x$	$2p_y$	$2p_z$		$2p_x$	$2p_y$	$2p_z$

These configurations obey the Pauli exclusion principle but the most correct representation in the ground state is governed by *Hund's rule*. This rule states that *when a set of orbitals of equal energy is being filled with electrons, the electrons distribute themselves in these orbitals so as to retain parallel spin as far as possible*. The electronic configuration of carbon in the ground state, therefore, may be written as

↑↓	↑↓	↑	↑	
$1s$	$2s$	$2p_x$	$2p_y$	$2p_z$

or $\quad 1s^2\ 2s^2\ 2p_x^1\ 2p_y^1\ 2p_z$

This will continue upto neon ($Z = 10$) because p-orbitals can accommodate upto six electrons and so the overall electronic configuration of neon is $1s^2 2s^2 2p^6$. This completes the L-shell.

The next electron in case of sodium ($Z = 11$) is now added to $3s$ orbital and has the electronic configuration $1s^2\ 2s^2\ 2p^6\ 3s^1$. This electron is shielded from $+11$ unit of nuclear charges by ten inner electrons, and so loosely bound and can be easily removed. This process of filling the orbitals continues until we reach Argon ($Z = 18$), $1s^2\ 2s^2 2s^6 3s^2 3p^6$ where K and L shells are completely filled while s and p sublevels of M-shell are also completed. The next two electrons in Ca ($Z = 20$) enter 4s orbital giving an electronic configuration of $1s^2 2s^2 2p^6 3s^2 3p^6 4s^2$. After calcium, the incoming electrons enter $3d$ orbitals. It continues until we reach zinc ($Z = 30$) where the $3d$ orbitals are completely filled. The series of elements from scandium to zinc, in which preferential filling of $3d$ orbitals results is known as the first transition series of elements. The next six electrons will successively occupy the $4p$ orbitals giving krypton ($Z = 36$) having the electronic configuration $1s^2 2s^2 2p^6 3s^2 3p^6 3d^{10} 4s^2 4p^6$.

After this, two electrons will go into the $5s$ orbital. From this onwards, $4d$ orbitals are being filled up since $4d$ levels are lower than $5p$ orbitals. So from elements yttrium ($Z = 39$) to cadmium ($Z = 48$) the 4d orbital levels are filled up. These elements constitute the second transitional series. From elements indium ($Z = 49$) to xenon ($Z = 54$) the $5p$ orbitals are completed. This is followed by the alkali metal caesium ($Z = 55$) with one $6s$ electron and barium with two $6s$ electrons.

At lanthanum ($Z = 57$), an electron goes into the $5d$ orbital but the next electron is cerium ($Z = 58$) does not enter the $5d$ orbital instead it goes into the $4f$ orbital. The maximum number of electrons that an f-orbital can accommodate is 14. This starts the beginning of a new series called *the lanthanide series* La (57) - Lu (71), where 14 electrons are successively put into $4f$ orbitals. All these 14 elements have an outer configuration $5s^2 5p^6 6s^2$. Since the chemical characteristics largely depend on the outer valence electrons, these elements are therefore alike in their behaviour.

After Lu ($Z = 71$), the incoming electrons are progressively added into $5d$ orbitals producing the third transitional series. It is completed at mercury ($Z = 80$). At actinium ($Z = 89$), a similar series like lanthanides results; $6d$ orbitals starts but is incomplete. The incoming electrons go into the $5f$ orbitals up to 103. This series is called *the actinide series*. Table 21.3 gives the electronic configuration of elements.

21.9 CLASSIFICATION OF ELEMENTS BASED UPON ELECTRONIC CONFIGURATION OF THEIR ATOMS

Based on the similarity of electronic configurations of atoms, elements are classified into four groups. These are (*i*) inert gas elements, (*ii*) representative elements, (*iii*) transition elements and (*iv*) inner transition elements.

Inert Gas Elements: These are elements which have completed electronic groups, *i.e.*, all the subsidiary quantum levels are filled to their capacity. Except helium, where the configuration is $1s^2$, each atom of this type has a general configuration of ns^2np^6 of the outermost shell. The chemical inertness of these elements is ascribed due to the presence of completed electronic groups. The inert gas elements embrace helium, neon, argon, krypton, xenon and radon.

Representative Elements: These are also known as *normal* or *typical elements*. These are characterised by atoms in which the levels of maximum principal quantum number are incompletely filled but all inner levels are completely filled to capacity. The general electronic configuration of the outermost shell of these elements ranges from ns^1 to ns^2np^5. All the nonmetallic elements (IIIb to VIIb) and the elements of I and II periodic groups are classed as representative elements. The reactivity of these elements is due to their tendency to achieve the electronic configuration of the nearest inert gas element by the gain or loss of electron(s).

Table 21.3 Arrangement of Electrons in Various Elements

Element	1s	2s	2p	3s	3p	3d	4s	4p	4d	4f	5s	5p	5d	5f	5g
1. H	1														
2. He	2														
3. Li	2	1													
4. Be	2	2													
5. B	2	2	1												
6. C	2	2	2												
7. N	2	2	3												
8. O	2	2	4												
9. F	2	2	5												
10. Ne	2	2	6												
11. Na	2	2	6	1											
12. Mg	2	2	6	2											
13. Al	2	2	6	2	1										
14. Si	2	2	6	2	2										
15. P	2	2	6	2	3										
16. S	2	2	6	2	4										
17. Cl	2	2	6	2	5										
18. Ar	2	2	6	2	6										

(Contd.)

Element	1s	2s	2p	3s	3p	3d	4s	4p	4d	4f	5s	5p	5d	5f	5g
19. K	2	2	6	2	6		1								
20. Ca	2	2	6	2	6		2								
21. Sc	2	2	6	2	6	1	2								
22. Ti	2	2	6	2	6	2	2								
23. V	2	2	6	2	6	3	2								
24. Cr	2	2	6	2	6	5	1								
25. Mn	2	2	6	2	6	5	2								
26. Fe	2	2	6	2	6	6	2								
27. Co	2	2	6	2	6	7	2								
28. Ni	2	2	6	2	6	8	2								
29. Cu	2	2	6	2	6	10	1								
30. Zn	2	2	6	2	6	10	2								
31. Ga	2	2	6	2	6	10	2	1							
32. Ge	2	2	6	2	6	10	2	2							
33. As	2	2	6	2	6	10	2	3							
34. Se	2	2	6	2	6	10	2	4							
35. Br	2	2	6	2	6	10	2	5							
36. Kr	2	2	6	2	5	10	2	6							
37. Rb	2	2	6	2	6	10	2	6			1				
38. Sr	2	2	6	2	6	10	2	6			2				
39. Y	2	2	6	2	6	10	2	6	1		2				
40. Zr	2	2	6	2	6	10	2	6	2		2				
41. Nb	2	2	6	2	6	10	2	6	4		1				
42. Mo	2	2	6	2	6	10	2	6	5		1				
43. Tc	2	2	6	2	6	10	2	6	6		1				
44. Ru	2	2	6	2	6	10	2	6	7		1				
45. Rh	2	2	6	2	6	10	2	6	8		1				
46. Pd	2	2	6	2	6	10	2	6	10						
47. Ag	2	2	6	2	6	10	2	6	10		1				
48. Cd	2	2	6	2	6	10	2	6	10		2				
49. In	2	2	6	2	6	10	2	6	10		2	1			
50. Sn	2	2	6	2	6	10	2	6	10		2	2			
51. Sb	2	2	6	2	6	10	2	6	10		2	3			
52. Te	2	2	6	2	6	10	2	6	10		2	4			
53. I	2	2	6	2	6	10	2	6	10		2	5			
54. Xe	2	2	6	2	6	10	2	6	10		2	6			

(Contd.)

Element	K	L	M	4s	4p	4d	4f	5s	5p	5d	5f	5g	6s	6p	6d	6f	6g	6h	7s
55. Cs	2	8	18	2	6	10		2	6				1						
56. Ba	2	8	18	2	6	10		2	6				2						
57. La	2	8	18	2	6	10		2	6	1			2						
58. Ce	2	8	18	2	6	10	2	2	6				2						
59. Pr	2	8	18	2	6	10	3	2	6				2						
60. Nd	2	8	18	2	6	10	4	2	6				2						
61. Pm	2	8	18	2	6	10	5	2	6				2						
62. Sm	2	8	18	2	6	10	6	2	6				2						
63. Eu	2	8	18	2	6	10	7	2	6				2						
64. Gd	2	8	18	2	6	10	7	2	6	1			2						
65. Tb	2	8	18	2	6	10	9	2	6				2						
66. Dy	2	8	18	2	6	10	10	2	6				2						
67. Ho	2	8	18	2	6	10	11	2	6				2						
68. Er	2	8	18	2	6	10	12	2	6				2						
69. Tm	2	8	18	2	6	10	13	2	6				2						
70. Yb	2	8	18	2	6	10	14	2	6				2						
71. Lu	2	8	18	2	6	10	14	2	6	1			2						
72. Hf	2	8	18	2	6	10	14	2	6	2			2						
73. Ta	2	8	18	2	6	10	14	2	6	3			2						
74. W	2	8	18	2	6	10	14	2	6	4			2						
75. Re	2	8	18	2	6	10	14	2	6	5			2						
76. Os	2	8	18	2	6	10	14	2	6	6			2						
77. Ir	2	8	18	2	6	10	14	2	6	7			2						
78. Pt	2	8	18	2	6	10	14	2	6	9			1						
79. Au	2	8	18	2	6	10	14	2	6	10			2						
80. Hg	2	8	18	2	6	10	14	2	6	10			2						
81. Ti	2	8	18	2	6	10	14	2	6	10			2	1					
82. Pb	2	8	18	2	6	10	14	2	6	10			2	2					
83. Bi	2	8	18	2	6	10	14	2	6	10			2	3					
84. Po	2	8	18	2	6	10	14	2	6	10			2	4					
85. As	2	8	18	2	6	10	14	2	6	10			2	5					
86. Rn	2	8	18	2	6	10	14	2	6	10			2	6					
87. Fr	2	8	18	2	6	10	14	2	6	10			2	6					1
88. Ra	2	8	18	2	6	10	14	2	6	10			2	6					2
89. Ac	2	8	18	2	6	10	14	2	6	10			2	6	1				2
90. Th	2	8	18	2	6	10	14	2	6	10			2	6	2				2

(Contd.)

Element	K	L	M	4s	4p	4d	4f	5s	5p	5d	5f	5g	6s	6p	6d	6f	6g	6h	7s
91. Pa	2	8	18	2	6	10	14	2	6	10		2	2	6	1				2
92. U	2	8	18	2	6	10	14	2	6	10		3	2	6	1				2
93. Np	2	8	18	2	6	10	14	6	2	6	10	5	2	6					2
94. Pu	2	8	18	2	6	10	14	6	2	6	10	6	2	6					2
95. Am	2	8	18	2	6	10	14	6	2	6	10	7	2	6					2
96. Cm	2	8	18	2	6	10	14	6	2	6	10	7	2	6	1				2
97. Bk	2	8	18	2	6	10	14	6	2	6	10	8	2	6	1				2
98. Cf	2	8	18	2	6	10	14	6	2	6	10	10	2	6					2
99. Ea	2	8	18	2	6	10	14	6	2	6	10	11	2	6					2
100. Fm	2	8	18	2	6	10	14	6	2	6	10	12	2	6					2
101. Md	2	8	18	2	6	10	14	6	2	6	10	13	2	6					2
102. No	2	8	18	2	6	10	14	6	2	6	10	14	2	6					2
103. Fm	2	8	18	2	6	10	14	6	2	6	10	14	2	6	1				2

Transition Elements: Atoms of these elements are characterised by the presence of an inner incompletely filled d orbital. The general electronic configuration of these elements may be represented by $(n-1)\,d^{1-9}ns^2$ or $(n-1)\,d^{1-10}\,ns^1$. Thus in transition elements, the two outermost shells are incomplete and the incoming electrons preferentially occupy d orbital. There are four transition series corresponding to the occupancy of $3d$, $4d$, $5d$ and $6d$ orbitals. All the series begin with group IIIa elements, namely, scandium $(3d^1\,4s^2)$, yttrium $(4d^1\,5s^2)$, lanthanum $(5d^1\,6s^2)$ and actinium $(6d^1\,7s^2)$. By definition, the first three transition series end at nickel, palladium and platinum, respectively, the fourth series being incomplete. Elements of periodic group I b and II b are quite analogous to the transition elements and are often classified with them. In Table 21.1, the electronic configuration of chromium $(Z = 24)$ is $3d^5\,4s^1$ and that of copper $(Z = 29)$ is $3d^{10}\,4s^1$. However, one would have expected these to be as $3d^4\,4s^2$ and $3d^9\,4s^2$ for chromium and copper respectively. This irregularity results from the increased stability of the half filled $(3d^5)$ and completely filled $(3d^{10})$ orbitals.

The energy differences between $(n-1)d$ and ns electrons are small and it results in variable valency of transition elements, formation of coloured ions, which are paramagnetic. They form many complexes and often possess marked catalytic activity.

Inner Transition Elements: They may be regarded as the members of the transition series within the transition series. Atoms of these elements have three incomplete outermost shells in addition to incompletely filled d orbitals; they have incompletely filled f orbitals as well. The incoming electrons in these elements preferentially go to f orbitals. There are two inner transition series, *viz.*, lanthanides and actinides corresponding to the filling of $4f$ and $5f$ orbitals. The actinide series includes transuranic elements. The f electrons are shielded by s and p electrons and hence they do not participate in bond formation.

21.10 IONIZATION POTENTIAL OR ENERGY

This is defined as *the energy required to remove an electron completely from an isolated gaseous atom of an element in its lowest energy state forming a gaseous positive ion.* The process may be written as

$$M(g) + \text{Energy} \rightarrow M^+(g) + e^-$$

Smaller the value of the ionization potential easier it is for the neutral atom to form the positive ion. However, on supplying extra energy the cation so formed can lose another electron to form $M^{2+}(g)$.

The energy necessary to remove the second electron from the gaseous cation is called the second ionization potential of the element. Likewise, third and higher ionization potentials may be defined and the ionization processes may be expressed as

$$M(g) + IE(1) \rightarrow M^+(g) + e^-$$

$$M^+(g) + IE(2) \rightarrow M^{2+}(g) + e^-$$

$$M^{2+}(g) + IE(3) \rightarrow M^{3+}(g) + e^-$$

where IE (1), IE (2) and IE (3) are the first, second and third ionization potentials respectively. Experimentally, this can be measured by spectroscopic methods. Usually ionization potentials are expressed in eV or kJ. The ionization energy depends on

    (*i*)   the size of the atom
    (*ii*) the charge on the nucleus
    (*iii*) how effectively the inner electron shells screen the nuclear charge
    (*iv*) the type of electrons involved (*s, p, d,* or *f*).

In small atoms, the electrons are tightly held, while in larger atoms, the electrons are less strongly held. Therefore, the ionization potential decreases with the increasing size of the atom. It is also observed that the second ionization energy is larger than the first ionization energy because the second electron is to be removed from a positively charged ion where the ratio of charges on the nucleus to the number of orbital electrons increases and hence reduces the size.

The shielding effect of other electrons: The inner electrons partially decrease the force of attraction between the loosely bound electrons and the nucleus thereby shielding the outer electron from the nucleus. This shielding effect of the inner electrons lowers the ionization potential. An *s* electron penetrates nearer to the nucleus and is therefore more tightly held than a *p* electron. For the similar reasons a *p* electron is more tightly held to the nucleus than a *d* electron and so on. Other factors being equal, the ionization energies are in the order of $s > p > d > f$.

To sum up, it can be stated that in a given row in the periodic table the ionization potential generally increases with increasing atomic number in a period. The ionization potential decreases from top to bottom in a group of the periodic table. Furthermore, smaller the number of electrons to be ionized lower will be the ionization potential.

21.11 ELECTRON AFFINITY

The energy released when an electron is added to a neutral gaseous atom to form a negative ion is known as electron affinity. Usually only one electron is added forming a uninegative ion. The process may be written as

$$M(g) + e^- \rightarrow M^-(g) + E_a$$

where M (g) is the gaseous element, e^- is an electron, M^- (g) is the gaseous anion and E_a the energy released in the process is known as electron affinity of the element M.

Addition of a second electron to a negatively charged ion is always opposed by the repulsive forces. This results in the input of the energy rather than its release, and the process is less likely to occur. Table 21.4 gives the value of the electron affinity of some typical elements. It should be noted that the negative value for the electron affinity indicates that the energy is released when an electron is added to the atom and the positive value shows that the energy is added to overcome the electrostatic repulsion.

Table 21.4 Electron Affinity of Some Elements

Element	Process	E_a (eV)
F	$F + e^- \rightarrow F^-$	−3.45
Cl	$Cl + e^- \rightarrow Cl^-$	−3.61
Br	$Br + e^- \rightarrow Br^-$	−3.40
I	$I + e^- \rightarrow I^-$	−3.10
O	$O + e^- \rightarrow O^-$	−2.20
O	$O + 2e^- \rightarrow O^{2-}$	+7.20
S	$S + e^- \rightarrow S^-$	−2.40
S	$S + 2e^- \rightarrow S^{2-}$	+3.40

Only halogens release energy when they acquire electrons to become negatively charged ions. All other elements, however, absorb energy in the formation of an anion.

The electron affinity of an element, in fact, may be regarded as the ionization potential of a negative ion with opposite sign. Therefore, the factors influencing the ionization potential may be extended to electron affinity.

For example, the addition of an electron to a halogen atom produces a stable noble gas configuration Cl^- ($1s^2\ 2s^2\ 2p^6\ 3s^2\ 2p^6$); Ar ($1s^2\ 2s^2\ 2p^6\ 3s^2\ 3p^6$).

21.12 FINE STRUCTURE OF HYDROGEN ATOM SPECTRUM

Electron spin has a further implication for the energies of atoms. Since an electron has spin angular momentum and the moving charges generate magnetic fields, and therefore an electron has a magnetic moment that arises from its spin. Similarly, an electron with orbital angular momentum is in effect a circular current, and possesses a magnetic moment that arises from its orbital momentum. The interaction of the spin and orbital magnetic moments is called spin-orbital coupling.

The orbital angular momentum L and spin angular momentum S of an electron are given as

$$|L| = \sqrt{l(l+1)}\ \frac{h}{2\pi} \qquad \qquad ...(21.28)$$

$$|S| = \sqrt{s(s+1)}\ \frac{h}{2\pi} \qquad \qquad ...(21.29)$$

where $|\ |$ sign represents the magnitudes of L and S; l denotes the angular momentum quantum number and can have values from 0 to $(n-1)$ and s represents the spin quantum number. The total angular momentum (J) of the electron is the vector sum of the orbital and spin momenta as

$$J = \vec{L} + \vec{S} \qquad \qquad ...(21.30)$$

Thus, when the spin and orbital angular momenta are parallel, the total angular momentum is high; when the two angular momentum are antiparallel (opposed), the total angular momentum is low. The orbital angular momentum of an electron is to be completely described by its magnitude and direction. The magnitude is given by equation (21.28) and is always quantised. The quantum theory says that a reference direction can be specified by applying magnetic or electric field and the angular momentum vector can have only those directions whose components along the reference direction are integral

multiple of $\frac{h}{2\pi}$. Such a reference direction is usually taken as z-axis. If L_z is the component of angular

momentum along z-axis, then

$$L_z = m_l \frac{h}{2\pi}$$ ...(21.31)

where m_l is an integral number and is called magnetic quantum number having values l, $(l-1)$, ... 0 ..., $-(l-1)$, $-l$. When $l = 0$, $m_l = 0$ and the angular momentum (by equation 21.28) will be zero. For $l = 1$, $m_l = +1, 0, -1$, the value of z component of angular momentum can be obtained from equation (21.31), as

when $\qquad m_l = +1, \qquad L_z = 1 \cdot \frac{h}{2\pi} = \frac{h}{2\pi}$

$$m_l = 0, \qquad L_z = 0 \cdot \frac{h}{2\pi} = 0$$

$$m_l = -1, \qquad L_z = (-1)\frac{h}{2\pi} = -\frac{h}{2\pi}$$

The angular momentum L as given by equation (21.28) is

$$|\mathbf{L}| = \sqrt{l(l+1)}\,\frac{h}{2\pi}$$

$$= \sqrt{1(1+1)}\,\frac{h}{2\pi}$$

$$= \sqrt{2} \cdot \frac{h}{2\pi}$$ ...(21.32)

Thus the magnitude of angular momentum vector $|\mathbf{L}|$ for $l = 1$ is $\sqrt{2} \cdot \frac{h}{2\pi}$. It should be noted that the

energy of the electron depends on the magnitude of the angular momentum and not on its direction. Thus one can conclude that all the values of m_l (corresponding to a particular l) have same values of L and have equal energy and are, therefore, degenerate.

The spin quantum number s is equal to 1/2. The spin angular momentum S can take only those directions for which its components (S_z) are half integral multiples of $h/2\pi$. Thus

$$S_z = m_s \frac{h}{2\pi}$$ ...(21.33)

where m_s is known as spin magnetic quantum number and is equal to +1/2 or −1/2.

Similarly, we can represent J, the total angular momentum, in terms of angular momentum quantum number, j as

$$J = \sqrt{j(j+1)}\,\frac{h}{2\pi}$$

where $j = |l+s|,\ |l+s-1|,\ \ldots\ldots|l-s|$

For an s-electron, j can be calculated as follows:

For $l = 0,\ s = \dfrac{1}{2}$

Therefore,

$$j = \left|\left(0+\frac{1}{2}\right)\right|,\ \left|\left(0+\frac{1}{2}-1\right)\right|,\ \ldots\ \left(\left|0-\frac{1}{2}\right|\right)$$

$$= \left|\frac{1}{2}\right|,\ \left|\left(-\frac{1}{2}\right)\right|$$

$$= \frac{1}{2}$$

Because the orbital angular momentum is zero in this state, the spin-orbital coupling energy is zero. Hence,

$$J = \sqrt{j(j+1)}\,\frac{h}{2\pi}$$

$$= \sqrt{\frac{1}{2}\left(\frac{1}{2}+1\right)}\,\frac{h}{2\pi}$$

$$= \frac{\sqrt{3}}{2}\frac{h}{2\pi}$$

For a p-electron, $l = 1$ and $s = 1/2$, therefore

$$j = \left|\left(1+\frac{1}{2}\right)\right|,\ \left|\left(1+\frac{1}{2}-1\right)\right|$$

$$= \frac{3}{2},\ \frac{1}{2}$$

For these two values of j will give two values as

$$J = \frac{\sqrt{15}}{2}\frac{\hbar}{2\pi}\ \text{and}\ \frac{\sqrt{3}}{2}\frac{\hbar}{2\pi}$$

These two values of J represent two values of energies as shown in Fig. 21.9. It may be emphasised here that all p-levels will be split into two energy levels corresponding to $j = 1/2$ and $3/2$ irrespective of whether they are $2p$, $3p$, $4p$ states. The strength of the spin-orbit coupling depends on the nuclear charge.

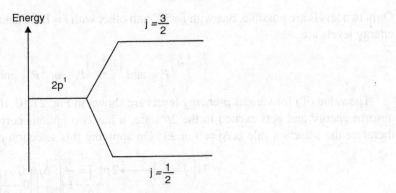

Fig. 21.9 Energy levels arising for a p-electron (spin-orbit coupling)

Similarly, for a d-electron, when $l = 2$, and $s = 1/2$, as done earlier, we can have two levels in configuration as

$$j = (2 + 1/2) \text{ and } (2 - 1/2)$$
$$= 5/2 \text{ and } 3/2.$$

Term Symbols

The energy levels of an atom are called terms. A term can be designated by a term symbol which is denoted as $^{2S+1}L_J$

where L is the total orbital angular momentum quantum number and can have values of 0, 1, 2, 3, 4, ...
The superscript $2S + 1$ gives the multiplicity of the energy state and the subscript J is the total angular momentum quantum number. The states designated for a given L are

L	=	0	1	2	3	4	... ...
State	=	S	P	D	F	G	... ...

For an s electron, $l = 0$ and $s = +1/2$,

therefore, $j = l + s = 0 + 1/2 = 1/2$

Only one level is possible.

The term symbol will be

$$^{2S+1}L_j = \left(2 \times \frac{1}{2} + 1\right)S_{1/2} = {}^2S_{1/2}$$

For a p-electron,

$$l = 1, s = 1/2$$

and

$$j = |l + s|, |l + s - 1|, ... |l - s|$$

$$= \left|1 + \frac{1}{2}\right|, \left|1 + \frac{1}{2} - 1\right|$$

$$= \frac{3}{2}, \frac{1}{2}$$

Only two levels are possible, one with $j = 3/2$ and other with $j = 1/2$. Hence the term symbols for the two energy levels are

$$\left(2 \times \frac{1}{2} + 1\right) P_{1/2} \text{ and } \left(2 \times \frac{1}{2} + 1\right) P_{3/2} \text{ or } {}^2P_{1/2} \text{ and } {}^2P_{3/2}$$

The value of j for various p-energy levels are shown in Fig. 21.10. If an electron in 1s energy level absorbs energy and gets excited to the 2p state, it has two options corresponding to two j levels and therefore the selection rule is $\Delta j = 0$ or ± 1. On applying this selection rule, we get

$$1s\left(j = \frac{1}{2}\right) \longrightarrow 2p\left(j = \frac{1}{2}\right); \ \Delta j = 0$$

$$1s\left(j = \frac{1}{2}\right) \longrightarrow 2p\left(j = \frac{3}{2}\right); \ \Delta j = +1$$

Thus both these transitions are allowed and the spectrum of hydrogen shows one line for each of these transitions.

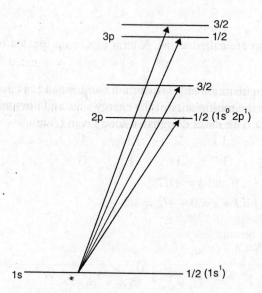

Fig. 21.10 Splitting of p states into two energy levels corresponding to two values of j

Multi-Electron Systems

Here we will discuss the spectrum of multi-electron atoms which have more than one electron in their outermost orbit. In such cases, the energy states are effected because of interelectronic interactions. We shall discuss only the Russel-Saunders coupling, also known as L-S coupling. This method is applicable to lighter elements.

In this method, it is assumed that the orbital angular momenta of all the electrons combine to give the total orbital angular momentum, L. Similarly, the spin angular momenta of the electrons combine to give the total spin angular momentum S. The resultant angular momentum and spin angular momentum for electrons 1 and 2 are given by Clebsch-Gordan series as

$$L = \left|(l_1 + l_2)\right|, \left|(l_1 + l_2 - 1)\right|, \ldots \ldots \left|(l_1 - l_2)\right| \qquad \ldots(21.34)$$

$$S = \left|(s_1 + s_2)\right|, \left|(s_1 + s_2 - 1)\right|, \ldots \ldots \left|(s_1 - s_2)\right| \qquad \ldots(21.35)$$

For two p electrons (p^2 configuration) for which $l_1 = l_2 = 1$, can combine in three ways as shown in Fig. 21.11.

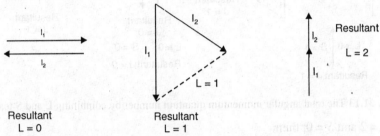

Fig. 21.11 The total angular momentum for two p electrons (p^2 configuration)

Since each electron has $s = 1/2$, therefore (Fig. 21.12) $S = 1$ and 0. The state $S = 1$ is usually described by saying that the two vectors are parallel and the state $S = 0$ by saying that they are antiparallel.

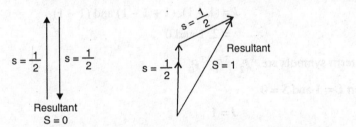

Fig. 21.12 For two electrons ($s = 1/2$) only two total spin states are permitted

It has been shown that for a p^2 configuration, the resultant orbital quantum number values of $L = 2$, 1 and 0 and the resultant spin quantum number values of $S = 1$ and 0 are obtained. The different values of L and S may now be coupled to give the total angular momentum quantum number J whose permitted values are given by the Clebsch-Gordan series as

$$J = |L + S|, |L + S - 1|, |L + S - 2|, \ldots .|L - S|$$

The total angular momentum quantum number J may also be obtained by coupling L and S (Fig. 21.13).
The vectors S and L can combine in various ways as follows:

(*i*) When $L = 2$, and $S = 1$,

$$J = |L + S|, |L + S - 1| \ldots \ldots |L - S|$$

$$= 3, 2, 1$$

Therefore, the term symbols are $^3D_3$, $^3D_2$ and $^3D_1$.

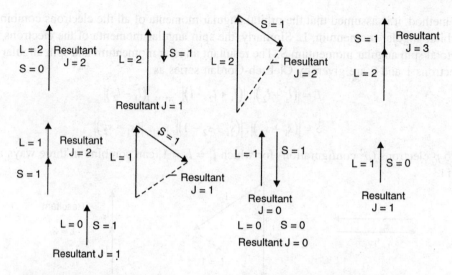

Fig. 21.13 The total angular momentum quantum number by combining L and S terms

When $L = 2$ and $S = 0$, then

$$J = 2 + 0 = 2$$

The term symbol is $^1D_2$

(ii) When $L = 1$ and $S = 1$

$$J = (1 + 1), (1 + 1 - 1) \text{ and } (1 - 1)$$
$$= 2, 1 \text{ and } 0$$

The term symbols are $^3P_2$, $^3P_1$, $^3P_0$

When $L = 1$ and $S = 0$

$$J = 1$$

The term symbol is $^1P_1$

(iii) When $L = 0$, $S = 1$

$$J = 1$$

The term symbol is $^3S_1$

When $L = 0$, $S = 0$

$$J = 0$$

The term symbol is $^1S_0$

Thus the total spectroscopic term symbols for p^2 configuration are

$$^3D_3, {}^3D_2, {}^3D_1, {}^1D_2, {}^3P_2, {}^3P_1, {}^3P_0, {}^1P_1, {}^3S_1, {}^1S_0.$$

All the spectroscopic terms derived from p^2 configuration may occur in the excited state of carbon in which two p electrons occupy different subshells (say $2p^1$ and $3p^1$). However, in the ground state, the number of states are restricted by Pauli Exclusion Principle, according to which, no two electrons in an atom can have all the four quantum numbers identical. In the ground state C is $1s^2\ 2s^2\ 2p^2$, the p

electrons have the same value of $n = 2$ and $l = 1$, so they must differ in at least one of the other quantum numbers m_l or m_s. This restriction reduces the number of terms for p^2 from six ($^1S, {}^1P, {}^1D, {}^3S, {}^3P, {}^3D$) to three ($^1S, {}^3P, {}^1D$) only.

The stability of various Russel-Saunders states resulting from the same electron configuration can be described by means of a set of rules, which are as follows:

1. Of the Russel-Saunders state arising from a given electron configuration those with the largest value of S lie lowest, next with the next largest and so on. In other words, the states with the largest multiplicities are most stable, *i.e.*, it is the lowest energy state.

2. The group of terms with a given value of S, those with the largest value of L lies lowest. Thus ^3P state is of lowest energy and is the ground state. The next higher state is ^1D (because it has greater L value) and then comes ^1S state.

3. The state with given values of S and L in a configuration consisting of less than half the electrons in a completed subgroup, the state with the smallest value of J is usually the most stable, and for a configuration consisting of more than half the electrons in a subgroup the state with the largest value of J is the most stable. Thus out of $^3P_2, {}^3P_1$ and $^3P_0$ states, $^3P_0$ will be having lowest energy.

If we apply these rules to p^2 configuration of carbon atom which are $^1S, {}^3P$ and ^1D, we observe that ^3P is the state with triplet multiplicity ($2S + 1 = 3$). This is the ground state. Between the ^1S and ^1D states, according to second condition, ^1D state (with $L = 2$) is more stable than ^1S state (with $L = 0$ and $S = 0$). Therefore, the order of energy is $^3P < {}^1D < {}^1S$. The ^3P state has three terms *viz.*, $^3P_0, {}^3P_1$ and $^2P_1$ because of J values are 2, 1 and 0. For the third condition, $^3P_0$ is the lowest energy (P^2 configuration of C is less than half filled). This arrangement of energy level is shown in Fig. 21.14.

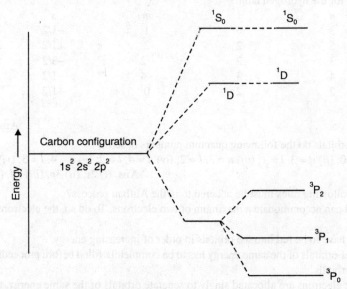

Fig. 21.14 Splitting of terms in carbon ground state

EXERCISES

1. For subatomic particles, which of the following statements concerning the uncertainty principle are correct?
    (*i*) When we try to gain precise information about the position of the particle, its momentum becomes uncertain.
    (*ii*) If we attempt to determine its exact momentum, the position becomes uncertain.
    (*iii*) Simultaneous accurate determinations of both the position and the momentum are possible.
    (*iv*) None of these.

    Ans. (*i*) and (*ii*) are correct.

2. Which of the following statements concerning the wave function ψ are correct?
    (*i*) ψ must be finite and single valued for all values of the coordinates.
    (*ii*) ψ must be continuous function of the coordinates.
    (*iii*) $\int \psi^2 d\tau$ must be finite when the integration is carried out over the whole of space, of which $d\tau$ is a small volume element.
    (*iv*) $\dfrac{d\psi}{dx}, \dfrac{d\psi}{dy}, \dfrac{d\psi}{dz}$ must be continuous functions of x, y and z respectively.

    Ans. All of them.

3. Which of the following statements concerning the function of two quantum numbers n and l with respect to an orbital are correct?
    (*i*) n determines the shape of an orbital.
    (*ii*) l determines the size of an orbital.
    (*iii*) n determines the size of an orbital.
    (*iv*) l determines the shape of an orbital.
    (*v*) n determines the number of lobes of electron density in orbital.

    Ans. Correct statements: (*iii*) and (*iv*).

4. Which of the following combinations of quantum numbers represent permissible solutions of the Schrödinger wave equation for the hydrogen atom?

	n	l	m	s
(*i*)	3	0	1	−1/2
(*ii*)	5	2	2	+1/2
(*iii*)	3	2	−2	−3/2
(*iv*)	4	3	−4	−1/2
(*v*)	2	2	0	+1/2

    Give reasons.

    Ans. Only (*ii*) is correct.

5. What type of orbitals do the following quantum numbers describe?
    (*i*) $n = 2, l = 0$; (*ii*) $n = 3, l = 1$; (*iii*) $n = 3, l = 2$; (*iv*) $n = 4, l = 2$; (*v*) $n = 4, l = 3$; (*vi*) $n = 5, l = 2$.

    Ans. (*i*) 2*s*, (*ii*) 3*p*, (*iii*) 3*d*, (*iv*) 4*d*, (*v*) 4*f*, (*vi*) 5*d*.

6. Which of the following rules must be adhered to in the Aufbau process?
    (*i*) An orbital can accommodate a maximum of two electrons. To do so, the electrons must be of opposite spin.
    (*ii*) Electrons have to be fed into the orbitals in order of increasing energy.
    (*iii*) Each set of orbitals of the same energy has to be completely filled before proceeding to the next orbital or set of orbitals.
    (*iv*) Whenever electrons are allocated singly to separate orbitals of the same energy, the electrons must all have the same spin.

    Ans. All of them.

7. (a) Would a spectral line be observed in the following transitions?
   (i) $2s \rightarrow 1s$, (ii) $3p - 2p$, (iii) $2p_x \rightarrow 2p_y$, (iv) $2p \rightarrow 2s$.
   (b) How many unpaired electrons are there in the electronic structure of Mn, Fe, Co, Ni and Zn?
   Ans. Mn-3, Fe-4, Co-3, Ni-2, Zn-0.

8. Explain, giving reasons, the following:
   (i) In a period, the átomic radius decreases with increasing atomic number.
   (ii) Ground state electronic configuration of copper ($Z = 29$) is [Ar] $4s^1 3d^{10}$ and not [Ar] $4s^2 3d^9$ while that of Cr ($Z = 24$) is [Ar] $4s^1 3d^5$ and not [Ar] $4s^2 3d^4$.
   (iii) The first ionization potential of Al ($Z = 13$) is less than that of Mg ($Z = 12$).
   (iv) The atomic radii of Zr ($Z = 40$) and Hf ($Z = 72$) are nearly equal.
   (v) In a group, ionization, energy and electron affinity decrease from top to bottom while in a period they increase from left to right.
   (vi) Chemical periodicity is a consequence of Pauli's exclusion principle.
   (vii) The 18-electron fluorine molecule is more reactive than the 18-electron molecule of argon.
   (viii) The ionization energy of nitrogen is greater than that of oxygen.
   (ix) If each is travelling at the same velocity, an electron has a larger wavelength than a proton.
   (x) Fe^{3+} ion is more stable than Fe^{2+} ion.
   (xi) First ionization energy of B is less than that of Be but the third ionization energy of Be is much higher than that of B.

9. (a) The ground state electronic configuration of an element with atomic number 32 is given by [Ar] $3d^{10}$ $4p^4$ or [Ar] $4s^2 3d^{10} 4p^2$ or [Ar] $4s^2 3d^9 4p^3$ or [Ar] $3d^6 4s^2 4p^6$. Select the correct configuration.
   (b) What is the ground state configuration of Cu^{2+} ion?
   Ans. (a) [Ar] $4s^2 3d^{10} 4p^2$ (b) [Ar] $3d^9$.

10. How many electrons can be accommodated into the orbitals that comprise (i) the second and (ii) the third quantum shells?   **Ans.** (i) 8, (ii) 18.

11. List the principal and azimuthal quantum numbers of electrons in the following orbitals:
    (i) 4s, (ii) 2d, (iii) 3f, (iv) 3p, (v) 5f.

    Which of these are not permissible? Explain.
    Ans. (i) $n = 4, l = 0$; (ii) $n = 2, l = 2$;
    (iii) $n = 3, l = 3$; (iv) $n = 3, l = 1$;
    (v) $n = 5, l = 3$. 2d and 3f are not permissible.

12. Arrange the following sets of atoms in order of increasing atomic radius:
    (i) Na, Mg, K and Rb;   (ii) Mg, Ge, Si, Ca and Sn;
    (iii) Br, Cl, C and O;   (iv) Li, B, N and F;
    (v) Be, N, F and Ca.
    Ans. (i) Mg < Na < K < Rb, (ii) Si < Mg < Ge < Ca < Sn, (iii) O < C < Cl < Br,
    (iv) F < N < B < Li, (v) F < N < Be < Ca.

13. Which one of the following pairs will have a larger radius?
    (i) Li^+ or Be^{2+}, (ii) Na or Na^+, (iii) O^{2-} or O^-, (iv) O^- or F, (v) B^{3+} or Be^{2+}.
    Ans. (i) Li^+, (ii) Na, (iii) O^{2-}, (iv) O^-, (v) Be^{2+}.

14. Arrange the following sets of atoms in order of increasing ionization energy.
    (i) Mg, Si, S and Cl, (ii) K, Cs, Rb and Ca, (iii) Li, Be, K and Rb, (iv) Cs, W, Cr and Fe.
    Ans. (i) Mg < Si < S < Cl, (ii) Cs < Rb < K < Ca.
    (iii) Rb < K < Li < Be, (iv) Cs < W < Cr < Fe.

15. Elements with unpaired electrons are paramagnetic in behaviour. In the series: N, O, Al, K, He, Ca, Ba, Co, Fe and Na, list out the elements which are expected to be paramagnetic.
    Ans. N, O, Al, K, Co, Fe and Na.

16. M^+ is a monovalent cation containing 18 electrons.

   (*i*) Write down the electronic configuration of M^+ and M.

   (*ii*) Indicate the position of M in the periodic table.

   (*iii*) Compare the ionization energies and sizes of M^+ with X and Y^-, where X is an atom and Y^- a monovalent anion. X and Y^- both contain 18 electrons.

   Ans. (*i*) $M = 1s^2\,2s^2\,2p^6\,3s^2\,3p^6\,4s^1$,

   $M^+ = 1s^2\,2s^2\,2p^6\,3s^2\,3p^6$.

   (*ii*) M is a member of first group in the periodic table.

   (*iii*) Ionization energies decrease in the order $Y^- < X < M^+$.

17. What is wavelength of a car with a mass of 1.3×10^3 kg moving at a speed of 10 ms^{-1}?

   Ans. 5.1×10^{-38} m.

18. If the wavelength of an electron is 0.5 nm, what is the velocity of the electron? **Ans.** 1.4×10^6 ms^{-1}.

19. Calculate λ for an electron moving with a velocity equal to one-tenth of light. In which region of the electromagnetic spectrum would this value of λ fall? Use 9.1×10^{-31} kg as the rest mass of the electron.

   Ans. 2.42×10^{-2} nm, γ-ray region.

20. The α-particles emitted from radium have an energy of 4.8 MeV. What is the de Broglie wavelength of these α-particles? **Ans.** $\lambda = 6.6 \times 10^{-15}$ m.

21. Consider a particle having a mass m located in a one-dimensional potential energy well with infinitely high walls. The wave function describing this system is given by

$$\psi_n(x) = K \sin \frac{n\pi x}{a} \quad \text{for } 0 \le x \le a.$$

   where K is a constant and $n = 1, 2, 3, \ldots$ Determine KK^*. **Ans.** $KK^0 = a/2$.

22. Show that the wave functions $\psi_{n'}(x) = K' \cos \dfrac{n\pi x}{a}$ and $\psi_n(x) = K \sin \dfrac{n\pi x}{a}$ are orthogonal.

23. (*a*) Calculate the permitted energies of an electron confined in a box 0.1 nm wide.

   (*b*) If the box is 1 cm wide, what are the permitted values of electron energies?

   Ans. (*a*) $E_1 = 38$ eV, $E_2 = 152$ eV, $E_3 = 342$ eV and $E_n = 38\,n^2$ eV.

   (*b*) $E_1 = 38 \times 10^{-16}$ eV, $E_2 = 152 \times 10^{-16}$ eV and $E_n = 38 \times 10^{-16}\,n^2$ eV.

24. A steel ball weighing 10 g is rolling on a smooth floor of a 10 cm wide box with a speed of 3.3 cms^{-1}. Calculate the quantum number of the energy level. Would you consider energy of the ball to be continuous or discontinuous? Give reasons. **Ans.** $n = 10^{29}$, energy would be continuous.

25. What is the degeneracy of the level for which $E = \dfrac{14h^2}{8ma^2}$? **Ans.** 6 fold.

26. The electrons in a vacuum tube are confined in a box between filament and plate which is 0.1 cm in width. Compute the spacings between energy levels in this situation. **Ans.** $\Delta E = 6.0 \times 10^{-32}$ J.

27. What does the term degenerate orbitals mean? How many degenerate orbitals are there in oxygen? Does helium have any degenerate orbitals?

   Ans. Three $2p$ orbitals in oxygen are degenerate orbitals. In helium there is none.

28. What is ψ? What informations are conveyed by ψ and ψ^2? Represent ψ^2_{2s} in two different ways.

29. Distinguish the following:

   (*i*) Matter waves from electromagnetic waves.

   (*ii*) Orbit from orbital.

(*iii*) Significance of ψ and ψ².

(*iv*) Motion of a particle in a box from the motion of a free particle.

(*v*) Hund's rule from Pauli's exclusion principle.

30. Write down the Schrödinger's wave equation. Explain the significance of the terms involved.

31. Write notes on:

(*i*) de Broglie rule; (*ii*) Uncertainty principle; (*iii*) Pauli's exclusion principle; (*iv*) Aufbau principle; (*v*) Hund's rule; (*vi*) Ionization potential; (*vii*) Electron affinity; (*viii*) Screening effect.

The Chemical Bonding

22.1 INTRODUCTION

One of the fundamental questions in chemistry is the nature of the forces which hold the atoms together to form a molecule. The first attempt in this direction was made by Berzelius in 1812 who suggested that all chemical combinations take place between atoms having opposite charges. In 1952, Frankland suggested that an atom of an element had a certain combining capacity known as the valence of the atom. Thus chlorine, oxygen, nitrogen and carbon have valencies of 1, 2, 3 and 4 respectively. In 1904, Abegg pointed out that in the periodic table a large number of elements could be assigned a negative valency and a positive valency, the sum of which was eight. Drude in 1905 pointed out that the number of loosely bound electrons in an atom gives the positive valency of the atom while the number of electrons that an atom can accept represents the negative valency. Thus it was necessary to know the number of electrons in each atom, *i.e.*, the atomic number of the element. This knowledge became available by the work of Moseley in 1913. It was noted in the development of the structure of atom that the inert gases have electronic configuration $s^2 p^6$; all the inert gases contain eight electrons in their valence shell (except helium which contains only two electrons). This electronic configuration represents a state of maximum stability and hence minimum energy.

Element	Atomic number	Electronic configuration
He	2	2
Ne	10	2, 8
Ar	18	2, 8, 8
Kr	36	2, 8, 18, 8
Xe	54	2, 8, 18, 18, 8
Rn	86	2, 8, 18, 32, 18, 8

Atoms of all other elements have a tendency to acquire this configuration of eight electrons in their outermost shell. They do so either by the transfer of electrons from one atom to another, or by mutual sharing of electrons. This is the fundamental idea of the electronic theory of valency.

In dealing with the combination of atoms of elements generally the bonds are classified into three types, *viz.*, (*i*) ionic or electrovalent bonds, (*ii*) covalent bonds, and (*iii*) metallic bonds.

22.2 IONIC OR ELECTROVALENT BOND

Kossel and Lewis in 1916 independently suggested that all atoms tend to attain the inert gas configuration either by gaining or losing the electrons. Thus in sodium chloride, the sodium atom has the electronic configuration $1s^2 2s^2 2p^6 3s^1$. This can acquire an inert gas configuration by losing an electron from the outermost shell to become Na^+. Since the sodium atom has a small ionization energy of about 5 eV and a small electron affinity of about 0.5 eV, therefore it easily loses an electron to form Na^+

$$Na \rightarrow Na^+ + e^-$$

On the other hand, chlorine atom has the electronic configuration $1s^2 2s^2 2p^6 3s^2 3p^5$. It may acquire the stable inert gas configuration by accepting an electron. Since the chlorine atom has a large ionization energy of more than 10 eV and a large electron affinity of about 4 eV, so it can easily gain an electron

$$Cl + e^- \rightarrow Cl^-$$

Thus when sodium and chlorine atoms are brought together sodium atom donates an electron to chlorine atom, and the resulting ions combine as Na^+Cl^-. These ions are held together by strong electrostatic attractions between the oppositely charged ions. The bond so formed between these two ions is known as the ionic or electrovalent bond. This may be represented as follows:

$$Na + \cdot \overset{\cdot\cdot}{Cl} : \longrightarrow [Na^+] \begin{bmatrix} \overset{\cdot\cdot}{:} \overset{\cdot\cdot}{Cl} : \end{bmatrix}^-$$

In a similar way, a calcium atom ($1s^2 2s^2 2p^6 3s^2 3p^6 4s^2$) may lose two electrons to two chlorine atoms ($1s^2 2s^2 2p^6 3s^2 3p^5$) forming a calcium ion Ca^{2+} and two chloride ions, Cl^-, that is, calcium chloride. Showing the valence electrons only, this may be represented as

$$\begin{matrix} \cdot \overset{\cdot\cdot}{Cl} : \\ \\ Ca + \qquad \longrightarrow [Ca^{2+}] \\ \\ \cdot \overset{\cdot\cdot}{Cl} : \end{matrix} \qquad \begin{bmatrix} \overset{\cdot\cdot}{:} \overset{\cdot\cdot}{Cl} : \end{bmatrix}^- \\ \begin{bmatrix} \overset{\cdot\cdot}{:} \overset{\cdot\cdot}{Cl} : \end{bmatrix}^-$$

Hence, the ionic bonds are formed by the transfer of one or more electrons from one atom to another and the ions so formed are held together by electrostatic attractions. Because of this electrostatic nature of the bonds, the bond between the ions is called ionic or electrovalent bond.

22.3 BORN-LANDE EQUATION—CALCULATION OF LATTICE ENERGY

In a diatomic molecule, if there is a large difference in electronegativities of atoms, a complete transfer of electrons from atom with lower electronegativity to the atom with higher electronegativity takes place. This results in the formation of an ionic bond. This is the case with gaseous alkali metal halides. In crystalline sodium chloride one cannot, however, think of NaCl molecules since the stable arrangement is a three-dimensional crystal structure of Na^+ and Cl^- ions. The existence of a sodium chloride molecule can be visualised only in the vapour phase in which Na^+ ions and Cl^- ions are bounded by electrostatic attractions between oppositely charged ions. If Z_1e and Z_2e are the charges on a pair of ions in a single molecule which are separated by a distance r, then the electrostatic potential energy is given by $-Z_1Z_2e^2/r$. The effect of this term is to draw the ions together, *i.e.*, the system tends to attain lower potential energy. If the ions are brought so close together that their electron clouds begin to overlap, a mutual repulsion between the two nuclei becomes evident. The repulsive forces increase rapidly as r increases. The potential energy due to repulsion has been given by Born and Meyer as

$$U_{\text{rep}} = \frac{b}{r^n}$$

where b is an empirical constant and depends on the structure and n is a constant called the Born exponent and is a large number usually between 6 and 12. Thus, the total energy holding the crystal together is U, the lattice energy and may be written as

$$U = -\frac{Z_1Z_2\,e^2}{r} + \frac{b}{r^n} \qquad \ldots(22.1)$$

In Fig. 22.1, the potential energy U is plotted against the internuclear distance between the ions. The figure shows that the total potential energy is zero when the two ions are infinitely separated from each other, *i.e.*, $U = 0$, when $r = \infty$. As the ions are brought closer (r decreases), the attractive forces come into play and the potential energy decreases as shown by the dotted line. When the two ions are brought so close to each other that their electron clouds begin to overlap appreciably, the repulsion sets in and it increases the potential energy markedly as indicated by the dotted line in the figure. The net potential energy is the sum of attraction and repulsion potentials and is shown by the solid line in the curve. The solid line shows a minimum in the curve corresponding to a distance r_0 and the lowest potential energy U_0. At this position the minimum potential energy becomes numerically equal to the lattice energy of the crystal which is defined as *the energy released when requisite number of gaseous ions of opposite charges are brought from an infinite distance to form a mole of an ionic crystal*. It is thus equal in magnitude but opposite in sign to the *energy of dissociation of the crystal*.

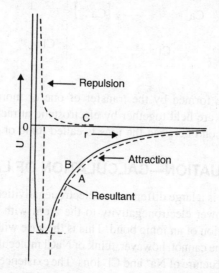

Fig. 22.1 Potential energy diagram for ionic bonding

Equation (22.1) gives the potential energy of interaction of an isolated pair of ions and is different from the energy of a pair of ions in a crystal lattice. Therefore, in order to calculate the total potential energy, one must consider the mutual interaction of other ions from a given ion pair. When these interaction energies are summed up over all the pairs of ions, then the total energy is given by

$$U = -\frac{AZ_1Z_2e^2}{r} + \frac{B'}{r^n} \qquad ...(22.2)$$

where A is a constant called *the Madelung constant*, and B' is another empirical constant. The Madelung constant is the geometric correction factor which takes into account the geometry and spacing of the ions in the crystal lattice. For a mole of ions, Eq. (22.2) becomes

$$U = -\frac{N_A AZ_1Z_2e^2}{r} + \frac{B}{r^n} \qquad ...(22.3)$$

where N_A is the Avogadro constant and B is equal to $N_A B'$. The value of B is calculated using the fact that U is minimum at $r = r_0$, the equilibrium distance in the crystal, *i.e.*,

$$\left(\frac{dU}{dr}\right)_{r=r_0} = 0$$

Differentiation of Eq. (22.3) with respect to r gives

$$\frac{dU}{dr} = +\frac{N_A AZ_1Z_2e^2}{r^2} - \frac{nB}{r^{n+1}}$$

Setting this equal to zero at $r = r_0$ and solving for B, we obtain

$$B = \frac{N_A AZ_1Z_2e^2}{n} r_0^{n-1}$$

Substituting the value of B in Eq. (22.3) gives

$$U = -\frac{N_A AZ_1Z_2e^2}{r_0} + \frac{N_A AZ_1Z_2e^2}{nr_0^n} r_0^{n-1}$$

$$U = -\frac{N_A AZ_1Z_2e^2}{r_0}\left(1 - \frac{1}{n}\right) \qquad ...(22.4)$$

This equation is called the Born-Lande equation. It allows the lattice energy to be calculated from the knowledge of the geometry of the crystal and hence Madelung constant, Z_1, Z_2 and the inter ionic distance. In SI units, equation (22.4) becomes

$$U = -\frac{N_A AZ_1Z_2e^2}{4\pi\varepsilon^0 r_0}\left(1 - \frac{1}{n}\right)$$

If n is about 10, then this equation shows that the repulsive forces reduce the attractive forces between the ions by about 10%.

For alkali metal halides, $Z_1 = Z_2 = 1$, hence from Eq. (22.4), we get

$$U = -\frac{N_A Ae^2}{r_0}\left(1-\frac{1}{n}\right) \qquad \qquad ...(22.5)$$

The experimental determination of the crystal energy is somewhat difficult to measure. However, this can be calculated from the thermochemical data by a cyclic process called *Born-Haber cycle*. It is based on the first law of thermodynamics and assumes that the ionic crystal may be formed either (*a*) by the combination of the respective constituent elements, or (*b*) the reactants are vapourized, the gaseous atoms are converted into ions and the gaseous ions are then combined to form the crystal. The process may be explained by considering the energetics of the formation of sodium chloride

$$Na(s)+\frac{1}{2}Cl_2(g)\xrightarrow[\Delta H_f]{-410.5\ kJ} Na^+Cl^-(s)$$

$$\frac{1}{2}Cl_2\xrightarrow[121.3\ kJ]{+D/2} Cl(g)\xrightarrow[-380.4\ kJ]{E_a} Cl^-(g)$$

$$Na(s)\xrightarrow[108.6\ kJ]{+S} Na(g)\xrightarrow[497.8\ kJ]{+I} Na^+(g)$$

$$-U_c = 757.8\ kJ$$

The enthalpy of formation (ΔH_f) of a mole of solid sodium chloride from its constituents, Na(*s*) and $1/2\ Cl_2(g)$ is -410.5 kJ mol^{-1}. In the second process the different steps involved in the formation are as follows:

(*i*)   Formation of the gaseous sodium atom from solid sodium. This process is known as sublimation and the energy required is referred to as the sublimation energy (S).

(*ii*) Removal of the outermost valence electron from gaseous sodium atom producing gaseous sodium ion. For this process a certain amount of energy, called the ionization energy (I), is supplied.

(*iii*) The diatomic chlorine molecules are dissociated producing gaseous chlorine atoms. The energy supplied for this process is the dissociation energy (D).

(*iv*) The electron is added to a gaseous chlorine atom to form a chloride ion. The process is accompanied by the liberation of energy and is called the electron affinity E_a.

(*v*)   The final step is the formation of solid crystal from gaseous ions. In this process a certain amount of energy called the crystal or lattice energy (U_c) is given out.

Thus from the above cycle we have

$$\Delta H_f = S + I + \frac{1}{2}D + E_a + U_c \qquad \qquad ...(22.6)$$

$$U_c = \Delta H_f - \left(S + I + \frac{1}{2}D + E_a\right)$$

$$= -410.5 - (108.6 + 497.8 + 121.3 - 380.4)\ kJ\ mol^{-1}$$

$$= -757.8\ kJ\ mol^{-1}$$

The value computed for U_c from the experimental values of the quantities on the right hand side of Eq. (22.6) has been found to be -757.8 kJ mol^{-1} and agrees fairly well with the value of -754.1 kJ mol^{-1} predicted by Eq. (22.5).

Lattice energies of some typical alkali metal halides and alkaline earth oxides and sulphides are given in Table 22.1. As can be seen from the table that the magnitude of the lattice energy depends both on the charge and size of the ions. On comparing the lattice energy of a series of alkali or alkaline earth compounds having same anion, we find that the lattice energy decreases as we move down a group.

Table 22.1 Crystal Energies $(-U_c)$ for the Alkali Metal Halides, the Alkaline Earth Oxides and Sulphides (kJ mol^{-1})

Alkali metal cation	F$^-$	Cl$^-$	Br$^-$	I$^-$	Alkaline earth metal cation	O^{2-}	S^{2-}
Li$^+$	994.8	802.6	760.8	710.6	Be^{2+}	4514	3734
Na$^+$	894.5	748.4	714.8	668.8	Mg^{2+}	3929	3253
K$^+$	790.2	681.4	656.3	618.7	Ca^{2+}	3490	5018
Rb$^+$	756.7	660.6	631.3	597.7	Sr^{2+}	3307	2872
Cs$^+$	719.0	618.7	593.6	564.3	Ba^{2+}	3123	2743

On the other hand, it increases with increasing ionic charge as may be noted from its higher value for alkaline earth metal oxides or sulphides than those of alkali metal halides.

22.4 CHARACTERISTICS OF ELECTROVALENT OR IONIC COMPOUNDS

Some of the important characteristics of ionic compounds are:

(*i*) Due to strong coulombic forces between the ions, the electrovalent compounds are hard crystalline solids possessing low volatility and having high melting and boiling points. In general, the hardness increases with decrease in internuclear distances.

(*ii*) Since the ions in the solids are not free to move because of strong electrostatic forces amongst them, therefore, they are poor conductors of electricity in the solid state. However, they become good conductor of electricity in molten state or in solution.

(*iii*) They are soluble in polar solvents having high dielectric constant, *e.g.*, water. In these solvents the interionic attractions between the ions are weakened and they get separated from one another. In non-polar solvents, however, the ionic compounds are insoluble.

(*iv*) Electrovalent compounds having the same electronic configuration exhibit isomorphism.

22.5 COVALENT BOND

We have stated in the last section that electron transfer from atom of lower ionization potential to atom of high electron affinity results in the formation of an ionic bond. However, such an explanation cannot account for the formation of simple diatomic molecules like H_2, N_2, Cl_2 etc. In such cases the atoms are identical and have the same ionization potential and the same electron affinity. To overcome this difficulty, G.N. Lewis in 1916 proposed that a bond between two atoms can be formed by mutual sharing of a pair of electrons. This sharing takes place in such a way that the participating atoms achieve the stable inert gas configuration. The bond thus formed is termed as a covalent bond. In hydrogen molecule, each hydrogen atom by sharing its electron can attain the stable inert gas configuration of helium resulting in the formation of a covalent bond. This is shown as

$$H_x + H^{\cdot} \rightarrow H \overset{x}{\cdot} H$$

A number of other examples can be cited. For example, in CH_4, carbon has four electrons in the outermost shell and thus needs four more electrons to complete its octet. These four electrons may be obtained from four hydrogen atoms as follows:

$$\underset{x}{\overset{x}{x}} C x + 4H^{\cdot} \longrightarrow H \overset{\cdot}{x} \underset{\cdot x}{\overset{H}{\underset{H}{C}}} \overset{x \cdot}{x} H$$

22.6 BORN-OPPENHEIMER APPROXIMATION

In this approximation it is supposed that the nuclei are much heavier than electrons and therefore electrons move much faster than nuclei in a molecule. We can therefore think of the nuclei as being stationary (fixed) while the electrons move relative to them. This approximation is quite good for ground state molecules. The total energy can be considered as the sum of the energies due to rotational, vibrational and electronic motions

$$E = E_{rot} + E_{vib} + E_{ele}$$

According to Born-Oppenheimer approximation, the kinetic energy term due to nucleus will be zero and the repulsion term between nucleus will be constant. This approximation allows us to write separate Schrödinger equation for electronic and nuclear motions. The electronic Schrödinger equation can be solved exactly and gives us how the energy of the molecule varies with bond length. The curve so obtained is called a molecular potential energy curve. A typical potential energy curve is illustrated in Fig. 22.2. Once the curve has been determined experimentally, we can identify the equilibrium bond length (at the minimum of the curve) and the bond dissociation energy D_o which is closely related to the depth of the minimum below the energy of the infinitely separated atoms.

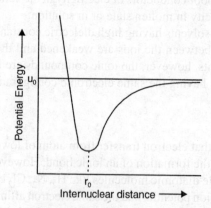

Fig. 22.2 Potential energy curve for the hydrogen molecule

22.7 THE VALENCE BOND THEORY

In valence bond theory the starting point is the concept of the shared electron pair. We see how to write the wave function for such a pair and how it is extended to account for the structures of a large number of molecules. This theory gives us the concept of σ and π bonds.

The system of hydrogen molecule consists of two electrons and two protons. Suppose the electron 1 is associated with proton A and the electron 2 with proton B. The corresponding structure would be represented by $H_A(1)\, H_B(2)$ and the orbital wave functions are given by $\Psi_A(1)$ and $\Psi_B(2)$ respectively. The electron in each hydrogen atom is in $1s$ orbital (lowest energy), the wave functions $\Psi_A(1)$ and $\Psi_B(2)$ are chosen as $1s$ functions. The total orbital wave function for the separated atoms is the product of the two wave functions

$$\psi_I = \psi_{1S_A}^{(1)}\, \psi_{1S_B}^{(2)} \qquad\qquad ...(22.7)$$

This wave function is exact for atoms so widely separated that the electrons do not interact with one another. The energy E of the system can be calculated using the equation

$$E = \frac{\int \psi_I H \psi_I d\tau}{\int \psi_I^2 d\tau} \qquad\qquad ...(22.7(a))$$

where Ψ_I is the wave function given by Eq. (22.7) and H is the hamiltonian given by

$$H = -\frac{h^2}{8\pi^2 m}\left(\nabla_1^2 + \nabla_2^2\right) + U \qquad\qquad ...(22.8)$$

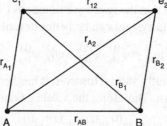

Fig. 22.3 Coordinates in the hydrogen molecule. The two protons are denoted by A and B

In this equation m is the mass of the electron, ∇_1^2 and ∇_2^2 refer to the coordinates of the two electrons and U is the potential energy of the molecule and is calculated from Fig. 22.3 as

$$U = -\frac{e^2}{r_{A_1}} - \frac{e^2}{r_{A_2}} - \frac{e^2}{r_{B_1}} - \frac{e^2}{r_{B_2}} + \frac{e^2}{r_{12}} + \frac{e^2}{r_{AB}}$$

The value of energy E thus obtained if plotted against the internuclear distance between the two atoms is shown in Fig. 22.4. However, the curve shows a minimum with a lowering of energy about 24 kJ mol^{-1}. The equilibrium interatomic distance is calculated to be 90 pm. The result indicates that the wave function Ψ_I gives a very poor agreement between the observed and the calculated values. This means that the assumption used in trial wave function Ψ that electron 1 resides on hydrogen atom A and electron 2 resides on atom B is not acceptable.

When the two atoms are within bonding distance of each other, the electrons interact with one another and the above wave function therefore is an approximation to the true wave function.

However, when the atoms are close, it is difficult to know whether the electron 1 resides on A or electron 2, because the electrons are indistinguishable. Therefore, an equally valid wave function is

$$\psi_{II} = \psi_{1S_A}^{(2)} \, \psi_{1S_B}^{(1)} \qquad \qquad ...(22.9)$$

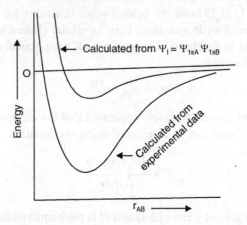

Fig. 22.4 The binding energy of the H_2 molecule based on the

wave function $\psi_1 = \psi_{1S_A}^{(1)} \, \psi_{1S_B}^{(2)}$

Here, electron 2 resides on atom A and electron 1 on atom B. This concept was introduced by Heitler and London in 1927. They pointed out that the two wave functions (Ψ_I and Ψ_{II}) given above are equally probable, therefore the true state of the system can be better described as

$$\psi_{VB} = \psi_{1s_A}^{(1)} \, \psi_{1s_B}^{(2)} \pm \psi_{1s_A}^{(2)} \psi_{1s_B}^{(1)} \qquad \qquad ...(22.10)$$

The + and − combinations are equally valid. However, it has been found that the combination with lower energy is the one with a +ve sign. Therefore, the valence bond wave function for H_2 molecule is

$$\psi_S = \psi_{1s_A}^{(1)} \psi_{1s_B}^{(2)} + \psi_{1s_A}^{(2)} \, \psi_{1s_B}^{(1)} \qquad \qquad ...(22.11)$$

$$\psi_A = \psi_{1s_A}^{(1)} \psi_{1s_B}^{(2)} - \psi_{1s_A}^{(2)} \psi_{1s_B}^{(1)} \qquad \qquad ...(22.11(a))$$

The wave function Ψ_S is called the symmetric wave function and does not change if indices 1 and 2 are interchanged. However, the wave function Ψ_A changes to $-\Psi_A$ when the indices are interchanged and is known as antisymmetric wave function.

Using these wave functions Heitler and London calculated the energy of the hydrogen molecule as a function of the internuclear distance between the two atoms. This is shown in Fig. 22.5. It is to be noted from the curve that the function Ψ_S leads to a minimum in the curve indicating the formation of a stable molecule. The curve obtained using the wave function Ψ_A fails to show a minimum, and as would be expected, it represents an unstable state. It is evident from these energy curves that Ψ_S represents a bonding state while Ψ_A represents a repulsive or non-bonding state.

It is thus clear that a covalent bond is formed between two atoms that share a pair of electrons (using the wave function Ψ_S). Since these two electrons are in $1s$ orbital (ground state), the Pauli exclusion principle demands that the spin of the two electrons must be opposite, *i.e.*, one must have the spin + 1/2 and the other −1/2. Hence the covalent bond is formed only when the spins are antiparallel.

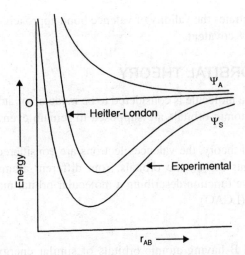

Fig. 22.5 The binding energy of the H_2 molecule based on the Heitler-London wave function

Thus the Pauli principle requires the wave function of two electrons to change sign when the labels of two electrons are interchanged. The valence bond wave function for electrons is

$$\Psi_{1,2} = \left\{ \Psi_{A(1)}\Psi_{B(2)} + \Psi_{A(2)}\Psi_{B(1)} \right\} s(2,1)$$

where s represents the spin component of the wave function. When the labels are interchanged, we get

$$\Psi_{2,1} = \left\{ \Psi_{A(2)}\Psi_{B(1)} + \Psi_{A(1)}\Psi_{B(2)} \right\} s(2,1)$$

$$= \left\{ \Psi_{A(1)}\Psi_{B(2)} + \Psi_{A(2)}\Psi_{B(1)} \right\} s(2,1)$$

However, the Pauli principle requires that $\Psi_{2,1} = -\Psi_{1,2}$
which is satisfied only if

$$s(2,1) = s(1,2)$$

The calculated bonding energy from valence bond treatment is 303.3 kJ mol^{-1} at an internuclear distance of 0.080 nm. This result is much better than that obtained using simple wave function as given by Eq. (22.7). This improvement in the result has been observed by introducing the concept of electron exchange between the two atoms. Thus the difference in energy calculated by using the wave function Ψ_S [Eq. (22.11)] and Ψ_I [Eq. (22.7)] is known as the exchange energy.

The value calculated above is still far below the expected value of 436.0 kJ mol^{-1}. Therefore, this trial wave function again requires modification. A new wave function is then designed keeping in mind the following features:

(a) The two electrons mutually shield one another from the nuclear charge. Hence the effective nuclear charge value Z^* must be used, instead of $Z = 1$.

(b) When orbitals overlap, they are no longer spherically symmetrical.

(c) Both the electrons may be simultaneously associated with one of the two nuclei thereby giving two possible ionic structures as $H_{A2}^{-1}H_B^+$ and $^+H_A H_{B2}^{-1}$

With these refinements, the bond energy and bond distance values are found to be 388 kJ mol^{-1} and 74.9 pm respectively. This brings the bond energy and bond distance values very close to experimental values. This clearly demonstrates the validity of valence bond approach. This theory also shows that no bond is 100% ionic or 100% covalent.

22.8 MOLECULAR ORBITAL THEORY

In the valence bond theory, a molecule is considered to be made up of atoms. Electrons in atom occupy atomic orbitals. Thus the atomic orbitals are supposed to remain even when the atom is chemically bonded in a molecule.

In the molecular orbital theory, the valence electrons are considered to be associated with all the nuclei in the molecule. Thus the atomic orbitals from different atoms must be combined to form molecular orbitals. The wave function describing a molecular orbital may be obtained by linear combination of atomic orbitals (LCAO).

LCAO Method

Consider two atoms A and B having atomic orbitals of similar energy and described by the wave functions Ψ_A and Ψ_B respectively. When atoms approach each other, the electron clouds of these two atoms overlap, then the wave function for the molecule (molecular orbital Ψ_{AB}) can be obtained by a linear combination of atomic orbitals Ψ_A and Ψ_B

$$\Psi_{MO, AB} = N(C_1\Psi_A + C_2\Psi_B)$$

where N is a normalising constant and C_1 and C_2 are constants so as to give a minimum energy for Ψ_{AB}. If atoms A and B are similar, then C_1 and C_2 will have similar values. If atoms A and B are same, then C_1 and C_2 are equal.

In hydrogen molecule, the electron 1 would be associated with both the nuclei (A and B) and the system is described by the sum of two $1s$ atomic orbitals

$$\psi_I = \psi_{1s_A}^{(1)} + \psi_{1s_B}^{(1)} \qquad \qquad ...(22.12)$$

Similarly, for electron 2

$$\psi_{II} = \psi_{1s_A}^{(2)} + \psi_{1s_B}^{(2)} \qquad \qquad ...(22.13)$$

The wave functions in Eqs. (22.12) and (22.13) are similar to atomic orbitals, but contain all the nuclei in the molecule and is, therefore, called molecular orbital (MO). An MO is constructed by the combination of two atomic orbitals. This method is usually known as *linear combination of atomic orbitals (LCAO)*. The product wave function is constructed to describe both the electrons

$$\psi_{MO} = \psi_I \psi_{II} = \left[\psi_{1s_A}^{(1)} + \psi_{1s_B}^{(1)} \right]\left[\psi_{1s_A}^{(2)} + \psi_{1s_B}^{(2)} \right]$$

$$= \psi_{1s_A}^{(1)} \psi_{1s_A}^{(2)} + \psi_{1s_A}^{(2)} \psi_{1s_B}^{(1)} + \psi_{1s_A}^{(1)} \psi_{1s_B}^{(2)} + \psi_{1s_B}^{(1)} \psi_{1s_B}^{(2)}$$

$$= \psi_{1s_A}^{(1)} \psi_{1s_A}^{(2)} + \psi_{1s_B}^{(1)} \psi_{1s_B}^{(2)} + \psi_S \qquad \qquad ...(22.14)$$

where Ψ_S is given by Eq. (22.11). The functions $\psi_{1s_A}^{(1)} \psi_{1s_A}^{(2)}$ and $\psi_{1s_B}^{(1)} \psi_{1s_B}^{(2)}$ represent the possibility of both electrons being associated with the same nucleus at the same time. That is, both electrons are placed in the same MO which is formed by the sum of two Ψ_{1s} atomic orbitals. Two electrons can go into such an orbital according to Pauli exclusion principle (provided they have antiparallel spins). The chemical structure corresponding to these two wave functions can be written as

$$H_{A(2)}^{-(1)}H_B^+ \text{ and } H_{B(2)}^{-(1)}H_A^+$$

These structures are known as ionic structures and contribute slightly to the overall structure of the hydrogen molecule.

The binding energy (258.7 kJ at 0.085 nm) calculated using Ψ_{MO} functions gives only a qualitative agreement with the experimental value (458.1 kJ at 0.0747 nm). The fact that the result yields stable molecule indicates that the model should be fairly reasonable. The simple LCAO-MO wave function given by equation (22.14) can be improved by introducing an effective nuclear charge and including the excited state wave functions.

22.9 COMPARISON BETWEEN VALENCE-BOND AND MOLECULAR ORBITAL METHODS

From the above discussions it is clear that the valence bond method starts with individual atoms and considers the interactions between them. Also, the electrons are indistinguishable and, therefore, the wave functions

$$\psi_{1s_A}^{(1)} \ \psi_{1s_B}^{(2)}$$

and

$$\psi_{1s_A}^{(2)} \ \psi_{1s_B}^{(1)}$$

for hydrogen molecule are equivalent. The valence bond wave function is given by

$$\Psi_{VB} = \psi_{1s_A}^{(1)} \ \psi_{1s_B}^{(2)} + \psi_{1s_A}^{(2)} \ \psi_{1s_B}^{(1)}$$

On the other hand, the molecular orbital approach of the molecules starts with two nuclei. The wave function of electron (1) on nuclei A and B is given as an LCAO

$$\psi_I = \psi_{1s_A}^{(1)} + \psi_{1s_B}^{(1)}$$

Similarly for electron 2

$$\psi_{II} = \psi_{1s_A}^{(2)} + \psi_{1s_B}^{(2)}$$

The combined wave function is the product of two wave functions

$$\Psi_{MO} = \Psi_I \Psi_{II}$$

$$= \left[\psi_{1s_A}^{(1)} + \psi_{1s_B}^{(1)} \right]\left[\psi_{1s_A}^{(2)} + \psi_{1s_B}^{(2)} \right]$$

$$= \psi_{1s_A}^{(1)} \ \psi_{1s_A}^{(2)} + \psi_{1s_B}^{(1)} \ \psi_{1s_B}^{(2)} + \psi_S \qquad \qquad ...(22.15)$$

Comparing Ψ_{VB} with Ψ_{MO} one notices that Ψ_{MO} gives more weightage to configuration that places both electrons on the same nucleus giving ionic structures. For example, in case of a molecule AB, the two ionic structures A^+B^- and A^-B^+ also contribute to the overall structure of the molecule. Such ionic contributions are neglected in valence-bond approach. In hydrogen molecule, since the results of VB approach are better than MO approach indicating that such terms are not of considerable importance and may not be included. However, in heteroatomic molecules, such ionic structures contribute to the structure of the molecule and are very important. Therefore these should be included in the wave functions. Thus one can say that VB approach considerably underestimates the ionic terms whereas the MO approach considerably emphasizes these terms. The true ionic contribution is actually somewhere between the two extremes. The VB wave function can be refined by including the contributions from these ionic structures, and MO wave function can be adequately improved by smaller contributions from such structures.

22.10 MOLECULAR ORBITALS FOR HOMONUCLEAR DIATOMIC MOLECULES

In case of a homonuclear diatomic molecule, the MO's are constructed from the linear combination of atomic orbitals. If Ψ_A and Ψ_B are two atomic orbitals, then the MO would be given by

$$\Psi_{MO} = C_1 \Psi_A + C_2 \Psi_B \qquad \qquad ...(22.16)$$

where C_1 and C_2 are the coefficients chosen to give the lowest energy for the molecular orbital. Since the molecule is symmetrical, so $C_1 = \pm C_2$, hence the two MO's are

$$\Psi_g = \Psi_A + \Psi_B \qquad \qquad ...(22.17)$$

and
$$\Psi_u = \Psi_A - \Psi_B \qquad \qquad ...(22.18)$$

In case of hydrogen molecule, the atomic orbitals are 1s and the two bonding and antibonding molecular orbitals are

$$\Psi_g = \Psi_{1s_A} + \Psi_{1s_B} \qquad \qquad ...(22.17(a))$$

$$\Psi_u = \Psi_{1s_A} - \Psi_{1s_B} \qquad \qquad ...(22.18(b))$$

The probability density of the electron in hydrogen molecule is proportional to the square of its wave function. This is given as

$$\Psi_g^2 = N^2 \left[\psi_{1s_A} + \psi_{1s_B} \right]^2$$

$$= N^2 \left[\psi_{1s_A}^2 + \psi_{1s_B}^2 + 2\psi_{1s_A} \psi_{1s_B} \right]$$

Since
$$\psi_{1s_A} = \left(\frac{1}{\pi a_0^3} \right)^{1/2} e^{-r_A/a_0}$$

where r_A is the distance of electron from A.

Similarly
$$\psi_{1s_B} = \left(\frac{1}{\pi a_0^3} \right)^{1/2} e^{-r_B/a_0}$$

It is easy to evaluate Ψ and hence Ψ^2, the probability density at any point.

From the above equation, it is observed that the probability density is proportional to the sum of

(i) $\Psi_{1s_A}^2$, the probability density if the electron confined to orbital on A

(ii) $\Psi_{1s_B}^2$, the probability density if the electron confined to orbital on B

(iii) $2\Psi_{1s_A}\Psi_{1s_B}$ is important and gives an extra contribution to the density as it arises because of the overlap between two atomic orbitals. This is sometime called overlap density. It represents an enhancement of the probability of finding the electron in the internuclear region. Since the electron is free to move over the whole nuclear framework, therefore the electron density increases in the internuclear region. This increase in the probability in this range amounts to constructive interference of the atomic orbitals. Each orbital has positive amplitude in this range so the total amplitude is greater than if the electrons were confined to a single atomic orbital.

The wave function Ψ_g is *symmetric, i.e.*, its sign or the magnitude remains unchanged by inverting through the mid-point of two nuclei. This wave function is therefore denoted by g, which stands for *gerade* (even). In this case Ψ is unchanged when the orbital is reflected about its centre (*i.e.*, axes x, y and z are replaced by $-x$, $-y$ and $-z$). The second wave function Ψ_u is *antisymmetric, i.e.*, it changes sign by inverting through midpoint of the two nuclei. It is denoted by u means *ungerade*. In Ψ_g the two orbitals that overlap are in the same phase in the region between two nuclei. This corresponds to the concentration of the electron density between the two nuclei resulting in an attractive interaction. Such orbitals are called bonding orbitals and are designated by 1s σ_g. On the other hand, Ψ_u results if the two atomic orbitals are in the opposite phase. It leads to a depletion of electron density between the two nuclei resulting in a strong repulsion between the nuclei. For antisymmetric wave function

$$\Psi_u = N\left[\psi_{1s_A} - \psi_{1s_B}\right]$$

The probability density for this wave function is written as

$$\Psi_u^2 = N^2\left[\psi_{1s_A}^2 + \psi_{1s_B}^2 - 2\psi_{1s_A}\psi_{1s_B}\right]$$

The last term in the above expression reduces the probability of finding the electron between the nuclei relative to its value if the electron were confined to one of the atomic orbitals. This reduction in probability density can be expressed in reduction in amplitude, *i.e.*, they interfere destructively where they overlap. Such interference helps to raise the energy of the molecule relative to the separated atoms. Such orbitals are called antibonding orbitals and are often labelled with an asterisk (*) to the orbital. These molecular orbitals are shown in Fig. 22.6.

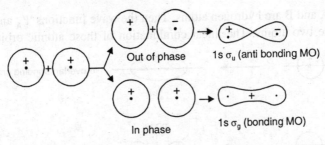

Out of phase   1s σ_u (anti bonding MO)

In phase   1s σ_g (bonding MO)

Fig. 22.6 Formation of MO's by linear combination of 1s orbitals

The relative energies of the two molecular orbitals and the atomic orbitals are shown in Fig. 22.7. The energy of the bonding MO is lower than that of the atomic orbital by an amount Δ, known as stabilization energy. Similarly, the energy of the antibonding MO is higher by the same amount Δ.

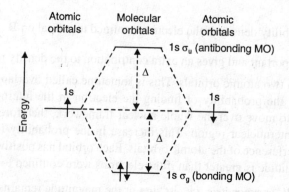

Fig. 22.7 Molecular orbital energy diagram for orbitals formed from $1s$ orbitals

The corresponding orbitals are added if the two orbitals of plus sign overlap; they are subtracted from one another if the positive region of one orbital overlaps with the negative region of the other. In Fig. 22.8, the probability density is plotted against the internuclear distance for bonding and antibonding orbitals. It is clear that the electron density calculated using the wave function ψ_g is higher in the region between the nuclei whereas the electron cloud is found to be very thin when ψ_u is used. Thus the build up of the electron density between the nuclei is the characteristic of bonding or attractive state while depletion of charge density between the nuclei corresponds to an antibonding or a repulsive state.

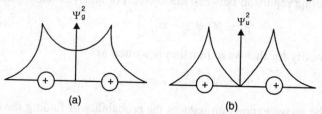

Fig. 22.8 Probability densities of (a) bonding and (b) antibonding states of H_2

22.11. OVERLAPPING OF ORBITALS

s-s Combination of Orbitals

Consider that atoms A and B are hydrogen atoms. Then the wave functions Ψ_A and Ψ_B describe the $1s$ atomic orbitals on the two atoms. The linear combination of these atomic orbitals give rise to two

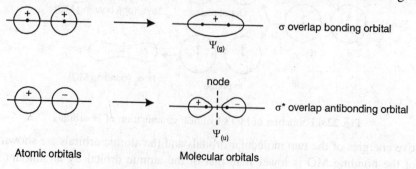

Fig. 22.9 Combination of s-s atomic orbitals

molecular orbitals; one bonding orbital (Ψ_g) and the other antibonding orbital (Ψ_u). The number of molecular orbitals produced must always be equal to the number of atomic orbitals involved. The bonding molecular orbital is lower in energy than the original atomic orbitals, whereas the antibonding molecular orbital is higher in energy. These MO's are depicted in Fig. 22.9.

s-p Combination of Orbitals

Let us study the molecular orbitals obtained by the combination of s and p atomic orbitals. An s orbital may combine with a p orbital provided that the lobes of p orbital are pointing along the axis joining the nuclei. When the lobes of s and p_x orbitals have the same sign, the molecular orbital produced is bonding molecular orbital with increased electron density whereas the antibonding molecular orbital results when the lobes are of opposite sign (Fig. 22.10). The antibonding MO are with a reduced electron density in between the nuclei.

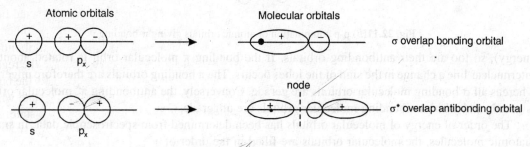

Fig. 22.10 Combination of s-p atomic orbitals

p-p Combination of Orbitals

As the two lobes of a p orbital are pointed along the axis joining the nuclei, lead to σ bonding as well as σ^* antibonding molecular orbitals. The formation of these orbitals depends on the nature of the signs of the wave function (Fig. 22.11(a)).

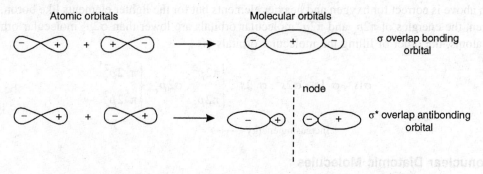

Fig. 22.11(a) p-p combination of atomic orbitals giving σ bonding

Now let us confine our attention to the combination of two p orbitals which are perpendicular to the internuclear axis and may overlap broad side on. The lateral overlap of these orbitals may be constructive or destructive and results in a π bonding or a π^* antibonding molecular orbitals (Fig. 22.11(b)). The two $2p_x$ orbitals overlap to give π_x bonding and π_x^* antibonding orbitals and two $2p_y$ orbitals overlap to give π_y bonding and π_y^* antibonding orbitals. The π_x and π_y bonding orbitals are degenerate (have

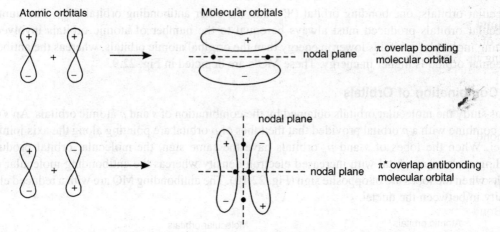

Atomic orbitals   Molecular orbitals

Fig. 22.11(*b*) p-p combination of atomic orbitals giving π-bonding

energy), so too are their antibonding orbitals. If the bonding π molecular orbit is rotated about the internuclear line a change in the sign of the lobes occurs. The π bonding orbitals are therefore ungerade, whereas all σ bonding molecular orbitals are gerade. Conversely, the antibonding π* molecular orbital is gerade and all σ* antibonding molecular orbitals are ungerade.

The order of energy of molecular orbitals has been determined from spectroscopic data. In simple diatomic molecules, the molecular orbitals are filled in the order of

$$\sigma 1s^2, \sigma^* 1s^2, \sigma 2s^2, \sigma^* 2s^2, \sigma 2p_x^2, \begin{cases} \pi 2p_y^2 \\ \pi 2p_z^2 \end{cases}, \begin{cases} \pi^* 2p_y^2 \\ \pi^* 2p_z^2 \end{cases}, \sigma^* 2p_x^2$$

Increasing energy ⟶

The energies of σ2p and π2p molecular orbitals are very close. The order of molecular orbitals shown above is correct for oxygen and heavier elements but for the lighter elements like boron, carbon, nitrogen, the energies of $\pi 2p_y$ and $\pi 2p_z$ molecular orbitals are lower than $\sigma 2p_x$ molecular orbital. For these atoms, the order of filling the molecular orbitals is

$$\sigma 1s^2, \sigma^* 1s^2, \sigma 2s^2, \sigma^* 2s^2, \begin{cases} \pi 2p_y^2 \\ \pi 2p_z^2 \end{cases}, \sigma 2p_x^2, \begin{cases} \pi^* 2p_y^2 \\ \pi^* 2p_z^2 \end{cases}$$

Increasing energy ⟶

Homonuclear Diatomic Molecules

Molecular orbitals are filled in with electrons according to Aufbau principle and Hund's rule, *i.e.*, the molecular orbitals having the lowest energy are filled in first while that having the highest energy are filled in at the end. Pauli exclusion principle is being obeyed while electrons are filled in the molecular orbitals.

H_2^+ molecule ion: It has only one electron and therefore its molecular orbital configuration can be written as σ1s^1. The electron occupies the σ1s bonding molecular orbital. The energy of this ion is lower than that of hydrogen atom (constituent atom) and therefore this species exists.

Bond order: Bond order is defined as the number of covalent bonds between the two combining atoms of a molecule and is equal to one-half of the difference between the number of electrons in the bonding molecular orbitals and in the antibonding molecular orbitals. Thus

$$\text{Bond order} = \frac{1}{2} \text{ (number of bonding electrons—number of antibonding electrons)}$$

The bond order for H_2^+ ion $= \frac{1}{2}(1-0) = \frac{1}{2}$

H_2-molecule: Each hydrogen atom contributes one electron. So the two electrons go to the lower energy $\sigma 1s$ bonding orbital giving electronic configuration as $\sigma 1s^2$. This can be represented in Fig. 22.12.

The Bond order for H_2 molecule $= \frac{1}{2}(2-0) = 1$.

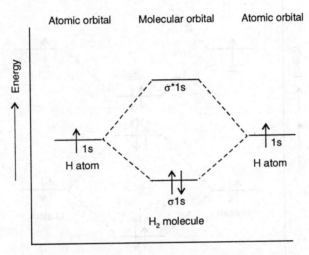

Fig. 22.12 Electronic configuration for hydrogen molecule

He_2^+ molecule: Since He_2^+ molecule has 3 electrons, which can be arranged in the molecular orbitals as $\sigma 1s^2 \cdot \sigma^* 1s^1$. The one electron is in antibonding orbital. Overall the molecule is stable and therefore He_2^+ molecule can exist.

The bond order for He_2^+ molecule is $\frac{1}{2}(2-1) = \frac{1}{2}$.

He_2 molecule: In He_2 molecule, each He atom contributes two electrons giving a total of four electrons. Two of the electrons can enter the bonding molecular orbital and the next two must enter the antibonding molecular orbital. The stabilization energy 2Δ derived from filling the bonding molecular orbital is cancelled by 2Δ destabilization energy derived from antibonding molecular orbital. The ground state electronic configuration of He_2 is $\sigma 1s^2 \sigma^* 1s^2$. The bonding and antibonding orbitals are equally filled and there is no net decrease in the energy as compared to helium atoms. Hence He_2 molecule does not exist.

The bond order for He_2 molecule is $\frac{1}{2}(2-2) = 0$.

Li₂ molecule: Each lithium atom has two electrons in its inner $1s$ orbital and one electron in the outer $2s$ orbital making a total of six electrons. These six electrons in lithium molecule can be arranged as $\sigma 1s^2 \, \sigma^* 1s^2 \, \sigma 2s^2$. The filled $\sigma 1s^2$ and $\sigma^* 1s^2$ do not contribute to the bonding (as shown in He₂). The electrons in these orbitals could be collectively represented as KK and hence the configuration of Li₂ is KK $\sigma 2s^2$. Now each lithium atom supplies one valence electron which filled the bonding $\sigma 2s$ orbital to give a bonding configuration. Li₂ molecule has been found to exist in the vapour state. This is shown in Fig. 22.13.

The bond order for Li₂ molecule is $\dfrac{1}{2}(2-0) = 1$.

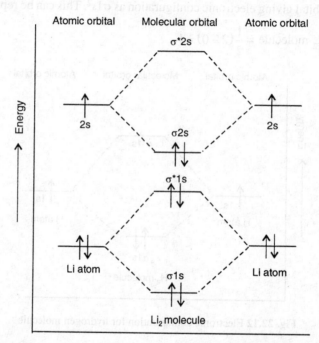

Fig. 22.13 Electronic configuration atomic and molecular orbitals for Li₂

Be₂ molecule: Each beryllium atom has four electrons; two electrons in the inner $1s$ orbital and other two electrons in the outer $2s$ orbital. Thus in Be₂ molecule there are eight electrons which can be arranged as $\sigma 1s^2 \sigma^* 1s^2 \sigma 2s^2 \sigma^* 2s^2$ or KK$\sigma 2s^2 \sigma^* 2s^2$. Again the effect of bonding $\sigma 2s$ and antibonding $\sigma^* 2s$ would cancel each other resulting in no net bond. Therefore, the molecule would not be expected to exist.

The bond order for Be₂ molecule $= \dfrac{1}{2}(2-2) = 0$.

B₂ molecule: Boron molecule has a total of 10 electrons and its molecular orbital configuration is

$$\text{KK } \sigma 2s^2 \cdot \sigma^* 2s^2 \begin{cases} \pi 2p_y^1 \\ \pi 2p_z^1 \end{cases}$$

Note that $\pi 2p$ orbitals are lower in energy than that of $\sigma 2p_x$ orbitals. Since $\pi 2p_y$ and $\pi 2p_z$ are degenerate, therefore they are singly occupied in accordance with Hund's rule (Fig. 22.14). The stabilization occurs due to the filling of $\pi 2p$ orbitals and hence B_2 exists. The bond order for B_2 molecule is $\frac{1}{2}(4-2) = 1$.

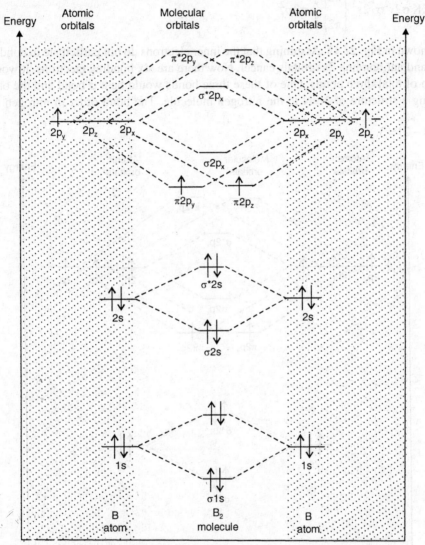

Fig. 22.14 Electronic configuration, atomic and molecular orbitals for boron

C_2 **molecule:** It has 12 electrons, each carbon atom contributes six electrons to the molecule. The

filling of molecular orbitals can be shown as $KK\,\sigma 2s^2 \sigma^* 2s^2 \begin{cases} \pi 2p_y^2 \\ \pi 2p_z^2 \end{cases}$. The molecule should be stable,

since two $\pi 2p$ bonding orbitals provide 4Δ stabilization energy. The bond order for C_2 molecule is

$\frac{1}{2}(6-2) = 2$.

N_2 molecule: In nitrogen molecule there are fourteen electrons which are arranged in molecular

orbitals as $KK \, \sigma 2s^2 \sigma^* 2s^2 \begin{cases} \pi 2p_y^2 \\ \pi 2p_z^2 \end{cases} \sigma 2p_x^2$

This is shown in Fig. 22.15. Assuming that the inner electrons do not participate in bonding and that the bonding and antibonding 2s orbitals cancel. Now there are six bonding electrons, it would result in the formation of total three bonds. One of these three bonds would be a σ bond and the other two are π bonds giving a structure of N≡N to the nitrogen molecule. The bond order in nitrogen molecule is

equal to $\dfrac{1}{2}(8-2) = 3$.

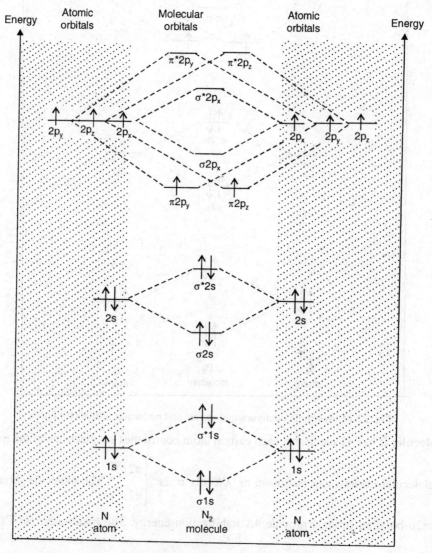

Fig. 22.15 Electronic configuration, atomic and molecular orbitals for nitrogen

O₂ molecule: In oxygen molecule there are 16 electrons in total. These are accommodated in the molecular orbitals as

$$KK\,\sigma 2s^2\sigma^*2s^2\sigma 2p_x^2 \begin{cases} \pi 2p_y^2 \\ \pi 2p_z^2 \end{cases} \begin{cases} \pi^*2p_y^1 \\ \pi^*2p_z^1 \end{cases}$$

This is shown in Fig. 22.16. According to Hund's rule π^*2p_y and π^*2p_z antibonding orbitals are singly occupied. Since the two unpaired electrons have parallel spins, therefore the oxygen molecule is paramagnetic in nature. A σ bond results from the filling of $\sigma 2p_x^2$. Since $\pi^*2p_y^1$ and $\pi^*2p_z^1$ are half-filled and therefore cancel half the effect of the completely filled $\pi 2p_y^2$ and $\pi 2p_z^2$ orbitals, thereby

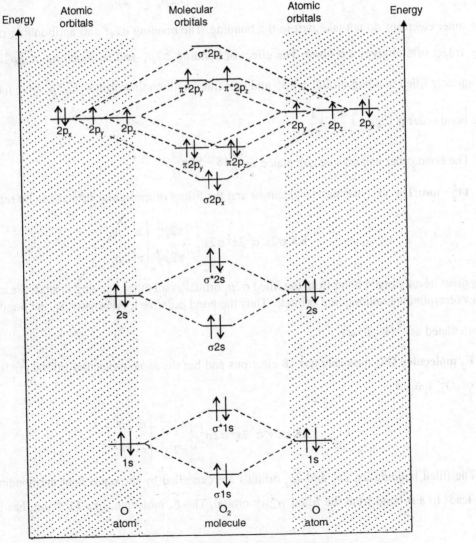

Fig. 22.16 Electronic configuration, atomic and molecular orbitals for oxygen

giving a 1 $\left(=\dfrac{1}{2}+\dfrac{1}{2}\right)$ bond. Therefore, the total bonds in oxygen molecule is 2. The bond order is equal

to $\dfrac{1}{2}(8-4)=2$.

O_2^- ion: O_2^- ion has $8 + 9 = 17$ electrons, one more than oxygen molecule. The extra electron occupies either π^*2p_y or π^*2p_z orbital. Since both these orbitals are degenerate (same energy), it does not matter in which it occupies. The molecular orbital configuration is therefore

$$KK\,\sigma 2s^2\sigma^*2s^2\sigma 2p_x^2 \begin{cases} \pi 2p_y^2 \\ \pi 2p_z^2 \end{cases} \begin{cases} \pi^*2p_y^2 \\ \pi^*2p_z^1 \end{cases}$$

The inner electrons do not take part in the bonding. The bonding $\sigma 2s^2$ and antibonding σ^*2s^2 cancel. The $\sigma 2p_x^2$ orbital gives a σ bond. The effect of bonding $\pi 2p_y^2$ and antibonding $\pi^*2p_y^2$ cancel. The completely filled bonding orbital $\pi 2p_z^2$ and half filled antibonding orbital $\pi^*2p_z^1$ give half a π bond.

The bond order is thus $1+\dfrac{1}{2}=1\dfrac{1}{2}$.

The bond order can also be calculated as $\dfrac{1}{2}(8-5)=\dfrac{3}{2}$.

O_2^{2-} ion: The O_2^{2-} ion has 18 electrons and the filling of molecular orbital can be represented as

$$KK\,\sigma 2s^2\sigma^*2s^2\,\sigma 2p_x^2 \begin{cases} \pi 2p_y^2 \\ \pi 2p_z^2 \end{cases} \begin{cases} \pi^*2p_y^2 \\ \pi^*2p_z^2 \end{cases}$$

This gives us only one σ bond from the filled $\sigma 2p_x$ orbital as all other bonding orbitals are cancelled by their corresponding antibonding orbitals. Thus the bond order is 1. Alternatively, the bond order may be calculated as $\dfrac{1}{2}(8-6)=1$.

F_2 molecule: This molecule has 18 electrons and has the same molecular orbital configuration as that of O_2^{2-} ion, i.e.,

$$KK\,\sigma 2s^2\sigma^*2s^2\,\sigma 2p_x^2 \begin{cases} \pi 2p_y^2 \\ \pi 2p_z^2 \end{cases} \begin{cases} \pi^*2p_y^2 \\ \pi^*2p_z^2 \end{cases}$$

The filled bonding $2s$, $2p_y$ and $2p_z$ orbitals are cancelled by the equivalent antibonding orbitals. This leads to a σ bond from the filled $\sigma 2p_x^2$ orbital. The F_2 molecule, like O_2^{2-} ion, has bond order one.

22.12   HETERONUCLEAR DIATOMIC MOLECULES

A heteronuclear diatomic molecule is a diatomic molecule formed from atoms of two different elements such as HF, HCl, CO, NO etc. The electron distribution, in such diatomic molecules in covalent bond, is not equally shared because the energies of their atomic orbitals are slightly different. This imbalance results in a polar bond. The bond in HF, for instance, is polar, with the electron pair closer to the more electronegative F atom. Because of this accumulation of electron pair near the F atom results in a net negative charge on the F atom. This negative charge is called a partial negative charge and denoted by δ^-. This is compensated by a partial positive charge δ^+ on the H atom.

HF molecule: The electronic configurations of the constituent atoms are

$$
\begin{array}{ll}
H & 1s^1 \\
F & 1s^2\, 2s^2\, 2p^5.
\end{array}
$$

The inner $1s$ and $2s$ electrons of fluorine do not participate in bonding since they are much lower in energy as compared to $1s$ orbital of hydrogen atom. The effective overlap is between $1s$ orbital of hydrogen and $2p_x$ orbital of fluorine, because $2p_x$ orbital being symmetrical about the internuclear axis. This results in the formation of a bonding and antibonding molecular orbital (Fig. 22.17). $\pi2p_y$ and $\pi2p_z$ orbitals have practically zero overlap with $1s$ orbital of hydrogen atom and are therefore non-bonding in HF. The molecular orbital configuration of HF molecule, having ten electrons, can be written as

$$
1s^2 2s^2 \sigma 2p_x^2 \pi 2p_y^2 \pi 2p_z^2
$$

The presence of 2 electrons in the bonding orbital results a bond order of one.

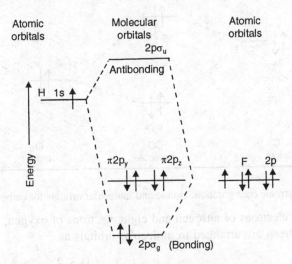

Fig. 22.17 Relative energeis of atomic and molecular orbitals in HF

CO molecule: The carbon atom (6 electrons) and oxygen atom (8 electrons) make a total of 14 electrons. The molecular orbital configuration can be represented as

$$
\sigma 1s^2 \sigma^* 1s^2 \sigma 2s^2 \, \sigma^* 2s^2 \sigma 2p_x^2 \left\{ \begin{array}{l} \pi 2p_y^2 \\ \pi 2p_z^2 \end{array} \right.
$$

This would result in the formation of one σ bond and two π bonds, thus giving a bond order of 3. This is shown in Fig. 22.18.

Due to different electronegativities of carbon and oxygen, the constituent atomic orbitals are of different energies, *i.e.*, the $2s$ atomic orbital of oxygen is lower in energy than the carbon orbital. Note that the bonding $\pi 2p$ orbitals of carbon monoxide are lower in energy than the $\sigma 2p_x$ orbital.

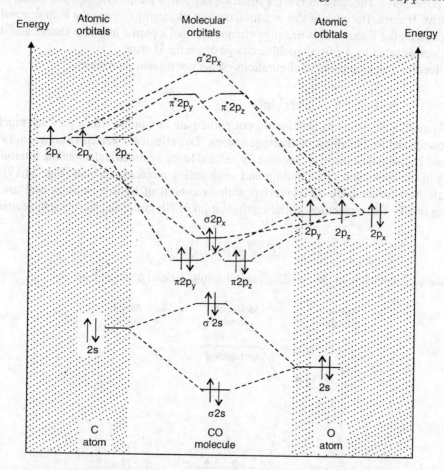

Fig. 22.18 Electronic configuration, atomic and molecular orbitals for carbon monoxide

NO molecule: Seven electrons of nitrogen and eight electrons of oxygen, making 15 electrons in NO molecule. These electrons are arranged in molecular orbitals as

$$\sigma 1s^2 \sigma^* 1s^2 \sigma 2s^2 \sigma^* 2s^2 \sigma 2p_x^2 \begin{cases} \pi 2p_y^2 \\ \pi 2p_z^2 \end{cases} \begin{cases} \pi^* 2p_y^1 \\ \pi^* 2p_z^0 \end{cases}$$

The inner shell is non-bonding. The bonding and non-bonding $2s$ orbitals cancel. $\sigma 2p_x^2$ results in the formation of a σ bond. A π bond is formed by the filled $\pi 2p_z^2$ orbital. The half filled $\pi^* 2p_y$ half cancels the filled $\pi 2p_y^2$ orbital, giving half a bond (Fig. 22.19). The bond order is thus $1 + 1 + \dfrac{1}{2} = 2\dfrac{1}{2}$

or $\dfrac{1}{2}(8-3) = 2.5$. The presence of an unpaired electron in $\pi^* 2p_y$ orbital is responsible for paramagnetic character of the molecule. This antibonding orbital weakens the bonding between nitrogen and oxygen and consequently, the bond in NO is weaker than in N_2 molecule.

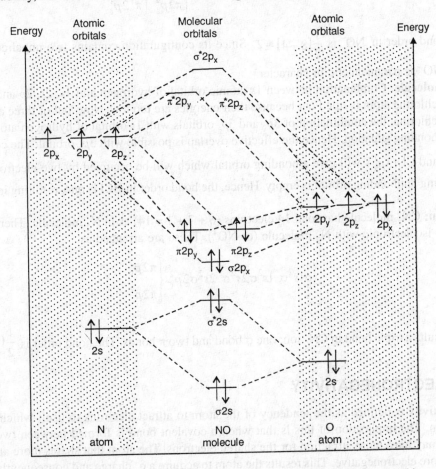

Fig. 22.19 Electronic configuration, atomic and molecular orbitals for nitric oxide

NO⁺ molecule: NO⁺ molecule has total 14 electrons. These electrons are arranged in molecular orbitals as

$$\sigma 1s^2 \sigma^* 1s^2 \sigma 2s^2 \sigma^* 2s^2 \sigma 2p_x^2 \left\{ \begin{array}{l} \pi 2p_y^2 \\ \pi 2p_z^2 \end{array} \right. \left\{ \begin{array}{l} \pi^* 2p_y^0 \\ \pi^* 2p_z^0 \end{array} \right.$$

The NO⁺ ion is isoelectronic with N_2 molecule. The inner shell is non-bonding. The bonding and non-bonding $2s$ orbitals cancel. $\sigma 2p_x^2$ gives a σ bond. One electron present in $\pi^* 2p^1$ in NO molecule is removed to give NO$^+$ molecule of the above configuration. Therefore, the bond order in NO$^+$ is $\frac{1}{2}(8-2)=3$ which represents one σ bond and two π bonds.

NO$^-$ ion: The additional electron in NO$^-$ will give an arrangement

$$KK\,\sigma 2s^2 \sigma^* 2s^2 \sigma 2p_x^2 \begin{cases} \pi 2p_y^2 \\ \pi 2p_z^2 \end{cases} \begin{cases} \pi^* 2p_y^1 \\ \pi^* 2p_z^1 \end{cases}$$

The bond order in NO$^-$ is $\frac{1}{2}[8-4]=2$. Since its configuration contains two unpaired electrons, therefore NO$^-$ is paramagnetic in character.

HCl molecule: Combination between 1s atomic orbital of hydrogen and 1s, 2s, 2p and 3s atomic orbitals of chlorine atom is ruled out because their energies are too low. Now, out of three available 3p orbitals of chlorine, the combination of $3p_y$ and $3p_z$ orbitals with 1s orbital of hydrogen atom will lead to the non-bonding situation. Hence the effective overlap is possible with $3p_x$ orbital. The combination of H $(1s^1)$ and Cl $(3p_x^1)$ will give a bonding orbital which will be occupied by two electrons; and the corresponding antibonding orbital is empty. Hence, the bond order in HCl is one, resulting in a stronger bond.

CN$^-$ ion: CN$^-$ molecule has total 14 electrons $(6 + 7 + 1 = 14)$ as in N$_2$ molecule. Therefore, CN$^-$ molecule is isoelectronic with N$_2$ molecule (or NO$^+$). These are arranged as

$$\sigma 1s^2 \sigma^* 1s^2 \sigma 2s^2 \sigma^* 2s^2 \sigma 2p_x^2 \begin{cases} \pi 2p_y^2 \\ \pi 2p_z^2 \end{cases}$$

This results a triple bond in CN$^-$ ion; one σ bond and two π bonds. The bond order is $\frac{1}{2}(8-2)=3$.

22.13 ELECTRONEGATIVITY

Electronegativity is defined as the tendency of the atom to attract electrons to itself which bind it to another atom. The implication of this is that when a covalent bond is formed between two different atoms, one may have more attraction for the shared electrons. The atom that shares more attraction is said to be more electronegative. This results the atom to acquire a δ^- charge and consequently the other atom will have a δ^+ charge. It should be noted that as the difference in the electronegativity between two atoms becomes greater, the ionic character of a chemical bond between these two atoms should also become greater. From our experience we can say that nearly pure ionic bonds are formed only between elements with extreme differences in electronegativity. Pauling pointed out that the electronegativity of an atom is a bond property and developed a scale based on bond energies. If E_{A-B} is the bond energy of a molecule AB and E_{A-A} and E_{B-B} are the bond energies of the homonuclear diatomic molecules A_2 and B_2, then Pauling defined Δ as the difference in energies between the actual bond energy of $A-B$ molecule and the geometric mean of the covalent energies of $A-A$ and $B-B$ molecules as

$$\Delta = (\text{actual bond energy}) - (E_{A-A} \cdot E_{B-B})^{\frac{1}{2}}$$

The quantity Δ is called the extra bond energy. If the bonding electrons were shared equally between two atoms, then Δ would be expected to be zero. However, the electrons are usually unsymmetrically distributed between the atoms and therefore the bond energy of AB molecule is always found to be greater than the geometric mean of the bond energies of A_2 and B_2. Pauling stated that the electronegativity difference between two atoms is equal to $0.208\sqrt{\Delta}$. This quantity $(0.208\sqrt{\Delta})$ was called the electronegativity difference between A and B by Pauling, *i.e.*

$$0.208\sqrt{\Delta} = X_A - X_B$$

where X_A and X_B are the electronegativities of atoms A and B respectively and factor 0.208 arises from the conversion of kcal to eV. It has been observed by Pauling that Δ values are not additive and therefore cannot be used to calculate the other values of Δ. However, Pauling noted that the values of $\sqrt{\Delta}$ were approximately additive. On Pauling's scale, fluorine is the most electronegative atom and is assigned a value of about 4 units. Caesium, on the other hand, is the least electronegative atom having a value of about 0.7 unit. Some of the values of the electronegativity of elements are given in Table 22.2. Pauling introduced the idea that the ionic character of a bond varies with the difference in electronegativity. It has been found that if the electronegativity difference between the atom is about 1.7, then the bond is about 50% in ionic character. Larger the difference in electronegativity, more ionic is the bond. When the difference in the electronegativity is less than 1.7, the bond is more covalent than ionic.

Table 22.2 Electronegativity Values on Pauling Scale

H						
2.1						
Li	Be	B	C	N	O	F
1.0	1.5	2.0	2.6	3.0	3.4	4.0
Na	Mg	Al	Si	P	S	Cl
0.9	1.2	1.6	1.9	2.2	2.58	3.1
K	Ca					
0.8	1.0		Ge	As	Se	Br
			2.0	2.2	2.55	2.9
Rb	Sr					
0.8	1.0		Sn	Sb	Te	I
			1.9	2.0	2.1	2.7
Cs	Ba					
0.7	0.9					

A more physical approach to the concept of electronegativity is due to **Mullikan**. He defined electronegativity in terms of ionization potential and electron affinity of an atom. According to him the electronegativity of an element is the arithmetic mean of the first ionization potential of atom and its electron affinity. Thus

$$A \rightarrow A^+ + e^- \; ; I_A$$
$$A + e^- \rightarrow A^- \; ; E_A$$

and Electronegativity $= \dfrac{I_A + E_A}{2}$

Ionization potential and electron affinity in this definition must refer to the valence states of the atom.

Mullikan and Pauling values of electronegativity are approximately related to each other by an expression

$$X_B^M - X_A^M = 2.78 \left(X_B^P - X_A^P \right)$$

where the superscripts M and P refer to Mullikan and Pauling scales respectively.

The percentage ionic character of a covalent bond can be calculated from the electronegativity values of the atoms using the empirical relation due to Hannay and Smyth

Percentage of ionic character $= 16(X_B - X_A) + 3.5 \, (X_B - X_A)^2$ (22.19)

It has been found that if $X_B - X_A \simeq 2.1$, the bond is 50% ionic in character. A larger difference in electronegativity leads to more than 50% ionic character, whereas a relatively small difference in electronegativity essentially leads to a covalent character of the bond.

22.14 DIPOLE MOMENT

When a bond is formed between two atoms of different electroneutrality, the more negative atom acquires a negative charge leaving a small positive charge on the less electronegative atom. Thus a heteronuclear diatomic molecule may be an electric dipole and will have a permanent dipole moment μ. If a charge $+q$ is separated from a charge $-q$ by an interatomic distance r, then the dipole moment μ is given by

$$\mu = qr$$

The dipole moment is a vector quantity and is represented by an arrow pointing from negative to the positive charge. For example, in HF molecule, the fluorine atom which is more electronegative than hydrogen acquires a small negative charge and hydrogen atom a small positive charge. This constitutes a permanent dipole as $H^{\delta+} \ldots\ldots F^{\delta-}$.

Larger the difference in the electronegativity of the two atoms, greater would be the polarity of the bond. The extent of polarity of a bond is expressed in terms of dipole moment. For more details see section 25.4.

22.15 STRUCTURE OF POLYATOMIC MOLECULES

So far we have studied the formation of a covalent bond by the overlapping of orbitals. The s orbitals are spherically symmetrical and hence there is no directional characteristic. Therefore, they overlap equally in all directions. However, when p or d orbitals are involved the electron density which is highest only along a particular axis, the maximum overlapping results if the bond is formed in that direction. Consequently, in such cases the directional characteristics of the bond formation are eminent and the molecules formed have characteristic shapes. As an example, consider first the formation of

water molecule. The electronic configuration of oxygen atom is $1s^2 \, 2s^2 \, 2p_x^2 \, 2p_y^1 \, 2p_z^1$. The two mutually perpendicular $2p_y$ and $2p_z$ orbitals are half filled and are available for bonding. Two bonding σ orbitals, each accommodating two electrons, are formed through the overlapping of these atomic orbitals with

$1s$ atomic orbitals of hydrogen atom. Because $2p_y$ and $2p_z$ orbitals lie at 90° to each other, the two σ bonds also lie at 90° to each other. We can therefore predict that H_2O molecule should be angular, which it is. However, the actual bond angle is 104.5° (Fig. 22.20). The discrepancy has been attributed to mutual repulsion between the hydrogen atoms. Due to the electronegativity difference between oxygen and hydrogen the O–H bonds are not pure covalent but possess partial ionic character. This makes hydrogen atoms slightly electron deficient leading to repulsion between them and extending the H–O–H bond angle from 90° to 104.50°. In other related molecules like H_2S, H_2Se and H_2Te the bond angles have been found to be 92.02°, 91° and 89.5° respectively fairly close to the predicted value of 90°. In these cases it is assumed that the repulsion between hydrogen atoms decreases due to the decrease in the electronegativity of the atoms and larger bond lengths.

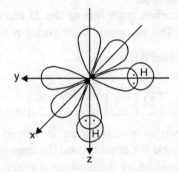

Fig. 22.20 Formation of water molecule by the overlapping of
$2p$ orbitals of oxygen and $1s$ orbitals of hydrogen

A similar reasoning explains the formation of NH_3 molecule. Nitrogen atom ($1s^2\, 2s^2\, 2p_x^1 2p_y^1 2p_z^1$) can form three equivalent mutually perpendicular bonds through the overlapping of its orbitals with three $1s$ orbitals of hydrogen atoms (Fig. 22.21). So we predict a trigonal pyramidal molecule with a bond angle of 90°.

The observed bond angle is 107.3° as against the predicted value of 90°. The enlargement of the H-N-H bond angle can be accounted for by the repulsion between the hydrogen atoms. Similar arguments are applied to other related molecules. In some cases the predicted structures may be different from the structures observed experimentally. The structures of these molecules can be predicted more precisely through the concept of hybridization of orbitals.

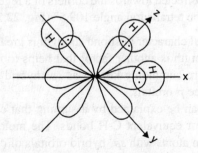

Fig. 22.21 Formation of NH_3 molecule

22.16 HYBRIDIZATION

An apparent deficiency of valence bond theory is its inability to account for tetravalency of carbon. In the ground state the electronic configuration of a carbon atom is $1s^2 2s^2 2p^2$ and can be represented as

$$1s \quad 2s \quad 2p_x \quad 2p_y \quad 2p_z$$

It has two unpaired electrons in p orbitals and on this basis one would expect the formation of a simple CH_2 molecule with a bond angle of 90°. In fact, CH_2 is very unstable and reactive. Furthermore, in most of the organic compounds carbon is tetravalent and all these four bonds are equivalent and directed towards the corner of a regular tetrahedron.

To explain the tetravalency of carbon atom one of the $2s$ electrons from $2s$ orbital is promoted (excited) to the vacant $2p$ orbital. The electronic configuration of the carbon atom thus becomes $1s^2 2s^1 2p_x^1 2p_y^1 2p_z^1$ and can be represented as

$$1s \quad 2s \quad 2p_x \quad 2p_y \quad 2p_z$$

The excitation of one of the $2s$ electrons to the vacant $2p$ orbital requires energy of about 272 kJ mol^{-1}. Since four electrons are available for bonding and the energy released during the formation of these four bonds is more than compensated for the promotion energy. When these four $2s$, $2p_x$, $2p_y$ and $2p_z$ orbitals overlap with $1s$ orbitals of hydrogen atoms to form a methane molecule, one would expect three bonds of one type—using $1s$ orbitals from hydrogen and $2p$ orbitals from carbon and one bond of another type—using $1s$ orbital of hydrogen and $2s$ orbital from carbon. Actually, all the four bonds in methane are known to be equivalent and are directed towards the vertices of a regular tetrahedron. To resolve this problem, Pauling and Slater introduced the concept of *hybridization* which means *mixing or combination of pure atomic orbitals*. In the process of hybridization various linear combinations of s and p orbitals are taken mathematically and the mixed (hybrid) orbitals with the greatest degree of directional character are found. The significant results that emerges from such calculations are:

(i) The best hybrid orbital is more strongly directed than either the s or p pure orbital. The shape of one of these hybrid orbitals is shown in Fig. 22.22(a).

(ii) The four hybrid orbitals are exactly equivalent to each other.

(iii) Because each sp^3 hybrid orbital has the same composition, all four σ bonds are identical.

(iv) The hybrid orbitals are directed towards the corners of a regular tetrahedron. The angle between two hybrid orbitals is the tetrahedral angle 109.5° (Fig. 22.22 (b)).

As a result of this directional character the bond strength is greater than for an s or p atomic orbital alone. This increased bond strength is another factor that helps to repay the promotional energy.

These equivalent orbitals are commonly known as sp^3 hybrid orbitals, since they arise from the mixing of one s orbital and three p orbitals.

The structure of methane can be explained by assuming that carbon atom in methane is tetrahedrally hybridized. There are four equivalent C-H bonds. The molecule is formed by the end to end overlap of s orbitals of hydrogen atoms with sp^3 hybrid orbitals of carbon atom resulting in the formation of four σ bonds. In these σ bonds the charge distribution is uniform. There are eight valence electrons (four from carbon atom and one from each of the four hydrogen atoms) to be distributed in the four localized bonding orbitals. These eight electrons account for the four equivalent localized electron pair bonds. Figure 22.22 (c) shows the localized MO configuration of methane.

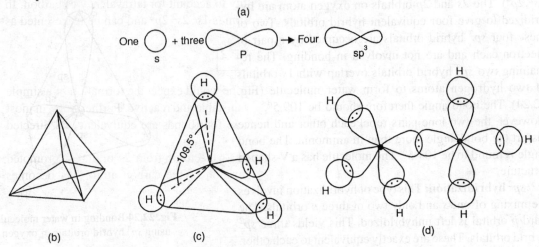

(a)

One ◯ + three ∞ → Four ∞

s   P sp^3

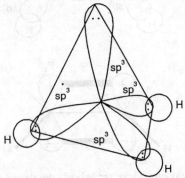

(b)

(c)

(d)

Fig. 22.22 (a) Tetrahedral hybrid orbital, (b) Set of four tetrahedral orbitals, (c) Structure of methane, (d) Structure of ethane

The structure of ethane can be illustrated in the same way as methane. Each carbon atom in ethane is sp^3 hybridized. Of the four hybrid orbitals on each carbon atom, three are overlapping with $1s$ orbitals of three hydrogen atoms and the fourth overlaps with the sp^3 hybrid orbital of the other carbon atom. This results in the formation of four localized σ MO's as shown in Fig. 22.22 (d). Free rotation about the central C-C bond in ethane appears to be possible and could lead to an infinite number of different arrangements of atoms in space called conformation.

The structure of ammonia and water can now be explained in a better way. The nitrogen atom in ammonia has the electronic configuration $1s^2 2s^2 2p^3$. It is assumed that the $2s$ and $2p$ orbitals hybridize to form four equivalent sp^3 hybrid orbitals. One of the sp^3 hybrid orbitals contains a lone pair of electron while the remaining three hybrid orbitals overlap with the $1s$ orbital of hydrogen atoms resulting in the formation of ammonia. The arrangement is again tetrahedral with the exception that one corner of the tetrahedron contains the lone pair of electrons. This structure is known as trigonal pyramidal (Fig. 22.23). Since the lone pair of electron occupies more space than any of the hydrogen atoms, therefore the bond angle compresses slightly from 109.6° to 107.3°.

Fig. 22.23 Bonding in NH_3 molecule using sp^3 hybrid orbitals of nitrogen

In water molecule the situation is similar to ammonia except that oxygen atom has two unshared electrons ($1s^2$ $2s^2 2p^4$). The $2s$ and $2p$ orbitals on oxygen atom are hybridized to give four equivalent hybrid orbitals. Two of these four sp^3 hybrid orbitals are occupied by a pair of electron each and are not involved in bonding. The remaining two sp^3 hybrid orbitals overlap with $1s$ orbitals of two hydrogen atoms to form water molecule (Fig. 22.24). The bond angle therefore should be 109.5°. However, the two lone pairs repel each other and hence distort the bond angle more than in ammonia. The bond angle is found to be 104.5°. The molecule has a V-shaped structure.

sp² **hybridization:** This type of hybridization involves the mixing of one *s* and only two of three *p* orbitals. The third *p* orbital is left unhybridized. This yields three sp^2 hybrid orbitals. These are exactly equivalent to each other.

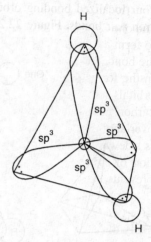

Fig. 22.24 Bonding in water molecule using sp^3 hybrid orbitals of oxygen

They lie on a plane and are directed to the corners of an equilateral triangle forming an angle of 120° between them (Fig. 22.25). This type of hybridization explains the structure of ethylene and other unsaturated hydrocarbons containing double bond.

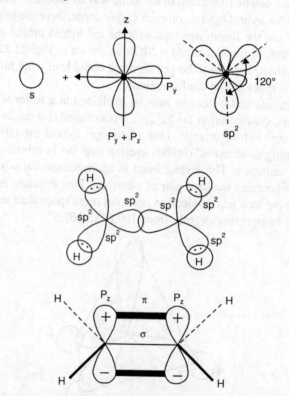

Fig. 22.25 Bonding in ethylene. Three sp^2 hybrid orbitals and one pure *p* orbital of each carbon atom are involved in bond formation

Two carbon atoms in ethylene are sp^2 hybridized, giving three equivalent hybrid orbitals in a plane and one $2p$ orbital perpendicular to it. One of these sp^2 hybrid orbitals from each carbon atom overlaps to form a σ bond between the two carbon atoms. The remaining two sp^2 hybrid orbitals on each atom are bonded to two hydrogen atoms resulting in four other σ bonds. Thus 10 out of 12 electrons are used in the formation of these σ bonds. The last pair of electrons involves the overlapping of two pure p orbitals sideways resulting in a π bond formation. Hence, in ethylene we get a double bond between two carbon atoms and these can be pictured as one σ bond and one π bond. The σ bond in which the overlapping is maximum along the internuclear axis is stronger than the π bond where the overlapping is sideways and electron clouds are arranged parallel to the internuclear axis (Fig. 22.25). The formation of a π bond increases the stability of the molecule and decreases the C-C bond distance and prevents the free rotation of the >CH$_2$ group around the C-C axis.

sp hybridization: This type of hybridization occurs when one s and p orbitals are hybridized to give two equivalent hybrid orbitals leaving two p orbitals uneffected. These hybrid orbitals are oppositely directed along a straight line that passes through the internuclear axis and the angle between the two hybrid orbitals is 180° (Fig. 22.26).

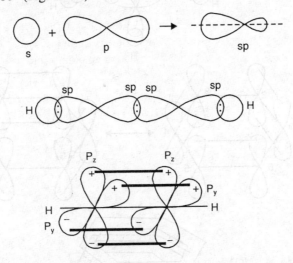

Fig. 22.26 Bonding in acetylene using two sp hybrid orbitals and
two pure p orbitals of each carbon atom

This type of hybridization explains the structure of acetylene molecule (CH≡CH) containing a triple bond. Each carbon atom has two sp hybrid orbitals and two pure p orbitals. Overlapping of one sp hybrid orbital of each carbon atom results one C-C bond of σ type. The other sp hybrid orbital from each carbon atom overlaps with 1s orbital of hydrogen atoms to give two C-H bonds. Electrons in the remaining two pure p orbitals on each carbon atom, which are perpendicular to the molecular axis, overlap sideways to form two perpendicular π-bonds. Thus the carbon-carbon triple bond in acetylene consists of one strong σ bond and two weak π bonds.

In benzene (C$_6$H$_6$) there are six carbon atoms and each has a pure p orbital and three sp^2 hybrid orbitals. Each carbon atom is attached to two other carbon atoms through the use of its two sp^2 hybrid orbitals forming a σ bond network of a regular hexagon as shown in Fig. 22.27(a). The third hybrid orbital of each carbon atom overlaps with 1s orbital of hydrogen atoms forming six C-H bonds. The unused pure p orbitals of each carbon atom perpendicular to the plane of the molecule now overlap sideways to form π bonds. These bonds are formed either between carbon atoms 1-2, 3-4, 5-6 or 2-3, 4-5, 1-6. The localized picture of the π bonding is shown in Fig. 22.27 (b). From this picture it would be expected that there are six C-C single bonds and three C-C π bonds. However, the C-C bond lengths in benzene have been found to be 1.39 Å which is in between the C-C and C=C bond lengths. In order to explain this it is assumed that the delocalization of π electrons results over all the six carbon atoms (Fig. 22.27 (c)).

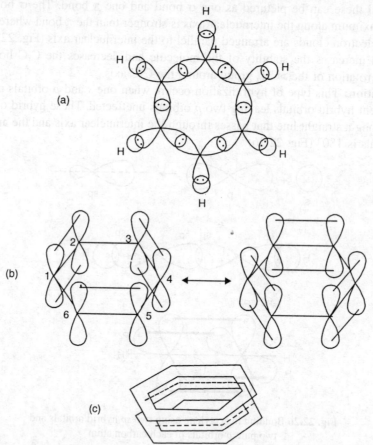

Fig. 22.27 Orbitals overlap in benzene (a) overlap of sp^2 hybrid orbitals forming σ bonds and (b) overlap of $2p_z$ orbitals, and (c) delocalization of the electrons in π orbitals

The delocalization renders the molecule more stable. The enthalpy of combustion of benzene may be calculated assuming that the molecule contains alternate single and double bonds. The calculated value exceeds the experimental value by about 150.6 kJ mol⁻¹ showing that the molecule is stable by 150.6 kJ mol⁻¹. This lowering of energy is called the *resonance energy* or *delocalization energy* and is due to the delocalization of electrons in π orbitals.

Hybridization Involving d-orbitals

Hybridization is not restricted to s and p orbitals only, but may involve the mixing of other types of orbitals, provided energy difference is not much. Hybrid orbitals involving d orbitals are quite common among the heavier elements and are of particular importance in complexes of transition elements. The structure of many of the coordination complexes and of molecules can be explained using the concept of hybridization.

(*i*) **sp³d hybridization:** Combination of one *s*, three *p* and d_z^2 atomic orbitals gives five sp^3d hybrid orbitals. Such types of mixing of atomic orbitals is called sp^3d hybridization. These hybrid orbitals are usually called trigonal bipyramidal hybrid orbitals because these are directed towards the apices of a trigonal bipyramid.

(*a*) **PCl₅ molecule:** The bonding in PCl₅ may be explained using hybrids of 3*s*, 3*p* and 3*d* atomic orbitals for phosphorus.

	3s	3p			3d				
Electronic configuration of phosphorus atom—ground state ($3s^2\,3p^3$)	↑↓	↑	↑	↑					
Electronic configuration of phosphorus atom—excited state ($3s^1\,3p^3\,3d^1$)	↑	↑	↑	↑	↑				

These five atomic orbitals now hybridize to form singly occupied sp^3d hybrid orbitals. These hybrid orbitals overlap with the singly filled *p*-atomic orbitals of five chlorine atoms to form five P–Cl σ bonds in PCl₅ molecule with trigonal bipyramidal shape as shown in Fig. 22.28.

| Phosphorus having gained five electrons from chlorine atoms in PCl₅ molecule. | ↑⇣ | ↑⇣ | ↑⇣ | ↑⇣ | ↑⇣ | | | | |

$$sp^3d \text{ hybridization}$$

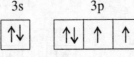

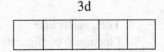

Fig. 22.28 Trigonal bipyramidal structure of PCl₅

(*b*) **SF₄ molecule:**
Electronic configuration of sulphur atom—ground state ($3s^2\,3p^4$)

	3s	3p			3d				
	↑↓	↑↓	↑	↑					

Electronic configuration of
sulphur atom—excited
state ($3s^2\ 3p^3\ 3d^1$)

These five atomic orbitals hybridize to give five sp^3d hybrid orbitals, one of which contains a lone pair of electrons. The remaining four hybrid orbitals contain one electron. These hybrid orbitals having one electron form σ bonds with four singly filled $2p_z$ atomic orbitals of four fluorine atoms. The presence of a lone pair in SF_4 molecule gives rise a distorted trigonal bipyramidal shape to the molecule. (Fig. 22.29)

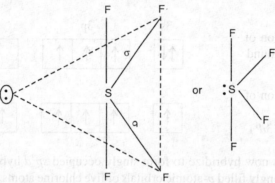

Fig. 22.29 Formation of distorted trigonal bipyramidal SF_4 molecule

(c) **ClF_3 molecule:**
Electronic configuration of
chlorine atom—ground
state ($3s^2\ 3p^5$)

Electronic configuration of
chlorine atom—excited
state ($3s^2\ 3p^4\ 3d^1$)

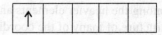
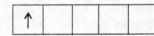

The five atomic orbitals hybridize to form five sp^3d hybrid orbitals. Three half-filled hybrid orbitals form three σ bonds by over-lapping with half-filled $2p_z$ orbitals from three fluorine atoms. The remaining two hybrid orbitals which contain lone pair of electrons do not participate in bonding.

Due to these two lone pair of electrons, the molecule gives distorted trigonal bipyra-midal shape. The molecule has T-shaped structure. The bond angle is reduced to 87.6° (Fig. 22.30).

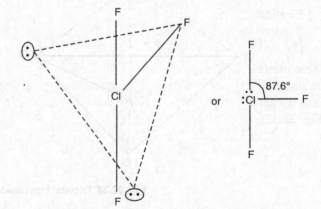

Fig. 22.30 Formation of T-shaped ClF_3 molecule

XeF_2 molecule:
Electronic configuration of
Xe atom—ground
state ($5s^2\ 5p^6$)

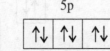

Electronic configuration of
Xe atom—excited state
$(5s^2\ 5p^5\ 5d^1)$

The five atomic orbitals hybridize to give five sp^3d hybrid orbitals. Two of these five hybrid orbitals contain one electron and are used to form two σ bonds (F–Xe–F) by overlapping two half-filled $2p_z$ atomic orbitals of two fluorine atomis. The remaining three hybrid orbitals which contain lone pair of electrons do not participate in bond formation. These lone pairs occupy the equatorial positions. Therefore XeF_2 molecule is linear in shape (Fig. 22.31).

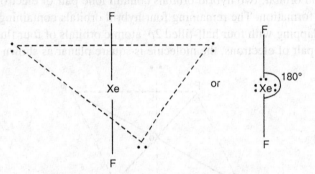

Fig. 22.31 Formation of linear XeF_2 molecule

(*ii*) **sp³d² hybridization:** Combination of one s, three p and two d-orbitals gives six equivalent sp^3d^2 hybrid orbitals. This type of mixing of atomic orbitals is called sp^3d^2 hybridization. These hybrid orbitals are directed towards the corners of a regular octahedron. It is for this reason that these are called octahedral hybrid orbitals.

(*a*) *SF₆ molecule:*
Electronic configuration of
S atom—ground state
$(3s^23p^4)$

Electronic configuration of
S atom—excited state
$(3s^1\ 3p^3\ 3d^2)$

These orbitals hybridize to form six equivalent sp^3d^2 hybrid orbitals. All the six hybrid orbitals which are single-filled overlap with singly occupied $2p_z$ orbitals of six fluorine atoms to form six S-F σ bonds. Thus we get an octahedral SF_6 molecule in which all S-F bonds are equal and S-F-S angle equal to 90° (Fig. 22.32).

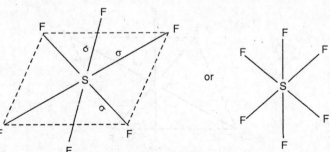

Fig. 22.32 Octahedral SF_6 molecule

(b) XeF₄ molecule:
Electronic configuration of
Xe atom—ground state
($5s^2\ 5p^6$)

Electronic configuration of
Xe atom—excited state
($5s^2\ 5p^4\ 5d^2$)

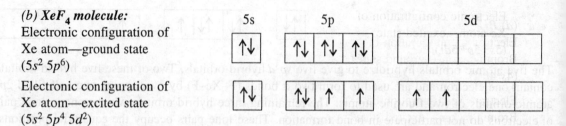

Of the six sp^3d^2 hybrid orbital, two hybrid orbitals contain lone pair of electrons and therefore do not take part in the bond formation. The remaining four hybrid orbitals containing one electron and form four σ bonds by overlapping with four half-filled $2p_z$ atomic orbitals of four fluorine atoms. Due to the presence of two lone pair of electrons, the molecule is square planar as shown in Fig. 22.33.

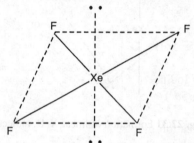

Fig. 22.33 Square planar XeF₄ molecule

(c) IF₅ molecule:
Electronic configuration of
Iodine atom—ground state
($5s^2 5p^5$)

Electronic configuration of
Iodine atom—excited state
($5s^2 5p^3 5d^2$)

The atomic orbitals on hybridization give six equivalent sp^3d^2 hybrid orbitals. Five of these hybrid orbitals containing one electron overlap with five singly filled $2p_z$ atomic orbitals of five fluorine atoms to form five σ bonds between I and F. Sixth hybrid orbital which is at axial position of the octahedron is occupied by a lone pair of electron. Due to the presence of a lone pair of electron the molecule is not a regular octahedral but is square pyramidal (Fig. 22.34).

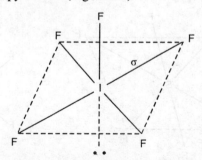

Fig. 22.34 Square pyramidal IF₅ molecule

(d) BrF₅ molecule:
Electronic configuration of
Bromine atom—ground state
$(4s^2 4p^5)$

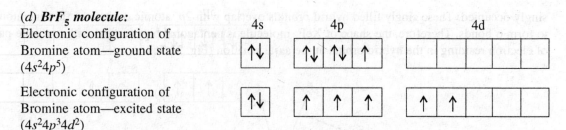

The shape of BrF₅ molecule is same as discussed in IF₅ molecule.

(iii) sp³d³ hybridization: Combination of one *s*, three *p* and three *d* orbitals gives seven sp^3d^3 hybrid orbitals which are directed towards the corners of a pentagonal-bipyramid.

(a) IF₇ molecule:
Electronic configuration of
Iodine atom ground state $(5s^2 5p^5)$

Electronic configuration of Iodine
atom—excited state $(5s^1 5p^3 5d^3)$

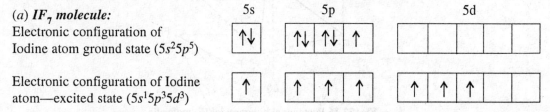

The atomic orbitals on hybridization give seven sp^3d^3 hybrid orbitals all of which are singly filled. These singly filled hybrid orbitals overlap with seven half-filled $2p_z$ atomic orbitals of seven fluorine atoms giving seven σ bonds between I and F. The molecule is therefore pentagonal pyramidal in shape as shown in Fig. 22.35.

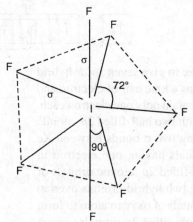

Fig. 22.35 Pentagonal pyramidal IF₇ molecule

(b) XeF₆ molecule:
Electronic configuration
of Xe—ground state $(5s^2\ 5p^6)$

Electronic configuration
of Xe—excited state $(5s^2\ 5p^3\ 5d^3)$

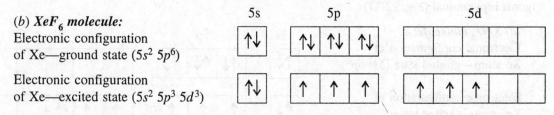

Of the seven sp^3d^3 hybrid orbitals, one is occupied by a lone pair of electron while the remaining six are singly occupied. These singly filled hybrid orbitals overlap with $2p_z$ atomic orbitals of fluorine atoms to form σ bonds. Therefore, the shape of XeF_6 molecule is pentagonal bipyramidal with one lone pair of electron residing in the hybrid orbital at the axial position (Fig. 22.36).

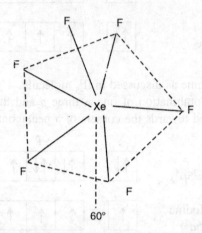

Fig. 22.36 Pentagonal bipyramidal IF_7 molecule

(c) XeO₂F₂ molecule:
Electronic configuration of
Xe atom—ground state $(5s^2\ 5p^6)$

Electronic configuration of
Xe atom—excited state
$(5s^2\ 5p^3\ 5d^3)$

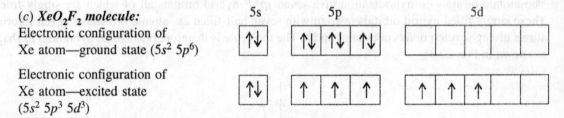

The seven atomic orbitals hybridize to give seven sp^3d^3 hybrid orbitals. One hybrid orbital contains a lone pair of electron and the remaining six hybrid orbitals contain only one electron each. The two hybrid orbitals overlap with two half-filled $2p_z$ atomic orbital of two fluorine atoms giving two σ bonds between Xe and F. The other two hybrid orbitals having one electron in each orbital overlap with two half-filled $2p_y$ atomic orbitals of two oxygen atoms. The remaining two hybrid orbitals overlap with remaining singly filled $2p$ orbitals of oxygen atom to form π bond (oxygen atom has two singly filled $2p$-orbitals) which is a $d\pi$-$p\pi$, π bond. The shape of the molecule is therefore trigonal bipyramidal (Fig. 22.37).

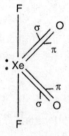

Fig. 22.37 Trigonal bipyramidal : XeO_2F_2 molecule

(d) XeO₃ molecule:
Electronic configuration of
Xe atom—ground state $(5s^2\ 5p^6)$

Electronic configuration of
Xe atom—excited state
$(5s^2\ 5p^3\ 5d^3)$

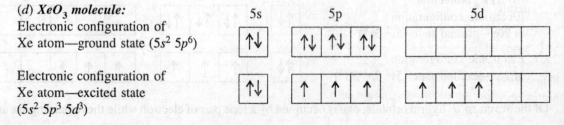

XeO_3 also involves sp^3d^3 hybridization. There are seven sp^3d^3 hybrid orbitals, with one hybrid orbital containing a lone pair of electrons which does not take part in the bond formation. The remaining six hybrid orbitals contain only one electron each. Out of these, three hybrid orbitals overlap with three half-filled $2p_y$, atomic orbitals of three oxygen atoms forming three σ bonds. The remaining three hybrid orbitals overlap with remaining singly-filled 2p-orbitals of oxygen atom to form π bonds, which is a dπ-pπ, π bond. The shape of the molecule is therefore pyramidal (Fig. 22.38).

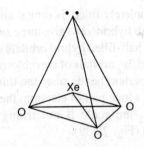

Fig. 22.38 Pyramidal XeO_3 molecule

Shapes of some common molecules

(i) **$BeCl_2$ molecule:**
Electronic configuration of
Be atom—ground state $(1s^2 2s^2)$

Electronic configuration of
Be atom—excited state $(1s^2 2s^1 2p^1)$

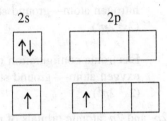

2s and $2p_z$ atomic orbitals on hybridization give two linear sp hybrid orbitals. Each of these hybrid orbitals is singly occupied and, therefore, overlaps with singly filled $3p_z$ atomic orbital of each chlorine atom to form two Be-Cl σ bonds. Both these bonds are coplanar and are at 180° to each other. Thus $BeCl_2$ molecule has a linear shape.

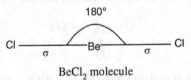

$BeCl_2$ molecule

(ii) **CO_2 molecule:**
Electronic configuration of
carbon atom—ground state $(2s^2 2p^2)$

Electronic configuration of
carbon atom—excited state $(2s^1 2p^3)$

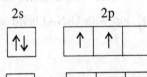

In CO_2, the central carbon atom is sp hybridized. Thus carbon has two sp hybrid orbitals and two 2p-orbitals. Two half-filled sp hybrid orbitals of carbon atom overlap with half-filled $2p_z$ orbitals of two oxygen atoms to form two σ bonds. The remaining two half-filled 2p orbitals of carbon atom overlap laterally with each of the two half-filled 2p orbitals of two oxygen atoms to give two π bonds which are $p_π - p_π$ bonds. Thus CO_2 molecule is linear in shape and has two σ and two π bonds as shown below:

$$:\ddot{O} \underset{\pi}{\overset{\sigma}{=\!\!=}} C \underset{\pi}{\overset{\sigma}{=\!\!=}} \ddot{O}:$$

(iii) **$SnCl_2$ molecule:**
Electronic configuration of
Sn atom—ground state $(5s^2 5p^2)$

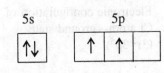

The completely filled 5s orbital and two half-filled 5p orbitals hybridize to give three sp^2 hybrid orbitals. The two half-filled hybrid orbitals overlap with two half filled $3p_z$ orbitals of two chlorine atoms to form two σ-covalent bonds since the third hybrid orbital contains a lone pair of electron, therefore the shape of $SnCl_2$ molecule is not triangular planar but distorted (Fig. 22.39).

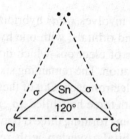

Fig. 22.39 $SnCl_2$ molecule

(iv) **NO_3^- ion:**

Electronic configuration of nitrogen atom—ground state $(2s^2\ 2p^3)$

Electronic configuration of oxygen atom—ground state $(2s^2\ 2p^4)$

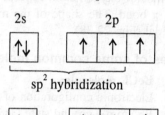

$2s$, $2p_x$ and $2p_z$ atomic orbitals of nitrogen atom hybridize to give three sp^2 hybrid orbitals. $2p_y$ orbital which contains only one electron does not participate in the hybridization. Hybrid orbitals containing an electron pair donates to an oxygen atom forming coordinate covalent N → O bond. Covalent σ bonds are formed by the overlap of half-filled hybrid orbitals with half-filled $2p$ orbitals of two oxygen atoms. The unhybridized electron of nitrogen atom then overlaps laterally with $2p$ orbital of oxygen atom to form a π bond ($p_\pi - p_\pi$ bond). Therefore the structure of NO_3^- ion would be

$$\overline{O} - N \longrightarrow O$$
$$\parallel$$
$$O$$

The double bond contains one σ and one π bond. This gives a planar trigonal and symmetric shape to NO_3^- ion with O-N-O bond angle of 120° (Fig. 22.40).

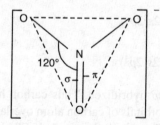

Fig. 22.40 Planar trigonal shape of NO_3^- ion

(v) **ClO_3^- ion:**

Electronic configuration of Cl atom—ground state $(3s^2\ 3p^5)$

  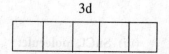

Electronic configuration of
Cl atom—excited state
$(3s^2\ 3p^3\ 3d^2)$

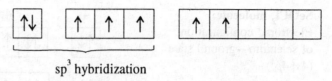

sp³ hybridization

The one 3s and three 3p orbitals hybridise to form four sp^3 hybrid orbitals. The three hybrid orbitals containing one electron each are used in the formation of three σ bonds with three oxygen atoms. The fourth sp^3 hybrid orbital, which contains a lone pair of electrons, is not used in the bond formation. The two electrons of the chlorine atom which are promoted to 3d orbitals overlap laterally with two oxygen atoms to form two π bonds $(p_\pi - d_\pi$ bond). This accounts for the pyramidal structure of the ClO_3^- ion (Fig. 22.41).

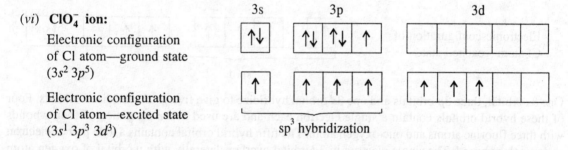

Fig. 22.41 Pyramidal structure of ClO_3^- ion

(vi) **ClO_4^- ion:**

Electronic configuration
of Cl atom—ground state
$(3s^2\ 3p^5)$

Electronic configuration
of Cl atom—excited state
$(3s^1\ 3p^3\ 3d^3)$

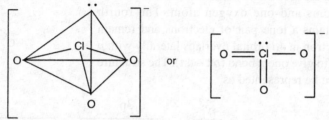

sp³ hybridization

The one 3s and three 3p electrons hybridized to give four sp^3 hybrid orbitals and there remains three electrons in 3d orbitals. These hybrid orbitals containing one electron each overlap with four electrons from each oxygen atom to give four σ bonds. The remaining three electrons from 3d orbitals overlap laterally with three electrons from oxygen atoms to form three π-bonds $(p\pi-d\pi$ bonds). This gives the structure of ClO_4^- ion as (Fig. 22.42).

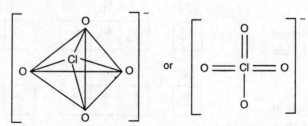

Fig. 22.42 Tetrahedrel structure of ClO_4^- ion

SeOCl₂ molecule:
Electronic configuration
of selenium—ground state
$(4s^2\,4p^4)$

Electronic configuration
of selenium—excited state
$(4s^2\,4p^3\,4d^1)$

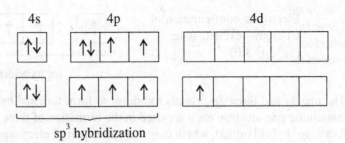

sp³ hybridization

The 4s and 4p atomic orbitals of selenium atom hybridize to give
four sp^3 hybrid orbitals. Three of these hybrid orbitals contain a
single electron each and are used in the formation of three σ bonds
with two chlorine atoms and one oxygen atom. The fourth
hybridized orbital contains a lone pair of electrons and remain
unused. The single electron in 4d orbital overlaps laterally with p
orbital of oxygen atom to give one π bond $(p\pi – d\pi)$. The structure
of SeOCl₂ can therefore be represented as

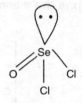

ClOF₃ molecule:
Electronic configuration of
Cl atom—ground state

Electronic configuration of
Cl atom—excited state

sp³d

One 3s orbital, three 3p orbitals and one 3d orbital hybridize to give five sp^3d hybridized orbitals. Four
of these hybrid orbitals contain a single electron each and are used in the formation of four σ bonds
with three fluorine atoms and one oxygen atom. The fifth hybrid orbital contains a lone pair of electron
and remains unused. The single electron in 3d orbital overlaps laterally with p orbital of oxygen atom
to form a π bond $(p\pi – d\pi)$. The structure therefore can be shown as

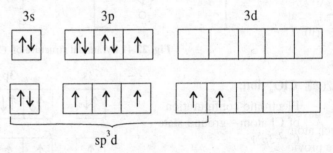

IOF₄⁻ ion:
Electronic configuration of
iodine atom—ground state
$(5s^2\,5p^5)$

Electronic configuration of
iodine atom—excited state
$(5s^1\,5p^3\,5d^3)$

sp³d hybrid orbitals

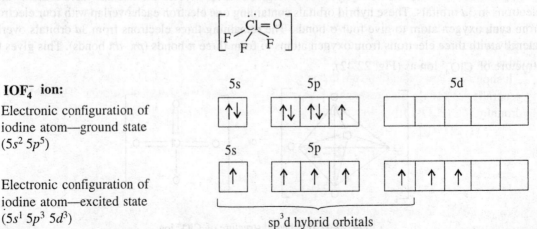

One 5s orbital, three 5p orbitals and one 5d orbital hybridize to give five sp^3d hybridized orbitals. These sp^3d hybrid orbitals contain a single electron each and are used in the formation of five σ bonds with four fluorine atoms and one oxygen atom. Of the two electrons in 5d orbitals, single electron is used in the formation of π bond ($p\pi - d\pi$).

$$\left[\begin{array}{c} \text{F} \longrightarrow \text{I} \longrightarrow \text{F} \\ \text{F} \quad \text{F} \\ \text{O} \end{array} \right]^{-}$$

22.17 CHARACTERISTICS OF COVALENT COMPOUNDS

   (*i*) Covalent compounds are generally held by weak intermolecular forces (van der Waals forces) and as a result these compounds have low melting and boiling points, *e.g.*, $SiCl_4$ (b.p. 58°C).
   (*ii*) Covalent compounds exist in molecular form and hence usually do not conduct electricity.
   (*iii*) These are generally soluble in nonpolar solvents such as benzene, carbon tetrachloride, etc., but are insoluble in polar solvents such as water etc.
   (*iv*) Covalent compounds have directional characteristics as they are formed by the overlapping of atomic orbitals. This enables the covalent compounds to exist in different spatial arrangements.
   (*v*) These compounds usually react slowly since the reaction usually involves breaking a bond and substituting or adding a group.

22.18 THE COORDINATE OR DATIVE COVALENT BOND

We have seen that in the formation of a normal covalent bond between two atoms, one electron from each atom is contributed in the bond formation. However, there are instances where both the electrons are provided by only one of the atoms involved in the bond formation. Such type of bond is called the dative or coordinate covalent bond and is often indicated by an arrow directed from the donor atom to the acceptor atom. Usually the atom that donates both the electrons possesses a pair of electrons in its outer valence shell and the acceptor atom has at least one vacant orbital. The formation of the dative covalent bond may be represented as

$$A{:} + B \rightarrow A{:}B$$
$$A^+ \rightarrow B^-$$

The symmetrical sharing of these two electrons which come from one of the atoms would result the donor atom to acquire a positive charge and the acceptor a negative charge. For this reason the dative bond is sometimes called a semipolar bond.

   It should be noted that the atom that supplies both the electrons for the formation of the dative bond is generally a strongly electro-negative atom such as oxygen, nitrogen or fluorine. The formation of hydronium ion (H_3O^+) from water and hydrogen ion may be represented as

$$\text{H} \longrightarrow \overset{\cdot\cdot}{\text{O}}{:} + \text{H}^+ \rightarrow \left[\text{H} \longrightarrow \overset{\cdot\cdot}{\text{O}} \longrightarrow \text{H} \right]^+$$
$$\quad \overset{|}{\text{H}} \qquad\qquad\qquad \overset{|}{\text{H}}$$

The oxygen atom in water molecule has two unshared pairs of electrons. When a hydrogen ion comes near the water molecule, it allows the proton to share one of the electron pairs to form H_3O^+ ion. Once this ion is formed all the OH bonds become indistinguishable and the positive charge is uniformly distributed over the entire molecule rather than on any hydrogen. $BCl_3 \cdot NH_3$, BF_4^-, Al_2Cl_6 etc., may be cited as some other typical examples of dative bond formation.

Instances of dative bonds are most common in the formation of complex ions. A complex ion is formed when a simple ion forms a covalent bond with other ions, molecules or atoms. These electron rich ions or groups or molecules give lone pair of electrons to the central atom forming a coordinate covalent bond, e.g.,

$$\left[\begin{array}{c} NC \\ \\ NC \end{array} \underset{\underset{CN}{\uparrow}}{\overset{\overset{CN}{\downarrow}}{Fe}} \begin{array}{c} CN \\ \\ CN \end{array} \right]^{3-} \quad \left[\begin{array}{c} H_3N \\ \\ H_3N \end{array} \underset{\underset{NH_3}{\uparrow}}{\overset{\overset{NH_3}{\downarrow}}{Co}} \begin{array}{c} NH_3 \\ \\ NH_3 \end{array} \right]^{3+} \quad \left[\begin{array}{c} H_2O \\ \\ H_2O \end{array} \underset{\uparrow}{\overset{\downarrow}{Cu}} \begin{array}{c} OH_2 \\ \\ OH_2 \end{array} \right]^{2+}$$

The ions or molecules which donate a lone pair of electrons to the central metal ion are called ligands.

22.19 METALLIC BOND

Metals are characterised by electrical and thermal conductivity. They have high co-ordination number, 12 for metals crystallizing either in hexagonal or cubical close packing and 8 for metals which crystallize in body centered cubes. These facts suggest that there is extensive overlap of the outer electron orbitals and the valence electrons cannot be associated with a particular nucleus. The valence electrons are relatively free and move through the entire crystal structure under the influence of an applied electric field. The localized electron pair bonding that one visualizes in the simple covalent molecules is obviously absent in metals. The theories regarding the bonding in metals are (*i*) classical free electron theory, (*ii*) valence bond approach, and (*iii*) the molecular orbital approach.

(*i*) The classical free electron theory is due to Drude and Lorentz. In this theory it is assumed that the valence electrons of the metal form a sea of negative charges and are free to move throughout the whole of the metal without any restriction. The metal is regarded as consisting of a positively charged residue with filled electron shells strongly bounded by the electron sea into a rigid structure. The force that binds a metal cation to a number of electrons within its sphere of influence is known as *the metallic bond*. This is, however, an oversimplification of the structure of metals, yet it provides explanation of metallic lustre, optical properties, malleability, ductility and high electrical and thermal conductivity. It also differentiates a metallic bond from ionic and covalent bonds.

(*ii*) *The valence bond approach:* The valence bond theory is due to Pauling. The metallic bond is treated essentially as covalent in character. However, the number of valence electrons is inadequate to form covalent bonds between each atom and its neighbours. It is, therefore, assumed that covalent bonds are not localized but are highly delocalized in the metal structure. The bonds resonate among alternate positions between each atom and its neighbours as shown below in lithium

$$\begin{array}{cc} Li-Li \\ Li-Li \end{array} \longleftrightarrow \begin{array}{cc} Li & Li \\ | & | \\ Li & Li \end{array}$$

The stabilization of the structure through this type of resonance would be expected to be relatively small, hence it is assumed that resonance involves ions, e.g.,

$$\begin{matrix} \text{Li} - \text{Li} \\ \text{Li} - \text{Li} \end{matrix} \quad \longleftrightarrow \quad \begin{matrix} \text{Li} - \overset{\text{Li}^-}{\underset{\mid}{\text{}}} \\ \text{Li}^+ \quad \text{Li} \end{matrix} \quad \longleftrightarrow \quad \begin{matrix} \text{Li} \quad \overset{\text{Li}^+}{\underset{\mid}{\text{}}} \\ \text{Li}^- - \text{Li} \end{matrix}$$

For effective stabilization the metal atoms must possess vacant orbitals of low energy. Larger the number of such vacant orbitals greater will be the number of resonating structures and more effective would be the stabilization.

(iii) *The molecular orbital approach:* The molecular orbital theory, also known as the band theory, was proposed by Block and provides a more detailed account of the bonding in metals. It is assumed that electrons in the completely filled levels are essentially localized while atomic orbitals containing the valence electrons interact or overlap to form a set of delocalized orbitals (molecular orbital) extending over the entire crystal lattice. Such a combination of atomic orbitals produces a large number of closely spaced energy states known as band of energy.

The electronic configuration of lithium is $1s^2\,2s^1$.

1s	2s	2p
↑↓	↑	

The Li_2 molecule exists in vapour state and bonding occurs using the 2s atomic orbital. The three 2p orbitals are vacant and their presence (empty 2p AO's) is a prerequisite for metallic properties.

The Li_2 molecule has been described earlier in MO treatment. The six electrons in Li_2 molecule are arranged in molecular orbitals as $\sigma_{1s^2}\,\sigma_{1s^2}^{*}\,\sigma_{2s^2}$. Ignoring the inner electrons, the 2s atomic orbitals on

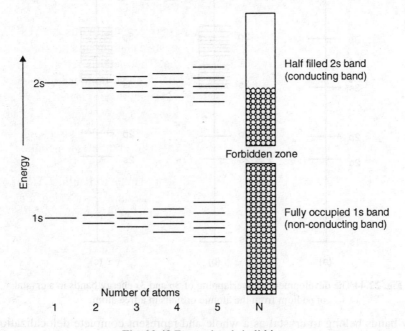

Fig. 22.43 Energy bands in lithium

each of the two lithium atoms combine to give two molecular orbitals—one bonding and another antibonding. The valence electrons occupy the bonding molecular orbital. If the third lithium atom is introduced to form Li_3, three $2s$ atomic orbitals would combine to form three molecular orbitals; one fully bonding, one fully antibonding and the intermediate non-bonding between neighbours. In Li_4, four molecular orbitals are formed—two bonding and two antibonding (Figure 22.43). As the number of electrons in the cluster increases, the spacing between the energy levels of various orbitals decreases. When there are large number of atoms the energy levels of the orbitals are so close together that they almost form a continuum.

In lithium, there are two energy bands, one of these bands originating from the $1s$ atomic orbitals is fully occupied; the other originating from the $2s$ atomic orbital is only half occupied. The fully occupied band is known as non conducting while the half occupied band is called the conducting band.

The energy gap between the two bands is so large that it effectively prevents the promotion of electrons from the lower to the higher bands. Such energy gaps are called *forbidden zones*.

In a similar way, we can consider the combination of s and p orbitals to form energy bands in metals. For sodium these energy bands are $1s^{2N}2s^{2N}2p^{6N}3s^N$. The $3s$ band is only half occupied and is the conducting band. It is found that the relative energies of successive bands depend on the internuclear distances and at shorter distances the adjacent bands may overlap. This situation is summarized pictorially in Fig. 22.44 where (a) shows the discrete energy levels of a free sodium atom, (b) shows the $3s$ and $3p$ bands developing as the sodium atoms are brought together and (c) shows the overlap of $3s$ and $3p$ bands when the atoms attain the equilibrium positions in the crystal.

The energy bands for magnesium are $1s^{2N}2s^{2N}3p^{6N}3s^{2N}$. The completely filled band distribution would predict that magnesium should be non-conducting and hence a nonmetal. However, $3s$ and $3p$ bands overlap and there is no forbidden zone between them, consequently, promotion of electrons from the $3s$ to empty $3p$ bands can take place readily.

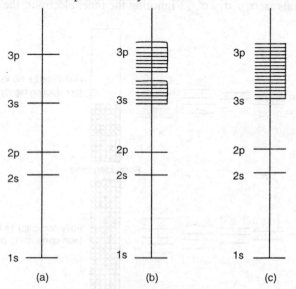

Fig. 22.44 The development of overlapping of $3p$ and $3s$ energy bands in a crystal
of sodium from the atomic orbitals in a free atom

The energy bands belong to crystal as a whole and represent complete delocalization. The result from the interactions of a large number of atomic orbitals of right energy and right symmetry. Electrical conductivity in metals is due to the movement of electrons from lower occupied to higher accessible unoccupied orbitals under the influence of an applied field. In nonmetals all the accessible energy states are occupied so they are poor conductors of electricity. In semiconductors the gap between the occupied and the unoccupied orbitals is not very large and the conduction of electricity is negligible at lower temperatures and appreciable at higher temperatures. At low temperature, the electrons in the occupied orbitals do not have sufficient energy and unable to move to the higher energy states. As the temperature is raised, the electrons acquire sufficient energy and the transition to the higher unoccupied state is possible.

22.20 RESONANCE

Sometimes the molecules and ions can be represented by more than one structures each having almost the same energy, approximately the same relative position of the nuclei and the same number of unpaired electron. For example, the hydrogen molecule can be represented by pure covalent structure H–H $\left(\text{or } H \text{\.{x}} H \text{ and } H \text{\.{x}} H \right)$ and also by the ionic structures $H^+ \text{\.{x}} H^-$ and $H^- \text{\.{x}} H^+$. The ionic structures are higher in energy and will not contribute appreciably to the overall energy of the hydrogen molecule. The pure covalent structures are equivalent in energy. None of these structures adequately describes the true state of affairs, and the actual structure of the hydrogen molecule is supposed to lie between these two extremes. In such a case, the actual structure is regarded as a resonance hybrid or resonating between the various possible structures. The total energy of the system will take the minimum value lying below that for any resonating structures. This gives rise to extra stability to the molecule and is measured in terms of resonance energy, which is equal to the difference in energy between the actual structures and the most stable of the resonating structures.

Some examples of resonance are given below. The structure of carbon dioxide can be described by three possible arrangements:

$$\ddot{\ddot{O}} :: C :: \ddot{\ddot{O}} \qquad \ddot{\ddot{O}} : C ::: \ddot{O} \qquad \ddot{O} ::: C : \ddot{\ddot{O}}$$
$$\text{I} \qquad\qquad\qquad \text{II} \qquad\qquad\qquad \text{III}$$

Each of the above three structures makes almost equal contribution and so the actual structure is given by the combination of the three structures. CO_2 molecule is, therefore, a resonance hybrid between forms I, II and III and is represented as

$$\ddot{\ddot{O}} :: C :: \ddot{\ddot{O}} \longleftrightarrow \ddot{\ddot{O}} : C ::: \ddot{O} \longleftrightarrow \ddot{O} ::: C : \ddot{\ddot{O}}$$
$$\text{I} \qquad\qquad\qquad \text{II} \qquad\qquad\qquad \text{III}$$

The double headed arrows are used to indicate resonating structures. The C—O bond distance in carbon dioxide is about 1.15 Å which is between the true C—O double bond and C—O triple bond. This shows the existence of resonating structures.

The nitrite ion $\left(NO_2^- \right)$ has two resonating forms and can be represented as

Both the forms contribute equally to the actual structure of the ion. In the above structures, one would expect two distinguishable N-O bonds, one single and one double. However, the structural studies show that both N-O bonds are indistinguishable. This again shows the existence of resonance.

In case of benzene molecule, C_6H_6 the resonating structures are:

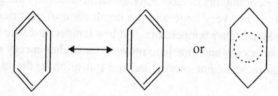

Both these structures show that the ring is composed of alternate single and double bonds. However, the structural studies reveal that all the carbon-carbon bond distances are equal.

In may be pointed out that in resonance, the actual electron distribution in the molecule cannot be represented by a single structure, but it can be regarded fairly accurately as an appropriately weighted combination of several possible configurations.

22.21 HYDROGEN BOND

A hydrogen atom when bonded to a highly electronegative atom such as F, O, or N, acquires a small positive charge which exerts an electrostatic attraction on other highly electronegative atom. This gives rise to a *dipole-dipole interaction* and is called the *hydrogen bonding*. Thus a hydrogen bond results when a hydrogen atom is shared by two electro-negative atoms and is represented as

$$X\text{———}H\text{........}Y$$

where X and Y are electronegative atoms like, F, N or O, and the broken line indicates the electrostatic interaction or hydrogen bond. It is sometimes also called a *hydrogen bridge* or *proton bond*. Since the hydrogen bonds are usually formed with atoms of high electron density, it is therefore recognised that these bonds are electrostatic in nature. The strength of such bonds increases with the increase in the electronegativity of the bonded atoms. Fluorine thus forms very strong hydrogen bonds; oxygen weaker ones; and nitrogen still weaker.

The hydrogen bond is a weaker bond and has in most cases, bond energies in the range of 8-42 kJ/ mole as compared to about 330-420 kJ/mol for ionic or covalent bonds. The bond length of a hydrogen bond has been found to be much greater than that of a pure covalent bond (O-H) except in FH_2^-. This means the hydrogen bond is weaker than the corresponding covalent bond. The lower bond energy and the ease with which it can rupture accounts for some anomalous properties observed in many compounds.

Liquid water shows many abnormal properties such as high boiling point, high enthalpy of vapourization, surface tension, etc. All these properties can be explained on the basis of hydrogen bonding. The boiling points of hydrides of elements of groups IV, V, VI and VII show that the first member of the hydrides of these group elements have abnormally high melting and boiling points because of the presence of hydrogen bonding in these compounds. This is shown in Fig. 22.45. The hydrogen bonding in ammonia is less pronounced than in water for two reasons. Nitrogen is less electronegative than oxygen, and ammonia has only one lone pair of electrons to attract the hydrogen from a neighbouring molecule.

Ice has a peculiar structure in which each water molecule is hydrogen bonded tetrahedrally to four others as shown in Fig. 4.29. This results in an open structure in ice with increase in volume. However, when ice melts the structure breaks down and there is a volume shrink and hence the increase in density.

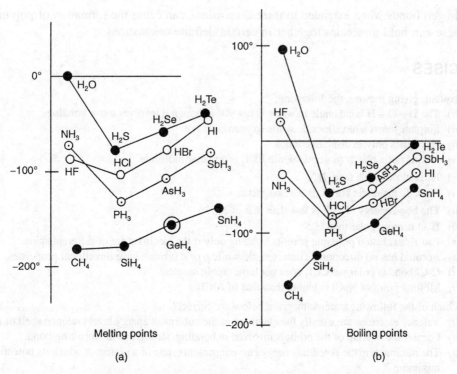

Fig. 22.45 Melting and boiling points of simple hydrides

Hydrogen bonding is often found in organic alcohols or carboxylic acids. For example, formic acid forms a dimer in non-polar solvents. The dimer is formed through intermolecular hydrogen bonding and has the following structure as determined by electron diffraction method. These hydrogen bonds have energies of 20 kJ mol⁻¹ each

$$H—C \begin{matrix} O —H \cdots O \\ \\ O \cdots H—O \end{matrix} C—H$$

0.136 nm   0.125 nm

0.27 nm

The intramolecular hydrogen bonding is possible in organic compounds such as salicyaldehyde or nitrophenols. It contains a hydroxyl and an aldehyde group adjacent to each other thereby forming a hydrogen bond between these two groups. The intramolecular hydrogen bonding does not show abnormal properties as observed in intermolecular hydrogen bonding.

Salicyaldehyde

O-nitrophenol

Hydrogen bonds when extended to three dimensions can cause the formation of polymeric structures. These can hold molecules together in certain definite orientations.

EXERCISES

1. Explain, giving reasons, the following:
    (i)   The H—O—H bond angle in water is not 90° although it involves a σ-p bonding.
    (ii) Sulphur forms a haxafluoride while oxygen does not.
    (iii) He_2 exists only in discharge tubes.
    (iv) NH_3 is not a planar molecule while BCl_3 is a planar molecule.
    (v) H_2 is more stable than H_2^+.
    (vi) N_2 is diamagnetic but O_2 is paramagnetic.
    (vii) The bond energy of N_2^+ is less than that of N_2.
    (viii) H_2O is more polar than H_2S.
    (ix) Pauli's exclusion principle permits bonding only if the electrons are of different spins.
    (x)   s orbital has no directional characteristic while p or d orbitals have directional properties.
    (xi) C-Cl bond is polar yet CCl_4 does not have dipole moment.
    (xii) Melting point of NaCl is higher than that of $AlCl_3$.

2. Which of the following statements given below are correct?
    (i)   Valence electrons are usually the electrons in the outermost energy level (valence shell of an atom).
    (ii)   Greater the overlap of the orbitals involved in bonding, stronger is the resulting bond.
    (iii) The minimum in the potential energy curve represents state of a system at which its potential energy is minimum.
    (iv)   Electron with same spins can also lead to bonding.
    (v)   Electron cloud overlap leads to equal electron density around both the nuclei.
    (vi)   s orbitals have no directional properties while p orbitals have directional properties.
    (vii) The geometry of a molecule can be approximated from the directional properties of atomic orbitals and their maximum overlap in bond formation.
    (viii) The bond angles where the central atom is sp^3 hybridized is 120°.
    (ix)   sp hybrid orbitals have equal s and p character.
    (x)   An atom with a large electronegativity has a small tendency to attract electrons.
                                         Ans. Correct statements: (i), (ii), (iii), (vi), (vii), (ix).

3. Distinguish the following:
    (i)   An atomic orbital from a molecular orbital.
    (ii) A bonding orbital from an antibonding orbital.
    (iii) A σ bond from a π bond.
    (iv) An ionic bond from a covalent bond.
    (v)   An ionic bond from a metallic bond.
    (vi) A polar bond from a nonpolar bond.
    (vii) Non-bonding electrons from antibonding electrons.

4. Which compound in the following series has the highest boiling point?
    (i) H_2O, H_2S, H_2Se and H_2Te.
    (ii) HF, HCl, HBr and HI.
    (iii) NH_3, PH_3 and AsH_3.
    (iv) CH_3OH and C_2H_5OH.
    (v)   Ar and Xe.
    (vi) C_2H_5OH and CH_3OCH_3
                    Ans. (i) H_2O, (ii) HF, (iii) NH_3, (iv) C_2H_5OH, (v) Xe, (vi) C_2H_5OH.

5. Arrange the following orbitals in order of increasing energy s, sp, sp^3 and p.

    Ans. $s < sp < sp^2 < sp^3 < p$.

6. Arrange the following molecular orbitals in order of decreasing energy.

    $$\sigma_s, \sigma_s^*, \pi_x^*, \pi_y, \sigma_z^*, \pi_x, \pi_y^*, \sigma_z.$$

    Ans. $\sigma_s < \sigma_s^0 < \pi_x = \pi_y) < \sigma_z < \left(\pi_x^* = \pi_y^*\right) < \sigma_z^*.$

7. (a) Write down the molecular orbital configuration of O_2, O_2^- and O_2^+.

    (b) Which one of these will have the highest bond dissociation energy? Explain.

    Ans. (a) $O_2 : \left[KK(\sigma_s)^2(\sigma_s^*)^2(\pi_{x,y})^4(\sigma_z)^2(\pi_x^*)^1(\pi_y^*)^1\right]$

    $O_2^- : \left[KK(\sigma_s)^2(\sigma_s^*)^2(\pi_{x,y})^4(\sigma_z)^2(\pi_x^*)^2(\pi_y^*)^1\right]$

    $O_2^+ : \left[KK(\sigma_s)^2(\sigma_s^*)^2(\pi_{x,y})^4(\sigma_z)^2(\pi_x^*)^1\right]$

    (b) O_2^+ has the highest bond dissociation energy.

8. On the basis of molecular orbital approach, which of the following species would be expected to be (i) paramagnetic and (ii) most stable.

    $$N_2^+, NO^+, O_2^+, Li_2^+, Be_2^+$$

    Ans. (i) N_2^+, O_2^+, Li_2^+ and Be_2^+ are paramagnetic, (ii) NO^+.

9. Write down the molecular orbital configurations of the following CN^+, CN^-, NO, NO^+, NO^-.

    Ans. $CN^+ : \left[KK(\sigma_s)^2(\sigma_s^*)^2(\pi_{x,y})^4\right];$

    $CN^- : \left[KK(\sigma_s)^2(\sigma_s^*)^2(\pi_{x,y})^4(\sigma_z)^2\right];$

    $NO: \left[KK(\sigma_s)^2(\sigma_s^*)^2(\pi_{x,y})^4(\sigma_z)^2(\pi_x^*)^1\right];$

    $NO^+: \left[KK(\sigma_s)^2(\sigma_s^*)^2(\pi_{x,y})^4(\sigma_z)^2\right];$

    $NO^-: \left[KK(\sigma_s)^2(\sigma_s^*)^2(\pi_{x,y})^4(\sigma_z)^2(\pi_x^*)^1(\pi_y^*)^1\right]$

10. Explain why the first ionization energy of NO is less than that of CO.

11. Explain why a lateral (sideways) overlap of an s and a p orbital is nonbonding, whereas a head-to-head overlap can be bonding or antibonding. Draw a schematic representation of each type of overlap.

12. Account for the fact that B-F bond distance in BF_3 is shorter than in BF_4^-.

13. The methyl radical $CH_3^{\cdot}$ is planar with three equivalent C-H bonds; discuss the nature of hybridization of the carbon atom and identify the orbital containing the unpaired electron. Explain the type of hybridization in CH_3^+ and CH_3^- and predict the shape of these ions.

    Ans. In $CH_3^{\cdot}$ and CH_3^+, carbon uses sp^2 hybrid orbitals while in CH_3^- carbon uses sp^3 hybrid orbitals.

14. Write the resonating structures for

    (*i*) N_2O,   (*ii*) NO_3^-,   (*iii*) SCN^-,

    (*iv*) CO_3^{2-},   (*v*) N_3^-,   (*vi*) H_2

    (*vii*) IBr,   (*viii*) O_3,   (*ix*) C_6H_6 and   (*x*) CO_2.

15. Predict the bond angle in the following molecules:

$$NH_3, H_2O, CH_4, C_2H_4, BeF_2, C_2H_2 \text{ and } BCl_3.$$

           Ans. NH_3, H_2O and CH_4–109°; C_2H_4, BCl_3–120°;
                                BeF_2 and C_2H_2–180°.

16. What type of hybridization would account in the following cases?
    (*i*) BF_3, a planar molecule with Cl-B-Cl bond angles of 120°.
    (*ii*) AsH_3, a tetrahedral molecule with H-As-H bond angles of 109°.
    (*iii*) $BeCl_2$, a linear molecule with Cl-Be-Cl bond angle of 180°.

17. Illustrate the shapes of the following molecules:

    (*i*) BeF_2,   (*ii*) BCl_3,   (*iii*) $SnCl_2$,   (*iv*) $SnCl_4$,

    (*v*) NH_3,   (*vi*) SF_6,   (*vii*) ICl_4^-,

    (*viii*) IF_5,   (*ix*) SiF_6^{2-},   (*x*) PCl_5 and   (*xi*) ClF_3.

           Ans. (*i*) Linear; (*ii*) Plane triangular; (*iii*) V-shaped; (*iv*) Tetrahedral;
           (*v*) Trigonal pyramid; (*vi*) and (*ix*) Octahedral; (*vii*) Square planar;
           (*viii*) Square pyrimidal; (*x*) Trigonal bipyramid; (*xi*) T-shaped.

18. Draw molecular orbital diagrams of N_2, O_2, HCl, $BeCl_2$, and BCl_3.

19. Show the distribution of valence electrons in the orbitals just prior to bonding with a H atom of
    (*a*) an sp^2 hybridized N atom,
    (*b*) an sp^2 hybridized B atom,
    (*c*) an sp^2 hybridized O atom,
    (*d*) an sp hybridized N atom and
    (*e*) an sp hybridized Cl atom.

20. Use the molecular orbital approach to predict the stability of the diatomic molecules Li_2, Be_2, B_2 and C_2.

21. Discuss the structure of hydrogen molecule on the basis of molecular orbital theory. Show how
    (*i*) the theory explains the nonexistence of He_2 and Ne_2 molecules and
    (*ii*) the difference in the reactivity of N_2, O_2 and F_2 molecules.

22. How can electronegativities of elements be used to predict the kind of bonds formed between elements. Give examples.

23. AB, CD, and EF are three compounds. The electronegativity difference between atoms in these compounds are 1.8, 1.5 and 0.1. Which one in these molecules would be expected to be
    (*i*) more polar,
    (*ii*) less ionic in character, and
    (*iii*) more covalent? Explain.

           Ans. AB more polar, EF less ionic and more covalent.

24. Which of the following compounds are essentially ionic and which are essentially covalent?
    (*i*) IBr, (*ii*) $SiCl_4$, (*iii*) MgO and (*iv*) KH.

                        Ans. Covalent (*i*), (*ii*) and (*iv*); ionic (*iii*).

25. Which of the following molecules would be expected to have zero dipole moment?
         O_2, HCl, CO_2, CCl_4, FBr, NH_3, H_2S and $BeCl_2$

           Ans. Molecules with zero dipole moment are O_2, CO_2, CCl_4 and $BeCl_2$.

26. Arrange the following compounds in order of decreasing dipole moments.
    HF, HCl, HBr, HI.

    Ans. HF > HCl > HBr > HI.

27. Bond energy of X–X bond is 200 kJ per mole and the bond energy of Y–Y bond is 300 kJ per mole. Calculate the bond energy of X–Y bond. Assume that the contributions to bond strength by X and Y atoms to be the same as in X_2 and Y_2 (equal sharing of electrons).

    Ans. 250 kJ mol^{-1}.

28. Discuss the relative merits and demerits of valence bond and molecular orbital approach to the bonding in hydrogen molecule. How can the two wave functions be improved?

29. What is meant by electronegativity of elements? Explain, giving reasons and suitable examples, how the electronegativity of elements changes
    (*i*) in a group and
    (*ii*) in a period of the periodic table

30. Explain and illustrate the concept of resonance.

31. Explain and illustrate the formation of molecular orbitals from atomic orbitals. Explain with the help of the energy diagram the significance of bonding and antibonding orbitals.

32. Define and illustrate each of the following terms:
    (*i*) Bonding and antibonding molecular orbitals; (*ii*) Hybridization;
    (*iii*) Resonance;   (*iv*) Delocalization energy;
    (*v*) σ and π bonds;   (*vi*) Bond energy;
    (*vii*) Electronegativity of elements and   (*viii*) hydrogen bonding.

23

Nuclear Chemistry

23.1 INTRODUCTION

Ordinary chemical reactions involve changes only in the outer valence electrons in an atom. The atomic nuclei remain unaffected, *i.e.*, the number of protons and neutrons is not disturbed. However, in nuclear transformations, there is a change in the number of protons or neutrons (or both) resulting in the formation of new nuclei. The study of nuclear transformations and their uses in chemistry is the subject matter of nuclear chemistry.

The energy released in ordinary chemical reactions is usually less and therefore, does not affect the stability of the nucleus. However, the energy released in nuclear changes is sufficiently high to break the chemical bonds and is used to induce chemical reactions. The vast energy released during nuclear transformation can be used either for the betterment of the society or for its destruction.

23.2 RADIOACTIVITY

The phenomenon of *radioactivity* was discovered by H. Becquerel in 1895. He observed that when a photographic plate wrapped in black paper was exposed to certain uranium salts, it was fogged. He concluded that fogging of the plate was due to the radiation emitted from the uranium salts. The emission of rays capable of producing these effects is a fundamental property of uranium atom. Subsequently, it was shown that radiation can cause ionisation of air and is not affected by factors like temperature, pressure, chemical environment, electrical and magnetic fields or the source of the uranium. The spontaneous emission of radiation of this type by an element is called radioactivity and the element which exhibits this behaviour is said to be radioactive.

In 1898, Pierre and Marie Curie undertook the systematic study of radioactivity of many substances. They noted that the chief source of uranium (pitchblende) contains elements which had greater activity than uranium. By chemical methods, Madam Curie succeeded in isolating from this mineral two new radioactive elements, polonium and radium. At the same time Madame Curie and G.C. Schmidt independently discovered a new radioactive element, thorium. Debierne in 1899 discovered a new element actinium which was also radioactive. Since then, the systematic investigation has brought to light about forty elements which show characteristics of radioactive elements. A large number of other elements have been found to become radioactive by special methods to be considered later.

In 1889, Rutherford began investigating the nature of the radiations emitted from radioactive elements. He showed that the radiation was composed of three types of rays; *the alpha rays, the beta rays* and *the gamma rays* (Fig. 23.1).

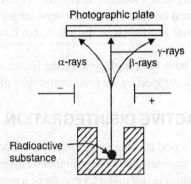

Fig. 23.1 Radiations emitted by a radioactive element

23.3 PROPERTIES OF α, β AND γ-RAYS

Alpha Rays

(i) *Nature:* The deflection of α-rays in electric or magnetic field shows that these are positively charged particles. Furthermore, it has been shown by Rutherford and T. Royds (1909) that an alpha particle carries two units of positive charge and has a mass approximately four times that of the hydrogen atom. In other words, the α-particle is a helium nucleus consisting of two neutrons and two protons ($_2He^4$).

(ii) *Velocity:* Alpha particles generally move with a velocity ranging from 1.4 to 2×10^7 m/sec.

(iii) *Ionization of air:* Since alpha particles have large mass and move with high speeds, they have therefore considerable kinetic energy. Due to this large energy, the alpha particles cause ionization when passed through a gas. The path of α-particles when photographed in the Wilson cloud chamber shows that they move in straight lines.

(iv) *Luminescence:* The α-particles cause luminescence when they strike a zinc sulphide screen.

(v) *Penetrating power:* Alpha rays have smaller penetrating power and are stopped by a sheet of paper or by a thin foil of aluminium.

Beta Rays

(i) *Nature:* The deflection of β-rays in an electric or a magnetic field shows that they are negatively charged particles. Their e/m ratio is the same as that of the electron indicating that β-particles are actually fast moving electrons.

(ii) *Velocity:* The velocity of β-particles is approximately equal to that of light. The average value being 2×10^8 m/sec.

(iii) *Ionization of air:* The small mass accounts for the low ionizing power of β-particles than α-particles.

(iv) *Penetrating power:* Due to their high speed β-particles are more penetrating than α-particles. Their penetrating power is about 100 times more than those of α-particles. β-rays are stopped by 3 mm of lead. Because of their small mass they are easily deflected from their path by electric or magnetic field.

Gamma Rays

(*i*) *Nature:* γ-rays are unaffected by electric and magnetic fields, hence they are not charged particles. γ-rays are electromagnetic radiation analogous to X-rays. Their wavelengths lie in the range of 10^{-10} to 10^{-13} m and hence have shorter wavelengths than X-rays.

(*ii*) *Ionization of air:* They cause ionization of the gases, but have proportionally weaker ionizing power.

(*iii*) *Penetrating power:* γ-rays have very high penetrating power and is about 10 to 100 times more than β-rays. These rays are stopped by several centimeters of lead.

23.4 THEORY OF RADIOACTIVE DISINTEGRATION

Rutherford and Soddy in 1903 proposed the theory of radioactive disintegration. It was suggested that radioactive elements with unstable nucleus undergo spontaneous disintegration with the emission of α-particles or β-particles. These emissions result in the formation of a new element which has both physical and chemical properties different from the parent element. The new element so formed may also be unstable and may emit radiation to form another new element. This may infact be a succession of transformation of each accompanied by the characteristic rays. For example, when uranium with atomic mass 238 and atomic number 92 emits an α-particle, it yields uranium X_1 of mass 234 and atomic number 90. In the formation of the new element the charge has decreased by two units and the mass by four units and the element is known as thorium.

$$_{92}Th^{238} \rightarrow {_{90}}Th^{234} + {_2}He^4$$

When an α-particle is emitted from the nucleus it must be accompanied by the loss of two planetary electrons so that the atoms remain electrically neutral. Thorium formed above is also unstable like uranium and it further emits a β-particle (an electron) from the nucleus. The new product so formed now has the same atomic mass but its atomic number (nuclear charge) is increased to 91. This new element now has an atomic mass 234 and an atomic number 91 and is called protactinium.

The loss of a β-particle from the nucleus should involve the gain of a planetary electron.

The loss of a β-particle (or an electron) is somewhat difficult concept in the sense that there are no electrons present in the nucleus. It is therefore assumed that the neutron in the nucleus first disintegrates into the protons and electrons, and then the electron is lost as β-particle.

$$_{90}Th^{234} \rightarrow e^0 + {_{91}}Pa^{234}$$

From the above example it is clear that the radioactive disintegration takes place in stages until a nonradioactive end product is obtained. Disintegration of a parent element produces another element (known as the daughter element) which is also radioactive. The radioactive decay of each succeeding daughter element gives rise to a series known as "radioactive series". For example, uranium I yields a whole series of consecutive disintegration products until eventually lead is obtained.

23.5 SODDY-FAJAN'S GROUP DISPLACEMENT LAW

Since the emission of an α-particle, which is helium nucleus of mass four and charge +2, from the nucleus of a radioactive element causes the mass number of the element to decrease by four units and the nuclear charge by two units, the new element so produced is, therefore, shifted to two periods to the left in the periodic table from its parent element. On the other hand, when a β-particle is emitted from the parent nucleus, the atomic number is increased by one unit and hence the new element so produced is shifted by one place to the right in the periodic table. These two changes are embodied in *the group displacement law* given by Fajan and Soddy. The law states *"when an α-particle is emitted from the radioactive element, the new element so obtained lies two places to the left of the parent element in the periodic table and an emission of a β-particle results in the displacement of the new element one place to the right of the parent element in the periodic table"*.

Isotopes, Isobars and Isotones

Isotopes (meaning same place in the periodic table) are *atoms of the same element which have different atomic masses (different numbers of neutrons) but same atomic number (same number of protons)*. Since isotopes have same extranuclear configuration they are therefore indistinguishable chemically and occupy the same place in the periodic table. Their physical properties, however, may differ slightly due to variations in masses. The variation is pronounced in lighter elements where the relative difference is large. $_{92}U^{238}$ and $_{92}U^{235}$ differ only in atomic masses and are isotopes of uranium. The three isotopes of hydrogen are protium ($_1H^1$), deuterium ($_1H^2$) and tritium ($_1H^3$).

Isobars, on the other hand, are nuclides *having different atomic numbers (Z) but same atomic masses*. $_{18}Ar^{40}$, $_{19}K^{40}$ and $_{20}Ca^{40}$ are isobars of the same mass number 40.

In addition to isotopes and isobars, there are nuclides which have different atomic numbers and different atomic masses but the same number of neutrons. These are known as the *isotones*. In $_{15}P^{31}$ and $_{16}S^{32}$ each has 16 neutrons and are therefore isotones.

23.6 RATE OF RADIOACTIVE DECAY

Like chemical reactions, nuclear reactions also proceed at certain specific rate, the rate of decay of a radioactive element does not depend on temperature, pressure or the nature of the compound in which it occurs. The rate of decay at any instant of time is proportional to the number of radioactive atoms present

$$-\frac{dN}{dt} = \lambda N \qquad \qquad ...(23.1)$$

where N is the number of atoms remaining at any time t, λ is a proportionality constant called *the decay constant* and is characteristic of the given element.

The above equation can be written as

$$-\frac{dN}{N} = \lambda dt \qquad \qquad ...(23.2)$$

This shows that the fraction of the nuclei, dN/N, that decays in a given time dt is constant. On integrating Eq. (23.2) between the limits $N = N_0$ at $t = 0$ and $N = N$ at $t = t$ yields

$$-\int_{N_0}^{N} \frac{dN}{N} = \int_0^t \lambda dt$$

$$\ln[N]_{N_0}^{N} = -\lambda [t]_0^t$$

$$\ln \frac{N}{N_0} = -\lambda t$$

$$t = \frac{1}{\lambda} \ln \frac{N_0}{N}$$

or
$$= \frac{2.303}{\lambda} \log \frac{N_0}{N} \qquad \qquad ...(23.3)$$

$$N_t = N_0 e^{-\lambda t} \qquad \qquad ...(23.4)$$

This equation is the rate equation for a first order reaction.

It is more convenient to use the half-life $(t_{1/2})$ of the process which is defined as the time in which the radioactive atoms are reduced to half of their initial amount. To obtain $t_{1/2}$, we substitute $N = 1/2\ N_0$ and $t = t_{1/2}$ in Eq. (23.3) to give

$$t_{1/2} = \frac{2.303}{\lambda} \log \frac{N_0}{N_0/2} = \frac{2.303 \log 2}{\lambda} = \frac{0.693}{\lambda} \qquad \qquad ...(23.5)$$

Equation (23.5) shows that the time necessary for half of the quantity of a radioactive element to disintegrate is constant and is independent of the initial amount of disintegrating element present and is characteristic of the element in question. Thus, if the half-life of a radioactive element is known, its decay constant can be calculated or vice versa.

The general equation for the number of atoms left at the end of n number of half life periods is

$$\left(\frac{1}{2}\right)^n N_0$$

If $t = \frac{1}{\lambda}$, then Eq. (23.4) becomes

$$\frac{N}{N_0} = e^{-1} = \frac{1}{e}$$

Thus the decay constant is the reciprocal of the time during which the original number of atoms of a radioactive substance falls to 1/e times its initial value.

Average or Mean Life of a Radioactive Element

The atoms of a radioactive substance are continuously in the process of disintegration. Some atoms have short life of the order of $10^{-11}\ s$ while others have exceedingly long life (10^{10} yrs.) and hence it is useful to determine the average or mean life of a radioactive substance. The average life of a radioactive substance is defined as *the ratio of the total life time of all the radioactive elements to the total number of atoms present in it.* It is estimated as follows:

From Eq. (23.1) and (23.4), we get

$$dN = -\lambda N_0 e^{-\lambda t} dt$$

which is the number of atoms disintegrating between t and $t + dt$. Each of these atoms has a life t and hence the sum of the life times of these atoms is $\lambda N_0 e^{-\lambda t} t\, dt$

The average life of the atoms is equal to the sum of all possible life times divided by the total number of atoms. That is,

$$\text{Average life, } \tau = \frac{\int\limits_0^\infty N_0 \lambda e^{-\lambda t} t\, dt}{N_0} = \lambda \int\limits_0^\infty t e^{-\lambda t} dt$$

$$= \lambda \left[\frac{te^{-\lambda t}}{-\lambda} \right]_0^\infty - \lambda \int\limits_0^\infty \frac{e^{-\lambda t}}{-\lambda} dt$$

$$= \int\limits_0^\infty e^{-\lambda t} dt = \left[\frac{e^{-\lambda t}}{-\lambda} \right]_0^\infty = \frac{1}{\lambda} \qquad \qquad ...(23.6)$$

Hence, the average life of a radioactive element is the reciprocal of the decay constant.

$$\text{Again } t_{1/2} = \frac{0.693}{\lambda} = 0.693\,\tau = 0.693 \times \text{Average life} \qquad \qquad ...(23.7)$$

The radioactivity of an element is expressed in units of *curie* (c). A curie is defined as *the quantity of the radioactive material in which 3.7×10^{10} disintegrations occur per second.* The smaller unit is *microcurie* (μc) having 3.7×10^4 disintegrations per second. The number of atoms present in one curie is then $(3.7 \times 10^{10})/\lambda$.

Problem 23.1: A certain radioactive element has a half-life period of 1590 years. Calculate the time during which 10^{-3} kg of the element would be reduced to 10^{-5} kg.

Solution: Since

$$t_{1/2} = \frac{0.693}{\lambda} = 1590 \text{ yrs.}$$

or

$$\lambda = \frac{0.693}{1590}$$

Again,

$$N = N_0 e^{-\lambda t} \text{ or } \frac{N}{N_0} = \frac{10^{-5}}{10^{-3}} = 10^{-2} = e^{-\lambda t}$$

$$\lambda t = 2.303 \log 100 = 2.303 \times 2$$

and

$$t = \frac{2.303 \times 2}{\lambda} = \frac{2 \times 2.303 \times 1590}{0.623} = 1085 \text{ yrs.}$$

Problem 23.2: The $t_{1/2}$ of a radioactive element X is 3 minutes. Calculate the amount left after 15 minutes if the initial amount was 3.2×10^{-2} kg.

Solution: Number of half-life intervals = 5

Hence, the amount left after 15 minutes $= \dfrac{1}{(2)^5} \times$ initial amount

$$= \frac{1}{32} \times 3.2 \times 10^{-2} \text{ kg} = 10^{-3} \text{ kg}$$

Problem 23.3: Calculate (*a*) the half-life period, and (*b*) the average life of a certain radioactive element Y (atomic mass 226 g mol^{-1}) if 1 g of it emits 3.7×10^{10} α-particles per second.

   Solution: Rate of decay = Rate of emission of α-particles

$$= \frac{dN}{dt} = \lambda N = 3.7 \times 10^{10} \text{ per second}$$

Now,

$$N = \frac{6.023 \times 10^{23}}{226} \text{ and } \lambda = \frac{0.693}{t_{1/2}}$$

Hence,

$$\frac{dN}{dt} = \frac{0.693}{t_{1/2}} \times \frac{6.023 \times 10^{23}}{226} = 3.7 \times 10^{10}$$

or,

$$t_{1/2} = \frac{0.693 \times 6.023 \times 10^{23}}{3.7 \times 10^{10} \times 226 \times 60 \times 60 \times 24 \times 365} \text{ yrs.} = 1580 \text{ yrs.}$$

The average life of the radioactive element,

$$\tau = \frac{1}{\lambda} = N \frac{dt}{dN} = \frac{6.023 \times 10^{23}}{226} \times \frac{1}{3.7 \times 10^{10}}$$

$$= \frac{6.023 \times 10^{23}}{226 \times 3.7 \times 10^{10} \times 60 \times 60 \times 365 \times 24} \text{ yrs.} = 2284 \text{ yrs.}$$

23.7 RADIOACTIVE EQUILIBRIUM

When a radioactive element (say *A*) disintegrates into another radioactive element (say *B*), then the rate of decay of *A* must represent the rate at which the product *B* is formed. The latter will itself disintegrate at a rate dependent on its amount present. It is apparent that a state of equilibrium is reached when the rate of formation of any element from its parent element is equal to that at which it itself disintegrates. Mathematically,

$$\frac{dN_A}{dt} = \frac{dN_B}{dt} \qquad \qquad ...(23.8)$$

   From Eq. (23.1), it follows that

$$\lambda_A N_A = \lambda_B N_B = ...$$

or

$$\frac{N_A}{N_B} = \frac{\lambda_B}{\lambda_A} = \frac{(t_{1/2})_A}{(t_{1/2})_B} \qquad \qquad ...(23.9)$$

where λ_A and λ_B are the rate constants for disintegration of *A* and *B*. At radioactive equilibrium, the amounts of different radioactive elements are inversely proportional to their rate constants of disintegration or directly proportional to their half-life periods.

23.8 RADIOACTIVE SERIES

There are three main radioactive series found in nature. These belong to either uranium, thorium or actinium series. In all the series the end products of final disintegration are isotopes of lead. These are shown in Table 23.1, 23.2 and 23.3 respectively.

It is to be noted that in thorium series the atomic mass of all the elements are whole number multiples n of 4. Therefore, this series is sometimes referred to as $4n$ series. For the uranium series the masses of the elements are $(4n + 2)$ and for this reason it is sometimes called $(4n + 2)$ series. In case of actinium series, the atomic masses of all the elements can be written as $(4n + 3)$. Therefore this is known as $(4n + 3)$ series.

23.9 MASS DEFECT, PACKING FRACTION AND NUCLEAR BINDING ENERGY

It has been found that the actual mass of an isotope of an element is smaller than the mass number, *i.e.*, sum of the masses of the protons, neutrons and electrons present in it. This difference between the two masses is known as the *mass defect*, ΔM. The mass defect which may be positive or negative is expressed in terms of *packing fraction* which is defined as

$$\text{Packing fraction} = \frac{\text{Isotopic atomic mass} - \text{Mass number}}{\text{Mass number}} \times 10^4$$

Packing fraction is therefore the mass defect per nucleon: A negative value of packing fraction implies stability while a positive value indicates the instability of the nucleus. However, more precise and quantitative approach to the stability of a nucleus is through the concept of *binding energy* which is defined as *the energy released per nucleon in the formation of a nucleus.* It is obtained from the mass

Table 23.1 The Uranium Series

Element	Symbol	Atomic mass	Atomic number	Particle emitted	Half-life period
Uranium	U	238	92	α	4.6×10^9 yrs.
Thorium	Th	234	90	β	24.9 days
Protactinium	Pa	234	91	β	1.15 min.
Uranium	U	234	92	α	2.7×10^5 yrs.
Thorium	Th	230	90	α	8.22×10^4 yrs.
Radium	Ra	226	88	α	1.60×10^3 yrs.
Radon	Rn	222	86	α	3.82 days
Polonium	Po	218	84	α	3.05 min
Lead	Pb	214	82	β	26.8 min.
Bismuth	Bi	214	83	β	19.7 min.
Polonium	Po	214	84	α	1.5×10^{-4} sec.
Lead	Pb	210	82	β	22 yrs.
Bismuth	Bi	210	83	β	4. 85 days
Polonium	Po	210	84	α	140 days
Lead	Pb	206	82	none	stable

defect. The binding energy in the nuclear structure has the same significance as bond energy in molecular structure. Just as high bond energy values signify the stability of the chemical bond, a high binding energy value points out the stability of the nucleus. Let us calculate the magnitude of the binding energy when an atom is formed from its constituent particles. If A is the mass number and Z the atomic number of the element then $(A - Z)$ is the number of neutrons. The mass M' of the atom is the sum of the masses of the constituents, $i.e.$, protons, neutrons and electrons

$$M' = Zm_p + Zm_e + (A - Z)m_n \qquad \qquad ...(23.10)$$

Table 23.2 The Thorium Series

Element	Symbol	Atomic mass	Atomic number	Particle emitted	Half-life period
Thorium	Th	232	90	α	1.4×10^{10} yrs.
Radium	Ra	228	88	β	6.7 yrs.
Actinium	Ac	228	89	β	6.15 yrs.
Thorium	Th	228	90	α	1.90 yrs.
Radium	Ra	224	88	α	3.64 days
Radon	Rn	220	86	α	54.4 sec.
Polonium	Po	216	84	α	0.15 sec.
Lead	Pb	212	82	β	10.6 hrs.
Bismuth	Bi	212	83	α	1 hr.
Thallium	Ti	208	81	β	3.1 min.
Lead	Pb	208	82	none	stable

Table 23.3 The Actinium Series

Element	Symbol	Atomic mass	Atomic number	Particle emitted	Half-life period
Actinium	Ac	231	89	β	13.4 yrs.
Thorium	Th	231	90	β	24.5 hrs.
Protactinium	Pa	231	91	α	3.2×10^4 yrs.
Actinium	Ac	227	89	β	13.5 yrs.
Thorium	Th	227	90	α	18.8 days
Radium	Ra	223	88	α	11.2 days
Radon	Rn	219	86	α	3.92 sec.
Polonium	Po	215	84	α	1.84×10^{-3} sec
Lead	Pb	211	82	β	36 min.
Bismuth	Bi	211	83	β	2.1 min.
Polonium	Po	211	84	α	5×20^{-2} sec.
Lead	Pb	207	82	none	stable

where m_p, m_e and m_n are the masses of proton, electron and neutron respectively. The above equation can be written as

$$M' = Z(m_p + m_e) + (A - Z)m_n = Zm_H + (A - Z)m_n \qquad ...(23.11)$$

where $m_H = m_p + m_e$ is the mass of the hydrogen atom which contains one proton and one electron. If M denotes the actual mass of the isotope determined experimentally, then the mass defect,

$$\Delta M = M' - M$$

or

$$\Delta M = Zm_H + (A - Z)m_n - M \qquad ...(23.12)$$

On C^{12} scale,

$$m_H = 1.00782$$

and

$$m_n = 1.00866$$

therefore

$$\Delta M = [Z(1.00782) + (A - Z)(1.00866)] - M \qquad ...(23.13)$$

This will be a positive quantity for stable nuclei. Thus the loss of mass in the formation of the nucleus is equivalent to the energy released in the formation of the given nucleus and is given by the Einstein relation

$$E = mc^2$$

where m is the mass which is converted into energy E and c is the velocity of light.

For a given ΔM, the energy evolved is very large. For instance the mass of an α-particle ($_2He^4$) should be 4.00260 and is equivalent to the combination of two hydrogen atoms and two neutrons. Using Eq. (23.13), we get

$$\Delta M = 2(1.00782) + 2(1.00866) - 4.00260 = 0.03036 \text{ g}$$

and hence the binding energy is given as

$$E_b = (0.03036)(3.0 \times 10^{10})^2 = 2.732 \times 10^{19} \text{ ergs per g atom}$$

$$= 6.530 \times 10^{11} \text{ cal per g atom} = 28.32 \text{ MeV}^* \text{ per g atom}$$

This enormous amount of energy would have to be supplied to 4 g of helium in order to disintegrate the nuclei into protons and neutrons. It is clear, therefore that the helium nucleus must be very stable. The binding energy per nucleon in the above example is

$$\frac{28.32}{4} = 7.08 \text{ MeV}$$

and would be expected to be same for all nuclides provided the interaction among the nucleons does not depend on the number of nucleons.

Figure. 23.2 shows the plot of binding energy per nucleon against mass number. After an abrupt rise among the lightest nuclei, the binding energy per nucleon changes slightly and attains a fairly

---

* Since 1 amu is equivalent to $(1.66 \times 10^{-24})(3.0 \times 10^{-10})^2 \text{ erg} = 1.492 \times 10^{-3} \text{ erg}$

and

$$1 \text{ eV} = 1.6 \times 10^{-12} \text{ erg};$$

$$1 \text{ MeV} = 10^6 \text{ eV}$$

therefore

$$1 \text{ amu} = \frac{1.492 \times 10^{-3}}{1.6 \times 10^{-12} \times 10^6} = 931 \text{ MeV}$$

constant value of about 8.5 MeV per nucleon corresponding to the stable nuclei, *i.e.*, those around iron. After the maximum is reached the curve falls off gradually showing that heavier nuclei are not as stable as the intermediates one. These stable nuclides contain an equal and even number of protons and neutrons suggesting a shell structure for the nucleus. Because of the maximum binding energy per nucleon that occurs near mass number 56, the fission of a heavier nuclide into two or more lower mass nuclides is a process that releases energy and increases their stability. Similarly, the nuclei of low mass number would increase their stability by fusing them to form heavier nuclides releasing large amount of energy. A large positive value of binding energy implies stability of the nucleus. However, in spontaneous disintegration the product nuclei is always of less energy than the parent nuclei and the difference appears as the kinetic energy of the product nuclei.

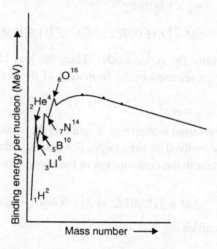

Fig. 23.2 Binding energy per nucleon as a function of mass number

Problem 23.4: Calculate (*a*) the mass defect, (*b*) the binding energy, and (*c*) the average binding energy of Li^7 nucleus. The lithium nucleus has a mass of 7.0160 amu.

Solution: (*a*) The lithium nucleus has 3 protons and 4 neutrons, therefore the mass defect can be calculated using Eq. (23.13).

$$\Delta M = 3\,(1.00782) + 4\,(1.00866) - 7.0160 = 0.04219 \text{ amu}$$

(*b*) The binding energy is given by

$$E_b = 931 \times \text{Mass defect} = 931 \times 0.04219 \text{ MeV} = 39.279 \text{ MeV}$$

(*c*) The average binding energy is

$$= \frac{39.279}{7} = 5.611 \text{ MeV}$$

Problem 23.5: The binding energy of $_{92}U^{238}$ per nucleon is 7.576 MeV. Calculate the atomic mass of this isotope.

Solution: Since the binding energy per nucleon is 7.576 MeV, therefore the total binding energy is equal to

$$7.576 \times 238 = 1803 \text{ MeV}$$

Hence the mass defect

$$\Delta M = \frac{1803}{931} = 1.936 \text{ amu}$$

But

$$\Delta M = 92(1.00782) + 146(1.30866) + M$$

or

$$M = 239.983 - 1.936 = 238.047$$

23.10 STABLE NUCLEI

A number of factors contribute to the stability of nucleus. A major factor that contributes towards the stability of the nucleus is its composition *i.e.*, the number of protons and neutrons. A stable nuclei is one which does not undergo spontaneous disintegration into another stable nuclide, or whose rate of disintegration is negligible.

For most stable nuclides, the number of protons (the charge Z) is plotted as a function of the number of neutrons N in Fig. 23.3. It is noted from the figure that the stable nuclides lie close in a definite belt of stability. This is called the stability belt. For nuclides lighter than $_{20}Ca^{40}$, the neutron-proton ratio (N/P) is very close to unity. However, as the nuclear charge increases beyond 20, the ratio N/P deviates from unity as the number of neutrons is larger than the number of protons ($N/P > 1$). In fact, all nuclides above atomic number 20 whether stable or unstable lie above the N-P line. The cause of this behaviour is due to the increase in the number of protons which tend to increase the repulsion between them and consequently, lower the stability of the nucleus. The forces of repulsion can be diminished somewhat by increasing the number of neutrons and increasing the nuclear size.

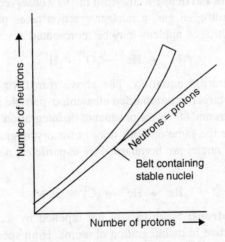

Fig. 23.3 Belt containing stable nuclei. Number of neutrons as a function of number of protons for nuclei

It may be noted that nuclei in which number of protons and neutrons are equal to 2, 8, 20, 28, 50, 82, 126 are more stable and abundant in nature. These numbers are sometimes called as magic numbers. The existence of these magic numbers suggested a "shell model" of the nucleus. It has been observed that nuclei with even numbers of protons and neutrons are more stable than these containing an odd number of the particles.

Unstable nuclide which lie above the region of stability ($N/P > 1$) will decay in such a manner that the ratio N/P becomes approximately equal to one to reach the region of stability. This may be achieved by the emission of beta rays $\left(_{-1}e^0 \right)$

$$_{11}Na^{24} \rightarrow {}_{12}Mg^{24} + {}_{-1}e^0$$

In this case the ratio of N/P falls from 13/11 to 12/12, i.e., from 1.18 to 1.0. However, in case of a nuclide lying below the stability belt, stability is attained by decreasing the number of protons. This decrease in the number of protons could be achieved by the emission of alpha particles ($_2He^4$). The loss of an alpha particle from a nucleus decreases the mass number by four units and atomic number by two units.

$$_{92}U^{238} \rightarrow {}_{90}Th^{234} + {}_2He^4$$

In this case, the N/P ratio increases from 146/92 to 144/90, i.e., from 1.58 to 1.60. The unstable nucleus continues to emit alpha particles until a stable nucleus is obtained.

23.11 ARTIFICIAL DISINTEGRATION OF ATOMS

The process of spontaneous transformation of a heavy nuclide led Rutherford, Curie, Joliot, etc. to find possible ways to bring about the disintegration of naturally stable elements by the relatively high speed atomic particles such as α-rays, neutrons, protons, deutrons and electrons. The conversion of one stable nuclide into another stable nuclide by artificial means is known as *artificial disintegration or artificial transmutation*. In some cases high energy γ-rays can also be employed.

(a) **Disintegration by Alpha Particles:** Rutherford in 1919 observed that when α-particles of high velocities are passed through nitrogen gas, a nuclear reaction takes place producing oxygen and a proton. The disintegration of nitrogen nucleus may be represented as

$$_7N^{14} + {}_2He^4 \rightarrow {}_8O^{17} + {}_1H^1$$

and is known as the disintegration equation. The above transformation can be represented as N^{14} (α, p) O^{17} where N^{14} is the target or bombarded element, α-particle is a projectile, p is the particle (proton) emitted from the nucleus and O^{17} is the product of disintegration. The sum of the mass numbers as well as the charges should be the same on both sides of the disintegration equation.

Similarly, when berryllium nuclei are bombarded by α-particles, neutrons are emitted and C^{12} is formed.

$$_4Be^9 + {}_2He^4 \rightarrow {}_6C^{12} + {}_0n^1$$

(b) **Disintegration by Neutrons:** Neutrons are not repelled by atomic nuclei as they carry no charge and hence are very effective in disintegration of atoms. High speed neutrons are not necessary for this case as they cause spallation, i.e., a process in which many nucleons are simultaneously given out. In fact, the slow moving neutrons are more effective. Four main types of behaviour have been obtained. These result in the emission of (i) a proton (ii) an α-particle, (iii) γ-radiation, and (iv) two neutrons respectively. Examples of these types are:

(i) $_{13}Al^{27} + {}_0n^1 \rightarrow {}_{12}Mg^{27} + {}_1H^1$ (n, p)

(ii) $_8O^{16} + {}_0n^1 \rightarrow {}_6C^{13} + {}_2He^4$ (n, α)

(iii) $_{11}Na^{23} + _0n^1 \rightarrow _{11}Na^{24} + \gamma \ (n, \gamma)$

(iv) $_{19}K^{39} + _0n^1 \rightarrow _{19}K^{38} + 2\,_0n^1 \ (n, 2n)$

(c) **Disintegration by Protons:** The nuclei could be disintegrated by means of fast moving protons and four main types of disintegrations have been observed. These are given as follows:

(i) $_3Li^7 + _1H^1 \rightarrow 2\,_2He^4 \ (p, 2\alpha)$

(ii) $_{20}Ca^{44} + _1H^1 \rightarrow _{21}Sc^{44} + _0n^1 \ (p, n)$

(iii) $_6C^{12} + _1H^1 \rightarrow _7N^{13} + \gamma \ (p, \gamma)$

(iv) $_4Be^9 + _1H^1 \rightarrow _4Be^8 + _1D^2 \ (p, d)$

(d) **Disintegration by Deuterons:** Some reactions induced by accelerated deuterons are

(i) $_{13}Al^{27} + _1D^2 \rightarrow _{14}Si^{28} + _0n^1 \ (d, n)$

(ii) $_1D^2 + _1D^2 \rightarrow _1H^3 + _1H^1 \ (d, p)$

(iii) $_{13}Al^{27} + _1D^2 \rightarrow _{12}Mg^{25} + _2He^4 \ (d, \alpha)$

(iv) $_4Be^9 + _1D^2 \rightarrow _4Be^{10} + _1H^1 \ (d, p)$

(v) $_{83}Bi^{209} + _1D^2 \rightarrow _{83}Bi^{210} + _1H^1 \ (d, p)$

(e) **Disintegration by γ-rays:** Disintegration of atomic nuclei by high energy γ-radiation has been observed in a few cases. Some examples are:

(i) $_4Be^9 + \gamma \rightarrow _3Li^8 + _1H^1 \ (\gamma, p)$

(ii) $_1D^2 + \gamma \rightarrow _1H^1 + _0n^1 \ (\gamma, n)$

The second reaction leads to the accurate determination of mass of the neutron, since the masses of the proton and deuteron are known.

23.12 ARTIFICIAL RADIOACTIVITY

F. Joliot and I. Curie in 1934 observed that when α-particles impinge on light metallic elements such as aluminium, magnesium and boron, there were two types of disintegrations, (a) the main one resulting in the emission of protons, and (b) emission of neutron and positron. It was found that the emission of protons ceased as soon as the α-irradiation was stopped. However, the emission of positron continued for sometimes, the intensity falling off exponentially. The most plausible explanation for this phenomenon is that the α-particle is first taken up by the bombarded nucleus to produce a complex which disintegrates instantaneously with the emission of neutrons. Thus with aluminium

$$_{13}Al^{27} + _2He^4 \rightarrow _{15}\overset{*}{P}^{30} + _0n^1$$

$_{15}\overset{*}{P}^{30}$ is not a stable isotope of phosphorus and decays into a stable isotope of silicon with the emission of positron $(_{+1}e^0)$

$$_{15}\overset{*}{P}^{30} \rightarrow {}_{14}Si^{30} + {}_{+1}e^0$$

This phenomenon of bombarding certain stable nuclei of elements with α-particles producing artificial radioactive elements is referred to as artificial or induced radioactivity. A few other examples of artificial radioactivity are

(i) $_{12}Mg^{24} + {}_2He^4 \rightarrow {}_{14}\overset{*}{Si}^{27} + {}_0n^1$

$$_{14}\overset{*}{Si}^{27} \rightarrow {}_{13}Al^{27} + {}_{+1}e^0$$

(ii) $_5B^{10} + {}_2He^4 \rightarrow {}_7\overset{*}{N}^{13} + {}_0n^1$

$$_7\overset{*}{N}^{13} \rightarrow {}_6C^{13} + {}_{+1}e^0$$

In the examples cited above, the induced radioactivity is brought about by α-particles with lighter elements; however, it is difficult to induce radioactivity in cases of heavier nuclei because of intense electrical repulsions.

Besides α-particles, the artificial radioactivity can be induced by protons, deuterons and neutrons.

Artificial Radioactivity by Protons and Deuterons: Accelerated particles such as protons, deuterons can bring about disintegration of nuclei in which the initial product is radioactive. The disintegration involving (d, α), (d, p) and (d, n) generally lead to radioactive species which are either positron or electron emitters. For example

(i) $_{11}Na^{23} + {}_1D^2 \rightarrow {}_{11}\overset{*}{Na}^{24} + {}_1H^1$

$$_{11}\overset{*}{Na}^{24} \rightarrow {}_{12}Mg^{24} + {}_{-1}e^0$$

(ii) $_{12}Mg^{26} + {}_1D^2 \rightarrow {}_{11}\overset{*}{Na}^{24} + {}_2He^4$

$$_{11}\overset{*}{Na}^{24} \rightarrow {}_{12}Mg^{24} + {}_{-1}e^0$$

(iii) $_8O^{16} + {}_1D^2 \rightarrow {}_9\overset{*}{F}^{17} + {}_0n^1$

$$_9\overset{*}{F}^{17} \rightarrow {}_8O^{17} + {}_{+1}e^0$$

Artificial Radioactivity by Neutrons: Fermi has shown that slow moving neutrons can react with almost all nuclei giving, in most cases, radioactive products. Bombardments with such neutrons leads to four types of reactions (n, α), (n, p), (n, γ) and $(n, 2n)$. The products of first three types of reactions are radioactive isotopes and emit electrons; those of $(n, 2n)$ reactions lead to positron and electrons. The (n, γ) is the most common of these reactions

(i) $\quad _{13}Al^{27} + _{0}n^{1} \rightarrow _{2}He^{4} + _{11}\overset{*}{Na}^{24}$

$\quad\quad _{11}\overset{*}{Na}^{24} \rightarrow _{12}Mg^{24} + _{-1}e^{0}$

(ii) $\quad _{15}P^{31} + _{0}n^{1} \rightarrow _{14}\overset{*}{Si}^{31} + _{1}H^{1}$

$\quad\quad _{14}\overset{*}{Si}^{31} \rightarrow _{15}P^{31} + _{-1}e^{0}$

(iii) $\quad _{18}Ar^{40} + _{0}n^{1} \rightarrow \gamma + _{18}\overset{*}{Ar}^{41}$

$\quad\quad _{18}\overset{*}{Ar}^{41} \rightarrow _{19}K^{41} + _{-1}e^{0}$

(iv) $\quad _{19}K^{39} + _{0}n^{1} \rightarrow _{19}\overset{*}{K}^{38} + 2_{0}n^{1}$

$\quad\quad _{19}\overset{*}{K}^{38} \rightarrow _{18}Ar^{38} + _{+1}e^{0}$

(v) $\quad _{37}Rb^{85} + _{0}n^{1} \rightarrow _{37}\overset{*}{Rb}^{84} + 2_{0}n^{1}$

$\quad\quad _{37}\overset{*}{Rb}^{84} \rightarrow _{38}Sr^{84} + _{-1}e^{0}$

23.13 NUCLEAR FISSION

It is the process in which a large nucleus breaks into two or more nuclei of medium size. Fermi (1934) studied the bombardment of uranium nucleus with neutrons and observed that products show several different types of strong β-rays activity and some strong products of decay. O. Hahn and Strassman (1939) showed that when uranium (U^{235}) was irradiated with slow moving neutron; the products so formed had an atomic mass and atomic number considerably lower than that of uranium. It was shown that the products of neutron irradiations were isotopes of barium and krypton.

$$_{92}U^{235} + _{0}n^{1} \rightarrow _{56}Ba^{144} + _{36}Kr^{89} + 3_{0}n^{1}$$

These results were interpreted by stating that the uranium nucleus is rendered highly unstable by capturing a neutron which then breaks up immediately into two nuclei of approximately equal size. Each fission reaction produces one nuclide with mass number near 90-95 and another with a mass number near 135-140. In the process of nuclear fission the mass of the products obtained is less than the mass of the disintegrating uranium atom and the projectile neutron, considerable amount of energy is liberated. Measurements indicate that there would be a mass defect of about 0.215 amu which is equivalent to about 200 MeV per uranium atom.

The fission of each uranium nucleus is accompanied by three neutrons which under suitable conditions cause fission of other uranium nuclei. This chain reaction of splitting would produce more and more energy and more neutrons.

It has been shown that only $_{92}U^{235}$ is fissioned under bombardment from slow neutrons. However, the more abundant U^{238} isotope absorbs slow neutrons, does not undergo fission but yields a series of transuranic elements (Np, etc.) as follows:

$$_{92}U^{238} + {}_0n^1 \rightarrow \left(_{92}U^{239} \right) \rightarrow {}_{93}Np^{239} + {}_{-1}e^0 \; ; \; t_{1/2} = 23.5 \text{ min.}$$

$$_{93}Np^{239} \rightarrow {}_{94}Pu^{239} + {}_{-1}e^0 \; ; \; t_{1/2} = 2.35 \text{ days}$$

Like $_{92}U^{235}$ nuclide, $_{94}Pu^{239}$ can also supply large amounts of energy through nuclear fission. With fast neutrons, $_{92}U^{238}$ suffers nuclear fission to a small extent. Plutonium like U^{235} is also fissionable. It has a longer half-life period and hence can be stored.

Another fissionable isotope is $_{92}U^{233}$ which can be obtained from $_{90}Th^{232}$ by irradiation with slow neutrons. The reactions are:

$$_{90}Th^{232} + {}_0n^1 \rightarrow {}_{90}Th^{233}$$

$$_{90}Th^{233} \rightarrow {}_{91}Pa^{233} + {}_{-1}e^0$$

$$_{91}Pa^{233} \rightarrow {}_{92}U^{233} + {}_{-1}e^0$$

23.14 NUCLEAR FUSION

The process in which two small nucleus come together to form a longer more stable nuclide is called nuclear fusion. It has been observed that tremendous amount of energy is obtained when lighter nuclei such as hydrogen, deuterium and helium are fused to form heavier nuclei.

Some examples of the nuclear fusion reactions are:

$$_1H^2 + {}_1H^2 \rightarrow {}_1H^3 + {}_1H^1 + 4.02 \text{ MeV}$$

$$_1H^2 + {}_1H^2 \rightarrow {}_2He^3 + {}_0n^1 + 3.26 \text{ MeV}$$

$$_1H^2 + {}_1H^3 \rightarrow {}_2He^4 + {}_0n^1 + 17.6 \text{ MeV}$$

$$_1H^2 + {}_2He^3 \rightarrow {}_2He^4 + {}_1H^1 + 1.83 \text{ MeV}$$

For the reaction

$$_1H^2 + {}_3Li^6 \rightarrow 2\,{}_2He^4$$

the mass defect $\Delta M = 0.0423$ amu. The energy change for this reaction is $\Delta E = 3.6278 \times 10^{12}$ J. This energy is for the formation of two molecules of $_2He^4$. For 1 molecule of helium $\Delta E = 1.8139 \times 10^{12}$ J.

The amount of energy released per unit mass of the atom is much greater in fusion processes than fission reactions. This is because of greater proportion of mass of the reaction is converted into energy.

23.15 SEPARATION OF ISOTOPES

Since isotopes have identical chemical properties, therefore their separation by chemical methods generally failed. However, physical methods may be employed for their separation. Some important methods are: (*i*) Diffusion method; (*ii*) Thermal diffusion method; (*iii*) Electromagnetic separation method; (*iv*) Evaporation method; (*v*) Electrolytic method; and (*vi*) Chemical exchange method.

Diffusion Method

The method is based on the principle of Graham's law of diffusion. The rate of diffusion of a gas or vapour is inversely proportional to the square root of the molecular mass (or its density). The mixture of isotopes in the gaseous form is allowed to diffuse through the porous membrane, e.g., a clay-pipe tube, when the diffused gas would be enriched in lighter isotopes. Larger the ratio of masses of the two isotopes, more efficient will be the separation. Thus, the method is more successful with lighter elements, e.g., in the separation of isotopes of hydrogen of mass number 1 and 2; the ratio of their diffusion rate is

$$\sqrt{\frac{2}{1}} \text{ or } 1.414 \text{ to } 1$$

The efficiency of a process for the separation is expressed in terms of *separation factor which is defined as the ratio of the concentrations of two species after processing to that before processing,*

$$S = \frac{C_1}{C_2} \Big/ \frac{C_1'}{C_2'}$$

where (C_1, C_2) and (C_1', C_2') are concentrations after and before processing. For effective separation, the value of separation factor should be large.

Aston used this principle for the first time to separate the isotopes of neon and succeeded in concentrating Ne^{22} to some extent. In 1932, Hertz was able to get 99% Ne^{20} and 1% Ne^{22} by using a cascade of 48 diffusion pumps in series. This method has been employed in atomic plants for separating $U^{235}F_6$ present to small extent (0.7%) from the predominant $U^{238}F_6$.

Thermal Diffusion Method

This method, used by Clausius and Dickel in 1936, involves a combination of thermal diffusion and convection. The apparatus consists of a vertical pipe about 36 metre in length, which is electrically heated to about 500°C or more (Fig. 23.4). The walls of the pipe are kept cold. The gas to be separated. into its isotopes is placed in the annular space and is thus situated between a hot and a cold surface. Due to thermal diffusion, concentration of the heavier isotope is greater in the cold region than in hot region.

Lighter isotope

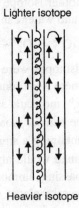

Heavier isotope

Fig. 23.4 Separation of isotopes by thermal diffusion

Moreover, due to thermal convection, the heavier isotope goes downward along the cold wall while the lighter isotope moves up along the hot walls. This method has been used for the rapid and effective separation of isotopes of chlorine, neon, carbon and argon.

Electromagnetic Separation

Positive rays containing mixture of isotopes of the element were first accelerated in an electric field and then deflected by a powerful magnetic field. The isotopes form group to different masses which separate out at different angles and are collected separately. The method is efficient one and was successfully applied in the separation of isotopes of light as well as heavy elements. The electromagnetic separation method has been employed in the large scale separation of U^{235} and U^{238}.

Evaporation Method

In this method use is made of the fact that the rates of evaporation of identical atoms or molecules from the surface of a mixture is inversely proportional to the square root of their masses. If the evaporated molecules are condensed immediately (at very low pressure) and are not allowed to return to the surface, the resulting condensate would be enriched in lighter isotope and the residue richer in heavier isotope. Brønsted and Hevesy allowed mercury to evaporate at very low pressure (highly evacuated space) and condensed the vapours by freezing it on a surface cooled in liquid air to obtain fractions differing appreciably in their densities.

Keeson used this method in separating heavy hydrogen. Ordinary liquid hydrogen containing 0.02% deuterium when subjected to fractional distillation with efficient rectifying column gave about 1.5% of deuterium.

Electrolytic Method

Washburn and Urey (1932) found that water obtained from an industrial electrolytic cell, which had been electrolysed several times had a density higher than the ordinary water. During electrolysis of aqueous solutions, the lighter isotope of water ($_1H^1$) is preferentially evolved, leaving an excess of heavier isotope ($_1H^2$) in the residual water.

Chemical Exchange Method

The rate of a chemical reaction depends somewhat on the atomic masses. The heavier isotope reacts more slowly than the lighter isotope. This fact has been used in separating the isotopes. In a reaction, an isotope of one compound exchanges with another isotope of the same element in another compound. For example, reaction involving oxygen gas and water can be written as

$$O_2^{16} + 2H_2O^{18} \rightarrow O_2^{18} + 2H_2O^{16}$$

If the chemical reactivities of both the isotopes were same, the equilibrium constant (K) of the reaction would be unity. But in actual experiment it is found to be more than unity (1.012). This result, therefore, shows that the reaction of the O_2^{16} molecule with H_2O^{18} is more rapid than the reverse reaction. In other words, the proportion of the heavier isotope O_2^{18} in the gas phase is greater than in the liquid phase. Thus, if gaseous oxygen containing a small amount of O_2^{18} is passed through liquid water continuously, the resulting gas so obtained would always be richer in O_2^{18}.

Urey and Thode concentrated N^{15} by passing ammonia gas through a solution of ammonium nitrate, when the following exchange reaction take place:

$$N^{15}H_3 + N^{14}H_4^+ \rightarrow N^{14}H_3 + N^{15}H_4^+ \; ; \; K = 1.033$$

23.16 RADIOACTIVE DATING

An estimate of age of materials can be made by measuring the activity of radioactive isotopes present in them. This technique can be used to measure the age of ancient objects and is called radioactive dating.

Carbon occurs largely as an isotope ^{12}C. In the atmosphere, nitrogen is bombarded by cosmic neutrons, which produces the isotope ^{14}C.

$$_7N^{14} + _0n^1 \rightarrow _6C^{14} + _1H^1$$

The carbon reacts with oxygen forming CO_2 which is used up by plants. All the plants therefore contain traces of C^{14}. Animals eat these plants and so they also contain traces of C^{14}. This isotope of carbon is radioactive, undergoes a slow β-decay and has a half life period ($t_{1/2}$) of 5720 years. In living plant, taking in carbon dioxide has the same $_6C^{14}/_6C^{12}$ ratio. When the plant is cut or the animal dies, intake of radioactive carbon stops and that C^{14} already present gradually decays (β-decay) and the ratio of $_6C^{14}/_6C^{12}$ decreases. By measuring the ratio of $_6C^{14}/_6C^{12}$ in the organic material and comparing it with that of the living ones, an estimate of the time at which the plant was cut or animal died can be made.

Let us calculate the age of a piece of wood for which the ratio $_6C^{14}/_6C^{12}$ is 0.4 times that of living plant and r_1 and r_2 be the ratio of $_6C^{14}/_6C^{12}$ of living and dead organic material respectively. Since half-life period, $t_{1/2}$ for $_6C^{14}$ is 5720 years, the value of λ is given by

$$\lambda = \frac{0.693}{t_{1/2}} = \frac{0.693}{5720 \text{ yrs.}} = 1.2 \times 10^{-4} \text{ yr}^{-1}$$

The age of the dead organic material is calculated using the rate equation

$$t = \frac{2.303}{k} \log \frac{r_1}{r_2}$$

$$= \frac{2.303}{1.2 \times 10^{-4} \text{ yr}^{-1}} \log \left(\frac{1}{0.4} \right)$$

$$= 7564 \text{ yr.}$$

It means that the sample of wood belongs to a tree which was alive before 7564 years.

EXERCISES

1. Select the correct statements from the following:
    (i) Nuclear forces are of short range type.
    (ii) Energy associated with nuclear processes are roughly a million or more times as great as the energies involved in chemical phenomena.
    (iii) Nuclei which lie outside the belt of stability are radioactive.
    (iv) Discovery of isotopes has been helpful in explaining fractional atomic masses.

(v) Nuclei for which $N/P > 1$ are unstable and β-ray emitters.

(vi) Disintegration of radioactive elements depends on the conditions prevailing in the surrounding atmosphere.

(vii) Emission of α-particles by the nucleus changes both the mass number and the atomic number.

(viii) A meson has the same mass as that of an electron.

(ix) Neutrons are regarded as more effective projectile than β-particles.

Ans. Correct statements: (i), (ii), (iii), (iv), (v).

2. Complete and balance the following reactions:

(a) $_5B^9 + _0n^1 = \text{.......} + _1H^1$

(b) $_3Li^7 + \text{.......} = _4Be^7 + _0n^1$

(c) $_8O^{19} + \text{.......} = _8O^{18} + _1H^3$

(d) $_{15}P^{30} + _2He^4 = _{16}S^{33} + \text{.......}$

(e) $_7N^{15} + \text{..........} = _6C^{12} + _2He^4$

(f) $_7N^{14} + _2He^4 = _8O^{17} + \text{........}$

(g) $_{13}Al^{27} + _2He^4 = _{15}P^{30} + \text{.......}$

(h) $_{92}U^{239} = _{93}Np^{239} + \text{...}$

(i) $_1H^2 + \gamma = \text{...} + _0n^1$

Ans. (a) $_4Be^9$, (b) $_1H^1$, (c) $_1H^2$, (d) $_1H^1$, (e) $_1H^1$, (f) $_1H^1$, (g) $_0n^1$, (h) $_{-1}e^0$, (i) $_1H^1$.

3. Complete the following:

(i) $Mg^{24}(_1H^2, \alpha)\text{.......}$,

(ii) $Ca^{40}(n, \alpha)\text{......}$,

(iii) $Au^{197}(n, \gamma)\text{......}$,

(iv) $H^3(\alpha, n)\text{.......}$,

(v) $Mo^{96}(p, n)\text{......}$,

(vi) $Al^{27}(\alpha, n)$ and

(vii) $Be^9(\alpha, n)\text{......}$

Ans. (i) Na^{22}, (ii) Ar^{37}, (iii) Au^{198}, (iv) Li^6 (v) Tc^{97}, (vi) P^{30}, (vii) C^{12}.

4. How the number of protons in a nucleus changes when:

(i) a γ-ray, (ii) a β-ray, (iii) an α-particle, is emitted from the nucleus?

Ans. (i) no change, (ii) increases by unity, (iii) decreases by two.

5. The overall equations for the disintegration of $_{89}Ac^{227}$, $_{90}Th^{232}$, $_{91}Pa^{233}$ and $_{92}U^{238}$ are as follows:

(a) $_{89}Ac^{227} \rightarrow 5\alpha + 3_{-1}\beta^0 + x$

(b) $_{90}Th^{232} \rightarrow 6\alpha + 4_{-1}\beta^0 + x$

(c) $_{91}Pa^{233} \rightarrow 6\alpha + 4_{-1}\beta^0 + x$

(d) $_{92}U^{238} \rightarrow 8\alpha + 6_{-1}\beta^0 + x$

Evaluate the mass number and atomic number of x in each case:

Ans. (a) $_{82}Pb^{207}$, (b) $_{82}Pb^{208}$, (c) $_{82}Bi^{209}$, (d) $_{82}Pb^{206}$.

6. Given the following nuclides:

$$_{18}Ar^{40}, _{18}Ar^{38}, _{19}K^{39}, _{19}K^{40}, _{19}K^{41}, _{20}Ca^{40}, _{20}Ca^{42}, _{20}Ca^{43}.$$

List out (a) the isotopes, (b) the isobars and (c) the isotones:

Ans. (a) Isotopes: $_{18}Ar^{40}$, $_{18}Ar^{38}$ and $_{19}K^{39}$, $_{19}K^{40}$, $_{19}K^{41}$ and $_{20}Ca^{40}$, $_{20}Ca^{42}$, $_{20}Ca^{43.}$

(b) Isobars: $_{18}Ar^{40}$, $_{19}K^{40}$, $_{20}Ca^{40}$

(c) Isotones: $_{18}Ar^{38}$, $_{19}K^{39}$, $_{20}Ca^{40}$ and $_{18}Ar^{40}$, $_{19}K^{41}$, $_{20}Ca^{42}$.

7. If $_8O^{16}$ has a mass of 16.00 amu, calculate the binding energy per nucleon for $_8O^{16}$. **Ans. 7.63 MeV.**

8. A certain isotope of an element X decays 1.0×10^5 atoms s^{-1} g^{-1}. Calculate its activity in (i) curies, (ii) millicuries and microcuries. **Ans.** (ii) 2.7×10^{-8} c, (ii) 2.7×10^{-3} mc, (ii) 2.7 μc.

9. Calculate the number of α-particles emitted per second by 1 g of pure thorium oxide. Half-life of $_{90}Th^{232}$ is 1.39×10^{10} years and molar mass of ThO_2 is 264 g mol^{-1}.
   Ans. 3.89×10^8 s^{-1}.

10. $_{92}U^{235}$, has a half-life of 7.1×10^8 years, and its daughter element $_{90}Th^{231}$, has a half-life of 24.6 hours. What is the mass of $_{90}Th^{231}$ in equilibrium with 1 g of $_{92}U^{235}$?
    Ans. 3.89×10^{-15} kg.

11. 1 g of radon produces 1.16×19^{18} α-particles in a minute. Calculate the fraction of radon disintegrated in this time. Molar mass of radon is 222 g mol^{-1}. **Ans. 4.28×10^{-4}.**

12. Calculate the mass (in g) of 1 curie of RaB (Pb^{214}, $t_{1/2}$ = 26.8 min). Also evaluate the specific activity (number of curies per unit mass or per unit volume) of the element.
    Ans. 3.1×10^{-8} g; sp. activity = 3.23×10^7 cg^{-1}.

13. The half-life of a certain radioactive element is 5760 years. In how many years would the activity fall to 90% of its initial value. **Ans. 877 years.**

14. The half-life of a certain radioactive element A (molar mass 108) is 2.30 min.
    (a) Calculate the decay constant.
    (b) If the sample had an activity of 3 μc, calculate the number of atoms and grams of the radioactive element A.
    Ans. (a) $k = 0.301$ min^{-1} (b) 2.21×10^7 atoms or 3.97×10^{-15} g of A.

15. The half-life of $_{11}Na^{24}$ is 14.9 hours and atomic mass is 24 g mol^{-1}. Calculate the activity of 1.00 g of Na^{24} in curies. **Ans. 8.74.**

16. $_{86}Rn^{222}$ emits α-particles and its half life period is 3.825 days. How many milligram of $_{86}Rn^{222}$ will remain after 8.83 days from 0.020 mg sample? **Ans. 0.0025 mg.**

17. (a) Calculate Δm, the difference in mass between the final and initial nuclei in g per mole of the emission of γ-ray of energy 2.6 MeV. **Ans. $\Delta m = -2.8 \times 10^{-3}$ g mol^{-1}.**
    (b) The emission of α and β-particles from the nucleus is frequently accompanied by the emission of γ-rays, the source of photons being the product nuclei. For example:

    $$_{82}Pb^{210} \rightarrow \, _{83}Bi^{210} + \beta \text{ and } _{88}Ra^{226} \rightarrow \, _{86}Rn^{222} + \alpha$$

    $$_{83}Bi^{210} \rightarrow \, _{83}Bi^{210} + \gamma \text{ and } _{86}Rn^{222} \rightarrow \, _{86}Rn^{222} + \gamma$$

    Are these particles and photons nucleons, *i.e.*, constituents of nuclei?

18. The half-life period of a radioactive element is 3.8 days. If it initially emits 7.0×10^4 α-particles per second and after a certain period it decreased to 2.1×10^4 α-particles per second, calculate the time interval.
    Ans. 6.6 days.

19. Calculate the age of an old sample of wood from chemical evidences if it possesses activity of 7.8 disintegrations per min. per gram of carbon. Assume that the activity of $_6C^{14}$ is 14.0 disintegration per min. g^{-1} of carbon and is also the value of the old wood sample, $t_{1/2}$ for $_6C^{14} = 5.73 \times 10^3$ yrs. **Ans. 4800 years.**

20.   A radioisotope decays at such a rate that after 68 minutes, only 1/4 of the original amount remains. Calculate the decay constant (μ) and the half-life of the radio isotope.   **Ans.** $\lambda = 0.0204$ min^{-1}, $t_{1/2} = 33.9$ min.

21.   (a) Show that the energy of a β-particle in the nuclear reaction

$$_{37}\text{Rb}^{87} \rightarrow _{38}\text{Sr}^{87} + \beta$$

expressed in g per mole, is equal to the difference between the atomic masses of Sr^{87} and Rb^{87}.

(b) What mass of $_6\text{C}^{14}$ ($t_{1/2} = 5760$ years) will make one curie of it?

Ans. 0.218 g.

22.   The only stable isotope of fluorine is $_9\text{F}^{19}$. What type of radioactivity would you expect from each of the isotopes $_9\text{F}^{17}$, $_9\text{F}^{18}$, $_9\text{F}^{20}$ and $_9\text{F}^{21}$?

Ans. F^{17}, F^{18} electron capture or positron emission. F^{20}, F^{21}-β-emission.

23.   The masses of $_{11}\text{Na}^{22}$ and $_{10}\text{Ne}^{22}$ atoms are 21.994435 and 21.991385 amu, respectively. Is it energetically possible for $_{11}\text{Na}^{22}$ to decay to $_{10}\text{Ne}^{22}$ by positron emission?   **Ans.** Yes.

24.   When an electron and positron encounter each other, they are annihilated and two photons of equal energy are formed. Calculate the wavelength of these photons.   **Ans.** 0.0024 nm.

25.   The most abundant isotope of helium is $_2\text{He}^4$ and may be regarded to be formed according to the reaction

$$4\,_1\text{H}^1 \rightarrow _2\text{He}^4 + 2\,_{+1}e^0$$

If the actual mass of the atom is 4.0026 amu, calculate the energy released in fusion of four hydrogen atoms to form a helium atom.   **Ans.** 25.9 MeV.

26.   Will the following radioactive nuclei be $_{-1}\beta^0$ or positron emitters?

(i) $_1\text{H}^3$, (ii) $_4\text{Be}^{12}$, (iii) $_6\text{C}^{11}$, $_{11}\text{Na}^{24}$ and (v) $_{12}\text{Mg}^{22}$.

Ans. (i) $_{-1}\beta^0$, (ii) $_{-1}\beta^0$, (iii) $_{+1}\beta^0$, (iv) $_{-1}\beta^0$, (v) $_{+1}\beta^0$.

27.   (a) Calculate the fraction of the total mass of a hydrogen atom contained in the nucleus.

(b) If the nuclear dimension were taken as 1.5×10^{-10} m and the atomic size as 0.529×10^{-19} m. What fraction of the total volume is occupied by the nucleus.   **Ans.** (a) 99.95 %, (b) 2.3×10^{-12} %.

28.   The mass of a nucleus is less than the sum of the masses of the individual nucleons (protons and neutrons). Do you consider this a violation of the conservation principle? Explain.

29.   A new element is always generated when the atomic number of the nucleus changes but a change in its mass number may not produce a new element. Comment on the statement.

30.   Explain and illustrate the following terms:

(i) Half-life period and average life period; (ii) Decay constant; (iii) Isotopes; (iv) Isobars; (v) Isotones; (vi) Group displacement law; (vii) Binding energy; (viii) Packing fractions; (ix) Fission; (x) Fusion; (xi) Artificial disintegration of atoms.

31.   What are the various types of radiations given off by radioactive elements. Discuss their main characteristics. How does the emission of each one of them effect the nucleus?

32.   Give an account of the methods available for the detection and separation of isotopes.

CHAPTER 24

Photochemistry

24.1 INTRODUCTION

We have seen in Chapter 16 that ordinarily reactions are initiated by activation brought about through molecular collisions. The average kinetic energy of translational motion $\left(\dfrac{3}{2} RT\right)$ is of the order of 4.184 kJ mol^{-1} and is not sufficient for chemical transformation. The energies required for chemical reactions are approximately of the order of 40-400 kJ per mole. Another way to provide the necessary activation is to bring the molecules into collisions with photons of ultraviolet light, X-rays or γ-rays. Besides photons, high energy particles like α-rays, β-rays or protons or neutrons may be used for activation. Thus, photochemistry comprises the study of the chemical reactions produced directly or indirectly by light where light includes the infrared and ultraviolet, as well as the visible region of spectrum, *i.e.*, the range of wavelength from about 10^2 nm to 10^3 nm. The energies of quanta in this range vary from about 90-900 kJ per mole. These energies are comparable with the strengths of the chemical bonds. In photochemical reactions, molecules are activated by the absorption of photons.

On the other hand, if high energy photons from X rays or γ-rays be used, innumerable molecules coming in their path would be ionized. These ionization would lead to chemical changes through secondary processes. The study of the effects of these radiations therefore comprise the subject matter of radiation chemistry.

24.2 THE GROTTHUSS-DRAPER AND LAMBERT-BEER LAWS

The Grotthuss-Draper law states that *only those radiations which are absorbed by the reacting systems are effective in producing a chemical change.* It does not necessarily mean that the absorbed light will always bring about the chemical reaction. When light passes through any medium, the amount of light absorbed depends upon the distance traversed in the medium. This principle was first stated in 1729 by P. Bouguer and later rediscovered by J.H. Lambert (1758), a German physicist. According to him when monochromatic light of intensity I passes through a medium of thickness dl, a decrease in the intensity of light results. The decrease in intensity, dI is proportional to the thickness and the intensity of the incident light, that is

$$dI = -\alpha\, I\, dl \qquad\qquad ...(24.1)$$

where α is a proportionality constant called the *absorption* or *extinction coefficient* and depends both on the nature of the medium and the wavelength of the light. The above equation can be rewritten as

$$\frac{dI}{I} = -\alpha\, dl \qquad\qquad ...(24.2)$$

Integration of equation (24.2) yields

$$\ln I = -\alpha l + C' \qquad\qquad ...(24.3)$$

where I is the intensity of emergent beam after passing through the medium of thickness l and C' is the integration constant. When $l = 0$, $I = I_0$, the intensity of the incident light. Therefore, $C' = \ln I_0$. Putting this value of C' in equation (24.3), we get

$$\ln I = -\alpha l + \ln I_0$$

$$\ln \frac{I}{I_0} = -\alpha l \qquad\qquad ...(24.4)$$

$$I = I_0 e^{-\alpha l} \qquad\qquad ...(24.5)$$

The intensity of the absorbed light is given by

$$I_{abs} = I_0 - I$$

Since I is given by equation (24.5), hence

$$I_{abs} = I_0 - I_0 e^{-\alpha l}$$

$$= I_0 (1 - e^{-\alpha l})$$

If α is large for the wavelength in question, then $e^{-\alpha l} \approx 0$ and $I_{abs} = I_0$, *i.e.*, all the incident light I_0 is absorbed.

Beer showed that for many solutions of absorbing substances in practically transparent solvents the constant α is proportional to the concentration of the solute, *i.e.*,

$$\alpha = \varepsilon C$$

where ε is *the absorption coefficient*. Equation (24.4) can be written as

$$\ln \frac{I}{I_0} = -\varepsilon C l$$

or

$$\log \frac{I}{I_0} = -\frac{\varepsilon C l}{2.303} = \varepsilon' C l \qquad\qquad ...(24.5(a))$$

where

$$\varepsilon' = \frac{\varepsilon}{2.303}$$

Hence

$$\frac{I}{I_0} = 10^{-0.4343\varepsilon C l}$$

or

$$\frac{I}{I_0} = 10^{-\varepsilon' C l} \qquad\qquad ...(24.6)$$

This is known as *the Lambert-Beer's law*. The ratio $\dfrac{I}{I_0}$ is the transmittance T and the quantity $\log \dfrac{I}{I_0}$ is referred to as absorbance A.

If the concentration is expressed in moles/dm^3, then ε' is called *the molar extinction coefficient* or molar absorption coefficient. The molar extinction coefficient depends on the frequency of the incident radiation and is greater where the absorption is most intense. Its dimensions are $\dfrac{1}{\text{conc} \times \text{length}}$ and is normally expressed as L mol^{-1}cm^{-1}. From equation (24.6) it is clear that if $I/I_0 = 10^{-1}$, then $\varepsilon'C\,l = 1$

or

$$\varepsilon' = \frac{1}{Cl}$$

and if $C = 1$ mole/dm^3, then

$$\varepsilon' = \frac{1}{l}$$

Hence ε' is defined as *the reciprocal of the thickness of the solution when the intensity of the incident radiation falls to 1/10 of its initial value*. The product $\varepsilon'Cl$ is called *the optical density* or *the absorbance* of the sample. It can be seen from equation (24.5 (*a*)) that the absorbance is directly proportional to the concentration C and the path length *l*. The proportionality constant is characteristic of the solute and depends on the wavelength of the light, the solvent and temperature. Since molar extinction coefficient depends on wavelength, the Lamber-Beer law is obeyed at all wavelength.

Equation (24.6) is the basic equation for various colorimetric methods of analysis. The extinction coefficient is determined by measuring the amount of light transmitted through a solution of known concentration and then plotting log (I/I_0) against C. The slope of the curve gives the value of $\varepsilon'\,l$, which is constant. This law is valid for dilute solutions. In concentrated solutions the absorption may be more than required by the equation.

Problem 24.1: 2.0×10^{-3}m thickness of a certain glass transmits 10% of the incident light of wavelength 300 nm. What percentage of light of the same wavelength will be absorbed by a 1.0×10^{-3} m thickness of the glass?

Solution: From equation (24.5) we have

$$\frac{I}{I_0} = e^{-\alpha l}$$

Here

$$I = 10\%, l = 2.0 \times 10^{-3} \text{m}$$

Therefore,

$$\frac{10}{100} = \exp(-2 \times 10^{-3}\alpha)$$

or

$$\alpha = \frac{2.303}{2.0 \times 10^{-3}}$$

Again

$$l = 1.0 \times 10^{-3} \text{ m}$$

Hence
$$\frac{I}{I_0} = \exp\left(-\frac{2.303 \times 1.0 \times 10^{-3}}{2.0 \times 1.0 \times 10^{-3}}\right) = \exp\left(-\frac{2.303}{2}\right)$$

or
$$\frac{I}{I_0} = 0.3162$$

or
$$I = 31.62\%$$

Thus the amount of light absorbed = 100 − 31.62

$$= 68.38\%.$$

Problem 24.2: Intensity of light of 260 nm when passed through a 1.0×10^{-3} m path length of a cell containing a 0.05 mol dm^{-3} solution is reduced to 15% of its initial value. Calculate the optical density and the molar extinction coefficient of the sample.

    Solution: From equation (24.6), we have

$$\frac{I}{I_0} = 10^{-\varepsilon'Cl}$$

Here
$$C = 5.0 \times 10^{-2} \text{ mol dm}^{-3}$$

$$l = 1.0 \times 10^{-3} \text{ m and } I/I_0 = 0.15$$

Therefore,
$$0.15 = 10^{-\varepsilon'\left(5.0 \times 10^{-2} \text{ mol dm}^{-3}\right)\left(1.0 \times 10^{-3} \text{ m}\right)}$$

$$\log 0.15 = -\varepsilon' \, 5.0 \times 10^{-5} \text{ mol dm}^{-3}\text{m}$$

or
$$\varepsilon' = 1.648 \times 10^4 \text{ mol}^{-1}\text{dm}^3\text{m}^{-1}$$

Hence the optical density = $\varepsilon'Cl$

$$= (1.648 \times 10^4)\,(5.0 \times 10^{-2})\,(1.0 \times 10^{-3})$$

$$= 0.824$$

24.3 THE STARK-EINSTEIN LAW OF PHOTOCHEMICAL EQUIVALENCE

The law of photochemical equivalence is in a sense simply a quantum mechanical statement of Grotthuss-Draper's law. This law states *that each molecule which takes part in a primary photochemical process absorbs one quantum of light causing the reaction*. If ν is the frequency of the irradiating light, then the energy of the corresponding photon is given by Planck relation

$$\varepsilon = h\nu$$

    This energy is absorbed by each reacting molecule according to Stark-Einstein law. The energy absorbed per mol is then $N_A h\nu$, where N_A is the Avogadro constant and is known as one Einstein of energy. Thus

$$E = N_A h\nu$$

$$= \frac{N_A hc}{\lambda}$$

where c is the velocity of light and λ is the wavelength of the absorbed light. Putting the value of $N_A =$ 6.023×10^{23}, $h = 6.626 \times 10^{-34}$ J s and $c = 3.0 \times 10^8$ m s^{-1}, we get

$$E = \frac{(6.023 \times 10^{23} \, \text{mol}^{-1})(6.626 \times 10^{-34} \, \text{J s})(3 \times 10^8 \, \text{m s}^{-1})}{\lambda}$$

$$= \frac{(6.023 \times 10^{23} \, \text{mol}^{-1})(6.626 \times 10^{-34} \, \text{Js})(3 \times 10^8 \, \text{ms}^{-1})}{(1000 \, \text{J kJ}^{-1})(\lambda \times 10^{-9} \, \text{m})} = \frac{119.73 \times 10^3}{\lambda} \, \text{kJ mol}^{-1}$$

where λ is in nanometers

For light of wavelength 600 nm the energy E is given as

$$E = \frac{(6.023 \times 10^{23} \, \text{mol}^{-1})(6.626 \times 10^{-34} \, \text{J s})(3 \times 10^8 \, \text{m s}^{-1})}{(600 \times 10^{-9} \, \text{m})}$$

$$= 199.55 \, \text{kJ mol}^{-1}$$

The quantity E is known as one Einstein of radiation of the given wavelength λ. It will be seen from above that the energy absorbed per mole is greater, shorter the wavelength of the light.

Problem 24.3: Calculate the energy per mole of light having wavelengths of (a) 85 nm, and (b) 300 nm.

Solution:
$$E = \frac{N_A hc}{\lambda}$$

$$= \frac{(6.023 \times 10^{23} \, \text{mol}^{-1})(6.626 \times 10^{-34} \, \text{J s})(3 \times 10^8 \, \text{m s}^{-1})}{(85 \times 10^{-9} \, \text{m})}$$

$$= 1.407 \times 10^6 \, \text{J mol}^{-1}$$
$$= 1.407 \times 10^3 \, \text{kJ mol}^{-1}$$

(b) When $\lambda = 300$ nm,

$$E = \frac{(6.023 \times 10^{23} \, \text{mol}^{-1})(6.626 \times 10^{-34} \, \text{J s})(3 \times 10^8 \, \text{m s}^{-1})}{(300 \times 10^{-9} \, \text{m})}$$

$$= 3.986 \times 10^2 \, \text{kJ mol}^{-1}$$

Problem 24.4: A certain photochemical reaction requires an activation energy of 30 kcal mol^{-1}. To what value does this correspond to in the following units (a) kJ per mol, (b) wavelength, (c) wave number and (d) frequency of light?

Solution: (a) Since 1 kcal = 4.184 kJ

Hence
$$30 \, \text{kcal mol}^{-1} = 125.52 \, \text{kJ mol}^{-1} = 125.52 \times 10^3 \, \text{J mol}^{-1}$$

(b) Since
$$E = \frac{N_A hc}{\lambda}$$

or
$$\lambda = \frac{N_A hc}{E}$$

$$= \frac{\left(6.023 \times 10^{23}\, \text{mol}^{-1}\right)\left(6.626 \times 10^{-34}\, \text{Js}\right)\left(3 \times 10^{8}\, \text{m s}^{-1}\right)}{\left(125.52 \times 10^{3}\, \text{J mol}^{-1}\right)}$$

$$= 9.528 \times 10^{-7}\, \text{m}$$

(c) We know that

$$\text{wave number } \bar{v} = \frac{1}{\lambda}$$

Hence

$$\bar{v} = \frac{1}{9.528 \times 10^{-7}\, \text{m}}$$

$$= 1.050 \times 10^{6}\, \text{m}^{-1}$$

(d) Since

$$E = N_A h v$$

Therefore,

$$v = \frac{E}{N_A h}$$

$$= \frac{\left(125.52 \times 10^{3}\, \text{J mol}^{-1}\right)}{\left(6.023 \times 10^{23}\, \text{mol}^{-1}\right)\left(6.626 \times 10^{-34}\, \text{Js}\right)}$$

$$= 4.149 \times 10^{14}\, \text{s}^{-1}.$$

24.4 THE QUANTUM YIELD OF A PHOTOCHEMICAL REACTION

When the law of photochemical equivalence is followed, then the quantum yield (ϕ) of the reaction must be unity. Studies on a large number of photochemical reactions indicate that some reactions follow photochemical equivalence law, whereas many other do not follow this law. Bodenstein pointed out that the photochemical equivalence law applies only to the absorption or primary photochemical processes where the products do not undergo further reactions, *i.e.*

$$A + hv \rightarrow A^{*}$$

Atom or molecule   excited species

If the primary reaction is accompanied by the subsequent reactions as happens in chain reactions, the absorption of photon might lead to the decomposition of several molecules and the simple 1:1 ratio between the photons absorbed and the molecules decomposed does not hold. To express the relationship between the number of molecules reacting with the number of photons absorbed, the concept of *quantum yield* or *efficiency,* ϕ is introduced. This is defined as *the number of molecules of reactants consumed or product formed per quantum of light absorbed, i.e.*,

$$\phi = \frac{\text{Number of molecules formed or decomposed in a given time}}{\text{Number of photons absorbed in the same time}}$$

If we measure the rate of formation of product in molecules per second then the quantum yield can also be written as

$$\phi = \frac{d[\text{Product}]/dt}{\text{Number of photons absorbed per second}}$$

$$= \frac{d[\text{Product}]/dt}{I_{abs}}$$

where I_{abs} is the number of photons absorbed per second.

According to the law of photochemical equivalence, the quantum efficiency will always be equal to one. But reaction with low and high quantum yields are known.

For a primary photochemical reaction the quantum yield is one. It is the secondary process which changes the overall quantum yield of the reaction. Hence the determination of the quantum yield helps in understanding the nature of the secondary process.

Experimental Measurement of Photochemical Reactions

An experimental arrangement for the study of a photochemical reaction is shown in Fig. 24.1. Radiation emitted from a source of light L is passed through a condenser system A when parallel beams are formed. The parallel beams are then passed through a filter or monochromator B, which yields beam of the desired wavelength. The light from the monochromator enters a radiation cell D immersed in a thermostat and containing the reaction mixture. Finally the light transmitted through D falls on a detector X which measures the intensity of radiation.

The intensity of radiation is generally measured with the help of thermopile or actinometer. The thermopile is essentially a multijunction thermocouple which is previously calibrated against a standard source of light. Instead, a commonly used actinometer is the uranyl oxalate actinometer consisting of 0.05 molar oxalic acid and 0.01 molar uranyl sulphate in water. On exposure to radiation the reaction

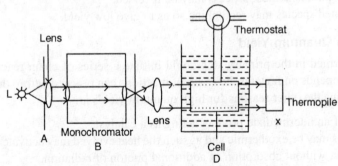

Fig. 24.1 Apparatus for the study of photochemical reactions

$$UO_2^{2+} + h\nu \rightarrow \left(UO_2^{2+}\right)^*$$

$$\left(UO_2^{2+}\right)^* + H_2C_2O_4 \rightarrow CO_2(g) + CO(g) + H_2O(l)$$

takes place the extent of which can be ascertained by titrating the remaining oxalic acid with potassium permanganate. The uranyl ion is not affected by the manganate ion. This reaction has a quantum yield of about 0.50.

The quantum yield of a photochemical reaction is calculated as follows: First the empty cell or the cell filled with solvent in case of a solution is exposed to radiation and the reading is recorded. This gives the total energy incident in a given time. Next, the cell is filled with the reactants and again the reading is recorded. Difference in the two readings will give the total energy absorbed by the reacting mixture in a given time. The reaction rate is measured by the usual methods. Small quantities of samples are pipetted out from time to time and analysed, or the change in some physical property such as refractive index or absorption or optical rotation etc., is measured. Thus from the data of the chemical reaction and the light intensity it is possible to calculate the quantum yield of the reaction.

High and Low Quantum Yield

The following conditions should be fulfilled by the reacting molecules in a photochemical reaction:

  (*i*) All the molecules of the reactants should be initially in the same energy state and hence equally reactive.
  (*ii*) The molecules in the activated state should be largely unstable and decompose to form the products.
  (*iii*) The reactivity of the molecules should be temperature independent.

Reasons for Low Quantum Yield

In the case of reactions having low quantum yield, the number of molecules decomposed by the absorption of one photon of radiation is less than one. The probable reasons for the low quantum yield are

  (*i*) The excited species formed by the primary process may be deactivated by collisions before the product is formed. This process is called quenching.
  (*ii*) One or more of the reactions in the secondary process

$$A^* \rightarrow \text{Products}$$

  may be endothermic. High energy requirement could decrease the reaction rate.
  (*iii*) The primary photochemical process may be reversed.
  (*iv*) The dissociated species may recombine so as to give low yield.

Reasons for High Quantum Yield

The excited atom formed in the primary step could initiate a series of chain reactions. The quantum yield in such cases depends on how far the chain of reactions can proceed before the chain terminating step. In addition to this the other reasons for high quantum yields are

  (*a*) Formation of an intermediate product acting as a catalyst.
  (*b*) The reactions may be exothermic and as such the heat evolved may activate the other molecules and thus react without absorption of additional photon of radiation.
  (*c*) The active molecule produced after absorption of radiation may collide with other molecules and activate them which in turn activate other reacting molecules.

Problem 24.5: In the photochemical reaction

$$CH_2ClCOOH + H_2O \xrightarrow{h\nu} CH_2OHCOOH + HCl$$

it was found that after irradiating the solution at 253.7 nm for 837 minutes 3.436×10^8 ergs of energy was absorbed and 2.296×10^{-5} mol of HCl were formed. Calculate the quantum yield of the reaction.
  Solution: Number of moles of HCl formed

$$= \text{Number of moles of chloroacetic acid decomposed}$$
$$= 2.296 \times 10^{-5} \text{ mol}$$

$$= 2.296 \times 10^{-5} \times 6.023 \times 10^{23} \text{ molecules}$$

$$= 1.38 \times 10^{19} \text{ molecules}$$

Number of quanta absorbed—

Elementary quantum corresponding to wavelength 253.7 nm

$$h\nu = \frac{hc}{\lambda}$$

$$= \frac{\left(6.626 \times 10^{-34}\,\text{Js}\right)\left(3 \times 10^{8}\,\text{m s}^{-1}\right)}{\left(253.7 \times 10^{-9}\,\text{m}\right)}$$

$$= 7.83 \times 10^{-19} \text{ J}$$

Number of quanta absorbed $= \dfrac{E}{h\nu} = \dfrac{3.436 \times 10^{1}\,\text{J}}{7.83 \times 10^{-19}\,\text{J}}$

$$= 4.39 \times 10^{19}$$

Quantum yield ϕ of the reaction $= \dfrac{1.38 \times 10^{19}}{4.39 \times 10^{19}}$

$$= 0.314$$

Problem 24.6: The quantum efficiency for the photochemical reaction

$$H_2(g) + Cl_2(g) \xrightarrow{h\nu} 2HCl(g)$$

is 1.0×10^6 with a wavelength of 480 nm. Calculate the number of moles of HCl (g) produced per joule of radiant energy absorbed,

Solution: The energy corresponding to 480 nm $= \dfrac{N_A hc}{\lambda}$

$$= \frac{\left(6.023 \times 10^{23}\,\text{mol}^{-1}\right)\left(6.626 \times 10^{-34}\,\text{J s}\right)\left(3 \times 10^{8}\,\text{m s}^{-1}\right)}{\left(480 \times 10^{-9}\,\text{m}\right)}$$

$$= 2.492 \times 10^{5} \text{ J mol}^{-1}$$

Since 2.492×10^5 J form 2.0×10^6 moles of HCl (g) (∴ one photon produces 2 moles of HCl (g))

$$1\text{J will form} = \frac{2.0 \times 10^{6}}{2.492 \times 10^{5}} = 8.02 \text{ mol}$$

24.5 PRIMARY PROCESSES IN PHOTOCHEMICAL REACTIONS

The first step in a photochemical process is the absorption of a photon of radiation by the molecule. This absorption of radiation is the primary process. In the primary process the energy absorbed from the photon in the visible or ultraviolet region raises the molecule to an excited state. This excitation is also accompanied by an increase in the rotational and vibrations energy levels. The excited molecule may then behave in different ways. There are four distinct possibilities of excitation of the molecule as shown in Fig. 24.2.

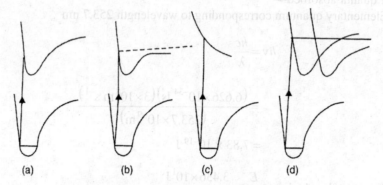

Fig. 24.2 Primary photochemical processes

(*i*)   In Fig. 24.2 (*a*) the electronic transition is from a stable ground state to a stable excited state. There will be no direct dissociation of the molecule. This is revealed from the spectrum which consists of discontinuous bands with a fine structure of closely packed lines.

(*ii*) The energy may raise the molecule to an electronic state which is unstable and the corresponding potential energy curve does not show any minimum as shown in curve (*b*). The molecule breaks up into atoms or radicals immediately on absorption of photon. The dissociated fragments are produced with different kinetic energy and a continuous spectrum is obtained without any fine structure.

(*iii*) If the molecule is raised to a higher stable quantum state and the energy acquired is more than the binding energy, it would undergo dissociation (curve c). The spectra will show continuum.

(*iv*) In this case the initial transition of the molecule is from a stable state to a higher stable state. Sometimes the higher state is intersected by the potential energy surface of an unstable state. When the molecule is vibrating in the excited state, it may be possible that the molecule may shift from the stable state to the unstable state, curve (*d*). When a shift of this type takes place, the molecule would dissociate producing atoms or radicals. The spectrum would show fine structure at lower levels of vibrations followed by a continuum. This type of phenomenon is known as predissociation.

24.6 SECONDARY PHOTOCHEMICAL PROCESSES—EXCITED STATES

Here we shall discuss only transitions between electronic energy levels. To understand the nature of electronic transitions, it is essential to know the concept of spin multiplicity. A molecule with electrons paired and with opposite spins is said to be in singlet ground state usually denoted by S_0. An excited molecule with two of its electrons unpaired and with opposite spins is said to be in the excited singlet state represented by S_1, S_2, ... An excited molecule in which the two of its electrons are not paired is said to be in the triplet states represented by T_1, T_2, ...

When a molecule in S_0 state absorbs a quantum of light, it gets excited, and its paired electrons become unpaired. Excitation generally leads to singlet excited states S_1, S_2,.... rather than to triplet states T_1, T_2, ... etc. Transition from $S_0 \rightarrow T_1$ is highly forbidden because it involves a change in spin multiplicity. After the molecule is excited to some vibrational level of an excited state, it generally loses vibrational energy very rapidly until it reaches the zeroth vibrational level of that electronic state. In other words, absorption of energy by the molecule in the ground state leads to allowed transition such as $S_0 \rightarrow S_1$, $S_1 \rightarrow S_2$, $S_2 \rightarrow S_3$ and so on. The various processes by which an excited molecule loses energy subsequently while reaching the ground state are shown by Jablonski diagrams (Fig. 24.3). In these diagrams, solid line represents radiative process, *i.e.*, a molecule discards its excitation energy as a photon. The wavy horizontal line denotes the transition between the excited singlet and triplet states without loss of energy. The wavy vertical lines denote the transition between singlet-singlet or triplet-triplet levels without loss of energy. Such transitions are sometimes called non-radiative transitions.

(*i*) An excited molecule may undergo a very rapid radiationless transition from a higher electronic state (S_2) to a lower electronic state (S_1) of same multiplicity. This process is called internal conversion (IC). The rate constants for conversion of S_3 to S_2 and S_2 to S_1 are in the range of 10^{-11} to 10^{-13} s^{-1}.

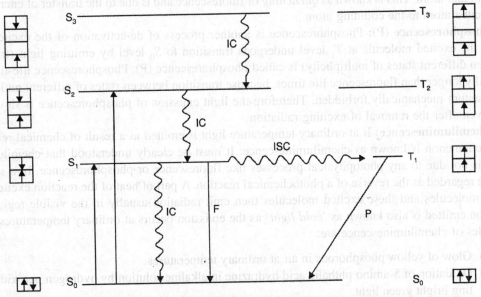

Fig. 24.3 Jablonski diagram

(*ii*) **Intersystem crossing (ISC):** It refers to a radiationless transition between states of different spin multiplicities. The excited molecule could cross over to the first triplet state through $S_1 \rightarrow T_1$ transition. Because of the spin interchange in intersystem crossing, the rate constant for this process is 10^{-2} to 10^{-6} as fast as internal conversion.

(*iii*) **Fluorescence (F):** The excited molecule could undergo the transition $S_1 \rightarrow S_0$, the radiation emitted in a transition between states of same multiplicity (i.e., singlet-singlet transition or triplet-triplet transitions). This phenomenon is called fluorescence and occurs in 10^{-8} sec. Fluorescence occurs at a lower frequency than the incident radiation because the emissive transition occurs after some vibrational energy has been discarded to the surroundings. Organic dyes like eosin, fluorescence compounds like chlorophyll, ultramarine etc., shows fluorescence in the visible or U.V. region. Once the exciting radiation is stopped, fluorescence stops.

The radiation emitted in fluorescence has a lower frequency (lower energy) than the incident radiation. This is due to the fact that the absorbing molecules initially in their lowest vibrational energy states may acquire higher vibrational energy states. Since atoms do not possess vibrational energy and in returning to their initial state from the excited state, they emit radiation of exactly the same frequency which they absorbed. This phenomenon is known as *the resonance fluorescence*. Thus, mercury vapours at low pressure with atoms in their normal state, when exposed to radiation of wavelength 253.7 nm, are excited and subsequently return to their normal state emitting radiation of same frequency which they absorbed.

In the above example, if the mercury vapours are mixed with the vapours of silver, thallium, lead or zinc which do not absorb radiation at 253.7 nm and then exposed to the radiation, a part of the excitation energy from mercury atoms is transferred to the atoms of the foreign substance. These are raised to higher energy states. As the excited atoms return to their lower energy states, they emit radiation. This is known as *sensitized fluorescence*.

The intensity of fluorescent radiation is diminished when a photochemically excited atom collides with another atom. This is known as *quenching* of fluorescence and is due to the transfer of energy from the excited atom to the colliding atom.

Phosphorescence (P): Phosphorescence is another process of de-activation of the excited state. When the excited molecule at T_1 level undergoes transition to S_0 level by emitting light (transition between different states of multiplicity) is called phosphorescence (P). Phosphorescence life-times are generally longer than fluorescence life times, because transition between states of different multiplicity are quantum mechanically forbidden. Therefore the light emission of phosphorescence is slow and it lasts even after the removal of exciting radiation.

Chemiluminescence: If at ordinary temperature light is emitted as a result of chemical reactions, the phenomenon is known as chemiluminescence. It must be clearly understood that chemiluminescence is not due to any photophysical processes like fluorescence or phosphorescence. In a sense, it may be regarded as the reverse of a photochemical reaction. A part of heat of the reaction excites some of the molecules and these excited molecules then emit radiation usually in the visible region. The radiation emitted is also known as *'cold light'* as the emission occurs at ordinary temperatures. Some examples of chemiluminescence are:

   (*i*) Glow of yellow phosphorous in air at ordinary temperatures.
   (*ii*) Oxidation of 5-amino phthalic acid hydrazine in alkaline solution by hydrogen peroxide emitting bright green light.
   (*iii*) Glow of fireflies is due to the aerial oxidation of a protein (luciferin) in the presence of an enzyme.

Thermoluminescence: It has been found that certain crystals when exposed to X rays release electrons. These electrons are trapped in negative ion vacancies of the crystal lattice. On heating, the irradiated crystal releases the trapped electrons from a higher energy level to a lower energy level emitting radiation. This is known as *thermoluminescence*. Limestone and fluorites are some examples which exhibit thermoluminescence.

24.7 SOME PHOTOCHEMICAL REACTIONS

(i) Decomposition of Hydrogen Iodide

Decomposition of hydrogen iodide is brought about by the radiation in the region 200-330 nm. The primary photochemical step can be written as

$$HI \xrightarrow[k_1]{h\nu} H + I \qquad\qquad (i) \ \ \text{rate} = I_{abs} \text{ or rate} = k_1[HI]$$

This is followed by secondary processes

$$H + HI \xrightarrow{k_2} H_2 + I \qquad\qquad (ii) \text{ rate} = k_2 [H][HI]$$

and

$$I + I \xrightarrow{k_3} I_2 \qquad\qquad (iii) \text{ rate} = k_3 [I]^2$$

Possibility of other elementary reactions of the type

$$I + HI \longrightarrow I_2 + H$$

$$H + H \longrightarrow H_2$$

$$I + H \longrightarrow HI$$

is ruled out as they involve either high activation energy or require third body collision. The overall reaction is therefore obtained by adding reactions (i), (ii) and (iii)

$$2HI \xrightarrow{h\nu} H_2 + I_2$$

The overall rate of this reaction is given by

$$-\frac{d[HI]}{dt} = I_{abs} + k_2 [H][HI] \qquad\qquad\qquad ...(iv)$$

and the rate of formation of H atoms is $\dfrac{d[H]}{dt} = I_{abs} - k_2 [H][HI]$

In the steady-state,

$$\frac{d[H]}{dt} = 0$$

$$I_{abs} - k_2 [HI][H] = 0$$

or,

$$[H] = \frac{I_{abs}}{k_2 [HI]}$$

Substituting the value of [H] in equation (iv), we get

$$-\frac{d[HI]}{dt} = I_{abs} + I_{abs} = 2I_{abs}$$

This shows that absorption of one photon leads to the decomposition of two molecules of HI, the quantum efficiency is therefore two. Experimental results confirm the proposed mechanism.

(ii) Photochemical Combination Between Hydrogen and Bromine

When a mixture of H_2 and Br_2 is exposed to light in the continuous spectrum of Br_2 ($\lambda < 510$ nm), dissociation of Br_2 molecules occurs

Primary Step: $\qquad\qquad\qquad Br_2 \xrightarrow{h\nu} Br + Br \qquad\qquad\qquad ...(i)$

The reactions which follow are

Secondary Steps: $\qquad\qquad Br + H_2 \xrightarrow{k_2} HBr + H \qquad\qquad\qquad ...(ii)$

$$H + Br_2 \xrightarrow{k_3} HBr + Br \qquad \qquad ...(iii)$$

$$H + HBr \xrightarrow{k_4} H_2 + Br \qquad \qquad ...(iv)$$

$$Br + Br \xrightarrow{k_5} Br_2$$

The mechanism is similar to the one that has been proposed for the thermal process. The rate of formation of HBr is given by

$$\frac{d[HBr]}{dt} = k_2[Br][H_2] + k_3[H][Br_2] - k_4[H][HBr] \qquad ...(a)$$

Applying steady state approximations for H and Br atoms, *i.e.*,

$$\frac{d[H]}{dt} = 0 = k_2[Br][H_2] - k_3[H][Br_2] - k_4[H][HBr] \qquad ...(b)$$

and $\qquad \frac{d[Br]}{dt} = 0 = 2I_{abs} - k_2[H_2][Br] + k_3[H][Br_2] + k_4[H][HBr] - k_5[Br]^2 \qquad ...(c)$

Addition of equations (*b*) and (*c*) yields

$$k_2[H_2][Br] - k_3[H][Br_2] - k_4[H][HBr] + 2I_{abs}$$

$$-k_2[H_2][Br] + k_3[H][Br_2] + k_4[H][HBr] - k_5[Br]^2 = 0$$

or

$$2I_{abs} = k_5[Br]^2$$

or

$$[Br] = \left(\frac{2I_{abs}}{k_5}\right)^{1/2}$$

Substituting the value of [Br] in equation (*b*), we get

$$k_2\left(\frac{2I_{abs}}{k_5}\right)^{1/2}[H_2] - k_3[H][Br_2] - k_4[H][HBr] = 0$$

or

$$[H] = \frac{k_2\left(\dfrac{2I_{abs}}{k_5}\right)^{1/2}[H_2]}{k_3[Br_2] + k_4[HBr]}$$

Putting the values of [Br] and [H] in equation (*a*) gives

$$\frac{d[HBr]}{dt} = k_2\left(\frac{2I_{abs}}{k_5}\right)^{1/2}[H_2] + k_3\frac{[Br_2]k_2\left(\dfrac{2I_{abs}}{k_5}\right)^{1/2}[H_2]}{k_3[Br_2] + k_4[HBr]} - \frac{k_4[HBr]k_2\left(\dfrac{2I_{abs}}{k_5}\right)^{1/2}[H_2]}{k_3[Br_2] + k_4[HBr]}$$

$$= \frac{k_2 \left(\dfrac{2I_{abs}}{k_5}\right)^{1/2} [H_2]}{k_3 [Br_2] + k_4 [HBr]} \left[k_3 [Br_2] + k_4 [HBr] + k_3 [Br_2] - k_4 [HBr] \right]$$

$$= \frac{2 k_2 k_3 \left(\dfrac{2I_{abs}}{k_5}\right)^{1/2} [H_2][Br_2]}{k_3 [Br_2] + k_4 [HBr]}$$

$$= \frac{2 k_2 \left(\dfrac{2I_{abs}}{k_5}\right)^{1/2} [H_2]}{1 + \dfrac{k_4}{k_3} \dfrac{[HBr]}{[Br_2]}} \qquad \qquad ...(d)$$

From this equation it is clear that HBr inhibits the rate of the reaction and the inhibition increases as the ratio [HBr]/[Br$_2$] increases. In spite of the chain mechanism, the quantum yield is very small and is approximately of the order of 0.01 at ordinary temperature. This suggests that most of the quanta are not used and the process is less efficient. At ordinary temperature, the reaction rate is so slow that most of the bromine atoms recombine to produce Br$_2$ molecules thus giving low quantum yield. As the temperature increases, the increase in k_2 increases the quantum yield.

(iii) Reaction Between Hydrogen and Chlorine

This is one of the most interesting photochemical reactions. When a mixture of hydrogen and chlorine is exposed to light in the continuous region of chlorine spectrum, i.e., wavelength less than 480 nm, the primary step is the photochemical decomposition of chlorine molecules

$$Cl_2 + h\nu \xrightarrow{\ I_{abs}\ } 2\,Cl \qquad \qquad ...(i)$$

This is followed by the secondary reactions

$$Cl + H_2 \xrightarrow{\ k_2\ } HCl + H \qquad \qquad ...(ii)$$

$$H + Cl_2 \xrightarrow{\ k_3\ } HCl + Cl \qquad \qquad ...(iii)$$

$$Cl + Cl \xrightarrow[k_4]{\text{Wall (M)}} Cl_2 \qquad \qquad ...(iv)$$

Instead of reaction (iv), the chain terminating step might be a recombination of chlorine atoms in the gas phase with the help of a third body (M or wall of the vessel) to carry away the excess energy. Reactions (ii) and (iii) are responsible for the conversion of a large quantity of H$_2$ and Cl$_2$ into HCl and the quantum yield of a reaction is exceptionally high usually of the order of 10^4 to 10^6. By setting up steady state expression for [Cl] and [H] in the usual manner, the rate of formation of HCl can be obtained and the final expression is given as

$$\frac{d[HCl]}{dt} = \frac{2 k_2 \phi I_{abs}}{k} [H_2]$$

If the chain termination step is the gas phase recombination of chlorine atoms with a third body as represented by equation

$$Cl + Cl + M \xrightarrow{k_5} Cl_2 \, (M)$$

and the rate expression has the form

$$\frac{d[HCl]}{dt} = k_2 [H_2] \left[\frac{\phi I_{abs}}{k_5 [M]} \right]^{1/2}$$

The reaction is sensitive to traces of impurities especially oxygen which acts as an inhibitor by removing H atoms.

$$H + O_2 + M \rightarrow HO_2 + M$$

(iv) Decomposition of Acetaldehyde

The decomposition of acetaldehyde by absorption of ultraviolet light ($\lambda < 300$ nm) is an example of photochemical process where the molecule is first excited to a higher quantum level and then it breaks up into radicals which start chain reactions. The primary stage can be written as

$$CH_3CHO + h\nu \xrightarrow{I_{abs}} CH_3 + CHO \qquad \qquad ...(i)$$

This is followed by the reactions

$$CH_3 + CH_3CHO \xrightarrow{k_2} CH_4 + CH_3CO \qquad \qquad ...(ii)$$

$$CH_3CO \xrightarrow{k_3} CH_3 + CO \qquad \qquad ...(iii)$$

$$CH_3 + CH_3 \xrightarrow{k_4} C_2H_6 \qquad \qquad ...(iv)$$

The radical may decompose as

$$CHO \longrightarrow CO + H$$

$$H + CH_3CHO \longrightarrow CH_3CO + H_2$$

At shorter wavelengths the quantum yield is high. At room temperature these steps are not fast enough to be of significance. However, at 300°C the quantum yield is more than 300 indicating that free radicals propagate the reactions. On applying steady-state approximations to rates of formation of CH_3CO and CH_3 radicals, the rate of formation of CO or CH_4 is obtained as

$$\frac{d[CH_3CO]}{dt} = k_2 [CH_3CHO][CH_3] - k_3 [CH_3CO] = 0$$

or

$$[CH_3CO] = \frac{k_2}{k_3} [CH_3][CH_3CHO]$$

and

$$\frac{d[CH_3]}{dt} = I_{abs} - k_2 [CH_3][CH_3CHO] + k_3 [CH_3CO] - k_4 [CH_3]^2 = 0$$

or
$$\left[CH_3 \right] = \left(\frac{I_{abs}}{k_4} \right)^{1/2}$$

Hence the rate of formation of CO is

$$\frac{d[CO]}{dt} = k_3 \left[CH_3CO \right]$$

$$= k_3 \frac{k_2}{k_3} \left(\frac{I_{abs}}{k_4} \right)^{1/2} \left[CH_3CHO \right]$$

$$= k_2 \left(\frac{I_{abs}}{k_4} \right)^{1/2} \left[CH_3CHO \right]$$

24.8 PHOTOSENSITIZED REACTIONS

Photosensitized reactions constitute an important class of photochemical reactions. In these reactions, the reactant molecules do not absorb the radiation to which they are exposed and no reaction occurs. However, if a suitable foreign substance that absorbs radiation is added to the reactant, the reaction takes place. The atoms of the foreign substance are excited during absorption and they pass on this energy to the reactants and thereby initiate the reaction. A process of this type is called *photosensitized reaction* and the foreign substance which absorbs the radiation is known as *photosensitizer*. Commonly used photosensitizers are cadmium and mercury vapours.

An example of photosensitization by mercury atoms is the synthesis of formaldehyde from carbon monoxide and hydrogen. When a mixture of carbon monoxide and hydrogen containing traces of mercury vapours are exposed to ultraviolet light of 253.7 nm, the mercury atoms are excited. These excited mercury atoms then transfer their energy by collisions to hydrogen molecules to dissociate them into hydrogen atoms. This initiates a radical reaction. The overall reaction is

$$Hg + h\nu \longrightarrow Hg^* \qquad \text{Primary stage}$$

$$Hg^* + H_2 \longrightarrow Hg + \dot{H} + \dot{H} \qquad \text{Energy transfer}$$

$$\left.\begin{array}{l} \dot{H} + CO \longrightarrow HC\dot{O} \\ HC\dot{O} + H_2 \longrightarrow HCHO + \dot{H} \\ 2HC\dot{O} \longrightarrow HCHO + CO \end{array}\right\} \qquad \text{Reaction}$$

The most familiar instance of photosensitization is the action of chlorophyll in permitting carbon dioxide and water to react in presence of sunlight to produce carbohydrates.

$$xCO_2 + xH_2O + nh\nu \rightarrow (CH_2O)_x + xO_2$$

chlorophyll absorbs strongly in the region between 600 to 700 nm. This region is most effective for photosynthetic reactions.

Decomposition of H_2, NH_3, H_2O etc., are sensitized by mercury vapours.

24.9 RADIATION CHEMISTRY

The photon used in photochemical reactions has energy of the order of 6.3×10^5 J mol^{-1} or 1.1×10^{-18} J/Einstein. In radiation chemistry, however, the radiations of sufficiently high energy (about 1 million electron volt) such as protons, α-particles, X-rays or γ-rays are used. In both photolysis and radiolysis, the primary process is the absorption of radiation to which the molecules are exposed. The primary effect of these high energy radiations is to produce ions, in addition to atoms and free radicals through which they pass. Thus, a typical photochemical reaction would be

$$M \rightarrow M^*$$

and in radiation chemistry it would be

$$M \rightarrow M^+ + e^-$$

In a secondary process, the slow moving heavier particles are more powerful ionizing agents than the lighter particles. It is due to the fact that the heavier particles have larger chance to collide with molecules and thus cause more ionization. In photochemical reactions each photon activates only one molecule whereas in radiolytic reactions the number of molecules ionized is quite large. The secondary processes are, therefore, quite complex.

In the study of overall reactions initiated by ionizing radiations, *ion pair yield or ionic yield and G-values* are of importance in providing informations about the mechanism of the reactions. The ion pair yield (M/N) is defined as *the ratio of the rate of formation of the product molecules to the rate of formation of ion pairs.* G-value is defined as *the number of molecules reacting for each 100 eV of energy absorbed*

$$G = \frac{\text{Number of molecules reacting}}{100 \text{ eV of energy absorbed}}$$

The irradiation of aqueous system has been widely studied. The steps involved in radiolysis are

$$H_2O \rightarrow H_2O^+ + e^-$$
$$H_2O^+ + H_2O \rightarrow H_3O^+ + OH$$

With slow moving particles (α-particles)

$$OH + OH \rightarrow H_2O_2$$

and with fast moving particles (β-particles)

$$H_2O + e^- \rightarrow OH + H + e^-$$
$$H + H \rightarrow H_2$$
$$H + OH \rightarrow H_2O$$

Polymeric substances like polyethylenes on irradiation yields cross-linked materials having greater rigidity and high melting points. This is due to the formation of free radical centres in polyethylene chains.

EXERCISES

1. Select the correct statements from the following:

   (*i*) In a reacting system only the absorbed radiation is effective in producing a chemical change.

   (*ii*) According to Einstein law of photochemical equivalence, each molecule which takes part in a photochemical reaction absorbs one quantum of radiation.

(iii) Molar extinction coefficient is the reciprocal of the thickness of the solution when the intensity of the incident radiation falls to 1/10 of its initial value.

(iv) The molar extinction coefficient is unitless.

(v) Quantum yield of any reaction is always unity.

(vi) Delayed fluorescence is phosphorescence.

(vii) Unless temperature changes are enormous, the rate of a photochemical reaction is almost independent of temperature.

(viii) Absorption of a photon by a molecule always leads to a chemical reaction.

Ans. Correct statements: (i), (ii), (iii), (vi) and (vii).

2. Distinguish the following:

(i) A photochemical reaction from a thermal reaction.

(ii) A primary photochemical reaction from a secondary photochemical reaction.

(iii) Fluorescence from phosphorescence.

(iv) A reaction with low quantum yield from a reaction with high quantum yield.

(v) Extinction coefficient from molar extinction coefficient.

3. Quantum yield of the reaction $H_2(g) + Br_2(g) = 2HBr(g)$ is low ($\simeq 0.01$) while that for the reaction $H_2(g) + Cl_2(g) = 2HCl(g)$, it is large ($\simeq 10^4 - 10^6$). Explain.

4. Explain the terms:

(i) Molar extinction coefficient;

(ii) Optical density;

(iii) Law of photochemical equivalence;

(iv) Quantum yield;

(v) Photosensitization;

(vi) Fluorescence;

(vii) Phosphorescence;

(viii) Photostationary state; and

(ix) Chemiluminescence.

5. State and explain Lambert-Beer's law. What are its limitations? Discuss its applications in analytical chemistry.

6. State the law of photochemical equivalence. How is the law verified experimentally? How do you account for the low and high quantum yields?

7. What are photochemical reactions? How do they differ from thermal reactions?

8. What prevents an excited atom or a molecule to absorb another photon to enhance its excitation?

9. List out the primary effects of absorption of radiation by molecules.

10. A certain substance in a cell of length l absorbs 10% of the incident light. What fraction of the incident light will be absorbed in a cell five times as long? **Ans.** 92.1%.

11. A 1.0×10^{-3} mol dm^{-3} solution of a certain substance absorbs 10% of an incident light beam in a path of 1 cm. What concentration will be required to absorb 90% of the incident light?

Ans. 2.20×10^{-2} mol dm^{-3}.

12. The following results were obtained in the spectrophotometric study of a complex at 570.0 nm in a cell of 1 cm thickness.

Concentration of the complex (mol dm^{-3}) × 10^5:	13.9	34.7	55.5
Percentage transmission:	62.4	30.9	15.2

Show that the Lambert-Beer's law is obeyed. Calculate the molar extinction coefficient for the complex.

13. A 2 mm thickness of glass is found to have a transmission of 70% for light of 253.7 nm. What will be the transmission of a 0.55 mm thickness of this glass? **Ans.** 90.7%.

14. A 0.01 molar solution of a compound transmits 20% of the sodium-D line when absorbing path is 1.5 cm. Calculate the molar extinction coefficient of the substance. The solvent is completely transparent.

Ans. 46.5.

15. A certain system absorbs 3×10^{18} quanta of radiation per second. On irradiation for 10 minutes, 3.0×10^{-3} mole of the reactant was found to have reacted. Calculate the quantum yield, ϕ.

Ans. $\phi = 1.003$.

16. In the photolysis of gaseous hydrogen iodide with light of 253.7 nm, it is found that absorption of 2.36×10^2 J of radiant energy causes decomposition of 1.0×10^{-3} mole of hydrogen iodide. Calculate the quantum yield (ϕ) for the decomposition of hydrogen iodide. What will be the quantum yield for the formation of molecular hydrogen and iodine?

Ans. ϕ for decomposition is 2.0 and for formation is 1.0.

17. Acetone vapours are exposed to light at $\lambda = 300$ nm. If the average bond energies of C—H, C—C and C = O bonds (expressed in kJ mol^{-1}) are 414, 347 and 732 respectively, discuss the reaction of acetone with the above light.

Ans. The energy of exposed radiation corresponds to 399 kJ mol^{-1}.
It will therefore break the C—C bond yielding CH$_3$ and CH$_3$ CO.

18. The bond energy of hydrogen is 431 kJ mol^{-1}. Calculate the wavelength of light necessary to photochemically break the H-H bond. As molecular hydrogen does not absorb in this wavelength so the reaction is carried out in the presence of photosensitizers. Which substance, Na(g) or Hg(g), would be an effective photosensitizer, if the primary absorption wavelengths are 330.3 nm and 253.652 nm respectively?

Ans. $\lambda = 277.0$ nm, Hg(g).

19. Hydrogen bromide is photochemically dissociated by light of 253.7 nm wavelength. Assuming that bromine atoms are in the ground state, calculate the kinetic energy of the hydrogen atoms produced by photodissociation. Bond energy of HBr is 364 kJ mol^{-1}.

Ans. 106.4 kJ mol^{-1}.

20. In the photobromination of cinnamic acid using blue light of 435.8 nm at 305 K, and intensity of 1.4×10^{-3} J s^{-1} produced a decrease of 750×10^{-5} moles of Br$_2$ during exposure for 1105 seconds. The solution absorbed 80.1% of the light passing through it. Bromine which reacted produced dibromocinnamic acid. Calculate the quantum yield for the photoreaction of bromine. **Ans. $\phi = 16.6$.**

21. A 0.1 dm^3 vessel containing hydrogen and chlorine was irradiated by light of 400 nm. It was found that 11 ergs of light energy was absorbed by chlorine per second. During irradiation of 1 minute, partial pressure of chlorine, as determined by the absorption of light and the application of Beer's law, decreased from 205 to 156 mm Hg. What is the quantum yield? **Ans. $\phi = 2.6 \times 10^6$.**

22. (a) The quantum yield for the gas phase photodecomposition of $2HI \rightarrow H_2 + I_2$ is approximately two. Calculate the number of grams of HI decomposed per joule of radiant energy absorbed when HI is irradiated with monochromatic radiation with wavelength, $\lambda = 207.0$ nm. (b) Suggest whether the following mechanism is consistent with the observed quantum yield? Explain.

(i) $HI + h\nu \rightarrow H + I$

(ii) $H + HI \rightarrow H_2 + I$

(iii) $2I \rightarrow I_2$ (third body)

Ans. (a) 4.4×10^{-4} g J^{-1}, (b) Yes.

23. When a mixture of chlorine and carbon monoxide is irradiated phosgene is formed according to the reaction.

$$CO(g) + Cl_2(g) = COCl_2(g)$$

The rate law for this reaction is, $\dfrac{d[COCl_2]}{dt} = k\, I_a^{1/2}\,[CO]^{1/2}\,[Cl_2]$

Devise a plausible mechanism consistent with the rate law.

24. The following mechanism has been proposed for the photo decomposition of hydrogen peroxide in the presence of carbon monoxide. Making the steady state approximations about OH and COOH, evaluate

$$-\frac{d[H_2O_2]}{dt}.$$

$$H_2O_2 + h\nu \longrightarrow 2OH$$

$$OH + CO \xrightarrow{k_1} CO_2H$$

$$CO_2H + H_2O_2 \xrightarrow{k_2} CO_2 + H_2O + OH$$

$$2CO_2H \xrightarrow{k_3} Products$$

Ans. $\dfrac{d[H_2O_2]}{dt} = -\phi I_a - \dfrac{k_2\left(2\phi I_a\right)^{1/2}[H_2O_2]}{k_3^{1/2}}$ where ϕ is the primary quantum yield and I_a is the Einsteins absorbed per second per dm^3.

Molecular Spectroscopy

25.1 INTRODUCTION

In this chapter, we take up the study of molecular spectra with a view to obtain more information about molecular structure. In chapter 20, we have seen that how atomic spectra is useful in the understanding of the electronic arrangement in atoms. The transition of electrons takes place from one electronic energy state to another electronic energy state results in emission or absorption of electromagnetic radiations. Corresponding to energy difference between the levels, the spectral lines occur in different regions giving the atomic spectra. As the atomic spectra gives information about the structure of the atom, molecular spectra gives information regarding the molecular structure, *i.e.*, the size and shape of the molecules, bond distance, bond length and dissociation energy of the molecule. The molecular spectroscopy may be defined as the study of interaction of electromagnetic radiation with molecules. The spectra produced by molecules are quite different and complicated from the atomic spectra.

In polyatomic molecules, the transition between various energy levels takes place in various possible ways. The total energy of a molecule is the sum of four different types of energy, viz., translational, vibrational, rotational and electronic. Therefore, the emission or absorption of energy may cause change in some or all of these types of energies.

1. Translational energy (E_{trans}): This is connected with the overall movement of the molecules along three axes. It is significant in gases.
2. Rotational energy (E_{rot}): It involves the spinning of the molecules about the axes passing through the centre of mass of the molecule. The transition between their rotational energy level leads to rotational spectra.
3. Vibrational energy ($E_{Vib.}$). It is associated with the vibrations within a molecule like stretching or bending of the bonds. The transition between vibrational energy levels give rise to vibrational spectra.

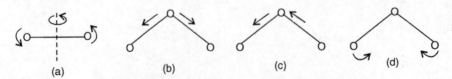

(a)   (b)   (c)   (d)

Fig. 25.1 (*a*) Shows rotation about two different axis, (*b*), (*c*) and (*d*) show vibrations
(*b*) and (*c*) show the stretching and (*d*) shows bending

4. Electronic energy (E_{elec}): It involves changes in the distribution of electrons by the promotion of the electrons to higher levels through absorption of energy.

The various modes of rotation and vibrations are shown in Fig. 25.1.

25.2 ROTATIONAL SPECTRA

Pure rotational spectra are observed in far infrared region. This spectra would be observed only with those molecules which are associated with a permanent electric dipole. A rotating diatomic molecule may be treated to a good approximation as a rigid rotator with an internuclear distance r.

Consider a diatomic molecule AB consisting of two atoms A and B of masses m_1 and m_2 respectively. Let the two atoms be joined by a rigid bond of length r. The two atoms A and B are at a distance of r_1 and r_2 from the centre of mass G of the molecule about which the molecule rotates end-over as shown in Fig. 25.2, so that

$$m_1 r_1 = m_2 r_2 \qquad \ldots(25.1)$$

and

$$r_1 + r_2 = r \qquad \ldots(25.2)$$

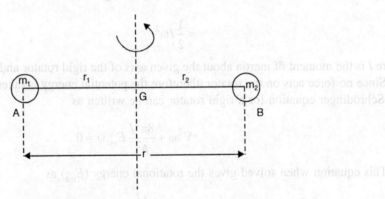

Fig. 25.2 Rigid rotator model for a diatomic molecule

The moment of inertia I with respect to a line (dotted as shown in Fig. 25.2) that passes through the centre of mass is

$$I = m_1 r_1^2 + m_2 r_2^2 \qquad \ldots(25.3)$$

Eliminating r_1 and r_2 between equation (25.1), (25.2) and (25.3) yields

$$I = m_1 \left(\frac{m_2}{m_1 + m_2} \right)^2 r^2 + m_2 \left(\frac{m_1}{m_1 + m_2} \right)^2 r^2$$

rearranging, we get

$$I = \frac{m_1 m_2}{(m_1 + m_2)^2} r^2 (m_1 + m_2)$$

$$= \frac{m_1 m_2}{m_1 + m_2} r^2$$

$$= \mu r^2$$

where μ is the reduced mass of the diatomic molecule and is equal to $\frac{m_1 m_2}{m_1 + m_2} \left(\frac{1}{\mu} = \frac{1}{m_1} + \frac{1}{m_2} \right)$.

The rigid rotator has only kinetic energy and is given as

$$K.E. = \frac{1}{2} m_1 v_1^2 + \frac{1}{2} m_2 v_2^2$$

where v_1 and v_2 are the linear velocities of mass m_1 and m_2 respectively. Since r_1 and r_2 are supposed to be constant (unchanged) during the rotation, therefore

$$K.E. = \frac{1}{2} m_1 \left(r_1 \omega \right)^2 + \frac{1}{2} m_2 \left(r_2 \omega \right)^2$$

$$= \frac{1}{2} I \omega^2$$

where I is the moment of inertia about the given axis of the rigid rotator and ω is the angular velocity.

Since no force acts on the rotator, therefore the potential energy is taken equal to zero, *i.e.*, $V = 0$. The Schrödinger equation for a rigid rotator can be written as

$$\nabla^2 \psi + \frac{8\pi^2 I}{h^2} E_{rot} \psi = 0$$

This equation when solved gives the rotational energy (E_{rot}) as

$$E_{rot} = \frac{h^2}{8\pi^2 I} J(J+1) \qquad \qquad ...(25.4)$$

where J is the rotational quantum number having integral values 0, 1, 2, ... and I is the moment of inertia of the molecule.

Since $E = hc\bar{v}$, therefore equation (25.4) can be written as

$$\bar{v} = \frac{h^2}{8\pi^2 Ihc} J(J+1)$$

$$= \frac{h}{8\pi^2 Ic} J(J+1) \qquad \qquad ...(25.5)$$

$$= BJ(J+1) \qquad \qquad ...(25.6)$$

where $B = \frac{h}{8\pi^2 Ic}$ is a constant and is generally referred to as the rotational constant and is expressed in cm^{-1} (or m^{-1}).

In order to predict the rotational spectrum, one needs to consider the difference between the rotational energy levels. The energy difference between two levels is given by

$$\Delta E_{rot} = E_{J'} - E_J$$

$$= \frac{h^2}{8\pi^2 I} J'(J'+1) - \frac{h^2}{8\pi^2 I} J(J+1) \qquad \qquad ...(25.7)$$

where J' is the higher quantum number and J is the lower quantum number ($J' > J$).

When a molecule moves from one rotational energy level to another, the rotating molecule may absorb or emit radiation, and only those transitions are allowed for which $\Delta J = \pm 1$. In absorption $\Delta J = + 1$ while in emission $\Delta J = -1$. Equation (25.7) can be rewritten in terms of wave number as

$$\overline{v}_{J \to J'} = \frac{\Delta E_{rot}}{hc} = \frac{h^2}{8\pi^2 Ihc} \Big[J'(J'+1) - J(J+1) \Big]$$

$$= \frac{h}{8\pi^2 Ic} \Big[J'(J'+1) - J(J+1) \Big]$$

$$= B \Big[J'(J'+1) - J(J+1) \Big] \qquad \qquad ...(25.8)$$

When $J = 0$ and $J' = 1$, equation (25.8) becomes

$$\overline{v}_{0 \to 1} = B \Big[1(1+1) - 0(0+1) \Big] = 2B$$

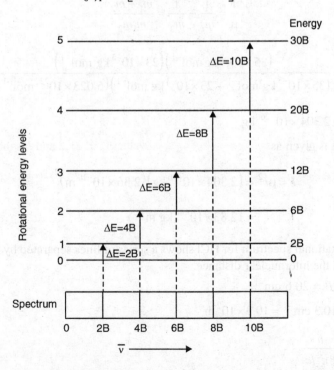

Fig. 25.3 Transitions between the various rotational levels and spectral lines arising from these transitions

Thus, for $J = 0$ and $J' = 1$ transition, an absorption line will appear at $2B$. Again, if the molecule is raised from $J = 1$ to $J' = 2$ level by the absorption of more energy in microwave region, then

$$\bar{v}_{1 \to 2} = B\left[2(2+1) - 1(1+1)\right]$$

$$= 4B$$

It means that corresponding to this transition ($J = 1$ and $J' = 2$), an absorption line will appear at 4B. In general, when the molecule is raised from the level J to $J + 1$, the wave number for the transition is

$$\bar{v}_{J \to J+1} = B\left[(J+1)(J+2) - J(J+1)\right]$$

$$= B(J+1)[J+2-J]$$

$$= 2B(J+1) \qquad \qquad \qquad ...(25.9)$$

From equation (25.9) it is clear that stepwise, raising of rotational energy results in an absorption spectrum consisting of line at 2B, 4B, 6B, etc., with a constant separation of 2B. (Fig. 25.3).

Problem 25.1: Calculate (a) the reduced mass and (b) the moment of inertia of NaCl using the mean internuclear distance of 2.36 Å. The atomic masses are Cl = 35×10^{-3} kg mol^{-1} and Na = 23×10^{-3} kg mol^{-1}.

Solution: The reduced mass is given as

$$\frac{1}{\mu} = \frac{1}{m_1} + \frac{1}{m_2} = \frac{m_1 + m_2}{m_1 m_2}$$

or $\qquad \mu = \dfrac{\left(35 \times 10^{-3}\,\text{kg mol}^{-1}\right)\left(23 \times 10^{-3}\,\text{kg mol}^{-1}\right)}{\left(35 \times 10^{-3}\,\text{kg mol}^{-1} + 23 \times 10^{-3}\,\text{kg mol}^{-1}\right)\left(6.023 \times 10^{23}\,\text{mol}^{-1}\right)}$

$$= 2.304 \times 10^{-26}\ \text{kg}$$

The moment of inertia is given as

$$I = \mu r^2 = \left(2.304 \times 10^{-26}\,\text{kg}\right)\left(2.36 \times 10^{-10}\,\text{m}\right)^2$$

$$= 12.83 \times 10^{-46}\ \text{kg m}^2$$

Problem 25.2: The rotational spectrum for HCl shows a series of lines separated by 20.6 cm^{-1}. Find the moment of inertia and the internuclear distance.

Solution: Since $2B = 20.6$ cm^{-1}

$$B = 10.3\ \text{cm}^{-1} = 10.3 \times 10^2\,\text{m}^{-1}$$

Also $\qquad B = \dfrac{h}{8\pi^2 Ic}$

$$I = \frac{h}{8\pi^2 Bc} = \frac{\left(6.626 \times 10^{-24} \text{ kg m}^2\text{s}^{-1}\right)}{8 \times \left(\frac{22}{7}\right)^2 \times \left(10.3 \times 10^2 \text{ m}^{-1}\right)\left(3 \times 10^8 \text{ ms}^{-1}\right)}$$

$$= 2.655 \times 10^{-47} \text{ kg m}^2$$

Now

$$I = \mu r^2$$

or

$$r = \sqrt{\frac{I}{\mu}}$$

Since

$$\mu = \frac{m_1 m_2}{m_1 + m_2} = \frac{\left(1.008 \times 10^{-3} \text{ kg}\right)\left(35.5 \times 10^{-3} \text{ kg}\right)}{\left(1.008 \times 10^{-3} \text{ kg} + 35.5 \times 10^{-3} \text{ kg}\right)\left(6.023 \times 10^{23} \text{ mol}^{-1}\right)}$$

$$= 1.628 \times 10^{-27} \text{ kg}$$

Therefore

$$r = \sqrt{\frac{I}{\mu}}$$

$$= \sqrt{\frac{2.655 \times 10^{-47} \text{ kg m}^2}{1.628 \times 10^{-27} \text{ kg}}}$$

$$= 1.276 \times 10^{-10} \text{ m}.$$

25.3 VIBRATIONAL SPECTRA

Now consider the theoretical basis of vibrational spectra. To understand the vibrations of a diatomic molecule consider a system of two balls of masses m_1 and m_2 joined together by a spring having a force constant k. This model of vibrating diatomic molecule is similar to that of a simple harmonic oscillator as shown in Fig. 25.4.

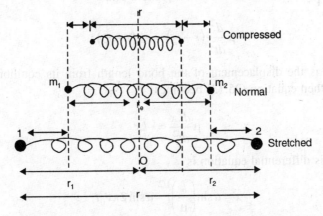

Fig. 25.4 Stretching and compresson of two particles joined by a spring

Point O in the figure indicates the centre of mass and r_1 and r_2 denote distances of ball 1 and 2 respectively from point O. If the bond is distorted from its equilibrium length r_e to a new length r, then the restoring forces on each atom are $-k(r - r_e)$. These forces are equated in terms of Newton's second law of motion ($F = ma$) as

$$m_1 \frac{d^2 r_1}{dt^2} = -k(r - r_e)$$

...(25.10)

and

$$m_2 \frac{d^2 r_2}{dt^2} = -k(r - r_e)$$

...(25.11)

Since $r_1 + r_2 = r$ and $m_1 r_1 = m_2 r_2$, therefore

$$r_1 = \frac{m_2}{m_1 + m_2} r \text{ and } r_2 = \frac{m_1}{m_1 + m_2} r$$

Using these expressions for r_1 and r_2, equations (25.10) and (25.11) reduces to

$$\frac{m_1 d^2 \left(\frac{m_2 r}{m_1 + m_2} \right)}{dt^2} = -k(r - r_e)$$

or

$$\frac{m_1 m_2}{m_1 + m_2} \frac{d^2 r}{dt^2} = -k(r - r_e)$$

$$\mu \frac{d^2 r}{dt^2} = -k(r - r_e)$$

...(25.12)

Since $\frac{d^2 (r - r_e)}{dt^2} = \frac{d^2 r}{dt^2}$ because r_e is a constant, we substitute $\frac{d^2 (r - r_e)}{dt^2}$ for $\frac{d^2 r}{dt^2}$ in equation 25.12 for having similar variables on both sides of the equation. Thus

$$\mu \frac{d^2}{dt^2} (r - r_e) = -k(r - r_e)$$

...(25.13)

The term $(r - r_e)$ is the displacement of the bond length from its equilibrium position. If we introduce $x = (r - r_e)$ then equation (25.13) becomes

$$\mu \frac{d^2 x}{dt^2} = -kx$$

The solution of this differential equation is

$$x = a \sin \left(\frac{k}{\mu} \right)^{1/2} t = a \sin 2\pi \nu_0 t$$

When a is a constant and is equal to maximum value of x, *i.e.*, it is the vibrational amplitude. If $x = 0$ when $t = 0$ and

$$\nu_0 = \frac{1}{2\pi}\left(\frac{k}{\mu}\right)^{1/2} \qquad \qquad ...(25.14)$$

is the fundamental vibration frequency.

Vibrational energy of a harmonic oscillator

It is more convenient to state Hook's law in terms of the potential energy of the vibrating particle. The potential energy (V) at the equilibrium position can be arbitrarily taken as zero. Displacement of the particle by a distance dx requires a force to be exerted to overcome that of the spring. The work done, all of which is stored in the system and is therefore potential energy, is equal to this applied force times the distance dx through which it acts. Thus

$$dV = (\text{Applied force}) \times (\text{Distance})$$

$$= (-f)(dx)$$

$$= (kx)\,dx \qquad \left[\because -f = kx\,(\text{Hook's law})\right]$$

Integration of this equation gives

$$V = \frac{1}{2}kx^2 \qquad \qquad ...(25.15)$$

Since the potential energy varies directly with the square of the displacement, a plot of V versus x gives a parabola shown in Fig. 25.5.

The Schrödinger equation for this system is given as

$$\frac{d^2\psi}{dx^2} + \frac{8\pi^2\mu}{h^2}\left(E - \frac{1}{2}kx^2\right)\psi = 0 \qquad \qquad ...(25.15a)$$

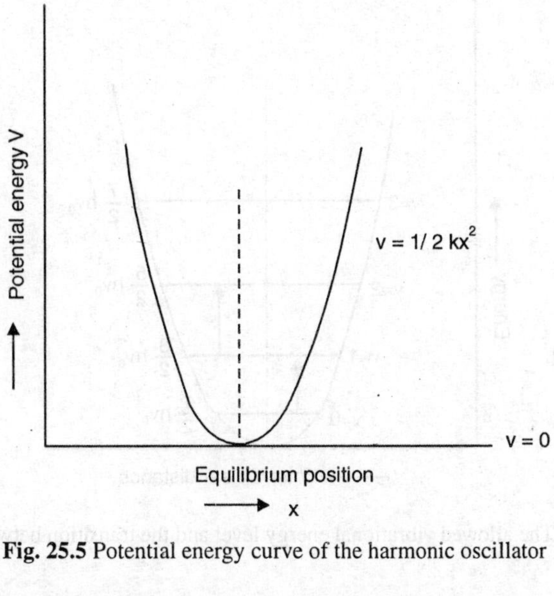

Fig. 25.5 Potential energy curve of the harmonic oscillator

The solution of this equation gives the energy E_{vib} as

$$E_{vib} = \frac{h}{2\pi}\sqrt{\frac{k}{\mu}}\left(v+\frac{1}{2}\right) \qquad ...(25.16)$$

where v is an integer and can have values 0, 1, 2, ... and is known as vibrational quantum number. Using equation (25.14), equation (25.16) can be written as

$$E_{vib} = hv_0\left(v+\frac{1}{2}\right) \qquad ...(25.17)$$

It may be noted from equation (25.17) that even in the ground state ($v = 0$) the molecule would have vibrational energy equal to $1/2\ hv_0$, called the zero point energy. But, according to classical mechanics, at the ground state oscillator may be at rest and have there zero energy, and the oscillator may have any energy. This is contrary to the quantum mechanics. According to quantum mechanics, the vibration still persists and the molecule will not at be rest, even at absolute temperature. At ordinary temperature, kT is rather small as compared to the vibrational energy spacing and hence it follows from Boltzmann distribution that majority of the molecules will be in vibrational quantum state, $v = 0$.

The vibrational spectra of a homonuclear diatomic molecule will not be observed as there would be no change in the dipole moment during the stretching of bond between the two atoms. However, in case of a heteronuclear diatomic molecule there is a change in the dipole moment during the vibration and hence will exhibit vibrational spectra.

Let us consider a molecule which undergoes a vibrational transition from the state v to state $v + 1$, the energy required is given by

$$\Delta E = E_{v\rightarrow v+1} = \left(v+1+\frac{1}{2}\right)hv_0 - \left(v+\frac{1}{2}\right)hv_0$$

$$= hv_0 \qquad ...(25.18)$$

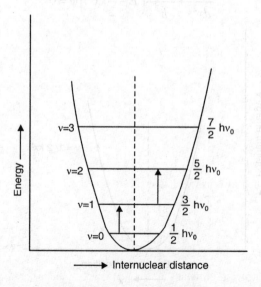

Fig. 25.6 The allowed vibrational energy level and the transition between them

The selection rule for a harmonic vibrational transition, according to the solution of Schrödinger equation is $\Delta v = \pm 1$. This means that the decrease or increase in the vibrational quantum number is by one unit only. The selection rule $\Delta v = \pm 1$ indicates that the energy difference (ΔE) between two vibrational levels involved in a transition are equally spaced as shown in Fig. 25.6.

From equation (25.18) we have

$$\Delta E = h\nu_0$$

or

$$h\nu = h\nu_0$$

or

$$\nu = \nu_0$$

This shows that the frequency of absorbed radiation is the same as the fundamental frequency of vibration of the molecule. If follows that the vibrational spectrum should consist of a single line provided that there are no rotational energy changes. However, the vibrational spectra consists of a number of bands each with a fine structure of closely spaced lines. The presence of a number of bands is due to the fact that in the lowest state of vibration the diatomic molecule behaves as a simple harmonic oscillator, but at higher quantum levels there is a deviation from simple harmonic oscillator and the vibration becomes anharmonic. Because of this anharmonicity, the vibrational transitions do not confine to adjacent levels but also occur at different levels. If we add anharmonic term, we get an expression for vibrational energy in the form.

$$E_{vib} = \left(v + \frac{1}{2}\right)h\nu_0 - x_e\left(v + \frac{1}{2}\right)^2 h\nu_0 \qquad \text{...(25.18 (a))}$$

where x_e is the anharmonicity constant. The second term represents a decrease in energy of the successive vibrational levels below those expected for a simple harmonic oscillator. The energy levels are therefore not evenly spaced but lie closer as the quantum number increases.

25.4 VIBRATION-ROTATION SPECTRA

Molecules do not have a pure vibration spectrum due to the accompanying rotational transitions. This is shown by the fact that the selection rule ($\Delta v = \pm 1$) governing vibrational transitions is not obeyed at higher energy levels. As a result of this, the infrared region of spectrum is the vibration-rotation spectrum. The appearance of bands in the infrared region can thus be interpreted by supposing that the vibrational and rotational energies are additive and the energy of a linear molecule can be expressed as

$$E_{vib-rot} = E_{vib} + E_{rot}$$

$$= \left(v + \frac{1}{2}\right)h\nu_0 + BchJ(J+1)$$

For anharmonic oscillator and non-rigid rotator

$$E_{vib-rot} = \left(v + \frac{1}{2}\right)h\nu_0 + h\nu_0 x_e\left(v + \frac{1}{2}\right)^2 + BchJ(J+1) - DchJ^2[J+1]^2 + ...$$

where D is the centrifugal distortion constant and is given $D = \dfrac{4B^2}{\omega^2}$.

In the transition from energy level E to energy level E',

$$(\Delta E)_{v-j} = (E' - E)_{vib\text{-}rot}$$

$$= \left[\left(v' + \frac{1}{2}\right)hv_0 + BchJ'(J'+1)\right] - \left[\left(v + \frac{1}{2}\right)hv_0 + BchJ(J+1)\right]$$

$$= \left[(v' - v)hv_0\right] + \left[J'(J'+1) - J(J+1)\right]Bch$$

The selection rule for vibrational transition is $\Delta v = +1$, hence we have

$$\Delta E_{v-j} = hv_0 + \left[J'(J'+1) - J(J+1)\right]Bch$$

or

$$v = \frac{\Delta E_{v-j}}{h} = v_0 + \left[J'(J'+1) - J(J+1)\right]Bc$$

and the wave number is given as

$$\bar{v} = \frac{v}{c} = \frac{\Delta E_{v-j}}{hc} = \bar{v}_0 + \left[J'(J'+1) - J(J+1)\right]B \qquad \text{...(25.19)}$$

The selection rule for rotational transition is

$$\Delta J = \pm 1 \ (J' = J + 1 \text{ or } J' = J - 1)$$

The transitions for which $\Delta J = -1$ $(J' = J - 1)$ produce the lines denoted as P branch of the spectrum (Fig. 25.7). The wave number of these lines is given by

$$\bar{v}_p = \bar{v}_0 - 2BJ \qquad \text{...(25.20)}$$

where J is the rotational quantum number of the initial state and have values of 1, 2, 3, ... etc.

The transitions which produce a set of lines arising from $\Delta J = 1$ $(J' = J + 1)$ constitute the R branch of the spectrum as shown in Fig. 25.7. The wave number of the lines in R branch is given by

$$\bar{v}_R = \bar{v}_0 + 2B + 2BJ \qquad \text{...(25.21)}$$

where

$$J = 0, 1, 2, ...$$

Equations (25.20) and (25.21) clearly show that the vibration-rotation bands are made up of two sets of lines P and R $(J \neq 0)$ and there will not be a line with the fundamental vibration frequency. Therefore the actual origin of the band is marked by a gap. The lines so obtained would be equally spaced and the adjacent lines on either side would be separated by a distance $2B$.

Since $\Delta J = 0$ is not allowed, the transitions with $\Delta E_{v, j} = hv_0$ is not observed under these conditions. This is referred to as Q branch (Fig. 25.7). This appears as the origin of the band. The infra red spectrum of a diatomic molecule with this model will have two rotational vibrational band.

Equations (25.20) and (25.21) indicate that the spacing of lines in the P and R branches are equal to $2B$, $i.e.$, same as in pure rotational spectra. Hence from vibration-rotation spectra, the moment of inertia and from it the internuclear bond distance can be calculated. The fundamental vibration frequency v_0 is obtained from the centre of the fundamental absorption band, $i.e.$, $v = 0$ to $v' = 1$. The fundamental vibration frequency can then be used to calculate the force constant (k) which is a measure of the stiffness of the bond.

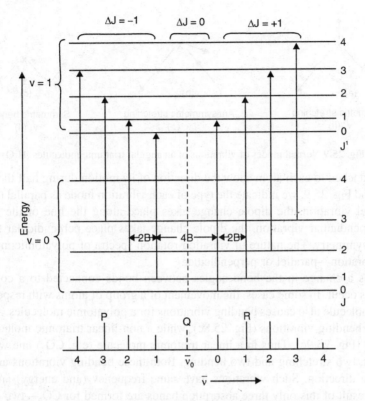

Fig. 25.7 Schematic energy levels showing structure of P, Q and R branches

Normal modes of vibrations: A molecule generally vibrates only in certain modes known as normal modes. Each normal mode corresponds to a vibrational degree of freedom. In general, a normal vibration is one in which all the atoms in a molecule vibrate with the same frequency and are in the same phase.

For a polyatomic molecules, the normal modes of vibrations are of two types. (*i*) Stretching vibrations and (*ii*) bending vibrations. The linear and non-linear molecules have $(N–1)$ stretching vibrations and $(2N–4)$ and $(2N–5)$ bending vibrations respectively. In stretching vibrations, the atoms move along the bond axis so that the bond length increases or decreases at regular intervals. The stretching vibrations again are of two types viz., symmetric and antisymmetric stretchings. In symmetric stretching of a triatomic molecule, both the bonds connected to a common atom can simultaneously either elongate or contract. This is shown in Fig. 25.8.

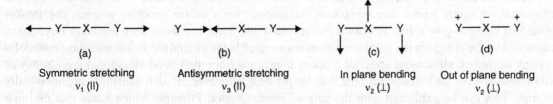

Fig. 25.8 Normal modes of vibration of a linear triatomic molecule (CO_2)

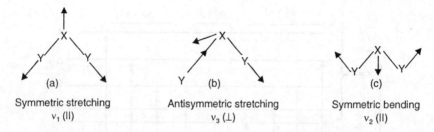

Fig. 25.9 Normal modes of vibrations of an angular triatomic molecules (H_2O)

The arrows attached to each atom show the direction of its motion during half the vibration. In the above Fig. 25.8 and Fig. 25.9, we indicate the type of each vibration mode as parallel (||) or perpendicular ($\perp$). In parallel vibration, the dipole change takes place along the line of the principal axis of symmetry. In perpendicular vibration, the dipole change takes place perpendicular to the line of the principal axis of symmetry. The nature of vibration-rotation spectra of polyatomic molecules depends on the type of vibration—parallel or perpendicular.

When there is a change in the bond angles between bonds connected to a common atom, the bending vibrations occur. In some cases, the movement of a group of atoms with respect to the remaining atoms in the molecule also causes bending vibrations for a polyatomic molecules. A linear triatomic molecule has two bending vibrations (Fig. 25.8c), while a non-linear triatomic molecule has only one bending vibration (Fig. 25.9c). Thus in a linear triatomic molecule (e.g. CO_2) one would expect four vibrational modes, two stretching and two bending. Both these bending vibrations are identical in all respect except the direction. Such vibrations have same frequency (and energy) and are said to be degenerate. As a result of this only three absorption bands are formed for CO_2—two corresponding to stretching vibrations and one corresponding to bending vibration. A non-linear angular triatomic molecule like H_2O also has three vibrational modes – two due to stretching modes and one due to the bending mode. The difference between the linear and non-linear triatomic molecule lies in the degeneracy of the bending mode of the former.

25.5 ELECTRONIC SPECTRA

The electronic spectra involves the promotion of electrons from an occupied molecular orbital to an empty or partially filled higher molecular orbital. The radiation required for the electronic transition lies in the visible or ultra violet region. A molecule in each stable electronic level can execute vibrational and rotational motions. The total energy E_t of the molecule can be written as

$$E_t = E_{elec} + E_{vib} + E_{rot}$$

Each electronic level consists of a number of vibrational levels and each vibrational level consists of several rotational levels. The vibrational transitions give a coarse structure whereas the smaller rotational changes give a fine structure. For an electronic transition there is no quantum mechanical restriction on the change in the vibrational quantum number. In the ground electronic state most molecules occupy the lowest vibrational level, all types of transitions from the lowest vibrational level to any of vibrational level of the higher electronic state are possible. However, all such transitions are not equally intense. This can be explained with the help of Frank-Condon Principle which states that the time required for a molecule to execute vibration (10^{-12} s) is longer than that required for electronic transition (10^{-15} s). To a good approximation it may be stated that during electronic transition the nuclei which are massive do not change their positions. This means that the internuclear distance remains unchanged during transition. This principle of Frank-Condon can be understood by considering the potential curve as shown in Fig. 25.10. Let us consider that the molecule is initially in the ground electronic state where it is most likely to be at its equilibrium internuclear separation corresponding to the minimum of the potential energy curve. On absorption of radiation, the transition occurs and the molecule is excited to the state represented by the upper curve (Fig. 25.10). According to Frank-Condon principle the nuclear framework remains constant during excitation and therefore the transition may be represented by a vertical line.

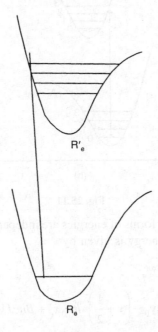

Fig. 25.10 Electronic transition based on the Frank-Condon principle

The nature of the electronic spectrum depends on the internuclear separation of the molecule in the excited state relative to that in the ground state. The internuclear separation in the excited state is slightly larger than those in the ground state. This gives rise to the depth in the potential energy diagram of the excited state slightly displaced towards the larger internuclear distance.

It can be shown by quantum mechanical calculations that the intensity of a band is related to the difference in the nuclear separation R_e and R_e' for the ground and excited electronic states respectively. Three cases of electronic spectra arise depending on the relative values of R_e and R_e'.

Case I: When $R_e = R_e'$. Fig. 25.11 (a) shows the near ultraviolet spectrum of CN^-. The curve shows $0 \to 0$ band has maximum intensity whereas others ($1 \to 0$, $2 \to 0$, $3 \to 0$) decrease in intensity.

Case II: Fig. 25.11 (b) shows the spectrum of CO. The minimum of the upper curve B lies at a moderately greater R_e value than the lower curve A. The $0 \to 3$ band has maximum intensity and other bands on both sides have decreased intensity.

Case III: The minimum of the upper curve B lies at a larger distance away from that of the lower curve A (Fig. 25.11(c)). In this case, the transition takes place to a very high vibrational level in the upper curve B, which leads to the dissociation of the molecule. In such cases, the line spectra would be followed by continuous spectra. The $0 \to 0$ band is absent in this spectrum. This spectrum is useful in obtaining the dissociation energy of the molecule in the ground state.

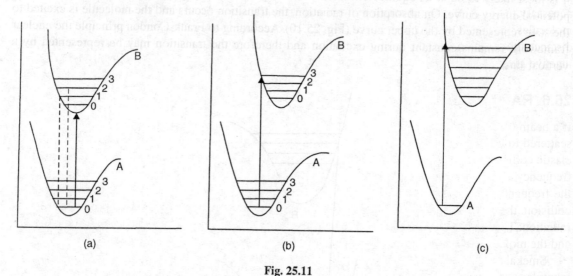

Fig. 25.11

Assuming that the three different forms of energies are independent of one another, the total energy of a molecule excluding its kinetic energy is given by

$$E_t = E_{elec} + E_{vib} + E_{rot}$$

$$= E_{elec} + \left(v + \frac{1}{2}\right)h\nu_0 - \left(v + \frac{1}{2}\right)^2 h\nu_0 x_e + BhcJ(J+1) \qquad \text{...(25.22)}$$

The frequency of any line resulting from a transition from one state to the other is given as

$$\nu = \left\{ \nu_{elec} + \left(v' + \frac{1}{2}\right)\nu_0' - \left(v + \frac{1}{2}\right)\nu_0 - \left(v' + \frac{1}{2}\right)^2 \nu_0' x_e' \right.$$

$$\left. + \left(v + \frac{1}{2}\right)^2 \nu_0 x_e \right\} + B'J'c(J'+1) - BJc(J+1) \qquad \text{...(25.23)}$$

where v, ν_0, B, J and x_c refer to one state and v', ν_0', B', J' and x_e' refer to the other state.

The term within the parenthesis corresponds to the frequency of the centre of the band ν_0 to which a fine structure is contributed by the rotational transitions. There is no restriction on the change in vibrational quantum number in electronic transitions and may have values $\Delta v = 0, \pm 1, \pm 2, ...$ Restricting the rotational transitions for the vibrational bands to $\Delta J = \pm 1$, we obtain P and R series of lines as

$$\nu_p = \nu_0 + B'cJ(J-1) - BcJ(J+1)\,;\ \Delta J = -1, \qquad \text{...(25.24)}$$

and

$$\nu_R = \nu_0 + B'cJ(J+1) - BJc(J-1)\,;\ \Delta J = +1 \qquad \text{...(25.25)}$$

Using various integral values of J in these equations, the fine structure of the lines in each branch can be investigated. These lines are apparently not equispaced and the spacing continuously decreases and beyond a certain position, the line structure disappears and a continuous emission results. The position of the limit beyond which a continuous emission occurs gives the frequency of radiation necessary to dissociate the molecule. From a careful study of the electronic spectra of simple diatomic molecules, v_0, x_e and B can be calculated. From these quantities moment of inertia, anharmonicity, bond distance, bond flexibility and bond dissociation energy can be obtained. Molecules which are infrared inactive give vibrational bands with rotational fine structure in electronic spectra.

25.6 RAMAN SPECTRA

If a beam of monochromatic light is passed through a medium, a small fraction of the incident light is scattered in all direction. The interaction of monochromatic radiation with matter may result in an (*i*) elastic collision or (*ii*) inelastic collision. In elastic collision, the resultant radiation will have the same frequency as that of incident radiation and is known as Rayleigh scattering. Thus in Rayleigh scattering, the frequency of resultant radiation is the same as that of the incident radiation. In case of inelastic collision, the direction and the frequency of the resultant radiation would be different from the incident radiation. Thus in inelastic collision, there is a transfer of energy between the electromagnetic radiation and the molecule of the medium.

Smekal in 1923 predicted that when monochromatic light falls on the substance, the scattering will take place and some of the scattered radiation should have different frequencies than that of incident radiation. In 1928, Raman experimentally showed the existence of such frequencies below and above of the incident beam. This effect is known as Raman scattering. The mechanism of Raman scattering can be explained as follows:

Consider the interaction of a photon of frequency v with a molecule. The molecule absorbs radiation and is raised from lower energy level E_A to higher energy level E_B. This state is an unstable state and photon is immediately emitted as scattered radiation, while the molecule returns to one of the states associated with the molecule. The frequency v' of the scattered radiation is obtained from the law of conservation of energy

$$E_A + hv = E_B + hv'$$

$$\left(E_B - E_A\right) = h\left(v - v'\right) = hv_{Raman} = ch\,\overline{v}'_{Raman} \qquad \text{...(25.26)}$$

If $E_B = E_A$, then the scattering radiation will have the same frequency as the incident radiation ($v = v'$), and the scattering is of Rayleigh Type (Fig. 25.12 (*a*)).

If $E_B > E_A$, then the frequency of scattered radiation v' is less than the frequency of the incident radiation v (or the wavelength of scattered radiation λ' will be more than the wavelength of the incident radiation). Such scattered lines which are observed on the higher wavelength side are called Stokes lines (Fig. 25.12 (*b*)). In other words, some portion of the energy is transferred from the incident radiation to the molecules and thus scattered radiations appears at a lower frequency in the spectrum.

If $E_B < E_A$, the frequency of scattered radiation v' is higher than the frequency of the incident radiation. Such scattered lines which are observed on the short wave length side are called anti-Stokes lines (Fig. 25.12 (*c*)). The frequency difference between the Rayleigh line and a Raman line is independent of the frequency of the incident line, but is characteristic of the scattering substance. The difference is called the Raman Shift.

Since the transfer of energy to and from the molecules follows the same quantum laws, both Stokes and anti-Stokes lines appear at equal spacing from the Rayleigh line. In order to give a common expression for Stokes and anti-Stokes lines, we can write in terms of wave numbers,

$$\bar{v}' - \bar{v} = \pm\Delta\bar{v}.$$

where $\vec{v}'$ and $\bar{v}$ are wave numbers of the scattered and incident radiation respectively and $\Delta\bar{v}$ is the rotational or vibrational, or rotation-vibration wave number of the molecule. $\Delta\bar{v}$ is known as the Raman shift. The plus sign on the above equation refers to anti-Stokes lines whereas negative sign refers to Stokes lines.

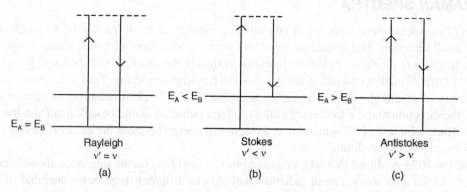

Fig. 25.12 Interaction which give rise to Rayleigh, Stokes and Antistokes lines

Rotational-Raman Spectra

Rotational transitions may also be observed by Raman effect if the polarizability of a molecule depends on the direction in which the applied field lies. Since the polarizability of a molecule returns to its initial value twice on every revolution, the rotational selection rule in Raman spectra is therefore $\Delta J = \pm 2$ in contrast to the corresponding selection rule for microwave spectroscopy, $\Delta J = \pm 1$. When a molecule makes transitions with $\Delta J = +2$, the scattered light emerges with a lower frequency and we get Stokes lines in the spectrum. The frequency of the Stokes lines is given by

Stokes lines $(\Delta J = +2)$: $v_{Raman} = v_0 - Bc(4J+6)$; for $(J+2 \longleftarrow J)$

$$-\Delta v_{rot} = -\left[v_{Raman} - v_0\right] = Bc(4J+6), \text{ for } (J+2\longleftarrow J) \qquad ...(25.27)$$

where v_0 is the frequency of the incident light. The frequency separation of the first Stokes line $(J=0)$ from the exciting line is $6B$ cm^{-1}. However, the separation between the successive lines is $4B$ cm^{-1} (Fig. 25.13). The intensity falls off for the line corresponding to high values of J. The equation for the anti-Stokes lines in the spectrum is $(\Delta J = -2)$.

Anti-Stokes lines $(\Delta J = -2)$: $v_{Raman} = v_0 + Bc(4J+2)$, for $J \longrightarrow J - 2$.

$$v_{Raman} - v_0 = BC(4J+2), \text{ for } (J \longrightarrow J-2) \qquad ...(25.28)$$

These lines are shifted by $4B$, $10B$, $14B$, ... to high frequency side of the incident light (Fig. 25.12).

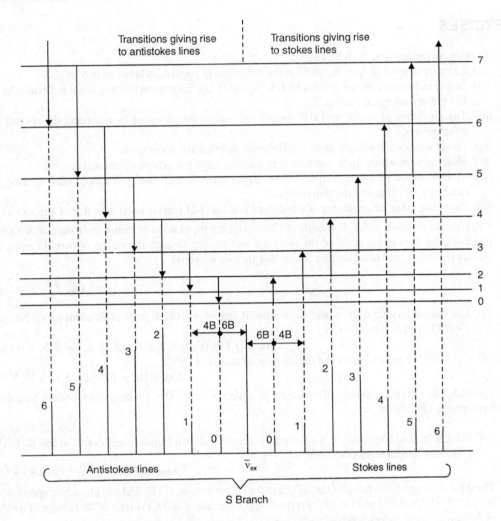

Fig. 25.13 Stokes and anti-Stokes rotational Raman lines

Vibrational-Raman's Spectra

The selection rule for vibrational Raman effect is $\Delta v = \pm 1$. The lines corresponding to $\Delta v = -1$ are on the high frequency side of the incident light and are called anti-Stokes lines and are usually weak. The lines corresponding to $\Delta v = +1$ are on the low frequency side of the incident light and are Stokes lines.

From the constant separation of $4B$ cm^{-1} between the neighbouring lines in Stokes and anti-Stokes series, B can be calculated. Evaluation of B allows the determination of the moment of inertia of the molecule perpendicular to the symmetry axis. From this, the bond distances and bond angles can be calculated. Molecules which are microwave inactive can produce rotational Raman spectra provided they possess anisotropic polarizabilities.

EXERCISES

1. Explain, giving reasons, the following:
    (*i*) Intensity of spectral lines depends on the difference in population between two levels.
    (*ii*) Homonuclear diatomic molecules such as N_2 and O_2 are microwave inactive while molecules like HCl, CO etc. are microwave active.
    (*iii*) The resolution of visible and UV spectra can usually be improved by recording the spectra at low temperatures.
    (*iv*) Lower rotational levels are more thickly populated than the upper ones.
    (*v*) Molecules for which dipole moment varies during vibration exhibit vibrational spectra.
    (*vi*) Vibrational and rotational energies can be added to give the total energy of a molecule exhibiting simultaneously vibration and rotation motion.
    (*vii*) Stretching vibration frequency of a hydrogen bonded O–H bond is lower than that of a free O–H bond.

2. BF_3 is planar molecule with F-B-F angle of 120°. Calculate the moment of inertia about each of two mutually perpendicular axes in the plane of the molecule and passing through the centre of mass in terms of the masses m_B and m_F and bond length r. Show that the two are equal.

    Ans. $I_X = I_y = \dfrac{3}{2} m_F r^2.$

3. (*a*) List out the number of translational, rotational and vibrational degrees of freedom for (*i*) Ne, (*ii*) O_2, (*iii*) CO_2, (*iv*) SO_2 and (*v*) CH_4.

    Ans. (*i*) 3, 0, 0; (*ii*) 3, 2, 1; (*iii*) 3, 2, 4; (*iv*) 3, 3, 3; (*v*) 3, 3, 9.

    (*b*) Calculate the reduced mass and the moment of inertia of $D^{35}Cl$.

    Ans. 3.162×10^{-27} kg, 5.14×10^{-47} kg m^2.

4. Calculate the zero point energy of hydrogen in joule per mole. The fundamental vibration frequency of hydrogen is 4395.24 cm^{-1}.

    Ans. 26.36 kJ mol^{-1}.

5. (*i*) What vibrational frequency in wave numbers corresponds to a thermal energy of kT at 298 K? (*ii*) What is the wavelength of this radiation?

    Ans. (*i*) 2.07×10^4m^{-1}, (*ii*) 4.83×10^{-5}m.

6. The typical energy differences for transitions in the (*i*) microwave, (*ii*) IR and (*iii*) electronic spectroscopies are 5×10^{-22}J, 5×10^{-19}J and 1×10^{-18}J respectively. Calculate at 300 K the ratio of the number of molecules in the two adjacent energy levels in each case.

    Ans. (*i*) 0.89, (*ii*) 5.7×10^{-6}, (*iii*) exp (–241.5).

7. How would the rotation and vibration spectra of HCl be affected if the internuclear distance were to be 12.90 Å instead of the actual value 1.29 Å?

8. Calculate the frequencies in m^{-1} for the pure rotational lines in the spectrum of $H^{35}Cl$ corresponding to the following changes in rotational quantum number: (*i*) $J = 0 \rightarrow 1$. (*ii*) $2 \rightarrow 3$.

    Ans. (*i*) 2.11×10^3m^{-1}, (*ii*) 4.22×10^3m^{-1}.

9. Which of the following three modes of vibration of a linear triatomic molecule AB_3 are IR active.

    (*i*) $B \rightarrow A \leftarrow B$ (*ii*) $B \rightarrow \leftarrow A \leftarrow B$ (*iii*) $\underset{\downarrow}{B} — \overset{\uparrow}{A} — \underset{\downarrow}{B}$

    Give reasons in support of your answer.

    Ans. (*ii*) and (*iii*).

10. In the infrared spectra of HBr, a series of lines having a separation of 16.94 cm^{-1} are obtained. Calculate the moment of inertia (*I*) and the internuclear separation (*r*) of HBr. (at. mass of Br = 79.92 amu).

    Ans. $I = 3.302 \times 10^{-47}$ kg m^2, $\nu = 0.141$ nm.

11. The molecule $^{12}C^{32}S$ undergoes $J = 0 \rightarrow 1$ transition and absorbs energy at a frequency of 491.70 MHz. Calculate the bond length. If the fundamental frequency is at 1285 cm^{-1}, calculate the force constant.

    Ans. 0.154 nm, 8.51×10^2 N m^{-1}.

12. The microwave spectrum of CN shows a series of lines separated by 3.7978 cm^{-1}. Calculate the internuclear distance in the molecule.

    Ans. 0.1172 nm.

13. Find the rotational energy corresponding to $J = 1$ for the hydrogen molecule, $r_e = 0.74$ Å.

    Ans. 2.4×10^{-21} J.

14. Typical fundamental vibration frequencies of HCl is 8.67×10^{13} Hz. Find (i) the corresponding value of a quantum of vibration energy $\hbar\omega$, (ii) the force constant (k) for the molecule.

    Ans. (i) 3.3×10^{-20} J, (ii) $k = 4.83 \times 10^2$ N m^{-1}

15. The fundamental vibration frequency for D^{35}Cl is given by $\nu = 208.1$ cm^{-1}. Calculate the force constant k and compare this value with the force constant obtained for H^{35}Cl in the previous problem. Comment on the result.

    Ans. 4.84×10^{-3} N m^{-1}.

16. In the infrared spectrum of HCl, the spacing for each branch of line corresponds to 20.8 cm^{-1}. Calculate (i) the bond distance and (ii) the moment of inertia.

    Ans. (i) 0.129 nm, (ii) 2.69×10^{-47} kg m^2.

17. At what wavelength and frequency will the 0, 2 band of HCl be found?

    Ans. 1.673×10^{-6} m, 5.978×10^5 m^{-1}.

18. The equilibrium bond length of nitric oxide (^{14}N^{16}O) is 1.15 Å. Calculate (i) the moment of inertia and (ii) the energy for the $J = 0 \rightarrow 1$ transition, (iii) How many times does the molecule rotate per second in the $J = 1$ level?

    Ans. (i) 1.65×10^{-46} kg m^2, (ii) 6.75×10^{-23} J, (iii) 1.02×10^{11} s^{-1}.

19. The bond length in CN$^+$ is 0.129 nm. Predict the position of first three lines in its microwave spectrum.

    Ans. $\nu_1 = 3.133$ cm^{-1}, $\nu_2 = 6.267$ cm^{-1}, $\nu_3 = 9.40$ cm^{-1}.

20. If one of the Raman lines appears at 460 nm when excited by light of wavelength 435.8 nm, at what frequency will it show absorption in the infrared region.

21. Explain Born-Oppenheimer approximation. What is its utility? When does the approximation break down?

22. What is Raman effect and how does it differ from phosphorescence and fluorescence?

23. What are Rayleigh, Stokes and anti-Stokes lines? Is the intensity of Stokes lines different from that of the anti-Stokes lines? Explain.

24. Explain (i) Franck-Condon principle and (ii) polarizability of a molecule and (iii) Phosphorescence and fluorescence with suitable examples.

25. Discuss the effect of temperature on (i) rotational spectra, (ii) vibrational spectra.

26. The wave number of pure rotational lines of HBr are represented by the equation $\bar{\nu}_J = 16.9 J$ cm^{-1}, where J is an integer. Calculate (i) the moment of inertia, (ii) internuclear bond distance of HBr, (iii) rotational frequency and (iv) rotational energy level that has the highest population at 298K.

27. The bond length of NO molecule is 1.151×10^{-10} m. Calculate the frequencies for pure rotational lines in the spectrum of NO corresponding to the following changes in the rotational quantum numbers (i) $0 \rightarrow 1$; (ii) $1 \rightarrow 2$; (iii) $2 \rightarrow 3$; (iv) $3 \rightarrow 4$.

    Ans. (i) 3.33×10^2 m^{-1}, (ii) 6.65×10^2 m^{-1}.
    (iii) 9.98×10^2 m^{-1} (iv) 13.3×10^2 m^{-1}.

28. The fundamental vibrational frequency of CO molecule is 2170.2 cm^{-1}. Calculate the force constant (k) of CO molecule.

    Ans. $k = 277.97$ Nm^{-1}.

Electrical and Magnetic Properties

26.1 INTRODUCTION

Physical properties of a system may be defined as those properties which can be investigated without any chemical change in it. These properties are divided into two categories, *viz.*, *additive* and *constitutive*. An additive property is given by the sum of the corresponding properties of the system. Mass is an example of additive property as the total mass of the system would be given by the sum of the individual masses of the constituents. A constitutive property, on the other hand, depends primarily on the arrangement of the constituents. Refractive index, surface tension, viscosity etc., are some examples of constitutive property.

The problem of establishing the structure of a molecule has two main aspects—qualitative and quantitative. The qualitative aspect deals with the general relationships of the positions of atoms to one another, types of internal atomic and molecular motions, etc. The quantitative aspect yields information on bond distances, numerical values of bond angles, extent of polarity of bonds and the extent of interactions between atoms in the molecule.

Chemical analysis and determination of molar masses provide informations concerning the composition of molecules. From studies of chemical properties, one can ascertain the sequence of atoms or group of atoms in the molecule. These investigations are, however, inadequate and do not give direct information required for the elucidation of the structure of molecules. To obtain an insight into the problem of structure determination, more refined techniques have to be employed. Some of the commonly used methods involve measurements of refractive index, optical activity, dipole moment, analysis of absorption and emission spectra and investigations of electric and magnetic properties. Sometimes a single technique is not enough and combinations of these techniques, depending upon the nature of the molecule, have to be employed.

26.2 OPTICAL ACTIVITY

Ordinary light is a transverse wave motion and is considered as an electromagnetic vibration of different wavelengths vibrating in many different planes at right angles to the direction or propagation of light. If light is made to pass through a nicol prism, the emergent light then consists of vibrations in one plane only, and is said to be plane polarized light. The prism that produces the polarized light is called the polarizer. If a second prism, called analyser, is placed in the path of the emergent light in such a way that the axis of both the prisms are parallel, then the light passes through completely and the field of view is visible. If, however, the axis of the two prisms are at right angles to each other (cross position), then no light passes through and the field of view is dark. If in between these two prisms a glass cell containing some liquid is placed, the polarized light that emerges through the second prism has to be rotated through some angle such that the light is completely visible. The substances that show such effects are called *optically active*. An optically active substance is, therefore, one that rotates the plane of polarized light. Optical activity is measured in degree of rotation angle.

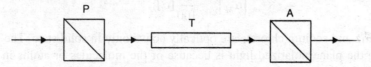

Fig. 26.1 Schematic diagram of a polarimeter

Measurement of Optical Activity

The rotation of plane polarized light is measured by means of a simple instrument called polarimeter (Fig. 26.1). It consists of two nicol prisms. The first prism (P) is called *the polarizer* and the second prism (A), which is used to detect the direction of polarized light, is called *the analyser.* T is a sample tube in which the substance whose optical activity is to be measured is taken and placed between two prisms. To start with, the zero position of the polarimeter is set, *i.e.*, the light is passed through the tube when it is empty and the field of view is either completely bright (or dark). The reading is taken from the circular disc provided with an angular scale. The sample of the liquid is placed in the sample tube and rotation of the plane of polarization of light by the sample is measured by rotating the analyser. If the substance rotates the plane of polarized light to the right or clockwise as viewed looking towards the light source, it is said to be *dextrorotatory*. On the other hand, if the rotation of the plane polarized light is to the left (anticlockwise), the substance is called *laevorotatory,* the symbols (+) and (−) are used to indicate the rotations to the right and to the left respectively.

Specific Rotation

The amount of rotation α depends on the concentration of the substance and on the length of the sample tube. Generally, the observed rotation is expressed in terms of *specific rotation* [α] given by the relation

$$[\alpha] = \frac{\alpha}{lC} \qquad \qquad ...(26.1)$$

where α is the observed rotation of polarized light, l is the length in decimeter of the sample tube through which light passes and C is the concentration in g/cm^3 of the solution. If in equation (26.1) we put $l = 1$ dm and $C = 1$ g/cm^3, then we get

$$[\alpha] = \alpha$$

that is, the specific rotation is defined as *the rotation observed by a solution containing 1g/cm³ of the sample in a 1 dm sample tube.* Since [α] varies with the temperature (T), wavelength (λ) of the light source and the solvent used; hence these variables must be specified. Therefore, the specific rotation is denoted as $[\alpha]_{\lambda}^{T}$.

If the solution of an optically active substance contains C' g of the substance per 100 cm^3 of the solution, then the specific rotation is given by

$$[\alpha] = \frac{\alpha 100}{l C'} \qquad ...(26.2)$$

The *molar rotation* is defined as *the product of specific rotation and the molar mass (M) of the substance and is denoted by* $[\alpha_M]_\lambda^T$.

$$[\alpha_M]_\lambda^T = \frac{M}{100}[\alpha]_\lambda^T \qquad ...(26.3)$$

Substances like quartz and sodium chlorate are optically active only in solid state. The ability of these substances to rotate the plane polarized light is because of the molecules or atoms in the crystal are arranged in the form of either a right handed or a left handed spiral. On melting, this structure disappears and therefore the liquid shows no optical activity. On the other hand, there are other variety of substances in which the optical activity is due to a particular arrangement of atoms and groups within the molecule. These substances show optical activity in solid, liquid, gas or in solution phase. This property of optical activity in the compounds is related to the molecular structure.

The optical activity is a property linked with the asymmetry of the molecules and is usually shown by organic substances. van't Hoff and Le Bel independently pointed out that those organic substances, which contain one or more carbon atoms attached to four different atoms or group of atoms are called Chiral carbon atoms. The chiral carbon atom is indicated by an asterisk (*) mark. The simplest organic compound that contains one chiral carbon atom is lactic acid.

$$H_3C - \overset{\overset{\displaystyle OH}{|}}{\underset{\underset{\displaystyle H}{|}}{C^*}} - COOH$$

Tartaric acid contains two such carbon atoms as shown below

$$HO - \overset{\overset{\displaystyle H}{|}}{\underset{\underset{\displaystyle H}{|}}{\overset{\overset{\displaystyle |}{C^*}}{\underset{\underset{\displaystyle |}{C^*}}{}}}} - COOH$$
$$HO - OH \;\; COOH$$

The four valencies of the carbon atom are directed towards the four corners of a regular tetrahedron with carbon atom at the centre. If only one chiral atom is present, then there are two ways of arranging them in space such that one is the mirror image of the other but these are not superimposable as shown in Fig. 26.2.

Substances whose molecules are related as two nonsuperimposable mirror images are called enantiomers. It will be further seen that when these tetrahedral structures are viewed through the same positions, the groups W, Z and Y are arranged clockwise in one case and anticlockwise in the other case. Thus, an optically active substance exists in two forms. These forms resemble in their chemical and in

to promote the molecule to higher excited electronic energy states but may cause a perturbation of the electronic configuration of the molecule. This kind of interaction causes the electric field of light to change its direction of oscillation. Symmetrical molecules such as methane, ethane etc. do not rotate the plane of polarized light as rotation in one direction is cancelled by an equal rotation in the opposite direction. However, asymmetric molecules like lactic acid etc., will produce a net effect on the incident polarized light. The electromagnetic interactions do not average to zero and the substance is optically active.

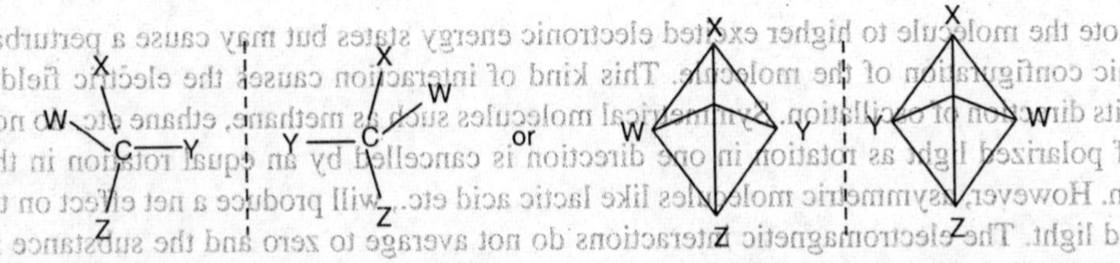

Fig. 26.2 Two nonsuperimposable arrangements of a chiral carbon atom

most of their physical properties except that one turns the plane of polarized light to the left (laevorotatory) and the other to the right (dextrorotatory). An equimolar mixture of the two enantiomers would not show any optical activity as the effect due to one will be counterbalanced by the other. Such a mixture is called a racemic form and can be separated into its active components by mechanical, chemical and biochemical methods. In case of lactic acid, we have three forms, namely, dextrolactic acid, laevolactic acid and racemic lactic acid. Dextro and laevo forms of lactic acid are shown below:

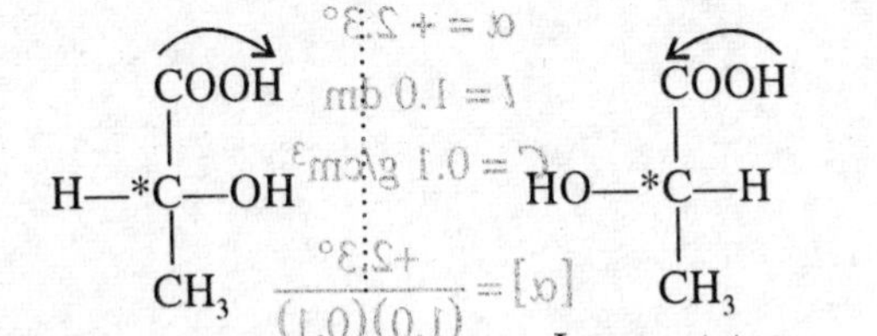

COOH H—*C—OH CH₃ Dextrorotatory

COOH HO—*C—H CH₃ Laevorotatory

If in a compound more than one chiral carbon atoms are present, then the mirror image isomers are called enantiomers and those, which do not have a mirror image relationship are called diastereomers. For example in 2:3 dichloropentane there are four isomers; I and II as also III and IV are two pairs of enantiomers

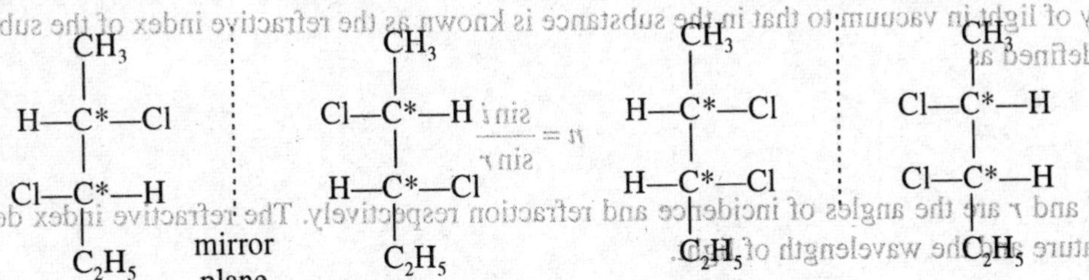

CH₃ H—C*—Cl Cl—C*—H C₂H₅ (I)

mirror plane

CH₃ Cl—C*—H H—C*—Cl C₂H₅ (II)

CH₃ H—C*—Cl H—C*—Cl C₂H₅ (III)

CH₃ Cl—C*—H Cl—C*—H C₂H₅ (IV)

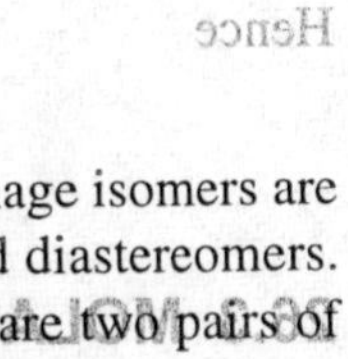

It is interesting to note that, if in a molecule there are two or more chiral carbon atoms, and if one half of the molecule is a mirror image of the other half, then the molecule would be optically inactive. Such an isomer is called a meso isomers. It will be noted that the above and below the dotted line in this structure there is an identical arrangement. In such a case optical rotation by one part of a molecule is cancelled by the other part. Thus in tartaric acid we have four forms, viz., dextro, laevo, meso and racemic.

COOH H—C*—OH H—C*—OH COOH

An oversimplified explanation to the optical activity exhibited by molecules which lack symmetry may be suggested in terms of interactions of the oscillating electric field of the light with the electrons within the molecule. When a light beam impinges on a molecule, the radiant energy may not be able to promote the molecule to higher excited electronic energy states but may cause a perturbation of the electronic configuration of the molecule. This kind of interaction causes the electric field of light to change its direction of oscillation. Symmetrical molecules such as methane, ethane etc. do not rotate the plane of polarized light as rotation in one direction is cancelled by an equal rotation in the opposite direction. However, asymmetric molecules like lactic acid etc., will produce a net effect on the incident polarized light. The electromagnetic interactions do not average to zero and the substance is optically active.

Problem 26.1: If 0.1 g of an organic compound is dissolved in 100 ml of ethanol, the observed optical rotation at 298 K was found to be +2.3° in a polarimeter having a sample tube of length 1.0 dm. Calculate the specific rotation, [α] of the compound.

   Solution: The specific rotation is given by equation (26.1),

$$[\alpha] = \frac{\alpha}{lC}$$

Here

$$\alpha = +2.3°$$

$$l = 1.0 \text{ dm}$$

and

$$C = 0.1 \text{ g/cm}^3$$

Hence

$$[\alpha] = \frac{+2.3°}{(1.0)(0.1)}$$

$$= +23°$$

26.3 MOLAR REFRACTION

Refractive Index: When a ray of light passes from one medium to another, it refracts. The ratio of the velocity of light in vacuum to that in the substance is known as the refractive index of the substance (n) and is defined as

$$n = \frac{\sin i}{\sin r}$$

where i and r are the angles of incidence and refraction respectively. The refractive index depends on temperature and the wavelength of light.

Molar Refraction

H.A. Lorenz and L.V. Lorenz in 1880 independently deduced the following relation between refractive index (n) and the density of the medium (d)

$$R_s = \left(\frac{n^2 - 1}{n^2 + 2}\right)\left(\frac{1}{d}\right) \qquad ...(26.4)$$

The term R_s is called *the specific refraction* of the substance and is independent of the temperature. Multiplying both sides of equation (26.4) by the molar mass of the substance, we get

$$R_M = R_S \times M = \left(\frac{n^2 - 1}{n^2 + 2}\right)\left(\frac{M}{d}\right) \qquad ...(26.5)$$

Here M/d is the molar volume and the quantity R_M is *the molar refraction* and has the unit of volume. The molar refraction is nearly independent of temperature, pressure and the state of aggregation of the substance. However, it depends on the number and the nature of atoms present and also on the binding between the atoms. This property has been found to be partly additive and partly constitutive. The molar refraction of a large number of compounds have been determined. These values show that atoms and group of atoms contribute to the molar refraction of the compound. A comparison of the observed and calculated values of the molar refraction helps in elucidating the structure of the molecules. Table 26.1 shows the values of the molar refraction of some atoms and structures.

Table 26.1 Molar Refraction Contribution at 589 nm, R_m (in cm^3 mol^{-1})

C	2.418	O (in carbonyl)	2.211
H	1.100	O (in hydroxyl)	1.522
Cl	5.967	O (in ether)	1.644
Br	8.865	Double bond (C=C)	1.733
I	13.960	Triple bond (C≡C)	2.398
N (in primary amines)	2.322	3 membered ring	0.710
N (in secondary amines)	2.499	4 membered ring	0.480
N (in tertiary amines)	2.840		

Let us take the example of C_2H_5OH. The calculated value of molar refraction is

$$2 \text{ C atoms} = 2 \times 2.418 = 4.836$$

$$6 \text{ H atoms} = 6 \times 1.100 = 6.600$$

$$1 \text{ O atom} = 1 \times 5.22 = 1.522$$

$$\text{Total molar refraction} = 12.958 \text{ cm}^3 \text{ mol}^{-1}$$

The observed value is calculated from the relation

$$R_M = \frac{n^2 - 1}{n^2 + 2} \frac{M}{d}$$

Here

$$M = 46 \text{ g mol}^{-1}$$

$$d = 0.78 \text{ g cm}^{-3}$$

$$n = 1.348$$

Therefore

$$R_M = \frac{(1.348)^2 - 1}{(1.348)^2 + 2} \frac{46}{0.78}$$

$$= 12.64 \text{ cm}^3 \text{ mol}^{-1}$$

The calculated value agrees fairly well with the observed value.

For open chain molecules with conjugated double bonds where the electrons of the π bonds are free to move over the entire molecule and are easily deformed the calculated value is different from the observed value. This behaviour is referred to as the *optical exaltation, i.e.,* the observed value is generally higher than the calculated value. If the double bonds constitute a closed ring, such as benzene, the optical exaltation disappears, but naphthalene, anthracene, and other polynuclear systems exhibit marked exaltation.

The molar refraction values of gases are generally identical with those of liquids. The molar refraction of a mixture in a solution is given by

$$[R_M]_{1,2} = \left(\frac{n^2-1}{n^2+2}\right)\left(\frac{X_1 M_1 + X_2 M_2}{d}\right) \qquad ...(26.6)$$

where X_1 and X_2 denote the mole fractions of the components in the solution, M_1 and M_2 are the molar masses of the solvent and solute and d is the density of the solution. It has been found that $[R_M]_{1,2}$ is related to the individual molar refraction, R_{M_1} and R_{M_2}, i.e.

$$R_M = X_1 R_{M_1} + X_2 R_{M_2}$$

$$= X_1 \frac{n_1^2-1}{n_1^2+2}\frac{M_1}{d_1} + X_2 \frac{n_2^2-1}{n_2^2+2}\frac{M_2}{d_2} \qquad ...(26.7)$$

Problem 26.2: Using the data of Table 26.1, calculate the molar refraction of butane (C_4H_{10}) and acetone (CH_3COCH_3).

Solution: The molar refraction of butane is given as

$$4\ C\ atoms = 4 \times 2.418 = 9.672$$
$$10\ H\ atoms = 10 \times 1.1 = 11.000$$
$$Total\ molar\ refraction = 20.672\ cm^3\ mol^{-1}$$

The molar refraction of acetone is given as

$$3\ C\ atoms = 3 \times 2.418 = 7.254$$
$$6\ H\ atoms = 6 \times 1.1 = 6.600$$
$$1\ O\ atom\ in\ carbonyl\ group = 1 \times 2.211 = 2.211$$

Total molar refraction = 16.065 cm^3 mol^{-1}

26.4 DIELECTRIC CONSTANT

When two charges q_1 and q_2 are separated by a distance r in a vacuum, the potential energy between the two is

$$V = \frac{(q_1 q_2)}{4\pi\varepsilon_0 r} \qquad ...(26.8)$$

where ε_0 is the permitivity of the vacuum.

When the charges are immersed in a medium such as air or a liquid, then their potential energy is reduced to

$$V = \frac{q_1 q_2}{4\pi\varepsilon r} \qquad ...(26.9)$$

where ε is the permitivity of the medium. The relative permitivity ε_r, which is also called the dielectric constant of the medium is written as

$$\varepsilon_r = \frac{\varepsilon}{\varepsilon_0} \qquad \text{...(26.10)}$$

From elementary electrostatics, the relative permitivity of a substance is measured by comparing the capacitance of a capacitor with the same and without the sample present (air), C and C_0, i.e.,

$$\varepsilon_r = \frac{C}{C_0} \qquad \text{...(26.11)}$$

Alternatively, the dielectric constant of a material can be defined as the ratio of the electric field in the vacuum to that in a given material. The dielectric constant is a dimensionless quantity. The dielectric constant is unity for vacuum while for any other material it is greater than unity. The Dielectric constant of a substance is large if its molecules are polar and highly polarizable.

26.5 DIPOLE MOMENT

When a bond is formed between two homonuclear molecules such as H_2, N_2, O_2 etc. there is a uniform charge distribution around each nucleus. On the other hand, if the bond is formed between two atoms of different electronegativity such as HF, HCl, NH_3, H_2O etc. the charge distribution is not uniform. The more electronegative atom has a greater tendency to attract the electrons thereby leaving an excess of negative charge on the more electronegative atom and an excess of positive charge on the less electronegative atom. The bond so formed between the two atoms would be polar and the molecule may be *an electric dipole* and will have a dipole moment μ. The permanent dipole moment would arise from the fact that the centre of gravity of the positive and the negative charges may not coincide. When a positive charge q is separated from a negative charge $-q$ by a distance r, then the magnitude of the dipole moment is given by

$$\mu = qr \qquad \text{...(25.8)}$$

Dipole moment is a vector quantity. It has both direction and magnitude and it is denoted by an arrow directed from the negative to the positive charge (Fig. 26.3). In nonpolar molecules there is no charge separation and hence $r = 0$ so that the dipole moment is zero.

When a charge q (4.8×10^{-10} esu) is separated by a distance 1 A°(10^{-8} cm), then the dipole moment is given by

$$\mu = (4.8 \times 10^{-10} \text{ esu}) (10^{-8} \text{ cm})$$
$$= 4.8 \times 10^{-18} \text{ esu cm}$$

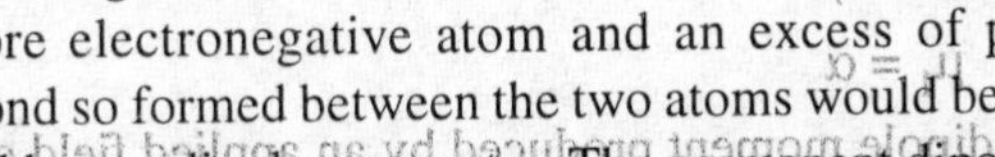

$$q \bullet \!\!\!-\!\!\!\!\!\!-\!\!\!\!\!\!\!\!\overset{\displaystyle r}{\longrightarrow} \bullet p$$

Fig. 26.3 Definition of dipole moment

The quantity 10^{-18} esu cm is called a debye and is denoted by D. Thus, the magnitude of dipole moment is 4.8 D. In SI units, the debye is expressed as follows:

$$1D = \frac{(10^{-18}\,\text{esu cm})(1.602 \times 10^{-19}\,\text{C})(10^{-2}\,\text{m cm}^{-1})}{(4.80 \times 10^{-10}\,\text{esu})}$$

$$= 3.336 \times 10^{-30}\,\text{C m}$$

Permanent and induced dipole moments: A polar molecule has permanent electric dipole moment. The permanent dipole moment arises from the partial charges on the atoms in the molecule that arises from differences in the electronegativity. Non polar molecules may acquire an induced dipole moment in an electric field on account of the distortion that the field causes in their electronic distributions and nuclear positions. The magnitude of this induced dipole moments is directly proportional to the strength of the electric field and can be written as

$$\mu_i = \alpha\, E_i \qquad\qquad ...(26.12)$$

where α is a characteristic of the molecule and is called the polarizibility of the molecule. Greater the polarizability, larger the induced dipole moment for a given applied field. The polarizability has the dimensions of volume. This can be seen using SI units as follows:

$$\alpha = \frac{\mu_1}{E} = \frac{\text{Cm}}{(\text{Fm}^{-1})(\text{Vm}^{-1})} = \frac{\text{Cm}^3}{\left(\dfrac{C}{V}\right)(V)} = \text{m}^3$$

When $E = 1$,

$$\mu_1 = \alpha$$

i.e., the polarizability is the dipole moment produced by an applied field of unit strength.

Molar polarization: Polarization for a mole of the substance is called molar polarization. The three types of polarization are

(*i*) **Orientation Polarization:** In the absence of an electric field, due to thermal motions, the molecular dipoles are generally distributed randomly. When an electron field is applied, it causes the molecular dipoles to orient along the direction of the field. For this reason it is called orientation polarisation. It is given by

$$P_0 = \frac{N_A \mu^2}{9\varepsilon_0 kT} \qquad\qquad ...(26.13)$$

where N_A is the Avogadro constant, μ is the dipole moment of the molecule, ε_0 is the permitivity of the vacuum, k and T stand for Boltzmann constant and temperature.

(*ii*) **Distortion polarisation:** This is due to the distortion of the electronic charge cloud in a molecule by the applied electric field. The polarization is independent of the temperature and is proportional to the electric field strength. The proportionality constant (α_e) is called the mean molecular electronic polarizability. It is given by

$$P_D = \frac{N_A \alpha_e}{3\varepsilon_0} \qquad\qquad ...(26.14)$$

(*iii*) **Vibrational polarization:** This is due to the deformation of the nuclear skeleton of the molecule by the electric field. Its value depends on the vibrational polarizability. Vibrational polarizability for one mole is given as

$$P_v = \frac{N_A \alpha_v}{3\varepsilon_0}$$

The total molar polarization P_M, which includes all the three contribution, is equal to

$$P_M = \frac{N_A}{3\varepsilon_0}\left(\alpha_e + \alpha_v + \frac{\mu^2}{3kT}\right) \qquad \text{...(26.15)}$$

Equation (26.15) is known as the Debye equation.

Clausius and Mosottii derived an equation to calculate the total molar polarisation of the molecules without permanent dipole moment as

$$P_M = \frac{\varepsilon_r - 1}{\varepsilon_r + 2}\left(\frac{M}{d}\right) = \frac{4}{3}\pi N_A \alpha \qquad \text{...(26.16)}$$

where N_A denotes the Avogadro constant, M the molar mass and d the density of the substance. From the equation (26.15) or (26.16) the polarizability and permanent dipole moment of the molecule in a sample

can be determined by measuring ε_r at a series of temperature. Calculating P_M and plotting against $\frac{1}{T}$

would yield a straight line, having slope equal to $\frac{N_A\mu^2}{9\varepsilon_0 k}$ and intercept $\left(\text{at } \frac{1}{T} = 0\right)$ equal to $\frac{N_A\alpha}{3\varepsilon_0}$. This

is shown in Fig. 26.4. From the slope and intercept, the dipole moment μ and the induced polarization of the molecule can be calculated. In case of nonpolar molecules like H_2, CH_4, CCl_4 etc., the dipole moments are zero and the line will be parallel to $1/T$ axis. The graphs for $CHCl_3$ and HCl show that P_M varies linearly with $1/T$ indicating that these substances possess permanent dipole moments.

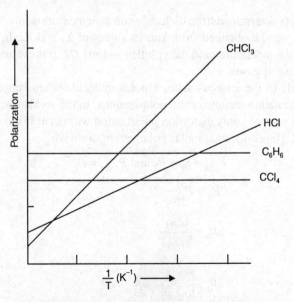

Fig. 26.4 Temperature dependence of molar polarization

Determination of Dipole Moment

Several methods are available for determining the dipole moments. A few of them will be discussed below:

(*i*) **Temperature method:** In case of gases, the total molar polarization, P_M (equation 26.15), when plotted against $1/T$ yields a straight line with slope equal to $\dfrac{N_A \mu^2}{9\varepsilon_0 k}$. So the dipole moment

$$\mu = \sqrt{\frac{9\varepsilon_0 k \cdot \text{slope}}{N_A}}$$

(*ii*) **Dilute solution method:** Dipole moments of substances in solution can be determined using nonpolar solvents such as benzene, carbon tetrachloride etc. In these experiments, dielectric constants and densities are measured at several concentrations. The measurements are repeated at a number of temperatures. The total molar polarization of the solution ($P_{1,2}$) if dilute, is given by the sum of the polarization of the constituents. e.g.,

$$P_{1,2} = \left(\frac{\varepsilon - 1}{\varepsilon + 2}\right)\left(\frac{X_1 M_1 + X_2 M_2}{d}\right) \qquad \text{...(26.17)}$$

where X_1 and X_2 are the mole fractions of the solvent and solute in the solution, M_1 and M_2 their respective molar masses and d is the density of the solution. $P_{1,2}$ is defined as

$$P_{1,2} = X_1 P_1 + X_2 P_2$$

where P_1 and P_2 are the molar polarization of the solvent and the solute respectively. Hence

$$\left(\frac{\varepsilon - 1}{\varepsilon + 2}\right)\left(\frac{X_1 M_1 + X_2 M_2}{d}\right) = \left(\frac{\varepsilon - 1}{\varepsilon + 2}\right)\frac{M_1 X_1}{d_1} + \left(\frac{\varepsilon - 1}{\varepsilon + 2}\right)\frac{M_2 X_2}{d_2} \qquad \text{...(26.18)}$$

The value of P_1 is determined from dielectric constant measurements of the pure solvent. Hence the value of P_2 can be obtained from known values of X_1 and X_2. In this manner P_2 is determined at several temperatures and then plotted against $1/T$. μ is evaluated from the slope of the line as in the case of gases.

(*iii*) **Eberts method:** In the gaseous state, a polar molecule when subjected to an electric field suffers both orientation and distortion polarizations. In the solid state where orientation of the molecule is not possible only distortion polarization will occur if the molecule were subjected to electric field. Hence for total molar polarization, we have

$$P_{\text{gas}} = P_i + P_0 \quad \text{and} \quad P_{\text{solid}} = P_i$$

or

$$P_0 = P_{\text{gas}} - P_{\text{solid}}$$

But

$$P_0 = \frac{N_A \mu^2}{9\varepsilon_0 kT} \qquad \text{...(26.19)}$$

Hence

$$P_0 = \frac{N_A \mu^2}{9\varepsilon_0 kT} = P_{\text{gas}} - P_{\text{solid}}$$

Fig. 26.4 Temperature dependence of molar polarization

From which we get

$$\mu = \sqrt{\frac{9\varepsilon_0 kT \left(P_{gas} - P_{solid}\right)}{N_A}} \quad \ldots (26.19(a))$$

As the quantities on the right hand side are known, the value of μ can be calculated.

Values of dipole moments for some substances are given in Table 26.2.

Table 26.2 Dipole Moments of Some Substances (in debye units)

Compound	Dipole moment	Compound	Dipole moment
H_2	0.00	CH_4	0.00
N_2	0.00	CCl_4	0.00
CO_2	0.00	CH_3Cl	1.87
CO	0.12	CH_3Br	1.81
HCl	1.03	CH_3I	1.65
HBr	0.79	CH_3OH	1.70
HF	1.91	C_2H_5OH	1.69
H_2O	1.85	C_6H_5OH	1.68
NH_3	1.46	$C_6H_5NO_2$	4.06
SO_2	1.61	C_6H_5Cl	1.55
H_2S	1.10	$C_6H_5CH_3$	0.36

Dipole Moment and Structure of Molecules

Dipole moment measurements provide valuable informations regarding the extent to which a bond is polarized and the structure of molecules. Some typical examples may be mentioned here.

In case of nonpolar molecules like H_2, Cl_2, O_2 etc. the dipole moments are zero indicating that the bonding electrons are symmetrically distributed between the atoms. Bonds in molecules like carbon dioxide or carbon disulphide are polar due to the difference in the electronegativities of the atoms. However, the net dipole moment is zero suggesting that the molecules are linear, the two bond moments counter balance each other (Fig. 26.5). Molecules like CX_4 ($X = H$, Cl, Br and I) possess no net dipole moment indicating that they possess symmetrical structures, the bond moment of any C—X bond is exactly counter balanced by the resultant bond moment of the remaining three C—X bonds.

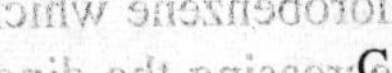

Fig. 26.5

A linear symmetrical structure for water molecule is ruled out from the fact that it possesses appreciable dipole moment (1.85 D). The molecule has an angular structure with each O—H bond moment of 1.60 D and the bond angle of 104.5°. Similarly dipole moments of NH_3, PCl_3 can be explained by assuming a triangular pyramidal structure for these molecules. In ammonia, nitrogen atom lies at the apex of the regular pyramid and the three hydrogen atoms are at the other three corners and lie in one plane. In BCl_3, although B—Cl bonds are polar but the dipole moment is zero indicating a planar configuration for the molecule in which chlorine atoms lie at the three corners of an equilateral triangle with boron at the centre of the triangle.

In aromatic compounds, benzene has zero dipole moment confirming a planar structure for the molecule. When a hydrogen atom in benzene ring is replaced by substituent like X (Cl, Br, I), R (CH_3, C_2H_5, etc.), NH_2, OH, NO_2 or SO_3 etc., the resulting molecule possesses dipole moment.

In disubstituted benzene derivatives if two substituents are identical and lie in the plane of the ring, the dipole moment is found to be zero for the symmetrical p-derivatives while unsymmetrical o- and m-derivatives possess appreciable dipole moments. An o-derivative being more unsymmetrical than the m-derivative hence possesses a higher value of dipole moment. In p-dihydroxy benzene the dipole moment is not zero indicating that the two hydroxyl groups are not in the plane of the ring. When two substituents in the ring are different, e.g., $C_6H_4NO_2Cl$, then all the three isomers possess dipole moments and the dipole moment increases in the order para < meta < ortho.

Dipole moment measurements can also be used to predict resonance in molecules. Chlorobenzene has a dipole moment of 1.7 D while for ethyl chloride the value is 2.05 D. Actually one would expect that the π electrons of the ring in chlorobenzene to be pulled by the electro-negative chlorine atom and thereby increasing the negative charge on it. The molecule should, therefore, possess a large dipole moment. This is, however, contrary to the observed low value of 1.7 D. It is explained by assuming that resonating structures are possessed by chlorobenzene which lead to a lowering of the negative charge on the chlorine atom and consequently decreasing the dipole moment.

From dipole moment one can estimate the percentage of ionic character in a covalent bond. In HCl, if the bond were purely ionic then the dipole moment would be

$$\mu = 1.26 \times 4.8 \times 10^{-10} = 6.05 \text{ D}$$

However, the observed value is only 1.03 D. Hence the percentage ionic character is given as

$$\% \text{ ionic character} = \frac{\mu_{obs}}{\mu_{calc}} \times 100$$

$$= \frac{1.03}{6.05} \times 100$$

$$= 17\%.$$

26.6 MAGNETIC PROPERTIES OF MOLECULES

If two magnetic poles of strength m_1 and m_2 are separated by a distance r in any medium, the force F acting between the two poles is given as

$$F = \frac{m_1 m_2}{\mu r^2}$$

...(26.20)

where μ is the *magnetic permeability* of the medium. It is a measure of the tendency of the magnetic lines of force to pass through the medium relative to the tendency for a vacuum. For vacuum or air, μ is unity. When $\mu < 1$, the substance composing the medium is said to be the *diamagnetic* and the lines of force tend to pass less readily through the substance than in vacuum or air. In case $\mu > 1$, the substance is known as *paramagnetic* and the lines of force prefer to pass more readily through the substance than the vacuum or air. Substances like Fe, Co, Ni, etc. with $\mu \gg 1$ are said to be *ferromagnetic* and the lines of force pass very readily through the ferromagnetic substances.

When a substance is placed in a magnetic field of strength H, the observable effects depend upon the magnetic induction or magnetic flux density B ($= \mu H$) inside the medium and is given by

$$B = H + 4\pi M \qquad \qquad ...(26.21)$$

where M is *the magnetization* of the substance and is defined as *the magnetic moment per unit volume*. In SI system, the unit of B is kg s^2 A^{-1}, called *the tesla* (T) and is equal to 10^4 *gauss*. Equation (26.21) can be written as

$$\mu H = H + 4\pi M$$

$$\mu = 4\pi \frac{M}{H} + 1$$

$$= 4\pi\chi + 1 \qquad \qquad ...(26.22)$$

where $\chi \left(= \dfrac{M}{H} \right)$ is *the magnetic susceptibility* per unit volume.

The magnetic susceptibility χ is a dimensionless quantity. It is sometimes more convenient to use the molar susceptibility which is obtained by multiplying χ by the molar volume M/d, hence

$$\chi_m = \chi \frac{M}{d}$$

Substituting the value of χ in equation (26.22) we get

$$\mu = 4\pi\chi_m \left(\frac{d}{M} \right) + 1 \qquad \qquad ...(26.23)$$

For paramagnetic and ferromagnetic materials μ is greater than 1 and hence χ_m is positive. For diamagnetic substances μ is less than unity and χ_m must be negative. Examples of these two types of magnetic behaviours are shown in Fig. 26.6. The figure represents the path of magnetic lines of force passing through the two kinds of substances.

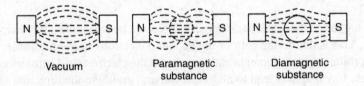

| Vacuum | Paramagnetic substance | Diamagnetic substance |

Fig. 26.6 Behaviour of paramagnetic and diamagnetic substances. Lines of force are drawn into a paramagnetic substance and pushed out of a diamagnetic substance

The susceptibility can be measured experimentally with a magnetic balance. The material under investigation is suspended from one arm of the balance, known as Gouy's balance, in such a way that it is half inside and half outside the magnetic field. When the magnetic field is switched on and if the substance is diamagnetic its energy is less if it is outside the field so it is repelled by the field. In case of a paramagnetic sample its energy is lowered if it is inside the field and so the sample is drawn into the field. The force necessary to maintain the original equilibrium is given as

is known as paramagnetic and the lines of force prefer to pass more readily through the substance than the vacuum or air. Substances like Fe, Co, Ni etc. are said to be ferromagnetic substances.

$$F = mg\frac{\chi_1 - \chi_2}{2}AB^2. \qquad \qquad ...(26.24)$$

where χ_1 and χ_2 are the susceptibilities of the sample and the surroundings, A is the area of cross section of the sample and B is the magnitude of the magnetic induction. The apparatus is generally calibrated against a sample of a known susceptibility, usually water. Values of molar susceptibilities of a few substances at 298 K is given in Table 26.3. It has been shown that molar susceptibility in a diamagnetic substance is an additive and a constitutive property, like molar refraction.

Table 26.3 Molar Magnetic Susceptibilities at 298 K

Substance	$\chi_m \times 10^6$	Substance	$\chi_m \times 10^6$
Water	−12.98	$CuSO_4 \cdot 5H_2O(s)$	+ 1,459
Carbon tetrachloride	−66.60	$NiCl_2(s)$	+ 6,145
Benzoic acid	−70.20	$FeSO_4(s)$	+10,200
Benzene	−54.70	$CoCl_2 \cdot 6H_2O(s)$	+ 9,710
Ammonia	−18.00	$MnSO_4 \cdot 5H_2O(s)$	+14,700
Acetylene	−12.50	$FeF_3(s)$	+13,760
Cyclohexane	−68.10		

Diamagnetism

The diamagnetic effects are produced by the orbital motion of the electrons around the nuclei. It can be understood if one imagines the electrons moving about the nucleus to be like a current in a circular wire. When a magnetic field is applied the velocity of the electrons is altered and as a consequence, a magnetic field is induced. This induced magnetic field opposes the applied field in accordance with the Lenz's law. Thus the diamagnetic susceptibility is always negative. The diamagnetic effects are independent of temperature and physical state of the substance. However, it depends on the state of the electrons. The diamagnetic effects are exhibited by all substances but are small in magnitudes.

Paramagnetism

Langevin in 1905 suggested that each paramagnetic molecule behaves like a tiny magnet with a definite magnetic moment. This is due to the spin of the unpaired electrons in the molecule. Paramagnetism is thus related to the orbital angular momenta and the spins of the electrons in a substance. When a magnetic field is applied these tiny magnets tend to align themselves parallel to the direction of the applied field. But this alignment is opposed by the thermal motions of the molecules. Thus the alignment depends on the temperature.

Pierre Curie in 1895 showed that the magnetic susceptibility of paramagnetic substances varies with temperature as

$$\chi_m = A + \frac{C}{T} \qquad \qquad ...(26.25)$$

where A and C are constants. From the theoretical considerations Langevin showed that

$$C = \frac{N_A \mu_m^2}{3k} \qquad \text{...(26.26)}$$

where μ_m is the permanent magnetic dipole moment, k is the Boltzmann constant and N_A is the Avogadro constant. This quantity is sometimes known as the *Curie constant*. Substituting the value of C in equation (26.26), we obtain

$$\chi_m = A + \frac{N_A \mu_m^2}{3kT} \qquad \text{...(26.27)}$$

The permanent magnetic moment can be obtained from the susceptibility measurements at various temperatures and then plotting χ_m against $1/T$. From the slope of the line $\left(= \mu_m^2 N_A / 3k \right)$, μ_m can be calculated.

The motion of an electron in an orbit corresponds to an electric current in a loop wire. It is known that when a current is passed through a coil it produces a magnetic field perpendicular to the coil. The magnetic fields so produced is equal to that of a magnet with magnetic moment μ_m, such that $\mu_m = AI$, where A is the area of the coil and I is the current. The current corresponding to an electron moving with a velocity v in an orbit of radius r is given by

$$I = \frac{-ve}{2\pi r} \qquad \text{...(26.28)}$$

The negative sign indicates that the electronic charge is negative. The cross sectional area of the coil is πr^2. Thus the magnetic moment in the lowest Bohr orbit is obtained as

$$\mu_m = AI = -\frac{\pi r^2 ev}{2\pi r}$$

$$= -\frac{vre}{2}$$

$$= -\frac{m_e vre}{2m_e}$$

$$= -\frac{h}{2\pi} \frac{e}{2m_e} \qquad \left(\text{Since } m_e vr = \frac{h}{2\pi} \right)$$

$$= -\frac{eh}{4\pi m_e} \qquad \text{...(26.29)}$$

This quantity of magnetic moment is known as *Bohr magneton* and is denoted by μ_B. In SI units its value is

$$\mu_B = \frac{eh}{4\pi m_e}$$

$$= \frac{\left(1.602 \times 10^{-19}\,\text{C}\right)\left(6.626 \times 10^{-34}\,\text{J s}\right)}{4\pi \left(9.109 \times 10^{-31}\,\text{kg}\right)}$$

$$= 9.2732 \times 10^{-24} \text{ JT}^{-1}$$

$$= 9.2732 \times 10^{-28} \text{ J G}^{-1} \ (1\text{T} = 10^4 \text{G})$$

$$= 9.2732 \times 10^{-21} \text{erg G}^{-1}$$

The ratio of magnetic moment to orbital angular momentum (L) is the *gyromagnetic ratio* γ

$$\gamma = \frac{\mu_m}{L} = -\frac{evr}{2m_e vr} = -\frac{e}{2m_e} \qquad \qquad ...(26.30)$$

The negative sign indicates that the magnetic moment is antiparallel to the angular momentum.

Since the electron possesses an intrinsic angular momentum or spin this gives rise to a permanent magnetic moment. The spin angular momentum is quantized and is given as

$$S = \sqrt{s(s+1)} \ \frac{h}{2\pi}$$

Since
$$s = \frac{1}{2}$$

therefore
$$S = \frac{\sqrt{3}}{2} \frac{h}{2\pi} \qquad \qquad ...(26.31)$$

The spinning electron behaves like a tiny magnet and its gyromagnetic ratio is given by $-\dfrac{e}{m_e}$, just twice

the magnetogyric ratio for the orbital magnetic moment. The extra factor 2 arises from a correct relativistic approach to the problem. This factor is not exactly two but 2.0023. This is called *Lande-splitting factor* and is denoted by g_e, the g-factor of the electron. Thus the magnetic moment of the electron is

$$\mu_m = 2\mu_B \ [s(s + 1)]^{1/2} \qquad \qquad ...(26.32)$$

If there are several electron spins in the molecule they may combine to give a total electron spin angular momentum with a magnitude given by quantum number S.

Since
$$\gamma_s = \frac{\mu_m}{S}$$

where γ_s is the magnetogyric ratio of the spinning electron and S is the total spin angular momentum

$$\mu_m = \gamma_s S = \frac{e}{m_e} \frac{\sqrt{3}}{2} \frac{h}{2\pi} \qquad \qquad ...(26.33)$$

Consequently, the magnetic susceptibility is given by

$$\chi_m = \frac{N_A \mu_m^2}{3kT} = \frac{N_A}{3kT} \Big[2\mu_B \sqrt{s(s+1)} \Big]^2$$

$$= \frac{4 N_A \mu_B^2 \ s(s+1)}{3kT} \qquad \qquad ...(26.34)$$

This quantity is positive, and therefore this permanent spin momentum contributes to the paramagnetic susceptibility of the system. Since the thermal motion randomizes the orientations of the individual spin magnetic moment at high temperatures, hence the contribution to the susceptibility vanishes at these temperatures.

26.7 NUCLEAR PARAMAGNETISM

Protons and neutrons present in the nuclei of atoms spin about their own axes. The nuclei with odd mass number have spins, designated by I and is always an odd integral multiple of 1/2. Nuclei with even mass number that have odd number of protons also have spins, and the spin quantum number in these cases is an integer, 1, 2, 3,... Thus, ^1H, ^{11}B, ^{19}F, etc., have magnetic moments having spins of 1/2, whereas ^{12}C, ^{16}O have no magnetic moment.

Many nuclei possess spin angular momentum due to the spinning of the nucleus about its axis. The spin angular momentum of a nucleus is a vector combination of the spin angular momentum of the protons and neutrons. The spin characteristics of the nucleus is denoted by I and is called the nuclear spin quantum number. The magnitude of the spin angular momentum |I| is related to the spin angular momentum quantum number I as

$$|\mathbf{I}| = \sqrt{I(I+1)}\,\frac{h}{2\pi} \qquad \qquad ...(26.35)$$

If the nucleus has a spin angular momentum $I \neq 0$, then this corresponds to a spinning positive charge and this will generate a magnetic momentum (μ). The magnetic moment, μ of any nucleus is proportional to the spin angular momentum, I and is expressed as

$$\mu_m = \frac{g_N e}{2m_p}\mathbf{I} \qquad \qquad ...(26.36)$$

where g_N is the nuclear g-factor which is characteristic of the particular nucleus, e is the charge on a proton and m_p is the mass of the proton. The quantity $\dfrac{g_N e}{2m_p}$ is called the gyromagnetic ratio, γ. Hence we can write the above equation (26.36) as

$$\mu_m = \gamma\,\mathbf{I} \qquad \qquad ...(26.37)$$

$$= \gamma\sqrt{I(I+1)}\cdot\frac{h}{2\pi} \qquad \qquad ...(26.38)$$

When the charge of the particle is positive, the magnetic moment vector $(\vec{\mu}_m)$ and the angular moment vector $(\vec{I})$ point in the same direction. But when the particle is negatively charged (electron), these two vectors point in the opposite directions. Equation (26.36) can also be rewritten as

$$|\mu_m| = \frac{g_N e}{2m_p}\sqrt{I(I+1)}\cdot\frac{h}{2\pi}$$

$$= g_N\,\mu_N\sqrt{I(I+1)} \qquad \qquad ...(26.39)$$

where $\mu_N = \dfrac{e}{2m_p} \cdot \dfrac{h}{2\pi} = \dfrac{eh}{4\pi m_p}$ and is called nuclear magneton and has a value 5.051×10^{-27} JT^{-1}.

A nucleus with spin quantum number I can take (2I + 1) orientations in the external magnetic field. If $I = 1/2$, then it can take two $(2I + 1 = 2 \times 1/2 + 1 = 2)$ orientations only in an external field. We shall consider spin 1/2 nuclei, which are nuclei with $I = 1/2$. These spin 1/2 nuclei can align parallel or anti parallel to the external field. No other orientation is permitted.

The component of the magnetic moment of the nucleus in the direction of the applied magnetic field, μ_Z is given by

$$\mu_Z = \frac{|g_N| e}{2m_p} I_z \qquad\qquad ...(26.40)$$

where I_z is the component of the spin angular momentum in the direction of the applied magnetic field. Also I_z can be expressed as

$$I_Z = m_I \frac{h}{2\pi}$$

where m_I is the quantum number for Z-component and can take values $-I ... +I$.

The different values of m_I give different values of I_z and μ_Z.

Thus, for $I = \dfrac{1}{2}$, $m_I = -\dfrac{1}{2}$ and $+\dfrac{1}{2}$ and

$$I_Z = -\frac{1}{2}\frac{h}{2\pi} \quad \text{and} \quad +\frac{1}{2}\frac{h}{2\pi}$$

Substituting the values of I_Z in equation (26.40), we have

$$\mu_Z = -\frac{|g_N| e}{2m_p} \times \frac{1}{2}\frac{h}{2\pi} = -\frac{1}{2}|g_N|\mu_N \qquad \left(\because \mu_N = \frac{e}{2m_p}\frac{h}{2\pi} \right)$$

and

$$\mu_Z = \frac{|g_N| e}{2m_p} \times \frac{1}{2}\frac{h}{2\pi} = \frac{1}{2}|g_N|\mu_N$$

The energy of the magnetic dipole in a magnetic field of strength B_Z is given as

$$E = -\mu_Z \beta_Z$$

$$= \frac{1}{2}|g_N|\mu_N B_Z \quad \text{and} \quad -\frac{1}{2}|g_N|\mu_N B_Z$$

The energy separation of the two states of spin $-1/2$ nuclei (Fig. 26.7) is

$$\Delta E = E_\beta - E_\alpha = \frac{1}{2}|g_N|\mu_N B_Z - \left(-\frac{1}{2}|g_N|\mu_N B_Z \right)$$

$$= |g_N|\mu_N B_Z$$

$$\nu = \frac{\Delta E}{h} = \frac{|g_N|\mu_N B_Z}{h}. \qquad \qquad ...(26.41)$$

The β state lies above the α state and corresponds to $m_I = -\frac{1}{2}$ and $m_I = +\frac{1}{2}$ as shown in Fig. 26.7.

The splitting of the nuclear energy into $(2I + 1)$ levels for a nucleus spin I is known as the nuclear Zeeman effect and is the primary phenomenon in NMR Spectroscopy

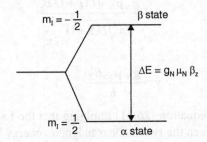

Fig. 26.7 Splitting of energy level of a proton in presence of magnetic field

If an electromagnetic radiation of frequency ν as given by equation (26.41) is allowed to interact with the nuclei, then the nuclei from lower energy level may absorb energy and go to higher energy level.

The difference in energy between nuclear spin states in a magnetic fields that can be produced in the laboratory is very small at room temperature and therefore, the populations in the various states are nearly equal. According to the Boltzmann distribution

$$\frac{N_\beta}{N_\alpha} = e^{-\Delta E/kT} \approx 1 - \frac{\Delta E}{kT} + ...$$

or
$$\frac{N_\alpha}{N_\beta} = 1 + \frac{\Delta E}{kT} = 1 + \frac{g_n\mu_n B_Z}{kT} \qquad ...(26.42)$$

Thus the excess population in the low-energy state is extremely small. Only the spins in the low-energy state can absorb radiation.

In a magnetic field, because of the interaction between the magnetic moment of the charged particle and the applied field, the charged particle experiences a torque λ which makes the angular momentum precess around the direction of the applied field (Fig. 26.8). This precessional frequency is called Larmor frequency and is directly proportional to the applied field, *i.e.*,

$$\omega = \gamma B_Z \qquad ...(26.43)$$

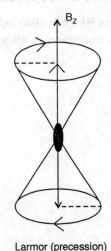

Larmor (precession)

Fig. 26.8 Larmor (precession) frequency

where γ is the gyromagnetic ratio and B_Z is the strength of the applied magnetic field felt by the proton.

From Equation (26.37) we replace γ by $\frac{\mu_m}{I}$ to get

$$\omega = \frac{\mu_m}{\mathbf{I}} \cdot B_Z = 2\pi\nu$$

So

$$\nu = \frac{\mu_m B_Z}{2\pi\mathbf{I}}$$

Substituting the value of μ_m and $\mathbf{I}$ we obtain

$$\nu = \frac{g_N\mu_N \sqrt{I(I+1)}\, B_z}{2\pi\sqrt{I(I+1)}\, \dfrac{h}{2\pi}} \qquad\qquad ...(26.44)$$

$$\nu = \frac{g_N\, \mu_N\, B_Z}{h} \qquad\qquad ...(26.45)$$

Equation (26.45) is identical with equation (26.41) implying that the Larmor frequency is equal to the angular frequency separation between the two nuclear magnetic energy levels.

When the radiofrequency is applied at right angle to the magnetic field it produces a rotating magnetic field. It is necessary that the frequency of rotation of the rotating magnetic field be exactly the same as Larmor frequency. Only when such a condition is met, *i.e.*, the two frequencies are in resonance, the nuclei will absorb energy. This is the reason why this phenomenon is called nuclear magnetic resonance and the condition for resonance is

$$h\nu = g_N\, \mu_N B_Z \qquad\qquad ...(26.46)$$

26.8 NMR SPECTROMETER

Purcell and Block in 1946 independently developed an experimental technique for studying the nuclear magnetic resonance. A diagram for nuclear magnetic resonance is shown in Fig. 26.9. The sample,

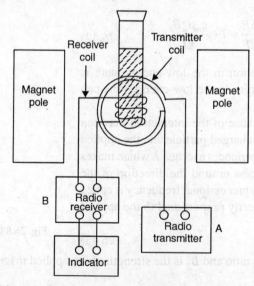

Fig. 26.9 Schematic diagram of a nuclear magnetic resonance spectrometer

usually a liquid or a solid to be investigated, is taken in the tube placed between the poles of an electromagnet of strength B. The field of the magnet is varied from 0 to 1.0 T. The radio-frequency oscillator A sends a preset frequency v in the coil located between the magnetic poles. Another coil around the sample tube, called receiver coil, picks up the signal from the sample, carries it to the receiver B and is amplified. The amplified signal then goes to a cathode ray oscillograph indicator or recorder. The field strength is gradually increased and the radiation is absorbed only when the right hand side of equation (26.41) is satisfied for a given frequency. At this stage the strength of the oscillating field equals the transition frequency. In other words, the sample is in resonance with the applied frequency and absorption takes place. The recorder at this point shows a peak. When the field strength is further increased the peak disappears as there is no absorption. Another peak will result only when the correspondence is reached again.

26.9 THE CHEMICAL SHIFT

NMR spectra can distinguish protons in different environments. The environment surrounding the nucleus has a little but definite measurable effect on the field experienced by the proton. This effect is extremely useful in elucidating the structure of molecules and the nature of the chemical bonds. Protons, whether in hydrogen atoms or molecules, are surrounded by electronic charge cloud. The applied magnetic field induces an electronic current in the molecule in a direction which opposes the applied field. The induced field is directly proportional to the applied field B and so can be represented by σB where σ is *the screening* constant of the order of 10^{-6}. The effective magnetic field B_{eff} experienced by a nucleus is given by

$$B_{eff} = B(1 - \sigma)$$

Thus in presence of the extra nuclear environment, the resonance condition (equation (26.46) has to be modified as

$$hv = g_N \mu_N B_Z(1 - \sigma) \qquad ...(26.47)$$

A positive value of σ means that the nucleus is shielded by the electronic environment whereas a negative value of σ corresponds to deshielding of the nucleus. In shielding $B_{eff} < B_Z$ hence B_Z must be increased to bring the nucleus in resonance. In deshielding $B_{eff} > B_Z$ resulting in the resonance at lower field. So due to shielding (or deshielding) identical nucleus having different chemical environments resonate at different values of the applied field. These values being characteristic can be used to identify various types of environments in which the nucleus is present. Since the shift in the position of resonance is due to difference in chemical environments, it is called chemical shift and is denoted by δ. This is expressed relative to some standard substance. $(CH_3)_4$ Si tetramethyl silane (TMS), is usually chosen as the reference.

$$\delta = \frac{B_{sample} - B_{ref}}{B_{ref}} \times 10^6 \qquad ...(26.48)$$

This is multiplied by 10^6 to express it as parts per million (ppm).

The advantages of using tetramethyl silane (TMS) are:

(*i*) it gives a single sharp peak, as all the twelve nuclei are equivalent.

(*ii*) its resonance peak occurs at very high field, and

(*iii*) it dissolves without reaction in many systems and hence can be readily recovered from most samples after use.

Resonance shifts are indicated on the δ-scale, with δ = 0 being the arbitrary value chosen for TMS. An alternative scale is τ-scale where δ values shift by 10 ppm; and then most values are positive. Table 26.4 gives the chemical shifts on the τ-scale.

NMR spectrum for ethanol at high resolution is shown in Fig. 26.10. Here the peak for CH_2 group splits into four lines (fine structure) and the peak for CH_3 splits into three lines. This fine structure is due to the interactions of the nuclear spins of one set of equivalent protons with another set. This is known as spin-spin splitting. The absorption line of CH_3 group is first split into two by the two orientations of one of the methylene (CH_2) protons; each line is further split due to the interaction of the second methylene proton. The absorption line of CH_3 is thus split into three lines of intensities 1 : 2 : 1. Similarly, the absorption line of the methylene protons is split into four lines due to the three protons of the neighbouring methyl group. The intensities of these lines are 1 : 3 : 3 : 1. However, it should be noted that a hydroxyl proton does not show splitting as it undergoes chemical exchange rapidly with protons in other molecules.

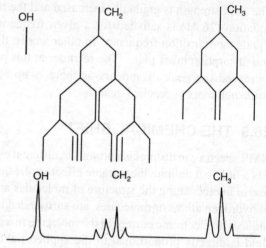

Fig. 26.10 NMR spectrum of ethanol

Table 26.4 Proton Chemical Shifts

Compound	Shift (τ) (ppm)	Compound	Shift (τ) (ppm)
Methyl protons			
$(CH_3)_4Si$	10.00	**Acetylenic protons**	
CH_3CH_2OH	8.83	$CH \equiv CCH_2OH$	7.67
CH_3CN	8.03	**Aromatic protons**	
CH_3COCH_3	7.92	C_6H_6	2.73
CH_3CHO	7.85	$o-C_6H_5NO_2$	1.78
CH_3OH	6.62	$m-C_6H_5NO_2$	2.52
Olefinic protons		$p-C_6H_5NO_2$	2.40
$CH_2 = CH_2$	4.16	Naphthalene	2.27
$(CH_3)_3 C = CH_2$	5.40		
Cyclohexane	4.43		

Problem 26.3: Calculate the magnetic field required for nuclear magnetic resonance at 220 MHz (g_N = 5.585, μ_N = 5.051 × 10^{-31} JG^{-1}).

Solution:

$$B = \frac{hv}{g_N\mu_N} = \frac{(6.626 \times 10^{-34} \, Js)(220 \times 10^6 \, s^{-1})}{(5.585)(5.051 \times 10^{-31} \, J \, G^{-1})} = 51.67 \times 10^3 G$$

26.10 ELECTRON SPIN RESONANCE (ESR)

The systems containing unpaired electrons can be studied by a technique called Electron Spin Resonance (ESR) in the same manner as NMR.

As nuclei have spin and magnetic moment, the electron also has spin and magnetic moment. When the electron is introduced in a magnetic field, the electron magnetic dipole will precess about the axis of the applied field with the frequency called Larmor precession similar to the case of a nucleus. If the same treatment is applied as in NMR we will get two spin states differing in energy (Fig. 26.11) *i.e.*,

$$\Delta E = E_2 - E_1 = g_e \mu_B B$$

When the sample is exposed to electromagnetic radiation of frequency ν, resonant absorption occurs when the resonance condition

$$\Delta E = h\nu = g_e \mu_B B \qquad \qquad ...(26.49)$$

is fulfilled.

Equation (26.49) shows that the energy of separation between the two levels and the frequency of the radiation absorbed (ν), is proportional to the applied field (B). Thus ESR spectra can be studied by using the radiation of any frequency provided an appropriate field is applied. Magnetic fields of about 0.34T correspond to resonance with an electromagnetic field of frequency 10 GH_Z ($10^{10}H_Z$) and wavelength 3 cm. The frequency 10 GH_Z lies in the X-band of the microwave region of the electromagnetic spectrum, ESR is a microwave technique.

Substances which show ESR spectra must have one or more unpaired spins. These include free radicals, paramagnetic transition metal complexes and molecules in the triplet states. Multiplicities of lines (hyperfine structures) observed in ESR are due to the interactions between the spin of the odd electrons and the magnetic nuclei of the molecule. The splitting of the lines and line widths may be used as a valuable source of information regarding the structure of molecules and electron distributions in the molecules.

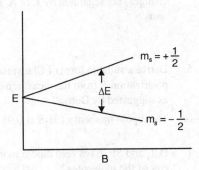

Fig. 26.11 Energy levels of an electron in a magnetic field

Problem 26.4: Calculate the precessional frequency of electrons in a 15,000 G field. $g_e = 2.0$, $\mu_B = 9.273 \times 10^{-28}$ J G^{-1}.

Solution:

$$\nu = \frac{B g_e \mu_B}{h}$$

$$= \frac{(15000 \text{ G})(2.0)(9.273 \times 10^{-28} \text{ J G}^{-1})}{(6.626 \times 10^{-34} \text{J S})}$$

$$= 41980 \text{ MHz}$$

EXERCISES

1. Explain, giving reasons, the following:

   (i) Molar polarizability of CCl_4 is independent of temperature whereas that of $CHCl_3$ changes with temperature.

   (ii) Both NMR and ESR spectroscopy differ from other branches of spectroscopy in one important respect.

   (iii) Dipole moment of CO_2 is zero but for SO_2 it is not zero.

   (iv) The dipole moment of o-dinitrobenzene is greater than that of m-dinitrobenzene.

   (v) ^{12}C and ^{16}O do not exhibit NMR spectra.

   (vi) Tetramethyl silane (TMS) is chosen as a reference compound in NMR studies.

   (vii) ESR signal becomes stronger at lower temperatures.

2. The molar refraction of $CHCl_3$ for the D-line of sodium at 293K is 21.25 cm^3 mol^{-1}. Calculate the refractive index of chloroform vapours at a hypothetical pressure of 1 atm 293 K.   **Ans.** 1.00333.

3. The refractive index, $n_{D^{293}}$ of CCl_4 is 1.4573 and the density at 293K is 1.595 kg dm^{-3}. Calculate the molar refraction.   **Ans.** 26.28 cm^3 mol^{-1}.

4. Calculate the dipole moment of HCl assuming that the proton and the chloride ion (considered to be point changes) are separated by 1.27 Å. How do you account for the fact that the experimental value is 1.03 debye units?

                                                              Ans. 6.1 debye units. The charges in the molecule are not
                                                                                                completely separated.

5. Derive a suitable form of Clausius-Mosottii equation which can be used for calculating the molar distortion polarization P from the measurements of dielectric constant (ε). What is the modified form of the equation as suggested by Debye?

6. The dipole moment of H_2S is 0.95 D. If the bond angle is 97°, calculate the S—H bond moment.
                                                                                                       Ans. 0.72 D.

7. PCl_5 and SF_6 have zero dipole moments in gaseous phase. What conclusion can be drawn about the geometry of the molecules?

8. The dipole moment of $C_6H_5NO_2$ is 3.93 debye, and the dipole moment of toluene is 4.39 debye. Predict the dipole moments of (i) o-nitrololuene and, (ii) p-nitrotoluene.

                                                                             Ans. (i) 4.2 debye, (ii) 3.8 debye.

9. The dipole moments of chloro- and nitrobenzene are 1.55 D and 3.80 D. Calculate the dipole moment of (i) m-dichlorobenzene and (ii) o-dinitrobenzene.

                                                                             Ans. (i) 1.55 D and (ii) 6.58 D.

10. The NMR signal for a compound is found to be 240 Hz downfield from TMS peak using a spectrometer operating at 60 MHz. Calculate its chemical shift in ppm relative to TMS.   **Ans.** 4 ppm.

11. How many ESR lines are observed if an unpaired electron, when closed to two non equivalent protons is placed in a magnetic field?   **Ans.** 4 lines.

12. If two equivalent protons are considered in problem (11) above, calculate the number of lines observed.
                                                                                                       Ans. 3 lines.

13. What is understood by the terms spin-spin coupling and chemical shift? Give suitable examples of each.

14. Sketch out the high resolution NMR spectra of the following compounds (i) ethanol, (ii) methyl ethyl either.

15. Calculate the value of Bohr magneton β_N for a proton.

                                                                             Ans. 5.051 × 10^{-31} JG^{-1}.

16. What is understood by molar magnetic susceptibility? What are its units? How can it be determined experimentally?

17. Calculate the frequency ν, required to excite a proton from $m_I = \dfrac{1}{2}$ to $m_I = -\dfrac{1}{2}$, given $g_N = 5.585$ and magnetic field applied = 14000 G.

    Ans. $5.97 \times 10^7 \text{ s}^{-1}$.

18. Calculate the (*i*) angular momentum and (*ii*) magnetic moment values for a proton. Given that the g value is 5.585.

    Ans. (*i*) 9.14×10^{-35} JS, (*ii*) 2.44×10^{-26} JT^{-1}.

Macromolecules

27.1 INTRODUCTION

Macromolecules are defined as giant molecules formed by large number of small structural units joined together by covalent bonds with molar masses greater than 10,000. The particle size lies in the range 1 nm-1000 nm. The small structural units may be atoms, or small molecules as such or their modified form. Hence we have the following classes of macromolecules:

1. When structural units are atoms–diamond, quartz, etc. are the examples of this class where one or more kinds of atoms are interlinked throughout the macromolecules. In quartz, a three-dimensional network of Si and O atoms gives rise to the formation of macromolecules which accounts for the hardness, non-volatility etc.

2. The other class of macromolecules are those where the structural units are one or more small molecules as such or in modified form. This class of macromolecules are called polymers. Some naturally occurring polymers are polysaccharides, such as cellulose, polypeptides such as enzymes, and nucleic acids such as DNA. The synthetic polymers are nylon, PVC, polystyrene etc.

The polymer is defined as a compound with very high molar mass, composed of a large number of one or more small molecular units (called monomers) which occur repeatedly and joined together by covalent bonds. The process of joining together of monomers to give polymer is called polymerisation. If X be the monomer unit then

$$\underset{\text{monomer}}{nX} \longrightarrow \underset{\text{polymer}}{(X)_n}$$

where n is the number of monomer units that unite together to form the polymer (macromolecule).

27.2 CLASSIFICATION OF POLYMERS

It is based on their mode of formation

(*i*) An addition polymer is one in which all atoms in the monomer are also present in the polymer. Some examples are polyethylene, PVC, Teflon, etc. These are formed by a free radical or ionic mechanism.

(*ii*) A condensation polymer is formed by combination of monomers with the elimination of H_2O or CH_3OH. Some examples are terylene, nylon-6 etc.

(*iii*) Copolymers are produced by polymerizing two or more different monomers, e.g.

$$nA + nB \longrightarrow [-A-B-]_n$$
Alternating copolymer

$$nA + nB \longrightarrow -A-A-B-A-B-B-$$
Random copolymer

27.3 MOLAR MASSES OF POLYMERS

Synthetic high polymers, and some naturally occurring polymers have a distribution of molar masses. The properties of macromolecular solutions depend to a great deal on the size and distribution of macromolecules in a sample. A synthetic polymer is a mixture of molecules with various chain lengths and molar masses. Thus the determination of average molar mass becomes important in the study of polymers. The average molar mass can be defined in different ways and the experimentally obtained values depend on the method of determination. The two most commonly used ways to define the average molar mass are discussed below:

The Number Average Molar Mass ($\bar{M}_n$)

The number average molar mass is equal to the mass of the whole sample divided by the number of molecules in it.

$$\bar{M}_n = \frac{\sum\limits_i N_i M_i}{\sum\limits_i N_i} \qquad \qquad ...(27.1)$$

where N_i is the number of molecules of molar mass M_i. If we divide each term in the denominator and numerator by Avogadro constant (N_A) in equation (27.1) we get

$$\bar{M}_n = \frac{\sum\limits_i \dfrac{N_i}{N_A} M_i}{\sum\limits_i \dfrac{N_i}{N_A}} = \frac{\sum\limits_i n_i M_i}{\sum\limits_i n_i} \qquad \qquad ...(27.2)$$

where $n_i = \dfrac{N_i}{N_A}$ is the amount (number of moles) of a species having molar mass M_i. The number average molar mass is sensitive to the species having low molar mass. This type of molar mass is obtained from the measurements of the osmotic pressure of solutions containing the polymer.

The Mass Average Molar Mass ($\bar{M}_w$)

The molar mass (M_i) of any particular molecule (*i*) is multiplied by its mass (m_i). The sum $\Sigma m_i M_i$ for all the molecules is then divided by the total mass of the sample $\sum_i m_i$. The mass average molar mass

$(\bar{M}_w)$ is then given as

$$\bar{M}_w = \frac{\sum_i m_i M_i}{\sum_i m_i} \qquad \qquad ...(27.3)$$

As $m_i = n_i M_i$, where n_i is the number of moles of the ith species, so

$$\bar{M}_w = \frac{\sum_i n_i M_i^2}{\sum_i n_i M_i} \qquad \qquad ...(27.4)$$

Also

$$n_i = \frac{N_i}{N_A}$$

Therefore,

$$\bar{M}_w = \frac{\sum_i N_i M_i^2}{\sum_i N_i M_i} \qquad \qquad ...(27.5)$$

The mass average molar mass is always greater than the number average molar mass. The ratio of $\bar{M}_w / \bar{M}_n$ is known as polydispersity index.

27.4 DETERMINATION OF MOLAR MASS

It has been pointed out that in macromolecular solutions, the distribution of macromolecules is not uniform. Therefore, some kind of average molar mass value is obtained. These values can be determined by using a property of the sample which is directly related to the molar mass. Some of the methods used are discussed below;

Osmotic pressure method: This method is used for determining the molar mass of polymers of molar mass upto 500,000 g mol^{-1}. The van't Hoff equation for the osmotic pressure of an ideal solution resembles the perfect gas equation of state

$$\pi = [P]\, RT \qquad \qquad ...(27.6)$$

where $[P]$ is the molar concentration of the macromolecule and π is the osmotic pressure. The above equation can also be written as

$$\pi = \frac{nRT}{V} = \frac{w}{\bar{M}_n} \frac{RT}{V} \qquad \qquad ...(27.7)$$

where w and M are the mass and molar mass of the polymer and V is the volume of the solution. Equation (27.7) can be written as

$$\pi = \frac{d\,RT}{\bar{M}_n} \qquad \left(\because d = \frac{w}{V} \right)$$

Also

$$\pi = \frac{C\,RT}{\bar{M}_n}$$

or

$$\frac{\pi}{C} = \frac{RT}{\bar{M}_n} \qquad \qquad \qquad \qquad \text{...(27.8)}$$

where $C\left(= \dfrac{w}{V} \right)$ is the concentration of the solution given in kgm^{-3} (mass concentration). The molar

concentration $[P]$ is related to C by $[P] = C/\bar{M}_n$. Equation (27.8) is applicable only to dilute solutions.

As these huge molecules dissolve to produce solutions that are not ideal (non-ideal solution), therefore equation (27.8) can be rewritten as

$$\frac{\pi}{C} = \frac{RT}{\bar{M}_n} \left(1 + \frac{B}{\bar{M}_n} C + ... \right) \qquad \qquad \text{...(27.9)}$$

where B is an osmotic virial coefficient and depends on polymer-polymer interaction. By plotting $\dfrac{\pi}{C}$

versus C and extrapolating to zero concentration ($C = 0$), the value of $\bar{M}_n$ can be obtained from the intercept at $C = 0$ and B can be obtained from the slope (Fig. 27.1).

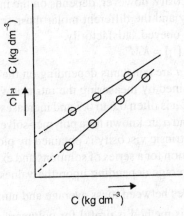

Fig. 27.1 The plot of π/C versus C

The viscosity method: Viscosity measurements of solutions have been widely used in the determination of molar masses of macromoles. Macromolecular solution have high viscosity even at low concentration due to (*i*) either the high solvation of the polymer molecules which do not allow the solvent to move freely. (*ii*) The macromolecules get entangled with each other due to their large size and thus restricting the movement of the solvent.

If η and η_0 are the coefficients of viscosity of the solution and pure solvent, then the relative viscosity is defined as

$$\eta_r = \frac{\eta}{\eta_0}$$

The *specific viscosity* η_{sp}, is defined as

$$\eta_{sp} = \eta_r - 1$$

$$= \frac{\eta}{\eta_0} - 1$$

$$= \frac{\eta - \eta_0}{\eta_0}$$

A plot of $\dfrac{\eta_{sp}}{C}$ versus C is a straight line and the limiting value of $\left(\dfrac{\eta_{sp}}{C}\right)_{C \to 0}$ is known as the *intrinsic viscosity* $[\eta]$ and is given as

$$[\eta] = \lim_{C \to 0}\left(\frac{\eta_{sp}}{C}\right) = \lim_{C \to 0}\left(\frac{\eta_r - 1}{C}\right)$$

$$= \lim_{C \to 0}\left(\frac{\eta - \eta_0}{C\eta_0}\right) \qquad \text{...(27.11)}$$

$[\eta]$ represents the fractional change in the viscosity of a solution per unit concentration of polymer at infinite dilution. The intrinsic viscosity, however, depends on the molar mass. The following empirical relationship between the viscosity and the different molar mass fraction of the polymer at a constant temperature has been found to be obeyed satisfactorily.

$$[\eta] = KM^a \qquad \text{...(27.12)}$$

Here M is the molar mass, K and a are constants depending on the solvent, polymer and temperature. The values of K and a are determined by measuring the intrinsic viscosities of a series of samples of known molar masses. The value of a is often 0.6 to 0.7 and increases to 1 to 2 depending upon the shape of the polymer molecule. Once K and a are known for a polymer-solvent combination, M can be calculated from measurements of $[\eta]$. The intrinsic viscosity is obtained by plotting the ratio of specific viscosity to concentration against concentration for a series of solutions and extrapolating it to zero concentration. The molar mass obtained is an average depending upon the values of a. If $a = 1$, M is mass average molar mass, $\bar{M}_w$ and if $a < 1$, M lies between mass average and number average molar masses.

Light scattering method: This method is useful for polymers of very high molar masses usually above 10,000 g mol^{-1}. The results obtained are quite accurate. This method is based on the scattering of light by a colloidal solution *i.e.*, tyndall effect. When a ray of light enters the solution, it suffers scattering in all directions thereby giving the solution a turbid appearance. If the intensity of the incident light is I_0 then the intensity of the scattered light I after passing through a solution of length l is given by

$$I = I_0 e^{-\tau l} \qquad \text{...(27.13)}$$

where τ is the turbidity and is defined as the fraction of the incident light scattered per centimeter length of solution through which it passes.

Turbidity of a solution is related to the molar mass of the polymer by the equation

$$\tau = HC\bar{M}_w$$

where

$$\frac{HC}{\tau} = \frac{1}{\bar{M}_w} \qquad\qquad ...(27.14)$$

$$H = \frac{32\pi^3 n_0^2 \left(\dfrac{n-n_0}{C}\right)^2}{3N_A\lambda^4}$$

where N_A is the Avogadro constant, λ the wavelength of the incident light, n_0 is the refractive index of the solvent and n is the refractive index of the polymer solution. Equation (27.14) is valid when $C \to 0$, so, we get

$$\left(\frac{HC}{\tau}\right)_{C\to 0} = \frac{1}{\bar{M}_w}$$

In order to determine $\bar{M}_w$ of the polymer we find out τ values at different dilutions of the polymer solution. Thus, quantity $\dfrac{HC}{\tau}$ is calculated for different concentrations. When a graph is plotted between $\dfrac{HC}{\tau}$ and C, a straight line is obtained as shown in Figure (27.2). Extrapolation of the line to zero concentration gives intercept on Y-axis as $\dfrac{1}{\bar{M}_w}$. Thus $\bar{M}_w$ can be calculated.

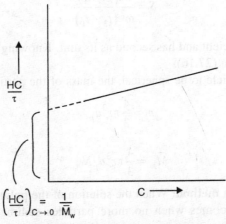

Fig. 27.2 Determination of molar mass by light scattering method

Sedimentation Method: When a colloidal solution is left in a vessel, the colloidal particles settle to the bottom under the influence of gravity. This phenomenon is called sedimentation.

The rate of sedimentation can be greatly accelerated if the solution is put under very large gravitational force which can be artificially created by means of ultracentrifuge. The polymer solution is kept in an ultracentrifuge and the rate of sedimentation is noted. Knowing the rate of sedimentation, the molar mass of the polymer can be calculated. This can be done by

(*i*) Sedimentation velocity method, and
(*ii*) Sedimentation equilibrium method.

Sedimentation velocity method: The velocity of sedimentation $\left(\dfrac{dx}{dt}\right)$ under centrifugal field is given as

$$\frac{dx}{dt} = \frac{2}{9}\frac{r^2\left(d_p - d_m\right)\omega^2 x}{\eta} \qquad \text{...(27.15)}$$

where r is the radius of the particle, d_p and d_m are the densities of particle and medium respectively and η is the viscosity of the medium and ω is the angular velocity and x is the distance from the centre of rotation. Rearranging and integrating equation (27.15), we get

$$\int_{x_1}^{x_2}\frac{dx}{x} = \frac{2}{9}r^2\frac{\left(d_p - dm\right)\omega^2}{\eta}\int_{t_1}^{t_2}dt$$

or

$$\frac{\ln\left(\dfrac{x_2}{x_1}\right)}{\omega^2\left(t_2 - t_1\right)} = \frac{2}{9}r^2\frac{\left(d_p - d_m\right)}{\eta} \qquad \text{...(27.16)}$$

If we denote right hand side of equation (27.16) by S, then we have

$$S = \frac{\ln\left(x_2/x_1\right)}{\omega^2\left(t_2 - t_1\right)} \qquad \text{...(27.17)}$$

S is called sedimentation coefficient and has second as its unit. Knowing S, the radius of the particle r can be calculated using equation (27.16).

Assuming the polymer particle to be spherical, the mass of the particle is given by

$$m = \frac{4}{3}\pi r^3 d_p$$

$$\bar{M}_w = \frac{4}{3}\pi r^3 d_p N_A$$

Sedimentation equilibrium method: When the solution of the polymer is rotated for a long time in an ultracentrifuge, a stage comes when no more particles sediment. This stage is called the sedimentation equilibrium. At this point the rate of sedimentation and the rate of diffusion back to medium are equal and opposite. Therefore,

$$\ln\left(\frac{C_2}{C_1}\right) = \frac{\bar{M}_w \omega^2 \left(d_p - d_m\right)\left(x_2^2 - x_1^2\right)}{2RTd_p}$$

$$\bar{M}_w = \frac{2RT \, d_p \, \ln\left(\dfrac{C_2}{C_1}\right)}{\omega^2 \left(d_p - d_m\right)\left(x_2^2 - x_1^2\right)} \qquad \qquad ...(27.18)$$

where C_1 and C_2 are the concentrations of particles at points x_1 and x_2 from centre of rotation respectively. R and T have their usual significance.

EXERCISES

1. Distinguish the following:
    (i) Number average molar mass from mass average molar mass.
    (ii) Relative viscosity from specific viscosity.
    (iii) A condensation polymer from an addition polymer.
    (iv) A homopolymer from a copolymer.
    (v) An alternate copolymer from a random copolymer.

2. Show that for an equimolar mixture of two substances

    $$M_1 = \bar{M}_n + \left(\bar{M}_n \bar{M}_w - \bar{M}_n^2\right)^{1/2}$$

    $$M_2 = \bar{M}_n + \left(\bar{M}_n \bar{M}_w - \bar{M}_n^2\right)^{1/2}$$

3. Explain the terms: monomers, macromolecules, addition and condensation polymers, random copolymers.

4. Why must average molar be defined for macromolecules and not for small molecules?

5. At 298 K, the molar mass and intrinsic viscosities of sodium polyphosphate were determined in 0.35 M NaBr for samples of different molar mass. The data were

$\bar{M}_w$	111,000	123,000	249,000	420,000
η (100 ml/g)	0.195	0.213	0.326	0.472

    Determine K and a values in the $|\eta| = K\bar{M}_w^a$

    Ans. $|\eta| = 6.5 \times 10^{-5} \bar{M}_w^{0.69}$.

6. What will be the ratio of the equilibrium concentration of a polymer with $\bar{M}_w = 50.0$ kg mol^{-1} at a distance of 5.0 cm compared to a distance of 4.0 cm in an ultracentrifuge operating at 1×10^4 min^{-1}? Assume $d_p = 1.25 \times 10^5$ kg m^{-3}.

    Ans. $\dfrac{C_2}{C_1} = 62$.

7. A polymer was prepared by condensing the monomer $HO-(CH_2)_5-COOH$. The mass average molar mass of the polymer was 44.1 kg mol^{-1} and the number average molar mass was 22.1 kg mol^{-1}. Calculate the

(i) polydispersity index and (ii) the extent of reaction (p). The extent of reaction is defined as $p = \dfrac{\bar{M}_w}{\eta_n} - 1$.

Ans. (i) 1.995, (ii) 0.995.

8. A polymer sample was found to be heterogeneous with respect to molar mass. It was found that a polymer sample contains a mole fraction of 0.2 with a molar mass of 100,000 g mol, a mole fraction of 0.7 with a molar mass of 1,25,000 g mol^{-1} and a mole fraction of 0.1 with a molar mass of 200,000 g mol^{-1}. Calculate number and mass average molar masses.

Ans. $\bar{M}_n = 1.2 \times 10^5$ g mol^{-1}, $\bar{M}_w = 1.3 \times 10^5$ g mol^{-1}.

9. A solution contains equal number of molecules with molar masses 10,000 g mol^{-1} and 20,000 g mol^{-1} respectively. Calculate $\bar{M}_n = \bar{M}_w$

Ans. $\bar{M}_n = 15,000$ g mol^{-1} and $\bar{M}_w = 16,666.7$ g mol^{-1}.

10. A solution contains 1:2 ratio of masses of particles of two substances with molar masses 10,000 g mol^{-1} and 20,000 g mol^{-1} respectively. Determine the number average $(\bar{M}_n)$ and mass average $(\bar{M}_w)$ molar masses

Ans. $\bar{M}_n = 15,000$ g mol^{-1} and $\bar{M}_w = 16,670$ g mol^{-1}.

11. The osmotic pressure of a solution of rubber in an organic solvent was determined by measuring the height (h) of the rubber solution in a capillary osmometer at 300 K for different concentrations

C (g cm^{-3})	0.0050	0.0179	0.0267	0.0354
h (cm)	2.2	13.0	24.6	39.4

Assume that the density of each rubber solution is 0.74 g cm^{-3}. Determine the number average molar mass of the rubber.

Ans. 120,000 g mol^{-1}.

12. Using the following relative viscosity data for solution of polystyrene in toluene at 298 K to determine $|\eta|$

C (10^3 kg m^{-3})	0.002	0.004	0.006	0.008	0.01
η_r	1.102	1.208	1.317	1.43	1.548

Calculate $\bar{M}_v$ (kg mol^{-1}) for this polymer using $a = 0.69$ and $K = 1.7 \times 10^{-3}$ m^3 kg^{-1}.

Ans. $\bar{M}_v$ (kg mol^{-1}).

14. What is understood by sedimentation equilibrium? How is the molar mass of a polymer determined by using the technique of ultracentrifuge sedimentation?

Index